The Great Masters

THE GREAT MASTERS

Quantum Books

A QUANTUM BOOK

This book is produced by
Quantum Publishing Ltd
6 Blundell Street
London
N7 9BH

This edition printed 2003

ISBN 1-86160-757-1

QUMEOTG

Manufactured in Singapore by
Universal Graphics (Pte) Ltd
Printed in Singapore by
Star Standard Industries (Pte) Ltd

CONTENTS

TITIAN 14

INTRODUCTION 16

LIFE CHRONOLOGY 26

THE PAINTINGS

MAN WITH A BLUE SLEEVE 28

THE PESARO ALTARPIECE 32

BUCCHUS AND ARIADNE 36

THE ENTOMBMENT 42

THE VENUS OF URBINO 46

DANAË 50

THE DEATH OF ACTAEON 54

Bruegel 60

Introduction 62
Life Chronology 72

The Paintings

The Battle Between Carnival and Lent 74
Children's Games 78
The tower of Babel 82
The procession to Calvary 86
The Corn Harvest 90
The Numbering at Bethlehem 94
A Peasant Wedding 98

Rubens 102

Introduction 104
Life Chronology 118

The Paintings

The Judgement of Paris 120
Samson and Delilah 124
The Arrival of Marie De' Medici at Marseilles 128
The Duke of Buckingham Conducted to the temple of Virtus 132
Allegory of Peace and War 136
The rape of the Sabine Women 140
Autumn Landscape with a View of Het Steen 144

REMBRANDT 148

INTRODUCTION 150

LIFE CHRONOLOGY 158

THE PAINTINGS

JEREMIAH LAMENTING THE DESTRUCTION OF JERUSALEM 160

BELSHAZZAR'S FEAST 164

SELF PORTRAIT 168

THE NIGHT WATCH 172

THE ADORATION OF THE SHEPHERDS 178

YOUNG WOMEN BATHING 182

SELF-PORTRAIT WITH MAULSTICK, PALETTE AND BRUSHES 186

GOYA 190

INTRODUCTION 192

LIFE CHRONOLOGY 202

THE PAINTINGS

A WALK IN ANDALUSIA: MAJAS AND THE MUFFLED MAJOS 204

THE BEWITCHED: PRIEST POURING OIL ON THE DEVILS LAMP 208

A MIRACLE OF ST ANTHONY 212

CHARLES IV AND HIS FAMILY 218

DOÑA ISABEL CORBOS DE PORCEL 222

THE BURIAL OF THE SADINE 226

TWO OLD PEOPLE EATING 232

Turner 236

Introduction 238
Life Chronology 248

The Paintings

The Shipwreck 250
The Fall of an Avalanche in the Grisons 254
Ulysses deriding Polyphemus 258
The Evening Star 262
Interior at Petworth 266
Norham Castle, Sunrise 270
Peace: Burial at Sea 274

Pissarro 278

Introduction 280
Life Chronology 290

The Paintings

View of l'Hermitage at Pontoise 292
Lordship Lane Station, Dulwich 296
The Little Bridge, Pontoise 300
The Shepherdess 304
The Quays at Rouen 308
The Boulevard Montmartre at Night 312
Self-Portrait 316

MANET 320

INTRODUCTION 322

LIFE CHRONOLOGY 330

THE PAINTINGS

MUSIC IN THE TUILERIES GARDENS 332

DEJEUNER SUR L'HERBE 336

OLYMPIA 340

PORTRAIT OF EMILE ZOLA 344

THE SEINE BANKS AT ARGENTEUIL 348

GIRL SERVING BEER 352

BAR AT THE FOLIES BERGERE 356

WHISTLER 362

INTRODUCTION 364

LIFE CHRONOLOGY 374

THE PAINTINGS

HARMONY IN GREEN AND ROSE: THE MUSIC ROOM 376

SYMPHONY IN WHITE NO.2: THE LITTLE WHITE GIRL 380

VARIATIONS IN FLESH COLOUR AND GREEN: THE BALCONY 384

HARMONY IN FLESH COLOUR AND RED 388

NOCTURNE IN BLUE AND GREEN: CHELSEA 392

HARMONY IN GREY AND GREEN: MISS CICELY ALEXANDER 396

NOCTURNE IN BLACK AND GOLD: THE FALLING ROCKET 400

BATHING POSTS, BRITTANY 404

DEGAS 408

INTRODUCTION 410
LIFE CHRONOLOGY 420

THE PAINTINGS

IN THE ORCHESTRA PIT 422
DANCER CURTSEYING 426
ABSINTHE 430
AT THE TERRACE OF THE CAFE 434
CARRIAGE AT THE RACES 438
MISS LALA AT THE CIRCUS 442
THE TUB 446

CÉZANNE 450

INTRODUCTION 452
LIFE CHRONOLOGY 462

THE PAINTINGS

PORTRAIT OF ACHILLE EMPERAIRE 464
SELF-PORTRAIT 468
THREE BATHERS 472
MOUNTAINS IN PROVENCE 476
POT OF FLOWERS AND FRUIT 480
MONT SAINTE-VICTOIRE 484
THE RED ROCK 488

MONET 492

INTRODUCTION 494
LIFE CHRONOLOGY 504

THE PAINTINGS

WOMEN IN THE GARDEN 506
IMPRESSION, SUNRISE 510
AUTUMN AT ARGENTEUIL 514
THE GARE SAINT-LAZARE 518
BOATS AT ETRETAT 522
POPLARS ON THE BANKS OF THE EPTE 528
MORNING WITH WILLOWS 532

RENOIR 538

INTRODUCTION 540
LIFE CHRONOLOGY 548

THE PAINTINGS

LA GRENOUILLERE 550
THE DANCER 554
BALL AT THE MOULIN DE LA GALETTE 558
THE UMBRELLAS 564
THE BATHERS 568
GIRLS AT THE PIANO 572
PORTRAIT OF MISIA 576
LES GRANDES BAIGNEUSES 580

GAUGUIN 584

INTRODUCTION 586
LIFE CHRONOLOGY 596

THE PAINTINGS

PONT D'IENA 598
VISION AFTER THE SERMON: JACOB WRESTLING WITH THE ANGEL 602
VAN GOGH PAINTING SUNFLOWERS 606
MANAO TUPAPAU: THE SPIRIT OF THE DEAD KEEPS WATCH 610
NEVERMORE 616
WHERE DO WE COME FROM? WHAT ARE WE? WHERE ARE WE GOING TO? 620
THE WHITE HORSE 626

VAN GOGH 630

INTRODUCTION 632
LIFE CHRONOLOGY 646

THE PAINTINGS

THE POTATO EATERS 648
KITCHEN GARDENS IN MONTMARTRE 652
NIGHT CAFE 656
VINCENT'S CHAIR WITH HIS PIPE 660
SELF-PORTRAIT WITH BANDAGED EAR 664
ROAD WITH CYPRESS AND STAR 668
CROWS IN THE WHEATFIELD 672

Toulouse-Lautrec 676

Introduction 678
Life Chronology 688

The Paintings

The Ball at the Moulins de la Galette 690
A La mie 694
Jane Avril Dancing 698
The Salon at the Rue des Moulins 702
portrait of Paul Leclercq 706
Mme Poupoule at her Toilet 710
At the Rat Mort 714

Index 718
Acknowledgements 736

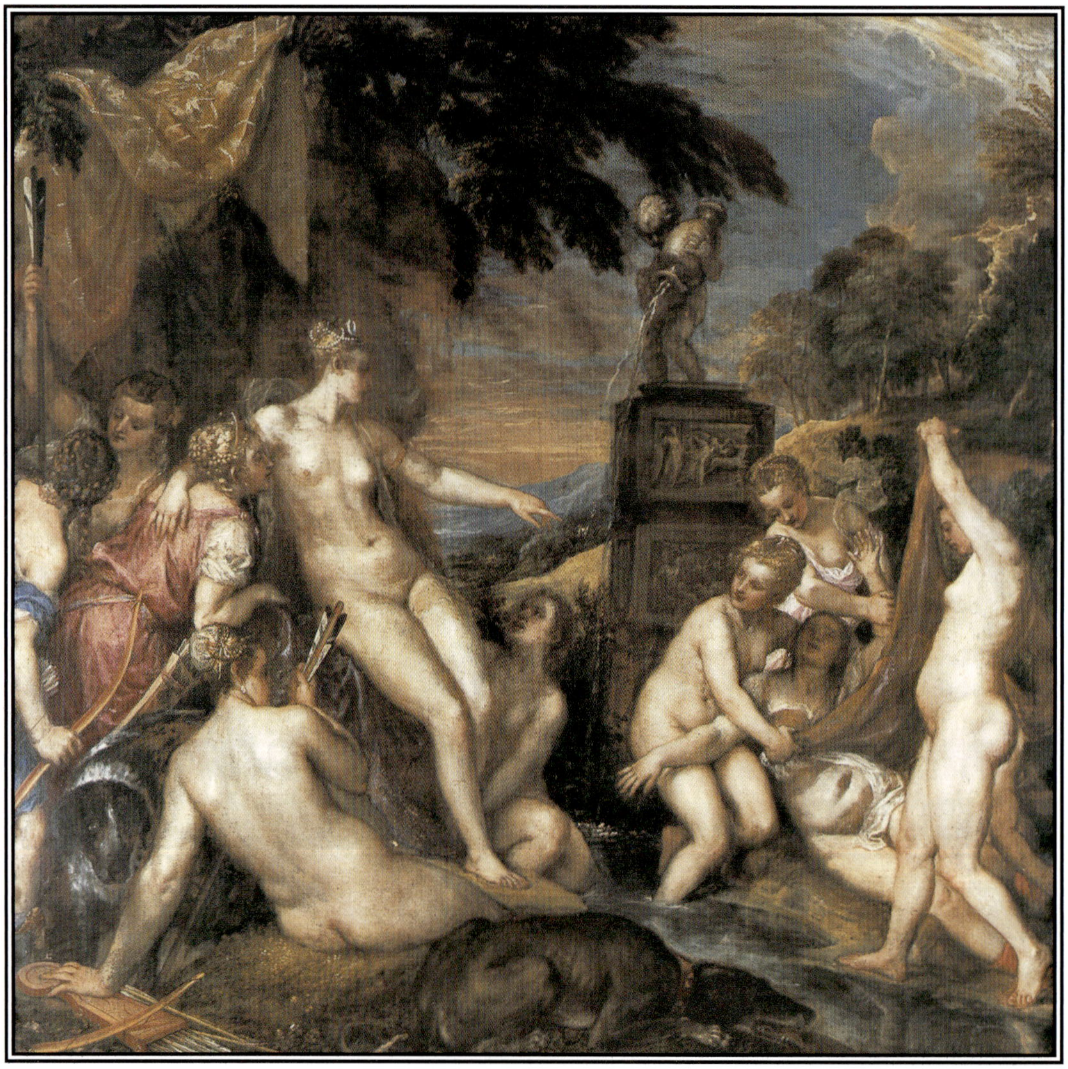

TITIAN

Introduction

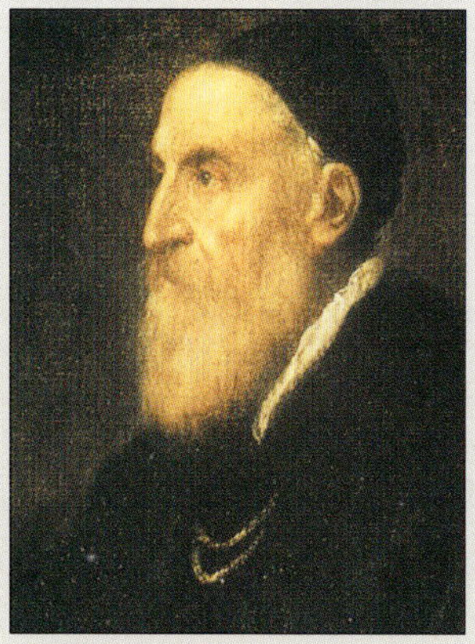

Titian
Self-portrait
c 1565-70, Prado, Madrid

"Titian walks alone as the equal of Nature," wrote his friend and biographer Ludovico Dolce in 1557, "so that each of his figures is alive, moves, its flesh quivering. He has displayed in his works no empty grace, but colors appropriate to their task." For Titian this task was that "the painter... must always aim at what is suited to each subject, and represent each person with his true character and emotions, which practice will gratify the beholders amazingly."

Titian's greatness lies in his ability to use color to catch nature's shimmering surface, while also penetrating this surface to illuminate the psychological aspects of human nature. His name is synonymous with color, light and mood, and although similar concerns had occupied earlier Venetian painters, Titian took them a step further, translating them into a visual metaphor for the very stuff of nature. In Titian's paintings, brushstrokes are used as the outer expression of an inner response, describing physical and emotional nuances in a way that had never been done before, and was to mold the vision of his contemporaries and later European painters until this day.

Oil paint: the "new" medium

The innovation that helped the Venetian painters to catch the characteristic properties of light was oil paint, not a totally new medium, but one which was beginning to be exploited in new ways. Oils had been perfected by early 15th-century Flemish painters, such as Jan Van Eyck (who is often credited as their inventor) and were introduced to Venice by artists such as Antonello da Messina. Unlike the water-based medium, tempera, they were ideally suited to reflect and soak up light, dissolving forms and contours.

Venice, a dominant port surrounded by sea, was well placed to absorb ideas both from the East on one side and the Italian peninsula on the other. Previously, the influence of Byzantine art from the East had been paramount, with its emphasis on color and flat, stylized pattern as a means of spiritual expression, but now the northern Gothic painting showed the Venetians a different approach, in which oil paint was used to capture the subtleties and intricate details of the visual world. This new naturalism was taken further with the rise of Humanism, particularly in Florence, when artists and architects combined in a return to Classical ideals of balance and harmony, treating human subjects with an increased understanding of their individual emotions and characteristics.

By the middle of the 16th century, Venice was the only one of the Italian states to maintain its independence, and consequently was far less disturbed by the political and economic troubles that were to unsettle Rome, Florence and Italy in general. She was still a major center for commerce, and artists were in the fortunate position of being able to take first pick from a wide range of high-quality pigments before they were sent to other parts of the country. In Venetian painting these superior pigments were combined with a greater flexibility of technique to give warmth and humanity to Renaissance ideals, celebrating the sensory pleasures of life with light and color.

Tempera, which had been used both for church frescoes and paintings on wooden panels, imposed severe limitations on the artist, and in Venice both pigment and surface were adversely affected by the city's humidity. Oil was far more stable as well as more convenient, as it enabled artists to work in their studios, for prolonged periods if necessary, on canvases which could then be transported easily to their destinations. They could also work from live models under controlled lighting conditions. In addition to the technical innovations, there were changes in the subject matter available to artists. Religious paintings were still needed, but more and more learned and scholarly patrons were demanding secular works with themes drawn from antiquity and mythology, subjects suitable for more intimate, private and domestic settings.

The Venetian legacy

This legacy of innovations in both materials and subject matter was the one inherited by Tiziano Vecellio, born between 1477 and 1490 in Pieve di Cadore, high in the Italian Dolomites. His grandfather, Count Vecellio, had been an important official in the garrison at Pieve, and his father Gregorio was captain of the same garrison, later becoming supervisor of the mines at Cadore. While still a child, Titian was sent to the house of a relative in Venice, and then became an apprentice to the mosaicist Zuccato, who quickly recognized his talent, and in about 1500 sent him to study with Gentile Bellini. As an apprentice he would have begun by cleaning brushes and palettes, then learned to grind colors and prepare surfaces before eventually being allowed to paint small areas for his master.

Gentile Bellini's linear and rather anecdotal approach evidently did not appeal to the impatient young man, and it seems his master did not think highly of him either – he is recorded as saying that his pupil painted too rapidly and would never amount to anything. Titian left to study under Gentile's less conservative brother, Giovanni. According to the contemporary art historian Vasari, both Giorgione and Sebastiano del Piombo were also in the studio at this time, when Giovanni must have been about seventy – his dates are uncertain. He must have had a powerful effect on the three young painters, for as Dürer said in 1506, "though he is old he is still the best in painting."

To appreciate Titian's paintings to the full it is helpful to look first at the work of his master, the artist who influenced him the most in his early years. At the end of the 15th century, Giovanni Bellini was the leading Venetian painter, and in his work the glowing impact of the earlier mosaics and gilded panels was translated into oil. His paintings are based on visual observation, but light and color are reinterpreted in a way that expresses the Divinity though the subtle illumination of diffused light. Unlike the Florentines, he saw line as artificial, and he rejected linear perspective, which creates depth by presenting things in an orderly progression. Instead he painted color and space as we actually perceive them. In such paintings as the *Sacred Allegory*, he built up a rich surface pattern (not unlike the earlier mosaics) which, rather than separating the various objects, seems to fuse them together through related colors, producing an almost palpable sensation of air and atmosphere.

With Bellini, landscape became a major concern of Venetian art, and this can be seen in the work of both Titian and Giorgione. Titian's early religious paintings also reflect the influence of Bellini, whose characteristic half-length Madonnas, often set against a curtain backdrop with a glimpse of landscape to the side, find an echo in Titian's *Gipsy Madonna*.

Painted poetry

In the landscape to Titian's painting, however, the lone armored figure sitting beneath a tree adds a sense of mystery, implying a narrative, but revealing nothing but an enigmatic and indefinable mood. This type of painterly analogy to poetry seems to have been created by

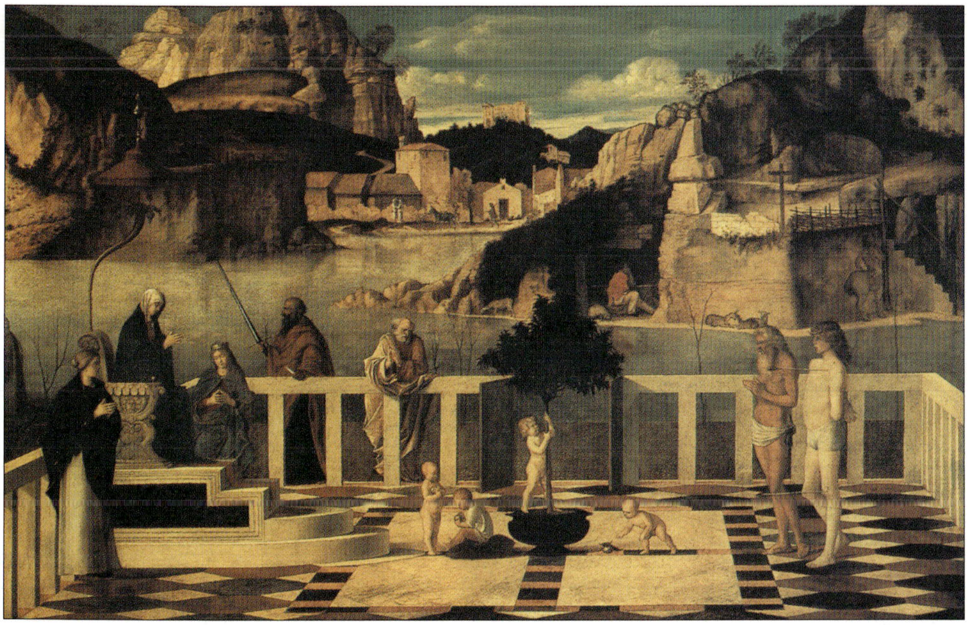

GIOVANNI BELLINI
Sacred Allegory
c 1490, Uffizi, Florence

This work, once thought to be by Giorgione, creates a dreamlike world in which the allegorical references of the title remain elusive. On a cushion in the center sits the Christ-child, holding an apple that may symbolize original sin. Beneath a vine (referring to the blood of Christ) sits the Virgin Mary, blessing or in judgment, between two women who may possibly stand for Mercy and Justice. The landscape setting is hauntingly real, creating a hallucinatory stillness that seems to make the hidden ritual all the more tantalizing.

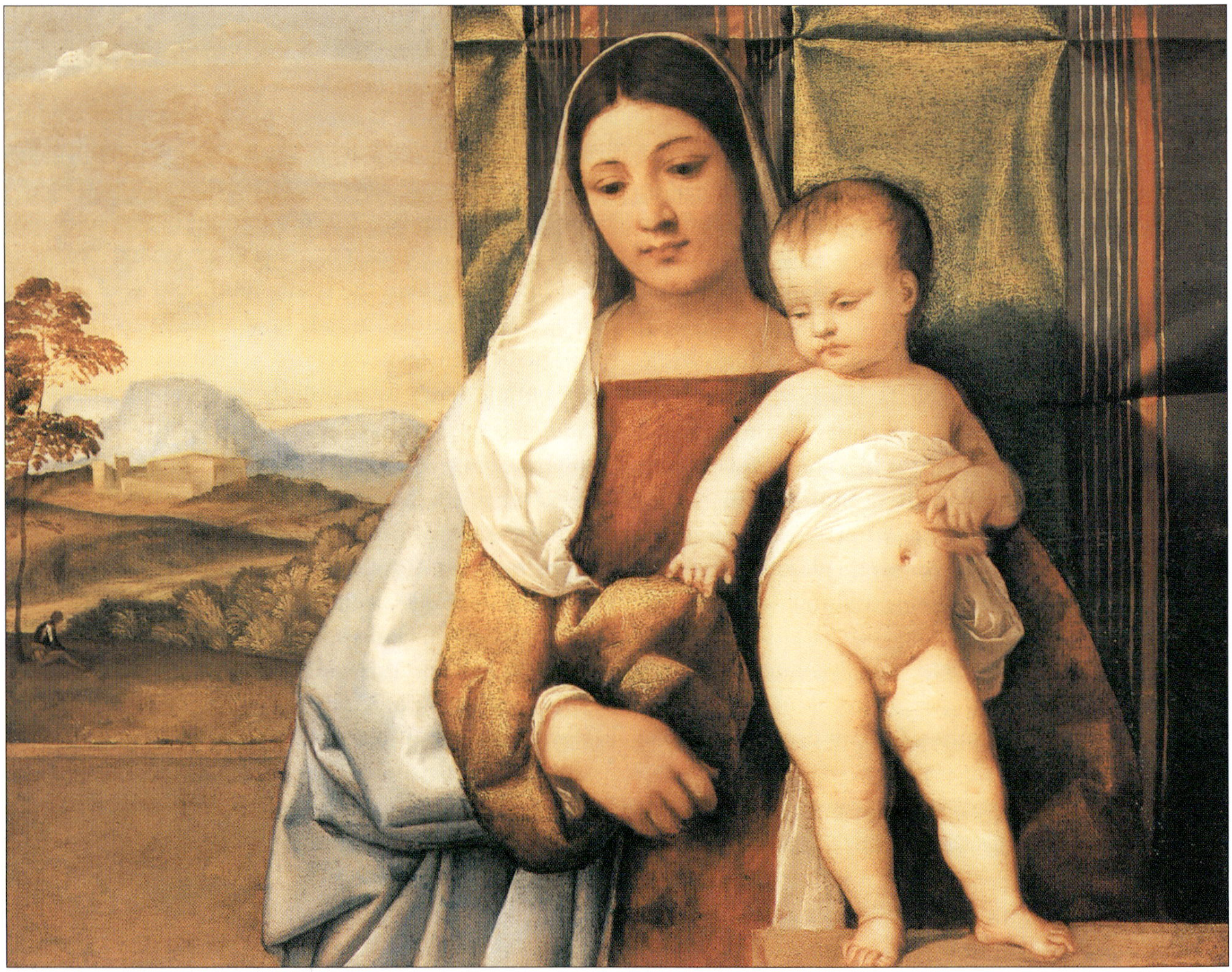

TITIAN
The Gipsy Madonna
c 1510, Kunsthistorisches Museum, Vienna

The Madonna set against a curtain derives from Bellini's half-length Madonnas, but in Titian's painting there is a fullness to the forms and their mass is complemented by the spatial delicacy of a "Giorgionesque" landscape. Rich color harmonies are heightened by the green balancing the touches of red that model the Madonna's face. The pyramidal composition, with the face at its peak, is typical of the High Renaissance.

Giorgione, who was another powerful influence on Titian in his early years. In works such as *The Tempest* Giorgione exploited the new secular subject matter in a way that created a poetic response to natural phenomena, working up a tonal structure from dark to light and using a *sfumato* technique (soft, edgeless gradations of tone and colour) to give his forms a brooding, atmos-

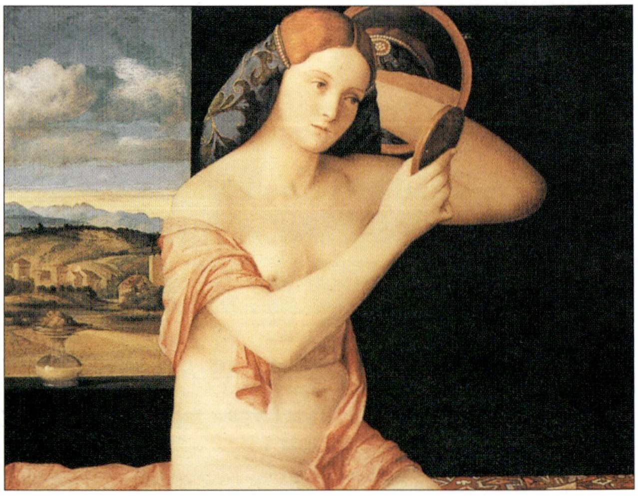

GIOVANNI BELLINI
Young woman with a Mirror
1515, Kunsthistorisches Museum, Vienna

Bellini's characteristic composition of a Virgin before a curtain backdrop, with a landscape behind, is here given a secular interpretation as a mortal Venus is molded by soft, filtering light. Her fullness is perfectly balanced against exquisite detailing. Titian was to draw upon both the sacred and the earthly variants of Bellini's works in such contrasting works as the *Gipsy Madonna* (above) and the *Danaë* (see page 51).

pheric presence. Here air both unites and confuses boundaries of form and meaning, and one feels the presence of the artist hovering over the surface of the canvas. The oil technique, emphasizing the marks of the brush, made the artist a less anonymous figure.

The Venetians tended to favor a fairly coarse canvas that encouraged an inventive use of paint, which could be dragged across the grain, producing texture and broken touches of color. This emphasized their enjoyment in manipulating pigments in a sensuous and painterly manner. This relish for the tactile quality of paint comes across very strongly in Titian's paintings. He was the first artist to really exploit the brushstroke as an expressive force in its own right, as important, in its way, as the subject itself. His emphasis on brushwork, stressing coloring as a means of describing form, in contrast with the Florentine preference for line, is made much of by Vasari in his anecdote about a visit in 1546 by Michelangelo to Titian's studio in Rome. Michelangelo had remarked on leaving that he liked the coloring, but that "it was a pity that in Venice one was not taught from the beginning to draw well."

The state painter

In 1510, possibly to avoid the plague that caused Giorgione's premature death, Titian went to Padua, where he painted a series of frescoes, and his work matured in both conception and technical ability. On returning to Venice, with a confidence that might be seen as bordering on arrogance, he offered in 1513 to paint a battle

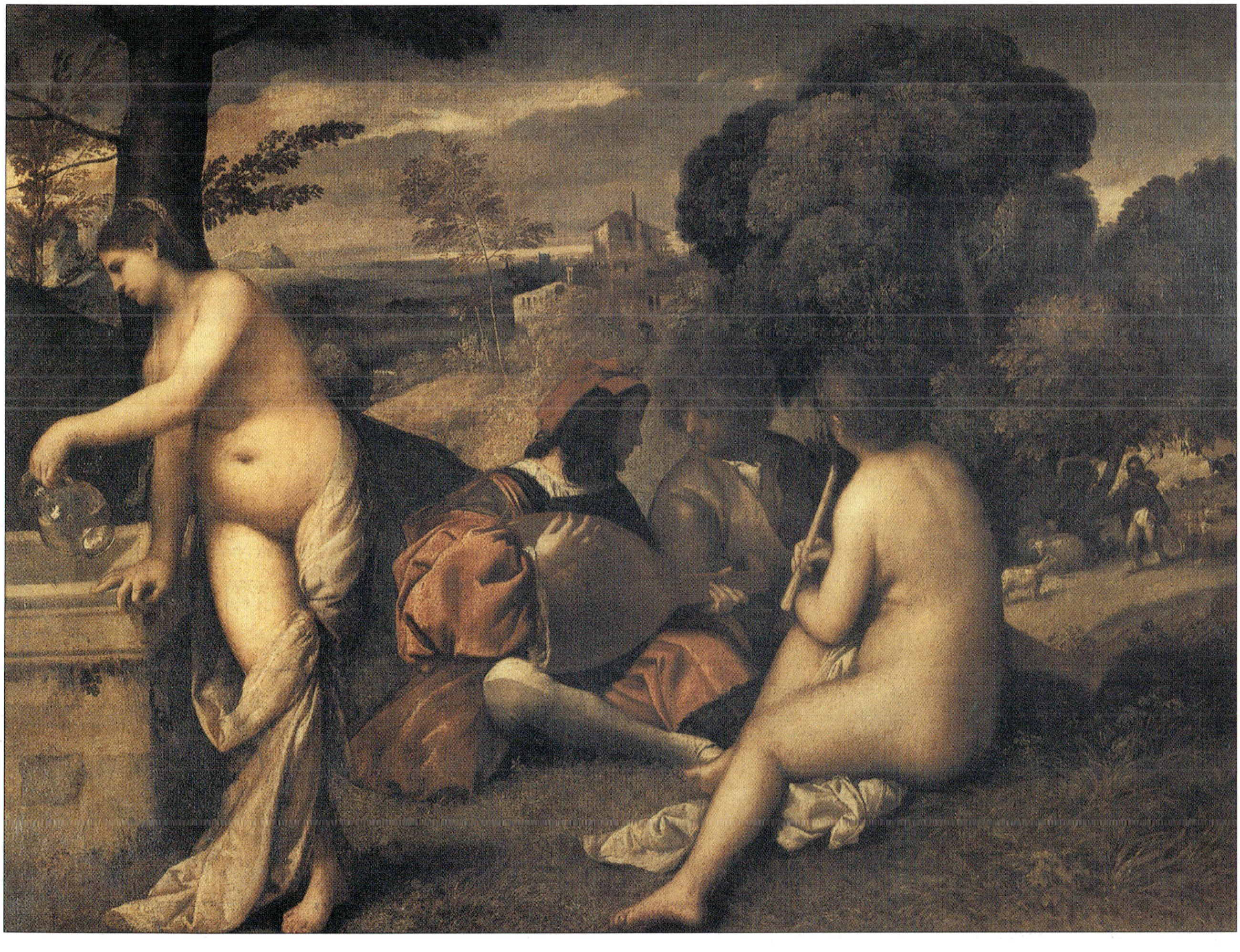

GIORGIONE and/or TITIAN
Concert Champêtre
c 1510, Louvre, Paris

Titian and Giorgione had worked together in the studio of the elderly master Giovanni Bellini, and for many years the attribution of this work has been the subject of much controversy. Believed at first to be by Giorgione, it was then thought to have been completed by the young Titian after his friend's premature death. In recent years, however, it has been increasingly attributed to Titian himself. The confusion underlines two artists' common concerns and the debt owed to Giorgione by Titian. As the figures harmonize to make music together, their notes linger on the warm air, as ephemeral as the sound of the water being poured into the well.

scene to replace a badly deteriorated 14th-century fresco. In return for this he asked to be granted the next *senseria,* the broker's patent reserved for the official state painter, then held by the aging Giovanni Bellini. After some to-ing and fro-ing, the offer was accepted, and when Giovanni died in 1516, Titian became the new state painter.

This official recognition gave his career a new impetus, and with Giorgione's death and the departure of Sebastiano del Piombo for Rome, the field was open to him. In the same year he began his first great masterpiece, the *Assumption* for the Frari Church, completed in 1518 . This was followed by the *Pesaro Altar piece* for the same church (see page 35) and the *Death of St Peter Martyr* (no longer extant, but known to us through engravings). These were innovatory works in which Titian firmly established his own personal style, and they justly brought him widespread fame. The compositional and technical brilliance achieved at this period were to be fully developed in the series of visionary masterpieces he painted in his later life.

But it was with portraits that Titian first achieved recognition in other parts of Europe, and he received commissions from the Emporor Charles V, the pope and countless princes, dukes and statesmen — his portraits illustrate generations of the European nobility. His engagements after receiving the coveted *senseria* are a testimony to his ever-growing reputation, and he quickly gained the patronage of the dukes of Ferrara, Mantua and Urbino.

In 1525 he married the woman with whom he had been living for some years, Cecilia, the daughter of a barber in Cadore, thus legitimizing their first two sons. It was to be a sadly brief marriage: Cecilia, already ailing, recovered to bear two further children, only one of whom survived, but she died in 1530. The artist was

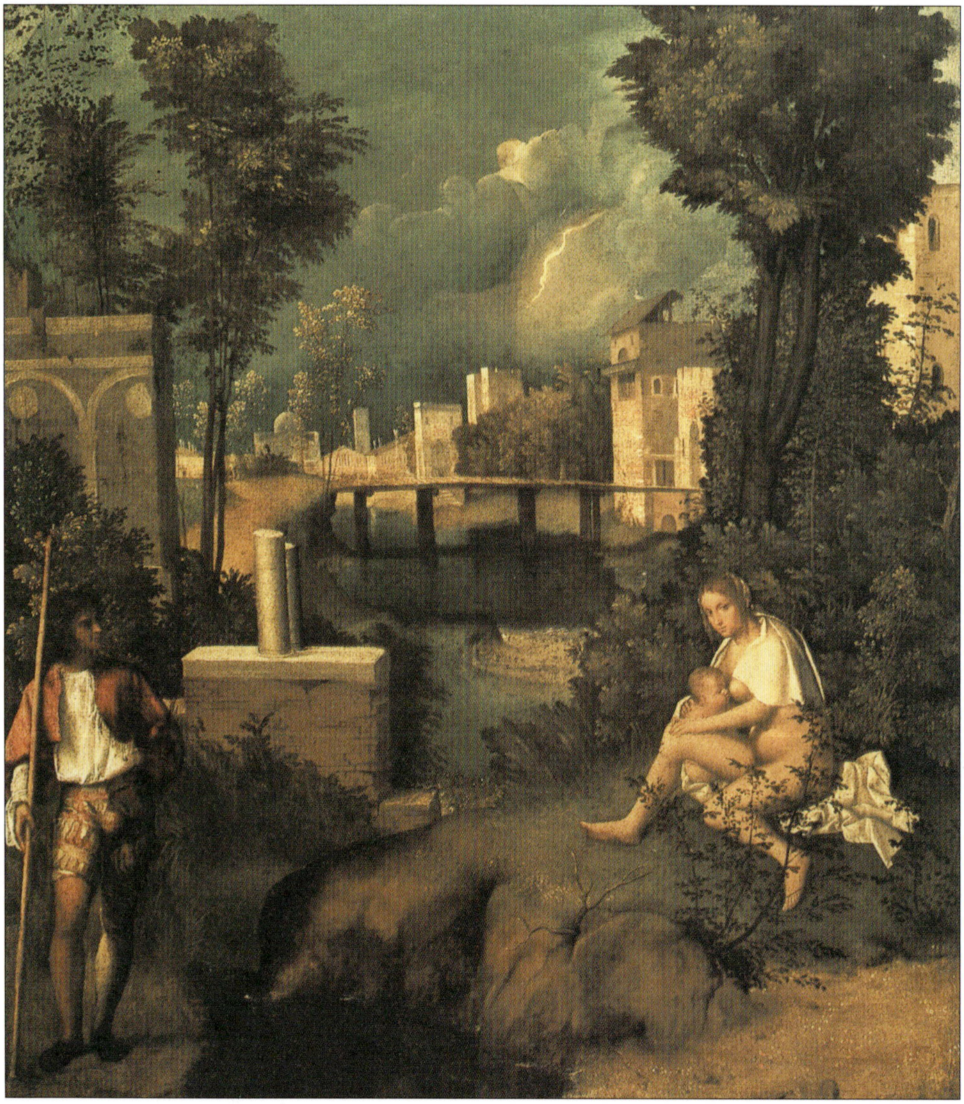

GIORGIONE
The Tempest
c 1505-08, Accademia, Venice

Giorgione, whose life was cut short by the plague in 1510, is an artist about whom very little is known. His enigmatic personality is reflected in works such as this, where images were improvised as the mood developed: X-ray photography has revealed that a nude woman originally sat in the left-hand corner where the young man stands. What the painting actually symbolizes can only be a matter for speculation. The landscape and sky seem to echo the figures' strange relationship and, as we try to decipher its enigmatic meaning, we are drawn into the scene as creative participants.

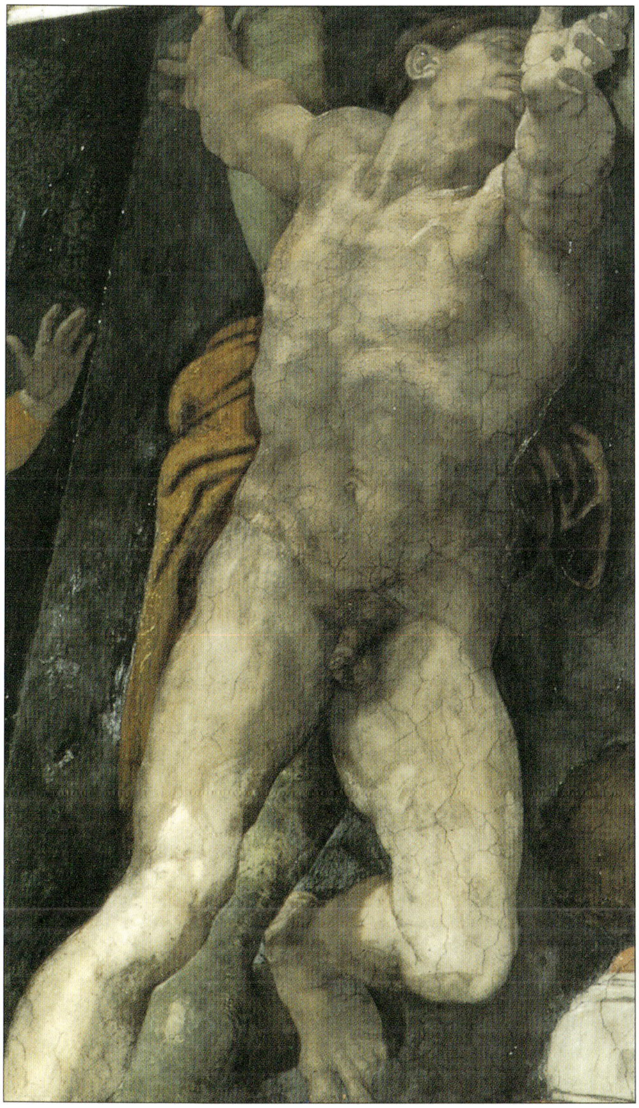

MICHELANGELO
The Punishment of Haman
1508-12, Sistine Chapel, Vatican, Rome

Michelangelo's masterful ability to position figures in the most complicated of poses is seen here, as the figure is twisted on its axis to create a vital sense of dynamic energy. His profound understanding of human anatomy and his ability to manipulate figures for dramatic effect were to be an inspiration to Titian, although the latter added a quality of asymmetrical, often informal, design that was very much his own.

devastated by the loss, was unable to work for a time, and moved away from their home, with its unhappy associations, to the district of Birri Grande. He remained devoted to his daughter Lavinia, and painted her several times, but he outlived her also – she died in childbirth in 1560.

Painter of kings and princes

In 1532 Titian met the man who was to become the most prestigious of all his patrons, Charles V, Holy Roman Emperor, ruler of Spain and the Netherlands. Charles conferred a knighthood upon Titian in 1533 and made him court painter, their relationship of mutual respect gradually ripening into a close friendship. This might seem unsurprising today, but in the 16th century, artists were seldom on an equal footing with kings. When Charles decided to abdicate in 1556 it was in front of one of his friend's paintings that he prayed for salvation.

In 1545/6 Titian visited Rome, where he was honored with Roman citizenship, and began a series of portraits

MARTINO ROTA
Engraving after Titian's *The Death of St Peter Martyr* 1530, British Museum, London

This engraving can only give an indication of how impressive this painting, one of Titian's most admired and influential works, must have been. Destroyed by fire in 1867, it was painted for the church of SS Giovanni e Paolo in Venice. The innovatory manner in which the landscape has been made a dramatic and inseparable part of the narrative set a new standard for altarpieces. The dynamically asymmetrical figure of the saint's companion surging out of the frame shows how Titian has absorbed other influences, drawing inspiration both from Michelangelo's work (left) and the dramatic pathos of classical sculptures such as the *Laocoön* (see page 31).

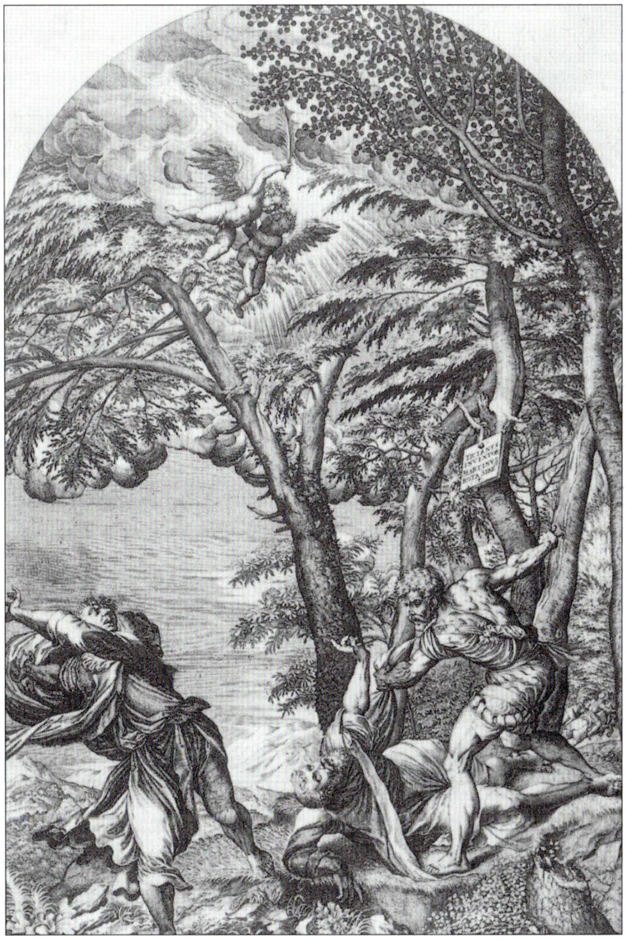

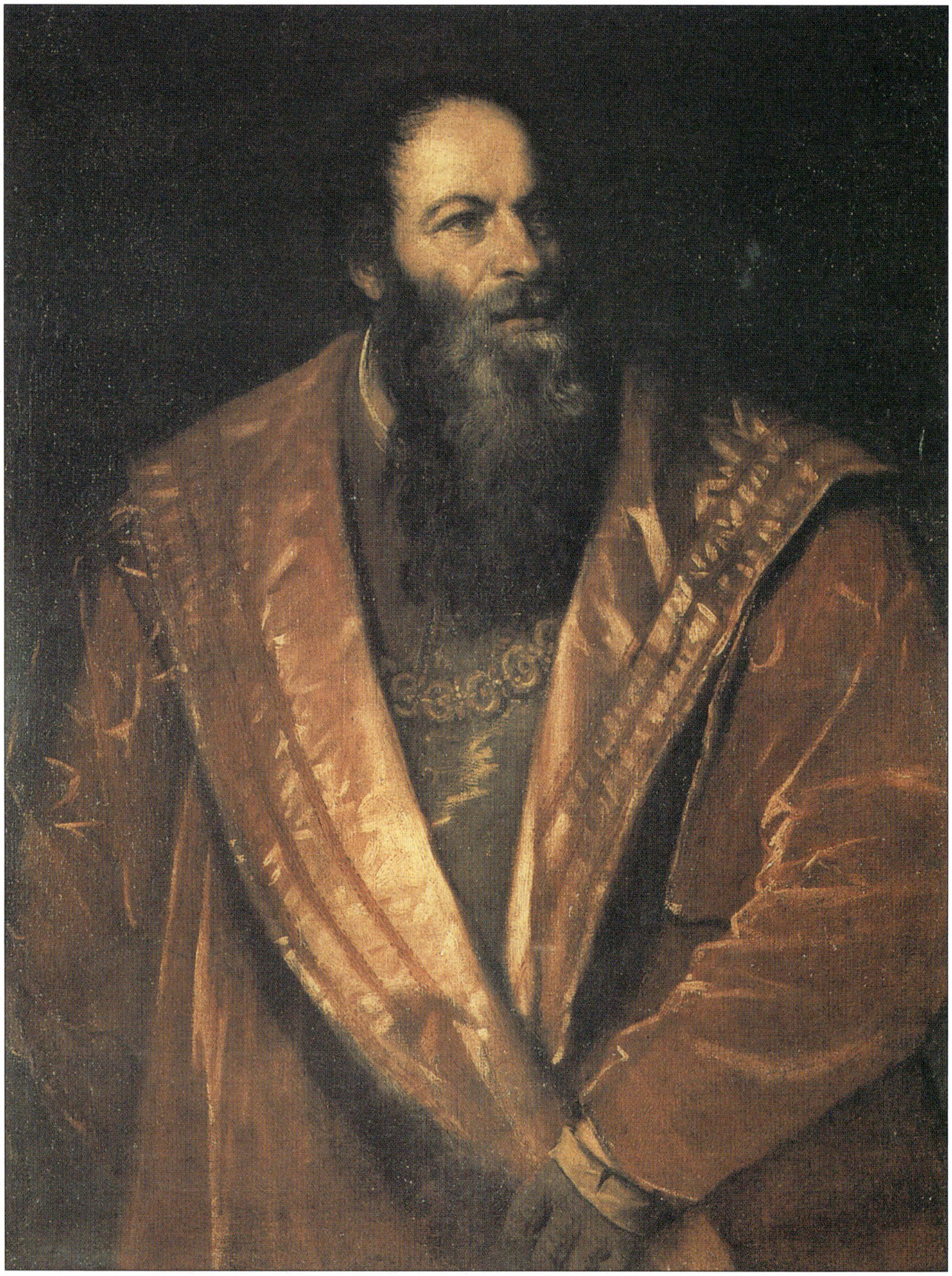

TITIAN
Portrait of Pietro Aretino
1545, Pitti Palace, Florence

Aretino, poet, playwright, and libel-monger, nicknamed "the scourge of princes," used innumerable contacts to gain commissions for his lifelong friend Titian. The artist has shown him filling the canvas, as befits a larger-than-life character, wearing the gold chain given to him by King Francis I, and radiating an arrogant intelligence. He himself summed up the portrait as "an awesome marvel."

of Pope Paul III and his family, and in 1556 he was elected to the Florentine Academy — truly an international celebrity courted by the rich and powerful of Europe But in spite of his fame and the esteem in which he was held, he was constantly reduced to haggling about money while procrastinating over the completion and delivery of works — the protracted communications between him and his patrons make for fascinating and amusing reading. The Duke of Ferrara, however, was not amused. "We thought that Titian would some day finish our picture — but he seems to take no account of us whatsoever . . . he must finish it under all circumstances or incur our greatest displeasure." The same patron was to be kept waiting for three years before being able to enjoy his *Bacchus and Ariadne* (see page 31).

Titian continued to paint until the last, although he withdrew from public life, having outlived most of his friends. He secured the future for his son Orazio, also a painter, by arranging for the transfer to him of the *senseria* and pension. In the late 1580s the elderly master offered to paint a *Pietà* for the Frari Church in return for a burial place in the chapel there, but he died in August 1576 before he could finish the painting The Guild of Venetian Painters were unable to give him the magnificent funeral they had planned because of the plague that was once again ravaging the city, but the artist was buried, as he wished, in the Frari chapel, the scene of his first great artistic triumph.

TITIAN'S PAINTING METHODS

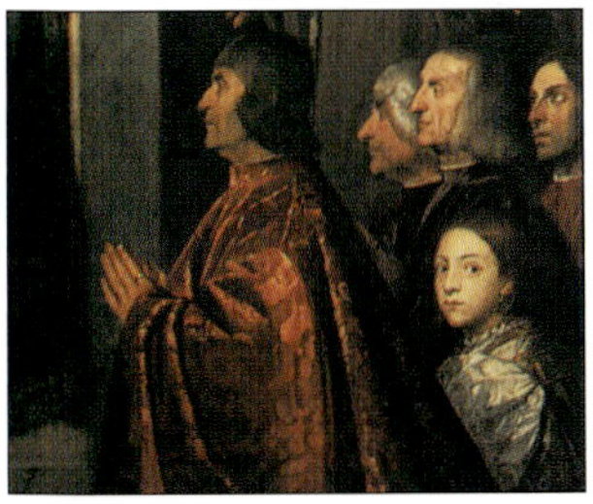

A comparison of this detail from the *Pesaro Altarpiece* (begun in 1519) with the one on the right shows the difference in style and treatment between Titian's early and late works.

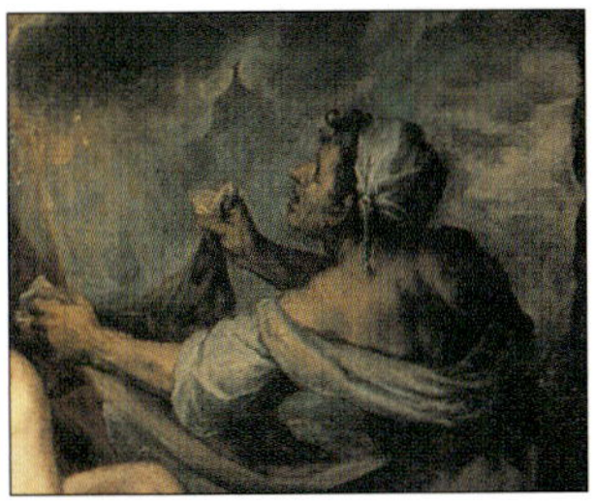

By 1553, when the *Danaë* was begun, the brushwork had become looser, freer and more expressive.

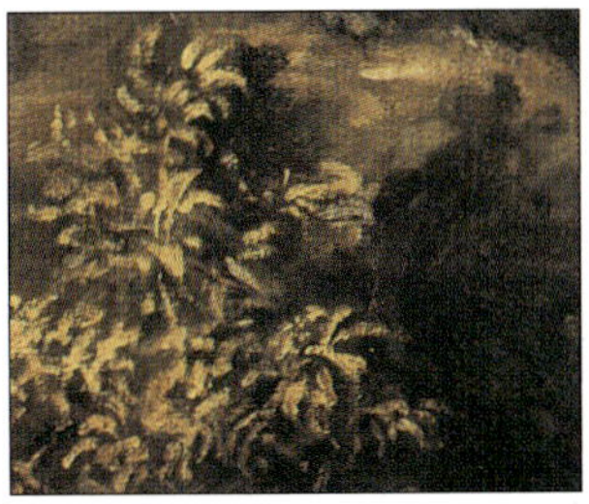

In the foreground foliage of *Death of Actaeon* form is suggested by directional strokes of a paint-laden brush.

Titian was an innovator, both in composition and in technique, and his impact on the subsequent history of painting has been enormous. His later works, at one time regarded as the careless and slapdash efforts of an artist past his prime, are now particularly admired for their bold brushwork and freedom of handling; like many artists he found the means to express his personal vision most fully in his maturity. The contemporary art historian Vasari, who visited Venice in 1566, was struck by the contrast between the careful, meticulous painting of Titian's early works and the vigorous brushwork of the later ones, which were best seen from a distance for maximum effect.

Instead of beginning with a detailed tonal underdrawing, which was the usual practice, we know from X-radiographs that Titian worked his compositions directly in paint, integrating the drawing and painting processes. One of his pupils, Palma Giovane, noted that "he laid in his pictures with a mass of color, which served as the groundwork for what he wanted to express . . . With the same brush dipped in red, black or yellow he worked up the light parts, and in four strokes he could create a remarkably fine figure . . ."

Titian used a variety of different weights and weaves of canvas during his career, but in his later works he favored a fairly rough, course-grained surface, which gave him an opportunity to exploit the texture to create broken-color effects. The first stage in the preparation of the canvas was the stitching together of two or more widths of fabric, which was usually about a meter wide. It was then stretched and sized, and finally a gesso ground was laid. This, made from gypsum and animal-skin glue, was applied thinly and smoothly so that it filled the gaps between the fibers while retaining the texture.

Titian's achievement

The majestic range of Titian's output, encompassing the universal and the particular, the spiritual and the physical, can be grouped into three main areas: portraits, religious works and the *poesie,* mildly erotic paintings with subjects drawn from mythology. His striking portraits range from the early *Man with a Blue Sleeve* (see page 29) of c 1512 – somewhat Giorgionesque in style although the sitter is presented in a new and more forceful manner – to later works such as *Pope Paul III and his Grandsons* , where the sitters' personalities and the interaction between them are caught with dramatic intensity. A comparable deepening of insight can be seen in the religious works. The early compositional innovations of the *Assumption* and the *Pesaro Altarpiece* are developed still further in later works to involve us increasingly in the spiritual experience, and paintings such as the *Entombment* (see page 43), the *Mocking of Christ* and the *Pietà* are profoundly moving. In the poesie a similar trend can be seen, with the boisterous sensuality of the early *Bacchus and Ariadne* developing into the sublime works of the 1550s. In paintings such as *Diana and Callisto,* one of the series painted for Philip II of Spain after the abdication of Charles V, or the *Death of Actaeon* (see page 55), a deeply personal awareness of humanity's suffering is transcended and ennobled through paint.

Perhaps Titian's greatest achievement was his ability to make the physical stuff of paint transcend its humble origins. Looking at one of his paintings we sense the enjoyment with which he dragged, swirled and scumbled his colors across the rough-grained canvas, using its texture to evoke radiant forms and colors that seem to be almost a metamorphosis of life itself. Titian was an innovator in both technique and composition, but none of his innovations was made for superficial effect; they were the means of expressing deeply felt emotions and experiences, and for this reason he is sometimes described as the "father of modern painting." His emphasis on the brushstroke was to be a vital factor in the development of European painting, a source of inspiration to many of the great masters, particularly Rembrandt, whose works share the same quality of emotion at one with the medium. In the modern period, Paul Cézanne's declaration that "where color is at its richest, form is at its fullest" gives a fresh insight into the continuing relevance of Titian's work.

Titian, who began his career celebrating in paint the sensual pleasure of life, ended it by achieving a profound vision of the contrasting, and complementary, side of the human experience. His paintings continue to move us with their ability to encompass the gamut of emotions, and redeem tragedy through a celebration of change, radiating a fundamental optimism. He reminds us that art is not a luxury but an essential – like air, it enables us to grow. This must surely have been his conviction when he chose the wording for his motto (or *impressa*): "Art is stronger than Nature."

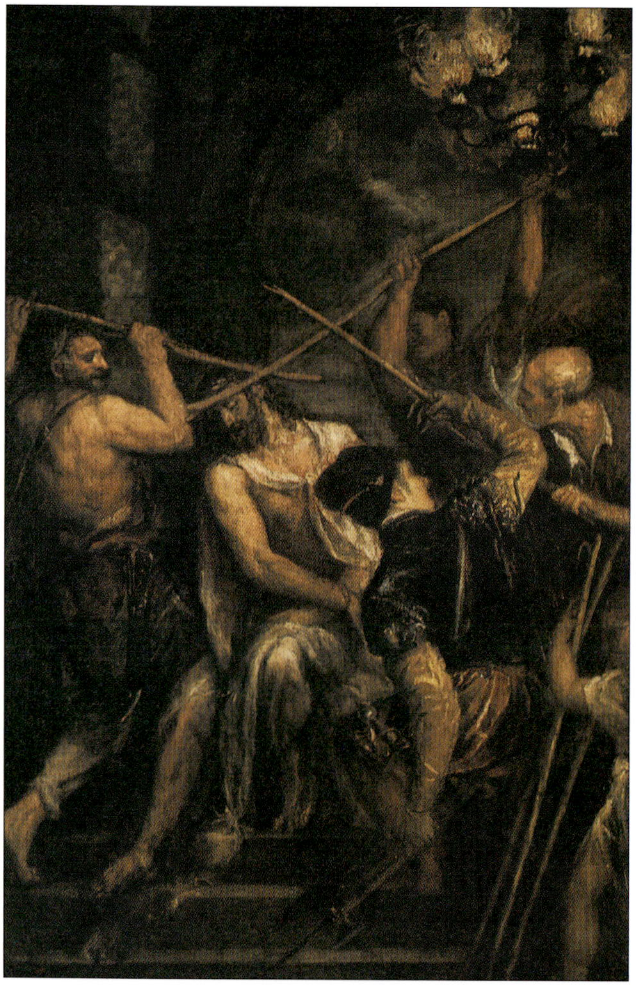

TITIAN
The Mocking of Christ
c 1570-76, Alte Pinakothek, Munich

This work is derived from a composition of the 1540s, now in the Louvre, but painted for the church of Santa Maria delle Grazie in Milan. In the early version, the violence of Christ's torture is treated with a classically heroic pathos drawn from the *Laocoön.* In this version, Christ is attacked from all sides by jabbing diagonals, but his physical torment is understated to emphasize his emotional anguish.

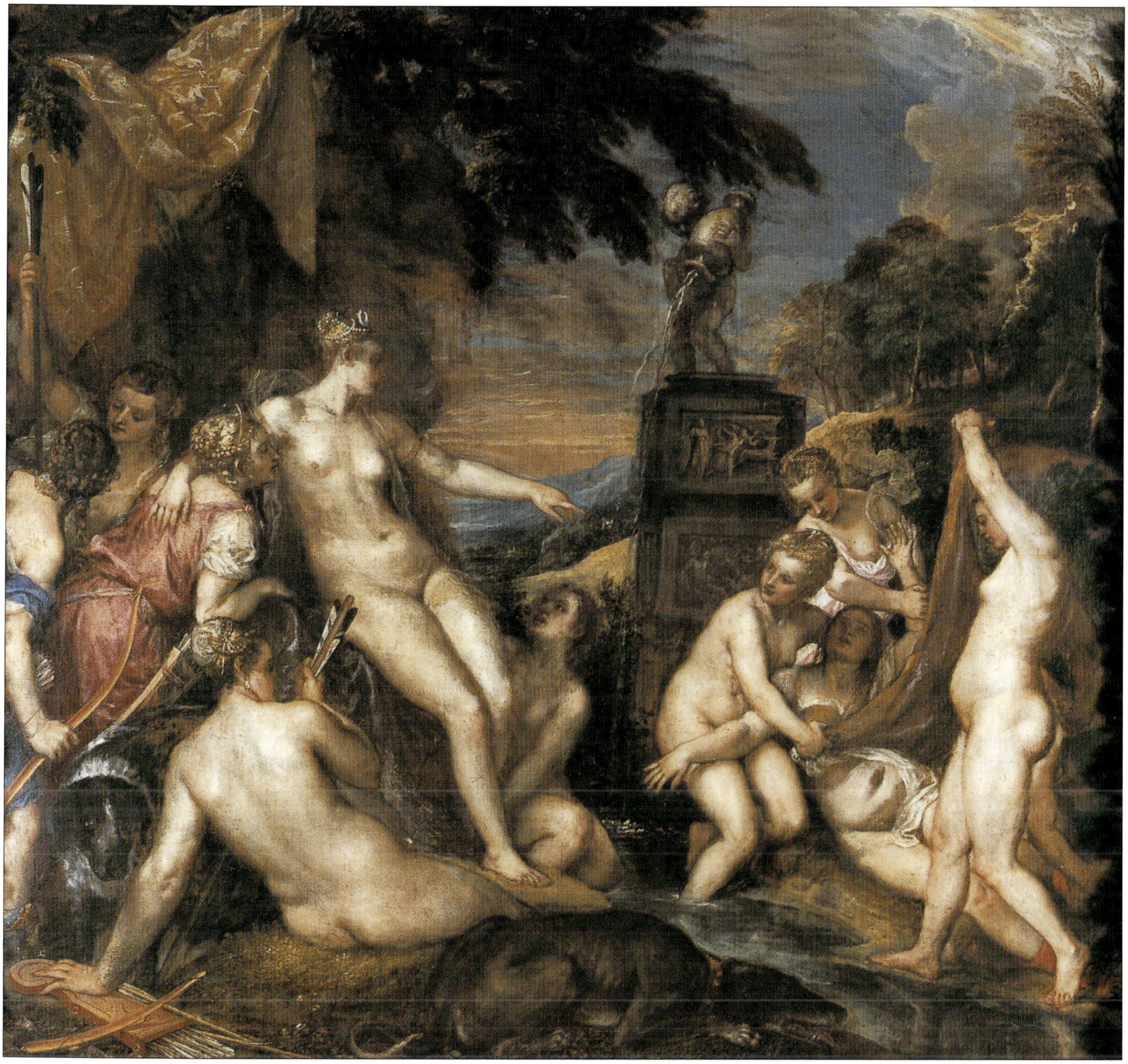

TITIAN
Diana and Callisto
c 1556-59, National Gallery of Scotland, Edinburgh

This is one of a series of paintings based on mythological subjects, commissioned by Philip II of Spain. The nymph Callisto, after being made pregnant by Jupiter, is banished by the goddess Diana. Titian uses a unity of surface texture and color to suggest a flickering light, dissolving the figures into a landscape which seems to reverberate with Callisto's sense of loss.

CHRONOLOGY OF TITIAN'S LIFE

c1477-90 Titian born in Pieve di Cadore to Gregorio di Conte Vecellio and Lucia.

c1497 Apprenticed to Zuccato in Venice.

c1500 Enters workshop of Gentile Bellini and then Giovanni Bellini

1508 Assists Giorgione with murals at the Fondaco dei Tedeschi

1510-11 To Padua: paints three frescoes in the Scuola del Santo

c1512 Paints *Man with a Blue Sleeve.*

1513 Invited to join Papal Court in Rome but declines Offers to replace 14th-century fresco in Sala del Maggior Consiglio, Venice, in return for next vacant *senseria* (broker's patent)

1514 March: Offer rejected (after complaints from other painters) but, by November, regains commission

1516 At the court of Ferrara. Giovanni Bellini dies.

1517 Awarded *senseria.*

1516-18 Paints *The Assumption.*

1519 Given contract for *Pesaro Altarpiece.*

1520-23 Paints *Bacchus and Ariadn*

1523 Contact with Gonzaga Cou Mantua.

1525 Marries Cecilia: three childre Pomponio, Orazio, and Lavini

c1525-32 Paints *The Entombment.*

1526 Completes *Pesaro Altarpiece.*

1530 Attends coronation of Charles V in Bologna. Paints copy of portrait of Charles by Seisenegger. August 5: Cecilia dies.

1531 Moves to Birri Grande.

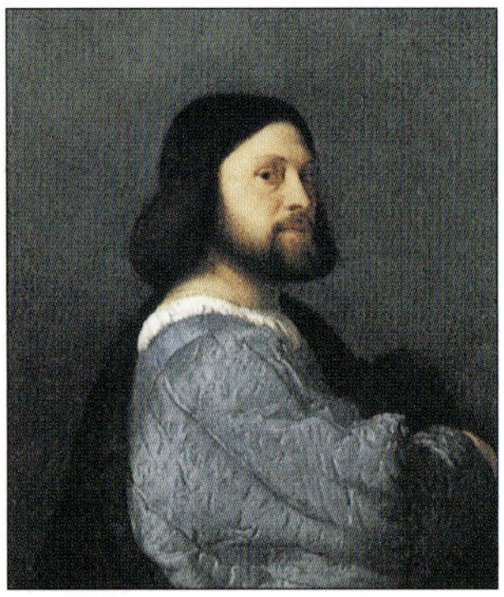

Man with a Blue Sleeve

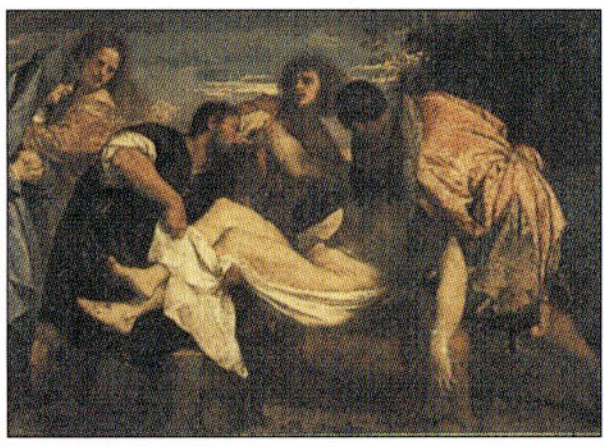

The Entombment

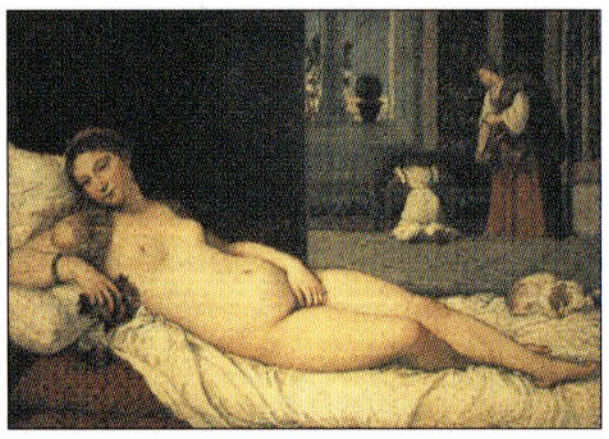

The Death of Actaeon

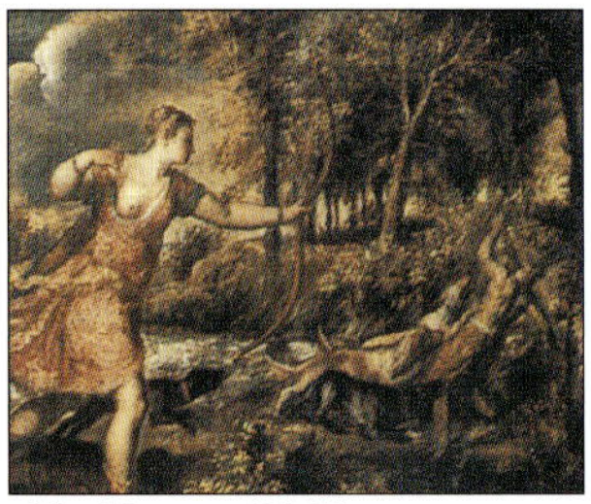

The Venus of Urbino

1532 Beginning of relationship with the Duke of Urbino.

1533 Knighted by Emperor Charles V.

1538 Paints *Venus of Urbino.* Sala del Maggior Consiglio commission eventually finished, but *senseria* taken away because of his procrastination.

1539 *Senseria* restored.

1543 In Ferrara for meeting between Charles V and Pope Paul III.

1545-6 In Rome. Meets Michelangelo; sees his and Raphael's works. Receives honorary Roman citizenship. Paints *Pope Paul III and his Grandsons.*

1548 Meets Philip II in Milan.

c1550 In Germany working on first portrait of Philip II.

1553-4 Paints *Danaë* (late version, Prado).

1555 Daughter Lavinia marries.

1556-9 Paints *Diana and Callisto.*

c1562 Paints *Death of Actaeon.*

1565 To Pieve di Cadore to supervise the execution of his designs in the local church.

1566 Granted copyright to engravings from his work. Elected to membership of Florentine Academy.

1569 Has *senseria* transferred to his son Orazio.

1571 Writes a letter to Philip II from whom he received a state pension. The king transfers the pension to Orazio.

1576 August 27: Titian dies. His *Pietà,* unfinished at his death, is completed by Palma Giovane.

THE PAINTINGS

Man with a Blue Sleeve

c1512
32×26in/81.3×66cm
Oil on canvas
National Gallery, London

This portrait, once believed to be of the poet Ludovico Ariosto, has also been thought to be of Titian himself, as the letters "TV" are signed on the parapet. We may never be sure of the sitter's identity, but he is certainly a confident and commanding figure, as was Titian, who was sufficiently sure of himself to make an offer for the highly prized *senseria* in 1513 (see page 20).

By the beginning of the 16th century, portraiture, both in the Netherlands and central Italy, had moved towards a greater realism. In the Netherlands the sitter was often shown in a room, sometimes with a glimpse of landscape seen through a window behind the head. A different convention was used in central Italian portraiture, where there was usually little indication of a specific interior. Instead, the wall behind the sitter, a surface parallel to and not far behind the picture plane, was a pictorial device to create shallow space, within which the subject was placed with a platform-like parapet just in front of him. This may perhaps have been a suggestion of a windowsill, but more importantly it created a distance between subject and viewer, thus imparting a sense of formality. In such portraits the subject was usually shown full-face, taken to just above the waist and with the head high up in the composition, forming a triangle secure on the steady base of the body.

Venetian portraiture developed in much the same way as in central Italy, although Giorgione, possibly influenced by Leonardo, brought to the formula his own personal form of sensual but elusive poetry. In this early masterpiece of Titian's there is still a strong Giorgione influence, particularly in the blurred and softened edges seen in some areas, and in the use of the parapet, which gives a dramatic twist to the body (*contrapposto*). But there is also a strength and sureness which is Titian's own, and he uses the traditional device of the parapet to project the forceful, almost intimidating personality of the sitter forward into our space. The marvellously fashioned blue sleeve presses out over the parapet, seemingly beyond the picture plane. Its very texture gives a sense of physical presence in the real world, and creates a little breakthrough in the barrier between him and us. The quilted sleeve and the edge upon which it rests indicate tangible space, yet the overall integrity of the canvas' flat surface is maintained.

An underlying sense of aloof detachment, a removed containment, is echoed in the color scheme and handling of the paint. Although there is a soft warmth in some areas, the dominance of blue creates a cool climate, both pictorially and emotionally. Light, falling upon the pyramidal structure, is used to illuminate and clarify the tones and forms, yet at the same time it blurs definitions, losing some contours in shadow and implying rather than stating the passage of one form or texture to another. The dark cloak, its fur lining rubbing against the satin sleeve, creates a resonant silhouette punctuated by accents of light, the crisp edge of the white border echoing the curve of the hairline to the left of the eye, which in turn echoes the overall shape of the pose. Although the man is turned away from us, with his left eye softly shielded in shadow behind the sharpness of the nose, we feel that in a moment he might turn toward us, or tire and look away. His keen, perceptive gaze creates a psychological dilemma: his eyes invite us to approach across the narrow space – but can we be sure that we would dare to?

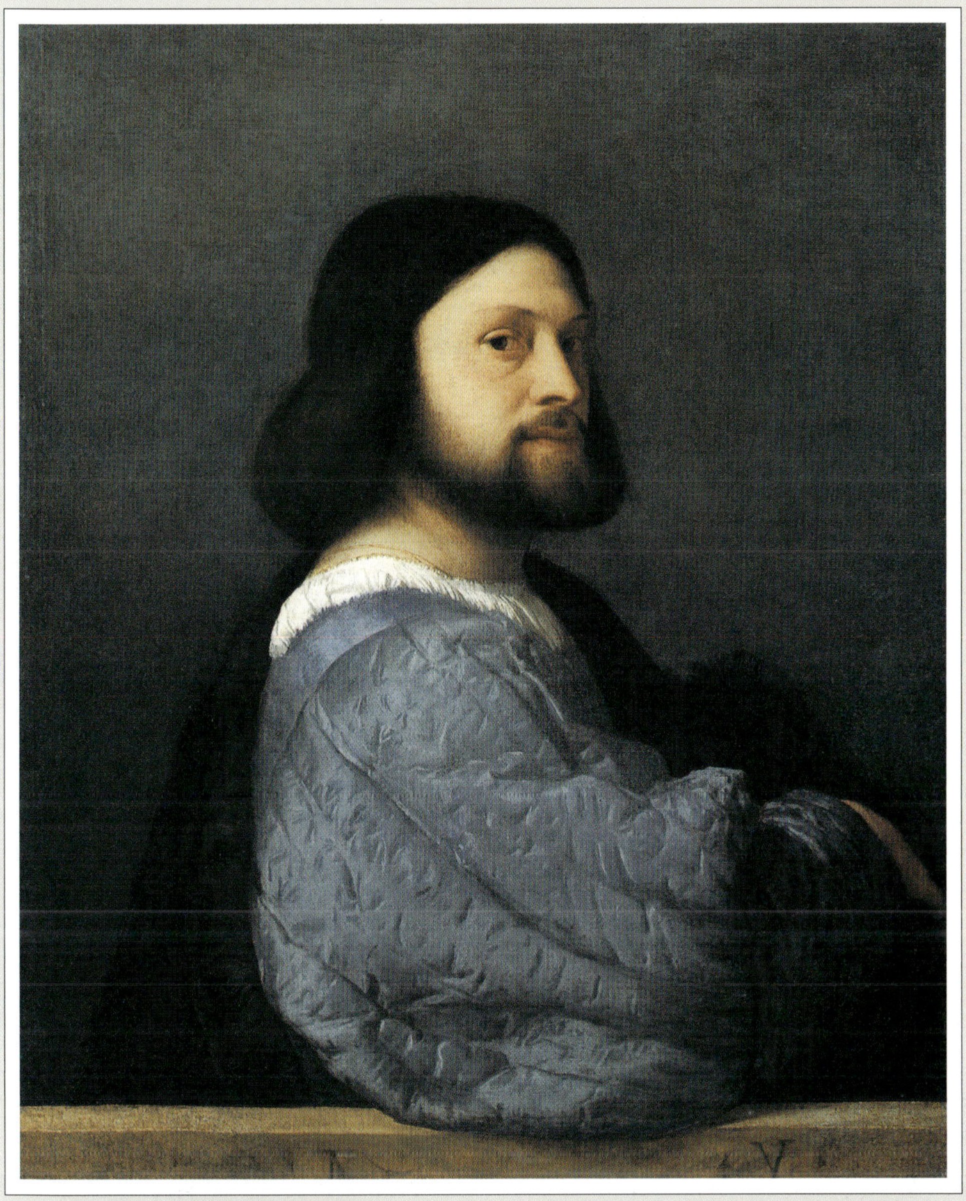

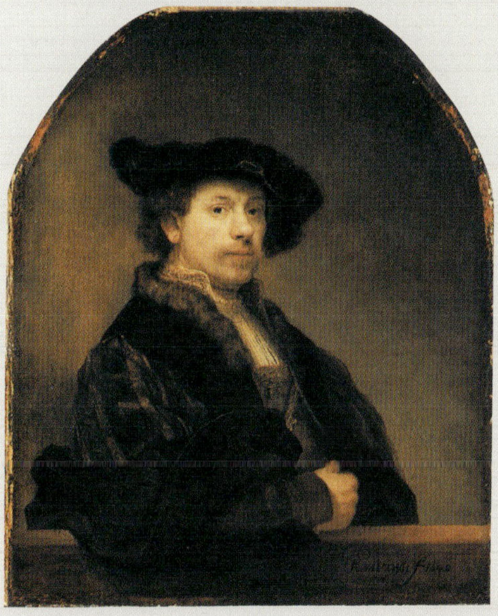

This painting can be seen as being essentially about contrasts — near and distant; hard and soft; cool and warm; intimate and detached. The quilted blue sleeve and the clear edge upon which it rests create a definite tangible space, yet the overall integrity of the flat surface of the canvas is maintained. The sitter's air of aloofness is echoed in the color scheme and the handling of forms; although there is a soft warmth in some areas, the predominant color is blue, creating a cool, restrained climate. The painting established a new canon in portraiture, and Rembrandt admired it so deeply that he based a self-portrait on it (left), using virtually the same composition but with modifications of lighting and color.

REMBRANDT
Self-portrait
1640, National Gallery, London

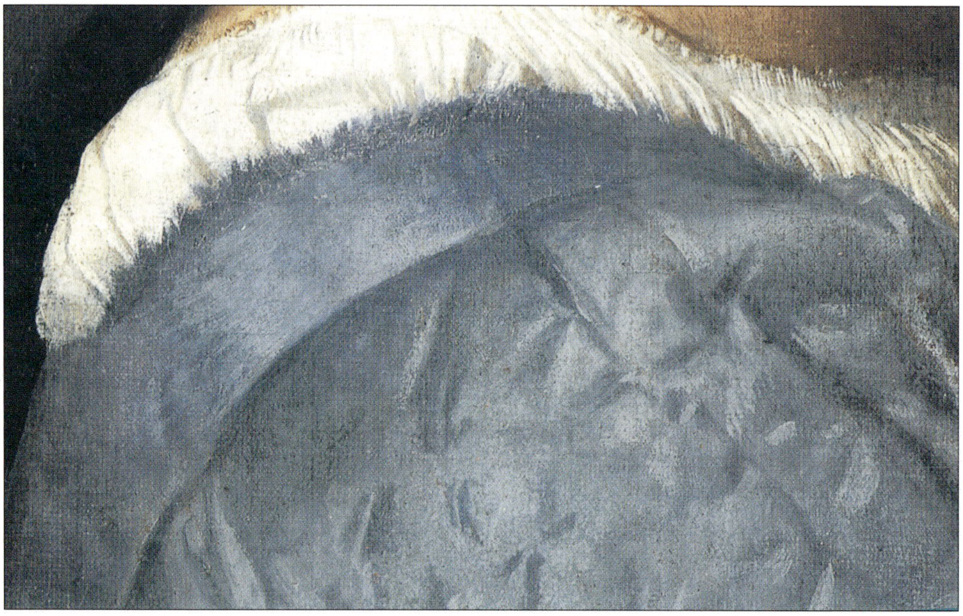

1

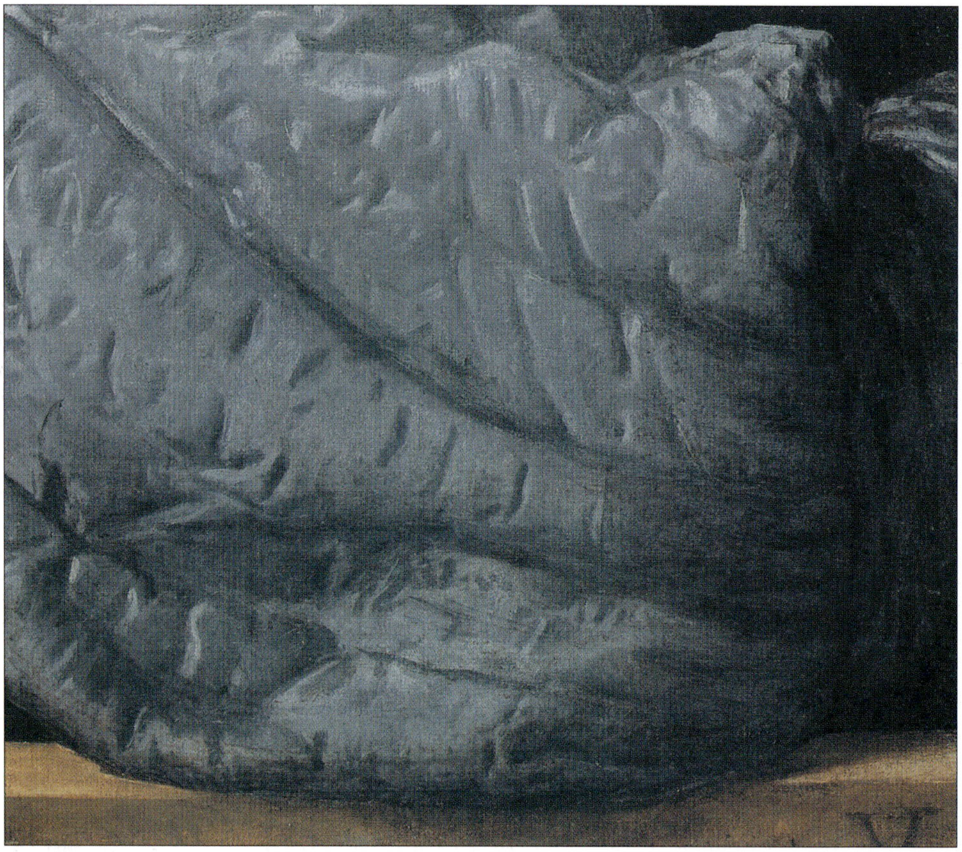

2

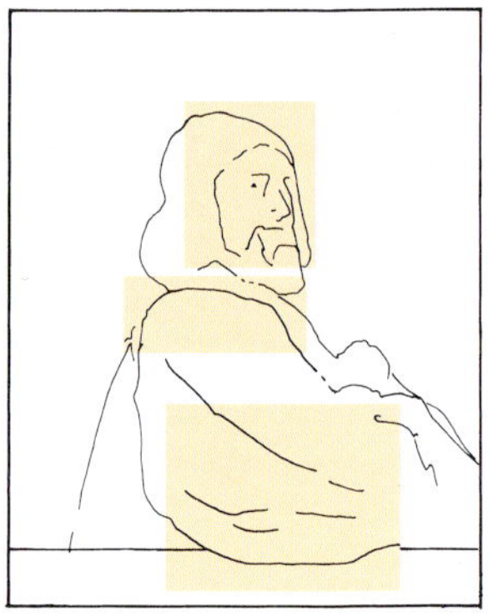

1 The white of the shirt's edge, applied with short, brisk strokes, blends tonally at the top side with the high key of the flesh, while the white edge below contrasts with the cooler blue. White is carried into this blue to indicate light moulding the direction of form, and this is enhanced by the fine line of golden yellow indicating the chain. This, applied thickly over a series of thin glazes, creates a ridge that physically catches light, adding an extra crispness to the definition.

2 Alternating touches of darkened blue and white are dabbed into the broadly applied blue of the sleeve. Canvas, glimpsed in some places through the blue, gives a violet tint to the material, its warmth linking with the surrounding browns.

3 *Actual size detail* Light flesh hues have been thinly applied to reveal the subtle planes of the bone structure. The delicate pink of the lips adds warmth to the shadow on the sitter's left cheek and to the corner of his right eye, the lids and sockets of which are strongly but delicately defined by single lines of brown. The beard and hairline, applied gently with a soft brush, are in places barely discernible from one another, with brown being worked across the flesh, allowing individual hairs to spread and trail to create an indistinct edge. In contrast to these softly blurred areas, fine lines have been used to define the nostril, creating a sharpness that accentuates the alert intelligence of the face.

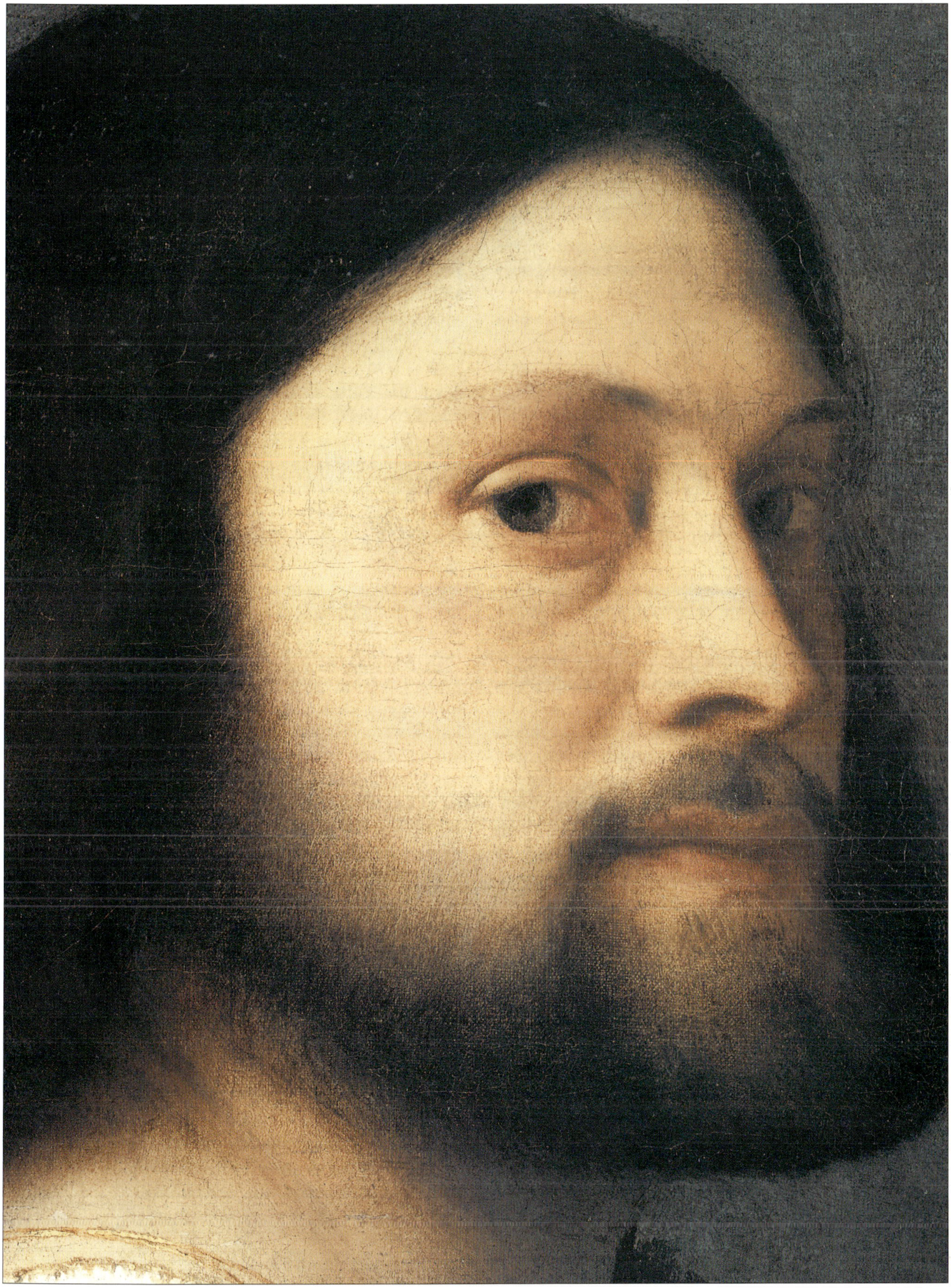

3 *Actual size detail*

The Pesaro Altarpiece

1519-26
15ft 8in×8ft 10in/4.78×2.68m
Oil on canvas
Santa Maria Gloriosa dei Frari, Venice

The year after the completion of the *Assumption*, Titian was commissioned by the Pesaro family to paint another work for the Frari church, but the painting was not completed until seven years later. This altarpiece was to be even more innovatory than the previous work, taking the traditional subject of a *sacra conversazione* ("holy conversation"), but blending the holy with the secular, so that there is as much emphasis given to the donor family as to the Madonna, Child and saints. The donor was Jacopo Pesaro, Bishop of Paphos and commander of the Christian fleet that defeated the Turks in 1502. The church was also his burial place, and we see him kneeling in prayer on the left of the picture. Behind him, a flag bearing the Pesaro emblem and the Borgia coat of arms, alluding to Pope Alexander VI, is carried by St Maurice, the patron saint of the crusaders, who pulls behind him two vanquished prisoners, a Negro and a Turk. The Frari is a Franciscan church, and on the right are the two main saints of the order, St Francis and St Anthony, with some members of Jacopo's family. At the top of the painting is the cross of the Church Triumphant, while above Jacopo, at the tip of the banner, is an olive branch symbolizing its peace. Directly below the cross is St Peter, holding the scriptures, his hand positioned at the crossing of two strong opposing diagonals that introduce a type of dynamic composition quite new in a subject like this.

The painting is situated above one of the side altars in the left aisle, and again Titian has organized his design in relation to its location. As one approaches diagonally from the nave, the painting has the effect of extending the interior space obliquely by means of the asymmetrical arrangement of the forms. The perspective vanishing point is located to the left, outside the picture area, thus drawing the spectator into the drama, and the Madonna and Child, who would previously have been shown in the center, are here placed to the right. A diagonal running from the heads of the Madonna and Child to Jacopo is crossed by another one descending from the olive branch to the kneeling figure in red, and these are stabilized by the two vertical columns — almost certainly derived from those separating the aisles from the nave in the church itself.

In the midst of the drama, Titian soothes us with harmonies of color, creating an atmosphere of warm tenderness, and tempering the violent diagonal movement of the figures with a settling triangle of strong color with the blue and golden yellow of St Peter's robe at its tip. St Peter unites the picture, not only in terms of color and composition, but also in terms of the earthly and the divine. The diagonal arrangement of the Madonna and other figures evokes the spiritual and the heavenly, while the color reminds us of the painting's two-dimensional surface, and hence of the worldly and the particular. In the upper sphere of the Madonna's realm a canopy of cloud hovers, casting its shadow on one of the massive columns that leads us down to the donor's family, who are depicted in various ways to emphasize the temporal realm. The elders are shown in strict profile, as though caught on a coin of the past, while at the far right a young man is seen from a less formal three-quarter view. Just in front of him is the youngest of the family, Giovanni, the only one of the figures to look straight at us. His presence is compelling and immediate, a mirror image of the reality of our own concrete world. He seems to invite us in to join his family in their joyous and respectful homage.

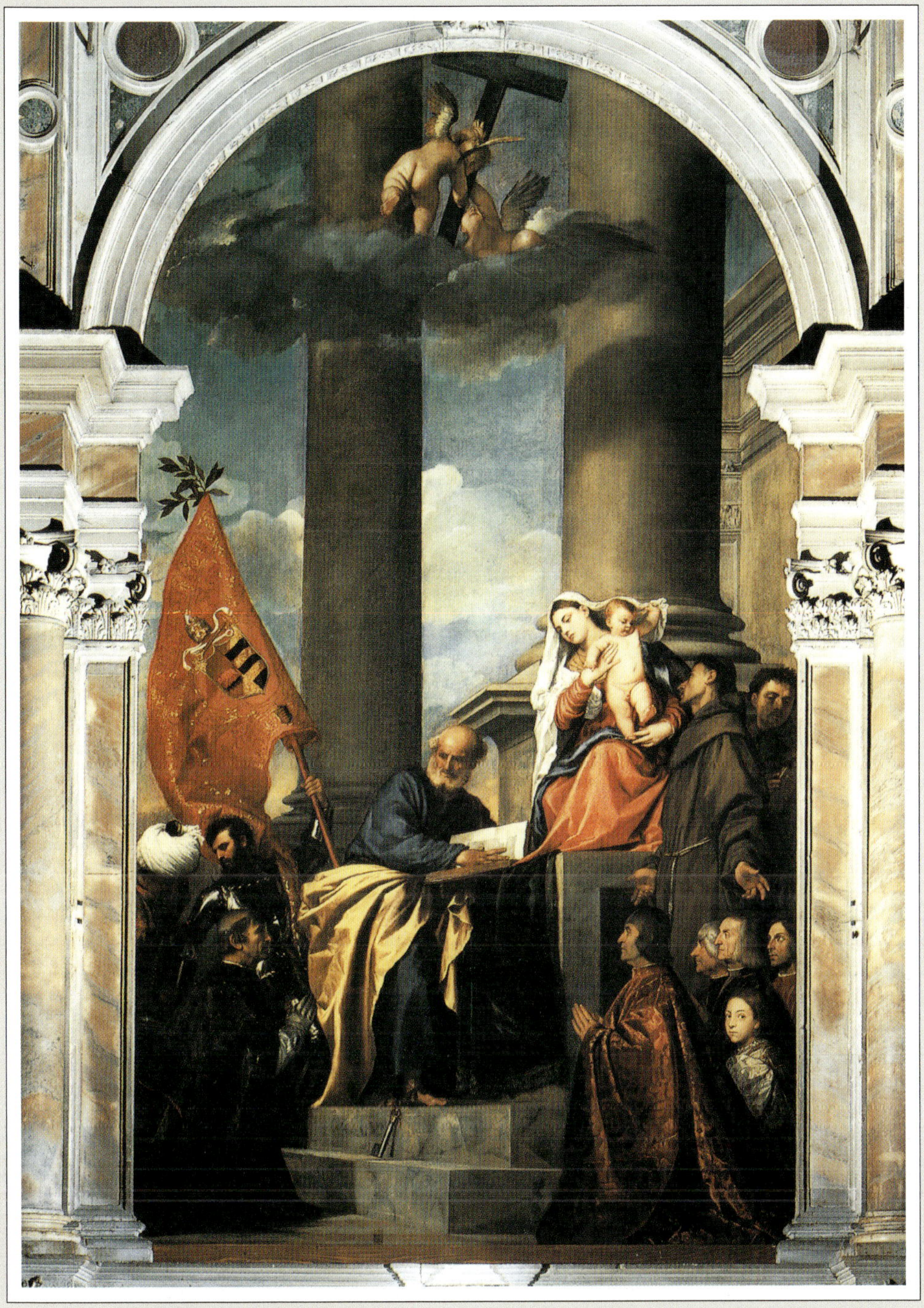

This work, departing radically from the traditional type of composition, marked a turning point in Venetian painting. Instead of placing the Madonna and Child in an obviously dominant position at the center of a secure triangular structure, which had hitherto been the convention, they are here placed obliquely to one side, balanced by the opulence of the donor family. Some years earlier, in 1508, Titian had painted the donor, Jacopo, Bishop of Paphos, being presented to St Peter by Pope Alexander VI. The latter was a member of the powerful Borgia family, and Titian clearly thought it diplomatic to include the Borgia coat of arms above Jacopo's head in this work. There is a new sense of informality in the painting, particularly in the realistic treatment of the younger members of the donor family, that seems to make their experience more personal.

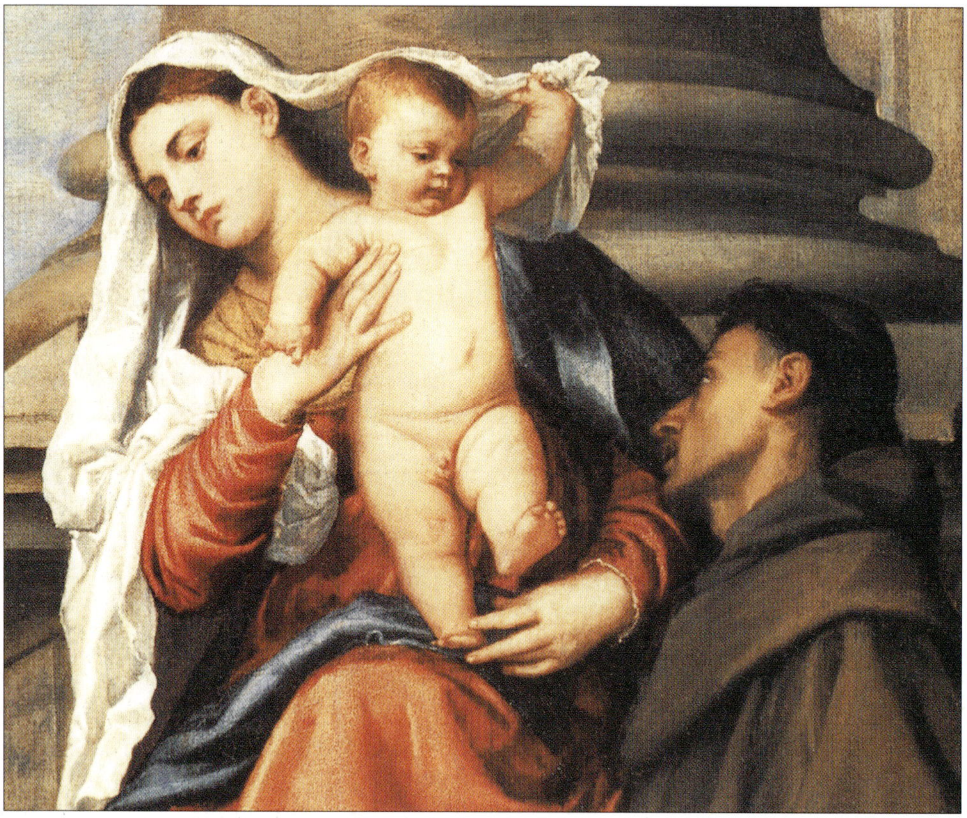

1

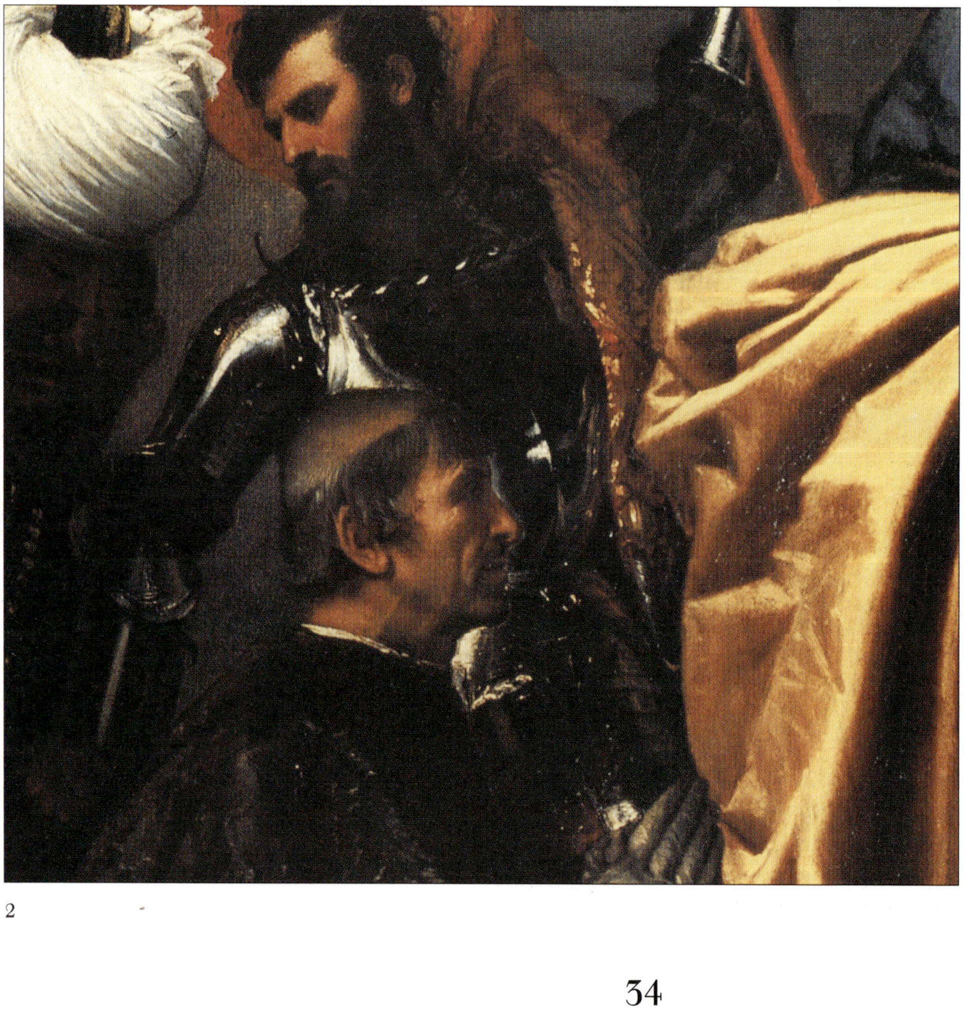

2

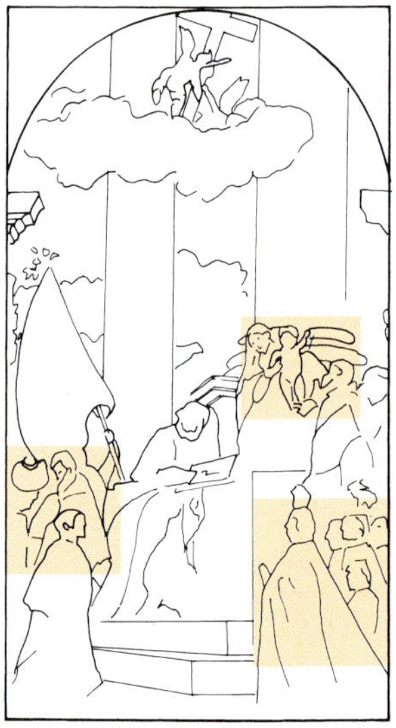

1 The light cream of the high-keyed flesh focuses our attention on the Madonna and Child, while the relatively small tonal gradation gives their forms a gentle fullness and harmony. The strongly defined shapes of the Madonna's crisp white veil frame the two heads in a translucent white glazed over blue, and the child's limbs reflect the intense red of her gown through lightly blurred strokes. These gentle touches soften the contours of his form, and provide a contrast with the face of the adoring saint. This is much earthier in both color and application, linked with his more coarsely textured robes.

2 The flesh hues of Jacopo and the standard bearer both reflect and are modeled with the warm golden-yellow of St Peter's robe and the orange-red of the swirling banner. Speckled impasto dabs of reflected yellow are deftly brushed into the banner, creating a lovely flicker of light that animates the gold-embroidered surface. The armour is molded with smooth black glazes, given life and sparkle by sharp, darting slashes and dots of thickly applied white.

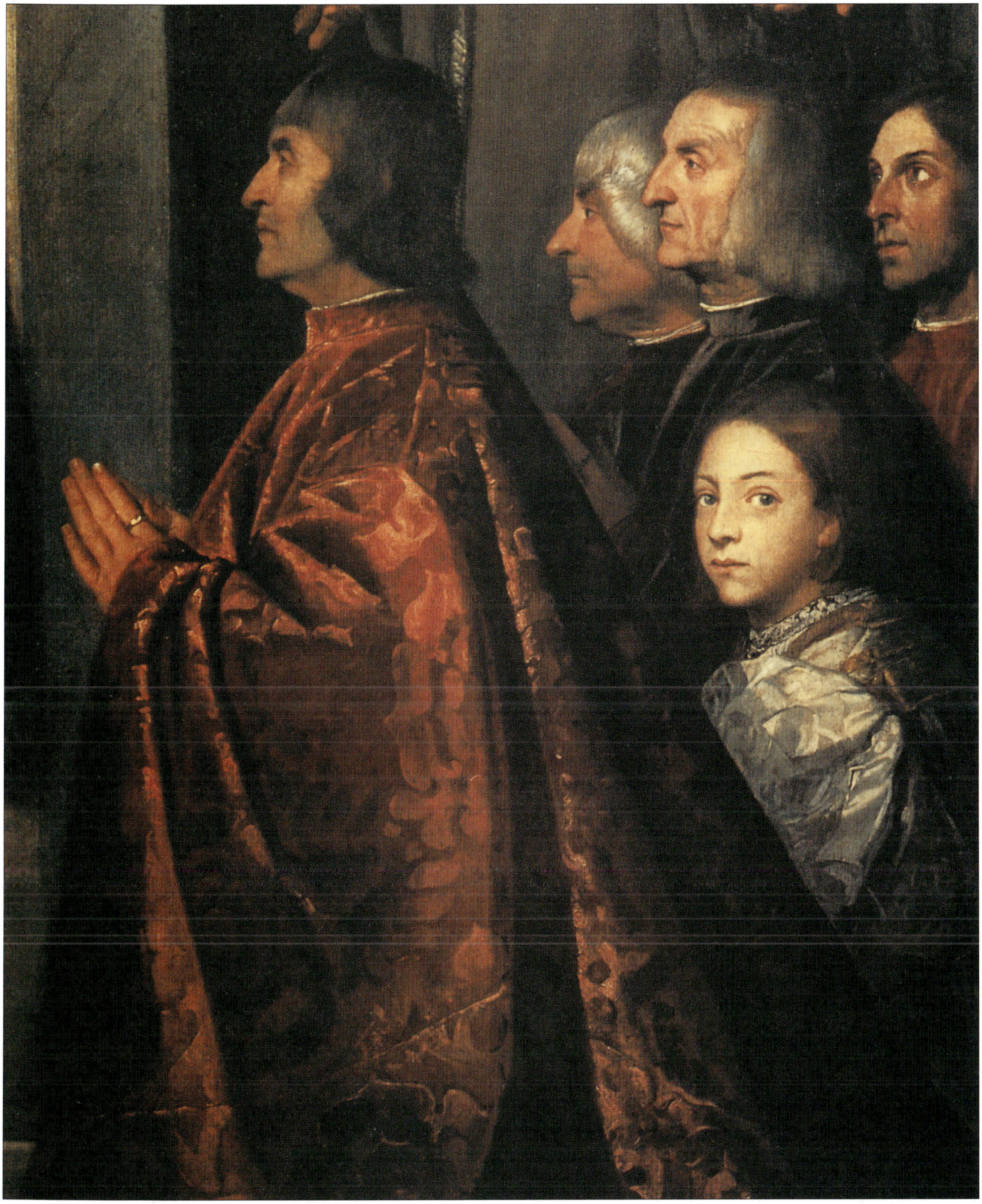

3

3 Over a pyramid of red, fairly loose but coherent touches of yellow-orange and a darker wine-red are applied across the basic glaze to animate the play of light within the triangular shape. Individual facial types are carefully described with fine descriptive brushwork. The young boy's face is the highest in tonal key, and this, combined with the white of his puckered sleeve, makes it shine out from the surrounding warm colors to create a focal highlight.

Bacchus and Ariadne

1520-23
69×75in/175×190cm
Oil on canvas
National Gallery, London

When Alfonso d'Este (husband of the infamous Lucrezia Borgia) became the Duke of Ferrara in 1505, he decided to use his newly acquired fortune to enhance his status by becoming a collector-patron of art. In his castle at Ferrara there was a series of small rooms known as the "alabaster chambers" because the marble in them was of such a lustrous white, and he decided to decorate these with paintings of subjects from the classical world. From the writings of Ovid, Catullus and Philostratus, the Duke chose several episodes involving Bacchus, the god of wine, and asked Raphael to paint a Triumph of Bacchus for the series. Raphael, however, declined and Alfonso then decided that Titian should paint three works for him, of which this picture is one. *Bacchus and Ariadne* is one of the first of Titian's mythological works, which he described as *poesie*, in which mood is conjured, as always by Titian, through color as an expressive entity in itself. Colors are applied as though they were precious stones, creating a rich enamel-like surface where individual hues sing out brilliantly, yet are orchestrated into a unified whole by the tonal arrangement of the composition.

Ariadne awoke on the island of Naxos to find she had been deserted by Theseus — in the painting, a tiny boat on the horizon can be seen disappearing to the left of her shoulder. As she dejectedly wanders the shore, Bacchus sees her and, leaping from his chariot, consoles her and offers her immortality through his love. The painting is full of movement and jostling tension as Bacchus is drawn compulsively towards Ariadne at the extreme left — and we with him. Ariadne is like a magnet, attracting all the figures from Bacchus onwards, but just as her gaze meets his their bodies are drawn into opposing directions, like corkscrews, creating a tension that continually sparks both their expectations and our own. Like Bacchus, we are kept hovering in mid-air; the space between them is electrically charged, crackling over the heads of the big cats whose supple, contained litheness underlines the sensuality of that magnetic attraction. A diagonal running from Ariadne's foot, up to the right through Bacchus' cloak and then up into the trees, is balanced by another from his back foot through to his head. This divides the composition into two interlocking triangles of which Bacchus is the motivating link, drawing together the color orchestration of the painting. His lower limbs are part of the earthy color scheme, uniting the exuberant procession — orange, browns, ochers and greens pulsing in their physical mass — while his cloak, a beautiful clear, scintillating pink, seems to materialize out of the warm blue of the sky. Ariadne's gesture acts as a pivot to the revelers, checking and resolving their pressing weight with her spiraling movement, and is taken up by the bacchante just behind the god himself. This echoing of the poses forms a link between the figures, stabilizing the boisterous throng, as does the tonal interplay of light and dark. The ecstatic writhing of the figures in the earthly lower half, building into a rising crescendo as Bacchus and Ariadne's eyes meet, finds release in the sky, where clouds curve and peak toward the top left corner to culminate in a constellation of stars, while the horizontal cloud above Bacchus meets and pierces the one that echoes Ariadne's vertical twist. The stars not only symbolize Ariadne's future in the heavens, since she is made immortal through Bacchus' love, but also bring completion to the pent-up rhythms of the painting and an end to the touching narrative that it illustrates. As so often in Titian's work, he has resolved conflicting elements on two separate levels through a unified harmony of color and design.

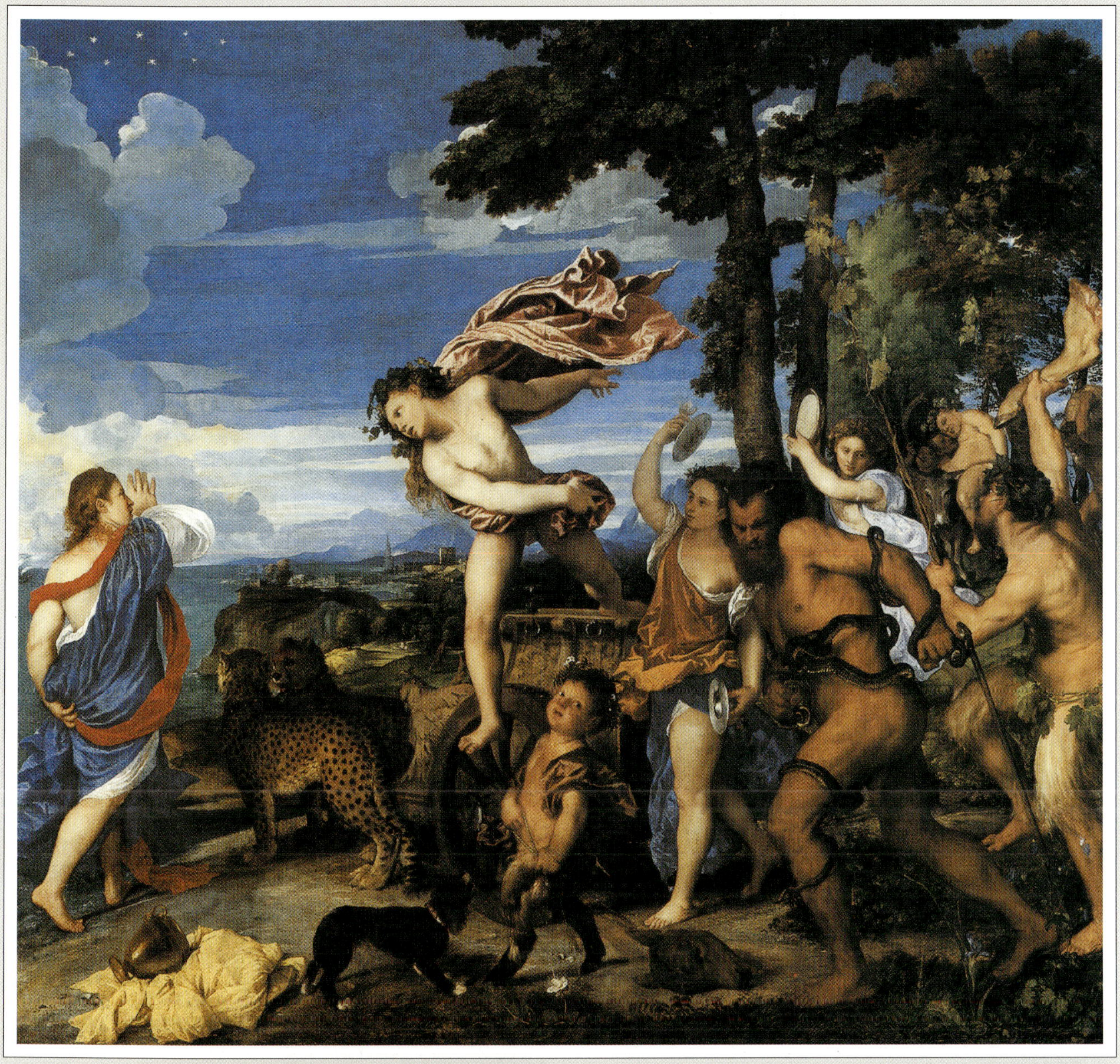

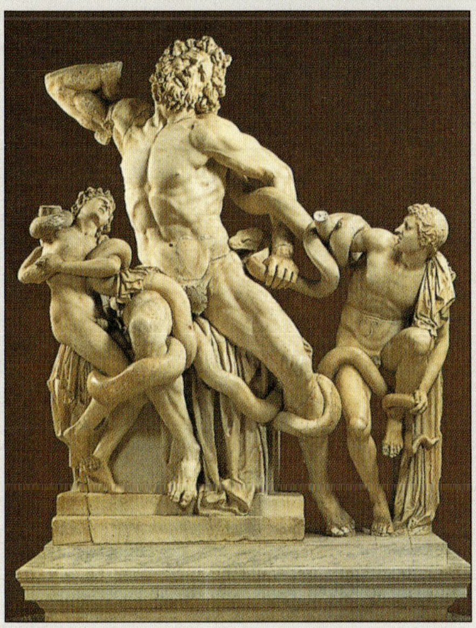

The contrasting blue and red and the billowing movement of Ariadne's clothing increase the drama of her twisted *(contrapposto)* pose, while her dejection as she gazes after her departing lover Theseus is suggested by the way she is placed – isolated on the edge of the composition. But as Bacchus leaps toward her, her body turns back to him, and he simultaneously twists away, his movement leading the eye to the mass of drunken revellers. The bearded figure with the snakes owes much to the late-Hellenistic sculpture *Laocoön*, one of the major classical works rediscovered in the Renaissance, and interestingly, Titian's painting was listed simply as the *Laocoön* in a late 16th-century inventory. Laocoön was a Trojan priest who had disobeyed Apollo by warning the citizens against the Greeks' wooden horse, and the sculpture (left), shows him and his sons struggling against serpents sent as punishment by the god. Its drama and monumentality were an inspiration to generations of painters and sculptors.

Laocoön
2nd century BC
The Vatican, Rome

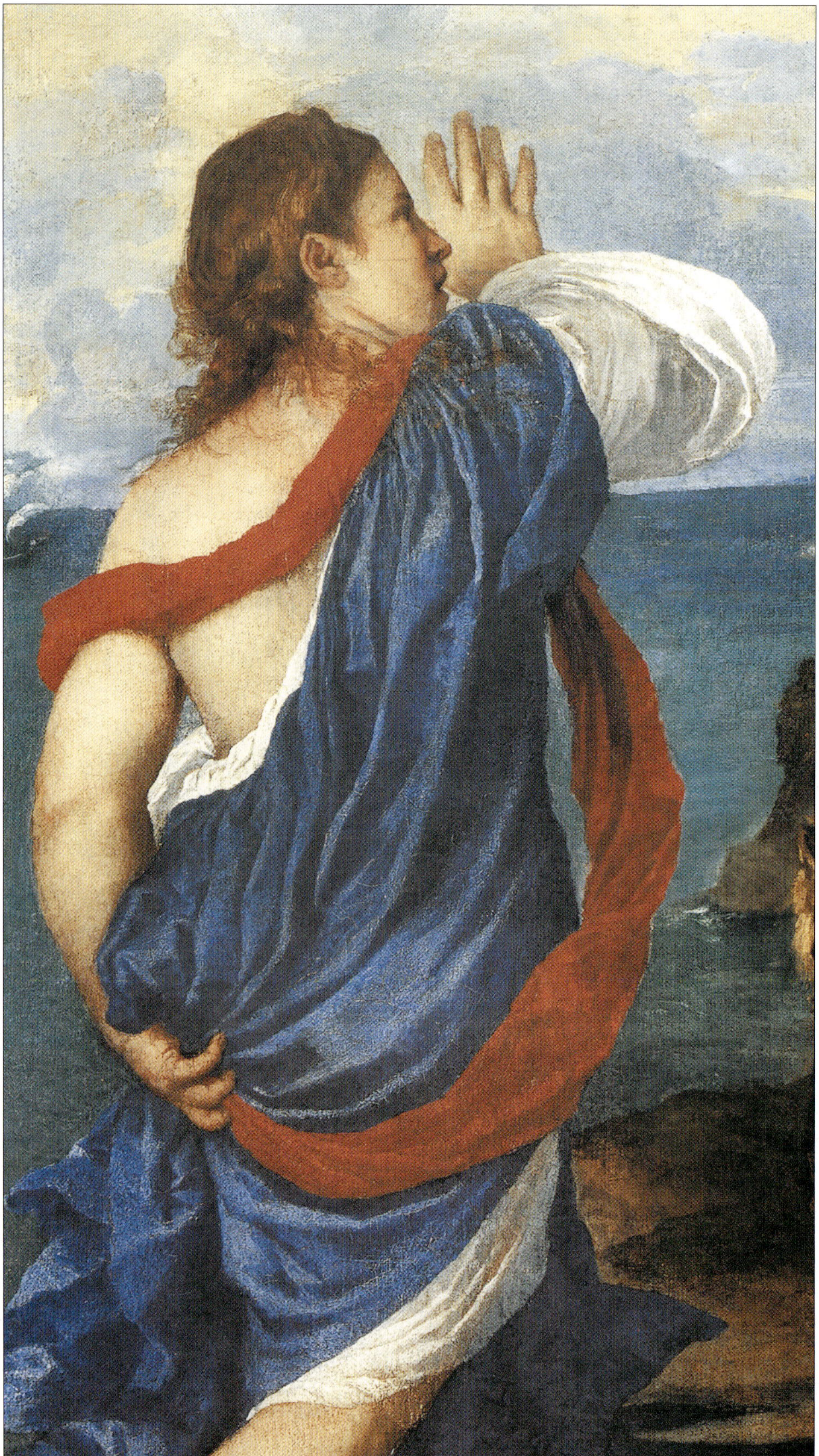

1

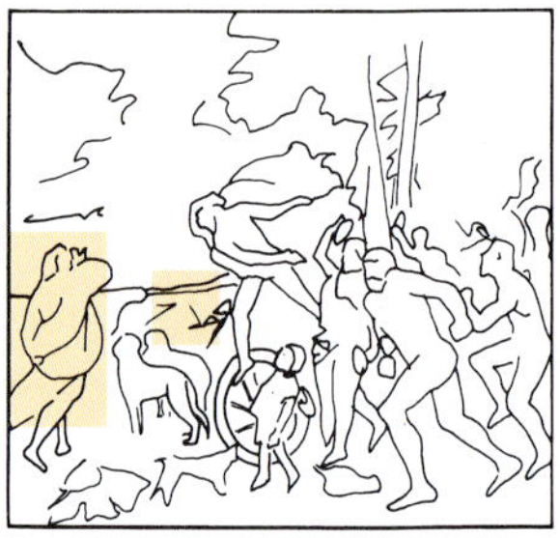

1 Ariadne's dress of precious ultramarine, linking with the greenish azurite of the sea, is strongly contrasted with a vibrant, intensely saturated red. This hot red, less varied in its tonal modelling, finds a muted echo in the wavy open strokes of the hair, brushed lightly over both red and blue across her shoulder. The white of the boat's sail, picking up some of the blue of the sea and clouds, seems almost to have been blown onto the canvas in deft strokes that follow the curve of the billowing cloth.

2 Layers of green glazes build up a spatial recession that is deepened by the cool blues that become more and more dominant towards the horizon. Warm light pinpoints forms with broadly touched-in strokes of yellow-green among the deep verdant greens. The distant spire is washed in with transparent paint so that it only partly covers the enamel-like surface of the glazed shapes beneath.

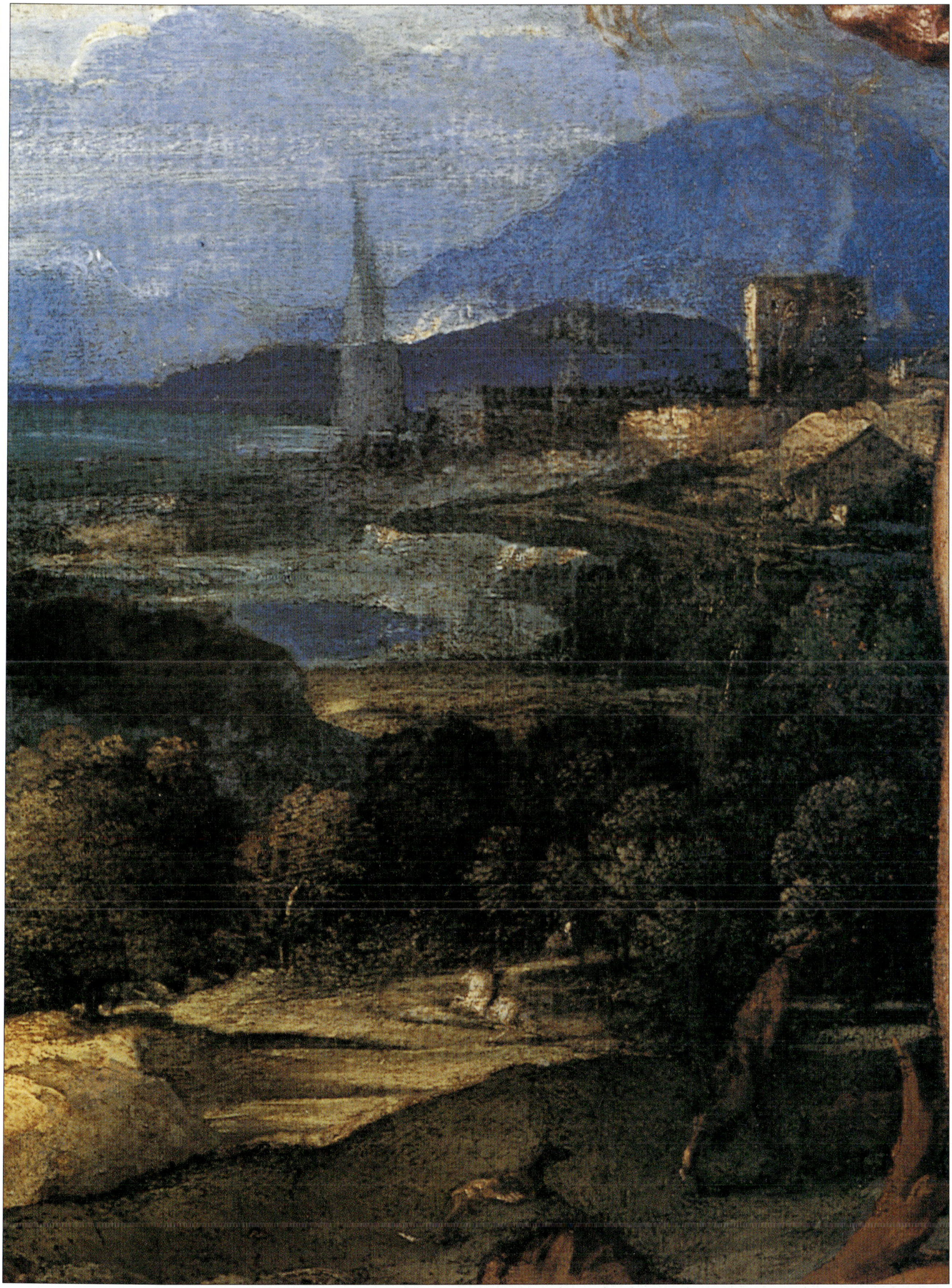

2

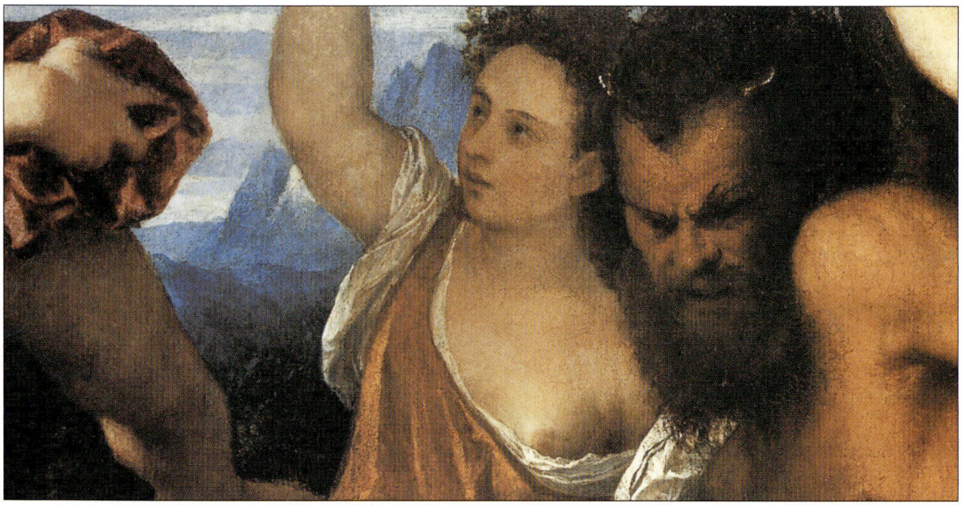

3

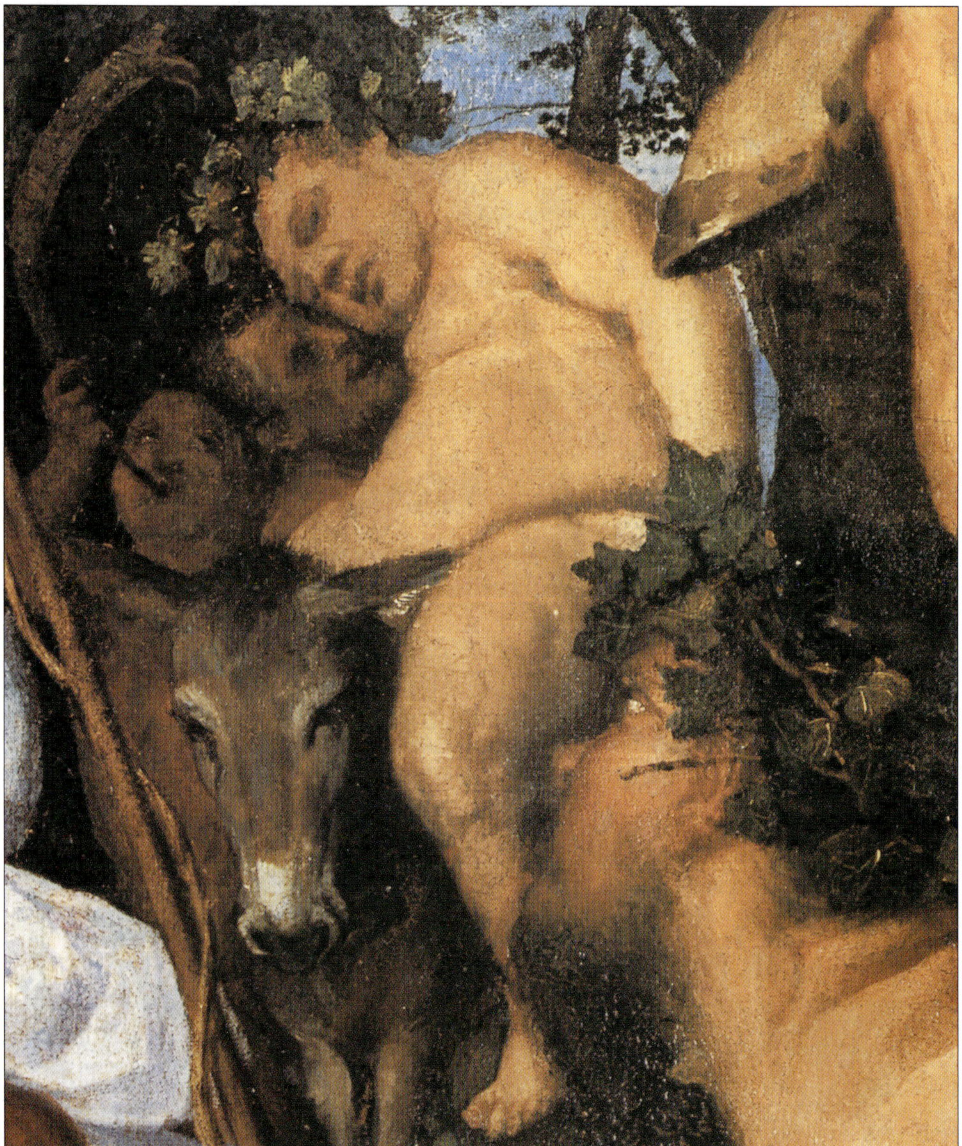

4

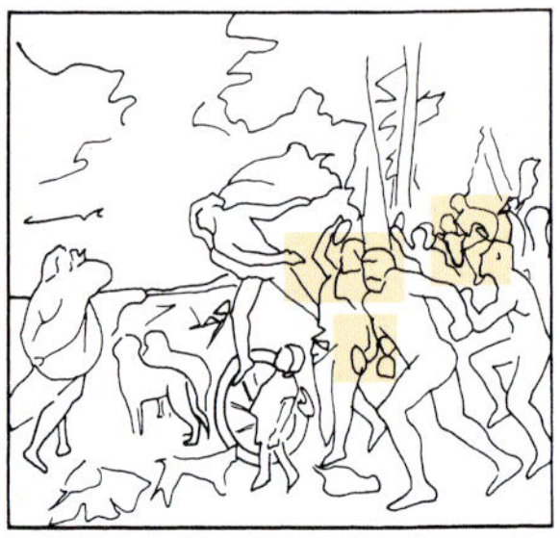

3 The clear translucent blue of the glazed sky contrasts with the diffused light that falls across the figures, who are in turn contrasted both in their flesh tones and by the manner of their modeling. For the gentle bacchante in the centre, paint is applied with a smooth, softly gradated touch, while the drunken reveler is described with an appropriate sketchy brusqueness. Bacchus' firmly blocked-in wrist is linked by its high tone to the sky, whilst his swirling robe is boldly described with short, abrupt strokes of sugar pink and deep wine-red that resonate against the cool airy blue.

4 Soft, dappled touches give an impression of drowsiness appropriate to the reveler's drunken state, and the creamy flesh tones are blurred and indistinct. By freely allowing the small brush to spread as it is turned, Titian has given a soft fullness to the plump forms, contrasting with the crisp treatment of the foliage. Loose speckled touches of yellow-green give a lively animation to the vine-leaf headdress.

5 *Actual size detail* The deep translucent glow of the glazed ultramarine is contrasted with the smooth milky-cream of the bacchante's firmly modeled flesh. A sharp edge of white gives a metallic dazzle to the cymbal, which is drawn into with fine black linear detailing. This crisp definition contrasts with the robes, which are freely painted with loose, fluid glazes, a painterly equivalent to the swirling movement.

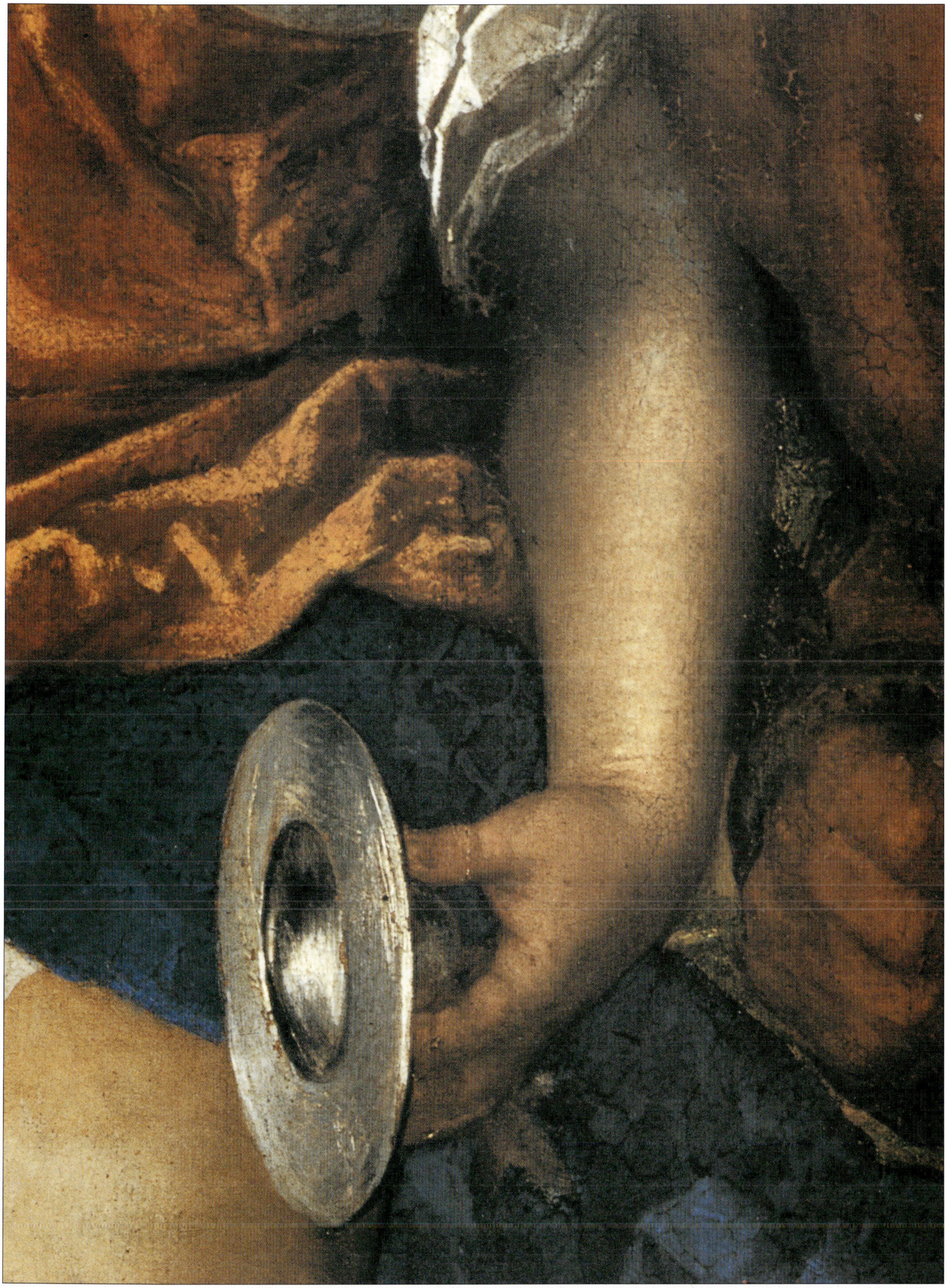

5 *Actual size detail*

The Entombment

c1525-32
$58^1/_4 \times 80^3/_4$in/148×205cm
Oil on canvas
Louvre, Paris

The dating of this work is somewhat uncertain, but it is generally believed to have been painted between about 1525 and the early 1530s for the Duke of Mantua. It is a deeply moving work, with a profound sense of pathos, rendered in a manner that combines an observed realism of human gesture with the powerful dramatic unity of both form and colour. It is possible that it was painted after the death of Titian's wife in 1530, and was therefore affected by his grief.

The central group of male figures creates an arch that shelters the shadowed Christ, their forms seeming to provide a cave-like hollow suitable for an entombment. This is augmented on one side by a dark, foreboding space and on the other by the responses of the women, the older ones showing a restrained acceptance of death and the young ones a fiery anguish. John, at the center (whose *chiaroscuro* treatment is reminiscent of Giorgione) links the male group to the female as he looks back at the two Marys. His head is inclined to balance the younger Mary's, while the semicircle between their heads echoes the hanging bulk of Christ. The overall grouping maintains the relief qualities of a carved sarcophagus, the shallow space occupied by the figures seeming to confine them, adding to the sense of brooding emotion. Through this space, its smallness underlined by the way the figures are placed up to the edge of the canvas, there is a very gentle rocking motion – like an achingly slow pendulum. This movement, initiated by the bent arm of Mary Magdalene, flows through the arm of the man in green (believed by some to be a self-portrait) through the legs and sagging torso of Christ, to be then turned back towards John by the bent figure of the man on the far right. This somber death-knell is given a poignant counterpoint by a variety of facial expressions and actions: these people are no longer classical "ideals" but touchingly human. In contrast, Christ's face and upper torso are set in deep shadow, as though to protect us from the full impact of the tragedy while allowing him a deep sense of privacy even among those closest to him. Against the grave horizontal swing of these elegiac rhythms, two verticals act as hanging weights, emphasizing the gravitational pull down to the earth. One vertical is implied by the crown of thorns below Christ's knees, indistinct at first, but, once seen, impossible to ignore, and pointing up his humiliation. The second is provided by his hanging arm – limp, drained of life, and trailing pathetically behind as the mourners struggle to move the inert body with dignity.

Around the ashen form, color resonates: the body in its white winding sheet is made yet more tragic by the vivid, living hues that surround it, from the red of John's clothing and the complementary green of Joseph of Arimathea's tunic to Mary's orange dress. The yellow in the dress is taken up in the olive-greens and then cooled by the blues of the Virgin Mary's robes and the sky, where all the colors reappear in the gathering clouds, which echo the mood of desolation. Titian seems deliberately to play off surface textures – of flesh, clothing, foliage and the ground, from which the earth colors seems to emanate – with brilliant sureness and sensitivity of touch. The range of brushwork is remarkable, from a careful clarity, seen especially in areas of tonal contrast, to a bold, free treatment, with broken, loose strokes giving a rich and scintillating shimmer to areas such as the clothing of the bending man on the right, whose long, trailing scarf echoes Christ's hand. Such passages, which evoke an almost sensual response, draw us into the tragedy in a way that no words could – we, like the mourners, move gravely across the scene with heavy steps. In this great work, Titian has used color and design to involve us completely, so that we participate in a moving yet enriching spiritual experience.

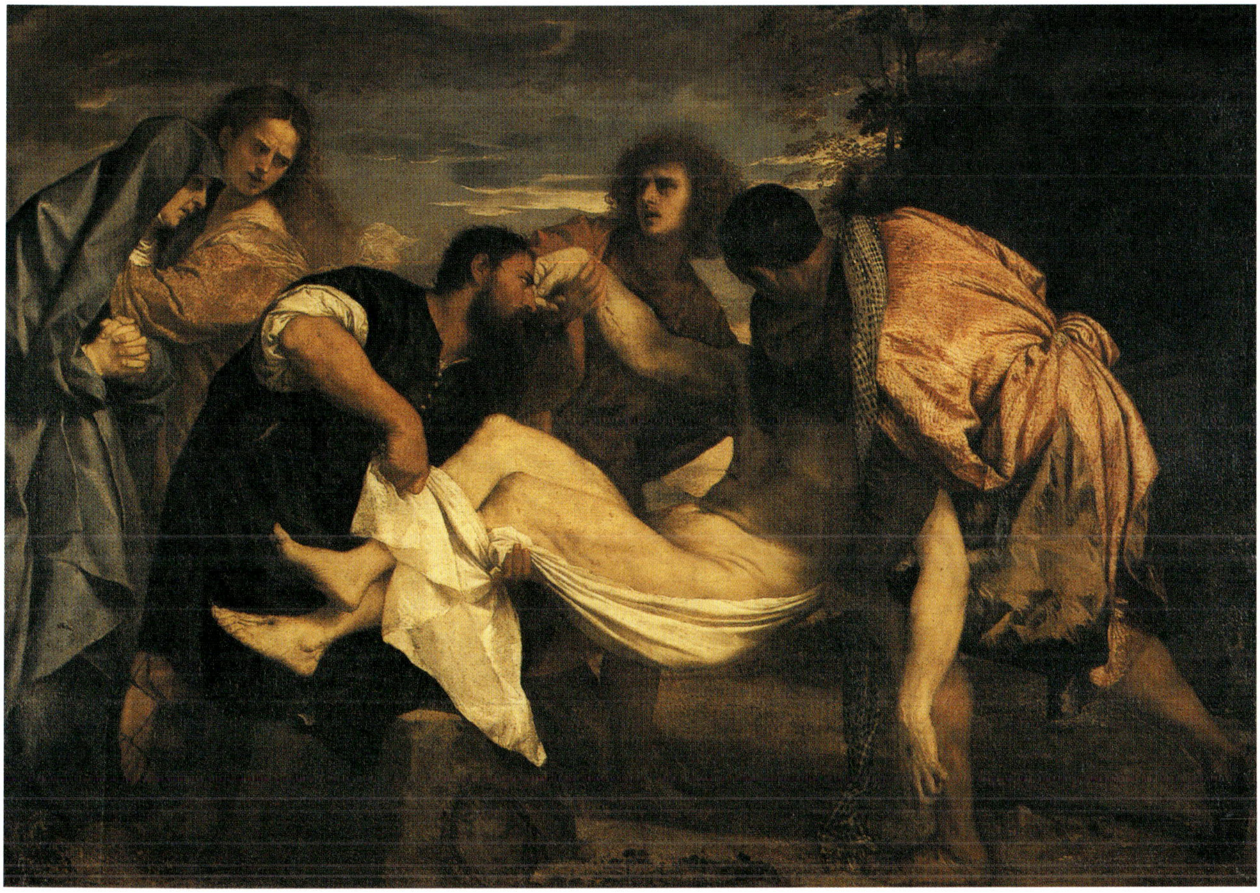

While much of the grouping is enveloped by heavy shadow, we are never in any doubt as to what is happening or what the participants are feeling. The horizontal format seems to stress the mortality of the mourners surrounding the ashen body of Christ, but even though they are in movement, actively gesticulating in their terrible grief, it is the still body that dominates the scene. Titian probably based his design on the death scenes carved on early Christian *sarcophagi* (stone coffins), constructing a frieze-like composition that, although derived from a controlled classical structure, is here made personal and human, with all the figures seen as individuals coping with loss in their own way.

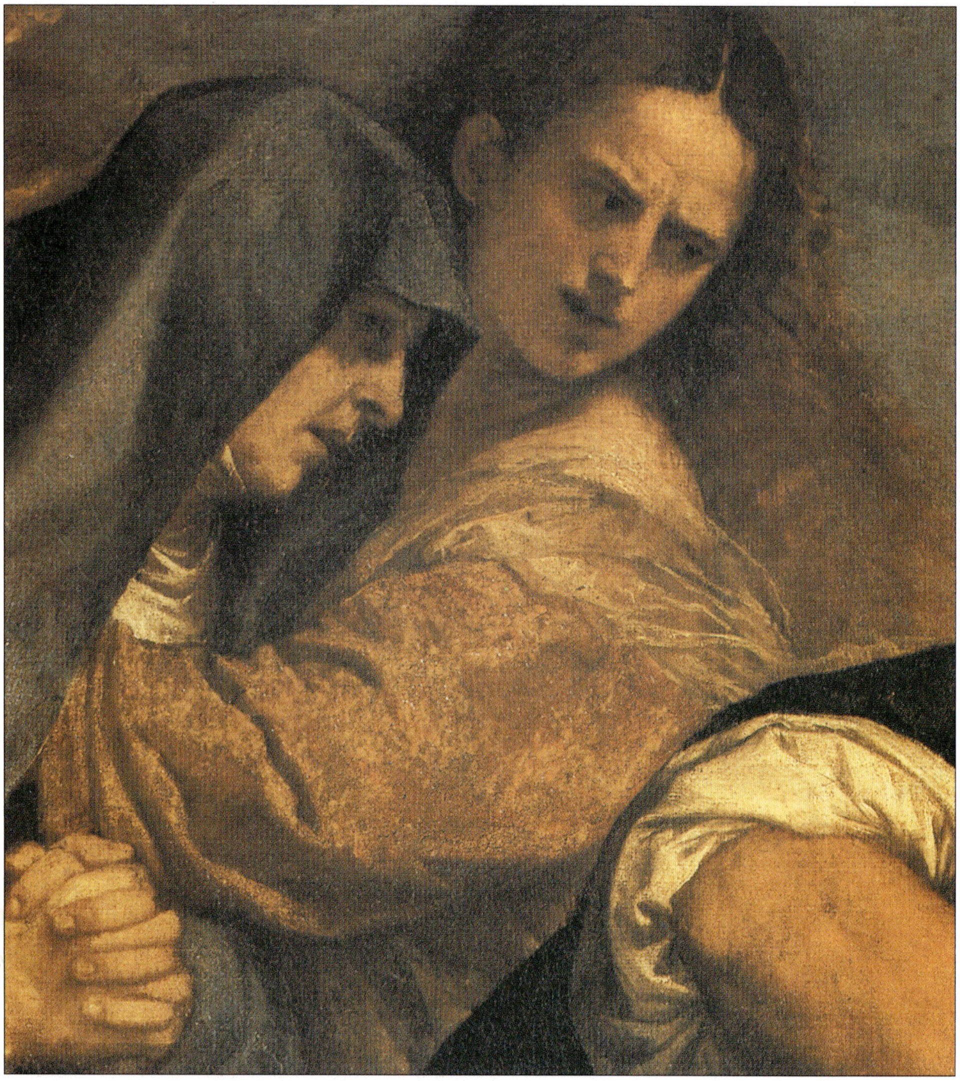

1

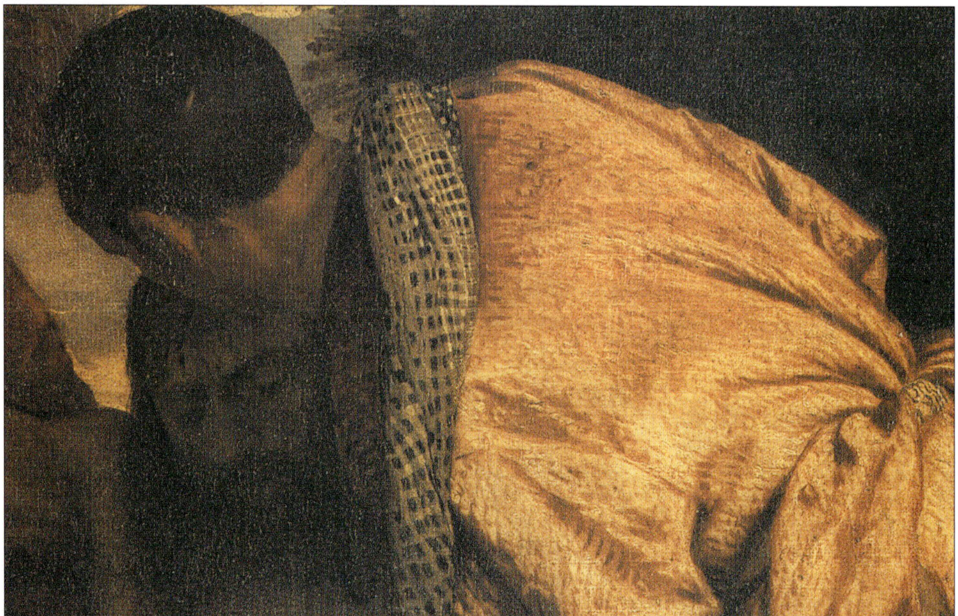

2

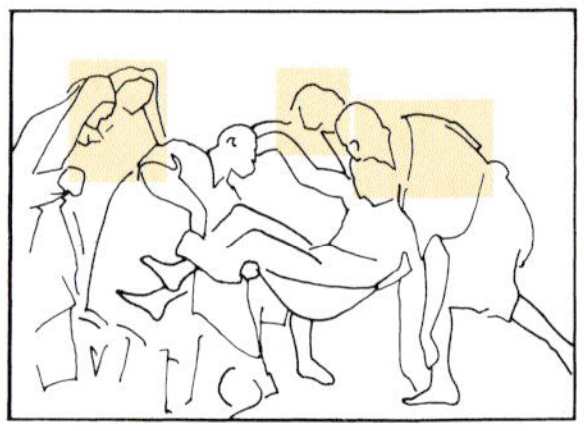

1 The blue of the sky, warmed by touches of golden yellow, is also used for the shawl of the elderly Mary, its smooth treatment and muted coolness contrasting with the brown-red of Mary Magdalene's roughly brushed-in hair, flesh and sleeve. The lightness of her diaphanous scarf is suggested by freely brushed, directional strokes and transparent glazes of creamy-white.

2 Loosely cross-hatched strokes of golden-orange and red are applied freely to describe the shimmering fabric of the bending man's garment. Directional strokes of darker red mould the shadow between creases and give some structure to the broad handling, which contrasts with the regularity of the checked scarf. Set against the light mass of the background, Christ's face is enveloped in dark shadow, his features made almost invisible by the subtle tonal variations of the understated dark-brown drawing.

3 *Actual size detail* The high-keyed patch of light flesh tone is softened at its edges, blending into the dark framing silhouette of the hair, which is brushed in gently with strokes following the direction of the curls. The blurred edge of the hair merges into the blue of the sky on the extreme left, but a creamy-white cloud gives accent to its form, with a single curl of reddish brown highlighted against the more substantial layer of white. The soft, wiry facial hair and the dramatic pocket of warm brown shadow that submerge the eyes and mouth, are prevented from completely dissolving the features by the fine modeling of the light side of the face, where delicate, angular touches accent the nose, chin and furrowed brow.

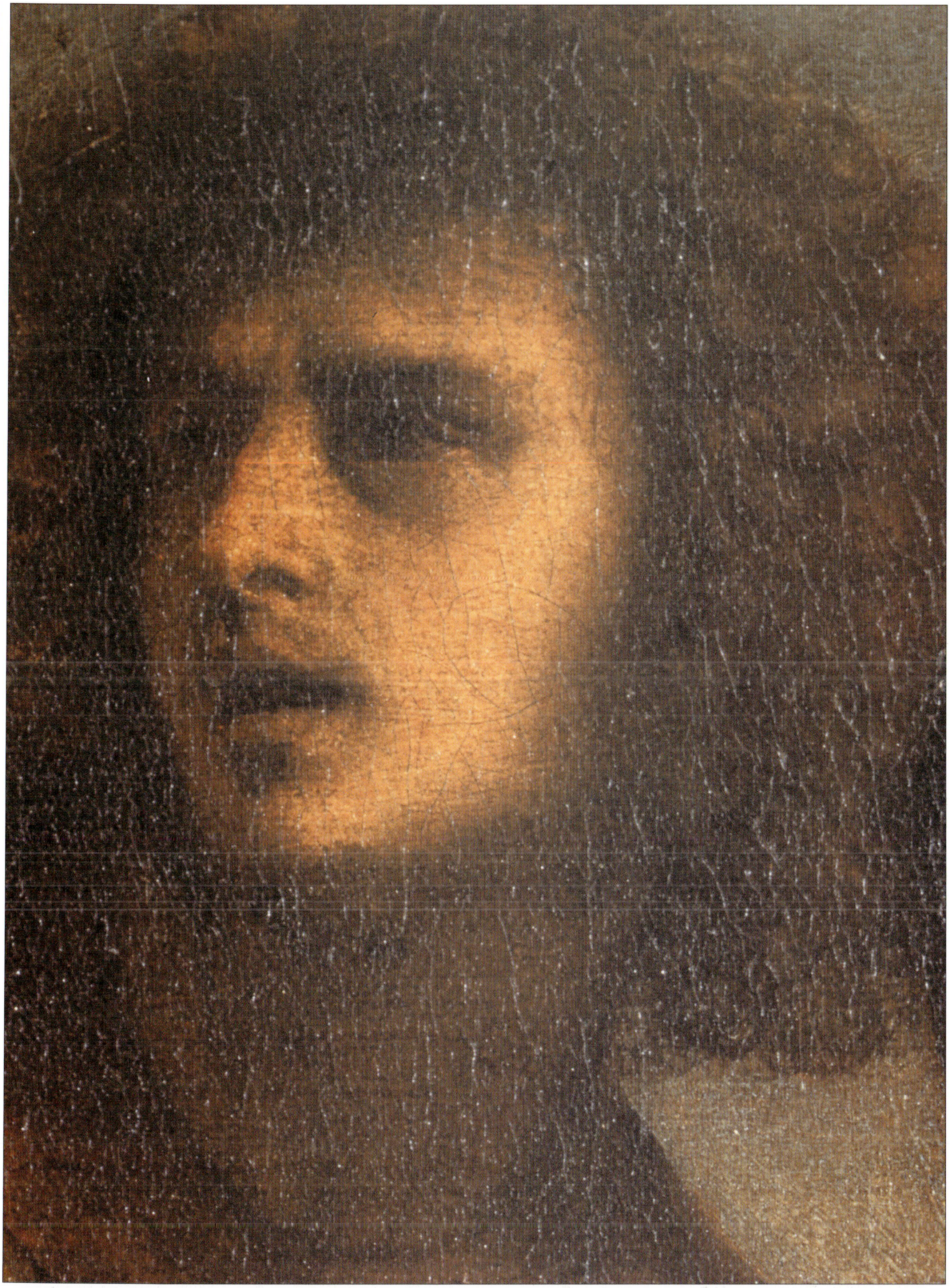

3 *Actual size detail*

The Venus of Urbino

1538
47×65in/119×165cm
Oil on canvas
Uffizi Gallery, Florence

In 1509 Giorgione had painted a *Sleeping Venus* (Dresden) showing the goddess in an idyllic landscape, lying naked with her eyes closed, asleep or deep in reverie. We see her beauty but she does not see us, thus remaining pure and uninvolved. Titian's work is more physical. Although his Venus is shown with the symbolic attributes of a goddess – a posy of roses and a myrtle tree silhouetted in the background – he has moved her into the intimate setting of a domestic interior, where she lies in comfort with open eyes and an air of pampered luxury. We sense her as a mortal, physical woman for whom nudity is not a constant state, as it might be for an idealized goddess in a divine realm. She is enjoying her nakedness, the warm air across her body and the ministrations of her maids, who go about their tasks in the background with professional efficiency. By her feet her little dog, a symbol of devotion and fidelity, snuggles contentedly. At any moment, we feel, it may wake and frisk around, perhaps investigating what the maids are doing before returning to its special, cosseted place in its mistress's world.

Lying back, at one with her setting, Venus's body is modeled – almost caressed – with ochers and pale rose tints, soft yet full and firm against the crisp, ruffled sheets. The smooth openness of the forms is in exquisite contrast with the delicacy of the red pattern below, its angle creating a diagonal that both raises her to acknowledge her audience and sets up a rhythm with the foreground horizontals and the verticals that make up the background. The dark drapery, which not only frames Venus's beauty but also increases the sense of intimacy, combines with the regularly tiled floor and the precise treatment of architectural space to create an ordered structure surrounding her. This measured order sets off her attitude of casual ease, a gently sensual ease that speaks of affection rather than carnality, and is reflected in her complete lack of self-consciousness. But although comfortable, she is deeply alluring, her flowing curves voluptuous against the stabilizing regularity of the room's right-angles. Titian has made his nude even more alluring by allowing her to retain her jewelry. Her hair, provocatively disarrayed, flows across her shoulder to her wrist, where a single bracelet adds an air of luxury and contrasts with the soft, rounded forms of the arm. The earring provides a focus for our eye, and from it we follow the line of the body down through the excitement of the reds and greens at either side, until finally the vertical of the drapery takes us to her nestling hand. This hand both shields and draws our attention to the most intimate area of her femininity, and the ring on her finger seems to make the gesture even more tantalizing. With tilted head, she gazes almost flirtatiously at us from the corner of eyes which, set beneath heavy lids, smoulder with a sultry langour echoed in the warm, heady Venetian sky behind her.

This kind of painting, providing, as it were, a "private audience" to sit and wonder in close proximity with a beautiful nude woman, was to appear frequently in the history of art, two notable later examples being Goya's *Naked Maja* and Manet's *Olympia.* It undoubtedly has a sexual content, but is more about the detached adoration of beauty than active sexual desire. We can sense this worship of beauty in the way Titian has applied the paint and orchestrated his color harmonies. The strong red and green, golden-brown and whites that set off the flesh tones in the foreground are taken up and repeated with equal intensity throughout the composition. Thus, although we are given the impression of tangible objects in three-dimensional space, the tapestry-like colors are a constant reminder of the flat surface of the canvas, allowing us to become spectators rather than participators in the visual splendor.

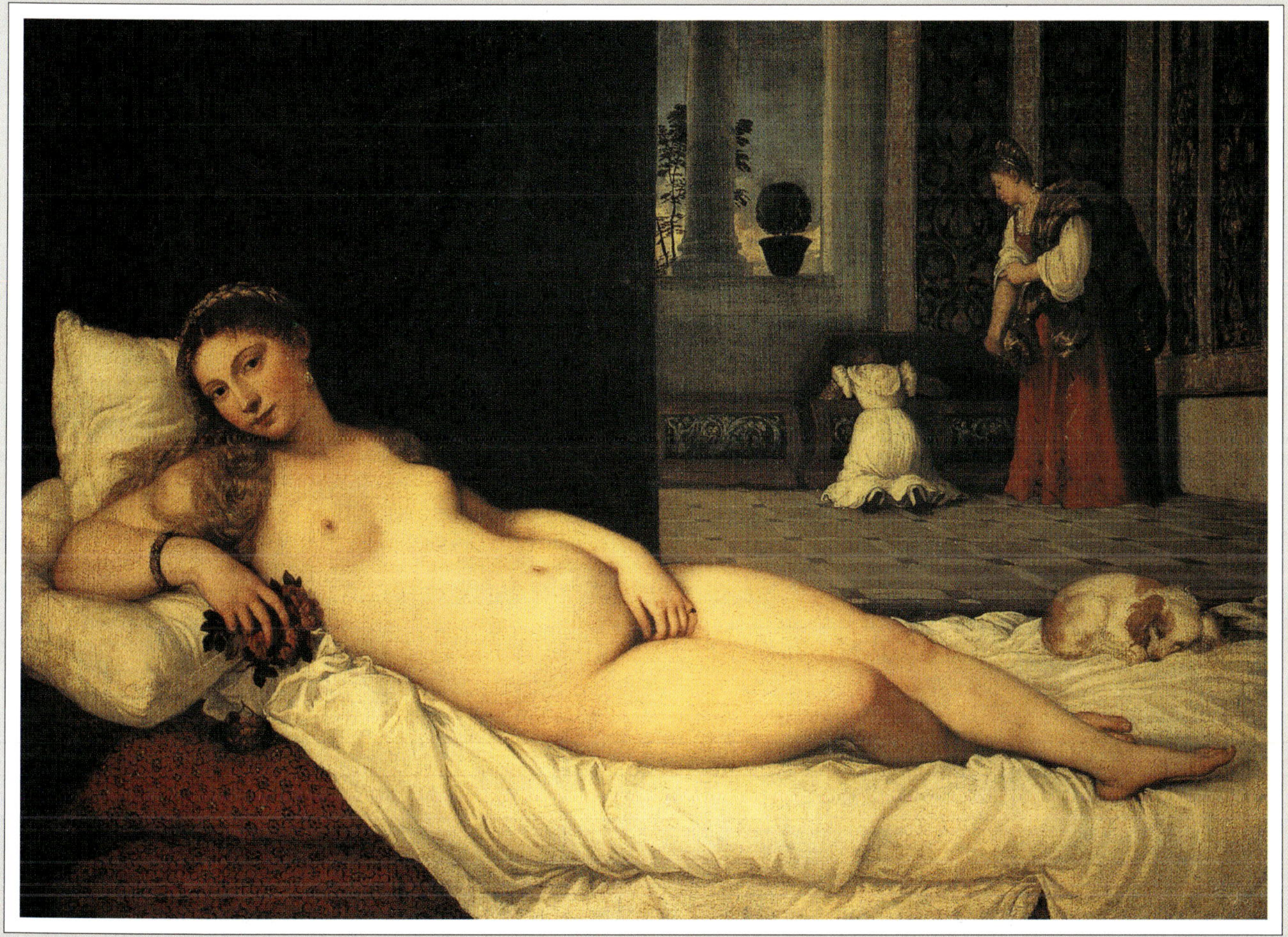

The painting originally belonged to Guidobaldo della Rovere, son and heir of Francesco, Duke of Urbino, at which time it seems to have been referred to simply as *La Donna Nuda* (the naked lady). Guidobaldo had married in 1534, and may possibly have commissioned the work to celebrate the occasion; the *cassone* (marriage chest) in the background seems to support this assumption. Whether it is an intimate celebration of marriage or a depiction of a mistress or courtesan, the painting remains a constant source of delight, and it is tempting to see it as a symbol of the union of a physical and emotional bond — an enchanting allegory of love and marriage.

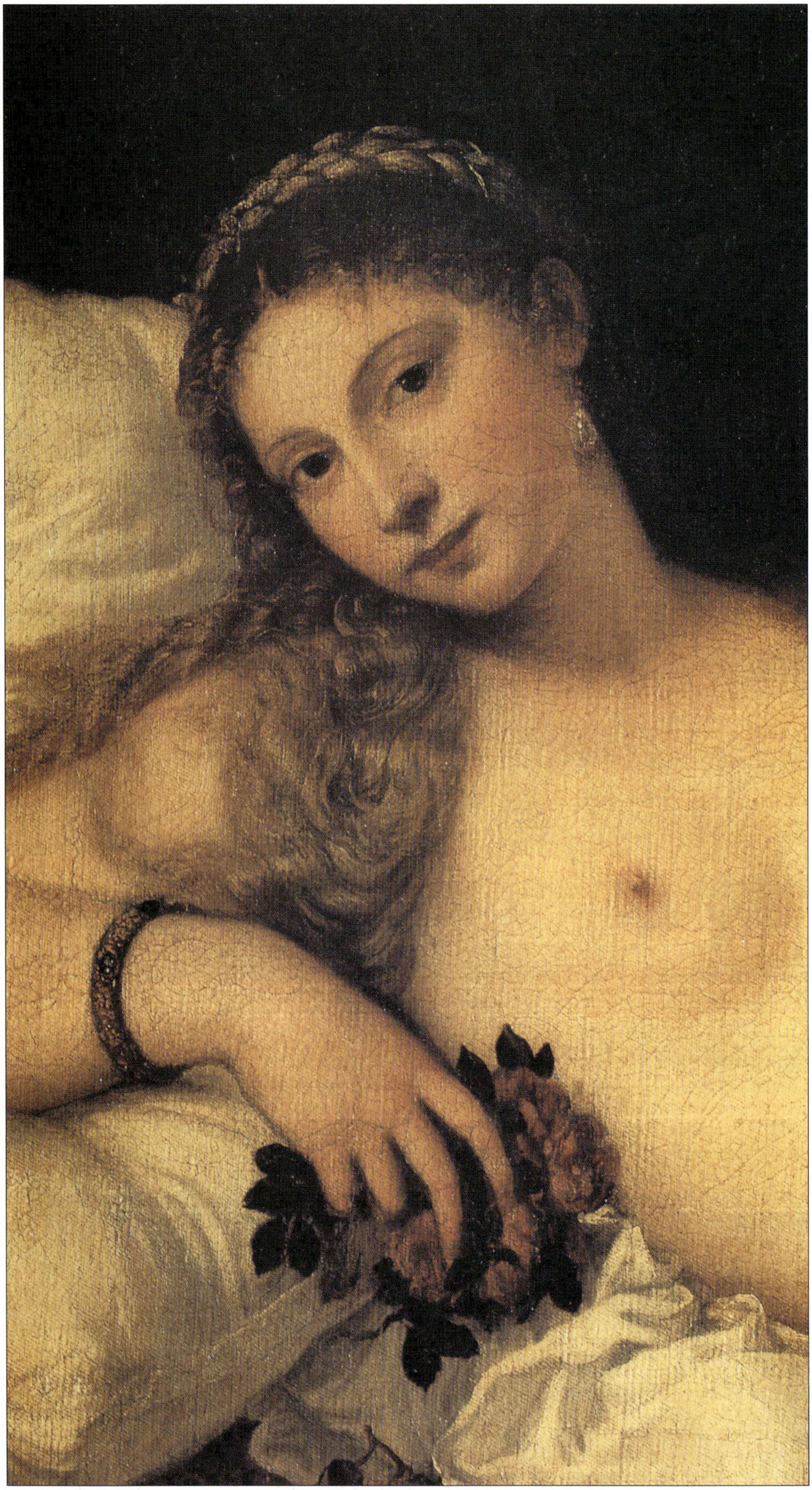

1

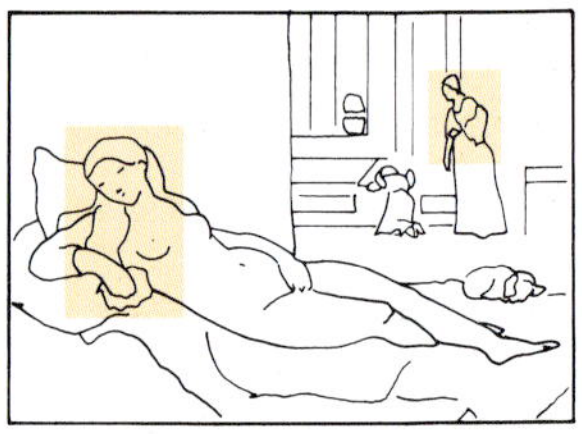

1 The deep red that clearly defines the shape of the lips is lightly brushed across Venus' cheeks and then taken down to her fingers and the posy of flowers. Softened to a delicate rose tint, the red is then used to hint at her nipple, lightly touched into the gently gradated flesh tones of creamy-white ochres and warm siennas. The contours of the ear and head are blended tonally into the hair and pillow, and fine wisps of dark brown paint, applied with curling linear strokes, tease her forehead and then flow in langorous rivulets across her shoulder. Heightened and warmed with golden brown streaks, these cascading waves of paint are contrasted with the undisturbed expanse of the chest, which is lightly molded by barely perceptible brushstrokes. Fine, detailed brushwork is used for eyelids, brows, bracelet and hair braid, with small pointed touches giving emphasis and a physical presence. This is especially noticeable in the treatment of the earring, where a tiny blob of impasted white is delicately dropped onto a silvery-gray glaze.

2 *Actual size detail* Touches of white and ocher, loosely trailed over the strong red to indicate the pattern of the skirt, are flicked up into the material across her shoulder. From there, browns, dark greens, and the cream and white of her flesh and sleeve, are brought down again into the skirt, the serpentine brushstrokes creating a lively and animated surface pattern. Browns and ochers are thinly applied to build up the pattern of the wall behind, while a thicker, shorthand-like notation of white enlivens her hair and the edging of the scarf around her neck.

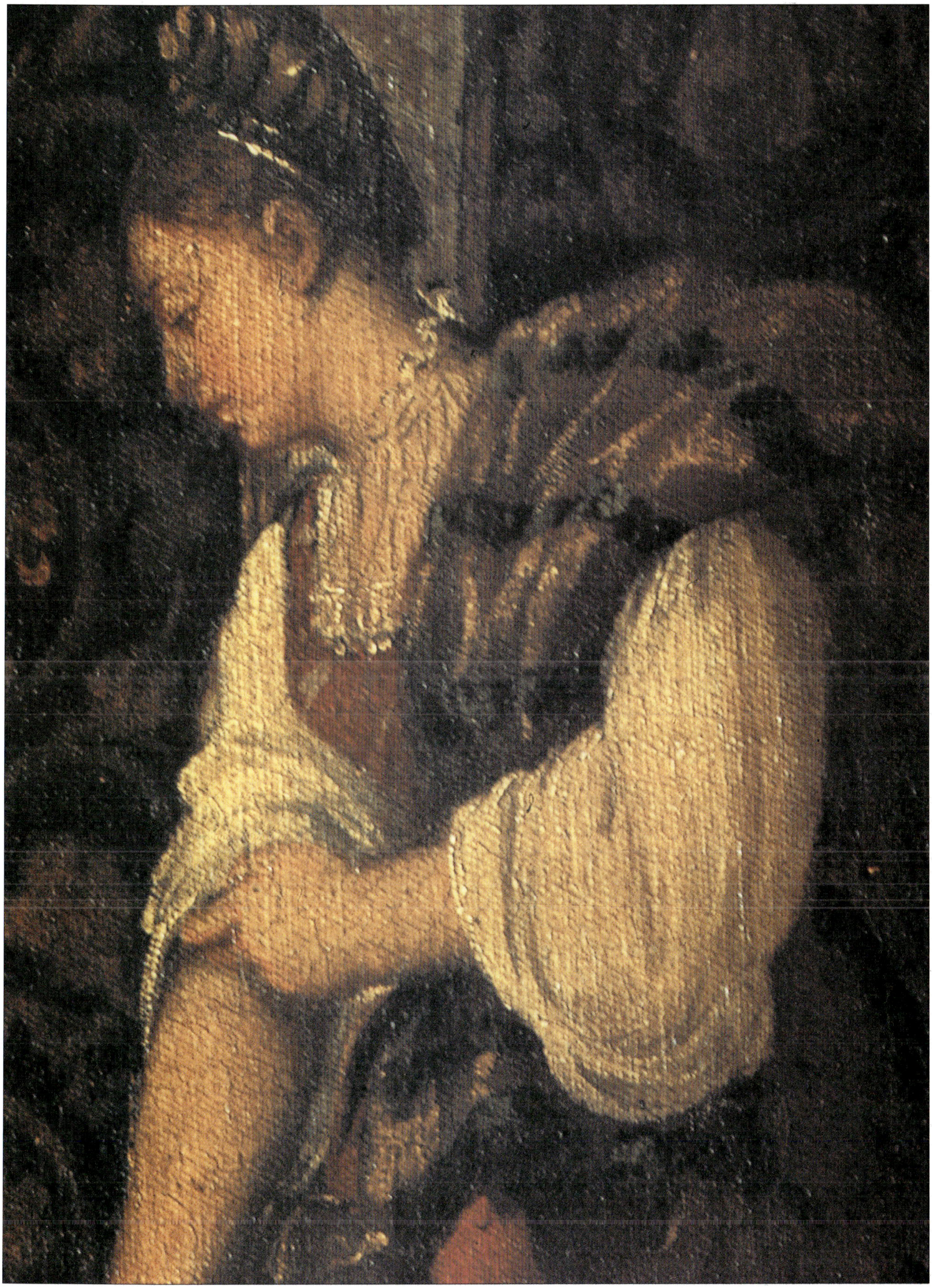

2 *Actual size detail*

Danaë

1553-54
$50\frac{1}{2}\times 70$in/128×178cm
Oil on canvas
Prado, Madrid

One of Titian's most important patrons in later life was Philip II of Spain, son of the Emperor Charles V. Philip, as befitted the Defender of the Catholic Faith, commissioned various religious paintings for the royal palace at Madrid, but at the same time Titian was to paint for him a series of loosely mythological scenes taken from the anthology of stories about the gods and goddesses of classical antiquity compiled by the poet Ovid. These paintings, which Titian called his *poesie,* were distinctly erotic by the standards of the day, and were hung in a private room for Philip's personal delectation. It was this work, the *Danaë,* delivered in 1554, which probabaly encouraged the king to commission the series (see also page 54), which were to be among Titian's greatest achievements in the twenty or so remaining years of his life.

Danaë, the daughter of the king of Argos, is imprisoned by her father in a bronze tower because an oracle had predicted that a son of hers would kill him. Zeus, transforming himself into a shower of gold, pays court to her, and she bears his son Perseus, who eventually fulfills the prophecy by accidentally killing the king while throwing a discus. The earlier version of the subject (below opposite) was painted in Rome during Titian's stay there, and is in some ways a Venetian challenge to the art of that city, both classical and contemporary, and especially to Michelangelo, whose *Leda and the Swan,* together with his sculptures for the Medici tomb, may well have been a source of both influence and rivalry.

In the earlier painting, the recumbent nude, no longer beguilingly in control as in *the Venus of Urbino* (see page 47), lies back passively, the sprightly animation of the cupid who accompanies her acting as a counterpoint to her inert form. In the later version the cupid of classical myth has been replaced by an aging mortal. The old woman tries to gather the golden coins for herself by holding open her apron, as though in a desperate attempt to clutch the sensual blessings of which passing time has deprived her, thus bringing the story at least partially out of the realm of myth and into the real, mortal world. In both paintings the expectant, abandoned pose of Danaë is set against stabilizing elements: the vertical drapery to the left and the horizontal of the couch. Twisting from the hips — her legs are at one with the picture plane — her torso is pulled round to imply her physical receptiveness, as her head sinks drowsily back into warm shadow. In the later version, however, the limbs are drawn out still further, expressing her aching desire, and the brushwork seems to dissolve the color into a fusion of canvas surface and implied forms that makes the earlier work seem almost sculptural by contrast. From the dramatically stormy sky, a shower of thick dabs of color burst forth, glistening and flashing in the light which also illuminates the flesh of Danaë, delicately colored against the creamy white of the sheets. These broad touches of paint, applied with free brushstrokes that are suggestive of form rather than literally descriptive, create a wonderfully tactile paint surface, the forms seeming to dissolve into one another with a sense of abandon — a visual metaphor for physical sensuality. As in *the Venus of Urbino,* we can sense the three-dimensionality but cannot quite grasp it because the color and brushwork always brings us back to the two-dimensional picture surface. This emphasis on rich surface tensions built up by relating touches of color to one another on the picture plane itself, rather than using colors to give the illusion of space, is more fully developed here. Titian has created an interlocking mesh of touches of color, in which each one resonates against its neighbor, producing an effect of homogeneity that absorbs the voluptuous beauty of the figure into an overall oneness of sensory delight.

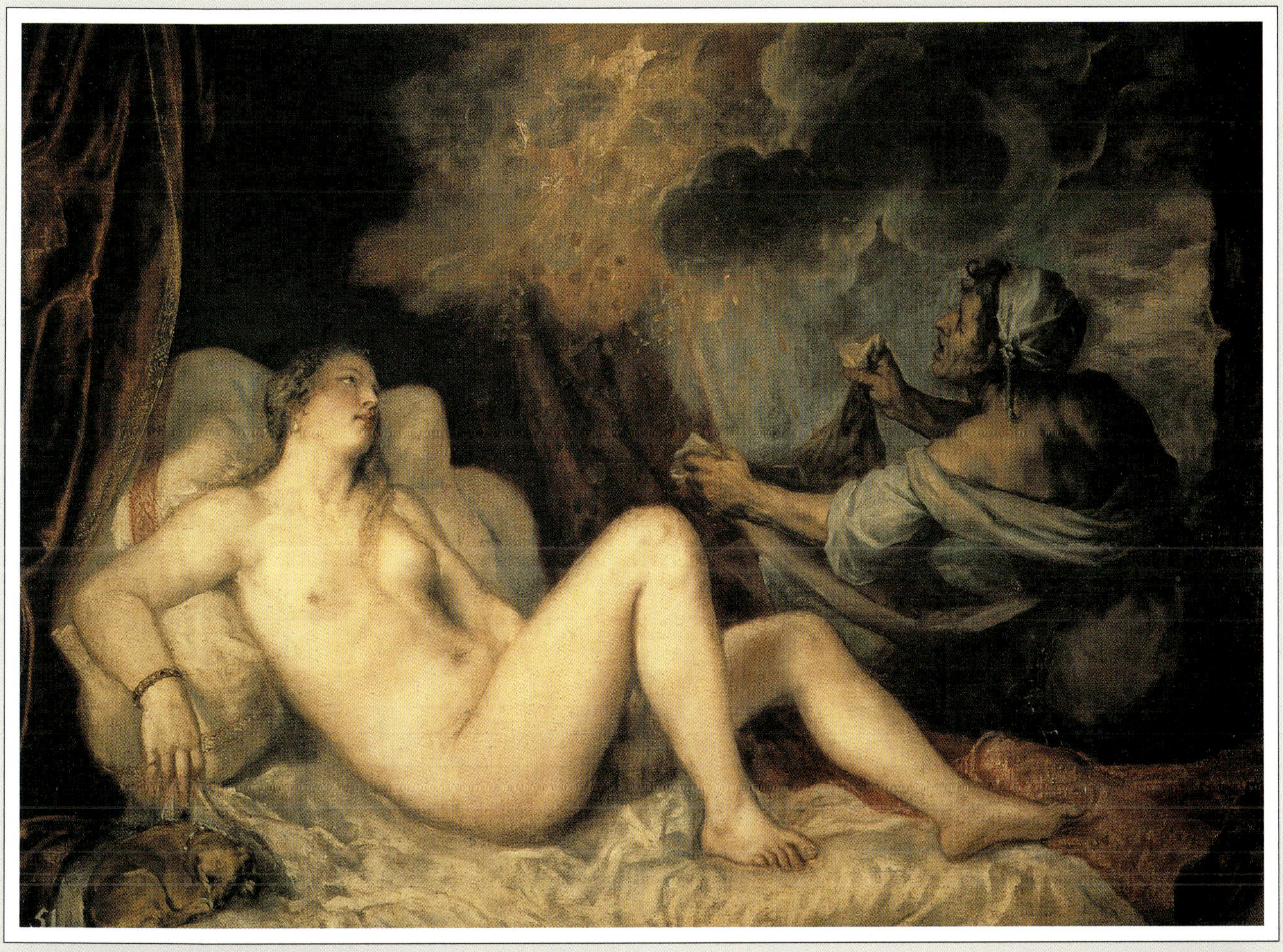

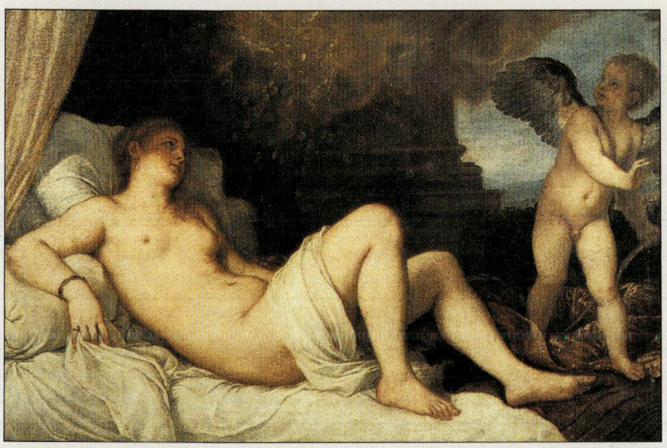

The subject of Danaë was popular with Renaissance painters because it could be used as a symbol for the transforming powers of divine love, and there are versions by both Tintoretto and Correggio. Rembrandt, in the 17th century, also painted the subject, which clearly appeals to painters partly because of the inherent visual possibilities in the shower of gold descending from the heavens. Titian's early *Danaë* (left) was commissioned by Cardinal Alessandro Farnese, and completed eight years before the version painted for Philip II (above). The earlier work shows a tendency that Titian had developed while in Rome, that of restricting his palette to two or three warm colors, thus intensifying the feeling of warm air on soft forms through almost monochromatic harmonies.

TITIAN
Danaë
1545-46, Capodimonte Gallery, Naples

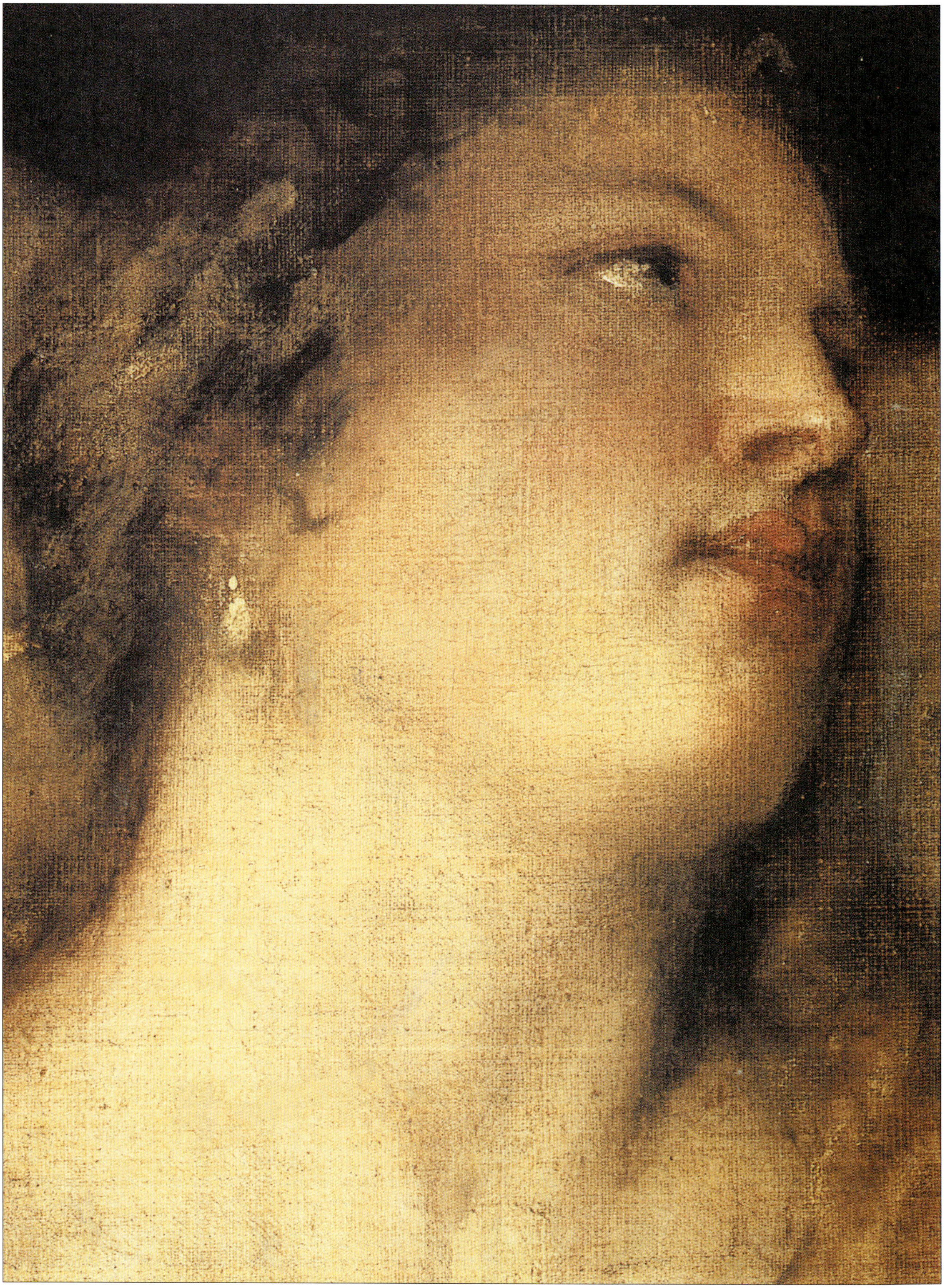

1 *Actual size detail*

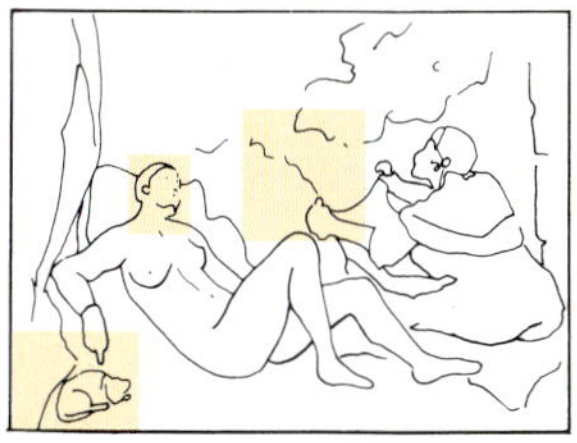

1 *Actual size detail* The paint is drily brushed into the grain of the canvas, emphasizing both the forms of the head and the canvas surface. The rose-pink of Danaë's lips and the gray-blues seen in the broad strokes of the pillow's folds are lightly brushed around her cheek, and liquid droplets of white give a sparkle to her eye and earring. Similar touches are used to bring the tip of her nose and jaw out of the warm blue shadow of the pillow.

2 Deep wine-red and warm turquoise are broadly applied for the backdrop, across which drier, creamy gray strokes, lightly dragged and flicked across the gain, convey a sense of movement. A grayed variant of the turquoise, applied in sinuous, fluid lines, indicates the veins of the clutching hand. From the muscular arm flesh tones are darted over the backdrop in flickering touches, heightened by dabs of white, pink and gray, to give an opulent, material presence to the coins.

3 The lightly trailed and stippled pinks and reds give a broad impression of the pattern of the embroidered bolster, and the tactile quality is emphasized by the way these same colors are brushed lightly into the fingers and then teased into the sheets. Loose white strokes, flurried and scumbled across the grain of the canvas, hint at light catching on the ruffled folds of fabric. The dog is painted boldly, with square-ended brushes following the directions of the forms to conjure the animal from broad fluid strokes of brown and black lightened by white. The white is formed into thick highlights for the collar.

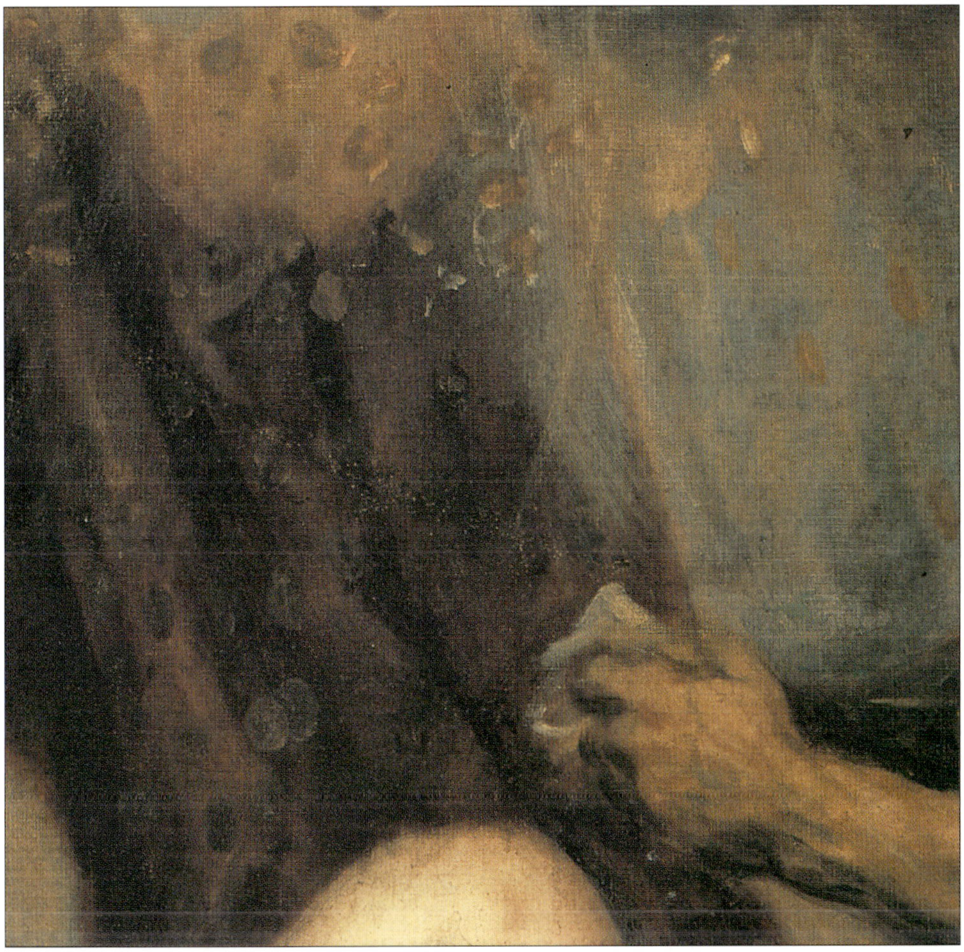

2

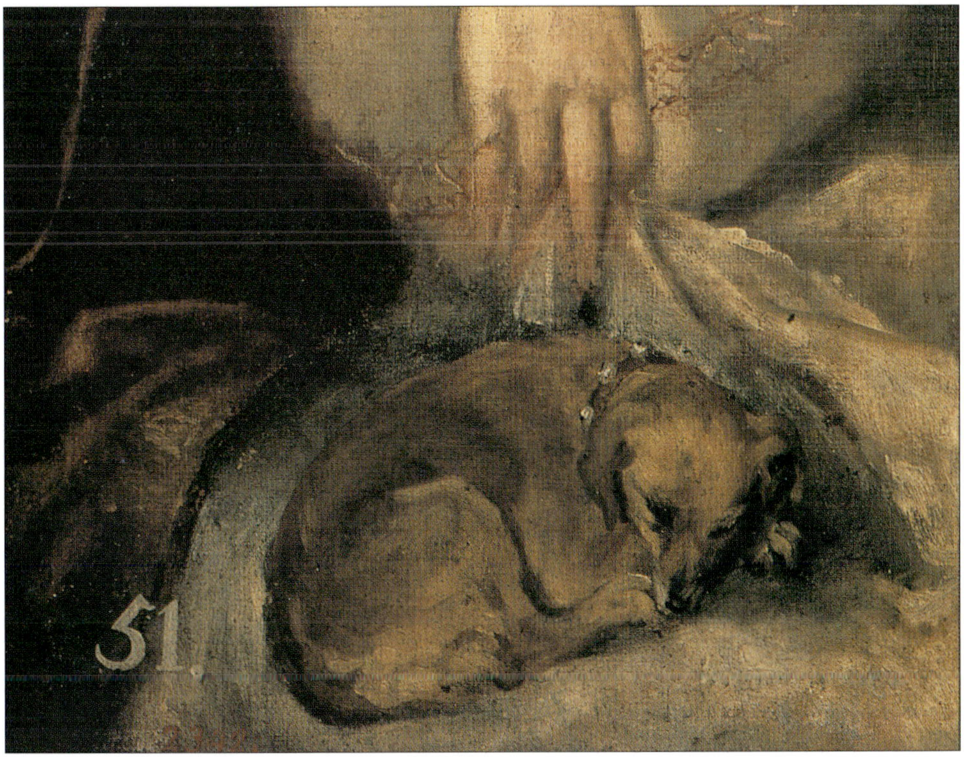

3

The Death of Actaeon

1559-c1562 (and possibly reworked in the 1570s)
$70^{1}/_{2}\times78$in/179×198cm
Oil on canvas
National Gallery, London

In 1559 Titian sent a pair of paintings, *Diana and Actaeon* and *Diana and Callisto* (both now in Edinburgh's National Gallery) to Philip II, who had become Titian's principal patron in the 1550s. In the letter from Titian telling of their completion, mention is also made of another work that the had just begun. This is the *Death* (or *Punishment*) *of Actaeon,* but it appears that the painting was never sent to Philip, as it is not included by Titian in the list that he made in 1576 of works delivered to the Spanish court.

In this painting and others from the late 1550s we see how Titian has developed the joyous, open exuberance of early mythological works such as *Bacchus and Ariadne* (see page 37) into a smouldering, atmospheric evocation of radiant forms glowing in a flickering light, qualities that typify all the later *poesie.* Titian's name for them was well-chosen – they are truly mood poems in paint.

The belief held in the classical world that painters and poets shared basically the same functions was taken up again during the Renaissance, poets being referred to as articulate painters, and painters as mute poets. This is particularly evident in Venetian painting: Giorgione and Titian both use paint to evoke sensory sensations and mood as a poet would use words, rather than merely illustrating a literary theme. In one of the Greek classics popularized in the age of Humanism, Philostratus the Elder (3rd century BC), discussing some ancient paintings, had asked, "Do you catch something of the fragrance hanging over the garden, or are your senses dull?" Titian, who knew these writings, drew on them, but in a highly expressive and personal manner, in his later *poesie.*

In the story taken from Ovid, Acteon, while out hunting, accidentally chances upon Diana bathing. She takes her revenge by transforming him into a stag, with the result that he is set upon by his own hounds. The pinks, blues and golds of the earlier paintings, such as *Diana and Callisto* (see page 25) are replaced here by a somber monochrome — a tendency first seen during Titian's visit to Rome in 1545. A sense of brooding unease is caught both through the brushwork, which ranges from thin washes and glazing to thick impasto, and the use of what seems to be a very limited palette of only two colors, dark red and brownish green, accented by touches of white, yellow and black. Diana dominates, majestic on the left, her body and limbs drawn out larger than life to emphasize her superhuman power.

Her profile, stormy as the sky that echoes her mood, has a formidable quality of smoldering anger that radiates through every flickering brushstroke, taking us across to the unfortunate Acteon, who disintegrates under a welter of snarling dogs and dissolving paint-strokes. The landscape is shadowy, its details no longer described with botanical clarity, and the clear air of the earlier *Bacchus and Ariadne* has now become dense and "heady," as though nature itself were reverberating with the horrors that are being perpetrated. In *Bacchus and Ariadne* a horseman can be seen rearing in the open, spacious landscape between the two lovers, but here the space between the two protagonists presses claustrophobically forward to the surface of the canvas, and in the ominous and murky wood a wraith-like specter seems to hover fleetingly, to witness Actaeon's death before dissolving back into the undergrowth. In the late *poesie,* the paint is often glowing and radiant, but here it is brooding and clotted, manipulated with brush and often fingers to form clusters that eloquently describe the tensions of the figures and their relationship to one another before fusing into an overall oneness of color and surface texture.

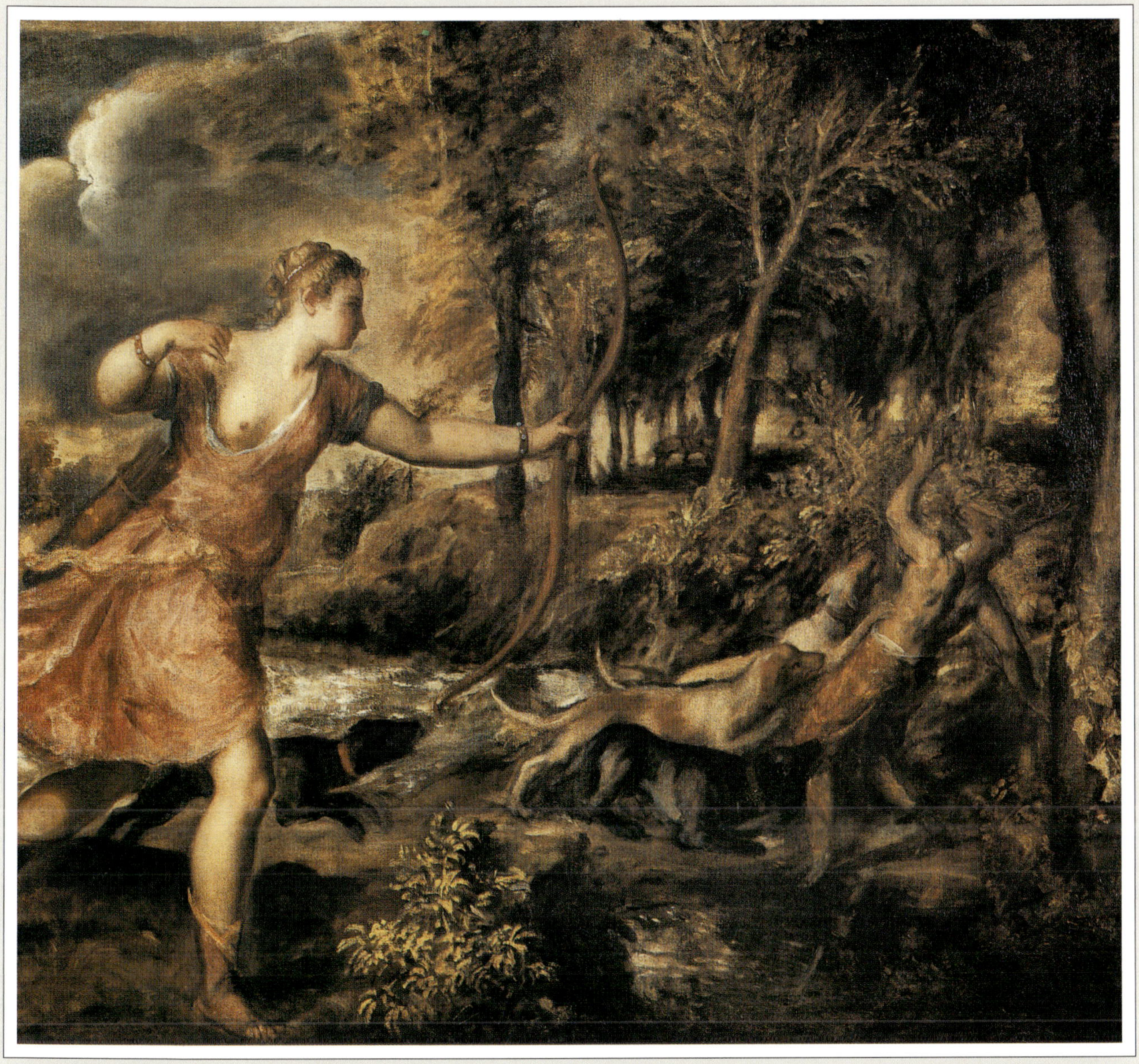

Unfortunately dark tones of the painting have been exaggerated by deterioration. It was once thought that Titian had used a dark oil ground, but recent examination reveals that it was painted on a white gesso priming, which has become translucent through the impregnation of a heavy lining paste, so that the original color of the canvas shows through. In addition to this, fugitive colors and discolored varnish prevents us from now seeing much of the ultramarine used for the sky, the bright greens of the foliage and the vermilion, crimson lake, and various yellows that originally enlivened the surface. But even without this deterioration, the painting would certainly have been darker and more somber than the earlier works, and the application of the paint here more than ever before emphasizes the tactile element of Titian's work — a rich surface of clotted pigment that suggests form rather than literally describing it. The elongation of Diana's body may owe something to the influence of the Mannerist painters, who distorted and exaggerated forms, making much use of tapering limbs and stylish gestures.

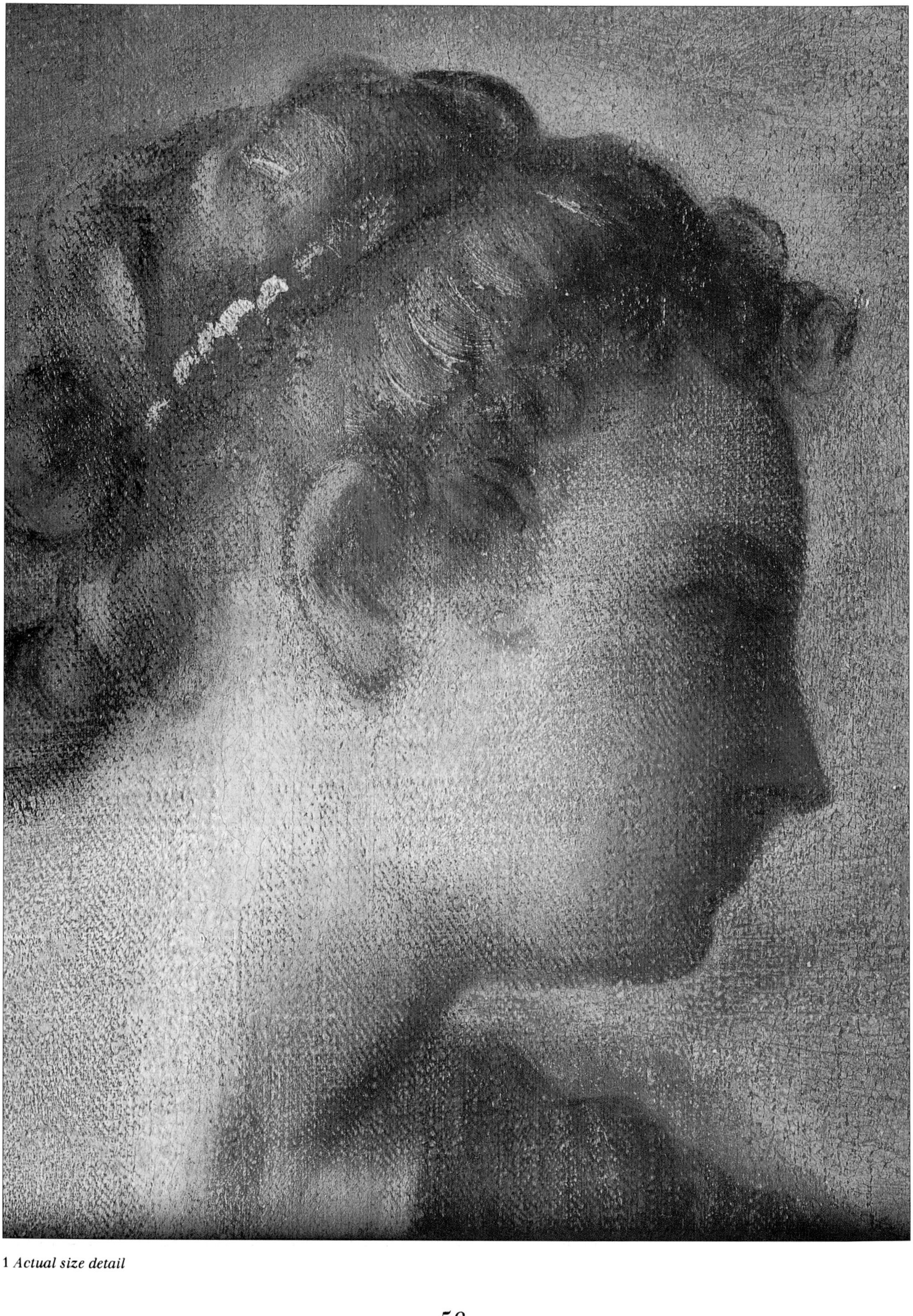

1 *Actual size detail*

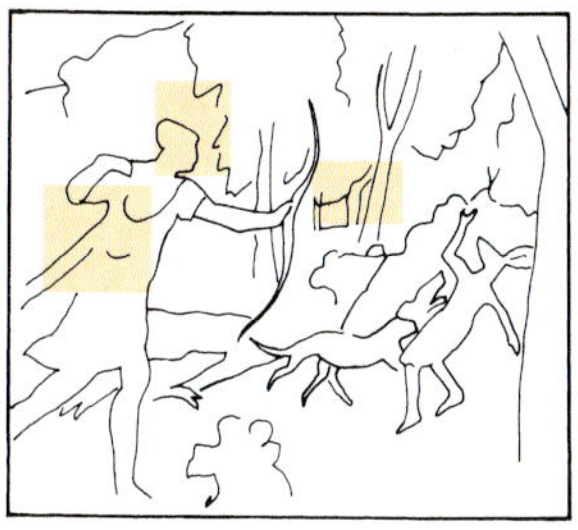

1 *Actual size detail* The opaque flesh hues, smoothed over the canvas grain, give form to Diana's face and emphasize her stormy profile by being the most clearly defined area of the painting. The smooth handling of her flesh is deliberately contrasted with the thin glazes used for her clothing. Earth colors, which sketch out the overall composition, give definition to her facial features and to her hair, which is wispily applied over the solid, opaque surface, with touches of white flicked into it for accents.

2 Diana's robe has been loosely built up from thin, roughly applied glazes. Across this translucent surface pinks and whites with a slight greenish tint have been freely applied, with flowing strokes indicating the movement of the floating sash. Fluid brown lines and softly touched-in ochers have been drawn or washed into these broadly massed areas, creating soft, flickering shadows.

3 Loose washes of dark and light color are dragged and scrubbed over the canvas, blurring edges of forms and shadows. Splatters and trickles of fluid, dilute paint sketchily hint at a figure on horseback, appearing to be glimpsed fleetingly before dissolving back into the shadows.

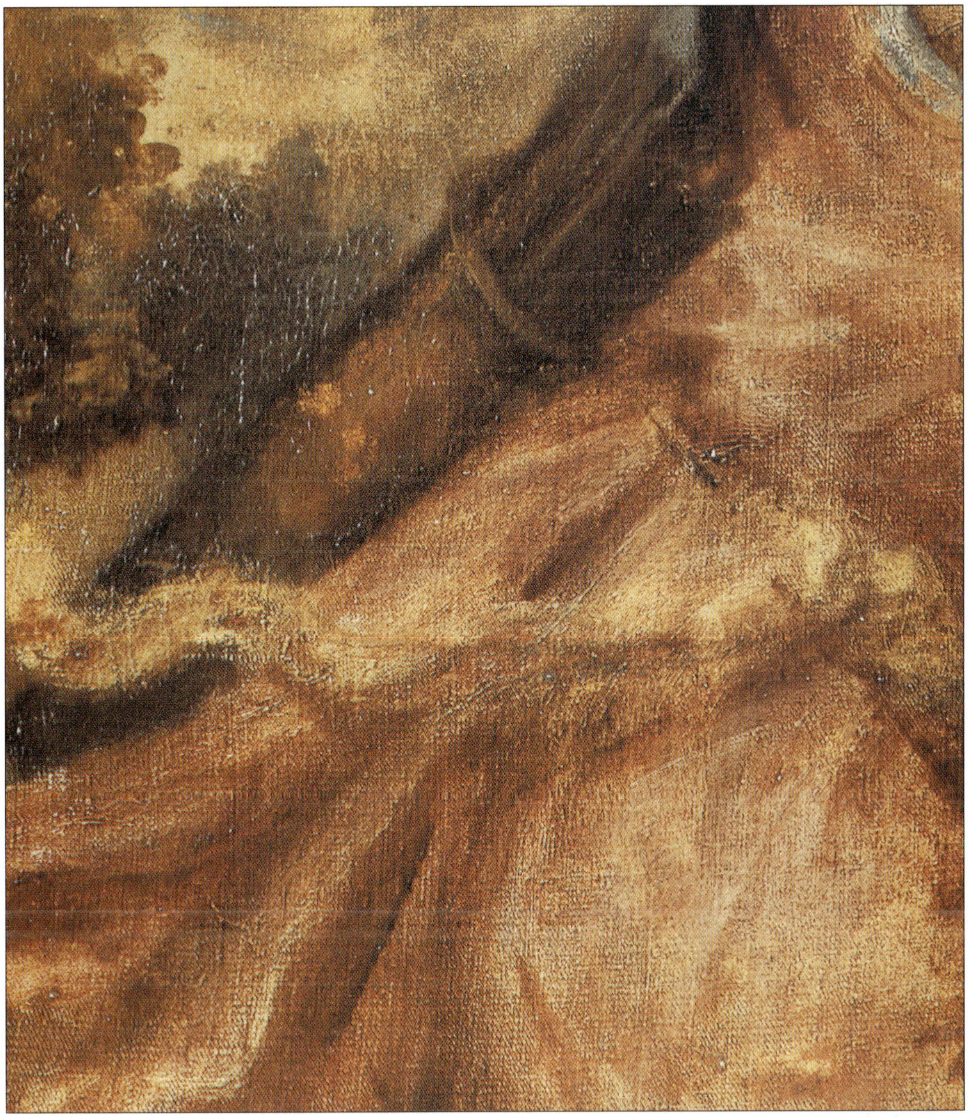

2

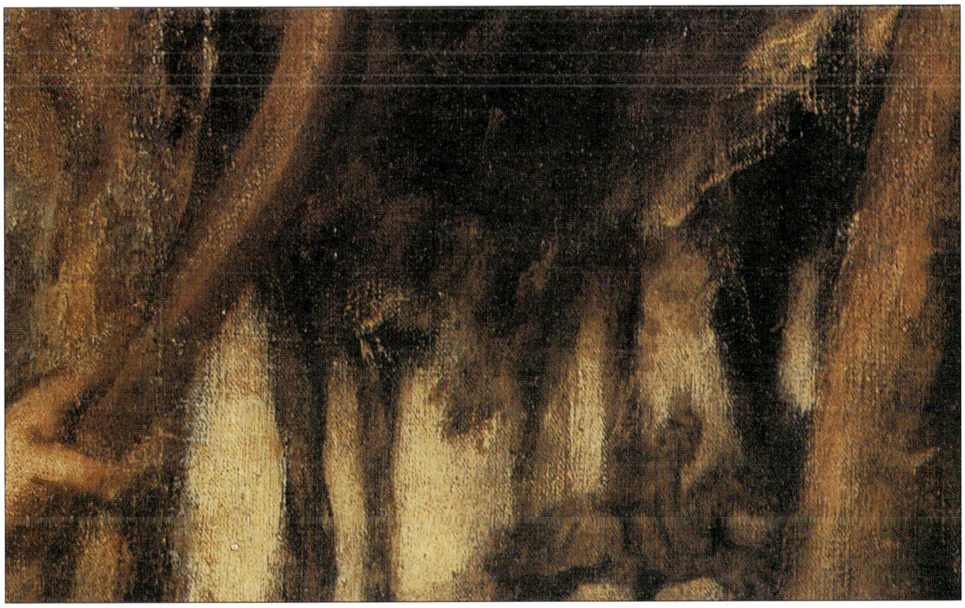

3

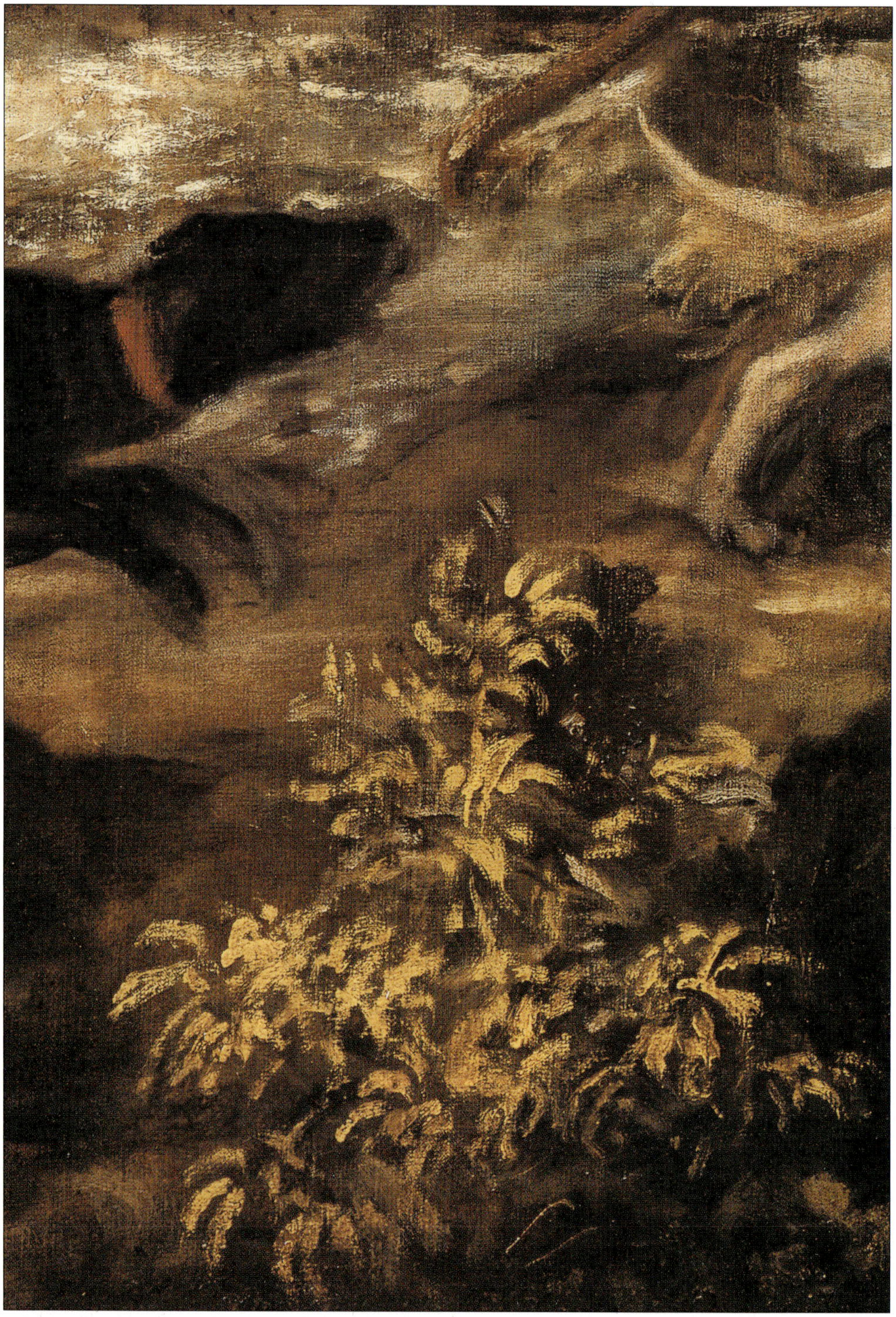

4

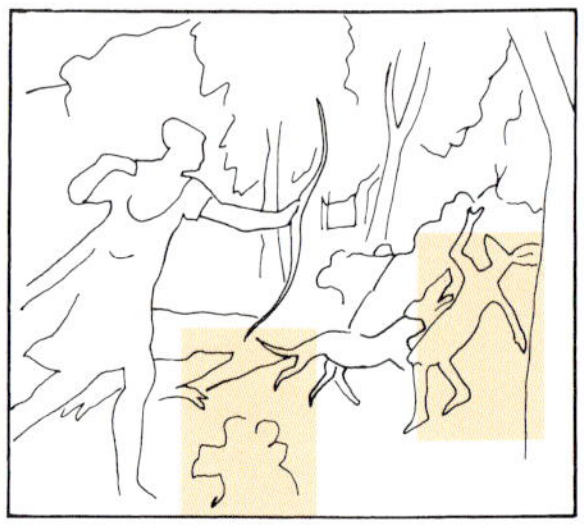

4 This is a fine example of Titian's later approach to handling paint, when he either applied it freely with a large brush or molded impressions of organic form with his fingers. The bright red used for the dog's collar catches our eye, while strong color and tonal contrasts animate its moving silhouette. Tactile blobs of white and yellow, dabbed rapidly across the rough canvas grain, not only hint at natural forms but communicate the painter's sensual enjoyment of manipulating pigments.

5 Broken, dissolving brushwork is used appropriately to suggest disintegrating form, as Actaeon, now transformed into a stag, is torn apart by his own hounds. Creamy-white, used for the solid physical bulk of the dogs, is slashed onto his waist and up onto his stag's neck. The dark browns and blacks used for the surrounding foliage are here dragged across the canvas grain, hinting at the torso yet also breaking it down. In contrast, lightly slashed curving diagonals of red, pink and orange give substance to the wrap, and the sinewy arm is treated with fine linear definition. On the right, between the arm and the back, is a shape into which are flashed two bold strokes of white which clarify the shadowed side of the torso and prevent the body from merging completely into the ground.

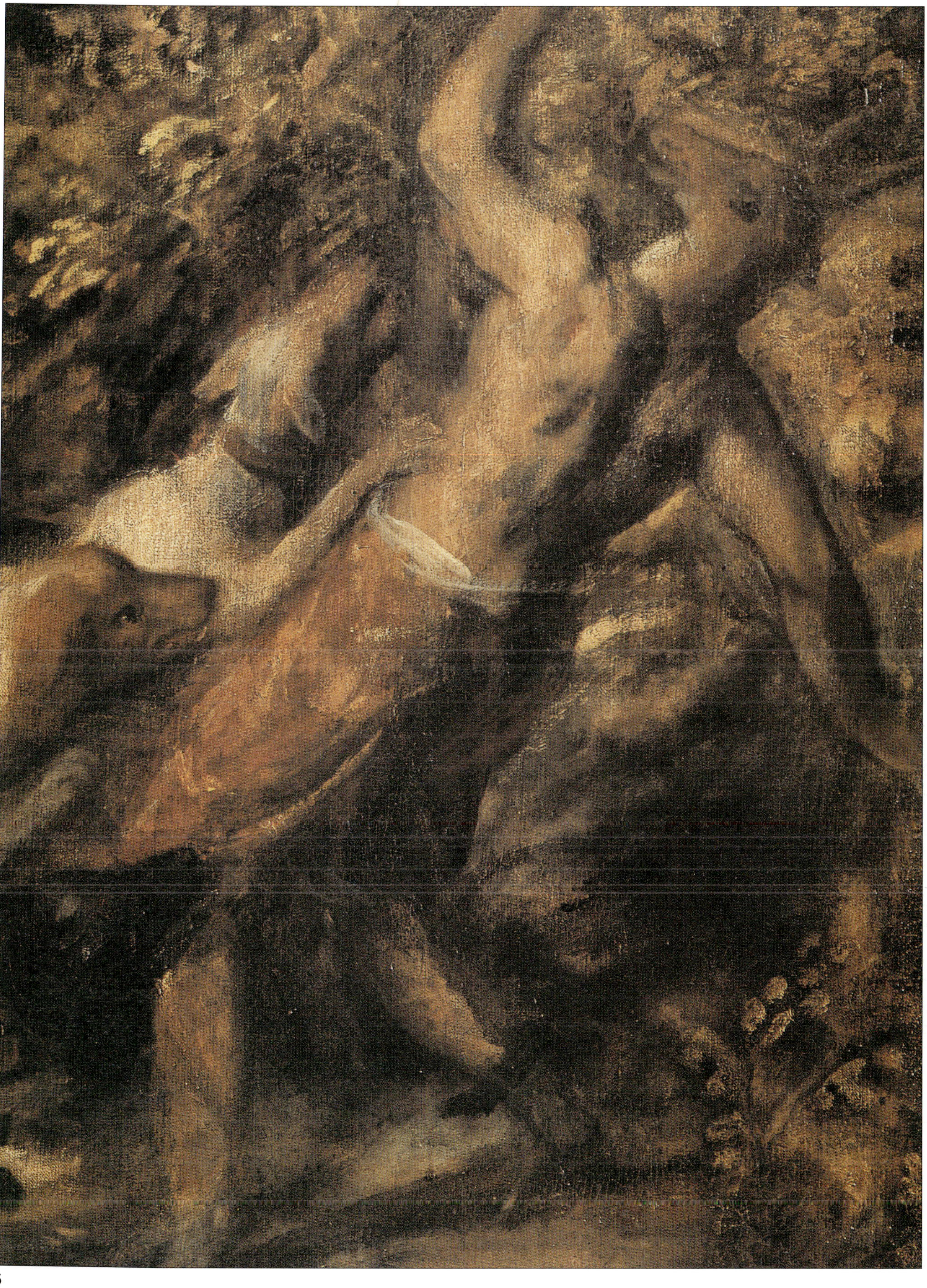

5

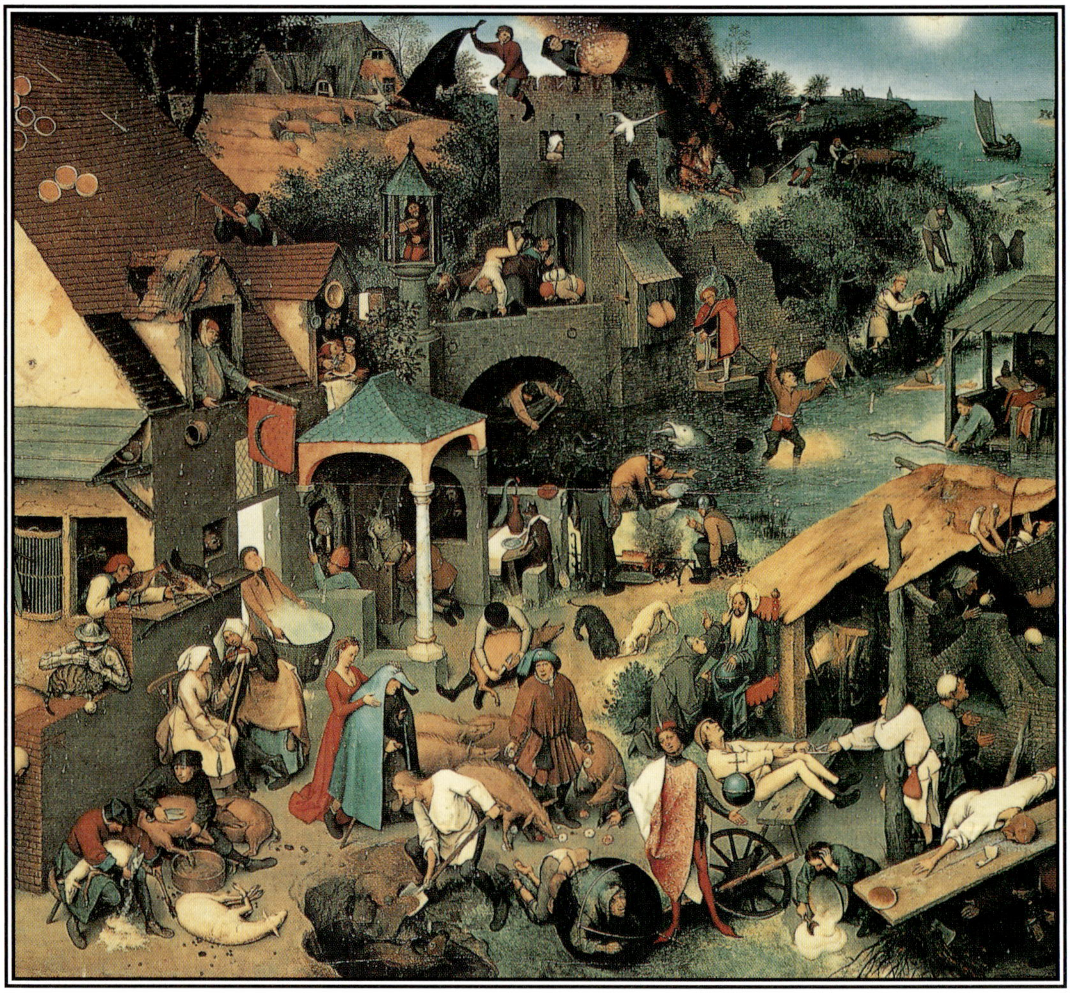

BRUEGEL

Introduction

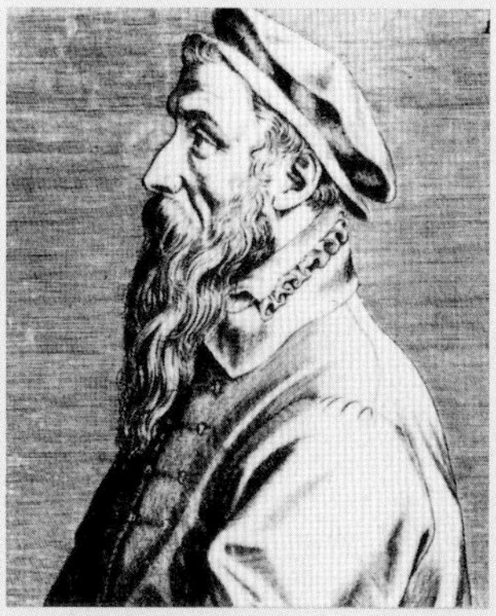

Pieter Bruegel The Elder
(artist unknown)
c 1569

"On his journeys Bruegel did many views from nature, so it was said of him when he traveled through the Alps that he had swallowed all the mountains and rocks and spat them out again, after his return, onto his canvases and panels, so closely was he able to follow nature here and in his other works." The quotation is from Karel Van Mander's *Het Schilder-Boek (The Painter's Book)* published in 1604, nearly forty years after Pieter Bruegel's death. It is still a major source of information on his life, about which very little is otherwise known. Our knowledge of the career of this much-reproduced artist has to be built around this biography and reinforced by some mentions in contemporary documents and letters and Bruegel's own work, which is frequently signed and dated.

Van Mander's vivid description of Bruegel's interpretation of nature was in fact extremely apt, for it was through a series of landscape drawings, published as engravings soon after his return from a long journey to Italy, that Bruegel first became known. His later paintings of the *Months* (see page 91), which fuse landscape and keen observation of human activity in a way that was totally new in the 16th century, are among his most memorable images.

Although Van Mander described many of Bruegel's paintings accurately, he characterized the artist himself as a somewhat droll and peasant-like person, which does not accord with other accounts. Two contemporaries of Bruegel – the Italian Ludovico Guiccardini, who published a *Description of the Low Countries* in 1567, and Dominico Lampsonius, a poet, painter, and historian from Liège – described him as a second Hieronymus Bosch. The latter (who died in 1516) was still famous, and the comparison was a compliment as well as being to some extent accurate. Bruegel drew on Bosch's imagery for some of his paintings and for the subject matter of the many popular engravings designed for the leading Antwerp print publisher, Hieronymus Cock. Van Mander's view of him is unfounded: modern scholarship has shown that he was in fact connected with a highly intellectual circle in Antwerp, which included the great geographer and cartographer Abraham Ortelius and other leading figures of the time, such as the publisher Christopher Plantin.

Apprenticeship and formative years

Pieter Bruegel's birth date is not precisely known and nor is his place of birth, but it is generally thought that he was born toward the end of the 1520s in Breda, Northern Brabant, in the modern Netherlands. In 1551 he became a Master in the Antwerp Guild of St Luke (the painter's guild) meaning that he had completed his training as a painter, and during this year he collaborated with an older painter named Pieter Baltens on an altarpiece in Malines. This town was at the time a center for tempera painting on linen, a technique which Bruegel later used for several paintings. Van Mander tells us that Bruegel's actual apprenticeship was with Pieter Coecke van Aelst (1502-50) a distinguished and intellectual Antwerp artist who had traveled in Italy and Turkey and who ran a large workshop producing tapestries and sculpture as well as paintings. Although Bruegel's early work in no way resembles Coecke's Italianate style, the fact that he later married Coecke's daughter confirms a connection.

Although Bruegel's work does not initially show reliance on the Italian style, he would have been keen to travel to the South, as were all aspiring Northern painters. In the 16th-century Netherlands, Italy was regarded as the source both of the admired style of the Italian Renaissance and of the world of antiquity from which the Renaissance in part derived. Prints after the work of Italian masters were widely circulated, and by Bruegel's day earlier visitors to Italy, such as the painter Frans Floris, had absorbed the Italianate figure style based on Raphael and Michelangelo, while Maerten van Heemskerck had made drawings of ancient Roman

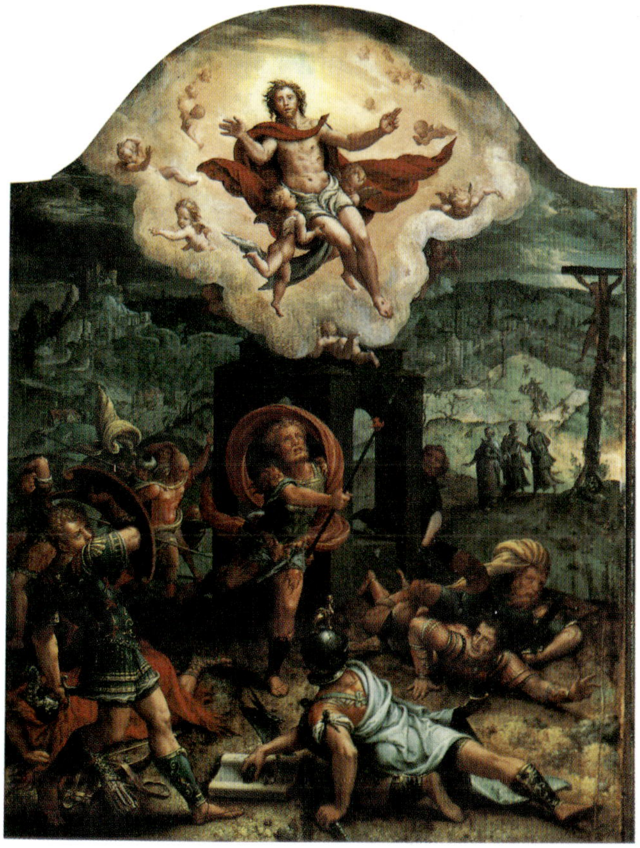

PIETER COECKE VAN AELST
The Resurrection of Christ
date unknown, Staatliche Kunsthalle, Karlsruhe

This painting, the central panel of a triptych, gives an idea of Coecke's Italianate style. Like other leading Flemish painters of his day, he was strongly influenced by Raphael and his school. Coecke, who visited Rome, was active as a painter from 1527, first in Antwerp and later in Brussels. According to Van Mander, he was also Bruegel's teacher but this is not substantiated by any document, and Bruegel's early paintings in no way resemble those of Coecke. Coecke died in 1550, and Bruegel married his daughter in 1563.

monuments and sculpture which were engraved in Antwerp.

Dated drawings and records show that Bruegel made the vital journey between 1552 and 1554, visiting Lyons in France and then going on to Italy – to Reggio in Calabria, Messina and Palermo in Sicily, to Naples, Rome, and possibly Bologna. In Rome he met the famous miniaturist Giulio Clovio (to become the patron of El Greco). Clovio was later to own four paintings by Bruegel, including one of Lyons (probably a tempera painting on linen) and a painting on ivory – presumably a miniature – of the Tower of Babel, a subject Bruegel was to use again for two large paintings. It was probably also in Rome that Bruegel produced in 1553 his first dated painting, *Christ Appearing to the Apostles at the Sea of Tiberias.* Its high viewpoint and pointed rock formations recall the work of two earlier Flemish landscape painters, Joachim Patinir (d. 1516) and Herri met de Bles (c 1500/10-after 1550).

Landscape and the role of printing

On his way back from Italy Bruegel spent a considerable time in the Alps making landscape sketches. The drawings, which reveal keen observation and a sensitive handling of the shapes and textures of mountains and trees, were to furnish motifs for later compositions such as the series of large landscape drawings on which he worked when he returned to Antwerp. These, engraved by Hieronymus Cock, demonstrate his outstanding mastery of landscape composition.

In the prosperous city and port of Antwerp with its large international population – by 1550 it numbered 100,000 people – pictures and prints were big business. Guiccardini describes the traffic in oriental spices, grain, French wines, German metals, and English cloth, as well as the prosperous picture market in the center of Antwerp. Three hundred qualified masters were at work; pictures were often purchased "sight unseen" before delivery, and whole cargoes were dispatched to Spain. Printing was an equally important activity; more than half the books published in the Low Countries were printed in Antwerp, and there was a thriving trade in prints, which were exported to all parts of Europe and imported from Italy and Germany. Hieronymus Cock had established his large publishing house, the Four Winds, in about 1550, and was a leading printer. He produced a variety of subjects, including maps and topographical scenes, as well as prints after leading Netherlandian and Italian masters.

Since the beginning of the century there had been an important tradition of landscape painting in the Netherlands. The Alps were then just beginning to be explored, and it is possible that it was Cock who had encouraged Bruegel not only to go to Italy but to record the Alpine landscape with a view to creating the large-scale engravings which he now produced after Bruegel's drawings. The landscapes are not topographical records of actual places, but a skillful mixture of motifs drawn from Bruegel's own on-the-spot sketches. These were blended with imaginative ideas, some of which look back, as Bruegel's first landscape painting had done, to Joachim Patinir's rocky landscapes and to the sweeping panoramas introduced by Herri met de Bles.

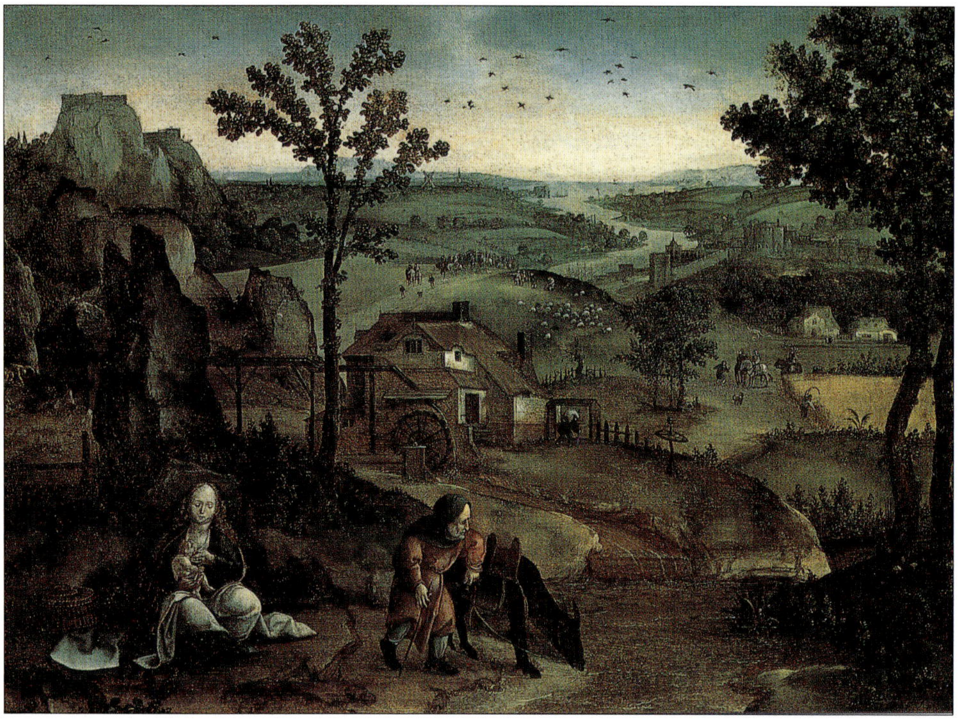

JOACHIM PATINIR
The Flight Into Egypt
c 1515-20, Musée Royale des Beaux-Arts, Antwerp

Patinir's concept of a panoramic landscape, surveyed from a high viewpoint, had already appeared in the work of an earlier Flemish artist, Hans Memling. But Patinir is the first-known landscape specialist. In this tiny panel, one of his few signed works, the figures of the holy family, dwarfed by towering rocks, are less important than the landscape stretching away to its far horizon. Patinir had many immediate followers, the principal one being Herri met de Bles, and was an important influence on Bruegel.

Bruegel's graphic work

In 1556 Bruegel began work on satirical or moralizing figure compositions, also intended for engraving by Cock. The first of these was based on a well-known proverb, "Big fish eat little fish." Proverbs, and a delight in categorizing aspects of the world's folly, were endemic to the Netherlands of this period. *Ship of Fools* (1494), by the German scholar Sebastian Brandt, a satirical comment on contemporary folly and vice, was well known, as was Erasmus's *In Praise of Folly* (1509), which had many themes in common with it. As early as 1500 Erasmus had published a collection of Greek and Latin proverbs, and the first Netherlandian collection appeared in 1549. Bruegel's subject was one which everyone would have known.

The drawing shows a huge fish, mouth gaping, with its inside split to reveal a myriad of increasingly smaller fish inside it. The boat and the human beings in the foreground emphasize the size of the biggest fish. The engraving made from the drawing extends the meaning of the proverb, with a legend printed in Latin, French, and Flemish: "Oppression of the poor; the power of the rich controls you." Cock published this engraving as "designed by Hieronymus Bosch," perhaps capitalizing on Bosch's enduring popularity to ensure its success; Flemish painters such as Jan Mandyn and Pieter Huys had already produced paintings in Bosch's style in the previous decade, while the great collector Cardinal de Granvella — later to be a patron of Bruegel — commissioned tapestries after his work. Bruegel was to follow the Bosch fashion in some of his paintings, and also in the series of drawings of the Seven Vices and the Seven Virtues, which he now produced for engraving by Cock.

The conflict between vices and virtues had been used by the medieval Church to teach moral lessons, and cycles personifying them were common in medieval art. In the *Allegory of Lust,* from the Seven Vices series, Bruegel represented Lust as a nude woman being caressed by a half-lizard, half-human creature. The rotting tree beneath which they shelter is topped by an embracing couple in a transparent bubble set into a half-open mussel shell, both motifs which appear in Bosch's *Garden of Earthly Delights.* Just below, a branch turns into an antlered stag, traditional symbol of sexual passion, while on the left two dogs echo the central couple (an idea which re-appears in a more restrained form in William Hogarth's *Marriage à la Mode* of 1743). The large-headed monster in the foreground breaks an egg (regarded as an aphrodisiac at the time) over himself. Bruegel's fantastic creatures, like Bosch's, are a mixture of animal, bird, and human parts extended by straight invention, the kind of creations which were to fill his later painting *The Fall of the Rebel Angels.* The subject matter, style, and composition of Bruegel's graphic work are often echoed or extended in his paintings and a knowledge of it contributes enormously to our understanding of him.

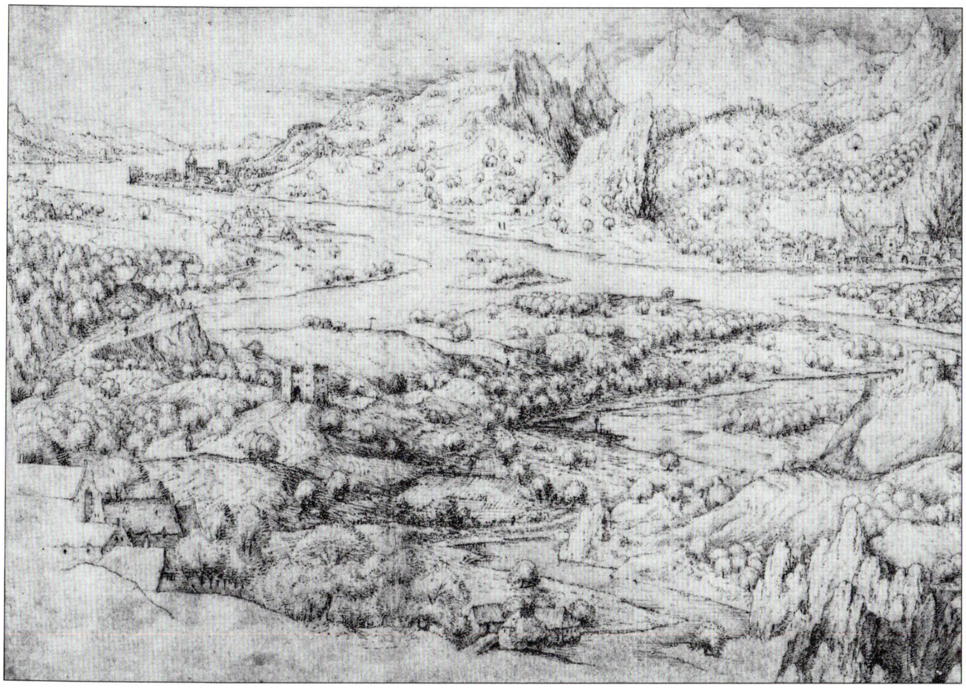

PIETER BRUEGEL
Country Concerns (Solicitudo Rustico)
c 1555, British Museum, London

This beautiful drawing, in pen and ink over black chalk, is the only surviving preparatory work for the series of engravings known as *The Large Landscapes.* Its composition resembles the part-imaginary landscapes of Joachim Patinir, but the sensitive draftsmanship reflects Bruegel's careful study of the real world. Note the delicate, tentative outlines of river and mountains, the variety of strokes used to differentiate rocks, trees, and buildings.

The influence of Bosch

In parallel with his work for Cock, Bruegel was also producing paintings, and *The Netherlandish Proverbs* of 1559 introduced a new compositional device – a village setting viewed, like the landscapes, from high up. This is also used for *The Battle between Carnival and Lent* (see page 75) and *Children's Games* (see page 79). These paintings combine some of the weirdness and drollery of Bosch with Bruegel's own amazing eye for recording the multifarious activities of human beings, also demonstrated in his figure drawings, sometimes inscribed *nar het lieven* (from the life).

Two years later Bruegel's painting becomes more obviously Bosch-like with *The Fall of the Rebel Angels, Dulle Griet* and *The Triumph of Death.* In the latter Bruegel sets his scene of the living battling against the dead in a vast landscape luridly lit by flaming fires. The concept recalls the Northern theme of the Dance of Death, where the dead rise from their tombs, dance, and go off to find new victims among the living. There is also

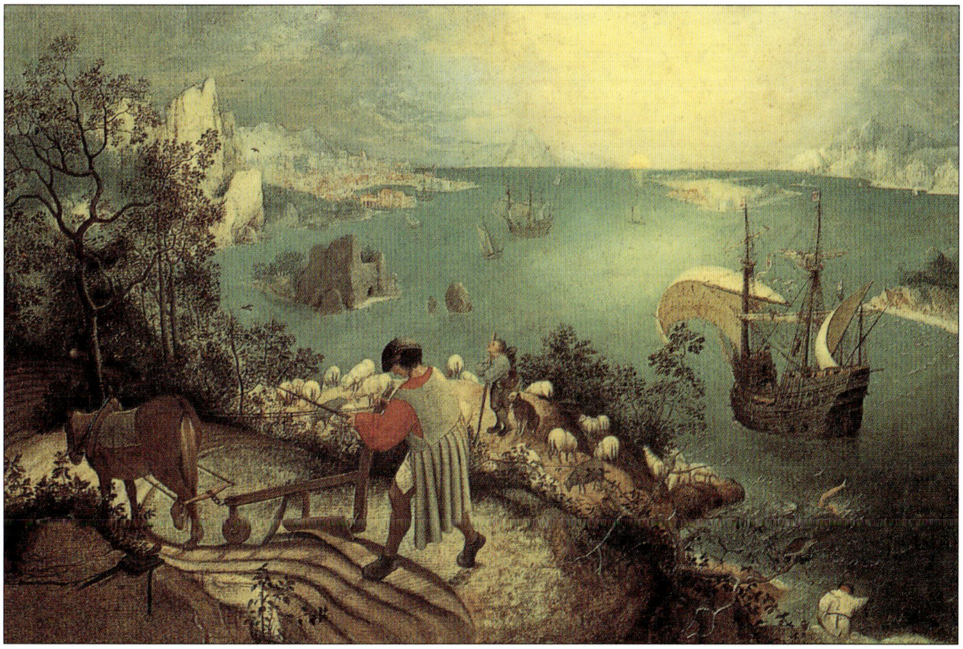

PIETER BRUEGEL
Landscape with the Fall of Icarus
c 1555, Musée Royaux, Brussels

At one time it was thought that this painting had been done on wood and then transferred to canvas, but laboratory examination has now shown that canvas was the original support. Bruegel had worked at Malines, a centre for tempera painting on canvas, in 1550. The work is undated, but is usually considered to have been produced around 1555 after his return from Italy, although there is now some degree of doubt as to whether the painting is by Bruegel.

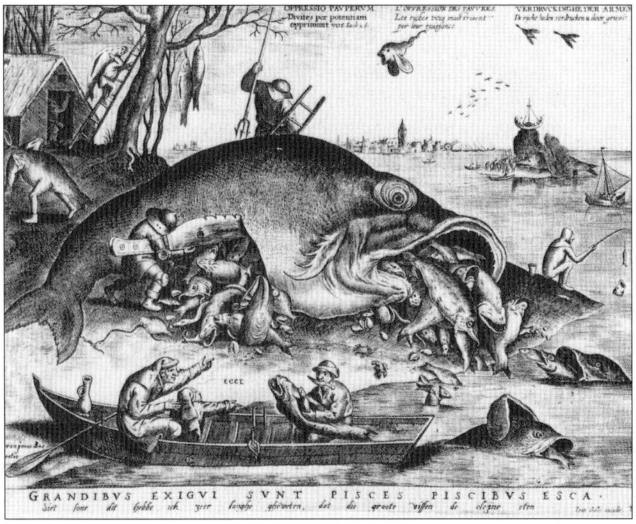

PIETER VAN DER HEYDEN
(after a drawing by Pieter Bruegel)
Big Fish Eat Little Fish
1557, British Museum, London

Although the original design was by Bruegel, the publisher Cock had the words "Hieronymus Bos—inventor" (lefthand corner) added to help sell this engraving. The word ECCE (behold) was also added to draw attention to the contrast between the soldier tackling the biggest fish and the ordinary man freeing a small one. The soldier's enormous knife carries the Christian symbol of the orb and cross, suggesting that dealing with evil must involve spiritual as well as human strength. On the bank a fisherman supplies the antithesis to the main subject: he uses a small fish to catch a bigger one.

a parallel with the Italian Triumph of Death, where three living princes encounter three dead ones. Bruegel could have seen such paintings on his Italian journey. It is interesting to consider this picture in the context of the troubled state of the Netherlands at the time. The country had been ruled since the beginning of the century by governors appointed first by the Holy Roman Emperor, Charles V, and then (from 1555) by Philip II of Spain, and increasing measures against religious heresies (i.e. non-Catholic) were provoking local resentment. But there is no evidence to link his portrayal of sacking and looting with contemporary events, and Bruegel himself was a Catholic. Perhaps it is more apt to view the picture as a powerful and universal statement about the helplessness of humanity in the face of the inevitability of death.

In 1563 Bruegel moved to Brussels, where he married Mayken, the daughter of his former teacher Pieter Coecke. He continued to work there until his death, both on paintings and on designs for Hieronymus Cock. His first son Pieter, who also became a painter (Pieter Bruegel the Younger), was born in 1564, by which time Bruegel had produced two versions of *The Tower of Babel* (see page 83), a subject he had already treated in Rome several years earlier. As well as showing extraordinary understanding of the complex construction of an intricate building, the painting exhibits a new tenderness in the delicate treatment of light and shade in the landscape background, presaging the profound revelation of

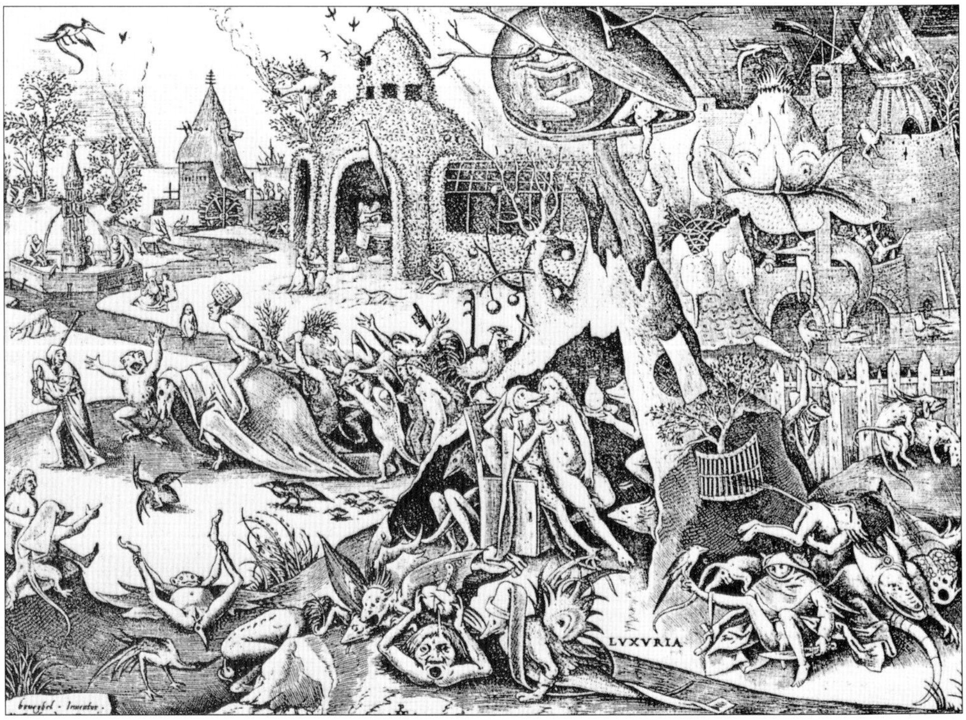

PIETER BRUEGEL
Allegory of Lust
1557, Bibliothèque Royale, Brussels

This small drawing was engraved by Pieter van der Heyden and published by Cock in the *Seven Deadly Vices* series. Bruegel's debt to Bosch can be seen in the way the pictorial field is crammed with variations on the same theme (in this case Lust). The rotting tree trunk and other "love pavilions" dotted around, and the fountain of love in the distance, derive from Bosch's *Garden of Earthly Delights* and, ultimately, from the famous medieval love garden described in the 13th-century allegorical poem *The Romance of the Rose*. The couple making love in the center parody the seduction of Adam by Eve as seen in 15th century engravings.

landscape in the later paintings of the *Months* (see page 91).

The later religious paintings

In 1564 three religious paintings underline the variety of Bruegel's painterly conceptions. The large *Procession to Calvery* (see page 87) combines vivid observation of contemporary manners with large foreground figures derived from early 15th-century Flemish painting; *The Adoration of the kings* shows his awareness of the elongated figures of 16th-century Mannerism, while *The Death of the Virgin*, painted for his friend Abraham Ortelius in *grisaille* – with grayish tonalities worked on a yellowish background – is notable for its subject matter. This necessitated an interior setting, unique in Bruegel's painting, and the subtlety of its light effects anticipate those of Rembrandt. *Grisaille,* or monochrome painting, had been used in Flemish painting since the 15th century, often on the wings of altarpieces, and was a technique Bruegel also used for a small panel of *Christ and the Woman taken in Adultery,* which he kept with him until he died.

The subject of the Virgin's death as presented in the painting was derived from the 13th-century *Golden Legend* of Jacobus de Voragine, who wrote an account of the patriarchs, confessors, and holy virgins present at the Virgin's death. This is supposedly recorded in an apocryphal book of St John the Evangelist, who is shown in the left foreground of the painting with eyes closed as though imagining the miracle of the resurrection. Four separate sources of gentle light – including the candle which according to an old custom is being placed in the hands of the dying Virgin, its light a symbol of Christian faith – are dimmed by the radiance which flows from the Virgin herself. The painting can be seen as a triumphant statement of belief in Christian salvation. In 1574 Ortelius had it engraved for some of his friends, one of whom, the poet and engraver Dierick Volckhertzoon Coornhert, testified to the power of Bruegel's art when he wrote from Haarlem to thank Ortelius: "I examined it

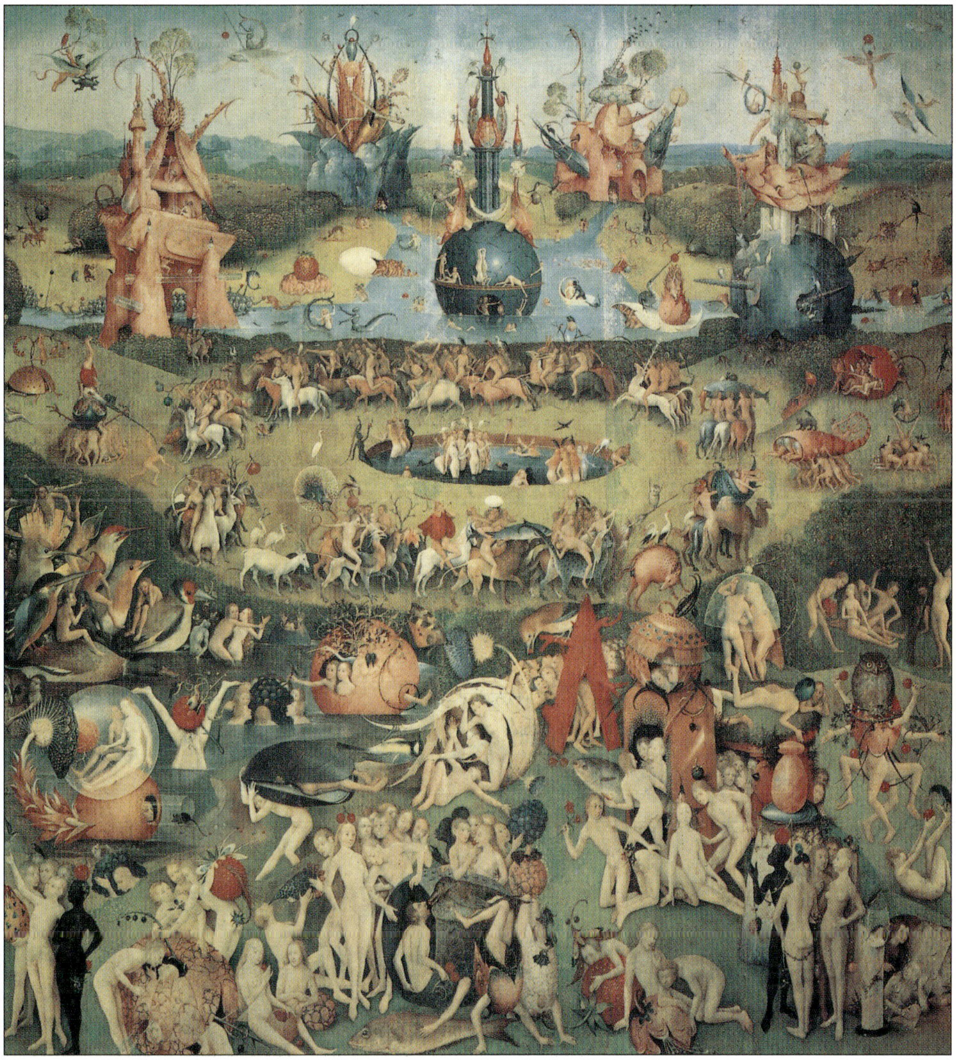

HIERONYMUS BOSCH
The Garden of Earthly Delights
(central panel)
c 1505-10, Prado, Madrid

Bosch, intensely religious, produced both altarpieces and moralizing works, such as this painting, packed with the symbolic subtleties that appealed to contemporary Flemish taste. The scene – a garden of lust rather than love – forms the center of a triptych, and is flanked by depictions of the Garden of Eden and Hell. Many of Bruegel's paintings look down in the same way on a panorama crowded with small figures, and his *Allegory of Lust* includes specific details from this composition. Probably executed for a lay patron, *The Garden of Earthly Delights* was eventually acquired by Philip II of Spain.

with pleasure and admiration from top to bottom for the artistry of its drawing and the care of the engraving . . . methinks I heard moaning, groaning and screaming and the splashing of tears in this portrayal of sorrow." Other letters from Ortelius's intellectual friends also bear witness to the high esteem in which Bruegel was held.

Bruegel's other *grisaille* panel, *Christ and the Woman Taken in Adultery* (stolen from the Courtauld Institute Galleries, London, in 1982), can be interpreted as a plea for religious tolerance, an attitude endorsed by Abraham Ortelius and others in his circle. Some of the figures in the painting, particularly that of the woman turned toward Christ, show an Italianate style, and can be related to the famous cartoons designed by Raphael in 1515-16, which could have been seen by Bruegel in Brussels, where they had been sent for weaving. These figures pave the way toward the more monumental style which Bruegel was to adopt in his later paintings.

New departures

Another characteristic belonging to many of the later paintings is an increasing interest in movement which Bruegel had already shown in the small *Landscape with the Flight into Egypt* of 1563 (Courtauld Institute Galleries, London). This painting is one of the few that can be precisely traced to the prestigious collection of Cardinal de Granvella, who in 1560 had been created archbishop of Malines and appointed by Philip II chief counsellor to the regent of the Netherlands, Margaret of Austria. Granvella's regard for the unrestricted authority of the monarch led to conflict with the freedom-loving group that emerged under the leadership of William of Orange in 1564. Forced to leave the Netherlands and his art collection, he is recorded as being particularly worried about his Bruegels.

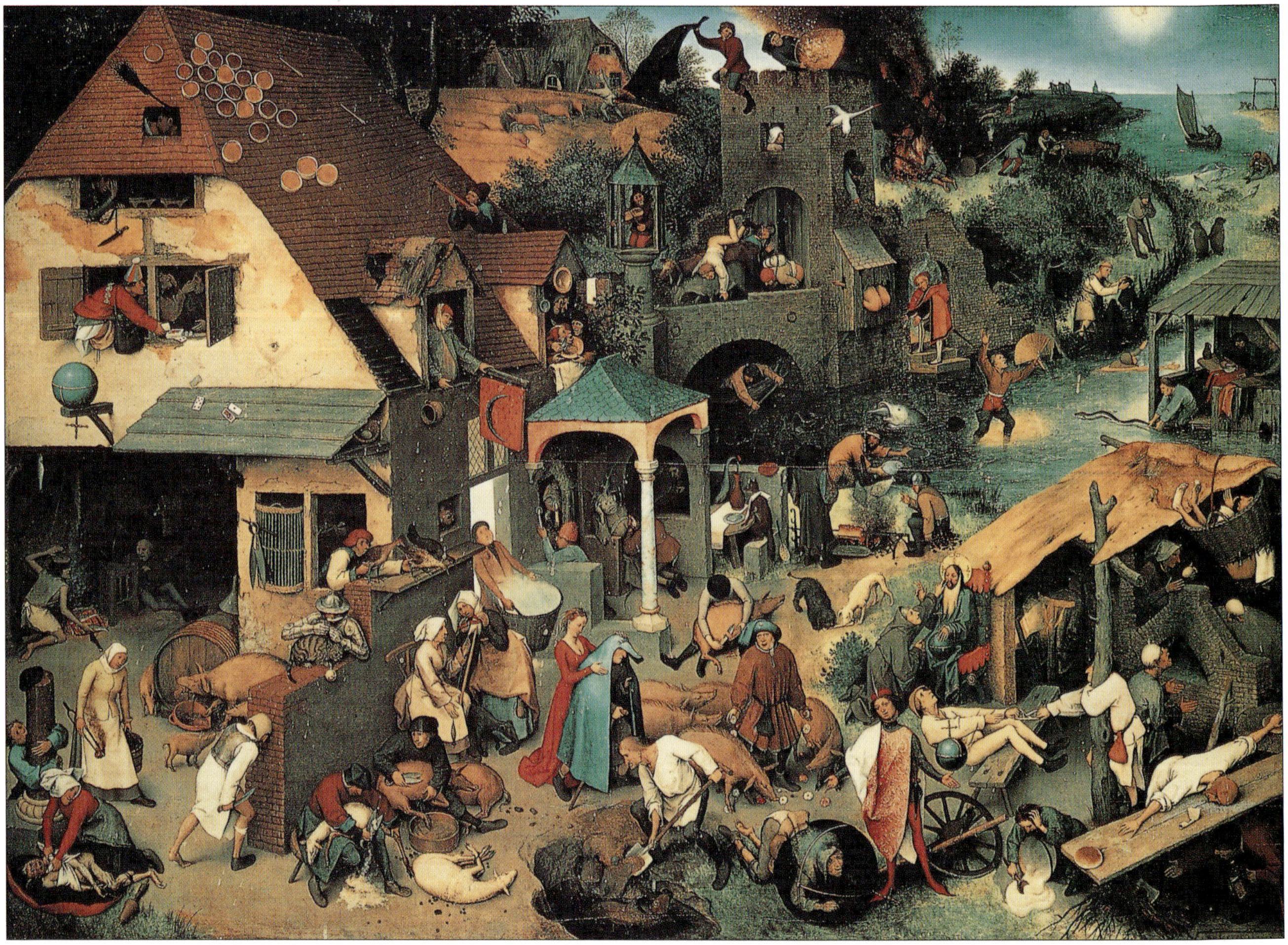

PIETER BRUEGEL
The Netherlandish Proverbs or *The Blue Cloak*
1559, Staatliche Museen, Berlin-Dahlem

Over eighty-five popular proverbs are acted out here, and acts of folly spread out to the horizon, where three tiny figures represent the parable of the blind. Spiritual blindness and the foolishness of the world is further emphasized by the orb and cross held by the seated Christ. An elegant man (foreground) balances it on his thumb and indicates the cripple who can't see it for looking. It reappears on the inn, upside down.

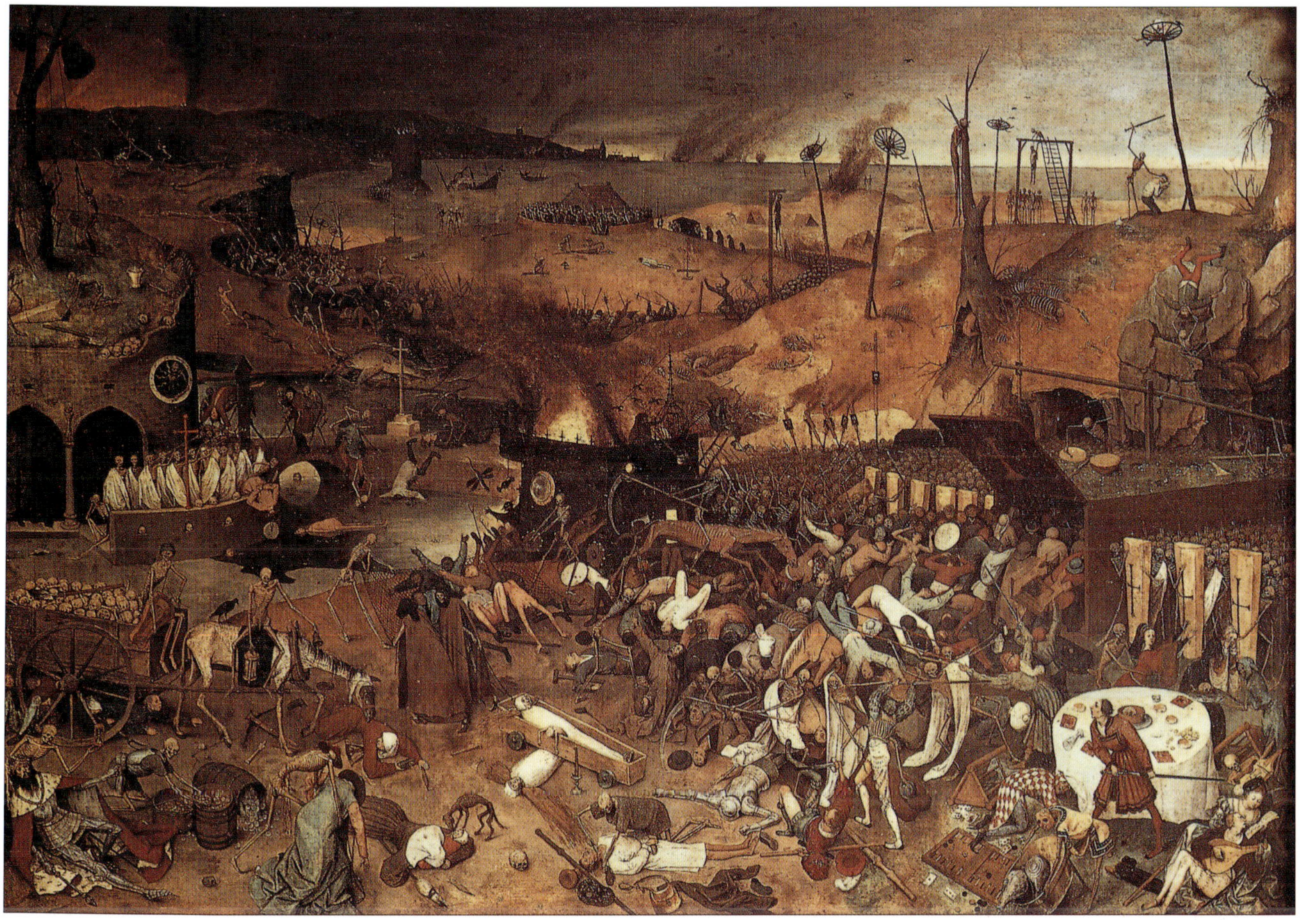

PIETER BRUEGEL
The Triumph of Death
c 1562, Prado, Madrid

Vividly rendered incidents of death and disaster are backed by a smoke- and flame-filled landscape. Skeletons toll the bell of death (left); high wheels hold rotting corpses (a contemporary reference), and, in the left-hand corner, a falling ruler cannot stay a looting skeleton. On the right, a woman stumbles before a cartload of skulls drawn by an emaciated horse. The skeleton with a scythe represents death cutting life short, and the horse he rides – almost a skeleton itself – is the red horse of war described in the Book of Revelations.

The new feeling for movement and the increasing ability successfully to combine figures and landscape culminated in the large paintings of the *Months* which Bruegel produced for the Antwerp banker, Niclaes Jonghelinck, in 1565. Using a combination of superb landscape panoramas, acutely and sympathetically observed figures, and a palette chosen in each case to epitomize the major colors of the season depicted, Bruegel achieved a presentation of landscape which was completely new in its evocation of atmosphere and its seemingly close relation to nature. His way of painting also changed, shifting from the more precise execution of earlier works to a rapid, spontaneous – sometimes almost sketchy – technique, with the paint often applied quite thinly and the underpainting sometimes left visible. This is a technique that the great 17th-century Flemish painter Rubens, who owned several Bruegel paintings, obviously studied closely.

The years between 1566 and 1569 saw the continued production of both paintings and drawings by Bruegel and the birth of Bruegel's second son Jan (in 1568), who was to become a still life and landscape painter. Bruegel's paintings were as varied as ever in both subject matter and approach, ranging from biblical subjects to peasant scenes and proverbs and from dazzling landscape panoramas to close-ups of monumental figures. The *Peasant Wedding* (see page 99), *The Parable of the Blind* and *The Conversation of St Paul* are among the products of these years. According to Van Mander, Bruegel was also commissioned by the City Council of Brussels to do a series of "pieces" celebrating the construction of the new Brussels Antwerp canal, but he died in 1569 before they could be done.

This was a period which saw an increase in the hostility felt in the Netherlands for the ideas of Philip II.

Although William of Orange had succeeded in removing Cardinal de Granvella, a request in 1564 for the withdrawal of the Inquisition (established in the Netherlands since 1522) and of the more rigorous anti-heretical edicts was countered by the arrival in 1567 of the Spanish Duke of Alva, who established a reign of terror. Van Mander says that Bruegel had his wife destroy some of his drawings before he died because they were "too biting and sharp" and might have brought her trouble. This may or may not be true; it is unlikely that any of Bruegel's paintings of these years was intended to reflect current events, but it is possible that his modern-dress presentations of subjects such as *The Numbering at Bethlehem* (see page 95) and *The Massacre of the Innocents* might have been seen by contemporaries as a general comment on governmental restrictions and an endorsement of the growing demands of the Protestants for freedom from persecution.

Bruegel died in September 1569, and his wife Mayken in 1578. They were buried in the church in which they had been married, Notre Dame de la Chapelle in Brussels. It was there that their son Jan put up a memorial to them adorned with a painting of *Christ Giving the Keys to St Peter* by Rubens, a fitting tribute from the next great Flemish painter and perhaps a reminder of Bruegel's personal faith and belief in spiritual salvation. While that can only be guessed at, Bruegel's paintings – totaling less than fifty and mostly produced between 1555 and 1569 – remain as an incontestable and vital testimony to his personal vision and technical brilliance. They are as fresh and exciting today as they must have been in the 16th century, and their indefinite capacity for interpretation only serves to underline the richness of the genius that created them.

PIETER BRUEGEL
The Death of the Virgin
1565, Upton House (National Trust), Banbury, Oxfordshire

Bruegel painted this tiny *grisaille* panel (only $14\frac{1}{2} \times 22$ inches/36×55 cm) for his friend Abraham Ortelius. Although it was engraved after Bruegel's death, its tonal subtleties make it unlikely that it was designed with engraving in mind. The almost palpable reverence and sorrow which emanate from the mourning group epitomize Ortelius' words about Bruegel – that "he painted many things that cannot be painted."

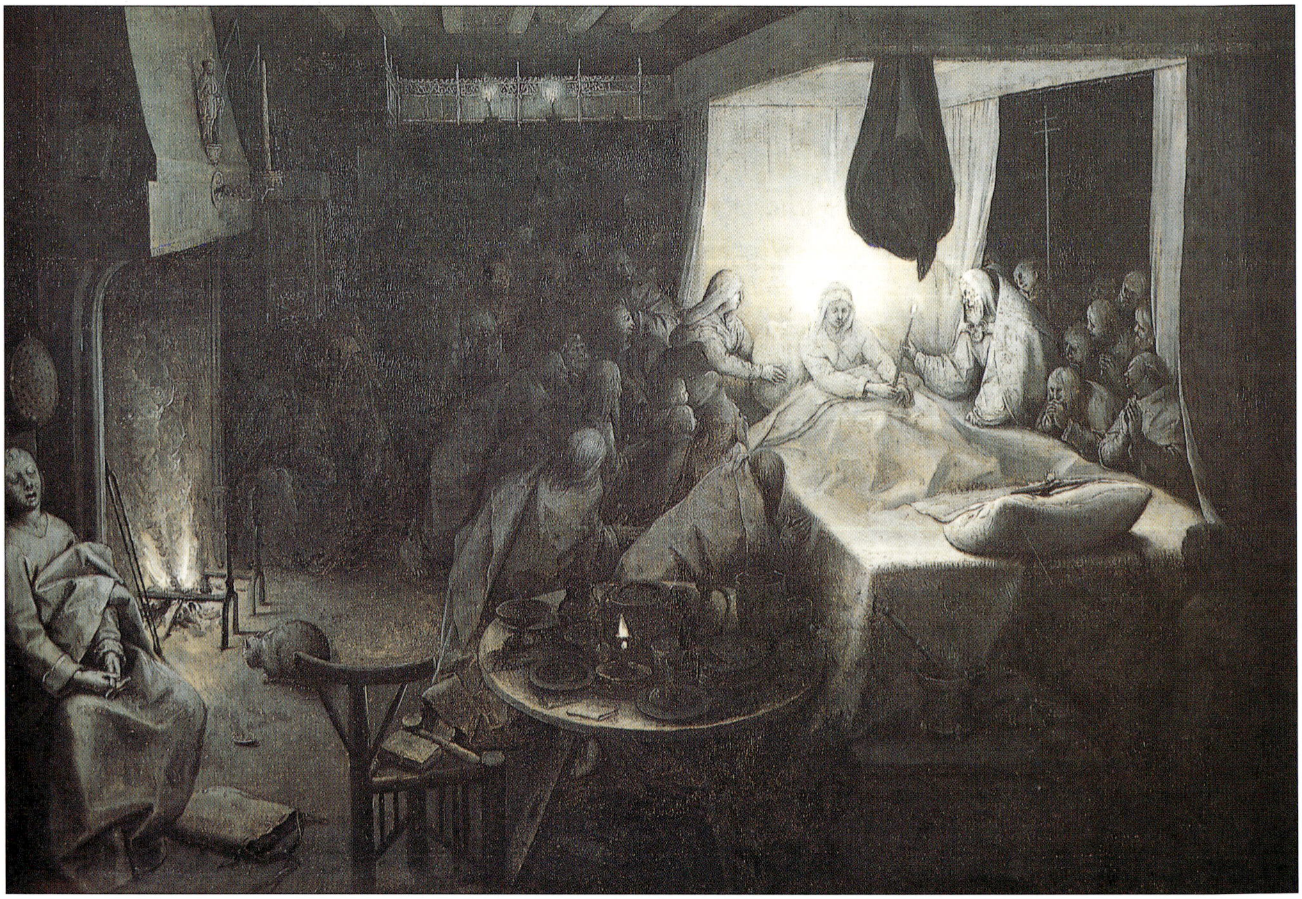

BRUEGEL'S PAINTING METHODS

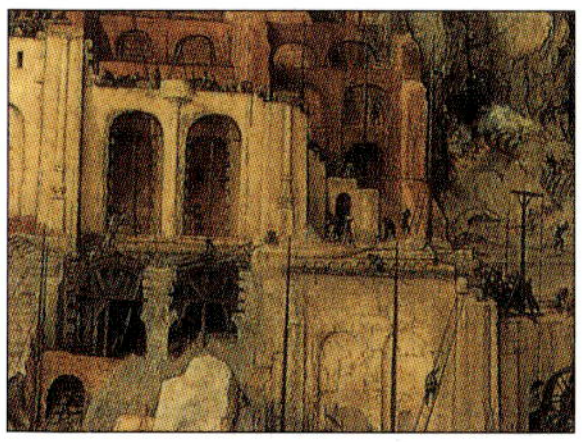

This detail from *The Tower of Babel* shows both Bruegel's amazing skill in rendering architectural detail and the variety of his brushwork.

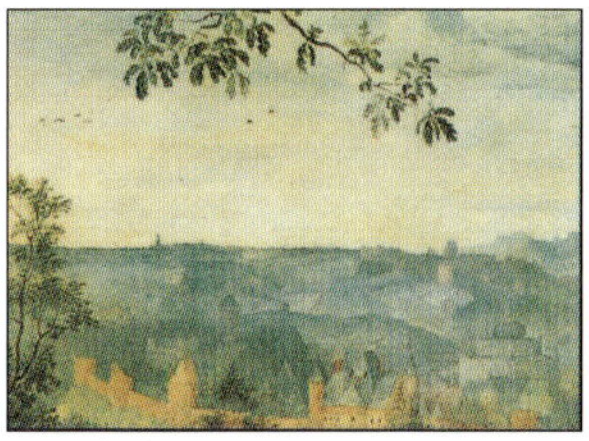

The luminous effect of light in the background of *The Procession to Calvary* is the result of successive applications of thin glazes over a white gesso ground.

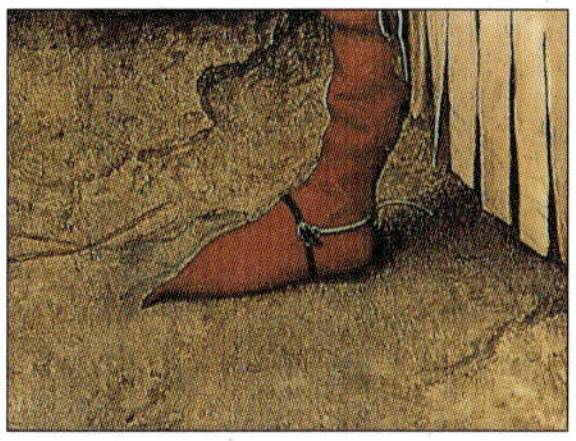

In this area of *The Adoration of the Kings* Bruegel's underpainting can be seen because the top layers of paint have thinned with age.

Bruegel was heir to the finely detailed techniques found in 15th-century Flemish painting, most of which, like his own, was in oil on wood panel. The panels for painting were made to order by specialist joiners from seasoned oak, probably imported from Poland. They were then prepared for painting, first being planed as smooth as possible and then covered with layers of a whitish ground made of chalk mixed with animal glue. The ground filled up any remaining unevenness in the wood and formed a foundation on which subsequent areas of color could be built up.

The next stage was to sketch out the final composition in an underdrawing (similar to the *sinopia* of a fresco). Bruegel's underdrawings (now visible through infrared photography and reflectography) were made with a thin paint line. They are particularly interesting because they show that he often changed his mind between a first and a final idea. A few extant drawings are evidence that he also worked out ideas on paper. Once the underdrawing was established, it was covered with an intermediate layer, probably of size or underpaint, before the actual painting was begun. For the final stage, pigments were ground up, mixed with linseed oil (and possibly turpentine) and applied, often fairly loosely, in thin layers. Details and highlights were added in tiny strokes, and Bruegel sometimes gave emphasis to his figures by delicately outlining them."

The brilliant reds and glowing orange-browns in paintings such as *A Peasant Wedding* are the result of the slow, careful technique of building up layers of thin paint over an underdrawing. Such brilliance is difficult, indeed almost impossible, to achieve with the opaque, buttery paint used by most oil painters today.

All pigments were ground by hand before painting, usually by apprentices or assistants, and the range of colors used was relatively small. Those used by Bruegel would have included the following:

Dark blue — azurite (apparently difficult to obtain because it had to be imported from Hungary, which was repeatedly invaded by the Turks).
Mid blue — smalt (used as a substitute for azurite and made from blue cobalt glass)
Green — malachite (green copper pigment)
Yellow — ocher and lead-tin yellow
Red — vermilion (a sublimation of sulfur and mercury)
White — lead white prepared by artificial means.

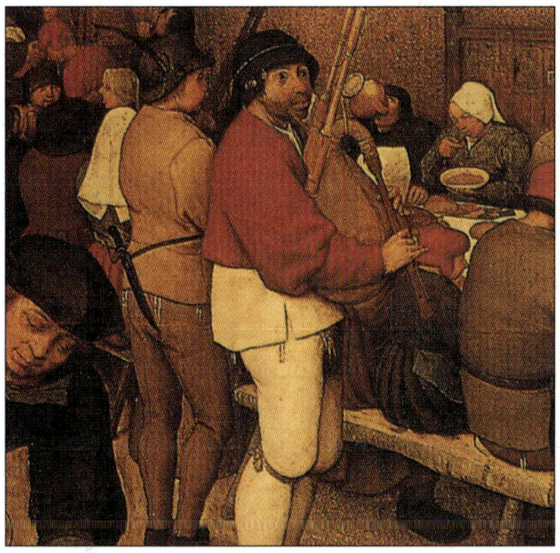

CHRONOLOGY OF BRUEGEL'S LIFE

Late 1520s Pieter Bruegel (the Elder) was probably born sometime between 1525 and 1530 in Breda, North Brabant.

1551 Bruegel becomes Master of the Guild of St Luke in Antwerp after an apprenticeship with (according to his biographer Karel Van Mander) the Antwerp painter Pieter Coecke van Aelst.

1552-4 Travels in France and Italy, visiting Lyons, Calabria, Sicily, Naples, Rome and possibly Bologna. Returns over the Alps. Works for the miniaturist Giulio Clovio while in Rome, and it is probably there that he paints in 1553 his first signed and dated painting: *Christ Appearing to the Apostles at the Sea of Tiberias.*

1555 Returns to Antwerp, where he lives until 1563. Produces only surviving drawing for the *Large Landscapes,* engravings published by Hieronymus Cock. Probable date of painting *Landscape with the Fall of Icarus.*

1556 Drawing for the print *Big Fish Eat Little Fish* published by Cock as the work of Hieronymus Bosch.

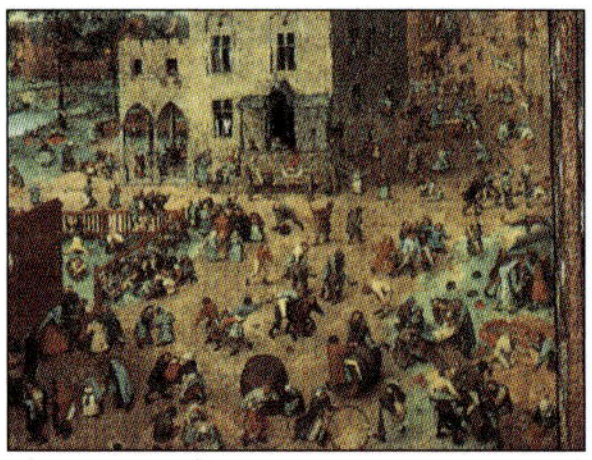

Children's Games

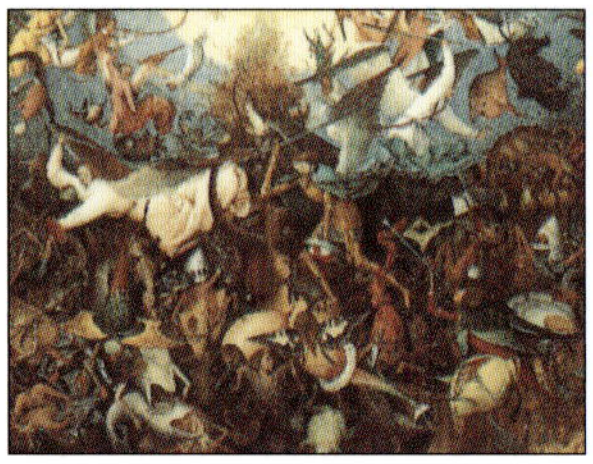

The Fall of the Rebel Angels

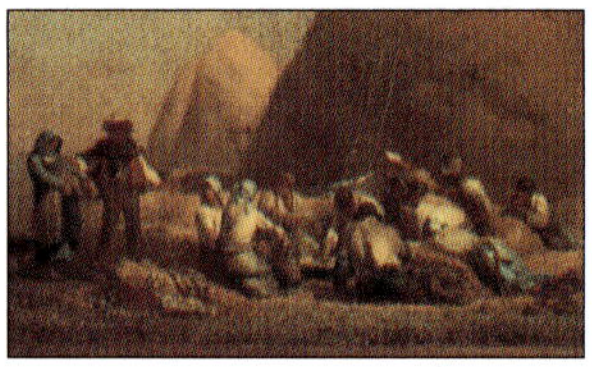

The Corn Harvest

1556-9 Works on drawings for engravings of *The Seven Vices* and *The Seven Virtues.* Paints *The Battle Between Carnival and Lent* (1559).

1560 Paints *Children's Games.*

1562 Paints *The Fall of the Rebel Angels.*

1563 Paints *The Tower of Babel.* Moves to Brussels, where he lives for the rest of his life. Marries Mayken, the daughter of Pieter Coecke van Aelst, and continues to produce designs for Hieronymus Cock.

1564 Birth of son Pieter (the Younger), who was also to become a painter, and frequently copied his father's work. Paints *The Procession to Calvary* and *The Adoration of the Kings.*

1565 Paints the cycle of the *Months* for the Antwerp banker Niclaes Jonghelinck.

1566 Paints *The Numbering at Bethlehem.*

1567 Probable date of *The Peasant Wedding.*

1568 Birth of second son Jan, to become a still life and landscape painter, sometimes called Velvet Bruegel. Paints *The Parable of the Blind.*

1569 Death of Bruegel in Brussels.

1578 Death of Bruegel's wife.

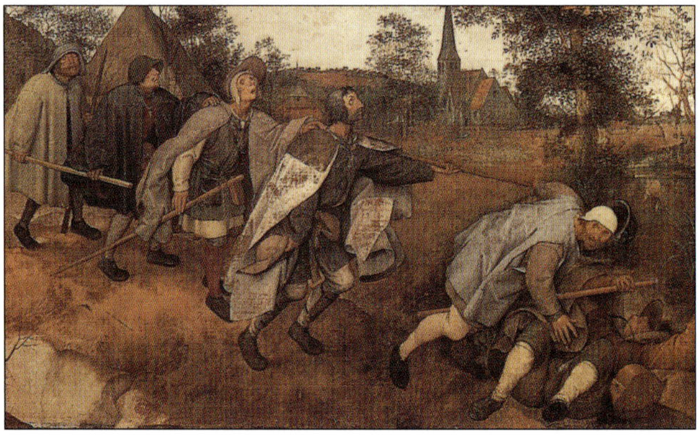

The Parable of the Blind

The Paintings

THE BATTLE BETWEEN CARNIVAL AND LENT

signed and dated 1559
$46\frac{1}{2} \times 64\frac{3}{4}$in/118×164.5cm
Oil on panel
Kunsthistorisches Museum, Vienna

In the foreground of the painting is the confrontation between feast and fast – figures representing Carnival (on the left) and Lent. This had already been the subject of a print by the Malines artist Franz Hogenberg, published by Hieronymus Cock the year before, and was a concept that might have been acted out in villages during the Carnival season. It was also the theme of plays produced by the *rederijker kamers* (chambers of rhetoric) which existed in most Netherlandian towns, and which performed plays and organized the allegorical floats used in religious processions. At the center of the scene a couple led by a jester – every *rederijker kamer* had one – underlines the *rederijker* connection and, by extension, the theme of the world as a stage.

Carnival, portrayed as a pot-bellied man, sits astride a barrel jousting with a spit loaded with rich meats, while the thin, sad figure of Lent is armed only with a griddle displaying two small fish – suitable Lenten fare. Carnival is crowned with a rich game pie; Lent wears a beehive surrounded by busy bees symbolizing (since St Ambrose) the Church and its Community. A broader comparison fills out the painting with the sweep of Carnival celebrations on the left and pious Lenten observances on the right. Two men gamble in the extreme left corner; a group in front of the inn watches a popular play, *The Dirty Bride*. This tells the story of a peasant who aped the ways of the rich – the hero is leading his untidy bride to the marriage bed inside a rickety tent. The inn sign with the words "In the Blue Boat" refers to the name of societies which organized Carnival festivities – but the phrase "Blue Boat" was also used to describe people who wasted their time on drinking and gambling. In front of the building behind the inn, another play, *Urson and Valentine* (the story of two twins separated at birth but finally reunited), is being performed while a procession led by bagpipers files up the street.

In contrast to the mindless revelry on the left, whose participants ignore the group of cripples in their midst, the crowd behind Lent is dutiful; the children's foreheads are marked with the penitential ash of Ash Wednesday, the first day of Lent; beggars are rewarded with alms; there is plenty of trade at the fish stall, and a group of people carrying chairs, showing they have just attended a sermon, comes out of the church. In contrast to the inn's sign, the church's trefoil window recalls the Trinity, while statues below its arch are already suitably draped for Lent.

Bruegel does not seem to favor one side more than the other, although he ensures that the main subject comes over clearly by making the figures of Carnival and Lent proportionately larger than all the others, an old-fashioned device which makes sense of the packed scene. One detail might indicate a deeply spiritual comment: the trees in the background are lightly greened in contrast to the bare branches behind the Carnival side, and it is tempting to read the greening as symbolic of the new life that believers would find reaffirmed in the Resurrection of Christ on Easter Sunday. But it is more likely to denote the passage of time: the practices of Carnival and Lent do not actually coincide, as here, but succeed one another. At the center of Bruegel's stage the jester, like the shepherd in *Landscape with the Fall of Icarus*, may be the clue to the underlying meaning of the painting. He leads toward the Carnival side of the painting, but the directions of the footsteps of the couple behind him – one to the left, one to the right – suggest both the eternal uncertainty of humanity and the possibility of choice between good and evil.

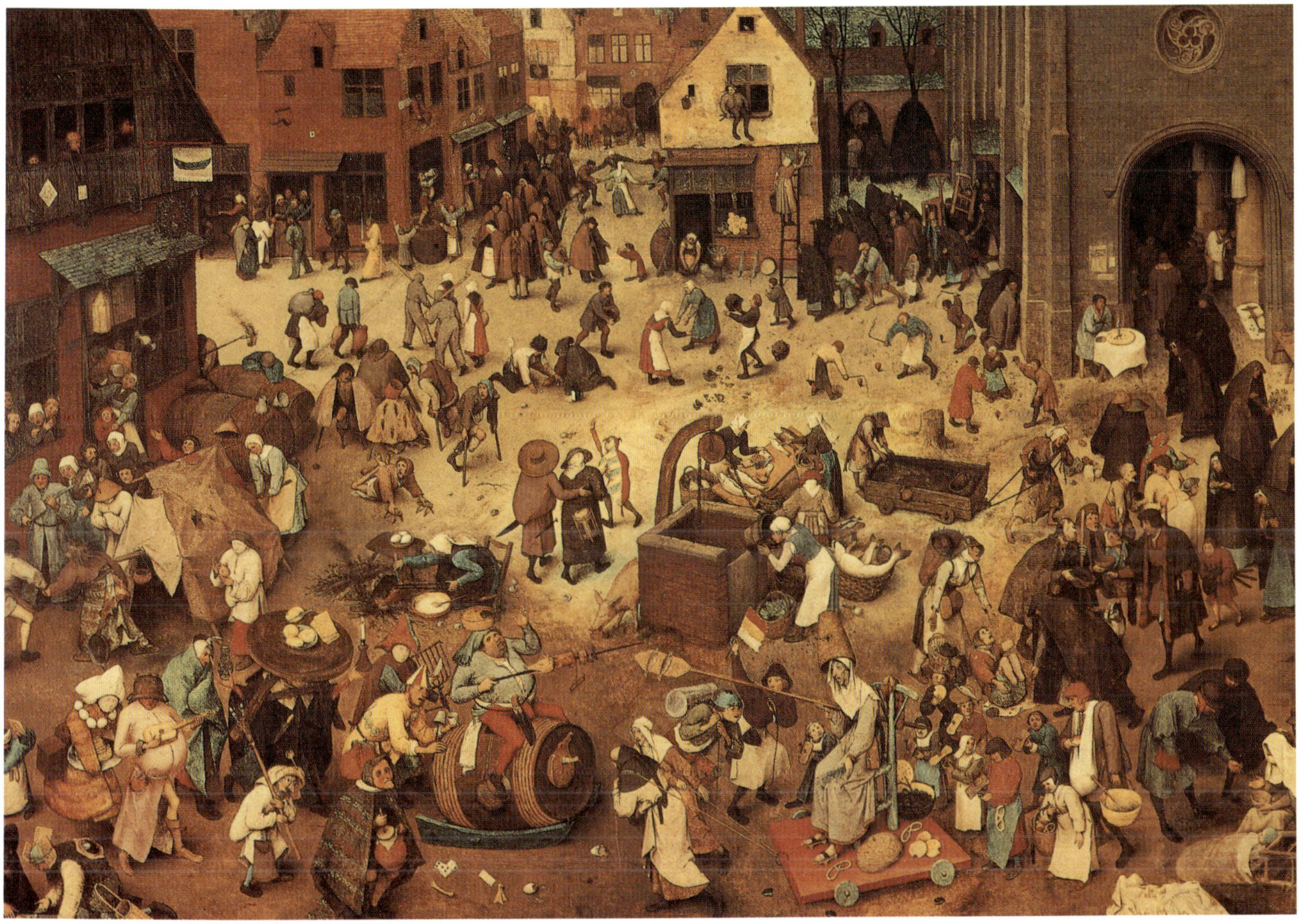

The high viewpoint, revealing a village setting crowded with figures, was also used by Bruegel in *The Netherlandish Proverbs* painted in the same year and in *Children's Games* of 1560 (see page 79). All three paintings can be related compositionally to Bosch's *The Garden of Earthly Delights* (see page 67), from which Bruegel had borrowed motifs for the engravings of *The Seven Vices* (1557). The concept of a world of absurd happenings spread out before the spectator as though on a stage can be connected with the idea of the *Theatrum Mundi* (Theatre of the World), derived from Classical antiquity and current in 16th-century thought.

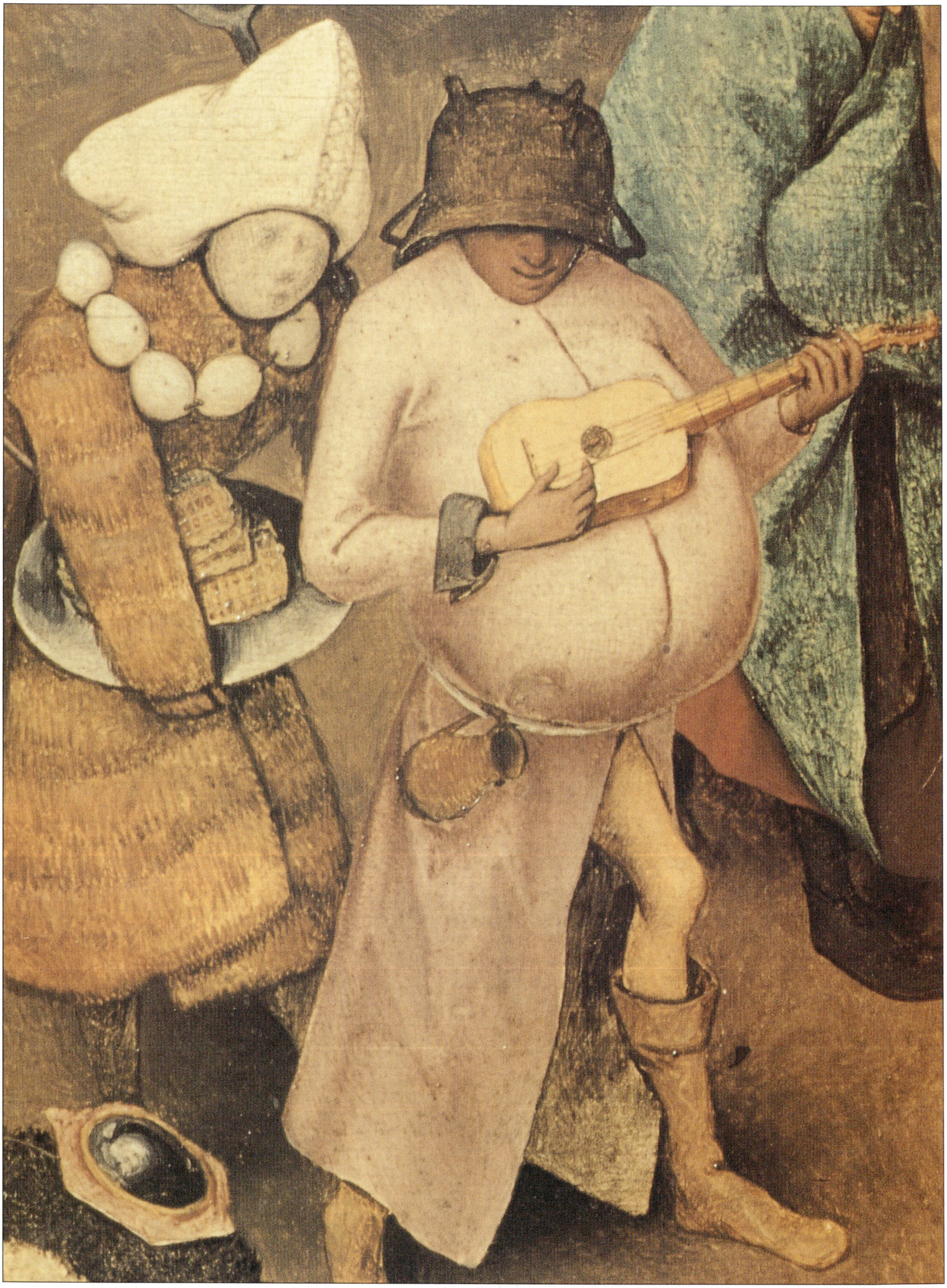

1 *Actual size detail*

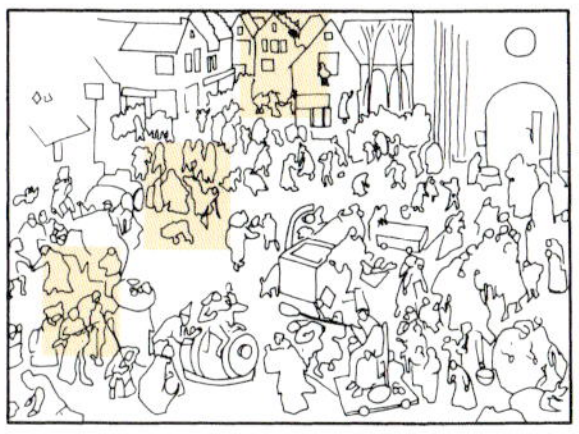

1 *Actual size detail* The coat of the man with the mandolin is painted in a delicate range of tones from the pale pink highlighting his pot belly to the subtle darks used for creases and folds. These tonal changes are made smoothly, while a different treatment is used for the garment of the clown-faced woman behind – tiny parallel brushstrokes of contrasting light and dark indicate the rough texture and structure of the material, possibly fur. Dark outlines applied with a fine brush to faces, fingers, and legs make these details stand out from a distance.

2 Bruegel has noted the contrasting light effects created by the glow of the flames on the broadly sketched figures around the fire and by the brightly lit doorway which throws the standing figures into relief. The architectural details of the houses above are precisely delineated; even the inset brick arches over the windows are suggested by controlled flicks of paint.

3 In this area of the painting six cripples exhibit their deformities. The one in the center is dressed up in a paper hat and has fox tails dangling from his cloak. The attitudes of the figures are clarified by dark outlines, and particular attention is paid to the cast shadows of the crutches. Thinly applied paint on garments and on the areas between the figures shows the underpaint and the underlying texture of the original chalk and glue ground.

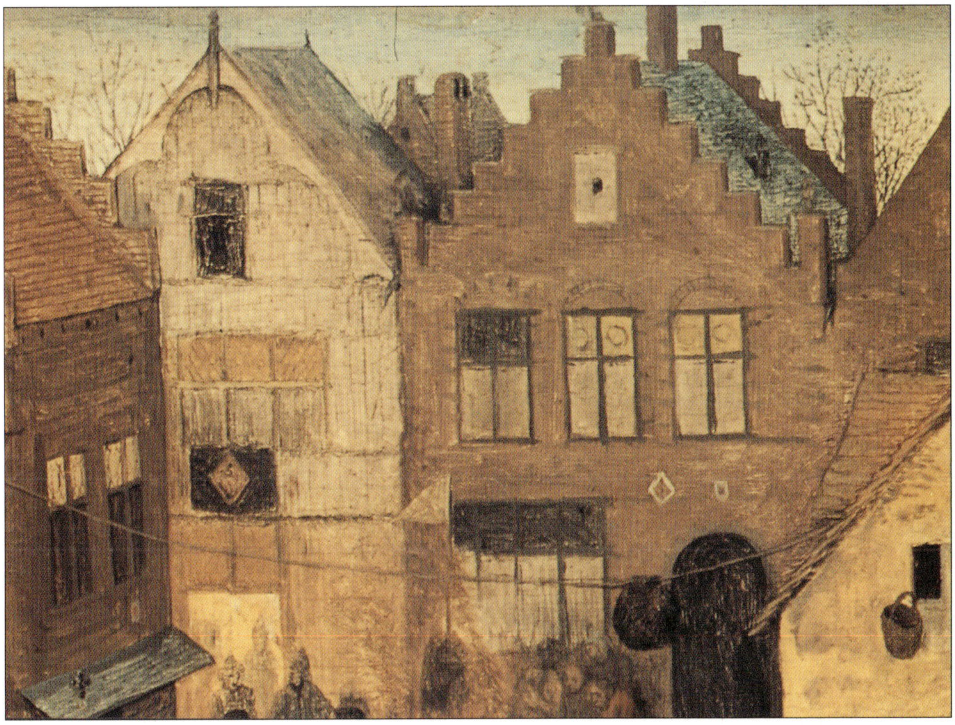

2

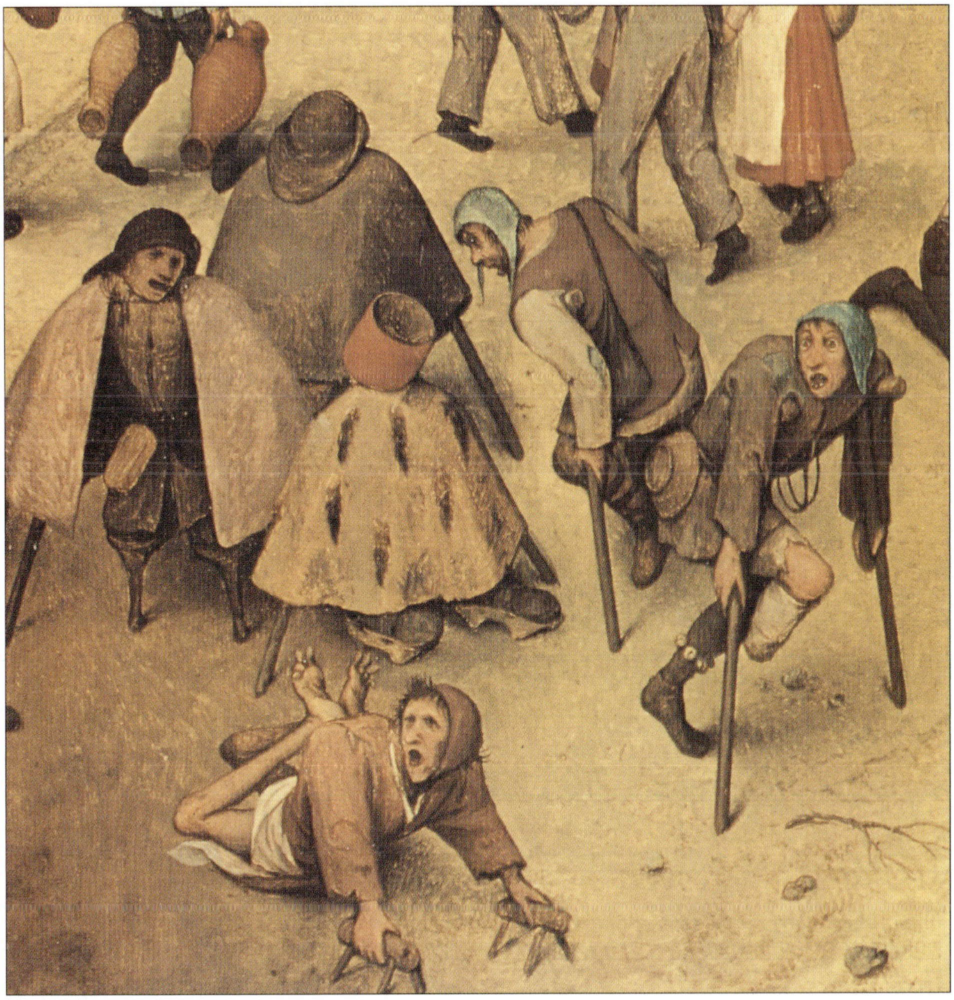

3

Children's Games

Signed and dated 1560
$46^1/_2 \times 63^3/_8$in/118×161cm
Oil on panel
Kunsthistorisches Museum, Vienna

Portraying as it does more than ninety contemporary children's games, the painting was probably designed to appeal to the passion for cataloging and classifying human behavior characteristic of Humanist cultures. Like *The Netherlandish Proverbs* (see page 68) and *The Battle Between Carnival and Lent* (see page 75) this scene would have been attractive to the Humanist collectors and scholars in Antwerp with whom Bruegel was associated.

Again the painting has a high viewpoint, and the world spread out before us shows over 200 children briskly engaged in diverse activities: hoop-rolling, playing knucklebones, leapfrogging, spinning tops, walking on stilts and so on. The games are portrayed with a precision that resulted from Bruegel's perceptive observation and drawings of the natural world and its inhabitants. As such, they are enjoyable just to look at, but deeper meanings can be looked for.

An anonymous poem published in Antwerp in 1530 had compared humanity with children who run and jump and fool around. The painting, like *The Netherlandish Proverbs,* could therefore be generally symbolic of folly, an interpretation which can be supported in various ways. The strongly indicated diagonals of the composition meet just where two children are turning upside down on a bench, suggesting a topsy-turvy world where foolishness is rampant. The large mask displayed at the upper window on the left suggests "playing at masks," but also represents the tragedy or folly of life itself. The marriage procession with a child dressed as a bride is a focal event; it draws attention to a 16th-century literary tradition which saw marriage as foolish because it permitted lust and meant that woman would eventually be dominated by man.

Other aspects of the painting introduce another concept: the idea that playing is connected with learning. Parallel to the picture plane, and so dominating the town square, is an important building, probably the town hall, seat of local authority and a reminder of the civic virtues to which children's upbringing should ideally lead. And while summer games go on within the delicately painted landscape on the left, the long street on the right takes the viewer to a distant horizon — possibly representative of the larger world into which the children will inevitably pass.

Finally, there are two interesting games which balance each other at each corner of the foreground. On the left is knucklebones, the game of chance which can suggest that all life is a lottery; on the right there is a girl playing at shop, a game which involves the artist himself. The funnel and scales on the girl's bench are to measure the red dust she is scraping from the brick in front of her, and this was used to make a special artist's pigment. When Bruegel's famous predecessor, Albrecht Dürer, visited the Netherlands in 1520-21, he bought some of this pigment, and noted in his diary that Antwerp was its exclusive source because it was made from new red bricks unique to the town. Bruegel has placed his own name and 1560, the date of the painting, at the end of the bench containing the precious dust. This could be a deliberate reference to his special role as the painter and visualizer of another version of the Theatre of the World and its spectacle of the absurdity of human life.

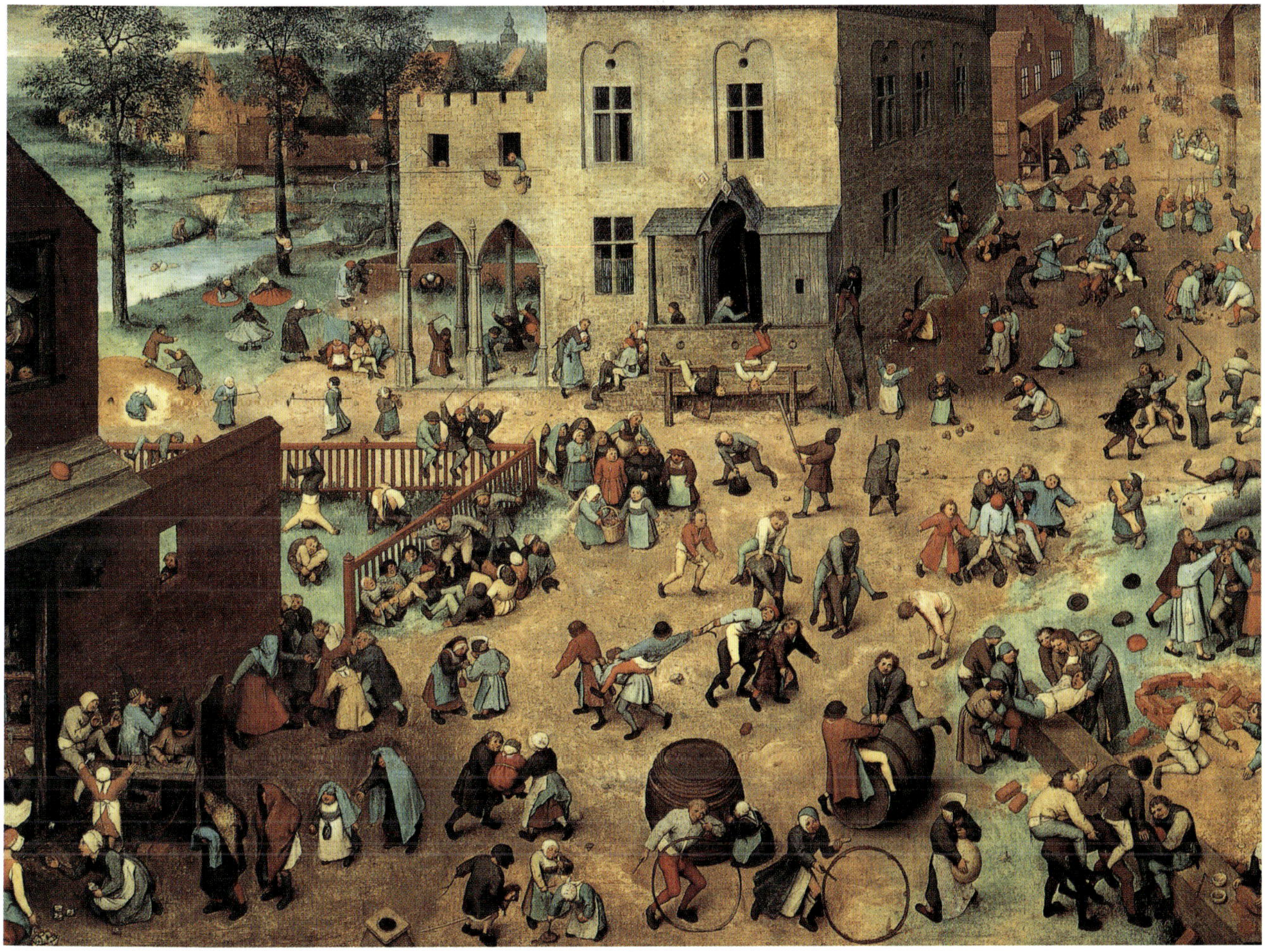

Mentioned in Karel Van Mander's account of Bruegel's life, *Children's Games* was one of the paintings which eventually passed into the collection of Archduke Ernst of Austria (Governor of the Netherlands 1593-95) towards the end of the 16th century. Artistic precedents for the subject already existed in calendar miniatures and in series of the Ages of Man. The latter interpretation has been suggested in connection with this painting, but is unlikely in view of the fact that there are no records of any other paintings by Bruegel which could have formed part of such a series.

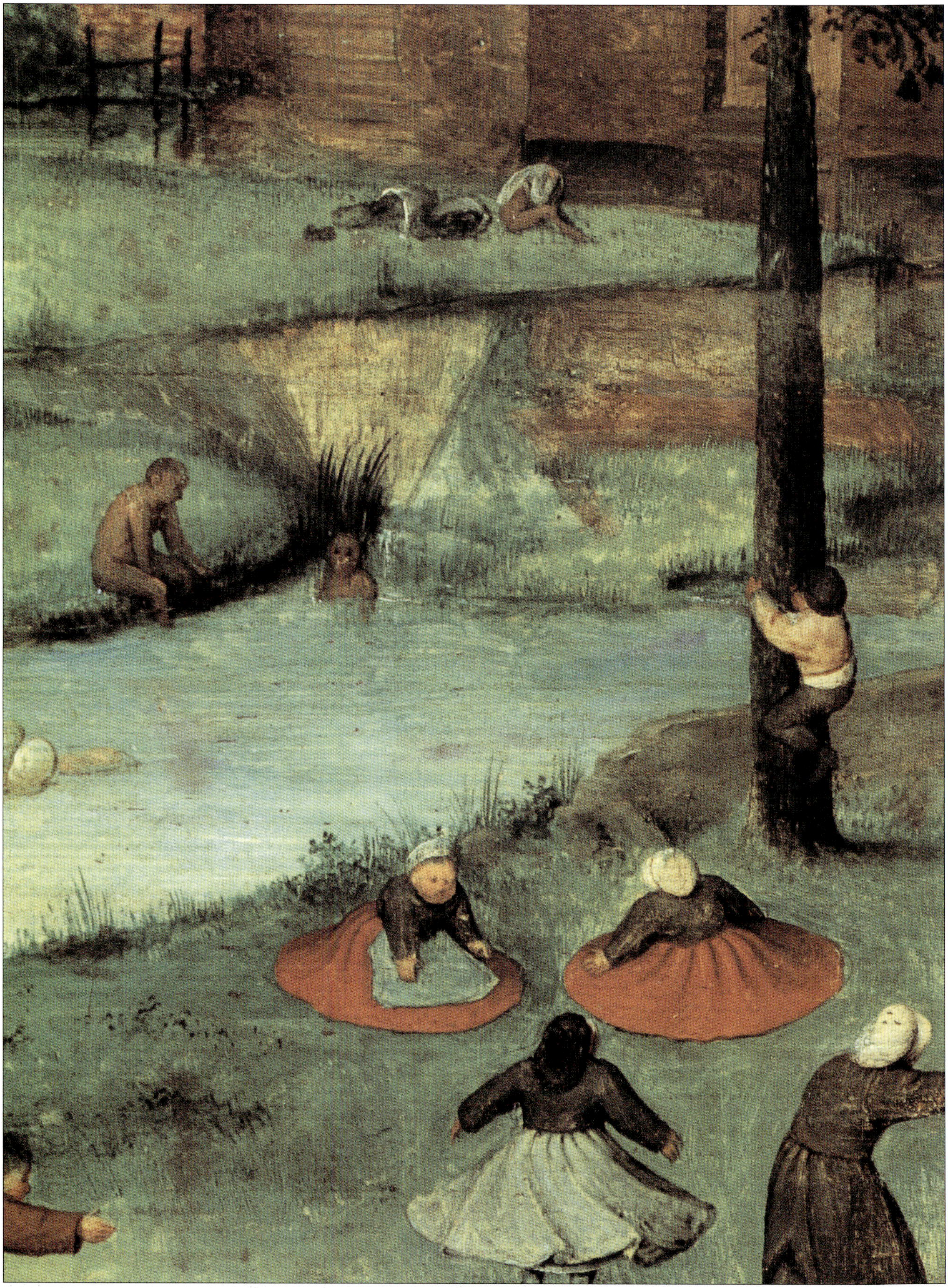

1 *Actual size detail*

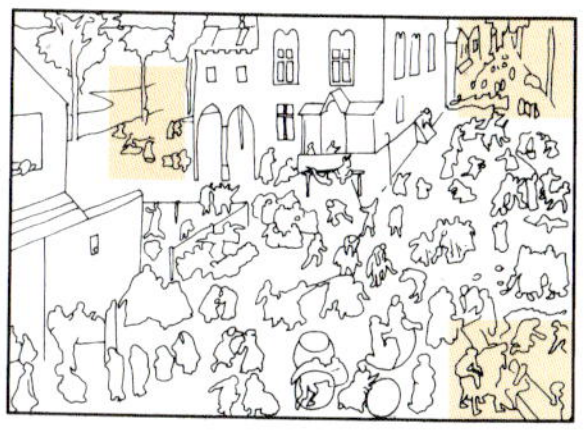

1 *Actual size detail* Horizontal strokes of blue, pale blue, and white, used for the water, contrast with the grassy areas where Bruegel has brushed on subtly mixed greens with varied brushstrokes, some vertical, some curved. Tiny strokes of darker greens are used for the reeds growing by the water's edge. The figures are simplified, but the girls' skirts include carefully placed shadows to give them volume and movement. The standing figure on the right is playing "whom shall I choose?"

2 Bruegel is following the laws of aerial perspective as he gradually diminishes the strength of color with which he depicts the buildings in the street. Details and figures get smaller as they move further away from the spectator's eye. Yet the clarity of detail is not lost; the tiny figures are clearly seen playing "follow the leader," "hare and hounds," "piggyback rides," and other games.

3 The big wooden beam that serves as a bench is painted thinly in dark brown dragged over a lighter tone to suggest graining. But the figures are painted in fairly thick, rich paint, with details such as the hanging laces of jerkins and the highlights on hands added in with tiny strokes of paint. Bruegel has signed his name on the end of the bench. Until 1559 he had spelt it "Brueghel," but then changed it, for no known reason, to Bruegel.

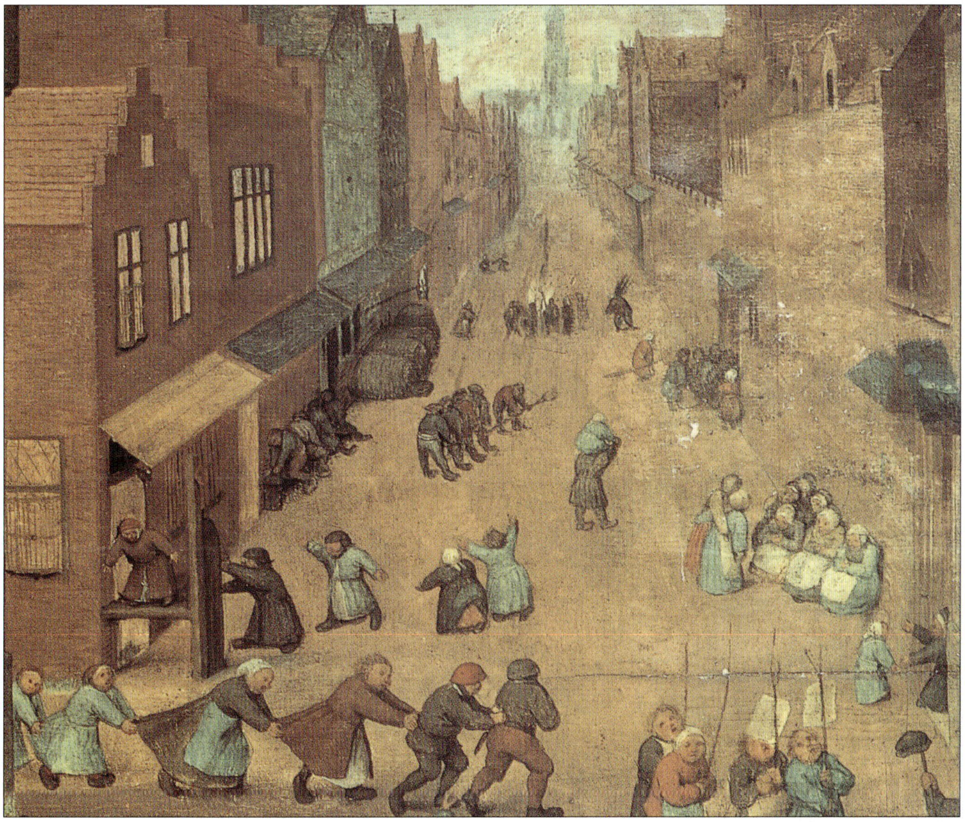

2

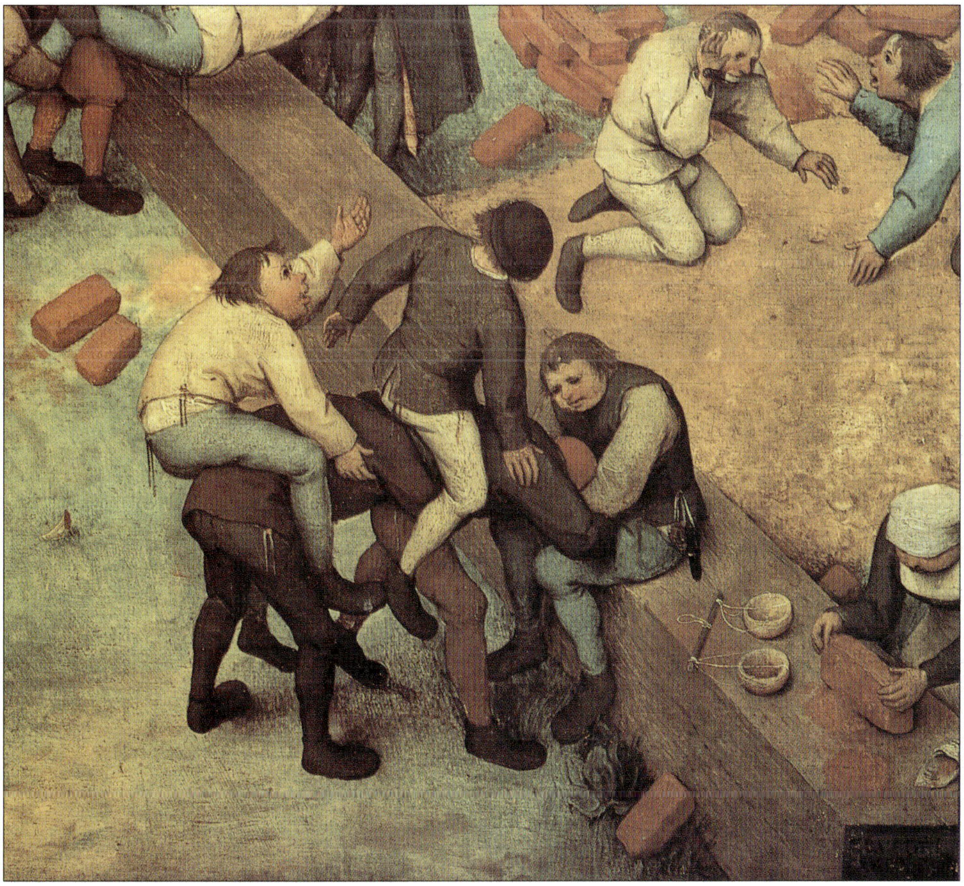

3

THE TOWER OF BABEL

Signed and dated 1563
$44^{7}/_{8} \times 61$in/114×155cm
Oil on panel
Kunsthistorisches Museum, Vienna

The building of the tower of Babel is described in the Old Testament (Genesis 11:1-9). The descendants of Noah baked bricks and built a town, and a tower with its top reaching heaven, on a plain in the land of Shinar (Mesopotamia). God then punished the people's pride in their achievement by muddling up the common language that they spoke, so that they could no longer understand one another, and scattered them over the earth. The physical origin of the tower was the ziggurat, a large brick temple-tower which was a real feature of the ancient cities of Mesopotamia where Babel (Babylon) was located. Babel is described in the Bible as part of the empire of Nimrod (a legendary ruler of the second millennium BC), and the 1st-century Jewish historian, Flavius Josephus, expanded the account of the building of the tower to suggest that Nimrod had actually supervised it, as in this painting.

The subject had been treated by earlier Flemish artists, and one composition, which Bruegel could have known, uses all the same details: the group of people around Nimrod, the ships and the landscape. In Bruegel's version the crowned ruler, elegantly clad in a fur-lined cloak and holding a scepter, appears in the left-hand corner; the workmen who have seen him are either down on their knees in front of him, or hastily getting onto them. Bruegel uses the figures, the houses around the base of the tower and the subtly lit landscape to emphasize the tower's enormous size, and he gives both the workmen and the town a realistically contemporary appearance which makes a telling contrast to the fantasy of the tower.

The tower itself is inspired by Bruegel's memories of the Colosseum in Rome and by prints of Roman ruins produced by the printer and publisher Hieronymus Cock, which Bruegel would have known. It shows a masterly understanding of building construction; the layered arches and the buttresses look completely believable, as do the various winches which are hauling up the big building blocks. The tower has an inner core built of red brick, but it is faced with creamy colored stone, as were the great buildings of ancient Rome.

Making the tower reminiscent of ancient Roman buildings is a reminder that although they had been built to last for ever they had fallen into ruins. The tower is thus a symbol not only of pride punished, but also of the transience of man's earthly achievements. Literary comments echo such interpretations: Nimrod had been picked out in Dante's *Divine Comedy* as an example of punished pride, and writers contemporary with Bruegel used the ruins of Rome as an example of the fleetingness of man's work.

Bruegel produced three versions of this subject: this one, which was at one time owned by the Antwerp banker Niclaes Jonghelinck; a version on ivory painted for Giulio Clovio when Bruegel was in Rome; and a second smaller panel painting. The latter is usually thought to be dated about a year later than this, which it resembles except for the substitution of a contemporary stone quarry for Nimrod and his group.

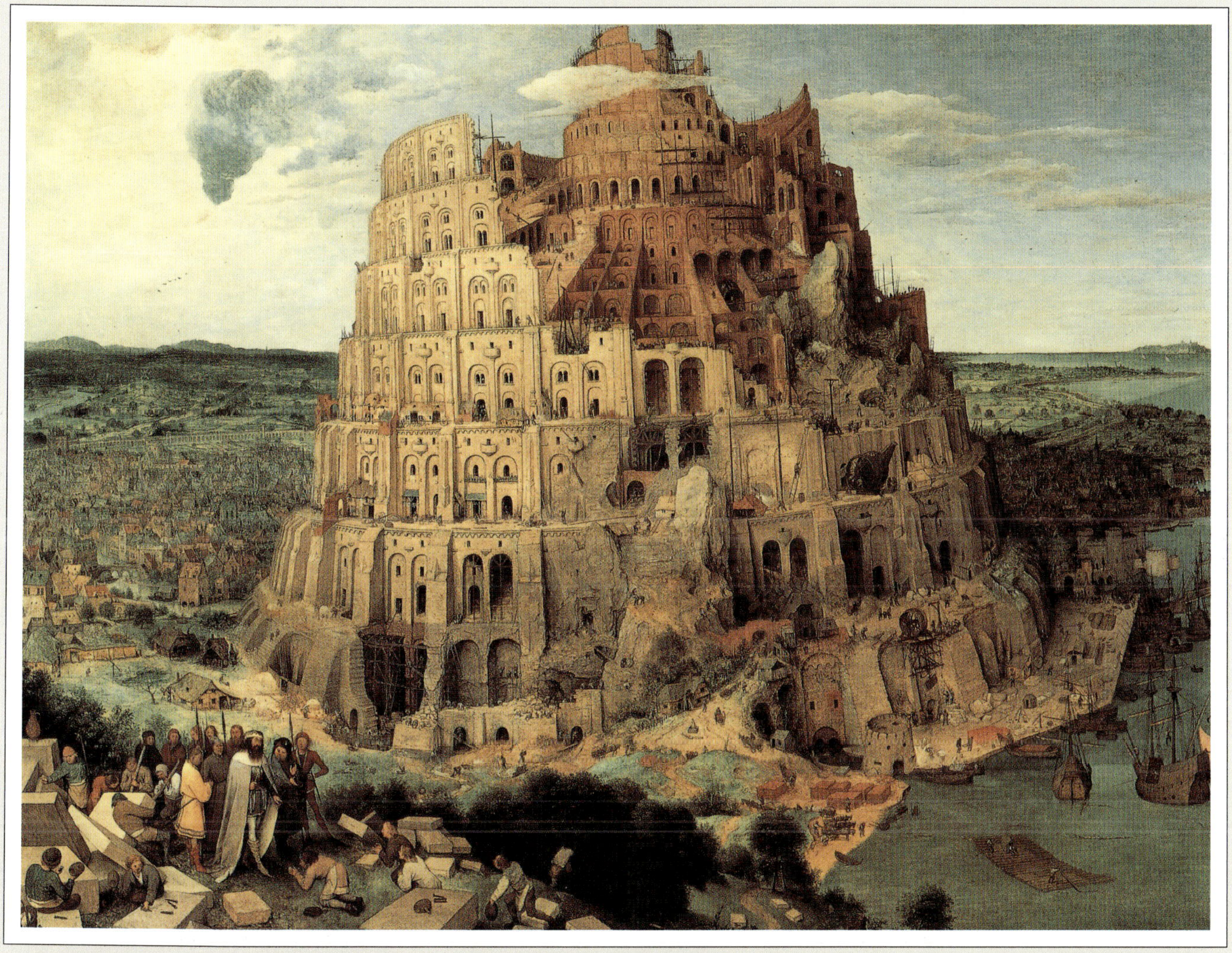

This subject allowed Bruegel to display his amazing skill in rendering complex architecture in precise detail – a skill that lends support to Karel Van Mander's statement that Bruegel was asked shortly before his death to produce work celebrating the construction of the new Brussels-Antwerp canal. But the painting is also memorable for the way in which the landscape, with its intermittent sun and shade, catches the essence of the light of the Low Countries. In this respect, the picture anticipates the Dutch landscape painters of the 17th century, such as Jacob van Ruisdael.

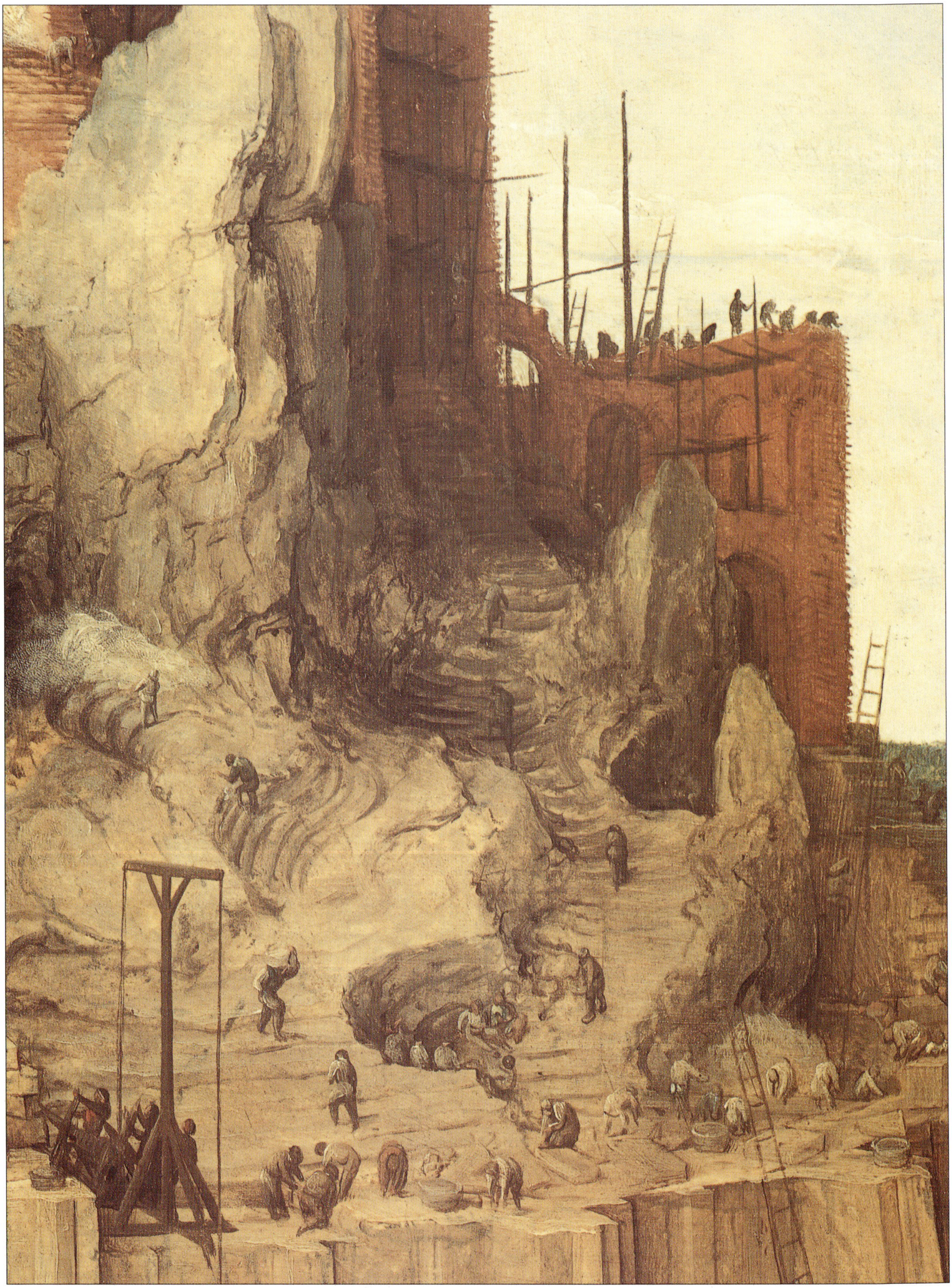

1 *Actual size detail*

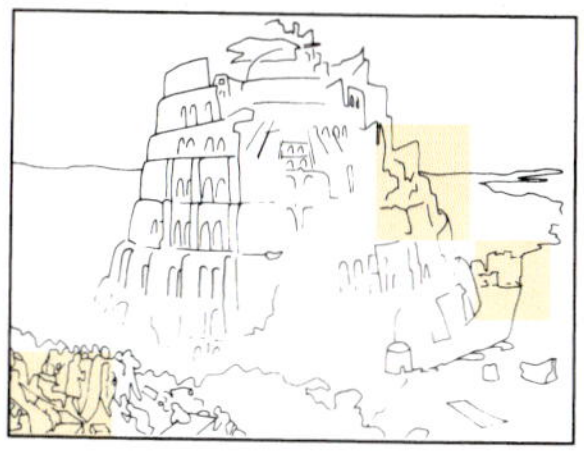

1 *Actual size detail* Swirling dark strokes are used to indicate the roughly hewn steps up the side of the living rock on which the Tower of Babel is being built. Minute traces of dark brown, creamy brown, and white create the figures – more than forty of them in this area alone. The brick structure being erected is painted in reddish brown, with minuscule marks in black and yellow to indicate detailing. Very thin strokes of dark paint are used to draw the ladders and poles against the luminous sky.

2 Amid the crowded roofs of the town, Bruegel has inserted tiny light patches of yellow and pale brown, anticipating the subtle light effects of 17th-century Dutch landscapes. The reddish brown of the houses are darkened to set off the gray-green of the castellated town entrance whose walls and arches are echoed by reflections in the sea. In the foreground of this detail Bruegel has shown how a large crane is worked, having included the two men who are turning it from the inside, as if on a treadmill.

3 The sharp angled shapes of the blocks of marble show a delicate range of cream to gray tones. In some of the shadowed areas the brush-marks are clearly visible. The rounded figures of the two stonemasons are painted in contrasting gray-green hues that pick up the colors of the ground on which the blocks are positioned. Tiny white highlights emphasize the tops of the pointed punches that are being used together with mallets to work the stone.

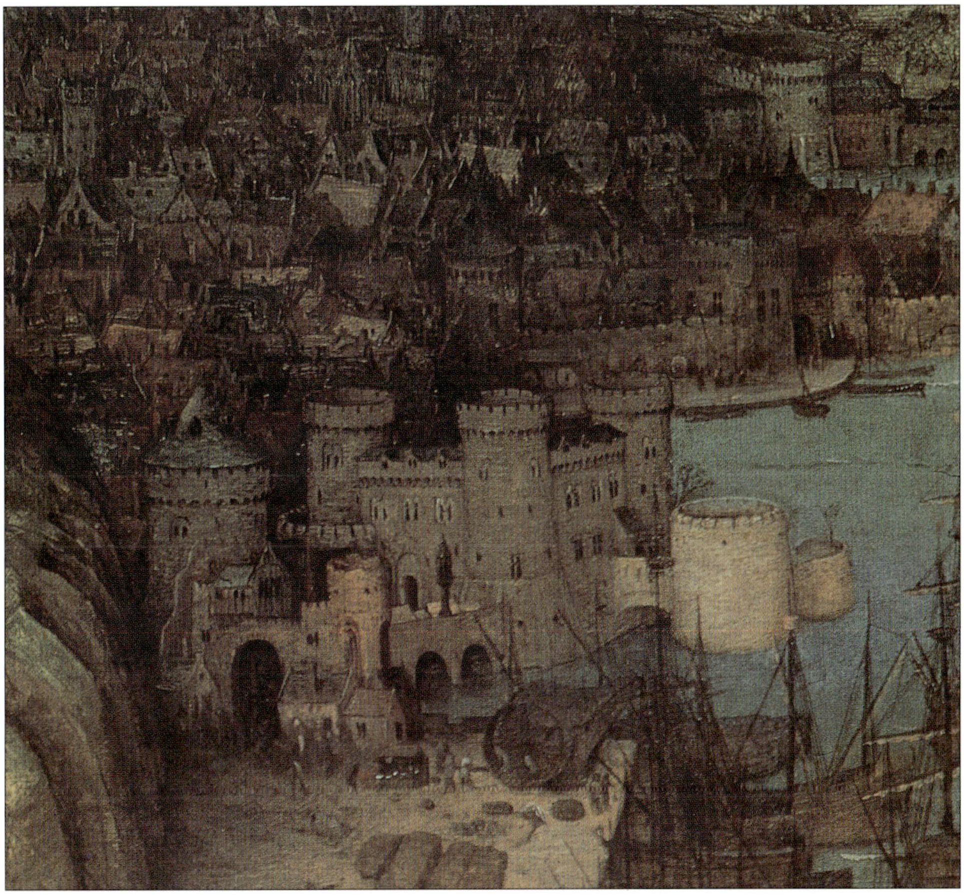

2

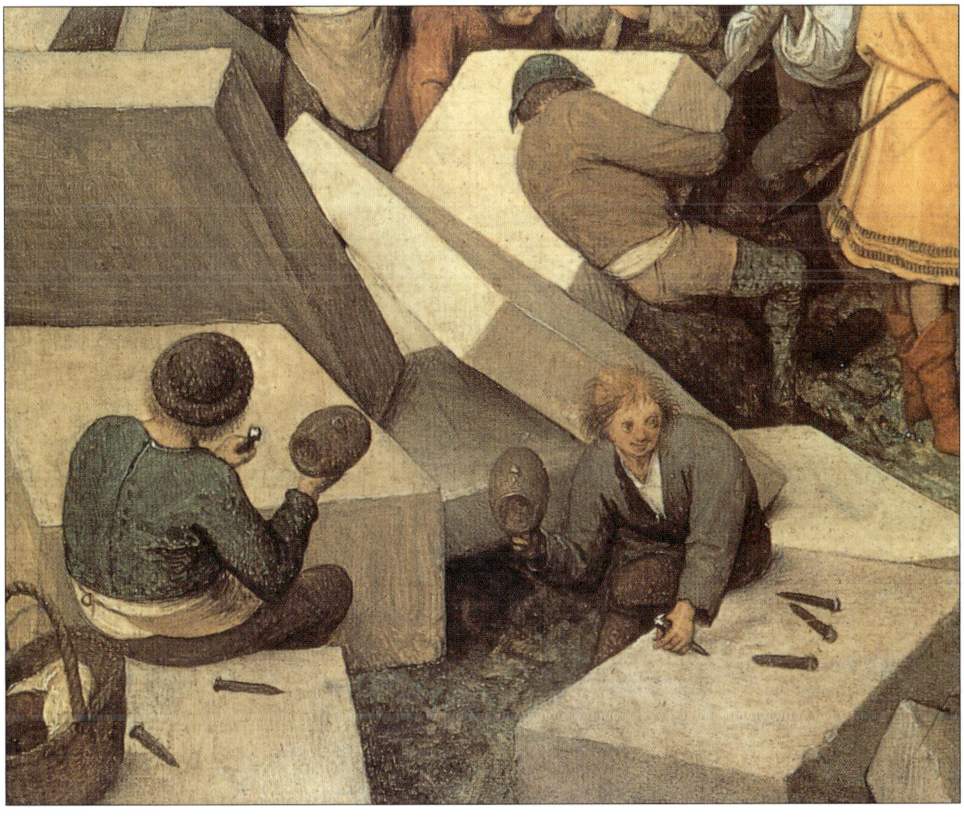

3

THE PROCESSION TO CALVARY

Signed and dated 1564
$48\frac{3}{4} \times 66\frac{7}{8}$in/124×170cm
Oil on panel
Kunsthistorisches Museum, Vienna

The subject of the procession to Calvary was familiar in Northern painting: there are versions by Herri met de Bles, Pieter Aertsen, and others. The grieving foreground figures provide a moving commentary on the scene, and also introduce a diagonal which leads across to the high, Patinir-like rock, through the tiny figure of Christ struggling under the cross. The device of making the key figure very small is something Bruegel had used in earlier paintings such as *Landscape with the Fall of Icarus* (see page 65) and *The Battle Between Carnival and Lent* (see page 75). But once the figure of Christ is found it can be seen that he is linked with the holy figures in the foreground by the timeless garments they wear – all the figures in the crowd, including Simon of Cyrene, who is refusing to help carry the cross, are in 16th-century dress. This, and the fact that Bruegel includes rich details of contemporary life – such as the two thieves attended by priests or monks who are jolting along in a cart, the high wheels on which bodies were left to rot, and the general air of festivity that would have attended a public execution in the 16th century – point up the contrast between the crowd which is unaware of the significance of the event and the figures of the Virgin, St John, and the two Marys who are deeply aware of it. Of the figures in the crowd, only the woman immediately behind the right-hand kneeling figure is grieving, and by turning toward the holy group, she makes a connection for the viewer.

Bruegel distances the foreground figures still more from the crowd not only by making them large but by modeling them on earlier 15th-century work, as he had previously done for the principle music-making angels in *The Fall of the Rebel Angels*. They are particularly akin to the mourning figures in Rogier van der Weyden's *Descent from the Cross* (opposite below). This painting was no longer in the Netherlands at this time, but Bruegel could have known it from copies or from preliminary drawings for a print published by Hieronymus Cock. The print features a structure similar to the building with a bulbous dome that is visible in the blue-green background to the left of the large rock. Being completely un-Netherlandian, it represents the Temple at Jerusalem. The oddly placed windmill, where wheat would have been ground, may have been intended as a symbol of the Eucharistic bread, and taken together with the mourning group, would emphasize the true religious meaning of the scene and the lack of spiritual awareness evidenced by the crowd.

Bruegel's use in the foreground of a style derived from earlier Flemish work may have reflected a growing interest in the 15th century on the part of both painters and their patrons. The existence of the print after *The Descent from the Cross* is evidence of this interest, as is the fact that Domenico Lampsonius – who later wrote a poem about Bruegel – was corresponding in about 1559 with the Italian art historian Giorgio Vasari. He supplied details of both earlier and contemporary Flemish painters for the second edition of Vasari's *Lives of the Most Excellent Painters, Sculptors, and Architects*, which was to appear in 1568.

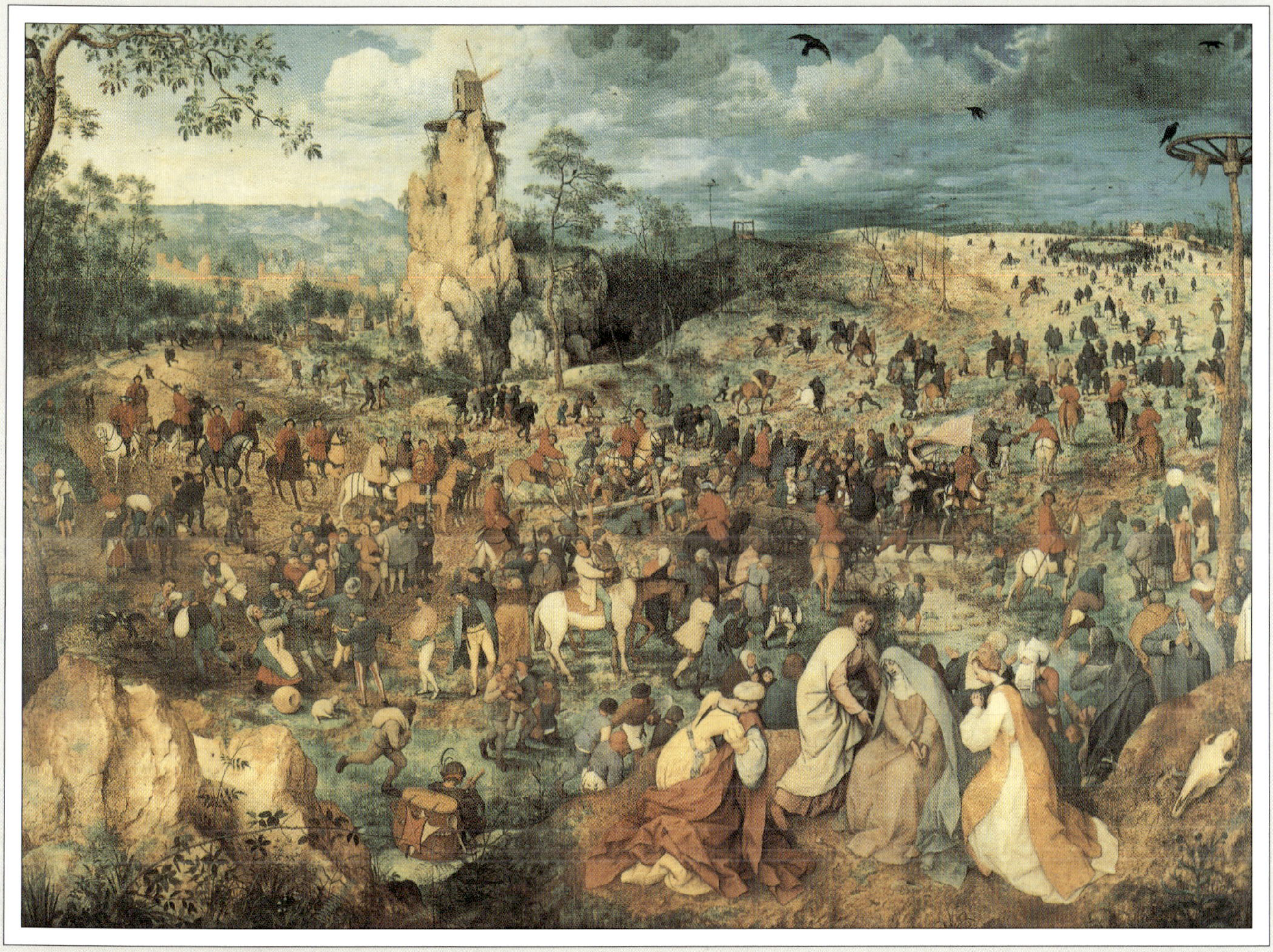

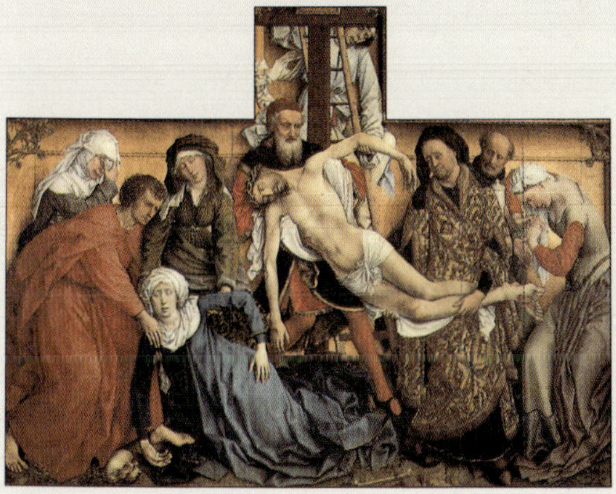

ROGIER VAN DER WEYDEN
The Descent from the Cross
c 1438, Prado, Madrid

This is one of the paintings that was owned by Niclaes Jonghelinck, who may even have commissioned it, and it is one of the few works for which known preparatory drawings for some of the figures exist. It is the largest of Bruegel's panels, and its combination of prominent foreground figures with a packed crowd scene against a landscape background is new, looking forward to the combination of large figures and landscape which Bruegel was to use for the paintings of the *Months* in the following year. Also new is the greater emphasis on movement, seen in the running people and the red-jacketed soldiers who sweep in a great arc toward Golgotha.

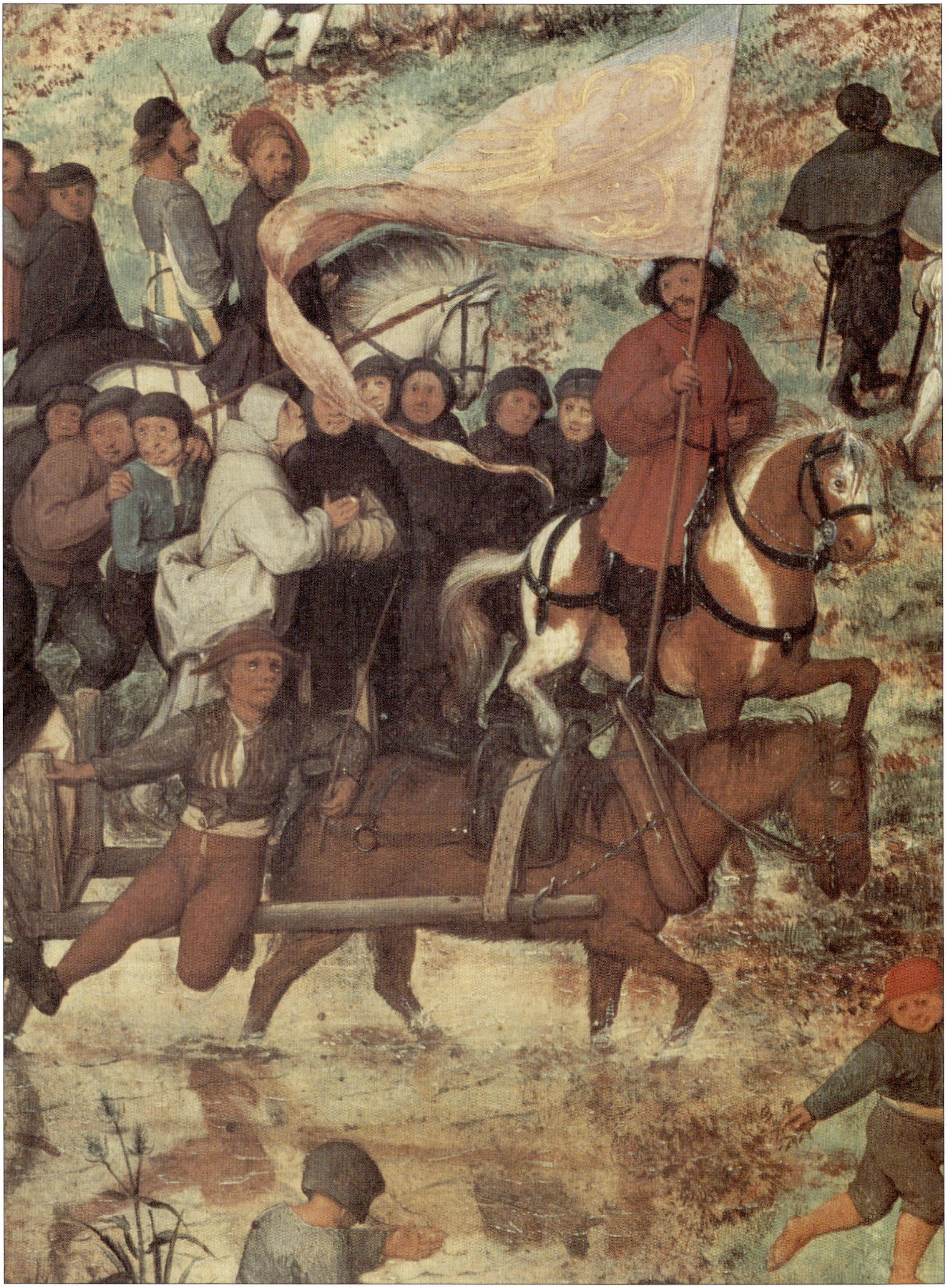

1 *Actual size detail*

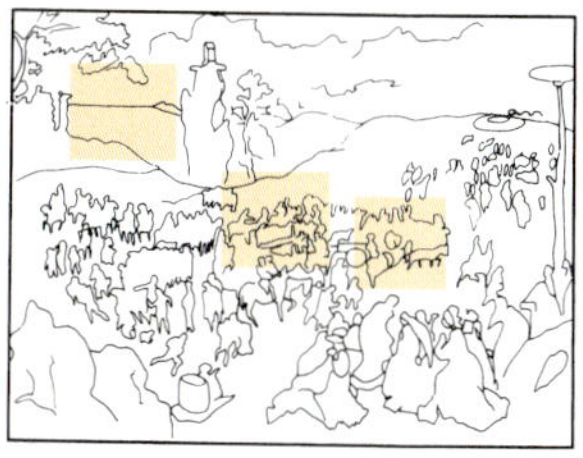

1 *Actual size detail* This detail demonstrates Bruegel's acute observation. He differentiates between the stolidness of the onlookers and the liveliness of the standard-bearer, and also between the plodding gait of the brown horse pulling the cart and the prance of the skewbald horse behind. Very thin paint is used for the hooves of the horse in the water and for the reflection of the man in red seated on the cart, and traces of white describe the water splashing up. Although this group is in the middle distance rather than the foreground, Bruegel has expressed the different emotions of each face with economy and precision, placing small, accurate marks for eyes, noses, and mouths.

2 Bruegel has used very small brushes and a range of subtle color gradations derived from the then conventional landscape colors – brown, blue, and green – to achieve the effect of distance. The blue-greens melt into each other, contrasting with the golden, turreted walls of what, in the context of the painting's subject, has to be the city of Jerusalem. The three tiered domed building representing the temple is an imaginary structure, but the other buildings would have been those that Bruegel saw around him in his own time and country.

3 Pale green and brownish yellow was brushed on first, with the figures built up over it. Christ has been dramatically silhouetted against the diagonal of the cross. Its texture is rendered with tiny dabs of mixed grays and cream, the greys toning with Christ's robe.

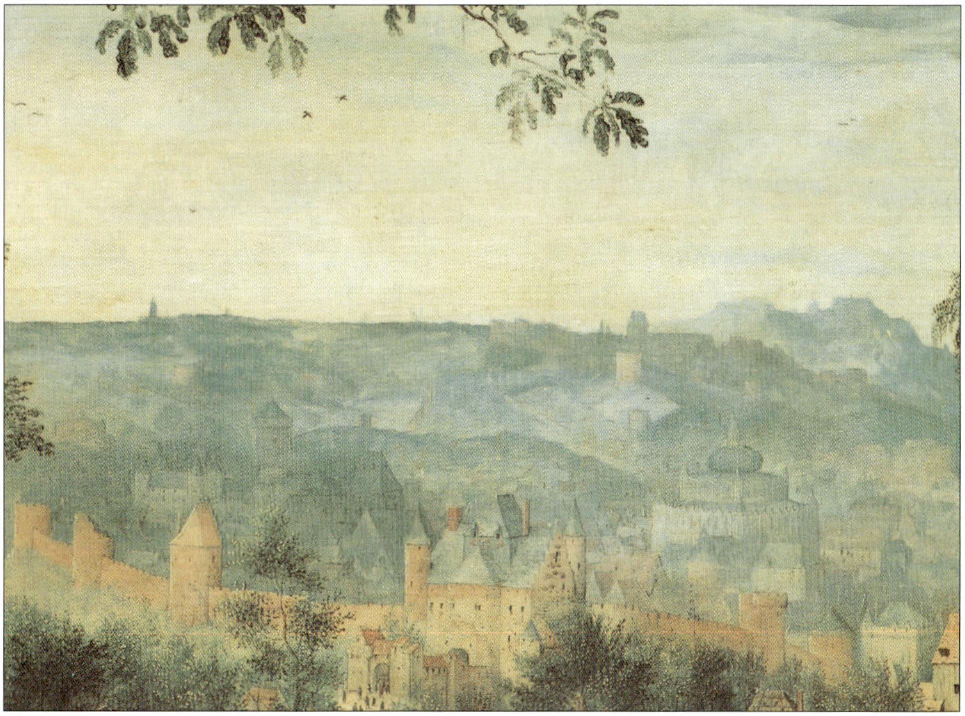

2

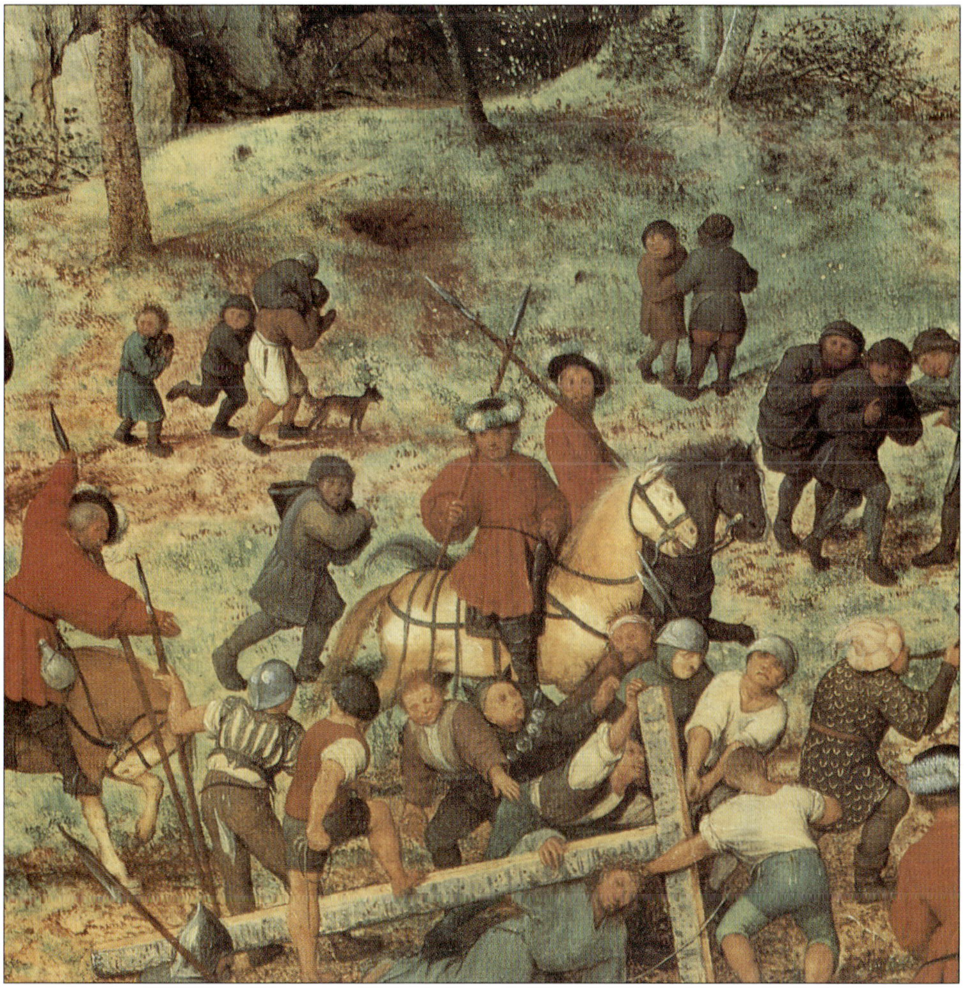

3

The Corn Harvest

1565

$46\frac{1}{2} \times 63\frac{1}{4}$in/118×160.7cm

Oil on panel

Metropolitan Museum of Art, New York

All five of the surviving paintings of the *Months* which Bruegel produced for Niclaes Jonghelinck passed into the collection of Archduke Leopold Wilhelm in the 17th century and thence to Vienna, where only three remain today. This panel representing August with the harvesting of the corn – harvesting was also used for August in earlier Books of Hours – provides a marvelous contrast to the freezing atmostphere of January's subject, *The Hunters in the Snow*. The heat of high summer is communicated firstly by the overall tones of rich yellows and browns, and secondly by the exhausted group gathered under the shade of the pear tree. Other workers who continue to cut the corn and stack the sheaves emphasize the harvest's relentless demand for labor. Their beautifully observed gestures were to reappear 400 years later in the peasant subjects of Jean-Francois Millet (opposite below).

Away to the left the landscape stretches away until it becomes lost in the hazy distance. Full of minutely observed details, it is so realistic that it is difficult to accept that it is imaginary, a made-up but convincing panorama. As with *The Hunters in the Snow*, the landscape and atmosphere form the real subject of the painting.

As with the first panel in the series, the design here leads the eye into the picture from the left-hand corner – a compositional layout designed to make the eye "read" the whole cycle of the Months from left to right and chronologically, as they would have been hung. The zigzag line of thick uncut corn continues toward an untidy hedgerow behind which lies an elegantly rendered church. The same church reappears at a slightly different angle in one of Bruegel's last paintings, *The Parable of the Blind*, so it seems likely that Bruegel used an actual church as a model, although there is no known drawing of it. Down below the cornfield the countryside changes to gentle green and huddled trees beyond which lies a far field of corn in which yet more figures appear to be laboring; the loaded haywain provides a glowing color link between the foreground and this distant paler field.

Bruegel's figures are economically depicted: he depends more on precisely observed contours than on modeling to give them reality. None of his drawings of figures supposedly done from life can be related to this painting, but since the figure of the sleeper is used again in slightly different form in *The Land of Cockaigne*, painted two years later, it is possible that there was a common source in a drawing now lost. Bruegel is also sparing in his recording of shadows. Although accurate where they do appear, they are used only here and there – just often enough to remind us of the midday heat.

The painting shows Bruegel's complete mastery of landscape painting, with the keen powers of observation and the profound knowledge of nature initiated on his journey to Italy now developed to the full. The entire scene appears natural, but the delineation of the figures, both in action and in rest, the way in which textures of trees or corn are unerringly indicated, the quality of the light and the subtlety of the palette, all reveal enormous technical skill. The picture's apparent simplicity conceals a brilliance of composition and of technique which ensures that it yields more and more to us the longer we study it. And its message is unmistakable: man is subservient to the relentless progress of the season – it is nature that dominates.

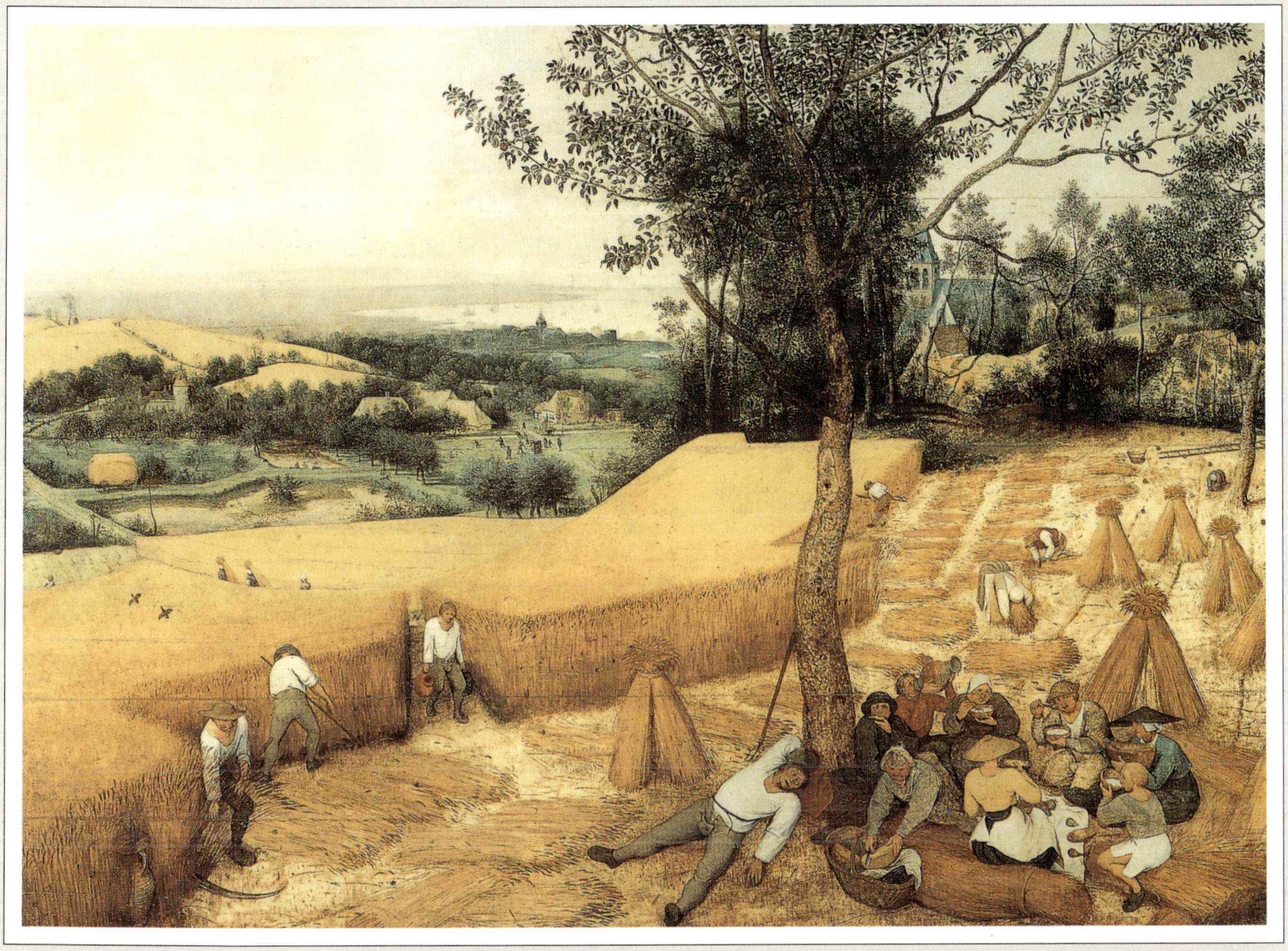

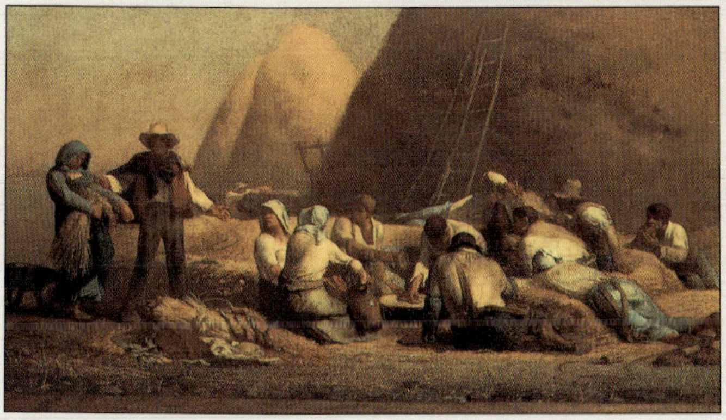

The fluid actions of the working figures in this scene contrast with the abandonment of the figures beneath the tree, who are occupied with rest and refreshment. They demonstrate the ultimate purpose of the harvest — to give sustenance to humanity — both by slicing into their loaves and by reclining on the sheaves. Against the intensity that emanates from the figures, whether they are in action or repose, the landscape itself seems calmly indifferent.

JEAN FRANÇOIS MILLET
Harvesters Resting
1851-53, Museum of Fine Arts, Boston

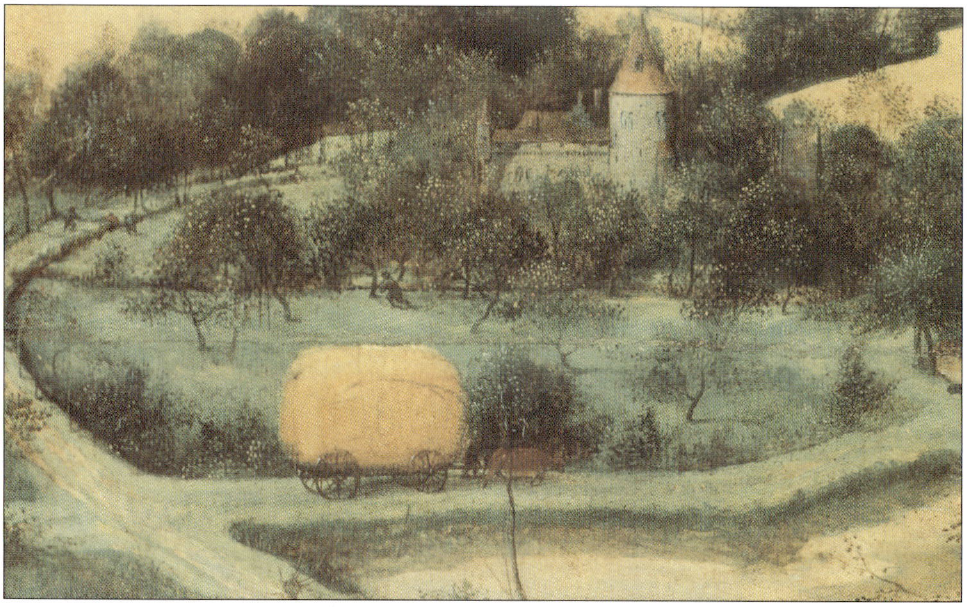

1

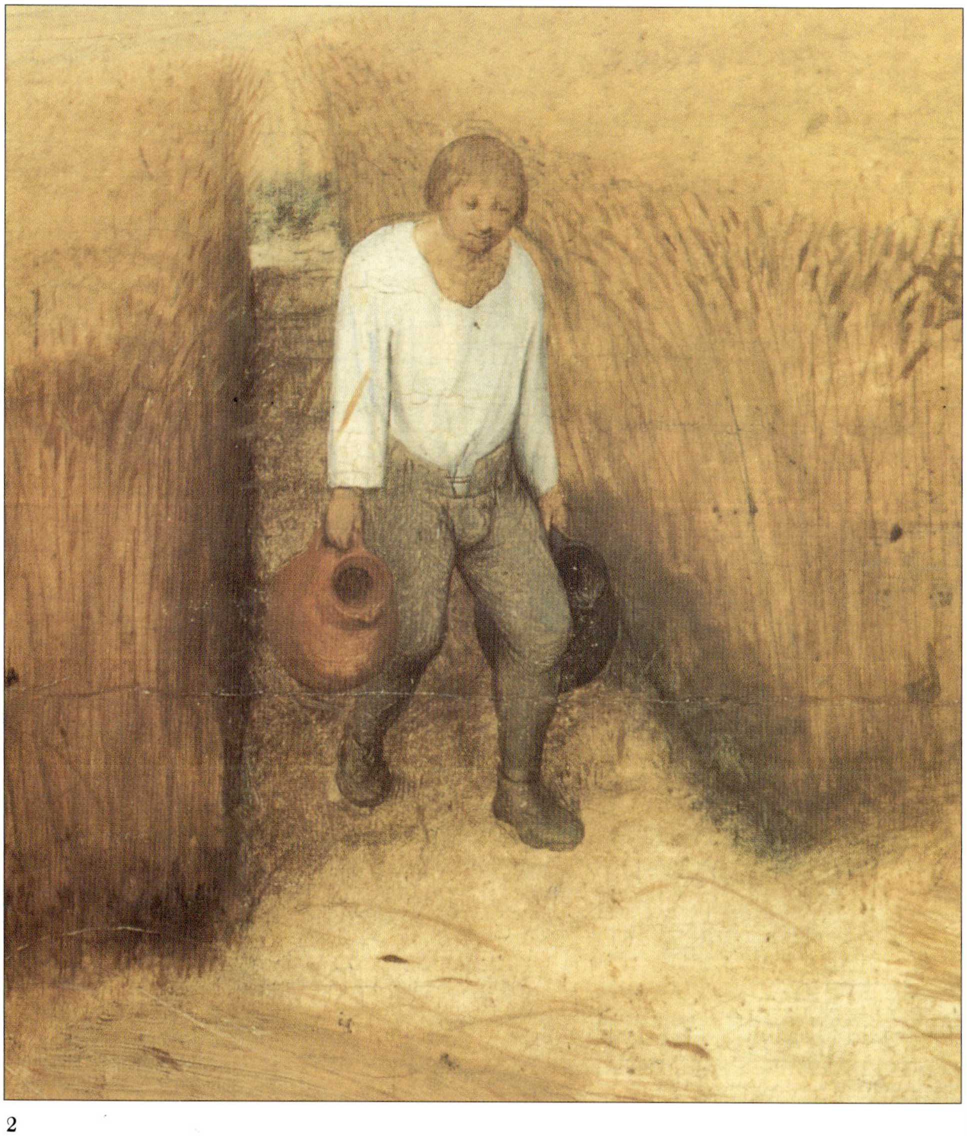

2

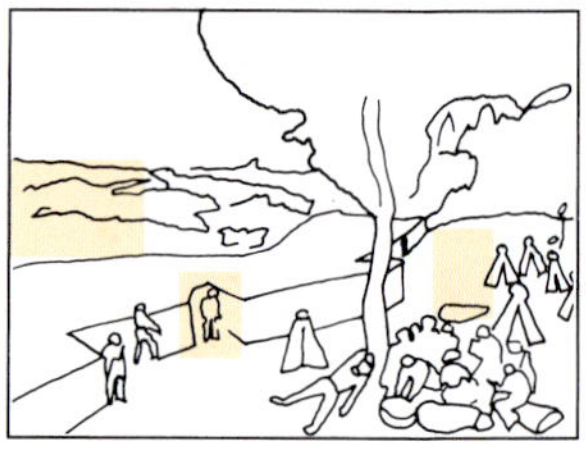

1 In the middle distance a loaded cart is on its way back to the farm. The block of yellow provides a color link between the wheatfield in the foreground and the uncut corn on the hill beyond, and contrasts with the light-toned greens around it. Clusters of trees are noted with brief lines and flecks of paint, and soft flecks are used for the window details of the turreted house set in the midst of the trees.

2 The figure bringing provisions to the harvesters trudges between thick blocks of standing wheat. This is detailed with thin lines and dots of dark paint and emphasized by thicker dark paint to the left of the figure and at the bottom of the wheat on the right.

3 *Actual size detail* The two figures tying up the sheaves of wheat are indicated with thin paint — almost the consistency of watercolor — which shows the layer of underpaint beneath. The white cap of the bending woman contrasts with the rich deep yellow of the wheat she is tying and the pale area to each side of her. Bruegel has set off the broad washes of color he has used for the simplified shapes of her figure and that of the man behind her with more precise strokes used for the stalks of wheat. These are accentuated in places with the point of the brush.

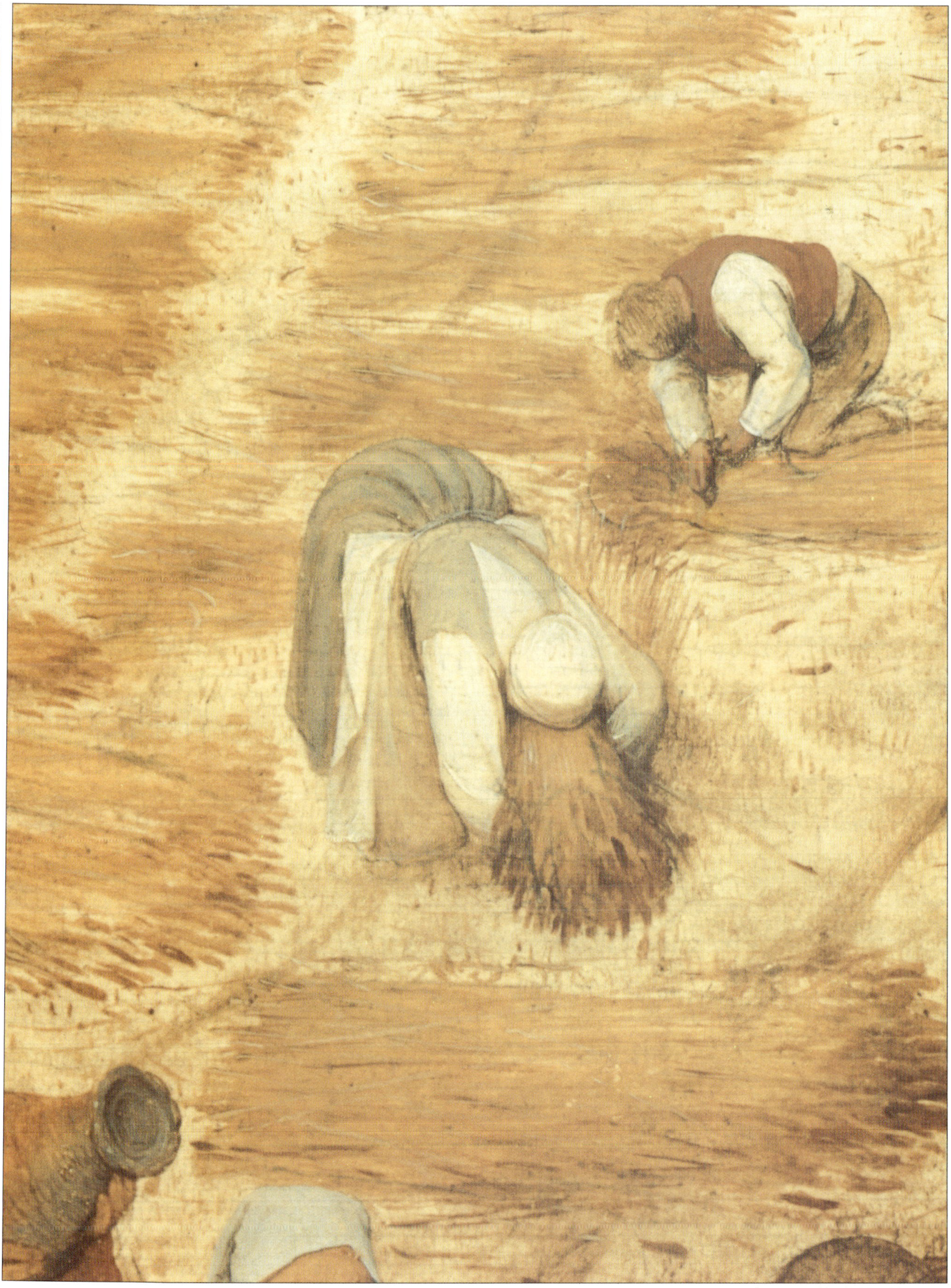

3 *Actual size detail*

The Numbering at Bethlehem

1566

$45\frac{5}{8} \times 64\frac{3}{4}$in/$116 \times 164.5$cm

Oil on panel

Musées Royaux des Beaux-Arts, Brussels

This is one of several snow scenes produced between about 1565 and 1567 and including two versions of *The Massacre of the Innocents*. The unusual subject is taken from the Gospel according to St Luke (2:1-5): "And it came to pass in those days, that there went out a decree from Caesar Augustus, that all the world should be taxed . . . and all went to be taxed, every one into his own city. And Joseph also went up from Galilee, out of the city of Nazareth, into Judaea, unto the city of David, which is called Bethlehem (because he was of the house and lineage of David) to be taxed with Mary, his espoused wife, being great with child." The account goes on to describe the birth of Mary's first-born son who was laid in a manger because there was no room at the inn.

As with *The Procession to Calvery* (see page 87), Bruegel has given the scene a contemporary setting. A Flemish crowd is lining up at the inn to register; an official is taking money from one man; another is noting the transaction. Pigs are being caught and killed for the travelers, people inside the inn enjoy the glow of a fire, a man opens an upper window, a pitcher and a wreath hang outside the inn. Mary and Joseph are singled out by the ass on which she rides and the ox alongside, both traditional in paintings of the Nativity. Mary has her face turned toward us while Joseph trudges by her side. He is identified by the carpenter's saw over his shoulder and by his large hat – this also appears in *The Adoration of the Kings*.

The painting, although full of the varied activity seen in earlier works, has the greater cohesion of design noticeable in the paintings of the *Months* (see page 91). Two important diagonals are set up by the stationary carts in the middle foreground. These are continued through the composition – one by parallel lines of houses and trees which lead to the ruined gate and fortifications of the town in the far right-hand corner, and the other by the line of figures crossing the ice, which leads to the precisely painted church in the left distance. Any implied symbolic meaning can only be guessed at, but Bruegel's deliberate positioning of things susceptible to symbolic interpretation in more than one of his religious paintings is unlikely to be pure coincidence: hidden symbolism was an important element in earlier Flemish painting. The ruined towers, which have been identified as the towers and gates of Amsterdam, might therefore refer to the time before the birth of Christ, while the little church could symbolize the era to come. Bruegel could also be making some kind of comment on the unsettled conditions in the Netherlands; in *The Massacre of the Innocents*, probably painted around the same time, Spanish soldiers are shown sacking a Flemish village. Other vivid details in *The Numbering* are the group warming themselves at an outside fire, people gathered round a tree "inn," indicated by the inn-sign swinging above, builders at work on a wooden structure and a variety of figures sporting in various ways on the ice. All are described economically, with only just as much paint as is necessary, used quite thinly and freely, noticeable in the marvelous detail of hens pecking and scratching in the foreground. The ramshackle building placed behind Mary and Joseph on a diagonal initiated by the bundle of straw in the immediate foreground has a cross on its roof, and so might represent the stable where Mary will give birth.

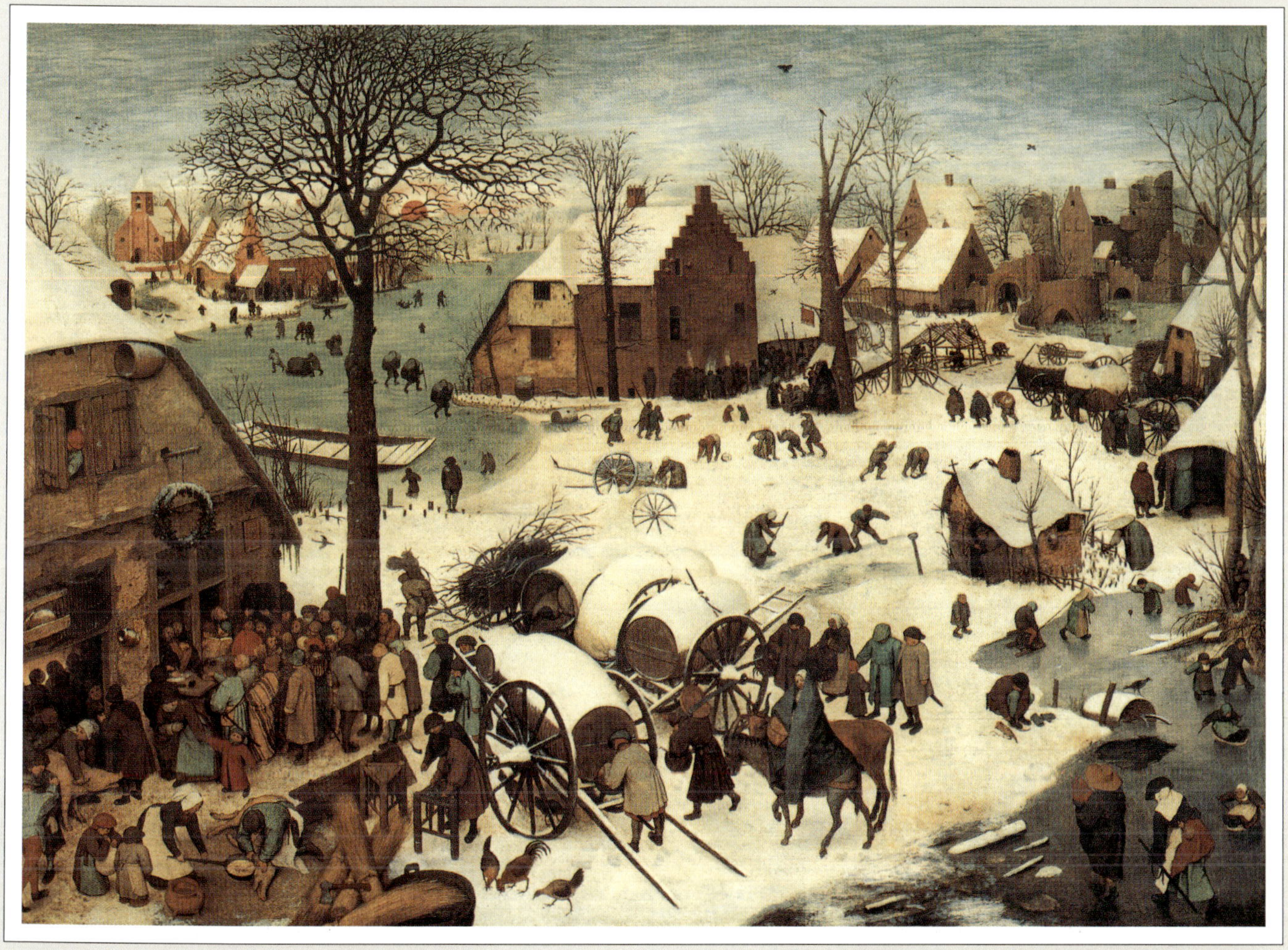

Bruegel's restrained palette of cream to brownish tones is enlivened only here and there by soft red. The painting has a biblical content, and the setting is a village rather than a landscape one, but the atmosphere of a particular kind of wintry day, encapsulated by the red ball of sun just setting behind the stark branches of the tallest tree, is communicated every bit as tellingly as in the paintings of the *Months*.

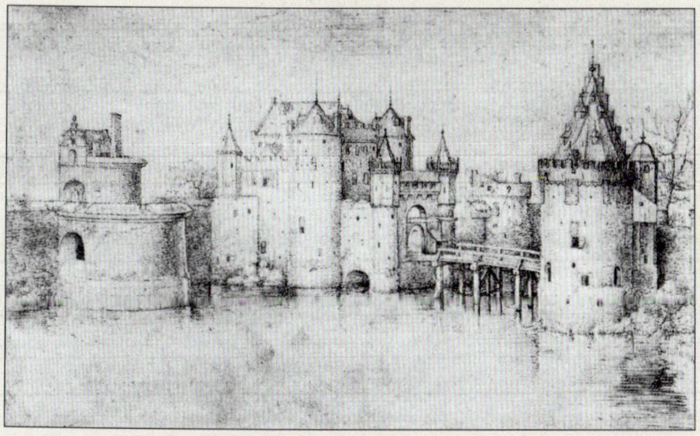

JACOB SAVERY
The Amsterdam City Gates
Museum of Fine Arts, Boston

The city gates that appear in Bruegel's painting here depicted by a contemporary.

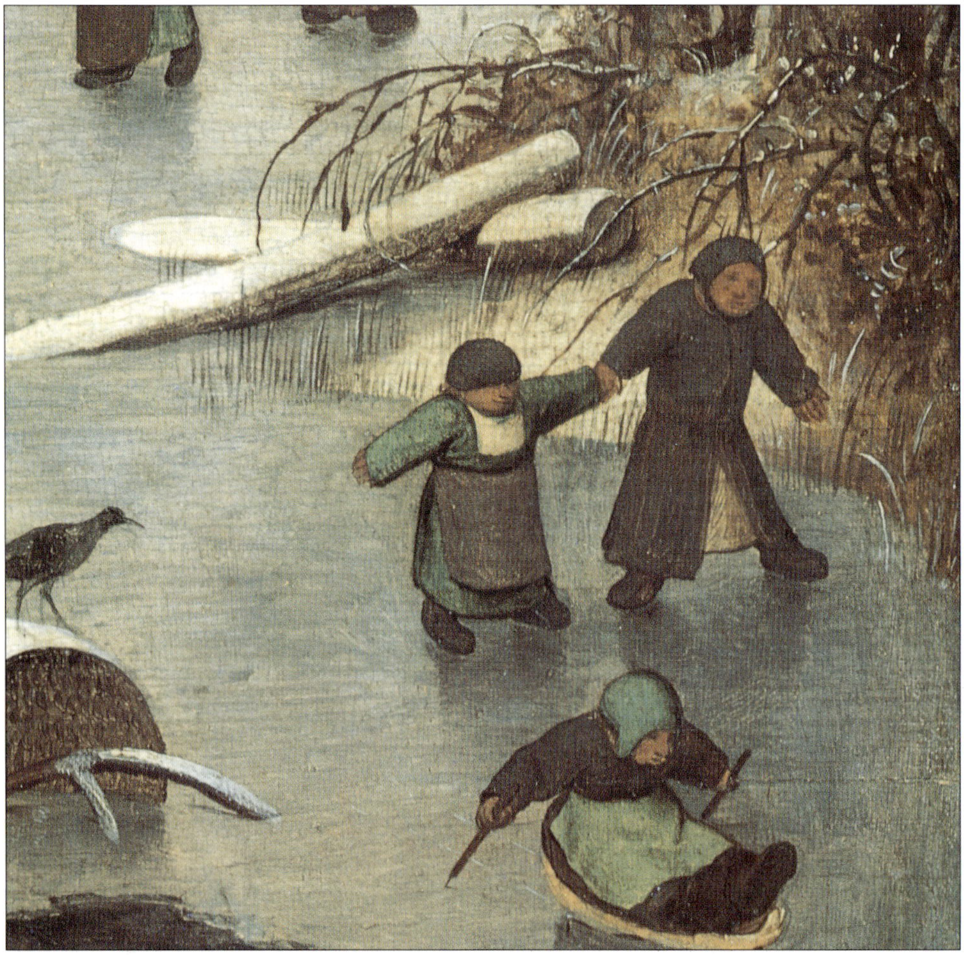

1 *Actual size detail*

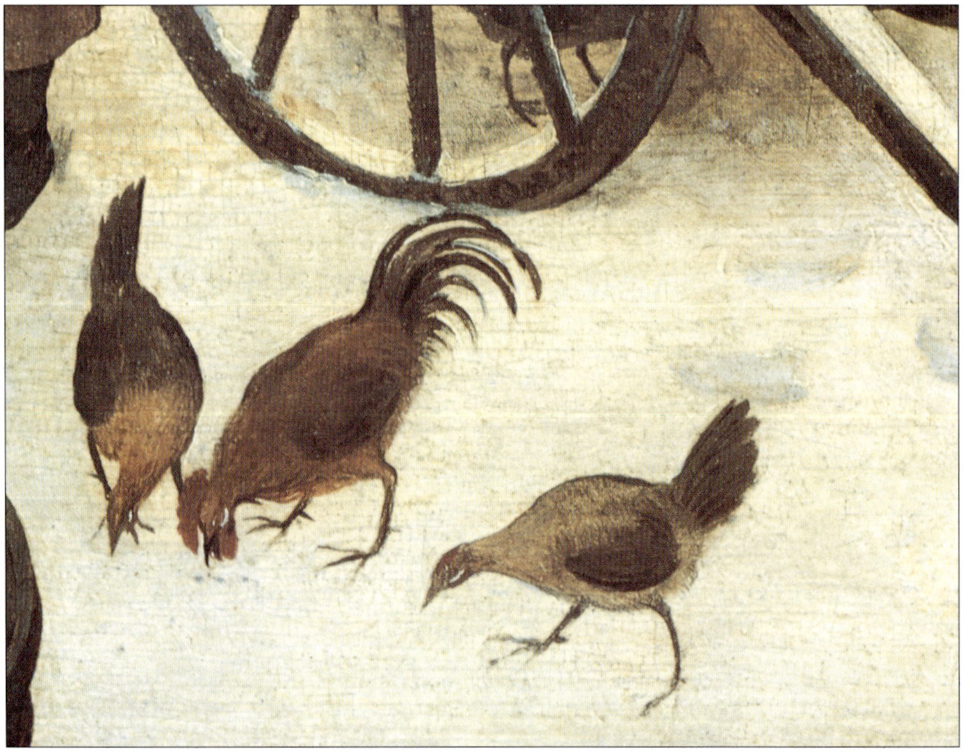

2

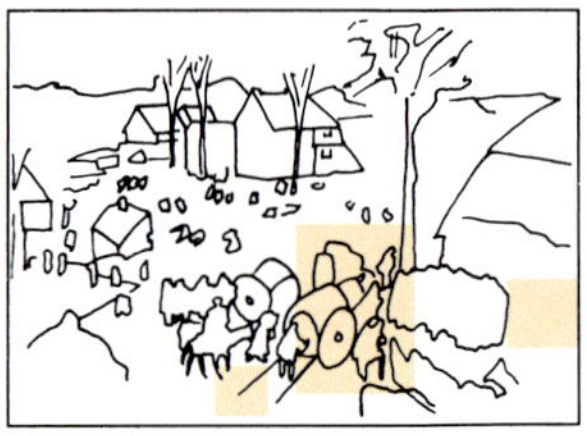

1 *Actual size detail* The precariousness of the two children walking on the ice is indicated by their outstretched arms and slightly splayed feet, reflected by darkened areas beneath. The figures, and that child in front of them, are outlined for added emphasis, perhaps because they are relatively small. Quiet color and precise observation of shapes gives this little group a vivid feeling of movement.

2 The rooster with two hens, one eating, the other searching for food, are painted with thin fluent strokes over the light ground. Bruegel contrasts the stiff tail feathers of the hens with the elegant plumes of the rooster, and indicates the springiness of the birds' legs and feet with delicately placed strokes. Details such as the shapes of the wings, the sharpness of the beaks, the spurs and comb of the rooster, are all accurately described with a minimum of paint.

3 The turn of the ox's head toward the spectator and the highlighting of its eyes seems deliberate and may have been intended to recall the Old Testament prophecy: "The ox knows its owner and the ass its master's stall but Israel, my own people, has no knowledge, no discernment." This was understood as a foretelling of the fact that the Jews did not recognize Christ as the Messiah. Bruegel notes the ordinary activities of the villagers with his usual economy – they are unmoved by the arrival of strangers – and he successfully conveys the quality of packed snow which has been lying for some time.

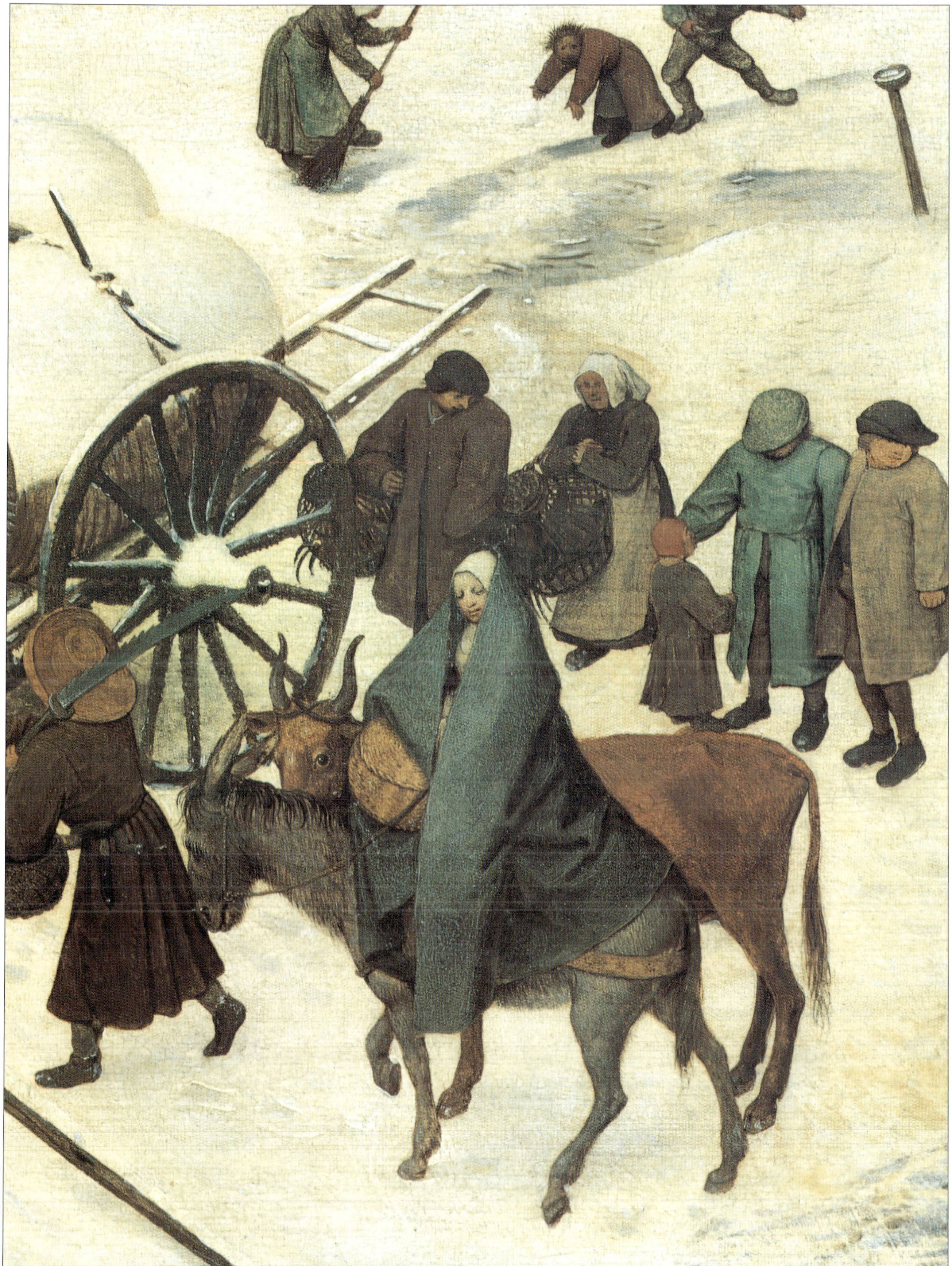

3

A Peasant Wedding

c 1567

$44\frac{7}{8} \times 64\frac{1}{8}$in/114×163cm

Oil on panel

Kunsthistorisches Museum, Vienna

According to Karel Van Mander, Bruegel and his friend Hans Franckert, a German merchant, used to disguise themselves as peasants and go out into the country to attend rustic celebrations of various kinds, and Bruegel "delighted in observing the droll behavior of the peasants, how they ate, drank, danced, capered or made love, all of which he was able to reproduce cleverly and pleasantly in watercolor or oils, being equally skilled in both processes." There may be a certain amount of truth in this account, for Bruegel's vivid representation of the wedding feast suggests first-hand observation. The richly dressed man seated in the right-hand corner on an upturned churn is sometimes thought to be the painter himself, based on the man's resemblance to the engraving of Bruegel which accompanied Domenicus Lampsonius' poem about him published in 1572. But perhaps it is more likely that the figure is the local landowner; the fact that his hands are posed in the same way as those of the bride (towards the center of the picture) provides what seems a deliberate visual link, but is unexplained. Bruegel's peasant subjects were once regarded as straightforward genre scenes, but it is now considered that they contain a degree of symbolism, like much of his work. Therefore the wedding feast, in spite of the generally sympathetic portrayal of the characters, may also refer to the sin of gluttony, and the absorption of the child licking his finger seems to point up this underlying theme.

The dramatic diagonal thrust of the composition is one that is found in earlier Flemish representations of the biblical story of the Wedding Feast at Cana. Here it also provides a useful device for including the entire group in Bruegel's preferred horizontal format. Twenty guests – the maximum allowed by a decree issued by the Emperor Charles V in 1546 – are grouped around a long table backed by high-stacked hay and the last wheat sheaves of the harvest. These are pinned up with a wooden rake, while a hay-fork supports the improvised cloth of honor behind the bride. Although one of the bagpipers is motionless – his longing gaze toward the food echoed by the dog scenting scraps from under the table – the painting as a whole is full of activity. Every figure is reacting to something or somebody, and the urgency felt in the two servers' brisk tread is extended by the twisting movement of the man handing out the shallow dishes of sweet rice porridge from their improvised tray. This red-hatted man, right arm reaching toward the bride, may be the groom – not otherwise identified – as it was apparently a tradition for the groom to serve the bride and her family at such a feast.

Although the white aprons of the servers and the tray of food draws the attention initially, the group in the left-hand corner provides a powerful balance. The face of the man pouring wine is painted with particular sensitivity, and the controlled urgency of his action complements the movement of the groom. The colors, textures, and shapes of the pile of jugs provide a memorable still life. Apart from the creamy white of cloth and clothing, this group also contains the basic palette of the entire scene, one in which Bruegel shows an assured handling of composition, modeling, and color, and an outstanding ability to record a wide variety of human expressions and poses both with sympathy and with penetrating truth.

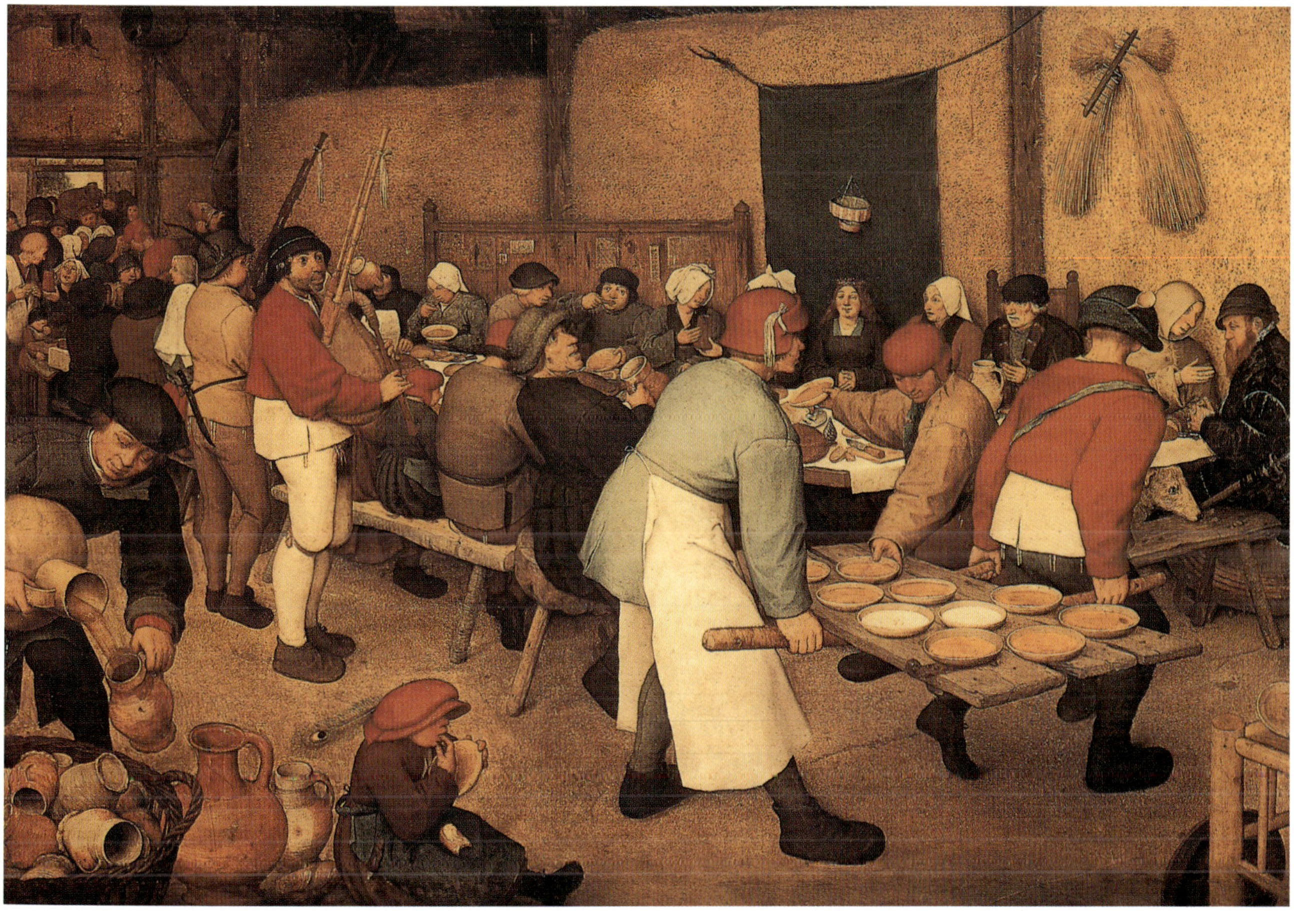

In his biography of Bruegel, Karel Van Mander describes seeing three of the artist's paintings of peasant subjects in private collections in Amsterdam. This one, however, was acquired in 1594 by Archduke Ernst of Austria, brother of the Emperor Rudolf II and Governor of the Netherlands in 1593-95. The picture is undated, but is thought to have been painted around 1567 together with the similar-sized *Peasant Dance* which is now also in Vienna. Both compositions introduce monumental figures seen in close-up from a lower viewpoint than hitherto and are notable for the newly powerful, almost sculptural way in which the figures are modelled.

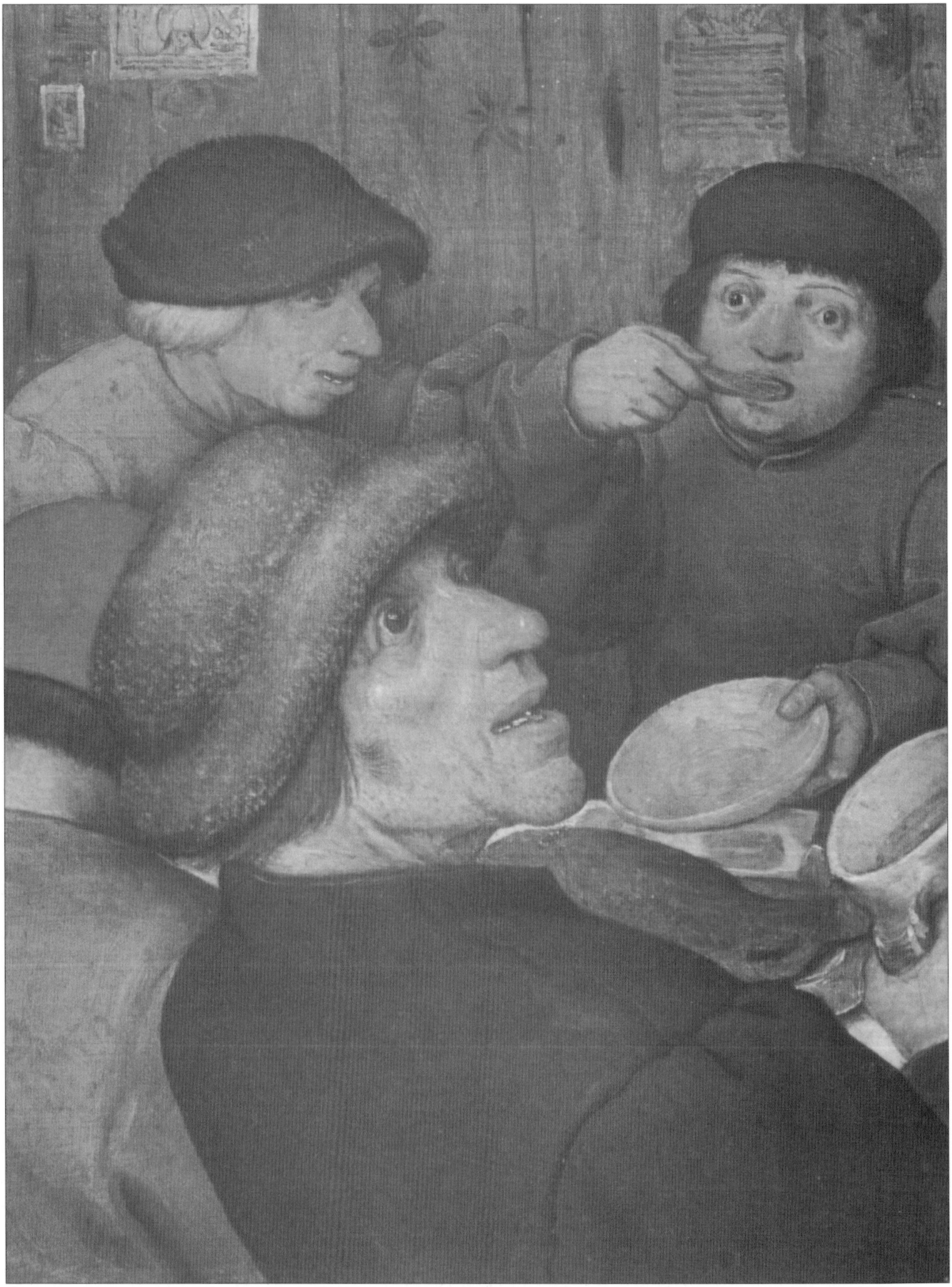

1

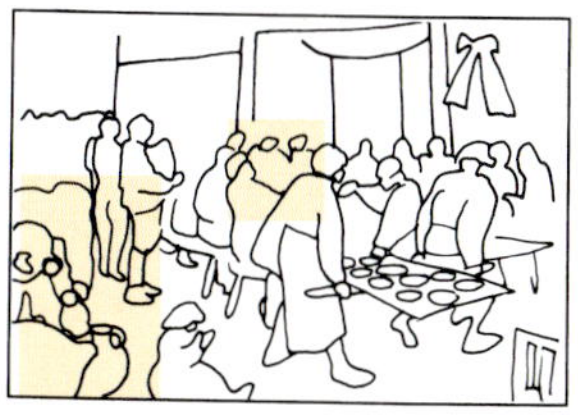

1 Irregular brushstrokes around the heads of the two men at the back suggest that Bruegel drew in the outlines of the figures before filling in the background color of the wooden bench. The faces of the three wedding guests are carefully modeled in shades of cream to reddish brown, with details such as lines around noses and mouths painted in with darker brown. The face of the nearest man is modeled with paler tones and small white highlights on nose, cheekbone, and the center of the eye. The three-dimensional quality of the faces of the two men in profile is emphasized by the dark value used around eyes, noses and chins. Subtly related values of lighter and darker gray have been used on the gray tunic of the man who is eating, to convey the thickness of the material and the fullness of the raised sleeve.

2 Traces of underdrawing – on the neck of the small pitcher on the right and on the hands of the man pouring the wine, for example, and some *pentimenti* ("ghost" images formed by a lower layer of paint showing through the upper one) suggest that Bruegel drew in figures and objects on his ground before using any color. The jugs show traces of the creamy color also visible on floor areas beneath the darker colors which have been superimposed. The jugs have been painted with rounded, sweeping lines, as befits their shapes, and touches of white have been used to show a faint gleam on the sides and tops of some of them.

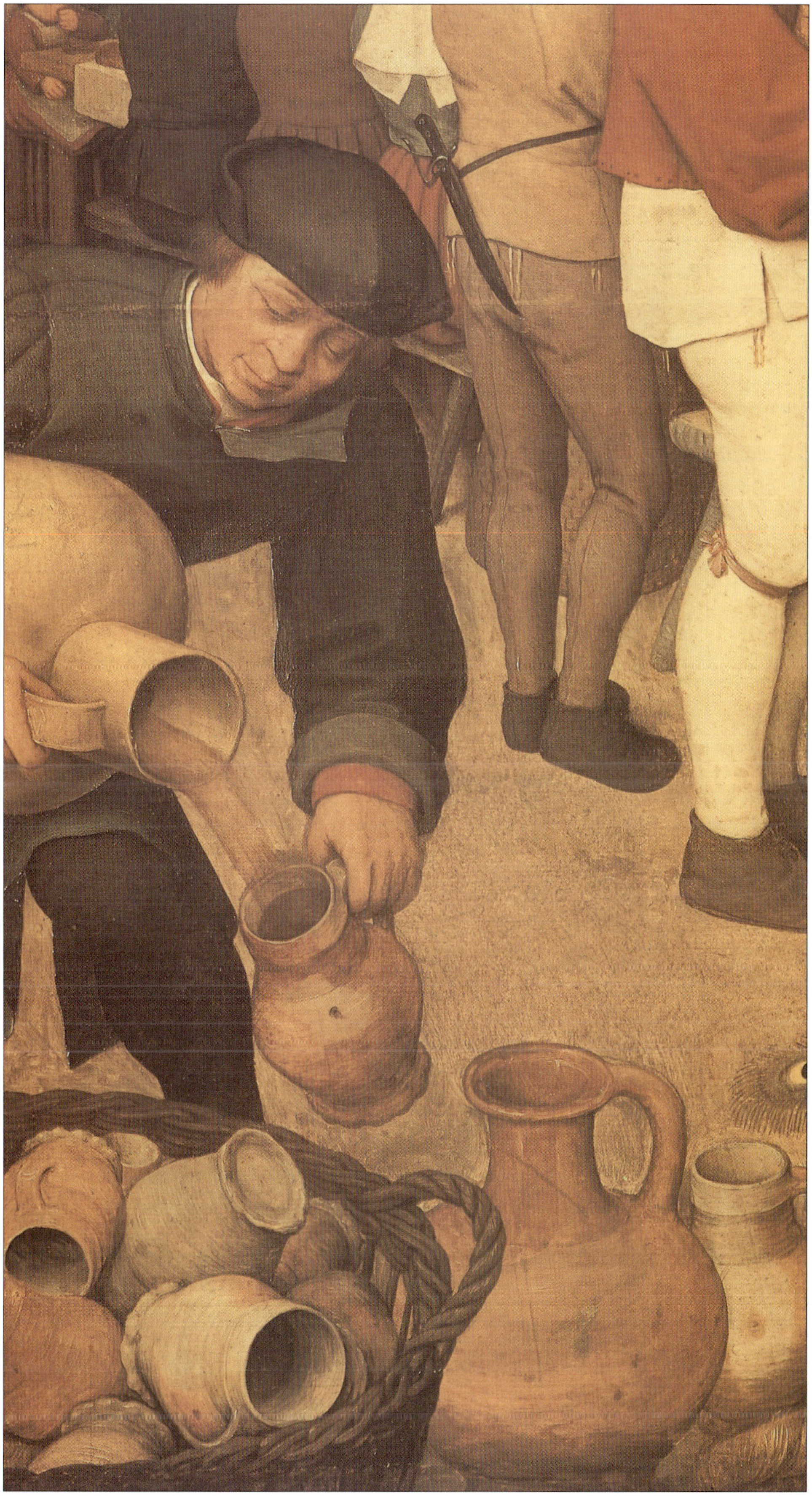

2

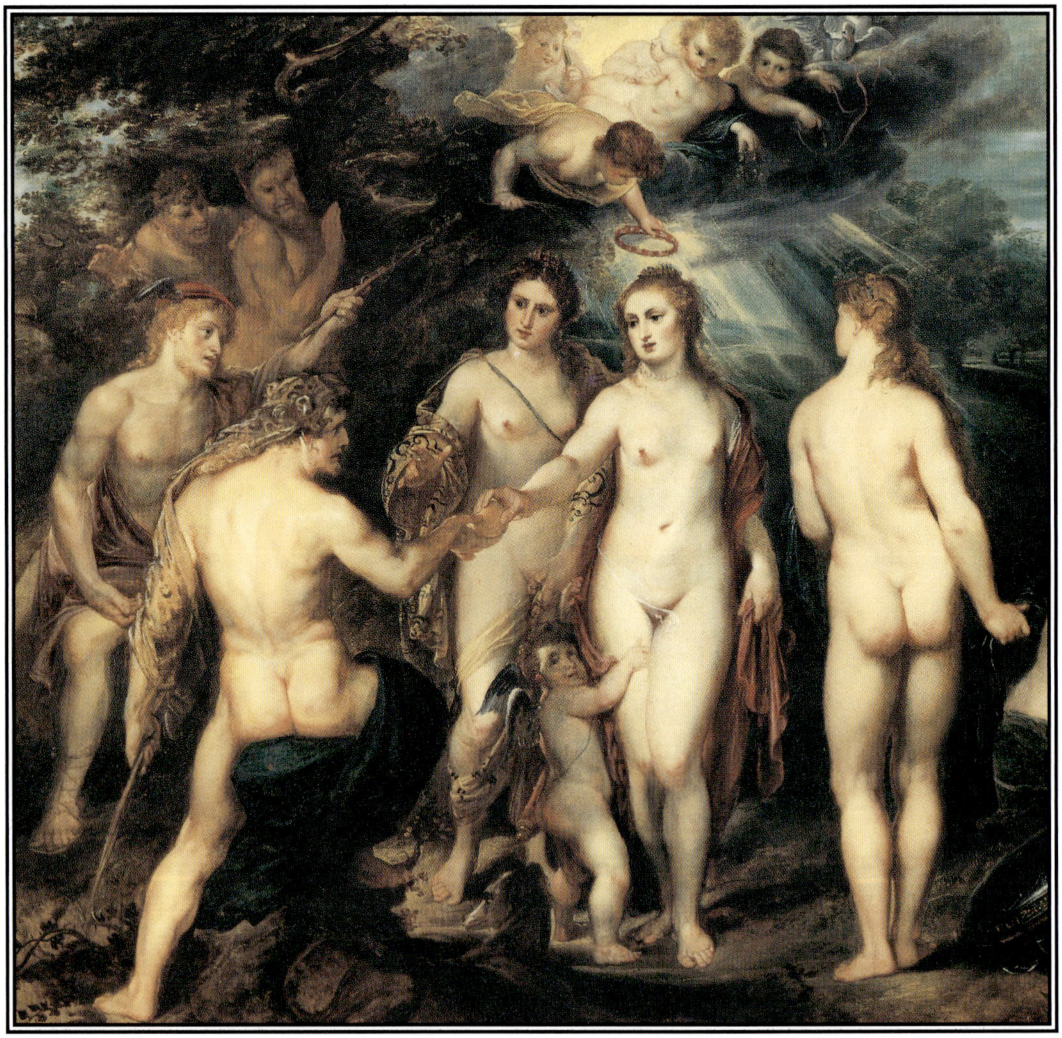

RUBENS

Introduction

Peter Paul Rubens
Self-portrait (detail)
c1639
Kunsthistorisches Museum, Vienna

The life and work of Peter Paul Rubens embody the character and qualities of his age. He seems to have been entirely in harmony with the values and aspirations of his society, and his protean talents, which were to make him as much diplomat as painter and give him the ear of the most powerful figures in Europe, afforded him a position of significance as much on the stage of world affairs as in the history of art. In this sense his career seems, more than that of other great seventeenth-century artists, to be intimately linked to the central political and cultural issues of his time.

Social and political background

Rubens was born into a Europe which, although rent by religious discord, witnessed within the Catholic nations a tremendous upsurge of spiritual confidence accompanied by a period of great wealth for the papacy. Beginning in Rome, vast rebuilding and refurbishing programs were begun, encouraged by new evangelizing orders such as the Jesuits, which spread to all parts of Europe and far beyond. Gradually a new kind of religious imagery emerged that expressed this buoyant, zealous mood. As laid down as early as 1563 at the Council of Trent, the purpose of religious images was both to instruct and to involve the laity emotionally. The hallmarks of the new style were accordingly legibility, realism, and a concern with moving, dramatic and spirtually uplifting themes.

The seventeenth century also witnessed the emergence of absolute monarchies: Louis XIV in France, Charles I in England and Philip IV in Spain; and the rhetorical, emotional and overblown idiom that was developed to extol the Martyrdom of the Saints was recognized as equally appropriate in celebrating the Divine Right of Kings. Rubens played a central role in the creation of this style. As a devout Catholic who celebrated Mass every day he could paint with total conviction the monumental decorations for the Jesuit church in Antwerp; as courtier and diplomat he could paint with equal facility the grand ceiling of the Banqueting Hall in Whitehall, glorifying the reign of James I. His art becomes the expression of a precise historical moment; even the contradictions of his art are those of the age, as for example the overt and enthusiastic sensuality that went hand in hand with a sincere piety.

The first decades of the century, when Rubens came of age as an artist, were a time of positive and creative reaction to the styles of the preceding century. These, with a few great exceptions, had degenerated into a highly stylized, anti-naturalistic aestheticism in which elegant and attenuated forms were favored at the expense of content or expressive value – the style known today as Mannerism. Like other great artists of the day, Bernini and Caravaggio in Rome, Velazquez in Spain and Rembrandt in nearby Holland, Rubens broke with this tradition – in which he was initially trained – by means of a direct and fresh study of nature, modified in his case by a deep immersion in the art of antiquity and that of the High Renaissance. By education and temperament he was the natural heir to the Humanist classical tradition. Throughout his life he possessed a love of classical literature and thought that was to mold his whole outlook on life and determine the classical bias of his art. Stylistically he absorbed certain tenets of classical and High Renaissance art, namely a sense of monumentality and idealization of form; an idea of the clear relationship of the parts to the whole; and the grand tradition of *"disegno,"* the poised and balanced grouping of figures within a harmonious whole. Rubens' particular greatness lies in developing and extending these principles of style in conformity with the tastes and passions of his own day. His monumental works for Church and court alike sanctioned the pretension of his patrons by tying them to history and to tradition through stylistic and iconographical reference to the Renaissance and to the antique.

Early life

The circumstances of Rubens' birth demonstrate the religious uncertainty of the times. He was born on June 28, 1577, at Siegen in Westphalia, and spent the first ten years of his life in Cologne. His father Jan was a native of Antwerp, where he had been a respected lawyer and city alderman until he fell prey to the religious struggles of the time. As both part of the hereditary Catholic Spanish Empire and a continuing center of the Protestant Reformation, the Low Countries became engulfed in religious conflict after the death of the moderate emperor Charles V. Charles's son Philip II of Spain, championing a rigid Catholic orthodoxy, precipitated the opposition of the Flemish nobles, led by William of Orange-Nassau. They actively espoused the Protestant cause in their attempt to gain political and religious freedom. This led, in 1568, to a long and burdensome war, concluded only in 1648, but which resulted more immediately in the separation of the northern, Protestant, United Provinces from Catholic, Spanish, Flanders.

Originally a Catholic, Jan Rubens converted to Protestantism following the changing political and religious sympathies of Antwerp, only to hastily reconvert when the Spanish brought the city to heel in 1567. The following year he left the city together with his family and settled in Cologne, where he became legal advisor to Anne of Saxony, who had been left behind by her husband William of Orange in his struggle against the Spanish. In the course of his duties Jan unfortunately succeeded in getting his employer pregnant and was duly condemned to death for adultery. He was saved only by the magnanimity of his wife, who pleaded unceasingly for clemency. Though spared, and allowed eventually to live with his family, Jan was placed under

JOACHIM WTEWAEL
The Judgement of Paris
1615
National Gallery, London

This work, although painted fifteen years later than Rubens' version (see page 121), shows typically Northern Mannerest treatment of an Italianate subject. This is evident in the profusion of meticulously painted details, subsidiary figures and animals as well as in the harsh lighting and palette. The elegant insouciance of the poses shows the artist's concern for decorative sophistication at the expense of narrative power.

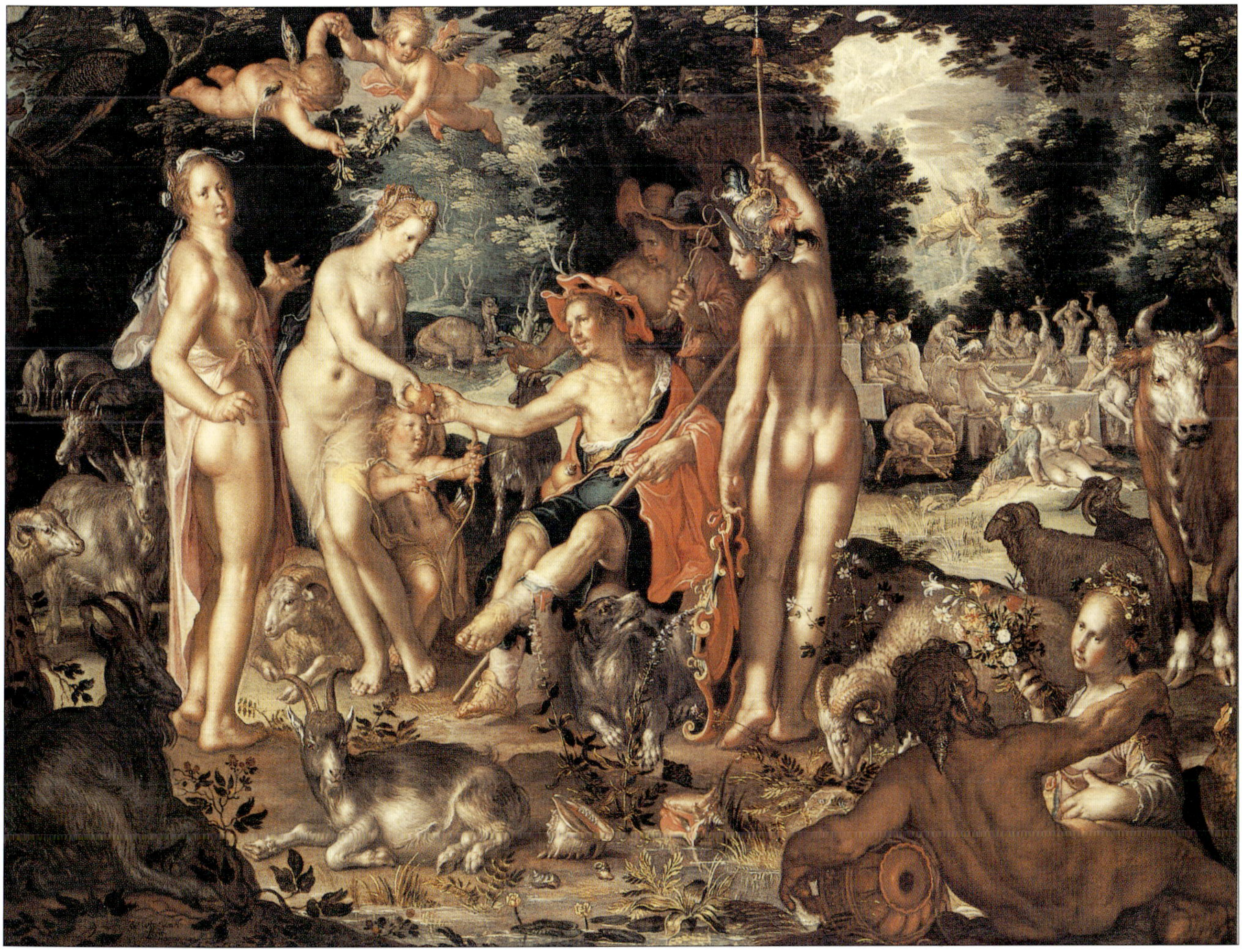

virtual house arrest in Siegen. There, with the resumption of normal family life, his wife gave birth to first Philip in 1576, then Peter Paul in 1577, followed by a sister in 1578. Only in that year was the family fully released and allowed to live anywhere except within the lands of Nassau. They moved back to Cologne and returned to the Catholic faith. Such was the capricious play of circumstances that made Peter Paul Rubens a Catholic and gave the Counter-Reformation one of its greatest propagandists.

Ten years later, on Jan's death, the family moved back to Antwerp, now permanently part of the Spanish Empire and Catholic in its allegiance. Though undergoing a steep economic decline, accelerated by the Dutch blockade of the mouth of the river Scheldt, which prevented access to its port, the city nonetheless continued to possess considerable financial and cultural resources. It became a focus of the Counter-Reformation in the north and witnessed a massive campaign of restoration of its churches, damaged or destroyed in the successive waves of iconoclasm that had swept over the city.

Rubens received a liberal classical education at a school run by a man named Rombout Verdonck. A love of classical literature, bred here and encouraged by his scholarly elder brother, bore fruit in a lifelong passion for the classical past. Through his brother, he was influenced by the Stoic philosophers, in particular Seneca and Plutarch, who advocated seriousness, moderation in all things, the pursuit of virtue, a belief in reason over the passions and an acceptance of fate. Such values were to become the guiding principles of his life.

PETER PAUL RUBENS
Ignudo (after Michelangelo)
c 1601-2
British Museum, London

Drawings of this type show how fast Rubens began to absorb the Italian Renaissance tradition. He shows the traits artists — the reluctance to generalize forms, the exact delineation of musculature and the specific, individual physiognomy that he gives the head. The violent torsions of Michelangelo's figures were important in forming the basis of Rubens' dynamic

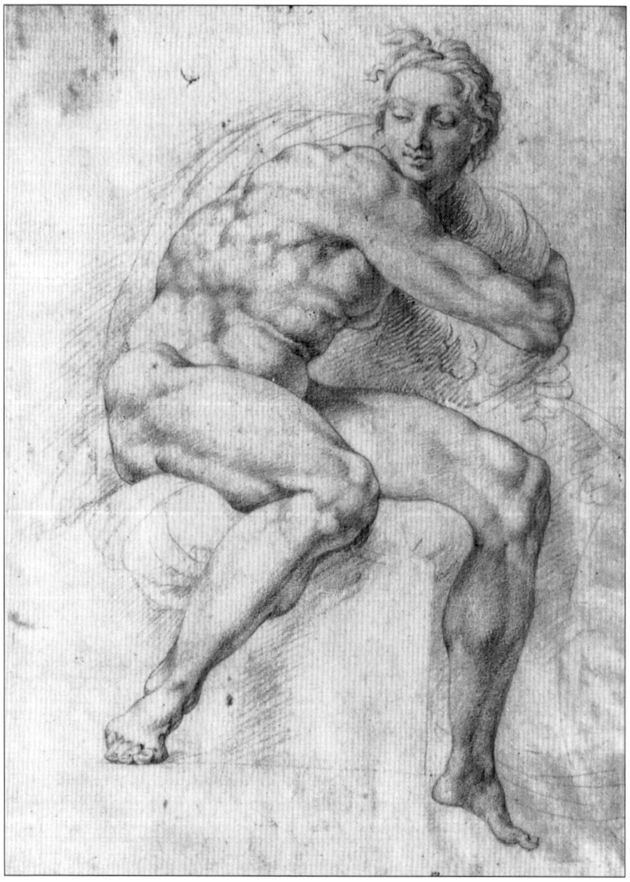

Artistic training

After serving briefly as a page to Marguerite de Ligne-Arenberg at Oudenarde, he entered, in about 1592, the studio of the landscapist Tobias Verhaecht, thereafter moving to that of Adam van Noort, who specialized in portraits. Here he stayed for four years of apprenticeship, and in about 1596 he moved to the studio of Otto van Veen, the most prestigious painter in Antwerp at the time. This master had travelled to Rome and knew at first hand the works of antiquity and of the Renaissance. Like his pupil he was interested in classical literature and, according to Humanist custom, had latinized his name to Octavius Vaenius. From him Rubens learned something of the principles of Renaissace figurative painting, and from his years of apprenticeship in general he learned the methods, techniques and palette of late Mannerist Flemish painting. By 1598 he had enrolled in the Guild of St Luke and had probably set up as an independent painter. Very few works have survived from this period, but the *Judgement of Paris* (See page 121), painted about 1600, shows the characteristics of his early style. The smooth, enamel-like flesh modelling and the palette of acid, discordant colours are entirely northern in conception, comparable to Joachim Wtewael's painting of the same theme. The figural composition, however, is derived from Italian prints, in particular Marcantonio Raimondi's engraving after Raphael's treatment of the same subject (see page 121). This well illustrates the chief means by which Rubens came into contact with the Italian tradition. Other sources that are known to have been available to him include the great northern graphic masters. He copied Dürer prints as well as Holbein's *Dance of Death* woodcuts, and thus absorbed certain northern characteristics, for example a dislike of smooth

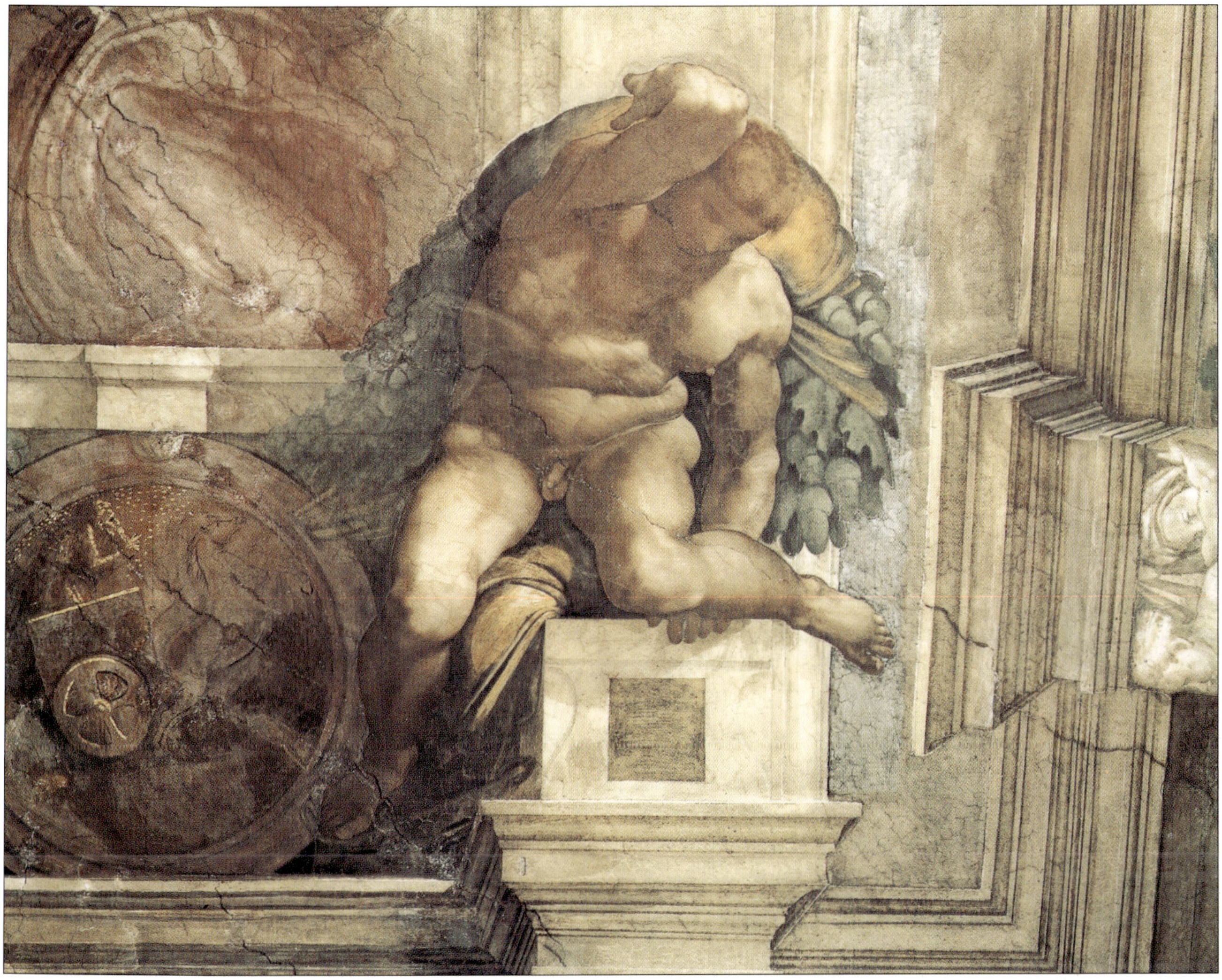

MICHELANGELO
Ignudo, detail of the Sistine Chapel ceiling

This is one of the idealized male nudes that flank the scenes of the Creation. They carry swags of oak leaves and acorns, the family insignia of the commissioning della Rovere pope, Julius II, but their further iconographical significance is unclear. Their elegant, serpentine poses were greatly admired by sixteenth-century artists and continuously emulated in succeeding centuries.

generalizations of form.

The *Judgement of Paris* was probably completed shortly before his departure for Italy in May 1600. With his apprenticeship finished, Rubens clearly felt that his education would remain incomplete until he had studied the art of Italy at firsthand. Like two other great northern artists of his century, Claude Lorraine and Nicolas Poussin, he felt the tug of the south, sensing the pull of a cultural and artistic tradition which he knew only incompletely. Once in Italy, he immediately recognized it as his spiritual home, leaving it only with great reluctance and with a lifelong desire to return, though this was to be denied him.

The court painter

Traveling initially to Venice, he soon found a position as a court painter to Vincenzo I Gonzaga, Duke of Mantua, and remained thus employed for the next seven years. His duties in Mantua were light, owing to the exiguous state of the duke's finances, and Rubens was therefore free to travel and to find commissions elsewhere. He was in Rome by July 1601, after already having witnessed the proxy marriage of Marie de' Medici to Henry IV of France in Florence in October 1600.

During the following years Rubens was to travel widely in Italy and to paint some forty works. Many more sketches and drawings survive from this period. A very large proportion of these were copies of things he had seen, and it is clear from their variety and number that he was quite deliberately forming a kind of personal reference library for his future use. That this was to be a fundamental part of his working process can be illustrated vividly by a copy of one of the *Ignudi* of Michelangelo's Sistine Chapel ceiling, made soon after his

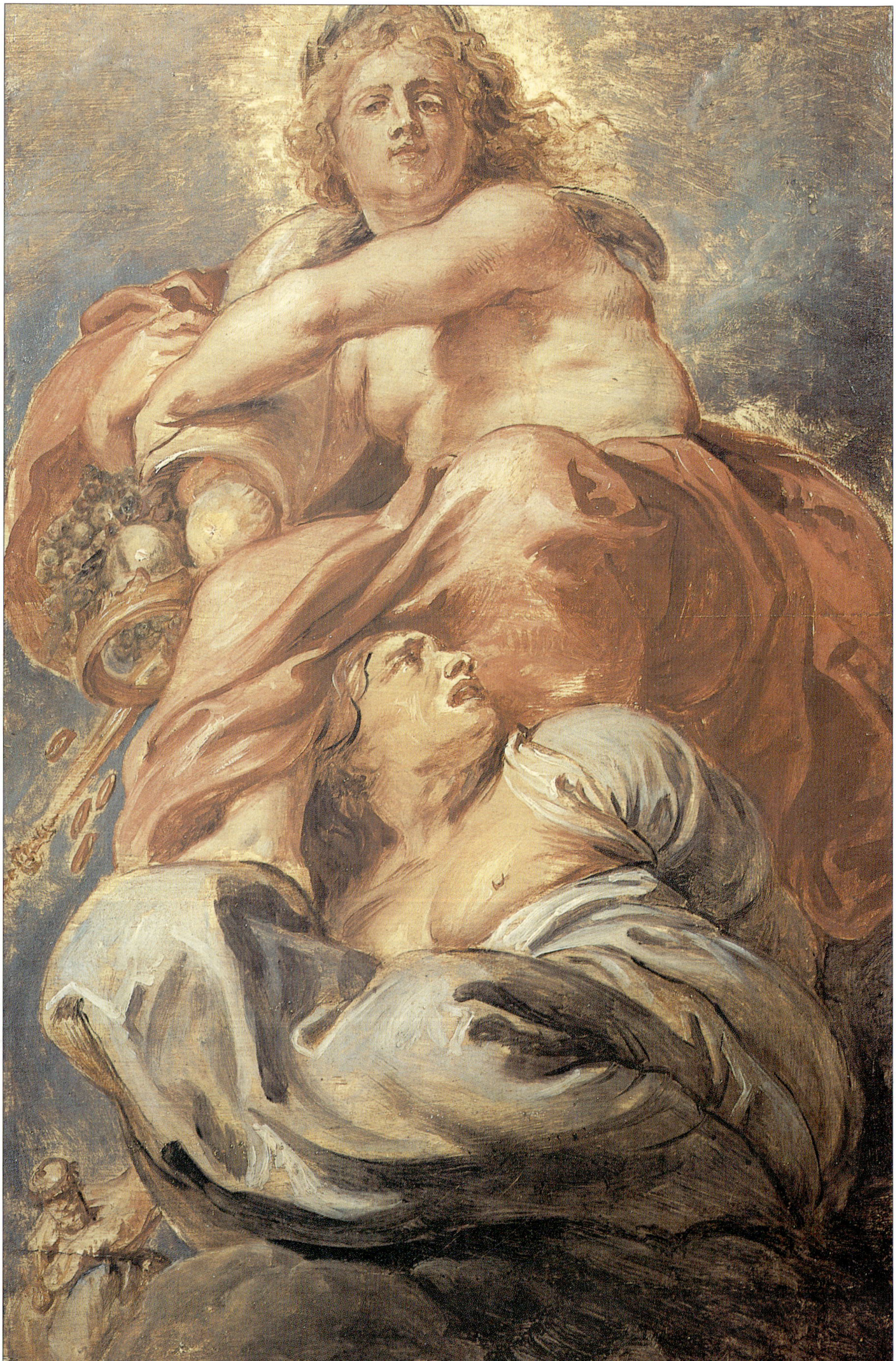

arrival in Rome. He has exaggerated the musculature and made the expression of the face more specific, thus losing the "spiritual" aestheticism of the original. That he kept this drawing and put it to later use is made clear by the existence of a counter-proof of the drawing with the figure extensively reworked that was used in the 1630s as a study for the figure of Bounty in the ceiling decorations of the Banqueting Hall in Whitehall, London. An oil-sketch for the same figure shows the same pose in reverse, now female and partially draped, the bend of the torso made less acute and the angle of vision more steeply foreshortened.

He also copied the most famous antique statues in the Roman collections, including the *Laocoön* group and the so-called "Belvedere torso." He made studies after Titian and Raphael as well as a host of other sixteenth-century artists as diverse as Tintoretto, Cigoli and Barocci. Rubens was also deeply interested in contemporary artistic developments. No sources exist that would prove that he was personally acquainted with Caravaggio, yet it was Rubens who persuaded the Duke of Mantua to buy Caravaggio's controversial *Death of the Virgin* altarpiece when the original commissioners rejected it on grounds of decorum. Variations he made on Caravaggio's *Entombment* demonstrate his interest in his contemporary and show the characteristic manner in which, although drawing inspiration for his own work from that of others, he could completely transform the original into a personal statement. Here he has increased the number of figures, widened the sense of space and unified the group by subordinating them to a single, generalized rhythmic flow of movement.

PETER PAUL RUBENS
Sketch for *Royal Bounty Overcoming Avarice*
c 1632-3
Courtauld Institute Galleries, London

Echoes of Michelangelo's *Ignudo* can be found in several of Rubens' compositions, but these are perhaps clearest in the figure of Bounty, destined for the ceiling of the Banqueting Hall, London, in praise of the unification of Scotland and England under James I. The figure has been reversed by taking a counterproof of the original drawing, and the oak-leaf swags of the original have been transformed into an overflowing cornucopia.

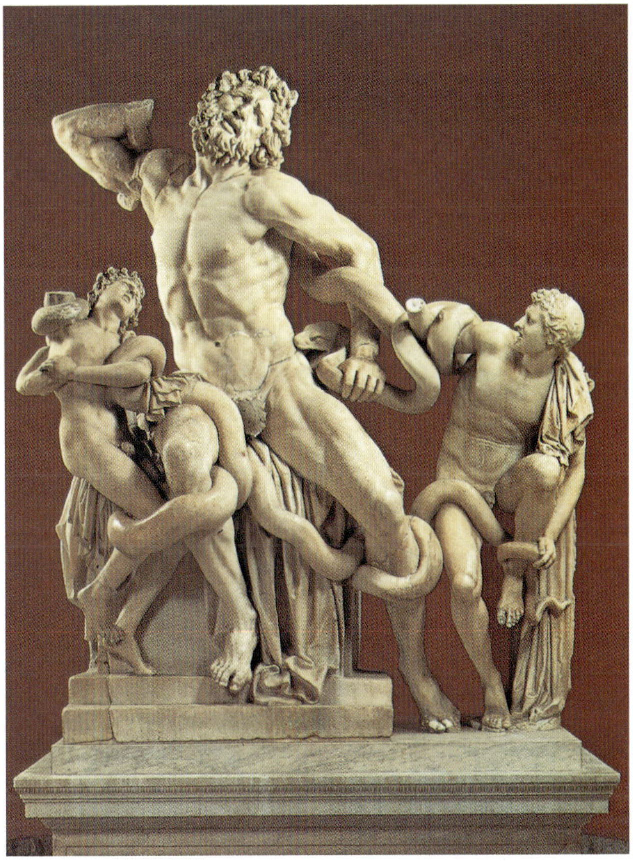

Laocoön
Second century BC
The Vatican, Rome

This famous late-Hellenic sculpture, excavated in 1506, was one of the major discoveries of the Italian Renaissance, and in its monumentality of form and pathos of mood it became a source of inspiration to many painters and sculptors. The subject is a Trojan priest and his sons being devoured by snakes after having warned the citizens of Troy not to bring the Greeks' wooden horse into the city.

Most great artists have drawn frequently on the art of the past for inspiration, but Rubens was exceptional in that, throughout his life, this habit was an almost necessary precondition for creation. He seems to have relied on study of other works of art in order to prompt formal ideas of his own. He was criticized for this even in his own day, but as Roger de Piles, the French seventeenth-century critic, sympathetically put it, he used "all that was most beautiful to stimulate his humor and warm his genius."

In 1603 the Duke of Mantua sent Rubens on a diplomatic mission to King Philip III of Spain, which was to initiate a highly successful career as a diplomat. He performed all his required duties, even restoring and in some cases repainting pictures that had been intended as gifts and which had been damaged en route. In Spain Rubens had the opportunity to study the great royal col-

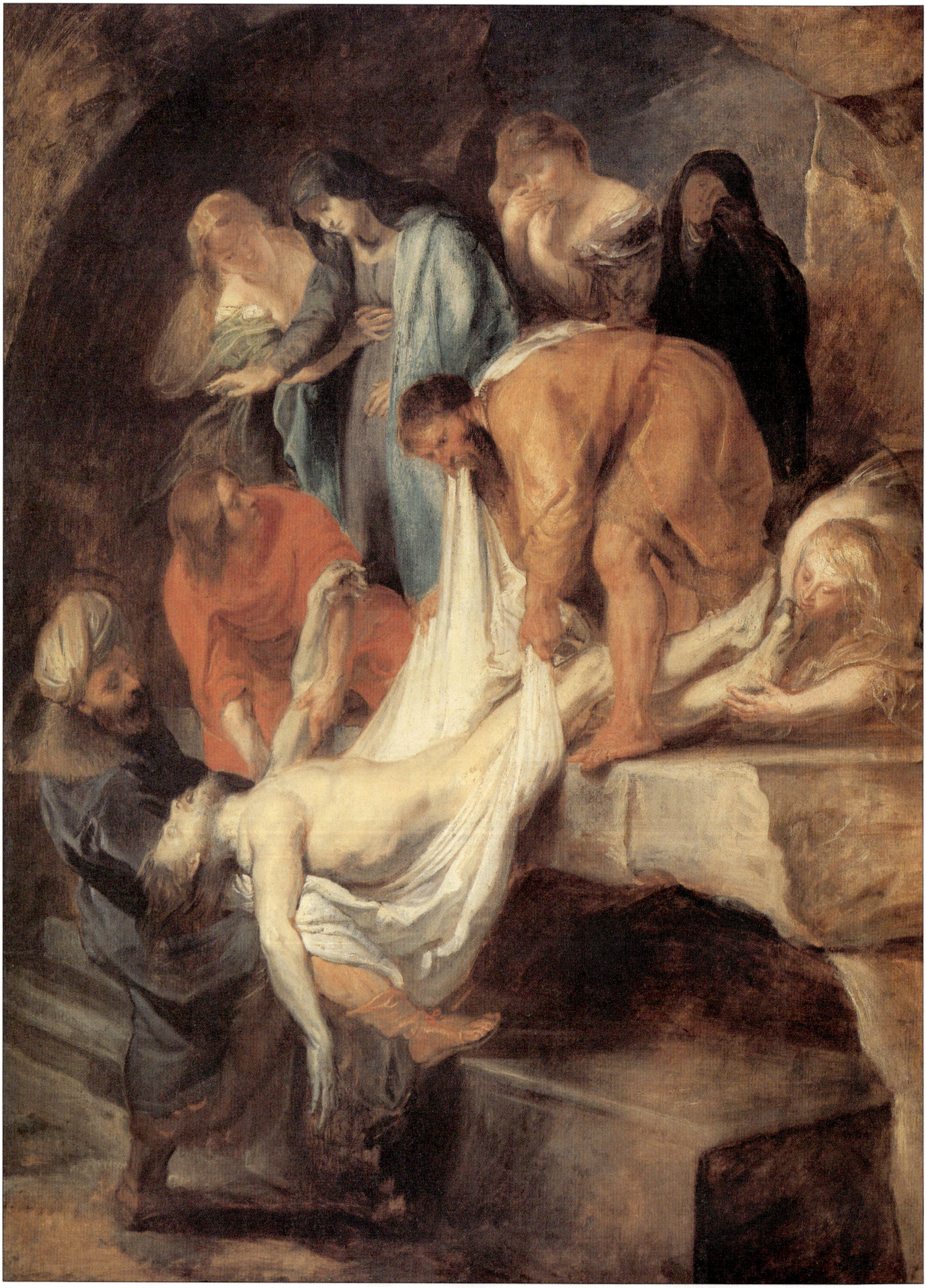

lection, and was particularly impressed by the number and richness of the Titians and Raphaels. By the end of his period away from home, he had had ample opportunity to study the greatest works of art in Europe. His style in this decade was eclectic and experimental; through intense study he broadened his technique, increased his facility with the paintbrush, widened his vocabulary of gesture, posture and expression and learned to paint on a large scale.

Rubens abruptly left the service of the Duke of Mantua in 1608, returning hurriedly to Antwerp upon hearing that his mother was very ill (she had in fact died even before the message reached him). He came back to his home town preceded by a considerable reputation, and quickly established himself as the leading painter of the city. He was commissioned by the city authorities to paint a large *Adoration of the Kings* for the chamber of state, and within a year of his return became court painter to the Regents of the Netherlands, the liberal Archduke Albert of Austria and his wife, Isabella, daughter of Philip II of Spain. He entered their service reluctantly, "bound," as he said, "with fetters of gold" to the tedious injunctions of court life. Yet the privileges that the position conferred were considerable. He was allowed to work in Antwerp (not at the court in Brussels), was exempted from guild regulations and dues and was given an annuity of 500 florins. Moreover, his duties at court were fairly light, consisting mainly of routine portrait painting.

Marriage and prosperity

In addition he married. His wife was Isabella Brant, the eighteen-year-old daughter of a secretary of the city and respected member of the burgher class. The double portrait that he executed as a momento of the wedding is interesting both as an example of his portraiture style in 1610 and as a revelation of how he saw himself, or how he wished himself to be seen – not as an artist but as a worldly and prosperous gentleman. He is elegantly dressed with ruff and jeweled sword, and sits in a pose of easy assurance, gallantly deferring to his wife, who clasps his hand with shy and unaccustomed intentness.

In November 1610 he began building a large and imposing house which also afforded plenty of studio space for his growing workshop. This house he gradually filled with art and antiques. He had begun to collect

PETER PAUL RUBENS
The Entombment
c 1616-18
Courtauld Institute Galleries, London

This oil-sketch illustrates the way in which Rubens developed the formal ideas of another painting into a personal creation of his own. He has retained the basic colors of Caravaggio's original as well as the protruding corner of the stone slab that seems to invade the spectator's space. Yet the figures are arranged dynamically within an overall shape, echoed by the curves of the cave roof.

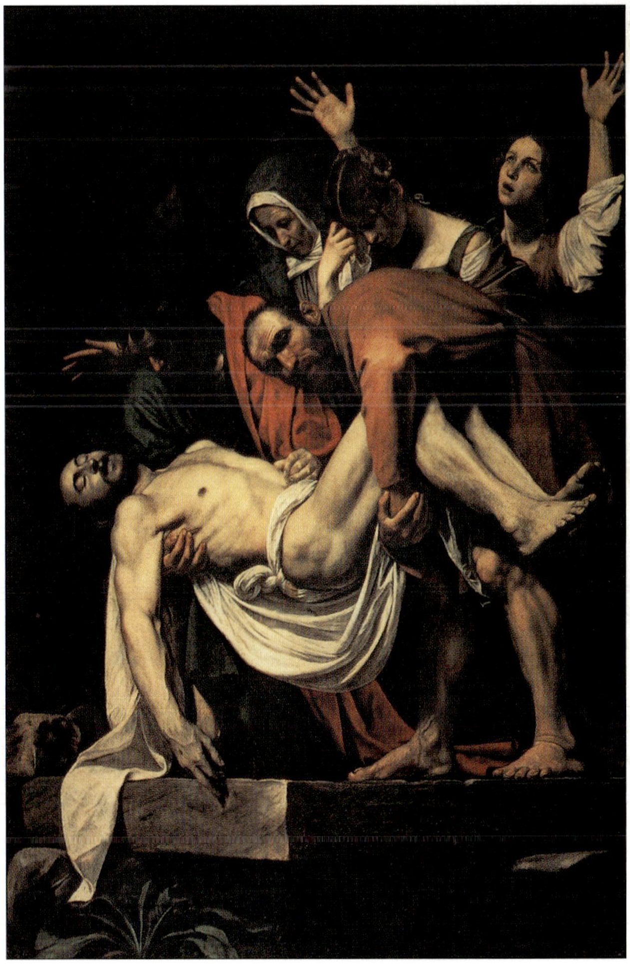

CARAVAGGIO
The Entombment
1602-4
The Vatican, Rome

This painting for a chapel in Rome shows Caravaggio's sharp, descriptive realism, dramatic lighting and use of "peasant types" to represent holy personages, all of which created a new tradition in painting in the early seventeenth century. Caravaggio's works were regarded as profane by many of the clergy and populace, and initially found favor only among a small circle of wealthy connoisseurs. Rubens immediately recognized his genius, and he made a copy of this work, subsequently elaborating it into a larger composition.

antique statuary while still in Italy, but the greater part of his collection was acquired in a transaction with Sir Dudley Carleton, an English diplomat, who between 1618 and 1620 exchanged some 129 pieces of classical sculpture and marble for six large paintings by Rubens. The result was the best collection of classical remains in northern Europe, and it became one of the sights for visitors to Antwerp.

Yet quite apart from the prestige value of such a collection, it is clear that sculpture was an important source of inspiration for his own work. Roger de Piles in 1708 published a verbatim account of the use and misuse of sculpture after notes from Rubens' notebooks that he had in his possession:

"To reach the highest perfection it is necessary to understand [statues], indeed to drink them in; but they must be used with judgement and care taken that painting does not take on the quality of stone. For many inexperienced and even experienced artists do not distinguish the material from the form, the stone from the figure, or the requirements of the marble from those of art."

Rubens' use of statuary as inspiration, as well as the extent to which he was able to disguise his source and translate it into the fluid paint medium is well illustrated by the *Descent from the Cross* altarpiece painted for Antwerp Cathedral between 1611 and 1614, where the figures of Christ, St John and Nicodemus are directly inspired by the figures of the Hellenistic *Laocoön* group which he had copied in the Vatican gardens. Both the unmistakable formal similarity and the distance Rubens achieves from the original demonstrate graphically not only his dependence on other art to prompt his own inventions but also the measure of his artistic independence.

As early as 1611 Rubens was having to turn away prospective students and to refuse commissions, so overwhelmed was he by requests for work. He very soon established a large and highly organized workshop in his new residence. Otto Sperling, a Danish medical student, visited the house in 1621 and left a valuable record of his working methods. He found the painter "just at work,in the course of which he was read to from Tacitus and moreover dictating a letter. As we did not disturb him by talking, he began to speak to us, carrying on his work without stopping, still being read to and going on with his dictation." There is no reason to suggest that this conjuring-trick facility was assumed. Sperling also saw the assistants at work, "...all painting different pieces which had been sketched out by Mr Rubens with chalk and a touch of paint here and there. The young fellows had to work up their pictures fully in oils until finally Mr Rubens himself would put the finishing touches with his own brushes. All this is considered Rubens' work; [and] thus he has gained a large fortune." Sperling clearly regarded Ruben's workshop as a kind of mass-production factory, and with some truth. Certainly Rubens had not time for the instruction of pupils in the strict sense. He employed apprentices to learn the trade step by step from the most menial tasks of grinding the colors and preparing the panels upwards. His most gifted assistants (including for a time the young Anthony van Dyck) were competent and sometimes very gifted painters in their own right, and Rubens was clearly dependent on them to a large degree in building up and thus interpreting, in a specifically "Rubenesque" manner, his initial designs. He would then alter or complete the top layers with a deft and personal hand, thus making them "autograph" (though he was always scrupulous in his business dealings in specifying the degree of studio help involved, and varied his prices accordingly).

In the years between 1610 and 1620 Rubens seems to have worked to the full, building up his reputation with a prodigious output which included altarpieces and whole cycles of paintings, as for example the decorations for the Jesuit Church in Antwerp, as well as smaller individually commissioned works, tapestry designs and even title pages of books.

The artist as diplomat

The next ten years might be characterized as Rubens' decade of diplomacy. In 1623 he was in Paris on behalf of the Regent Isabella; in 1626 he was again in France; in 1627 he visited Holland, and in 1628 Madrid, traveling thence in 1629 directly to England and returning home only in March 1630. During this time he succeeded in laying the basis for a peace treaty between England and Spain. Because of his singular position as painter first and diplomat second, his detachment from the courts and thus lack of political ambition, and his sincere desire for peace, he was trusted by all parties and acted as go-between in the delicate negotiations. He was knighted by both Charles I of England and Philip IV of Spain.

His wholehearted involvement in diplomatic activity and his continued absence from home was prompted by the death of his wife, probably of the plague, in 1626. His daughter, Clara Serena, had died three years earlier. Rubens wrote to a friend of his loss: "...since the true remedy for all ills is Forgetfulness, daughter of Time, I must without doubt look to her for help. But I find it very

RUBENS' PAINTING METHODS

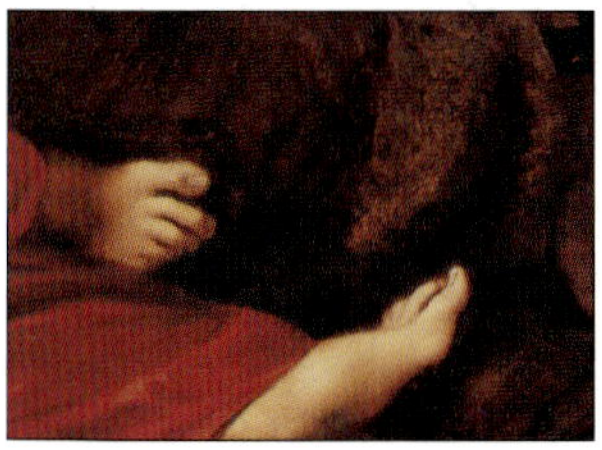

In this detail from Samson and Delilah *the transparent brown underpainting can be seen, left uncovered in places to form the middle ground.*

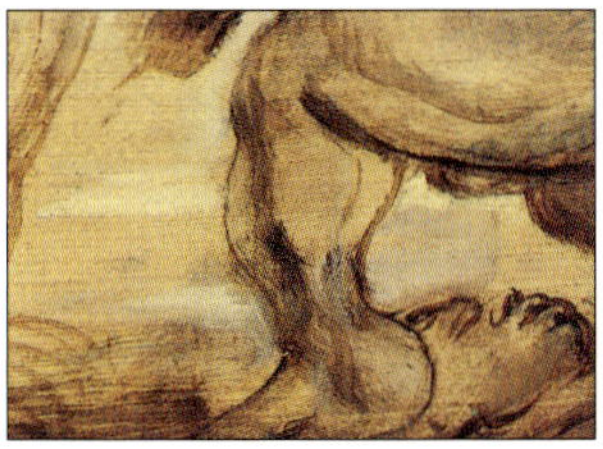

In the Lion Hunt, *one of Rubens' preliminary* modellos, *the white ground is visible beneath the yellow-brown under-painting.*

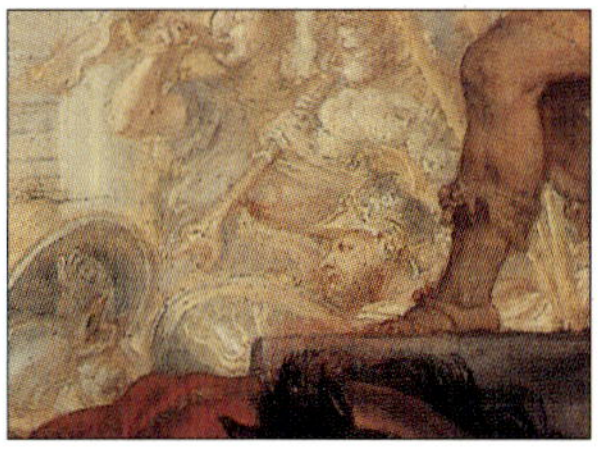

This detail of Rape of the Sabine Women *shows the contrast of brushwork, from thin washes to thick impasto.*

Although he sometimes used canvas, Rubens preferred to work on wooden panels, which gave a smooth surface and allowed his brush to move fluently. The panels, made by a professional panel maker, consisted of several oak planks glued together and then covered with a white ground made up of chalk bound with animal glue and impregnated with oil. This type of support was common at the time, but Rubens was distinctly innovative in his priming *(imprimatura)*, which consisted of very thin yellowish brown paint applied unevenly, usually in long, diagonal strokes from top right to bottom left. This underlayer, applied with a coarse bristle brush to create a striated effect and allow some of the white ground to show through, is clearly visible in Rubens' oil-sketches. It plays an important part in the color effects of the finished paintings, particularly in the flesh, where the transparent brown is sometimes left exposed to form the middle ground.

In general, Rubens did very little underdrawing on the support, since his practice was to execute a preliminary *modello* which provided the general layout for the painting. Instead, the composition was sketched in with thin, fluid paint, and the laying in of colors proceeded from this point, the lights being built up thickly to cover the ground priming and the shadows scumbled thinly over it. Rubens is described as painting with a pot of turpentine beside him, frequently dipping his brush into it to thin or work the paint (the first documented reference to turpentine as a diluent), which may help to explain the amazing variety of his brushwork.

This painting of Susanna Fourment, Rubens' first wife's sister, done about 1620, is one of his loveliest and most luminous portraits. His preference for wooden panels as a painting support allowed him considerably more latitude than canvas. The support for this painting consists of four oak planks made by a well-known panel maker, whose monogram is on the back. The composition appears to have expanded spontaneously from a central core, with two strips of wood added, one on the right to expand the sky and another at the bottom to give the figure more substance. Such a practice was not unusual for Rubens: ***in his*** **Autumn Landscape with a View of Het Steen** ***(see page 145), painted on a support made up of seventeen panels, he appears to have enlarged the composition in*** *several stages, adding strips to bottom, top and sides as he became more and more interested in the panoramic landscape.*

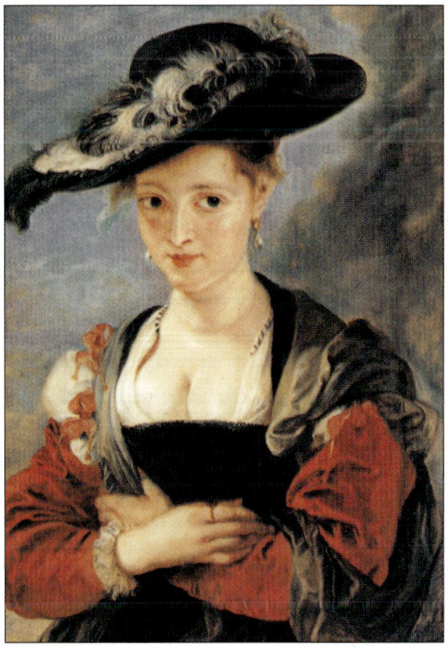

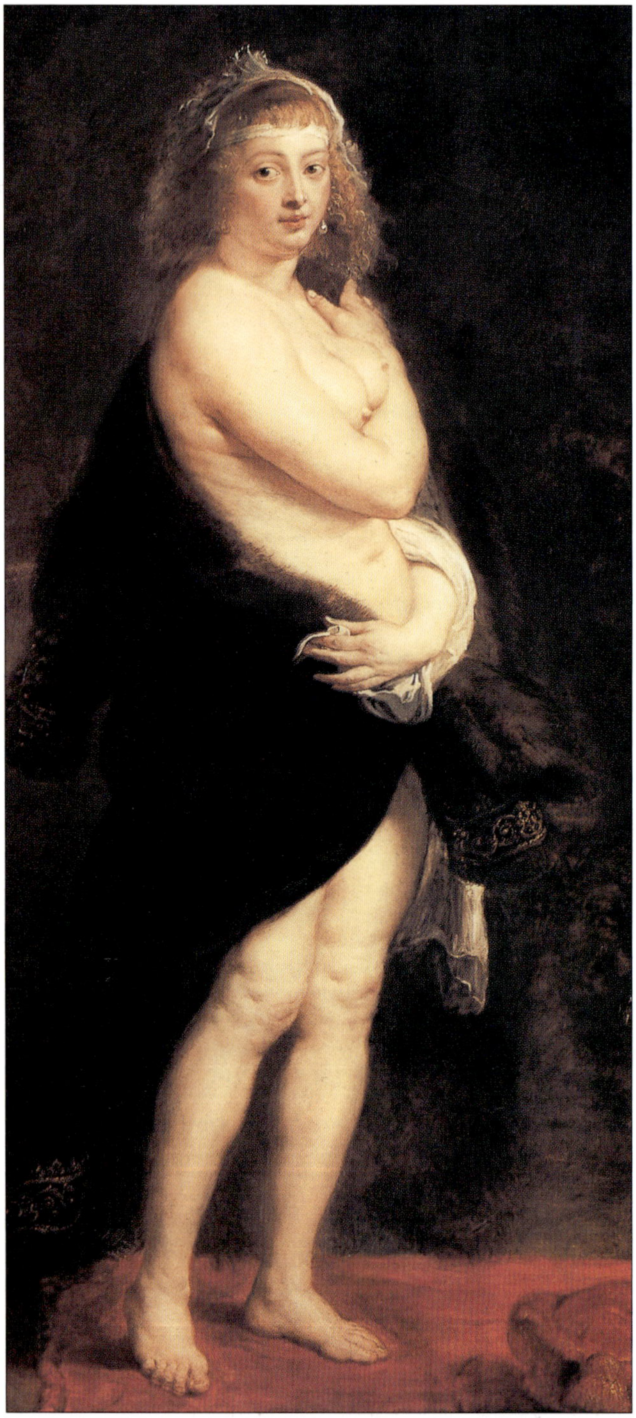

PETER PAUL RUBENS
Helena Fourment as Venus or *"Het Pelsken"*
c 1636-8
Kunsthistorisches Museum, Vienna

In this sumptuously painted image of his second wife, Rubens has posed her in the attitude of the classical "Medici Venus," and placed her in front of a fountain, just visible in the right background. The idea of the fur wrap was borrowed from Titian. Neither simply a portrait nor purely an image of a mythological deity, this intensely private work has ironically become one of the most celebrated erotic images in Western art.

hard to separate grief from the memory of a person whom I must love and cherish as long as I live."

The major works he painted during this period reflect his political role as arbiter of kings and princely propagandist. In 1622 he was summoned to France by Marie de' Medici, the widow of King Henry IV. After her husband's assassination in 1610 she had been appointed regent to her son, Louis XIII, until he ousted his mother from power and assumed the full position of king in 1620. Two years later Marie de' Medici commissioned Rubens to decorate two long galleries in the Luxembourg Palace with a series of twenty-one huge canvases, celebrating her life and virtues, a subject that clearly presented something of a challenge even to Rubens. In the largest surviving cycle of monumental canvases (see page 129) he skilfully conjoined pagan and Christian imagery, actual incident and allegory, to reinforce the somewhat sparse glories of her reign. The work took three years to complete, and assistants were used extensively in realizing the vast designs.

During this period his style loosened considerably, the hard outlines and sculptural modeling of form diminished and his treatment became more painterly, with the colors warmer and more saturated and the compositions more complex. All these tendencies are to be seen in the sumptuous *Allegory of Peace and War* (see page 136), which Rubens presented to Charles I before leaving England which neatly summed up the purpose of his mission.

The later years

On his return to Antwerp in March 1630 he made a clear decision to leave political life. Partly exasperated by the fickle and vacillating habits of negotiators and their masters, partly discomfited by personal slights and financial losses meted out to him by the Spanish bureaucracy, and partly spurred on by the promptings of the creative instincts that had had of necessity to lie fairly dormant, he persuaded the Regent Isabella to release him from further diplomatic assignments. In December of that year, at the age of fifty-three, he married again, taking as his wife Helena Fourment, the sixteen-year-old daughter of an Antwerp silk merchant. He frankly explained his reason for doing so to an old friend: "...since I was not yet inclined to live the life of a celibate thinking that, if we must give the first place to continence we may enjoy licit pleasures with thankfulness...I have taken a young wife of honest but middle-class family..." The many paintings of Helena in a variety of guises — as Venus or as Hagar in the Wilderness — as well

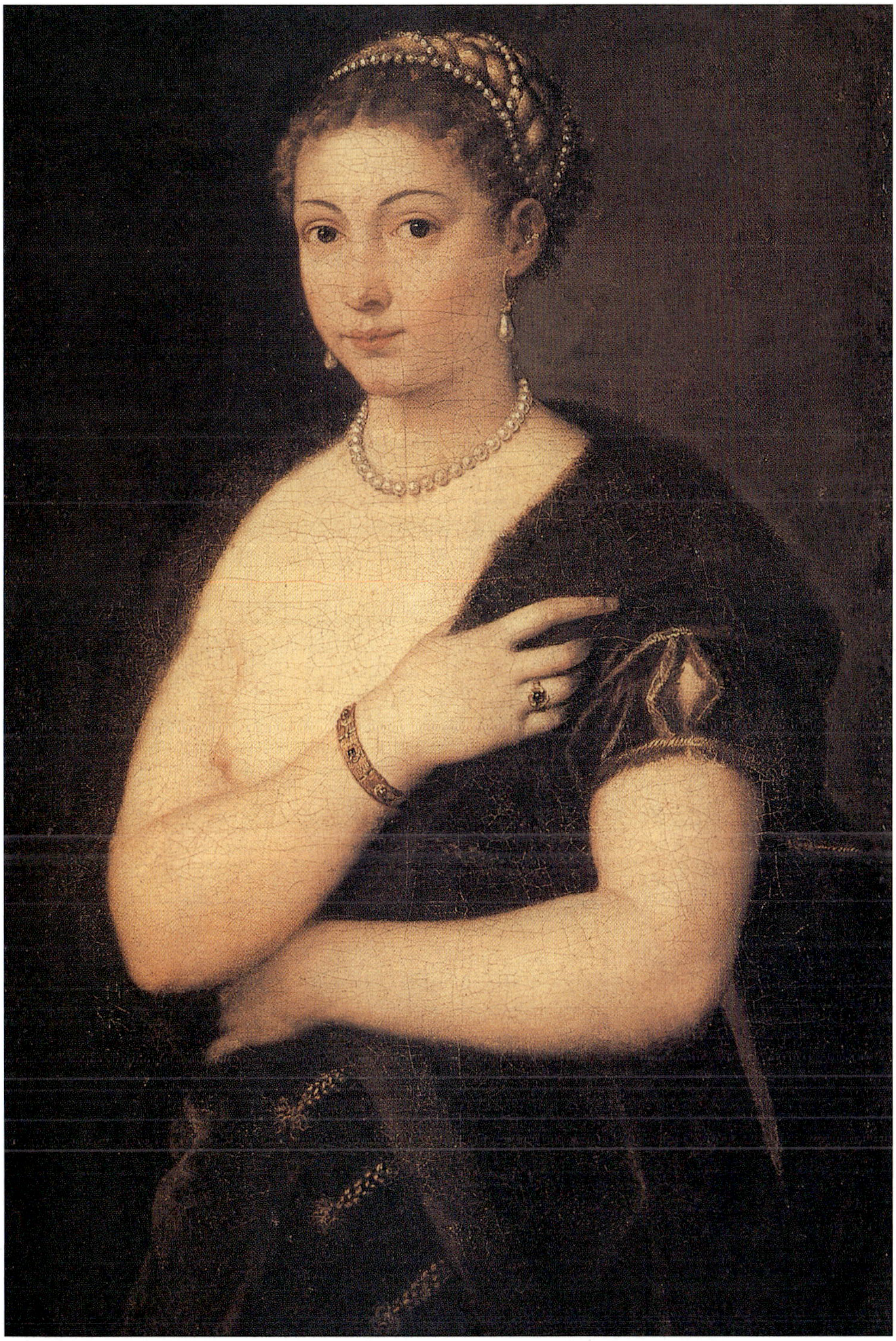

TITIAN
Girl in a Fur Wrap
1535-7
Kunsthistorisches Museum, Vienna

Rubens made a copy of this painting when he saw it in the collection of Charles I, and later used the erotic idea of a partially draped wrap for his own "*Het Pelsken*." The subject of the Titian painting was an anonymous girl, intended as a mildly erotic "pin-up" of a type readily available in his workshop. The same model reappears in a similar pose and wearing the same blue dress in a painting bought by Francesco Maria della Rovere in 1536, now in the Pitti Palace, Florence.

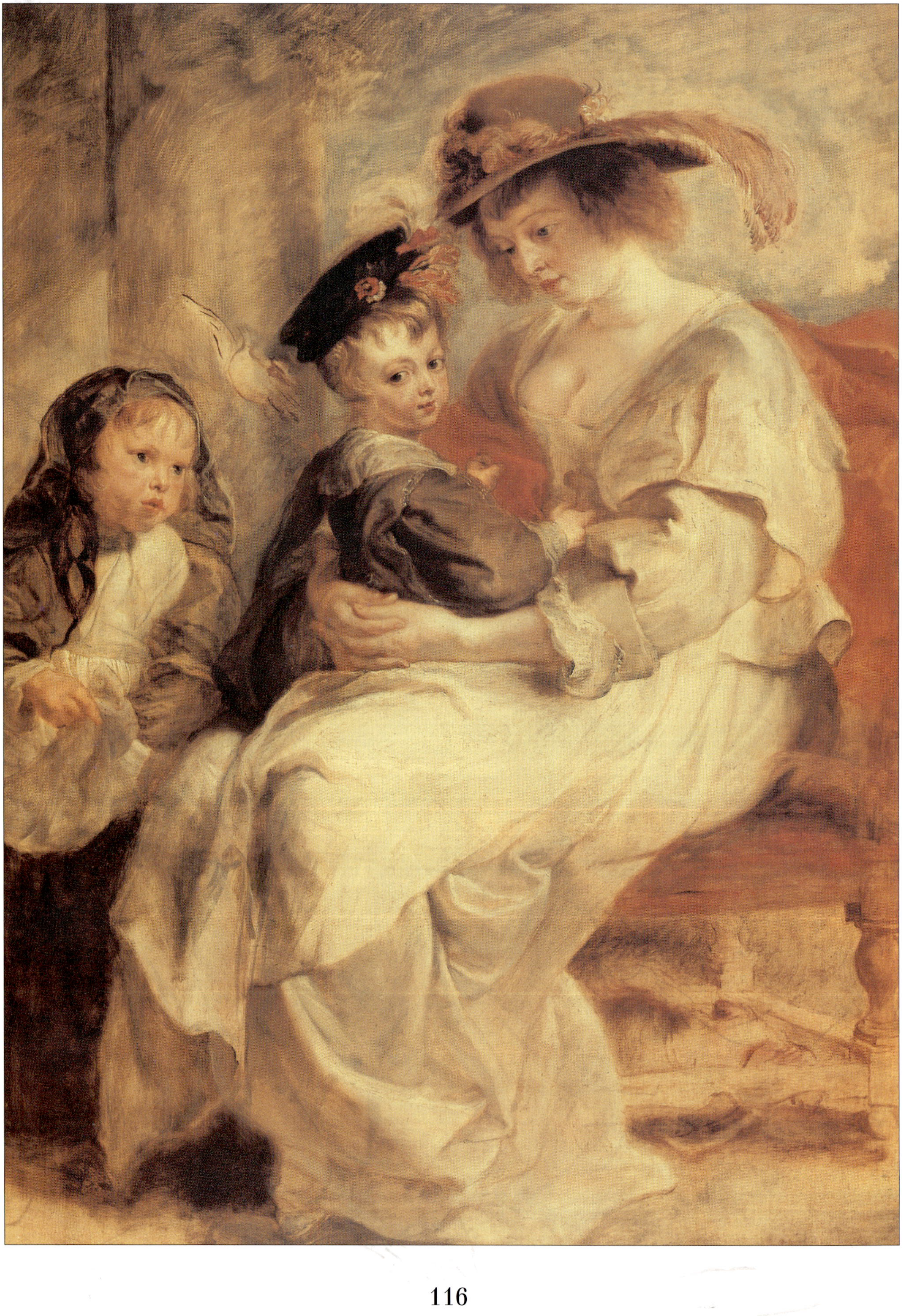

as straight portraits, clearly reveal the extent to which she was his inspiration and the object of an almost palpable physical passion.

Equally inspirational for his late paintings was the example of Titian, never far below the surface throughout his career, but a powerful instrument in the deepening of his own style in the last decade of his life. Like the late works of Titian or Rembrandt, his style becomes deeply personal, and though aided considerably by a renewed study of Titian, the loosening of style is the product of a lifetime's handling and experience with paint. The beautiful and sumptuous *Het Pelsken*, or *Helena Fourment as Venus*, shows the twin aspects of his passion: the physical beauty of his wife expressed in the warm diaphanous brushwork inspired by the Venetian master, which allows him to create the opalescent glow of soft skin. The subject has its basis in Titian's *Girl in a Fur Wrap*, but Rubens has made the idea completely his own. Unlike Titian, who generalizes his forms, Rubens sees no need to disguise the dimples and puckers of the knees or the folds of flesh under the arm. He combines the dignity of a goddess with a human and fleshly eroticism. This work had a special significance for the artist and his wife, for he expressly left it to her in his will, calling it "Het Pelsken" or "The Little Fur," and though she destroyed several nudes after his death, she spared this one.

In 1635 he bought the large castle of Steen, near Malines, and to all intents and purposes retired there. Though he was kept busy throughout the 1630s with "official" commissions, notably the finishing of the Whitehall ceiling canvases (1634), the city decorations for the triumphal entry into Antwerp of the Cardinal Infante Ferdinand (1635), and unceasing demands from the Spanish king, in general his subject matter becomes more personal, the style more relaxed, and he seems to be painting more for pleasure. The warm and vibrant landscapes of the countryside around his estate (see page 145) suggest an enjoyment in depicting the things closest to him, as do the group portraits of his family. Though increasingly hampered by gout, he lost none of his powers of invention or precision of touch. The *Rape of the Sabine Women* (see page 141) of c 1635 illustrates his skill in organizing large numbers of figures into an expressive and intelligible whole and by a brilliance of touch and colour, to endow the energy of his compositions with profound poetic vision.

His last great self-portrait (see page 104) must date from the last five years of his life. It combines the outwardly worldly — the pose, costume and background pillar show the traditional attributes of the distinguished statesman — with acute self-knowledge: the honesty with which he describes the tired and slackening features underlines the pervasive sense of gravitas and sharp intelligence. It constitutes a profound summation and testament of his life.

Rubens died in Antwerp on May 30, 1640.Though the use of allegory and frequent references to obscure classical myths or episodes from forgotten Roman history make his works today often difficult to digest, no other artist before or since has equaled his ability to employ brushstrokes both to describe form and to endow it with such a buoyancy and vibrant sense of energy. Above all, his idea of truth, his affirmation of human feelings and emotion is expressed in terms of movement, be it in the overall dynamic vehemence of his compositional formuli or in the rapid sequences of broken brushwork. Unlike his younger contemporary Rembrandt, who sought to express in his figures an idea of inner truth almost at the expense of the material world, Rubens, one might say, believed that truth lay not at the bottom of a well, but on the surface, traceable in the outward appearance of things. It is in the joyful apprehending of this sensual world that his peculiar greatness lies.

PETER PAUL RUBENS
Helena Fourment and her Children
c 1636
Louvre, Paris

This family group of Rubens' wife and children demonstrates the breadth and informality of his late work. It is unfinished, as can be seen from the lower part of the stool, which remains unpainted. The two hands that protrude into the right side of the picture belong to the third child, Isabella, as is known from a preparatory drawing in the Louvre, and reveal that the painting has been cut down at some later date.

CHRONOLOGY OF RUBENS' LIFE

1577 June 28: born at Siegen, Westphalia to Jan and Maria.
1578 Moves with family to Cologne.
1587 Father dies; family moves to Antwerp.
1590 Becomes page to the Countess de Ligne.
1591-2 Works in studio of Tobias Verhaecht, then apprenticed to Adam van Noort.
c 1596 Moves to studio of Otto van Veen (Vaenius).
1598 Master in Antwerp Guild of St Luke.
1600-3 Paints *Judgement of Paris*. Leaves Antwerp for Italy, then Spain. Attends proxy marriage of Marie de' Medici to Henri IV in Florence (1600).
1604 Returns to Mantua via Genoa.
1605 Completes paintings for SS. Trinita, Mantua.
1606-7 In Genoa and Rome. Completes first Chiesa Nova altarpiece.
1608 Leaves Rome on news of mother's illness, but mother dead on return.
1609 Paints *Samson and Delilah*, and *Adoration of the Kings* for Antwerp town hall. September: appointed court painter to the Regents. October: marries Isabella Brant. Twelve Years' Truce begins.
1610-12 Begins building new house and workshop. Commission for St Walburga altarpiece and *Deposition* altarpiece.

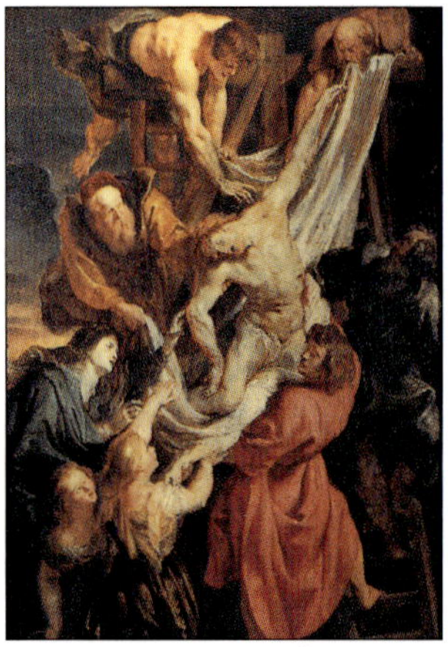

The Descent from the Cross

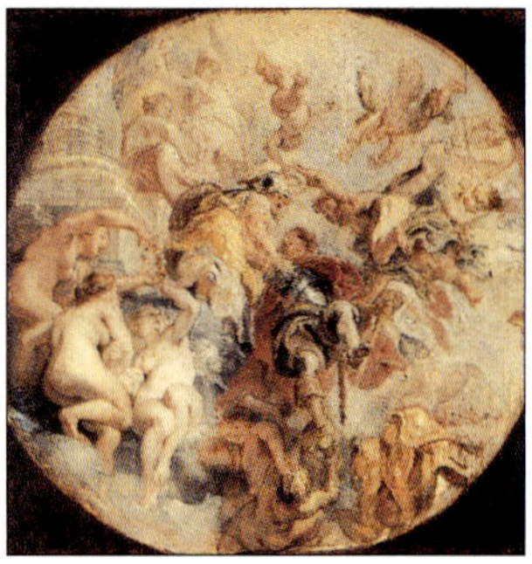

The Duke of Buckingham Conducted to the Temple of Virtus

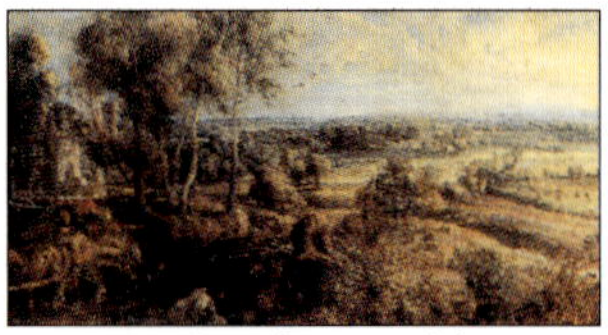

Autumn Landscape with a View of Het Steen

1620-1 Paints ceilings for Antwerp Jesuit church. Twelve Years' Truce ends.
1622 In Paris. Commission for *Marie de' Medici* cycle.
1623 In Paris again with nine completed *Marie de' Medici* pictures.
1624 *Adoration of Kings* for St Michael, Antwerp.
1625 Meets Duke of Buckingham and sells paintings to him.
1626 Isabella Brant dies.
1628 Paints *Madonna and Saints* for St Augustine, Antwerp. Leaves for Madrid.
1629 Brussels via Paris, then London. Paints *Allegory of Peace and War* for Charles I. Knighted by Charles I at Whitehall.
1630 Leaves political life. Marries Helena Fourment.
1634 Continues work on Whitehall ceilings. Paints *Rape of the Sabine Women*.
1635 Buys castle of Steen near Malines. Suffers increasingly from gout. Completes Whitehall ceilings and city decorations for entry into Antwerp of Cardinal-Infante Ferdinand. Paints landscapes.
1636 Appointed court painter to Cardinal-Infante Ferdinand.
c 1639 Paints last *Self-portrait*.
1640 May 30: dies in Antwerp, buried in St James'.

THE PAINTINGS

THE JUDGEMENT OF PARIS

c1600

$52\frac{3}{4} \times 68\frac{3}{4}$in/134×174.5cm

Oil on panel

National Gallery, London

This painting is one of Rubens' earliest surviving works, executed in about 1600, in all probability shortly before he left for Italy. It represents, in figure style and palette, the culmination of his apprenticeship in the idiom of late Flemish Mannerism.

The scene depicts the pastoral beauty contest between Juno, Minerva and Venus, judged by Paris, the son of King Priam of Troy, who had been abandoned to die on a hillside as a baby following a prophecy that he would bring about the ruin of Troy. Raised by a shepherd, he eventually married Oenone, the daughter of the river god Oneus, both of whom are to be seen on the right-hand side of the painting. Angered that she was not invited to the wedding, Eris the goddess of Strife threw down a golden apple among the guests, inscribed "To the fairest." Paris, decreed by Jupiter to be the judge, was offered lands and wealth by Juno, and victory in battle by Minerva, while Venus offered him the love of the most beautiful mortal woman, Helen of Sparta.

Though Rubens' initial idea, as preparatory drawings and an oil-sketch make clear, had been to show Paris in the process of choosing, instructing the goddesses to disrobe, he changed this first and more purely erotic conception to the dramatic and "historically" more crucial moment when Paris awarded the golden apple to Venus, thereby initiating the process that was to lead to his abduction of Helen and the Trojan War. The epic nature of this act is made clear by the *putti* who place a wreath upon Venus' head, amid a burst of celestial light.

Rubens used Marcantonio Raimondi's print (opposite) of Raphael's own *Judgement of Paris* as a starting point for the central figure group, although the figure of Venus has been much altered. It is possible too that Paris' muscular back implies some knowledge of the Hellenistic sculpture known as the "Belvedere Torso," perhaps through prints or plaster casts. These references show the artist attempting to come to terms with Italian and antique art, even at secondhand.

The artificiality of the stylized poses is increased by the vivid and discordant contrasts of color between the gleaming, marble-like flesh tones and the green-blue background, heightened by the harsh red and mauve accents at the extremities of flesh. The treatment of the river god and his daughter show clearly Rubens' method of building up the flesh tones. The thin striated umber underpainting is visible in the god's chest, running diagonally from top left to bottom right. The outlines and general musculature have been sketched in on top in a darker brown — probably raw umber. The flesh tints of pink, blue and an orange-yellow were then painted on top in fluid sequence. The outlines of the hands have been drawn in in bright red. These figures are the most thinly painted areas of the whole work, and allow the painting process to be clearly seen. The treatment of flesh is essentially the same in the main figures, although to a more developed degree. The colors used are startling in their range: from a turquoise-greenish blue to a dark red lake to lemon yellow. Hot reds are used in thicker accents for the nipples, navel outlines and shadows under the arms and around the buttocks.

The painting of the cloud and *putti* above Venus' head is very thickly applied and probably disguises earlier ideas painted out at a later stage. The disturbing contrast between the lemon yellow and purple is characteristically Flemish. To appreciate Rubens' adoption of a more Italianate palette and the maturing of his figure style, it is instructive to compare this early work with, for example, the *Allegory of Peace and War* (see page 136), painted some twenty-nine years later, both for the overall tonality and the treatment of flesh.

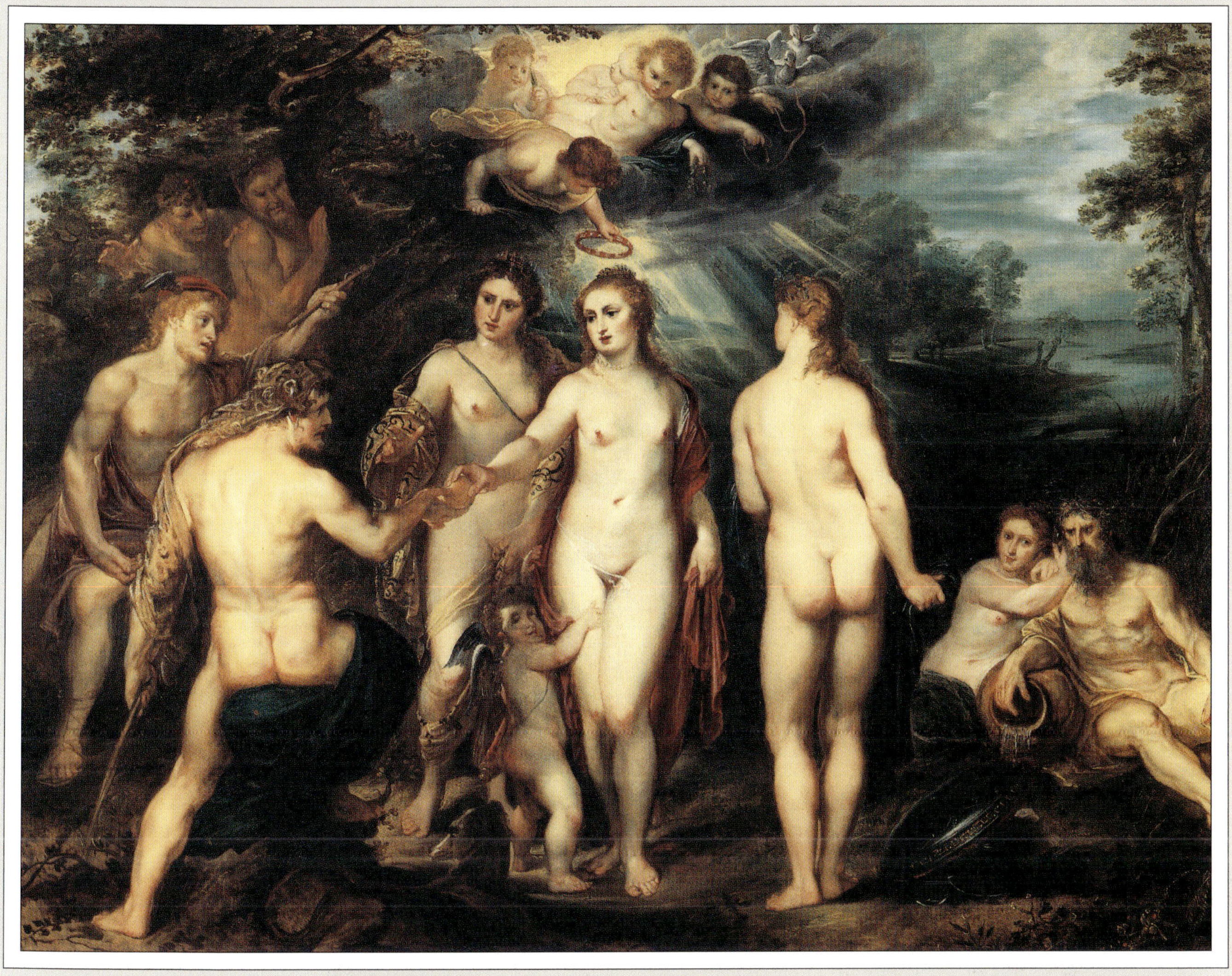

This is one of Rubens' earliest surviving works, and clearly shows the influence of Mannerist Flemish painting in the smooth, enamel-like modeling and the palette of acid and discordant colors. The figural composition is derived from Italian prints, especially the one shown here, an engraving after Raphael's treatment of the same subject. This formed the starting point for the painting, although the figure of Venus has been much altered.

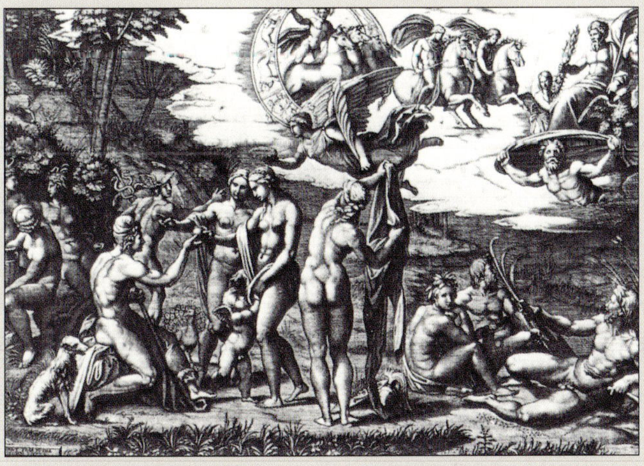

MARCANTONIO RAIMONDI
The Judgement of Paris
(after Raphael)
British Museum, London

Raimondi was one of the first Italian artists to make a living solely as an engraver. His career began in Venice, where he copied Dürer's prints, but he later moved to Rome and devoted himself to reproducing designs by Raphael. His engravings formed one of the main channels through which Italian ideas were transmitted to other parts of Europe.

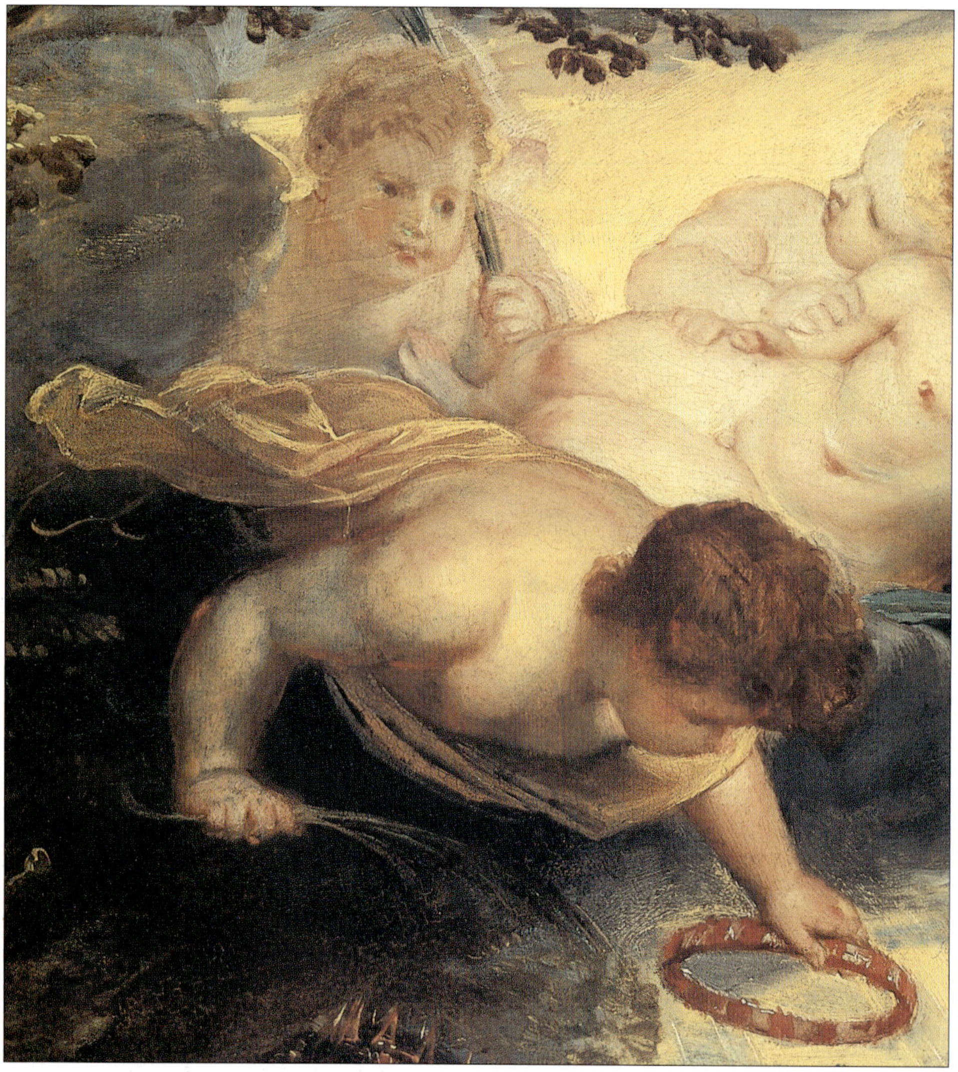

1

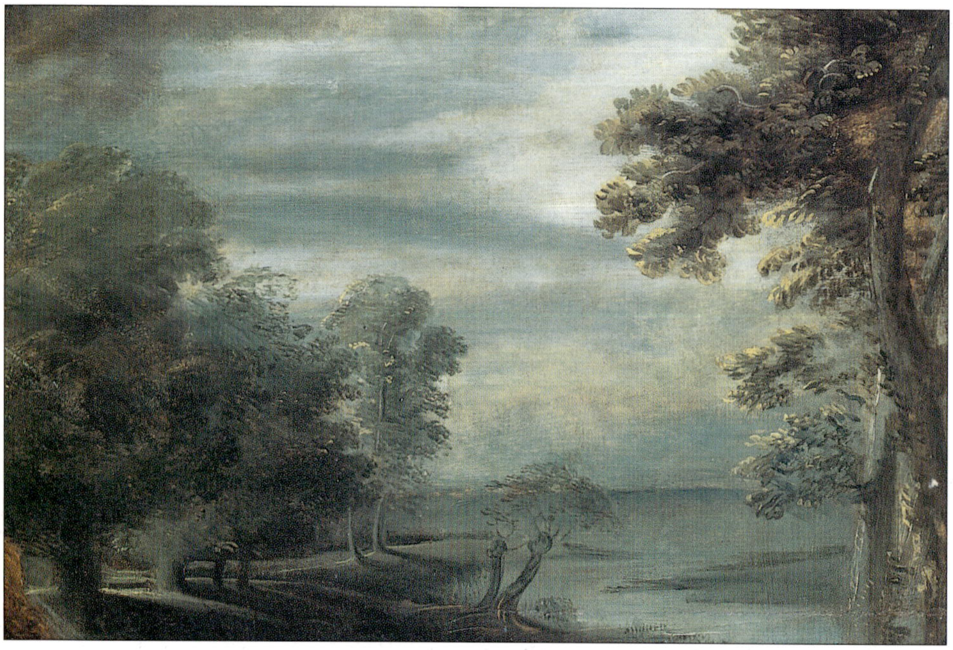

2

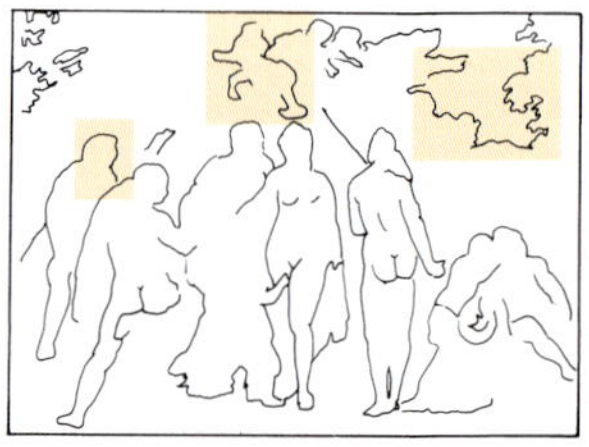

1 The flesh tones of the *putti* show the young Rubens' predilection for a rather loud palette. Here he has used a pale flesh tone in combination with a harsh turquoise green, a bright vermilion (in the nipples and outlines) and touches of yellow. The passage of bright lemon yellow behind the group sets off the colors in almost garish contrast. This area is very thickly painted, covering an earlier idea.

2 This combination of aqueous turquoise greens and blues is typical of the palette of the Flemish landscape painters of the later sixteenth century. Here the colors have been very thinly applied in broad washes, with details of the trees and river bank lightly sketched over this in brown or black paint. The foliage of the right-hand tree has been freely worked in loose dabs of varying tones of green and brown. The crack running horizontally through this section shows where the planks that make up the panel have parted slightly.

3 *Actual size detail* The head of Mercury clearly shows Rubens' early flesh-painting technique. It is very thinly painted in rather subdued tones, thus allowing the more brightly lit figure of Paris to assume greater prominence. The thin bluish gray colors have been applied over the umber underpainting and are set off by touches of bright crimson in the cheeks, lips and nostril.

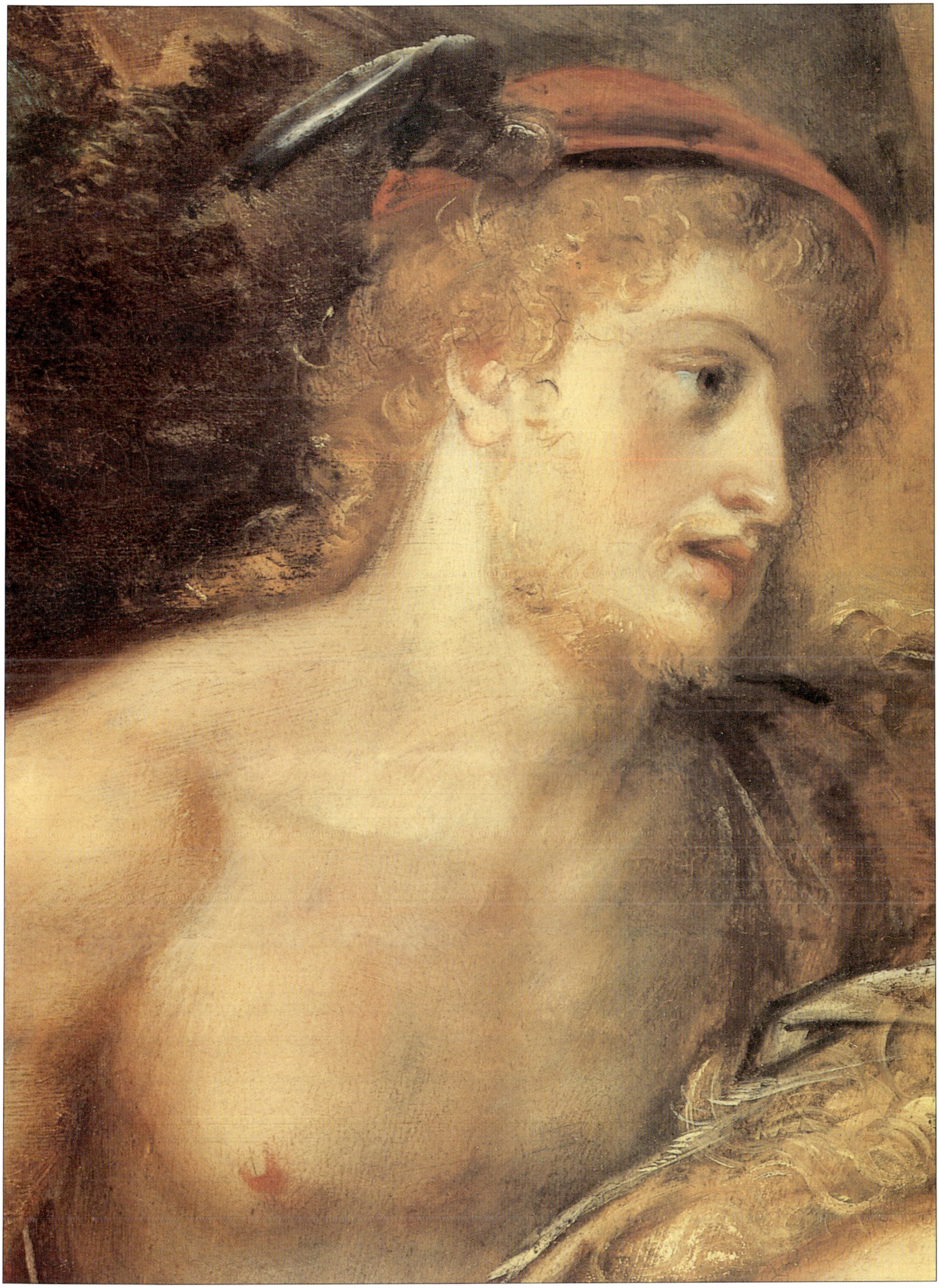

3 *Actual size detail*

Samson and Delilah

c1609
$72\frac{3}{4} \times 80\frac{3}{4}$in/185×205cm
Oil on panel
National Gallery, London

Rubens was commissioned to paint this large panel-painting in about 1609, shortly after his return from Italy. His patron was Nicholas Rickox, a prominent Antwerp citizen and personal friend of the painter, who as president of the Guild of Arquebusiers was probably responsible for Rubens' commission from that guild to paint the *Descent from the Cross* in Antwerp Cathedral. From an exant painting by Frans Francken the younger, it is known that the *Samson and Delilah* hung in a prominent position above the large mantelpiece in Rickox' salon, and from the general perspective within the painting, which necessitates a fairly low viewing point, it is clear that Rubens painted it with this location in mind.

The coloring is extremely rich although the range of colors is limited and a restricted palette has been used. The main areas of paint are thinly applied and have survived in almost pristine condition, with very little paint loss — a testimony to Rubens' craftsmanship and his use of old-established methods. The support is an oak panel, made up of six horizontal planks glued together, and supplied in all likelihood by a professional panel-maker. Following fifteenth-century Flemish precedent, Rubens generally preferred wooden supports, for unlike canvas, the smooth surface allowed his brush to move more fluently. This was then covered with a white ground made up of chalk bound in animal glue. Over it Rubens painted a thin *imprimatura* in light yellow-brown paint, which runs for the most part diagonally from top right to bottom left. It was applied very thinly, using a coarse hog-hair brush to create a striated effect, which allowed the white ground to show through. It is an effect particularly characteristic of his oil-sketches. This transparent brown is left exposed in the finished painting to form the middle ground in such areas as — most spectacularly — Delilah's right wrist and upper hand, Samson's right calf and upper leg, and passages of Delilah's yellow drapery.

There would have been very little underdrawing, as the preliminary *modello* provided the general layout. One or two bold strokes of black, visible for instance along Samson's wrist, his shadowed underarm and the folds of Delilah's white sleeve, were used to establish the general disposition of the figures. The laying-in of colors would have proceeded progressively from this point. The dark background is very sketchily painted, in striking contrast to the main foreground group, the architectural details mapped out in rough strokes of translucent reddish-brown, and painted directly over the thin priming, as are the local colors of the soldiers. Both the reflected highlights on the soldiers' armor and legs and the candle flame are applied in thicker impastoed strokes on top.

The same warm reddish-brown occurs in other areas of shadow, notably in Samson's back, and suggests that Rubens began with the background area and mapped out the areas of shadow with the same color in the foreground at the same time. The flesh tones were then thinly applied on top, modifying the shadowed areas. The basic pink flesh tones of Delilah's skin are made up of lead white tinted with vermilion, with the highlights a mixture of lead white and a little yellow ocher. Deeper effects of shadow, as between Delilah's breasts and along Samson's upper arm, are laid in with warm red-brown glazes similar to those of the background.

The passages of drapery are dazzlingly broad and direct in treatment. The red dress is made up of broad strokes of crimson lake mixed with tinges of vermilion, the deeper shadows created with glazes of crimson lake superimposed on top. The highlights are in strokes of lead white, softened also by crimson-lake glazes. Tinges of orange yellow to suggest reflections of the candle flame are visible in the folds of Delilah's lap.

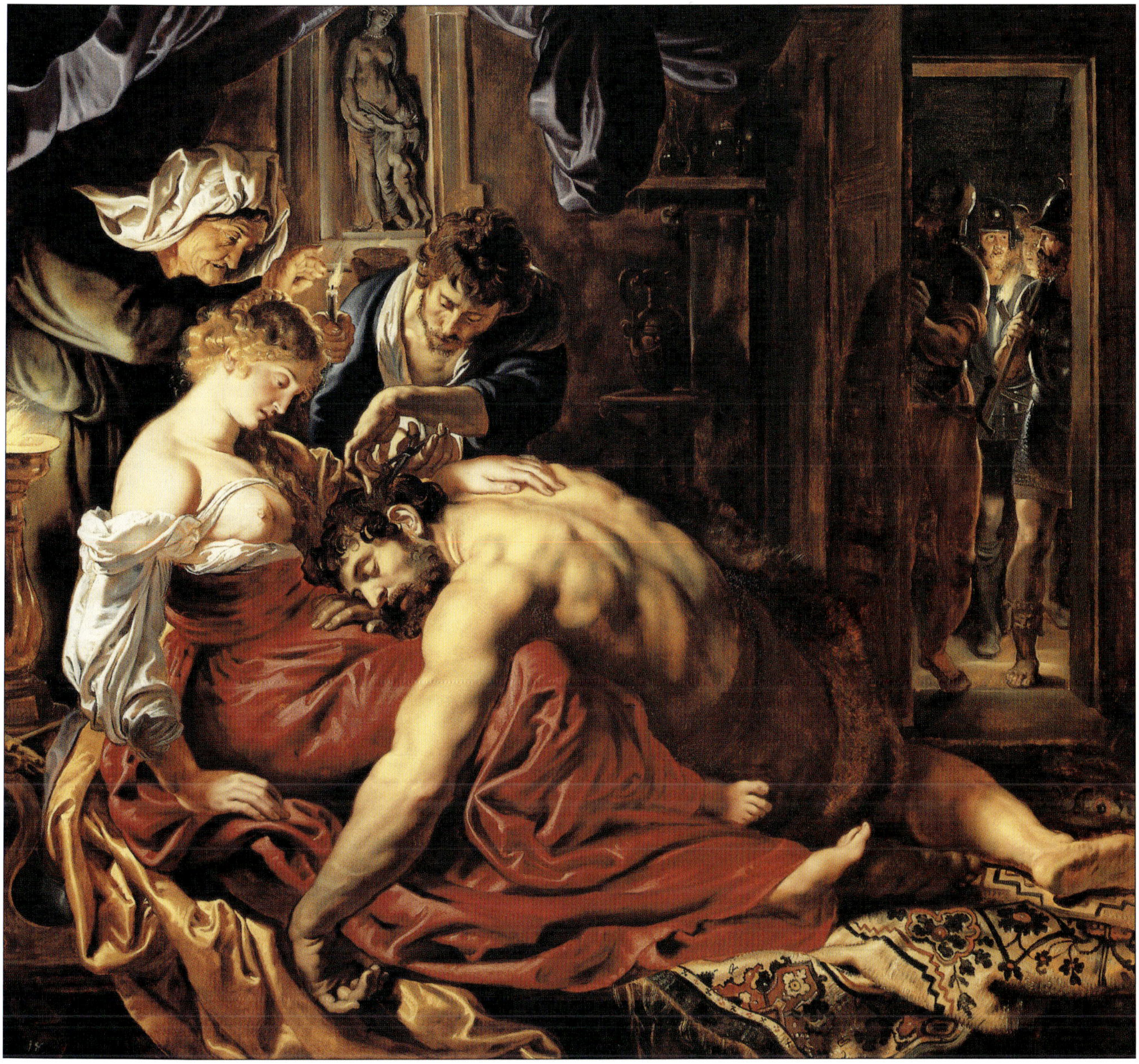

The painting illustrates Samson's betrayal by Delilah who, having elicited from him the knowledge that his superhuman strength lies in his hair, seduces him and has his hair shorn while he sleeps. The erotic treatment, emphasizing woman's power over man, is typical of the seventeenth century, and the statuette of a blindfolded Venus further comments on the theme of "blind love." The old woman holding the taper represents a procuress, thus locating the scene in a brothel. The forms of the central group reflect Rubens' study of Italian art. The figure of Delilah is derived from the pose of Leda in Michelangelo's lost work, *Leda and the Swan*, while Samson's massive, muscular back also contains echoes of Michelangelo and of the antique.

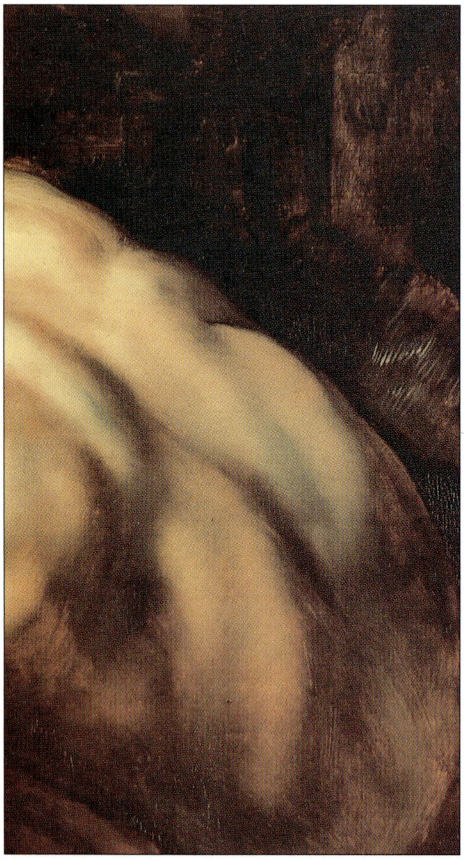

1

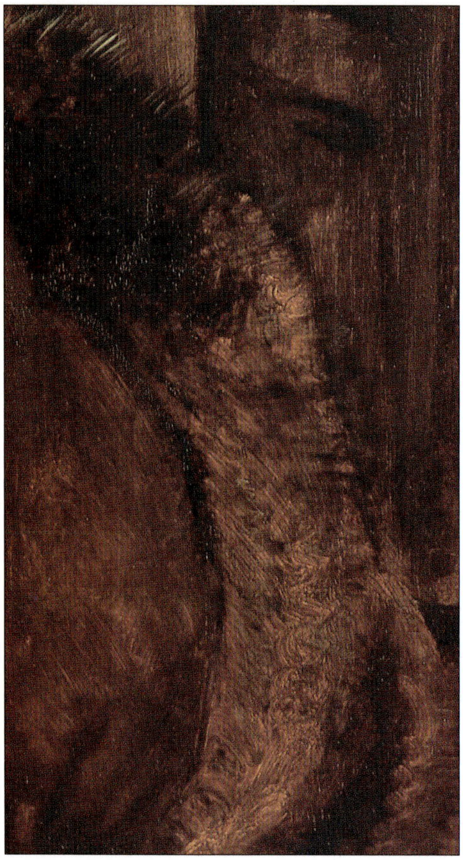

2

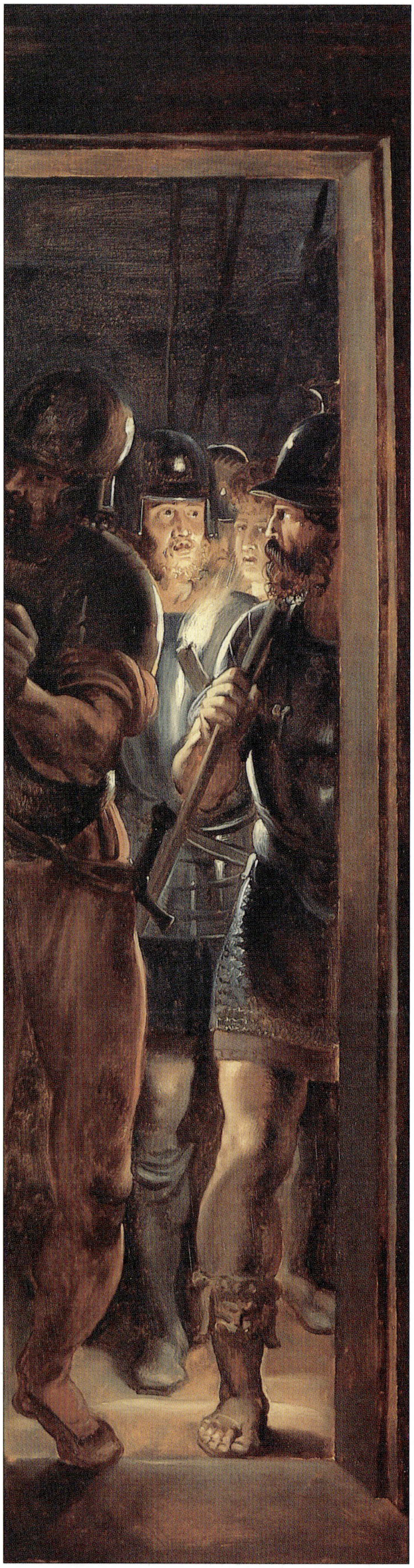

3

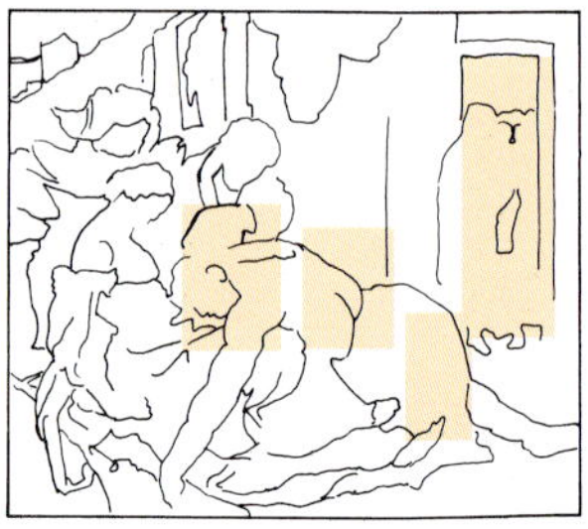

1 This detail illustrates Rubens' method of working up his form from a warm medium brown. The main planes of the back have been drawn in burnt umber, with the deep shadows applied around them in brown wash. Increasingly lighter flesh tones have then been built up, with the harsh transitions of tone modified with a neutral gray-green.

2 The outlines of the fur were first drawn in irregular streaks of burnt umber, after which the illusion of texture was created by dragging the same fluid paint in short, curling strokes, perhaps with a rag or broad brush. Strokes of dull, muddy green were laid on top, with individual hairs evoked by tiny strokes of yellow.

3 The whole area of the doorway and adjacent wall was initially painted in a warm brown, with the figures and the space they occupy suggested by bold streaks of color laid over it. The palette is muted and the tonality dark, in order to preserve the balance with the central figures.

4 The main planes of Samson's face were drawn in burnt umber, with a mid-tone applied over it and the brightest points confidently brushed in on top. The servant's jerkin appears to be blue, but is in fact made up of red lake, lead white and black, with no blue pigment used.

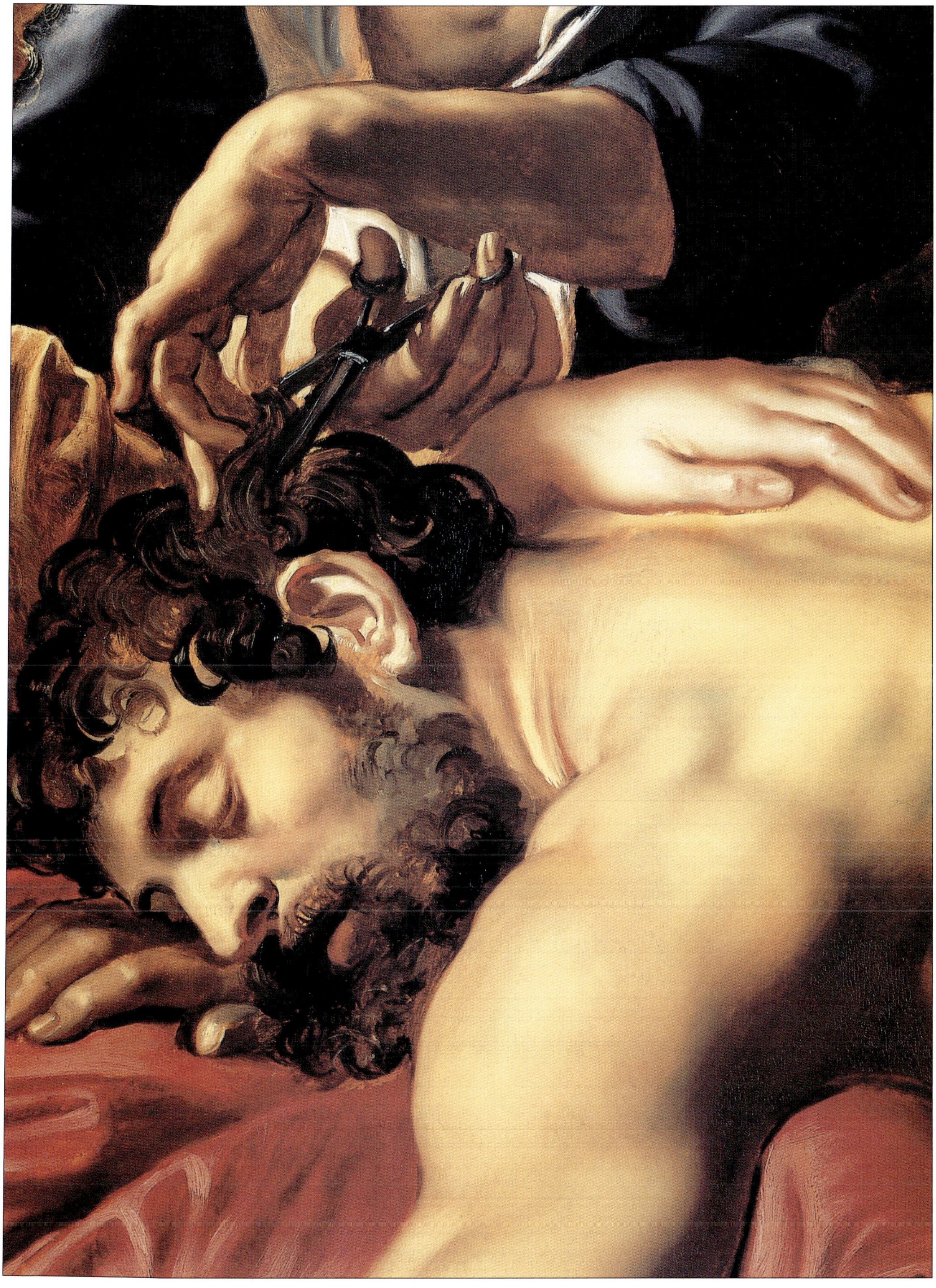

4

The Arrival of Marie de' Medici at Marseilles

1622-26
155×115¼in/394×293cm
Oil on canvas
Louvre, Paris

This vast work was one of twenty-one canvases that Rubens executed between 1622 and 1625 to decorate a long gallery in the Palais du Luxembourg, the new home of Marie de' Medici, widow of the assassinated king Henry IV and ex-regent to her son Louis XIII. Louis had come of age in 1614, quarreled with his mother and banished her from Paris for several years. She was allowed to return only in 1620, and occupied herself, in her new role as Queen Mother, in decorating her new residence. She wished to be seen as a patron of the arts, as her illustrious ancestors had been In commissioning Rubens to paint, as the contract states, her "heroic deeds," her intention was to provide, not only a sumptuous decorative scheme in the great tradition of palace decoration, but also a monumental pictorial justification of her life that managed to suppress the more ignominious aspects of her career. Indeed the choice of subjects, although carefully and diplomatically drawn up by Rubens, was ultimately determined by Marie de' Medici herself, who had the final power of sanction or veto over certain scenes. A projected scene of "The Flight from Paris," for example, was replaced by the innocuous and more general "Felicity of the Regency."

The scene depicting her arrival at Marseilles on November 3, 1600, provided no such problems. It shows the landing of the young queen in France, shortly after her proxy marriage to Henry IV (which Rubens had witnessed in Florence). Rubens has infused the scene with allegorical personifications and mythological figures to glorify the event. The new queen is greeted by a figure representing France, in helmet and fleurs de lys, as well as another figure personifying the City of Marseilles, in a crown made up of towers. Winged Fame flies overhead, heralding the event with a trumpet. In the foreground Neptune has assured her safe arrival, and Triton and three muscular nereids moor the elaborately carved hull to land. The spectator can be in no doubt as to the special nature of the event. The epic treatment of the subject together with the monumental handling of the forms, the richness of coloring and the beauty of detail combine to give an impression of energetic adulation and extreme magnificence.

It was stipulated in the contract that Rubens himself was to paint all the figures, and though he relied a good deal on the help of assistants for background work and the laying out of the designs, it is clear that the major parts of this work are his own. Particularly spectacular is the treatment of the nereids and of the waves in the lower right foreground, which particularly struck the great nineteenth-century painter Eugène Delacroix. In an entry in his *Journal* for June 1849, Delacroix wrote, "I thought the nereids seemed more beautiful than ever. Only complete freedom and the greatest audacity can produce such impressions on me." He made a copy of one of them and took his assistant, Andrieu, to study the iridescent color of the flying drops of water. In another part of the *Journal* he writes that Rubens "...for all his...unwieldly forms, achieves a most powerful ideal. Strength, vehemence and brilliance absolve him from the claims of grace and charm." Delacroix recognized and admired the highly original use of the female nude, unusual in the history of art, to express not only sensuality but a generalized sense of rampant energy conveyed as much by the twisting forms themselves. Flesh becomes the vehicle for the expression of energy, and thus transcends ordinary eroticism.

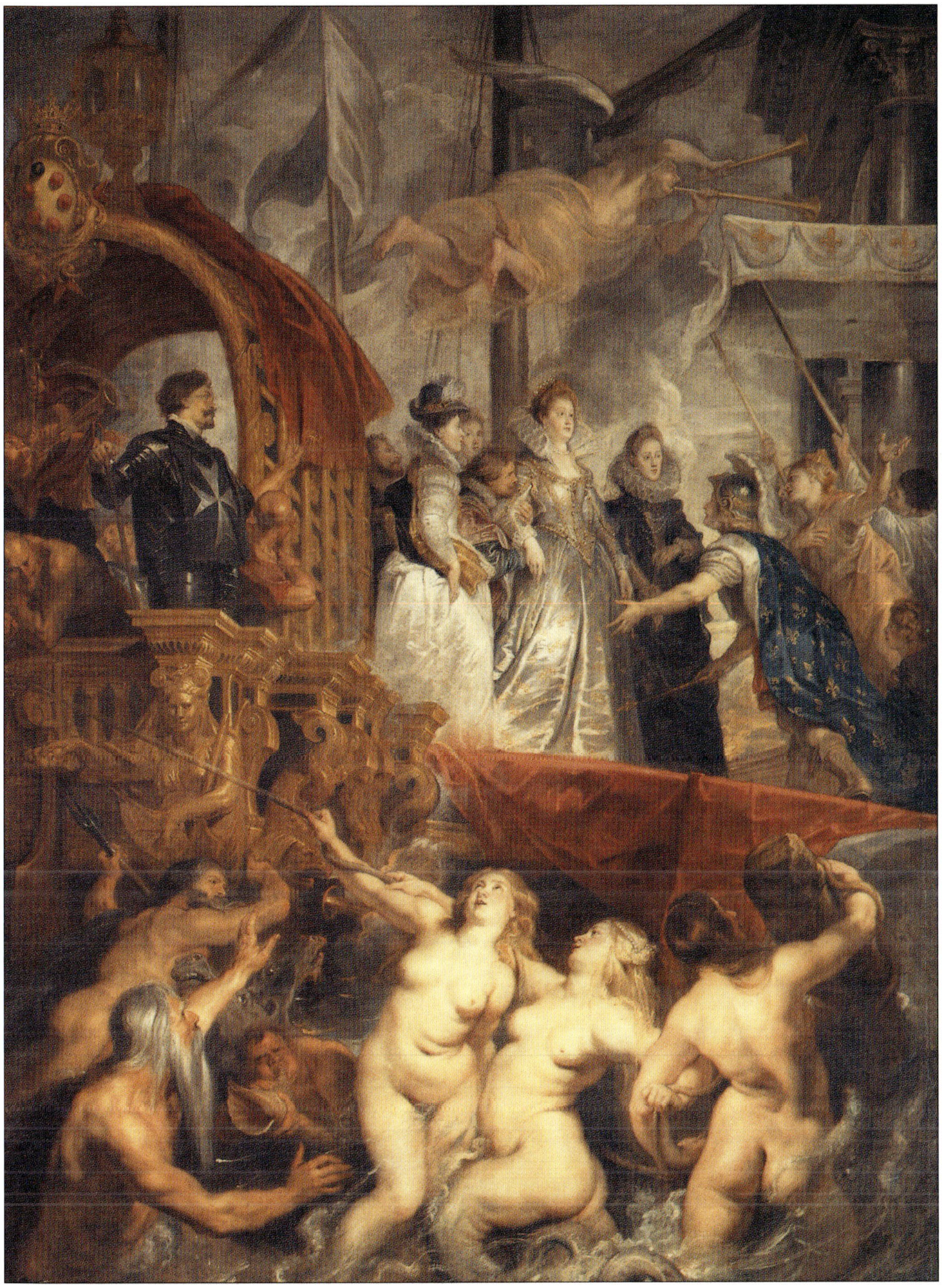

This painting, one of the twenty-one huge canvases that Rubens was commissioned to paint for Marie de' Medici's Luxembourg Palace, reflect his political role as arbiter of kings and princely propagandist. The works took three years to complete, and although Rubens' contract stipulated that he should paint all the figures himself, assistants were used extensively for background work and general laying out. The handling of paint is masterly, and shows Rubens' ability to render different surfaces with unfaltering sureness of touch.

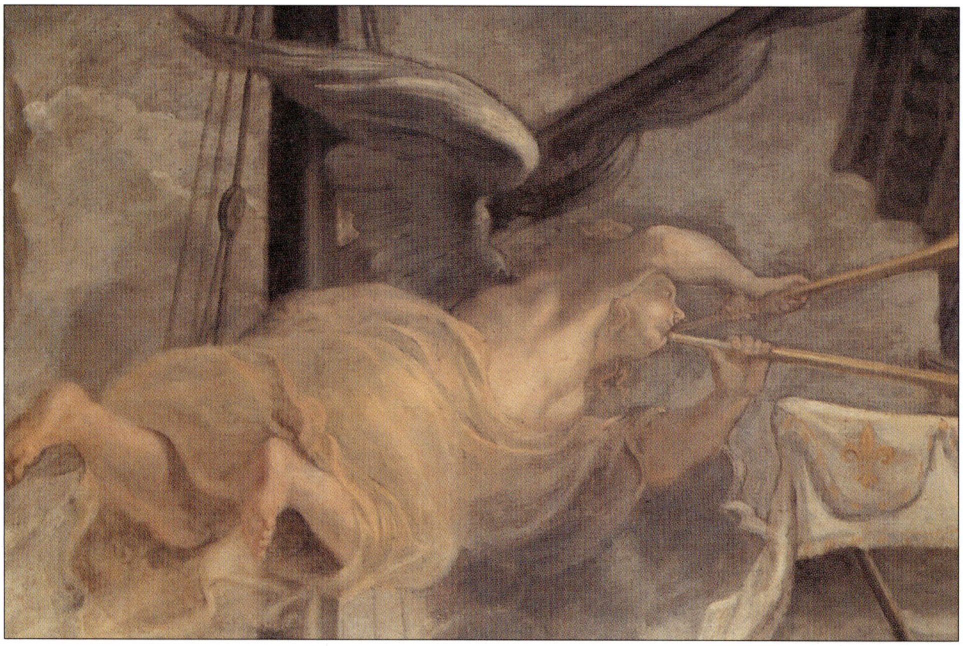

1

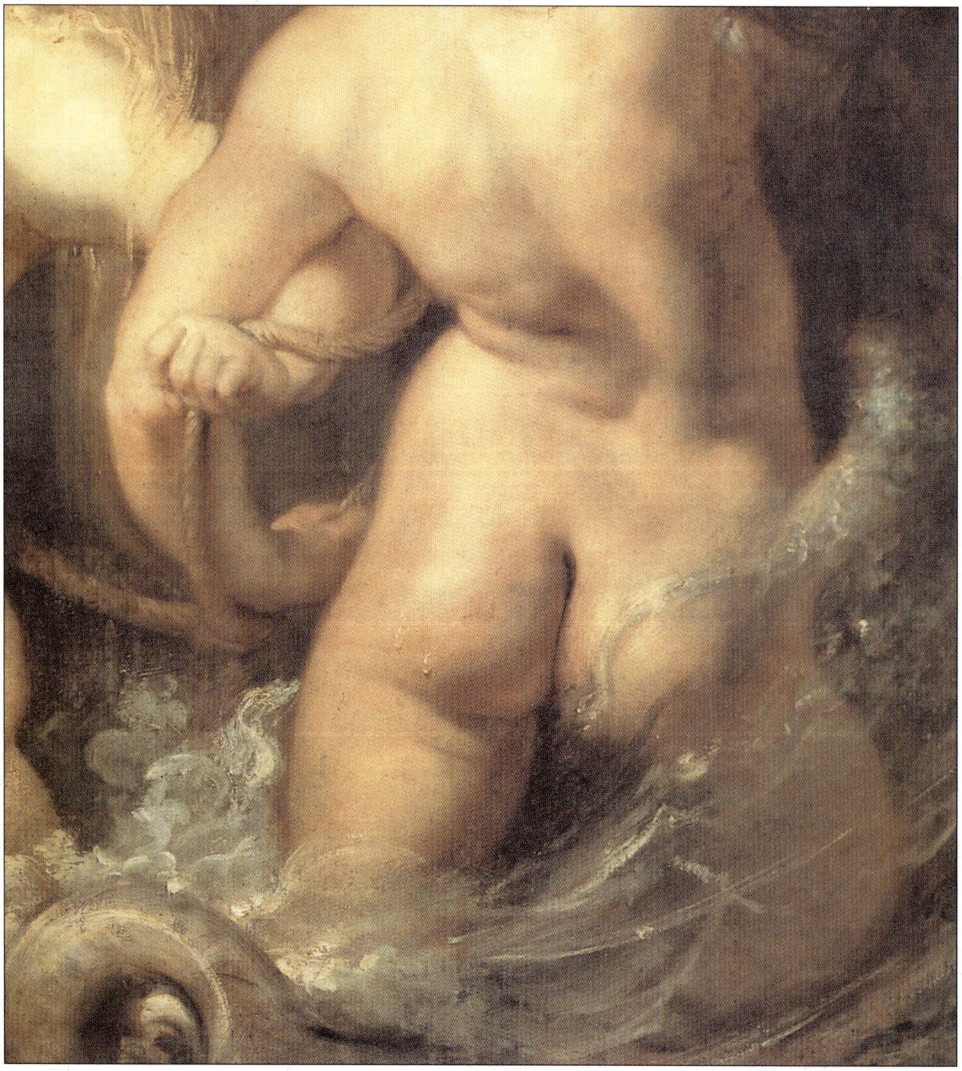

2

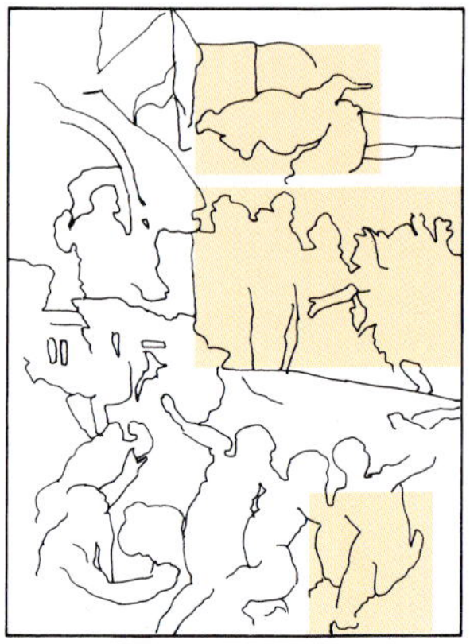

1 The winged victory is painted in dull colors in order not to disturb the formal prominence of the group of figures below. The limbs and drapery have been described in the most economical way, with highlights thickly applied in dry impasto.

2 This detail shows Rubens' amazing facility with his medium, not only in the flesh but also in the way he has translated the effect of the turbulent water into paint. This has been built up in a dull and dilute blue-gray over the medium-brown underpaint, with thin washes of white applied on top in streaks that mimic the movement of the water. The effects of spray have been marvelously achieved on top of this, using thick, rather dry strokes of white smeared on with a broad brush. The drops of water on the buttocks are rendered by the simplest of optical means — points of white impasto and a thin brown glaze to indicate the shadows they cast.

3 The stunning surface treatment seen in such passages as Marie de' Medici's dress show the quality of the brilliant final touches Rubens was accustomed to bestow on these large-scale works drawn up largely by assistants. It is difficult to ascertain the degree of studio participation, but there may be a slight difference in quality between the face of the dowager queen and those of her attendants on the left.

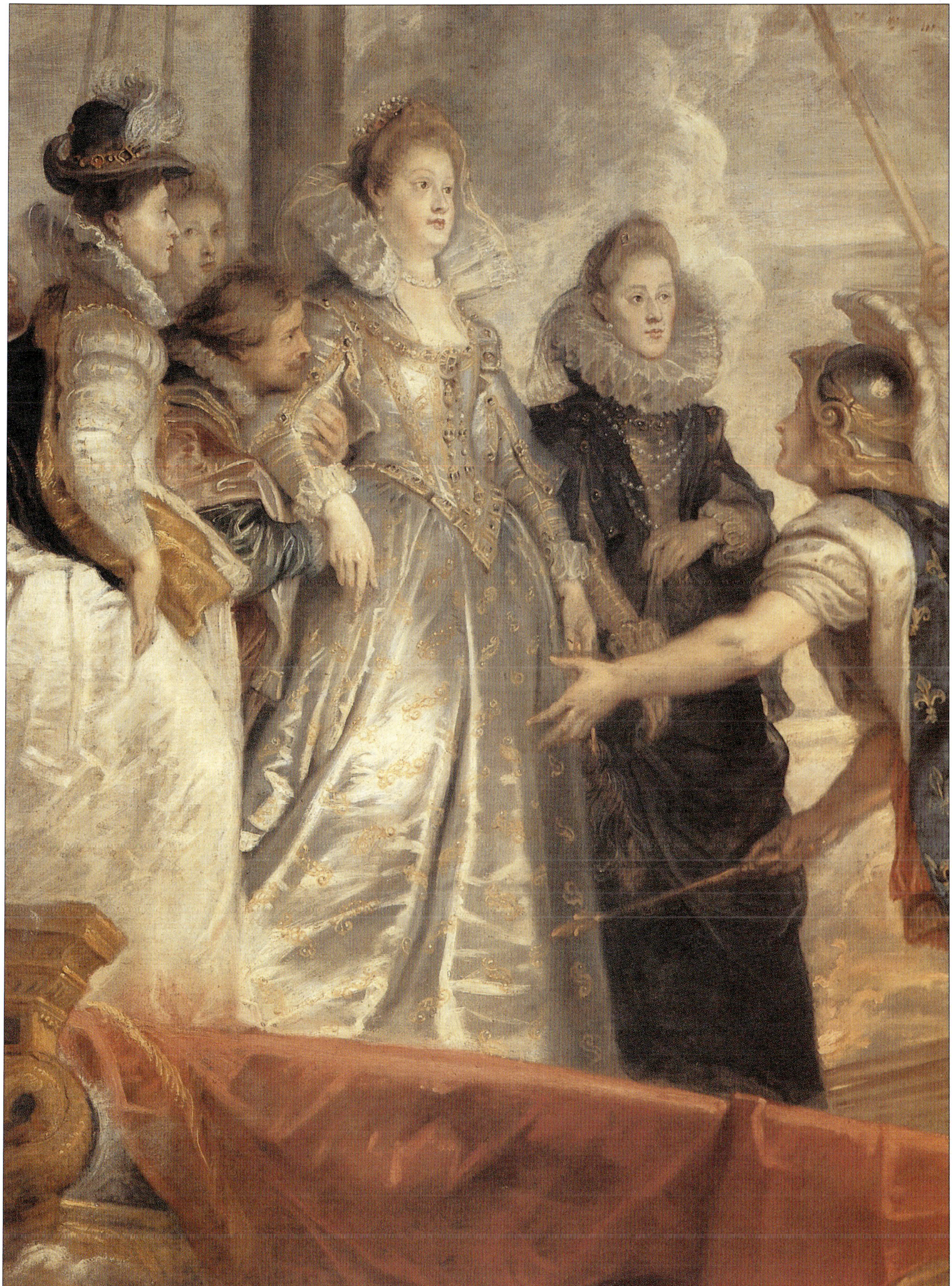

3

The Duke of Buckingham Conducted to the Temple of Virtus

c1625-7
25in/63.5cm square
Oil on panel
National Gallery, London

This small, brilliant oil-sketch is a preparatory work for a ceiling decoration, completed by 1627 for George Villiers, the 1st Duke of Buckingham, political advisor to Charles I of England. The finished ceiling, made for York House, the Duke's London mansion, was destroyed by fire in 1949.

Rubens first met Buckingham in Paris in 1625 when he was putting the final touches to the Marie de' Medici cycle. In the next two years he sold several paintings to the Duke, as well as the major part of his sculpture collection. Buckingham, as Rubens recognized, was an incompetent and unreliable diplomat, mistrusted abroad and unpopular at home. Rubens wrote of him: "When I consider the caprice and arrogance of Buckingham I pity the young king who, through false counsel, is needlessly throwing himself and his kingdom into such extremity. For anyone can start a war when he wishes, but he cannot so easily end it." In fact the duke was assassinated in 1628. Nonetheless Rubens apparently saw no contradiction in glorifying the virtues of the Duke in the grand monumental manner of Baroque ceiling painting. The notion of a figure being conducted heavenwards by attendant allegorical personifications originated in the church ceilings of Rome, where the figure was usually Christ or a saint. In taking over this device Rubens transforms the duke into something of a secular deity.

Rubens' mastery of allegorical storytelling is matched by his complete grasp of Baroque dynamic composition. Unlike the *Lion Hunt modello*, this represents a stage further in conception. Here the colors are fairly clearly mapped out, though the changes that have occurred in working up the sketch, obvious in the various *pentimenti* (places where the paint has worn thin, showing underpainting), show that it was not the working *modello* on which the actual full-scale painting was based.

Rubens uses differences in strength of color and tone to rationalize the space and organization of the composition. The central group is treated with the strongest accents, not only in the strongest colors – the red and black of the Duke and the yellow of Minerva's cloak – but also with the strongest contrasts of tone, which provide an appropriate focus for the eye. The paint is also thickest in this part. The three Graces on the lower left are smoothly painted to a considerable degree of finish, but executed in paler tones. The contrast of light flesh tone and the surrounding light blue clouds is also less dramatic. The palest colors and area of least tonal contrast is reserved for the columns and the figures of Abundance and Virtus. This system of diminishing tones and increasingly pale coloring is used to convey a sense of the distances between the groups, but also on a more general pictorial level to create a central focus and to provide greater legibility, allowing the eye to pass more easily from group to group.

The painting is in general very thin. The priming is clearly visible, particularly at the edges, indeed it stops short of the top left and right corners, perhaps indicating that a smaller painted surface was at first intended. The dark umber outlines are also very visible, particularly in the marvelously freely drawn *putti* at the top, and accompanied by a brown wash in the lion and the figure of Envy. A *putto* just above the lion has been suppressed by white overpaint, but can still be clearly made out.

The colors that Rubens employed in his oil-sketches are generally duller than those of his finished paintings, and obviously it would have been wasteful to use expensive pigments on workshop *modelli.* It is probable that he used a dull red ocher color rather than the expensive crimson lakes or vermilions that are used in his finished pieces. Nonetheless one can see in a sketch of this kind Rubens' instinctive surety of touch and brilliance and speed of execution.

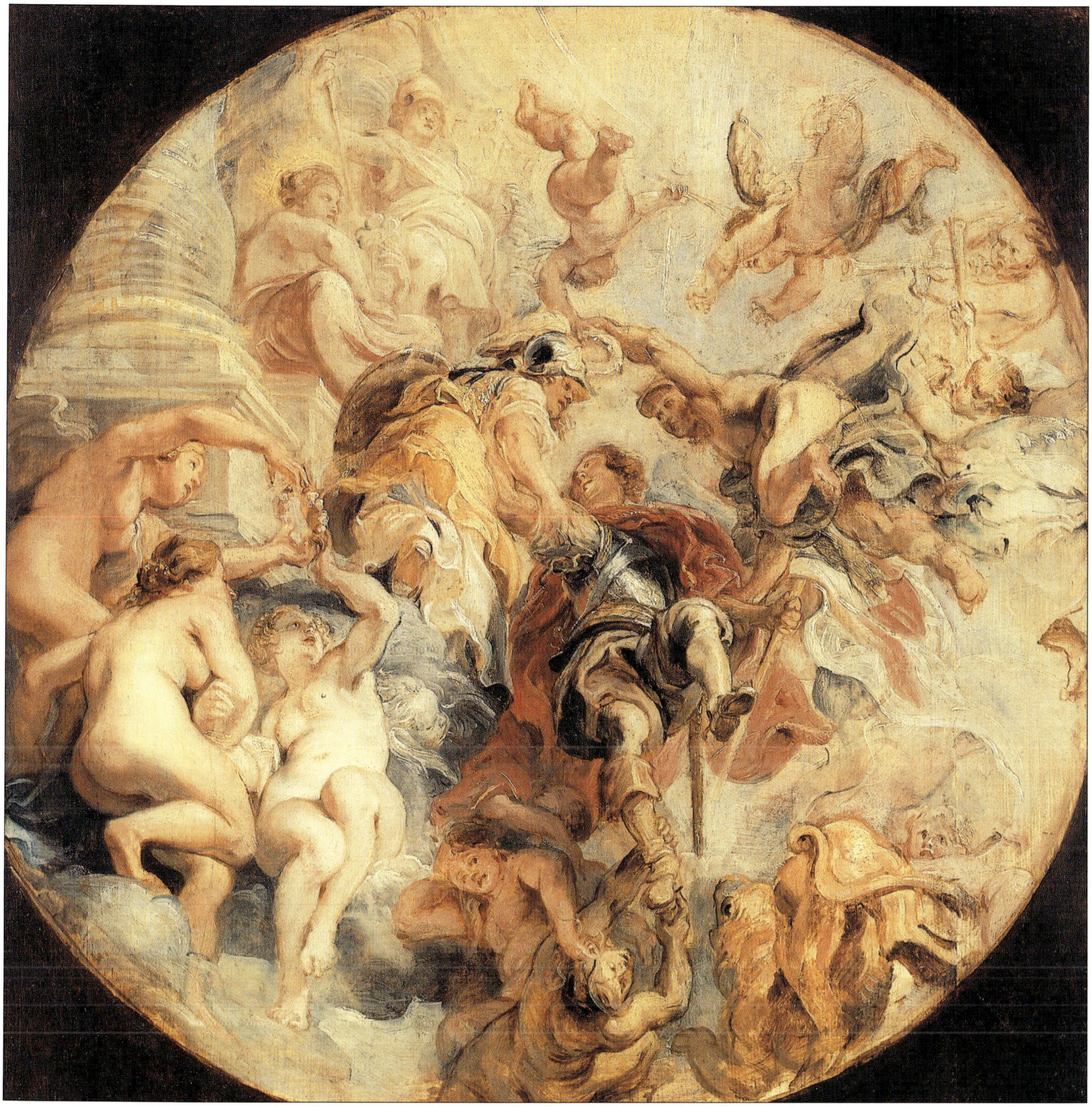

This is a preparatory oil-sketch for a ceiling decoration, now destroyed, for the Duke of Buckingham's London mansion. Rubens has glorified the Duke in the grand manner typical of Baroque ceiling paintings, showing him being borne heavenwards by Minerva and Mercury, who represent the Arts and Diplomacy. Above them is the entrance of a temple, indicated by the huge solomonic columns. The seated female with the cornucopia is probably Abundance, and the standing figure beside her the goddess Virtus. Below, a female figure with snakes in her hair (Envy) attempts to drag him down, and a lion (Anger) roars ineffectually. These figures are probably allusions to Buckingham's enemies, who sought to bring about his fall.

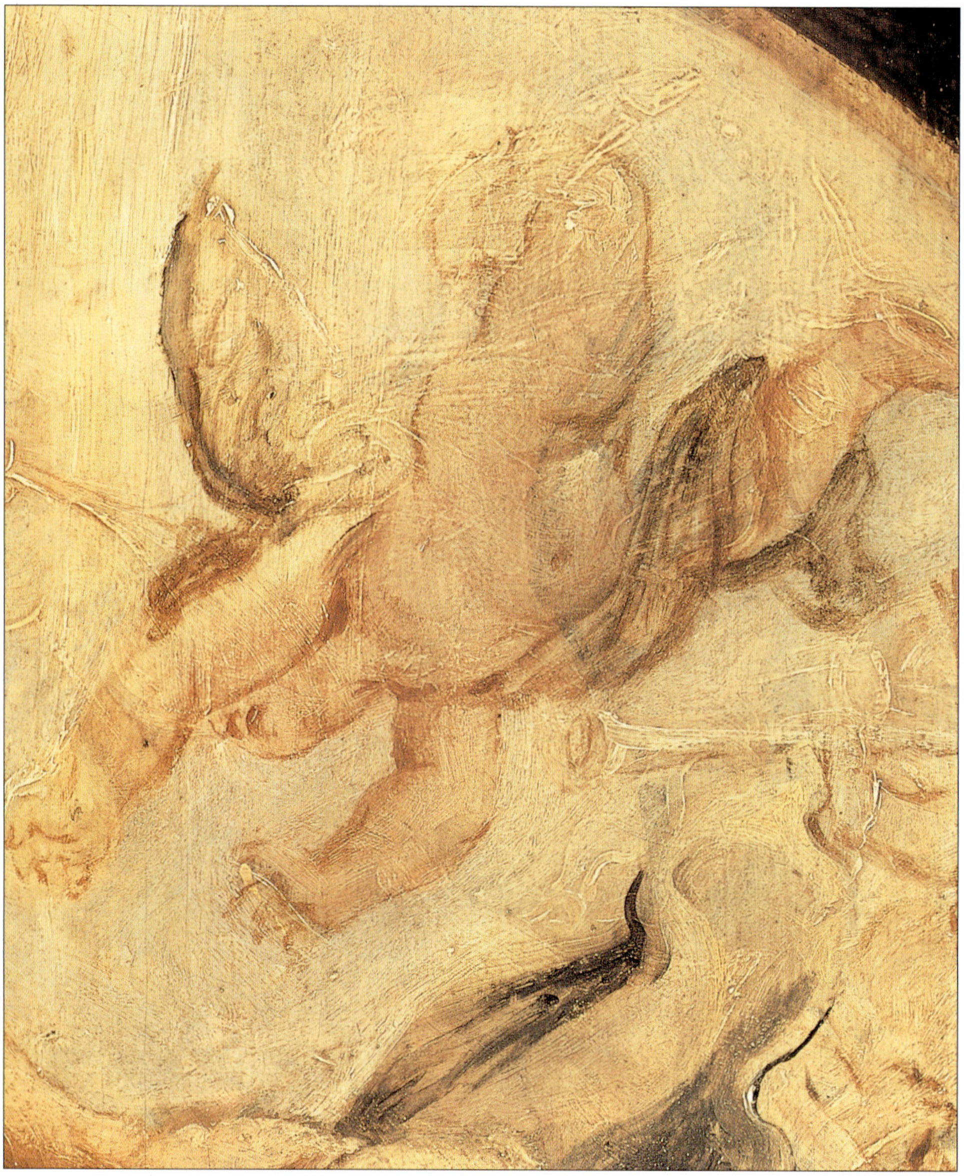

1

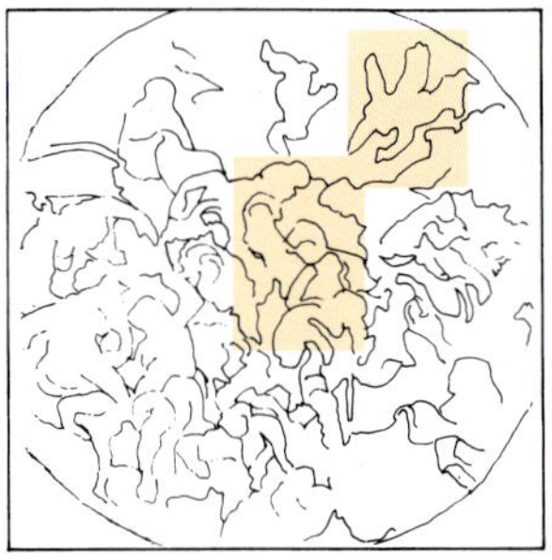

1 The outlines of the foreshortened *putto*, sketched in lightly in burnt umber, have been painted over a previous idea, touches of which are visible running through the stomach and upper leg. Thickly impasted brushstrokes, seen for example at the base of the wing and by the left knee and right heel, have no real relevance to the shape or form of the *putto*, and indicate the existence of a highly finished figure beneath the present one.

2 *Actual size detail* This part of the painting constitutes the area of the most thickly applied paint and the strongest color, but the freshness and spontaneity of the brushstrokes are nevertheless vividly illustrated. Changes in composition can be seen in the space above the Duke's head, where there are traces of an earlier arm beneath a thick layer of gray-ocher paint, and the original position of Mercury is visible to the left of his torso. The outlines of the figures, drawn in burnt umber, are quite clear, particularly that of Mercury. The Duke's armor has been suggested by black strokes over gray, and it is interesting to note the degree of attention Rubens has paid to reflected lights, even in a sketch. Thus the reflected highlight is a very thick dab of yellow-tinted white, with further touches of red for the reflection of the cloak.

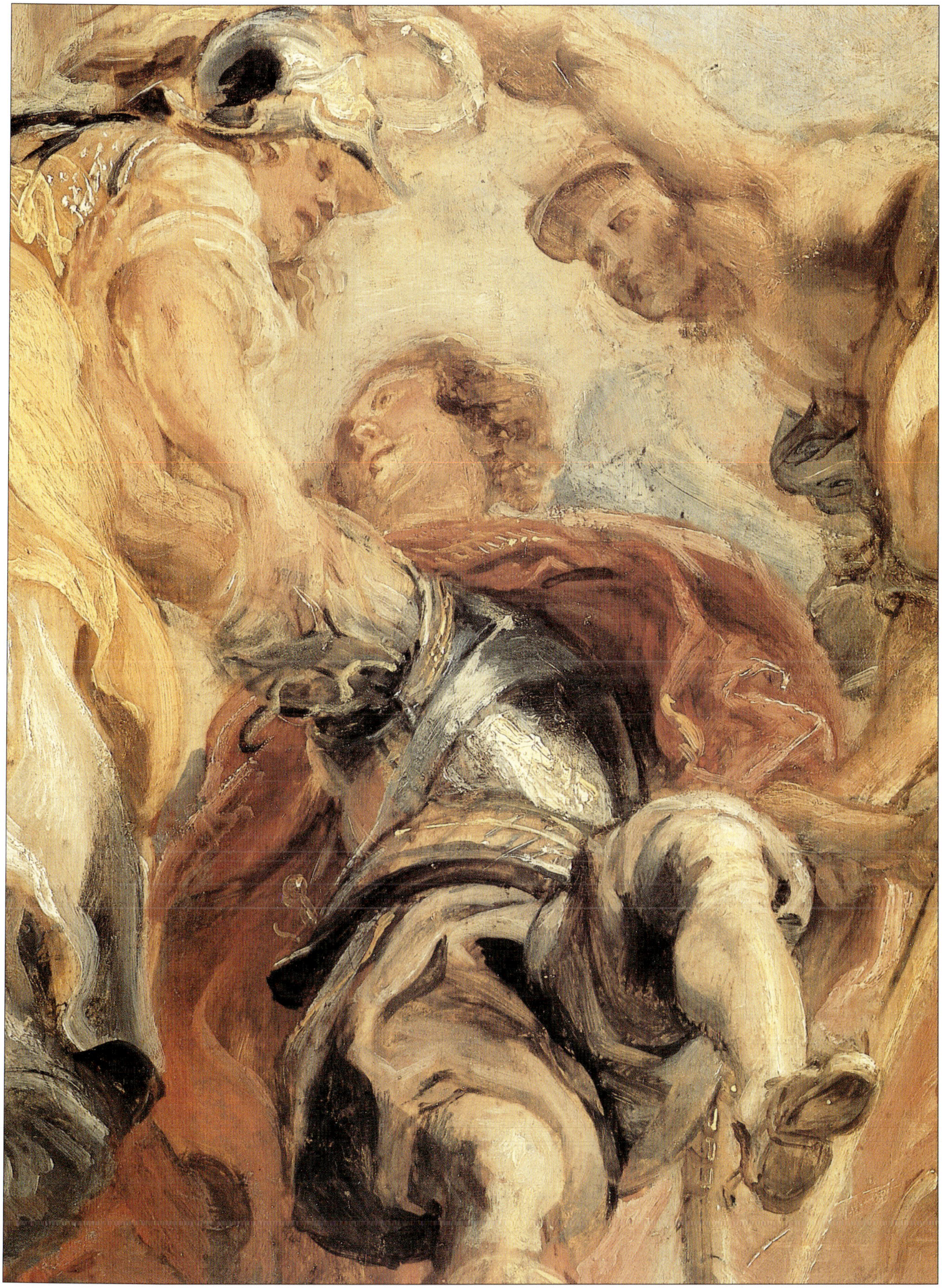

2 *Actual size detail*

Allegory of Peace and War

1629-1630
78×117in/198×297cm
Oil on canvas
National Gallery, London

Painted some time during Rubens' stay in England, the *Allegory of Peace and War* was made specifically as a presentation gift by the diplomat-artist to King Charles I. This followed the successful conclusion of a peace treaty between Spain and England, and was a gesture that honored Charles' role as a peacemaker among nations.

As part of an attempt to end the war that had existed between England and Spain since 1623, Rubens had been sent to England in 1629 by Philip IV of Spain as a secretary to the Spanish king's privy council in the Netherlands. His instructions were to offer a truce to England that did not include her ally, the United Provinces. After lengthy and delicate negotiations, peace was declared in December 1630.

The painting appropriately illustrates the benefits of peace threatened by war. In the center the figure of Pax gives milk from her breast to the infant Plutus, the god of wealth. In front of them a satyr, follower of Bacchus, the grower of vines and lover of plenty and of peace, offers an overflowing cornucopia to a group of children. The boy holding a torch is Hymen, god of marriage – which flowers and prospers in time of peace. He places a garland of flowers over the head of the elder girl. A female figure carrying golden vessels and jewels enters from the left, signifying the riches that peace brings, while the figure with the tambourine and the leopard are traditional ancillaries to Bacchus' train. A *putto* flies over the figure of peace with olive branch and caduceus, representing concord and prudence. Behind this group Minerva, goddess of Wisdom, drives out Mars, god of War, a fury and an attendant harpy.

The composition was partly inspired by Tintoretto's *Minerva and Mars* in the Palazzo Ducale in Venice, though there are echoes too of Titian's paintings, *Ecce Homo* and *Worship of Venus*. Indeed, the richness of color and the brilliance of handling are the result of Rubens' renewed study of Titian, many of whose works he had examined afresh and copied while in Madrid. The warmth of color and extension of the palette shown in the use of rich deep blues, crimsons, yellows and greens owes much to the example of the Venetian master.

The dark tonality is the result of dark brown underpainting. This work is on canvas, unusual for Rubens, who normally preferred a wooden panel primed with a light ground. He was perhaps unable to obtain a suitable panel in England, and was thus forced to use canvas and to follow the standard seventeenth-century practice of working the forms up from dark to light. The underpaint can be seen emerging on the surface at various points – in the blue of the sky where the top layers of paint have rubbed, or more spectacularly as the middle tone of Mars' shield and armor. Here the effect of polished steel has been brilliantly evoked by the use of broad passages of black, suggestive of the matte areas, thinning out to the brown underlayer in the areas of dullest shine, and overlaid with bold touches of white impasto in varying thicknesses for the reflected highlights.

Such marvelously suggestive passages are to be found in every part of the painting, for example in the luscious evocation of ripened fruit and the wonderful depiction of the leopard's fur. The right paw gives the impression of blurred, clawing movement, created by loose dashes of white impasto over a reddish brown underpaint. The spots are created with splashes of diaphanous black glaze, themselves brushed over with orange-yellow glazes. In such a work, intended for a king, and on which Rubens clearly lavished all his skill, we see the mature artist working at the full stretch of his inventiveness.

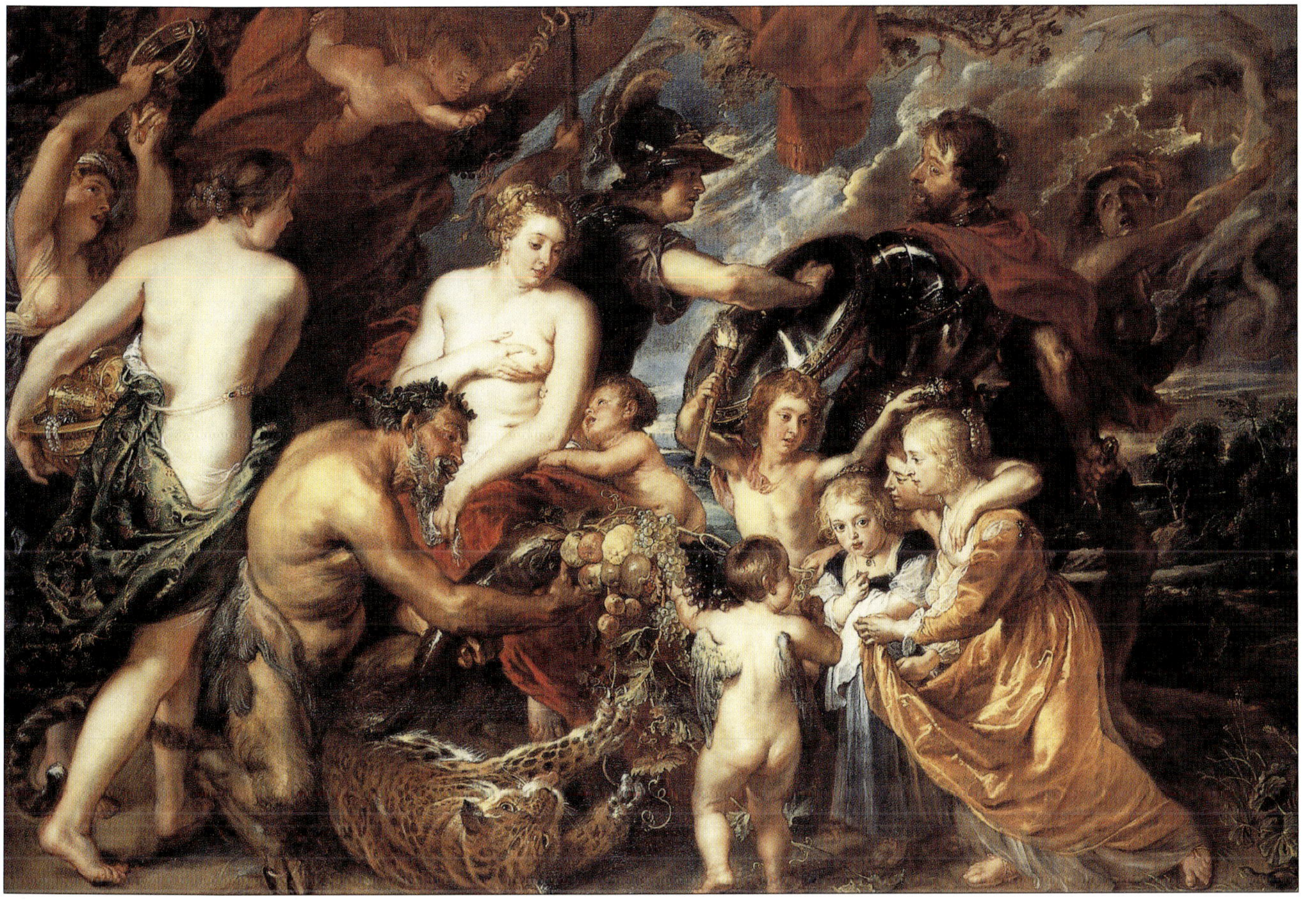

This sumptuous work, painted during Rubens' stay in England, was a presentation gift to Charles I in honor of his role as a peacemaker, and its subject is the appropriate one of the benefits of peace under threat of war. Unusually for Rubens, it is painted on canvas, not on a wooden panel, and the underpainting is darker than his normal one. It provides a wonderful example of his mature style, which by this time had loosened considerably and become more painterly, with less of the hard outlines and sculptural modeling of form that had characterized his earlier work. Once again, much attention has been paid to the skillful evocation of different textures and materials, seen for instance in the marvelously suggestive painting of the bowl of fruit, the leopard's fur and the polished steel of Mars' shield and armor.

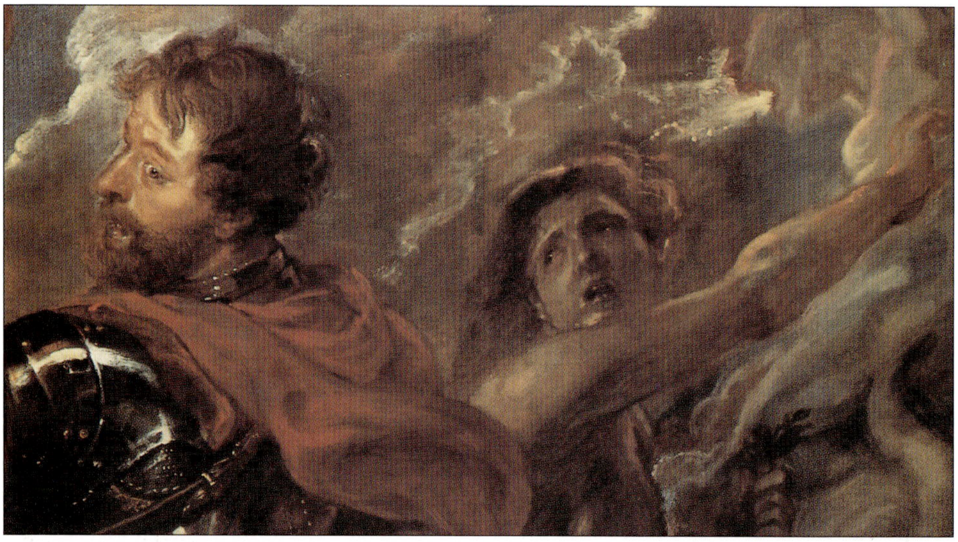

1

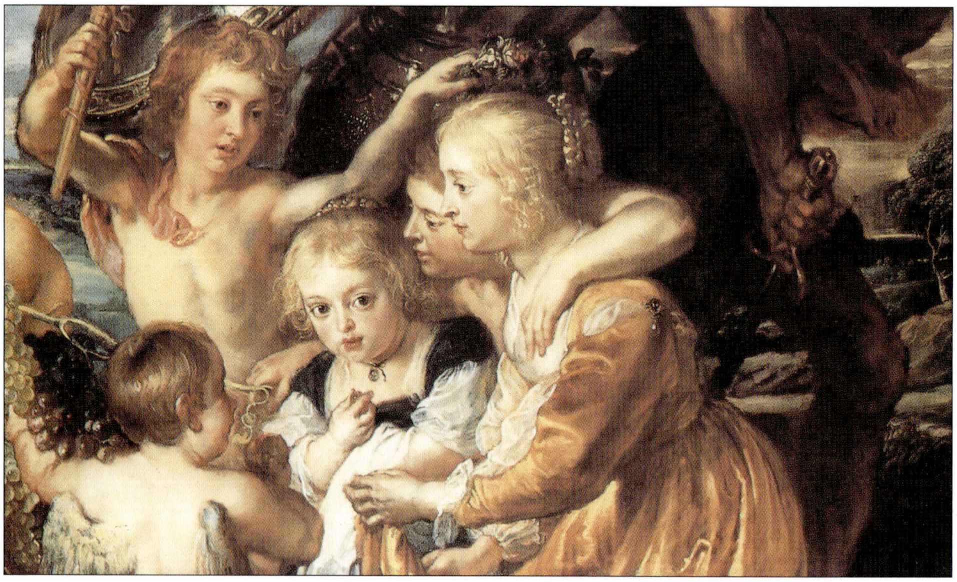

2

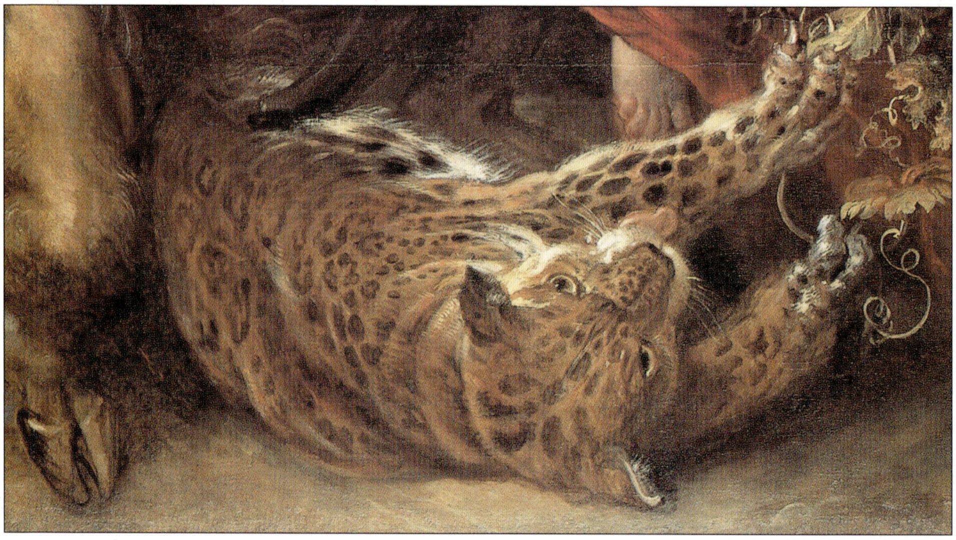

3

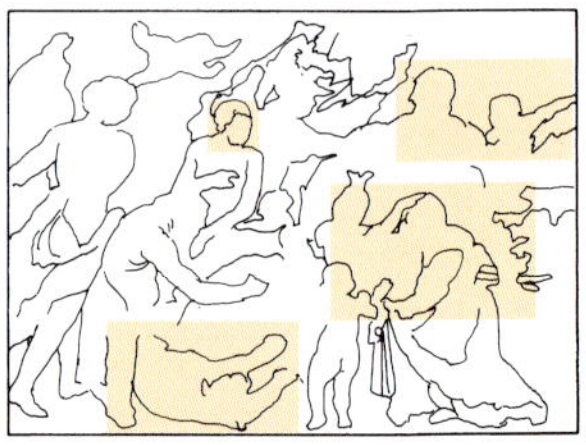

1 The head of Mars and a fury emerge only dimly from the dark brown underpaint, representing perhaps the least "finished" part of the painting. The effects of light reflected in the armor are created by working broad areas of black onto the brown underlayer, which stands as the middle tone between this and the brilliant streaks of white impasto, tinged at the ends with blue and a yellowish brown.

2 Rubens' use of warm, diaphanous glazes can be seen particularly clearly in the upper left torso of Hymen, where the pale skin tones and grayish shadow area have been overlaid with touches of transparent orange, pink and yellow.

3 The forms of the leopard have been built up very broadly, with yellow tones laid thinly on top of rough strokes of burnt umber and the spots painted in in thin dabs of dark brown and then glazed over with a modifying layer of yellow-brown varnish. Definition and a sense of texture have been given by thick strokes of impasted white tinged with yellow, and some touches of greenish blue.

4 *Actual size detail* Rubens' use of glazes was learned from Titian, and the head of Pax is very Titianesque both in type and in rendering. The broad areas of pale flesh tone are delicately glazed with transparent pinks, and gently highlighted with white at the brow and along the bridge of the nose.

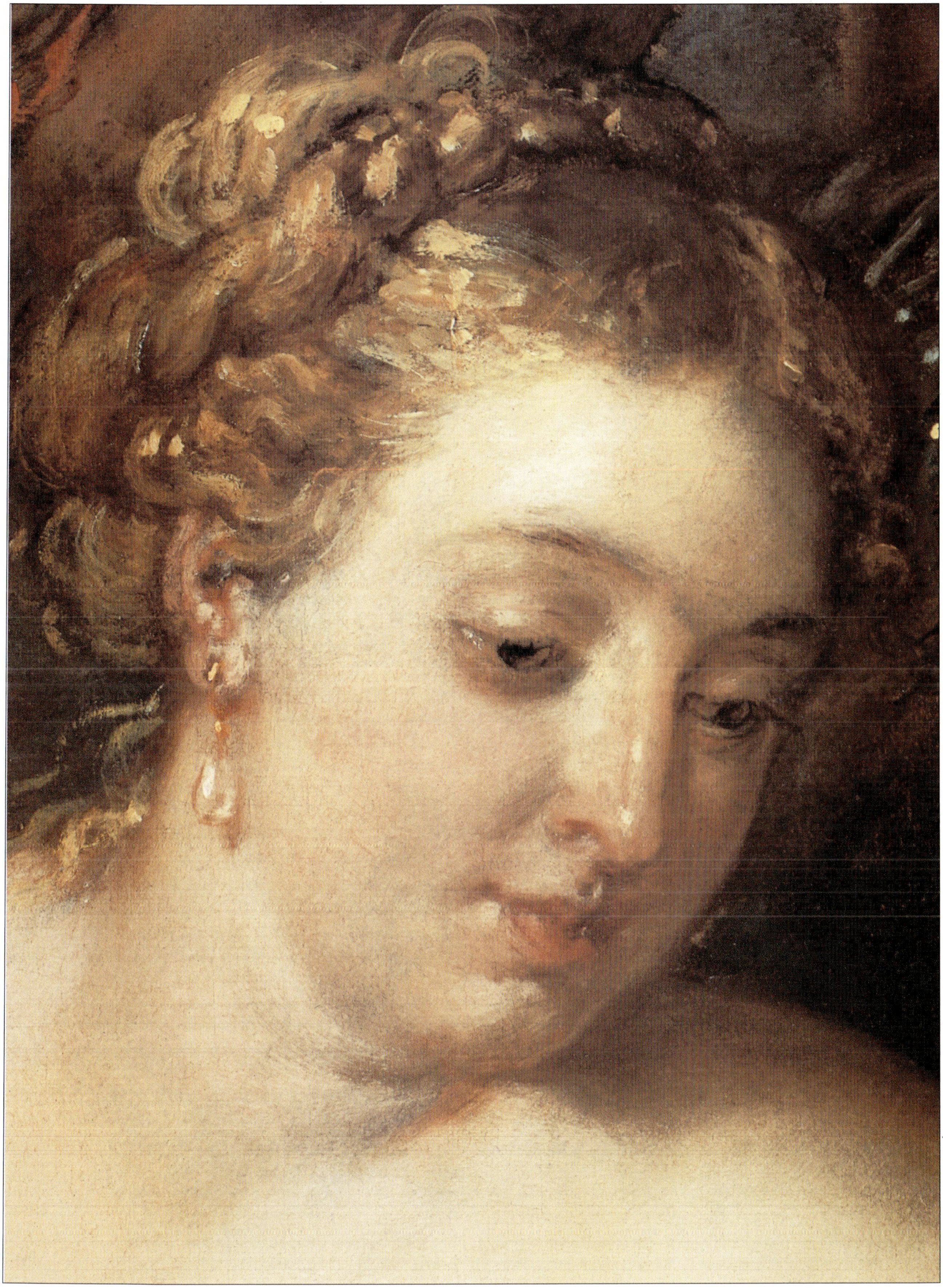

4 *Actual size detail*

The Rape of the Sabine Women

c1634
$66\frac{3}{4} \times 93$in/169.9×236.2cm
Oil on panel
National Gallery, London

The original purpose and location of this work remain unknown, although it was probably in the collection of Cardinal Richelieu in 1676. However, it is dateable on stylistic grounds to around 1634, and represents a fine example of Rubens' late style, particularly his ability to organize a huge number of figures into a satisfying whole.

The scene illustrates the famous episode in early Roman history, described by Plutarch, in which Romulus, in a ruse to increase the population of Rome, invited the Sabines, a tribe living near Rome, to attend some games, during which he ordered his soldiers to carry off a number of the unmarried women. The Sabines then attacked the Romans but were defeated. The Sabine women in the meantime accepted their lot, the population of Rome was duly increased, and peace was made with the Sabine tribe. Thus the story is not one of brutal violence: as Plutarch put it, the Romans "did not commit this rape wantonly, but with a design purely of forming alliance with their neighbors by the greatest and surest bonds." Although Rubens did not follow Plutarch literally on all points of story-telling, the painting follows the spirit of the literary account fairly closely. The women on the left-hand side are being carried off, having been separated from their menfolk, while behind, the Sabines rally to their defense, held off by Roman troops. The Roman soldiers in the foreground are setting about their task of abduction with the attitudes and expressions of noble and dutiful heroes rather than of lascivious seducers.

Formally, the composition is arranged into two dynamic masses held in precarious balance by the central foreground group and stabilized by the background architecture. Color and tonal arrangement are used in such a way that they clarify the narrative and unify the composition. The brightest point of the whole picture is the white flesh of the Sabine woman's exposed breasts in the center foreground, while the darkest is her deep blue drapery. This creates the area of greatest contrast of both color and tone, and provides an immediate focus for the eye, which is further strengthened by the strong modeling and close attention to descriptive details. The women in the left middle ground are treated in paler and more subdued colors, and the paint is thinner, without the plastic force of the foreground group. The background elements are paler still, with the colors even more washed out, the walls of the round vaulted building and the soldiers being just sketched in with very thin paint. This reduction in the intensity of the colors has been used more for reasons of pictorial unity than to indicate recession — according to the theories of aerial perspective, the distances implied by the relative sizes of the figures would not have been sufficient to merit such contrasts of tone and color. The "artificial" lightness of the background in fact has the opposite effect, of pushing it closer to the foreground, and the light area also provides a balancing contrast to the generally dark tonality of the foreground. This is an excellent example of Rubens' unique concern with unity and balance in all aspects of the composition, which was quite independent of conventional modes of perception or rules of perspective representation.

The handling of paint is breathtaking in its variety and suggestiveness of touch: for example the extreme thinness of paint in the figure of Romulus, who is drawn in with no more than a wash; the streaks of thick white impasto on the drapery of the central Sabine woman's shoulder; or the suggestion of a moving sword-blade in the fist of the left-hand soldier, evoked by the roughest smear of dry white paint over an undefined muddy brown ground. Despite attacks of gout, Rubens was still at the height of his powers.

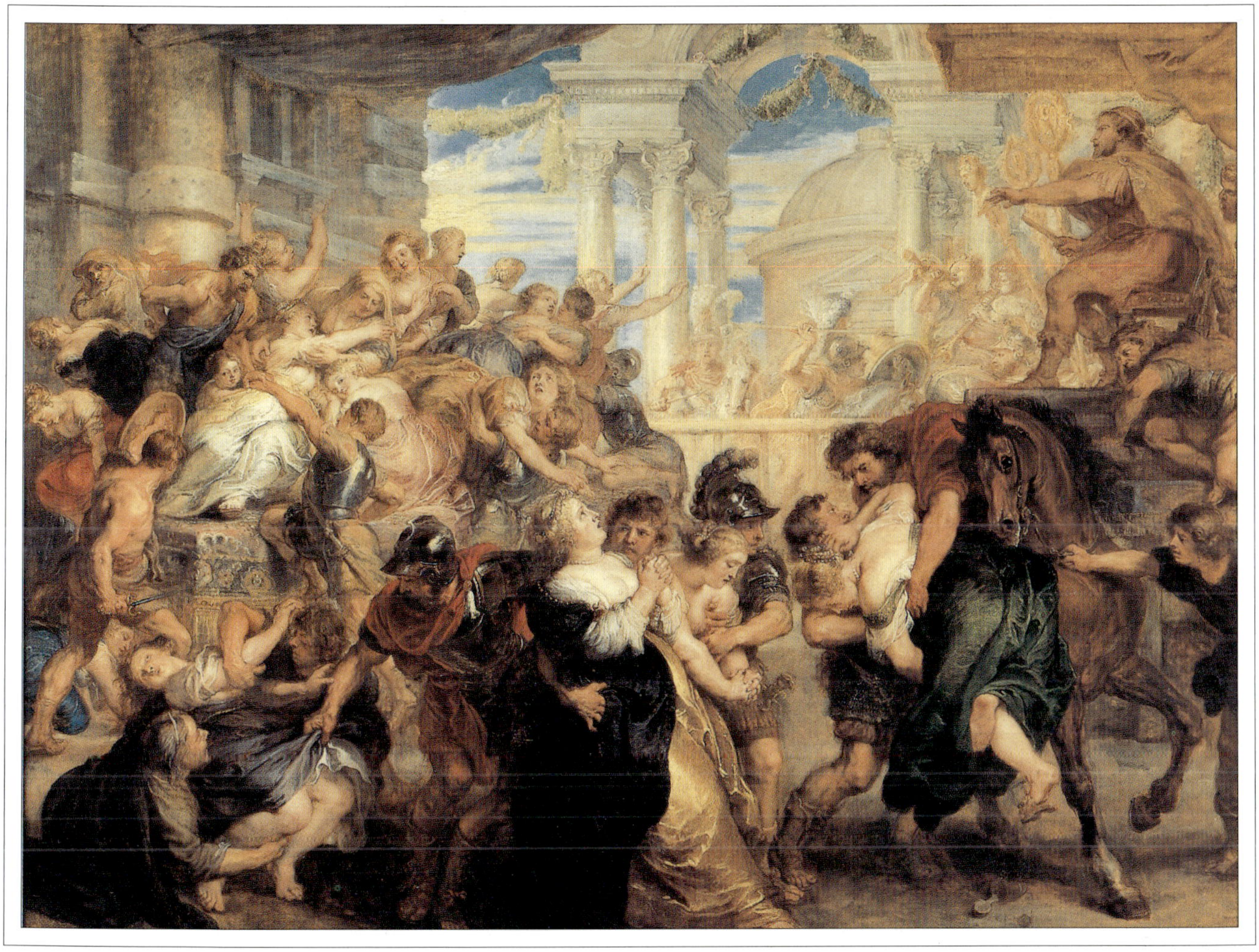

This is a particularly fine example of Rubens' late style, demonstrating both his expressive handling of paint and his ability to organize a large number of figures into a balanced but dynamic composition. Though increasingly hampered by attacks of gout, he had lost none of his brilliance of touch, and the variety and suggestiveness of the paint handling is breathtaking. Equally impressive is the way color and tone have been used to clarify the narrative as well as to unify the composition, for example the brightest point and area of greatest contrast is the Sabine in the center foreground, providing an immediate focus for the eye.

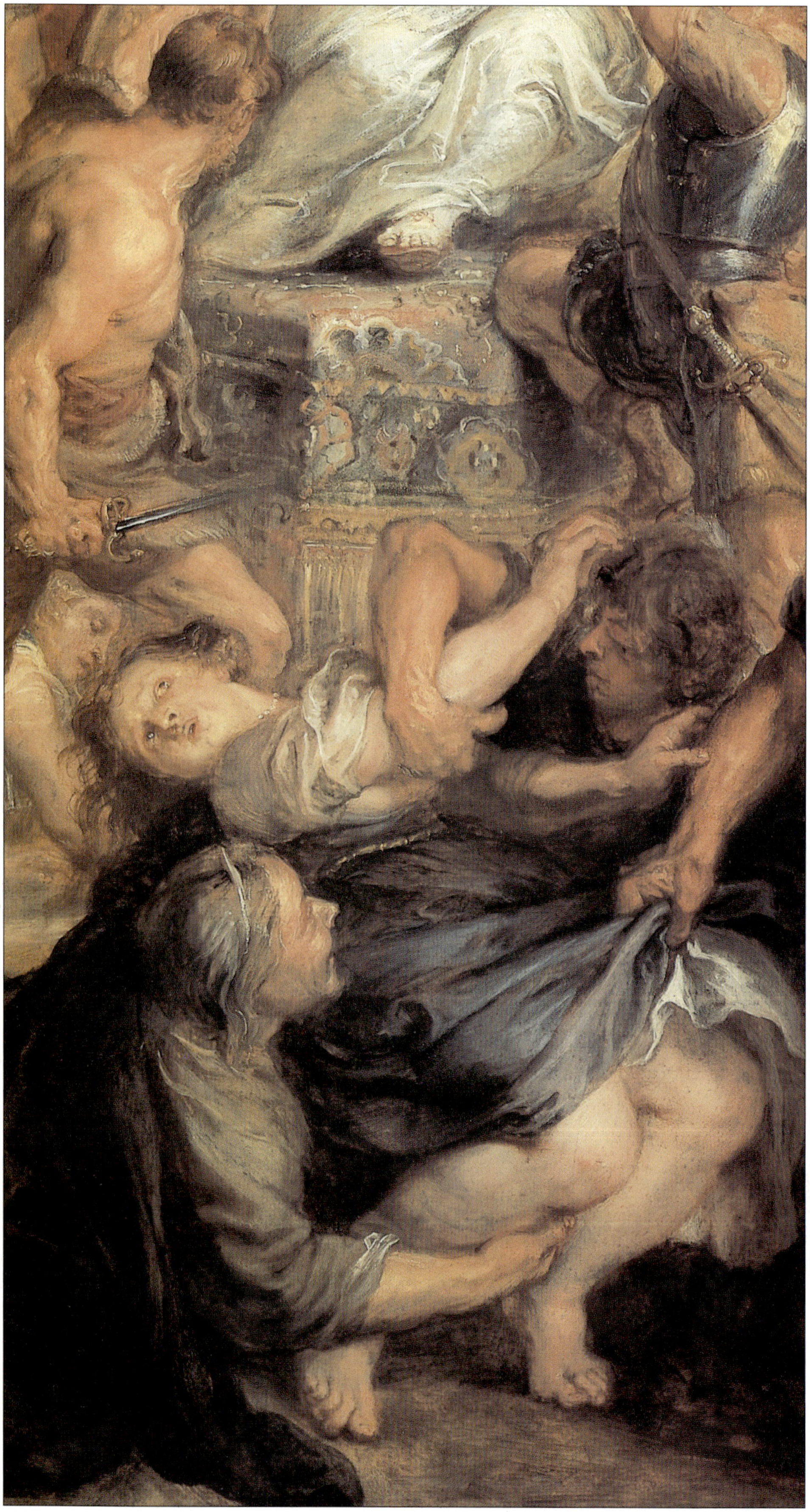

1

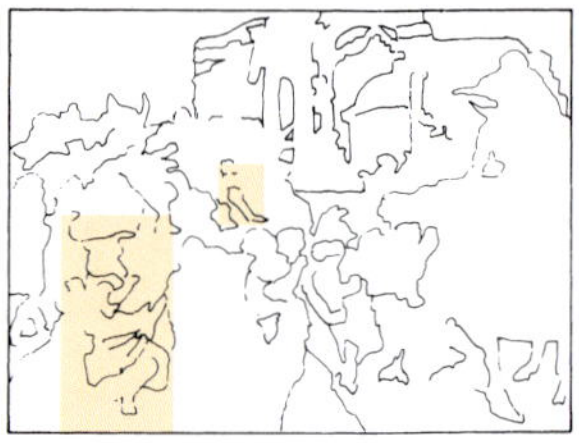

1 This detail shows a considerable range of colors employed in a relatively small space as well as illustrating the suggestiveness of Rubens' late style. The muscled arms and hands have been drawn in burnt umber and then vigorously brushed over in rich, thickly applied flesh tones, while the "white" drapery around the girl's upper arm is painted in a neutral green-gray repeated in the hair and arm of the old woman. This balances the brilliance of the central group. The girl's face is thinly painted, with touches of white impasto delicately suggesting tears in the eyes, and the blue dress is made up of a diaphanous dark brown layer over which rough strokes of black and blue articulate the folds.

2 *Actual size detail* The face of the Sabine woman in the middle ground is painted in paler colors and without the degree of definition given to those in the foreground group. Nonetheless, the feeling of her distress is clearly conveyed through Rubens' characteristic economy of drawing, demonstrating his ability to convey an emotion or expression in a brief "thumbnail sketch."

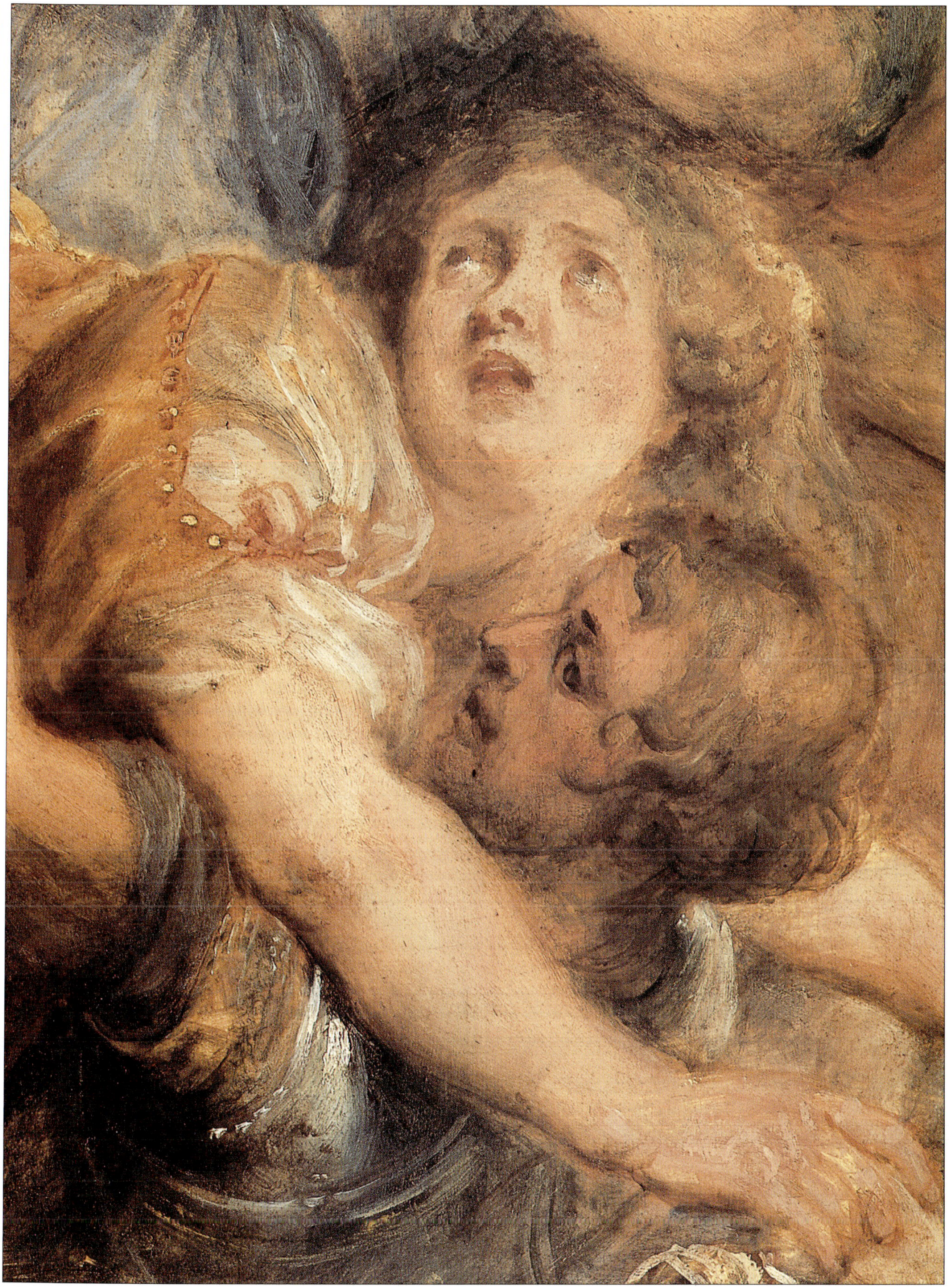

2 *Actual size detail*

AUTUMN LANDSCAPE WITH A VIEW OF HET STEEN

c1636
52×90½in/132×230cm
Oil on panel
National Gallery, London

Rubens painted relatively few landscapes in the course of his career, but they were most frequent in the last decade of his life. Though initially trained in the studio of a landscape specialist, Tobias Verhaecht, he clearly aspired in his early career to the more exalted status of "history painter." Indeed he often collaborated with landscape specialists like his friend Jan Brueghel the Elder, executing the figurative elements against a landscape background by another hand. What landscapes he did paint were done "informally," as it were, springing from his own interest rather than being constrained by the demands or tastes of patrons. His approach to landscape is thus very personal, and shows little awareness of, or interest in, his contemporaries the great Dutch landscape painters.

Autumn Landscape was painted in all probability in 1636, Rubens' first year of residence in his new country mansion. He bought the Château of Steen, visible on the left side of the painting, together with a sizeable estate, as a suitable country retreat, "rather far from the city of Antwerp and off the main roads," as he himself wrote. The property brought with it a title, that of Lord of Steen, which he evidently valued — he is thus named in the epitaph on his tomb.

The painting depicts the estate in early morning, with a farmer and his wife on their way to market and a hunter stalking some early prey. The house and copse are bathed in a sharp, horizontal dawn light. Just as the space in his figurative paintings is defined by the figures that fill it, so in this landscape the sense of space is dependent on the physical objects — bushes, shrubs, trees, buildings and so on — that lead the eye from point to point into the horizon. It is a fundamentally concrete conception of space — the complete antithesis of the large, empty spaces of sky and distance typical of the works of such Dutch contemporaries as van Goyen or Salomon van Ruisdael — and in this case it results in a slight lack of overall coherence.

The apparent evolution of the paintings seems to confirm this judgement. The support is made up of an astonishing seventeen panels that can be divided into three separate groups, suggesting (though by no means proving) that there were three stages of evolution. Beginning with the house, Rubens then seems to have extended the support to take in the landscape, and finally enlarged the whole composition by additional strips attached to top and bottom. *Pentimenti*, visible under X-ray, tend to confirm this view.

As with other landscapes by Rubens, it is not a true topographical reflection. The figure of the huntsman, the partridges, the magpies in the sky and the general layout of the composition are all derived from an engraving after Stradanus entitled "Duck Hunting." Moreover he has placed Het Steen in gently rolling countryside, whereas the land around it was in reality insistently flat.

The condition of the painting is generally good, though some passages of paint, especially around the wheel of the cart and the horses' legs, appear to be worn. The small figures close to the castle are not very characteristic of Rubens and may be later additions. The surface vibrates with color and movement, leading the eye in all directions to fresh pockets of interest. Rubens endows his plant forms with the same underlying energy that motivates his history paintings. The range of brushstrokes and the varied manipulations of paint are extraordinary — from the portrayal of the distant view, which was drawn in over the light ground in an extremely thin dark wash, and subsequently glazed over with greens and yellows — to the thick scumbles of dry paint that brilliantly suggest the tangle of blackberry bush and undergrowth; or the free strokes of smeared white impasto that evoke the reflected light on the tree trunks. This ability to suggest form by means of raw oil paint is equal to that of the late Rembrandt.

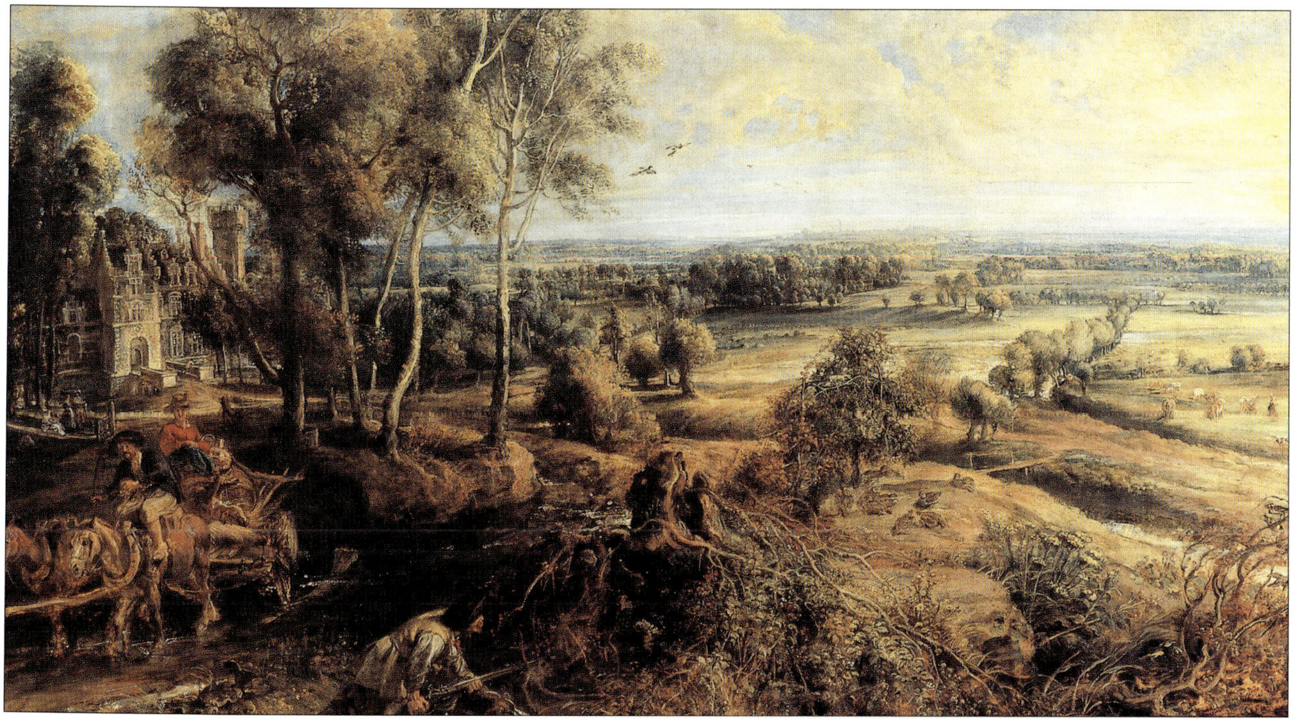

Although Rubens had trained in the studio of a landscape painter, Tobias Verhaecht, he painted relatively few landscapes himself, and in some of his works he would execute the figural elements while another artist painted the landscape background. However, he began to be more interested in landscape when he bought the Château of Steen as a country retreat in 1636. Now less constrained by the demands of patrons, he was free to explore more personal and private subjects. This work depicts the countryside around his new residence, which can be seen on the left-hand side, but like his other landscapes, it is not a true topographical representation. The general layout and some elements, such as the figure of the huntsman, are derived from an engraving of a duck hunt, and the countryside is shown as gently rolling while in fact it was quite flat.

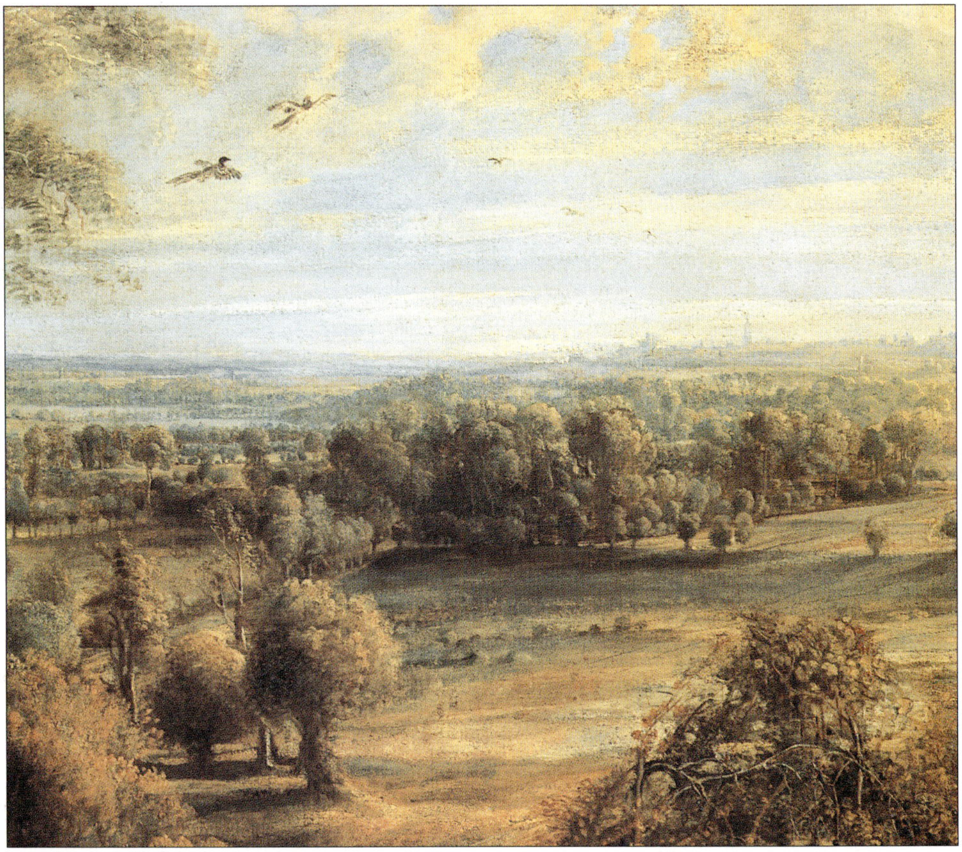

1

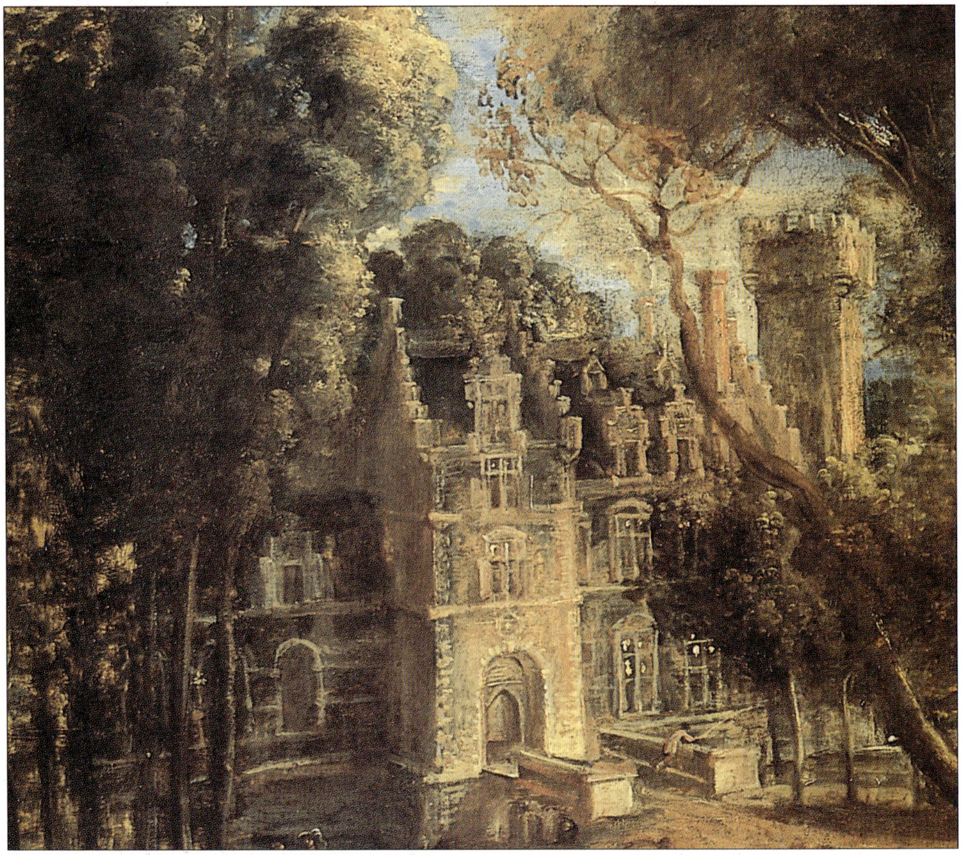

2

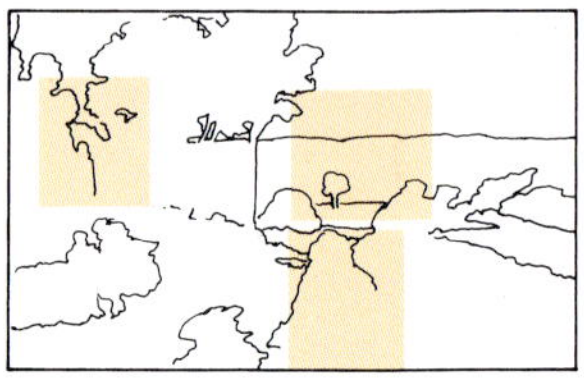

1 The distant landscape has been created by drawing the details of buildings, woodlands and shadowed hills in very dilute paint and then overlaying the drawing with successive layers of equally thin pale greens and yellows. Final touches were the small thick strokes of yellow to indicate the patches of sunlight.

2 The chateau, bathed in the sharp, angled light of early morning, is very thinly painted, the main walls mapped out by a glaze of green ocher and the detailing defined by dabs and touches of yellow and white impasto. Tiny drops of pure white impasto serve as the reflections of light in the glass windows.

3 The tangle of trees and undergrowth is one of the most thrilling passages in the painting. It is brilliantly worked up in a series of muddy greens, yellows, orange-browns and earth reds, all seemingly haphazardly imposed onto a loosely indicated network of tendrils and branches. The shadowed areas have been glazed over in dark brown, with definition provided by wedges of an orange hue, thickly applied. Viewed at close quarters, these streaks and dabs lose their identity as forms, but when seen from a distance they immediately become recognizable.

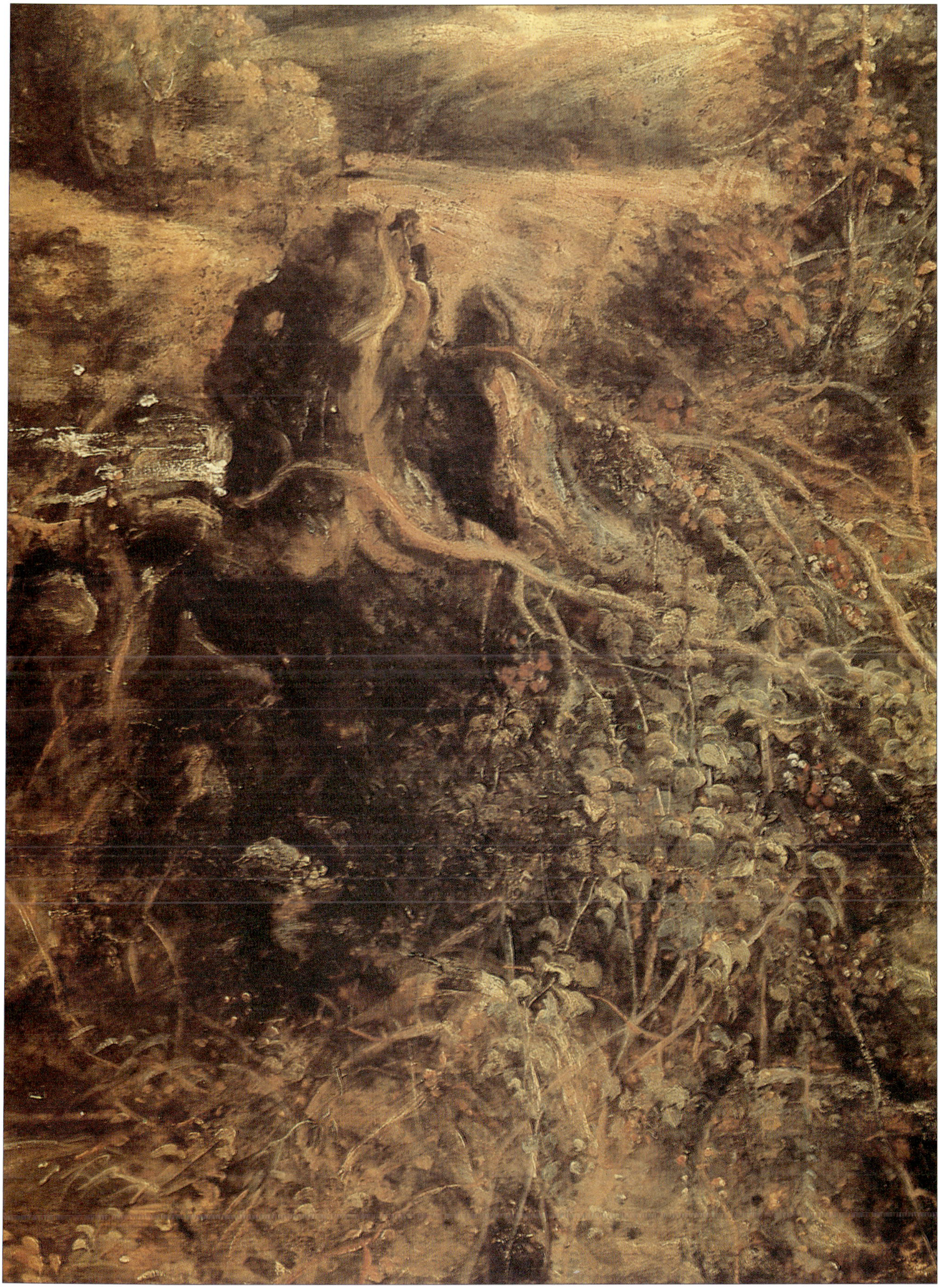

3

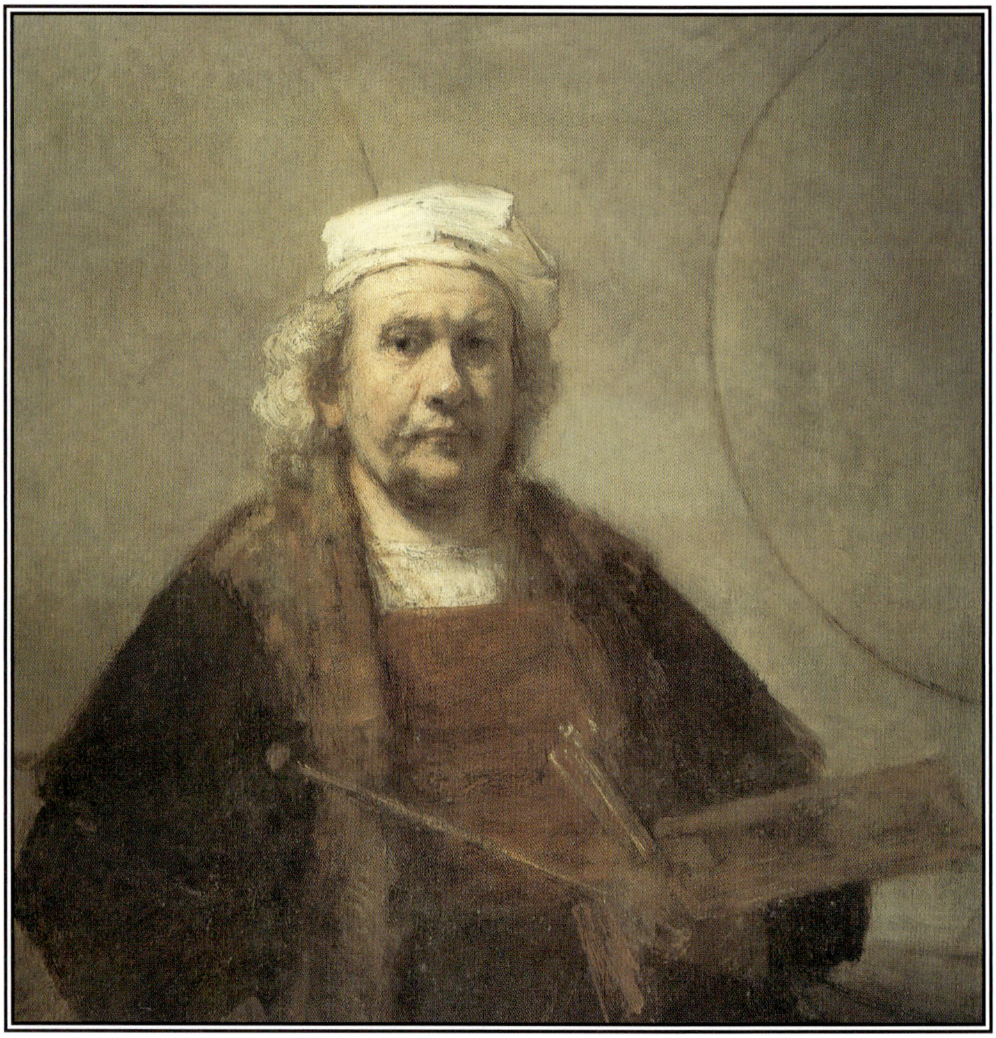

REMBRANDT

Introduction

REMBRANDT
Self-portrait
1640
National Gallery, London

Rembrandt van Rijn was undoubtedly the greatest interpreter of the human personality in the history of painting. Throughout a long and very productive career his two overriding interests were portraiture and Biblical narrative subjects. In the human face, and not least his own — over sixty self-portraits by him still exist — he could "study" character, personality and temperament, while the Bible provided him with a limitless range of subjects through which to explore powerful human emotions. Rembrandt saw the Bible stories as products of human experience, and more than any other painter, he interpreted them in bold, unidealized human terms. Equally his vision of human nature was colored to a considerable degree by his reading of the Bible; many of his portraits read almost as meditations, often seeming to carry the same sense of moral weight as his paintings of the Old Testament prophets. To these powerful depictions of human nature he brought a highly original technique which pushed the possibilities of the oil-painting medium to extraordinary limits. In terms of technique Rembrandt remains the greatest individualist of the seventeenth century, and the natural heir to Titian (c1487-1576), his great sixteenth-century forebear.

The content of his paintings cannot be separated from his style. His highly allusive commentaries on human life, time, age and experience demanded experiments in the medium that took him far beyond the limited vocabulary of contemporary practice. And as his attitude to his subject matter deepened over time, so his technique became increasingly personal, to the point at which, in his last years, he completely stepped outside the stylistic conventions of his day.

The young Rembrandt

Rembrandt was born in Leyden on July 15, 1606, at the start of what was to be for Holland an unprecedented period of peace and prosperity. Three years earlier, the Twelve Year Truce with Spain had been signed, which in effect signified Spain's recognition of the independence of the Dutch Republic and the end of a long and burdensome war. Rembrandt was thus born into a relatively young and optimistic culture, made resolute through its successful opposition to a larger power, economically vital, and relatively liberal in its political and religious practice. He was the son of a miller, Harman van Rijn — the family name derives from the mill that stood on the banks of the Old Rhine just outside Leyden — and was the eighth of nine children, only four of whom were to survive to maturity. Although in later life Rembrandt was to marry into the wealthy patrician class of Amsterdam and fully participate in the cultured, artistic world of the capital, he maintained throughout his life a brusqueness of manner and an impatience with social niceties that betrayed his modest origins. Filippo Baldinucci, writing in 1686, complained that the "ugly and plebeian face by which he was ill-favored, was accompanied by untidy and dirty clothes, since it was his custom, when working, to wipe his brushes on himself, and to do other things of a similar nature."

At the age of fourteen he was enrolled at the University of Leyden, a relatively unusual step for one of his class, and perhaps an indication that he was considered exceptionally bright. His inclination toward painting, however, must already have been strong, for after only a few months he left and became apprenticed to a local painter, Jacob van Swanenburgh, who specialized in both portraits and depictions of hell in the tradition of Hieronymus Bosch (c1450-1516). No trace of this artist's influence can be found in Rembrandt's subsequent work.

It was not until 1624 that Rembrandt, doubtless impatient with the provincial nature of Leyden's artistic circles, spent six months in the studio of the fashionable Amsterdam artist, Peter Lastman, and first came into contact with an artistic personality of real stature.

Lastman had been trained by the leading Flemish Mannerist artist, Cornelis Cornelisz van Haarlem, and had lived for some time in Rome, where he became familiar with the art of Adam Elsheimer (1578-1610) and the leading southern Baroque painters. He specialized in Biblical and mythological subjects, and his style, which combined the polished paint surfaces and stylized classicism of Flemish Mannerism with a vigorous and realistic attitude to his subject matter, left a deep impression on the young artist. Rembrandt's interest in Biblical subjects and realistic portrayal, as well as his taste for exotic and romantic settings and costume details both seem to have been stimulated by his contact with Lastman, and the paintings he executed on his return to Leyden reflect this debt. Works like *Anna Accused by Tobit of Stealing the Kid* display an almost over-emphatic realism, a desire for the exact delineation of expression and gesture to convey emotion, very close to the manner of Lastman.

The technique of chiaroscuro

The other major influence on Rembrandt's emerging style was that of the Utrecht School, the Dutch followers of the Italian artist, Caravaggio. Working principally in Rome and Naples at the beginning of the century, Michelangelo Caravaggio (1573-1610) had created a strikingly original style of painting that combined a vigorous "peasant" realism with violent contrasts of light and shade which conveyed an impression of intense drama. This technique, called chiaroscuro (literally "light-dark"), was adopted by artists all over Europe and became a major stylistic feature of seventeenth-century painting. The Utrecht "Caravaggisti" adopted the same deep tenebroso effects, but tended to use them for less violent subjects than Caravaggio himself. Gerrit van Honthorst's *Christ before the High Priest* shows this style very clearly, and also illustrates the common device of introducing some kind of light, often a burning taper, into the composition as the primary light-source.

Rembrandt adopted this chiaroscuro technique early in his career, and for the rest of his life it was to be the main expressive vehicle of his work. He recognized in this shadowy light – in the deep well of a darkened interior or in a flickering murk of half-tones and reflections – the power of suggestion, of metaphor, the ability to create mood and to suggest realms of thought and feeling beyond the concrete surfaces of the material world. By cloaking his figures in a veil of shadows and half-lights, he created a shift of attention from the tangible world of perceived objects to the intangible one of spirit and feeling.

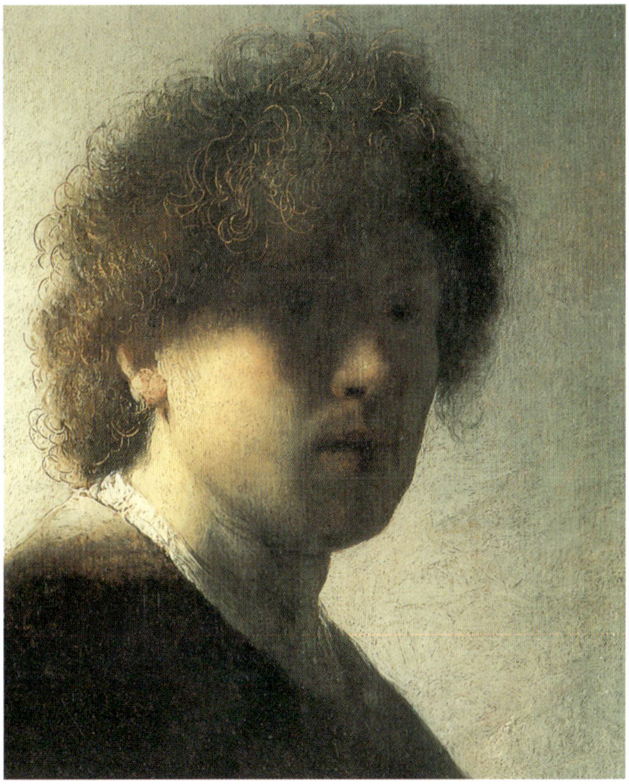

REMBRANDT
Self-portrait
c 1629, National Gallery, London

The deep shadow covering the face is an early and crudely forceful example of the device Rembrandt developed of using light and shadow to heighten the psychological suggestiveness of the image. Here the spectator is forced to complete the sitter's features in the imagination.

Clearly his painting technique was determined by his chosen style, and he early on adopted a method of painting from dark to light, beginning to work with a uniform underlayer of a fairly dark brown and building up the major forms in increasingly lighter tones, finishing with the highlights. (Generally in Rembrandt's work the thinnest areas of paint are found in the darkest areas and the thickest in the highlights.)

A boldly experimental approach can already be seen in the early *Self-portrait* painted about 1629. The shadow falls over the face so as to virtually conceal the expression, something no other artist had hitherto attempted. He is also experimenting with different effects of texture. There are expressive differences between the rough impasto of the collar and the thinner painting of the jerkin. The background has been achieved by dragging a brush loaded heavily with fairly dry paint over a darker background, allowing the darks to show through the pitted troughs left by the brush hairs and thus creating a sense of surface shimmer. The wild, unkempt curls of the hair have been created in part by using a blunt instrument, possibly the wooden end of his paintbrush, literally to carve the lines through the upper layer of paint and reveal the underlayer beneath.

Such a rough, vigorous treatment, such a deliberate lack of "finish," complements the unadorned and uncompromising realism of the portrait. Rembrandt seems at this point to be deliberately exaggerating his coarse, disheveled nature. The immediate impression created is of an extremely forceful individual and romantic temperament, and one that was attempting to flout the existing standards of portraiture. The serious, questioning expression, half-hidden in deep shadow, seems to have more in common with the nineteenth-century Romantic vision than with the urbane polish of fashionable seventeenth-century practice.

Success and prosperity

The originality of Rembrandt's art was evidently soon noticed, for by at least 1629 he had met Constantijn Huygens, secretary to the Prince of Orange. Huygens was a man who had traveled widely in his capacity as civil servant and diplomat, and was possessed of wide cultural interests, his great passion being painting. He was immediately struck by the work of this young miller's son and by that of another fellow Leyden painter, Jan Lievens; in his autobiography he stated that they already equaled the famous masters and would soon surpass them. It was almost certainly through the encouragement and connections of this man that Rembrandt was induced to move to Amsterdam in 1631, and there he embarked on the happiest and most successful period of his life. He quickly established his reputation as a skilled and accomplished portrait painter with *The Anatomy Lesson of Dr Tulp*, his first large-scale group commission, and thereafter he was in constant demand for portraits. For his commissioned works of this period he adopted the polished and elegant realism that characterized the style of other leading portraitists of the day, such as Willem de Keyser, holding back the freedom of technique he had developed at Leyden.

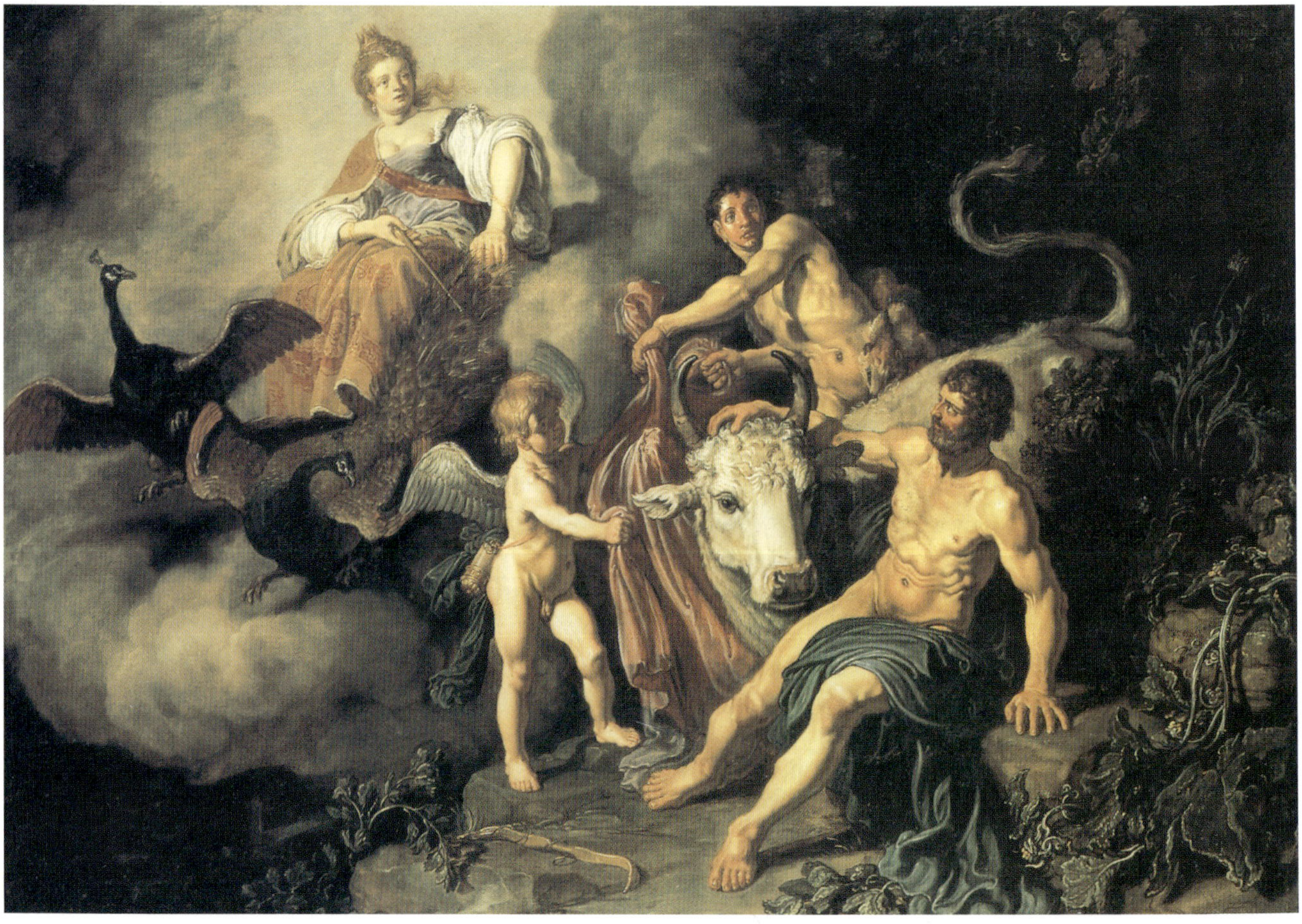

PETER LASTMAN
Juno Discovering Jupiter with Io
1618, National Gallery, London

Juno, on the left, descends to earth with crown, scepter and peacocks, and discovers her husband Jupiter with the nymph Io, whom he hastily turns into a heifer. Winged Cupid and Deceit, in mask and foxskin, casts a drapery over her. The classical subject and Italianate handling typify Lastman's mature style.

In 1634 Rembrandt married his landlord's first cousin, Saskia van Ulenborch. Saskia's family were of the professional class of Amsterdam, and she brought him a sizeable dowry as well as connections in wealthy patrician circles. Their marriage, though tragically short-lived, appears to have been extremely happy, and Saskia's pale, coquettish features appear repeatedly in paintings, etchings and drawings throughout the 1630s.

Rembrandt was now successful, popular and prosperous. By 1639 he and Saskia had bought themselves a large house in the Joden-Breestraat, and Rembrandt had begun to amass a large collection of paintings, drawings and prints of old masters and contemporaries, as well as a varied collection of exotic curios. What evidence there is suggests that the young couple lived a fashionable and extravagant lifestyle, and in Rembrandt's art at this time one also senses the same exuberance and self-indulgence. This is perhaps best seen in the extraordinary double portrait of himself and Saskia that must date from the mid-1630s. It shows the artist, extravagantly dressed, raising his glass with a wide, almost leering smile on his face, and with a much more sedate Saskia on his knee. While it is unlikely that this work was intended as a straight representation (the presence of a peacock, symbol of pride, possibly alludes to a scene from the life of the prodigal son), it shows the spirit with which Rembrandt was approaching his art and perhaps his life.

The work also shows the extent to which he was attempting to come to grips with the dynamic conception and rhetoric of the High Baroque style of the "Caravaggisti" and of Rubens, whose paintings Rembrandt was aware of through engravings. His other major paintings of the 1630s are no less extravagantly theatrical in both composition and conception. In *Belshazzar's Feast* (see page 165) he has taken over the Baroque device of catching a single moment of high drama and freezing his characters in split-second gestures of instantaneous reaction. The figures are pushed forward toward the picture plane within a cramped space, seeming as though about to burst the confines of the canvas. The effect is melodramatic and perhaps a little forced — instantaneity was not Rembrandt's chief forte.

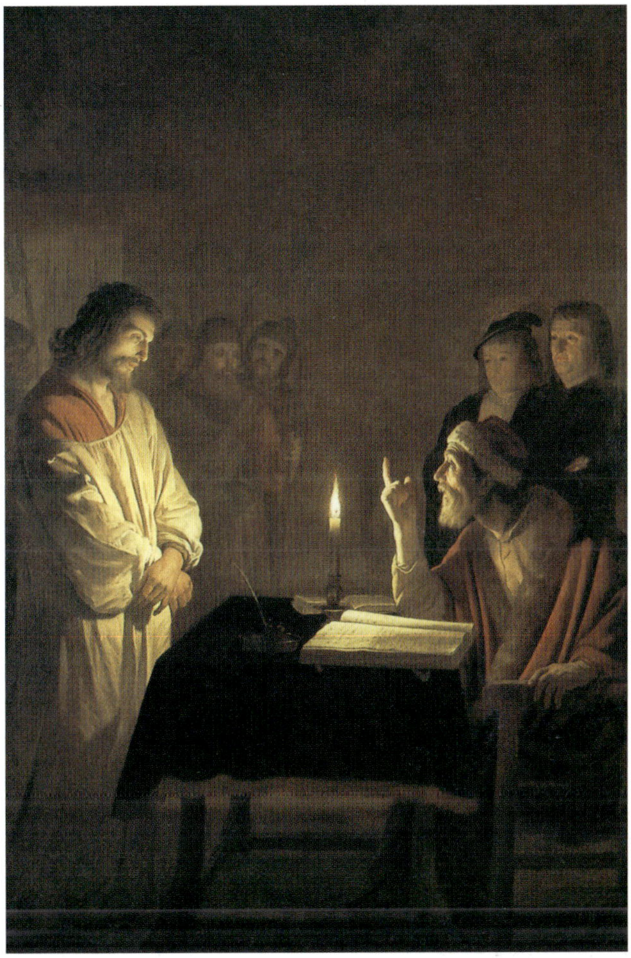

GERRIT VAN HONTHORST
Christ before the High Priest
c 1617, National Gallery, London

Honthorst was known as "Gherardo della notte," ("Gerard of the night") in Italy, where he lived from about 1610 to 1620, because of his interest in nocturnal or dimly lit scenes. He was important in transmitting the use of chiaroscuro from Italy to the Netherlands, and thus was an influence on Rembrandt.

Family tragedy and new directions

By the 1640s, as if aware that he had explored this theatricality to the full and recognized its limitations, he began to change his style in a process that continued throughout the next decade. He gradually dropped the violence, clamor and extravagance of gesture and adopted a tone of quieter, more restrained emotion. This change in his art is usually attributed to the tragic events of his personal life. Three children born to Saskia died in early infancy — only the fourth, Titus, was to live to early adulthood — and Saskia too was ailing, perhaps as a result of child-bearing. Numerous drawings and etchings show her sinking slowly from glowing health to a sickly, bed-ridden state. She died in June, 1642.

From this point onward Rembrandt was to be increasingly burdened by financial worries and a waning in popularity. The 1640s saw the rise in Amsterdam of a taste for the elegant, courtly portraiture of artists like van Dyck, a style for which Rembrandt had little sympathy and to which he refused to adapt. Commissions accordingly went in increasing numbers to his more flexible pupils, but his decline in popularity was by no means as dramatic as is often believed. His greatest

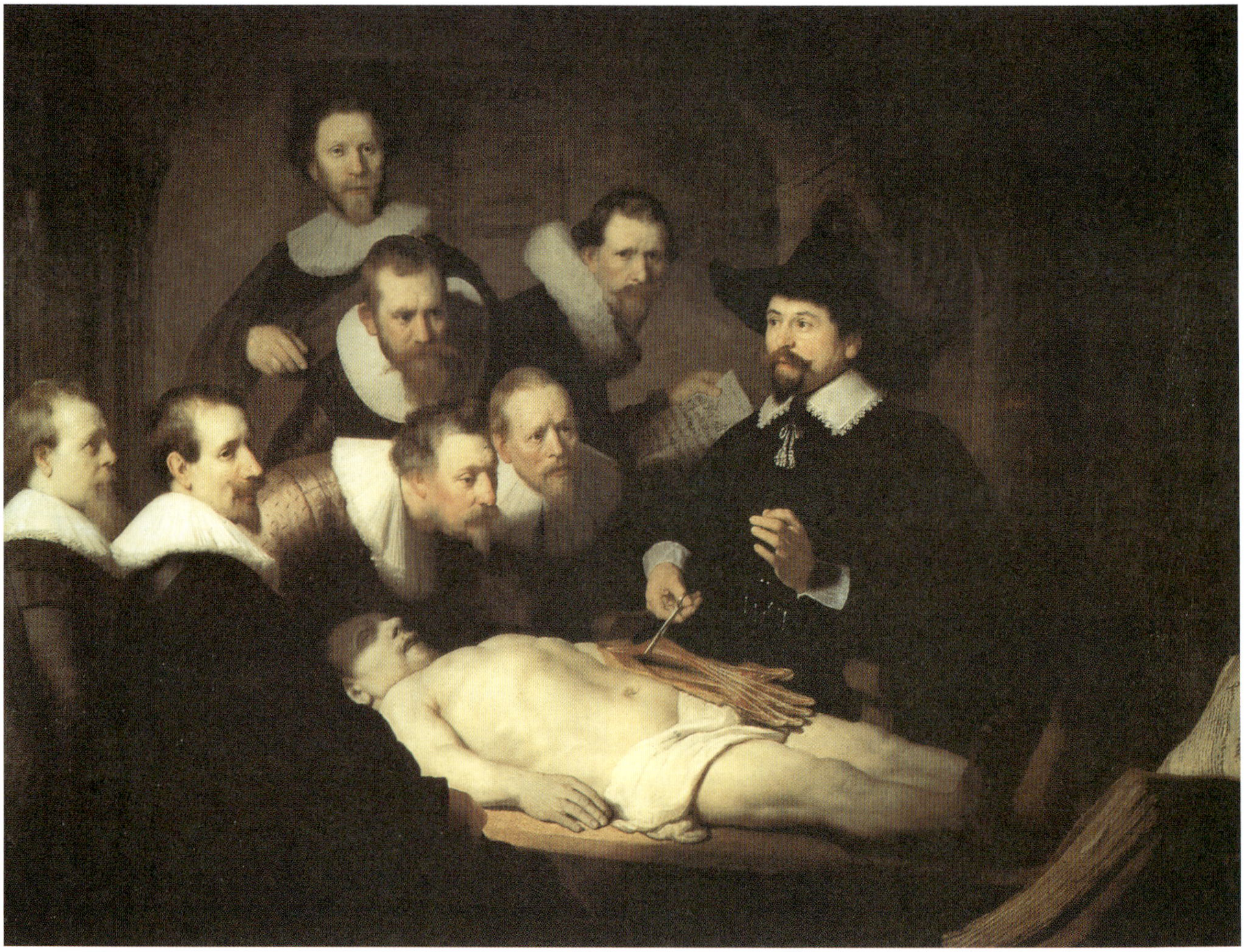

REMBRANDT
The Anatomy Lesson of Dr Tulp
1632, Mauritshuis, The Hague

In this early masterpiece Rembrandt solved the problem of group portraiture, namely how to reconcile interest, variety and compositional unity with faithful and suitably dignified likenesses. Attention has been focused on the corpse, with the onlookers arranged around it in varying attitudes of concentration.

showpiece of group-portraiture, the celebrated *Night Watch* of 1642 (see page 173), was very highly regarded even by his more classically minded critics, and he maintained a steady, if reduced, flow of commissions. His gradual rejection of fashionable taste should perhaps be regarded as a symptom of his deepening awareness of himself as an artist and of the nature and direction of his art. This new awareness is clear in the *Self-portrait* of 1640 (see page 169), in which he shows himself dressed expensively, as was appropriate to a successful painter, but in a mood that is sharply serious and quite at odds with the showy flamboyance of earlier self-portraits.

The new element of restraint signals a profound change in Rembrandt's artistic outlook, which partly found expression in an awakened sense of nature, witnessed by the many landscape drawings and etchings that he carried out in these years. Done with a wonderful economy of line, they show a very direct response to the fields and copses outside the city, together with a feeling for space and rolling skies quite unlike that of his earlier, less realistic and more romantic treatments.

The same directness can also be discerned in his handling of human subjects. He abandoned the theatricality of his earlier style and began to choose calmer, more serene subjects, especially those from the life of Christ, which allowed him to explore more generalized and more enduring human qualities. One senses a closing in of his social life, a reluctance to look beyond his family and immediate circle for inspiration. In a number of sketches and drawings that date from this period, such as the *Two Women Teaching a Child to Walk* one recognizes the same sense of domestic tenderness that can also be found in many small-scale works of the childhood of Christ, for instance the *Adoration of the Shepherds* (see page 179). His style in both drawing and painting shows an increasing impatience with descrip-

REMBRANDT'S PAINTING METHODS

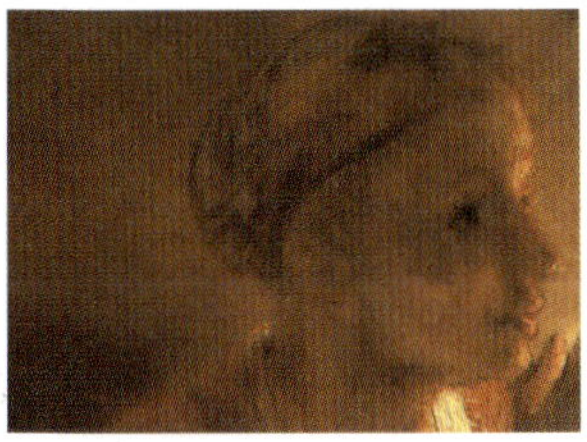

In Rembrandt's paintings the paint was always thinnest in the background, and here the color of the brown priming can be seen through the top layer.

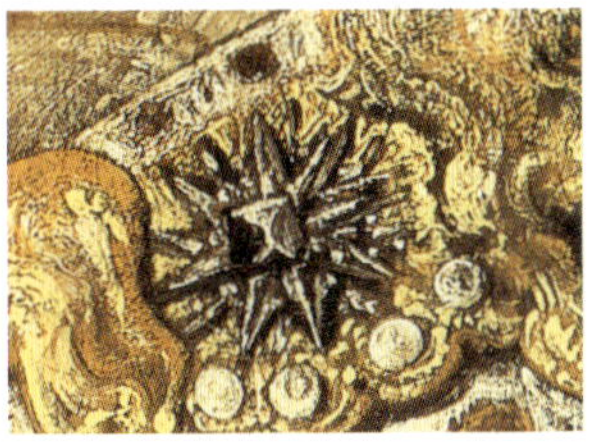

In parts of Belshazzar's Feast *the paint is built up thickly and then partially carved away with a sharp instrument.*

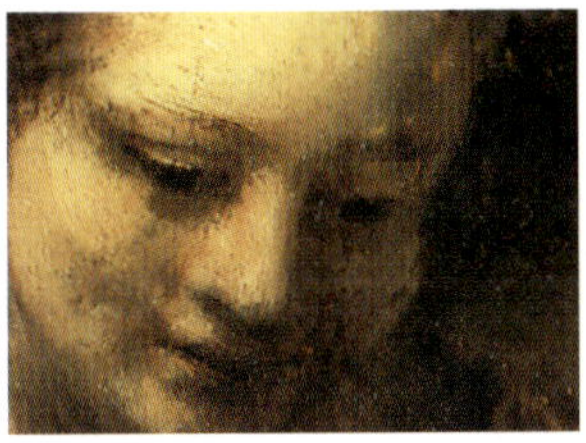

Rembrandt often used thin, transparent glazes over thick impastos, as in this detail of Woman Bathing.

In Rembrandt's day and before it, painting was a far slower and more laborious business than it is today, when paintings are often completed in one or two sessions. Advances in the manufacture of artist's materials have given us the boon of ready-primed canvases, pre-mixed, permanent colors and fast-drying mediums, but in the seventeenth century canvases had to be measured, stretched and primed, and pigments ground, mixed and stored before the real work could begin. Sometimes many of these preliminaries were done by artists' apprentices or studio hands, but a painting still had to be built up layer by layer, often with a long drying time between each one.

Rembrandt worked on a medium-brown ground consisting of ocher bound with resin and animal glue, a method introduced by Titian and used more or less universally until the nineteenth century, when white or light-toned grounds began to be favored by artists such as the French Impressionists. He has left no sketches or preliminary studies; his compositions were mapped out directly onto the canvas in a monochrome underpainting, producing what is known as a "dead-color painting" ready to be worked up. Over this he applied his body color, working from background to foreground, leaving the figures at the front as monochrome silhouettes until their turn came.

His palette was small even by seventeenth-century standards, but he was a superlative colorist, managing to retain a balance between color itself and tonality — the use of light and shade.

The range of colors Rembrandt used was quite small by modern standards. Those illustrated here, with the addition of lead white, were the ones used in Belshazzar's Feast.

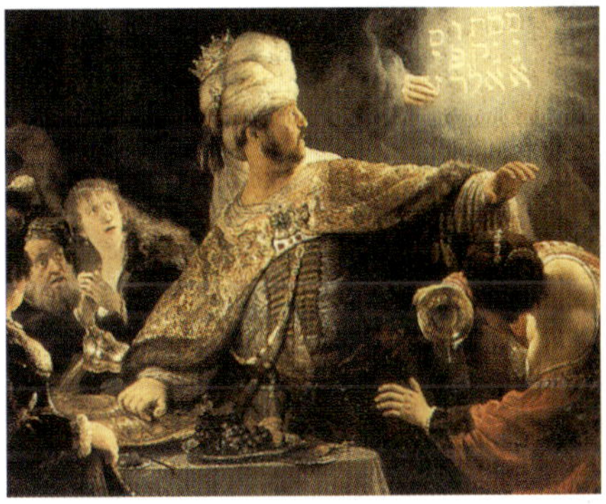

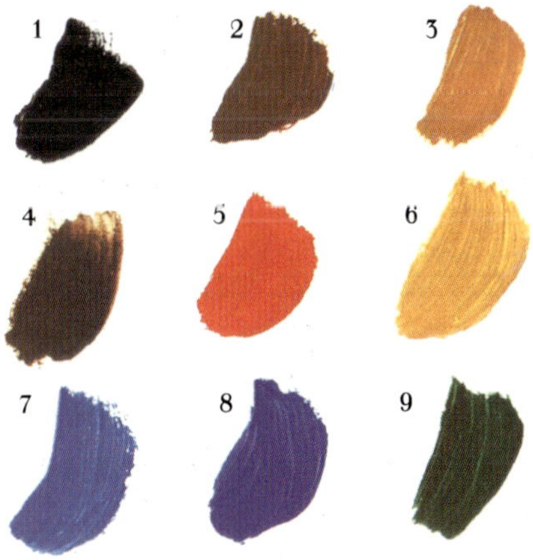

1 Black; 2 Brown (precise pigment not known); 3 Red ocher; 4 Transparent browns, probably Cologne earth and bistre; 5 Vermilion and organic red lakes; 6 Lead tin yellow, usually mixed with lead white; 7 Azurite; 8 Smalt; 9 Greens, made by mixing lead tin yellow with azurite and smalt

tive details and a desire to capture the expressive essence of an attitude or gesture with the greatest economy.

Part of this new harmony in Rembrandt's art was possibly due to the presence in his household of Hendrickje Stoffels, a peasant girl who in about 1645 had been taken on as a nurse for Titus, supplanting another woman, one Geertge Dix, both in her capacity as surrogate mother and in her employer's affections. (Geertge won an extremely bitter legal battle claiming unfair dismissal, but Rembrandt retaliated in a revealing display of obduracy, and managed to have her locked up in a house of correction in Gouda.) Thereafter Hendrickje became in effect his common-law wife, looking after his needs and eventually bearing him a daughter. They never married, possibly because Rembrandt would thereby have forfeited the small allowance left to him under the terms of Saskia's will. Hendrickje was the complete opposite of Saskia, yet it is clear from the many paintings and drawings in which she appears that she and Rembrandt settled down into a life of domestic contentment.

REMBRANDT
Self-portrait with Saskia
c1635, Staatliche Kunstammlungen, Dresden

One of the strangest of all Rembrandt's self-portraits, this was probably intended more as a general genre or narrative scene in the manner of the Dutch "Caravaggisti" than as a specific double portrait, though a personal level of meaning cannot be ruled out.

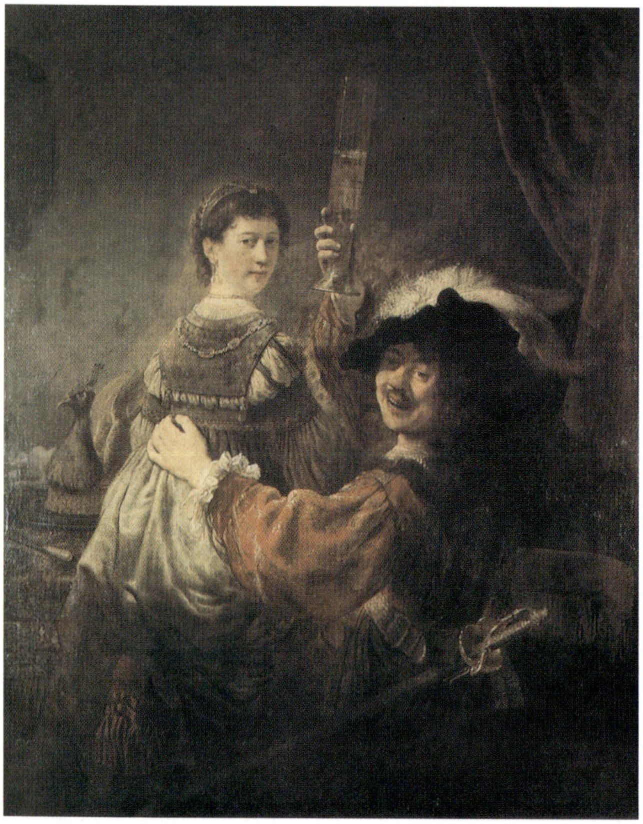

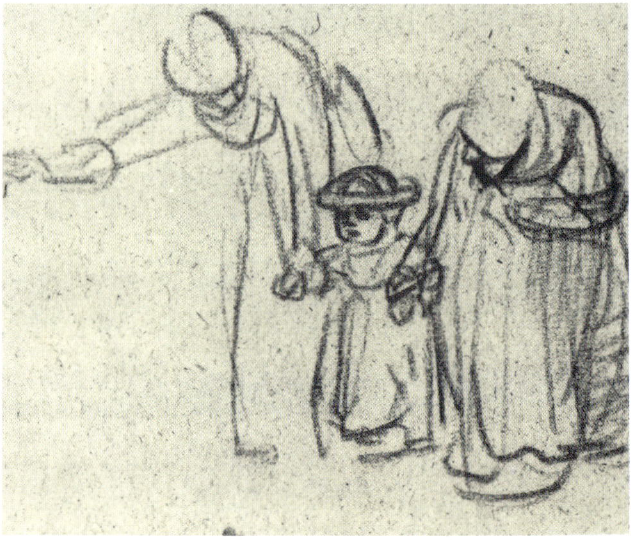

REMBRANDT
Two Women Teaching a Child to Walk
Pen and ink

In a few rapid strokes Rembrandt manages to convey a precise idea of personality in each figure, as well as a sense of the rapt absorption of the two women (perhaps mother and grandmother) in the child as it takes its first tentative steps.

The later years

The last twenty years of Rembrandt's life were nonetheless dogged by financial hardship and personal tragedy. Partly due to his natural acquisitiveness and extravagance, partly to the ever-dwindling income from commissions, and partly also to the generally worsening state of the Dutch economy, debts began to accumulate around his large house on the Breestraat. In 1656, in order to ensure an inheritance for Titus, he placed the house in his son's name and borrowed more in order to purchase another, smaller house. But a short time later he was forced to declare himself insolvent and to pledge all his belongings to pay off his debts. The liquidization of his property was ordered and an inventory of his goods drawn up and placed on public auction. This inventory still exists, providing an interesting insight into his tastes and collecting habits. It shows him to have been an extremely eclectic collector of works of art, listing paintings not only by contemporary masters such as Hercules Seghers, Jan Lievens and Porcellis, but also works attributed to such great names as Giorgione, Palma Vecchio and Raphael. In addition, there were literally thousands of prints and drawings, ranging from Renaissance masters to Persian miniatures. Other objects included a large collection of arms and armor, oriental costumes and bowls, and a miscellany of natural objects such as shells and stuffed birds.

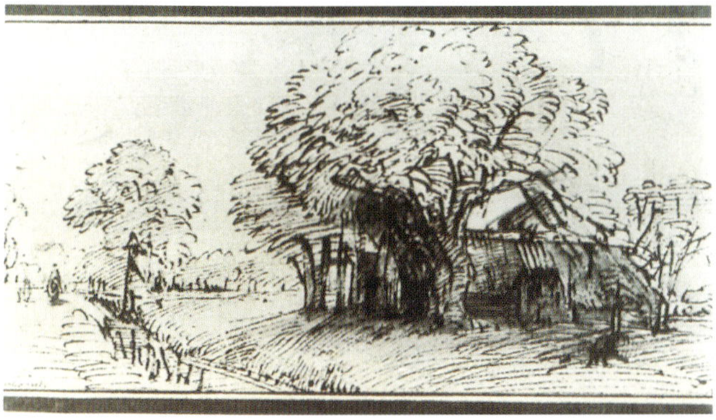

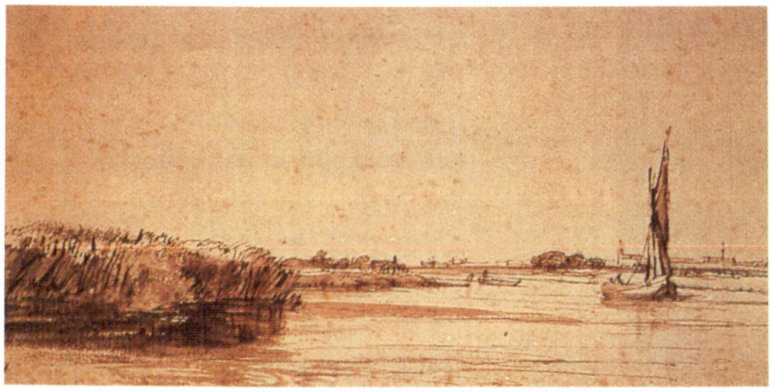

Above
REMBRANDT
View across the Nieuwe Meer near Amsterdam
Pen and brush, brown ink, on colored ground

In the 1640s, during long walks, Rembrandt recorded the countryside around Amsterdam in a series of drawings and etchings. Here he marvelously suggests the action of a light wind across its sluggish surface.

Top
REMBRANDT
Landscape with Trees
Pen and ink

Executed not with a quill but with a reed pen, which gives broad strokes and a softening effect, this drawing, with its rapid and rhythmical strokes, contrasts with the more deliberate and calculated use of tinted paper and broad, translucent washes of the later work illustrated above.

The sale of his effects did very little to pay off his creditors, and in an attempt to keep him at least minimally solvent, Hendrickje and Titus formed a company which in effect employed Rembrandt and paid him a salary out of his own earnings, thus preventing his creditors from taking away any money he made. In this manner he continued to survive, albeit in a meager way, but tragedy was to strike him further. In 1663 Hendrickje died, followed five years later by Titus. Rembrandt struggled on briefly with his young daughter, but he too died the following year, alone and in obscurity.

Despite the hardship and adversity of his last years, this final period of his life witnessed an important development of his art and an extraordinary extension of his technique. In his old age, indifferent to fashion and worldly opinion, he was free to abandon the conventions of contemporary art to develop so personal a manner of painting as to completely transcend all stylistic categories. Contemporaries often failed to understand his intentions, complaining that his works seemed unfinished, and Arnold Houbraken wrote in 1718 of a portrait by Rembrandt that "the colors were so heavily loaded that you could lift it from the floor by its nose." Certainly his manner became increasingly broad and his application of paint increasingly thick.

In the late portraits and self-portraits it is possible to discern a somber, rather pessimistic mood that may reflect the sad events of his personal life. Yet it was also in this period of his life that he could produce works of a depth and meaning unsurpassed in the whole history of art. In a work like *The Jewish Bride*, one sees the distillation of pure feeling, expressed in terms of an awesome solemnity that fully conveys both the grandeur of the human spirit and the power of human love.

REMBRANDT
Saskia Lying in Bed
Ink drawing

This is one of a number of drawings of Saskia in bed that witness her gradual decline from health. Here, accompanied by a nurse at the foot of the bed, she looks decidedly depressed, her chin resting dejectedly on her hand.

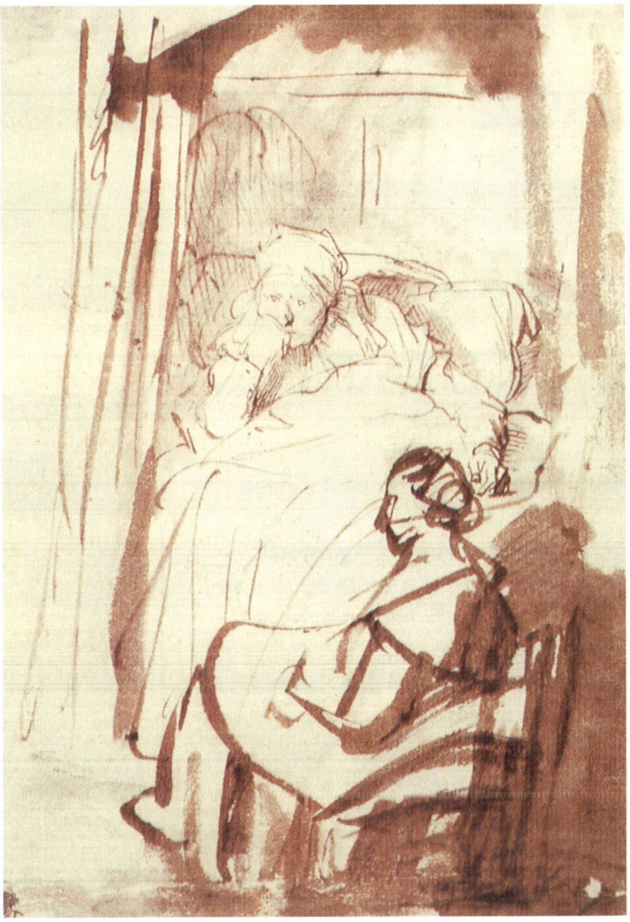

Chronology of Rembrandt's Life

1606 July 15th: Rembrandt born in Leyden.
1613-20 Attends the Latin School in Leyden.
1620 Enrolled at the University of Leyden.
1621-23 Apprenticed to the painter Jacob van Swanenburgh.
1624 Spends about six months in the studio of Peter Lastman in Amsterdam.
1626 Established as independent artist in Leyden. Paints *Tobit and Anna.*
1630 Favorably noticed by Constantijn Huygens. Paints *Jeremiah Lamenting the Destruction of Jerusalem.*
1631 Moves to Amsterdam.
1632 Establishes reputation with *The Anatomy Lesson of Dr Tulp.*
1634 July 22nd: marries Saskia van Ulenborch.
1635 December 1st: Saskia gives birth to Rumbartus, who dies shortly afterwards. *Belshazzar's Feast* painted around this time.
1638 July: birth of daughter, Cornelia, who dies within a month.
1639 Rembrandt and Saskia move into large house on the Jodenbreestraat.
1640 July: birth of second daughter, Cornelia, who also does not survive. Paints *Self-portrait.*
1641 July: birth of son, Titus, the only one of their children to reach maturity.
1642 June 5th: Saskia dies. Geertje Dix employed as nurse for Titus. Completes *The Night Watch.*
1646 Paints the *Adoration of the Shepherds*, perhaps to a commission from the Stadtholder, Frederick Henry.

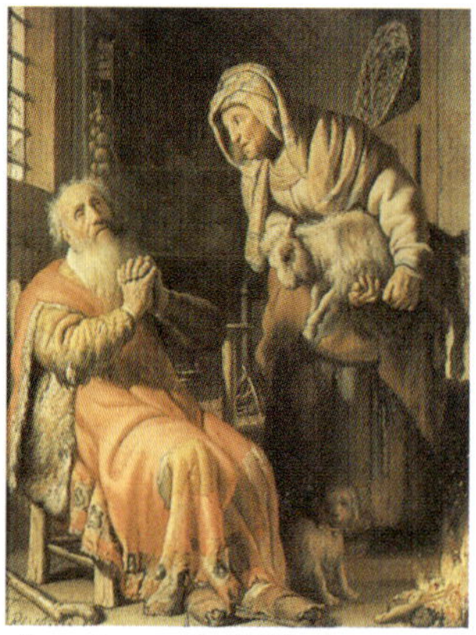
Anna Accused by Tobit of Stealing the Kid

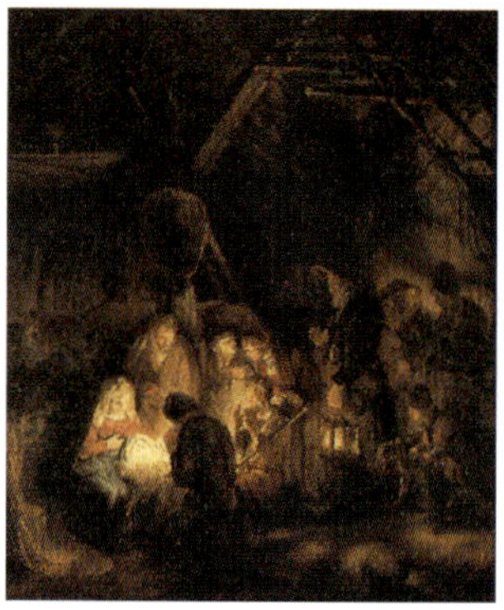
Adoration of the Shepherds

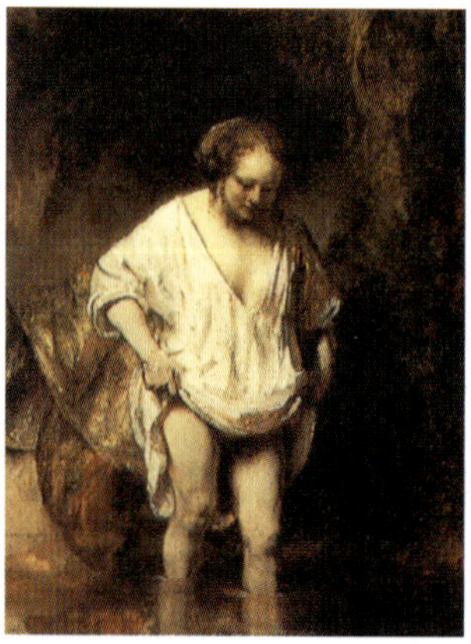
Young Woman Bathing

1648 Geertje Dix leaves Rembrandt's service and brings case against him for unfair dismissal. By this time Hendrickje Stoffels has entered Rembrandt's employ.
1654 Rembrandt and Hendrickje summoned before the Ecclesiastical Court, accused of concubinage.
1654 Hendrickje gives birth to a daughter, Cornelia.
1655 Paints *Young Woman Bathing.*
1656 To avoid bankrupcy, Rembrandt applies to the High Court for a "cessio bonorum," and declares himself insolvent. Liquidaton of his property ordered and inventory of his belongings made.
1657-8 Rembrandt's goods disposed of by public auction.
1660 Moves into smaller house in the more modest Rozengracht. Hendrickje and Titus form a company that "employs" Rembrandt, and receives all his work, in return for a salary, in order to keep the creditors at bay. Paints *The Denial of St Peter.*
1661 Painted the *Portrait of Margaretha de Geer.*
1663 July 21st: Hendrickje dies. *Self-Portrait with Maulstick, Palette and Brushes* painted about this time.
1664-68 The *Jewish Bride* painted about this time.
1668 September 4th: Titus dies.
1669 October 4th: Rembrandt dies. Four days afterward he is buried in the Westerkerk, beside Hendrickje and Titus.

THE PAINTINGS

Jeremiah Lamenting the Destruction of Jerusalem

Signed and dated 1630
$22\frac{3}{4} \times 18$in/58×46cm
Oil on panel
Rijksmuseum, Amsterdam

In this small jewel-like painting, executed four years after the previous example, a marked broadening of technique is evident, as well as a deepening of the artist's sense of color and a fuller understanding of the expressive uses of chiaroscuro. The aged prophet sits sunk in an introspective gloom below a dimly perceived pillar. To the left, the ruined city is in flames, above which, traced in very fluid paint, the Angel of the Lord can be seen, bringing down death and destruction as the prophet had foretold.

Throughout his life Rembrandt was fascinated by the portrayal of old age. He evidently used his parents as models at the start of his career, as the same elderly faces occur repeatedly in a series of early works. They, of course, provided him with free models whose features and characters he knew well, yet on a deeper level the whole theme of old age held a strong sway over his imagination and he turned to it repeatedly, portraying it in terms of the summation of a life's experience rather than as infirmity or senility. He was particularly attracted to the aged seers and prophets of the Bible, figures of great wisdom and moral stature; and his renderings of the deeply etched lines of a forehead or an absorbed and introspective stare, demonstrate a sympathy and an understanding that has more to do with an attitude to life itself than with the interpretation of any single individual. His aged figures seem to express a vision of profound human goodness, born of knowledge and experience.

It is the chiaroscuro that sets the emotional key of this painting. The deep shadows which encroach from above and from the side of the prophet contribute powerfully to his mood of hopeless despair. Once again Rembrandt has built up his composition from a dark background by using successive layers of lighter tones. The brushwork is broader and no longer so doggedly descriptive, and the transition from the deepest shadow of the background to the lighter tones of the middle ground has been achieved by a layer of broadly painted, thin, tawny yellow, overlaid in turn by a thicker passage of greenish gray. The murky form of the huge pillar has been picked out in the same thin yellow together with touches of a light gray. These broad areas contrast with the rich, vigorous brushwork of the robe and the firm modeling of the foot. The glinting highlights of the embroidered gown and the golden vessels have been applied in minute touches of thick lead-white impasto, while the shadows have been given greater depth and luminosity by additional glazes of tinted brown. In both the embroidery work on the prophet's chest and the treatment of the bush on the left, Rembrandt's technique of scraping away the top layer of paint with a sharp instrument is again visible. By these means an extremely sophisticated tonal range is created which, together with a more expressive use of deep colors, shows his increasing mastery of his medium.

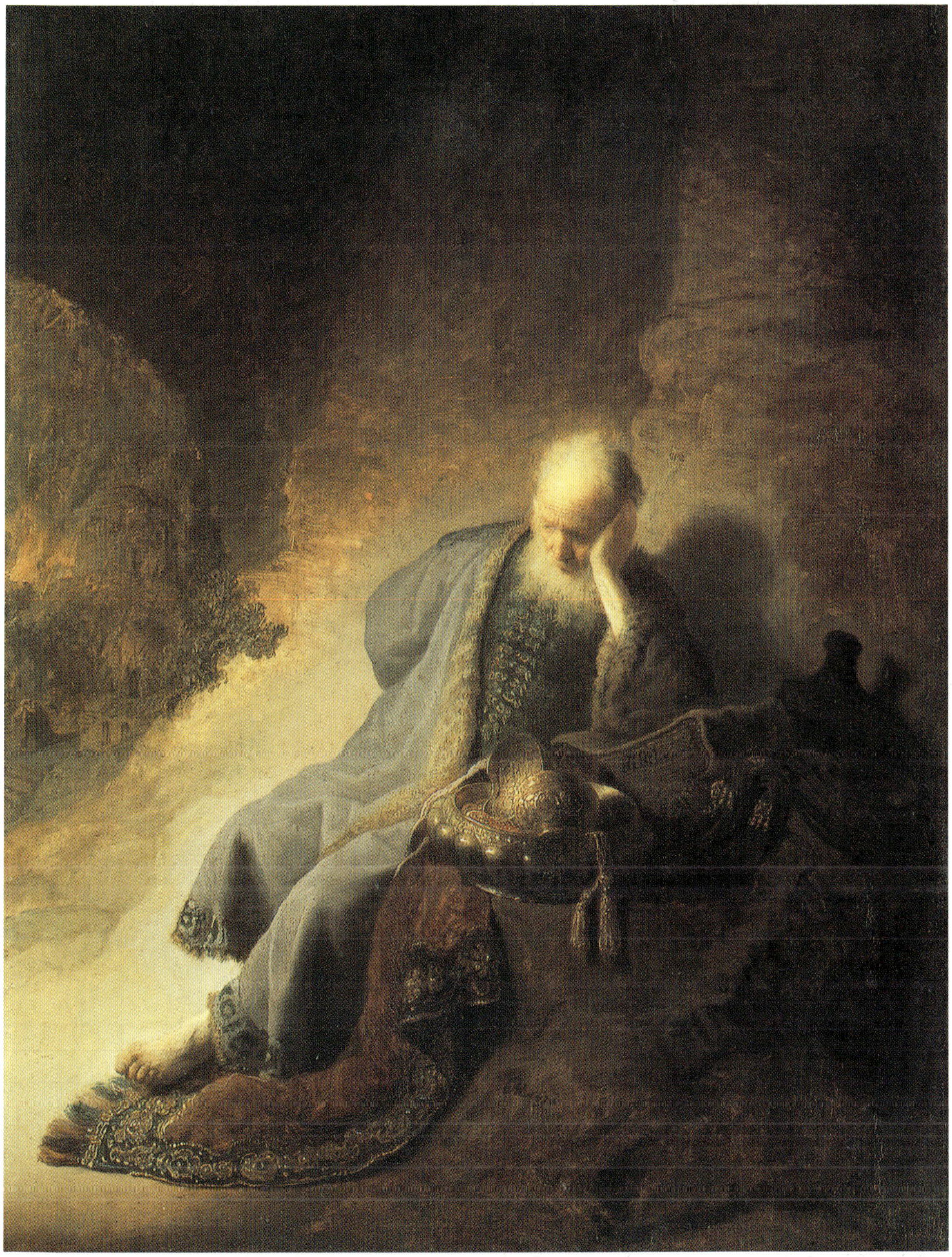

Rembrandt's artistic development can be gauged in the way he has moved away from the precise rendering of descriptive details in every part of the picture toward psychological and emotional emphasis by means of lighting, color contrasts and varied brushwork. Here he focuses attention on the prophet by placing him dramaticallay at the juncture of the light and shadow as well as by contrasting the detailed modeling, rich colors and thick impasto of the figure with surrounding passages of extreme thinness. This creates a sense of spatial depth also.

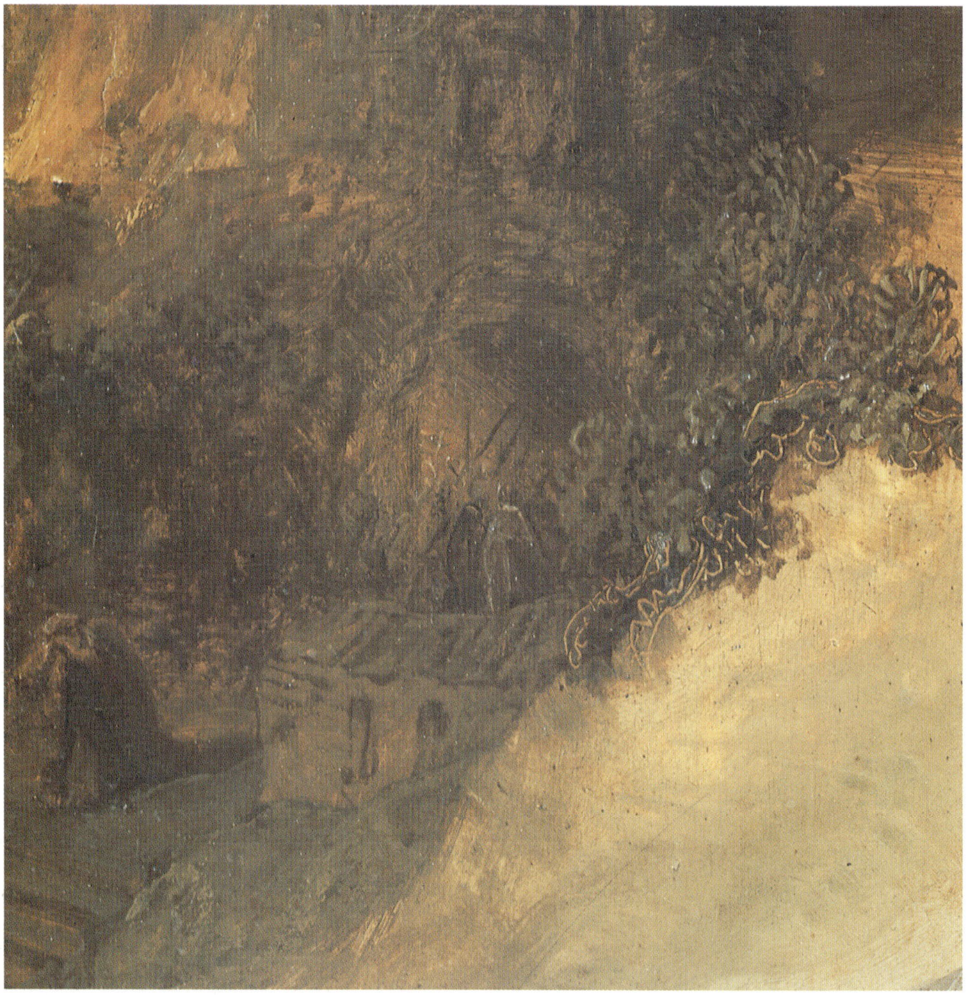

1

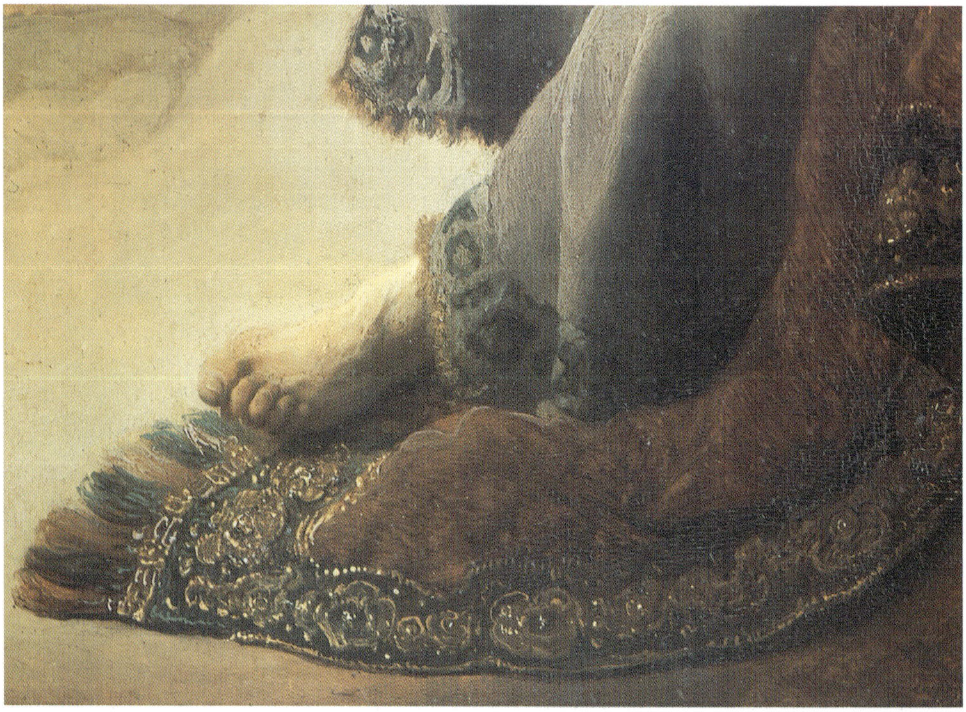

2

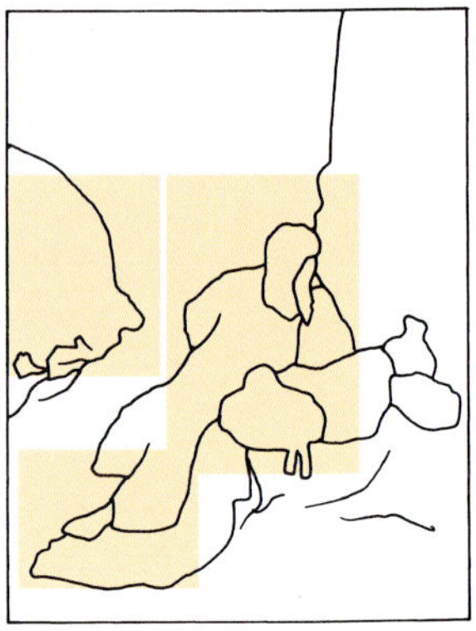

1 The ruins of Jerusalem, the flames and the huddled figures have been evoked with extreme economy, using four colors, each thinly laid over the other, in a fluid wet-on-wet technique. The green of the bush has been partially scraped away in rapid, scribbled strokes.

2 The prophet's foot has been modeled with great accuracy, and the subtle distribution of light and shade over the network of veins precisely recorded. Thin strokes of white follow the ridges of the folds of the gown, executed in minute hatchings, and the deepest areas of shadow are overlaid with glazes of deep black. The pale underlayer is plainly visible beneath the tawny crimson of the robe.

3 *Actual size detail* The bulbous forms of the golden bowl have been sketched in in dark brown outlines over a greenish-ocher middle ground, and the highlights filled in with tawny yellow. Thick drops of lead-white impasto, tinted with yellow, make up the points of reflected light. The technique of scratching through the top paint layer, used here to suggest embroidery on the prophet's chest, is clearly visible. The effect of the wrinkled skin on the arm has been suggested by an uneven, pitted surface of white impasto dragged across a darker underlayer. The deepest areas of shadow — beneath the Bible and on Jeremiah's left shoulder — have been created by the addition of dark brown, translucent glazes.

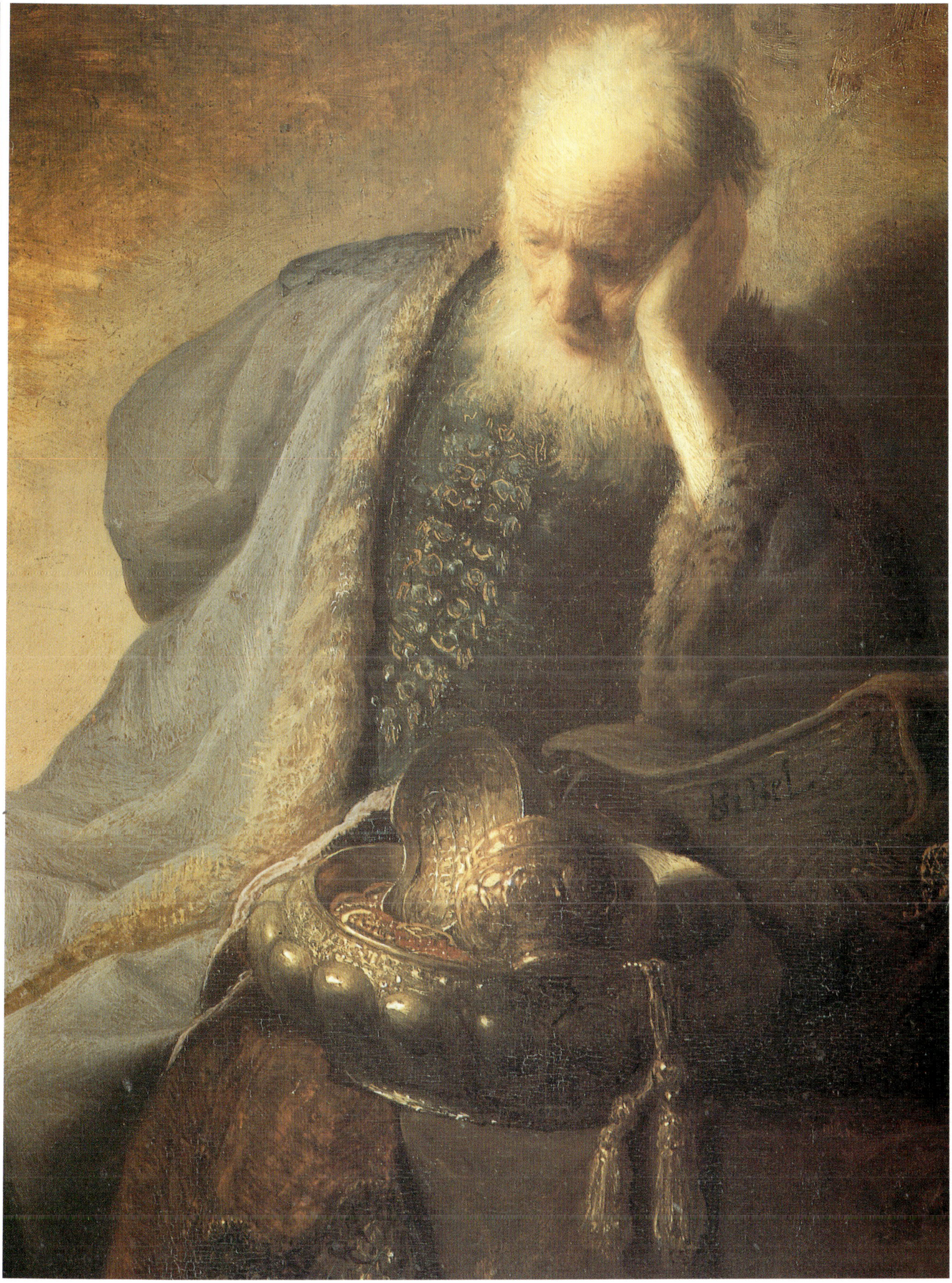

3 *Actual size detail*

BELSHAZZAR'S FEAST

Signed (with indistinct date) c 1637
66×82¼in/167.5×209cm
Oil on canvas
National Gallery, London

By the mid-1630s Rembrandt had established his reputation as a successful young painter in Amsterdam and set about coming to terms with the International High Baroque style. He was undoubtedly familiar with the work of Rubens and of monumental painting in Flanders and Italy, if only through engraved reproductions, and he now tried his hand at painting on a large scale himself, adopting all the stylistic "tricks" of the Baroque painters. Here he has chosen a story that allowed him to exploit to the full his love of exotic costumes and rich objects. Belshazzar, King of Babylon, has given a feast using precious vessels stolen from the Temple of Solomon. At the height of the banquet a mysterious hand appears and writes on the wall, portending the destruction of the city and the death of Belshazzar himself. Rembrandt shows the moment when the king turns around in terror and his guests are thrown into confusion, freezing his characters at the point of maximum drama. This theatrical approach to narrative painting is typical of much seventeenth-century Baroque painting, and has its roots in the work of Caravaggio. The same is true of the compositional device of showing the figures in half-length, pushed close to the picture plane and set against a neutral background.

Though the composition is rather derivative, particularly in the forms of the woman on the extreme right, Rembrandt demonstrates a stunning virtuosity in the range of different painting techniques, and one can see very clearly the stages by which he has built up the composition. He has begun with a brown underlayer, providing a unifying tone to the finished work, visible in the shadows beneath the king's outspread arm and the base color of the tablecloth. He then mapped out the general areas of his forms in cool, "dead" colors — tempera may have been used for these because of its quick-drying qualities. He seems in general to have dispensed with preparatory drawings (very few exist) and to have developed his forms directly in paint as he went along. In the greenish gray coloring of the shadowy flute player to the rear of the lefthand group, one can see the base color from which he fleshed out the skin tones in the other figures. The same green is visible beneath the flesh tints of the bearded man, and have also been used to define the broad outlines of the tablecloth. The dark brown underpainting is visible beneath the red of the woman's gown on the far right. Here one can see Rembrandt's skillful manner of mapping out the general form by "kissing" the dark undercoat with a thin layer of red and then building up a sense of volume by subsequent strokes of the same color, applied thickly enough to be only partially modified by the darker paint beneath. Additional thick dashes of the same red are applied last to suggest those lightest parts where light catches the folds of the material.

It is in the handling of Belshazzar's richly jeweled gown, however, that the virtuosity of handling is most obviously apparent. The effect of the encrustation of gold embroidery and precious stones is rendered in thick swathes of yellow impasto that have been literally modeled in relief with a pointed brush and then partly carved away with a sharp instrument. This method of descriptive modeling is in sharp constrast to the broad suggestion of form that can be seen in passages such as the small plate at the edge of the table on the left, which has been lightly suggested in a couple of loose sweeps of light gray against the original brown underpaint. Such variety of handling shows the young Rembrandt's complete mastery of his medium.

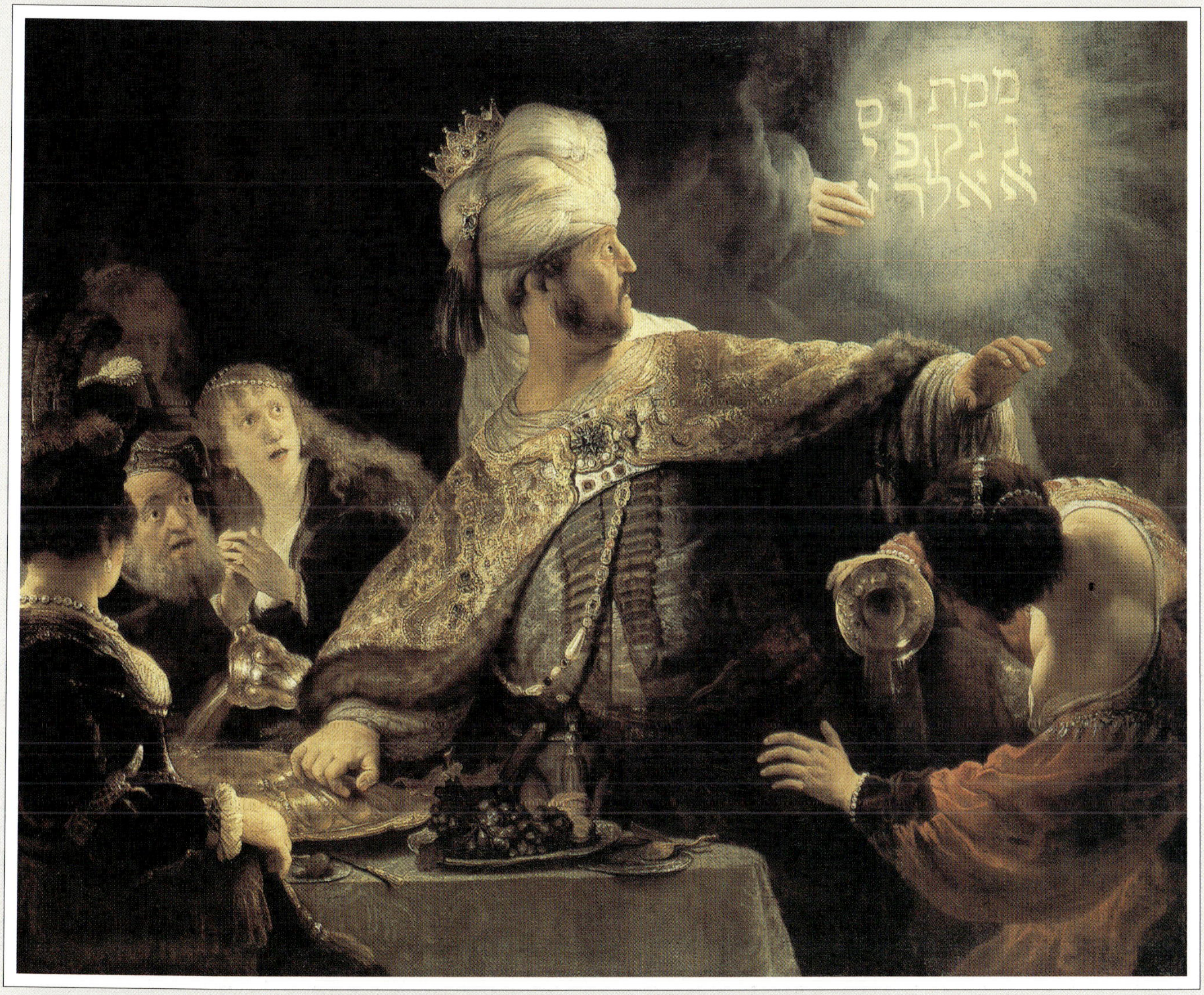

In this, the most theatrical of Rembrandt's paintings discussed here, one can follow very clearly the stages by which the artist has built up his composition. Few other works contain such a wide range of brushwork: from the modeling of the jeweled clasp in thick wet impasto to the rich glazing technique in the far lefthand figure or the broad and confident directional brushwork seen in the folds of the red sleeve.

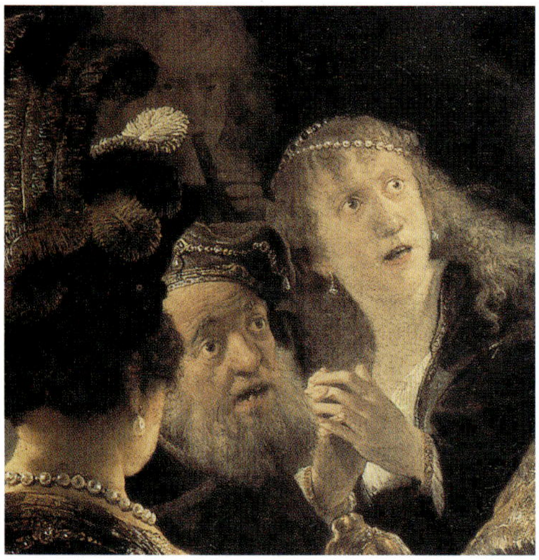

1

2

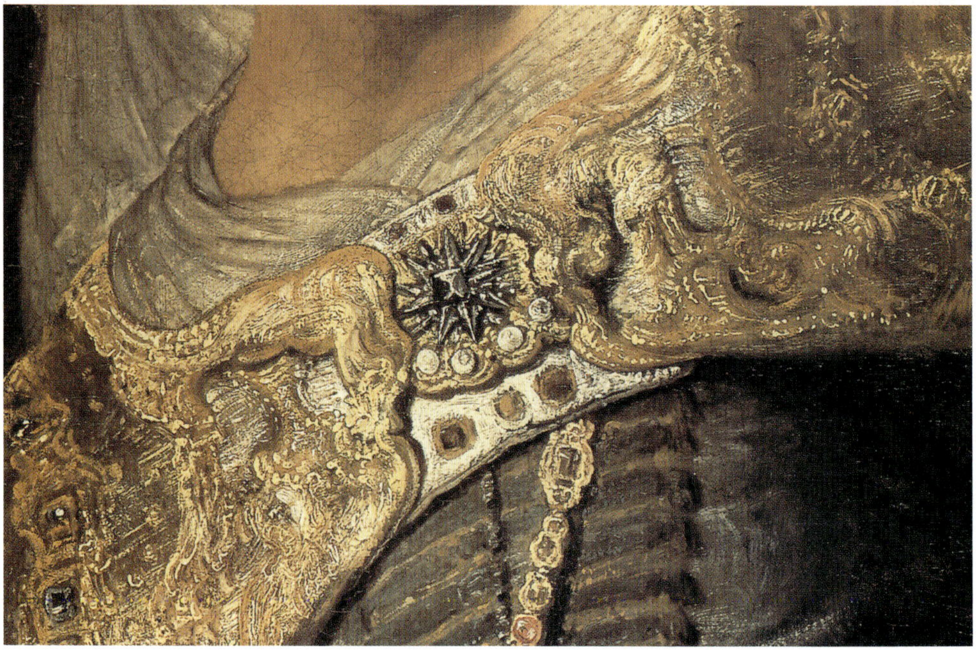

3

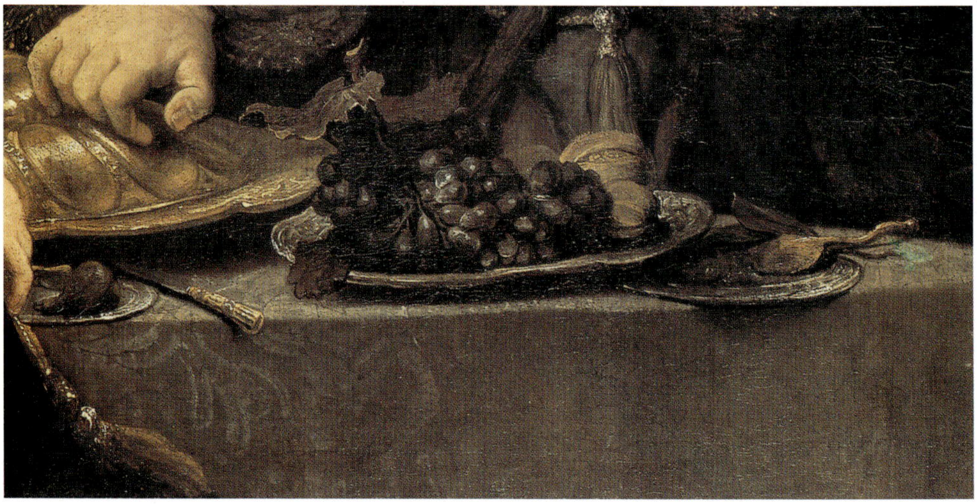

4

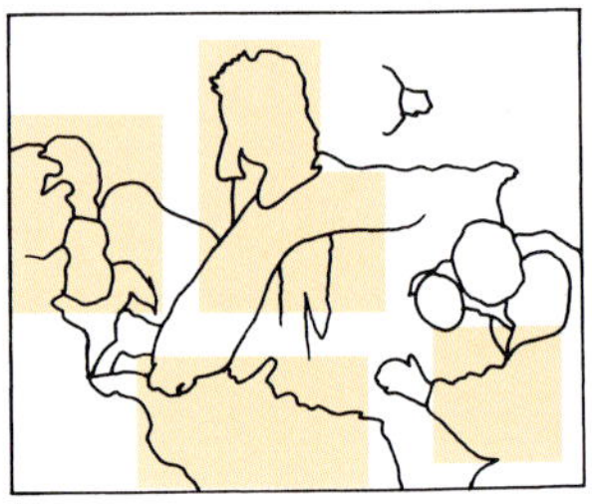

1 The ghostly face of the musician behind the main group shows the first stage of underpainting in dull green from which all the other figures have emerged.

2 The forms of the red sleeve have been achieved by using the same red but in differing degrees of thickness against the brown underpainting. The freely applied squiggles and loops of the drapery suggest the arm's implicit movement.

3 The decoration of the cloak and the jeweled clasp was achieved with two brushes: one thick and rounded, the other fine and pointed. The first was used to create broad grooves, perhaps also using the handle of the brush to create three-dimensional ridges. Touches of wet white were then applied with the pointed brush, with yellow to provide the highlights.

4 The tablecloth is painted in dull green over the brown underpaint, the pattern picked out in thin strokes of white. The plates are conceived with great economy, in rough, sweeping strokes of white or yellow which catch in the grooves of the underpainting, suggesting reflected highlights. The still life of grapes has been very simply drawn in a series of muddy half-tones, set off by touches of white highlight.

5 The head of Belshazzar has been firmly modeled in flesh tones, the highlights and half-shadows painted upon a tan middle ground, most obvious in the nose. Parts of the turban have been very thinly painted and have become transparent with age.

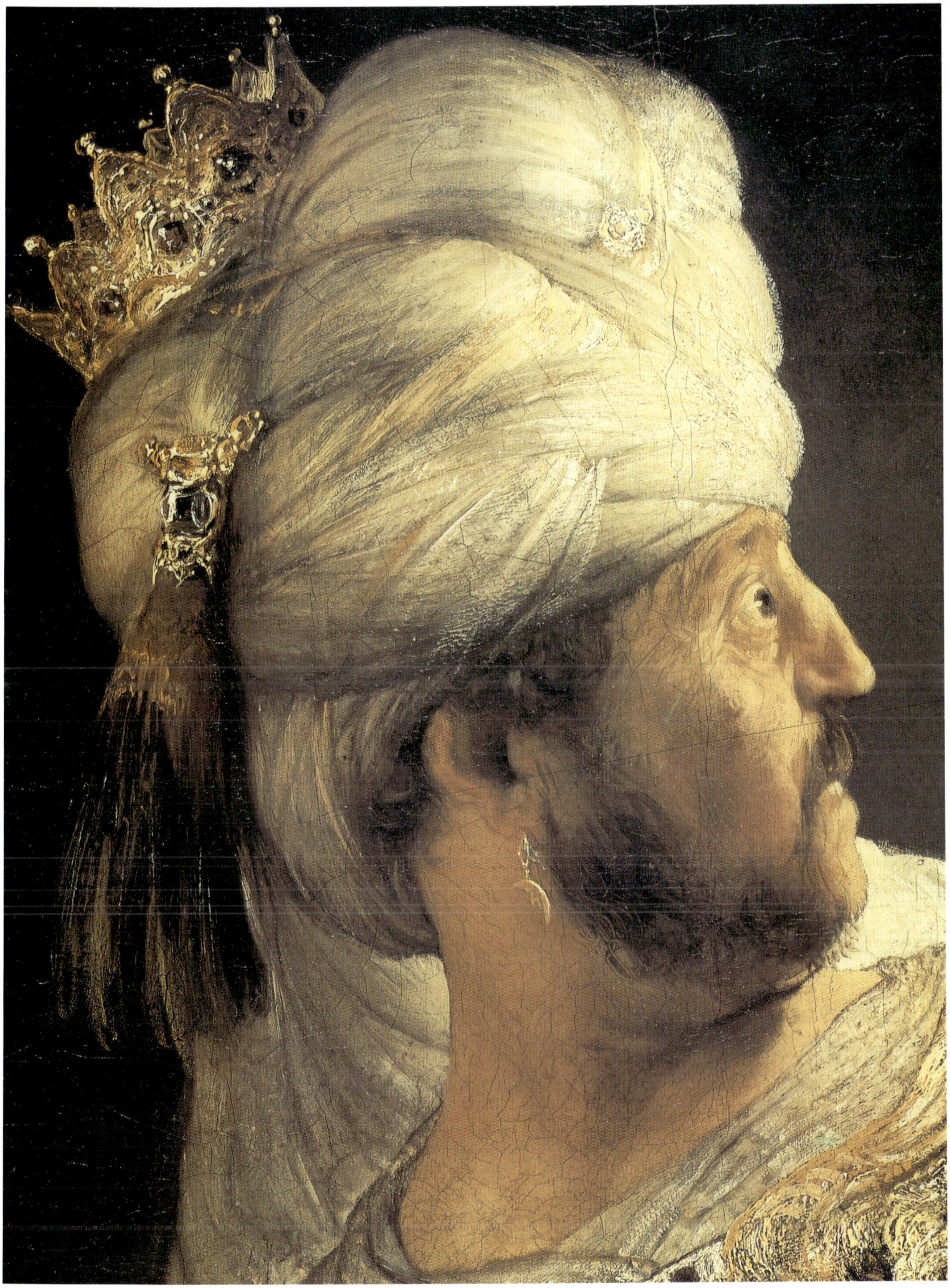

5

Self-portrait

Signed and dated 1640
$39\frac{3}{8} \times 31\frac{1}{2}$in/$100 \times 80$cm
Oil on canvas
National Gallery, London

Rembrandt here has depicted himself as the successful painter, dressed expensively and with an expression of calm assurance. The Baroque rhythms and exuberant outward show which had governed his work throughout the previous decade have been replaced by a sense of "gravitas," echoed in the stable triangular form and the stressed horizontals of cap and sill as well as by the alert but reserved expression. The idea of including the *trompe l'oeil* device of the parapet is a rather artificial convention that had been widely used in Renaissance art, and in fact Rembrandt based his composition on Titian's *Portrait of a Man with Blue Sleeve* (see opposite), widely believed at the time to represent Ludovico Ariosto, the famous Italian poet. At the time this painting was in the collection of Alphonso Lopez, a rich Spanish diamond dealer who also dealt in and collected works of art. He possessed an early Rembrandt, and from extant letters it is clear that they were acquainted with each other. Rembrandt saw in this work and in other Renaissance paintings a restraint and dignity which he found increasingly congenial to the tenor of his own art, but the borrowing from Titian may have a deeper significance as well. It has been suggested that in following Titian so obviously, Rembrandt was consciously comparing himself, the painter, with Ariosto, the poet, and thus claiming a status for painting equal to that of poetry, in the spirit of a theory of the arts that goes back to the Renaissance.

Perhaps taking his lead from Titian, the portrait is much more thinly painted than in the previous works examined here, and he has paid minute attention to descriptive details. The lighting is strong but quite diffuse, the intensity of the strongest lights on cheek, chest and hand softened by a subtle range of half-tones and transparent shadows. The background is relatively light, made up of delicately scumbled greenish yellow and light brown strokes laid over a darker brown underlayer, very obvious by the left cheek and sleeve. This helps to create a greater impression of space between the figure and the background. A sense of shimmering, diffused light is created by the interplay of the thin top layer and the darker tone beneath. The face is very delicately painted, with soft fluid colors built up from a greenish gray base in a series of slightly varying flesh tones blended delicately and almost imperceptibly together. Rembrandt has used at least three different kinds of red — a dullish pink for the cheeks, a more orange-red for the nose and a deeper crimson for the mouth. The passages around the eyes and mouth are made up of extraordinarily delicate touches, applied with a very thin pointed brush on a thin underlayer of wet paint. This delicate pattern of thin blended colors not only builds up the forms of the face, but describes the texture, the color and the exact tonal quality dictated by the fall of light.

The sleeve is more broadly painted in a sequence of browns and blacks, the darkest areas glazed over with additional layers of translucent black and the middle tones and highlights picked out in thicker passages of reddish browns and yellows.

Of all Rembrandt's self-portraits, this is perhaps his most overtly public statement, in its virtuosity of handling, its high degree of finish, and its assured, challenging, bearing.

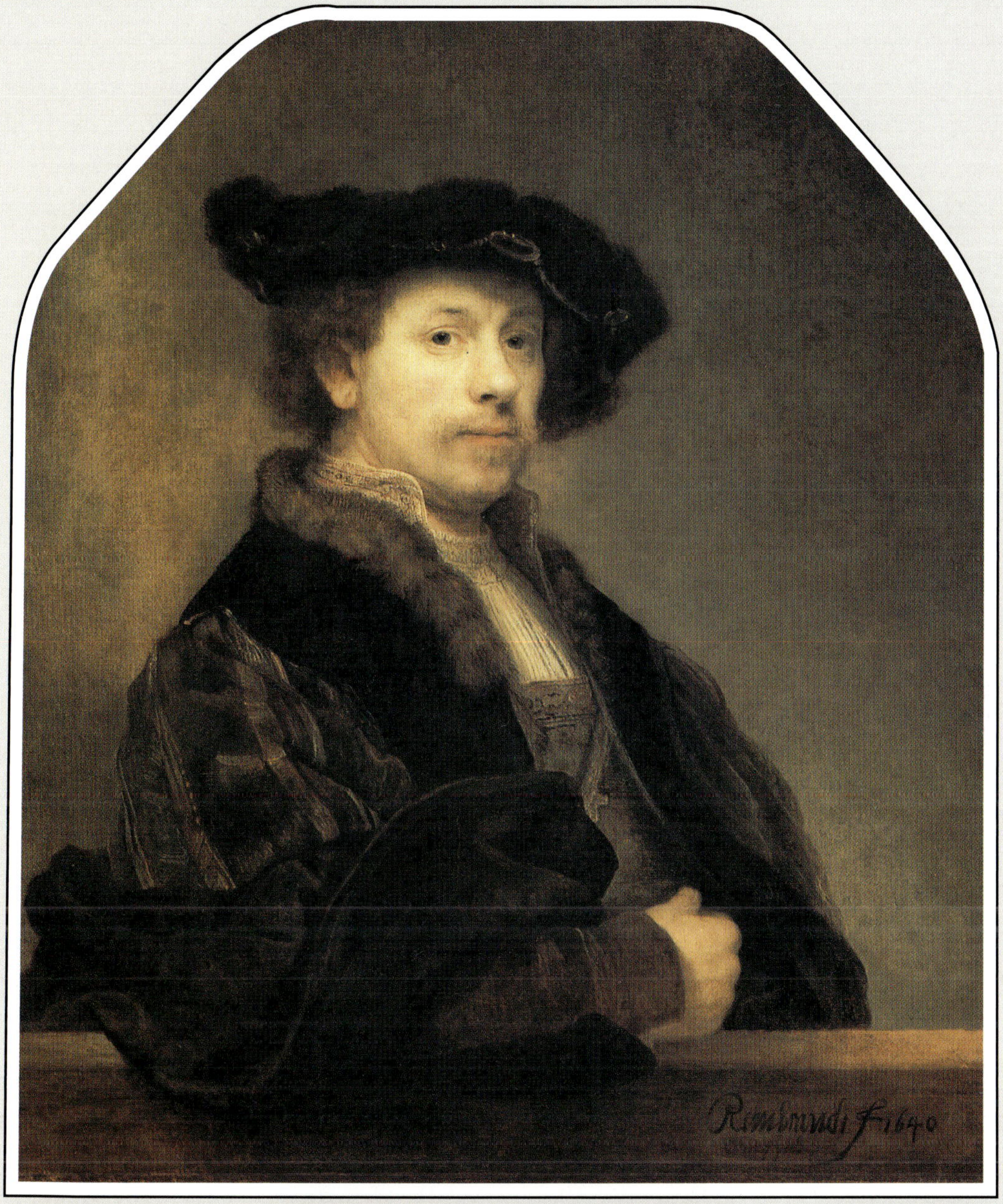

Comparison with Titian's *Man with Blue Sleeve* shows the artist's obvious debt to the Venetian master in terms of pose, the use of the parapet, and the prominence of the sleeve. Yet Rembrandt has made many modifications. The lighting is less dramatically focused and more diffuse than in the Titian, the pose is less in profile, and the sleeve has lost the rhetorical assertiveness of the earlier picture.

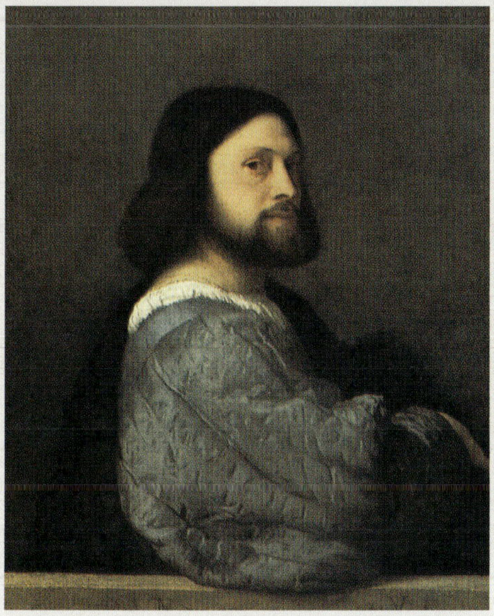

TITIAN
Man With Blue Sleeve
c 1512 National Gallery, London

Titian's youthful masterpiece transformed an older tradition of portraiture and established a new canon. Much greater prominence was given to the torso, and here its elegant *contrapposto* helps to convey the sitter's assured and confident personality. The splendid sleeve, the dramatic lighting and the proud assertive stare combine to make this work one of the epoch-making images in the history of portraiture.

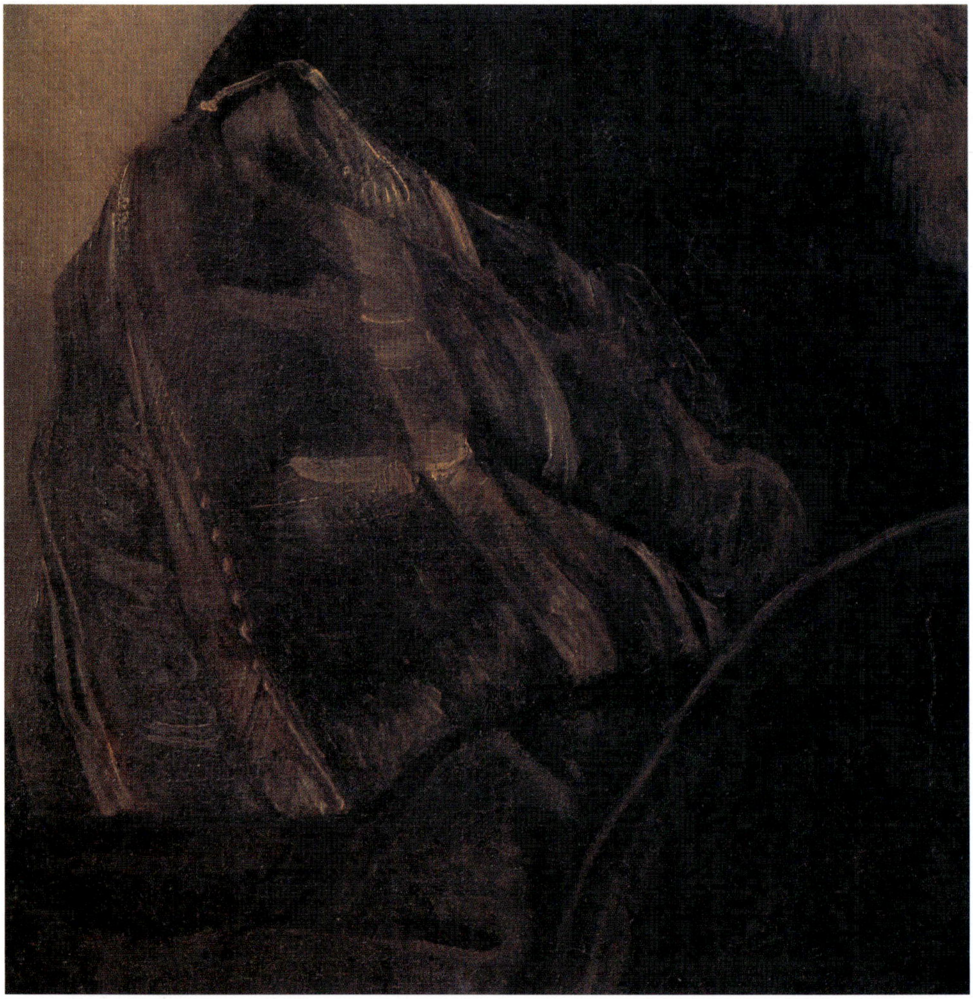

1

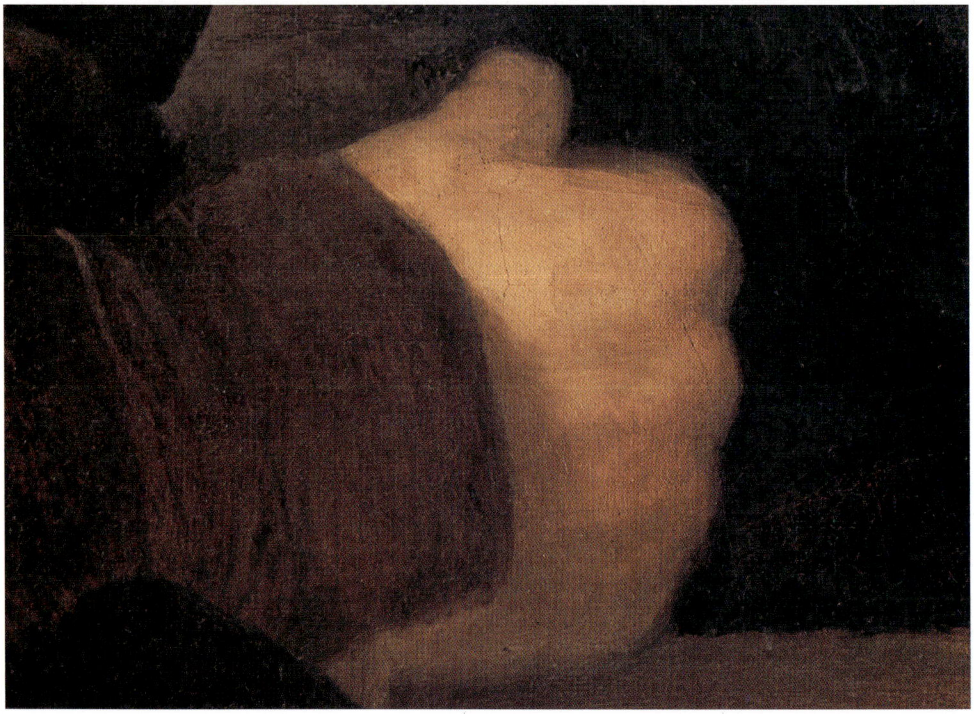

2

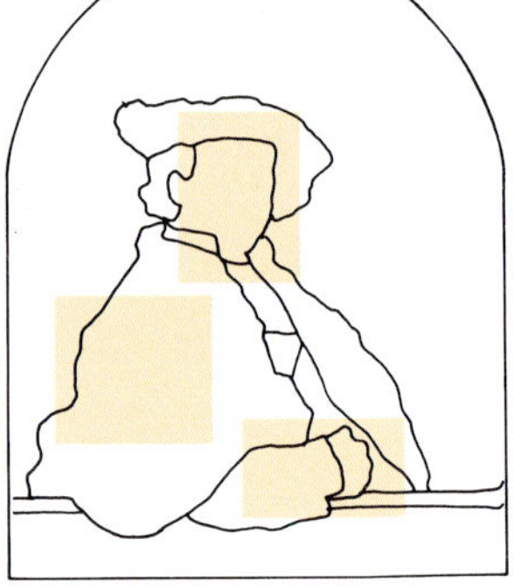

1 The sleeve is painted in a sequence of broadly applied glazes over a general area of brown, the darkest areas rendered in translucent black. The details of the running seams are picked out in lighter, muddy browns and touches of thick yellow impasto.

2 The brightly lit hand is handled in a very broad manner, the forms of the fist only very roughly drawn, and the lightest parts applied in a thick layer of pre-mixed flesh tones over the darker brown of the shadowed area.

3 *Actual size detail* The flesh tones of the face are built up in a series of glazes of the utmost subtlety, each blending all but imperceptibly into the wet layer beneath in a manner that calls for extreme precision of handling. The pouches and lines around the eyes – the part of the face that perhaps reveals most about the artist's character, creating a sense of vulnerability, even anxiety, around the alert stare – are minutely drawn. Very thin brown paint has been used, merging into the wet, lighter skin tone beneath so that they lose their quality as "lines," and assume the character of the shadowed declivities and puckers of the skin.

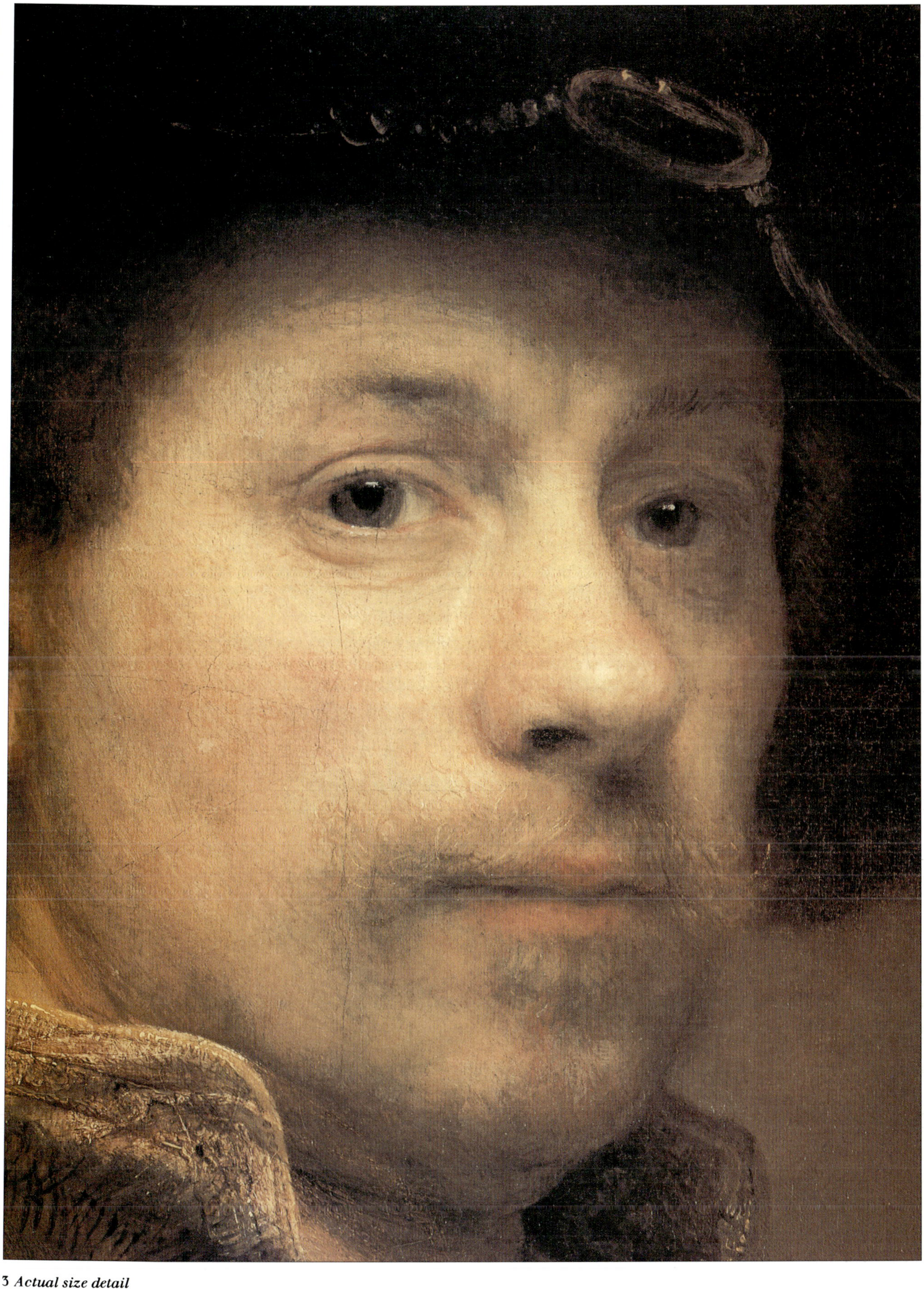

3 *Actual size detail*

The Night Watch

Signed and dated 1642
$141\frac{1}{4} \times 172\frac{1}{2}$in/$359 \times 438$cm
Oil on canvas
Rijksmuseum, Amsterdam

This is perhaps Rembrandt's most celebrated work, as famous among his contemporaries as it is today. Its name is in fact a mistitling, as after cleaning it was found to be a day scene, and it shows the Militia Company of Arquebusiers under the command of Captain Frans Banning Cocq and his lieutenant, Willem van Ruytenburch, preparing to march out. Each city in Holland had a number of militia companies, originally formed for defense in the war against Spain. By 1640, however, the threat to peace had largely evaporated and the companies had grown into societies of high-ranking citizens, somewhat resembling gentleman's clubs. This painting was commisioned to hang in the newly built wing of the company headquarters, along with seven other canvases of militia group portraits by other artists. But as Rembrandt's pupil Samuel van Hoogstraten wrote in a biography of his master, such was the picture's daring and originality of conception that "in comparison, according to some, all the other pieces there look like packs of playing cards."

The work represents the apogee of Rembrandt's treatment of the group portrait, for he has completely subordinated the demands of portraiture to those of large-scale narrative painting with unprecedented originality. (Each sitter paid a sum commensurate with his prominence within the painting.) The Captain is ordering his lieutenant to give the signal of departure, and the other members of the company adopt appropriate gestures in readiness, one loading a musket, another raising the standard, the drummer beating a roll on his drum and so on. The names of eighteen members of the company depicted are inscribed on the stone cartouche to the right of the portal, and the scene has been fleshed out with a number of peripheral figures, including dogs and children (Rembrandt's own features can be glimpsed to the immediate right of the standard-bearer's shoulder). Onto this complex arrangement of figures Rembrandt has imposed a lively pattern of chiaroscuro combined with a palette of rich color, both of which serve to emphasize the chief protagonists. The dominant combination of deep red, lemon yellow and black that make up the two central characters is repeated and echoed in touches throughout the whole composition, most notably in the red uniform of the musketeer and the bright yellow of the little girl to the right of the central group. Her prominence is explained by the claws of the chicken at her belt – claws were the symbol of the company — and this points up the fact that the scene is symbolic rather than a faithful representation of an actual event.

No other work shows quite such rich and varied handling of the brush: in the thin and schematic painting of the background architecture; in the rapid sequence of glazes that make up the standard-bearer's sash; in the minutely drawn "high-relief" modeling of the trimmings of the lieutenant's tunic; and finally, in the broad suggestion of velvet folds in the righthand musketeer's costume, done by free sweeps and clotted question-marks of thick red paint. Despite the fact that the work was cut down at the top and sides in the eighteenth century, it remains, in its ingenuity of composition and variety of technique, one of Rembrandt's most successful works.

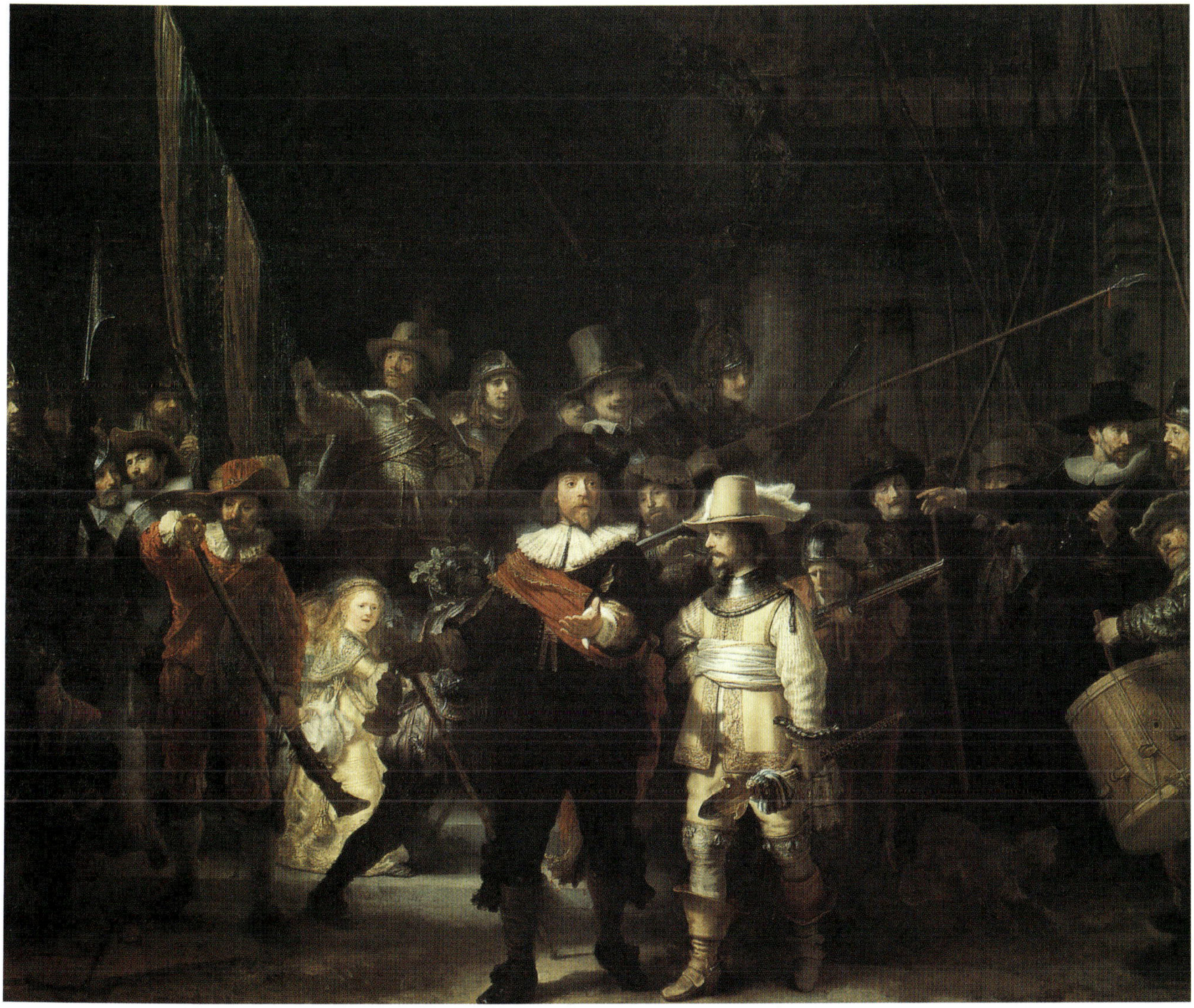

This is one of Rembrandt's largest extant works, and in few other paintings has he displayed such a wide range of brushwork. It acts as both a group portrait and as a narrative composition, and technique has been used in the service of both traditions.

Passages of highly detailed descriptive painting, combined with bright lighting, accentuate certain key figures and differentiate them from the mass, while other subsidiary figures — some are not actual portraits — are more generally treated.

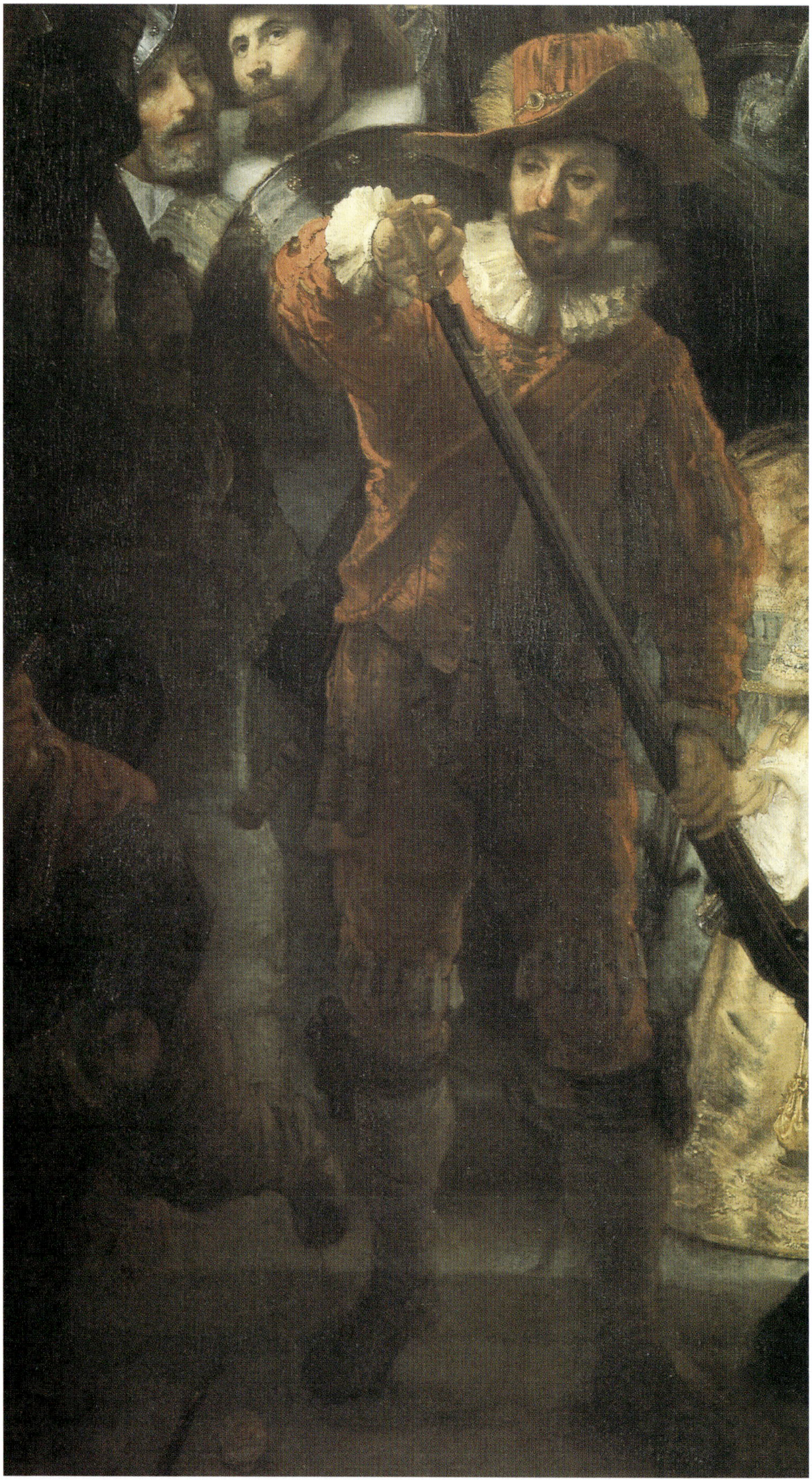

1

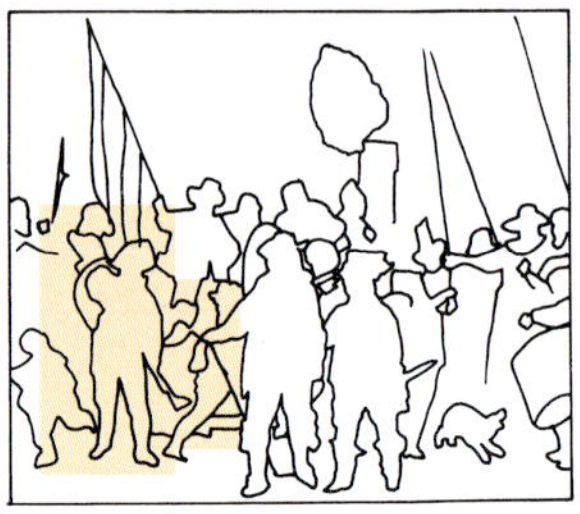

1 The handling of paint on the red-clothed figure presents a great contrast with that of the girl (see opposite); it is far less detailed and more loosely handled. The dark underlayer is traceable in the brown tinge of the shadows, and the colors have been worked up in a broad, thin red overlay that allows the brown to show through. Onto this were superimposed the bright reds and darks of the folds, the brushstrokes being particularly evident in the highlights beneath the right arm.

2 The strange, symbolic motif of a dead chicken hung from the waist of the small girl has been given a deliberate prominence by the use of bright colors that form a striking contrast with the darker tones of the surrounding figures, particularly the silhouette of the musket in front. The shimmering brightness of both the dress and the feathers of the chicken has been achieved by the application of closely painted lemon yellow against a darker ground layer, highlighted with thick lead-white impasto. The suggestion of rich embroidery on the collar has been achieved by a great variety of brushstrokes, from small descriptive dashes along the hem to thin glazes of blue and passages of thick white impasto for the brightest parts.

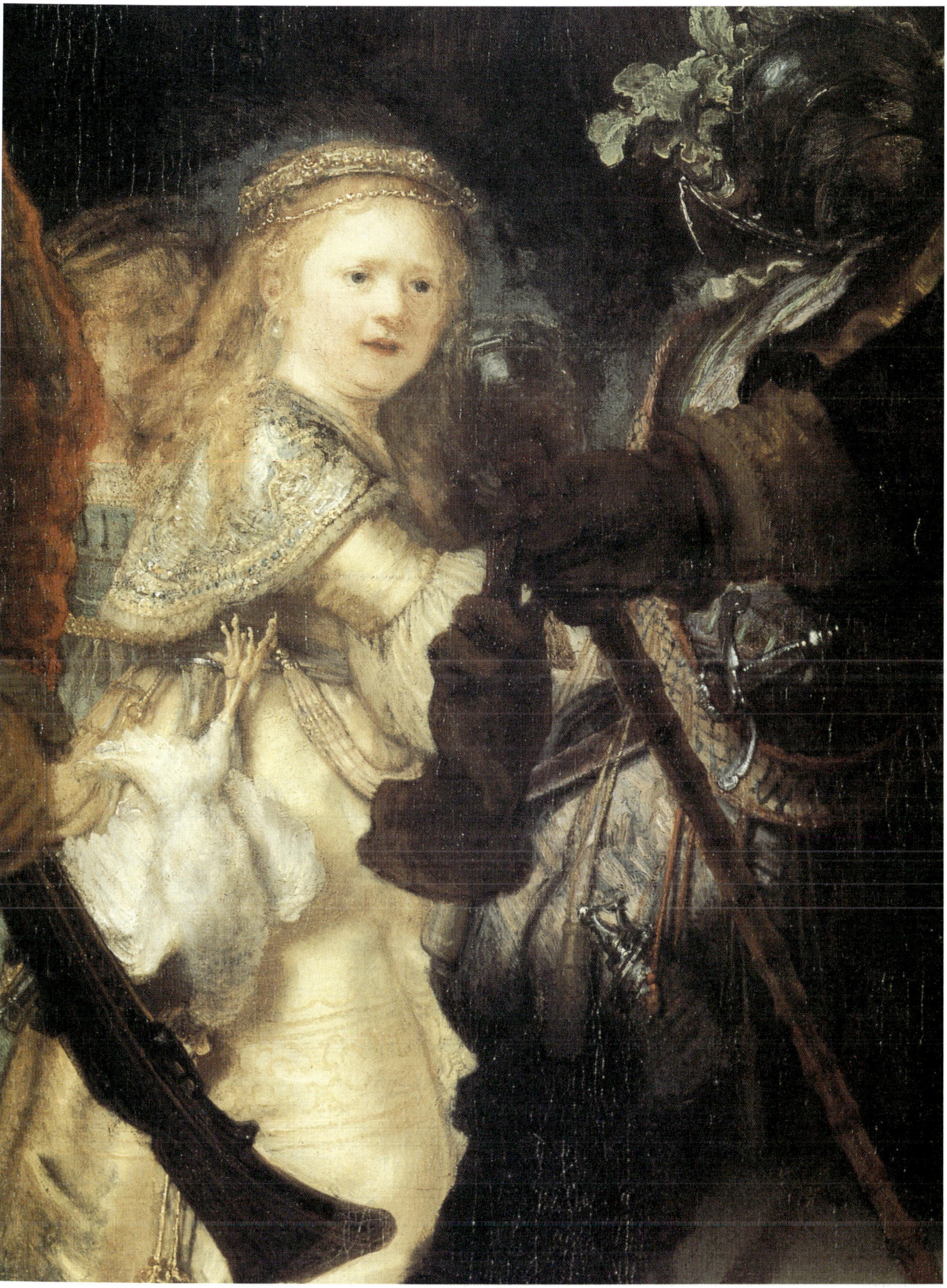

2

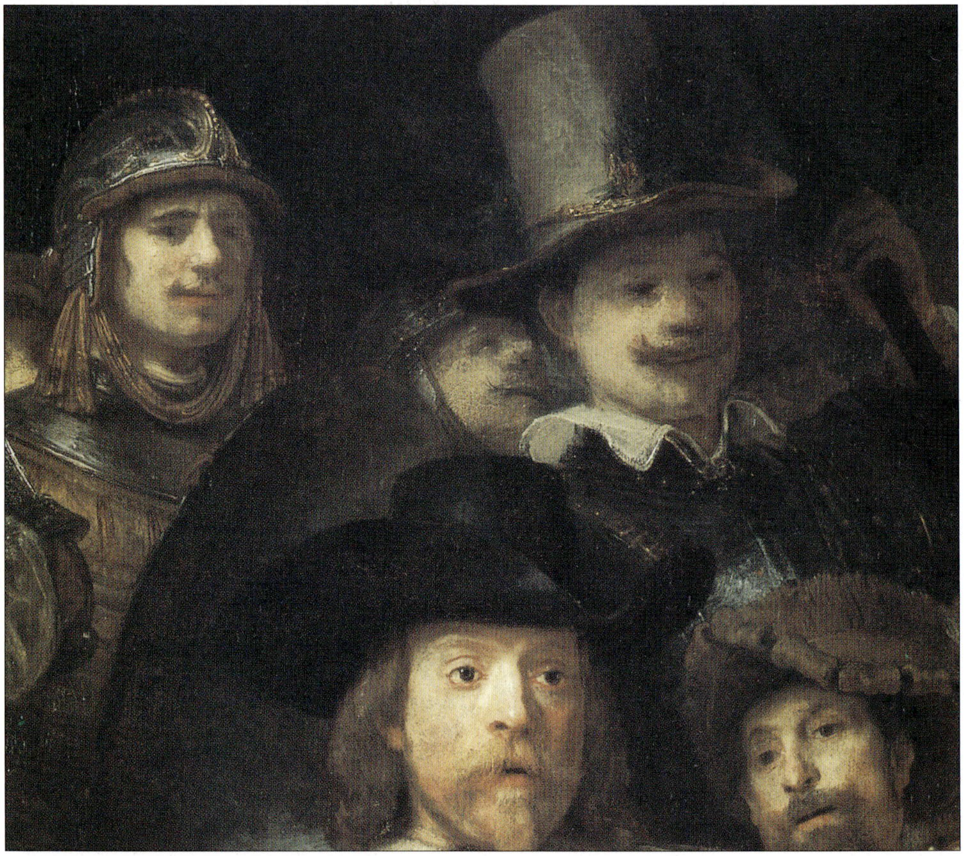

3

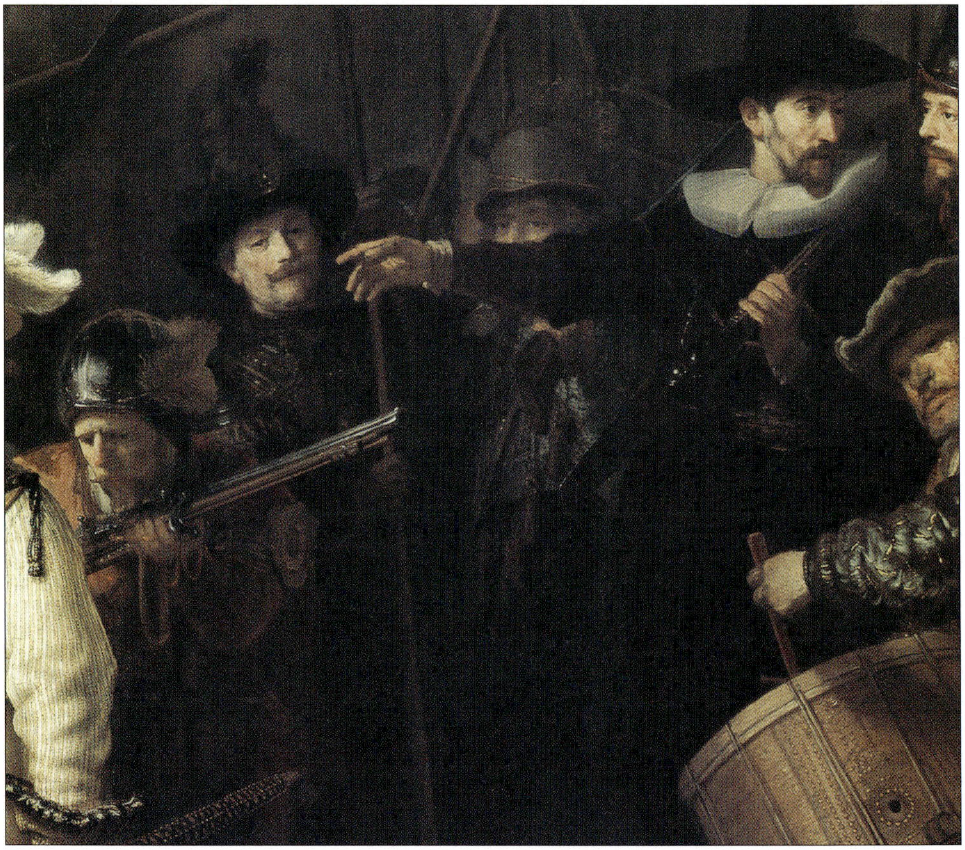

4

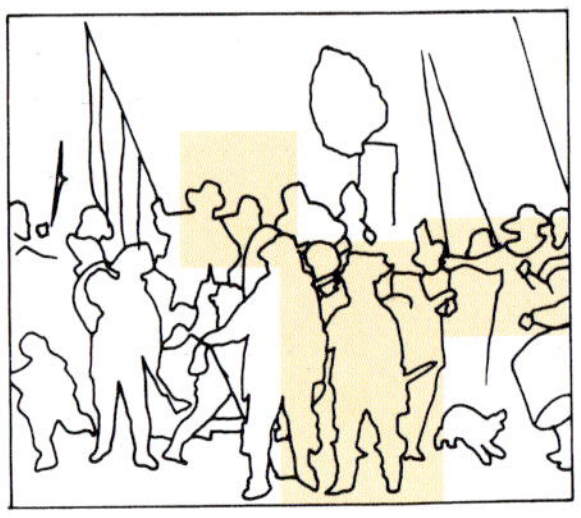

3 The head, or part of a face, glimpsed on the far left above the shoulder of the man in armor is traditionally supposed to be a self-portrait, although such is its obscurity that it is impossible to be certain. Given the nature of the commission – a large-scale figurative scene – it is possible that Rembrandt was aware of and was following a well-established self-portrait tradition that went back to the Italian Renaissance.

4 The painting was cut down at the sides at some point after its execution and the figure of the drummer and the man immediately above him have been seriously curtailed. The apparent lack of finish to the face of the drummer, as compared with the treatment of the other faces, is probably due to damaged paint surface rather than any deliberate device of the artist. His sleeve and drum are rendered with painstaking care.

5 The extremely high degree of finish of the passages of embroidery and in the ceremonial spear constitute the most detailed parts of the whole painting. In the treatment of the clasps securing the jacket there is a literal description of forms modeled in high relief that is comparable to the treatment of details in the earlier *Tobit and Anna*. The gold- and pearl-embroidered border and leggings have been executed over a broadly painted yellow ground in small loops and dashes of brown paint, with occasional stronger accents of the same color in the areas of shadow. These have been overlaid with touches of tawny yellow and tiny points of white impasto.

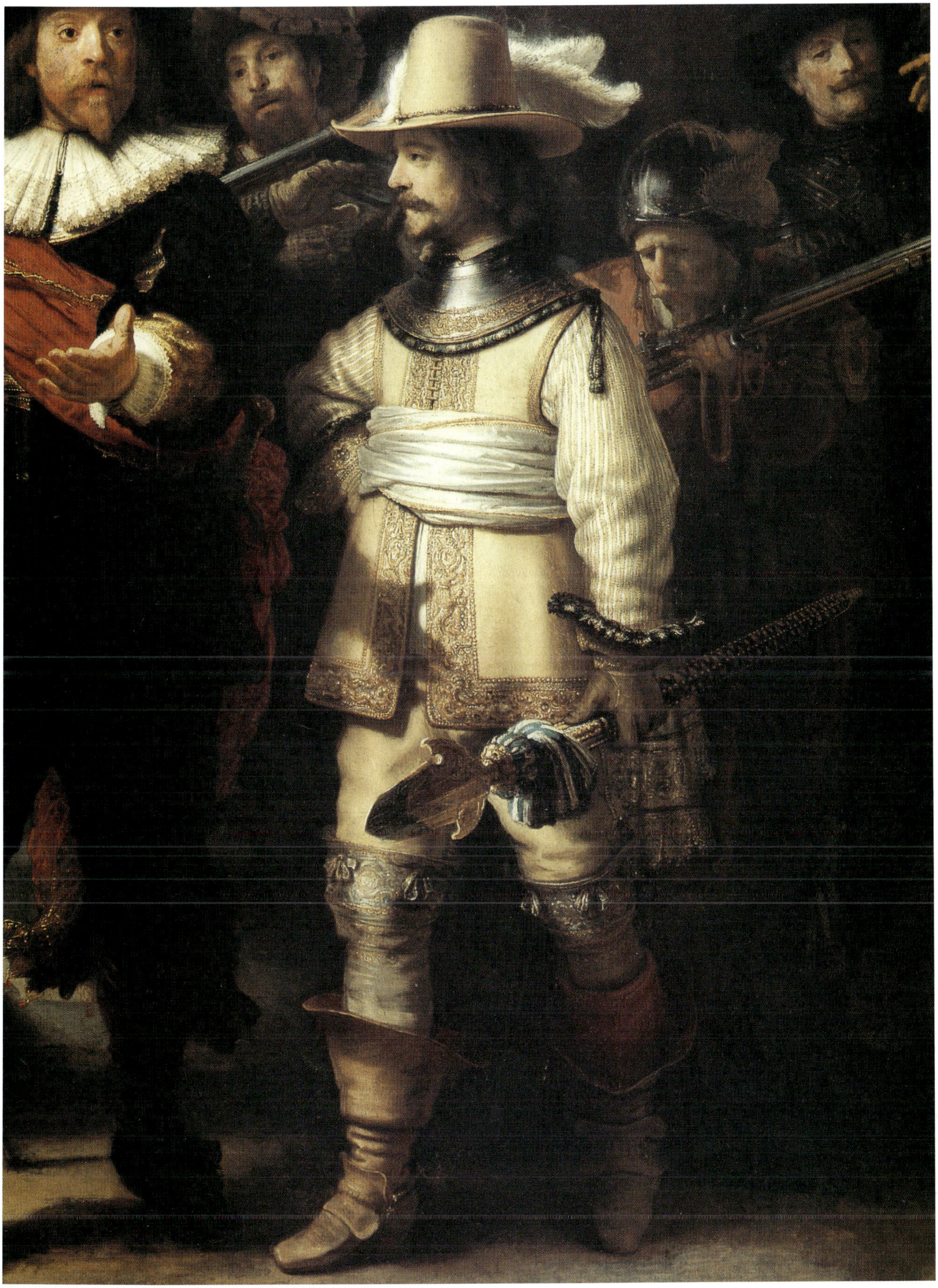

5

The Adoration of the Shepherds

Signed and dated 1646
25¾×21¾in/65.5×55cm
Oil on canvas
National Gallery, London

In this work one can see the sharp change in style that had become apparent in Rembrandt's work by the mid-1640s. The canvas is quite small, and the mood evoked is one of quiet and restraint. The gestures of the assembled figures are entirely natural, with none of the rhetoric of *The Night Watch* or *Belshazzar's Feast*, and they have clearly been studied carefully from life. Rembrandt approaches the mystery of the Nativity from a wholly human standpoint; indeed the only symbolic element that might suggest supernatural significance is the extraordinary light that seems to emanate from the Christchild, bathing the onlookers in a mysterious glow. This symbolic function of light is accompanied by a new breadth of technique. Rembrandt applies the colors in flat, succinct brushstrokes which now barely serve to model form or indicate texture. The Virgin's face, arm and torso, for example, are made up from a small number of dabs of unmodulated color, which only assume the suggestion of form when viewed from a distance. A single brushstroke of thick, creamy black suggests the forms of the ox's neck, the ridges of paint on either side of it reflecting light and thus giving an actual impression of three-dimensional form. The kneeling shepherd immediately in front of the Christchild has been created by a few strokes in black against the darker brown background which describe with the utmost economy his attitude of deep humility. This painting style is directly related to his manner of drawing at this time in which all extraneous details are sacrificed to the task of catching in its most concentrated form that attitude of a figure which best reveals its inner state. By suggesting form rather than carefully describing it Rembrandt bypasses the surface distractions of the external world and concentrates on the expression of pure feeling. The result is an image of extraordinary emotional power.

This is heightened by the lighting, which creates a warm, hazy, atmospheric effect which muffles features and mingles forms and shadows. The highlights that describe the Christchild contrast with the thinner treatment of the light shed by the lantern, falling in muted pools on the ground in the lower righthand side. This effect is created by a loose wet-into-wet technique in which touches of lighter color are painted onto a wet, dark brown undercoat, so that at times the lighter color is modified by mixing with the brown. The uneven, mottled effect made in this way provides a rich surface texture that, together with the range of carefully calculated half-tones and reflections, creates an atmosphere of hushed mystery in which the figures play out their solemn roles.

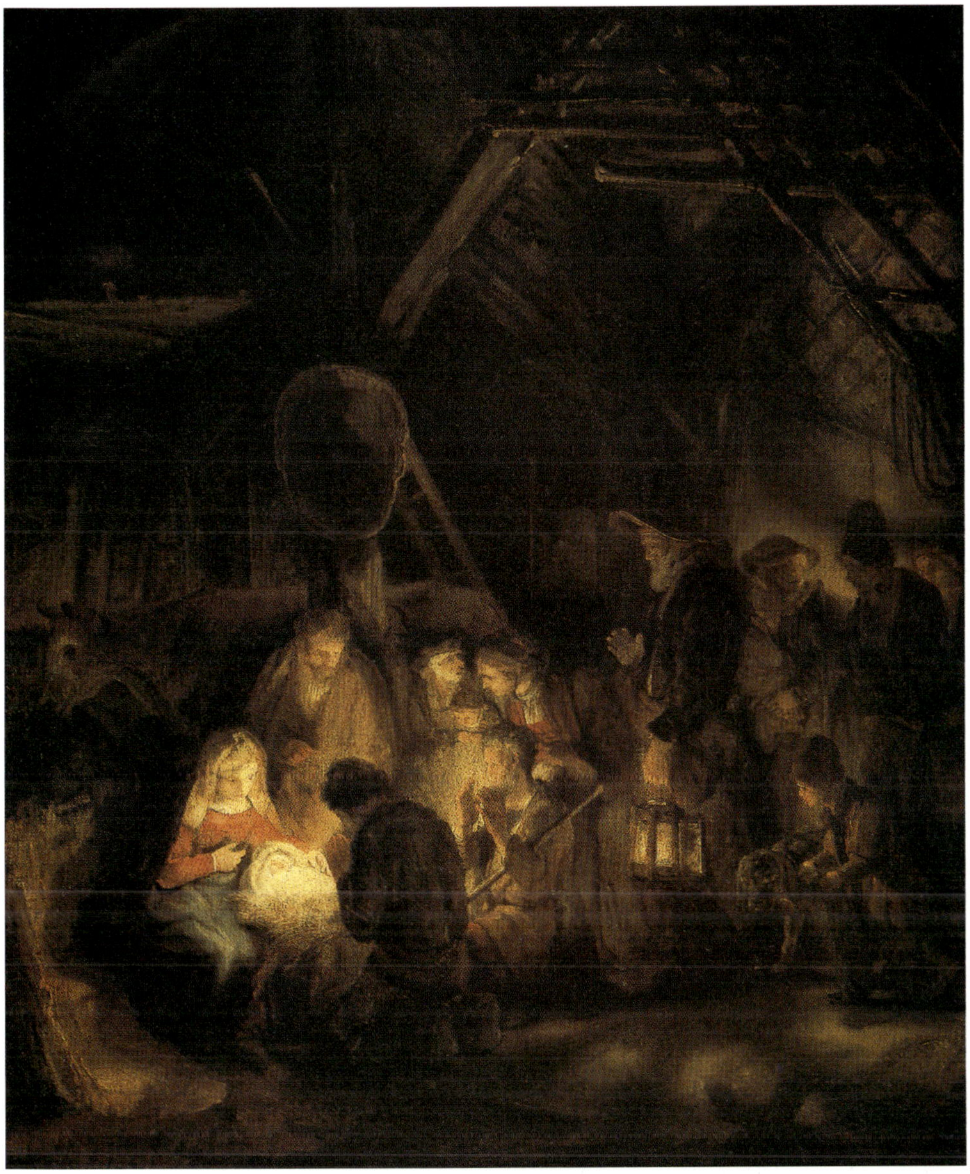

This is one of several small-scale Biblical works of the 1640s in which the figures are treated in the tradition of contemporary Dutch *genre* painting. It may possibly reflect the beliefs of the Mennonites, a Protestant sect which placed great importance on the Biblical injunction to "love thy neighbor" and with which Rembrandt is known to have been closely associated. This could have had some bearing on the way Rembrandt expressed divine events in everyday, down-to-earth terms, easily accessible to his contemporaries, and with an emphasis on individual humility and quiet devotion.

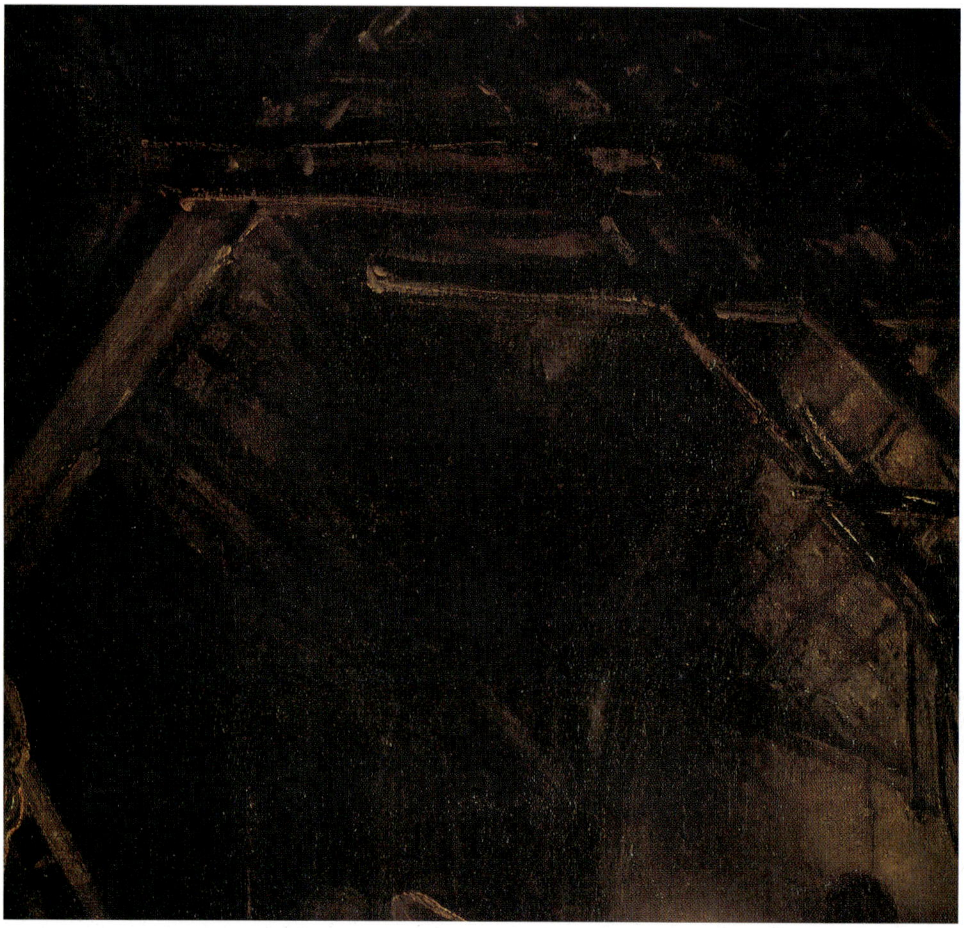

1

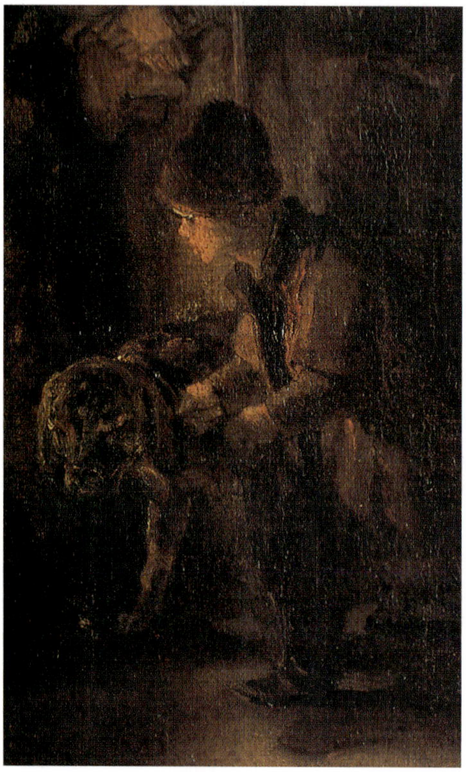

2

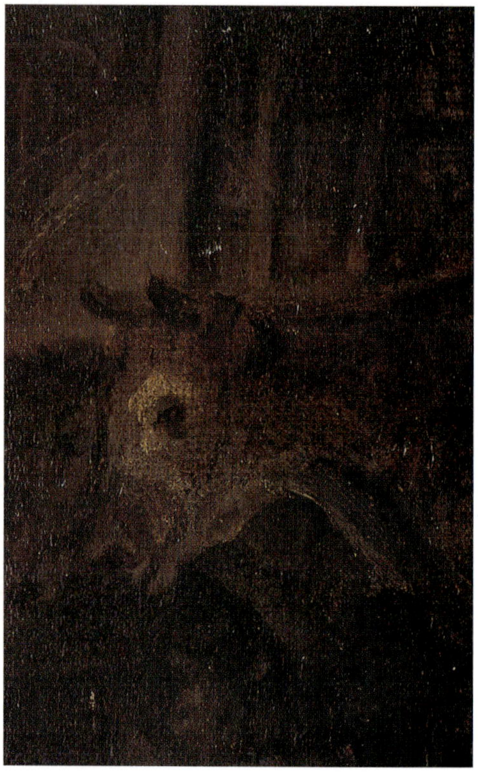

3

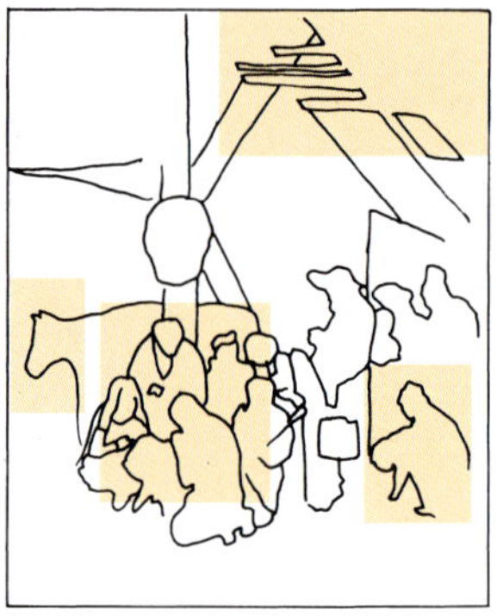

1 The warm atmosphere of the central group is extended even to the rafters in the outermost part of the composition, where the reflected lights are made up of touches of red and orange-yellow set against the deep brown of the shadows. Once again the broad handling is accompanied by a complex tonal range.

2 The details of boy and dog have been picked out over a brown underlayer of small, thin touches of paint. Tiny dabs of red indicate the local color of the tunic; touches of deeper brown and black articulate folds and shadows; the outlines of the dog have been picked out very simply in white highlight and touches of black against the dark ground.

3 The ox has been sketched in with great economy in a sequence of thin, warm browns; the collarbone, ears and front part of the head roughly outlined in black, while the throat and mouth have been picked out in lighter brown, palely reflecting the light of the central group. A single creamy brushstroke, applied so as to leave ridges on either side, suggests in almost literal three-dimensional form the shape of the neck.

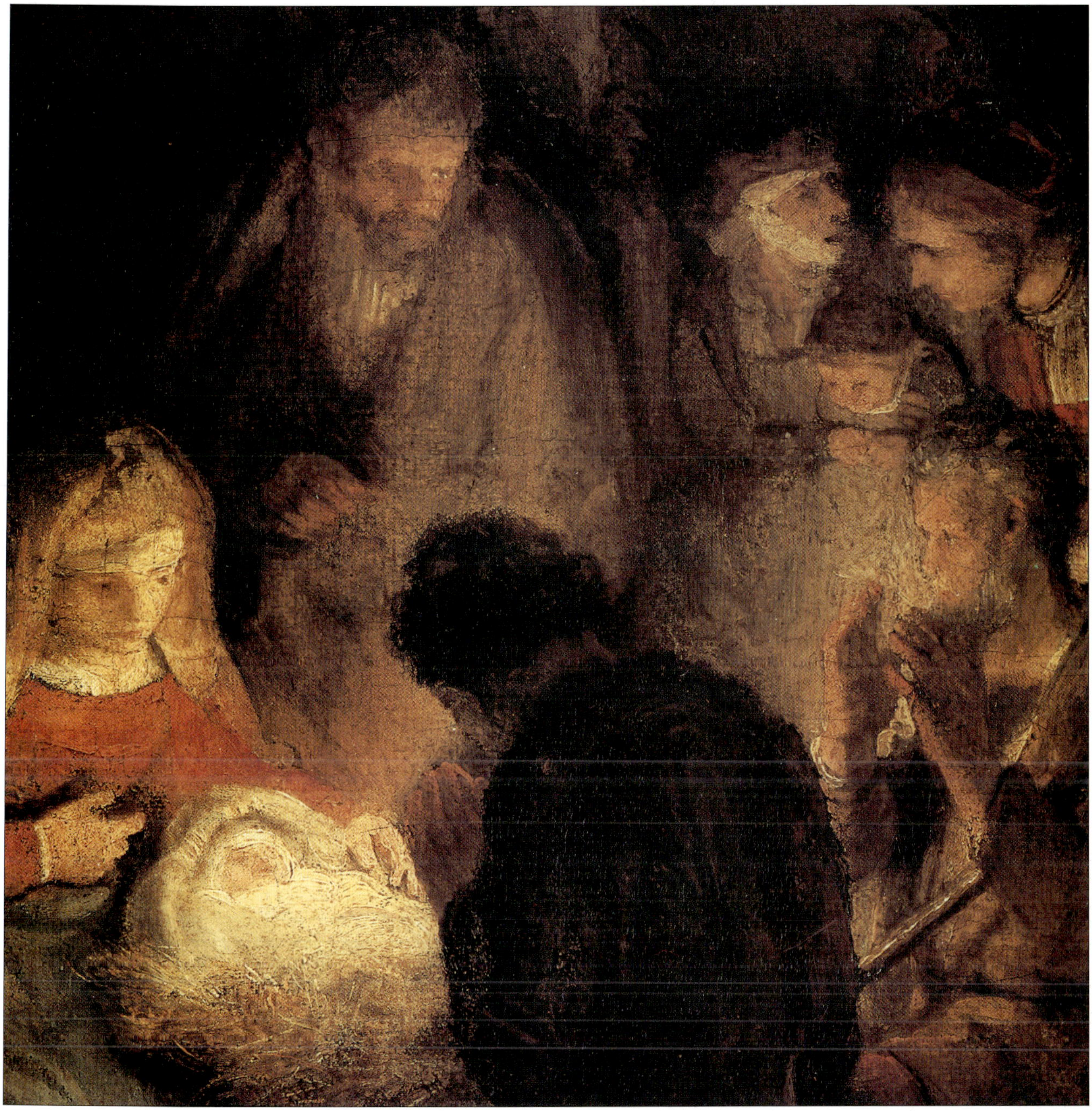

4 *Actual size detail* The simplicity and economy of Rembrandt's brushwork is very clearly shown in this detail, in which expressions are caught with the smallest touches of paint. The paint is very thin here, with the folds of drapery, half-tones and local colors indicated by small, free touches of tinted varnish over a medium-dark ground. The areas of thickest color are reserved for the most strongly lit parts, for instance the Christchild's swaddling clothes and the figure of the Virgin. The warm, hazy *sfumato* effect is achieved by an almost imperceptible mingling of yellows and browns of varying tone that charges the atmosphere and merges the figures and surrounding space.

Young Woman Bathing

Signed and dated 1655
$24\frac{3}{8} \times 18\frac{1}{2}$ in/62×47 cm
Oil on canvas
National Gallery, London

This work vividly demonstrates Rembrandt's growing ability to combine rich color harmonies with a complex chiaroscuro system and an astonishingly broad and sensual handling of paint. In certain passages, the brushstrokes have become almost independent of the forms they describe. The small scale and spontaneous quality of the painting suggests an oil sketch, although Rembrandt has chosen to sign and date it.

Any precise indication of the work's subject has been left unclear, although the richly embroidered garments on the river bank perhaps suggest the Old Testament subject of "Susannah Bathing." It shows a rather stockily built woman, traditionally thought to be Hendrickje Stoffels, carefully raising her undershirt as she wades into the water, apparently completely wrapped in thought. Her beauty lies in the unconscious way in which she unwittingly reveals her upper thighs, a potentially erotic gesture which is emptied of any lascivious content by its very naturalness. Rembrandt's conception of beauty lies, not so much in the idea of inherent beauty of form, but in the revelation, often in a private moment, of an unstudied attitude of grace which captures the inner, private character.

The variety of brushwork is dazzling. The outline of the figure has been roughly mapped out in dark brown strokes, which convey a marvelous sense of volume and of underlying bone structure, as for example in the definition of the right arm and hand. The flesh tones of the face and legs have been strongly modeled with fluidly applied directional brushstrokes of varying tinges of flesh color, blended wet-into-wet and applied so as to follow the shape of the forms they describe. These contrast vividly with the treatment of the shirt, which is made up of loose strokes of beige, light blue and yellow, laid beneath a thrilling sequence of thick impasto strokes of creamy white, smeared with extraordinary freedom with the brush and palette knife, and gouged in places with the brush handle, leaving ridges in high relief. These describe almost literally the three-dimensional form in the folds of the cloth.

The right forearm is articulated by a single flat brushstroke extending from elbow to wrist, which succeeds in conveying volume when viewed from a distance. The left shoulder and arm have been treated in a very abstract manner, the lines of the initial rapid sketch clearly visible, the sleeve of the shirt barely glazed over the light brown underpaint, and the arm composed merely of flat lozenges of highlights and darks. The background and righthand side of the painting have been thrown into deep shadow by a varnish of dark glazes that spills over onto the shoulder and partly obscures the face. Once again the shadows establish the mood of the work and deepen the sense of the young woman's rapt self-absorption. The same shadows seep into the colored reflections in the water, which are magically suggested by thin, fluid glazes of deep red, browns and golden yellows over a light beige underlayer, the gentle ripples picked out in touches of white impasto. In few other works does Rembrandt so skillfully interweave lights and darks with so suggestive and allusive a touch.

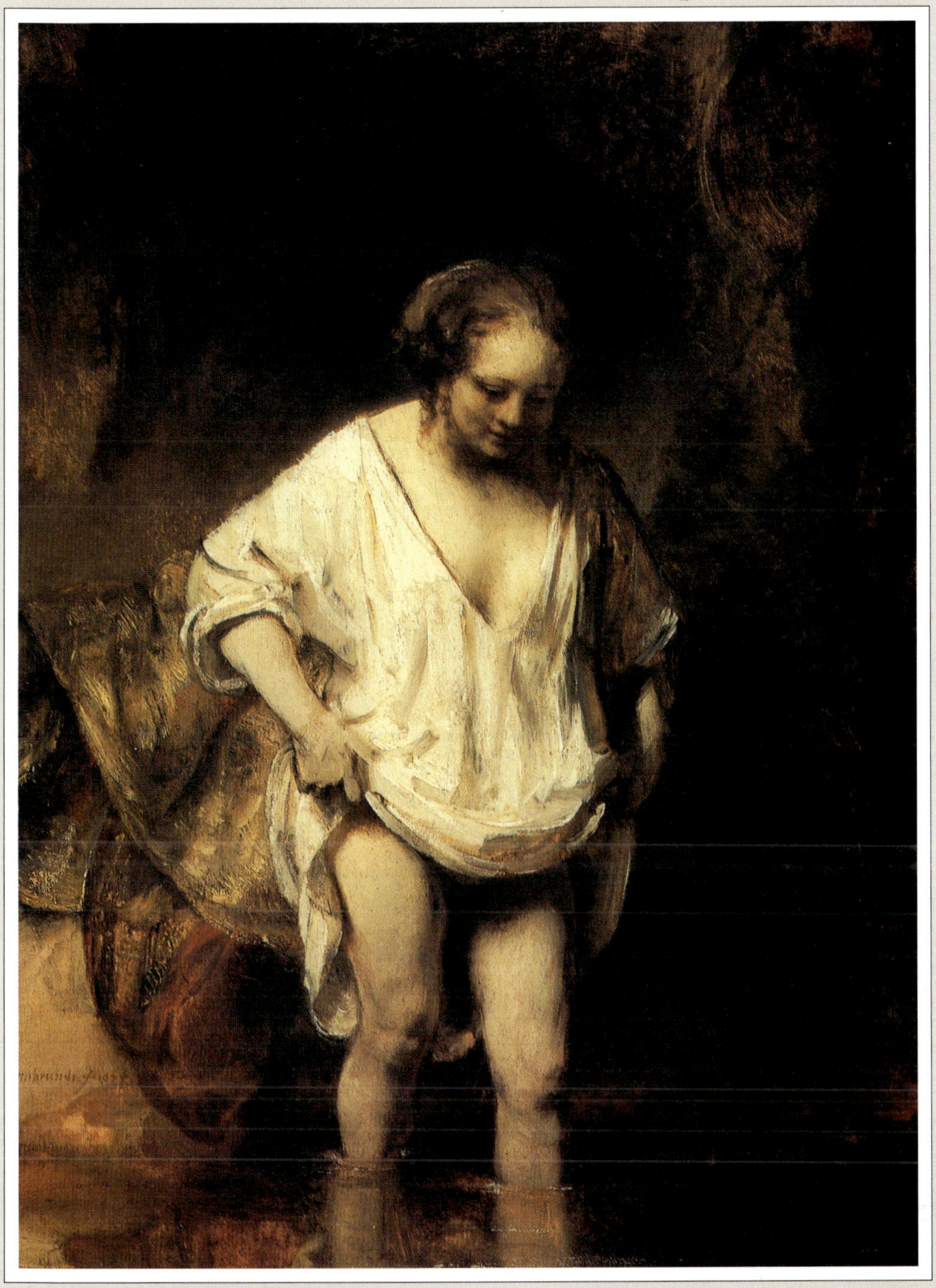

The breadth of handling, rishness of color and complex range of chiaroscuro in this small-scale, intimate work are the hallmarks of Rembrandt's style in the 1650s. The breathtaking variety of technique shows his complete mastery of the "suggestive" brushstroke. The broad, creamy strokes of the undershirt, the rounded, directional modeling of the legs, the flat, translucent glazes of the reflections of the pool and the abstract hatching of the left arm all precisely denote the quality of the elements they describe, and combine harmoniously.

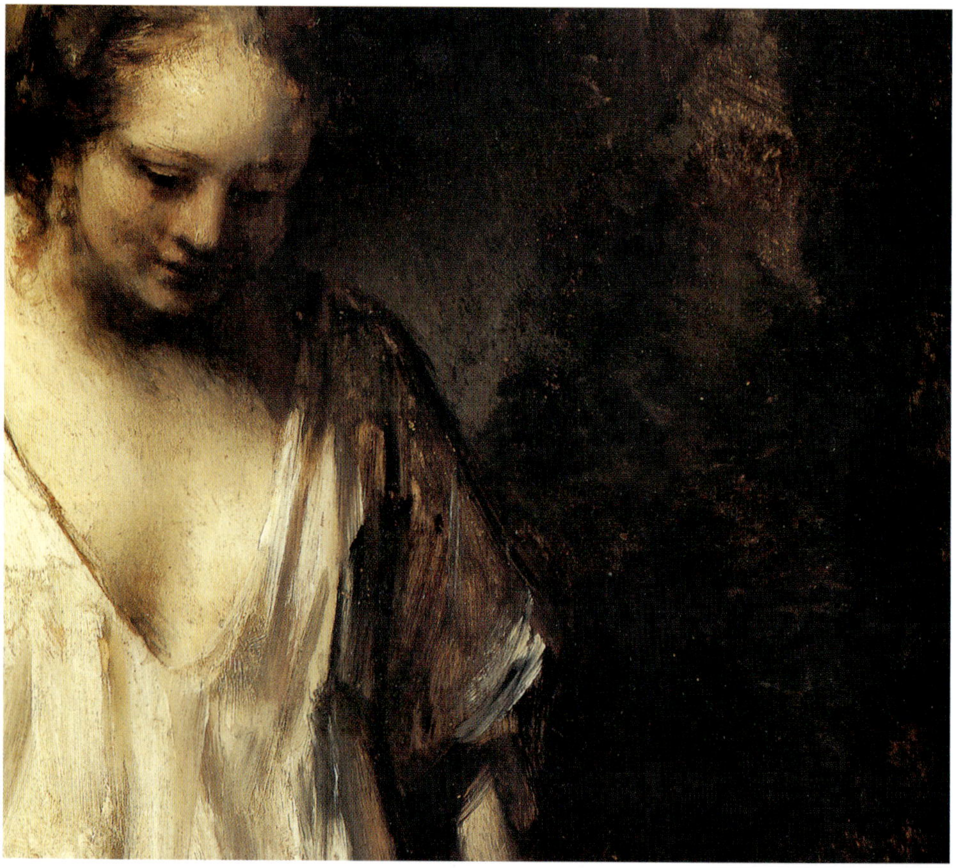

1

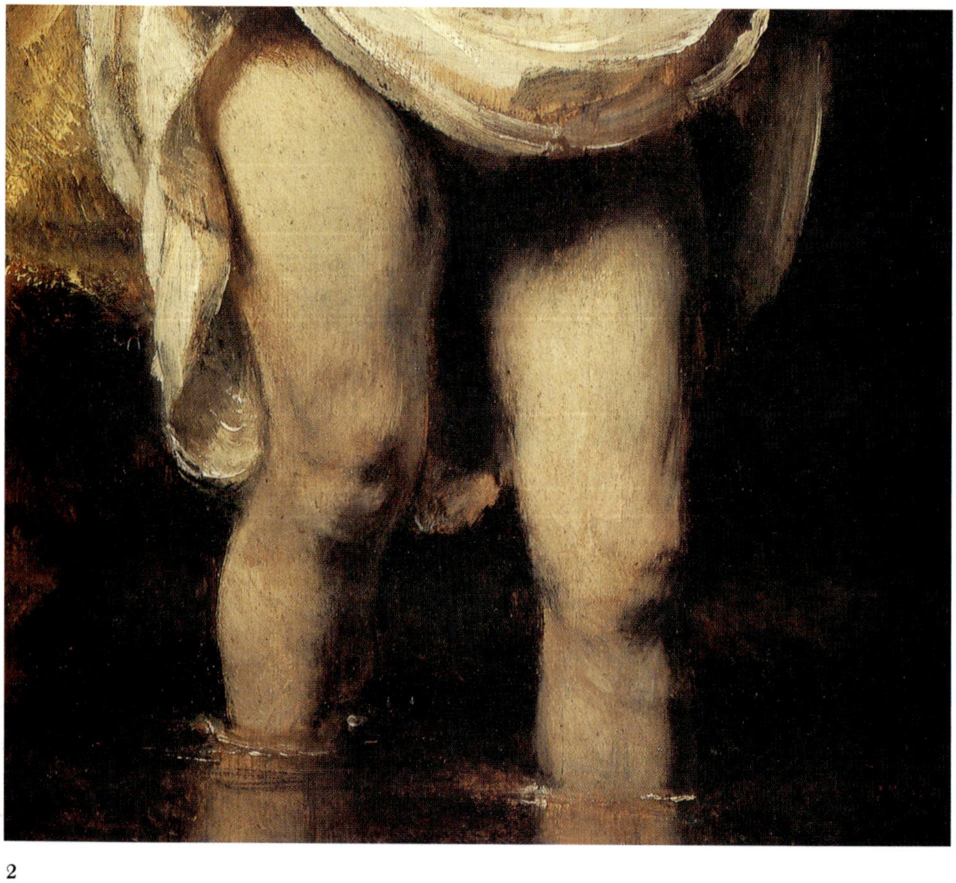

2

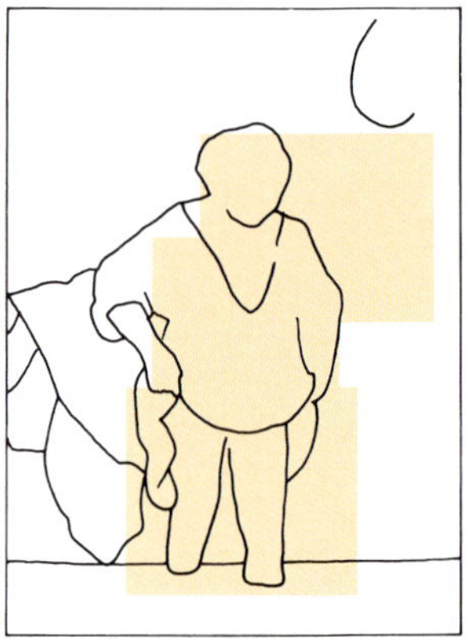

1 Divorced from its context the left arm appears almost abstract in its lack of descriptive modeling. A rough black outline defines the upper arm, and a thin brown glaze, sketchily applied, indicates the sleeve of the shirt in semi-shadow, set off by an errant touch of white at the edge. The forearm has been articulated solely by contrasting patches of white and dark brown paint. The background is equally undefined and for the most part left in rich brown shadow. The forms of a tree on the river bank have been roughly picked out in a very thin, tawny reddish-brown.

2 The firm, directional modeling of the legs and knees conveys the impression of heavy, dimpled flesh, and contrasts with the thin, diaphanous treatment of the water. Threads of thick, dry white paint mark the point where the legs break the surface of the water.

3 *Actual size detail* The rough outlining in brown is evident at the hem of the undershirt, and in the definition of the arm, wrist and knuckled hand. The ridged and smeared three-dimensional quality of the thick, white impasto strokes of the folds of the cloth is clearly shown above a beige ground. This contrasts with the more modeled areas of flesh, where the individual strokes are smaller and merge together more. The shadows of the neck and shoulders have been deepened with additional glazes of very dark brown.

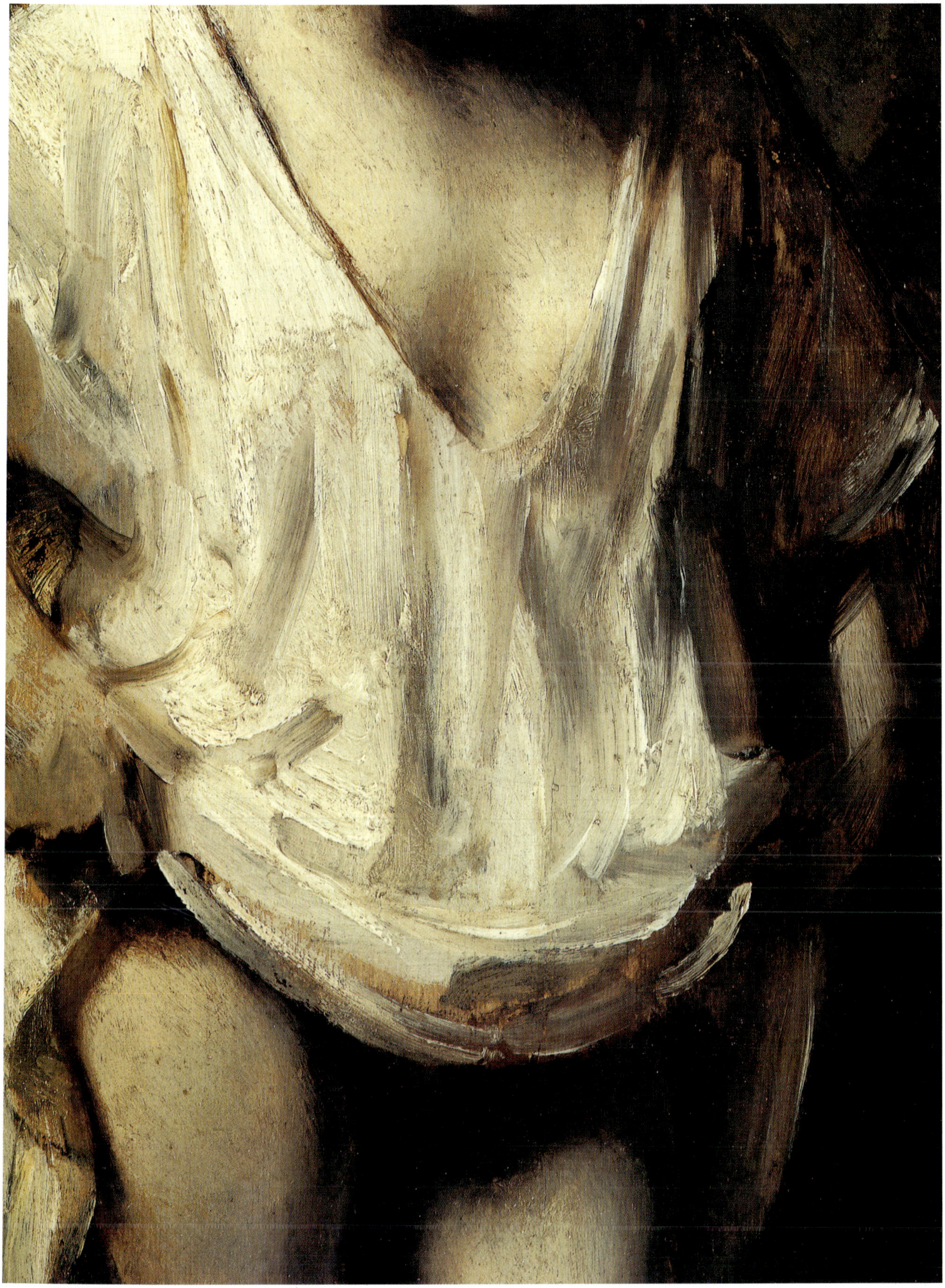

3 *Actual size detail*

Self-portrait with Maulstick, Palette and Brushes

c 1663

$28\frac{3}{8} \times 30$in/72×76cm

Oil on canvas

Iveagh Bequest, Kenwood House, London

This somber work is both a moving example of Rembrandt's late style and a revealing image of the artist in his late middle-age. In contrast to the self-portrait of 1640 (see page 169), this is an image of the artist at work, roughly dressed in simple tunic and painter's cap, holding his palette, maulstick and brushes as he surveys his canvas. While the portrayal of the artist in his studio, surrounded by the tools of his professions and often accompanied by exotic or "learned" studio props was by no means uncommon in seventeenth-century Holland, this work is exceptional in its stark, unadorned simplicity. There is no attempt to create a fashionable environment, or to make a case for the gentlemanly nature of the artist's profession. Instead it conveys a powerful sense of the rough simplicity of the painter's craft. In doing so Rembrandt has also endowed his image with a monumental grandeur equaled by few other self-portraits. This is achieved by the arrangement of the composition into stark geometrical forms of triangle and circles, as well as by the artist's imposing bulk, which takes up a large proportion of the picture surface. In addition, the searching, self-scrutinizing expression confirms the deep seriousness with which Rembrandt approaches his art.

Rembrandt painted his own features repeatedly throughout his career, sometimes in order to study different expressions and poses, sometimes dressing himself up in exotic costumes and posing as some Biblical character. There are, however, a large number of self-portraits which appear to have been made for their own sake, and which offer clues to the artist's real character. This work is one such.

It is painted with stunning breadth, and though the palette is restricted to a relatively limited range of colors, they are arranged in telling combinations and contrasts. The head is composed of a rich sequence of loose directional strokes and dabs which suggest the forms they describe, for instance the single brushstroke that follows the right side of the jaw or the tiny dabs of yellowish white that exactly describe the slight concavity of the skull to the left of the eye-socket. A marvelous interweaving of light and shadow is created by the application of dabs of differing color that also vary in tone. Thus the dull pink of the left cheek is a carefully calculated middle-tone, caught between deeper shadows, whereas the different flesh colors on the more brightly illuminated right cheek are chosen for their lighter tonal values.

The paint has been applied in thick, rich strokes of a heavily loaded brush, wet-on-wet, to provide a sensual mingling of the paint layers. The stiff hairs of the brush leave behind minute troughs and valleys that reveal the paint beneath and thus create a rich, broken surface texture that reflects actual light and conveys both an impression of three-dimensional form and the actual texture of skin. The effect of the mustache has been created by scribbling with a sharp instrument directly into the wet paint.

As in many of his mature portraits, a suggestiveness of mood is evoked by concealing the exact expression of the eyes in deep shadow so that the spectator is forced to use his own imagination to complete the expression. The fluctuation of the shadows, created by varying the degrees of dark tones, strengthens the impression of a somber inner mood. Rembrandt has brought an objectivity of approach, an intellectual honesty and a depth of insight to bear on his own features that place this painting among the greatest works of confessional autobiography of any age.

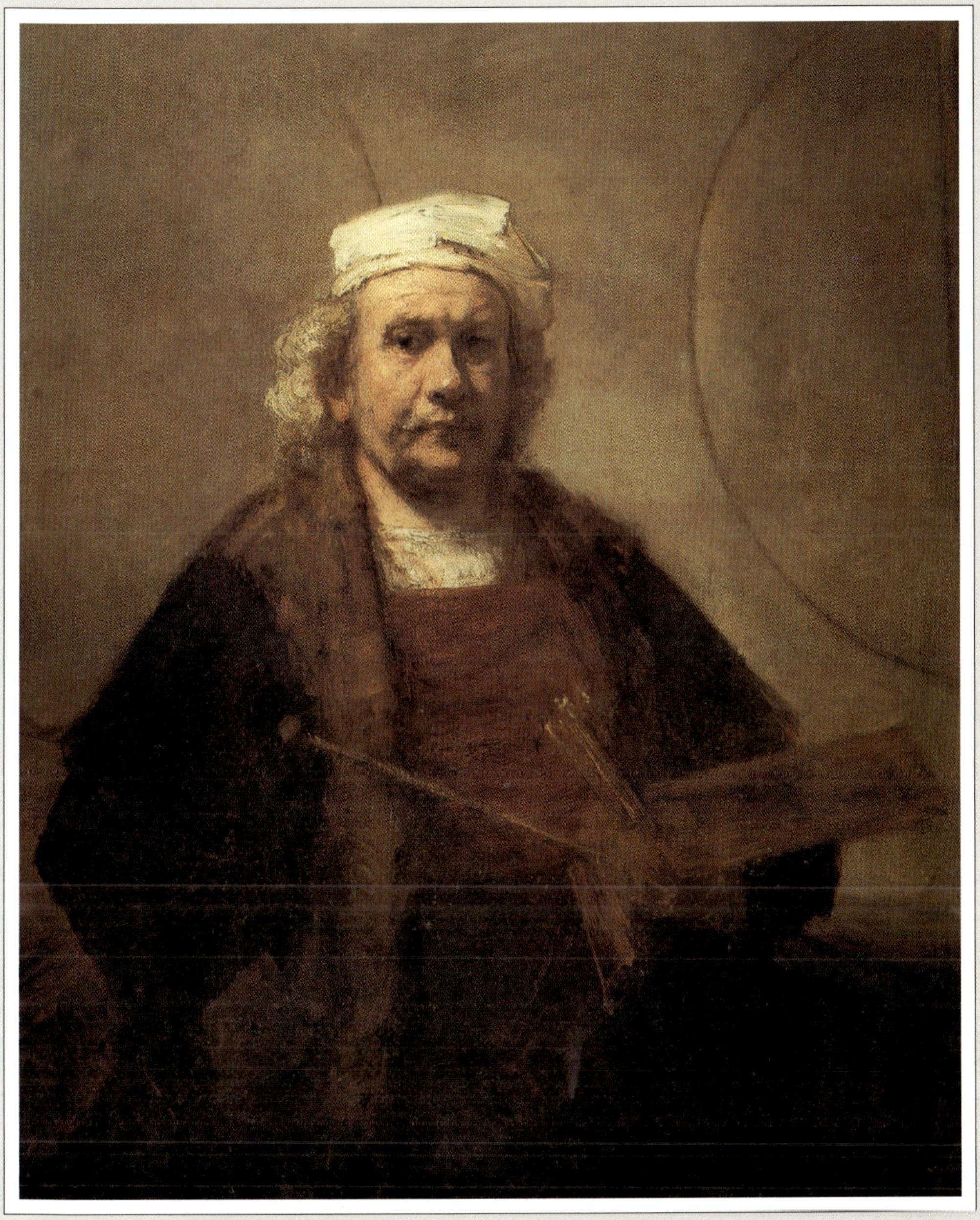

This self-portrait is of an additional, incidental interest because it shows the tools with which Rembrandt approached his craft: a rectangular palette, maulstick and a number of brushes. These last are too indistinctly drawn to be able to identify with any certainty the types of brush he used, but from the evidence of his canvases it is probable that he used stiff hog's-hair brushes with a blunt end for the broad passages, and a series of fine, pointed ones for more detailed work. The curious and unsual motif of the circles in the background of the painting has not been satisfactorily explained, but they combine with the triangular bulk of the figure to divide the picture into large, austerely simple geometric shapes, enhancing the feeling of brooding monumentality.

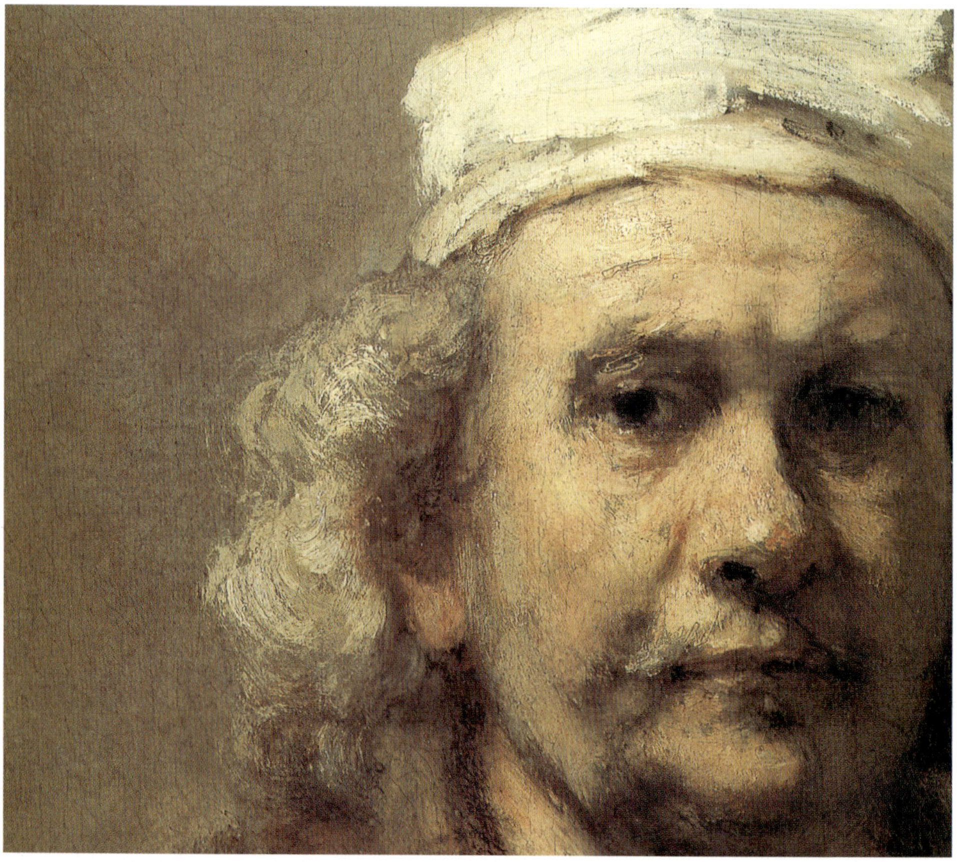

1

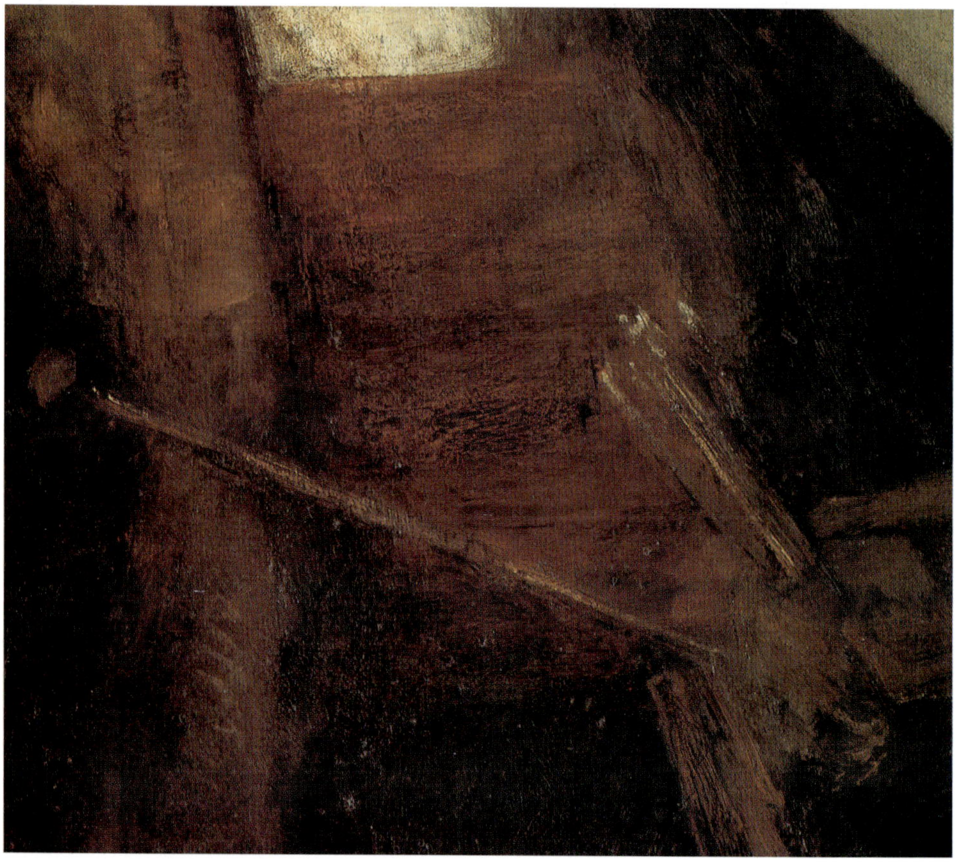

2

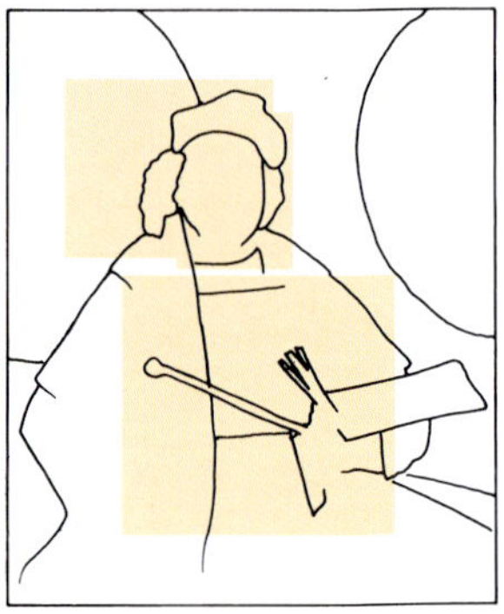

1 The impression of wild, unkempt curls of graying hair is achieved by small directional strokes of a dull ocher, applied with quite a thick brush, over which small amounts of white impasto have been dragged. The impression left by the hairs of the brush and the direction the stroke has taken are clearly visible. The large, thick, white rectangular strokes that make up the folds of the cap form a strong contrast with the dull green of the background.

2 No attempt has been made to define the hand holding the palette and brushes. The tools themselves are executed in swift strokes that lose definition when seen from close at hand. The palette has been roughly painted over the black of the artist's coat so that the latter is plainly visible beneath.

3 *Actual size detail* The breadth of handling, the density of the paint surface and the variety of colors are vividly displayed in this detail. A light, grayish-green underpainting is discernible in the middle tones of the face, onto which a range of dull reds, pinks, orange and even yellow have been worked, in overlapping, wet-on-wet layers to build form and color. A single line of black strengthens the right eyelid; another dimly defines the fold under the chin.

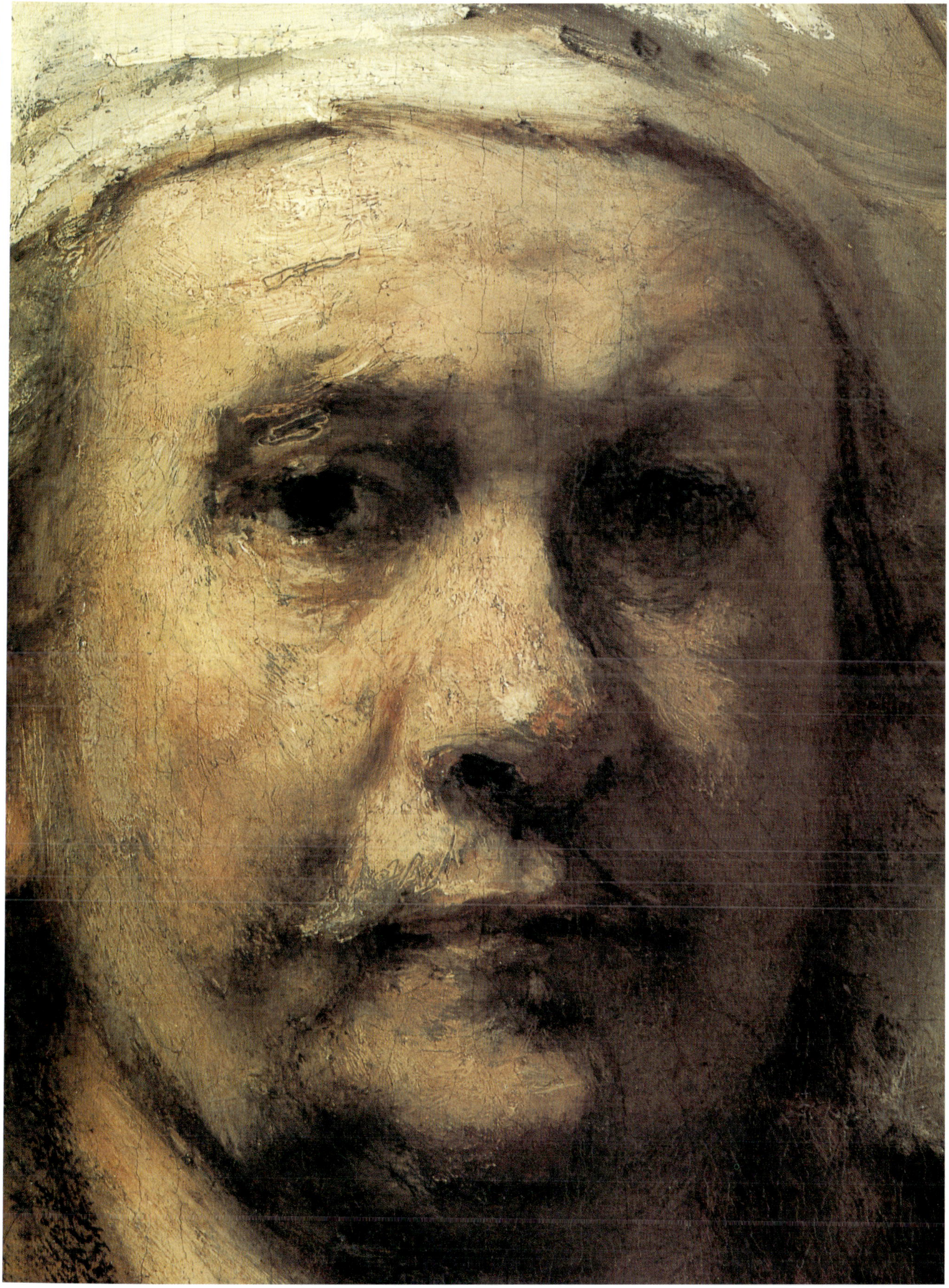

3 *Actual size detail*

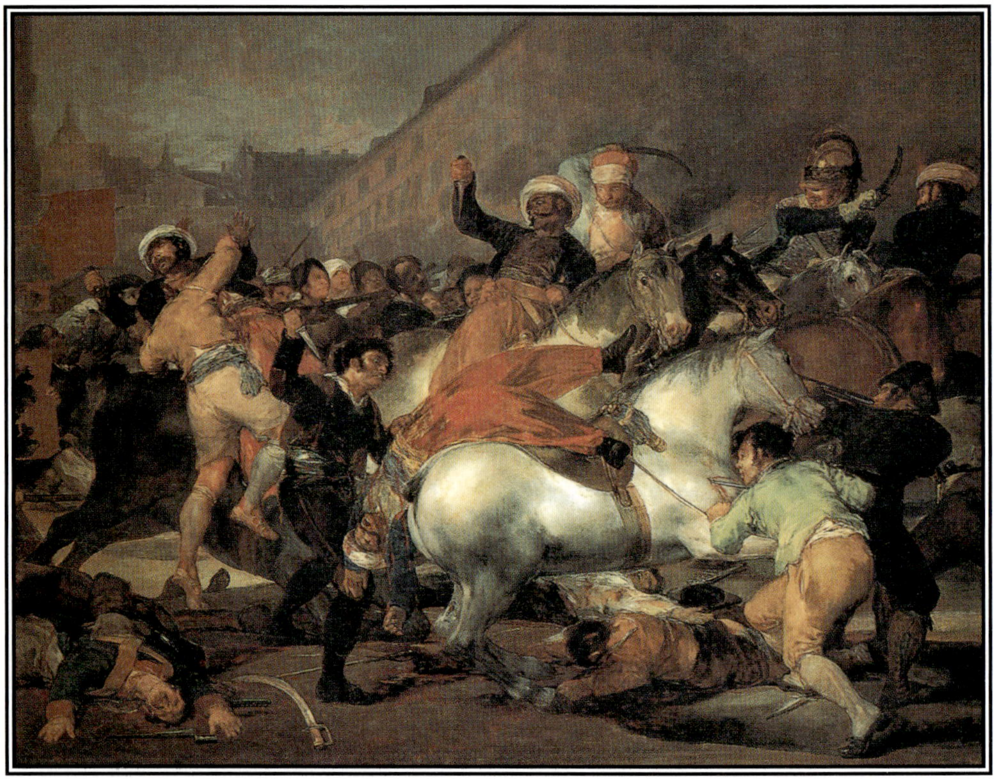

GOYA

Introduction

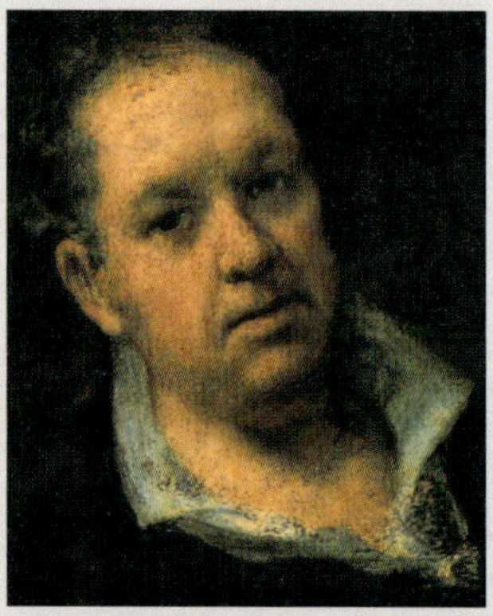

Francisco Goya
Self-Portrait
1815-16, Prado, Madrid

Since his death in 1828, Goya's art, personality, and even his technical and stylistic repertoire have been the subject of much controversy. His mastery of technique attracted the admiration of a wide variety of 19th-century artists, and continues to do so today, but his virtuosity as a painter and printmaker was never used as an end in itself, but always as a means to express the potential of his subject matter. Consequently, many of his images have become for us some of the most powerful in the whole of Western culture, and although his work is rooted firmly in his own historical period, his continued popularity suggests that it has a particular significance for the present age.

Goya's life coincided with one of the most confused and troubled times of modern European history, a period which helped shape the world we live in today. But his perception of this world was always mediated by his inner life. For him the world of dream was as real as that of waking, and his depictions of both realms possess the sense of immediacy, honesty, and sincerity that we recognize in the best work of the news photographers or cameramen of modern times — "I saw this" *(yo lo vi)* is the title of one of his most effective prints. But just as photographers study their techniques and plan their compositions, Goya's work was always the result of careful forethought: his *reportage* was far from being direct experience magically translated onto a canvas or copperplate. He has been called the last of the Old Masters and the first of the new; his people, whether aristocrats or plebeians, peasants, beggars, or beauties, are indisputably inhabitants of a world that we recognize — individuals unknown to us, but once seen never forgotten. It seems contradictory that this vision that speaks to us so directly should have been the product of a society that butchered humans and animals alike, a society based on hypocrisy and fear — the Spain of the Inquisition.

Although profoundly critical of human behavior at every level of society, Goya was fully aware of his need to remain outwardly loyal to the state, and there are many contradictions in both his work and his attitudes. The major political and social upheavals through which he lived, as well as his various illnesses, profoundly affected the nature of his art. He produced work for the state, the Church, private patrons, and for his own personal needs and pleasures, but these areas are not always as widely separated as they might seem: the many different elements of his art overlap and interweave, creating an *oeuvre* of considerable complexity. Among his private patrons was a small circle of influential intellectuals who longed to see their country lose the shackles that tied it to a superstitious and feudal past. Their wish was to introduce the spirit of the Enlightenment initially associated with France and the French Revolution and later personified by the charismatic figure of Napoleon. Much of Goya's mature work was deeply connected with such ideas, indeed it is clear that much of it was intended to function on various levels and to be open to a number of interpretations. This goes some way to explain its continued impact on an audience that is largely ignorant of the circumstances or social patterns that lay behind its production. But this is only one side of Goya's art: it has often been said that if he had died at the age of forty-five he would have been remembered as a talented painter of tapestry designs for the Spanish court, a craftsman with a fertile imagination and a bravura painting style, happy to remain within the bounds that his own social ambitions had set for him.

Early years

Until his mid-forties, when a mysterious illness caused a change of direction, Francisco José de Goya y Lucientes could be described as the epitome of the self-made man, proud of having found his own way in the world by means of his skill and wit. He was born on 30 March, 1746, in the poor agricultural community of Fuen-

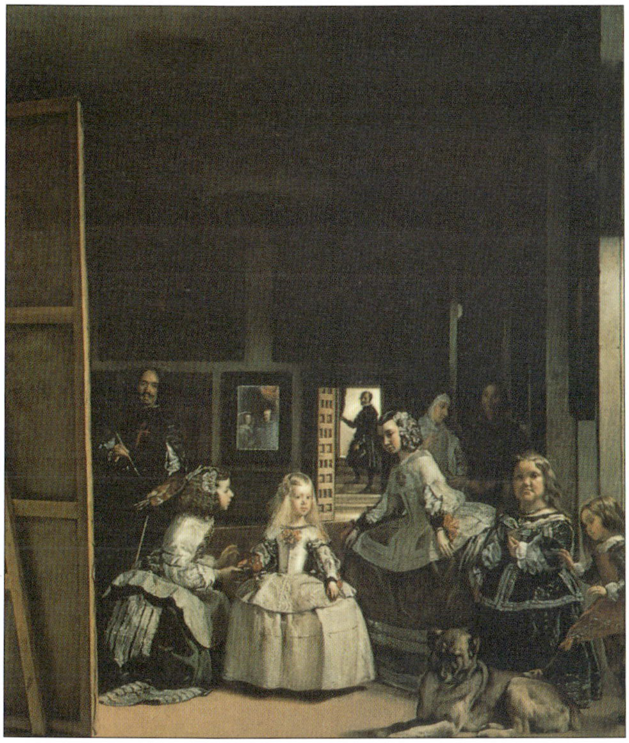

DIEGO VELASQUEZ
Las Meninas
1656, Prado, Madrid

During Goya's lifetime this painting was considered to be the most valuable work in the royal collection. Goya was deeply influenced by Velasquez; he was reported as having said that his only masters were Rembrandt, Velasquez, and Nature. Echoes of Velasquez' psychological penetration, his ease with paint, and his assured mastery of tone and composition recur in Goya's work throughout his career.

detodos, part of the province of Aragon, situated on the high arid plateau of central Spain. His family was not wealthy; his father, who had been a master gilder, died intestate, and the young Goya was left to make his own way in the world. At the age of fourteen he was apprenticed to a local painter, José Luzán y Martinez, who had been a pupil of the Neapolitan Francesco Solimena, one of the last great painters in the Baroque tradition. At Luzán's studio in Saragossa, Goya was trained to work in the grand and assured theatrical style that could then be seen in many of the churches and palaces of Spain.

In 1763, aged only seventeen, he attempted unsuccessfully to gain a scholarship to the Academy of San Fernando in Madrid. He made a second attempt three years later and was once again refused. There was not a single vote in his favor despite the presence on the committee of another artist from Aragon, Francesco Bayeu, who held the post of court painter to Charles III, King of Spain.

Goya returned to Saragossa and concentrated on establishing himself as the major painter of the area, carrying out a series of church frescoes. In 1770/1 he made a trip to Italy, the home of the Baroque style, and visited Rome, Naples, and Parma, where he saw the frescoes by Correggio, and must have been impressed by the art of the surrounding region. Writers of the 19th century, who did so much to build the popular idea of Goya's life and personality that still prevails today, record him climbing the dome of St Peter's, getting involved in brawls, and so on. Whether or not such stories are true, it

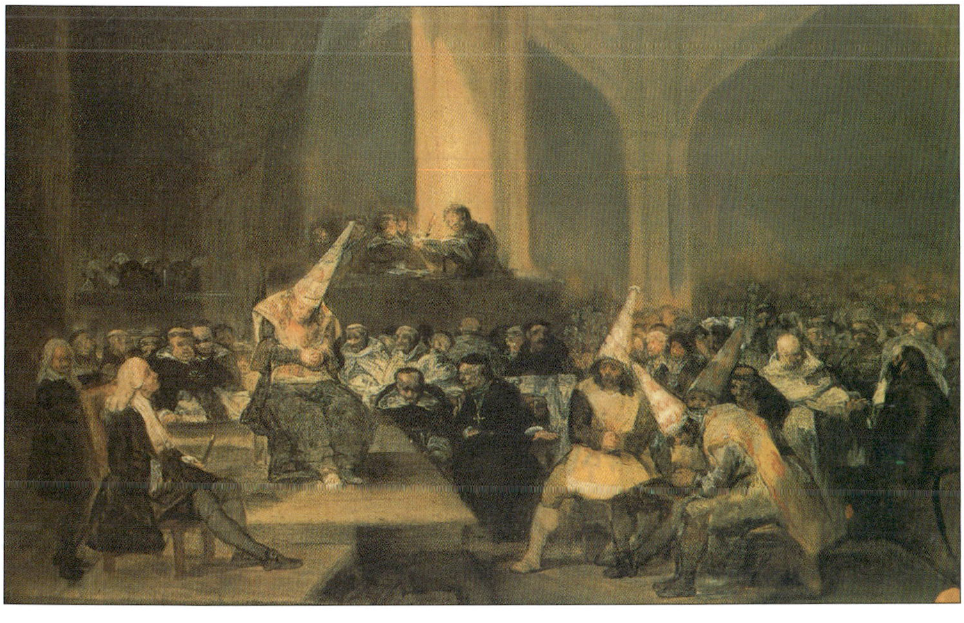

FRANCISCO GOYA
Inquisition Tribunal
c 1812-15, Academy of San Fernando, Madrid

The expressions, attitudes, and costumes of the participants in this tragic farce reveal the power and terror embodied by the religious courts of the Inquisition. The influence of this religious institution stretched far beyond the confines of the Church to form a living symbol of the brutal and repressive aspects of "Black Spain" – the still feudal country that was Goya's home.

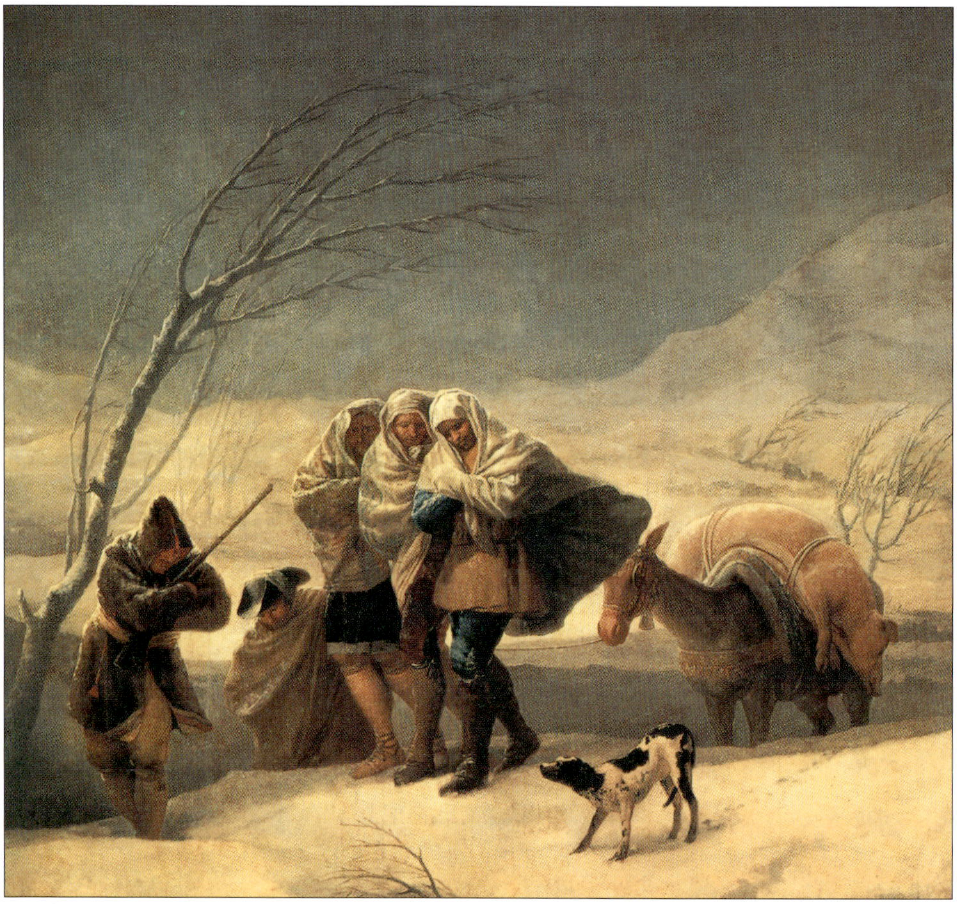

FRANCISCO GOYA
Winter (tapestry cartoon)
1786-9, Prado, Madrid

Goya has balanced a skillful evocation of atmospheric reality with the decorative qualities necessary for a tapestry cartoon. A group of figures, framed by the bare trees and set large against the stark snow-covered landscape, huddle to protect themselves from the intense cold of winter.

is certain that he did not neglect his professional concerns, and was commended by the Academy at Parma for his "fluent handling." This aspect of Goya's work and his exquisite sense of value and color were to become his dominant stylistic hallmarks.

In 1773 Goya married Josefa Bayeu, sister of the fashionable Francesco Bayeu who was himself the protegé of the Neo-Classical painter Antonio-Raphael Mengs, favorite of the king and virtual dictator of the Spanish art scene. Whether this was a shrewd piece of career building or a love match has been a matter of continued speculation. Goya was a man with a huge appetite for the pleasures of life; he loved hunting, attending the popular fiestas and, if we are to believe the legends, he was an active participant in bullfights. In 1774 Mengs, who was among other things director of the royal weaving mills, invited Goya to work under the direction of his brother-in-law at the royal tapestry factory of Santa Barbara in Madrid. The tapestry cartoons were the first works for which he became popularly known, and for almost twenty years between 1775 and 1792 they formed the basis of his professional activity. He produced sixty-three cartoons for the royal household, forty-three of which are now conserved in the Prado, Madrid.

Fame and success

In December 1778 Goya sent his childhood friend, the intellectual Martín Zapater, eighteen etchings which he had made after the paintings by Velasquez in the royal collection, and in 1780 he was unanimously elected to the Academy of San Fernando on the strength of a deliberately conventionally painted *Crucifixion* closely modeled on a Velasquez painting of the same subject. Goya was later to say that his only teachers had been Velasquez, Rembrandt, and nature.

By the 1780s he had a firmly established reputation as a skilled craftsman-artist. In the early years of the decade he had begun to paint society portraits, and these, together with royal commissions and paintings for the Church, continued to be the mainstay of his financial independence. By mid-decade he was free from financial worries and affluent enough to own an expensive English carriage, which he drove so recklessly that he killed a passer-by — he subsequently exchanged this vehicle for a luxurious four-wheeler drawn by two mules.

In 1785 he was appointed deputy director of the Academy, and the next year he became painter to the king *(pintor del rey)*. He was patronized by both the royal

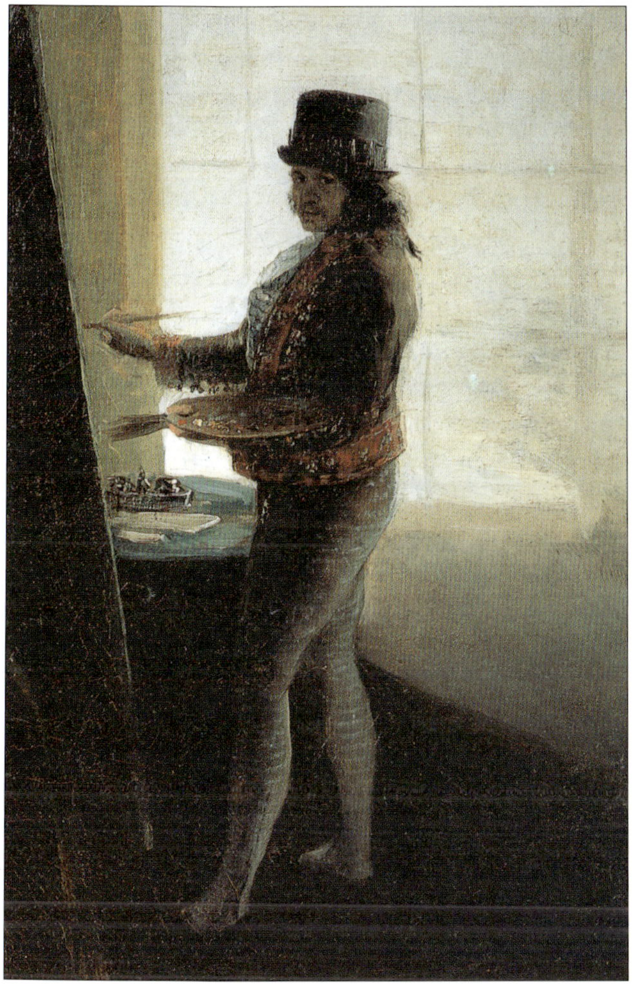

FRANCISCO GOYA
Self-portrait with Candles
c 1797-98, Academy of San Fernando, Madrid (Contessa de Villagonzalo Collection)

The painting forms an intriguing document of the artist at work. He has shown himself standing up, his favored position for working. The hat he wears supports a number of candles to allow him to work in artificial light. Despite the back-lighting provided by the large window behind him, his fashionable *majo* dress can easily be discerned. He has corrected the reversing effect of the mirror image that would have made him appear left-handed and given us the opportunity to study the colors laid out on his palette.

FRANCISCO GOYA
Portrait of Duchess of Alba
1795, Hispanic Society of America, New York

"There is not a hair of her head that does not excite desire," wrote a French traveler of the famed aristocratic beauty. The rings on her fingers bear the names "Goya" and "Alba," while in the sand at her feet is written "Solo Goya." These details could have been added at a later date, as the canvas remained in the artist's possession until 1812.

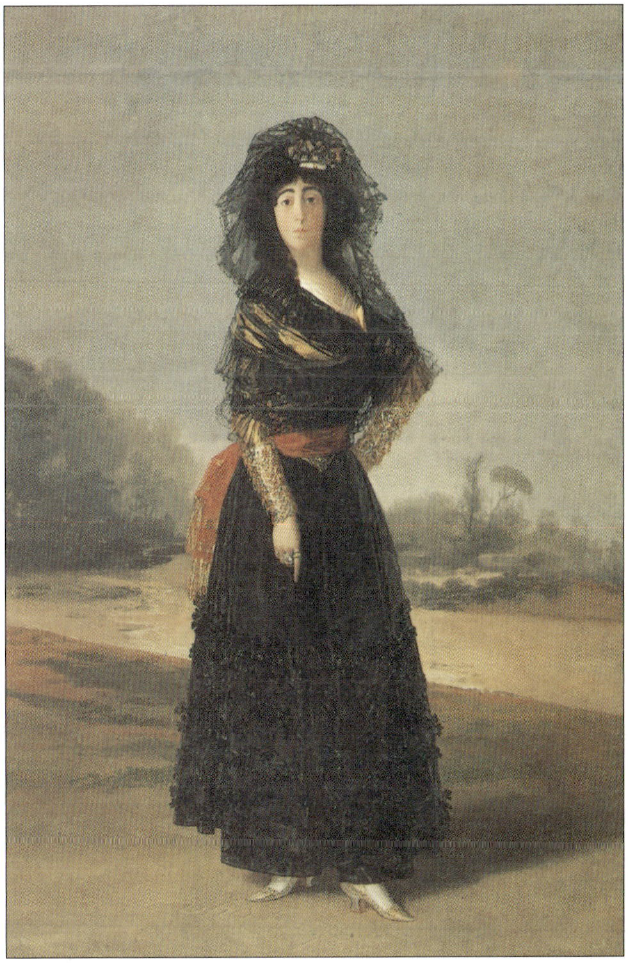

family and the influential and enlightened families of Spain, and through the patronage of wealthy liberals he was able to produce more personal works alongside those in the traditional genres. Religious themes were a staple of his artistic production – the most profitable in financial terms – but a large body of his work concerns the unacceptable face of religion. Subjects such as the courts of the Inquisition or the activities of witches were popular with his intellectual friends and patrons, who saw such themes as metaphors for the fear-ridden state of their country.

Commissions for tapestry designs also continued, but Goya's manner of handling them changed considerably, as may be seen by comparing *A Walk in Andalusia* of 1777 (see page 205) to *Winter*, of ten years later. Winter is more realistic in its treatment of pose, and the effects of atmosphere, and weather; it is much more lively and free in handling and less restricted by the limitations of its primary purpose – the cartoons took the form of patterns or models to be interpreted by the weavers of the Santa Barbara factory. By the 1790s Goya's dissatisfaction with producing these tapestry commissions was widely known. On April 25, 1789, aged forty-three, he was given by Charles IV, who had been crowned King of Spain a few months earlier, the prestigious post of *pintor del cámara del rey*, official painter to the court. He was now at the height of his popularity, and in 1792 he produced his last work for the tapestry factory.

Illness and introspection

1792 was a fateful year for Goya. En route to Cadiz, the seaport on the southwest coast of Spain, he became seriously ill. The exact nature of his illness is not known, but it lasted several months, brought him close to death, and left him profoundly deaf. Deafness is a disability which separates its victim irretrievably from easy communication with others, and this, together with his narrow escape from death, must have deeply affected Goya's view of himself and his position within society. In January 1794 he submitted eleven paintings for the Academy, and wrote to Bernardo de Iriate, the vice-protector of the Royal Academy in Madrid, that the pictures presented were executed "...to occupy my imagination, vexed by consideration of my ills, and to . . . make observations that normally are given no place in commissioned works which give no scope for fantasy and invention." Such themes were by no means unknown or unique to Goya: in the 17th century Philip II had collected the work of Bosch and Bruegel, both of whom were specialists to varying degrees in the weird and macabre.

Recuperation from his illness kept Goya away from the capital for almost a year, and this period formed the turning point in his work. He became more concerned with developing an art based on his personal interests and began, along with his portraits of the wealthy, to produce new works with an often disturbing subject matter. Simple and dynamic in composition, small in scale, these depicted scenes of natural disaster, gatherings of prisoners, lunatics, and witches, episodes of rape, murder, cannibalism, and disease.

In 1795 he produced a portrait of the great aristo-

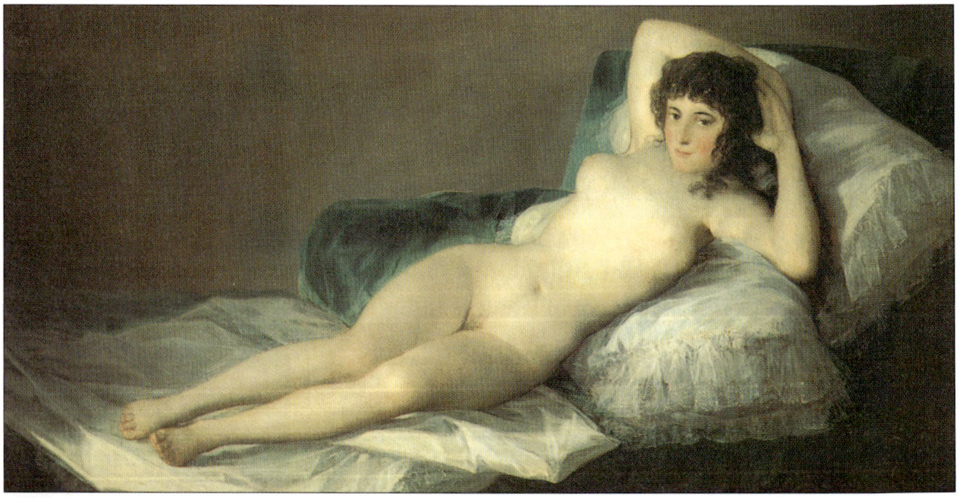

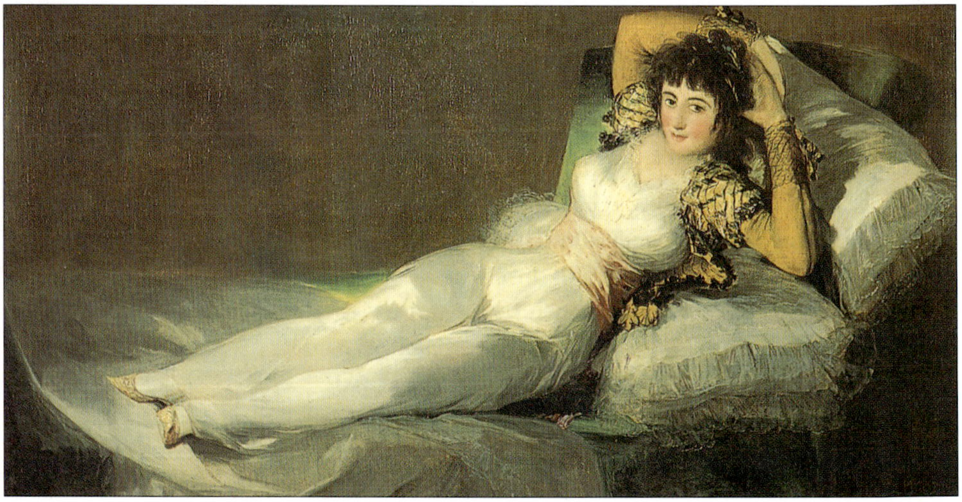

The Naked and Clothed Majas
c 1800, Prado, Madrid

These are two of the most enigmatic images in Western art. They were originally in the Duchess of Alba's own collection, but were subsequently owned by Manuel Godoy, who also possessed Velasquez' so-called *Rokeby Venus*. The nude was extremely rare in Spanish painting, and the unashamed eroticism of these works brought Goya before the Court of the Inquisition.

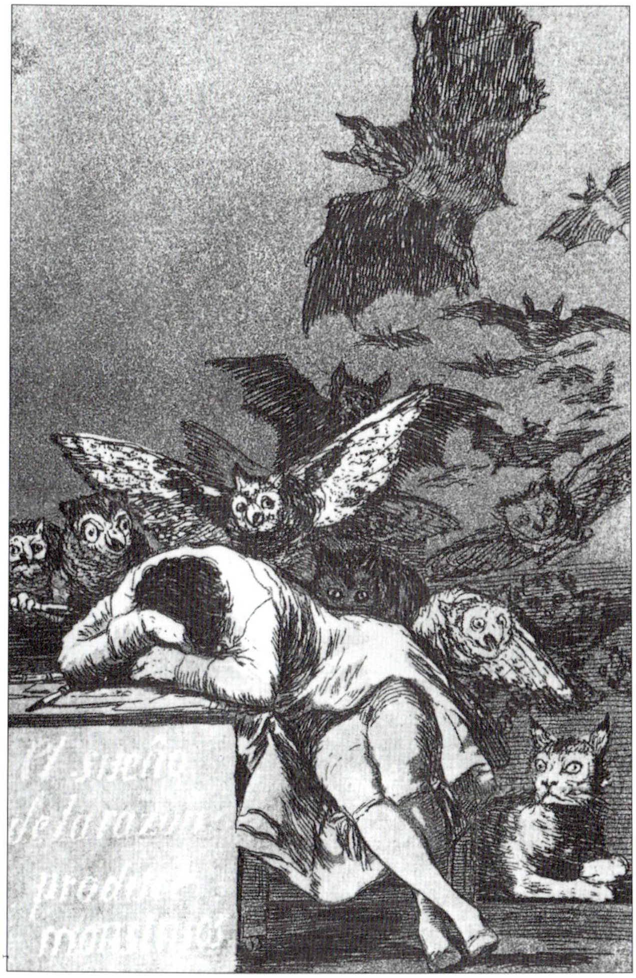

FRANCISCO GOYA
"The Sleep of Reason Produces Monsters"
1797-98, British Museum, London

Plate 43 of the book of etchings called *Los Caprichos* ("Follies") shows the artist asleep at his work desk, surrounded by the creations of his imagination. The text that accompanies this print – possibly the best-known of the series – is translated as follows: "Imagination abandoned by reason produces impossible monsters: united with her she is the mother of the arts and the source of wonders."

cratic beauty, the Duchess of Alba. A year later her husband died and Goya visited her residence at Sanlúcar de Barrameda, where he stayed for a number of months. He appears to have been deeply infatuated with her, although whether his feelings were reciprocated is unknown. Certainly she inspired some of his greatest works. After the death of his brother-in-law, Goya was appointed director of the Academy of Fine Arts, but his continuing ill health forced him to resign from this position two years later. In the spring of 1798, he painted the frescoes of San Antonio de la Florida in Madrid, one of his great achievements.

The graphic works

In the autumn of 1799 Goya was given the supreme position of first court painter *(primer pintor de cámara del rey).* The same year saw the publication of a suite of eighty-two etched and aquatinted plates entitled *Los Caprichos* ("Follies"), which firmly linked him with the liberal supporters of the Enlightenment. The etchings were based primarily on drawings he had made while staying with the Duchess of Alba at Sanlúcar, taken from scenes of everyday life at her residence, and revolving

FRANCISCO GOYA
The Forge
c 1812-15, Frick Collection, New York

Goya's originality was not merely a matter of technique: he also was one of the first artists to give a significant place in his work to the laboring classes. His depiction of these workers shows a deep understanding of the skilled co-ordination of movement their activity involves. This was one of the relatively few paintings by Goya to be seen in France – between 1838 and 1848 it was part of King Louis Philippe's "Spanish Gallery."

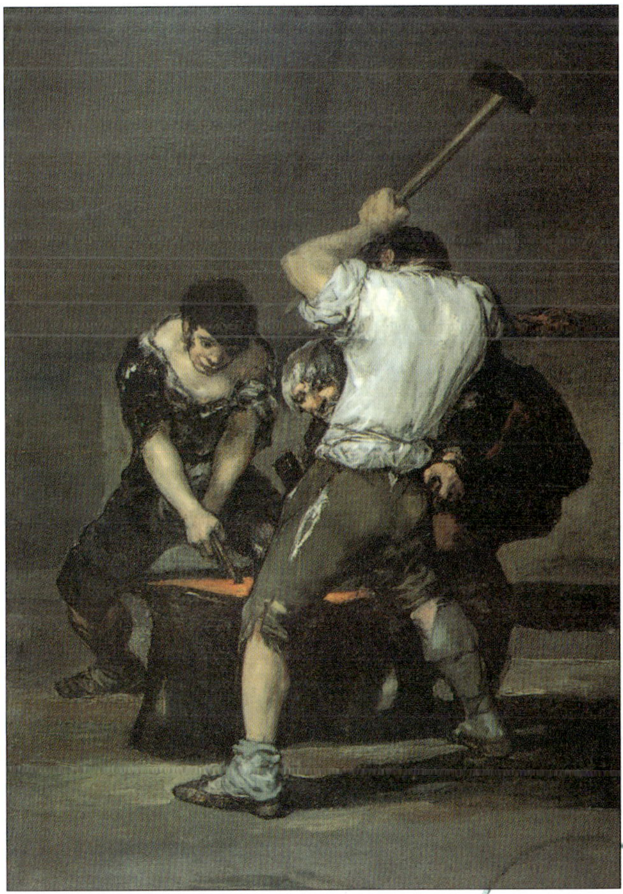

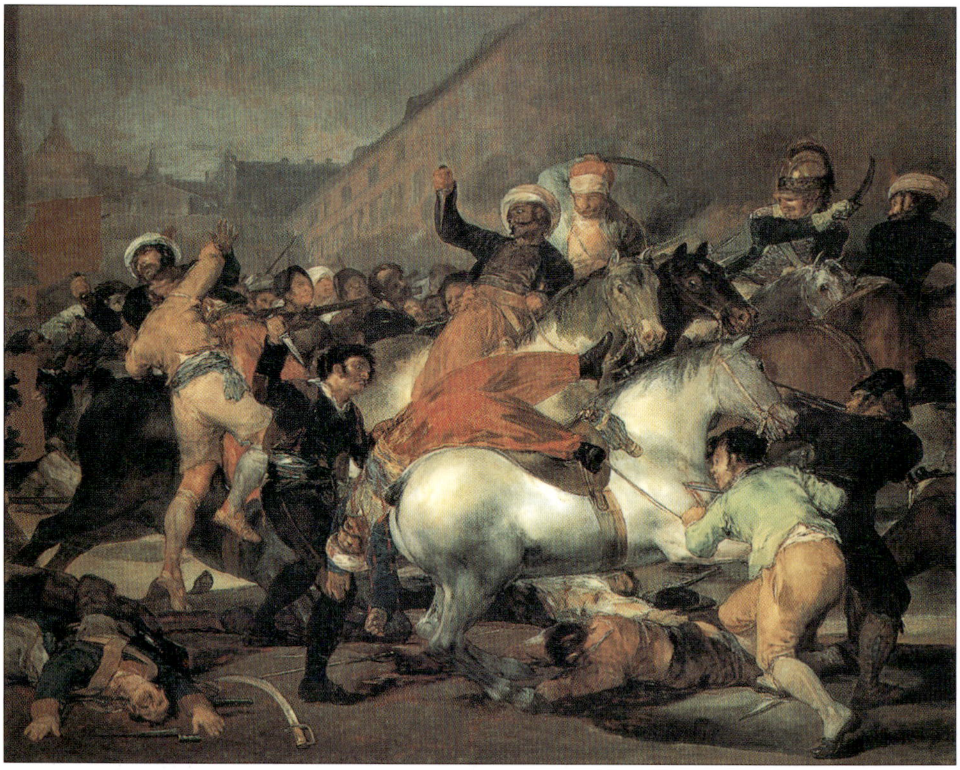

FRANCISCO GOYA
The Second of May 1808
1814, Prado, Madrid

The frenzy of killing is depicted with the frankness and vigor for which Goya is famous. This is not a propagandist glorification of war; it is a reaction to the horrific reality of violence and death. Goya takes no sides: the citizens fighting Murat's cavalry may be the heroes, but their savagery in the pursuit of their aims equals that of their oppressors.

scenes of everyday life at her residence, and evolving around the follies and superstitions of the Spanish people from every social sphere. He took enormous care with their production, and each plate is accompanied by a commentary and is given a succinct and evocative title that is at once comprehensible and disturbingly ambiguous. "No one knows himself," "There's plenty to suck," "And still they won't go," are just a few of the titles. As the introductory commentary makes clear, they represent "the follies and blunders common in every civil society as well as . . . vulgar prejudices and lies authorized by custom, ignorance or interest . . ." With startling economy of detail, Goya creates in these prints a murky urban wasteland fired with a theatrical tension and populated by a host of diverse individuals. It is at once specific and general, and the biting edge of his satire cuts many ways — even some of the institutions he attacked in the etchings praised the series as an edifying force. If Goya is to be believed, they were on sale for a mere two days and then withdrawn, possibly as a result of the intervention of the Inquisition. In 1803 Goya presented the king with the copperplates of *Los Caprichos* and 240 unsold copies of the printed book, receiving by way of compensation an annual pension of 12,000 reals for his son, Francisco Javier. The episode appears to have done him little harm. His Velasquez-inspired portrait of *Charles IV and his Family*, painted in 1800 (see page 219), ushered in a period of relative tranquility and wellbeing.

Political conflicts

On March 17, 1808, Ferdinand, Prince of the Asturias, heir to the Spanish throne, staged a *coup d'état* against his father Charles IV, whose reign had been repressive and consisted of an unparalleled series of disasters. The king and his corrupt minister Godoy were imprisoned, and on March 19 Charles abdicated in favor of his son, who became Ferdinand VII. Napoleon ordered the troops he had in Spain under a treaty made a year earlier, to occupy Madrid and six days later the French general Murat entered the city unopposed. On May 2, the populace reacted to the occupation by attacking a detachment of mamelukes and dragoons escorting Charles IV's brother in one of the city's main squares, the Puerta del Sol. Reprisal was merciless and swift: forty-three civilians were executed on the hill of Principe Pio just outside the city. Goya witnessed these events, which gave rise to two major canvases, painted after the final defeat of the French, when Spanish artists were given the opportunity to commemorate the uprising. Goya's versions were not popular with the government and were hidden away from public view for many years.

While Napoleon installed his brother Joseph Bonaparte on the throme (May 13), the anti-French revolt spread all over Spain. The Spanish royal family, held at the French town of Bayonne, sanctioned the *guerrilleros* and the first guerilla war had begun. It was this brutal and bloody conflict that Goya recorded in his powerful series of etchings, *The Disasters of War,* produced, ironically, at the same time as accepting the appointment of court painter to King Joseph.

The Duke of Wellington's forces slowly pushed the French out of Spain, and in 1814 Joseph abdicated. Ferdinand VII returned to the throne. He wasted no time in continuing the absolutist regime of his father, reinstituting the monastic orders and even restoring the Inquisition. From 1814 to 1820 some 12,000 Spaniards found guilty of French sympathies were arrested or sent into exile. Goya himself was tried for treason, but acquitted on a technicality.

It was a prolonged period of confusion, resulting in divided loyalties among liberals who, like Goya, had initially viewed France as the harbinger of reform. Goya's work records the travails of the time. The figure of the Colossus dominates his late painting and graphic work, much of which was meant as a private reacion to the futile horrors of war and its effects upon a civilian population. His views are ones we understand and are only too familiar with — there are few heroes, only victims. As a well-known former liberal and French sympathizer he was in real danger of persecution, and his prints connected with these years were not published until after his death.

Last years

Goya retired to the country, to a comfortable house on the banks of the river Manzanares near Madrid. His wife had died (in 1812), as had four of his five children. In 1819, aged seventy-three, he fell seriously ill but recovered and despite his age, began to experiment with the newly discovered medium of lithography, of which he is one of the most celebrated masters. He went on to produce some of his greatest works, those known as the "Black Paintings," executed directly onto the walls of his house. There are fourteen of these (now in the Prado), and with a certain sardonic humour, he placed the paintings of *Saturn Eating His Children* (inspired by an oil by Rubens of the same subject) and *Two Old people Eating* (see page 233) in his dining room. These magnificent and pessimistic productions were produced simultaneously with the equally enigmatic suite of etchings called the *Disparates* ("Absurdities"), reminiscent of the earlier *Caprichos.*

Goya had by now become a wealthy man, possessing substantial amounts of jewelry and property, and owning a collection of paintings by Rembrandt, Tiepolo, Velasquez, and Correggio as well as seventy-three of his own works. However, although his relationship with the despotic monarch appears to have been relatively stable, the outlook was not promising, and Goya wasted no time

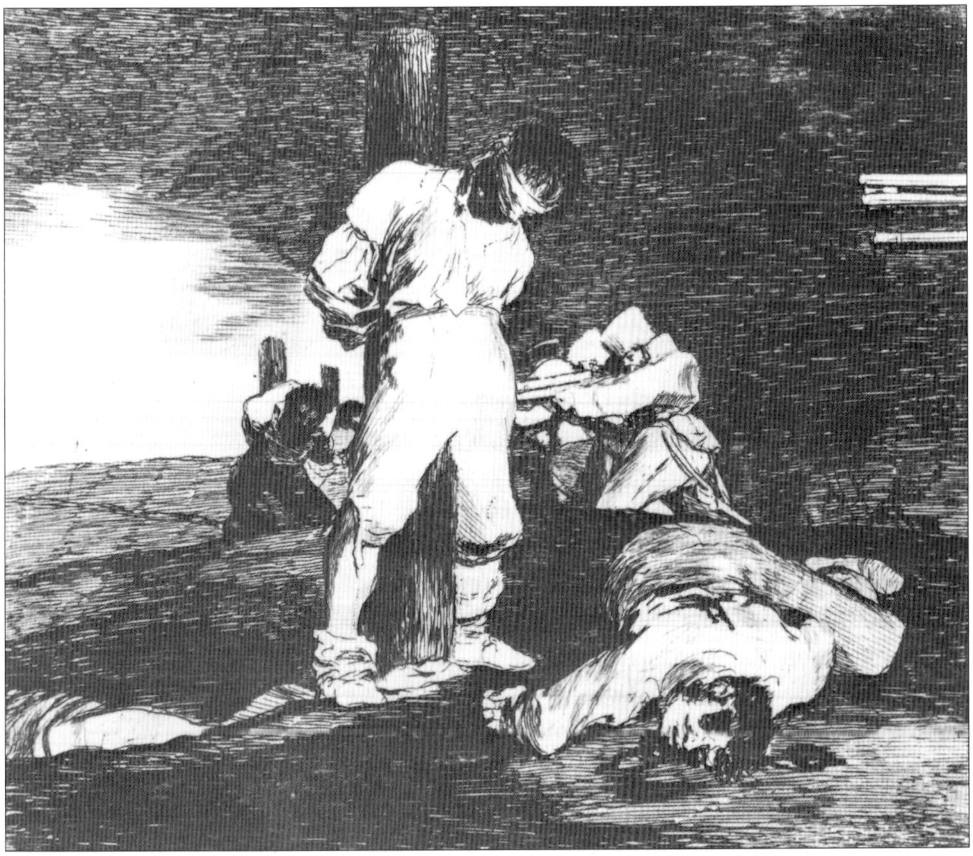

"There is no remedy"
1810-11, British Museum, London

This etching from Goya's *Disasters of War* series is a reduction to essentials of his painting *The Third of May.* Three stakes, like three crcifixes, stand out starkly from the darkness, the victims anonymous, their dead bodies supported only by the ropes that bind them. Like so many of Goya's images, these cross the boundaries of time and place to speak to us today as clearly as when they were first drawn.

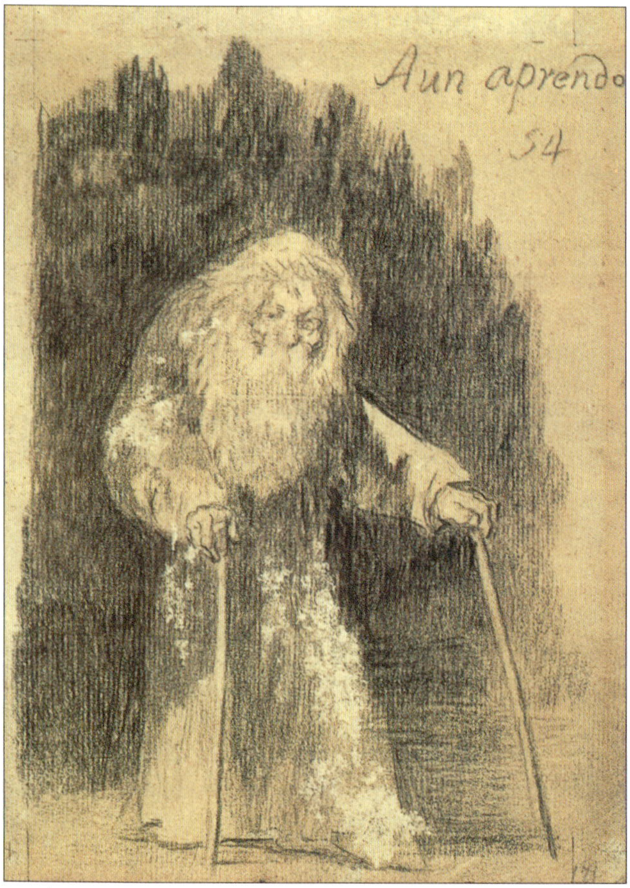

Still Learning
1824-28, Prado, Madrid

Goya continued to paint and draw, experimenting tirelessly with new media, until he died. This drawing, done when he was an eighty-year-old exile in France, is not an actual self portrait, but is surely a metaphorical one. Like the works of other aged masters, such as Titian and Rembrandt, it is a testament to the unquenchable curiosity and creative inventiveness of its executor.

arranging his exit from Spain. He requested leave, "to take the waters of Plombières" (in France), but he made no attempt to reach the spa town and settled instead in Bordeaux. "Goya has come," wrote his friend and fellow exile Moratin, "deaf, old, slow, and weak . . . but content and anxious to see the world." From June to the end of August 1824 he lodged in Paris, where he had a chance to see at the Salon the *Massacre of Chios* by the young Romantic painter, Eugène Delacroix – it is said that he was unimpressed. He returned to Bordeaux, and Moratin recorded that "Goya is full of himself and painting all that occurs to him, without ever spending time in correcting what he has already painted."

He continued to experiment with techniques and media, painting miniatures on ivory, and in 1823 producing the lithographs known as *Bulls of Bordeaux*. He seems to have been happy and content – certainly pictures like the *Milkmaid* suggest a certain ease with his lot. In May 1826 he returned to Spain, where he was well received by the court, but he stayed only long enough to ensure that his pension was secure and then returned to Bordeaux. He died on April 16, 1828, aged eighty-two, and was buried in France, fittingly, since it was there that his art was to make such an impact on both the avant-garde and the establishment painters of the 19th century. His body was not brought back to the country of his birth until 1901, when it was placed equally appropriately in the small church of San Antonio del Florida, which thirty years earlier he had decorated with images showing the full scope of his genius.

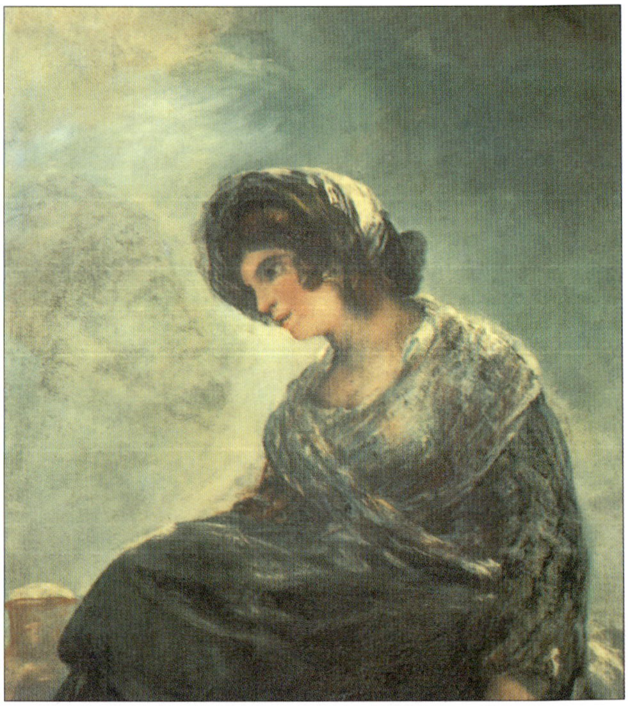

The Milkmaid of Bordeaux
c 1827, Prado, Madrid

This calm and assured portrait of a working girl was painted for the artist's own pleasure when he was living in France. He died a year after its completion. The young girl's shawl and blue-green dress palpitate with broken touches of color, the warm red ground breaks through periodically to add a warmth to the cool tones that serve as the basis of the composition.

GOYA'S PAINTING METHODS

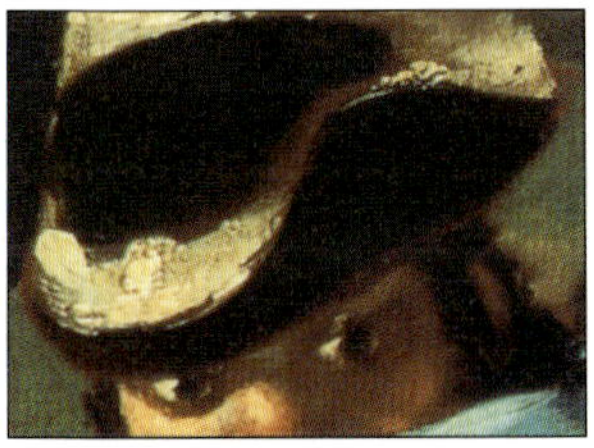

A Walk in Andalusia was painted, like many of Goya's works, on a warm reddish ground, which is allowed to show through to stand as the shadow area of the tunic.

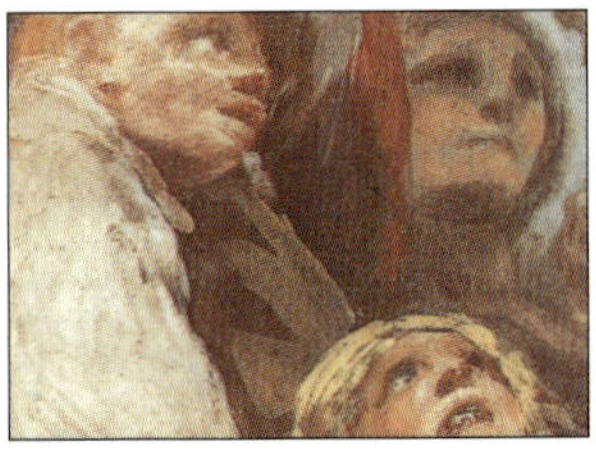

Goya's frescoes, such as a *Miracle of St Anthony*, were squarely in the tradition of Baroque painting. Each figure is formed with a few telling strokes to create a simple but powerful effect.

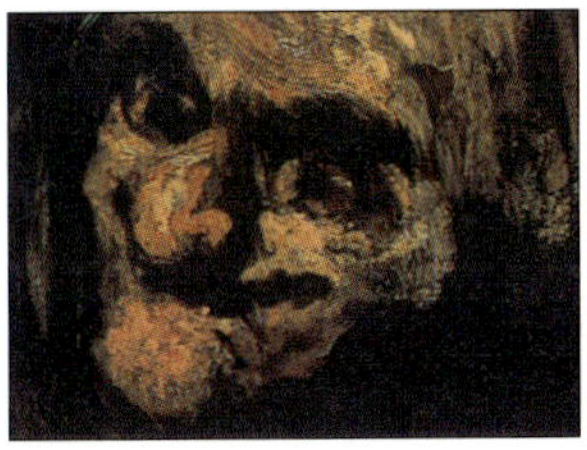

The Black Paintings show Goya's virtuoso brushwork at its most personal, with the details slashed on with thick impasto over a dark ground.

Goya was one of the great manipulators of paint, like Titian, Rubens, and Rembrandt. But the freedom of his technique, which made such an impact on 19th-century painters, was a direct continuation of the Baroque tradition, in which the fewest number of brushstrokes are exploited for maximum potential.

In Goya's time the traditional technique of building up the density of values and colors by working in successive layers over a monochrome underpainting was still the norm, and it is the method he would have learned in his apprentice years. But later, notably when he became so successful as a portrait painter that he had to work extremely rapidly, he perfected the method of direct (or *alla prima*) painting that most artists now use — paint is premixed on the palette so that each brushstroke is an approximation to the finished value and color. Goya sometimes employed both methods in one work, using layers of delicate glazes in one part and painting wet into wet in others. He varied the colors of his grounds, sometimes using a dark priming and sometimes allowing the warm color of a red priming to break through as a counterpoint to grays and cool colors. As he grew older his brushwork became more and more personal — we see dots, squiggles, lozenges, circles, narrow lines and thick ones, and he would apply paint with anything that was available, including his fingers.

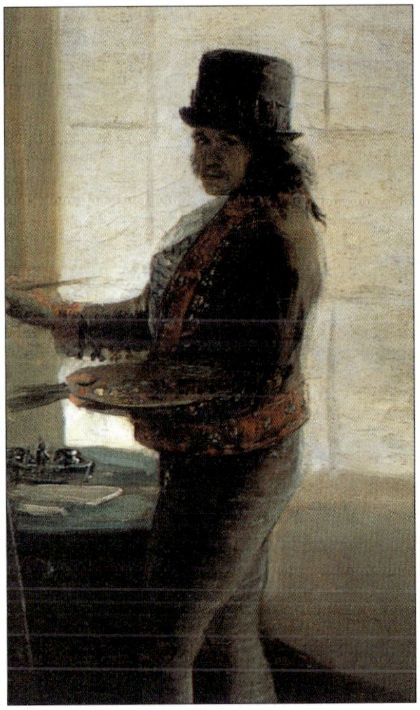

Goya's output was prodigious, and he worked very fast, often completing a painting in no more than an hour. He rarely made use of background detail, and tended to limit his color harmonies to two, or a clash of two main colors reconciled by harmonies. He particularly loved cool blue-grays and salmon pinks, and often used thinned black paint to establish details. In this self-portrait he has shown himself working with candles fixed around the band of his hat to provide a back-up light. This seems a somewhat bizarre device, but was evidently effective — it is recorded that he often finished his paintings by artificial light.

Chronology of Goya's Life

1746 30 March, Francisco José de Goya y Lucientes born at Fuendetodos.
1760 Begins four-year apprenticeship in the studio of José Luzán at Saragossa.
1763 Unsuccessful attempt to gain a scholarship to the Academy of San Fernando in Madrid.
1771 First commission: frescoes for the Pilar Cathedral at Saragossa.
1774 Invited by the Neo-classical artist, Raphael Mengs, to work for the Royal Tapestry works of Santa Barbara.
1775 First tapestry commissions.
1778 Begins a series of etchings after Velasquez's paintings.
1780 Successful reception of his painting *Christ on the Cross.* Unanimously elected a member of the Academy of San Fernando.
1784 Birth of his son Javier.
1785 Appointed assistant director of painting at the Academy of San Fernando.
1786 Appointed painter to the king.
1789 Coronation of Charles IV. Goya promoted to official court painter.
1791-2 Paints the last of his tapestry cartoons.
1792-3 Goya is stricken with a serious illness that leaves him profoundly deaf.
1795 Succeeds Francisco Bayeu as director of painting at the Academy of San Fernando.
1796 Stays with the recently widowed Duchess of Alba at her Sanlúcar estate.
1797 Announcement of the publication of *Los Caprichos.*
1798 Paints frescoes for the Church of San Antonio de la Florida, Madrid.

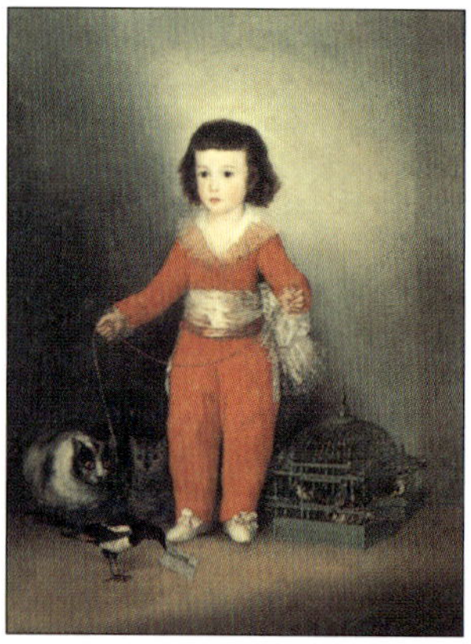

Don Manuel Osorio de Zuñiga

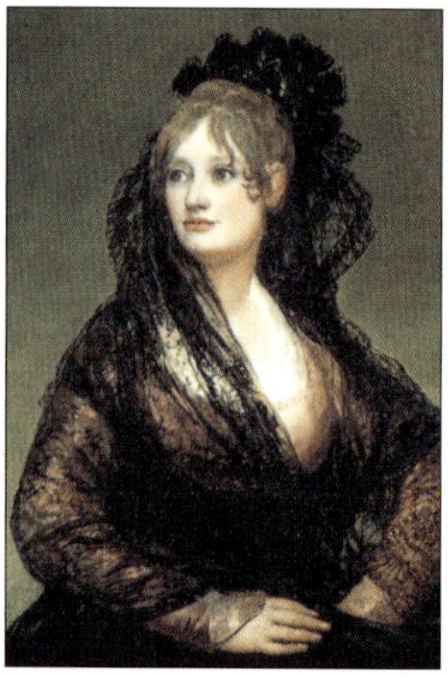

Doña Isabel Cobos de Porcel

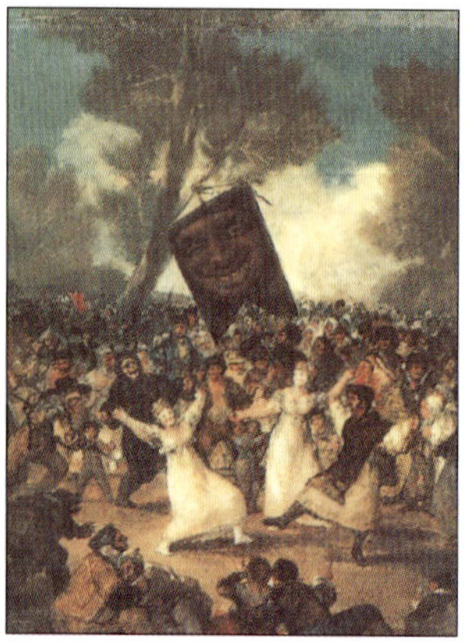

The Burial of the Sardine

1799 Publication of *Los Caprichos.* Appointed first court painter.
1808 Napoleon's troops enter Spain, Joseph Bonaparte made king. Uprising in Madrid on 2 May and subsequent executions on 3 May.
1810 Works on the *The Disasters of War* etchings.
1811 Awarded the Royal Order of Spain by Joseph.
1814 Restoration of Ferdinand VII to the Spanish throne
1816 Publication of the *Tauromachia* series.
1819 Purchases House of the Deaf Man. Falls ill at the end of the year. Recovers to make first experiments with lithography.
1800 Paints *Charles IV and his Family.*
1804-5 Probable date of *Portrait of Dona Isabel Cobos de Porcel.*
1812-9 Paints *The Burial of the Sardine.*
1814 Paints two canvases commemorating uprising of 1808: *The Second of May* and *The Third of May.*
1820-2 Paints Black Paintings on wall of house.
1824 Goya goes into hiding as liberals suffer persecution. On 30 May he is allowed to leave Spain. Stays in Paris and then (September) settles in Bordeaux with a young German widow, Leocadia Weiss.
1825 Set of lithographs: *The Bulls of Bordeaux.* Paints a number of ivory miniatures.
1826 Brief sojourn in Madrid to secure pension. The painter Vincent Lopez paints his portrait.
1827 Second visit to Madrid since self-imposed exile.
1828 Dies on 16 April.

THE PAINTINGS

A Walk in Andalusia: Majas and the Muffled Majos

(tapestry cartoon)
August 1777
$108\frac{1}{4} \times 74\frac{3}{4}$in/$2.75 \times 1.9$m
Oil on canvas
Prado, Madrid

The gestures and poses of the figures betray the theatrical origins of this scene, in which the mood is at once decorative and melodramatic. The setting, in spite of the title, is not Andalusia but one of the many parks of Madrid. Like the work of the 18th-century French artist Antoine Watteau, the painting was designed to appeal to the cultivated tastes of the aristocracy, and the tapestry woven from it was destined for the dining room of the princes of the Asturias in the Prado Palace. The values, colors, and forms are all clearly demarcated to help the weavers transform the work into a successful textile design, but in later cartoons Goya became progressively less constrained by these limitations.

The colorful characters inhabiting Goya's designs are often, as in this case, taken from the demi-monde of the *majas* and *majos,* whose flamboyant dress and behavior were often imitated by the upper and middle classes. They bore themselves with a haughty grandeur, the men wearing tight knee-breeches and stockings, ostentatiously buckled shoes, short jackets and a colorful *bandilero* around their waists in which lay hidden a *navaje,* or folding knife. The outfit was completed by the dark, dramatic swathes of a heavy black cloak and a low-brimmed hat. The women affected the same short jackets, and were potentially as dangerous as their partners, since a sharp dagger lay concealed beneath their wide skirts. The fiery romances of these people were popularized by the works of such dramatists as Roman de la Cruz, and by the time this painting was completed *majaism* had become a popular trend with the fashionable upper and middle classes.

In his paintings for the Santa Barbara tapestry works Goya's training in the Baroque tradition can clearly be seen. Effects are gained with the minimum of means and an apparent ease combined with an absolute mastery of technique. These canvases do not normally possess a particularly pronounced weave although the grain of the material is distinctly noticeable in the more thinly painted areas of the cartoon. The canvas was coated with a thin glue size, and on top of this was placed a coat of colored tempera. Over this ground a coat of fairly thick oil paint was brushed to create a comparatively smooth base for the painting.

The color of Goya's ground is easily discernible and was always used to give a warmth to the overall composition and to enhance the decorative effect of the image. Whenever he could take a short cut by using this warm ground as a positive element in his picture he did so. An example of this can be seen in the bodice of the *maja,* in which Goya has only applied the blue paint to denote the color of the velvet material, allowing the red ground to work most effectively as the shadowy area of her tunic. This practice allowed the overall coloration of the composition to remain light and airy. Goya used a red clay color for these initial stages — Seville earth which, when mixed with white, resulted in a brick-red tone that could be either left as a color in its own right or modified by the glazes that he used so inventively. In later works he lightened the value of this base color to a cool pinkish hue.

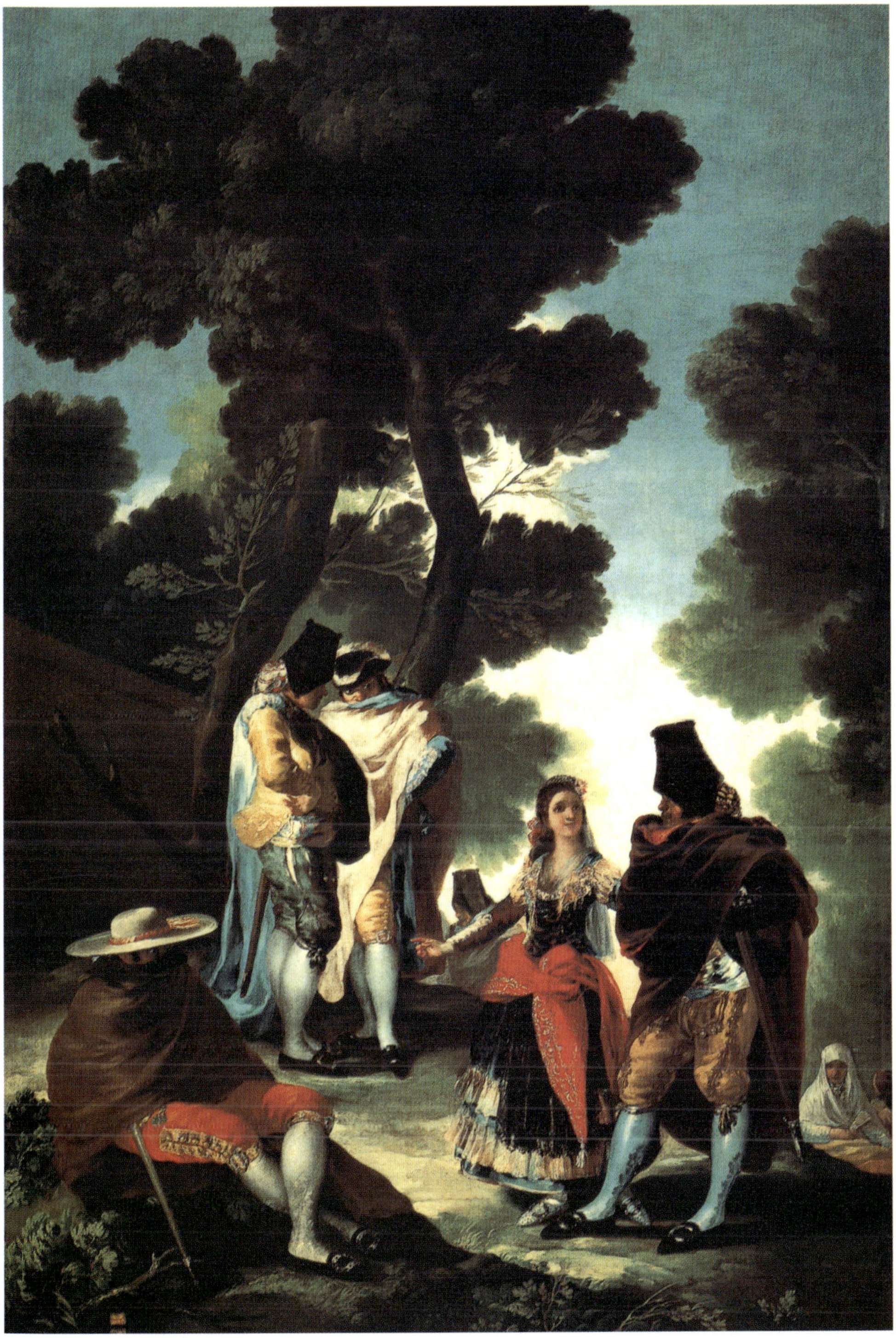

Goya was only one of a number of artists who produced works specifically designed to be translated into tapestries by the skilled workers of the Santa Barbara tapestry factory. Although the production of these cartoons was something of a chore for the artist, his work in this gave him a valuable grounding in technique and composition, which he turned to account in much of his later, more personal work.

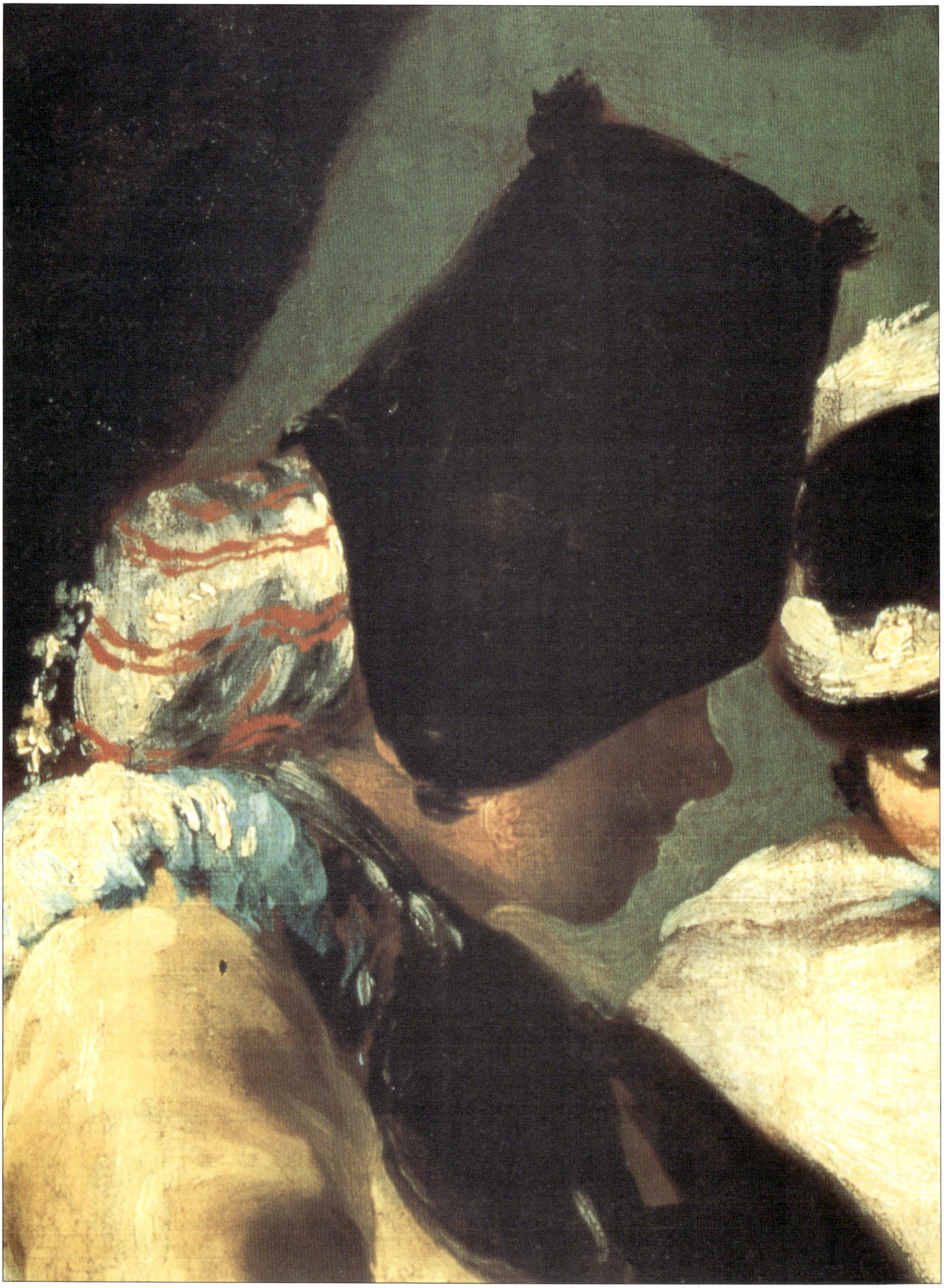

1 *Actual size detail*

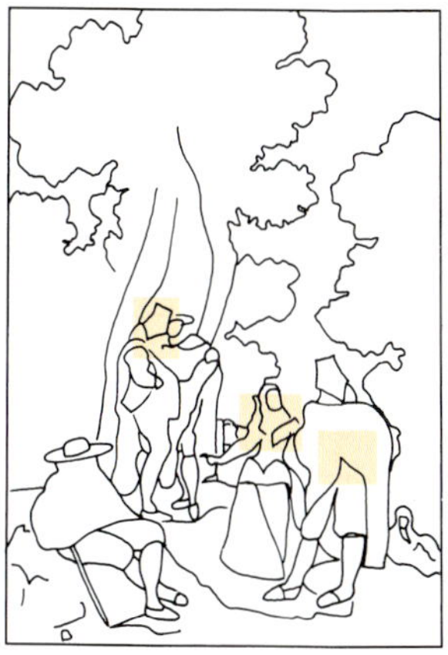

1 *Actual size detail* Goya's inventive-mark making, use of impasto and innovative freedom in use of color can be clearly seen in this detail, particularly in the *majo's* distinctive bandeau where the variously handled layers of pigment work together to create, at the right visual distance, a stunning sense of actuality.

2 Goya frequently painted on a pink ground, which allowed greater speed of execution. The way he uses the color within the composition constantly changes. Sometimes it helps to define objects, while elsewhere it is used to enhance the decorative qualities of the colors laid over it. Here it signifies not only the shadows in the heavily worked brocade, but also the more supple areas of the sleeve. Deft loops of paint added to the impastoed yellow combine to give a sumptuous and suitably gaudy richness.

3 In this area of the painting the pink ground color is clearly visible between the brushstrokes that define the material. So skillfully does Goya manipulate the presence of the ground color that it is sometimes difficult to ascertain where the underpainting is allowed to show. Separate slashes of green, blue, black, and white create the dazzling illusion of the sash.

2

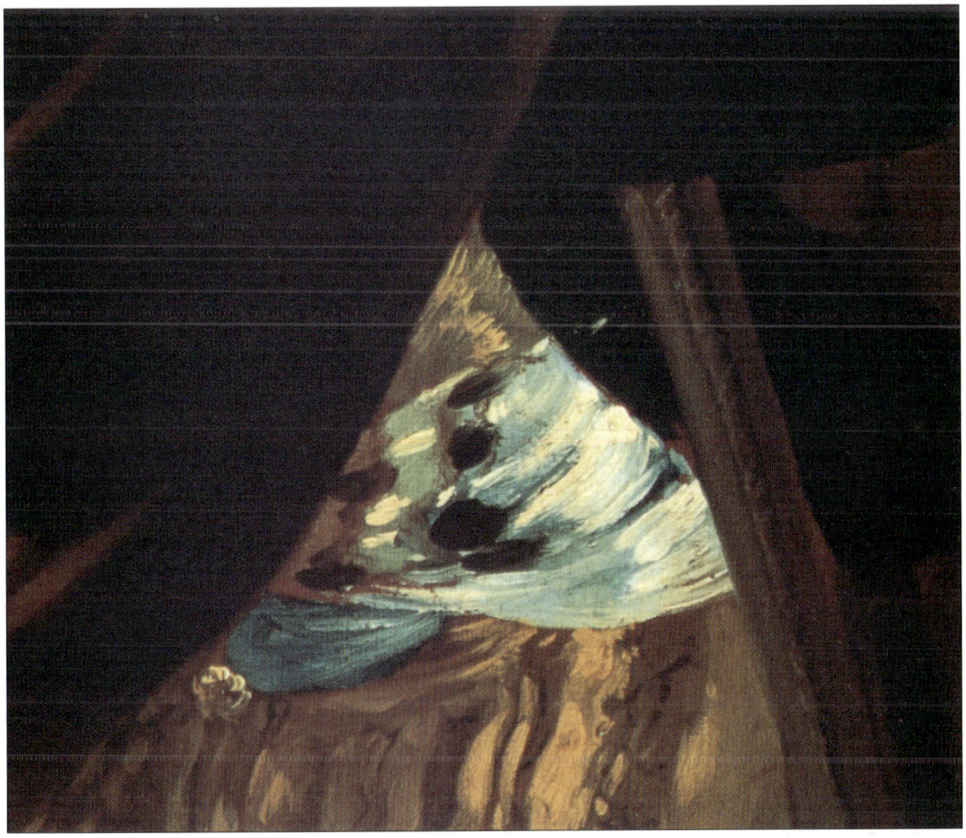

3

The Bewitched: Priest Pouring Oil on the Devil's Lamp

1797-98

$16\frac{1}{2} \times 11\frac{3}{4}$in/$42 \times 30$cm

Oil on canvas

National Gallery, London

This was one of six small witchcraft scenes commissioned by the Duke and Duchess of Osuna, for which the artist was paid 6000 reals, a considerable amount of money at the time. The Osuna family were among Goya's earliest and most supportive patrons. The duchess was a great lover of the arts, the theater and the bullfight, and it is likely that this series of paintings reflected her interests rather than those of the duke. In 1799 Goya sold to her no less than four sets of *Los Caprichos,* which consisted of eighty prints in the first edition. The paintings were produced at the same time that he was working on these etchings, and they and the paintings correspond in both subject and composition. Such scenes were highly fashionable in the liberal intellectual circles in which Goya and the Osunas moved. Eleven years earlier the Osunas had commissioned him to produce a large oil painting for the family chapel in the Cathedral of Valencia depicting St Francisco de Borja, an ancestor of the duchess, at the death-bed of a penitent. In this work, his earliest known depiction of the supernatural, blood flows miraculously from the crucifix proffered by the saint to save the dying man from the ghouls that surround his bed.

In its simple divisions of value and its use of a single somberly dressed figure, *The Bewitched* could be read as a parody on Velasquez's masterful paintings of philosophers that Goya had copied earlier in his career. The painting relates directly to a popular play written in the late 17th century by Antonio de Zamora. The book visible in the right-hand corner of the painting bears the inscription LAM DESCO, which is a reference to a speech in the play which begins "*Lámpara descomunal* [monstrous lamp] . . ."

The bewitched priest has the illusion that his life will only continue as long as the lamp in the painting remains lit. Quite sensibly, therefore, if with an understandable degree of fear, he pours oil to feed the flame. The brilliant color of the flame creates a dramatic contrast with the monochromatic treatment of the rest of the canvas, while the spotlight effect on the priest's almost caricatured features reveals the intensity of his terror. A horizontal dash of light draws attention to his feet, which are humorously juxtaposed with the cloven hooves of the hermaphrodite devil who holds out the lamp with mock servility. Behind the two figures, a group of donkeys rear out from the shadows to witness this strange scene. The light, almost farcical humor seen in the painting is absent from the gritty nightmare world of *Los Caprichos.*

Goya's concern with the supernatural remained a constant in his art. At the end of his life he returned to such subjects in his Black Paintings, in which, stripped of their anecdotal qualities, they reappear as some of the most powerful meditations on the human condition in Western art.

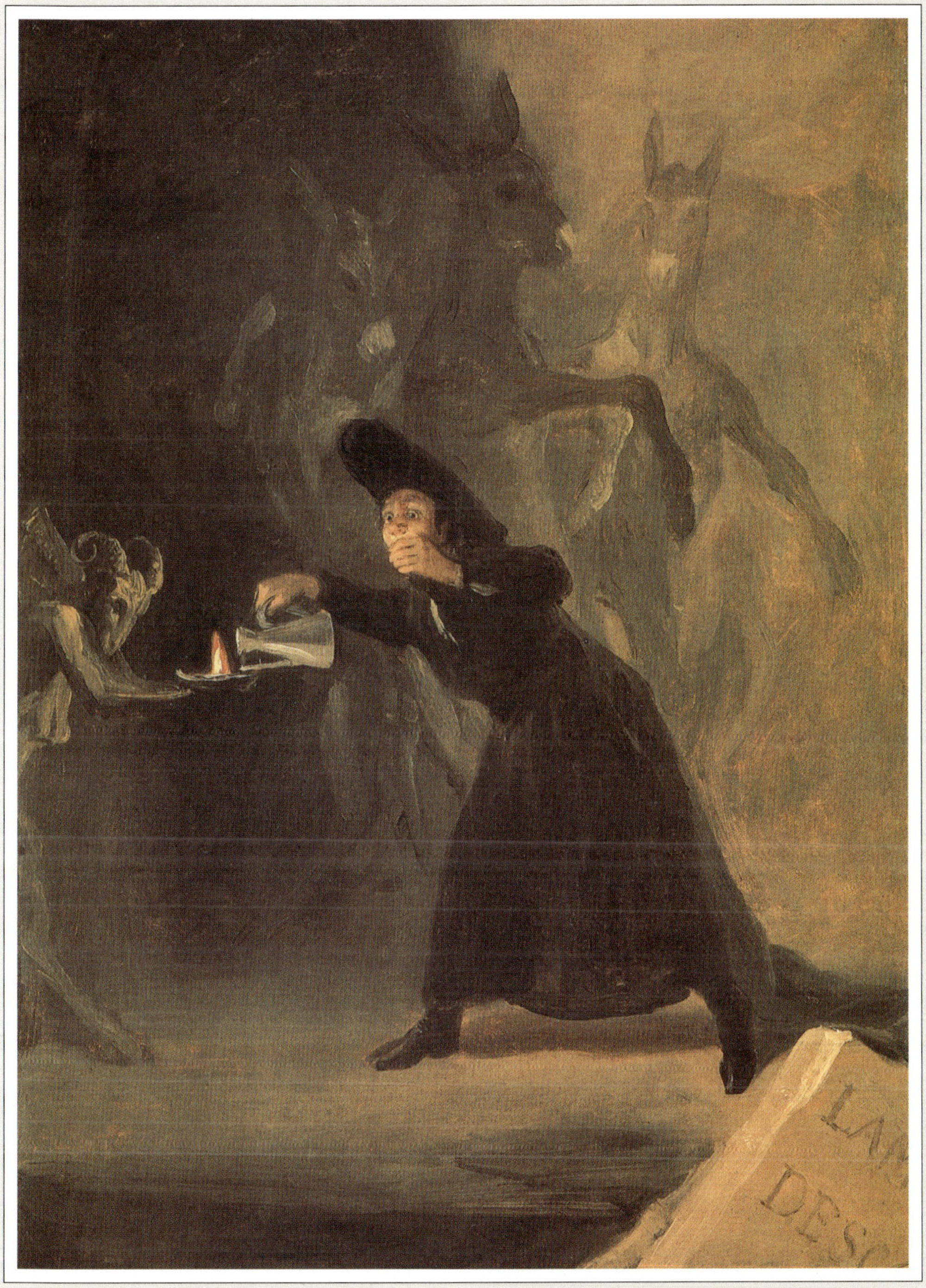

The humor of this small cabinet painting can still be appreciated today, but the obvious anecdotal quality of the work should not be allowed to obscure our appreciation of its painterly qualities. The construction is tightly knit, resting upon the meticulously balanced gradations of light and dark. The fresh and lively handling of the paint surface further unites the separate elements of the composition to create a pleasing decorative ensemble.

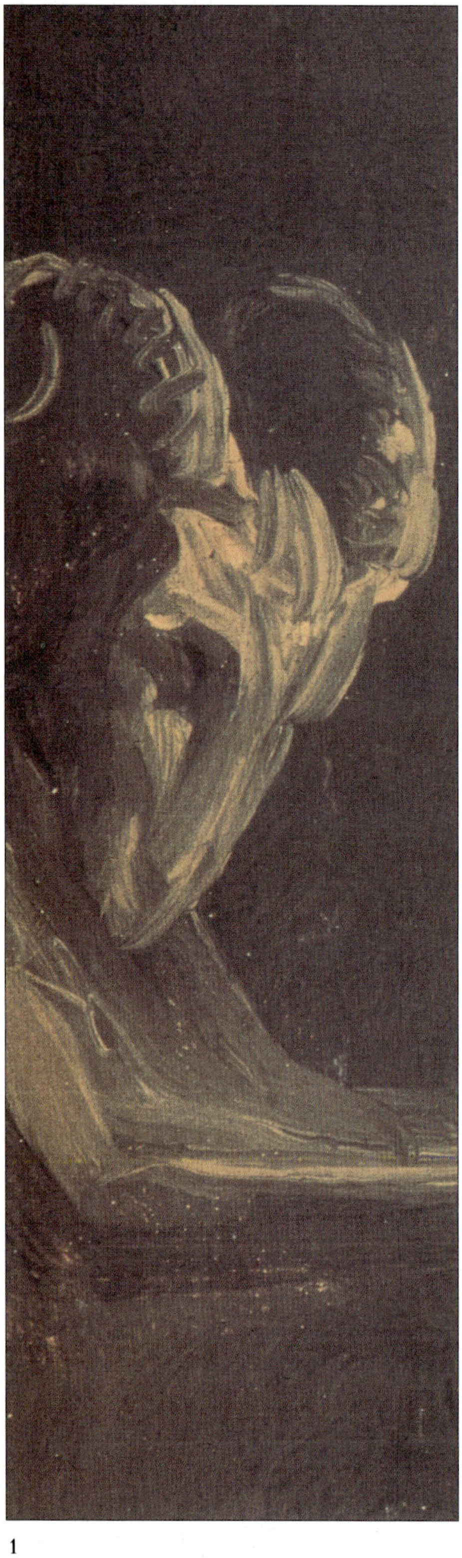

1

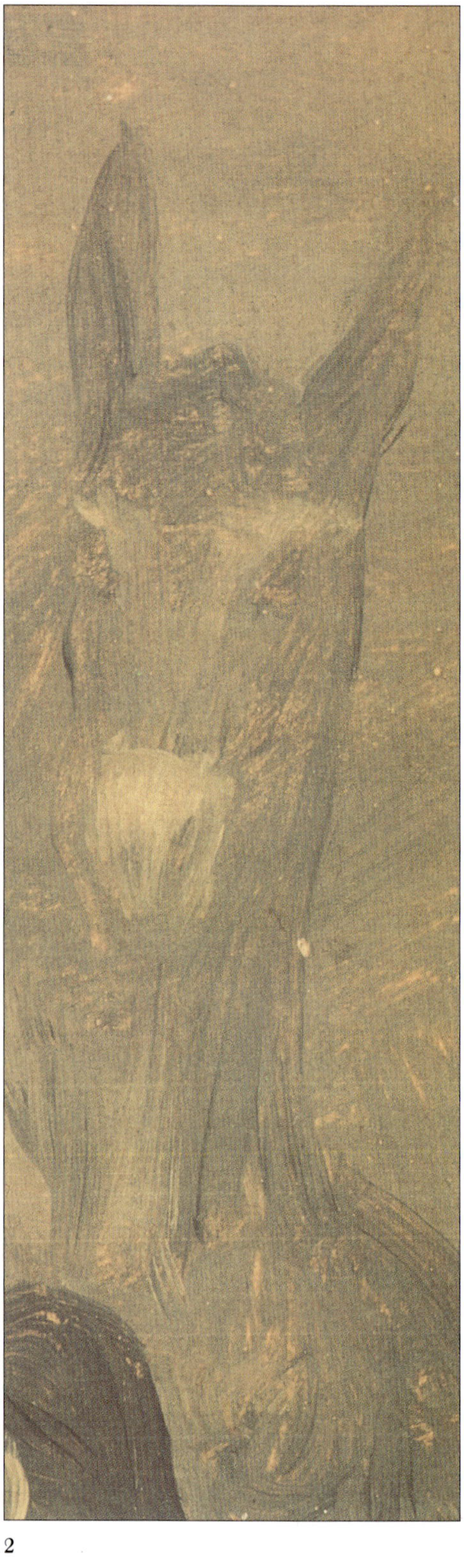

2

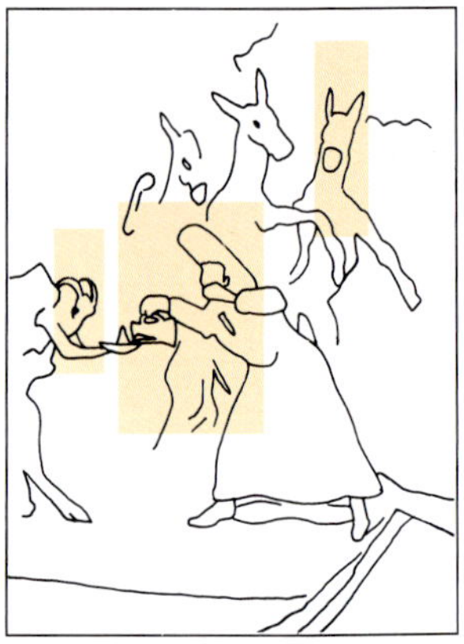

1 The devil's head emerges out of the darkness, indicated only by those parts of its anatomy which catch the somewhat unconvincingly powerful light emanating from the lamp.

2 The ghostly images of the rearing donkeys are lightly sketched in a few tones. The warm color of the ground and the gray of the underpainting allow the creatures to form a dominant part of the background, while at the same time giving the impression of melting into it.

3 A variety of Goya's techniques can be clearly seen in these details. Goya moves from the merest of indications to a more detailed working, as is evident in the handling of the priest's face, the dramatic center of this small painting. Carefully drawn details, such as the raised hand, suggest a sense of finish that is absent from the rest of the picture. The warm ground Goya liked to use can be clearly sensed in all parts of the painting, giving a richness and glow to the predominantly cool tones.

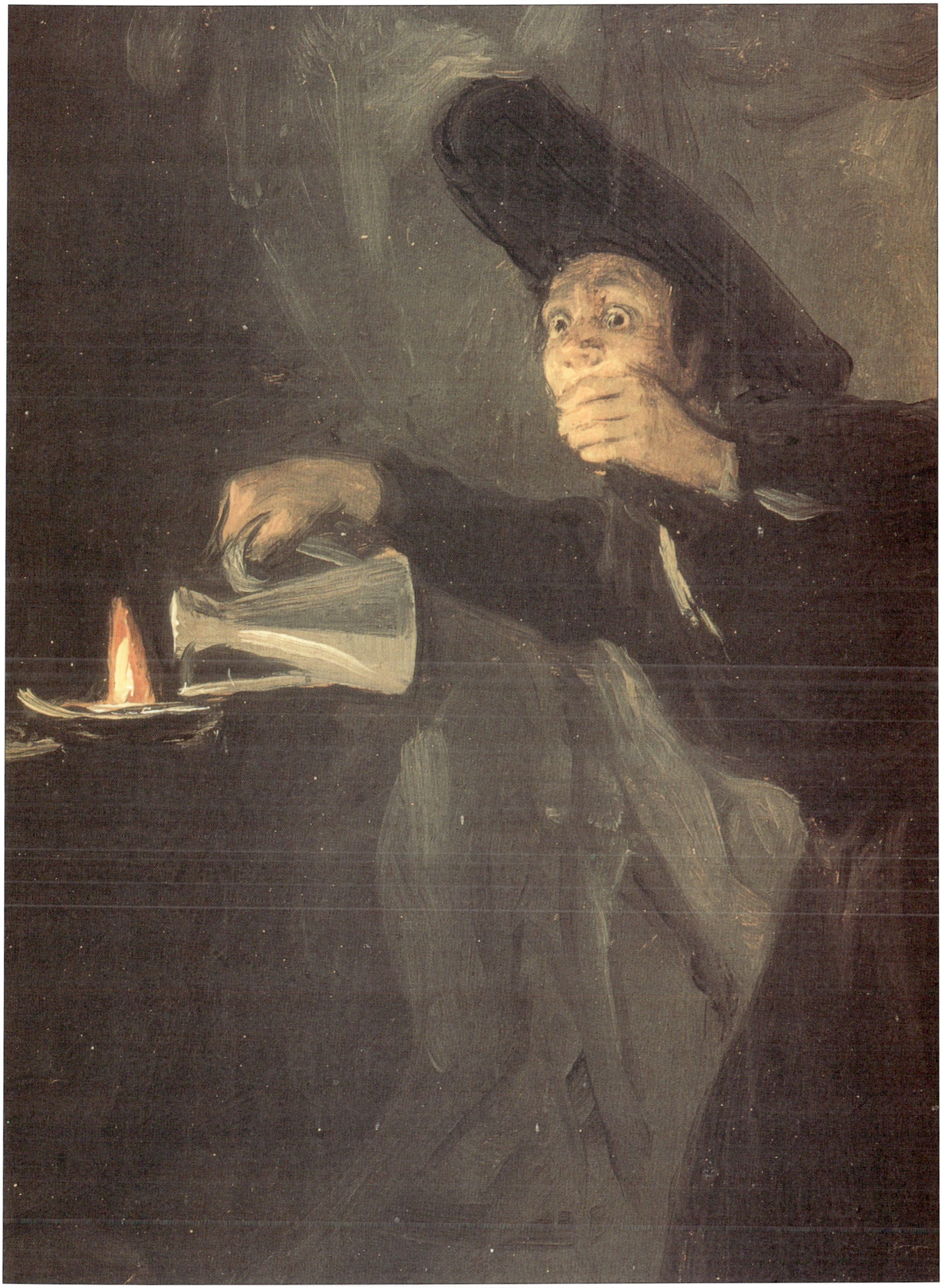

3

A Miracle of St Anthony

1798

(detail)

Fresco

San Antonio de la Florida

Goya and his assistant Asensi Juliá painted the cupola and supporting decorations of the hermitage of San Antonio de la Florida in 1798. In reverse of traditional practice, a heavenly throng of angels supports the all too human world that makes up the subject matter of the painting. The story is relatively simple. St Anthony's father had been accused of murder, and in order to prove his innocence the saint was prevailed upon to resuscitate the corpse of the murdered man. The fresco shows the very moment of the miracle, with St Anthony surrounded by about fifty figures of both sexes and various ages and social position. Each shows a different degree of interest in the unusual event. Some raise their hands and faces in ecstasy, while others, less easily impressed or perhaps unaware of the miraculous nature of the resuscitation, indulge in the more normal activities of a crowd. To the left of the saint, balancing the form of an old man in yellow who might be his father, is a man in a yellow jerkin and slouch hat who turns to force his way through the crowd – the murderer perhaps?

The first impression on entering the chapel of San Antonio is one of clarity and light. At the center of the dome is a lantern whose pierced sides form both the actual source of light and the imaginary illumination for the composition. In accordance with the architecture of the church, the coloration of the fresco is based around grays – almost unbelievable in their range – counterpointed by broad swathes of low-value color. The varied values of gray are activated by the presence throughout the fresco of black and white and by separate groups of various single colors that are placed in a rhythmical order across the composition. The painted balustrade continues the line of the architecture, and creates a vivid sense of space and actuality. The crowd leans, climbs, or falls away from this railing, while swathes of material, human limbs, or the falling folds of sleeves break up its stark geometry. The overwhelming sensation is one of movement and human drama. Once again Goya's training in the Baroque tradition and his experience as a tapestry designer has allowed him to work with an astonishing abbreviation of technique and a sureness of touch that places him firmly in the company of the 17th-century Italian painters, such as Luca Giordiano and Tiepolo. These great decorative painters were among many who had found employment in Spain, carrying out grand fresco schemes for the royal palaces.

Goya's technique was that of *buon fresco,* painting directly onto the still wet plaster in a free and spontaneous way, and forming the figures with a few expressive slashes of his brush. In each figure there are two or three major shifts of value; Goya's tonal accuracy allowed him to situate his figures in the imagined space of the dome using the minimal amount of detail, making the entire work, when seen from below, throb with the pulse of real life. The cupola is relatively small, and although the figures are over lifesize, the general effect is one of intimacy, with each figure clearly identifiable. Not least of Goya's achievements was that the fresco took him less than three months to complete.

In the Baroque tradition, the painting aims at creating a clear and powerful effect – such works were not produced to be seen as masterpieces of painting, but as dramatic narratives. The modern viewer, taking a close-up view with binoculars or telephoto lenses, can discern parallels with 19th- and 20th-century Expressionism, but for Goya such effects were simply the result of the methods employed to overcome technical problems. Nor were they unique to Goya, as is shown by a treatise on Spanish painting by Palomino written in the early 18th century.

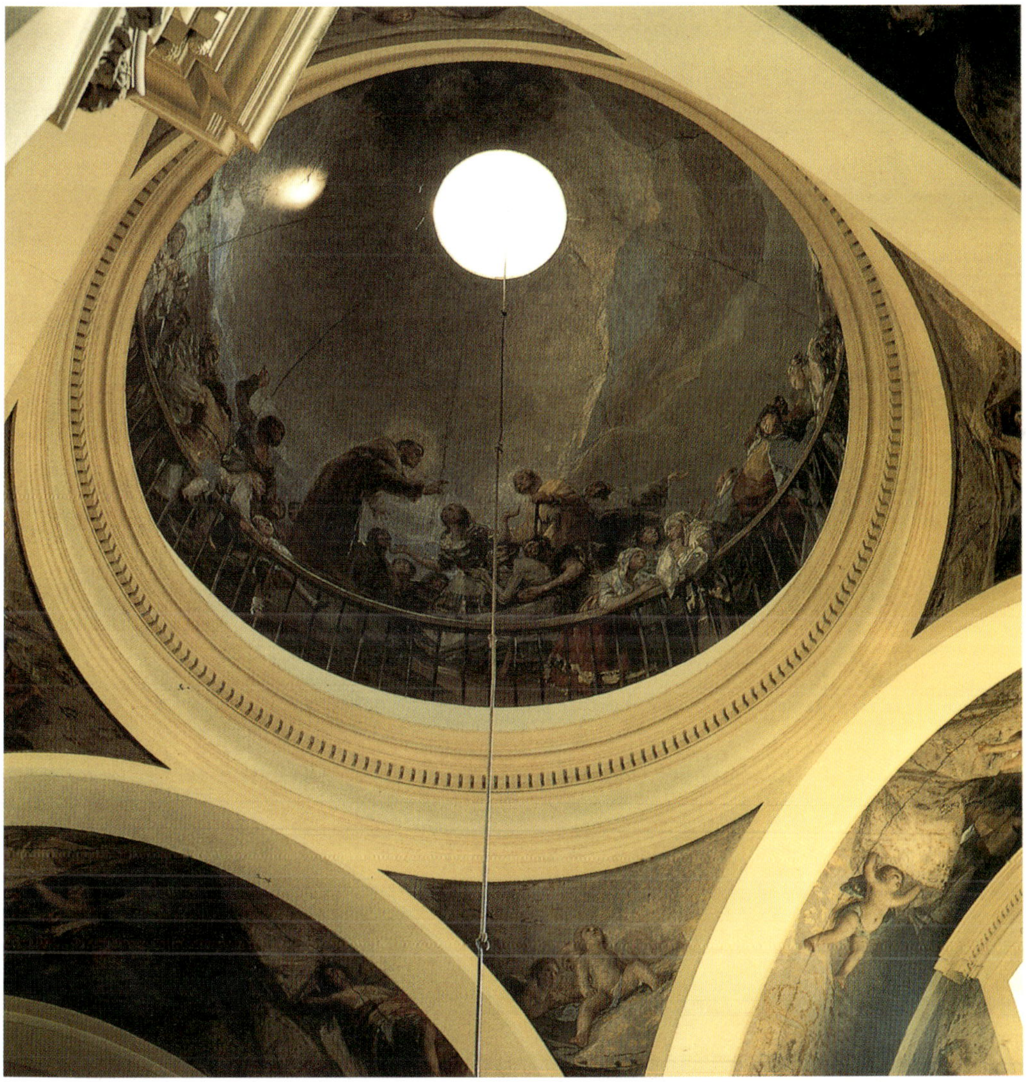

Goya produced a number of paintings for churches in his early career, and this is one of the finest examples in the whole of 18th-century church decoration. Goya, who had petitioned the king for the commission (San Antonio was owned by the crown), was in total artistic control of the project. Following customary practice, he claimed for enough painting materials to last him a number of years after the completion of the work. The small church, which now contains the artist's tomb, is one of his most secure claims to fame.

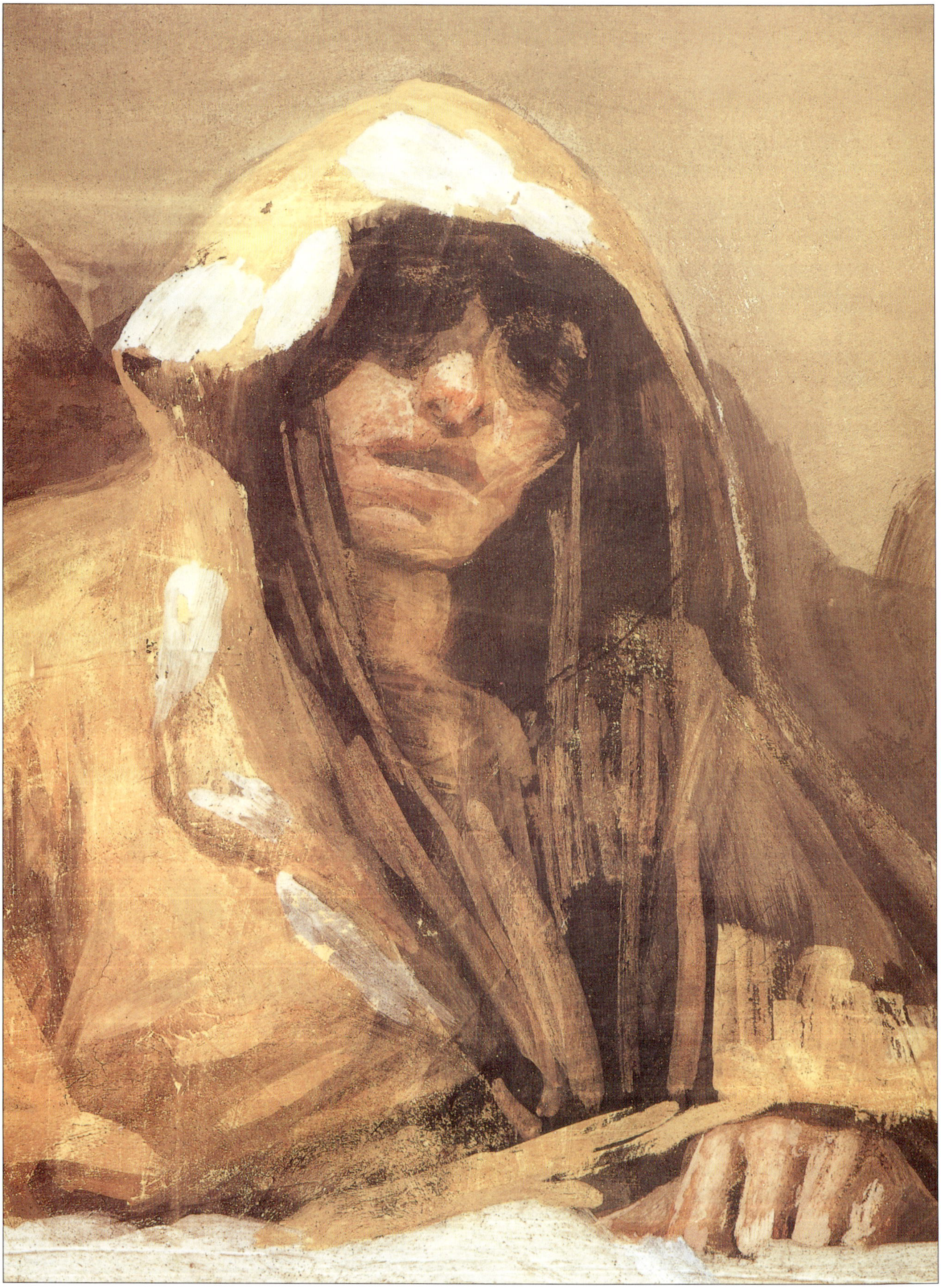

1

1 Fresco painting demands an absolute sureness of technique because few alterations can be made. Goya completed this commission within 120 days. It was painted *al fresco,* the pigments being dissolved in limewater and painted directly onto specially prepared wet plaster. This, as it dries, becomes part of the physical structure of the wall, with any underdrawing (or *sinopia*) obliterated in the process. Once dry, a few additional touches can be laid across the surface to define the image further. These details show that Goya treated all the various elements of his composition as painterly problems to be solved in the most direct and simple way possible. Such thinking allowed him to make the most extraordinary and effective "shorthand" notations for the people and other elements that fill his composition.

2 The dramatic rhythms of Goya's staccato brushstrokes have the vigor and force of a modern expressionistic painter, and his freedom in this recalcitrant medium equals that seen in his oil paintings. An interplay of simple masses and constructional marks creates a totally convincing image of these three women lost in reverie.

3 The most complicated of effects are translated into the simplest of technical operations involving an ever-changing use of over-painting with opaque or translucent paint.

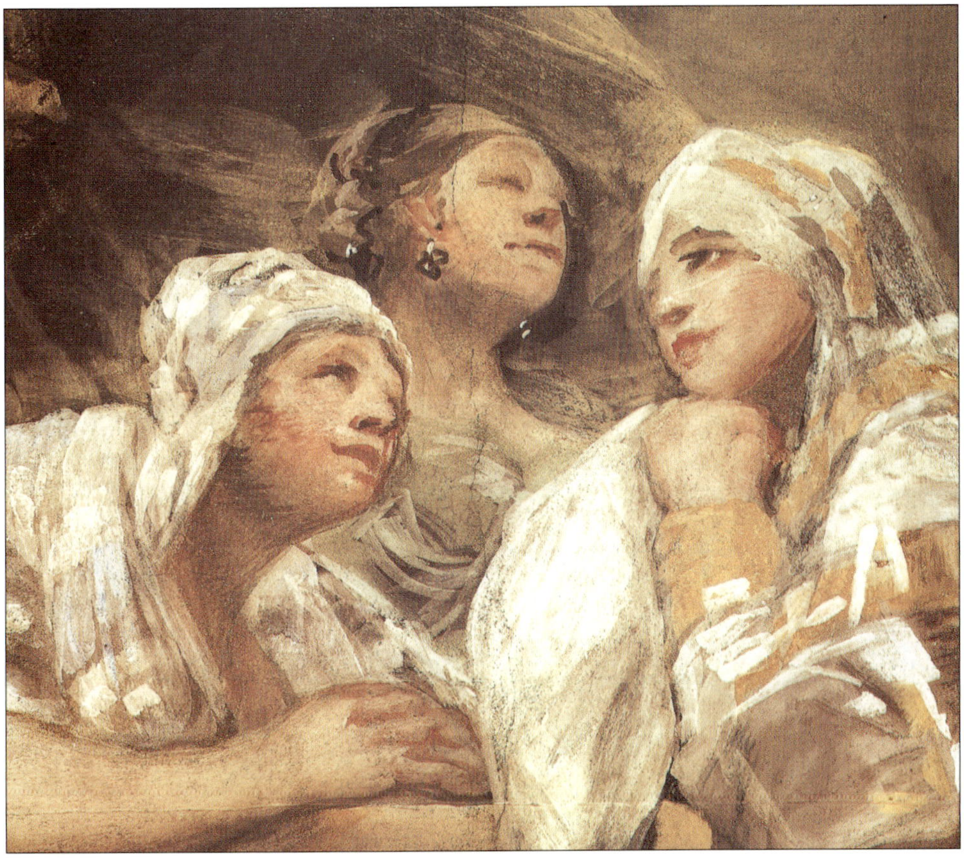

2

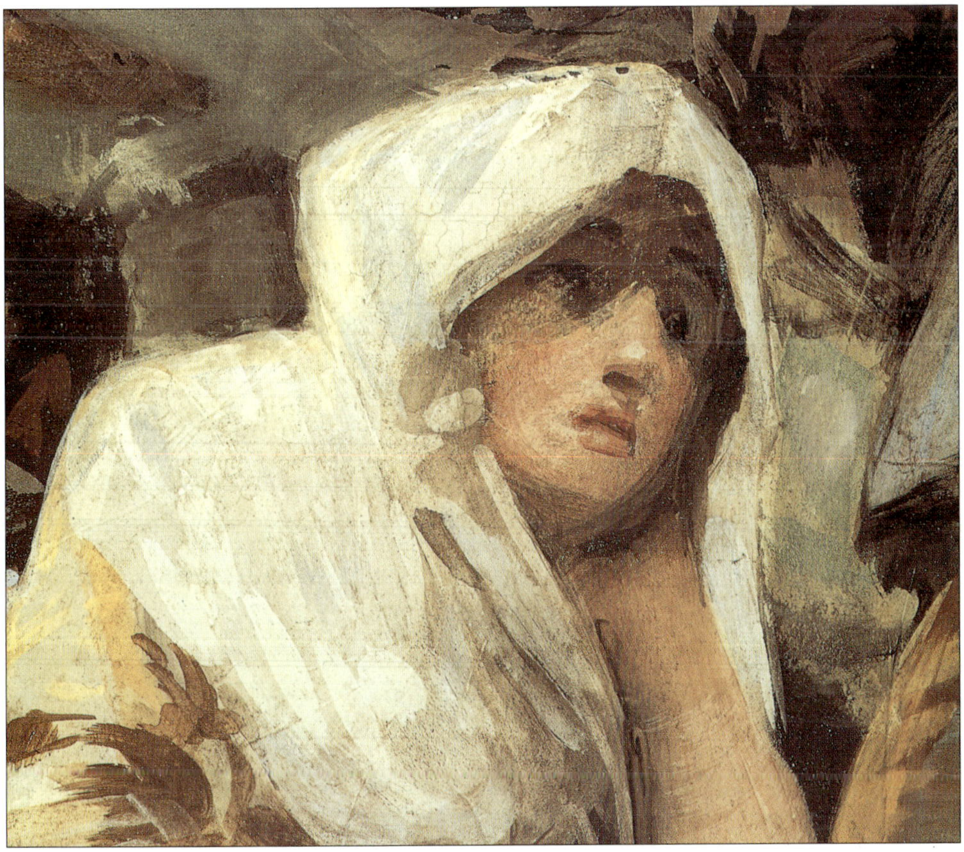

3

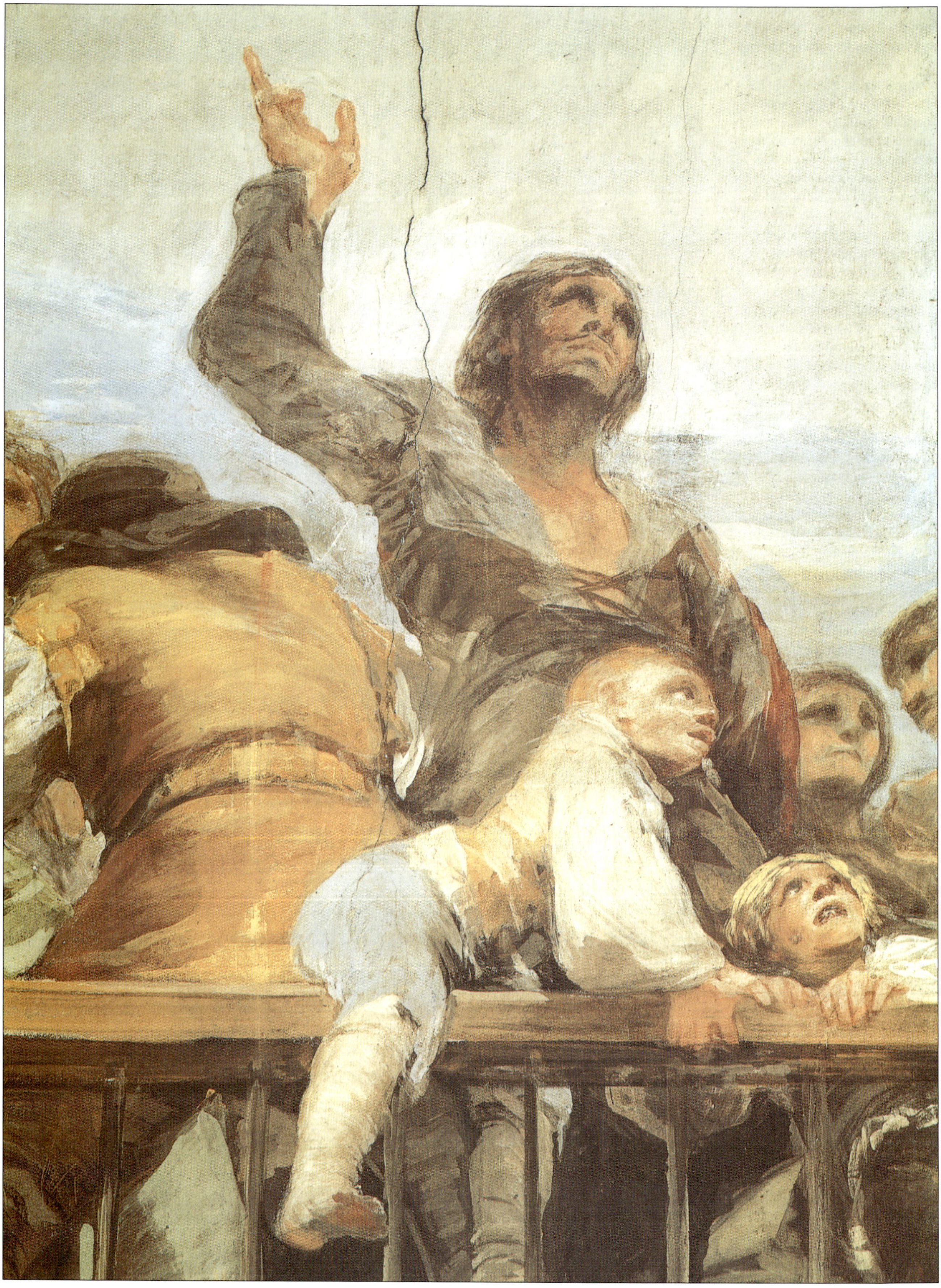

1

1 The limited color range of the fresco can be well appreciated in this detail. The basic blue-gray balance is counterpointed by dramatic touches of the primary colors. Goya's task was to paint a fresco that had to be read from a distance, hence his exaggerations and simple dramatic shifts of value and color. These, when seen from the floor of the church, are vivid and convincing, retaining the vitality of actual life.

2 The spectators each make their own reaction to the miracle taking place in their presence. This young boy's expression of awe and repulsion is brilliantly caught in a few deft brushstrokes. His upturned face is placed in space by the directional broken touches evident in the fair hair and in the single mark that defines his chin. The white overpainting of the sleeve and ragged leggings contrast with broad sweeps that indicate the larger masses of the painting, contrasts that add to the sense of vitality that permeates the composition.

3 Three simple areas of paint create the illusion of a fully rounded human being. Directional brushstrokes describe the anatomical structures of the figures with brilliant economy of means. The features are fixed with an equal freedom of technique, a few judicious white highlights scumbled across the surface with a dry brush bringing the whole into relief.

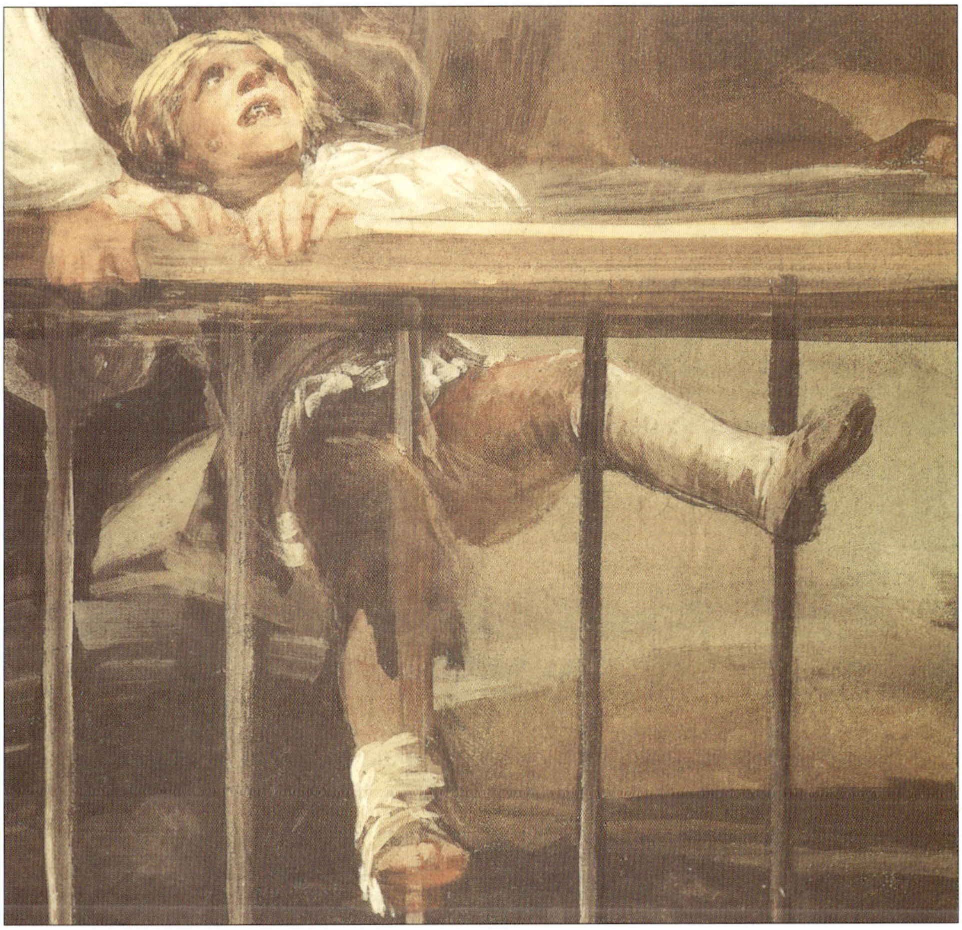

2

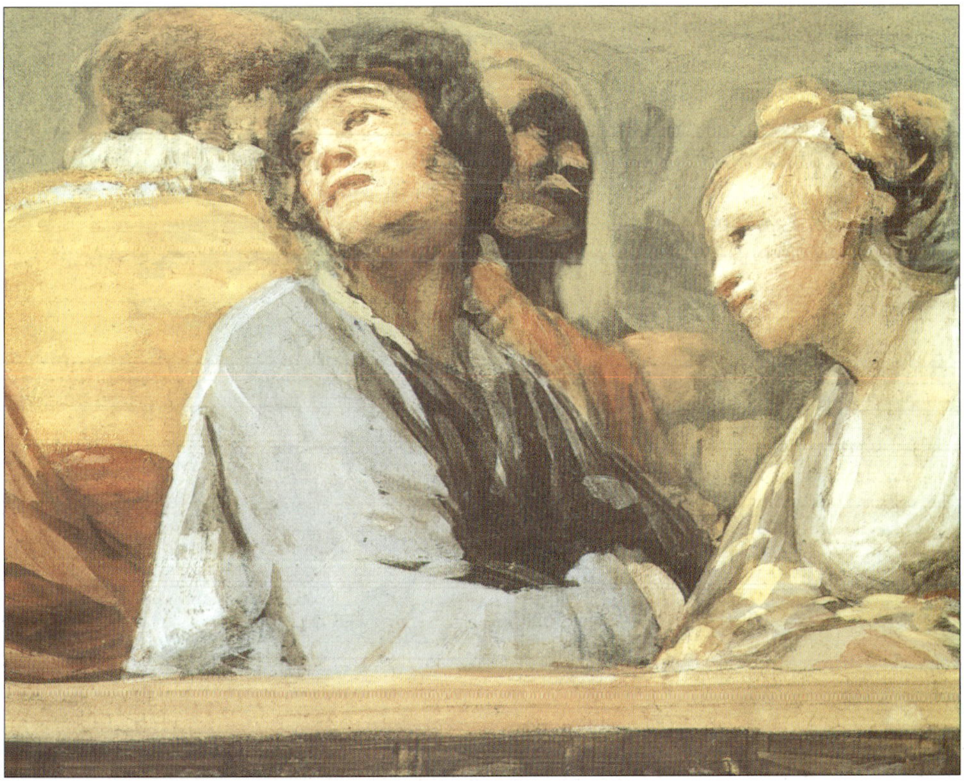

3

Charles IV and his Family

1800

100×132½in/254×336.5cm

Oil on canvas

Prado, Madrid

In an age like our own that tends to associate glamour with power, the apparent honesty of Goya's treatment of these obviously less than perfect human beings may come as something of a shock. There are few other royal portraits that can match the brutal frankness of this depiction of the realities of hereditary monarchy. And yet the royal family were apparently pleased with the painting; Queen Maria Luisa wrote of the sketches (which are even less flattering than the final version), "Tomorrow Goya is beginning another portrait of me. He has finished the others [for the family group] and they are all very well done." Nearly half a century later, the 19th-century French poet and critic Théophile Gautier described the king and his family as looking like "the corner baker and his wife after they have won the lottery."

The work has obvious parallels with Velasquez's famous *Las Meninas* (see page 193), which is, amongst other things, an informal portrait of the Infanta and her royal parents. Goya had copied the painting as a learning exercise earlier in his career, and the reference to the Velasquez family group would have been appreciated by the royal family, as it linked them through the painting to the illustrious "Golden Age" of Spanish history.

On April 22, 1800, the artist was summoned to the summer palace in order to paint the entire royal family, and less than two months later, on June 13, the work was finished. It is very much a studio concoction, produced from a number of rapidly painted portrait sketches. The standing figure in blue is the king's eldest son, Ferdinand, who was later to lead a successful *coup d'etat* against his father (see page 198). The girl who stands next to him, her face turned to the wall, could perhaps signify his as yet unidentified future bride. At the center of the painting is the real controller of Spain's destiny, the matriarchal figure of the Bourbon queen, flanked by her youngest children. To her left is her husband – king in name, but overshadowed, both in the painting and in real life, by the more dominant personality of his wife. The nature of the composition and the brilliant characterization of the individual personages ensure that the eye of the viewer returns again and again to the secondary members of the group. The eyes of the majority of the family are focused with varying degrees of intensity out from the canvas at the viewer, who now occupies the position originally taken by the artist. Part of the painting's chilling atmosphere comes from the way Goya has placed himself in a position which would in reality be impossible. We can see the corner of his canvas on the extreme left of the painting, while he stands facing us, half-hidden in the shadows, shrewdly surveying the motley group of humanity it is his job to immortalize.

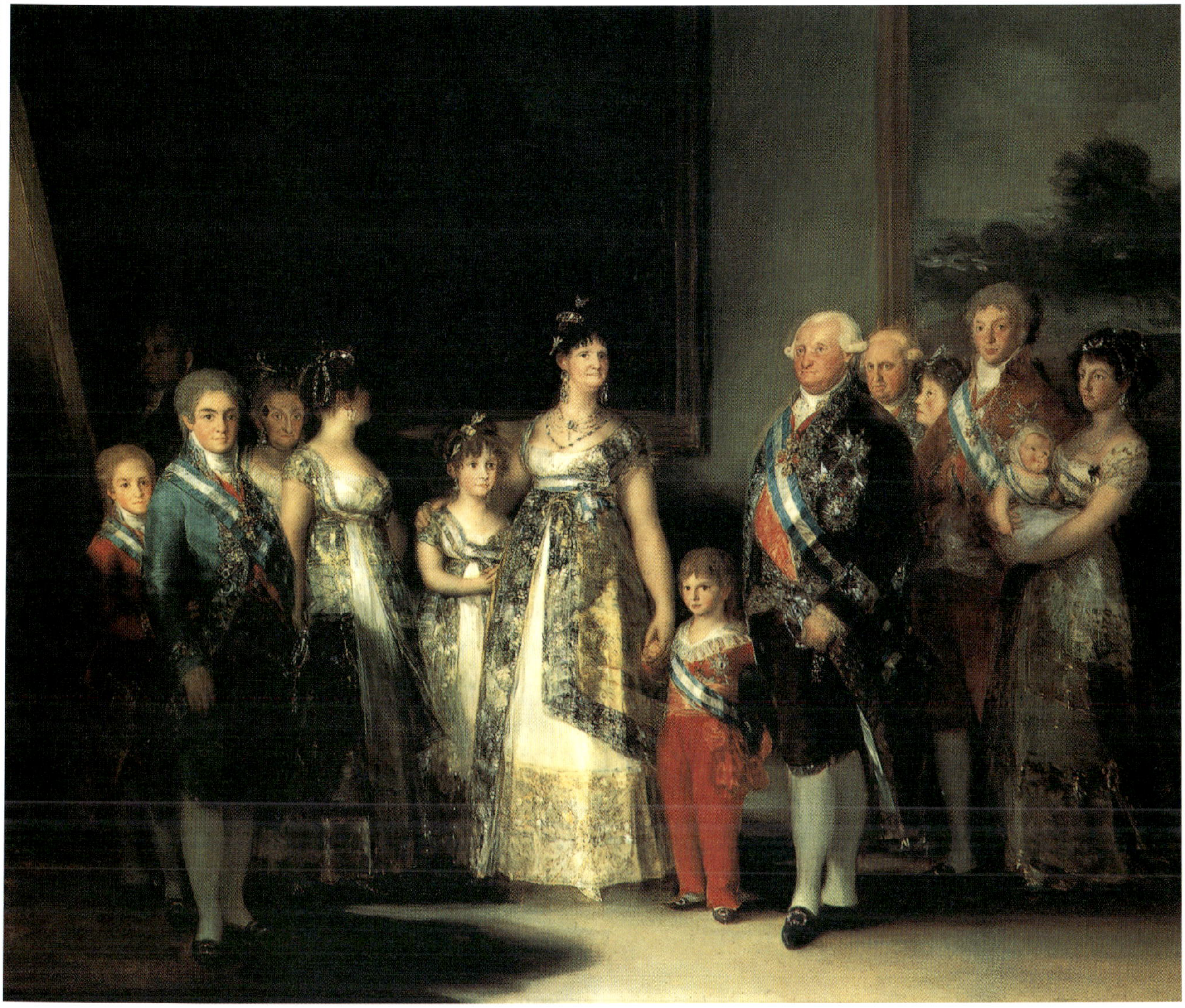

Even today, nearly 200 years after Goya "fixed" the Spanish royal family on canvas, the imperious stare of Queen Maria Luisa has enough regal power to stop casual strollers through the Prado in their tracks. Paintings such as these were the means by which royal authority could be disseminated via prints to a broader audience, and most were flattering portrayals. Goya, however, painted what he saw, and it is still a matter of some amazement that this disquietenly frank image of the Spanish Bourbon household was accepted by its sitters.

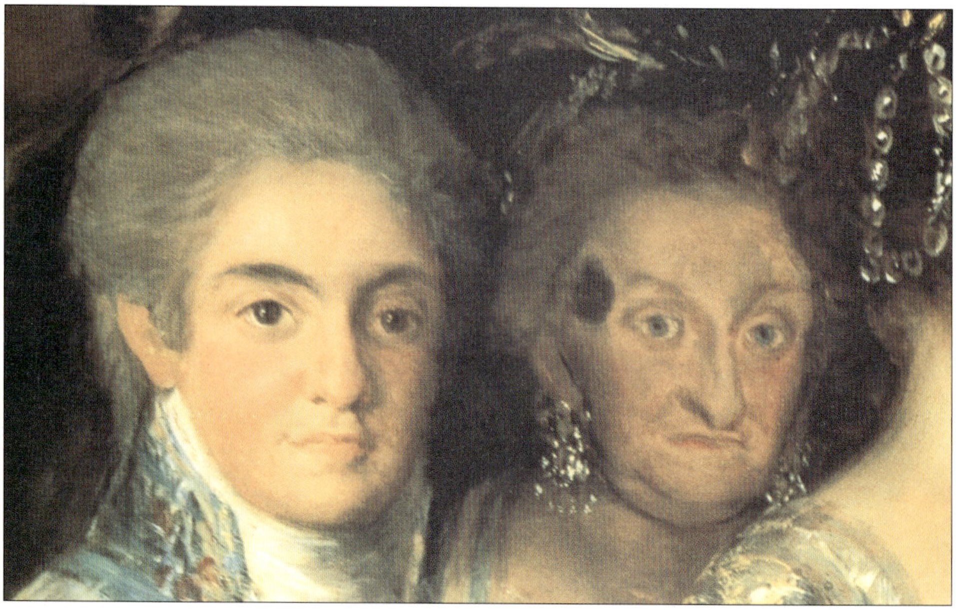

1

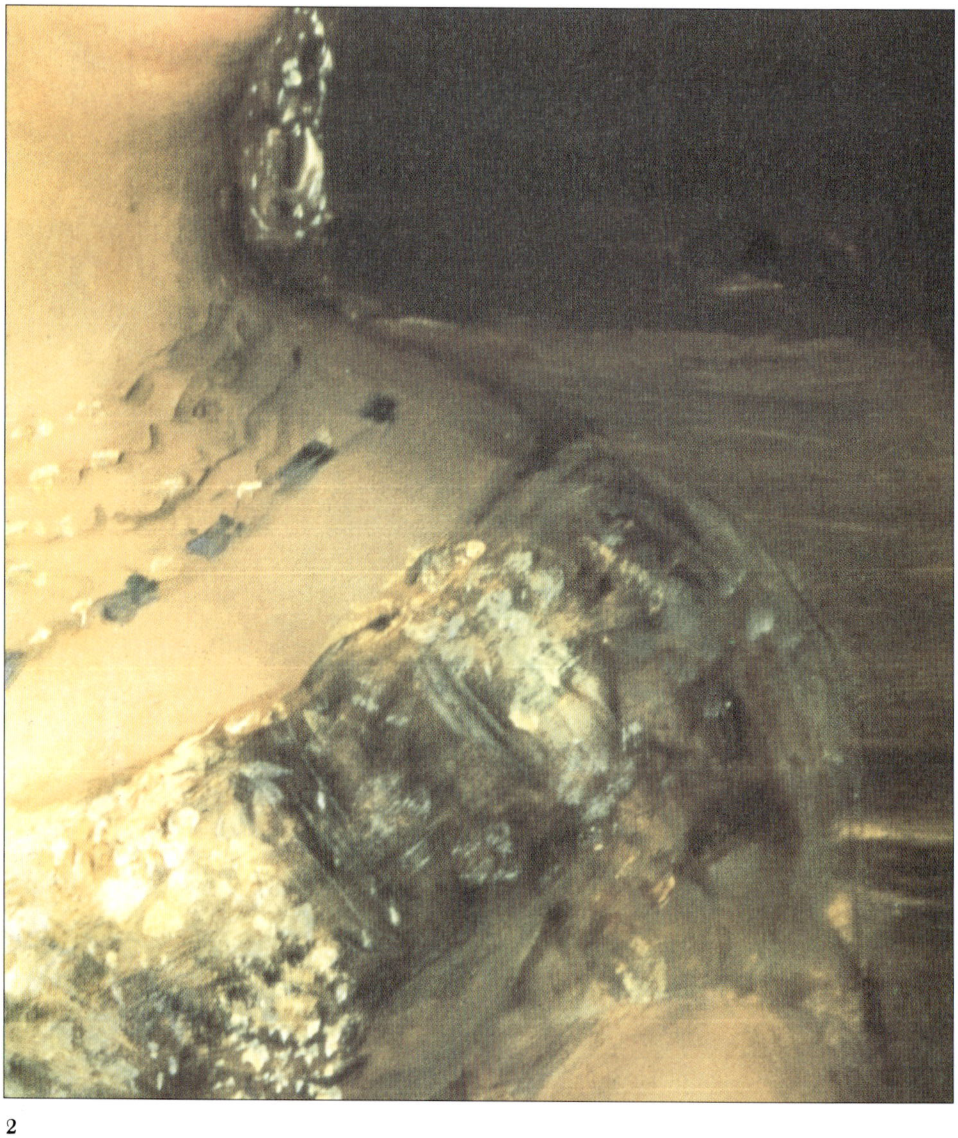

2

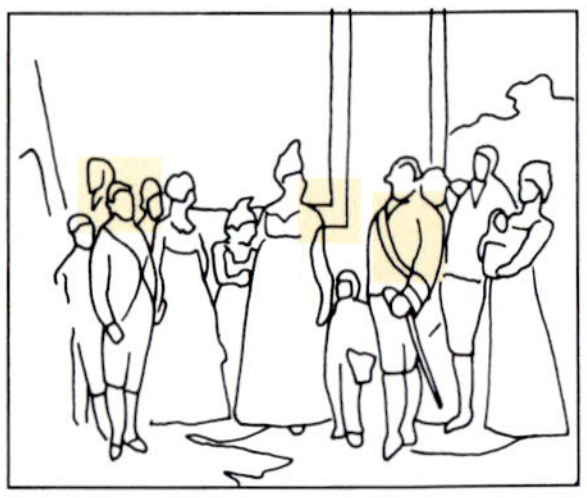

1 Certainly Goya's most flattering portrayal of the Prince of the Asturias, Ferdinand, monarch-to-be. The woman to his left is Doña Maria Josefa, the elder sister of the king, who died shortly after the painting was finished. Both figures, set in Hogarthian contrast to each other, are vivid examples of Goya's apparently objective stance and extraordinary powers of character analysis.

2 Goya's varied brushwork allows him to contrast the cosmeticized smoothness of the queen's flesh against the rich fabric of her dress. A few scribbles of dilute paint suggest her necklace and define her form, while a broken ribbon of rectangular marks of blue pigment are all that is needed to create the impression of glittering sapphires. Thickly impasted paint laid over the modulated browns of the background paint brings out the glitter of the earring.

3 *Actual size detail* The flashy gaudiness of Charles IV's decorations are perfectly matched by the explosive power of Goya's handling. Detail is sacrificed for effect, the sharp brightness of the medals described entirely by the surfaces that reflect the light. The thickly painted decorations are laid over thinly applied paint modulated by the warm ground color beneath, and this area is, in turn, surrounded by more solidly applied brown paint that describes the rest of the king's coat.

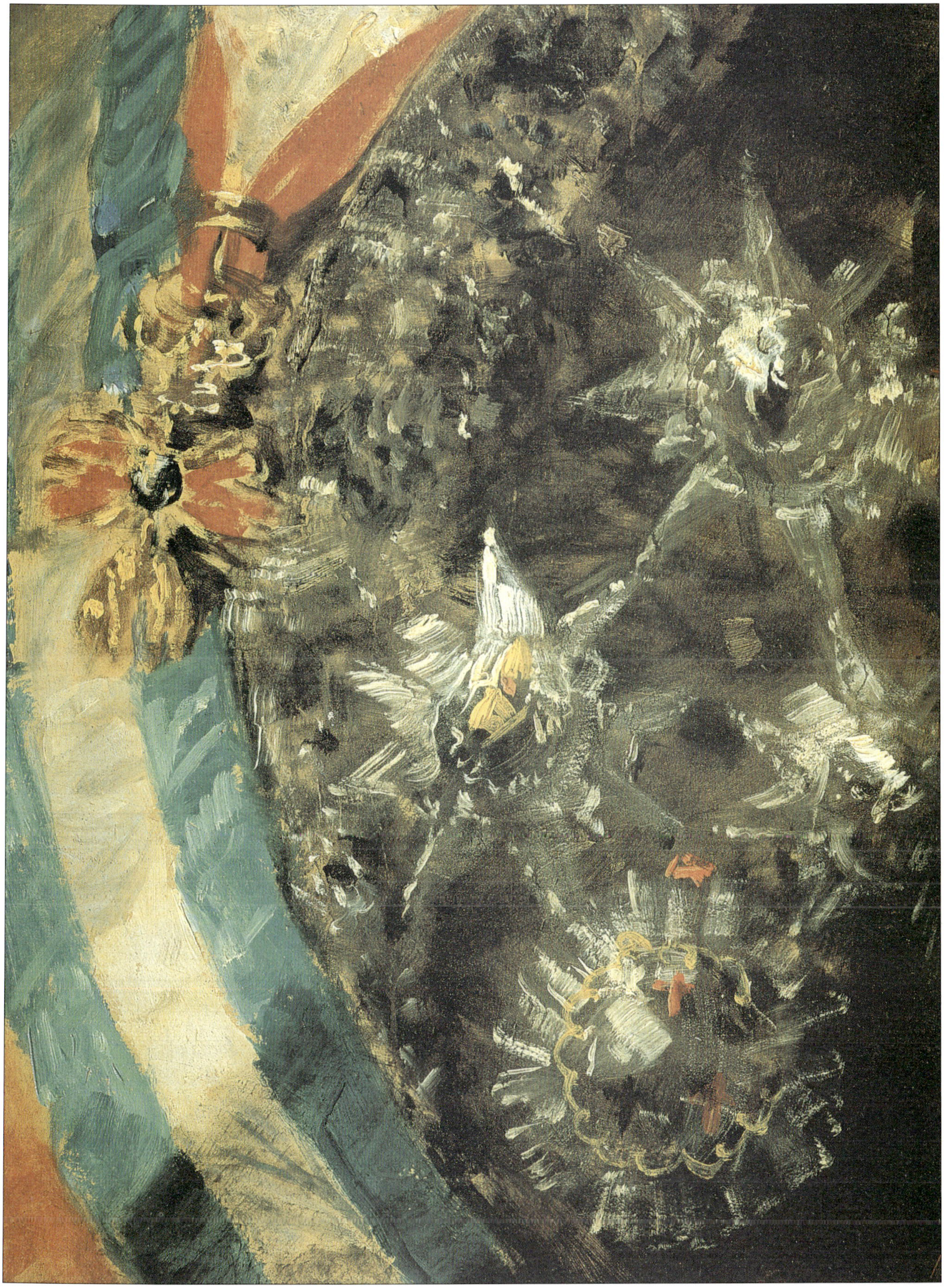

3 *Actual size detail*

Doña Isabel Cobos de Porcel

1804-5/6?
$32\frac{1}{4}\times21\frac{1}{4}$in/82×54cm
Oil on canvas
National Gallery, London

This is one of the most majestic of Goya's portraits. The magnificent aristocrat beauty is shown following the fashion of the time by dressing in the *maja* style, one associated with the inhabitants of the Madrid slums, but taken up by the rich and fashionable. The sitter, Doña Isabella Lobo y Mendieta, was the wife of Don Santonio de Porcel, a favorite of the all-powerful Manuel Godoy, the *éminence grise* of Spanish politics. The date of the painting is not absolutely certain, but it was probably the one that was exhibited at the San Fernando Academy in 1805; in 1806 Goya painted a companion portrait of her husband, which unfortunately no longer exists.

Many of Goya's portraits show acute psychological insights, but there is no place in this work for character analysis; the painting is concerned with the creation of an imposing image of confidence — in her sexuality and, most important, in her social position. This confidence is matched by the sumptuous brilliance with which the artist has constructed her image, one which sums up the spirit of the aristocratic class to which she belongs. Her figure fills the entire canvas, creating a marvelous glowing contrast of black and gold, enlivened by the artificial color of her heavily made-up face. Goya's choice of a half-length format has allowed him to make the most of the dynamic possibilities of the costume, but apart from this, there are no auxiliary props to indicate her position or interests. None is needed: the spiraling forms of her dark rose gown and her black mantilla rise up to support and frame her face and golden hair, and her form, melting into the neutral background, creates an image of strength and elegance.

Goya's son reported that "portrait painting came quite easily to him, and the most felicitous were those of his friends which he finished in a single sitting. He only worked for one session each day, sometimes ten hours at a stretch, but never in the afternoon. The last touches for the better effect of a picture he gave at night, by artificial light." The speed with which the artist worked has allowed the paint to form a single skin, the individual brushstrokes standing proud from each other in places, while in others they merge into each other to create a harmonious, unbroken paint surface.

The sitter's pose is rather unusual: the hands, half hidden by the sleeves of her *maja* jacket, suggest that she is either leaning on some kind of support or seated — it is difficult to decide which is the case. The tonality of the painting comes from the contrast between the warmth of the flesh tones and the rose pinks of her jacket and the magnificent black and green that dominates the rest of the canvas. The whites of the *fichu* are painted with heavy impasto, while the thin paint and light treatment of the black mantilla suggests the delicate, transparent quality of the lace, partially covering the rose satin jacket.

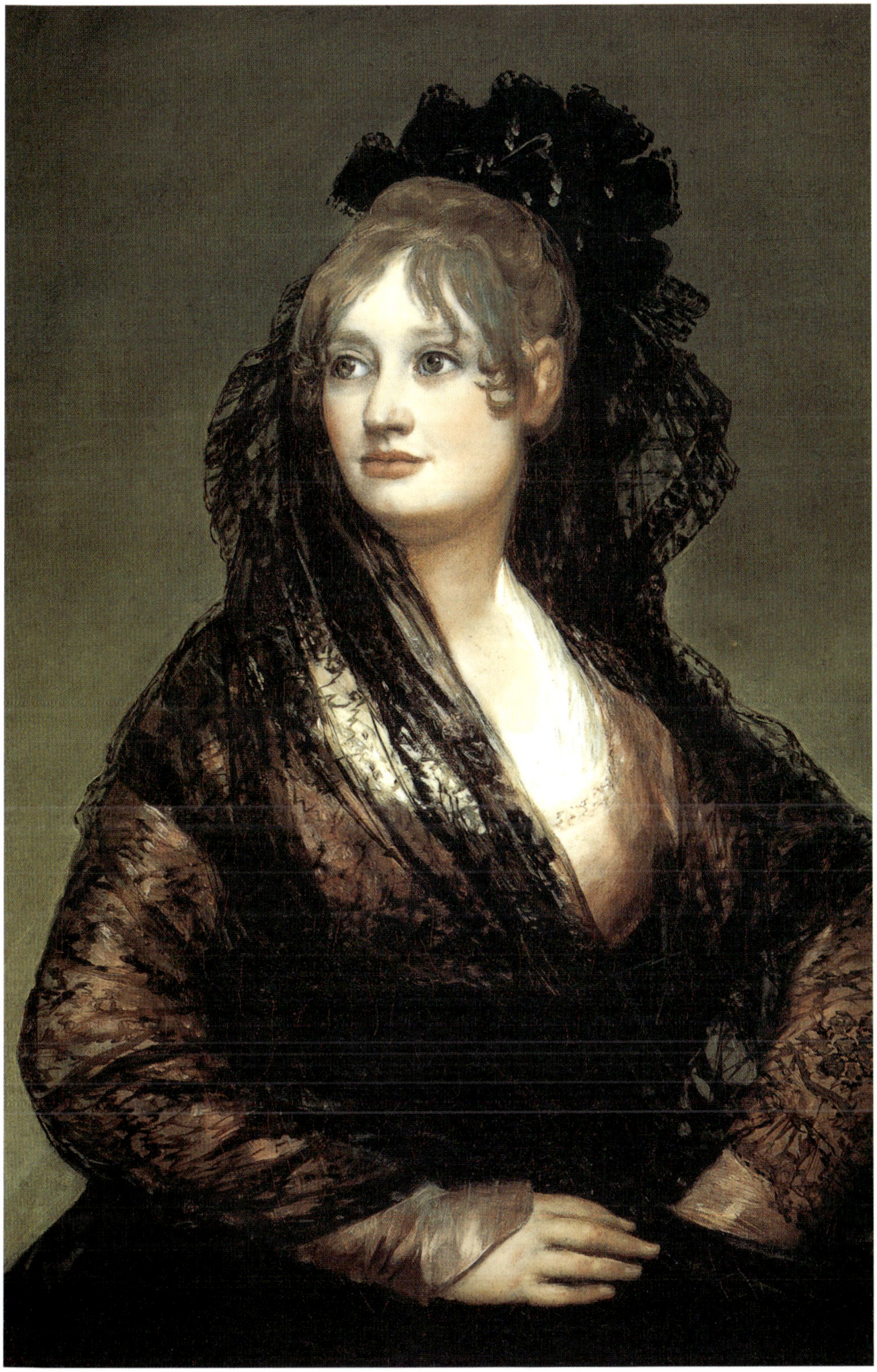

The almost overpowering presence of the aristocratic beauty, which almost threatens to spill out of its frame, disguises the fact that like so many of Goya's portraits it is very freely painted. Scribbles of paint overlay patches of color, the thinnest of glazes are placed adjacent to thick, flat areas of buttery paint, which in this case match perfectly the cosmetics that the sitter has applied to her face. Goya's supreme technical assurance can be judged by the fact that this portrait was painted directly over an earlier one of a man, traces of which can still be discerned today (left).

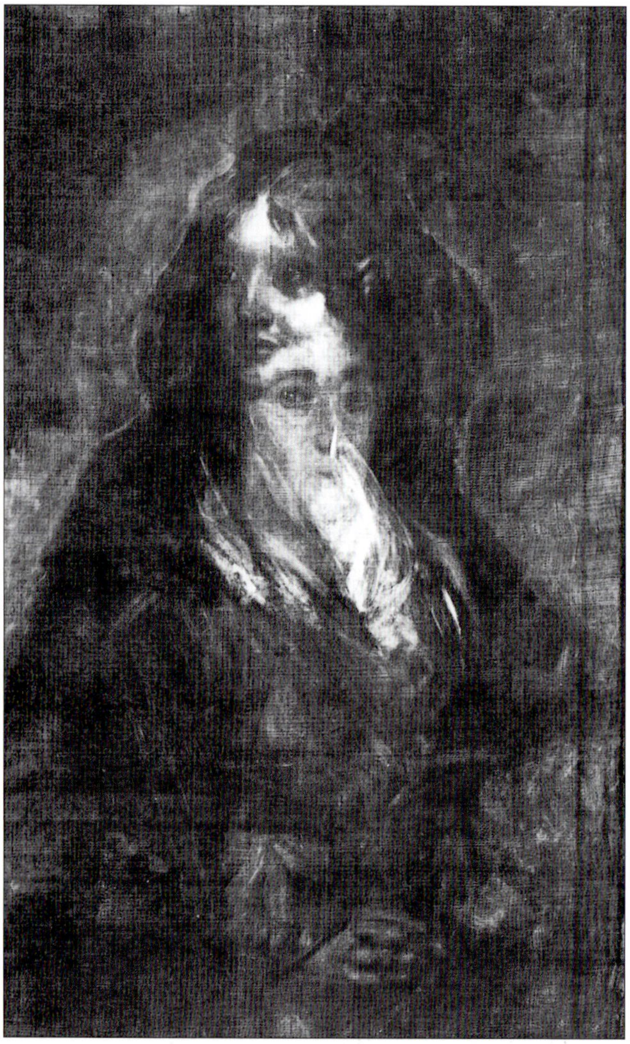

1

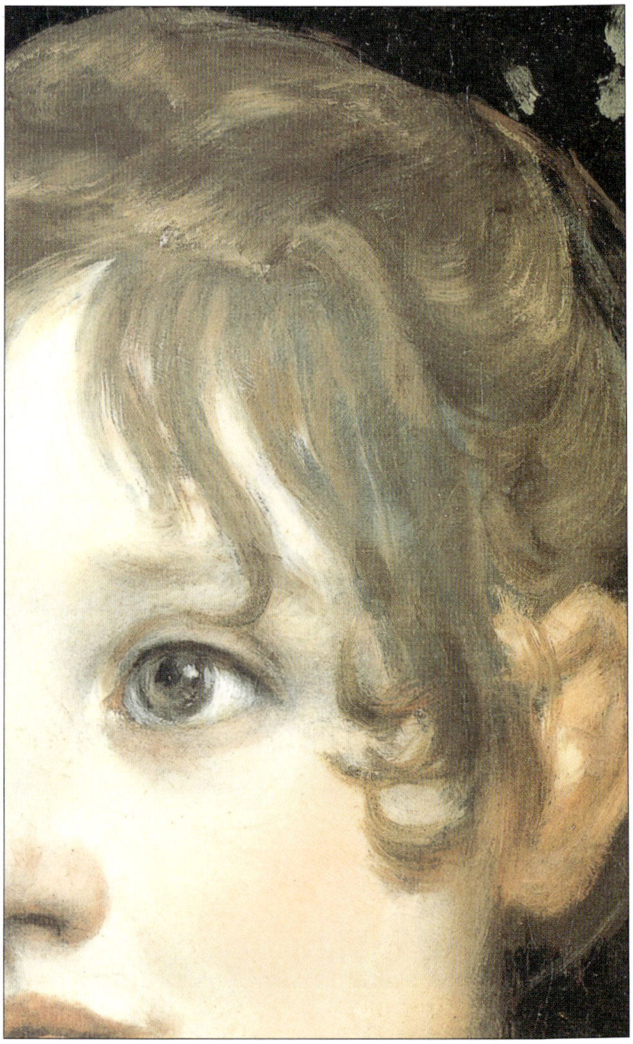

2

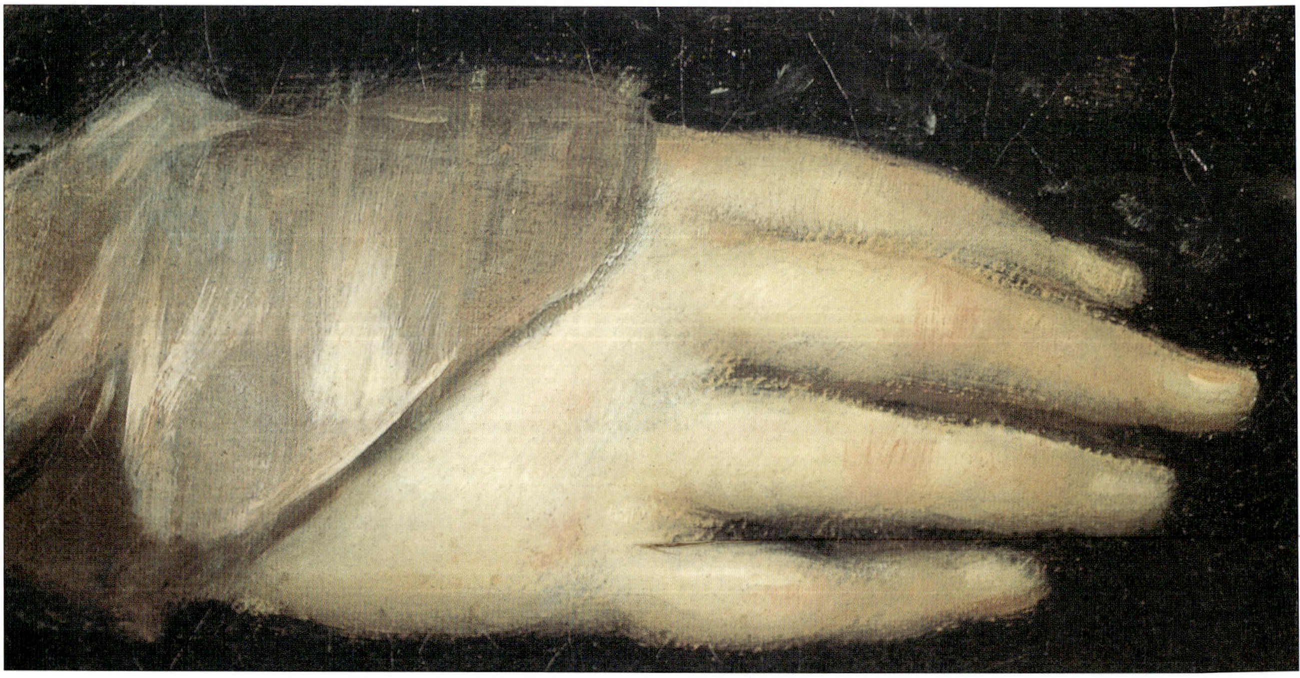

3

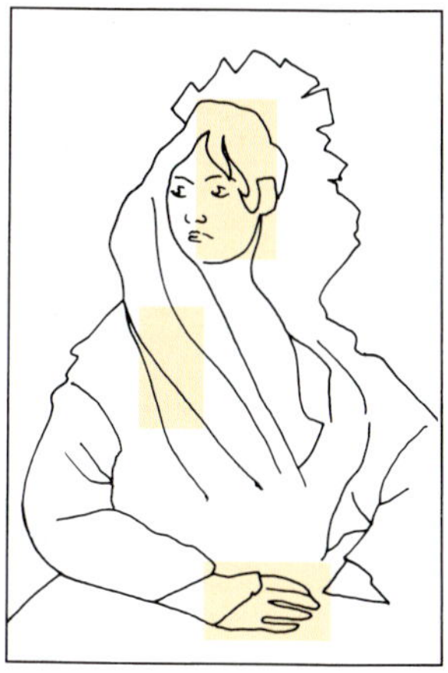

1 X-ray and infrared photography have been particularly helpful in studying the genesis and original state of Goya's paintings. Few can offer as spectacular a revelation as this example taken during a recent cleaning of the painting, and revealing the traces of a portrait of a man directly under the paint surface of the present work.

2 The thick paint denoting the broad areas of flesh on the sitter's face correspond to the cosmetics she wears, while more dilute paint is used to suggest the hollows and shadows. The handling gives a marvelous impression of the soft translucency of the sitter's skin, while her luxuriant coiffure is described with great economy.

3 The hand and sleeve are treated with wonderfully free, calligraphic brushstrokes, with a wide variety of subtle pinks, creamy yellows, and warm greens used to build up the forms.

4 *Actual size detail* The unflagging inventiveness of Goya's handling was much admired by later painters in England and France. These have sometimes been referred to as "twist of the wrist" painters in acknowledgment of their attempts to match the athletic brushwork of Goya and Velasquez. The effect of the black lace has been created by streaking thin paint over the impasto of the white *fichu* and rose-pink jacket.

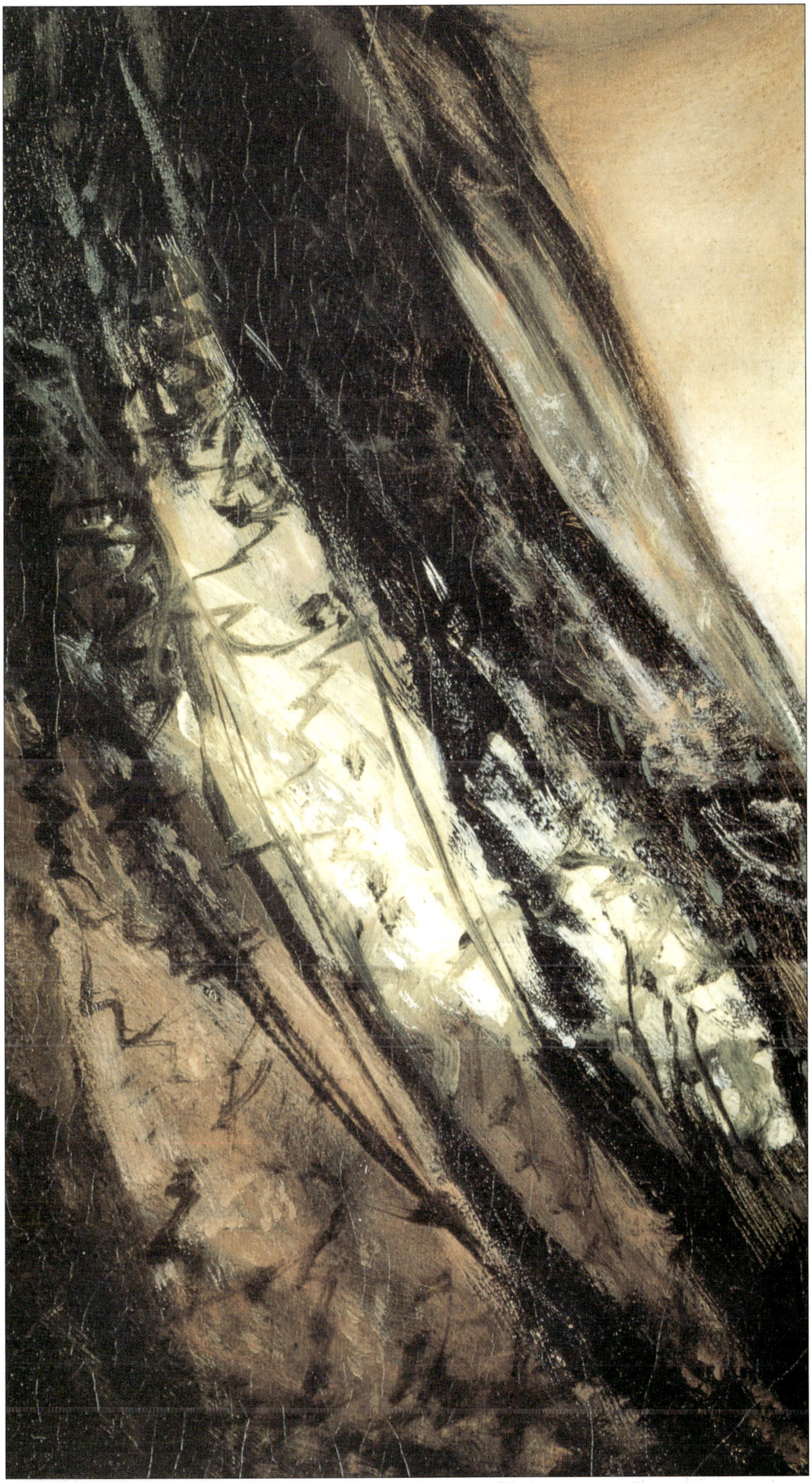

4 *Actual size detail*

The Burial of the Sardine

c 1812-19
$32\frac{1}{2} \times 24\frac{3}{8}$in/$82.5 \times 62$cm
Oil on panel
San Fernando Academy, Madrid

The date of this painting has been contested, but the period 1812-19 has now been generally accepted. It is a relatively small work, and depicts a procession that celebrates the Corpus Christi Festival on Ash Wednesday. The burial of a sardine, marking the end of Carnival time and the beginning of Lent, is a tradition that still continues in a modified form in the present day. In Goya's time, the celebrants would carry a puppet down to the bank of a river, where it was ceremonially burned. Like so many of his earlier tapestry designs, the work contains elements that were later to come to the fore in the Black Paintings (see page 233). Similar subjects had been painted by the Venetian artist, Giambattista Tiepolo, but Goya's knowledge of the work of the Northern European painters such as Hieronymus Bosch and Pieter Bruegel, who has treated similar themes in a more macabre way, stressing the inevitable triumph of death, has allowed him to instill this scene of bucolic entertainment with an all-pervasive atmosphere of terror.

Preliminary studies for the composition show that the banner originally bore the single word "Mortus" (death) in place of the huge grinning face that dominates the near-hysterical Carnival — "for remember dust thou art and to dust shalt thou return." In an attempt to arrest the inevitable progress of time, the celebrants dance in a frenzy; masks and disguises are worn and identities confused as individual responsibility is abdicated to the will of the crowd. *Picaros* and soldiers, animals and devils, mingle with those who look on, some of whom point out the more bizarre costumes, while others shudder in discomfiture at the unruly sight. From this swirling mass of movement the dancers are singled out by their white dresses. At first glance they appear to be radiantly happy, but closer examination proves this to be a false reading: the grins are not theirs but those of their masks, and one of their number — the figure on the right of the group — is, despite his dress, male. Shards of cool blue and blood red intermingle with a medley of ochers and grays. The brilliant patches of color contrast with the mass of the banner and the swept-in areas of blue and green that nonchalantly indicate the landscape and sky — a little more than a painted backdrop. Goya's rapid, summary handling of the procession gives an impression of unrestrained movement: figures are caught in mid-action, some painted in sharp detail; others merely suggested by free and sketchy brushwork. The animation of the crowd is matched by the technical means Goya uses to describe it. Calligraphic traces of thin black paint interweave over commas, patches, and blurs of pigment to create a balletic movement of brushstrokes across the canvas. Here we can see the roots of some of the startling innovations of Edouard Manet that were to have such consequences for French avant-garde art of the 19th century. Manet admitted a considerable debt to both Goya and Velasquez.

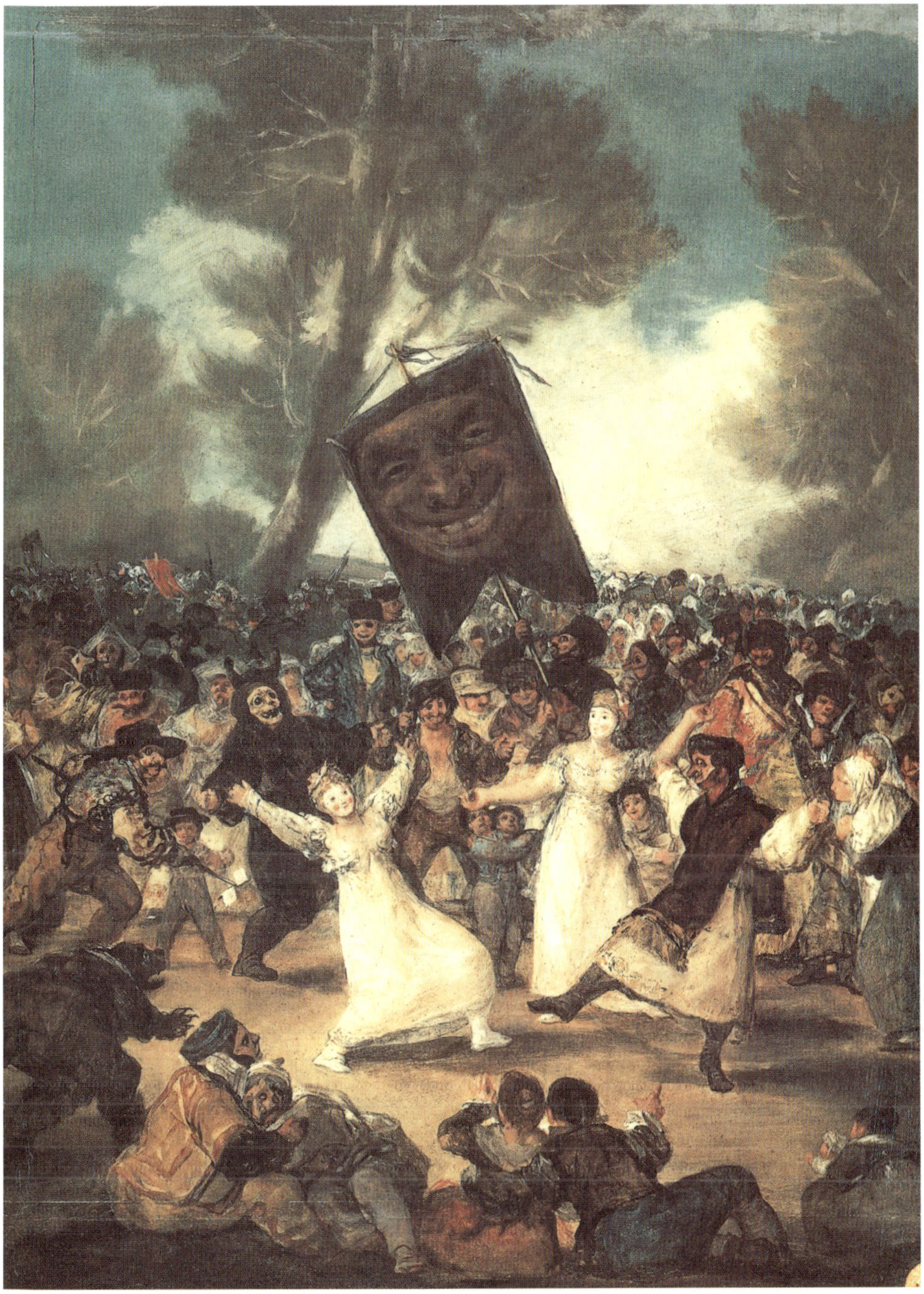

The world of 18th-century Spain was particular to itself, and it is wise to be wary of creating over-simplistic comparisons with the present day. However, in this painting, as in many of Goya's works, we can recognize the sense of the ordinary world on the verge of slipping, in the midst of celebration, into something monstrous and terrible, where the rules that govern normal existence no longer apply. Goya's use of courtly or ecclesiastical ritual and masquerade are metaphors that an audience of today can still understand.

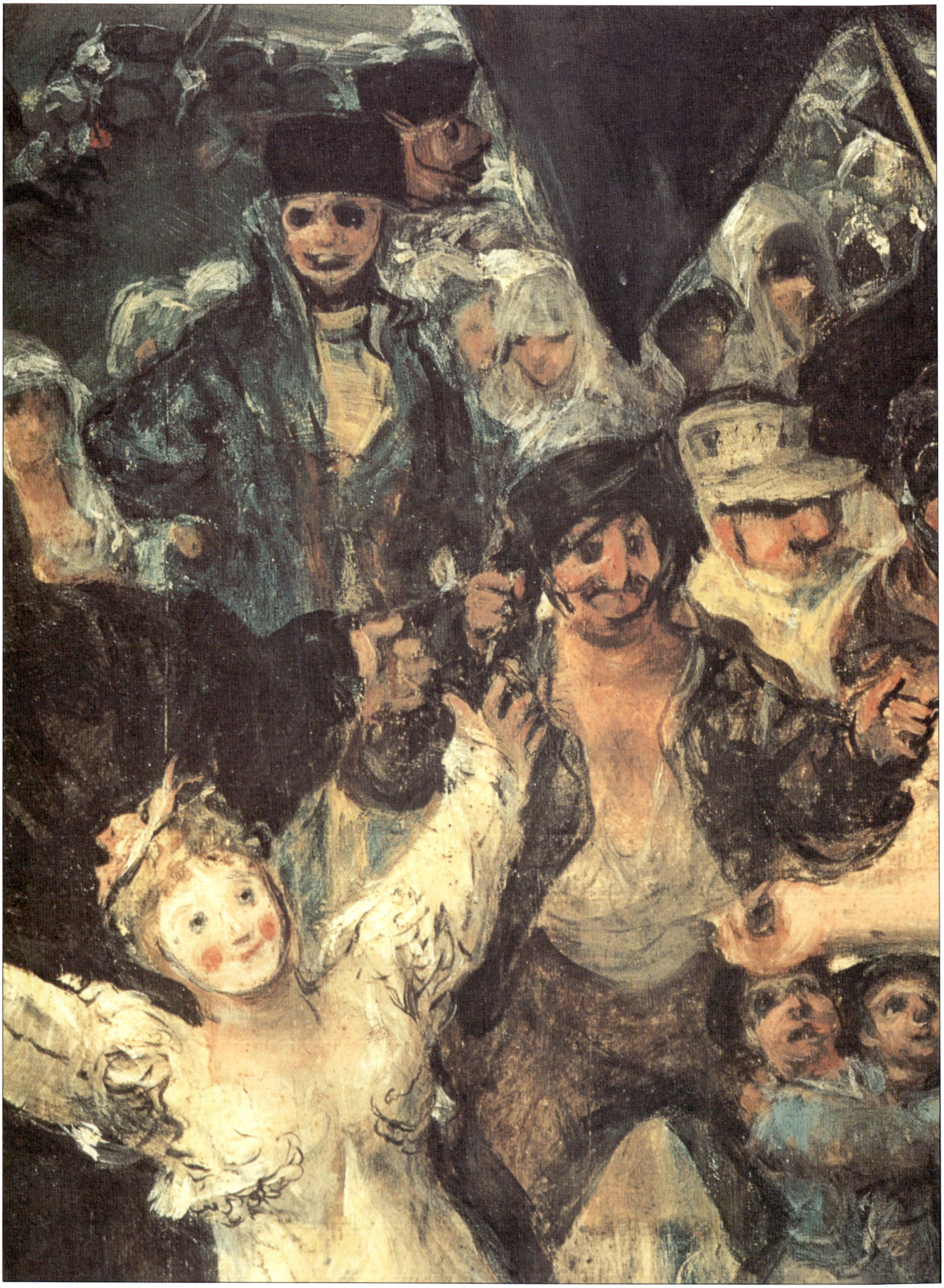

1 *Actual size detail*

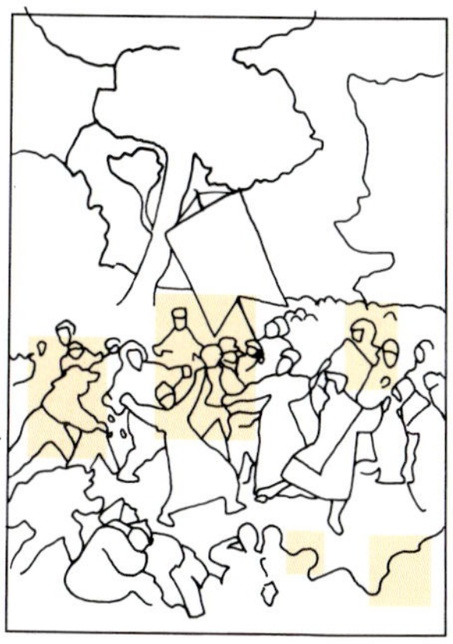

1 *Actual size detail* By using thin black paint drawn over loosely laid-in areas of color, Goya has created an impression of rich detail and enormous vitality. His calligraphic line weaves across the canvas defining and suggesting the heads and features of these grotesques. It is often difficult to decide whether Goya's creations are masked or otherwise, but what appears from a distance to be a happy smile on the left-hand dancer's face is clearly the fixed grin of a mask. The dancer could well be a man, despite the female costume.

2 This is one of the many ambiguous and possibly malevolent figures in the crowd whose identity and purpose defy definition. Goya has selected the degree of finish and detail in each area of the painting, thus creating a richness and sense of life that is analogous to real experience. As someone watching the event might search out a particular focus of interest, so peripheral areas of activity would fade out of focus.

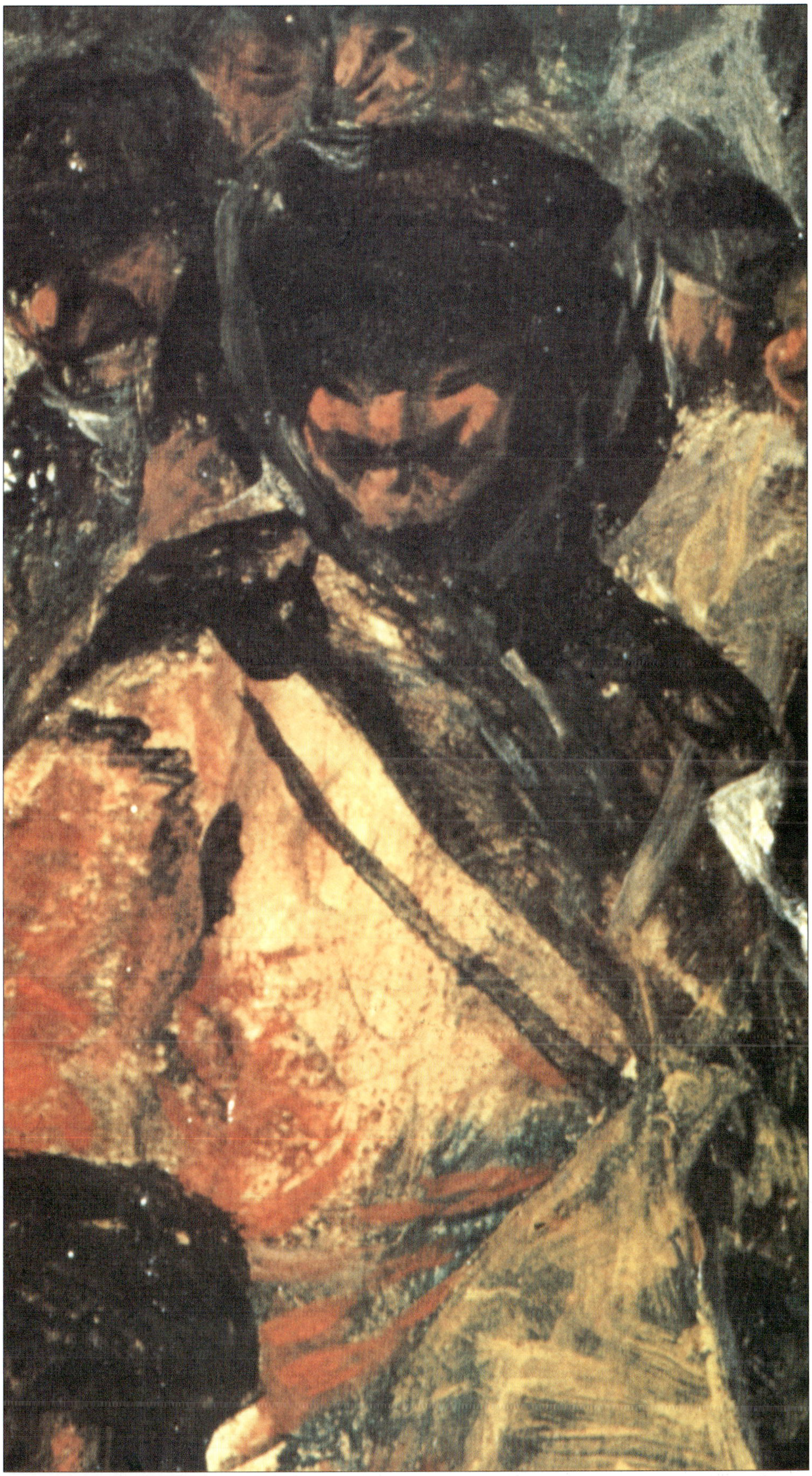

2

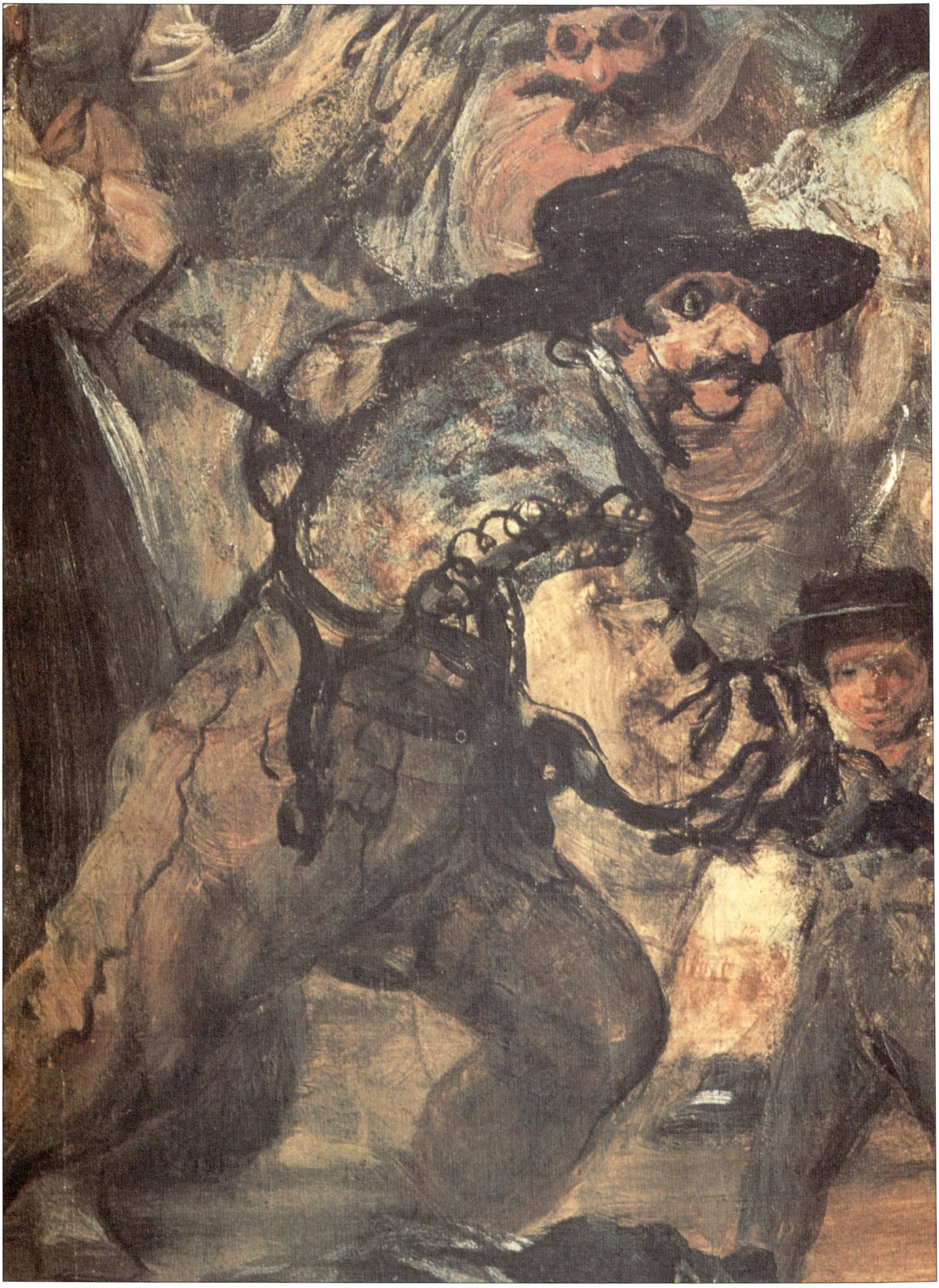

3

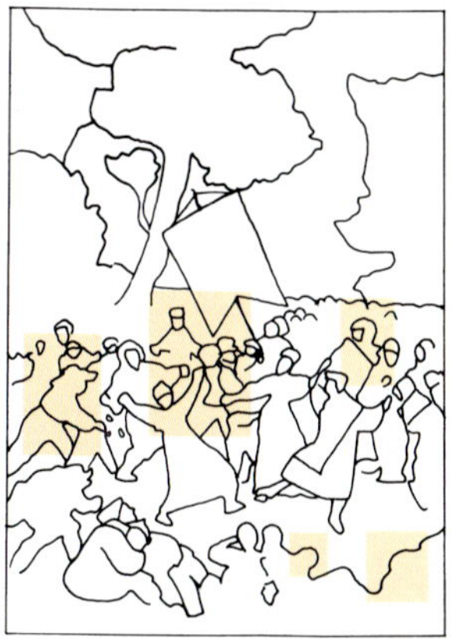

3 Goya exploits the color of the ground to great effect in his works. Here his assurance is evident in his economical handling. He allows the medium to describe all that is essential about the figure — his dress, and his aggressive and ambiguous posturing — but never allows himself to be beguiled by unnecessary details that could weaken his statement.

4 The rhythmic flow of Goya's line as it weaves in and out of patches of color has the effect of reinforcing the action it describes.

5 The drawing of this watching woman and child is a good example of the way in which Goya can develop a sense of character and movement with great economy of means.

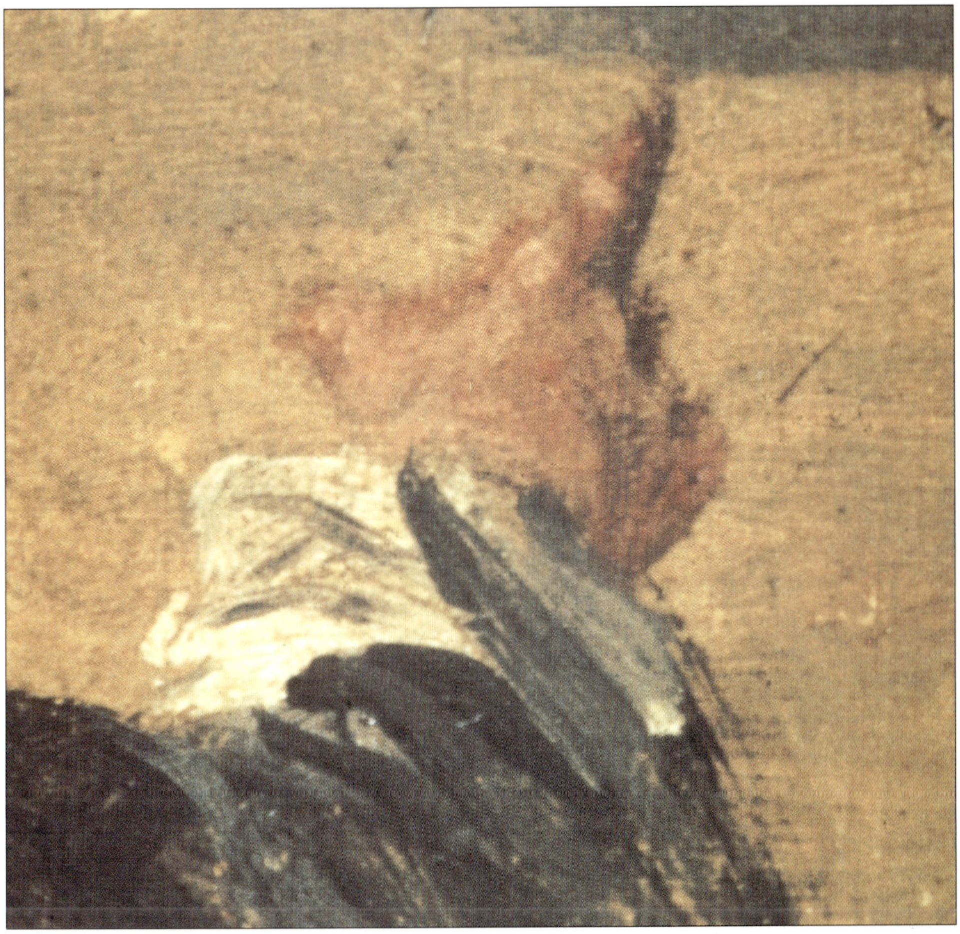

4

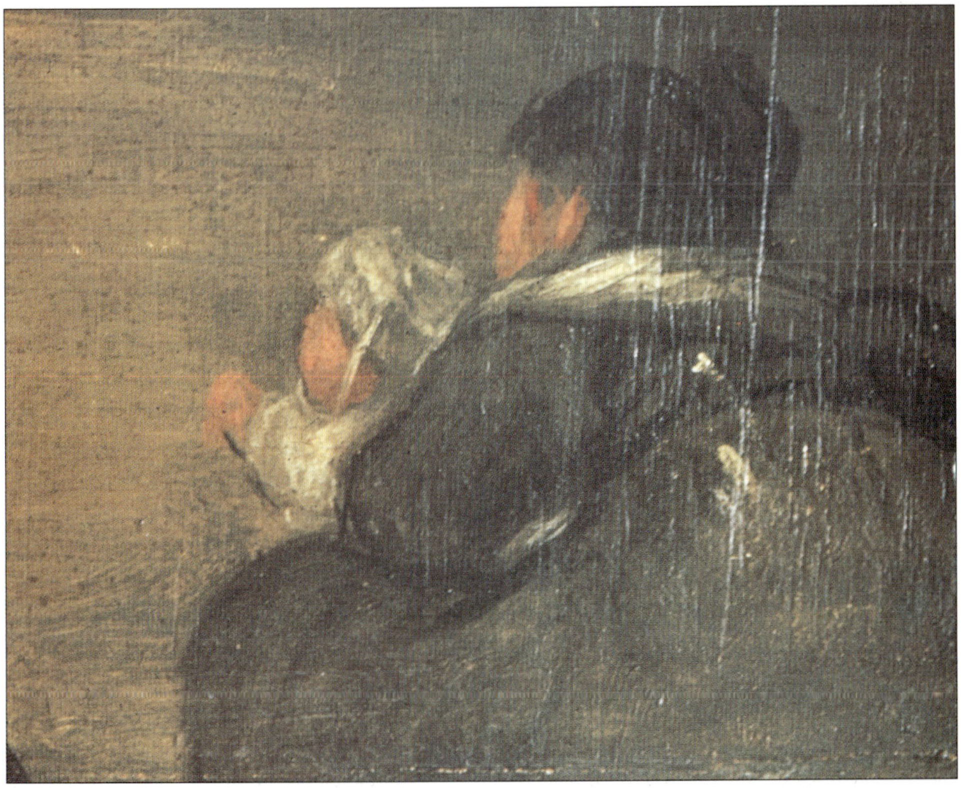

5

Two Old People Eating

1820-23

$20^{3}/_{4} \times 33^{1}/_{2}$in/$53 \times 85$cm

Oil on canvas (originally oil on plaster)

Prado, Madrid

This is one of the series of fourteen paintings Goya produced at the age of seventy-four to decorate the interior of his house, the Quinta del Sordo (the House of the Deaf Man). The name, oddly enough, refers not to Goya but to a previous occupant, also deaf. The paintings were worked directly onto the plaster of the wall, in the powerful "shorthand" style that is familiar to us from the San Antonio fresco and the backgrounds of Goya's smaller works. The subject matter of these works, now known as the "Black Paintings," is ambiguous and often occult, and no simple thematic link between them has yet been established, although they are obviously meditations upon old age and the incurable folly of humanity. The subjects are nightmarish and grotesque – dark scenes from mythology, witches' sabbaths, madness, and violence. This painting was the one Goya chose for his dining room. Despite – or perhaps because of – their ability to deflect the most scrupulous of scholarly research, these paintings have become some of the best known of all Goya's creations.

Thematically the individual Black Paintings refer back to ideas and images from earlier stages in Goya's *oeuvre,* his later work being an intensification of his lifelong obsession with the dark and irrational side of human life. They were painted on dark grounds and, as with the San Antonio fresco of twenty years earlier, the abiding effect, although on a more somber scale, is of a vast symphonic use of gray, the color which forms the *leitmotif* of each painting. It appears in every value, from the palest of nuances suggestive of early morning light to total blackness, as in the background of this painting.

As always with Goya, even the simplest of pictures lend themselves to a variety of interpretations. The image of a dog up to its neck in quicksand, the painting of the two men so intent on doing each other violence that they fail to realize that they too are sinking into a bog, the Sabbat and the Pilgrimage of St Isidro are all macabre references to his earlier tapestry cartoons or his various suites of etchings. The series of his etchings entitled *Los Disparates* ("Absurdities") were produced in the same years as these works. The paintings were done entirely for his own satisfaction, and their survival is the result of a stroke of good fortune. In 1873 a German banker bought Goya's house and had the paintings transferred onto canvas. In 1878 he sent them for exhibition to Paris, where, amazingly, they passed almost without comment. Finally they were presented to the Prado Museum in 1881 where they hang together as a group to this day. Their combined effect is breathtaking. Reproductions, however good, cannot replace the experience of direct confrontation.

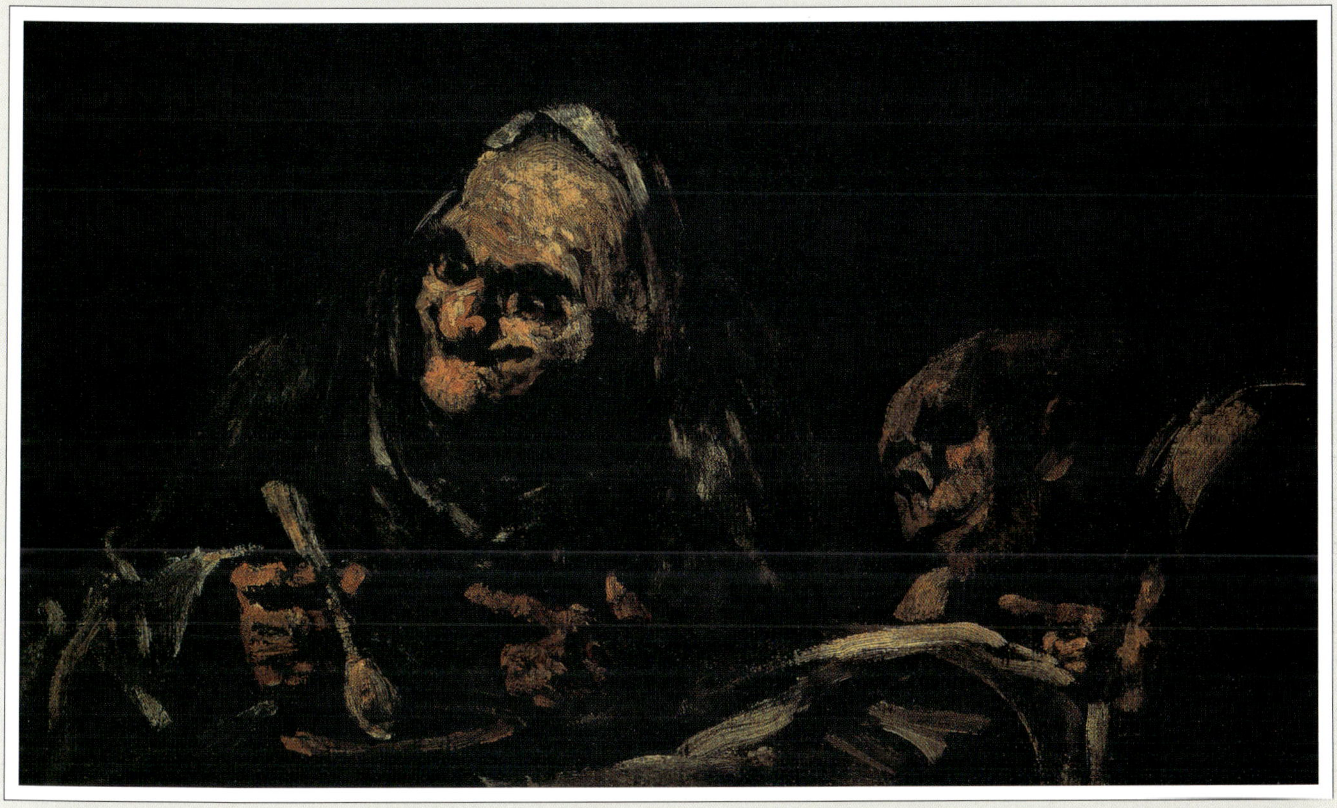

For whom is the mysterious repast being prepared? Are the two figures the consumers or the preparers of the food in the bowl? We do not know. The figure to the right of the old woman may be an earthly associate or — as in other works by Goya — may be a supernatural visitor of whose presence the woman is unaware. What is certain is that this is no simple genre scene but an image with a very personal and amblematic significance. This may be lost on the modern viewer, but we cannot fail to admire the masterly paint handling and expressionistic force of the work.

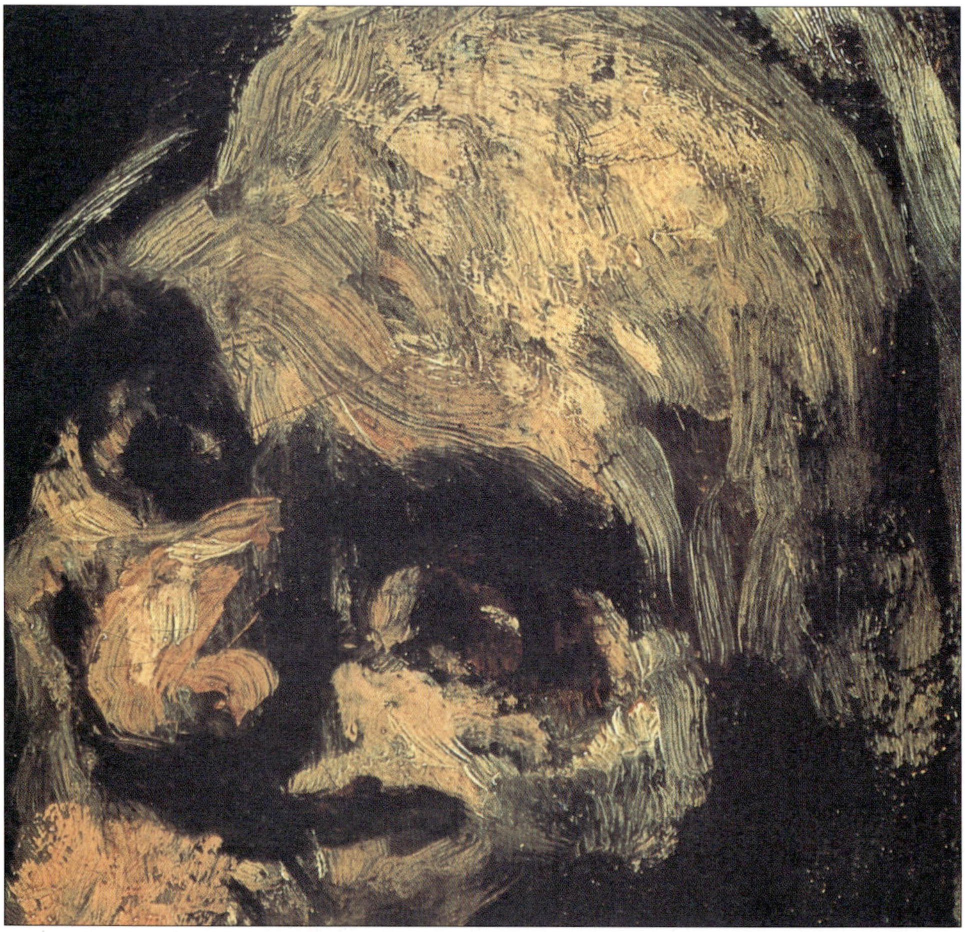

1 *Actual size detail*

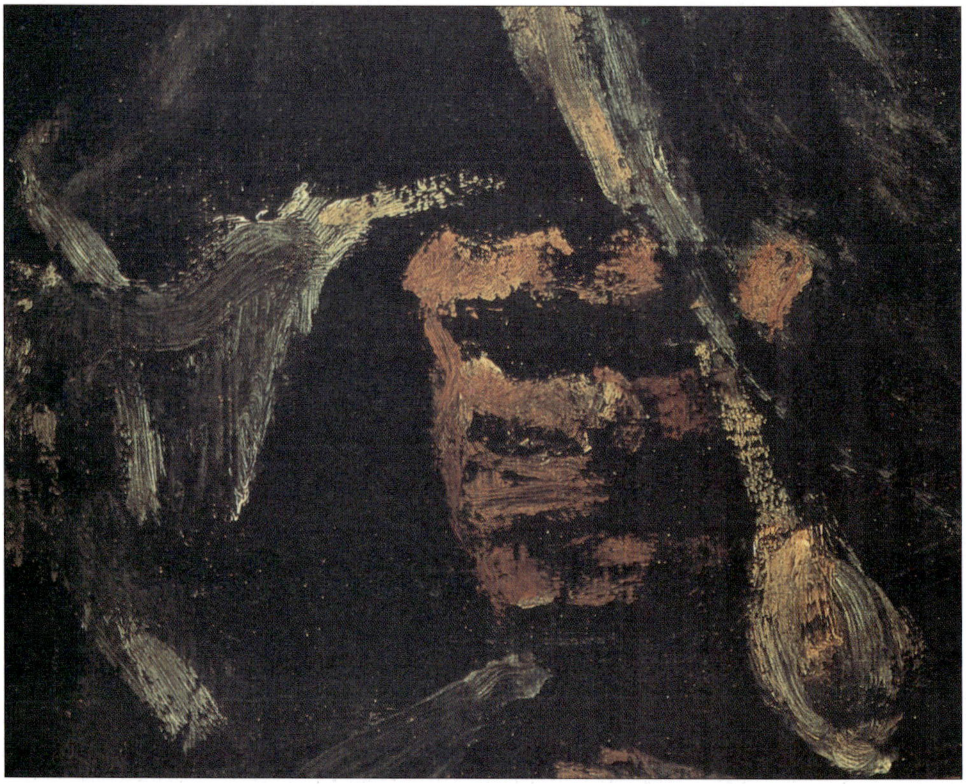

2

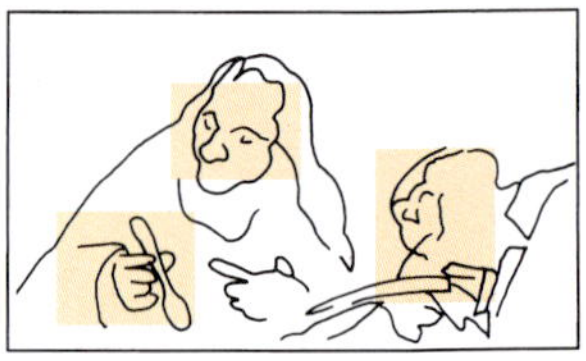

1 *Actual size detail* This is the smallest of the Black Paintings, and shares with the others a breadth and speed of handling allied with an absolute mastery of tone. Using a very restricted palette Goya modeled his bizarre forms from a black ground, working up toward the lighter values. The shadows and features are defined by the ground, the thick sweeps of paint creating sharp edges of richly modulated color.

2 The Black Paintings have been much restored. Now transferred to canvas, they were originally painted *al secco*, that is, onto a dry, specially prepared surface that allowed the artist to build up a considerable thickness of pigment. The surface was striated in order to receive the oil pigment, and traces of these indentations remain. However, they still convey a strong sense of spontaneity and freshness. Here, powerfully modeled paint describes the sleeves, with soft highlights and touches of red and brown in the hands and bowl. The surface pattern of this area is built up with strongly defined sweeps of paint, laid on with a twisting brush for dramatic effect.

3 The shrouded figure was originally much bulkier, and traces of the original silhouette can be made out above its head and shoulder. The light falling on the face is described in thick creamy paint over the dark ground. The structure of the nose is defined by leaving the black ground uncovered, while the impact of the eyes is strengthened with black overpainting.

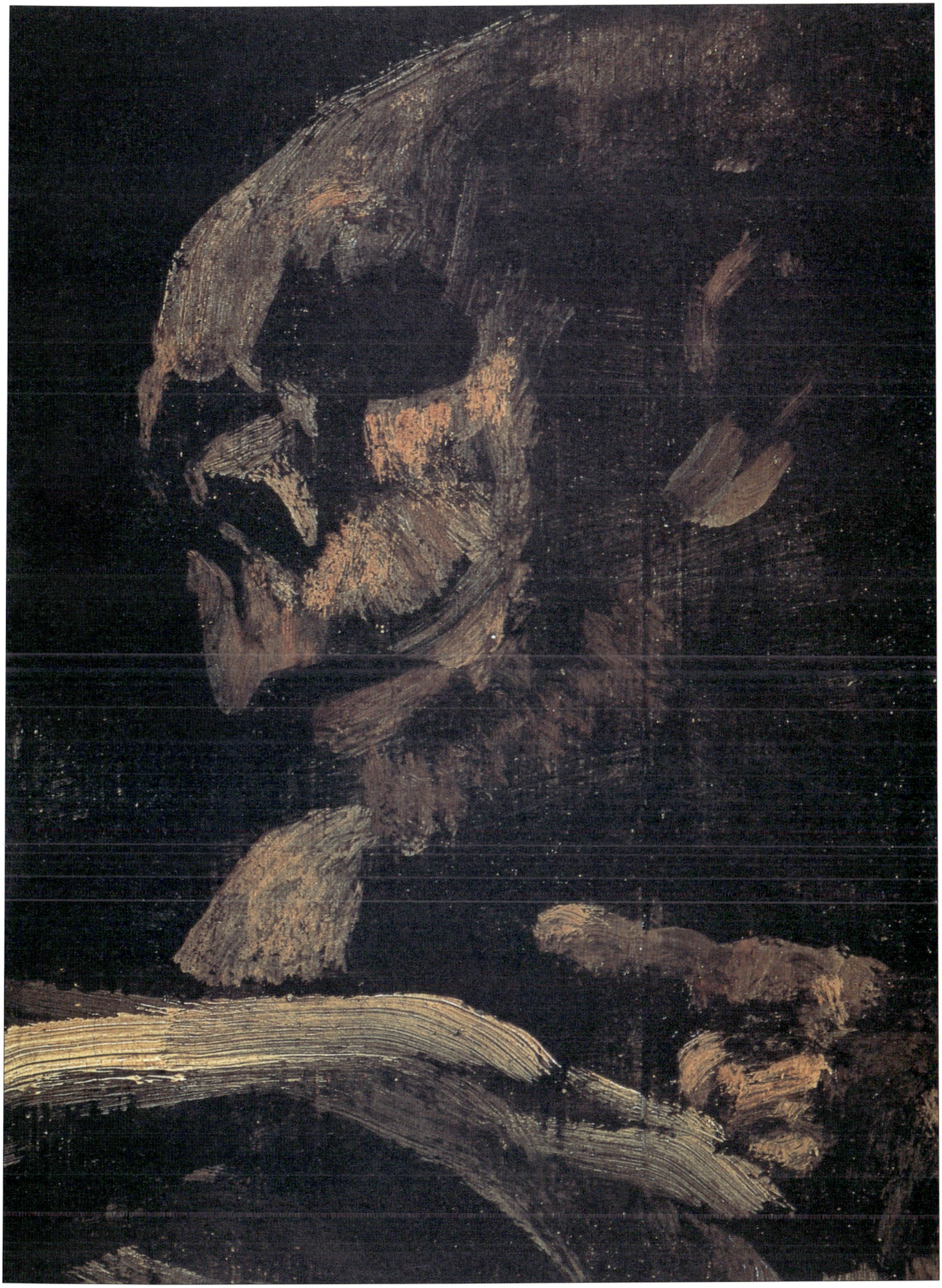

3

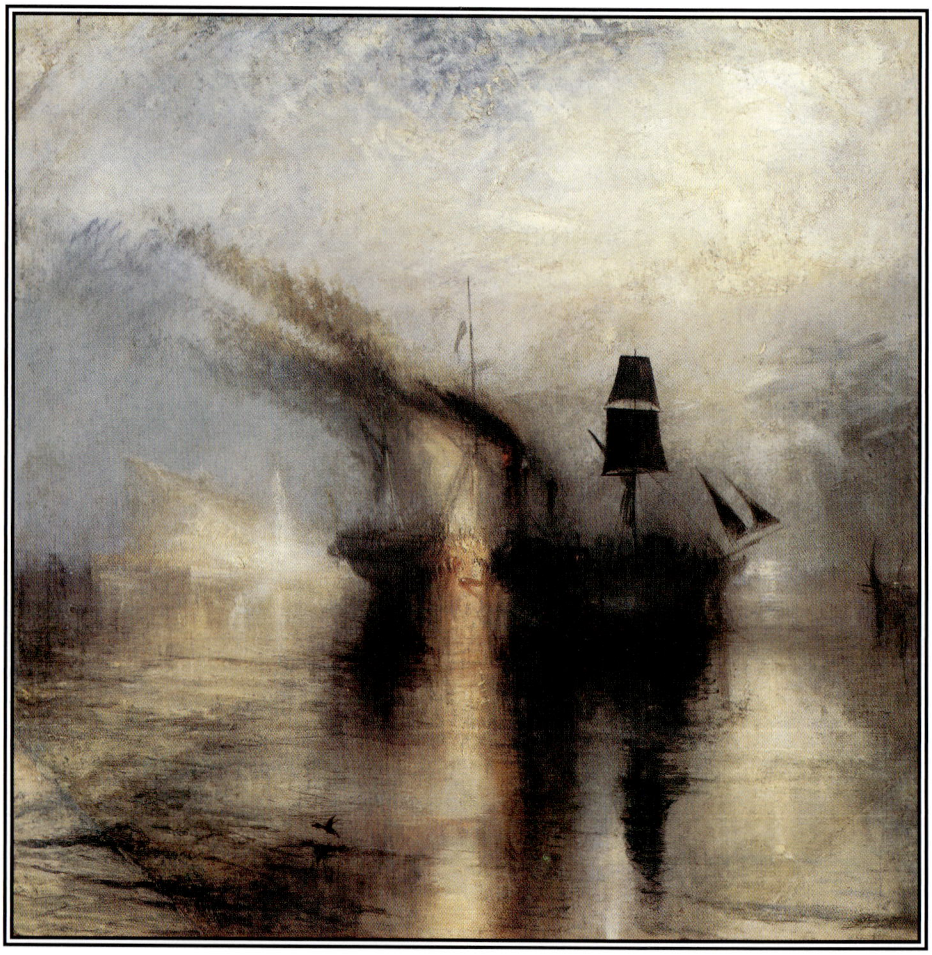

TURNER

Introduction

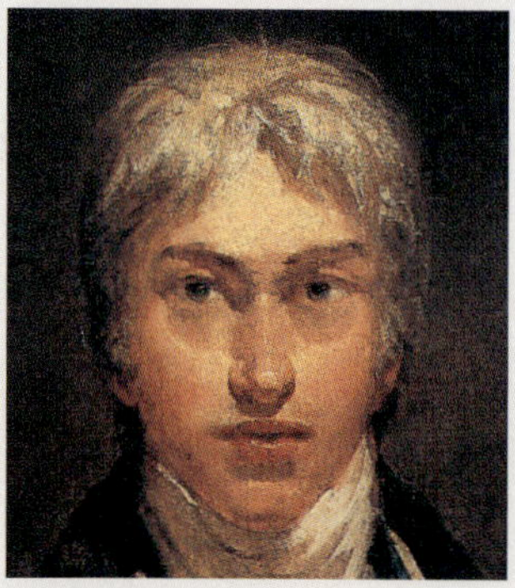

J.M.W. Turner
Self-portrait
c 1798
Clore Gallery for the Turner Collection, London

"All lookers on were amused by the figure Turner exhibited in himself, and the process he was pursuing with his picture. A small box of colors, a very few small brushes, and a vial or two, were at his feet, very inconveniently placed; but his short figure, stooping, enabled him to reach what he wanted very readily. Leaning forward and sideways over to the right, the left hand metal button of his blue coat rose inches higher than the right, and his head, buried in his shoulders and held down, presented an aspect curious to all beholders, who whispered their remarks to each other, and quietly laughed to themselves. In one part of the mysterious proceedings Turner, who worked almost entirely with his palette knife, was observed to be rolling and spreading a lump of half transparent stuff over his picture, the size of a finger in length and thickness."

This description of Turner completing a picture – one of his several versions of the *Burning of the Houses of Parliament* – on varnishing day before a Royal Academy exhibition tells us much about the way he worked. It also sums up a popular view of the artist, who appears as a mysterious figure, obsessed by his work and oblivious to events around him, producing as if by magic a picture of the swirling elements from an intense smearing, brushing, scratching, sponging and blotting. The technical mastery that enabled Turner to suggest every subtlety of nature and its effects was barely comprehended by most of his contemporaries. Even today, to eyes accustomed to the freedoms of contemporary art, Turner's late work seems to stand on the extreme limit of oil painting – the work of a revolutionary who broke all the conventions and canons of taste of his day. However, like many other great painters, Turner attained these heights of virtuosity from the most down-to-earth training in the conventions and craft of painting. "D--d hard work" was what he once gave as the secret of his success, and every technical effect that he brought to his work was the result of just this. In the production of the pictures he often referred to as his "children," all else was sacrificed to obsessive, continual work.

Early training in watercolor

Joseph Mallord William Turner came from a humble background, the son of a London barber in Covent Garden. His father quickly saw his son's talent and encouraged him by exhibiting and selling his drawings from his own premises. From this early beginning Turner acquired a keen business sense and an appreciation of the importance of financial success, which he realized was the only way to provide the freedom he needed to develop his work. He came to the notice of a well-to-do amateur painter, Dr Monro, who lived a few streets away and paid a group of young artists (among them Thomas Girtin) to make copies of his collection of watercolors. Through this mundane but valuable process the young Turner learned more or less at firsthand the techniques and style of the leading watercolor painters of the day. Although watercolor was considered a less elevated form of painting than oils, a thriving and highly skilled school of watercolorists had grown up in England by the late eighteenth century. These artists satisfied a strong and increasingly sophisticated public demand for "views" – of landscapes, towns and historical buildings, both at home and abroad. Engravers often worked alongside the painters, popularizing their work in a wider and more lucrative market through widespread reproduction.

Turner quickly mastered the dry descriptive style of topographic drawing and painting, where the principal concern was for accuracy. He became a skilled draftsman, able to produce faithful renderings of architectural detail, but also capable of conveying landscape and weather effects when necessary. These were favorite subjects of watercolorists, as the delicacy and subtlety of the medium is well suited to conveying effects of light and atmosphere, indeed, from the painters' point of view this was the principal virtue of the medium, and Turner's precursors had become increasingly fascinated by the challenge it presented. Watercolor is also a very demanding medium, requiring both skill and accuracy to control its extreme fluidity and to produce an effect which cannot easily be altered or repainted. Building up on the work of the previous generation, Turner and his contemporaries at Dr Monro's had developed a highly sophisticated technical vocabulary, and were increasingly interested in extending its conventions beyond the tradition of straightforward representation. An extremely subtle range of tones enabled them to depict the full range of atmospheric effects, thus enhancing their work with a sense of mood or even drama that made them more than mere "views."

The growth of the Romantic movement

This maturity in the English watercolor school as it reached toward a more expressive style was part of a universal and profound shift in taste throughout Europe toward the end of the eighteenth century. This is perfectly reflected in the development of Turner's art, which provides the clearest expression in the whole of English painting of this change in attitudes. A concern for order and harmony, qualities which articulated an optimistic view of a world run according to rational laws, was gradually being superseded by a new interest in an art that depicted creation as exciting, dynamic, even hostile. The old classical values — the preoccupation with perfectly poised, objective beauty created by an adherence to set rules of taste — had produced a certain blandness, and in reaction to this connoisseurs began to interest themselves in an art that could be a means of exploring emotions rather than presenting peace and harmony. The taste for the less rational, the more evocative and mysterious, grew throughout the eighteenth century, in reaction to the established reverence for the ordered art of ancient Greece and Rome, and by the end of the century had become almost universal. It was now coherent enough to be given a name — Romanticism.

Nature, as seen through landscape, was crucial to Romanticism, but now Nature was wild and unkempt, not placid and idealized as it had previously been. Turner's choice of landscape subjects was thus typical of the period, and both he and his contemporaries began to explore the mountains, hills and rugged coast of Britain. When a temporary peace was signed in the war against France he crossed the Channel to add the greater splendor of the Alps to his repertoire. The quality most admired in such scenes was the "Sublime," which was seen as the stimulus to an exciting and spontaneous sense of awe, awaking in the observer a thrilling sense of his own weakness in the face of the giant irrational power of nature. The concept of the Sublime was most fully developed by the English statesman and philosopher Edmund Burke (1729-97), who suggested that "darkness, vacuity and silence" were the qualities that attended it — qualities readily to be found in Turner's views of mountain scenery.

The sea fascinated Romantic artists in the same way as wild mountains did. Its vast scale dwarfed men and their ships, who were helpless before the power of the elements when traveling over it. It suggested the infinite, and by association, death, the great oblivion that held a particular fascination for the Romantics. Turner's first exhibited oil painting, *Fishermen at Sea off the Needles*, of 1796, showed a small boat on a rough sea at night, the moonlight increasing the drama of the scene, an image which introduced a series of works depicting storms and the perils of the sea.

Themes in painting

Turner's art combines the themes and motifs of Romantic painting and literature with more personal

S.W. PAROTT
Turner on Varnishing Day
c 1846
University of Reading, Ruskin Collection

Turner greatly enjoyed the sociability of the varnishing day before a Royal Academy exhibition. He sometimes transformed a roughly prepared canvas into a finished work in the space of a few hours, and he became a source of some amusement to his fellow artists, most of whom were content to simply apply the statutory coat of varnish to their paintings.

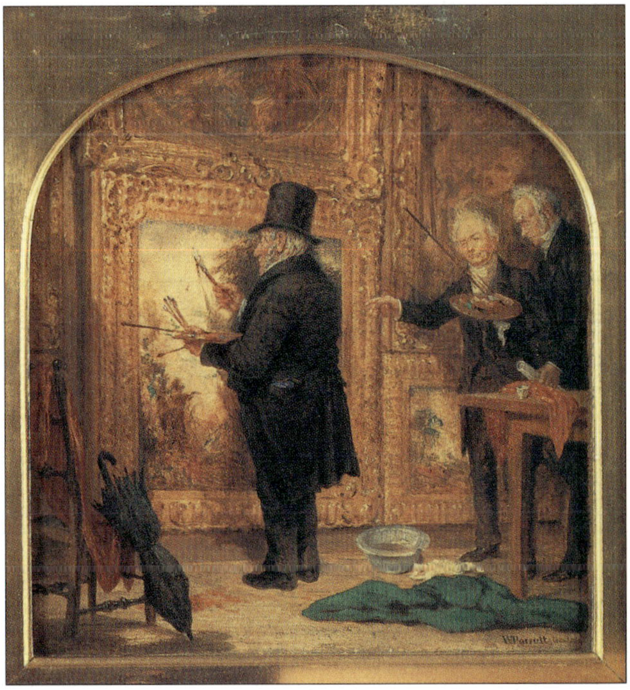

and often obscure concerns. This is not as paradoxical as it might appear, for Romanticism celebrated the individual view against the impersonal orthodoxy of the established, and its heroes were those who, because of the intensity of their private vision, were misunderstood or even rejected by the majority. Suffering and loneliness were seen to enhance the integrity of the artist. Turner's character and life can be seen within this context, since although he was convivial in the company of his fellow-artists and those with whom he felt at ease, he was not equipped for the kind of elegant society life that would have brought him fashionable recognition. Small, and with a strikingly large nose, shyness gave a gruffness to his manner that emphasized the curtness of many of his responses to uninformed enquiries. He was always extremely sensitive to criticism, and his strong desire to be understood was combined with a conflicting urge toward obscurity. His ineptness for expressing himself in words contrasted poignantly with his eloquence in paint. Thus John Ruskin, his most sensitive and perceptive champion, recounted how, "The want of appreciation touched him sorely, chiefly the not understanding his meaning. He tried hard one day, for a quarter of an hour, to make me guess what he was doing in the picture of 'Napoleon,' before it had been exhibited, giving me hint after hint, in rough way; but I could not guess and he would not tell me."

Turner was indeed obsessively private, to the point of developing elaborate veils of secrecy around certain aspects of his life, hiding his mistress and even his address from his contemporaries. To his neighbors in Chelsea in the 1840s he was known as a retired admiral, having taken for local convenience the surname of his mistress and landlady, Mrs Booth. This state of mind could only have been encouraged by the almost universally hostile criticism his work attracted from his early maturity onward. Even when such comments were clearly ignorant and expressed in the most vulgar idiom of the day they wounded Turner deeply. His paintings were said to be "soapsuds and whitewash," "cream or

J.M.W. TURNER
Transept of Ewenny Priory
1797
National Museum of Wales, Cardiff

The romanticism of this medieval subject is given extra drama by the depth of shadow Turner could bring to his watercolors. A contemporary critic compared this interior, with its gloomy grandeur and dappled light, to the work of Rembrandt, whom Turner came to admire later in his career.

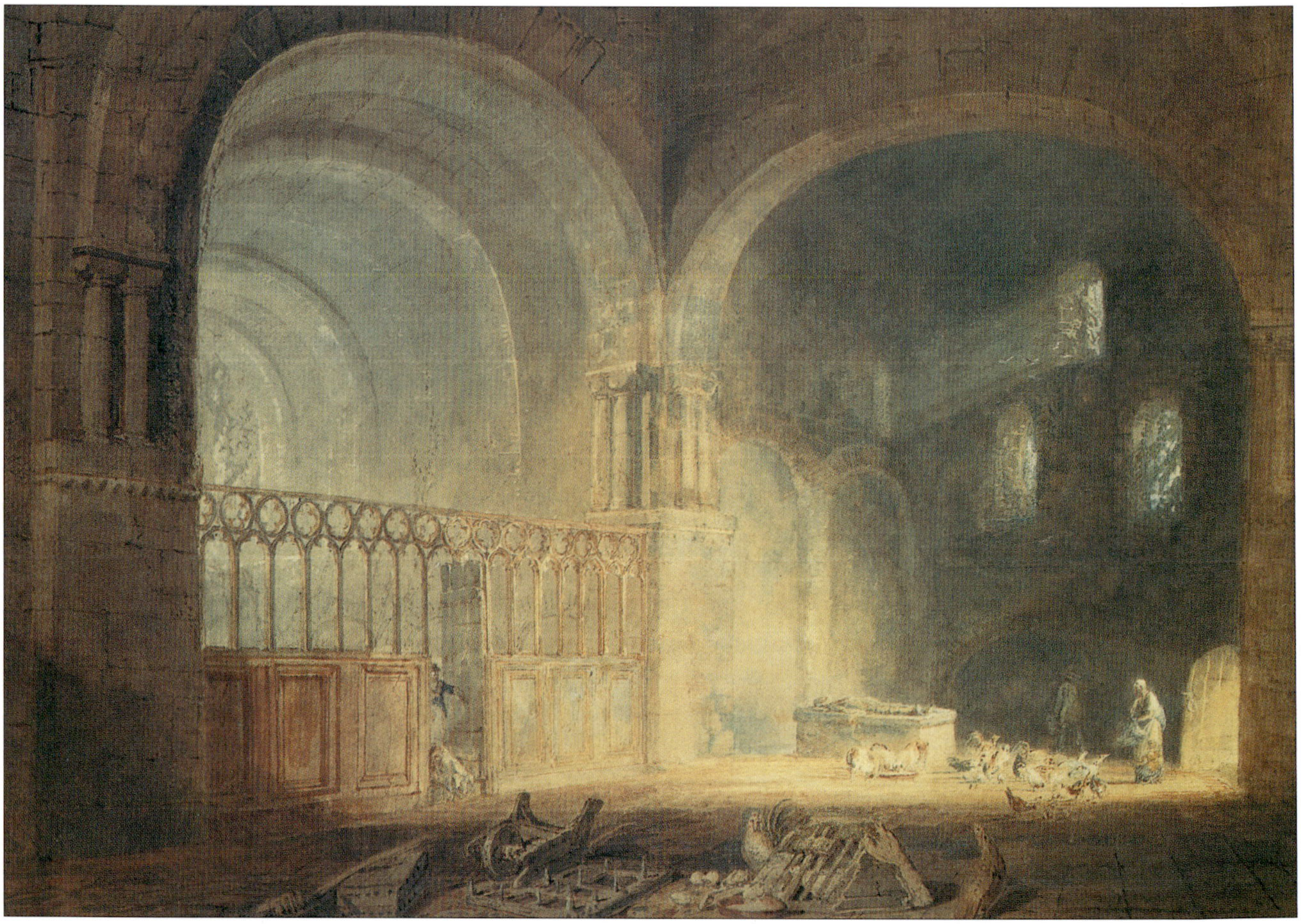

chocolate, or yolk of egg, or currant jelly," "eggs and spinach," "mustard," "produced as if by throwing handfuls of white and blue and red at the canvas, letting what chanced to stick, stick." The casual attribution of "mad" to his later style must have caused particular distress, since his mother had died in the Bethlem Hospital for the Insane. The epithet continued to be used after his death by French critics, applied to the passion and fury of his later works.

The isolation of the artist, and by extension, of man himself, was a recurring theme in Romantic art. Turner frequently used the plight of a great hero as the central theme of a picture, a hero frequently rejected, punished or set apart from his fellows by some remarkable and distinguishing powers. Examples are the lonely Napoleon in exile; the disgraced and blinded Regulus; Moses writing the book of Genesis (after the Flood, in Turner's confused biblical chronology); or Masaniello, the doomed leader of the Neapolitan rebellion. As the artist matured, his themes became more dramatically concerned with the futility of man's efforts, which could be eroded by the tide of history, as was the great empire of ancient Carthage, which sank into decadence, decline and eventual destruction. Carthage was the theme of several of his works. Man's efforts were similarly threatened by the savage elements, which could wreck simple fishing boats as easily as they could terrify the hardened troops of the Carthaginian general Hannibal as they crossed the Alps into Italy. Man could struggle against avalanches, storms and floods just as he struggled against the power of fate, but eventual defeat was inevitable. The theme of death – sometimes elegiac, as in *The Fighting Téméraire*, where the aged battleship is towed away, and sometimes violent and bloody, as in *Slavers Throwing Overboard the Dead and Dying*, where slaves are cast out to be devoured in the savage sea – increasingly dominated Turner's work, accompanied by a deep pessimism.

The role of literature

However, it is not only the lonely profundity of his work that connects him with the other isolated spirits of Romanticism. Apart from the common images of Romantic painting – Gothic ruins, lonely heroes, storms and gloomy skies – he was familiar with the work of the contemporary poets. Although he had no formal education, and his thoughts as they appear both in his writing and reported speech often appear unstructured and confusing, many contemporaries remarked upon the essential keenness of his mind. He eagerly assimilated any knowledge that was of practical benefit to him, for

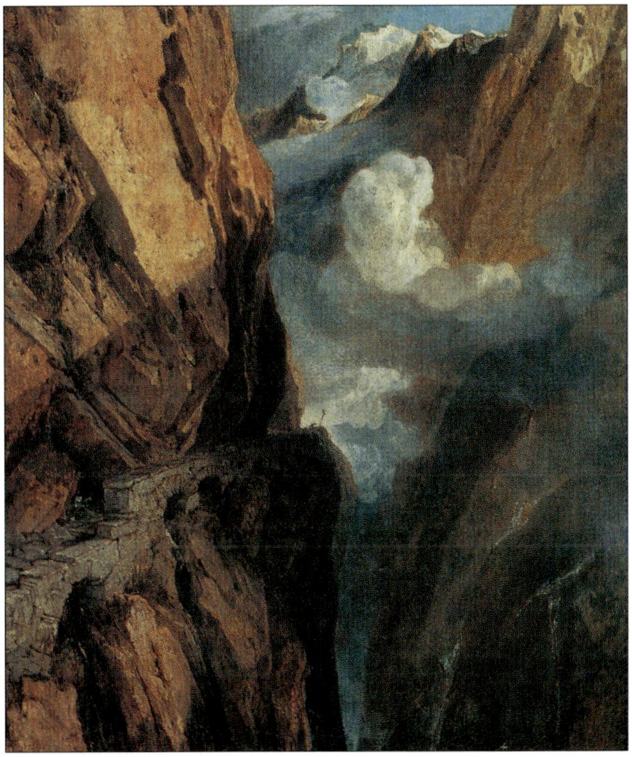

J.M.W. TURNER
The Passage of the St Gotthard
1804
Birmingham City Museums and Art Gallery

Turner first went abroad in 1802, going first to the Alps and returning via Paris and the Louvre. He painted several watercolors of the dramatic Alpine scenery, one of which, exhibited in his own gallery in 1804, formed the basis for this oil painting.

instance teaching himself the rudiments of French before his first trip abroad, and the importance of his reading is evident in his art. This is well illustrated in the close relationship between poetry and English landscape painting that had grown up during the eighteenth century. At this time poets had acted as a major stimulus to landscape painters through pastoral descriptions, themselves inspired by the Old Master Italian landscapes collected by the English aristocracy. James Thompson's *The Seasons*, for example, with its lengthy evocations of weather and landscape, enjoyed an enormous vogue, and the success of this work gave Thompson's selection of natural scenes an increased prestige as subjects for works of art in their own right. Thus Turner used lines from *The Seasons* to accompany many of his paintings, particularly his early oils, which he may possibly have felt needed some support to elevate them into fully fledged pictures rather than "views."

Progressing from Thompson, Turner began to exhibit his paintings with lines from a poem of his own, *The Fallacies of Hope*, an incomplete work whose title served to link together the various fragments he produced to rein-

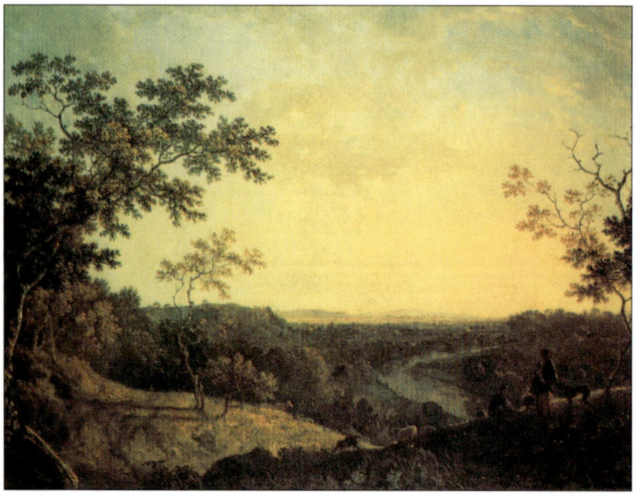

RICHARD WILSON
The River Dee
c 1762
National Gallery, London

Wilson began as a portrait painter, but his real interest was landscape, and it is for these that he is remembered. Like Turner, he was much influenced by Claude, and Turner saw him as his only major predecessor in the kind of art which successfully combined a sensitive rendering of the English landscape with the grandeur and drama of the Italian classical tradition.

force particular paintings. It may seem surprising to us in the present day that he felt the need for such addenda when his work can be appreciated for its purely visual qualities, but this was entirely in keeping with his ambition: deeply imbued with a respect for art in its traditional spiritual role, he wished his painting to be placed in the context of feelings and ideas and not just visual sensations. The *Aeneid*, the masterpiece of the Roman poet Virgil, was also among Turner's reading matter, particularly valued for its story of the Carthaginian queen Dido and its natural descriptions. He was equally familiar with the works of his contemporaries, Byron and Shelley, perhaps the most widely read of the English Romantic poets at the time, and several works were inspired by passages from Byron. This literary awareness brought him closer to the heart of the Romantic movement, which at the time was as much literary as visual.

Turner and the art establishment

Although this picture of Turner, the lonely, pessimistic artist painting landscapes of passionate turmoil, fits easily into an historical context of the Romantic movement, it is a portrait that the artist himself might not have recognized. Despite his innovations in technique, the visionary nature of his work and the mockery of some critics, Turner was in many ways a fervent upholder of tradition and the artistic establishment. His instinctive respect for the institutions of his profession had its origins in his humble beginnings, and it was of great importance to him to become an associate of the Royal Academy at the age of twenty-four (in 1799) and a full member three years later, not only financially, but in terms of security and recognition. His social awkwardness made him doubly appreciative of the company and support of his fellow painters, and he remained loyal to the Academy throughout his career. As a student he had learned life drawing in the Academy Schools, and had attended the last lecture of the great founder, Sir Joshua Reynolds (he may even have attended Reynolds' studio in the company of other young painters eager for informal instruction). Turner never failed to refer to Reynolds with great respect, partly for his painting style and technique and partly out of natural reverence for his professional achievement. When Turner was appointed professor of perspective at the Academy he took his obligatory course of lectures with great seriousness, no doubt aware of the weight of tradition supplied by the founder's famous discourses on art.

Turner's highly developed sense of history was, typically, the product of conflicting feelings: the insecurity caused by his humble background and a sense of his own value that enabled him to regard the great masters of the past as his equals and rivals. These feelings spurred on his well-developed professional ambition, and continually throughout his career he produced works that were in direct response to the success of a contemporary – works that enabled him to learn, assimilate and compete. His relationship with the Old Masters worked in very much the same way, and he produced what amounted to updated interpretations that were simultaneously homages and challenges.

Major influences

Turner's influences were catholic, but were fundamentally derived from the seventeenth century, the first heroic age of landscape painting. The two schools of this time were those of the Dutch and Italian. The Dutch had painted their landscape for its own sake, without the inclusion of any "storyline" other than the day-to-day activities of its inhabitants, and the interest of their work lies in the vivid depiction of nature and the changing effects of climate. These paintings were unpretentious works painted for a middle-class public, and were popular among English artists and collectors who found the straightforward depiction of landscape, as well as the landscape itself, compatible with their own outlook. By Turner's day the Dutch influence on British painting was well established, and is the primary source of the topo-

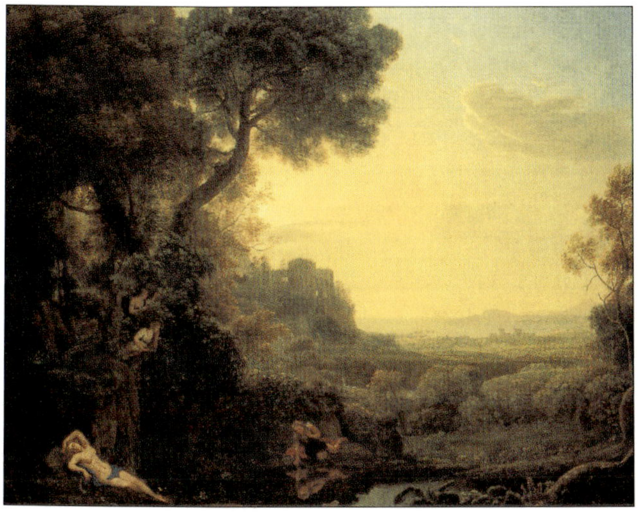

CLAUDE LORRAINE
The Embarkation of the Queen of Sheba
1648
National Gallery, London

On seeing this for the first time in his early twenties, Turner said, "I shall never be able to paint anything like this picture." Now, in accordance with his will, his own tribute to Claude, *Dido Building Carthage*, hangs next to it in the National Gallery. Claude painted many variations of the theme of a classical seaport, all of them featuring a rising or setting sun and its reflection.

graphical work with which he began his career. Of more direct importance to him were the Dutch seascape painters, to whom he was naturally drawn in his continual re-examination of his favorite subject. Again it was in a spirit of both homage and competition that Turner echoed in his own paintings the work of the Dutchman Van der Velde (see page 251).

A different tradition of landscape painting had arisen in seventeenth-century Italy, led by the Frenchman Claude Lorraine. He was inspired by the warm, even and unchanging light of the countryside around Rome, and used it in his carefully arranged and idealized landscapes. These, unlike the simple Dutch landscapes, had a "storyline," and although the landscape was the real subject, figures relating to a biblical, mythological or classical tale were always placed unobtrusively in the foreground. With these works Claude created the style of historic landscape that became much admired and was considered by the academies of Europe as more prestigious than the mere view painting of the Dutch. Claude's undisputed eminence in landscape had a powerful fascination for Turner, who was mesmerized in particular by the luminosity of the paintings, the way in which the subtle glows of morning, afternoon and evening were conveyed through the glazes of oil. After studying Claude's work in the collections of his patrons, Turner's first trip to Italy in 1819 took on the nature of a pilgrimage to the source of this ideal world.

Turner also studied the work of Claude's contemporary and compatriot Nicolas Poussin, whose paintings were a less lushly lit and more austerely controlled variant on the classical landscape. The clarity of Poussin's work, usually based on posed studio studies of models, seems distant from Turner's more dynamic approach taken from direct outdoor experience, yet the two shared a concern with theme, or content, in their landscapes. Turner's respect for the traditional view of how the business of art was to deal with the most elevated themes — very much the viewpoint of the academician — accords with his concern to give the maximum intensity to his own landscapes. His early admiration for Richard Wilson, his major precursor in English landscape painting, can also be seen in this context. Wilson had also traveled to Italy to see for himself the light that had inspired Claude, and his panoramic, balanced compositions and golden light effects were an important early influence on Turner, who described such works as being "replete with the aerial qualities of distance, aerial lights, aerial color." Wilson, who had begun as a portrait painter, had attempted to win the same level of prestige for landscape. In this he had only limited success, but his classical landscapes in the Claudian manner succeeded in transposing onto the familiar British scenery something of the grandeur and drama of the biblical or mythological scenes for which he used it as a setting. Thus he served as an important example to Turner just as the latter was breaking out from the particular of the watercolor genre to the broader stage of oils.

NICOLAS POUSSIN
The Deluge
c 1640
Louvre, Paris

Turner greatly admired the somber coloring of this work when he studied it in the Louvre on his first trip abroad. At this time his own coloring was still quite subdued. He was also drawn to the treatment of natural disasters, which became a strong theme in his work.

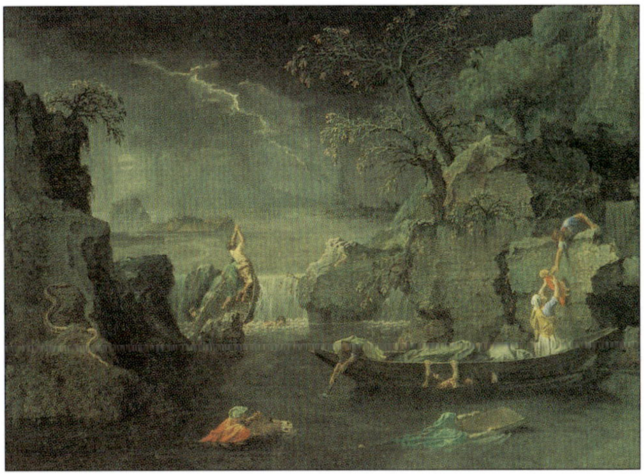

Recording and observation

But while Turner looked to Romantic literature and the Old Masters to give greater force to his work, the essential foundation for his painting always remained his concentrated observation and recording of nature itself. His visual memory was such that he could store the details of a particular weather effect to reproduce it exactly in a work produced years later, but despite this ability he relied also on painting directly from nature. On each trip he made, either at home or abroad, he filled sketchbooks with watercolors and drawings done on the spot, as had become usual for a topographic artist. At a later stage he classified the sketches by subject or theme and stored them until needed, so that he had a huge reference file of fresh impressions to be consulted when working on large canvases.

This was the normal working method of the oil painters of the day, who would use such sketches as the raw material for a work conceived and painted in the studio, but as so often in matters of technique, Turner took the practice one step further, producing small oil sketches as well as watercolors in the open air. He started this around 1806-7, just slightly before his contemporary Constable began the same practice. Both painters were using oils in a new way, to record impressions rapidly and accurately at firsthand, and this free and personal response to nature was to make a great impact on French painters (more stifled by academic tradition than the English) when they developed first the Realist movement and then the Impressionist movement later in the century. Turner subsequently returned to watercolors as his customary medium for recording color impressions, but his early oil sketches, painted from a boat in the Thames, remain an important step in establishing his own personality as a painter. His first biographer records how, later in life, he was fond of taking a bottle of gin with him on such occasions, a habit that discouraged the two boatmen who rowed him along the river from believing that their passenger had indeed been a great painter.

Turner's close observation of nature gave rise to an interest in natural science, and his obsession with light made him particularly interested in exploring the closely related problems of light and color as perceived by the human eye. He was familiar with Newton's earlier use of the prism and discovery of the spectrum, and he

J.M.W. TURNER
Snow Storm: Hannibal and his Army Crossing the Alps
1812
Clore Gallery for the Turner Collection, London

Here Turner evokes the imminent defeat of the great hero through the drama of the storm, said to have been based on one he had observed in Yorkshire two years earlier. The painting marks the beginning of his interest in the Carthaginian empire, while the way the paint is applied looks forward to the style which Turner himself termed "indistinct" and Constable described as "tinted steam."

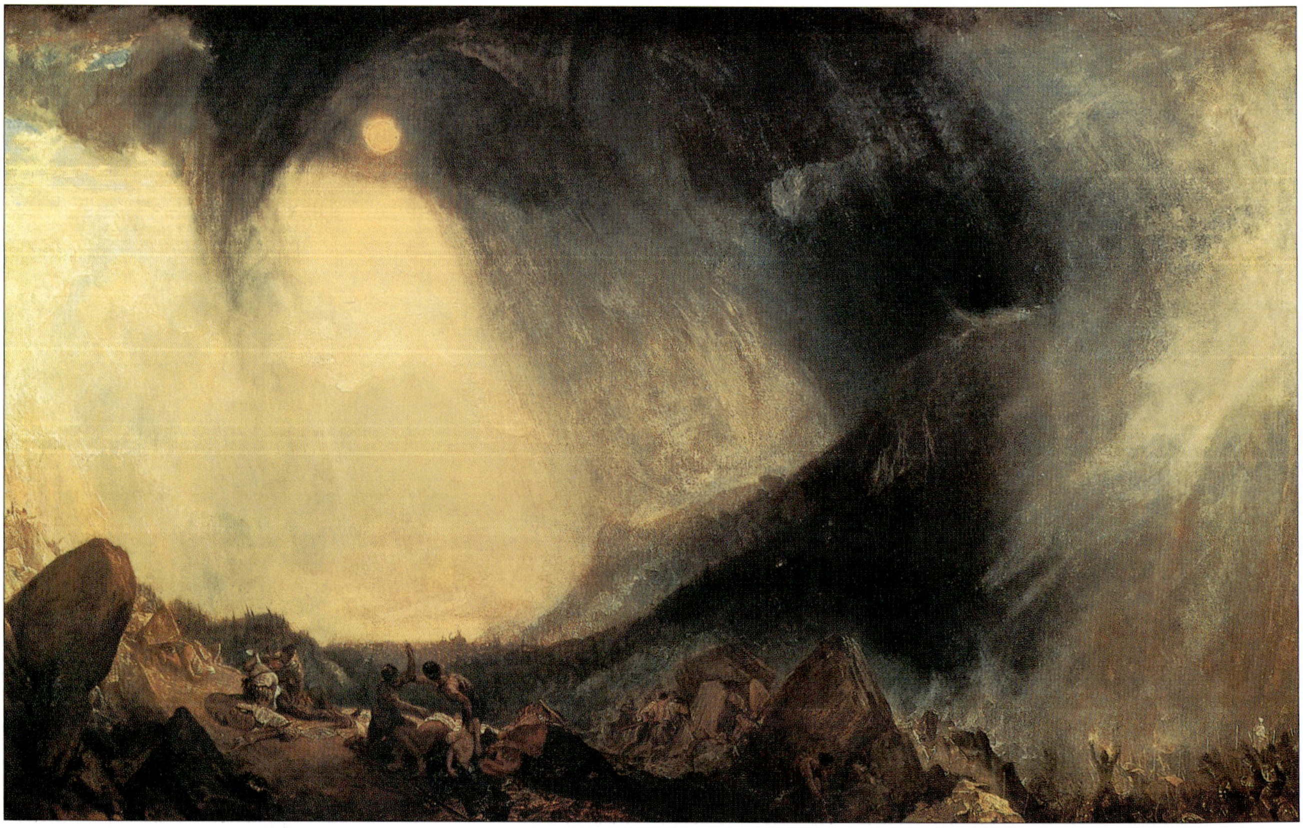

TURNER'S PAINTING METHODS

In this detail from The Dogana, San Giorgio *we see Turner's use of impasto to emphasize the clouds in the pale sky.*

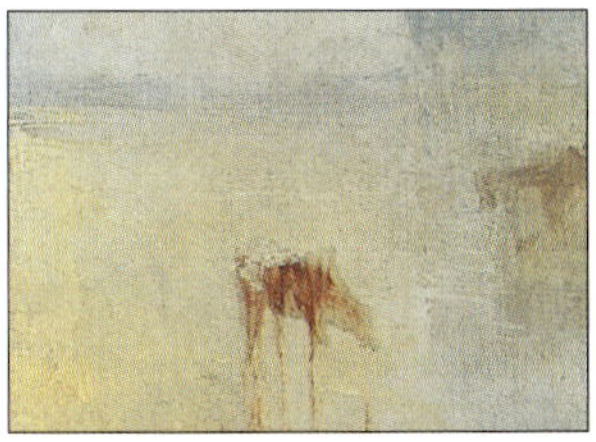

In Norham Castle, Sunrise *the thin paint applied over the brilliant white ground gives a luminous effect similar to watercolor.*

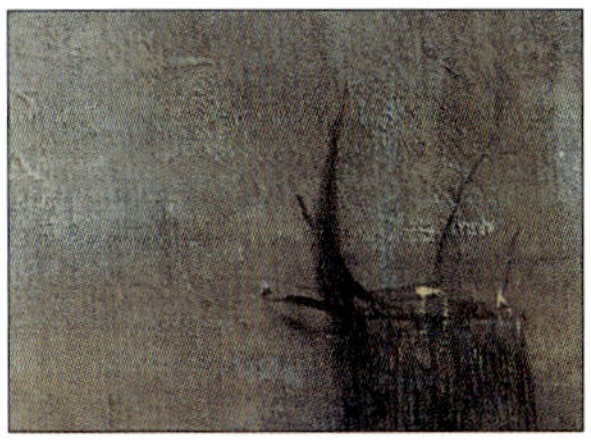

For details such as this, from Peace: Burial at Sea, *Turner used thin paint applied with a fine, pointed brush.*

Turner's oil-painting technique is dazzling, particularly in his later works. He was a true craftsman as well as a great artist, and was constantly pushing forward the frontiers of experience in his search for the means to convey drama, emotions and the effects of nature. As his career progressed, he began to use increasingly vivid and pure colors, preferring to work on a light ground that reflected back through the layers of paint to give a glowing luminosity to his work. From the start he adopted broad under-painting, but instead of the traditional mono-chrome brown or ocher he used pale washes of color, such as pinks, blues and yellows, which both established the composition and enhanced the effect of the colors added sub-sequently. These were laid over one another on the canvas rather than being premixed on the palette. He used a great number of dif-ferent techniques, such as knife-painting, scumbling, thick impasto and thin glazes, often combining all of them in one painting to give a marvelously varied paint surface.

His watercolor technique is no less revo-lutionary — in an age when the standard method was to apply a series of thin, pale washes over a careful pencil or pen drawing, Turner mixed his paint with gouache, gum arabic or pencil to give it more body, and then created highlights by removing areas of paint with blotting paper or a damp brush. Some-times, when working rapidly on the spot, he would allow the colors to mix into one another or drip down the paper, exploiting each effect as it occurred to create magical evocations of light and atmosphere.

Before the mid-nineteenth century, when ready mixed paints in metal tubes were introduced, paints were sold in powdered pigment form and stored in glass bottles prior to grinding and mixing with oil. The prepared paint was kept in small bladders — visible at the back of the box. Oil painting outdoors was a much more laborious process than it is today, but Turner, who was deeply committed to working from nature, was one of the first to use oil paint as an outdoor sketching medium. In general, however, he preferred watercolor or pencil, filling sketchbook after sketchbook with visual "notes" that were later used as reference for finished compositions.

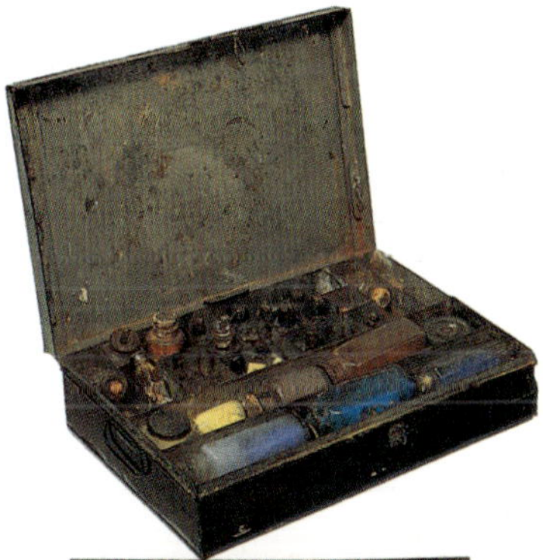

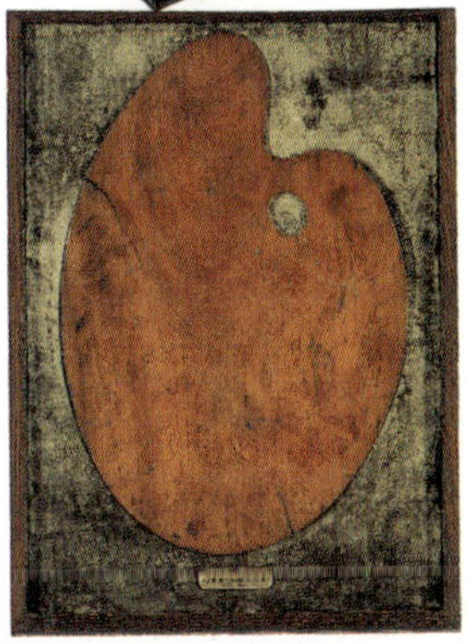

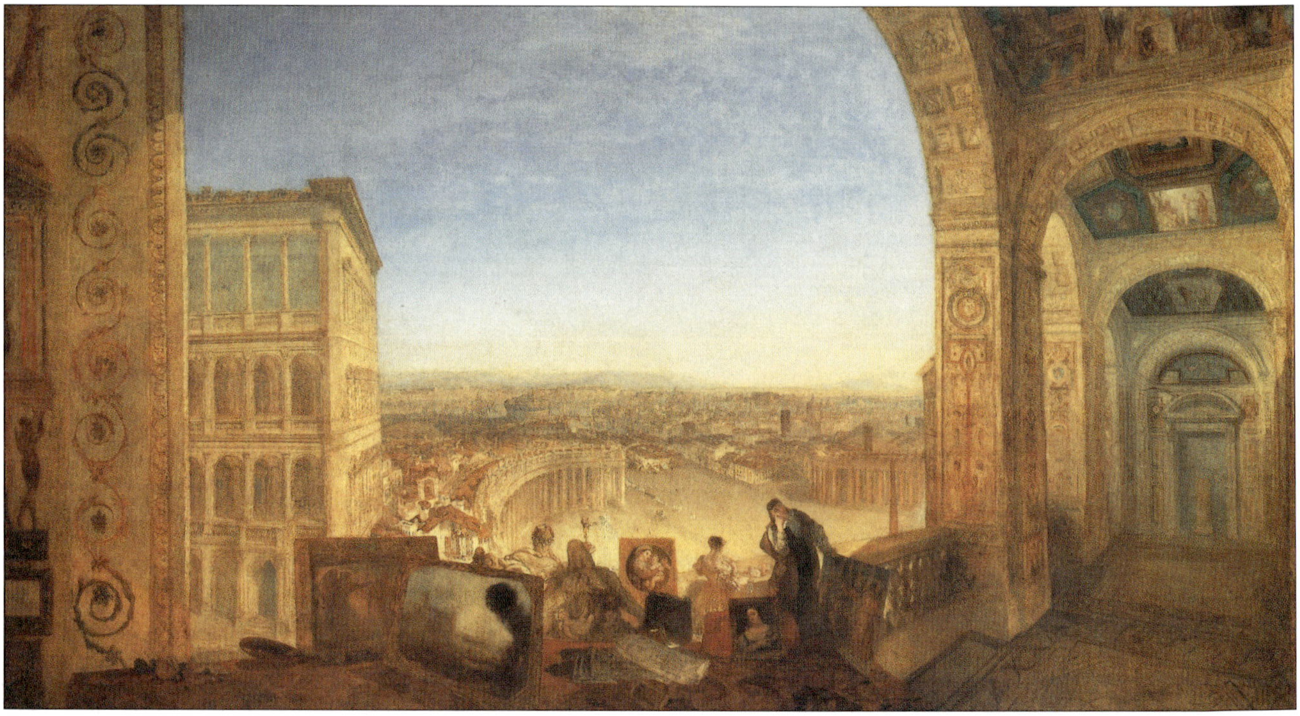

J.M.W. TURNER
Rome from the Vatican
1820
Clore Gallery for the Turner Collection, London

This was Turner's first oil to be directly inspired by his visit to Italy. An ambitious and slightly awkward composition, it shows Rome as though viewed by Raphael, who is shown in the foreground surrounded by his works. The art-historical theme emphasizes Turner's self-consciousness in approaching Italianate subject matter.

followed the contemporary studies on the same theme, reading the English translation of Goethe's book on color theory with close attention, and experimenting with some of its ideas in his work.

The Turner who was a painstaking and clearheaded observer of the world around him may seem to contrast with the Turner who was the creator of such highly personal and visionary works, but in his greatest work the two strands intertwine. In these we are presented with scenes that are immediately convincing as visual experiences, but are also filled with great drama and personal feeling. His genius amplifies the private drama of his characters or of his own emotions into a drama of nature itself, and the apparent opposites are united into a vision of the world which is both personal and universal. Indeed, much of the excitement of Turner's work is created by the attempt to combine disparate elements, with the tension between the revolutionary and the academician, the observer of nature and the inspired visionary, giving enormous vitality to an art that deals so eloquently with movement, conflict, change and the passing of time.

Turner's legacy

Turner died in 1851 at the age of seventy-six, and his estate included 350 oil paintings and 20,000 drawings and watercolors. These were only his unsold works, but when added to the considerable number sold throughout his career they give a good idea of the nature and scale of his lifetime of unceasing activity. Within this vast *oeuvre* there is tremendous variety, but also a strong thematic continuity, a quality Turner himself was well aware of. He tended to think of his work as a unity, a natural extension of the many series that it contained, and some works he refused to sell, while others were bought back by him from their first owners so that they might return to their place in the whole. This concern for completeness, an interesting complement to the theme of destruction and loss that appear in many of the paintings, extended to the terms of his will, in which he left all the works in his possession to the nation on the condition that they be displayed together. This condition understandably created grave problems, and has only recently been fulfilled with the establishment of the modern Turner gallery alongside the Tate Gallery in London. In this gallery, whose ancestor was the one the painter himself had added to his London house, it is possible to see the private, experimental and preparatory works alongside the more polished pieces to which they contributed, a unique collection which echoes and reinforces the artist's high estimation of his own work implicit in the terms of the bequest.

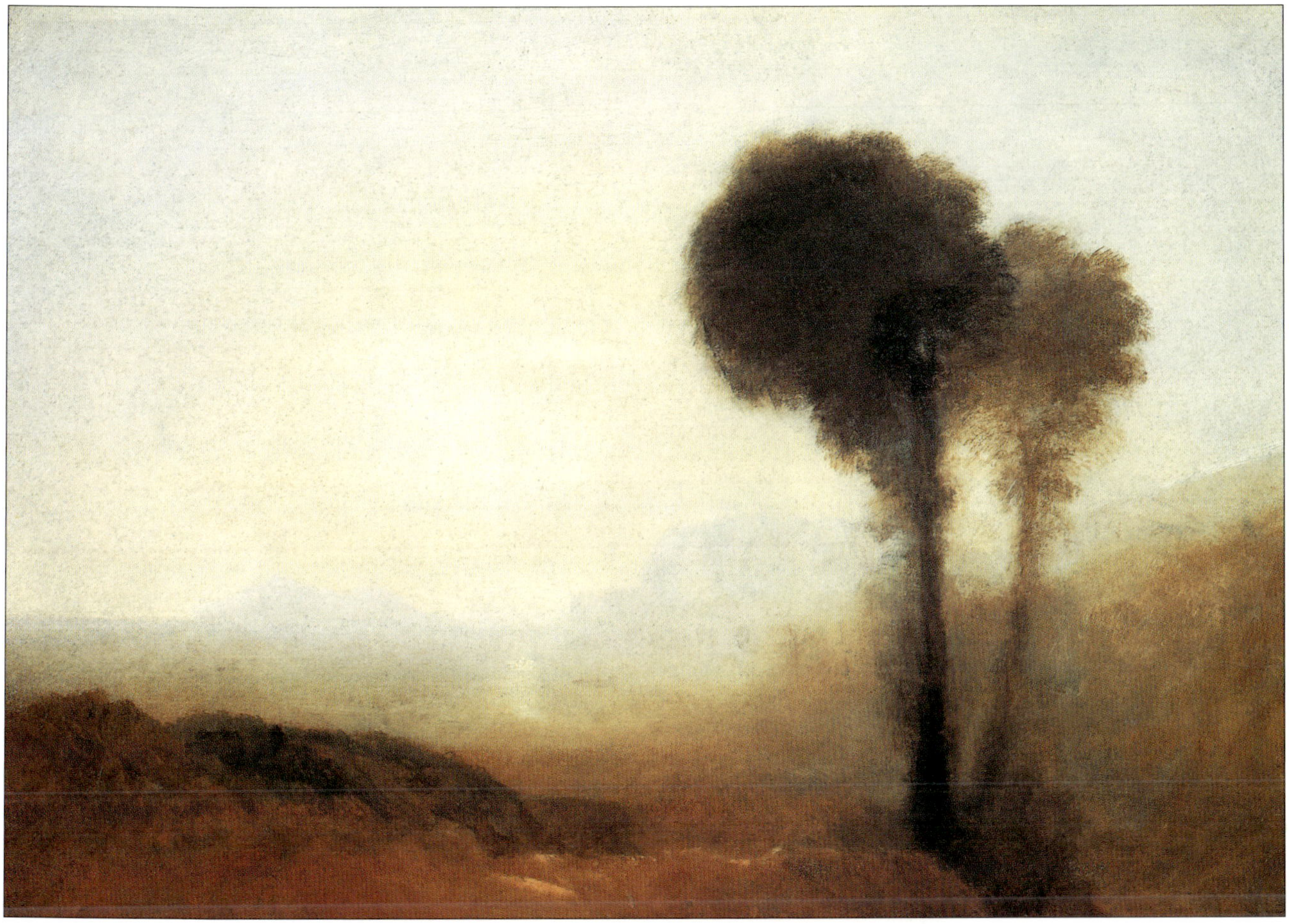

J.M.W. TURNER
Coast Scene near Naples
1828?
Clore Gallery for the Turner Collection, London

This is one of Turner's sketches, or "color beginnings," in which he tried to capture the exact hues of the sunlit landscape, regardless of detail. It is one of a group of ten such works, on board, probably done on his second visit to Italy. These truly Impressionist pieces, which would later be used as reference for a finished painting, show him concentrating on light and color as the essence of his work.

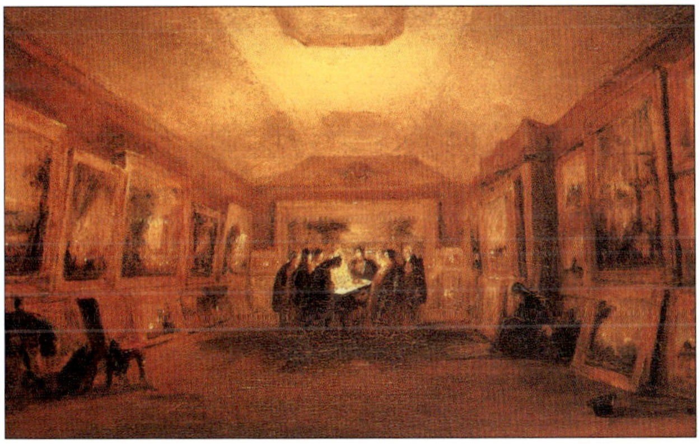

GEORGE JONES
Turner Lying in State in his Gallery
1852
Ashmolean Museum, Oxford

Turner had built his own gallery, an extension of his house, when he began to become successful, reserving it for his more private or experimental paintings. When he died he was laid out in the gallery, surrounded by the pictures he found it so difficult to part with. One of these, visible here, is *Dido Building Carthage,* which he had once expressed a wish to be buried with.

CHRONOLOGY OF TURNER'S LIFE

1775	April 23: born in Covent Garden, London.
1789	Admitted to Academy Schools.
1794-97	Works for Dr Monro copying his collection of drawings and watercolors.
1796	First oil painting exhibited at Royal Academy, *Fishermen at Sea off the Needles.*
1797	First tour of the north of England.
1799	Made associate of the Royal Academy. Receives commission for topographical watercolors.
1800	Mother admitted to Bethlem Hospital for the Insane.
1802	Elected full member of the Royal Academy. Earl of Egremont starts buying his work.
1804	Builds his own gallery as extension to house.
1805	Paints *The Shipwreck.* Mother dies.
1807	Made professor of perspective at Royal Academy Schools. First volume of *Liber Studorium* issued.
1810	Paints *The Fall of an Avalanche in the Grisons.*
1812	Paints *Hannibal Crossing the Alps.*

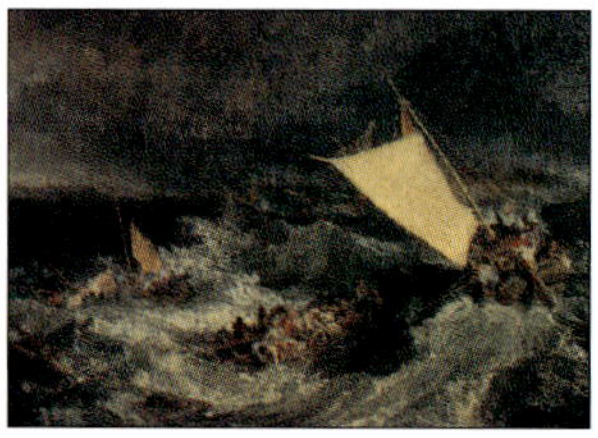

The Shipwreck

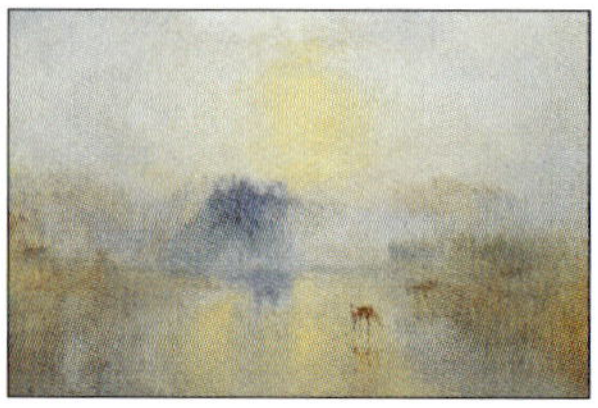

Norham Castle

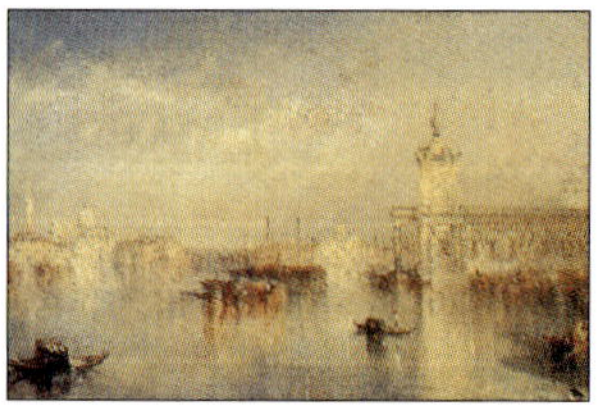

The Dogana, San Giorgio

1815	Paints *Dido Building Carthage.*
1817	Visits the Netherlands and Rhine valley.
1819-20	First visit to Italy; sees Rome, Venice and Naples.
1828	Travels to Rome via Paris.
1829	Paints *Ulysses Deriding Polyphemus.* Father dies.
1830	Paints *The Evening Star.* Begins to stay regularly with Earl of Egremont at Petworth.
1833	Second visit to Venice.
1834	Paints several versions of *Burning of the Houses of Parliament.* Exhibits illustrations to Byron's poetry.
1837	Death of Earl of Egremont. Probable date of *Interior at Petworth.*
1839	Takes cottage in Chelsea as retreat.
1840	Meets John Ruskin. Third visit to Venice.
1842	Paints *Peace, Burial at Sea* and *The Dogana, San Giorgio.*
1844	Paints *Rain, Steam and Speed.*
1850	Exhibits for last time.
1851	19th December: dies in Chelsea.

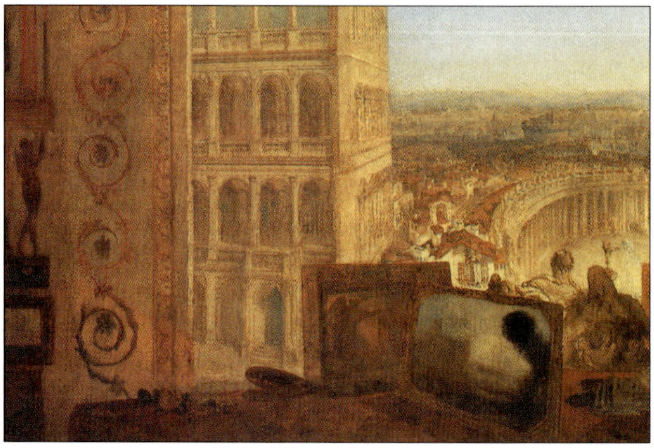

Rain, Steam and Speed

THE PAINTINGS

The Shipwreck

1805

$67\frac{1}{2} \times 95$in/171.5×241cm

Oil on canvas

Clore Gallery for the Turner Collection, London

Turner explained that "this made me a painter" when examining a print of a Van der Velde seascape with a friend. *The Shipwreck* is one of a series of paintings beginning with his first exhibited oil and continuing through the National Gallery *Calais Pier*, in which Turner expands and develops the Dutch genre of seascape. The Duke of Bridgewater, who owned a Van der Velde seascape, had stimulated this sequence by commissioning Turner to produce a matching work to hang with it. Growing up close to the banks of the Thames where the merchant and naval ships were moored. Turner had a detailed personal knowledge of the subject.

Here he extends the usually modest dimensions of the genre to the more monumental scale of a full-blown academic work, and an earlier theme begins to become more explicit. In his previous seascape treatments there had been a heavy swell, or rough sea, but this now becomes a life-threatening tempest, with endangered and clearly mortal man engaged in a struggle against the elements. The theme which emerges in this painting was one that was to reappear again and again in Turner's work. The wrecked ship itself is placed in the background, almost obscured by the sail of the largest boat; the foreground drama is that of the struggle of the survivors in their tiny craft. The composition perfectly evokes the turbulence of the water, a formless, ever-changing mass which allows Turner greater freedom than could the more defined and substantial features of land. An ellipse provides the focus of the picture, suggesting continual swirling movement and the depths into which the survivors are in danger of being drawn. From this point on Turner's imagination was to return continually to the form of the ellipse or vortex, which he used to represent the superhuman forces with which he became increasingly fascinated. Not only did the stormy sea give him a freer hand with composition, but his brushstrokes also became less inhibited when conveying the movement of water, and the oil paint itself, applied with enough vigor to suggest it had been splashed across the canvas, provided an equivalent to the spray from the waves. It was this kind of paint handling that first attracted the charge of a "lack of finish," but Turner's desire for more vivid realism surpassed that of Van der Velde (see opposite), whose technique was more polished, with a much more generalized treatment of the water's surface.

The Shipwreck was exhibited, not at the Royal Academy, but at Turner's own gallery which he had completed as an extension to his house in the spring of 1804, the previous year. This was a substantial room, seventy feet long, which demonstrates how successful Turner had already become in financial terms. He opened the gallery at a time when the future of the Academy seemed uncertain: it was bitterly divided between rival factions, either supporting or opposing King George III's attempts to encourage a more significant production of royal, "official," art. The turmoil had already encouraged the formation of two independent groups, the Society of Watercolour Artists and the British Institution. The creation by an artist of his own gallery was unusual for the time, but it was typical of Turner's concern for security and independence. He continued to use his gallery throughout his life, for the display of more private works, passing its management to his old father when he built another house for himself outside London, on the river at Twickenham.

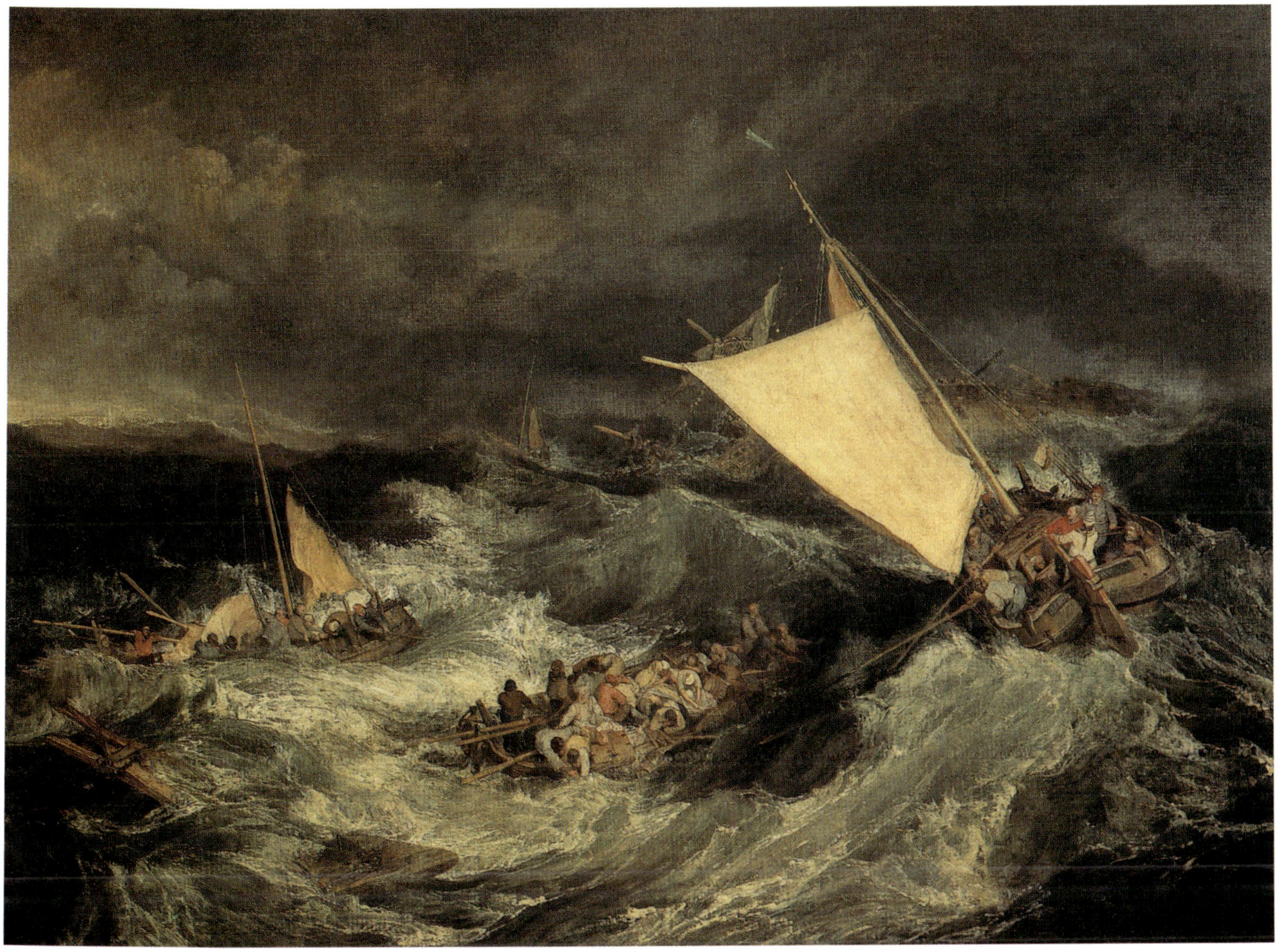

Turner's brushwork parallels the fluidity and movement of the sea in its direction and application. The looseness of handling seen in the details seems to anticipate his late style. But this is deceptive, for here speed and spontaneity of execution are combined with great care in building up the surface by means of many different hues and small, patient brushstrokes.The preference for a dark ground, from which the highlights are worked up, is also typical of his early work. This is a large painting, and from a distance the looseness of touch in some areas draws the eye in to the fine detail in others. Through the contrast in paint handling, Turner has given extra drama to the subject, his brushwork emphasizing the force of the water directed against the tiny, helpless figures.

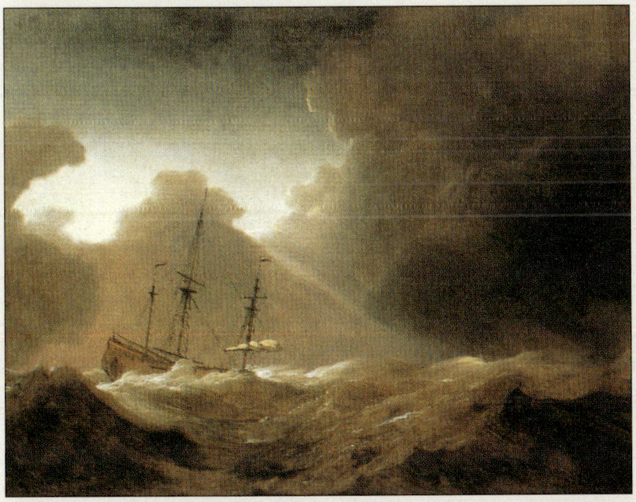

WILLEM VAN DER VELDE
1633-1707
Ship in a Storm
National Maritime Museum, Greenwich

Early in his career Turner was commissioned to paint a seascape to match a work by Van der Velde, a task which he was pleased to carry out, attempting to surpass the Dutch artist's realism. The Dutch seascape painters were of great importance to him, and he is supposed to have said, when looking at a print of such a painting, that "this made me an artist."

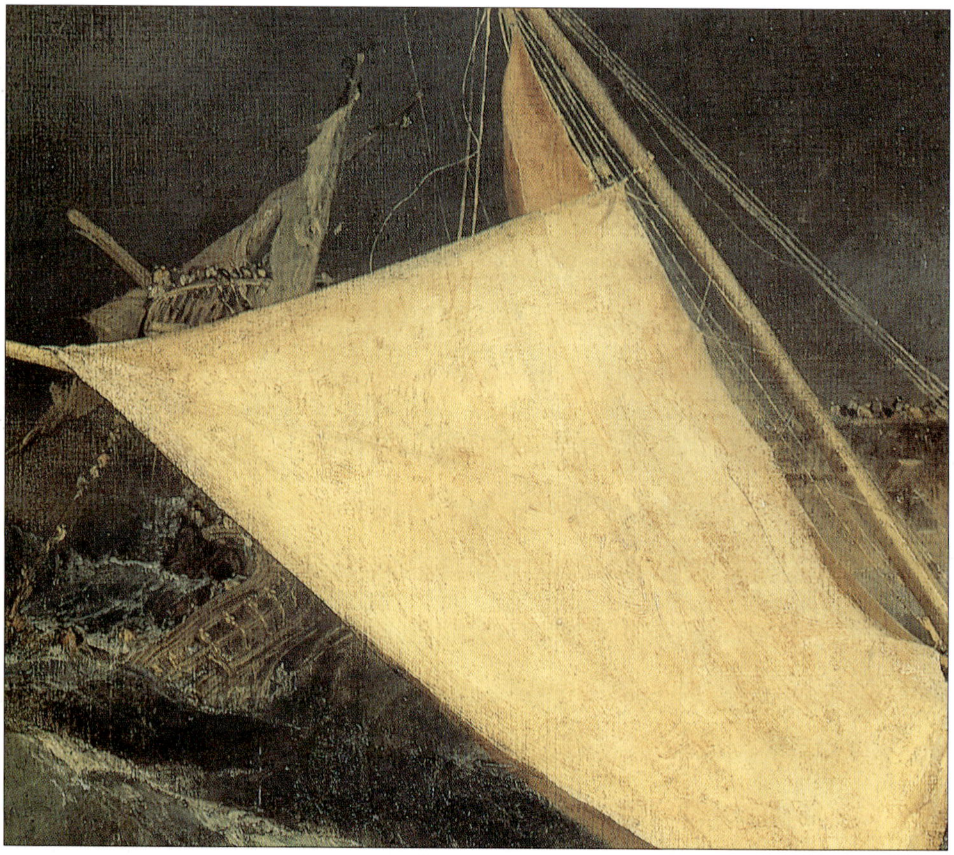

1

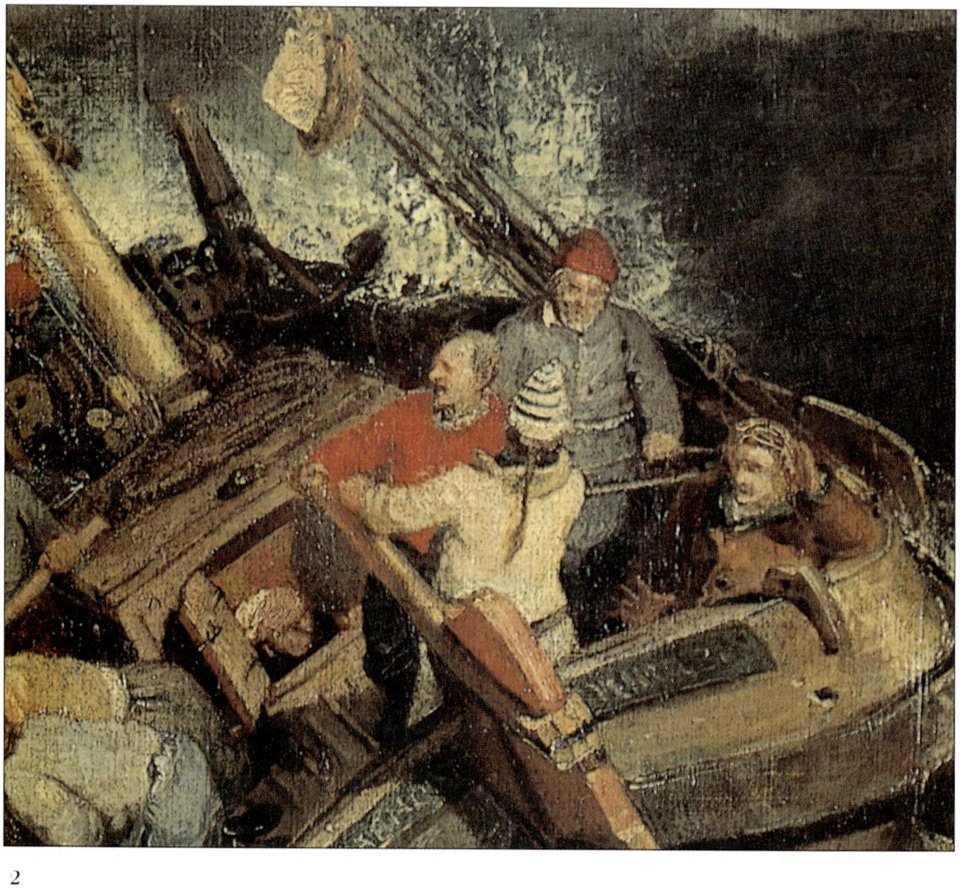

2

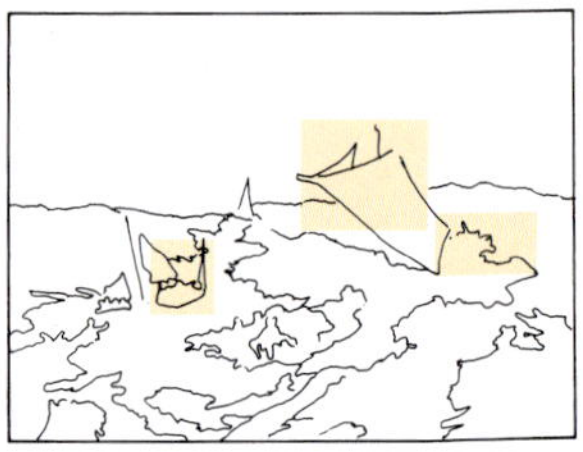

1 The sail is the area of the thickest and most opaque paint. The path of the brush through the pigment is clearly visible, with faint lines of underpainting showing through the marks of the hairs. Behind the sail lies a shattered fragment of the prow of the wrecked boat, whose details are sketched in with single strokes of umber.

2 Here the flexibility and originality of Turner's technique have been reined in. Paint is applied in thick dabs, and barely moved across the surface except in the pink used to describe the surface of the rudder. A series of discrete flat areas are juxtaposed in sharp, clear-cut contrasts, particularly in the red, white and black of the sailor's clothes.

3 *Actual size detail* Over the deep gray underpainting visible beyond the foam Turner draws strokes of pale gray-green leading to a vortex of foam just above the side of the boat. This is applied in dilute paint, so that its surface is relatively smooth, like a semi-transparent veil of water thrown into the air. Touches of white and a bluer green are mixed in in places, and over this, brief individual touches of white and blue-green suggest flecks of foam and spray. These are applied thickly toward the border with the boat, and thin and dry as they fade away over the background at the crest of the wave.

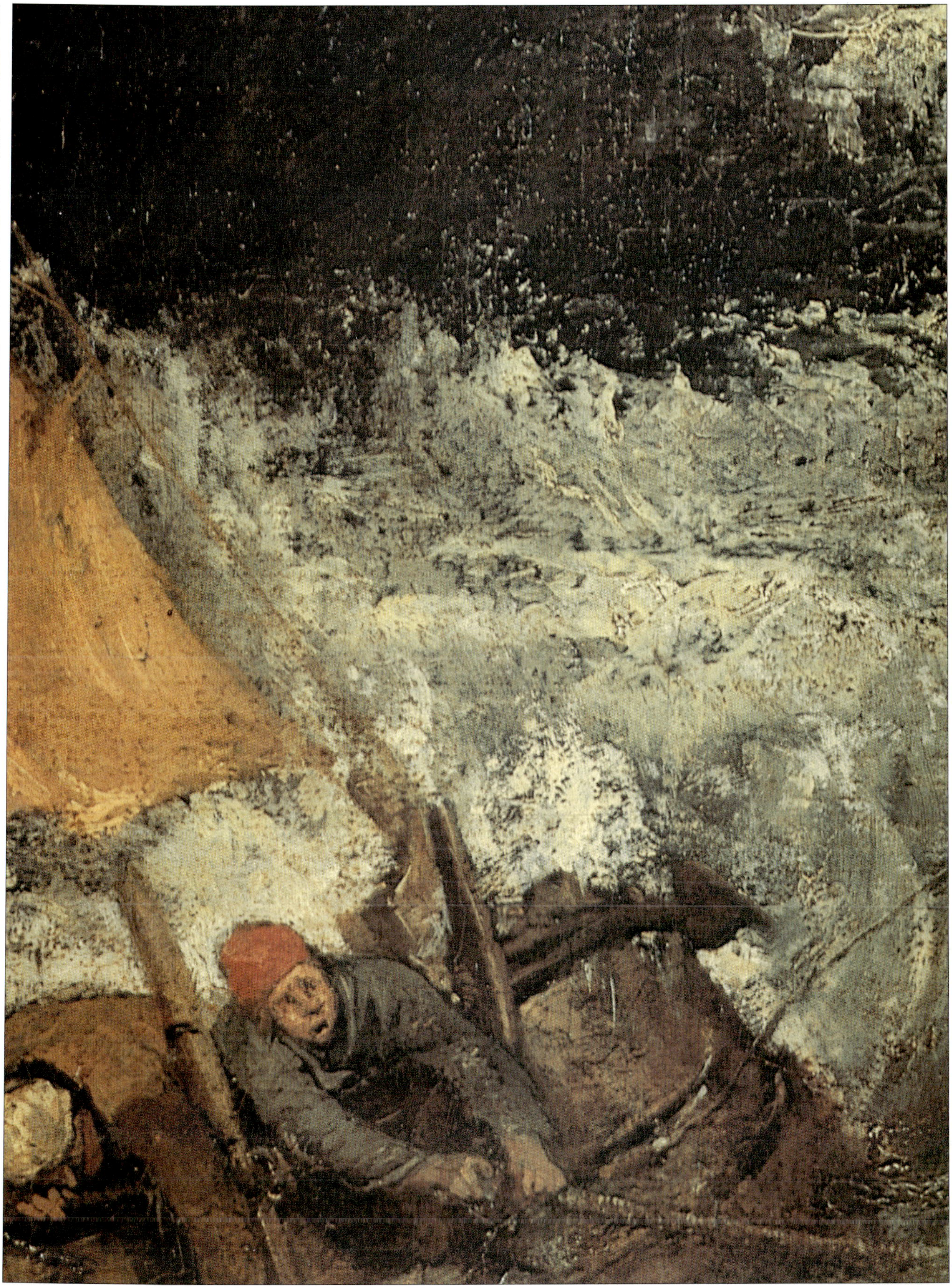

3 *Actual size detail*

THE FALL OF AN AVALANCHE IN THE GRISONS

1810

$35\frac{1}{2} \times 47\frac{1}{4}$in/$90.25 \times 120$cm

Oil on canvas

Clore Gallery for the Turner Collection, London

Turner had visited Switzerland eight years before this work was painted, and on the same trip had studied the Old Masters in the Louvre, Paris. Despite the somewhat muted enthusiasm implied by his comment that "the Country on the whole surpasses Wales, and Scotland too," the Alps clearly made a deep impression on him. They represented the apogee of the Sublime, and he drew and painted them with that quality in mind, emphasizing the deep ravines, huge cliffs and dangerous paths. By the time of this work Turner's interests had progressed beyond simply capturing the Romantic grandeur of the conventionally picturesque, and had become more ambitious and personal. The setting here is Switzerland, but it is a part which he had not visited, and neither had he witnessed an Alpine avalanche, although he had seen several dramatic thunderstorms which are clearly remembered in this work. Avalanches had, however, been painted by his contemporary Philip De Loutherbourg, from whom he had earlier learned to depict dramatic night effects. This type of synthesis, combining minutely recalled natural detail with a more open visual reminiscence of a fellow artist, is typical of Turner's way of thinking.

The fact that he was moving beyond the detached depiction of a natural phenomenon is stressed by the nine lines of verse he included with the work when it was exhibited. These close with the following:

And towering glaciers fall, the work of ages
Crashing through all! extinction follows,
And the toil, the work of man — o'erwhelms.

These are Turner's own lines, but they appear to be partly inspired by a passage describing an avalanche in the *Winter* poem of Thompson's *The Seasons.* In the painting, the agent of the destruction of the work of man is the massive boulder poised to crush the tiny foreground cottage. This powerful image expresses clearly and concisely the complete destruction of man's works, although no human being is in sight. The composition is pared down to a clash of conflicting diagonals, differentiated by tone and by the variety of surface treatment Turner gives to snow, rock and cloud. In both handling and composition it is an unusual work for this stage in Turner's career, and was shown in his own gallery as too unconventional for an academic context. It anticipates *Hannibal Crossing the Alps* (see page 244) which was to be painted two years later, where natural disaster echoes the destruction of the Napoleonic wars which at that time were threatening the canton of Grisons.

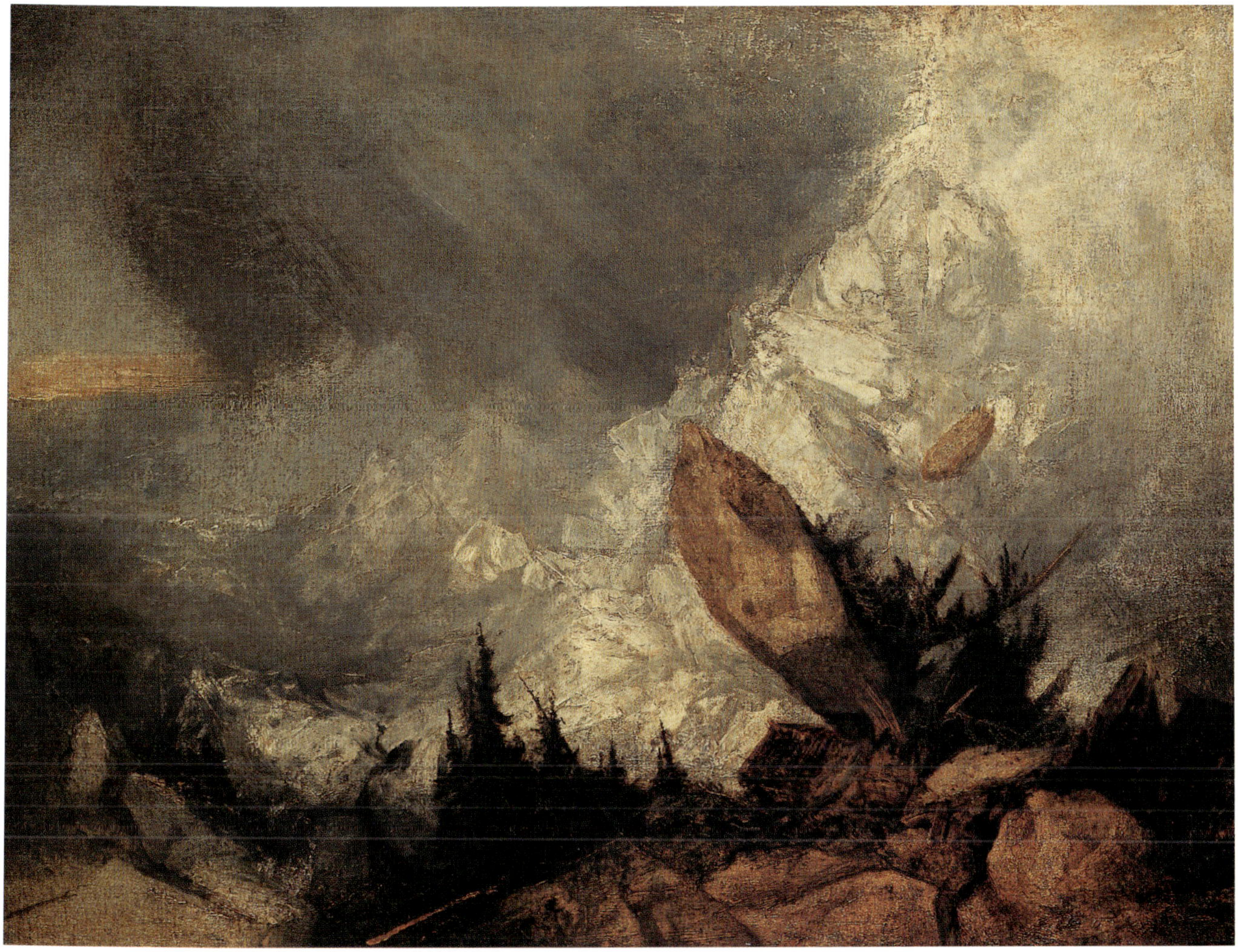

Typically for one of Turner's early oils, color is almost ignored here, except for the dull browns of the foreground rocks, and the whole composition is an exercise in the use of tonal relationships. A narrow range is used effectively to set off the brilliance of the snow, dramatically emphasized by the dark rock. The disregard for detail, however, is an unusual feature at this stage in Turner's career, and the broad areas of underpainting have an almost abstract impact. Such roughly painted areas occur in all Turner's paintings, but here they have been left more clearly visible to become imprecise suggestions of storm, sky and snow. The way the avalanche has been painted is also unusual; its boldness anticipates the late work, but lacks the variety of handling that Turner was later to develop.

1

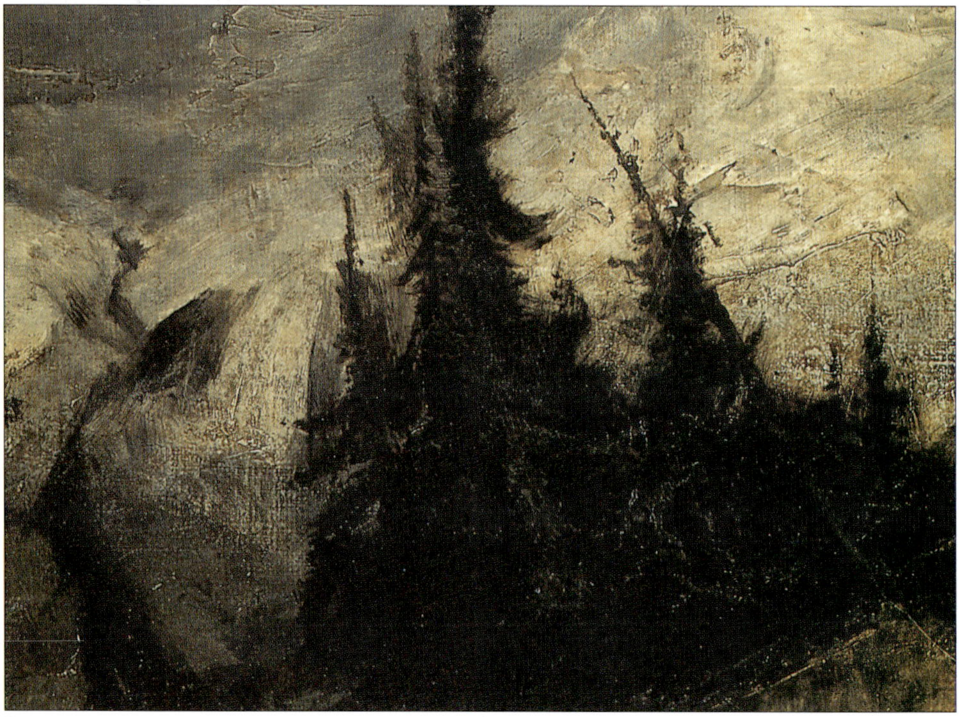

2

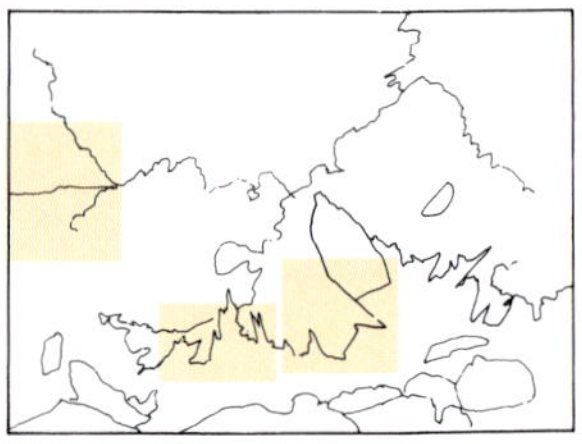

1 Turner's use of "long,"or heavily diluted oil paint can be seen clearly here. The underpainting is dark gray, seen in the extreme left where the bare canvas begins. Slashes of white cross it and are covered by a mid-tone gray, thinly applied and dragged down so that the canvas weave can be seen above the area of highlight. Toward the touches of white indicating the crest of the avalanche, more paint is applied, but still very fluid, so that tones blur together. The diagonal dark stormclouds are applied with long strokes, drier toward the margins.

2 The paler underpainting of the trees has been applied while the background was still moist, but the finer details of trunks and branches demanded a drier brush. To the left of the trees the direction of the brushstrokes follows the movement of the snow, with two rapid strokes producing a gash of dark gray. A very thin blue-gray, recalling a watercolor wash, has been drawn over the more solidly applied white.

3 *Actual size detail* The paint has been applied most loosely at the point where the avalanche buckles up on striking the ground, for here Turner was free from the demands of depicting solid forms. Slabs of thicker white are used near the cottage, and elsewhere they are applied flatly with the palette knife. Leaving patches of bare canvas between, the more fluid blue-gray has been vigorously brushed on, mixing with the white beneath. The reverse technique has been used on the boulder, where thick buff highlight areas are applied over a thin, dark umber ground.

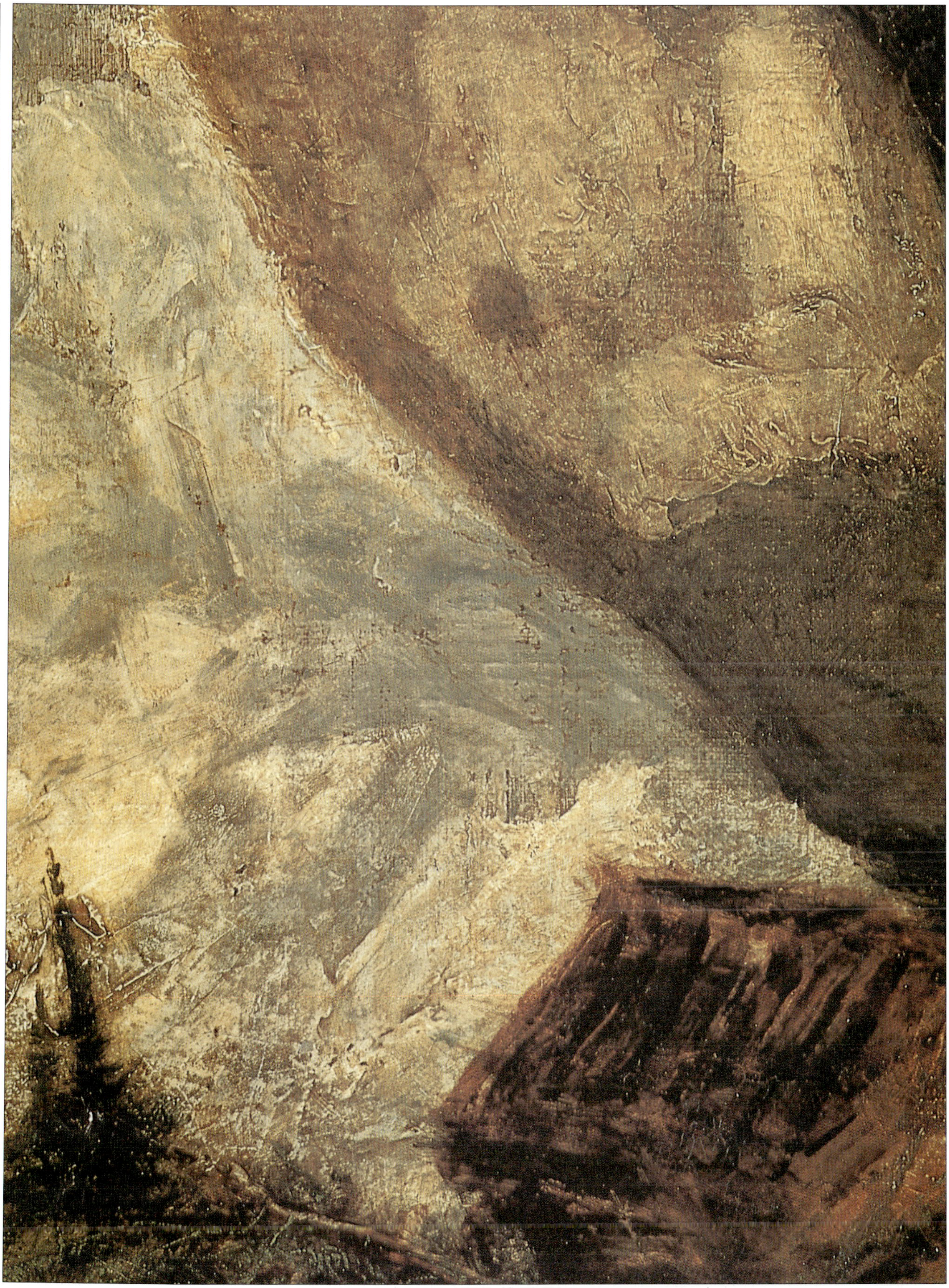

3 *Actual size detail*

Ulysses Deriding Polyphemus

1829

$52\frac{1}{4} \times 80$in/132.75×203cm

Oil on canvas

National Gallery, London

The critic and art historian John Ruskin saw this as "the central picture of Turner's career," and it marks the beginning of the last two decades of Turner's life when his work became increasingly assured and self-contained. The influence of his trips to Italy now emerges as the chief spur to his increasing originality. His private response to Italy had been expressed in watercolors that were concerned with the discovery of the new possibilities presented by the light and color, but for some time after his first visit in 1819 his preoccupations in oil-painting were as much with the traditional Claudian and classical view of the country as with his more vivid personal impressions. *Rome from the Vatican* (see page 246) showed him to be still in the earliest stages of absorbing what he had seen, and feeling inhibited by the depth of art history that lay before the modern traveler. It was not for some years after his first visit that he fully digested the experience.

Turner produced a sketch of *Ulysses Deriding Polyphemus* (see opposite) when in Italy on his second visit in 1828, and the painting itself was done the following year. The influence of Italy is more apparent in the painting technique than in the classical subject matter or in the setting, though the latter is perhaps reminiscent of the southern Italian coastline he had seen on his first tour. On his second trip to Italy, he experienced not only the vivid hues of the sunlit landscape, but also the pure colors of the Gothic and early Renaissance paintings that were becoming fashionable among young English and German painters working in Rome. He began to use purer colors, and he grew less and less reliant on the use of colorless tones to build up his picture. Finally, colors darkened by black disappeared altogether in favor of pure hues. This contrasted dramatically with the conventional academic technique, which aimed at an overall harmony of tone and hue at a much lower pitch, helped by the use of dulling glazes. This was in part a misconceived ideal based upon revered works of the past, many of which were only dark because they had grown so with age, but connoisseurs had become accustomed to this effect, and therefore valued subtle tones in a very narrow range, with little disturbance from strong color. Turner now rejected these values as positively as he also turned his back upon the academic requirement of "finish," a concept that included fine detail and a very smooth application of paint.

The change that was heralded by this work did not go unnoticed by his contemporaries. The critic of the *Morning Herald* noted that it marked "a violent departure from his old style" with "coloring run mad — positive vermilion, postive indigo, and all the most glaring tints of green, yellow and purple." The brightness of these colors conjures up the glowing heroics of myth and the pagan violence of the epic. The blinded giant Polyphemus is left alone on the island, his seated form seeming to blend into the landscape, masked in cloud suggestive of a volcano. Beneath him, the sea glows in the light of the sunrise — an effect partly inspired by the artist's reading of contemporary accounts of phosphorescence in tropical waters.

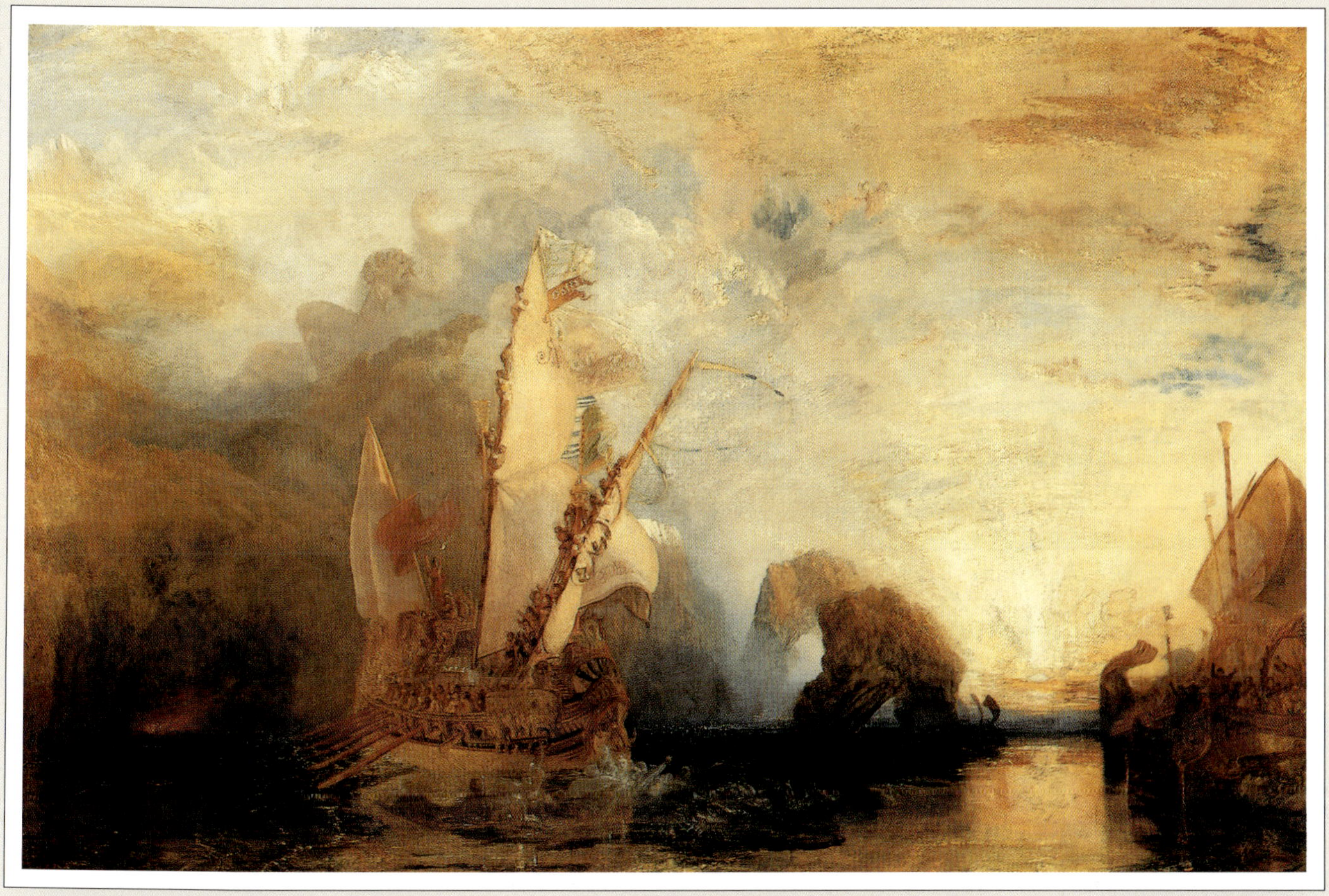

The color and brushwork here clearly show the artist in his maturity, moving confidently away from the traditions of the Old Masters toward the originality and modernity that were to lead to his critical isolation. Yet echoes of Claude, forever associated in Turner's mind with classical themes, remain strong. Cliffs, rocks and ships are all arranged around the sunrise in a manner reminiscent of the seaport scenes by Claude that he had studied so closely. The use of strong silhouettes set against the light, as in the ship's prow and the distant sail, are also traditional devices, and ones that Turner was to use less as his art developed.

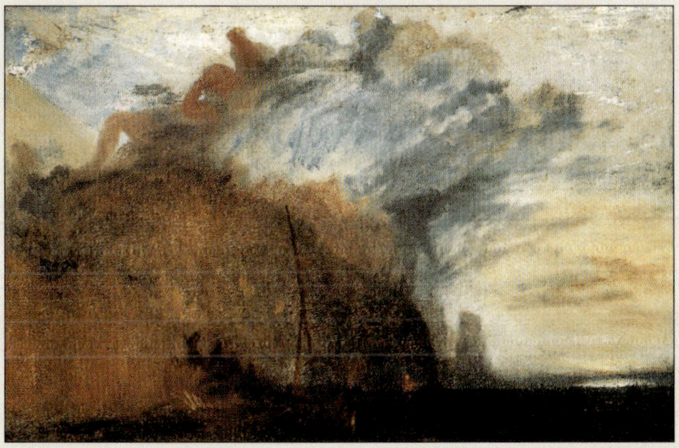

This is the first experimental oil-sketch made on the theme, painted while Turner was in Italy, a year before the painting itself was completed. Such sketches were executed rapidly and freely, using much-thinned paint, but all the main elements of the later composition are included, with the addition of a more clearly defined volcano behind the figure of the giant.

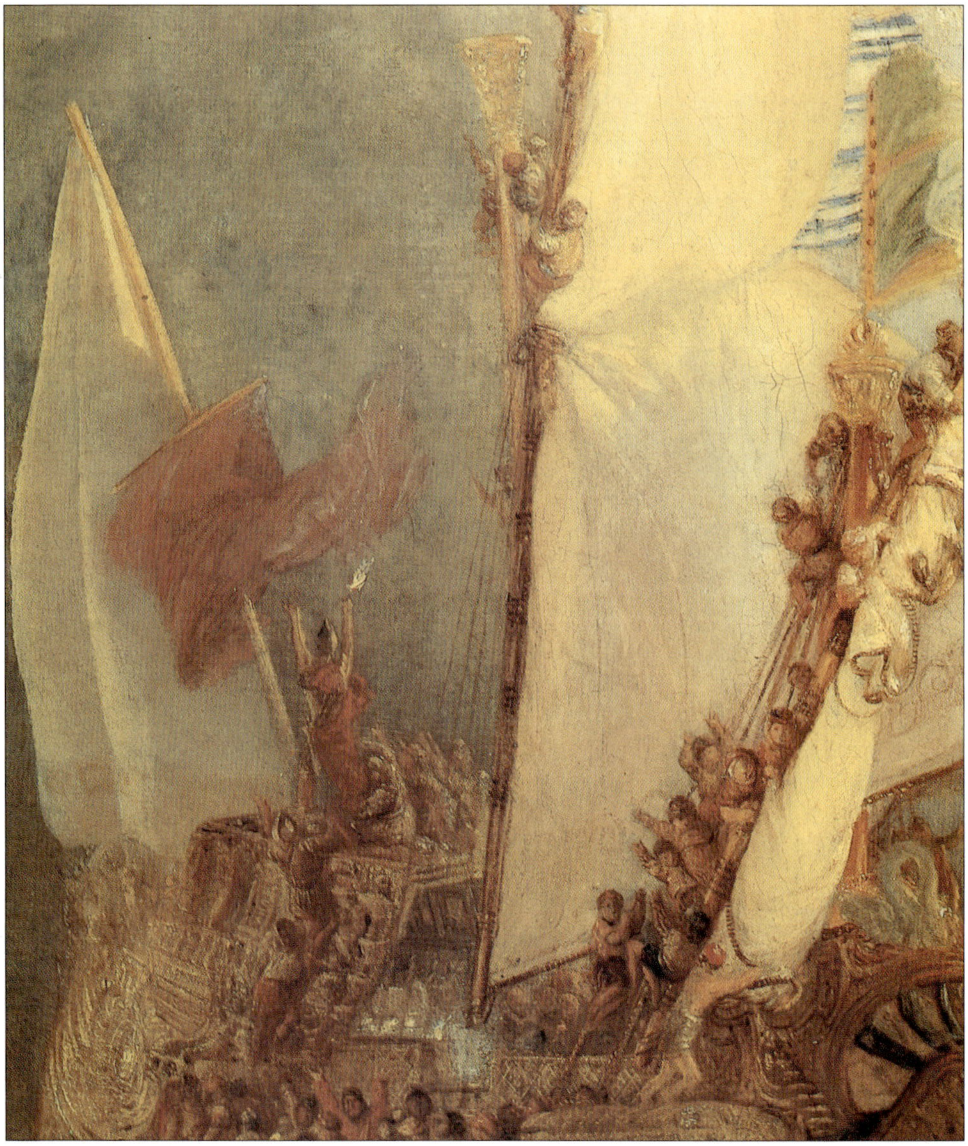

1

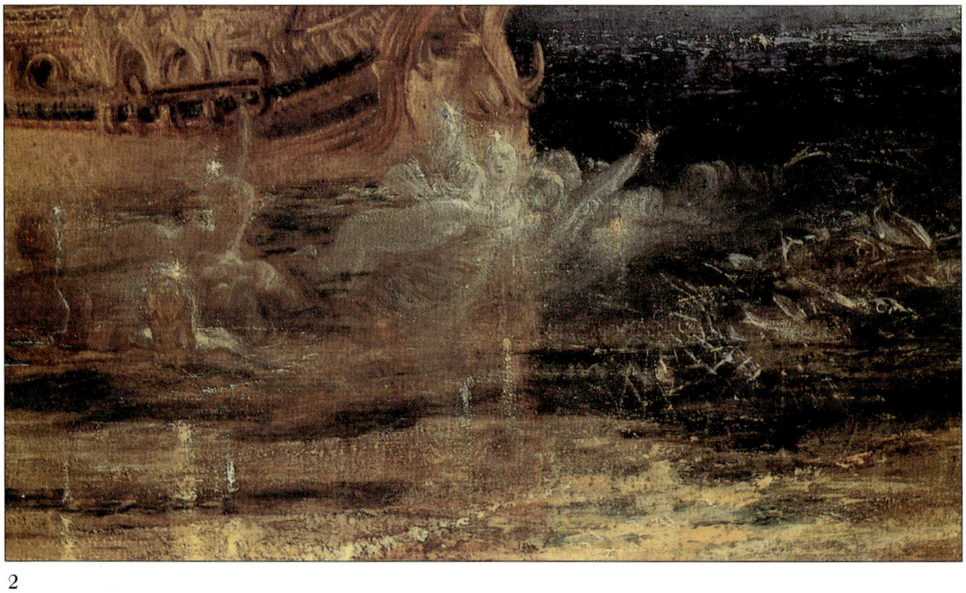

2

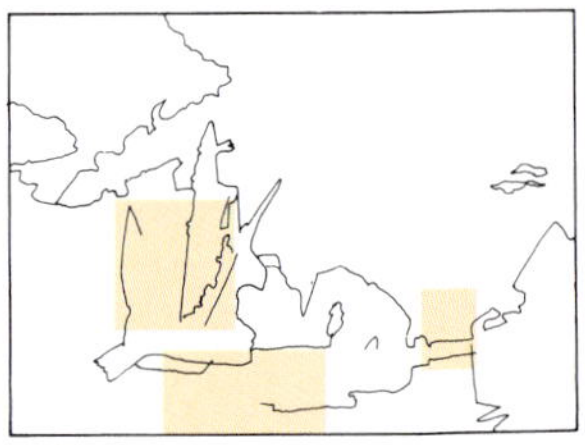

1 The area behind the ship is extremely smooth, so that the ship is pushed forward, and the division between the sails and the background is kept sharp. On the main sail, a pale application of blue is used to cool the shadow and echo the tones of the background cliffs. A few dabs of paint describe Ulysses, holding up a torch and highlighted by a fluttering scarlet above, a counterbalance to the blue-striped sail.

2 The sea-nymphs who accompany Ulysses' ship are painted in a gray-green monotone with tiny touches of white impasto for the star-like lights on their foreheads. Elsewhere, similar touches are used as the points of light on the water's surface, thus linking the nymphs with their medium.

3 *Actual size detail* The brightest, purest colors in the picture are also the areas of the thickest paint. The paler blue underpainting is built up by dark, dry horizontal strokes of deep blue that create the horizon, with below, a comparatively thin layer of pale yellow overlaid with even more transparent touches of pink forming the background of the sea. Over this, thickly applied white is partly scraped away to produce the reflected highlights of the sunrise. The sun itself is more thick white painted around an opaque bar of yellow, pulled into crimson at the right, while scratched white impasto and faintly opaque glazes form the diagonal rays of light.

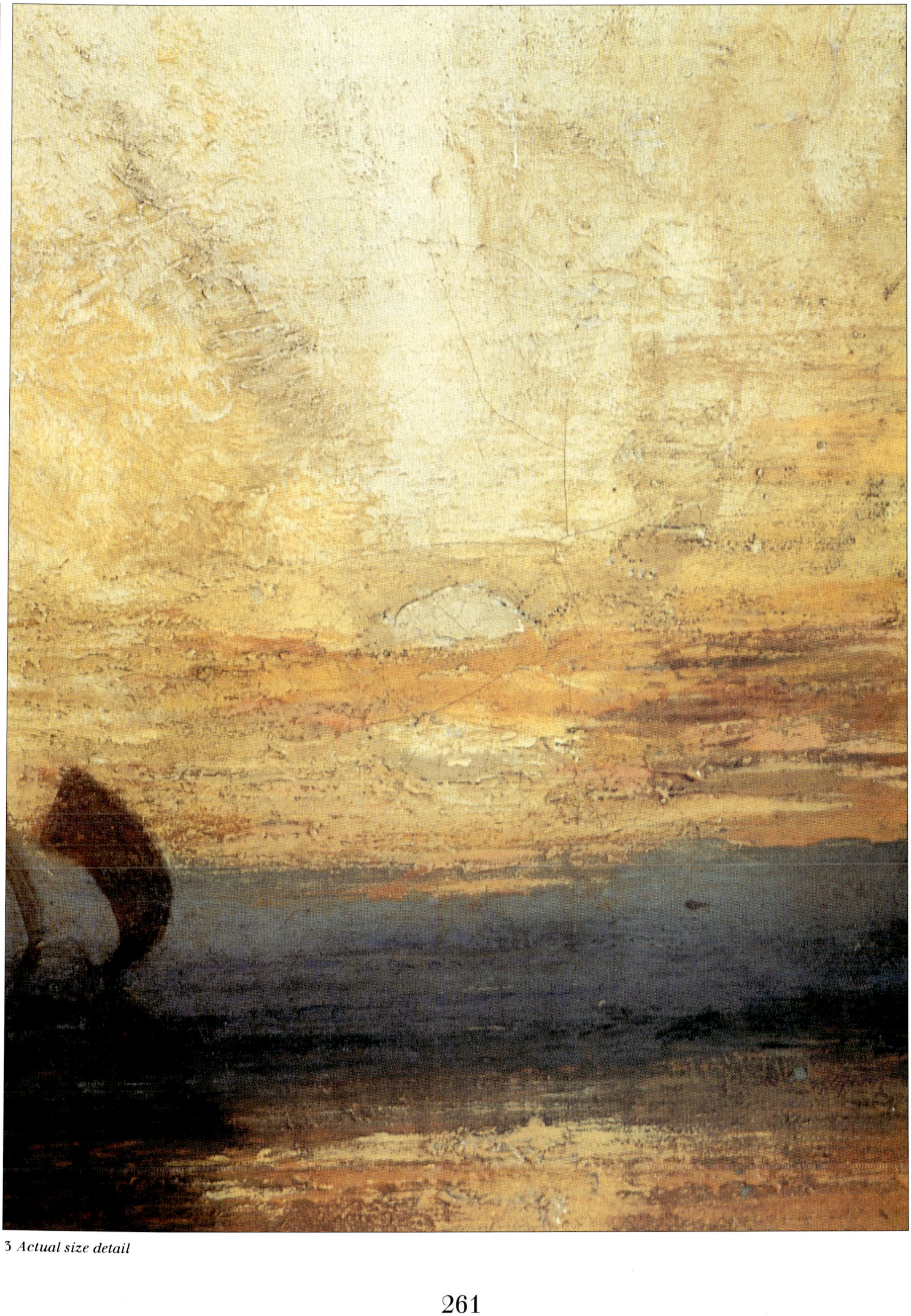

3 *Actual size detail*

The Evening Star

1830

36¼×48¼in/92×122.5cm

Oil on canvas

National Gallery, London

While working on his more ambitiously dramatic works Turner continued to paint the familiar and intimate English scenes that he knew so well. Certain themes and favorite landscapes he returned to at regular and sometimes protracted intervals throughout his life. He was particularly attached to the River Thames, beside which he lived, and he painted views of the river from the Berkshire valley to the estuary. *The Evening Star* can be traced back to a number of views of fishing in the Thames estuary, of around 1808, where the foreground clutter of fishermen and nets has been removed to create empty, airy compositions with only distant sails breaking the even line of the horizon. In *Calais Sands, Low Water, Poissards Collecting Bait*, he returned to the theme of a long bare expanse of beach, a bare canvas on which he could concentrate on atmospheric effects. This was painted in the same year as *The Evening Star*, and probably depicts the same scene, which he had revisited on a recent trip to northern France. A contemporary comment on the former work could apply equally to both: "it is literally nothing in labor, but extraordinary in art."

The Evening Star might well have been painted to balance the more full-blooded effects of *Ulysses Deriding Polyphemus* (see page 259), but although in a quieter, more somber key, it is just as much a pure-color painting from which colorless shading has been removed. The fanfare of the *Ulysses* is here replaced by an elegiac tone in which carefully controlled touches of red and gold are subtly harmonized into the prevailing purples and silvers. Turner's use of a subtly gradated tonality and a severely limited palette shows a painter in his maturity, creating his effects with the maximum of precision and economy. No brushstrokes are squandered in rhetorical embellishment, but the widest variations of textures of sky, sea and sand are suggested with the fewest possible strokes. The musical analogies of which Turner was fond seem especially apt for this work, where the solitary barking of the dog on the silent beach provides an auditory equivalent to the growing brilliance of the star setting in the dusk.

The note of elegy, although unforced, is deliberate and perhaps appropriate. Turner was keenly aware of young talent around him, and had been an admirer of the work of Richard Parkes Bonington, who had made his name painting the wide, empty beaches of northern France with a delicate attention to the nuances of atmosphere. Bonington had died prematurely — at the age of twenty-six — two years earlier, and it is natural that Turner should have thought of him while absorbed in a similar subject. Even without this specific reference a soft mood of acceptance and peace accompanies the end of day, and calls to mind a more intimate sense of loss, that of Turner's beloved father who had died the year before and whom he mourned deeply.

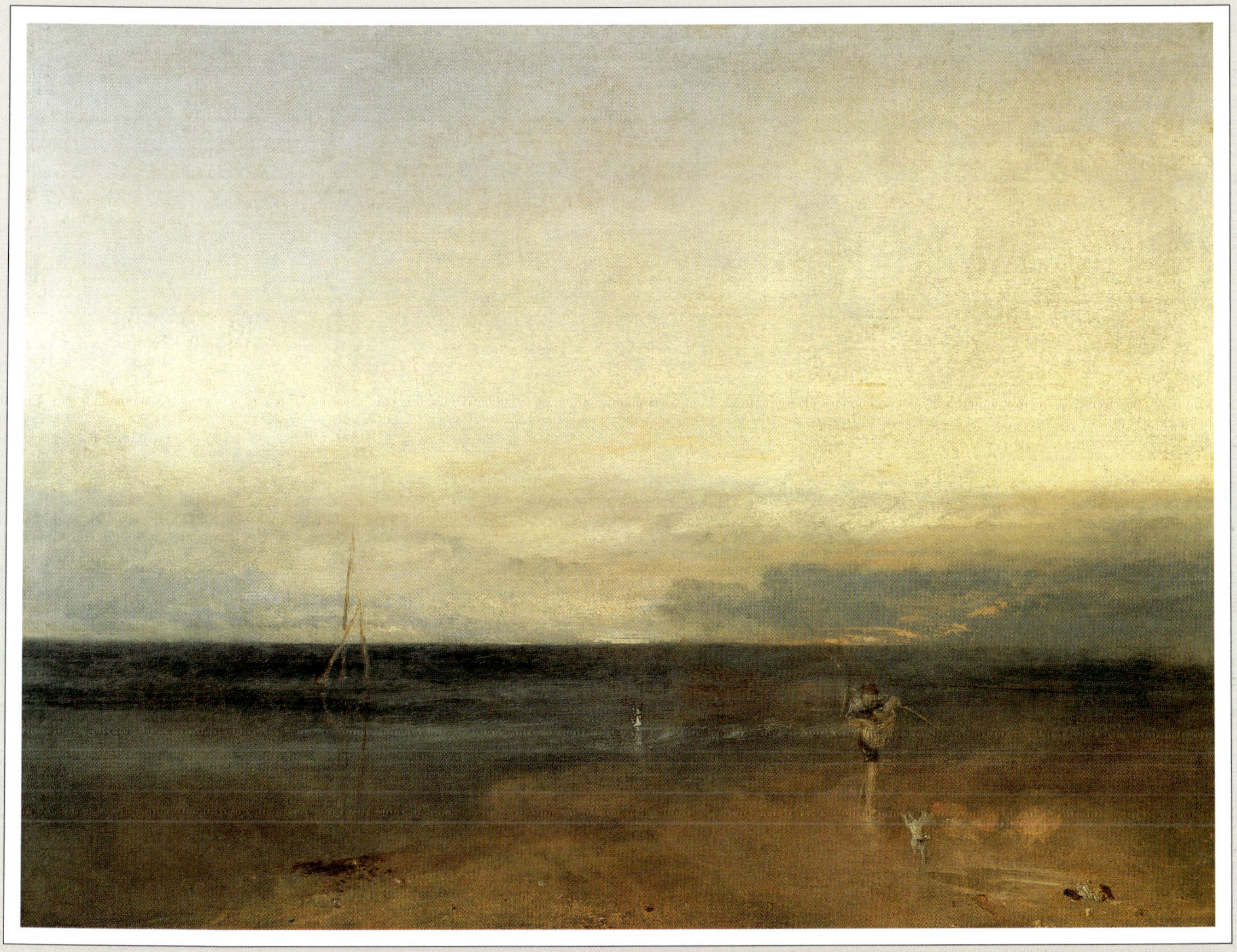

As an unfinished work, this gives us an insight into Turner's method of building up a painting. In particular, the lack of narrative incident concentrates the attention on the fundamentals of land, sea and sky. Great care has been taken with the translucence of the various layers of underpainting, best seen in the painting of the beach, where the relationship between the underlying warm brown and the blue-gray over it is particularly sensitively controlled. The changing opacity of both is carefully varied either by the amount of oil mixed with each pigment or by rubbing down after application.

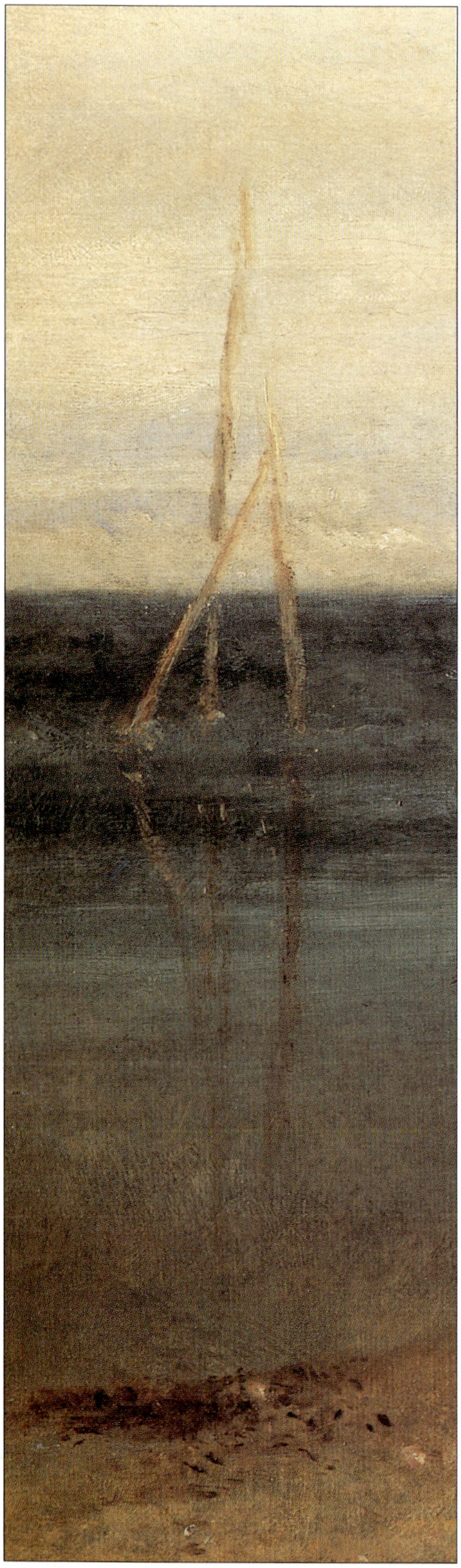

1

2

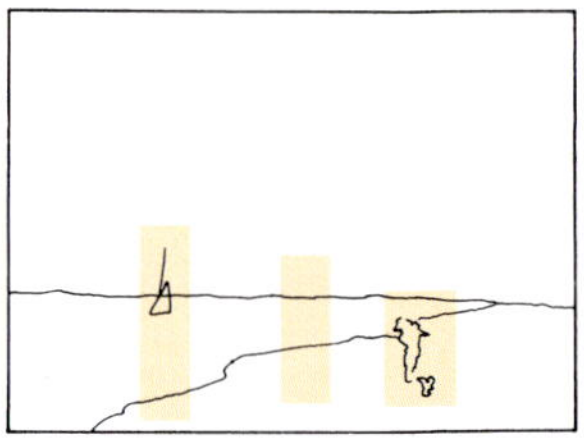

1 The tall spar set against the sky is drawn in several quick downward strokes, identifiable by the way the color fades as each stroke continues down. The surface of the distant water appears at first glance to be smooth, but in fact it owes its subtlety of color to densely applied small strokes of paler blue over the deep color beneath. A few horizontal bands of dark crimson are drawn across to separate the spars from their reflection in the shallow waters, which are single faint continuous strokes extending until the brush is cleared of paint.

2 A moist and quite thick gash of white is used above the horizon to emphasize the focal central area, with one scratch across it to give a further horizontal emphasis. The highlight of the reflected star is a single application of white, dabbed on with a few sharp jabs, then pulled down dry to mix with the touches of pale gray suggestive of pale reflections in shallow pools.

3 *Actual size detail* Thick touches of carmine across the horizon suggest the course of the sunset beneath the gathering clouds. A fine, dry brush has been used in continuous strokes for the outline of the boy's net and, more heavily loaded, for the highlights around the rim of his basket. To the right of the dog, some simple, rapid smears of a lightly loaded brush, applied with a sharp turn of the wrist, balance the pale glow of the vanishing sunset.

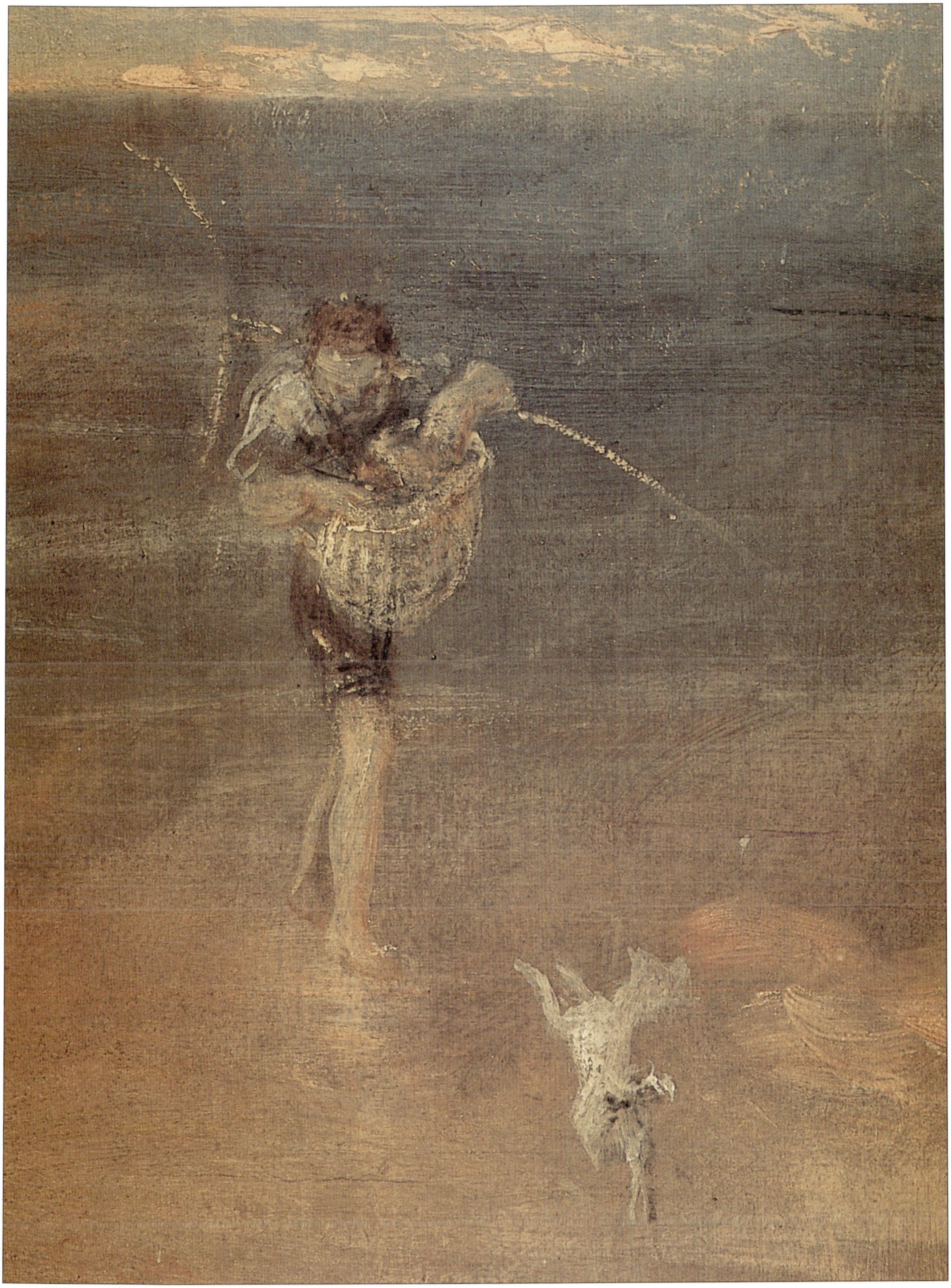

3 *Actual size detail*

INTERIOR AT PETWORTH

c1830-7

35¾×48in/90.75×122cm

Oil on canvas

Clore Gallery for the Turner Collection, London

Turner's most important patron in 1830 was the Earl of Egremont. He had been buying Turner's work since 1802, having commissioned a view of Petworth house, his country seat, and four landscapes specifically for one of the rooms there. Rather than continuing to buy Old Masters, the Earl had decided that his wealth was better spent patronizing living artists, and a large gallery had been built at Petworth to house his extensive collection. The Earl's forthright honesty, complete lack of concern for social convention, and easy-going hospitality made him the center of a large and motley household – reputedly consisting of mistresses and children as well as artists – over which he presided with aristocratic tolerance. From 1830 onwards, when Egremont was already an old man, Turner began to stay regularly at Petworth, and eventually a special room was set aside for him as a studio. Here, in the friendly and informal atmosphere, he felt at ease, and was allowed to work as he pleased. His watercolors of the bright Petworth interiors are among the most spontaneous and charming that he ever produced, capturing in bright colors on blue paper the atmosphere of rooms full of sunlight.

While working on these informal paintings, Turner also had an opportunity to look closely at the other works in Lord Egremont's collection. In a rare figure painting he did at this time he made a number of visual references to Van Dyck, the court painter to Charles I, some of whose aristocratic portraits hung at Petworth. He studied Rembrandt too. As an enthusiast of the sleeker Italianate style he had in his youth been slightly disparaging of the more homely Rembrandt, but as his interest in the manipulation of paint grew, so too did his appreciation of the great master. He noted the way Rembrandt applied paint with a palette knife and used the handle of his brush to scratch into the paint surface in places, and in the landscapes, Turner particularly admired the "streams of light floating over the surface of the middle ground" – a description that could equally be applied to his own work.

Something of the atmosphere of Rembrandt's warm and rather mysterious interiors with their glowing pools of light is recalled here. The subject of the painting is unclear, for it is not of any recognizable room at Petworth; it appears as a kind of composite of the many watercolors Turner had produced there, probably painted after the death of Lord Egremont in 1837. If this is so it can be seen as a tribute and a valediction to the great patron and to a way of life that had gone forever. It has been suggested that the form on the right is a coffin on whose side a coat of arms is discernible, surrounded by a jumble of objects and animals littering the silent room. The picture is a complex synthesis of things thought and things felt. One senses a semi-conscious symbolism in the light flooding into the room from an unseen source, but elsewhere, in the flecks of light dancing in the air or in the reflected glow on soft material, there is a strong sense of Turner painting rapidly and instinctively. The value of this instinctive approach in an artist who often seemed to back away from a full intellectual understanding gives a work such as this the full force of an art still warm and elusive, its impreciseness offering something fully felt and only half understood.

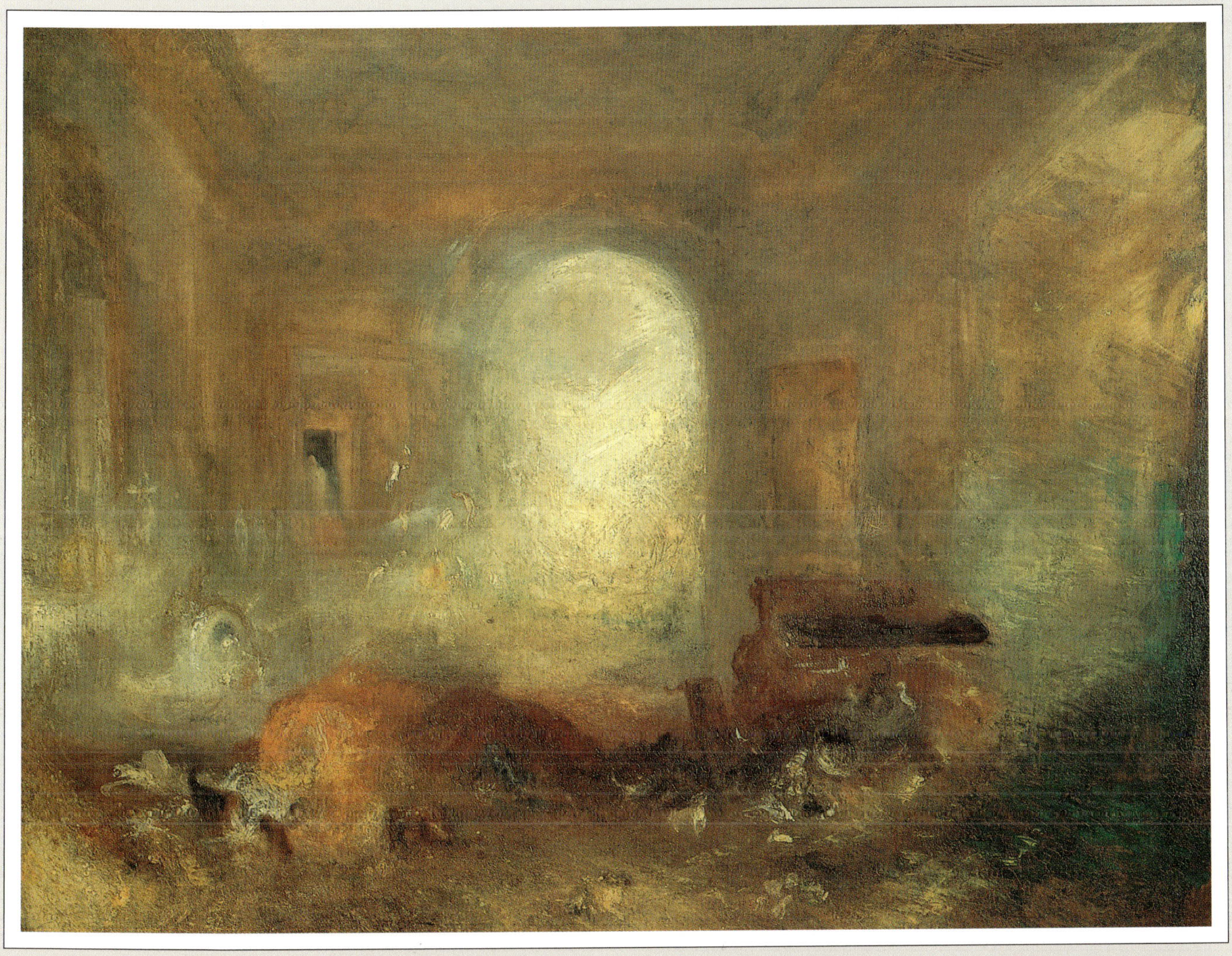

In conventional terms, this is an unfinished work, the sense of urgency and spontaneity in its execution helping to explain the different degrees of attention Turner has accorded to the various parts of the surface. Large areas of the upper canvas are covered with thin and roughly applied color, contributing to the feeling of lightness and space. In the foreground, the greater depth of handling results in a richer use of color as warm hues are mixed to produce a dull glow. Here the plain description of objects has been rejected in favor of a more suggestive evocation of atmosphere. Light and color are the two elements which unite the composition, and the central burst of light, clearly of deep significance for Turner, is echoed around the canvas by subsidiary highlights which help to illuminate the shadowy interior.

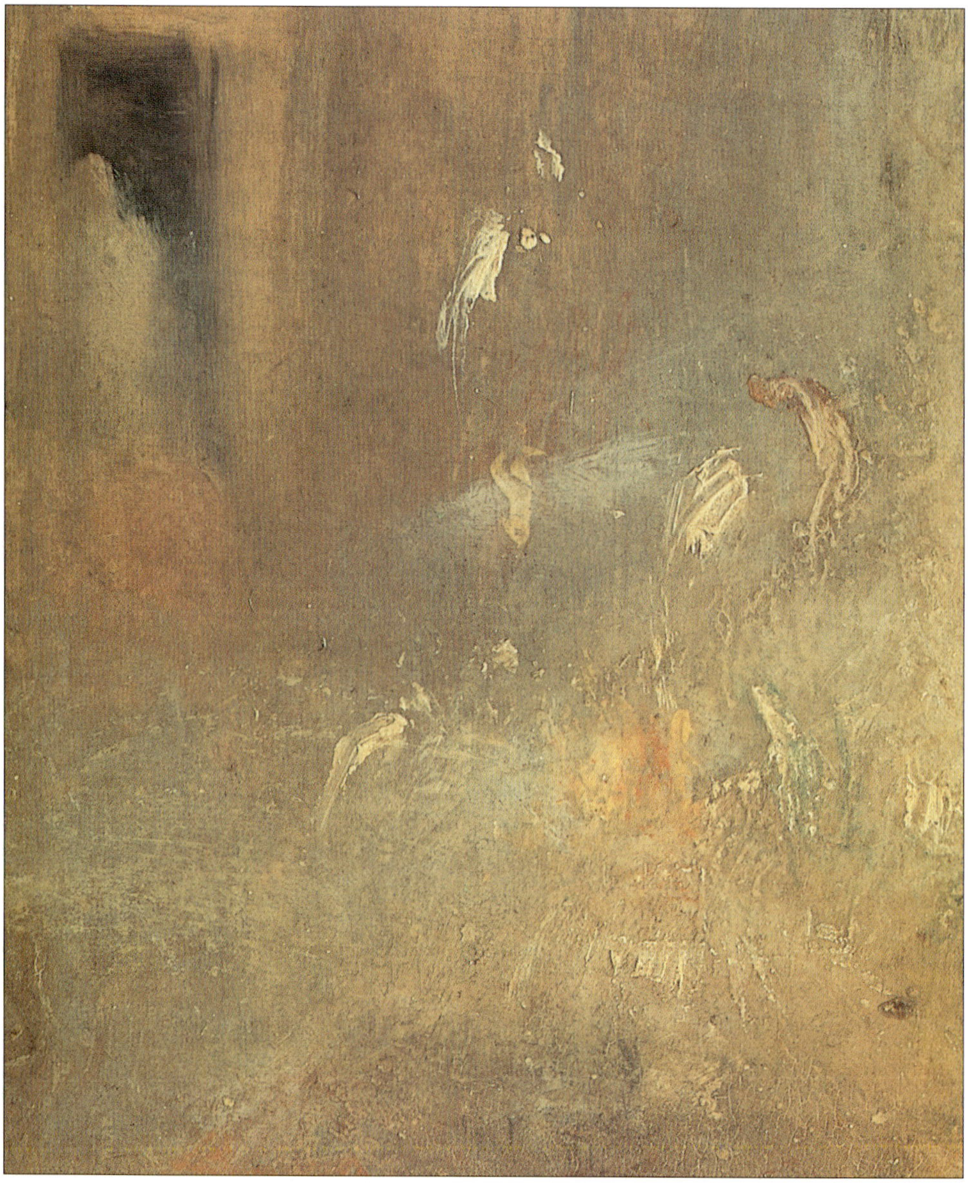

1

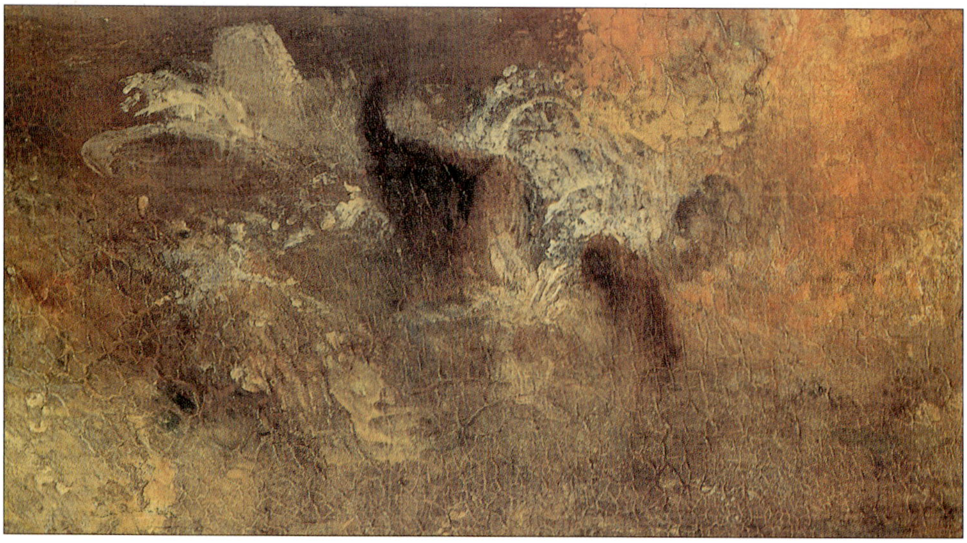

2

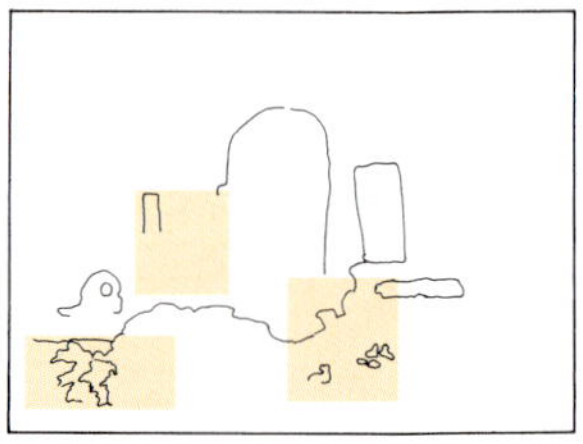

1 A pale tan ground has been overlaid by a deeper umber, itself overlaid by pale gray and white that toward the right have been wiped to create the impression of diffused light from the central arch. Rough strokes of white have been set over the smoothed layers, applied with a rapid twist of the wrist. In most cases the main thickness of paint has been scraped away using the handle of the brush to lessen the impasto and thus create a more insubstantial effect. This technique is carried through into the central area, where the thick paint has been scored and gouged with a sharp tool.

2 Here a form resembling a cornucopia provides the focus for a cluster of light and color, and paint has been applied more thickly and dryly than in the upper areas of the work, helping to give stability to the painting. A deep brick red provides a warm ground to a thick and vivid orange, sponged and blotted to evoke the texture of a rich fabric.

3 Turner has used single strokes of white with great simplicity to suggest reflective metallic objects clustered together in disarray. Here a variety of spontaneous strokes can be seen — dabs, smears and quick, sharp angular touches — all providing an area of highlighted detail to balance that on the left. Only the form of a small dog is recognizable by the touches of white on its chest, brought down to form the legs.

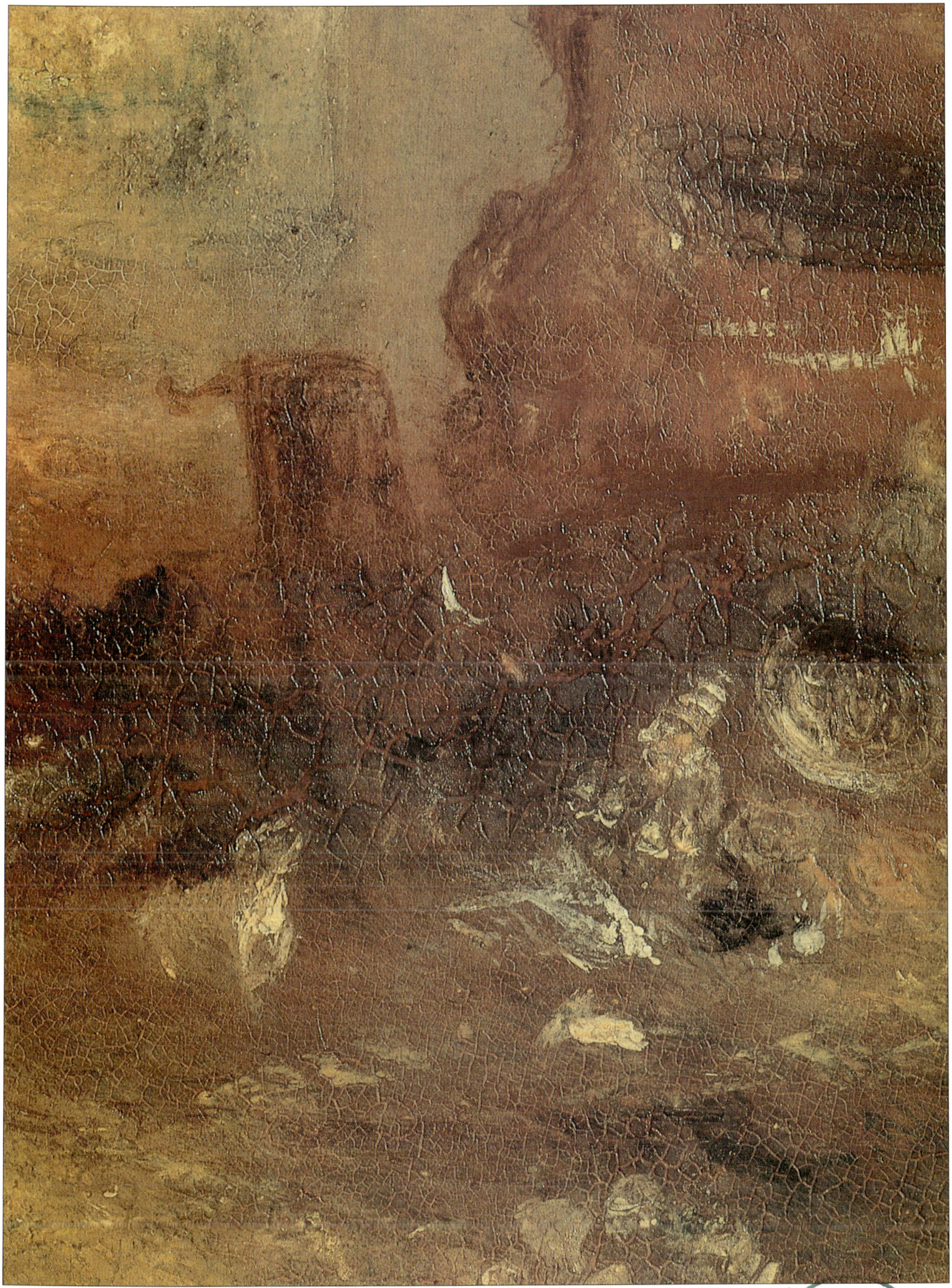

3

Norham Castle, Sunrise

c1835-40

$35^3/_4 \times 48$in/78×122cm

Oil on canvas

Clore Gallery for the Turner Collection, London

A scene such as this – a castle set against the skyline overlooking a meandering river and surrounded by rolling hills – was the epitome of the picturesque landscape which Turner sought when he had first discovered Norham Castle in 1797. The effect was completed by the sun rising behind the castle, emphasizing the dark romantic silhouette of the crenellated walls and illuminating the river below the reflected light. This was the theme of his watercolor, *Norham Castle on the Tweed, Summer's Morn*, which was shown at the Academy the following year. As one of his most successful compositions, he included it in his *Liber Studiorum*, a book of engravings produced from 1807-1819 in imitation of Claude's collection, *Liber Veritatis*. (This, like Turner's, was intended as a set of authenticated works produced as a safeguard against unauthorized reproduction.) From the *Liber Studiorum*, the subject was reworked as an illustration for the collection *Rivers of England* of 1824.

Turner's interest in Norham was developed by a further visit in 1833. Unexhibited and officially unfinished, this late version of the subject has clearly moved far from the conventions of the picturesque. Norham is unique in Turner's work as being a specific scene that recurs almost through his entire career, and his many treatments of it evidence the satisfaction it afforded him. As his work progressed, the fundamental components of the scene were stripped, as here, of all distracting detail, a tendency which occurred more and more. The theme of the single outcrop above water is repeated in watercolors of the peaks of Rigi and Pilatus above the Swiss lakes, or in the château of Amboise above the Loire in France, and in each case it seems to provide a central focus in a world of air and water, like a ship glimpsed through the mist.

As details are reduced to suggestions, so Turner has narrowed the range of colors to concentrate on variations of blue, yellow and red. These are laid onto a white ground, a departure from the academic tradition that Turner had learned in his youth from Reynolds. This made use of the ocher ground first developed by the great Venetian masters, which gave a warmth and an underlying deep tonality to the finished work. Ironically, Turner's own visits to Venice had hastened his rejection of this practice, and he had developed the use of white grounds to heighten the tonality of his work. The method enabled him to recapture in oils something of the translucence of watercolor by allowing the white ground to shine through the thin glazes of color just as in watercolors the paper reflects back through the wash. Once again, we see how Turner's expertise in the two media provides him with a greater flexibility of technique in both.

Here the white ground assumes the nature of the pure light from which Turner has extracted color, following the practice of obtaining colors from natural light via a prism, with which he was very familiar. The brilliance of the picture is achieved through this prismatic use of color, juxtaposing almost pure primary colors set against carefully controlled secondary harmonies. The effect of an all-enveloping light which creates for our eyes the features of the landscape is a technically complex parallel to the simple freshness of the sunrise which the picture shows us.

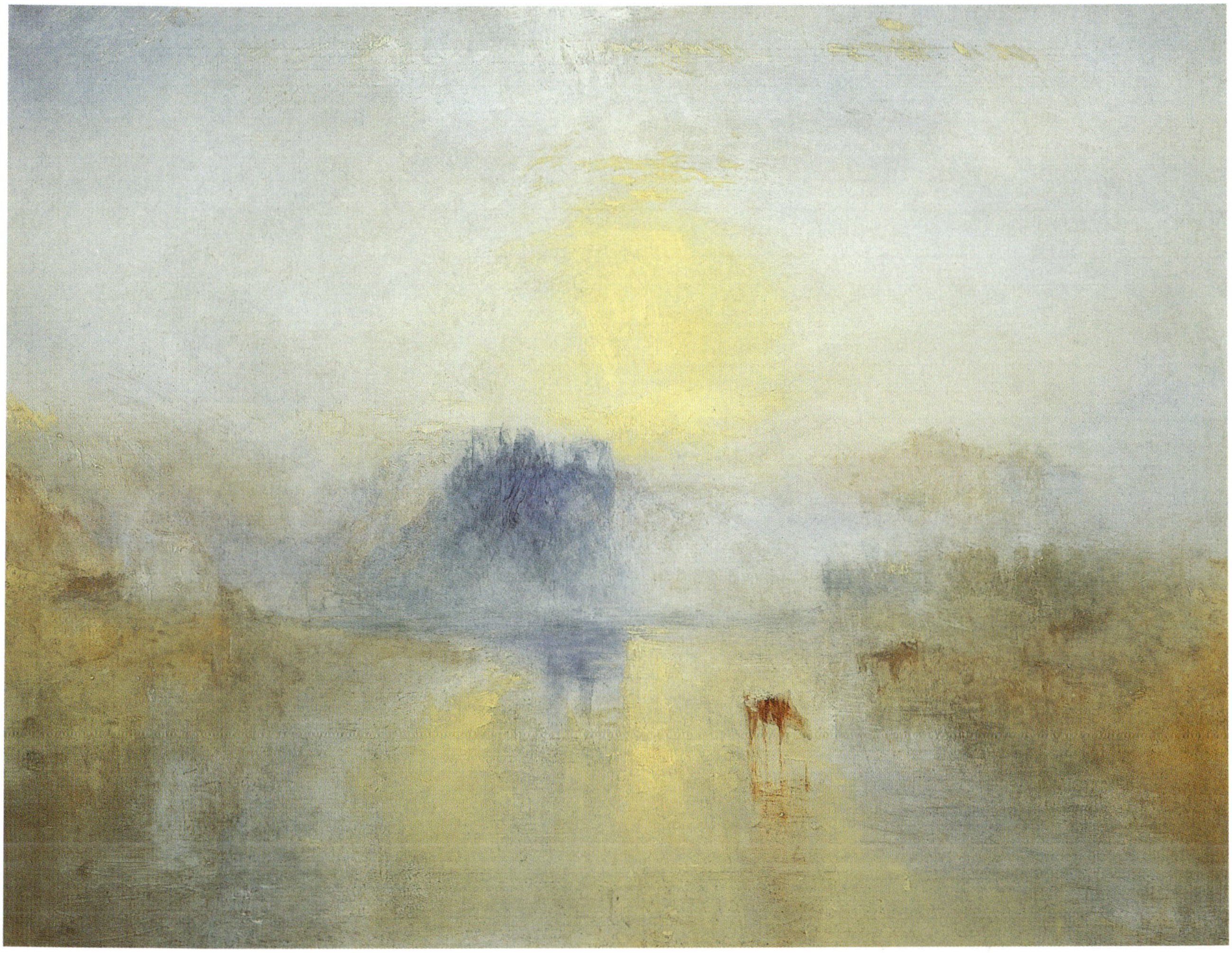

This final, unfinished version of the subject that Turner painted many times is taken from the same viewpoint as his first, dramatizing the scale of the castle and distant hills, but there the similarity ends. Only the castle itself and the foreground cow, necessary to suggest scale, are retained. In the lower part of the canvas the areas of pure color from which it is composed converge on the central motif like spokes around the hub of a wheel, suggesting the spectrum and the color theories that so fascinated Turner. In the upper half, a series of semi-transparent applications builds up a smooth, creamy surface over which the glow of the sunrise radiates.

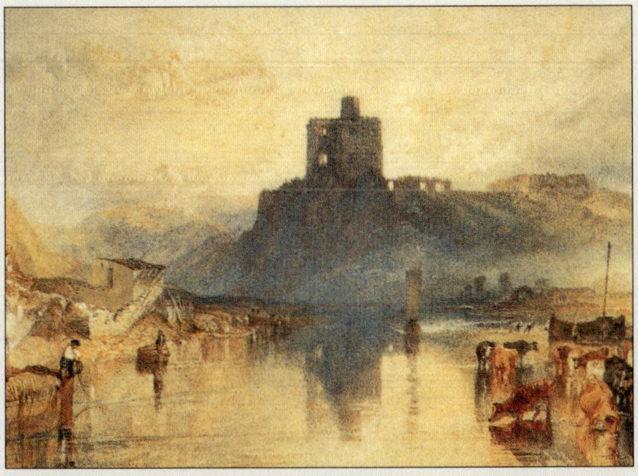

Norham Castle on the River Tweed, Summer's Morn
1897

This watercolor, shown at the Academy in 1898, was Turner's first painting of the scene, and was engraved for inclusion in his *Liber Studorium*, and later reworked for the collection *Rivers of England*. It includes all the anecdotal details appropriate to a "picturesque" illustration, all of which were stripped away in the later painting, where his interest lay in the essential combination of sunrise, water and hills.

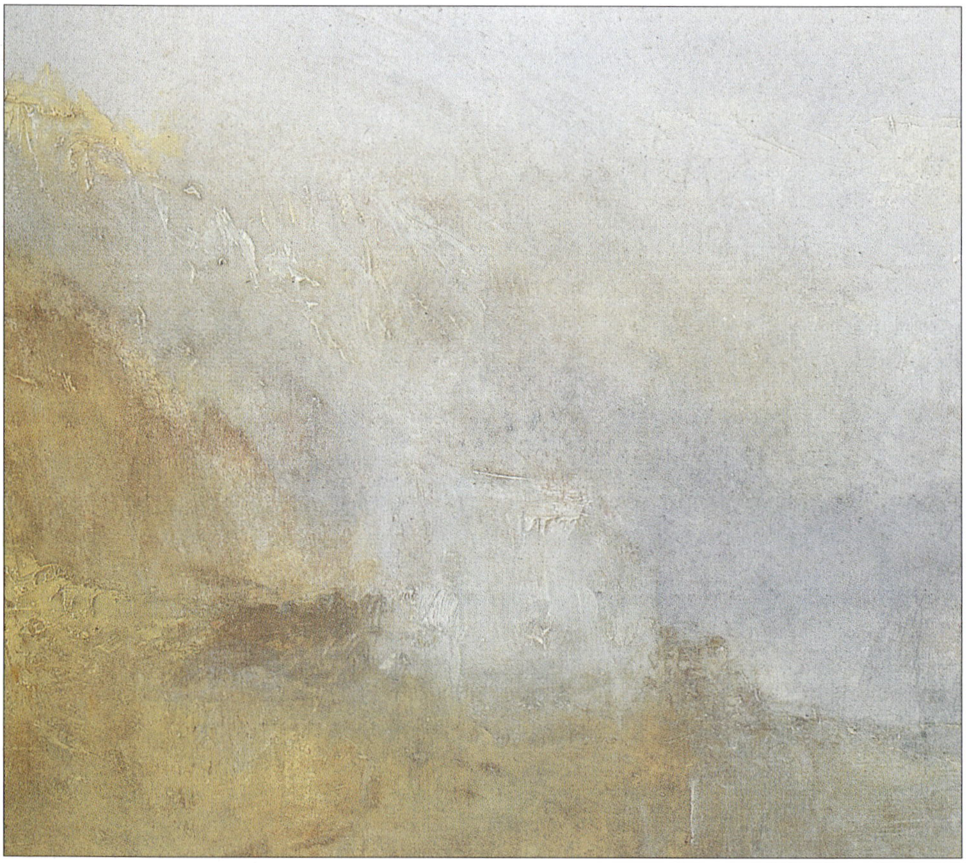

1

2

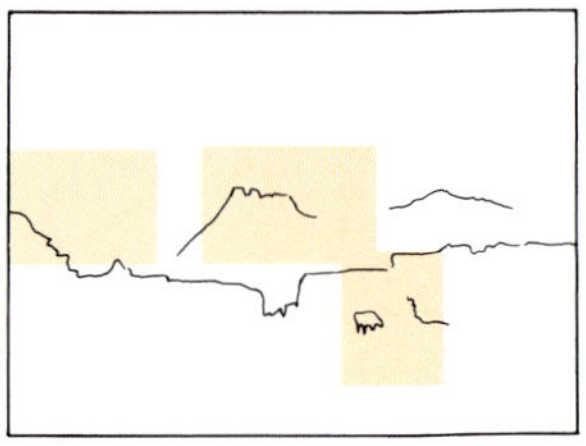

1 The crest of a line of hills is just suggested by thick strokes of pale yellow, applied with a fine brush but with enough vigor and pressure to push the paint out to form tiny lines and ridges of impasto. This was an effect that Turner often created by using the sharp handle of the brush. Beyond this, in the horizon caught in the light of sunrise, form is all but transparent, with only the faintest pale yellow glaze differentiating the hill from the sky.

2 The extreme fluidity of Turner's application is clearly revealed in the lines of blue allowed to run down to create small gullies of color forming the shadows beneath the walls. More regular touches suggest towers and battlements against the sky, and Turner has pressed the brush sideways to leave a horizontal imprint, a hint of regularity in the general insubstantiality.

3 *Actual size detail* The foreground cow is reduced to a pale, semi-abstract umber stain with a dab of off-white impasto over the haunch and touches of brown over this, at the belly and shoulder. A thin brush has been wiped dry over the canvas in a few vertical and horizontal strokes to suggest the reflection of legs and body. A transparent, matte chalky layer lies over the blue underpainting beyond the head, while below its outstretched neck a fluid area of pale yellow is brushed down to end in an impasto bar of reflection.

3 *Actual size detail*

Peace: Burial at Sea

1842

34¼×34⅛in/86.9×86.6cm

Oil on canvas

Clore Gallery for the Turner Collection, London

Shown in the same Academy exhibition as *The Dogana, San Giorgio*, this was one of a pair with *War, The Exile and the Rock Limpet*, a painting of Napoleon on St Helena. The latter was of the same dimensions as this work, and was a sunset scene painted in livid reds and yellows. The contrast with the cool blues of *Peace* was intentional, and illustrates Turner's conscious use of the emotional value of color. In the Napoleon picture, blood red was clearly a reference to the sanguine memories of the exiled soldier, while the blue used here creates a more elegiac mood. This contrast tallies with the theory of color developed by Goethe, whose book on the subject Turner had studied when it was translated into English the previous year. This proposed a division of colors into positive and negative groups, each associated with a range of appropriate emotions, which are echoed in the titles Turner used for these works. He accompanied both with lines from his fragmentary poem *The Fallacies of Hope.* The lines for this painting were:

The midnight torch gleamed o'er the steamer's side
And Merit's corpse was yielded to the tide

The midnight scene Turner has imagined was the burial at sea (off Gibraltar) of the painter David Wilkie, who died returning from Palestine. Wilkie had been the most successful painter of his generation, and his popular subject-matter of rural interior scenes had once been imitated by Turner in his vein of competitive tribute. This work was produced in something of the same spirit to complement another painterly homage by a friend, who chose to depict the burial from the ship's deck. The unremitting black of the ship's sails, for which even his champion Ruskin criticized Turner, has been seen as a further tribute to Wilkie, who was noted for the use of black in his later pictures. Turner's famous reply to criticism of the sails, that he wished he could have made them "even blacker," was a typically combative response to the harsh criticism both *War* and *Peace* received compared to the praise for the more seductive Venetian pictures.

This is one of Turner's most direct meditations on death, which Ruskin saw as being the ultimate concern of his art. Now aged 67, Turner had suffered the death of many of his friends and patrons, as well as his own father to whom he was so close and who had helped to manage his business affairs throughout his life. Contemporaries noted how solicitous Turner was during illnesses, and how keenly he felt a death. From the mood of peaceful acceptance and reverie of the *Evening Star* (see page 263) the tone here has become heavier and more tragic, perhaps because it celebrates an untimely end. Linked with the declining Napoleon, Wilkie's death is treated in a heroic vein, and Turner dramatizes by using the elements to emphasize the tragedy.

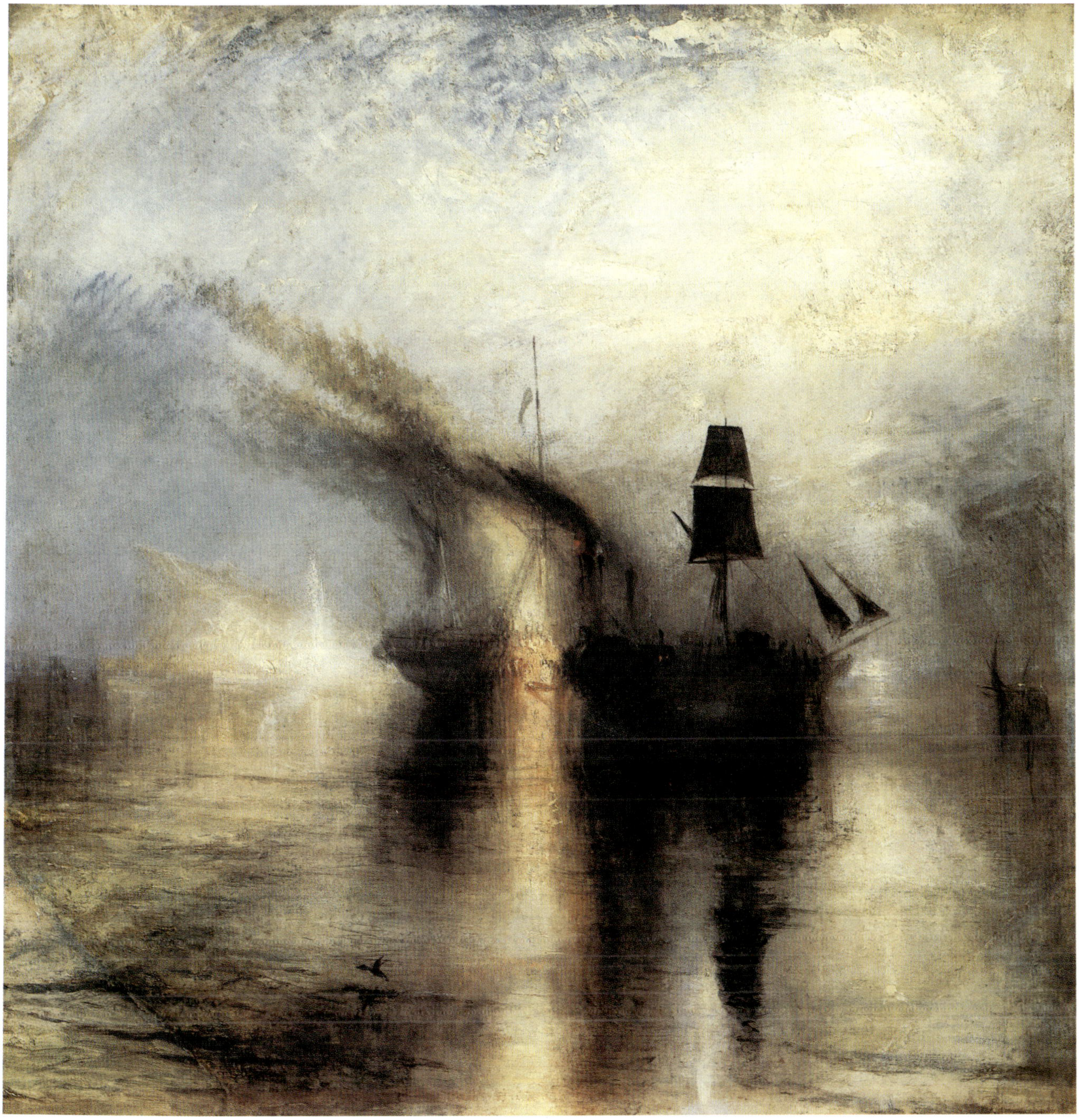

Turner planned this painting and its companion piece, *War*, as octagonal compositions, as can be seen from the painting of the bottom corners. The present frame reveals the glazing and overpainting intended for the finished work, sharply contrasted against the areas that remain undeveloped. The arrangement of the linear composition confirms the painter's intention, with the diagonals of smoke and the Rock of Gibraltar behind echoing what were to have been the original corners. Turner began to favor square and octagonal formats as he concentrated increasingly on a central motif, in particular the central vortex of light that became the main theme in many of his late works.

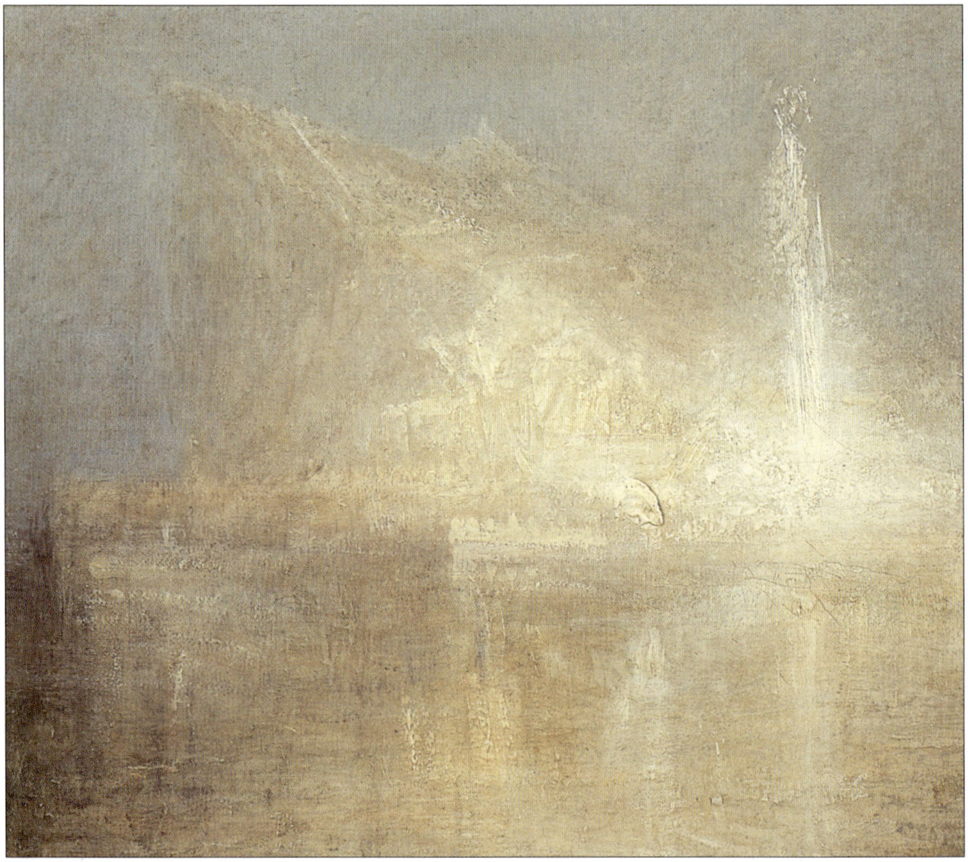

1

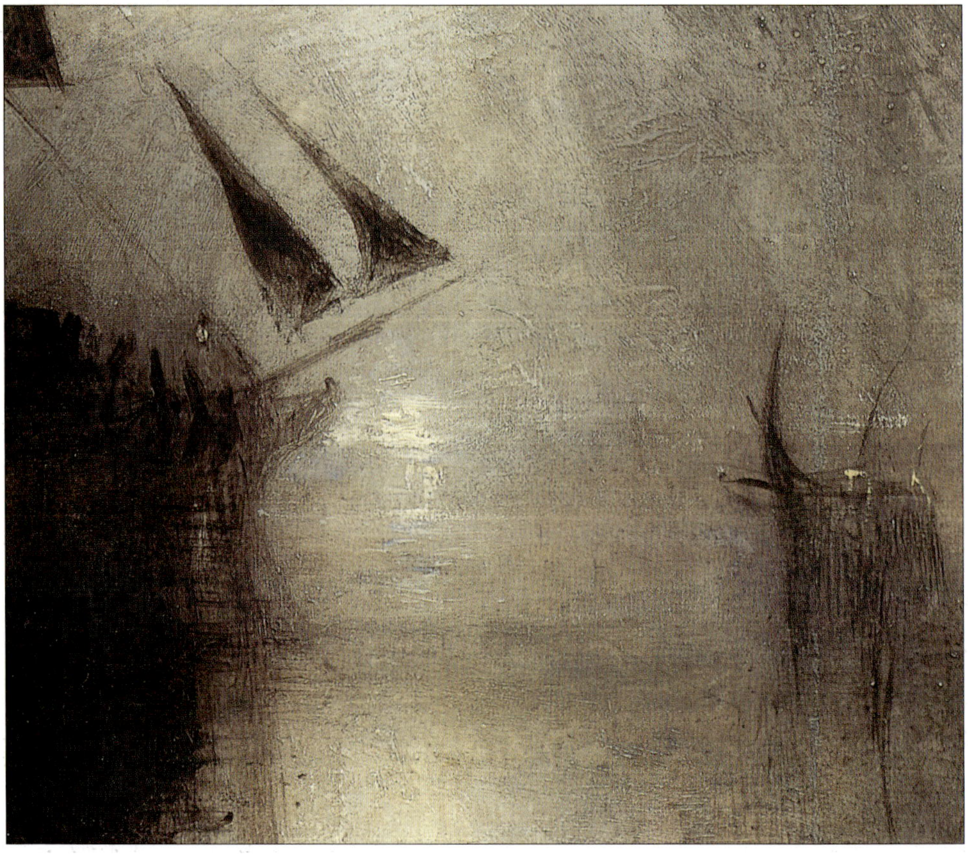

2

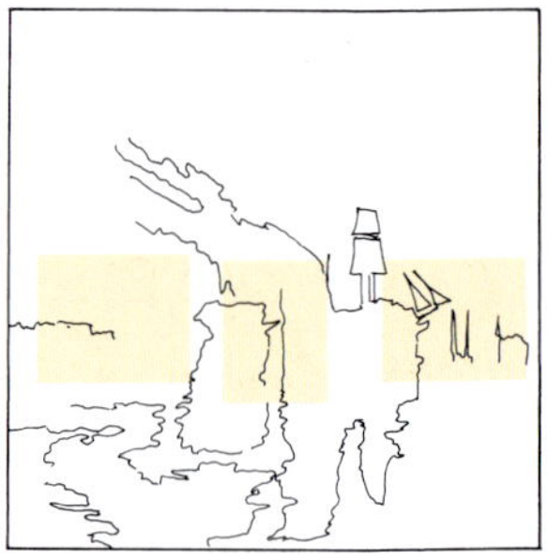

1 A soft gray has been smoothed over the blue underpainting to the right of the rock and on the cliff face itself, where long, elliptical strokes describe the curvature of the structure. Ocher has been used for both this and its reflection. The rock itself is firmly outlined, and on its lower slopes, strokes of white are applied over the moist underpainting and then scored with brush handle or fingernails. This has increased the surface movement, and the gray background beyond has also been given additional surface interest by light sponging.

2 The dark sails and rigging have been faintly outlined in dry paint, and black has then been used to fill out the shapes. A few moist touches of white suggest moonlight on the horizon and help to fix a sense of distance, pushing the boat toward the viewer.

3 *Actual size detail* Turner places the torchlit ceremony at the very center of the composition, a position of formal solemnity. The deep gash of light cutting through the somber silhouette of the ship is one of his most original and dramatic inventions. It is formed by a thin gold glaze over which the heavy shadow of the ship is drawn at each side like a curtain, giving faint glimpses of the painting beneath before the blackness becomes total. The highlights, applied with thick impasto, are echoed in the reflection in the water far below — a few rapid touches of the brush.

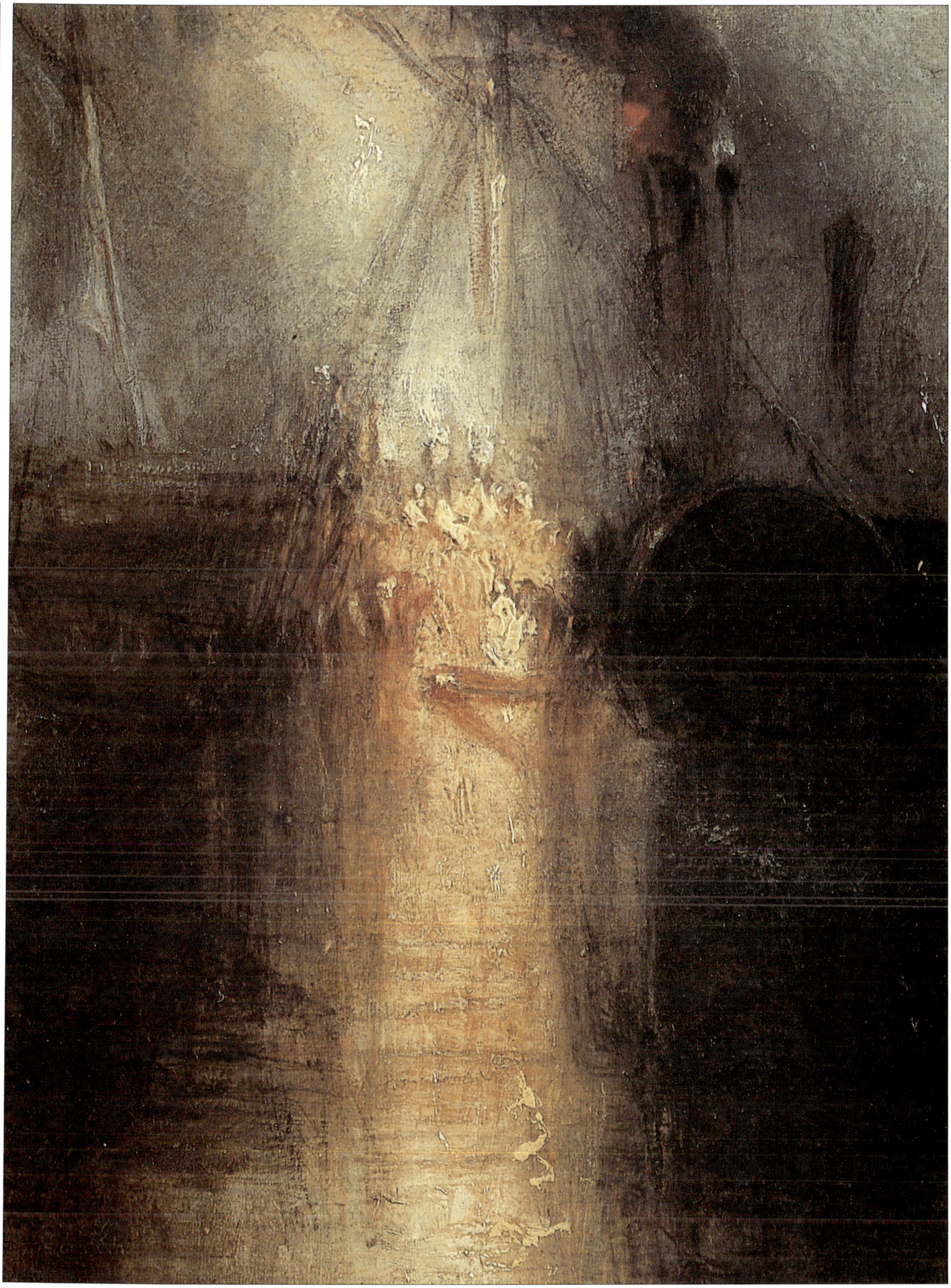

3 *Actual size detail*

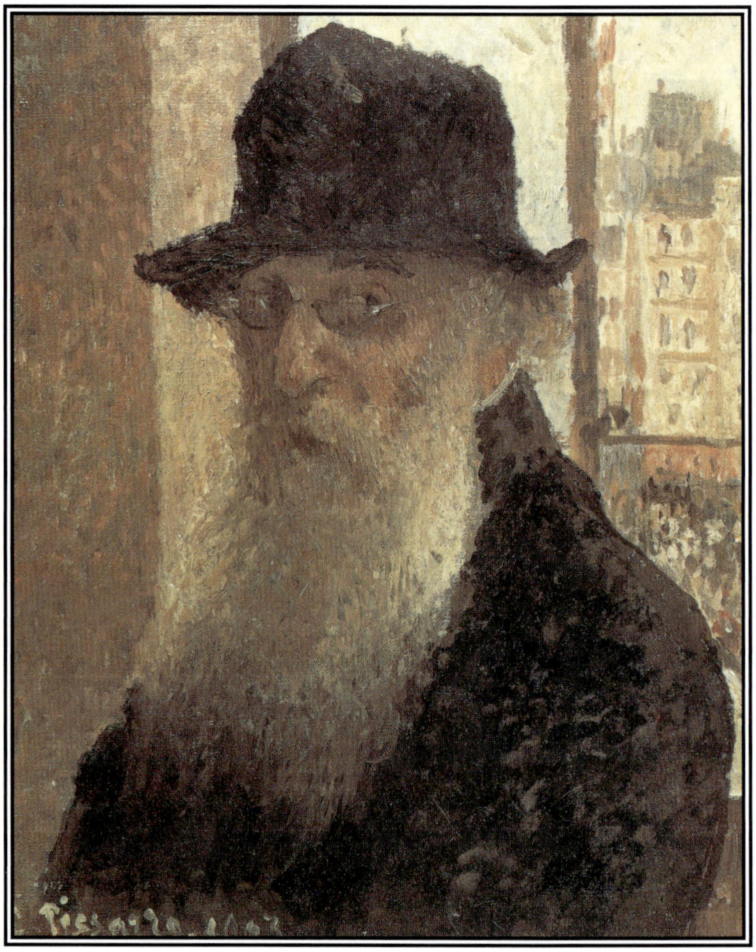

PISSARRO

Introduction

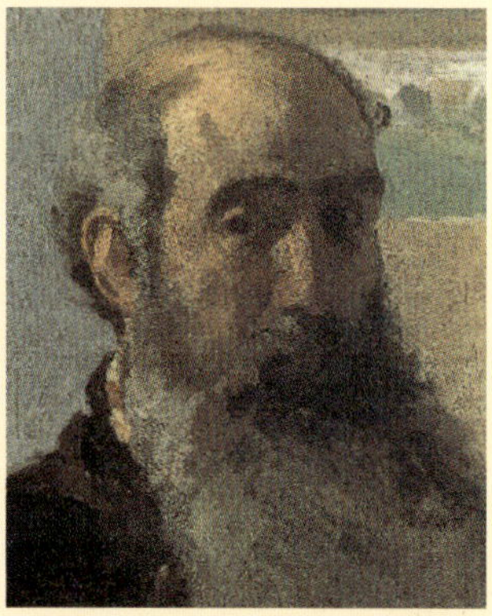

Camille Pissarro
Self-Portrait
1873, Musée d'Orsay, Paris

"Remember that I have the temperament of a peasant, I am melancholy, harsh and savage in my works." With these words Camille Pissarro tried to explain his single-minded search for truth in all that he painted. "It is only in the long run that I can expect to please," he continued, "and then only those who have a grain of indulgence." Pissarro's dedication to his work, his family, his friends, and his radical political beliefs caused him to choose an arduous route through life, which often found him in opposition to establishment views. Yet his solid good sense and the strength of his beliefs inspired loyalty among his friends – fellow painters, literary men and political thinkers – who regarded him as a patriarchal figure, a view no doubt prompted by his upright bearing and flowing beard, gray from his early forties. His role in the Impressionist and Neo-Impressionist movements (see page 287) was less that of the great man of ideas than that of the good counselor and appeaser

good sense helped to rationalize the aims of the group.

Pissarro's strengths and weaknesses are poignantly revealed in the correspondence with his eldest son Lucien, living in London from 1883. These letters recount his daily dealings with all those involved in his life and work. We hear of his extensive family, so important to him, and his reactions to his friends and their work. All the characters of Parisian cultural life are there – among them artists Claude Monet, Paul Cézanne, and Paul Gauguin; and writers and critics Emile Zola, Théodore Duret, and J.-K. Huysmans – and many more. We are kept abreast of the political situation and informed of Pissarro's opinions; we witness his continual reassessment of the aims and methods of his art, and we follow his labored progress toward recognition and financial stability.

Early life

The man who was to become an influential figure among the avant garde of Paris in the second half of the nineteenth century spent much of his formative years on a tiny island, that of St Thomas in the Virgin Islands, then a Danish colony. There he was born in 1830, son of a Jewish father and a Creole mother, and his childhood was spent in the small capital port of Charlotte Amalie, where his father was a merchant. His parents were ardently francophile, and sent their son over to Paris to school at the Savary Academy in Passy, where he would have had an opportunity to visit museums and to get to know the established masters of French art. According to later family accounts, Monsieur Savary gave him a traditional grounding in drawing and painting and implored his talented pupil on his return to St Thomas to draw the coconut palms from nature – a piece of advice that the young Pissarro duly followed.

It would appear that he returned to St Thomas with artistic ambitions, which did not meet with parental approval. His father found work for him in the family business checking cargo, where it is said he took every opportunity to practice his drawing skills. When he was twenty-one he took matters into his own hands, leaving his family and job with nothing but a note of farewell and sailing to Venezuela with a Danish artist, Fritz Melbye. In Caracas, the two young artists shared a studio for two years, establishing the first of many reciprocal artistic relationships which punctuated Pissarro's life. Drawings survive from this early period which testify to Pissarro's facility as a draftsman. Fine sketches, and more finished wash drawings and watercolors, demonstrate a confidence in his medium and a developed style in part influenced by drawing manuals on techniques available at the time. In Caracas, he drew everything around him: landscapes, village scenes, and sketchbooks full of figures – inside playing at cards or dancing outside in the market, fetching water, and washing clothes.

The few extant paintings from this time, some of the local people, others light-filled tropical views, although competent, show a more orthodox approach to composition and style, generally attributed to the influence of Melbye who trained at the Copenhagen Academy of Fine Arts. The strictures of academic demands, as is so often the case, can be seen to eradicate the life and spontaneity of his drawing. Fortunately, such worries did not crush the will of young Pissarro who determined to pursue his artistic career. After returning briefly to St Thomas, Pissarro decided to sail for Paris to continue his studies under Melbye's brother Anton.

Paris and new influences

It is difficult to imagine how Pissarro must have reacted to the seething cauldron of ideas represented by Paris at this time. His direct approach and easy way with people as well as his innate intelligence must have helped with his integration into the life of the capital, but he did not immediately launch himself into the truant ideologies of the avant-garde. He began, indeed, by doing just the opposite, striving in his thorough way to meet the standards of the Salon, the official body whose academic traditions dominated French artistic life. Until later in the century, the Salon was the only art marketplace, and even artists who were beginning to criticize its views as outmoded would submit works to the Salon Committee each year. As Anton Melbye's assistant, Pissarro settled down to working in the prescribed manner, producing the sizable and carefully planned oil paintings demanded by the committee. In 1859, to the delight of his father, his first painting was accepted and exhibited.

Those works that have survived from the period before 1865 certainly show Pissarro's debt to Camille Corot and the Barbizon School – particularly Daubigny, Courbet, and Millet – whose work he first fully appreciated on his arrival in Paris at the Great Exhibition of 1855. He is said to have called on Corot soon after this and later, after taking private lessons at the Ecole des Beaux Arts, became his pupil. As an old man, Pissarro looked back to "Claude Lorraine, Corot, the whole 18th century and Chardin especially" as early influences. He and Corot shared a love of rural scenes, painted from nature, which Pissarro, like his master, learnt to interpret with an underlying geometrical structure. But Corot's vision of landscape was principally idealized and sometimes stylized, and even though he painted with his easel set up in the countryside, he would work up his pictures in the studio into something which accorded with his preconceptions. A comparison of Corot's *Dardagny, Morning* of 1853 with Pissarro's *View from Louveciennes* of 1870 shows how alike the two artists appeared in their depiction of the countryside, but closer inspection reveals a fundamental difference between them. Corot is painting an image of arcadian bliss, whereas Pissarro's road is completely factual – rutted and edged with a sprawling hodgepodge of bushes, mounds of earth, and trees in various stages of development. To contemporary viewers this streak of honesty in Pissarro was regarded as vulgar, the equivalent of a painter today including the garbage and beer cans found on the side of a street.

Pissarro's desire to paint the countryside as he saw it, making it look real and without artifice, inevitably caused a rift between master and pupil. In 1859, at the free school, the Académie Suisse, Pissarro met a group of like-minded painters, among them Claude Monet and later Armand Guillaumin and Paul Cézanne. This younger generation of artists discussed their dissatis-

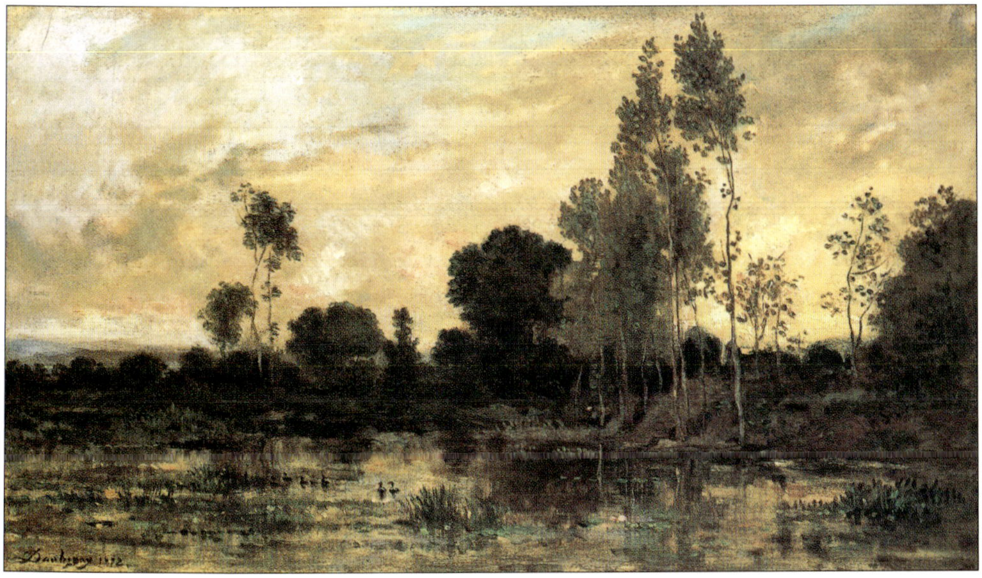

CHARLES FRANÇOIS DAUBIGNY
Alders
1872, National Gallery, London

In many ways Daubigny anticipated the work of the Impressionists, showing something of the immediate, sketchlike quality for which they were criticized. Pissarro would have first seen this work, along with those by other painters of the Barbizon school, at the Universal Exhibition in 1855, the same year that he arrived in Paris. Although he was initially more attracted to Corot's style, he was later to appreciate Daubigny's strong colors and bold brushwork.

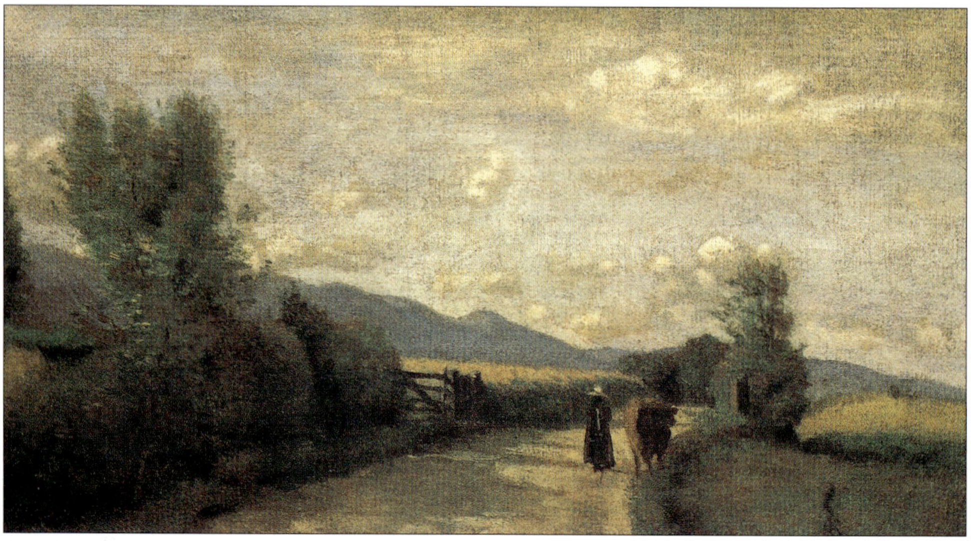

CAMILLE COROT
Dardagny Morning
National Gallery, London

Pissarro particularly admired a painting by Corot that he saw at the Universal Exhibition of 1855. He found the imaginary landscape "the stuff of dreams," but it seems that his own desire to render landscape more truthfully could not accommodate the poetic approach. The two artists eventually parted company, but Corot's influence can be found in almost every aspect of Pissarro's early painting.

faction with the stranglehold of the official Salon, and Pissarro also found that his political views, centered on the importance of the individual, truth to nature, and an abhorrence of artifice and false grandeur, coincided to an extent with the more fundamentally artistic aims of the group. In 1863 so many works were rejected by the Salon that Napoleon III ordered that the paintings turned away should be exhibited separately in an exhibition called the Salon des Refusés. Both Pissarro and Cézanne were included, but the show was dominated by the howls of protest over Manet's *Déjeuner sur l'Herbe*. The art establishment was as hostile to the show as the public, and it was not repeated, but it weakened the position of the Salon and established the notion of an alternative.

In the catalogs for the Salon exhibitions of 1865 and 1866, Pissarro acknowledges his debts to Anton Melbye and Corot, whom he cites jointly as his masters. But, by 1868, a more individual style had evolved and, recognizing this, Pissarro declared himself independent by citing no master in the catalog. After visiting the 1868 exhibition and viewing Pissarro's two landscapes, Emile Zola, author and critic and champion of the new art, declared "Camille Pissarro is one of the three or four true painters of this day . . . I have rarely encountered a technique that is so sure." Certainly, his works of this time still owe much to Corot and to the naturalism and expressive brushwork of Courbet but his work is showing the early signs of an approach to painting which in the following decade is labeled "Impressionism".

At the beginning of the 1860s Pissarro accepted a new role, that of the family man. He met and formed a relationship with his mother's maid Julie Vellay, a vinegrower's daughter from Burgundy, later (in 1871) to become his wife. In 1863, his son Lucien was born, the first of a rambling family of seven children to whom Pissarro was a fond and loving father. In 1866 he, Julie, and their small son established themselves at Pontoise outside Paris, later moving to Louveciennes. The countryside around the village, the river and woods became the inspiration for his painting in these years, but he retained a studio in Paris and kept in touch with developments in the city, occasionally attending Zola's "Thursdays" and also meetings with Monet, Renoir, Cézanne, and Bazille at the Café Guerbois, where they worked toward a manifesto for their new art.

London

In 1870 the peace of Louveciennes was shattered by the news of the outbreak of the Franco-Prussian war. Pissarro, who still held Danish nationality, and was therefore unable to fight, was forced to remove his family to safety, eventually taking refuge in London with his half-sister. He begrudged his forced exile, but soon settled down to continue his work, painting his surroundings where he stayed in Norwood, then a fast-urbanizing village outside the city, not unlike Pontoise. *Lordship Lane Station, Dulwich*, painted at this time, records the effects of urbanization on the landscape — the railroad and the newly built rows of red-brick houses. Writing home in 1871 to his friend and patron Théodore Duret he sadly records: "My painting doesn't catch on, not at all, a fate that pursues me more or less everywhere."

Possibly the most important incident of his London stay was his introduction to the Parisian art dealer Paul Durand-Ruel, who was to help sell Pissarro's work throughout most of his life. Durand-Ruel put him in touch with Monet, also in London to escape the war, and together they viewed the work of Constable and Turner. Pissarro later remarked that although these British landscape artists certainly influenced them – what was more important, they provided confirmation that they were working in the right direction, particularly with respect to painting in the open air, the depiction of light and the fugitive effects of light and atmosphere. Whether through the influence of the British painters or as a result of his close contact with Monet, Pissarro's paintings of this period reflect a lighter, brighter palette. The paint is applied more freely, with loosely blended brushstrokes of color and areas of impasto.

Pissarro and the Impressionists

Pissarro returned to Louveciennes to find that, during his absence, his home had been requisitioned as a slaughterhouse and his canvases torn from their stretchers and spread over the ground in the yard to protect Prussian uniforms from the mud. After this desecration, they were thrown out onto the manure heap, where Pissarro found them. Only forty out of 1500 paintings covering twenty year's work remained, apart from the few he had sold, a tragedy which makes it difficult to assess his artistic progress up to this date. What remain are primarily landscapes in the Corot style – undoubtedly his more popular works. Most important among the casualties were his early paintings – documenting the birth of Impressionism, such as those painted in 1869 at La Grenouillère with Monet and Renoir. Also lost were no doubt his more informal paintings, portraits of his family and flower studies similar to his *Pink Peonies* of 1873 and *Mme Pissarro Sewing Near a Window* of 1879.

But Pissarro quickly settled back into his former way of life, centered around his family, his work, and his friends. Soon he was embroiled in discussions with his artist friends, including Monet, Manet, Renoir, and Degas, on ways of providing an alternative to the Salon, which would enable them to exhibit and sell their work. In 1873 the Société Anonyme des Artistes, Peintres, Sculpteurs et Graveurs was set up as a joint stock company with fifteen artists with equal rights: Pissarro based the charter on the contract of the Pontoise bakers' union. His involvement in this group of artists is regarded as pivotal. Although he did not have the personal magnetism or the high-flying ideas of Monet, who could be seen as the guiding force, his well-respected strength and honesty did much to get things organized and hold the group together. The somber self-portrait painted at this time shows a man with a prematurely gray beard, looking somewhat older than his forty-three years: it is little wonder that the group regarded him as a wise elder and father figure.

The fruit of these labors was the first Impressionist Exhibition, held in 1874. The critical reaction to it is well known, but it is easy to forget what exactly it was that so horrified the critics. Firstly they found fault with the subject matter. The paintings admired by the Salon committee were mainly religious, historical, or mythological scenes, but here were "vulgar, commonplace" scenes of street people going about their everyday lives, or in Pissarro's case, the countryside as it really was – muddy, dirty, and unkempt. Secondly, the manner of painting

CAMILLE PISSARRO
View from Louveciennes
1870, National Gallery, London

This painting, done just before Pissarro and his family fled to London to escape the Franco-Prussian War, shows close links with his former mentor Corot. Further observation, however, reveals a more down-to-earth vision of nature. Unlike Corot, Pissarro insisted on painting what he saw – in this case a hodgepodge of trees, bushes, and mounds of earth along the country lane. Emile Zola said of Pissarro that, "He is neither a poet nor a philosopher but simply a naturalist."

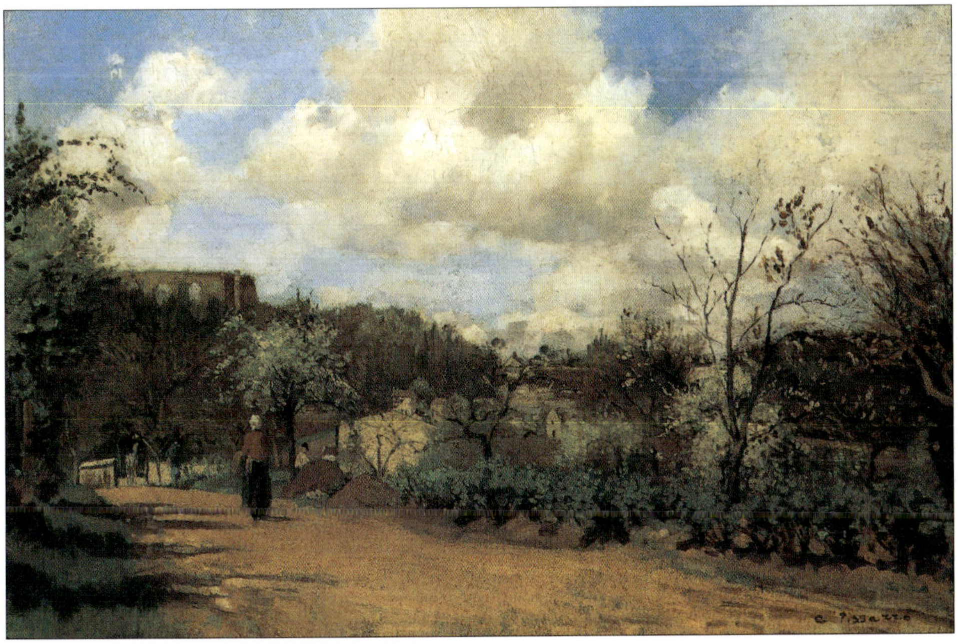

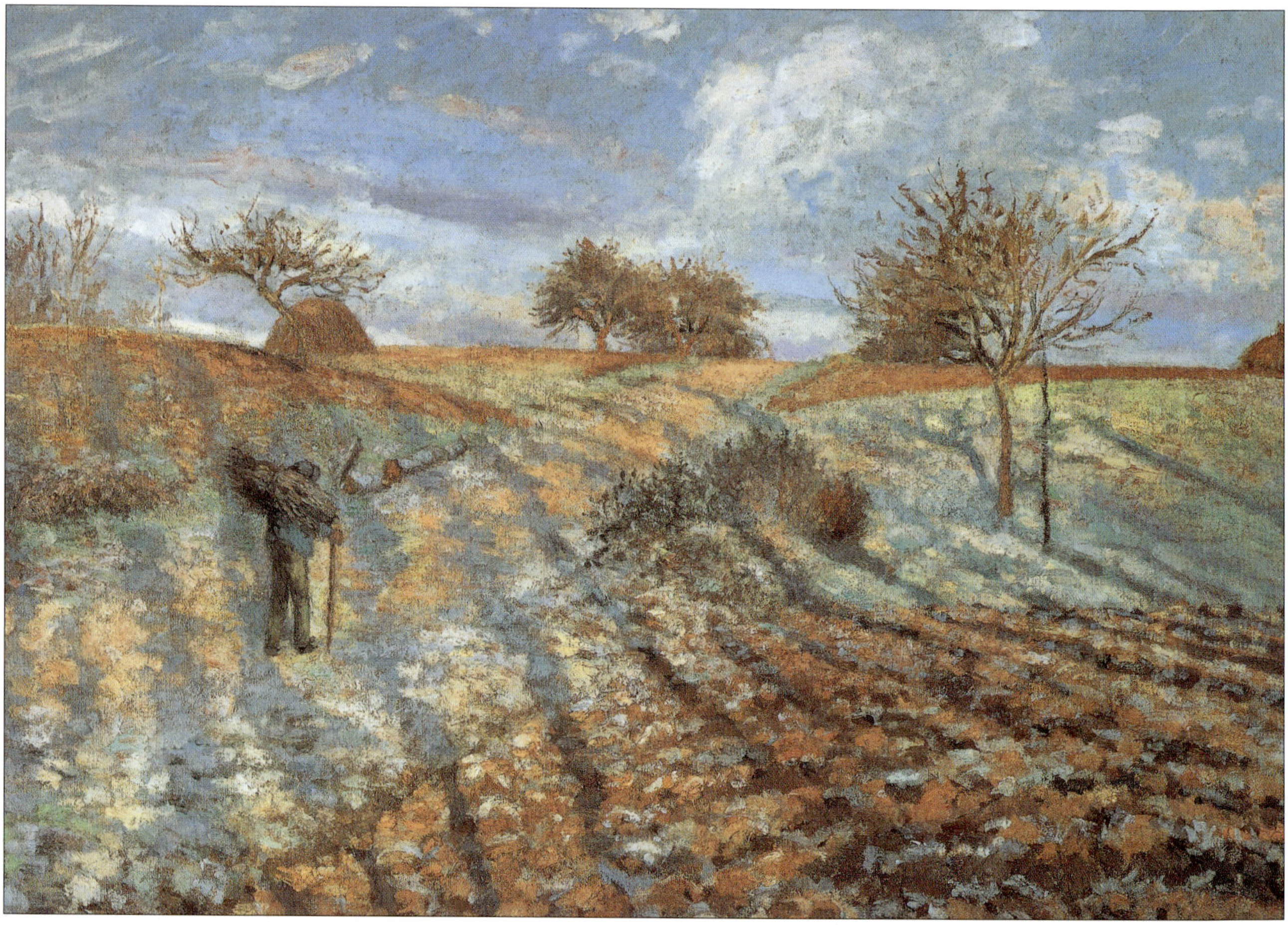

CAMILLE PISSARRO
Hoar Frost, the Old Road to Ennery, Pontoise
1873, Musée d'Orsay, Paris

One of five paintings exhibited by Pissarro at the first Impressionist exhibition in 1874, this painting clearly justifies his place in the group.

The strong diagonals of the road and the ploughed furrows, highlighted with frost, are crossed by the shadows of a row of trees outside the picture, an innovative compositional device that did not find favor with the contemporary critic A. J. Castagnary.

was found wanting by the traditionalists of the Beaux Arts school. They considered the pictures sketchy, like studies rather than finished works, with none of the qualities they saw as a *sine qua non* for good painting, such as academic organization of the composition or painstaking build-up of paint layers over an underpainting. Instead, the paint was often applied wet-in-wet, one brushload of paint applied into another, and the painting finished in one sitting. The expressive use of the paint, with brushstrokes visible on the picture surface, became part of the vocabulary of this group of painters, but the academics considered this an effrontery to the painter's craft; they expected a work to testify to weeks, if not years, of labor. Finally, the "Impressionist" painters shocked their critics with their new theories on color, particularly those used for shadows which they saw as modified by the reflected light of surrounding objects. There were, however, some enlightened critics, including Emile Zola, who braved public outcry and praised the new art.

Pissarro showed five landscapes in this exhibition. These may have appeared tame in comparison with some of the other entries, such as those by Monet or Manet – as he later said of his paintings, "Whoever is in a hurry will not stop for me" – but he was described by the critic Armand Silvestre as "basically the inventor of this [Impressionist] painting." Indeed his expressive brushwork and his approach to color shocked spectators, and were to continue doing so. In 1876 Albert Wolf in *Le Figaro* whined: "Try to make M Pissarro understand that trees are not violet, that sky is not the color of fresh butter, that in no country do we see the things he paints and that no intelligence can accept such aberrations." Pissarro was painting everyday aspects of the countryside and, under the influence of Monet, he was already by the late 1860s applying the paint loosely in unblended brushstrokes of color. His palette had become lighter and clearer, and in his pictures of this time small specks of red and viridian are left unmixed on the surface of the painting. In later years Cézanne was to refer to him as "the first Impressionist."

Friend and teacher

Pissarro's single-minded approach to his art may have something to do with the fact that, certainly in his early years, he found painting difficult. He was constantly searching for a solution to his methods of representing nature and this allowed him to reassess his work in the light of those around him. Back in Pontoise from 1872, he painted regularly with Cézanne, who, Lucien recalled later, often walked the couple of miles from Auvers-sur-Oise to join Pissarro. In a reappraisal of Courbet, both artists were exploring ways of representing space and unifying the painting, and there is evidence of a reciprocal exchange of ideas. Cézanne wanted to study the countryside through Pissarro's eyes, and was particularly interested in Pissarro's Pontoise landscapes of the late 1860s, where he first built up areas with refined blocks of color. Pissarro reassessed these developments, deliberately imitating the style of Cézanne, as in *The Little Bridge at Pontoise* of 1875 (see page 301). The two artists worked together from nature in the surrounding countryside, using the palette knife to help them broaden their approach and refine the composition to zones of color.

Cézanne, although not much younger than Pissarro, said of him that "he was a father for me. A man to consult and a little like the good Lord." Many of Pissarro's friends write in a similar vein; even Lucien, who was taught at home by his father, described him as a "splendid teacher, never imposing his personality on his pupil." Gauguin, who worked more with him at the end of the 1870s, and was greatly influenced by his peasant-girl studies of the early 1880s, refers to him as "one of my masters." The American Impressionist Mary Cassatt noted that he was "such a teacher that he could have taught the stones to draw correctly." Not only did he influence his own contemporaries but the next generation of artists too – particularly Henri Matisse and Francis Picabia.

As the decade progressed, Pissarro struggled more and more with his technique. After the mid-1870s he adopted a comma-like brushstroke to express himself, creating form and value from hatched and cross-hatched areas of small strokes, which built up to a textured impasto surface. *Kitchen Garden with Trees in Flower, Pontoise* of 1877 shows his early attempts with this new approach. Some of his canvases of this period became overloaded with superimposed strokes of thick paint, creating a densely painted, almost

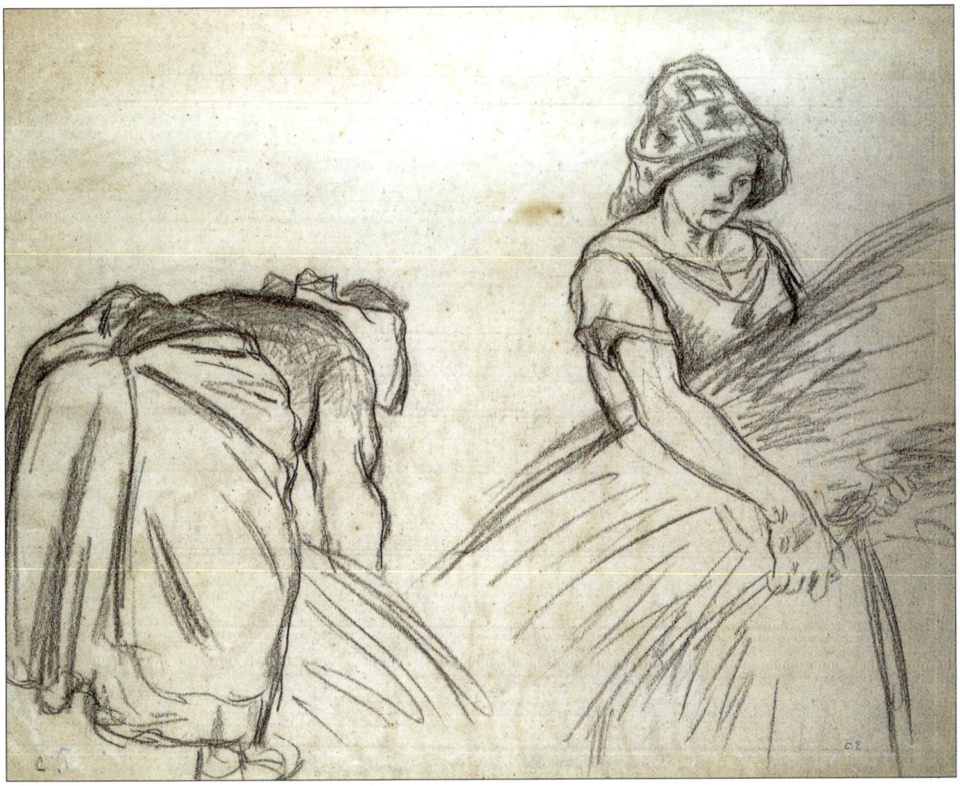

CAMILLE PISSARRO
Study of Two Female Harvesters
1890, Ashmolean Museum, Oxford

Pissarro was a skillful and prolific draftsman from his youth, when he had spent his time drawing the cargo-handlers in the port of Charlotte Amalie in the Virgin Islands. He used his drawings to record visual information which he would later incorporate into his paintings. This drawing in black chalk was among the careful preparations for a tempera painting, *The Harvesters*, shown in the seventh Impressionist Exhibition.

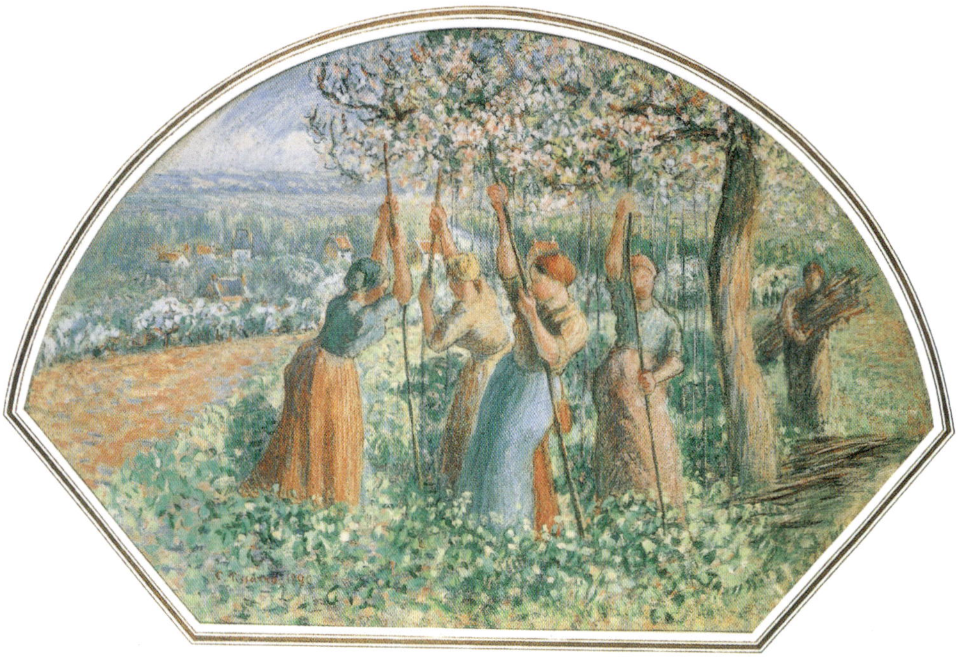

CAMILLE PISSARRO
The Pea-Pickers
1890, Ashmolean Museum, Oxford

This vibrant gouache of peasant women planting pea sticks is one of a number of fans Pissarro painted from 1879 onward. It is very different from the earthiness of his earlier paintings. The rhythmic curves of the figures impart something of the quality of a ritual dance to their arduous task, and the pale, luminous colors seem to conspire in distancing the scene from reality. A painting by Pissarro of the same composition was owned by Monet.

sculpted paint surface. At times the technique achieved a depth of color and a sense of form which can only be appreciated in the original. Close to, the paint is thick and sometimes smeared and matted; standing back, however, the pigments fuse and forms appear. By degrees, a painting of great penetration emerges. But Pissarro was unhappy with his work, feeling that it lacked clarity and structure.

Perhaps in reaction to these difficulties, Pissarro explored other media. A particularly successful venture was undertaken with Degas to publish a journal of original prints. The result of their partnership was a large group of fine etchings by both artists, exploring unconventional ways of creating texture and depicting light. Another new scheme, possibly inspired by Degas, was the decoration of fans. Painted in gouache and watercolor on silk or linen, Pissarro seemed to want to explore the effect of the shape on the composition and also the capabilities of the new medium. *Le Repas Champêtre*, painted later, in 1891, shows a charming scene of a harvesting picnic. The bleaching light of the midday sun contrasts with the subtleties of color and value in the shade, which Pissarro captures with delicate hatching strokes of pure color.

New themes and Neo-Impressionism

Perhaps in an effort to break out of what he considered a stylistic mire, Pissarro in the 1880s boldly explored new themes and new ways of expressing them. He was not alone in his stylistic dilemma: the same feeling of dissatisfaction, and perhaps stagnancy after the initial excitement of the early Impressionist years, was also being experienced by other members of the Impressionist group. Pissarro turned back to a theme which had always concerned him – the life of country people. It was not a new subject for him – his drawings, from his early Caracas market scenes, are peppered with sketches of women working the land. But in the early 1880s it is as if Pissarro focused in on the peasants in his country scenes and his attention is drawn to scenes such as the two female harvesters of 1882 shown here.

Similar scenes by Francois Millet must have influenced Pissarro, who shared his socialist beliefs, but Degas summed up the fundamental difference between them: "Millet? His *Sower* is sowing for Mankind. Pissarro's peasants are working to make a living." Pissarro had been reading anarchist literature since the 1860s, particularly works by P-J Proudhon, who encouraged painters to educate the public by painting people at work or at home as they were in reality, without idealizing their lives. Even in his earliest drawings, executed in St Thomas and Caracas, Pissarro had shown a fascination for the daily lives of the blacks and South American Indians, which he recorded with honest simplicity, so Proudhon's words must have struck a chord with him.

The overthrow of the Paris Commune in 1871, followed by the execution or exile of many supporters, decimated French left-wing politics, but at this time Pissarro, unlike Courbet who was exiled, was not involved. It was not until the 1880s, when the Anarchist movement gained strength and became more active, that Pissarro's views evidently began to harden. In 1882,

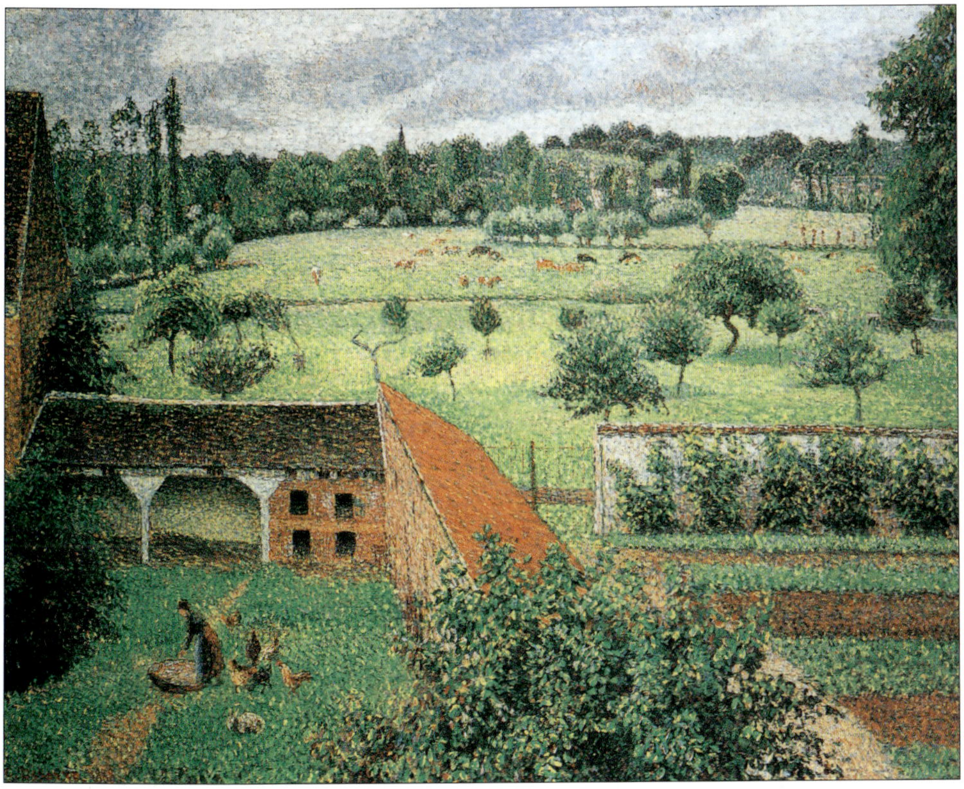

CAMILLE PISSARRO
View from my Window, Eragny-sur-Epte
1886-88, Ashmolean Museum, Oxford

This fresh, yet restrained view of the artist's garden from an upstairs window was painted at the height of his Neo-Impressionist phase. Like Seurat and Signac, he built up his paintings with dabs of pure color that were intended to mix optically in the eye of the viewer. In July 1886 he wrote about the painting to his son Lucien: "It appears that the subject is not popular. They [Durand-Ruel and his son] object to the red roof and the back yard, just what gives character to the painting."

Renoir referred to Pissarro as a revolutionary and alluded to his anarchist sympathies by writing that it would not be long before Pissarro invited the Russian Lavrof (a known anarchist) to exhibit with them. However, Pissarro seldom overtly used his art to preach a political message even though his sympathetic treatment of country people and his preference for more humble subject matter made his position clear. It is no accident that the châteaux at Pontoise and Louveciennes are never included in his rural views.

Pissarro's paintings of country figures, particularly peasant girls, in the first half of the 1880s, break new ground in terms of their spatial organization. He places the figure in an enclosed setting, preventing any recession into the picture space and thus focusing attention on the figure, which is treated more like a portrait. In *The Shepherdess* (see page 305) the wistful young girl is depicted against a backdrop of generalized foliage which spreads out like a tapestry behind her. In this peasant girl series Pissarro perfects the painting style he was working toward in the late 1870s, covering the canvas with a consistent network of small brushstrokes.

In the light of both the unified brushwork and his use of pure strokes of color in these paintings, his conversion to Neo-Impressionism later in the decade seems a less radical step. In 1884 Pissarro met Seurat and Signac, two young artists who had been working toward a new "scientific" theory for art, based on treatises by theorists, among them Charles Henry, Ogden Rood, and David Sutter. These painters set out to use pure pigments – no earth colours or black – premixed on the palette as set out in Hayet's color wheel shown on page 289. Shades of color and tonal value were built up by placing small patches, or dots, of pure color side by side, to be blended optically by the eye.

Pissarro's search for a more structured method of painting had also led him to Henry and Rood, so he was excited by Seurat's interpretation. In addition, the Neo-Impressionists, like Pissarro, supported the Anarchist cause, which was reflected in their theory. With typical industry, he threw himself into mastering the new techniques, but the system was time-consuming and laborious. From 1885 to 1888 he struggled with its limitations, producing some inspired examples of Neo-Impressionism, including *View from My Window, Eragny* and *Apple Picking at Eragny-sur-Epte*, both painted in 1888. Later, in 1896, he explained in a letter to Henry Van de Velde, the Belgian designer, how insensitive he found the system, making it impossible for him to follow his fleeting sensations and to give his work a sense of movement and life. It would appear that he also found the system created the very sense of artifice in his art which he had always avoided, making it difficult to record what were to him the all important transient details of nature.

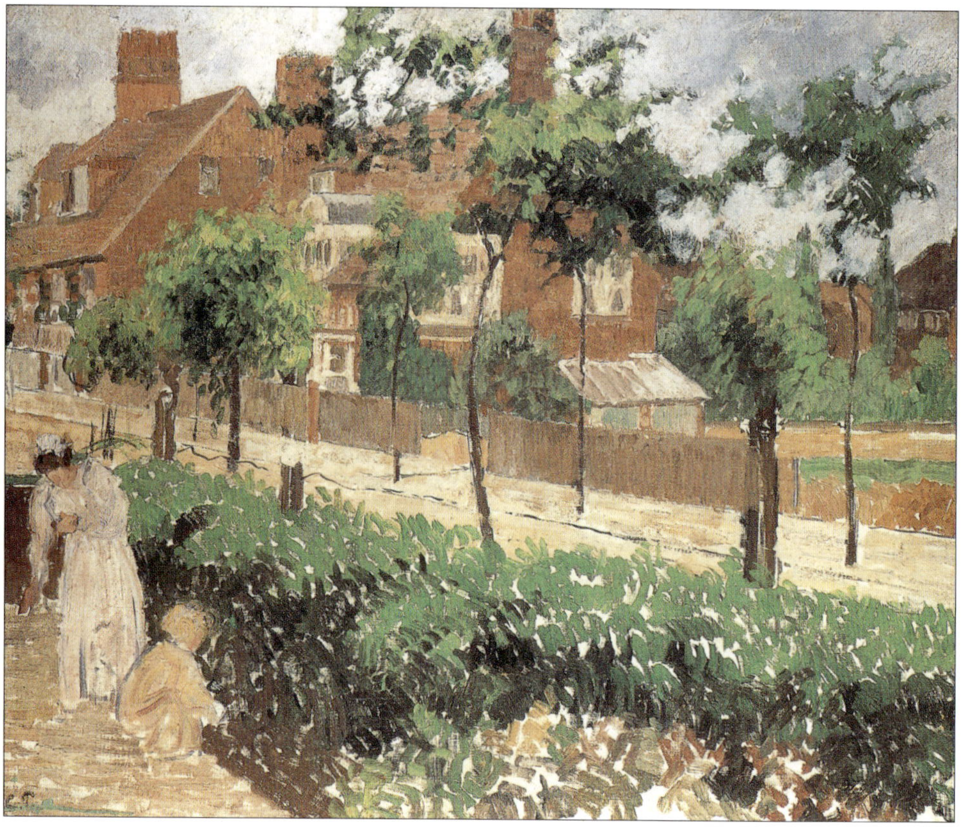

CAMILLE PISSARRO
Bedford Park, The Old Bath Road
1897, Ashmolean Museum, Oxford

This painting was begun, but not completed, during Pissarro's last visit to London to see his ailing son Lucien. Being unfinished, it shows how he built up his paintings: clearly visible are the blue lines of the underdrawing, done quickly and freely in dilute paint to map out the main components of the composition. The top part of the picture, with the red brickwork, is more finished, but the figures in the foreground are still at an early stage, as is the hedge, which has been built up with broad strokes of different greens applied from all directions.

Final years

Pissarro's later years were dogged by a recurring eye infection but this physical affliction in no way stopped him painting. In effect, it meant that he was no longer able to work outside, except in warm weather, and this turn of events encouraged him to reappraise both his working methods and his subject matter. A trip to Rouen earlier in 1883, when he painted *The Quays at Rouen,* perhaps reminded him of the busy life of the port in the Virgin Islands where he spent his youth. Pissarro found the town very stimulating, painting a number of views from the shelter of a hotel room. It is not surprising therefore that, after the onset of the eye infection, he returned to similar urban/portside themes all painted from upper-story hotel rooms. In his last years he produced series of paintings of the same urban view under different conditions of light and weather, returning to places and themes which had attracted the Impressionists in their early years. He moved around Northern France painting from hotel rooms in Rouen and Paris as well as Le Havre and Dieppe. He continued with the same urban themes when visiting London in the 1890s to stay with Lucien in Chiswick, painting holiday crowds in the botanical gardens at Kew, and also painting the parks, as Monet had done earlier. In his later style he reverted to the highly worked canvases of the late 1870s, often painting in forms of people or trees over the thickly built up impasto layer underneath.

Contrary to what might be expected, Pissarro as he grew older became increasingly active in his support for the Anarchist movement. His support ranged from involvement with the Anarchist newspaper *La Révolte* to his backing of Zola in the Dreyfus Affair, which developed from a burst of anti-semitism in France in the late '90s. After the murder of the French President in 1894 by an Italian Anarchist, Pissarro as a known Anarchist sympathizer was forced to flee to Belgium, where he stayed for four months. Even two weeks before his death, he was still ready to demonstrate his loyalties by joining a pilgrimage to Médan on the first anniversary of Zola's death.

In his self-portrait of 1903 (see page 317), we see Pissarro a few months before he died, an upright, dignified old man still with a sense of vitality. He continued to work up until the last moment, in good weather pushing his patent easel on wheels around the orchard at Eragny. In the summer he even sold five canvases, including two to the local museum. A few months later, in November, he died, revered by his friends and fellow painters as a great artist and a good man. Signac wrote to Lucien: "He will always be for me *le vieux Maître* . . . he leaves behind him one of the most beautiful painting *oeuvres* of our times and the memory of a life of impeccable distinction and utter dignity."

PISSARRO'S PAINTING METHODS

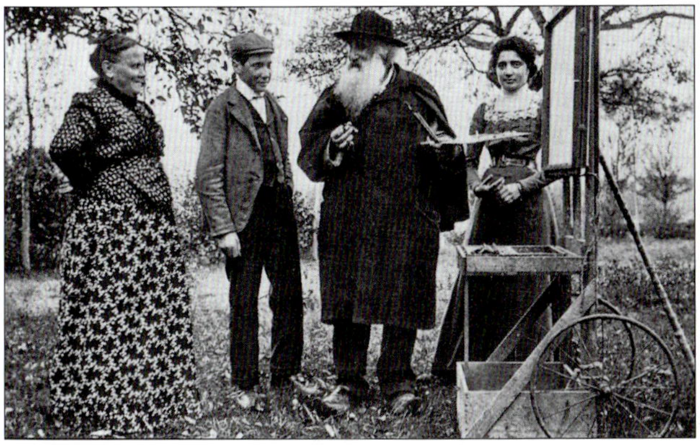

For outdoor work, Pissarro had a specially designed easel on wheels, which could be pushed along like a barrow until he found a suitable spot for a painting. Here he is seen with his wife Julie and two of his children, Paul-Emile and Jeanne (Cocotte). He is wearing his everyday working clothes — a loose jacket, wooden clogs (his country wear) and the wide-brimmed hat which seldom left his head.

Pissarro's palette and brushwork changed from one period of his career to another, but his general approach to his paintings was a constant factor. His philosophy of landscape painting is set out in a letter of about 1896 to a young painter.

"Look for the kind of nature that suits your temperament. The motif should be observed more for shape and color than for drawing . . . Precise drawing is dry and hampers the impression of the whole . . . it is the brushstroke of the right value and color which should produce the drawings . . . Don't work bit by bit, but paint everything at once by placing tones everywhere, with brush-strokes of the right color and value, while noticing what is alongside. Use small brush-strokes and try to put down your perceptions immediately . . . Cover the canvas at the first go and then work until you see nothing more to add. Observe the aerial perspective well, from foreground to the horizon, the reflections of sky, of foliage. Don't be afraid of putting on color, refine the work little by little. Don't proceed according to rules and principles, but paint what you observe and feel. Paint generously and unhesitatingly, for it is best not to lose the first impression. Don;t be timid in the presence of nature; one must be bold at the risk of being deceived and making mistakes. One must have only one teacher — nature; she is the one always to be consulted."

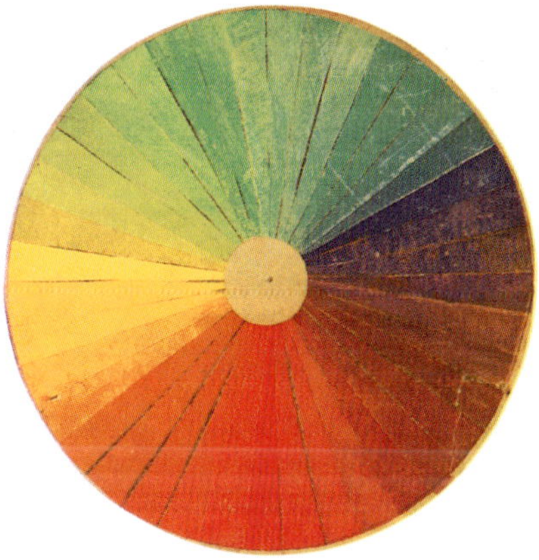

Louis Hayet, a friend of Pissarro, painted this color circle based on Ogden Rood's color wheel. Such charts were helpful to the Neo-Impressionist painters. For the idea of optical mixing to be really successful, colors had to be chosen with great care, the only hues premixed on the palette being those adjacent to one another on the circle.

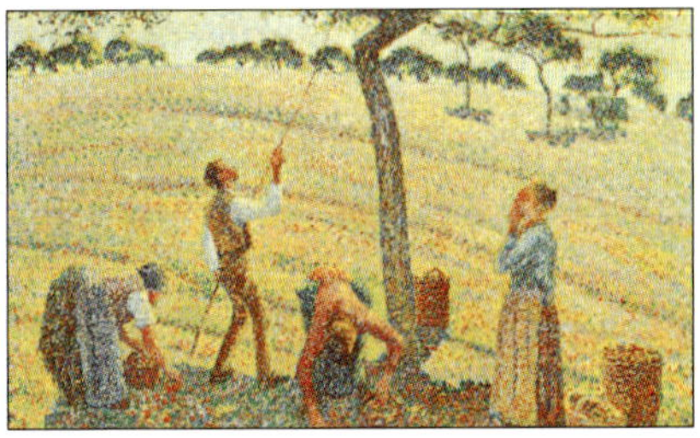

The colors Pissarro used for *Apple Picking at Eragny-sur-Epte* were probably similar to those used by Seurat. These were cadmium yellow, vermilion, madder lake, cobalt violet, ultramarine, cobalt blue, cerulean blue, viridian, emerald (Veronese) green, and cadmium yellow light.

CHRONOLOGY OF PISSARRO'S LIFE

1830	10 July – born on the island of St Thomas, Virgin Islands.
1842-7	At school in Passy outside Paris.
1847	Returns to St Thomas and joins family business.
1852-4	To Venezuela with Fritz Melbye, Danish painter.
1855	Travels to Paris. Visits World Exhibition.
1856-8	Works in Paris, with financial help from his parents.
1859	First picture accepted for Salon (exhibits in 1864, 1865, 1866, 1868, 1869, and 1870). Visits Académie Suisse, where he meets Monet.
1860	Meets Julie Vellay, later his wife.
1861	Registers as a copyist at the Louvre. Meets Guillaumin and Cézanne at the Académie Suisse.
1863	Three landscapes exhibited in the Salon des Refusés. Son Lucien born.
1866	Settles at Pontoise. Attends Zola's meetings and formative meetings of the Impressionist group at the Café Guerbois.
1867	Paints *View of l'Hermitage at Pontoise.*
1869	Moves to Louveciennes. Paints with Monet and Renoir at La Grenouillère.
1870	Franco-Prussian War drives Pissarro to London.
1871	Marries Julie. Paints *Lordship Lane Station, Dulwich,* London. Returns to Louveciennes.
1872	Settled back in Pontoise. Cézanne at Auvers-sur-Oise.
1873	Impressionist Society formed. Paints *Pink Peonies.*

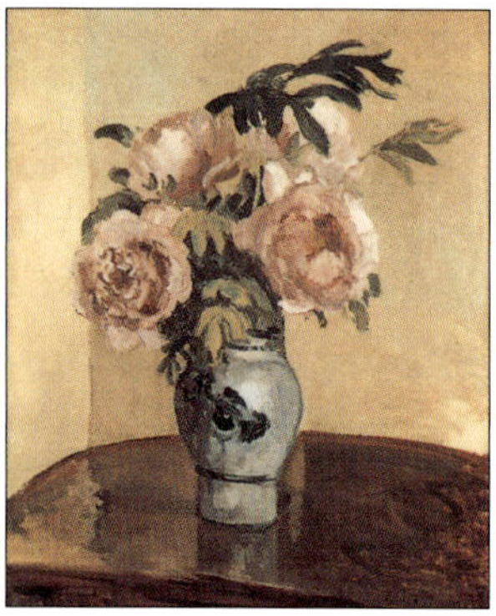

Pink Peonies

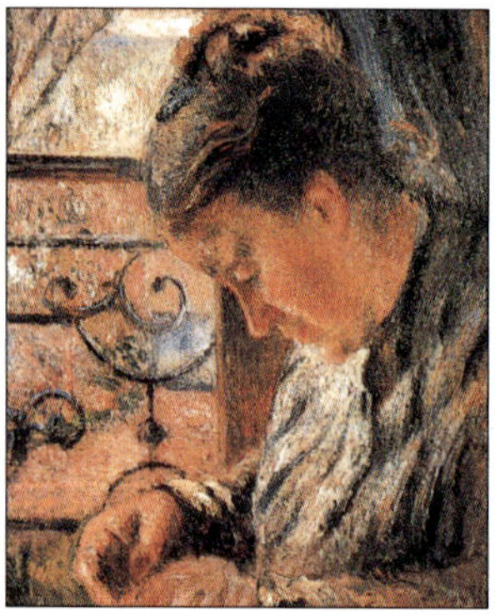

Mme Pissarro Sewing Near a Window

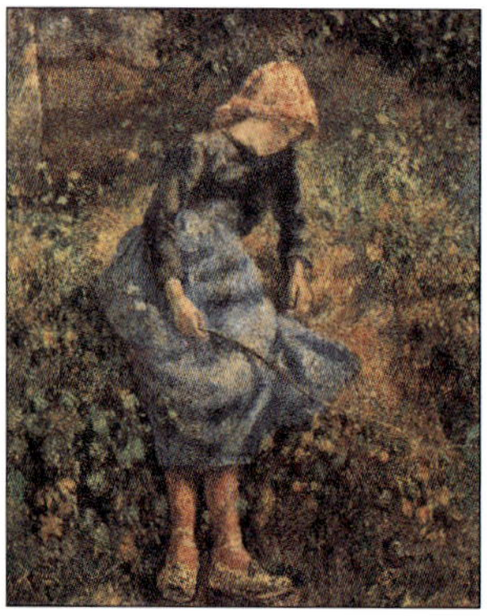

The Shepherdess

1874	15 April exhibits five landscapes in the first Impressionist exhibition (Pissarro exhibits in all of them – 1876, 1877, 1879, 1880, 1881, 1882, and 1886).
1875-80	Struggling to make a living (fourth son born 1878). Paints *The Little Bridge, Pontoise* (1875) and *Kitchen Garden with Trees in Flower, Pontoise* (1877).
1879	About this time, paints *Mme Pissarro Sewing near a Window.* Gauguin paints with Pissarro at Pontoise.
1881	Break-up of original Impressionist group. Paints *The Shepherdess.*
1883	Durand-Ruel organizes a one-man show for Pissarro. Lucien leaves for England. Visit to Rouen, painting *The Quays at Rouen.*
1884	Moves to Eragny.
1885-91	Joins Seurat and Signac in the Neo-Impressionist movement.
1888	Paints *Apple Picking at Eragny-sur-Epte.* In September contracts eye infection.
1890	Visits Lucien in London (and again in 1892 and 1897).
1892	Successful one-man show of a hundred paintings. Buys the house at Eragny.
1894	To Belgium to escape reprisals against Anarchists.
1893-1903	Paints urban views of Rouen, Le Havre, Dieppe, and Paris such as *The Boulevard Montmartre at Night,* 1897.
1903	13 November Pissarro dies in Paris.

THE PAINTINGS

View of L'Hermitage at Pontoise

1867

$35\frac{7}{8} \times 59\frac{1}{4}$in/91×1.505m

Oil on canvas

Wallraf-Richartz Museum, Cologne

Pissarro is perhaps best known for peaceful rural scenes such as this, painted when he was living in the small village of Pontoise just outside Paris. He had moved there in his mid-thirties with Julie Vellay, later to be his wife, and their young son Lucien. Although Pissarro kept a studio in Paris to stay in touch with his artist and writer friends and to try and sell his work, he was more at ease in the countryside, which provided him with the inspiration for his work. This view, showing L'Hermitage in the northeast part of Pontoise, is one of a series painted at this time, all of them exploring methods of composition and ways of depicting light and space.

The early paintings of Pontoise are larger than much of Pissarro's other work, being painted to the specifications of the Salon committee, which laid down stringent rules about submissions for possible inclusion in the annual Salon exhibition. Following the traditions of the time, artists were expected to begin by making sketches and oil studies of their subject from life. This information was then worked up in the studio into a full-sized oil sketch, and finally the painting was executed in slow stages with painstaking care. Although Pissarro was soon to find himself in strong opposition to the old-fashioned and increasingly outdated aims and methods of the Salon, he was, like his contemporaries, forced to comply with them through a need to sell his work. He exhibited views of L'Hermitage, Pontoise, in the Salons of both 1868 and 1869. Of the two landscapes shown in 1868, Emile Zola, the writer and critic, wrote in highly complimentary terms: "The originality here is profoundly human. It is not derived merely from a facility of hand or from a falsification of nature. It stems from the temperament of the painter himself and comprises a feeling for truth resulting from an inner conviction." Even at this early stage, Zola, who was to become a close acquaintance of Pissarro's, had an uncanny grasp of what the artist was trying to achieve in his painting.

It was really only in the mid-'60s that Pissarro evolved a truly individual style, as represented by this work. The evenly cast light in the painting allows the forms to be defined without the descriptive use of cast shadows. By reducing the walls and roofs to clearly defined shapes and defining them with solid directional strokes of color, the warren of buildings is boldly and unambiguously expressed. These early paintings were to provide an inspiration to Cézanne when the two artists worked together in Pontoise in the early 1870s.

Although the strong underlying geometric composition, with the small figures in the foreground, and the mute greens and brown earth colors, are reminiscent of Corot, the bold handling of the paint – both with hog bristle brushes and the palette knife – shows Pissarro's affinity with Courbet. He needed to use a well-loaded brush in this painting, as it covers another work underneath. In places the ridged brushstrokes of the painting beneath catch the light, working against those that are superimposed. The influence of Daubigny, who strongly supported the inclusion of Pissarro's work in the 1868 Salon, can also be seen in the lively working of the paint surface. But already there are signs of cross-fertilization between Pissarro and the younger artists later to form part of the Impressionist group, Monet and Manet particularly. Manet's *Déjeuner sur l'Herbe* had made a great impact on his circle after the outcry it created at the Salon des Refusés in 1863. One of the bitter criticisms leveled at it related to its "vulgar" or commonplace treatment of the subject, and the same complaint was also frequently made of Pissarro, who, it was considered, was unable to find anything elegant or poetic to paint in the countryside.

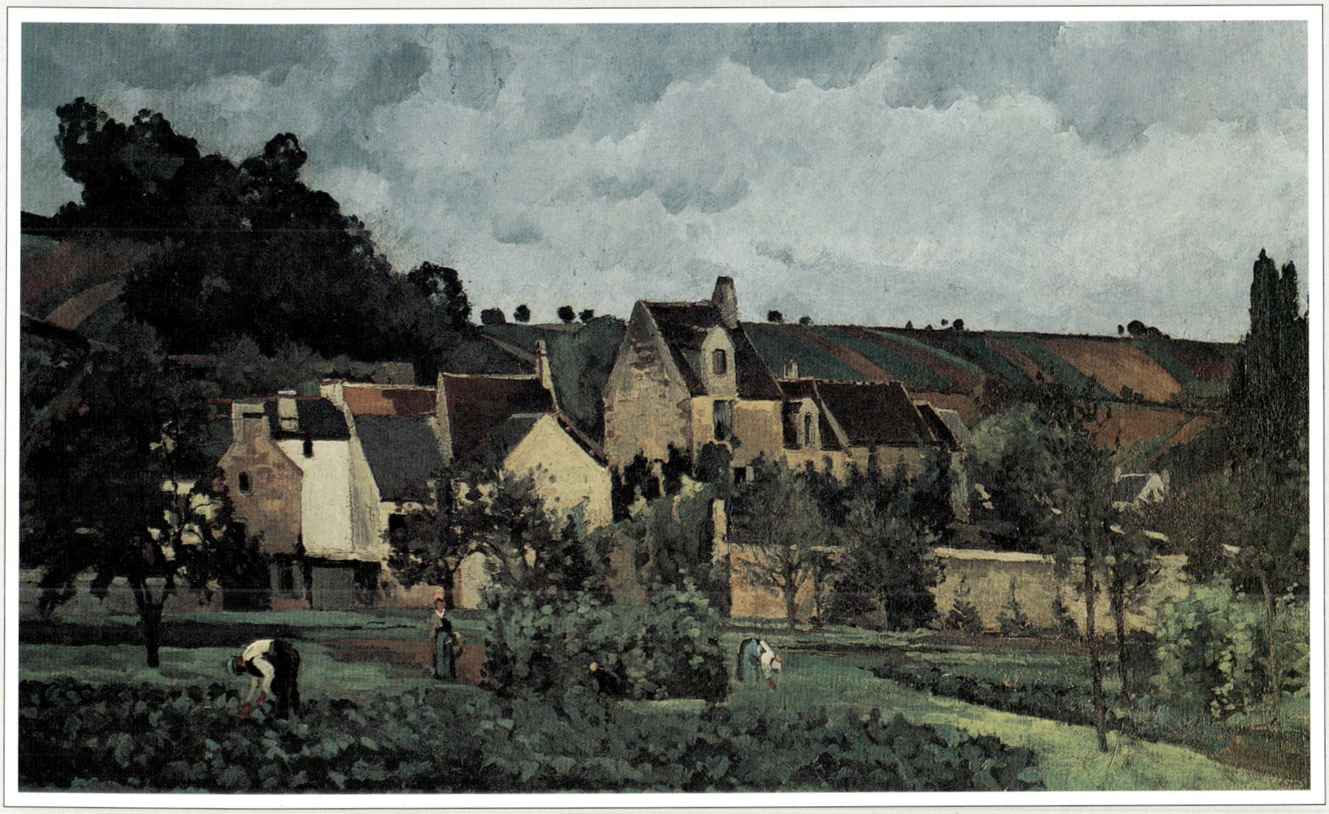

This painting is considered one of the most important works of Pissarro's early *oeuvre.* The underlying geometrical structure is a careful balance of horizontals – the vegetable patch in the foreground, the wall, the ridges of the roofs, and the background brow of the hill – with strong, punchy diagonals leading the eye from the foreground on the right and repeated in the eaves of the buildings and the stripes of the landscape up on the hill behind. This structure holds the composition together on the picture surface, and is reinforced by the handling of the paint, which makes a consistent pattern of brushstrokes over the surface. The canvas, barely visible through the thick layers of paint, is an unusual chevron-woven twill. In paintings such as *Hoar Frost* (see page 284), the diagonal weave is used to enforce the composition. In size the canvas is close to the standard "marine 80" often used by Corot and recommended for paintings submitted to the Salon. Normally Pissarro preferred much smaller canvases which were easy to carry on painting trips in the countryside and quicker to complete before the light changed.

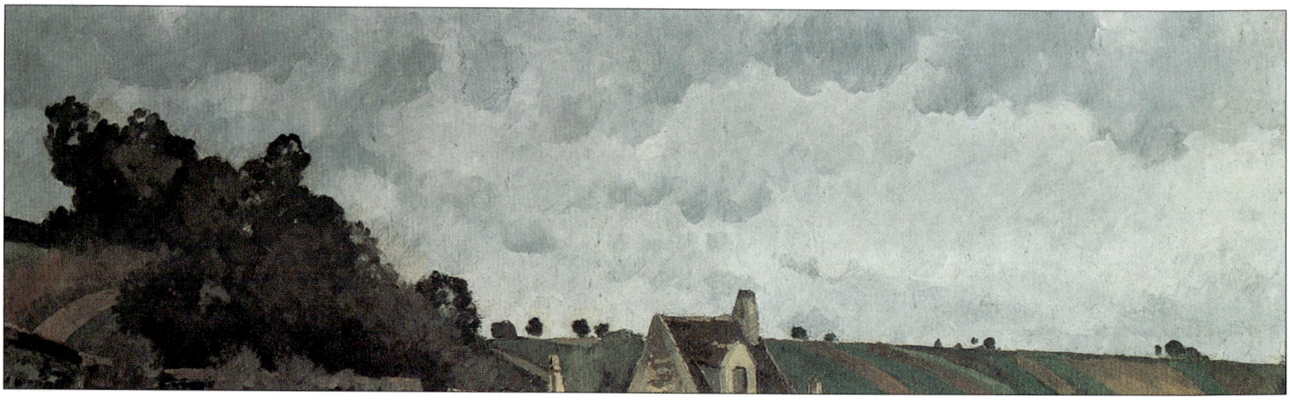

1

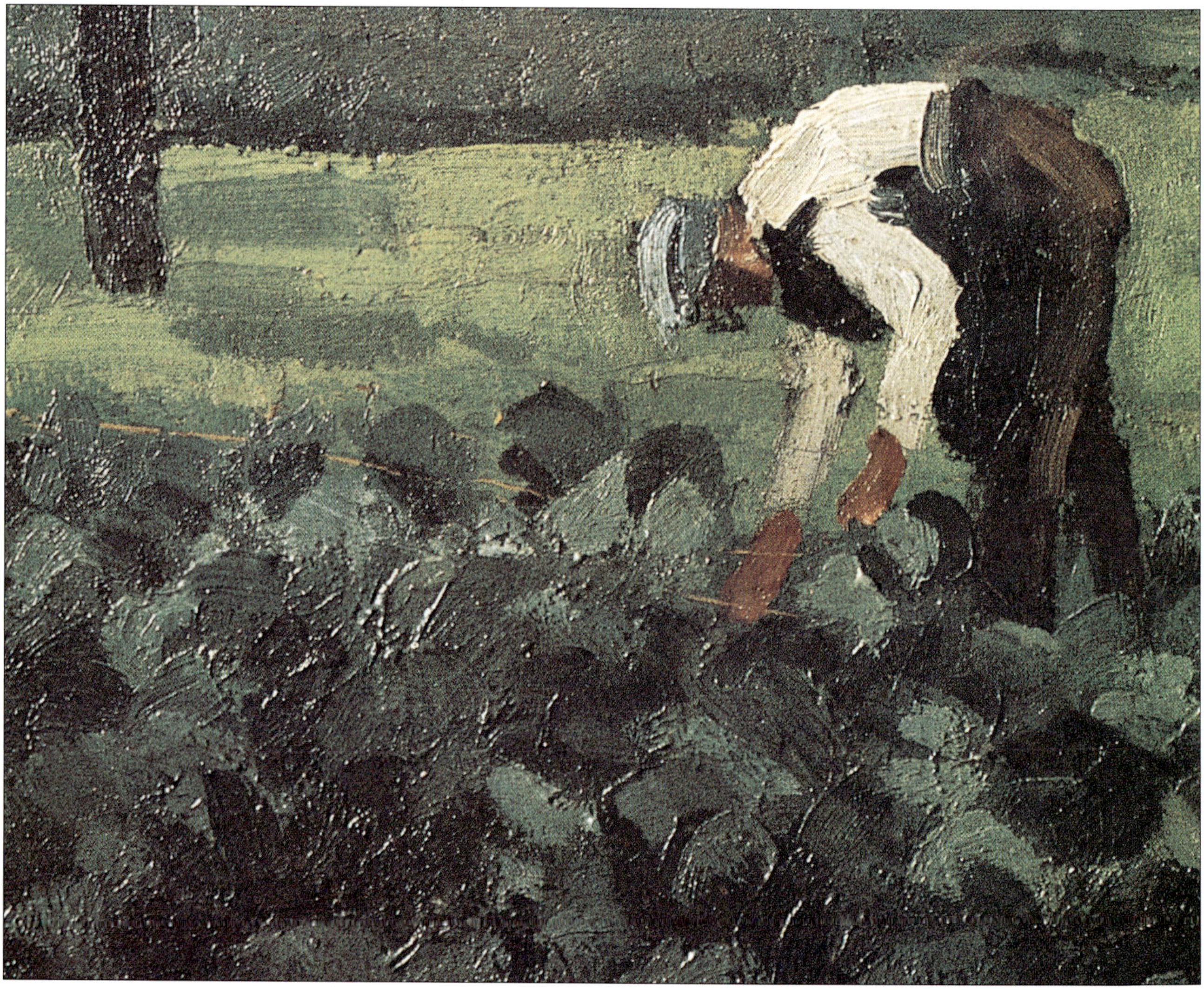

2

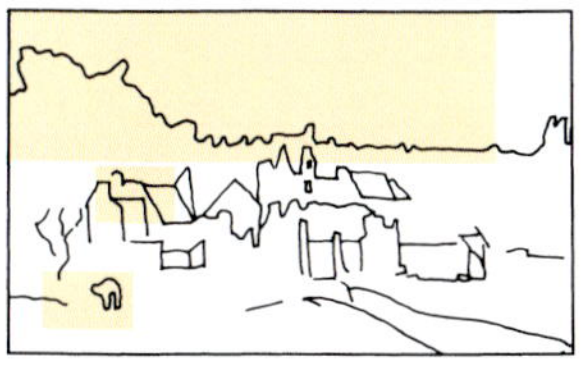

1 Pissarro was fond of the rather dull, even light usually cast on a gray day, which prevented high contrasts and deep shadows — he was later to find that the English climate could often provide him with these conditions. The sky area here has been applied in places wet-in-wet, with light, lively strokes that give a sense of movement to what is otherwise a still scene. In places, as on the skyline, the pinkish tones of the underpainting are allowed to show through the broken brushwork, warming the cool grays of the sky area.

2 Pissarro was described by one critic as "a painter of cabbages." Certainly he appeared to delight in the sense of order achieved in a kitchen garden, and the demonstration of good honest toil it afforded. Like Corot, he used figures in his early landscapes to give a sense of scale and often to enforce the vertical compositional lines. Here the line down the backs of the man's legs is a continuation of a clear vertical from the buildings and a chimney above, which helps to tie the foreground to the background. The eye is naturally drawn to this figure, painted in high contrast and remarkable economy. The same broad flat brush has been used as for the buildings. The waistband and trousers are given form by working ocher wet-in-wet into the dark umber below.

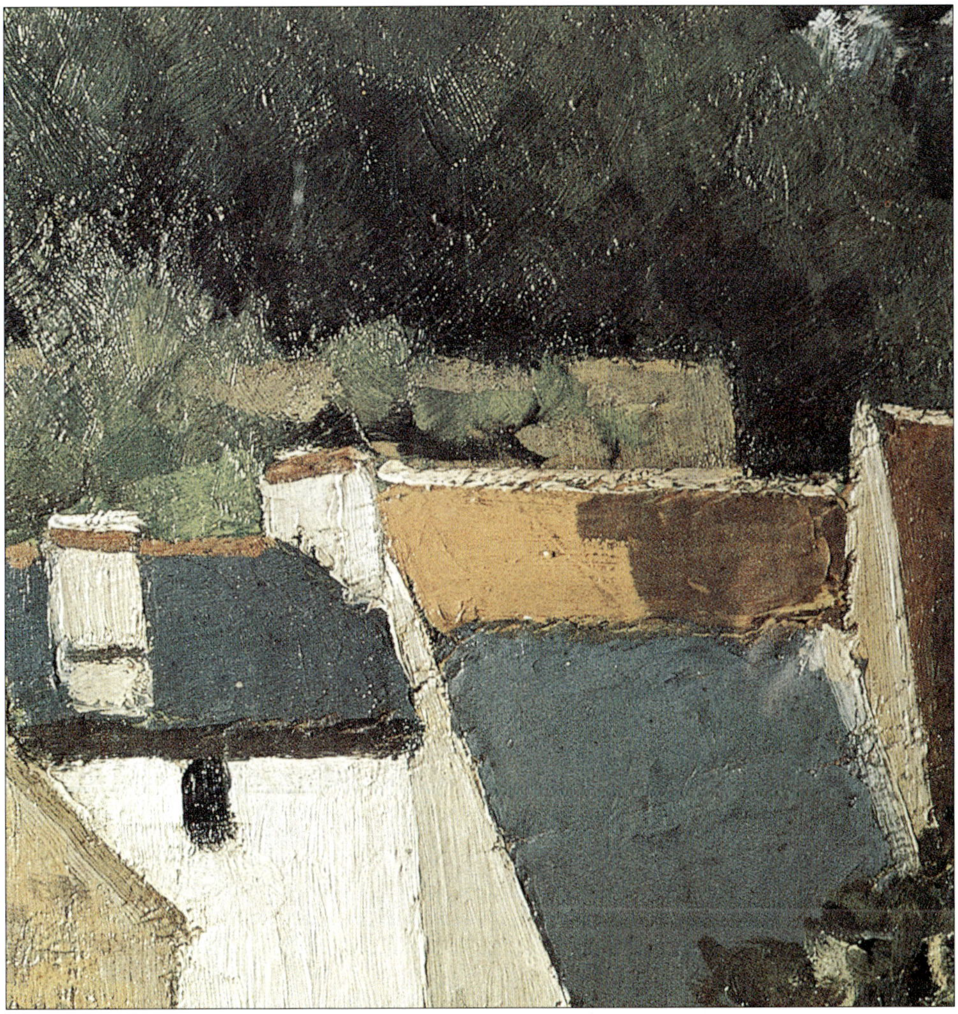

3

3 In this detail of the farm buildings in the left middle ground Pissarro's bold handling of the subdued earth colors forms an almost abstract composition of geometric shapes. The treatment of paint in this area of the painting shows the influence of Courbet and, in turn, was later to be a source of inspiration to Cézanne. Bold strokes leave the mark of a flat hog bristle brush in the thick juicy paint. These brushmarks help to enforce the different planes of the walls and roofs, which are otherwise merely described in flat colors, sometimes clarified with broken outlines with a dry brush, as on the eaves. The slate-gray roof in the foreground has been applied with a palette knife, giving a smoother appearance to the paint. But note how the dark underpainting is allowed to show through around the edges to help define the outline.

LORDSHIP LANE STATION, DULWICH

1871

$17\frac{1}{2} \times 28\frac{1}{2}$in/$44.5 \times 72.5$cm

Oil on canvas

Courtauld Institute Galleries, London

This scene of the newly built Lordship Lane Station, which served the crowds visiting exhibitions at Crystal Palace, was painted on Pissarro's first visit to London. In 1870 he brought his family to England to escape the Franco-Prussian War, and they stayed with his half-sister in Upper Norwood just outside the city. Pissarro had found himself in a difficult situation when the war broke out: he was unable to fight with the French as he still retained Danish nationality, and it soon became clear that his house at Louveciennes was in the path of the invading Prussians. Abandoning over 1500 paintings, the body of his early work, he first fled with his family to Montfoucault in Britanny to take refuge with his great friend, the painter Ludovic Piette, and from there in the fall they traveled to England.

Later in his life Pissarro was to visit London regularly, and he enjoyed it, but he begrudged this first visit, writing to his friend Théodore Duret in June 1871: "I am here for only a very short time. I count on returning to France as soon as possible . . . Here there is no art; everything is a question of business." Even so this London visit gave him a chance to reassess his work in the light of Constable and Turner, whom he viewed with Monet, also in London to escape the war.

The structure of the painting relies on a traditional compositional device, that of receding parallel lines which lead the eye into the picture space. Pissarro has effectively reversed the process, however, by depicting the train steaming toward the viewer, against the natural "entry" into the composition, but he ensures that the eye is taken back toward the rows of newly built houses on the left by using the fence, with its strong browns and blacks, to direct the way. Similarly the strong, swift gray line of paint on the brow of the bank prevents the eye from leaving the picture on the right.

The foreground of scrubland is an interesting area of paint, loosely executed in quick strokes in varying greens and browns. The movement here contrasts with the flat color of the buildings in the background, which although not as important as those in *l'Hermitage, Pontoise* (see page 295), are treated in the same manner. Although the overall palette reflects the dull light of the day, the warm red-brown of the buildings is taken through the painting, and helps to unify it. This color can be seen boldly painted into the green of the grass, in the track, and on the train, and it is also worked in to modify the whites and grays of the sky and the impasto of the cloud of steam. But there are also small patches of pure color which intensify the range of hues – a bright yellow in the grass on the right and vermilion painted wet-in-wet on the front of the steam engine.

Most of Pissarro's early paintings include small figures in the foreground, usually for compositional reasons and to help with the interpretation of scale. It is interesting that X-ray and infra-red photographs have shown a small figure standing in the foreground, on the bank to the right of the tracks, that Pissarro eventually painted out.

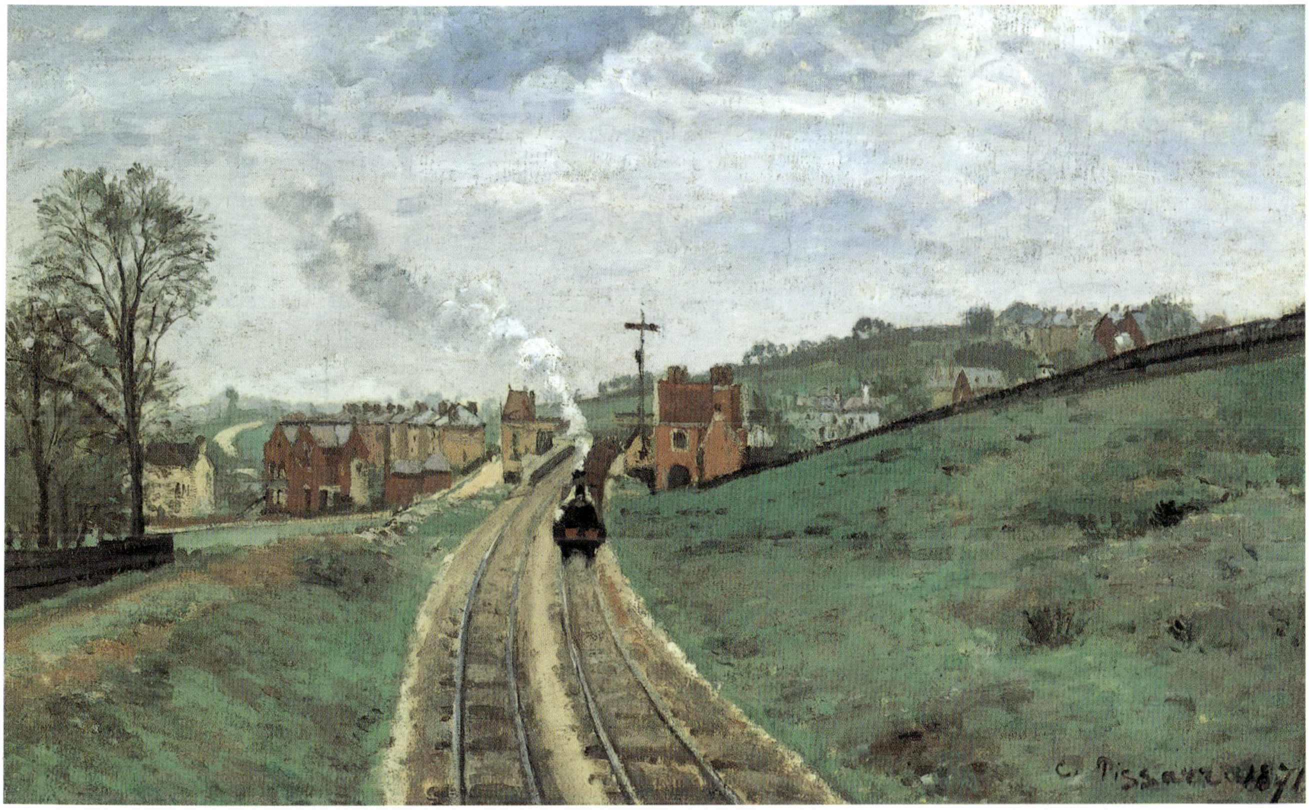

Pissarro painted this urban scene from a footbridge over the railroad to the south of Lordship Lane Station (now demolished), near Crystal Palace, London. His interest in recording what he saw as the threat of urbanization became an enduring theme in his later years. Turner's painting *Rain, Steam and Speed,* painted in 1844, would have been seen by Pissarro at the National Gallery, but even though they both depict an oncoming steam train, Pissarro's painting uses none of Turner's dramatic atmospheric effects. His own approach to nature is more humble.

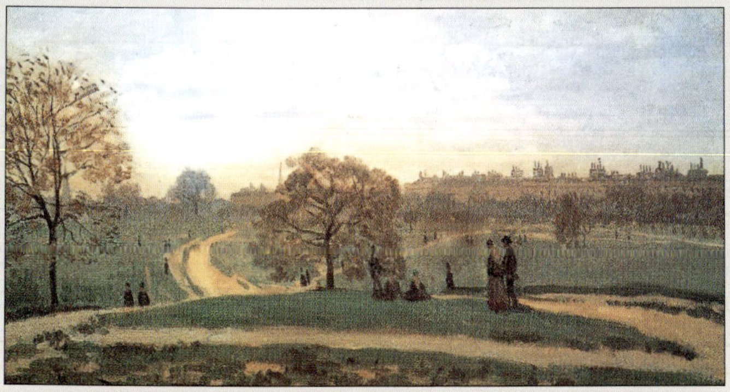

CLAUDE MONET
Hyde Park
1871, Museum of Art, Rhode Island School of Design

Also in London to escape the Prussian invasion of France, Monet met up with Pissarro, and together they viewed the Constables and Turners at the National Gallery. This view of Hyde Park, painted at the time, shows many similarities with Pissarro in style and coloration, although Monet's more "blond" palette was to influence his friend.

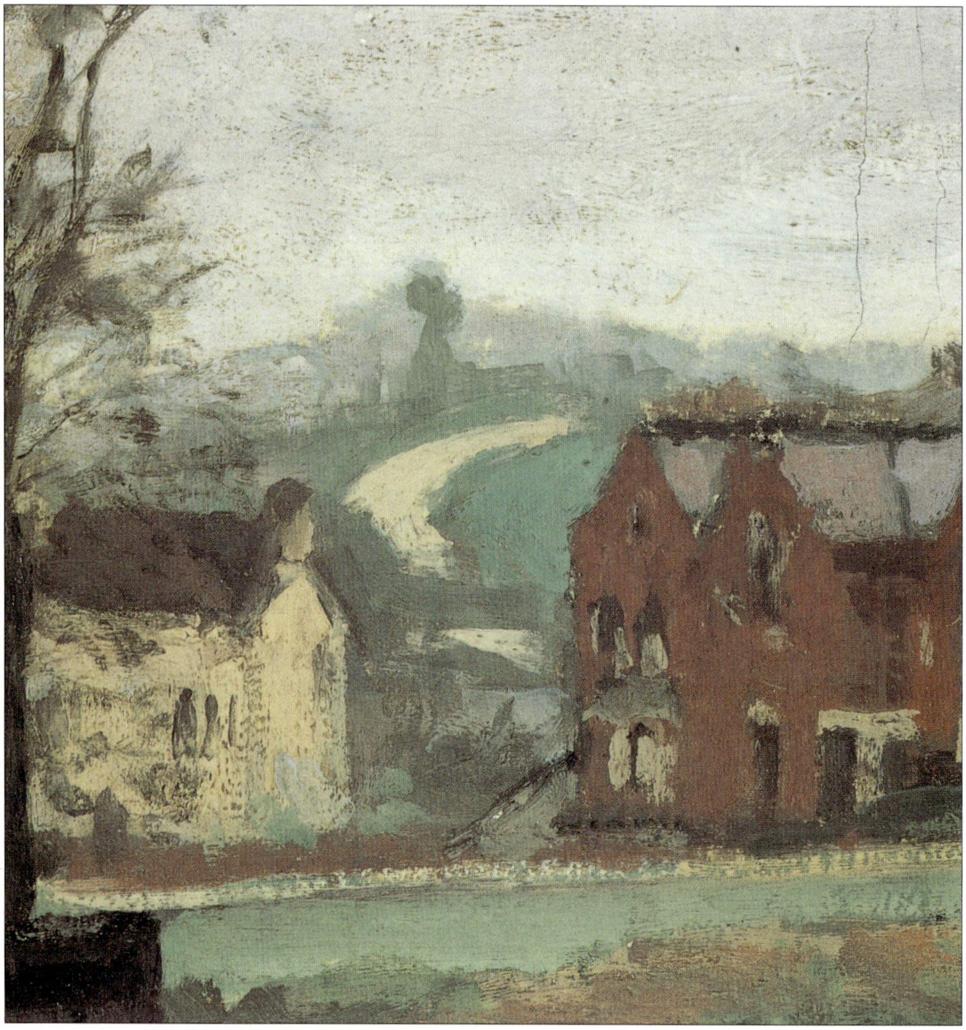

1

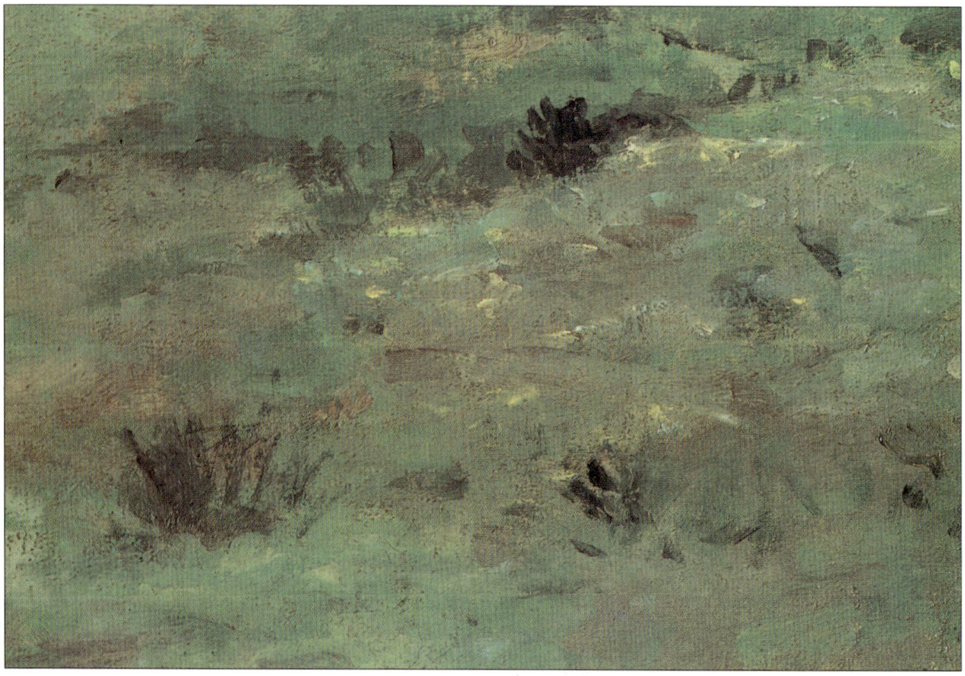

2

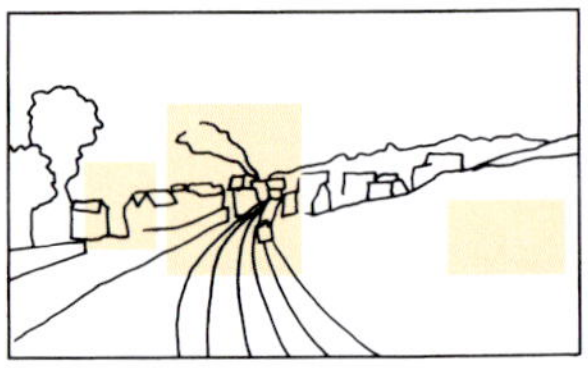

1 This perfectly conceived vignette in the left background demonstrates Pissarro's attention to detail. Although executed with small, economic dabs of paint, the intentions of the artist are absolutely clear, and he has also been concerned with recession. The colors, though of a surprisingly bright hue, are well knocked back with white in accordance with atmospheric perspective. The glimpse of the distant road disappearing over the hill helps to take the eye further into the picture space. Tiny patches of the white canvas have been allowed to show through on the eaves of the red houses to give sparkling highlight effects.

2 At first sight the stretches of scrubland on either side of the railroad track seem pointlessly barren; Pissarro's desire to produce an honest depiction of the scene would not allow him to compromise. But closer inspection shows a wide variation in the use of color and technique in this area. Working in small dabs with probably a fairly soft brush, he has applied the paint in places wet-in-wet, leaving the colors unblended, while the darker green clumps of grass have been added with a dry brush. The result is a patchwork of colors with a wide range of greens, areas of browny red which tie in with the buildings in the background, and accents of pure yellow.

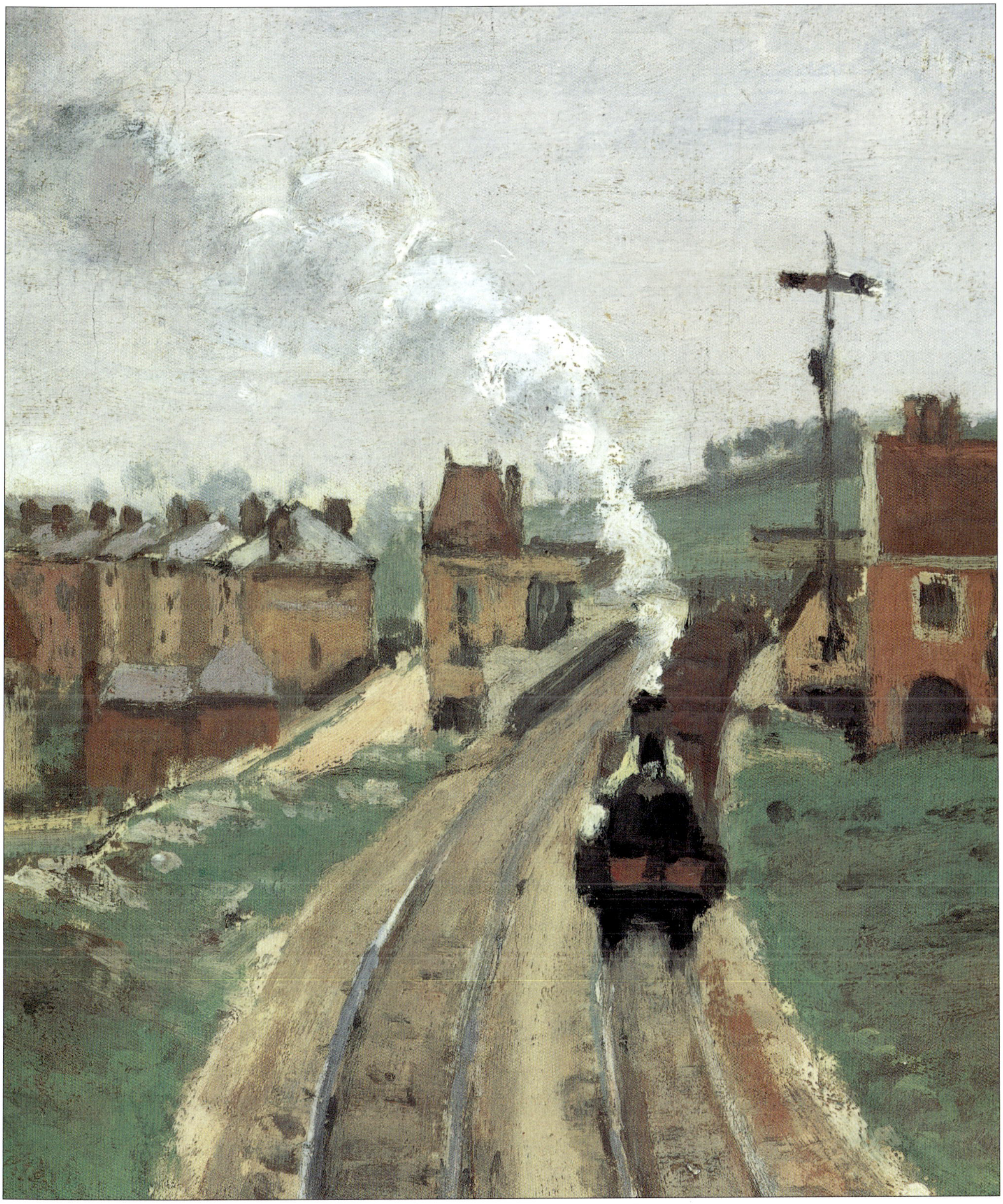

3

3 *Actual size detail* If Pissarro had wanted to produce a more dramatic composition, he would have focused in on the train as this detail does. But he was interested in other aspects of this scene — particularly the way in which the recently built railroad has carved this gentle landscape in half. As this detail shows, each element of the painting is treated separately: flat brushstrokes are used for the rows of houses, thick molded impasto for the angry puff of steam, horizontal wet-in-wet dabs for the sky, and sweeping directional strokes for the railroad track. The cruciform signal silhouetted against the sky is added with a dry brush over the sky color.

The Little Bridge, Pontoise

1875

$25^3/_4 \times 32^1/_8$in/65.5×81.5cm

Oil on canvas

Städtische Kunsthalle, Mannheim

In later years, Pissarro's son, Lucien, remembered how Cézanne used to trudge for about two miles from his house in Auvers-sur-Oise to paint with Pissarro at Pontoise. There are photographs of the two of them setting out to paint in the countryside with their painting equipment in backpacks – in winter wearing warm hats, thick dark capes and walking boots, and in summer, straw hats to keep off the sun. The two worked closely together during the 1870s, learning from and inspiring each other. At the beginning Cézanne wanted to learn to observe nature in the same manner as Pissarro but, in the course of their work, their combined interests led them to more important developments. Both artists were reassessing the realism and expressive style of Courbet, whom they admired both as a painter and for his radical politics. A sensitive portrait of Cézanne by Pissarro of 1874 has been shown to express their political beliefs and includes a cartoon of Courbet in the background as well as a caricature from the leftist paper *l'Eclipse.*

Cézanne's influence is very obvious in *The Little Bridge, Pontoise,* but the style which Pissarro is imitating here was itself derived from Cézanne's study of Pissarro's earlier Pontoise series, so the influence is not all one-way. In those early paintings, such as *l'Hermitage, Pontoise* (see page 293), Pissarro had explored methods of representing spatial depth, particularly in the architecture, through interlocking zones of flat paint. Here, under Cézanne's influence, he applies the same method overall to the full range of subject matter and particularly to nature, by simplifying forms, colors, and values.

To produce these flat areas of paint, both artists worked with large palette knives, which also helped to broaden their approach; Lucien Pissarro remembered a package arriving from Paris containing two large knives for his father and his friend. Although Pissarro had used a palette knife before, he had not considered using it over the whole picture surface. A comparison of Pissarro's painting with Cézanne's *Etang des Soeurs* of the same time (opposite below), shows that Pissarro's sensitivity to nature made it hard for him to reduce the composition to basic elements, as in doing so they lost their importance as natural forms. Consequently, although Pissarro learnt from Cézanne, he did not pursue this particular method. But these experiments of the early 1870s renewed his interest in the surface texture of paint and introduced the idea of a unifying approach to brushwork, which he went on to exploit in the late '70s and early '80s.

Pissarro's admiration for Cézanne's work never diminished. It was with Pissarro's support that Cézanne exhibited in the first Impressionist exhibition in 1874 and, as an old man, in 1895, Pissarro wrote to Lucien about Cézanne's show in Paris "in which there were exquisite things, still lifes of irreproachable perfection . . . landscapes, nudes and heads that are unfinished, but yet grandly conceived and so *painted*, so supple. Why? Sensation is there."

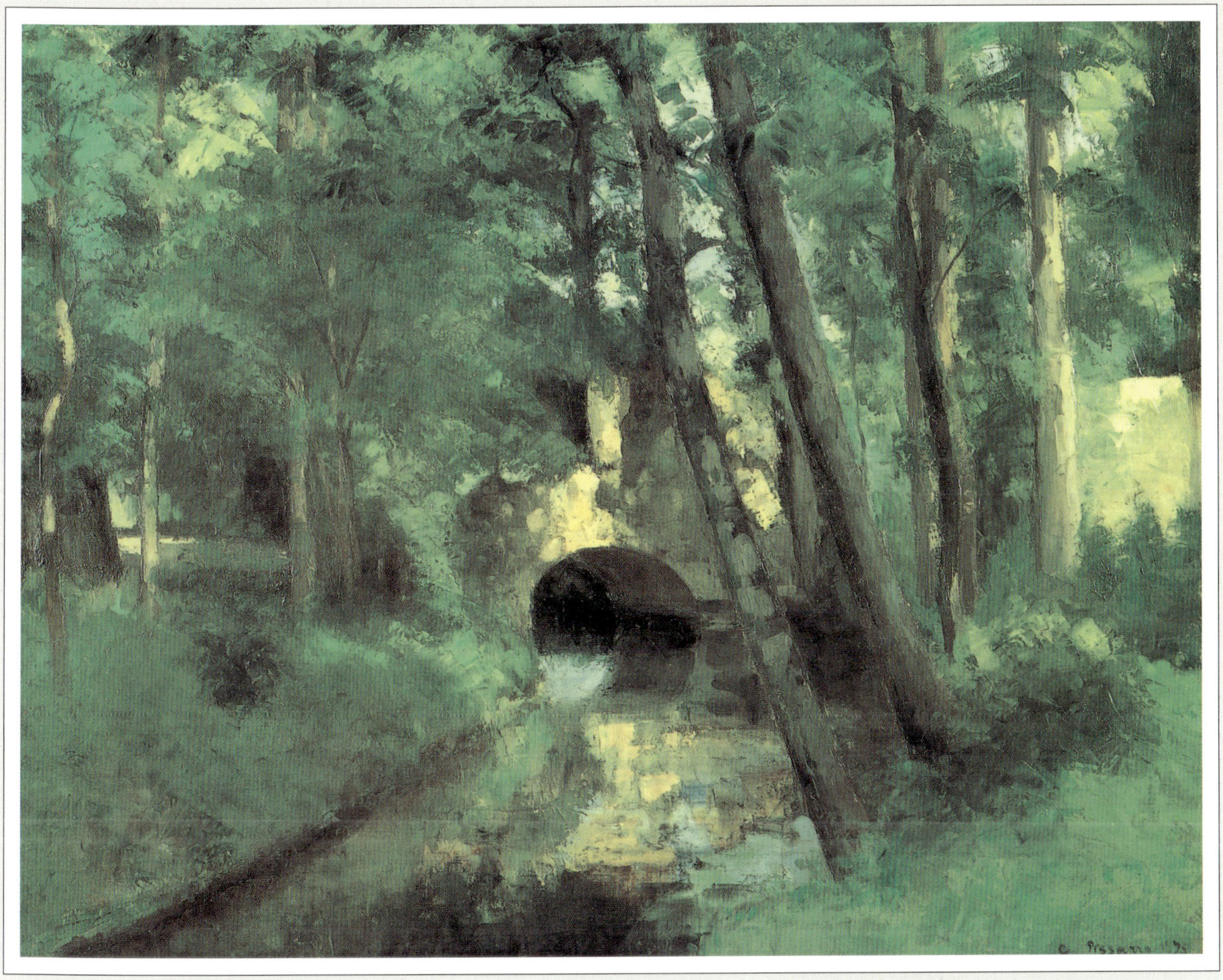

Painted at the height of Pissarro's close working relationship with Cézanne, *The Little Bridge, Pontoise* relates closely to a number of paintings by Cézanne of the same time, including *Etang des Soeurs, Osny* (below). Pissarro's sensitivity to the dappled light in this woodland scene has led him to use the painting knife and brush with more delicacy — but it could be said, less radically — than Cézanne. The forest greens are built up in layers from different directions, allowing the superimposed paint, like a scumble, to be qualified by that beneath. Pissarro is also more concerned with recession, leading the eye back by means of the stream. For Cézanne much of the interest centers on the surface pattern of knife marks. Such a study might have been painted *in situ* on a painting expedition and then touched up in the studio.

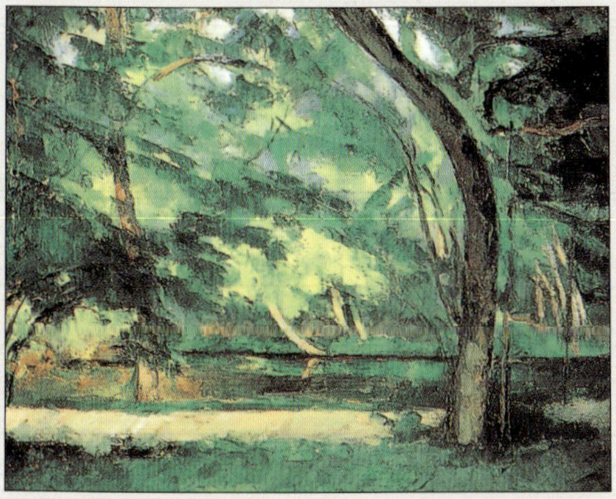

PAUL CÉZANNE
Etang des Soeurs, Osny
1875, Courtauld Institute Galleries, London

Cézanne in *Etang des Soeurs, Osny* (left), which was originally owned by Pissarro, uses the palette knife more rhythmically, unifying the painting with strong directional sweeps of the blade. After abandoning the palette knife, both artists eventually evolved a style of overall rhythmic strokes — Pissarro's juicy and shaped like a comma and Cézanne's more angular and constructivist.

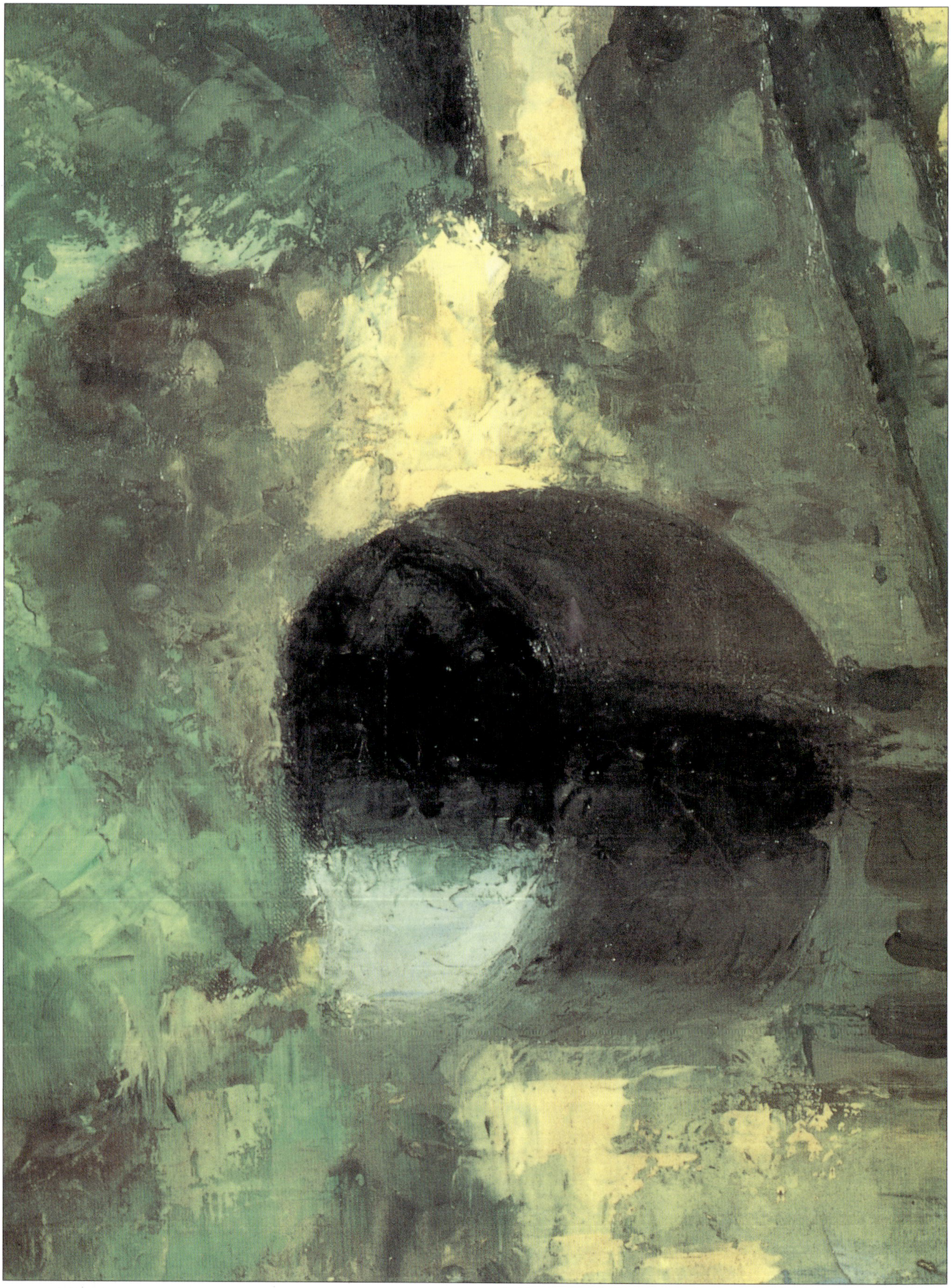

1 *Actual size detail*

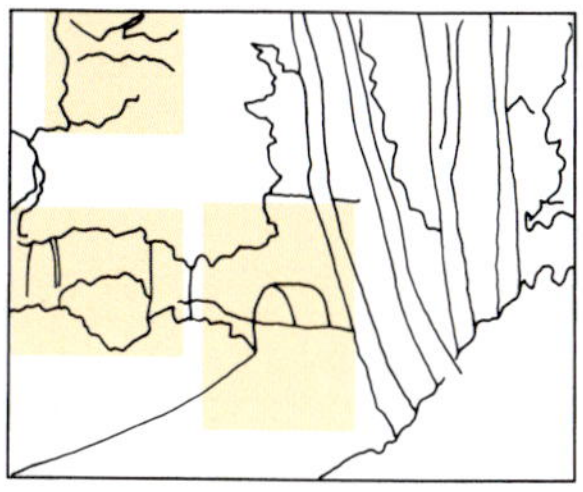

1 *Actual size detail* Perhaps under the influence of Cézanne, Pissarro's palette for this painting, although similar to that of earlier works with perhaps the addition of cadmium yellow, is used more boldly. In the central area of this painting, sizable blocks of strong color have been applied, skillfully capturing the fall of sunlight on the bridge and the reflections in the water. The bridge is a delicate merging of shades of ocher, working around a bright center of cadmium yellow. The yellow patches of reflection in the water are made by touching the edge of the knife on the canvas and then smearing the paint down. This merges with a strong ultramarine blue reflection of the sky.

2 The very intricacy of the build-up of greens in the foliage contrasts with Cézanne's broader sweeps of paint. Here the juicy smears are qualified with delicate patches of glazes applied with the knife, tips of opaque paint, and finally leaf-shaped dabs of the brush. The result is a rich area of texture and color.

3 A patch of sunlight in a clearing leads the eye through the mid-ground screen of trees into the background. The tree-trunks have been built up with thick paint using the edge of the knife and the brush. But note how ridges of paint which catch the light define the contours of the stylized curves of these trunks.

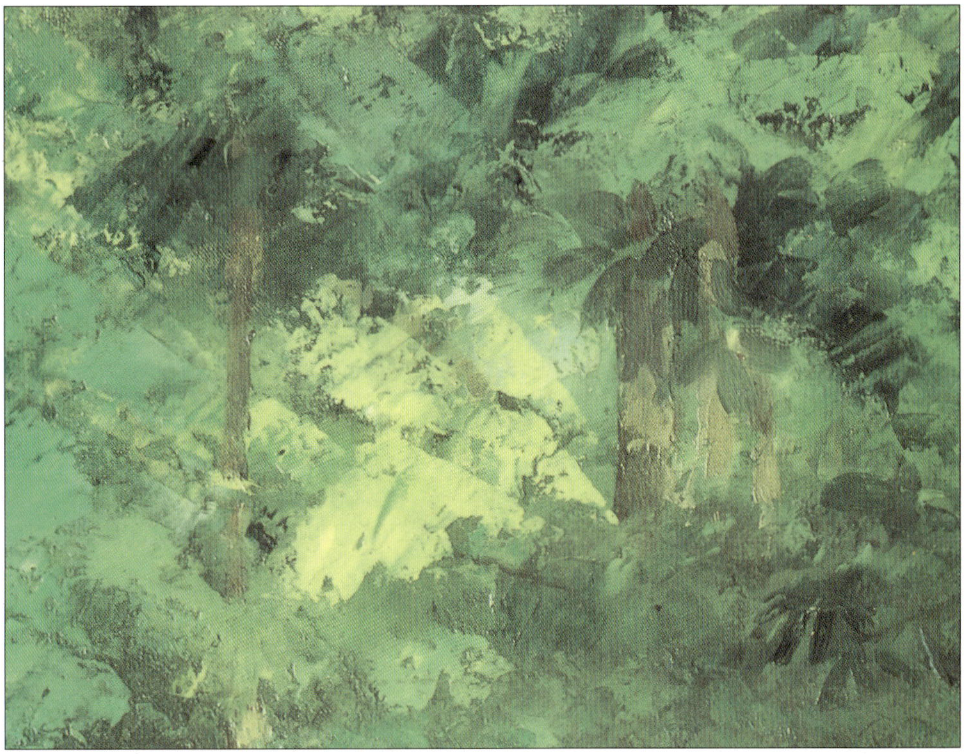

2

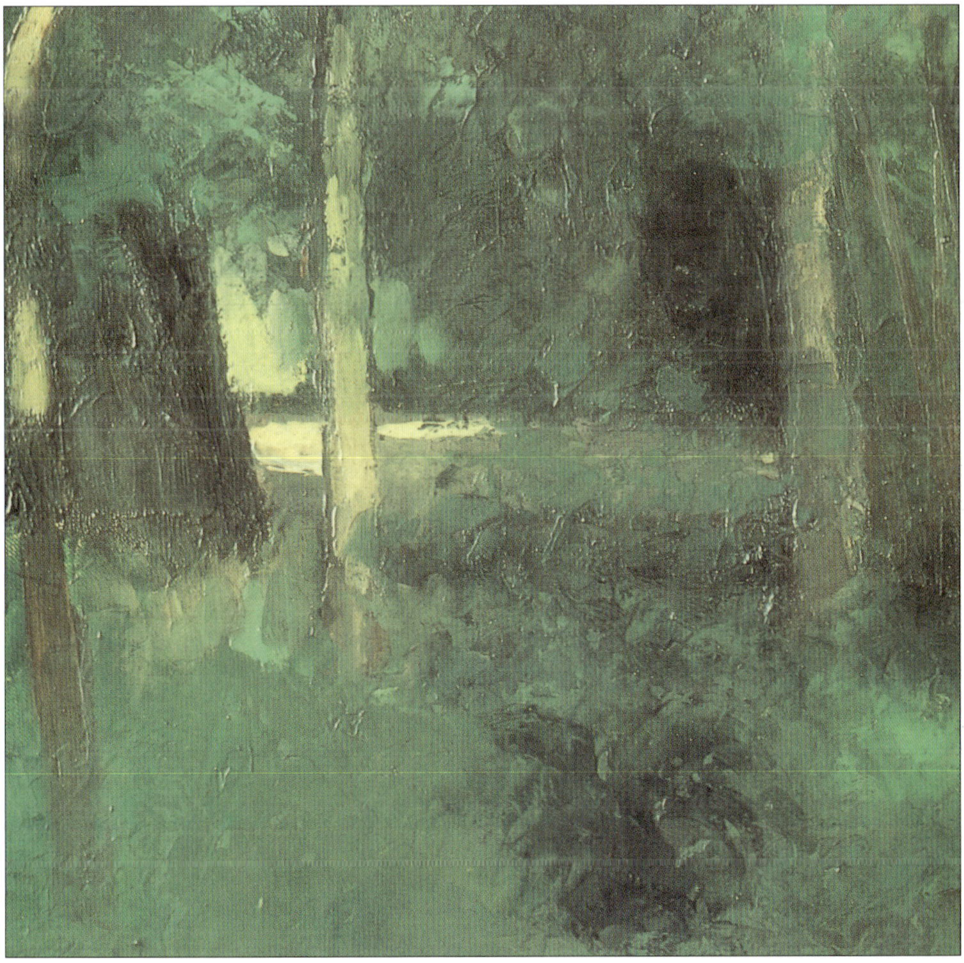

3

The Shepherdess

1881

$31^{7}/_{8} \times 25^{1}/_{2}$in/$81 \times 64.7$cm

Oil on canvas

Musée d'Orsay, Paris

Like other members of the Impressionist group, Pissarro, by the end of the 1870s, had become dissatisfied with his work and sought to introduce a more structured method to his painting. Perhaps in an effort to simplify the content of his compositions, he turned from the spatial problems inherent in landscape painting to portrait-like representations of peasant girls. These figures were usually set in an enclosed space, often against a backdrop of stylized foliage like that in *The Shepherdess.* During the early 1880s Pissarro concentrated on this theme, depicting peasants — mostly girls — talking, eating, working the land or, as in the case of *The Shepherdess,* just thinking. Although to the modern eye these peasant portraits appear more idealized and therefore more romantic than his work to date, at the time they were regarded as showing life at its most base.

Even in his earliest drawings, Pissarro showed a fascination for the everyday dreary drudge of peasant life. He loved the clamor of the marketplace and the dockside, drawing and painting the black cargo handlers in St Thomas and later the Indians in Caracas. In the countryside outside Paris, he found other, less picturesque, peasant tasks worthy of his attention — such as women digging, weeding, or washing dishes. It is not surprising that he found his ideas in tune with Anarchist ideology which upheld the work of the peasant — in harmony with nature and shared by others — as the ideal.

In his peasant girl paintings, Pissarro concentrates on the facial features and the detail of the clothing, focusing on the character of the person. *The Shepherdess* is a simple country girl, idling on a shady bank, but there is more to her than this: she is young and pretty and is shown in a wistful, rather sad mood. Some would say she was reflecting on the misery of her lot but Pissarro, with typical bourgeois misconception, would have seen her life as ideal. Pissarro's work of this time is often compared with that of Jean-Francois Millet. But although Millet also studied peasants at work, his paintings commenting on their plight, he did not have the same approach to realism as Pissarro, who saw the peasants as people rather than as symptoms of a social malady. Pissarro's peasant pictures are closer in conception to the figure paintings of Renoir and Degas. Pissarro was working with Degas in his studio in 1879, collaborating on a printing project, and it is possible that Degas' portrait-like studies of dancers at work inspired him, as his own were later to inspire Gauguin.

At the seventh Impressionist Exhibition of 1882 Pissarro exhibited thirty paintings, most of them figure studies, which were particularly admired by the influential critic J. K. Huysmans. But it was a different story the following year when *The Shepherdess* was exhibited in London by the dealer Durand-Ruel with ten other paintings by Pissarro and works by Renoir, Sisley, Morisot, Cassatt, Degas, Monet, and Manet. Despite the rantings of outraged critics, who thought Pissarro's work uncouth and unfinished, Lucien encouraged his father to exhibit again. "Alas, I shall never do more careful, more finished work," he lamented.

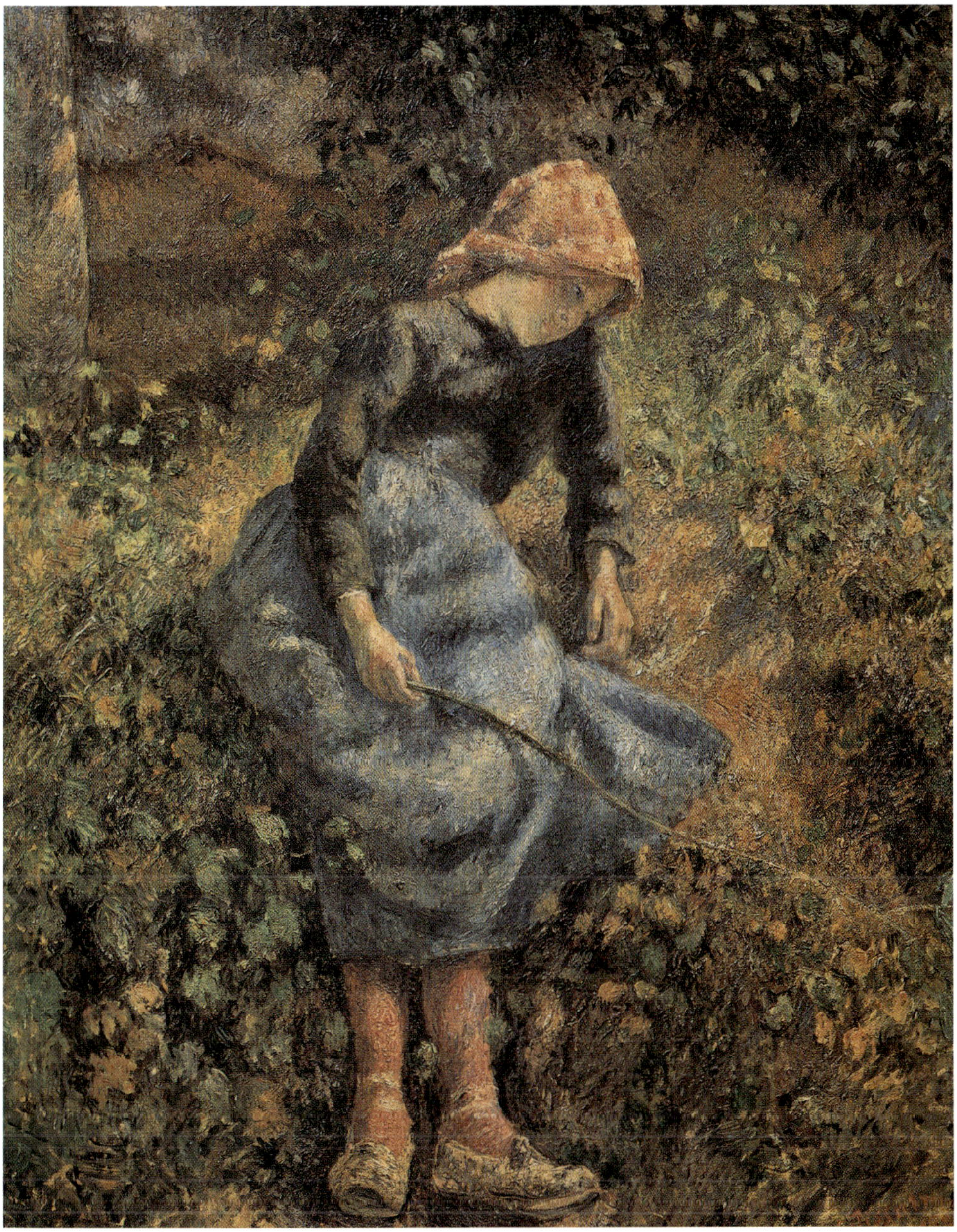

Pissarro's execution of *The Shepherdess* shows a development in his painting style from that of the late 1870s. The consistent comma-like brushstroke, formerly restricted to certain areas of the painting, now delicately fuses the picture surface, locking the figure into the background. Each area is built up from small strokes of color, sometimes worked wet-in-wet into the brushstrokes below to modify them, sometimes carefully placed alongside. In this way he captures the dappled sunlight playing on the pensive figure. The almost classical treatment of this figure in its solidity of form, dignity, and general restraint, combined with what was considered the base nature of the subject matter, proved a tantalizing combination for the younger generation of artists in Paris (in particular Gauguin) whom it was to influence greatly.

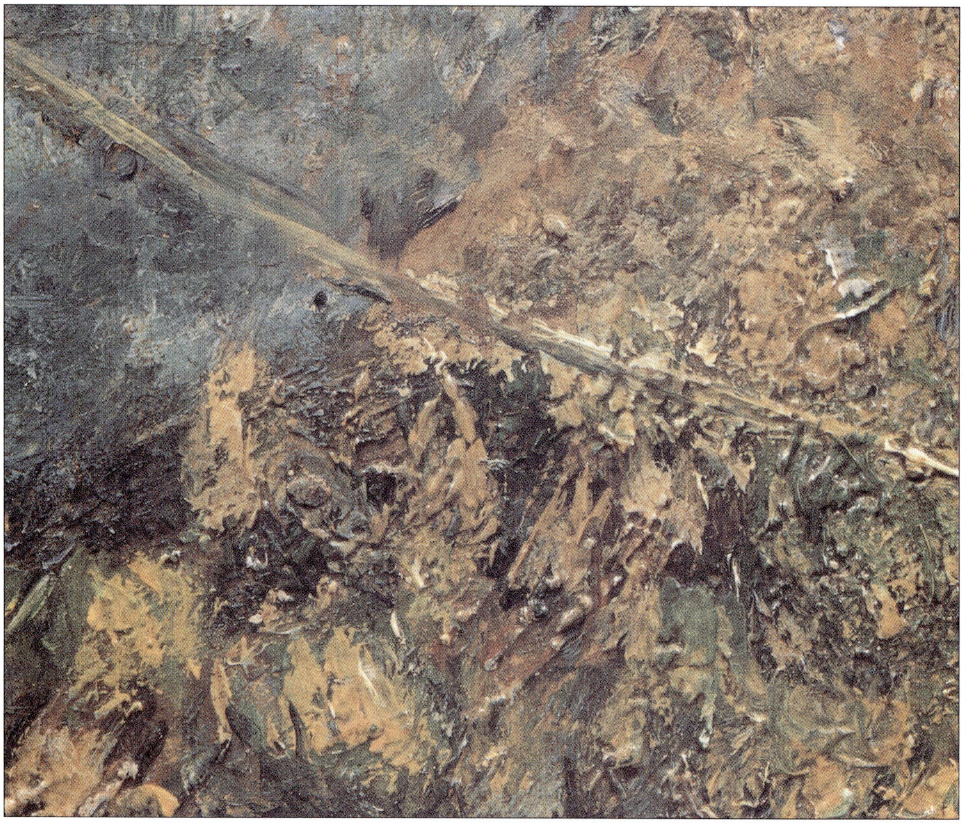

1

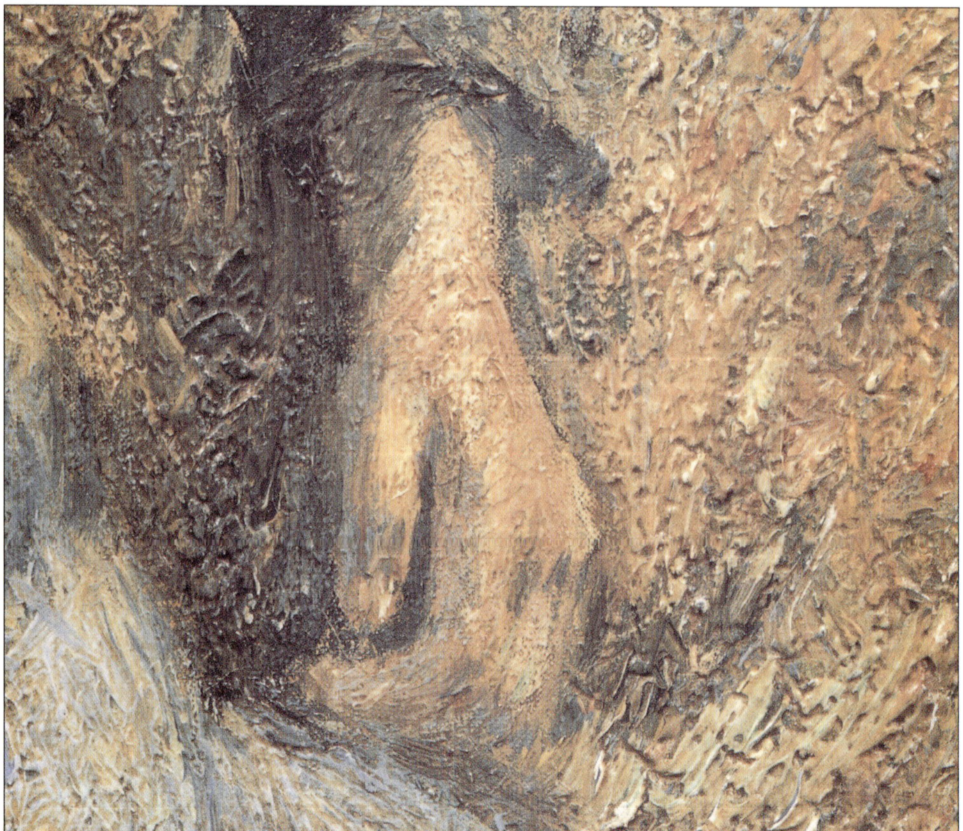

2

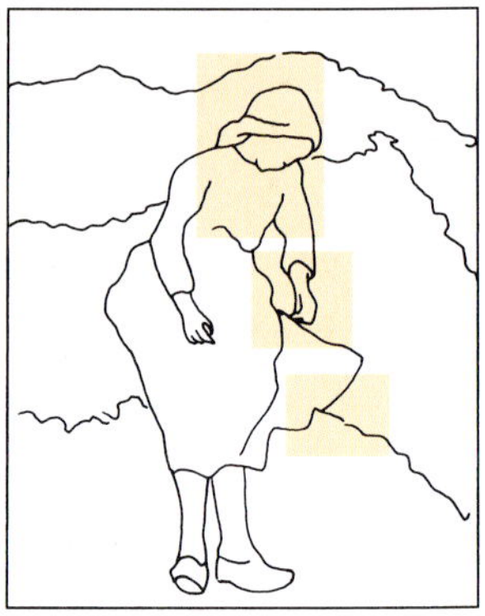

1 The glorious confluence of the painted background can be fully appreciated in this detail. A wide mixture of hues — sometimes pure greens, yellows, reds, blues, and blacks — are worked over and into each other. In places the dried impasto of an earlier layer appears contrary when superimposed on a thin stroke of color in another direction, but the result is a living area of paint of infinite depth.

2 Pissarro seems to dwell on the girl's overlarge peasant hands, but it is fairly likely that he admired them. Streaks of blue reflected from her skirt form the shadows on her fingers, whereas on her wrist the shadow is blacker, picking up the color of her shirt.

3 *Actual size detail* Pissarro is known to have kept a number of paintings going at the same time, allowing one to dry while working on another. In this way he could develop the exact color or tone he was seeking by working with wet paint on the dried surface below. Here the small hatched layers of strokes, crossing over one another to form a dense layer of paint, create a sense of solid form. However, the brushstrokes here, unlike those seen in his earlier work, do not describe the outline of the form but rather the play of light on it.

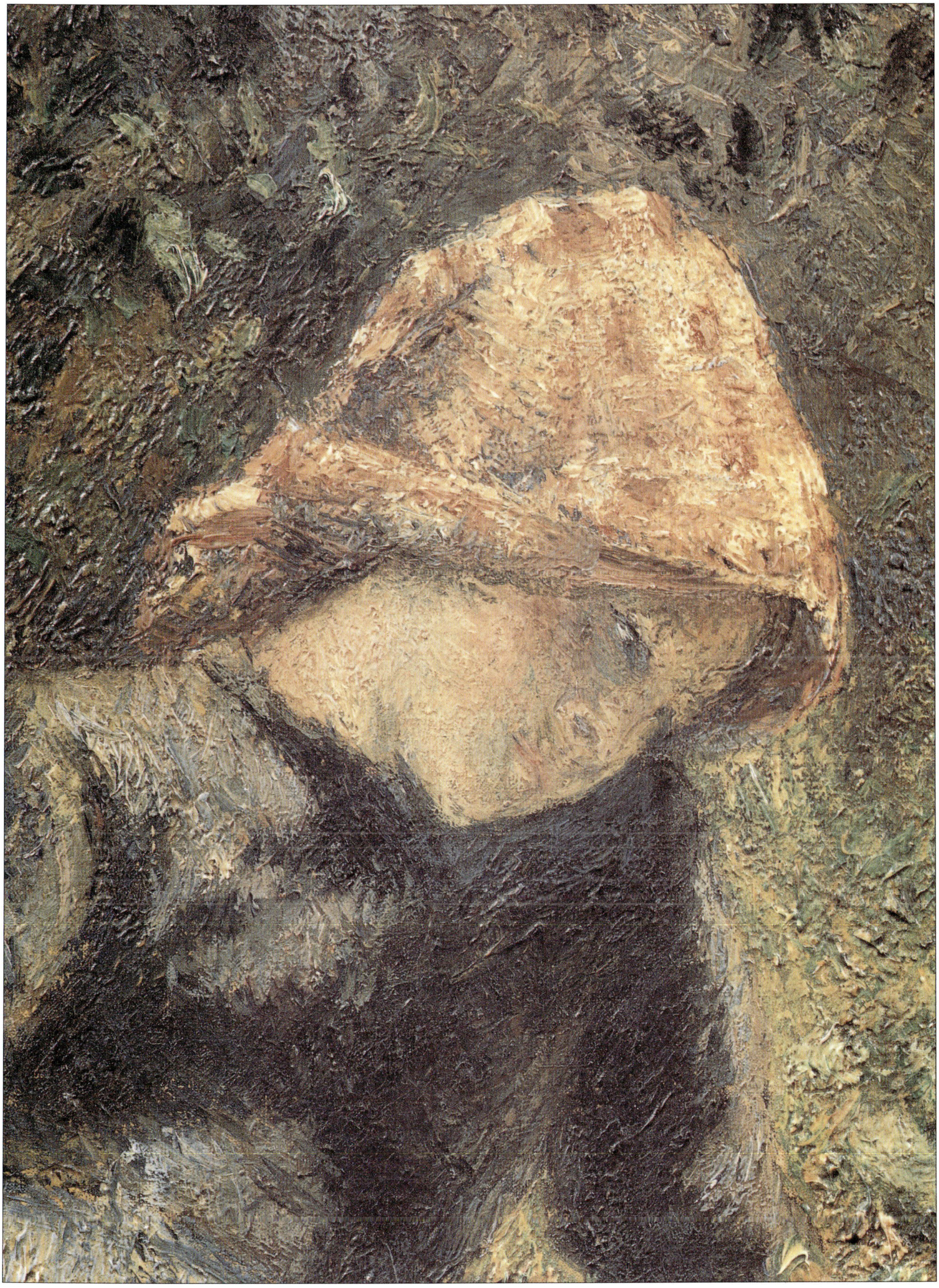

3 *Actual size detail*

The Quays at Rouen

1883

$18\frac{1}{4} \times 22$in/46.3×55.7cm

Oil on canvas

Courtauld Institute Galleries, London

Pissarro's visit to the city of Rouen in October 1883 was very important to him. It gave him a new perspective on life which inspired a large number of oil paintings, watercolors, drawings, and later etchings. This first visit may have been inspired by Monet's paintings of the façade of Rouen Cathedral of 1872, or it may have been encouraged by Pissarro's patron Eugène Murer, the Paris *restaurateur* and pastry chef, who befriended many of the Impressionists, in whose hotel in Rouen Pissarro stayed. Murer, by enticing the hard-up painters with his delicious food, had by the end of the 1870s collected many fine paintings including twenty-five by Pissarro.

Having concentrated on landscapes and the lives of country people up to this time, Pissarro's work from this first visit to Rouen, of which thirteen paintings survive, was to anticipate the major theme of the last twenty years of his life. These were scenes of Rouen, Paris, Le Havre, and Dieppe painted from the seclusion and shelter of an upstairs hotel room. This busy scene on the banks of the Seine, with barges lining the banks, loading and unloading their cargo, and smoking dock chimneys in the background, is typical of his later work. It is possible that the subject matter appealed to him because it related to his earliest drawings of cargo handlers in the port of Charlotte Amalie.

Unlike his intimate studies of country peasants painted at about this time, these descriptive paintings show his desire to remain aloof from the busy workings of the town. In contrast to Renoir's close-up figure paintings, showing Parisians at leisure and play, Pissarro's townscapes are populated with dark, faceless people – sometimes close to caricature – pursuing lives of drab monotony, many with the stooping shoulders of the world-weary.

In this painting, Pissarro comes close to perfecting the style of repetitive brushwork toward which he was working in the late 1870s. The picture surface is alive with closely worked small brushstrokes, yet in no place does the surface become overworked and muddled, as in some of his paintings of this period. The painting's unity is achieved firstly through the consistency of the brushwork over the surface and secondly by color, particularly dashes of strong viridian green and yellow ocher. There is much here that points toward Pissarro's imminent and radical change in style under the influence of the Neo-Impressionists. But his use of a consistent small brushstroke and pure color, always nascent in his work, shows that his style did not in fact have to change as fundamentally to accommodate their science-based theories as is sometimes supposed.

Writing to his son Lucien from Rouen in November, Pissarro expresses self-doubts: "I have just concluded my series of paintings. I keep looking at them. I who created them often find them terrible. I understand them only at rare moments." But not long afterward he writes in a more positive mood: "Result of my trip: I return with pleasure to my studio and look over my studies with greater indulgence with a better idea of what needs to be done to them." In *Bouquet of Flowers*, painted in 1898, Pissarro places this painting in the background, which shows he liked it enough to hang it, but also that it had not been popular with potential buyers.

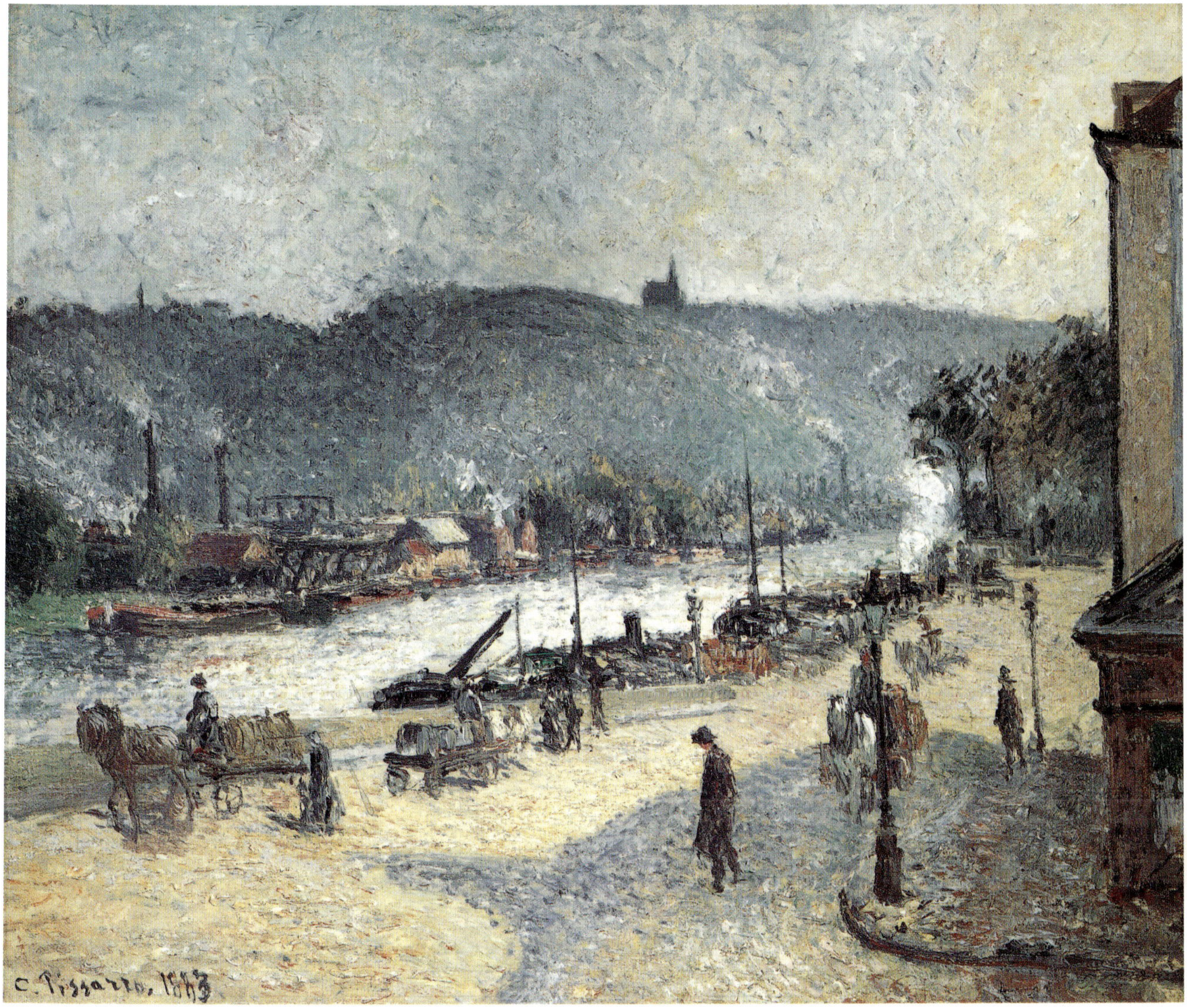

This scene of the quays at the cathedral city of Rouen was one of a series marking a new direction in Pissarro's work that was to absorb him fully in his later years. Painting unobserved from the upstairs window of a hotel room, he was able to make visual comments on the busy interchange of dock life. This bird's-eye view was in direct contrast to the closer viewpoint of his peasant girl "portraits" of the same time. The composition is divided into four horizontal areas of sky, hill, river, and road, broken with incidental verticals — chimneys, lampposts, masts, figures, and the strongly realized building on the right. The composition is unified, however, through the consistent brushwork over the whole surface of the painting. In addition, patches of white smoke and bright color throughout the painting — viridian, yellow, and vermilion in particular — help to integrate the disparate elements. Pissarro has cleverly broken up the expanse of road in the foreground with the shadow of a church spire and building out of the picture — a compositional device of which he was fond.

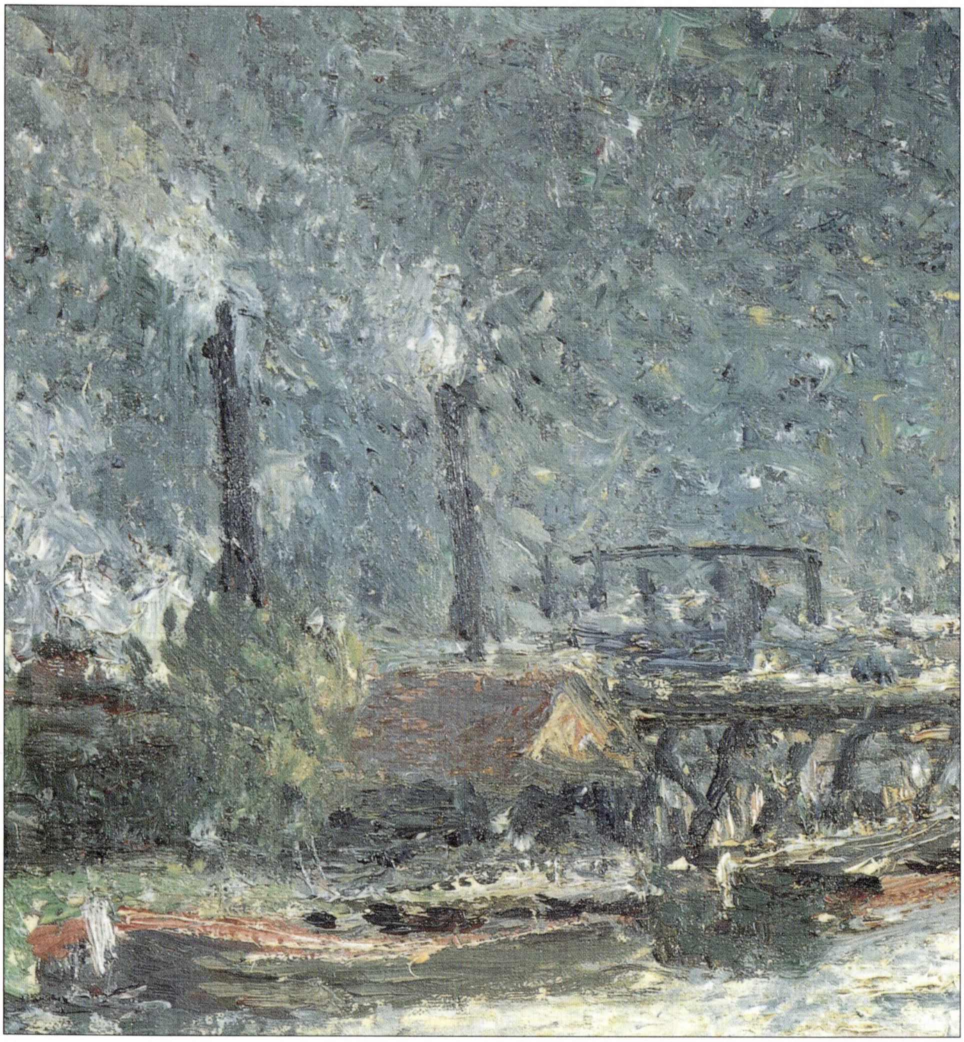

1

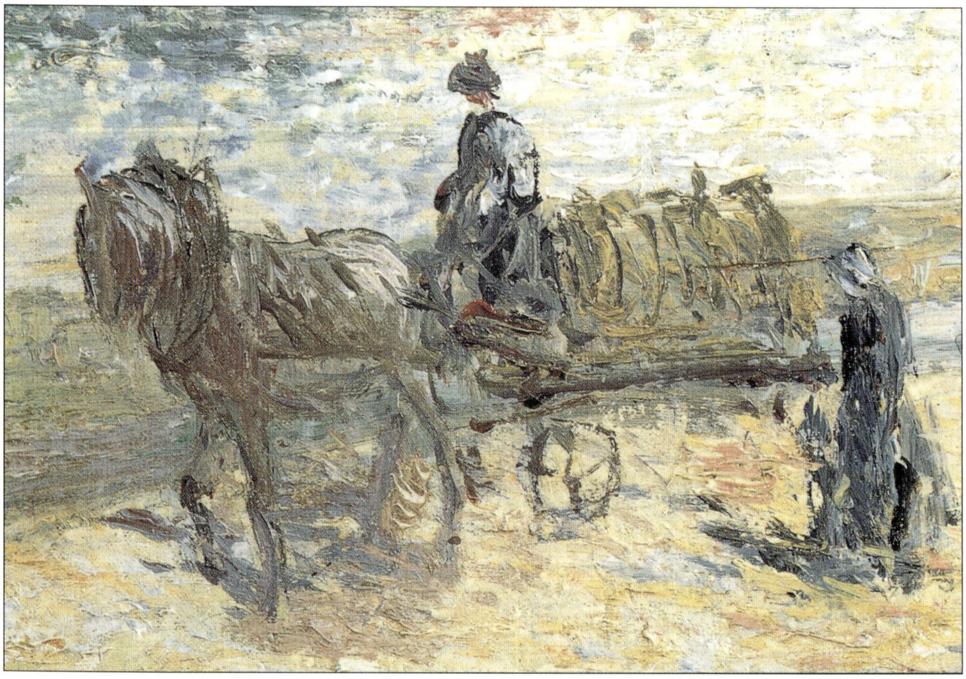

2

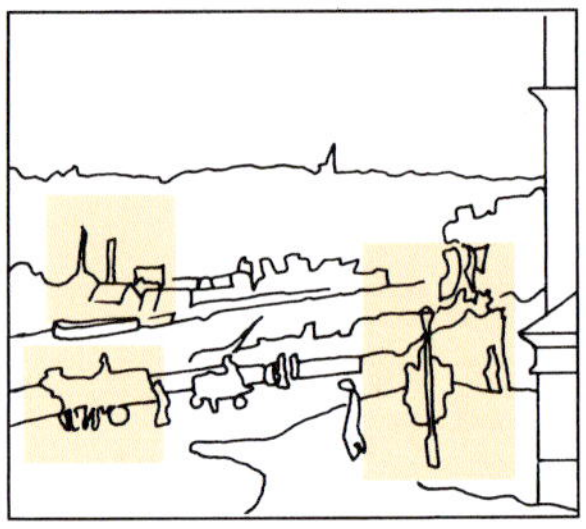

1 On the far bank of the river, the flat barges and belching factory chimneys contribute to the type of scene admired by Pissarro. Here the hues are reduced in strength with the addition of white, but the brushwork is no less lively.

2 The horse and cart and the small family group alongside, are skillfully portrayed, with admirable economy. Pissarro omits all unnecessary detail — the cart appears to have only one wheel and the horse no reins. Yet the eye fills in this information.

3 *Actual size detail* As if to draw attention to what might seem an insignificant part of the composition, Pissarro carefully explores the nuances of the shadow on the street corner. The deft brushstrokes, which appear to have been laid on with a small soft-haired brush, create a vibrant surface, while the street traffic is created with larger, more confident strokes — in higher contrast and more detail in the foreground than in the background. To emphasize the sense of recession, Pissarro has built up the foreground with layers of increasingly small strokes of strong color. In the background, the paint is more thinly applied and in bolder strokes.

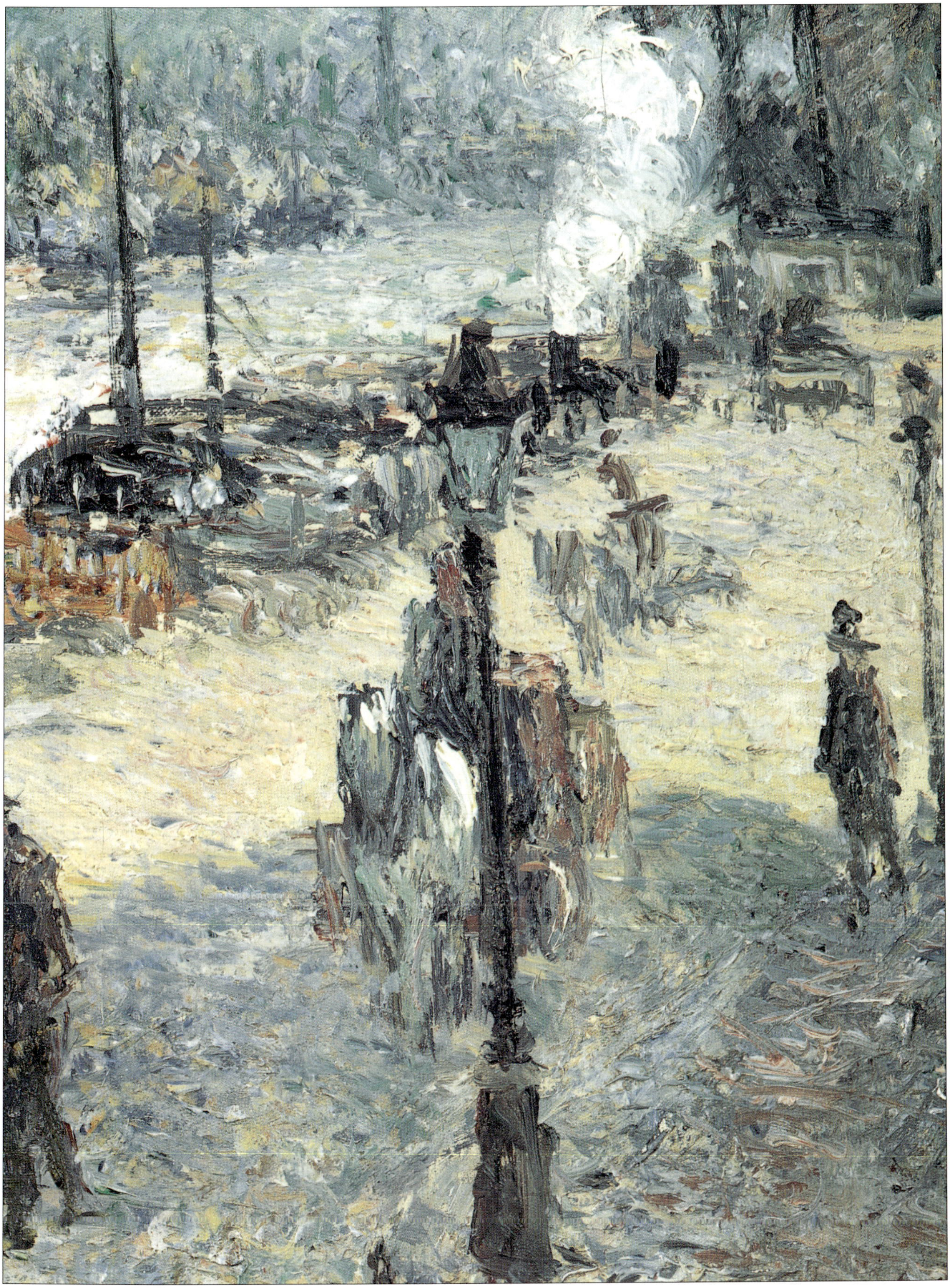

3 *Actual size detail*

The Boulevard Montmartre at Night

1897

$20^3/_4 \times 25^1/_2$in/53×65cm

Oil on canvas

National Gallery, London

Although living and working in the countryside for most of his life, Pissarro kept a studio in Paris when he could afford it. However, with a few exceptions, he showed no interest in the city as a subject for painting until the last twenty years of his life. It seems that the visit to Rouen in 1883 (see page 308) captured his imagination and , when in 1888 he contracted an eye infection which obliged him to reconsider his working methods, he decided to turn his attention to a study of urban themes. He had always considered painting from nature *(en plein air)* of the greatest significance to his art, but his eye was irritated by both light and cold, particularly wind. This meant that except on warm still days he had to work from the shelter of an interior, and finding such a room, with a view that could sustain his interest, led him back to the city. Monet also painted scenes of Waterloo Bridge from the Savoy Hotel in London in his old age.

Typically, Pissarro tackled his new-found subject with great enthusiasm, writing to Lucien in 1897: "I am delighted to be able to paint these Paris streets that people have come to call ugly, but which are so silvery, so luminous and vital." But he did not restrict himself to views in Paris; he also spied down from hotel windows on the lively streets and ports of Rouen, Dieppe, and Le Havre, painting many of the scenes depicted by the Impressionists in their early years. He even took up early Impressionist themes as well, studying the effect of weather and passing time in series of paintings, as Monet was doing at much the same time.

In early 1897 Pissarro established himself in the Grand Hôtel de Russie, Paris, close to his old studio in rue des Trois-Frères. Here, working from an upstairs room, he painted thirteen views of the Boulevard Montmartre (and later made a lithograph), showing it in different weather conditions and at different times of day, but only once at night. Here he captures in bold brushstrokes of color the fashionable life of this busy street on a wet night, the road a pattern of luminous grays and blues; and the sidewalk reflecting the lights of the cafés and restaurants.

For Pissarro these late urban themes solved one of the overriding problems of his early landscapes — that of depicting recession. The architectural structure of a Paris street gave his paintings a natural spatial depth, leaving him free to concentrate on other aspects of the painting. Here he leads the eye into the dark void with lines of dancing lights — the street lamps, the lines of carriages, and the watery reflections on the sidewalks. He enforces the receding lines of the street and buildings with tonal extremes — dark shadows and bright lights — and eliminates the detail of the boulevard buildings, even reducing the picturesque skyline of the rooftops on the right to a harsh black line.

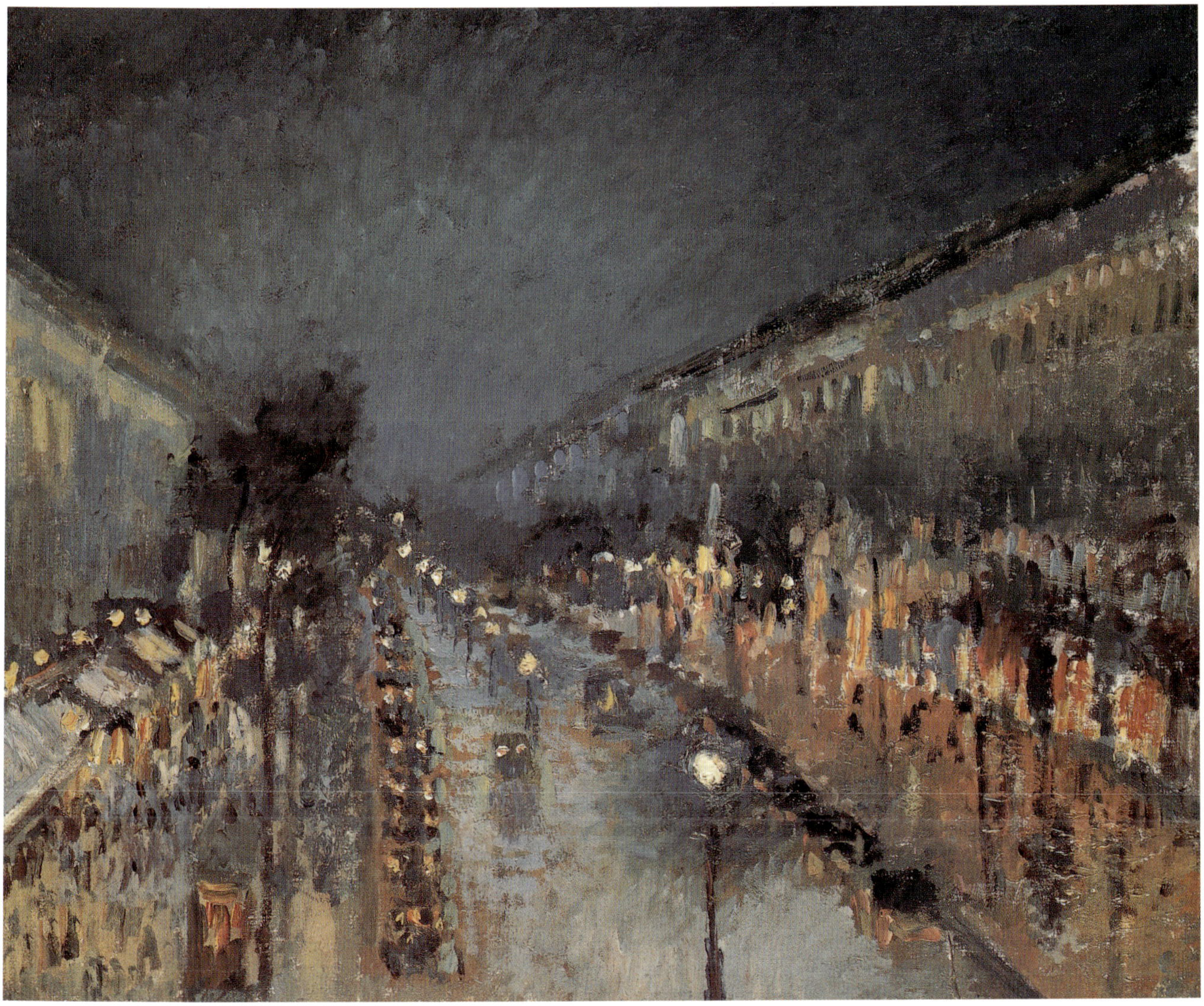

In the last two prolific decades of his life Pissarro suffered from a recurring eye infection and was forced to paint indoors. But the formula he had discovered in Rouen in 1883 of painting city life from the seclusion of an upstairs room continued to prove a source of inspiration. Like other members of the Impressionist group, notably Monet, Pissarro took to painting series of a single scene in different weather conditions. In 1897 he painted a series of the Boulevard Montmartre from a room in the Grand Hôtel de Russie. This lively night scene – the only one in his *oeuvre* – is more like an oil sketch than the others in the series, which are painted in the dense impasto typical of his later years; he seems to have worked quickly in an attempt to capture the lights and silvery reflections in the wet street before they disappeared.

1 *Actual size detail*

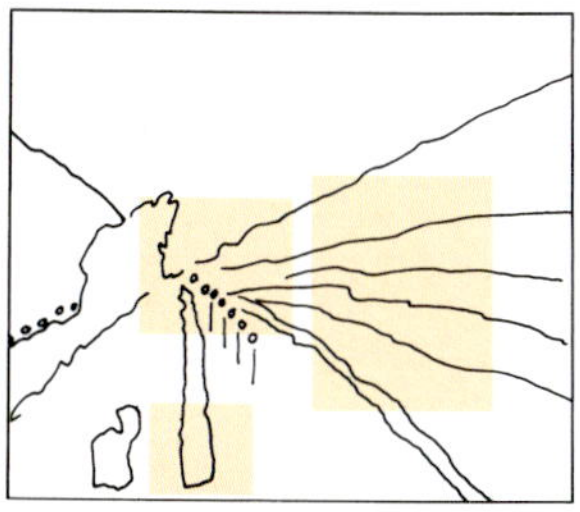

1 *Actual size detail* Pissarro seems to have battled with this perverse street lamp — it dominates the foreground of twelve of his thirteen views of the boulevard. (In his crowd-packed vision of the street at *Mardi gras*, he takes the unprecedented step of omitting it for "cosmetic" reasons.) The build-up of impasto and the surrounding circle of light draws the eye to the center of the canvas, to survey the scene in its entirety. The bright lights of nighttime Paris are boldly expressed in vertical strokes of juicy paint.

2 Pissarro was always concerned with recession into the picture space, and here the paint is in general more thinly applied in the background. The exception is the thick impasto of the street lamps, which help the illusion of space by leading the eye into it. The pulsating area of deep violet blue where the lines of the street converge also helps to draw the eye into the picture.

3 The silvery reflection of light on the wet surface of the boulevard is created with a scumble of pale blue over a layer of interwoven flat strokes of pinky browns. A few carefully placed strokes of color describe the line of oncoming carriages.

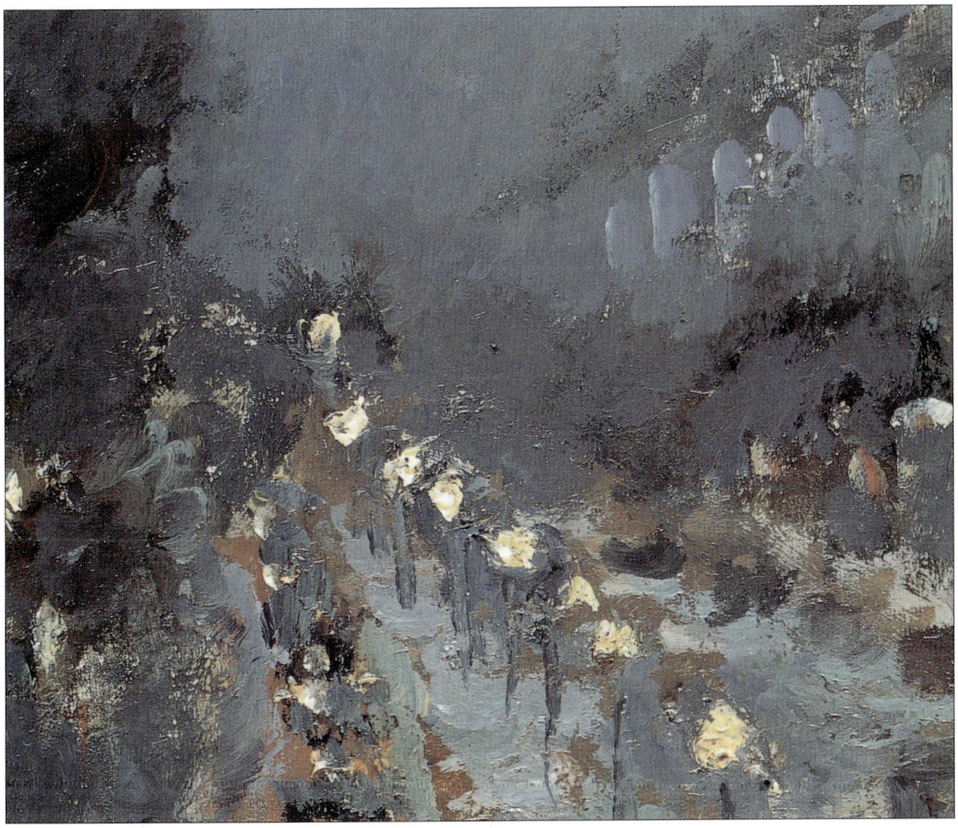

2

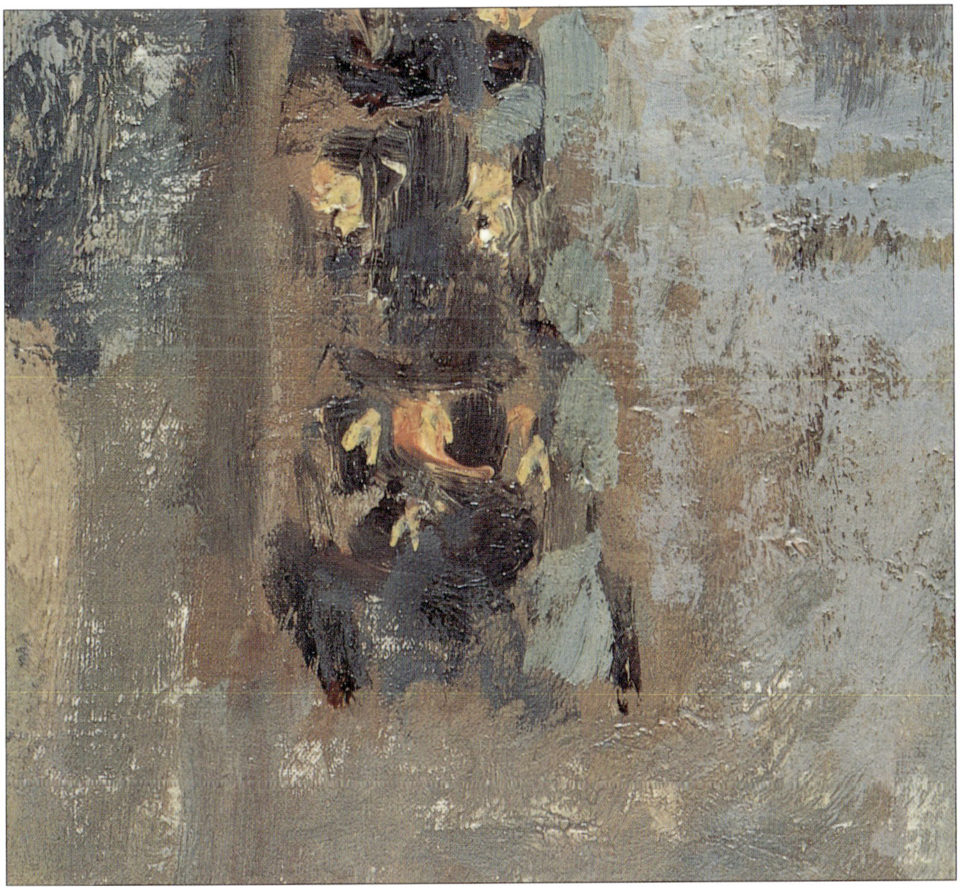

3

SELF-PORTRAIT

1903

$16^{1}/_{8} \times 13^{1}/_{8}$in/$41 \times 33.3$cm

Oil on canvas

Tate Gallery, London

Even in the last years of his life Pissarro never lost the impetus to work. "Work is a wonderful regulator of mind and body. In the joy of working, I forget all sorrow, grief, bitterness, I even ignore them," he said. So for this dignified self-portrait, which turned out to be his last, it is appropriate that he shows himself seated at the window of his Paris studio at 28 Place Dauphine, behind him the busy streets of the city which inspired the paintings of his last years.

Pissarro seems to have made no concessions to his old age. He spent each summer of his last years painting the docks from hotel windows; in 1901 and 1902 in Dieppe, in 1903 in Le Havre. He was as active selling his paintings as he was painting them, withholding the whole of his Dieppe series from his dealer Durand-Ruel when he found that the latter was conspiring with the Bernheim Jeune gallery to keep the prices down. In the summer of 1903 he sold two canvases to the Museum at Le Havre. By this time Pissarro had found acceptance, and his work was sufficiently highly regarded for forgeries to be on the market, signed with an inaccurate "Pissaro." His work had found its way into more respected museums; Gustave Caillebotte, an amateur painter and great organizer of the Impressionist exhibitions, bequeathed on his death his fine collection of Impressionists to the Musée du Luxembourg in Paris, who were unwilling to accept it. After a heated debate, they were exhibited in 1897, in effect the first public showing of the work of the Impressionists.

In October 1898 Pissarro traveled to Amsterdam, where he viewed the Rembrandt exhibition. It is possible that he drew inspiration from the self-portraits of the ageing artist, particularly in the attitude of the sitter, who seeks the attention of the viewer but at the same time remains aloof. Pissarro painted three self-portraits in these last years, and in addition was sculpted by the dentist-sculptor Paulin, and it is tempting to believe that he was motivated by similar feelings to those of Rembrandt's dignified elderly sitter Jacob Trip, who had his portrait painted at least six times, it is thought in an effort to provide as many as possible of his twelve children with something to remember him by.

Pissarro appears a little frail in this last portrait, but the glint in his eye is evidence of his unquenchable spirit. Here we see Pissarro the patriarch, as perhaps he wished his children to remember him: upright with a steady look, his white beard flowing over his chest. As in his portrait of Julie, he takes advantage of the window setting and the *contre-jour* light which forms strong contrasts, as well as the compositional arrangement offered by the frame, which breaks up the background.

The view through the window, seen in reverse because it is painted from the reflection in a mirror, is of the houses on the site of the present Samaritaine department store by the Pont Neuf. It is painted in muted, soft colors, in contrast to the dark interior, but the blurred image does not take attention away from the sitter.

Pissarro has executed this self-portrait with confidence and a facility which barely indicates his age. Except for the face and areas of impasto highlighting, the paint is applied in thin dabs, allowing small areas of the grayish primed canvas to show through. The winter coat and wide-brimmed hat, in which Pissarro was also sculpted by Paulin, is built up in superimposed brushstrokes of black, with blue and green, and even red.

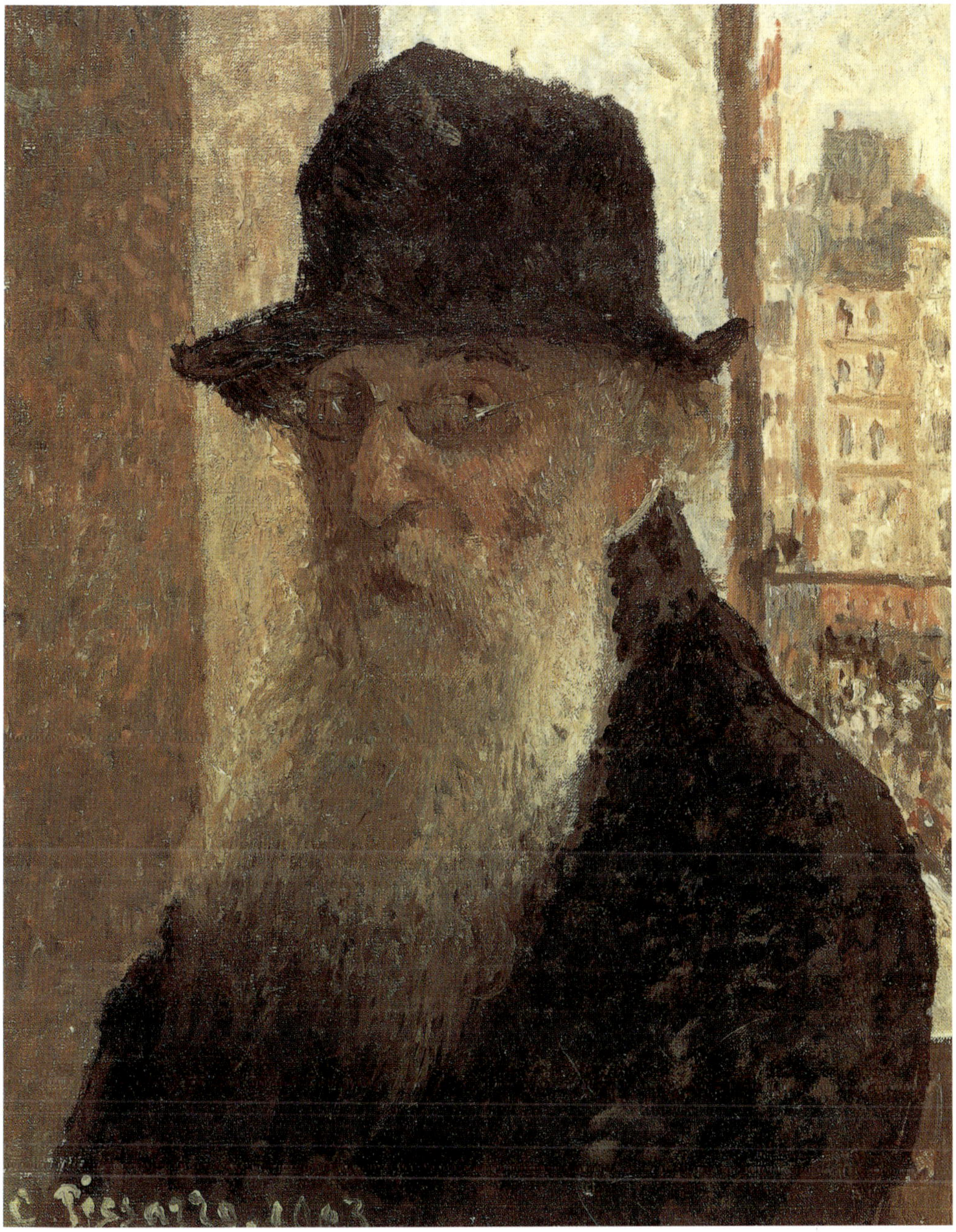

This touching self-portrait, executed in Pissarro's Paris studio at 28 Place Dauphine in the last months of his life, bears witness to his strength of purpose — at the grand age of seventy-three he was still painting continuously. His piercing eyes, here shown peering over his half-moon glasses, were evidently no less observant, and the precise and delicate brushwork is a testimony to the steadiness of his hands. The marvelous build-up of the flesh tones, with carefully placed strokes of pure color, and the precise placing of highlights demonstrate the facility and confidence with which he was painting at this time.

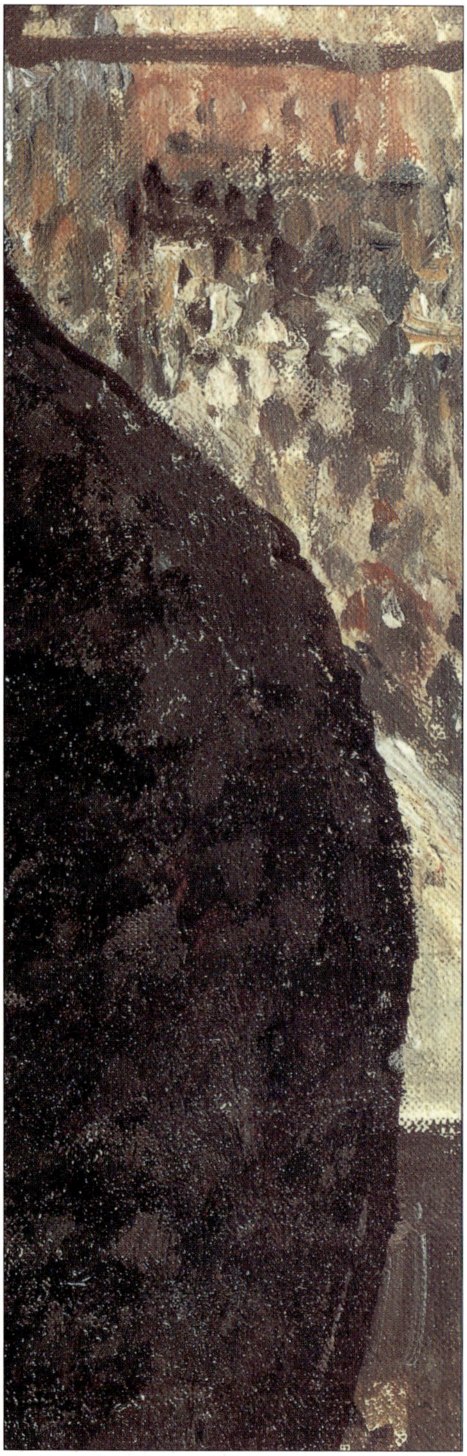

1

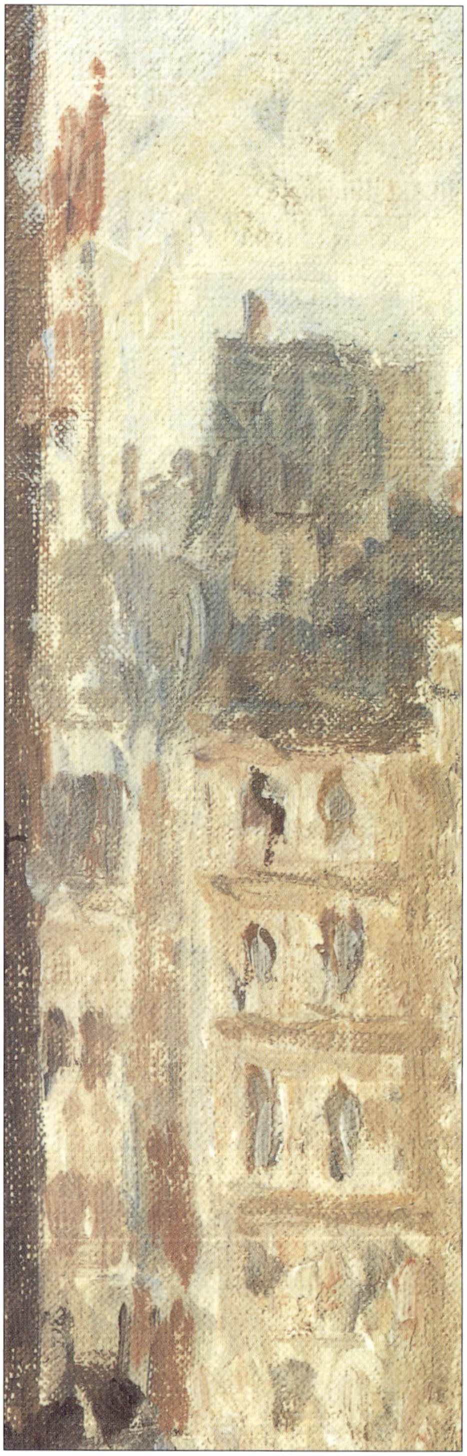

2

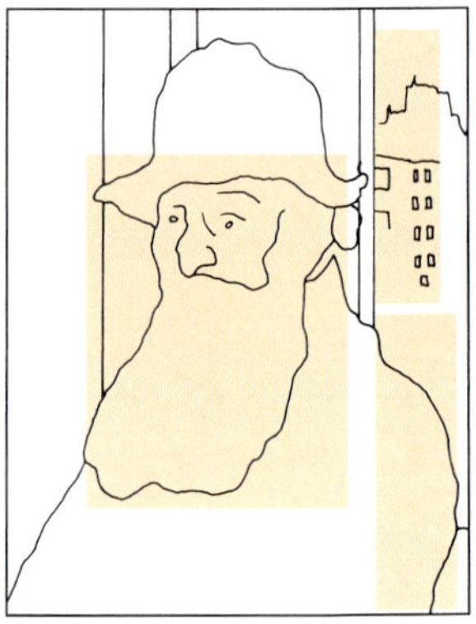

1 The strong outline of the first mapping out of the composition visible along the shoulder line shows Pissarro's confident grip. His coat is built up from a flat layer of dark gray stippled over with a darker layer of dabs with a flat hog bristle brush. Accents of vermilion and ultramarine spike this potentially dull area of black.

2 Through the window, the houses of what is now the Samaritaine store by the Pont Neuf are viewed in reverse, as painted in a mirror. By sketching them in muted, bleached colors, Pissarro has ensured that attention is not drawn away from the commanding portrait.

3 *Actual size detail* Areas of flat tone have been laid in on the face and then built up with delicate parallel strokes – mixtures of vermilion, white, umber, and ocher combined on the palette. The paint appears to have been diluted with medium except for the impasto highlights and the delicate lines of dark brown added with a very fine brush to delineate the features. Pissarro's bushy beard, which turned gray when he was forty-three, is cleverly conceived in layers of sparse dabs to evoke a sense of volume without substance. Except in a few strokes around the mouth and on the coat, Pissarro avoids the more obvious linear conception of the beard.

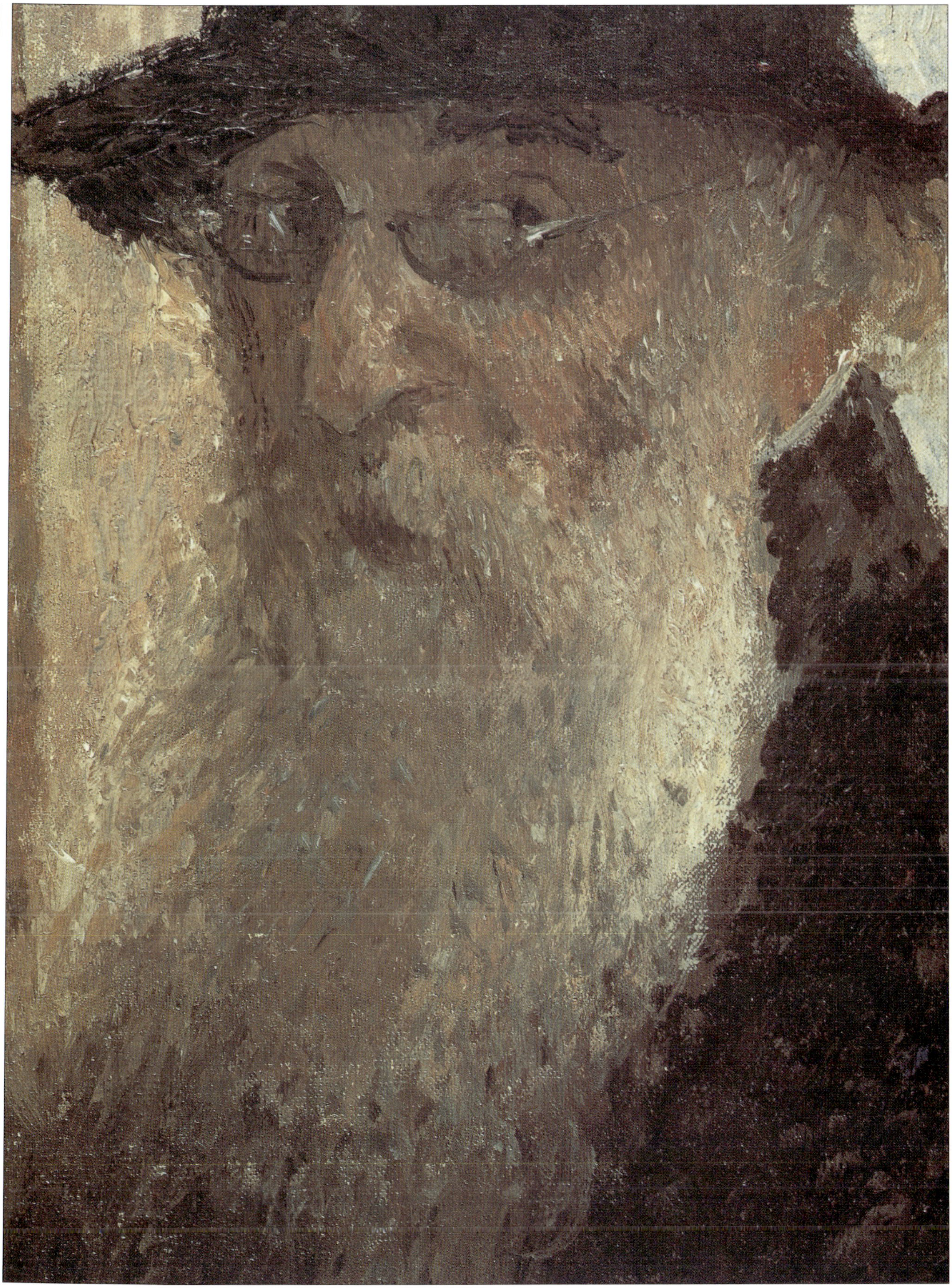

3 *Actual size detail*

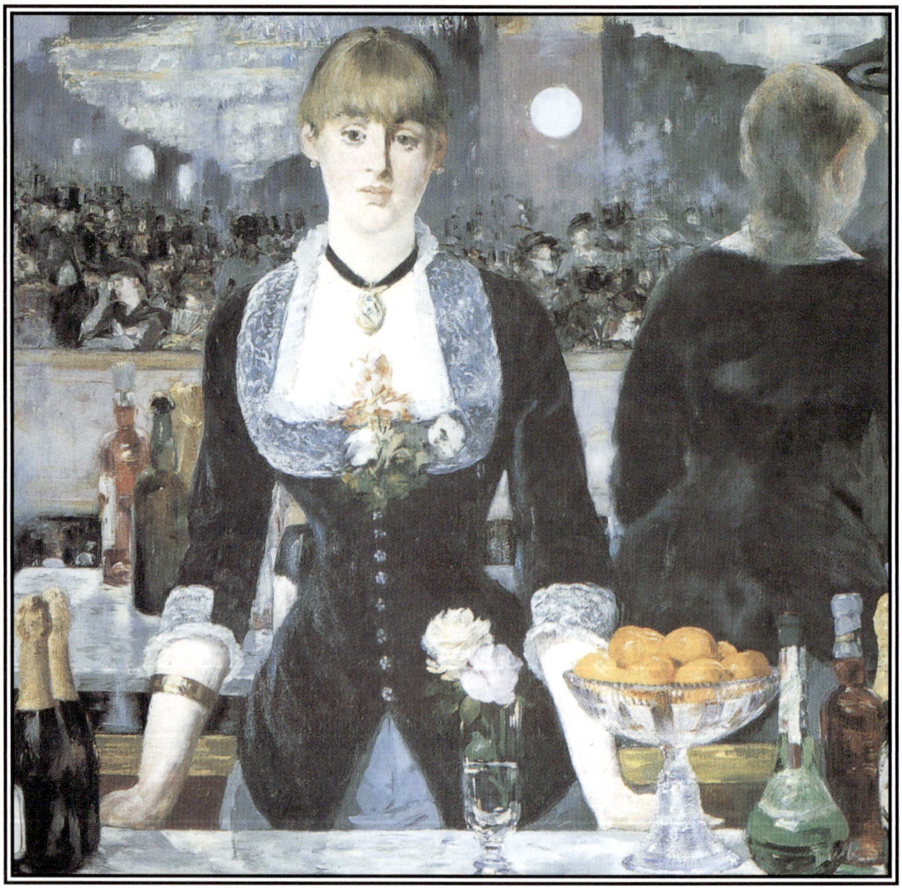

MANET

Introduction

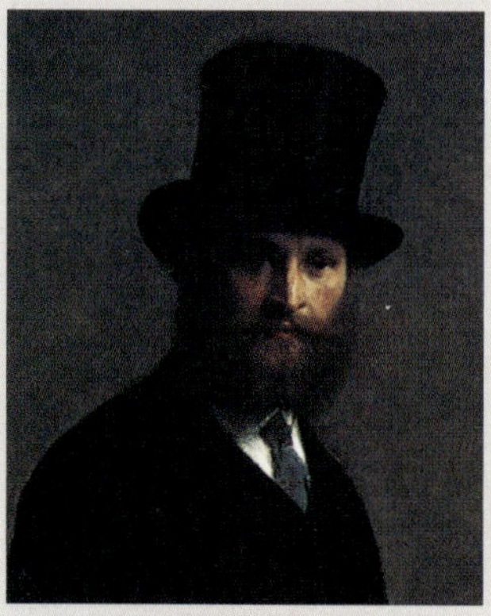

Henri Fantin-Latour
Portrait of Edouard Manet
1867, Chicago Art Institute

Modern art begins with Manet. His legacy to the latter half of the 19th century affected every artist of note, and as Renoir said, for the Impressionists he was what Giotto or Cimabue were for the artists of Renaissance. To the generation that succeeded him Manet seemed to have invented an entirely new kind of painting, completely breaking away from the earlier tradition of depicting the external world accurately within the accepted style of the day. Manet claimed to paint what he saw, but he introduced two elements that were to alter the history of painting for ever. The first was the transformation of the image into a highly personal vision, entirely at odds with the contemporary style, and the second was the recognition of the essential artifice of painting, which was also stressed by Edgar Degas. This was put into words by another artist, Maurice Denis, in 1890. "Remember that a picture — before being a war-horse, a nude woman or an anecdote — is essentially a flat surface covered with colors assembled in a certain order."

The new art

Manet's new approach encouraged other artists, particularly the Impressionists, to consciously interpret their sensations of nature, instead of merely reproducing an image with the greatest possible degree of accuracy. It also led to an entirely new way of seeing the role of painting, so that subsequent generations could acknowledge it as an autonomous and personal art form rather than a vehicle for public preaching, edification or storytelling. After Manet, a painting could be whatever the artist chose it to be.

By the middle of the 19th century both artists and writers had become increasingly aware that a new direction was needed in art. Painting had become sterile and irrelevant to modern life, and the poet Théophile Gautier spoke for many when he said that "Today art has at its disposal only dead ideas and formulas which no longer correspond to its need. Something must be done, but what?" A similar sentiment was expressed by Victor Hugo after the revolution of 1848. "Poor great France, unconscious and blind! It knows what it does not want, but does not yet know what it does want." The poet Charles Baudelaire, later to become Manet's close friend, shared this sentiment. "The great tradition is lost," he said, "and a new one not yet created."

Manet took on the role of pathfinder, pointing the way forward by rejecting the academicism instilled by traditional teaching. He painted, not historical or mythological subjects, but the world he saw around him. His technique, like his subject matter, broke all previously accepted rules: he radically rethought methods of composition, handling of color and tone, brushwork and the treatment of light. His paintings, with their acid, often disconcerting juxtapositions of strong color, their harsh lighting and elimination of half-tones, bold brushstrokes, absence of detail, deliberate flattening of form and inconsistencies of scale, combined with his choice of subject matter to outrage the gallery-going public. People were accustomed to highly "finished" works, in which colors were subtly blended together, brushwork was so smooth as to be virtually invisible, and nudes were given respectability by appearing in the guise or nymphs from classical myth or figures in biblical narrative. One has only to compare Cabanel's highly **acclaimed *Birth of Venus* (opposite) with Manet's *Déjeuner sur l'herbe* (see page 337) to see the difference between the old art and the new.**

Student years

Edouard Manet, the eldest of three sons, was born into the cultured Parisian bourgeoisie; his father was a prominent magistrate in the Ministry of Justice and his mother, the daughter of a diplomat, was an amateur musician. His father's first wish was for his son to follow his own footsteps into the legal profession, but the young

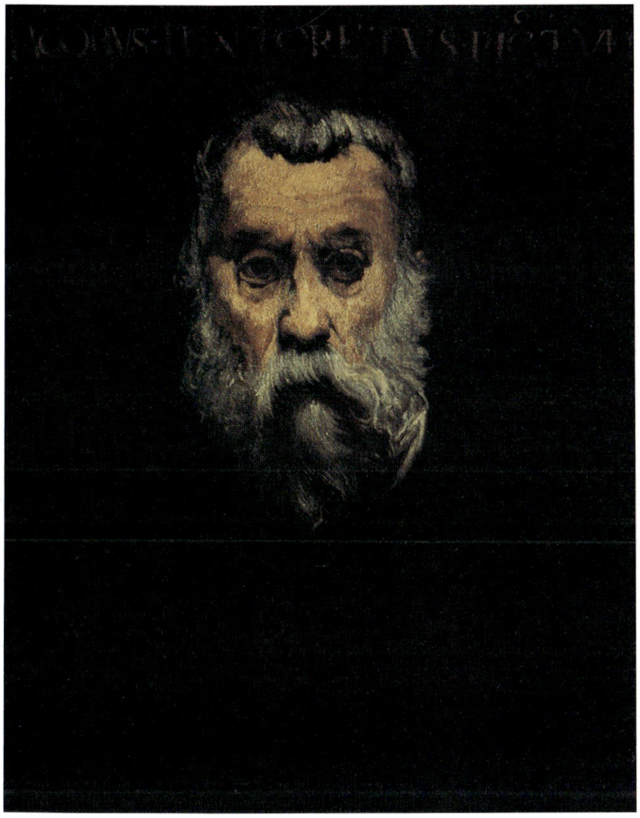

EDOUARD MANET
Self-portrait after Tintoretto
1854, Musée de Dijon

Manet's earliest known works are copies of the Old Masters. His teacher Thomas Couture guided his students towards the painterly techniques of artists such as Titian, Tintoretto, Velasquez and Delacroix. Manet considered Tintoretto's self-portrait the most beautiful portrait in the world, and always stopped before it in the Louvre.

Manet's enthusiasm for drawing had led to a neglect of his studies, and his scholastic record was indifferent. The second option was a career in the navy, but after failing two sets of naval exams Manet succeeded in persuading his father to let him study art.

In 1851 he entered the studio of Thomas Couture, a portrait and history painter, whom he had chosen in preference to the prestigious but stultifyingly academic Ecole des Beaux Arts. Unfortunately he found little inspiration with his chosen master, and studied under him with increasing frustration for six years. As at the Beaux Arts, the students were set to copy plaster casts of classical statuary, and when professional models were hired they were arranged in exaggeratedly heroic poses.

"Everything we are given to look at is ridiculous," Manet complained. "The light is false, the shadows are false. When I arrive at the studio I feel as if I were entering a tomb." A fellow student, Antonin Proust, described a quarrel with one of the male models. "What! Can't you be more natural?" Manet shouted at the naked man. "Is that the way you would buy a bunch of radishes at the greengrocers?" The model, choking with anger, reminded Manet that it was thanks to him that several artists had won the Prix de Rome, the highest and most coveted award, which gave young artists the opportunity of studying in Rome at the French Academy. Manet's retort – "We're not in Rome now and we don't want to go there. We're in Paris; let's stay here" – reveals his scorn for the blind acceptance of classically inspired tradition. A thoroughgoing Parisian, he sought inspiration from his own city, not from rules dictated by academies. "It's only too easy," he said, "to accept ready made formulas, to bow

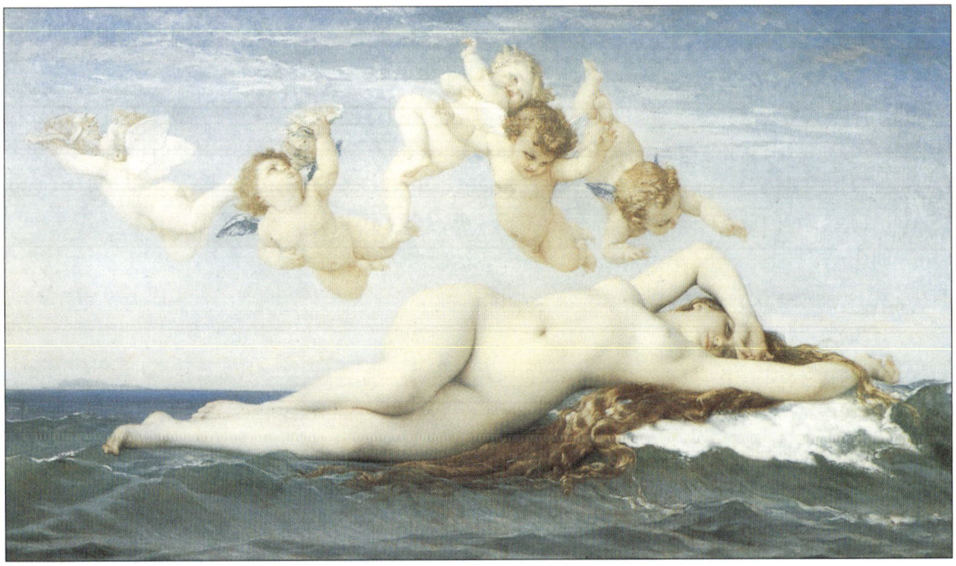

ALEXANDRE CABANEL
Birth of Venus
1862, Musée d'Orsay, Paris

Highly acclaimed by the Salon of 1863, this painting exemplifies the type of titillating nude, painted in a polished and highly finished style, appreciated by the gallery-going public in the mid-19th century. The eroticism of this Venus was acceptable because it was given respectability by the classical framework, while Manet's *Déjeuner sur l'herbe* (see page 337), exhibited the same year, was found shocking both in style and in content.

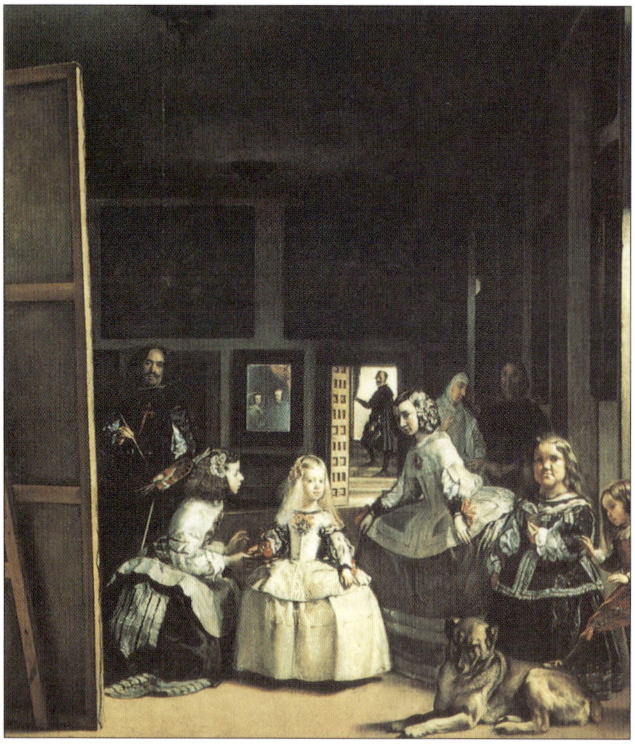

DIEGO VELASQUEZ
Las Meninas
1656, Prado, Madrid

Manet had a lifelong admiration for Velasquez, calling him "the painter to beat all painters." He described this work as an "extraordinary picture," and wrote that "I have found in the work of Velasquez the realization of my ideal in painting." He borrowed Velasquez' somber tonalities and his use of luminous blacks and grays, also imbuing his own canvases with the apparent spontaneity of the master's work.

down before what's called 'ideal classical beauty,' as though beauty were something constant. Beauty, of course is always changing . . . beauty is something malleable."

Unlike the majority of painters, Manet realized his personal style at an early age. Proust recalled the remark of a fellow student at Couture's that "There's a fellow called Manet who does some astonishing work but doesn't get on with the models." Even his earliest works show a boldness of composition and handling, with a preference for the single figure and a liking for the somber, dramatic arrangements of Tintoretto, Le Nain, Velasquez and Goya. But although he was admired by the students, he was a source of irritation to his master. On one occasion Couture, upbraiding him for posing the model in his own clothes instead of naked, and in a naturalistic rather than heroic pose, told him he would never be more than the Daumier of his day. Manet replied that he would rather be a Daumier (a painter of everday subject matter, a cartoonist and social satirist) than a Coypel (an 18th-century history painter).

The Parisian dandy

Manet spoke little and wrote less about his art, but it is a testimony to his culture, wit and intelligence that he was the intimate of three of the century's greatest literary figures, the poets Charles Baudelaire and Stéphane Mallarmé and the novelist Emile Zola. It is from Baudelaire, whom Manet had met by 1858, that we learn most about the artist, and he is often seen as Manet's spokesman, particularly in what he called the "heroism of modern life." The cult of the dandy, the stroller on the boulevard and frequenter of cafés, concealing his life of the imagination beneath an urbane and immaculate exterior, was also extolled by Baudelaire and practiced by Manet.

The young Manet of the 1850s personified the stylish, well-bred man-about-town, and Proust has left us an appealing description. "Edouard Manet was of medium height and physically very strong. There was a rhythm in the way he moved, added to which his particular rolling walk gave him a peculiar elegance. Even when he tried to exaggerate this rolling walk and assume the drawl of the Parisian street urchin, he could never succeed in being vulgar. One was always conscious of his breeding. His forehead was broad, his nose drawn in a bold straight line. His mouth, turned up at the corners, was mocking . . . Few men have been as attractive as he."

All his contemporaries agree that Manet was not only attractive but also immensely likable; he was reported as retaining his smile, "like a schoolboy in love," even in his final illness. And yet, as Renoir noticed, "the incomprehensible thing is that Manet, so gentle and affectionate, was always attacked, whereas Degas, so vitriolic, violent and uncompromising, was accepted by the Academy, the public and the revolutionaries." Discreetly generous financially to friends in need (he had some private means), Manet also appears to have done the decent thing by his Dutch mistress Suzanne Leenhoff. She had been brought into the Manet household to give piano lessons, and the young Edouard, only a year or two her junior, had begun a liaison with her. In 1852 she bore a child, whom she named Léon-Edouard, initially passing him off as her godson and later as her younger brother. It is generally assumed that he was Manet's son. His mother knew of the affair, though it was concealed from his father, and Manet married her in 1862, a year after his father's death.

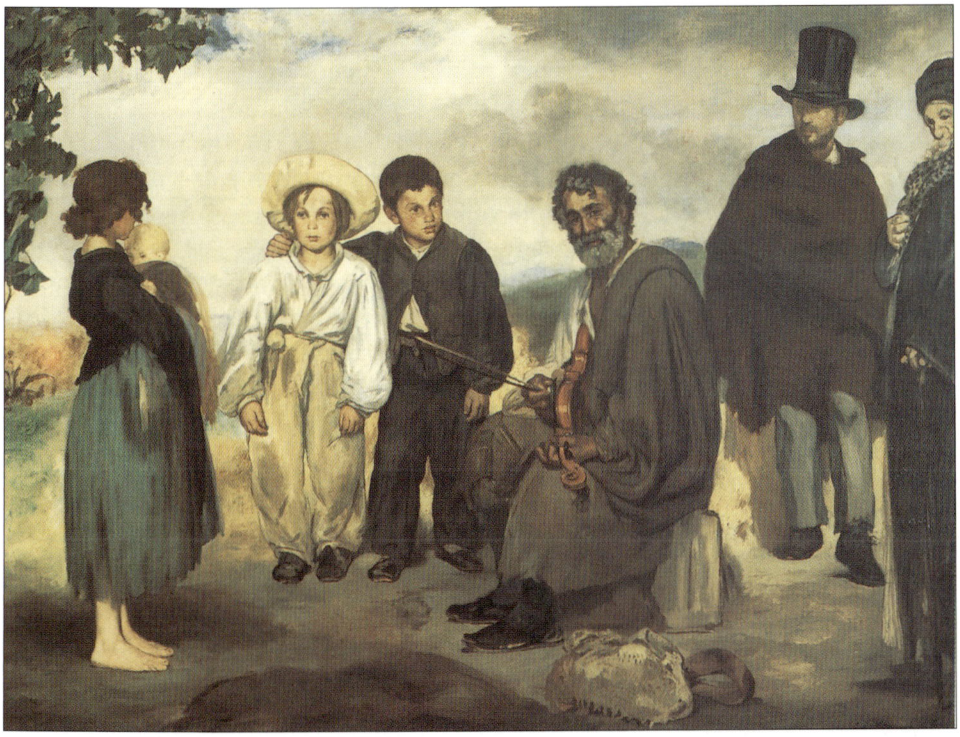

EDOUARD MANET
The Old Musician
1862, National Gallery of Art, Washington

Manet was working on this painting at the same time as ***Music in the Tuileries Gardens*** **(see page 333). The latter portrays the upper section of** society, while this work depicts its poorer members, whom the new city developments were uprooting. The figures of Manet's own *Absinthe Drinker* and the barefoot girl carrying a baby, someone who inhabited the "Little Poland" area around Manet's studio, are combined with those of the Wandering Jew, the Old Musician, and Gilles the sad clown character, derived from Watteau, here protected by a dark twin.

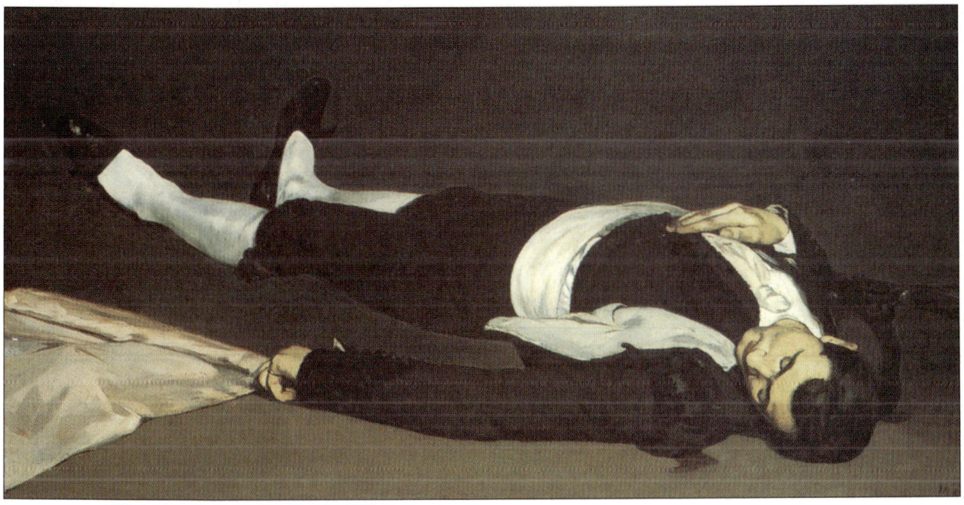

EDOUARD MANET
The Dead Toreador
1863, National Gallery of Art, Washington

This painting is the center of a much larger canvas which Manet cut down for dramatic effect, isolating the single figure spread diagonally across the canvas. The influence of Velasquez is clearly apparent; this work may even have been inspired by a painting in the National Gallery, London, formerly attributed to the master. It depicts a dead soldier in an identical pose executed in the same coloring, tonal values, lighting and brushwork.

The influence of Spanish painting

In 1856 Manet left Couture's studio and travelled to visit various collections of great masters, journeying first to Holland, Germany, Prague and Austria and then to Italy. Although he did not reach Spain until ten years later, Spanish painting had formed a powerful influence on him since the start of his career, and his earliest biographer, Edmond Bazire, explains that although "his travels abroad were interrupted, he contented himself with daily visits to the Louvre. There he was deeply impressed by the Spaniards. As soon as he had become thoroughly acquainted with the works of Velasquez and Goya, fresh perspectives opened up before his eyes. After studying these pictures, where black becomes luminous, he began to show a new awareness of the quality of light, and from that moment, all his former research was upset . . . But Spain was nagging at him now, and suddenly he grasped it with both hands. Whilst respecting its art, he wished at the same time to rejuvenate it, and from ancient moulds he fashioned something new."

By 1867 over half of Manet's work was on a Spanish theme, and he was dubbed the "Spanish Parisian." Velasquez was the artist he admired above all others, and he singled out the Spanish master's *Little Cavaliers* (now thought to be by the painter's son-in-law, Mazo). "Ah! That's clean. How disgusted one is with these stews and gravies." What attracted him was the robust handling of color, the bold brushwork and the dramatic contrasts, so very different to the dead colors and smooth polish of the paintings admired by the Ecole des Beaux Arts.

The *Absinthe Drinker* of 1859 demonstrates his radical departure towards a new means of pictorial expression. The Spanish flavor is evident in the somber coloring, the lack of background detail and the use of black, while the foreground bottle is a direct echo of Velasquez, who often included still-life detail in both his portraits and his religious paintings. Manet showed the picture to his erstwhile master, and although Zola maintained that Couture's influence could be seen in the "studio technique," Couture himself was unimpressed. "The only drunkard is you," he said, a sneer which marked the end of their relationship.

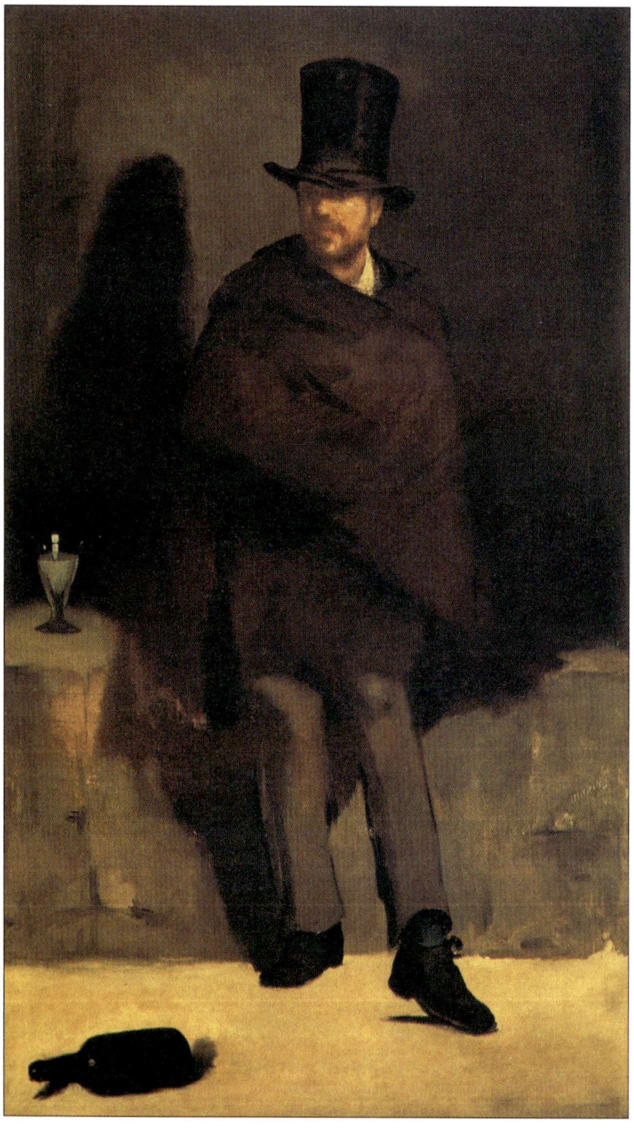

EDOUARD MANET
The Absinthe Drinker
1858-59, Ny Carlsberg Glyptotek, Copenhagen

This painting was rejected by the Salon of 1859. The influence of Couture is evident in the treatment of the face, and the somber coloring echoes that of the Spanish masters. Manet himself explained that, "I have made a Parisian type, observed in Paris, while putting into execution the technical naïveté I found in the painting by Velasquez. They do not understand. Perhaps they will understand better if I make a Spanish type." He made no reference to the bizarre arrangement of the sitter's left leg and foot, which has invited much complex interpretation.

This was the first painting that Manet sent to the Salon, but like so many of his later works, it was rejected, being criticized for the very features that were to become the hallmarks of his art. The jury objected to the dramatic coloring, innovatory treatment of space and eccentric choice of subject, the "cult of systematic exaggeration," as one jury member put it. But although the subject certainly contrasted with those found acceptable at the Salon, it was completely in accord with Baudelaire's advocacy of a new kind of art depicting contemporary themes.

New concepts of space

Manet always longed to be accepted by the art establishment, and continued to submit works to the Salon, but he never achieved the kind of fame he envisaged. His painting *Music in the Tuileries* (see page 333) caused an uproar, as did the two subsequent works, *Déjeuner sur l'herbe* (see page 337) and *Olympia* (see page 341). In 1863 the Salon rejected over 4000 paintings, including all Manet's entries, and the indignation of the artists was so vociferous that Napoleon III ordered the rejected works to be displayed in the galleries adjoining those of the Palais d'Industrie, which housed the Salon. It became a popular amusement to visit the Salon des Refusés and laugh at the Manets, whose flatness, lack of modeling, "brutal beauty" and unusual treatment of space became the talk of the town.

Such was the impact of Manet's rejection of the theory of perspective, an aspect of art dogma that had been unquestioned for five centuries, that it will be useful to look briefly at its history in the context of his work. The discovery of mathematical perspective is credited to the 15th-century Florentine architect Brunelleschi. Based on the assumption that receding parallel lines appear to meet at a vanishing point on the horizon, he demonstrated the use of a grid system to create the illusion of figures and objects receding in space. No one is sure whether Manet's denial of this time-honored system was deliberate or simply an unconscious result of the personal vision which was never destroyed or weakened by academic training. His

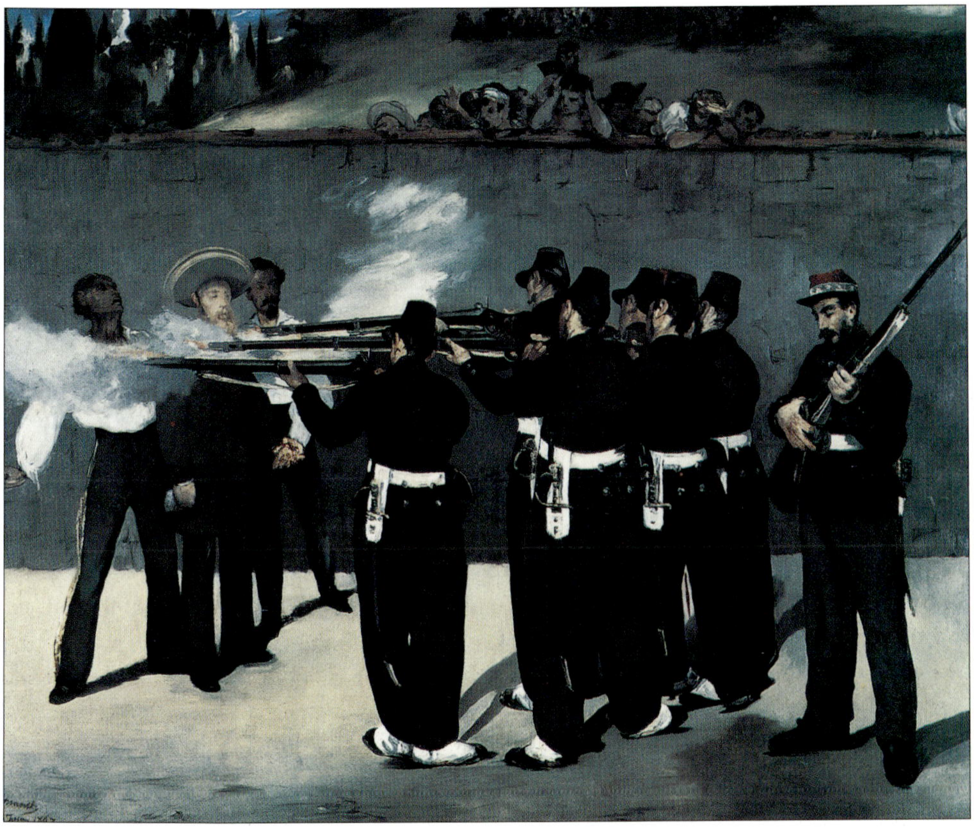

EDOUARD MANET
The Execution of Maximilian
1868, Kunsthalle, Mannheim

Manet borrowed freely from Goya's *Third of May, 1808,* which he had seen two years earlier in Madrid. He was interested in the idea of commemorating on canvas an event of modern history, and had been affected by the execution of Maximilian, the Austrian archduke who had been installed as emperor of Mexico by Napoleon III. Manet worked on the subject for over a year, producing four oil paintings and a lithograph. This work, the latest, is the largest and most finished.

treatment of space has baffled generations of critics, who either bewail his "compositional difficulties" or view his radical departures as the result of two influences that were to alter the aesthetic idiom in the latter half of the century – photography and the Japanese print.

Photography questioned the whole notion of how we see. The camera, termed the "petrified Cyclops," records with one static eye instead of the two moving ones with which we actually view the world, giving a flattened and sometimes distorted image of reality which many artists found intriguing. Japanese prints, which started to come into the country in large numbers in the 19th century, and were avidly collected by artists and connoisseurs, offered a totally new concept of spatial arrangement. Figures were cropped, form was suggested by line

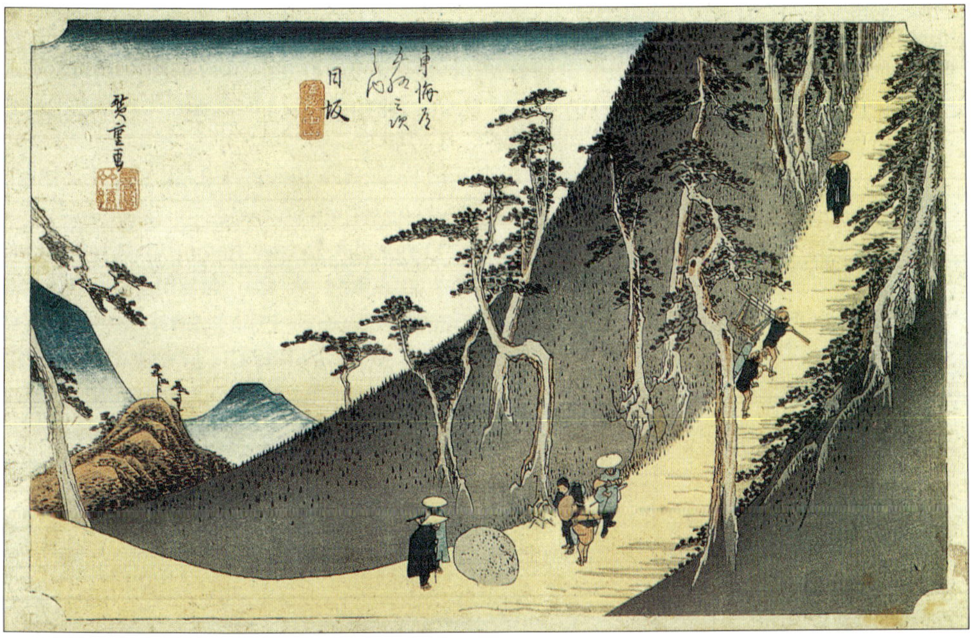

HIROSHIGE
Hisaka in the Sayo Mountains
1833-34

Manet was one of the earliest collectors of Japanese prints in Paris. The discovery of eastern art was a contributory factor in the revolution that challenged the dominance of the Western system of perspective in the second half of the 19th century. The flat, linear quality and absence of intermediate colors and tones, notable features of Japanese prints, are also evident in much of Manet's work.

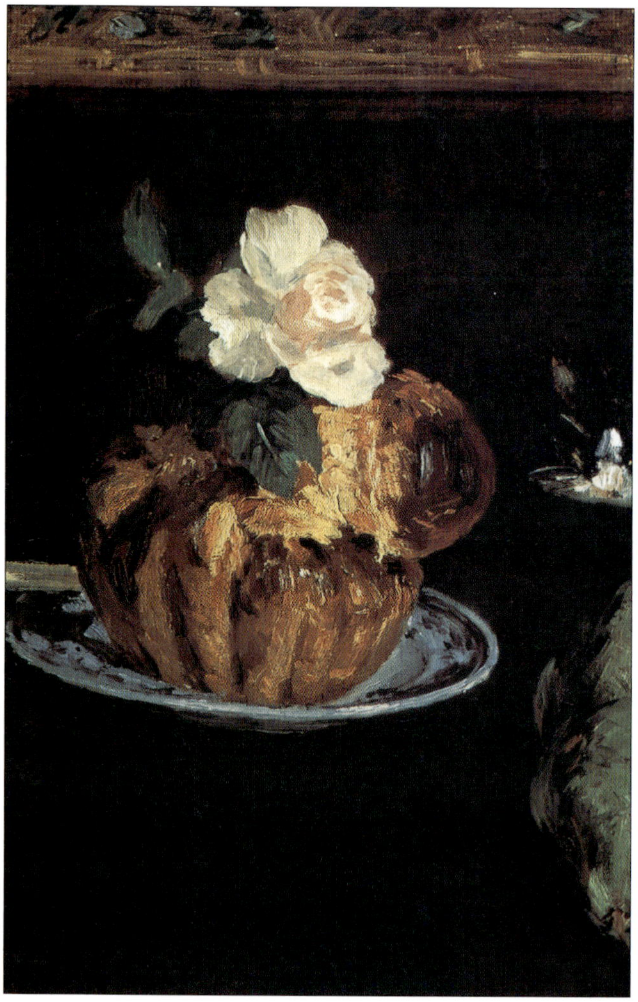

EDOUARD MANET
Still life with Brioche
c1880, Private collection

Manet was particularly interested in still lifes at two separate periods, the first being from 1864-65 and the second at the end of his life. Before the mid-19th century, still life had not been considered a subject worthy of critical attention, but by the 1860s it had become popular. Manet's still lifes were not painted for the official Salon, but for picture dealers in return for modest payment, or for friends and acquaintances.

instead of tonal modeling, and perspective by means of overlapping shapes. Although Manet did not make direct use of Japanese idioms, as artists like Edgar Degas and James Whistler were to, the Eastern system of perspective must have appeared as a viable alternative to the Western one and provided encouragement to an artist who, whether consciously or unconsciously, was challenging the accepted rules.

The quest for official acceptance

By 1865 Manet was generally regarded as the leader of an ever-growing group of non-conformist artists. They were nicknamed "Manet's band," and would all meet on Friday evenings at the Café Guerbois on the Boulevard Clichy, where two tables were set aside for them. These were the painters who were to become the Impressionists, and they all acknowledged a debt to Manet, yet when he was asked to exhibit with them at the first Impressionist Exhibition of 1874 he refused. "Instead of huddling together in a separatist group," he said, "you should put on a tailcoat and go out into the world." This remark shows his essential conservatism; others might have seen him as a bohemian and anti-establishment revolutionary, but this is not how he saw himself. Even while painting works that he knew would not find favor in the official Salon he still sought success within it.

The importance of the Salon cannot be over emphasized — until later in the century it was the only art market place, and it was virtually impossible for an artist to succeed without its seal of approval. In 1867, however, having failed to gain official recognition, Manet staged a show of his own work in a temporary building on the Place de l'Alma. Crowds arrived to laugh at the fifty paintings on show, but notice was beginning to be taken of him: a year later Zola maintained that his reputation was assured, and Degas jokingly told him he was "as famous as Garibaldi."

By 1870 he had ceased to be vilified, and by the 1880s works by other artists which showed his influence were also acceptable. Tragically, before he could develop into maturity, he was attacked by the debilitating disease locomotor ataxia, which caused his premature death at the age of fifty-one, ten days after the amputation of his left leg. But eighteen months before his death he had received the accolade coveted by every Frenchman who craves recognition — he was made a Chevalier of the Légion d'Honneur.

MANET'S PAINTING METHODS

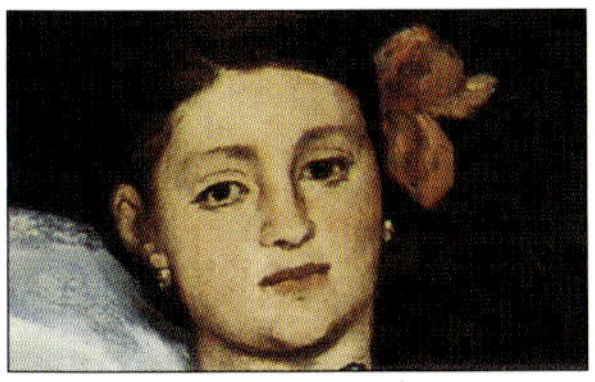

This detail from *Olympia* shows Manet's use of full-on lighting, giving strong contrasts of light and shade and no half-tones.

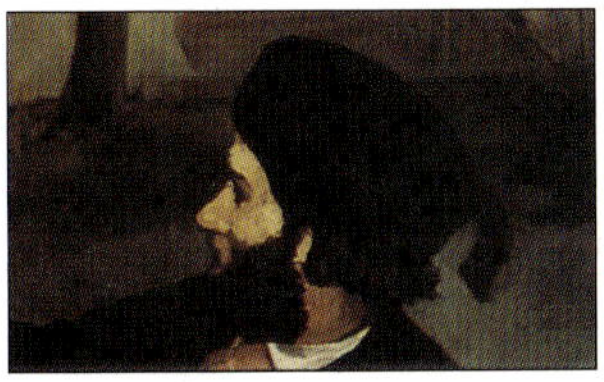

Detail from *Déjeuner sur l'herbe*. Manet's early paintings show the influence of Velasquez, whom he admired for his use of deep, rich blacks.

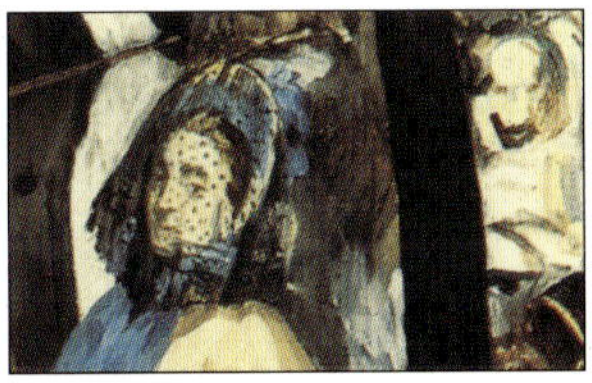

This detail from *Music in the Tuileries Gardens* shows Manet's use of bold brushwork and the wet-in-wet technique.

Manet developed his personal style early in his career, while still a student, using a slurred, wet-in-wet technique of mixing the colors directly on the canvas. The paintings admired by the art establishment of the day were highly finished, built up gradually in successive layers over a tonal foundation, with the color added last and the brushwork virtually invisible. Manet, in contrast, used only a single skin (or coat) of paint and suppressed middle tones to emphasize bold areas of light and dark. He liked a strong, direct light source, which helped to eliminate half-tones and created flattened planes of light and shade; his paintings were criticized for their harsh, flat appearance and lack of modeling.

One of the academic theories of the day was that bright colors should never be placed side by side without gradual transitions to blend one into another, but Manet boldly juxtaposed clear colors such as bright greens and acid yellows, exploiting pale grounds for their luminosity and flatness — also in direct contrast to academic practice. It is more difficult to create an illusion of depth on a pale ground than a dark one, and he used this to advantage to create a shallow pictorial space.

Surprisingly, Manet worked slowly and hesitantly. Manet said of his *Olympia* (see page 341) that "he had a laborious, careful method. He always wanted his paintings to have the air of being painted at a single sitting; but often . . . would scrape down what he had executed during the day. He kept only the lowest layer, which had great charm and finesse, on which he would begin improvising."

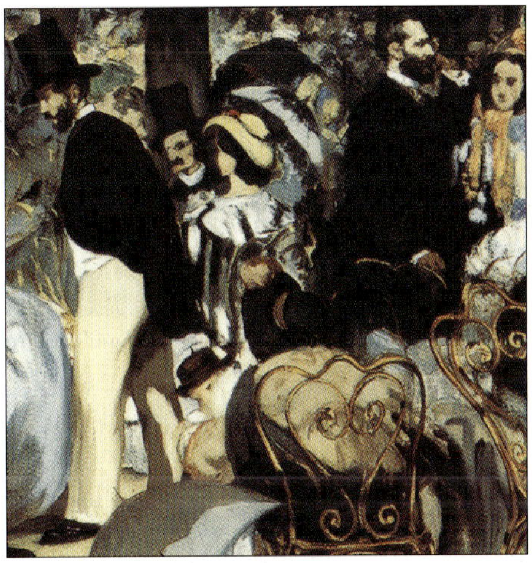

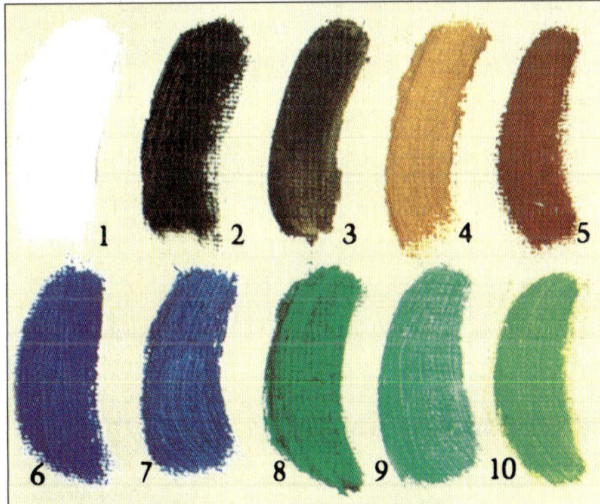

Manet's palette probably comprised lead (1) and zinc whites, black (2), raw umber (3), yellow ochre (4), red earth (5) or red lead, ultramarine blue (6), cobalt blue (7), viridian green (8), possibly cobalt green (9) and chrome (10) green.

In the 1860s, when he painted *Music in the Tuileries Gardens* Manet's palette probably comprised the following colors, with the addition of lead and zinc whites. 1 black; 2 raw umber; 3 yellow ocher; 4 red earth or red lead; 5 ultramarine blue; 6 cobalt blue; 7 viridian; 8 (possibly) cobalt green; 9 chrome green.

CHRONOLGY OF MANET'S LIFE

1832 Born in Paris, eldest of three brothers.
1839 Starts school in Vaugirard, then a suburb of Paris.
1842 Enters the Collège Rollin, where he meets life-long friend Antonin Proust. Takes course in drawing.
1848 December: joins navy and sails to Rio de Janeiro. Spends time drawing.
1849 July: Re-takes naval exams, but fails. Manages to convince father to allow him to study art.
1850 Enters the studio of Thomas Couture. Also attends the Académie Suisse in the evenings.
1852 Birth of a son to Suzanne Leenhoff, piano teacher to the Manet brothers, and Manet's future wife. The child is believed to have been his.
1853 Visits Italy, and makes copies of the old masters.
1856 Leaves Couture's studio, and travels widely, visiting various European collections of paintings in Belgium, Holland, Germany, Austria and Italy.
1859 Submits *The Absinthe Drinker* to the Salon jury, but it is rejected.
1861 *The Guitar Player* received with acclaim at the Salon. Manet meets Degas in the Louvre. The Galerie Martinet in the Boulevard des Italiens begins to show his paintings.
1862 Death of Manet's father.
1863 *Déjeuner sur l'herbe* rejected by the official Salon and shown at the Salon des Refusés, where it creates scandal. October 28, to Holland; marries Suzanne Leenhoff.
1865 *Olympia* shown at the Salon causes an uproar. Manet leaves for Spain.
1866 Zola publishes an article on Manet, singling him out as the greatest modern master.

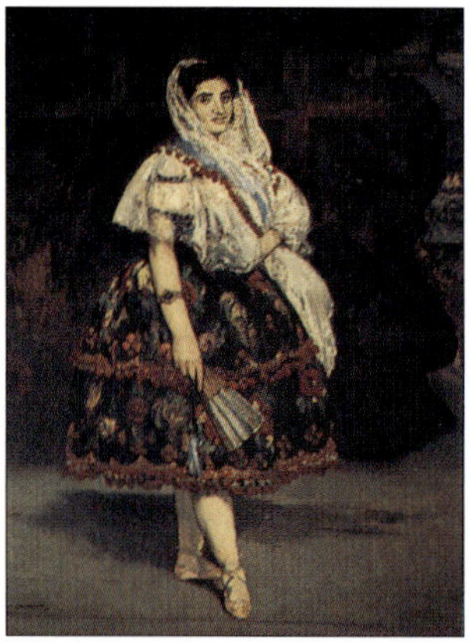

Lola de Valence

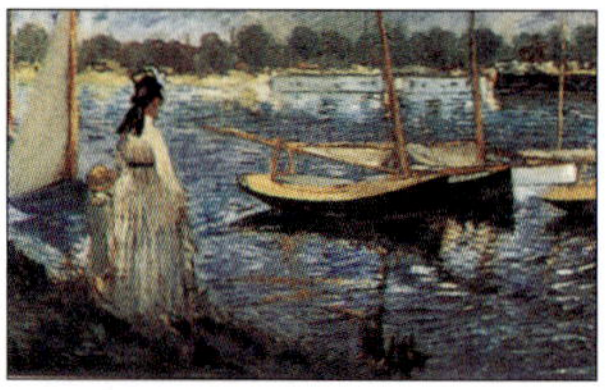

The Seine Banks at Argenteuil

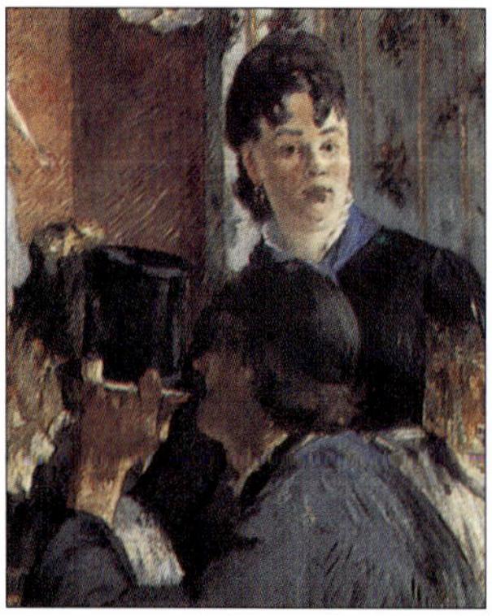

Girl Serving Beer

1867 Manet stages private exhibition of his most important paintings in a temporary building on the Place d'Alma. Meets Monet and Berthe Morisot, later to become his sister-in-law.
1868 Visits England briefly. Works with Berthe Morisot.
1870 July 19: outbreak of the Franco-Prussian war. Serves with Degas in the artillery of the National Guard during the Siege of Paris.
1871 February: war ends, Manet leaves Paris to join his family in Bordeaux.
1872 The dealer Durand-Ruel buys about thirty of his paintings. Spends summer in Holland. Dutch influence apparent in painting *Le Bon Bock*, greeted with approval at the Salon the following year.
1873 Beginning of friendship with the poet Stéphane Mallarmé.
1874 Declines to exhibit at the first Impressionist Exhibition. Spends Summer with Monet and Renoir at Argenteuil.
1875 September: makes trip to Venice.
1879 First symptoms of locomotor ataxia.
1881 Wins a second-class medal for a portrait, and is therefore entitled to exhibit at the Salon without submitting his work to the jury. Becomes very ill. His schoolfriend Antonin Proust, now Minister of Arts, secures for him the Légion d'Honneur, though the President of the Republic refuses to sign his confirmation.
1882 *Bar at the Folies-Bergère* well received at the Salon.
1883 April 20: bedridden, Manet's left leg is amputated to halt gangrene. Ten days later he dies.

THE PAINTINGS

Music in the Tuileries Gardens

1860
$30 \times 46\frac{3}{4}$in/76×119cm
Oil on canvas
National Gallery, London

This painting is an informal record of the artist's literary, artistic and musical friends enjoying an afternoon concert in the Tuileries Gardens in Paris. Working from both photographs and sketches of the group of well-to-do Parisians at leisure, Manet has given us a slice of contemporary life devoid of the heroic or dramatic content fashionable with the art establishment of the time. His friendship with the poet and occasional art critic Charles Baudelaire must certainly have influenced his development as the painter of modern life, although it seems that as a youth he had already exhibited signs of an interest in a new pictorial expression based on everyday subjects. Proust was later to comment on this, telling us how Manet reacted scathingly to Diderot's comments that the painting of contemporary dress would perforce render a picture old-fashioned, "How imbecilic," said Manet. "One must be of one's time, paint what one sees,without worrying about fashion." Baudelaire, Manet's constant companion during the early 1860s, had expounded his views on modern painting in *The Heroism of Modern Life* (1846). Here he maintained that "we have only to open our eyes to discover our own heroism." The French salon regarded contemporary life as too trivial a subject for painting.

It is hard for the modern audience to appreciate the anger this painting aroused; one visitor even threatened to attack it with his walking stick. It was not only that the subject matter was unusual and accorded ill with the Salon visitors' expectations; the technique was shocking too. Paintings chosen by the Salon jury always had a high degree of "finish," and Manet's lack of polish and bold brushwork, although virtues for the modern viewer, must have seemed slapdash and even impertinent. We see it as possibly the first modern picture, but the gallery-going public, from the mid-1860s on, took great pleasure in deriding Manet's work.

Having trained for six years in the studio of Thomas Couture, Manet had both received and practiced traditional lessons of academic painting. Couture advocated the method of building up a painting in successive thin layers, unifying tone and color by scumbling white pigment over a darker ground, or applying colored glazes over the painted surface. Manet soon discarded this technique in favor of a simpler, more direct application of pigment to create a more spontaneous effect. He did not always achieve this at the first attempt: visitors to his studio were surprised to see the way he "attacked" the canvas, often scraping off the image many times without dirtying the subsequent overpainting or diminishing the impression of spontaneity.

There is evidence to suggest that Manet intended to work further on this painting. A. C. Hanson in *Manet and The Modern Tradition* points out how the center of the picture (which would usually be the most detailed and carefully worked) is the part most loosely painted, and that while some portraits are clearly indentifiable, other figures seem to be waiting for the addition of significant features. "The paint itself," she observes, "is extremely thin in many areas and there is evidence of scraping as though in preparation for further layers of paint. The build-up of rich color relationships seems not to have yet taken place." The date of the painting is in a different color from the signature, which implies that it was probably not signed until just before it was shown in the Galerie Martinet in 1863. If it was only a partially finished sketch, Manet may have exhibited it to demonstrate an attempt "to capture the raw beauty and vivid reality of his own society."

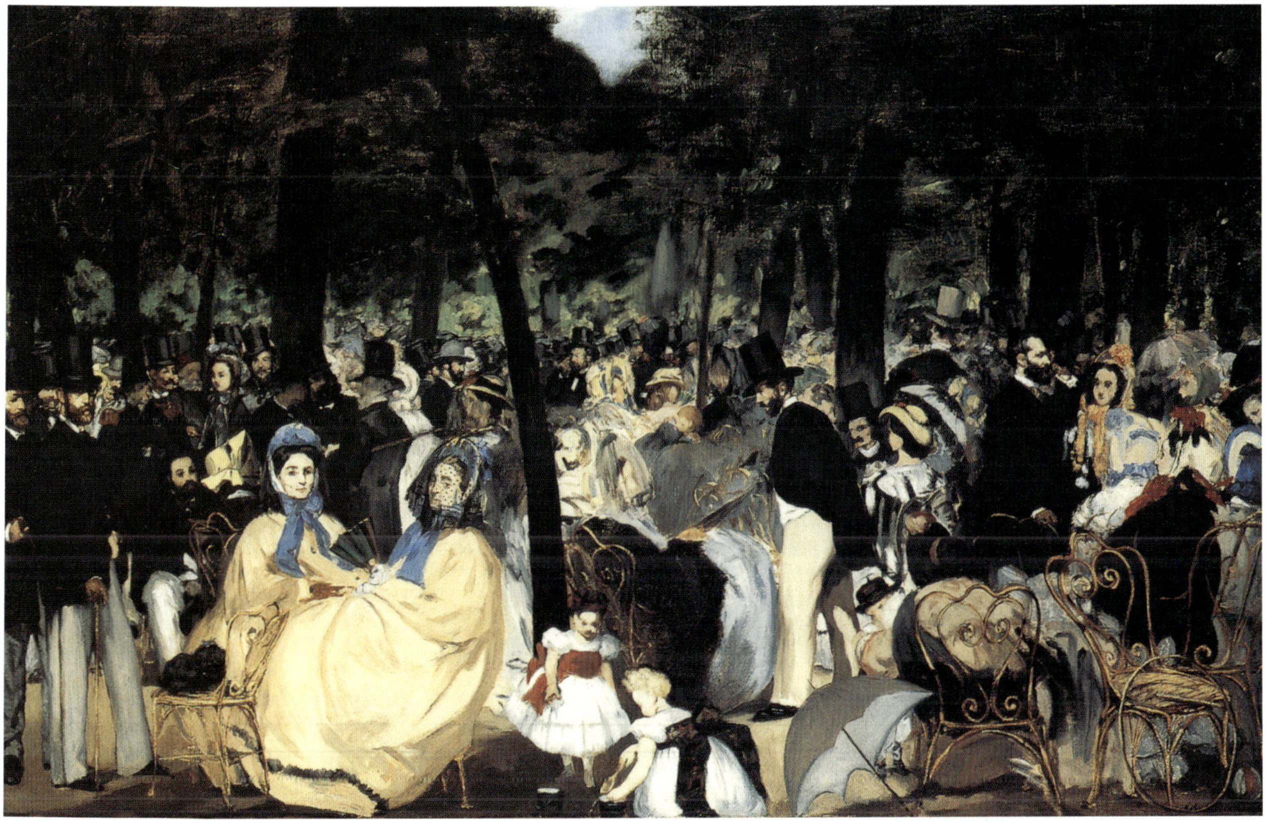

The use of a thinned light brown, evident in certain areas of the canvas, shows that Manet worked in a traditional way, creating an *ébauche,* or monochrome underpainting, before laying in color. The semi-transparency of the greenery in the upper half of the painting shows evidence of scraping, and reveals the white of the underlying primed canvas. The unfinished character of the picture, which is little more than an oil sketch, contributes to its vitality. But the apparent naturalism is misleading, for the way the figures are shown, looking outward as though to involve the viewer in the scene, was a device Manet was to develop in much of his later work. In contrast to the density of the crowd that occupies the central horizontal band, the area immediately at the foreground is unoccupied, allowing the foreground figures to stand out clear and unobscured.

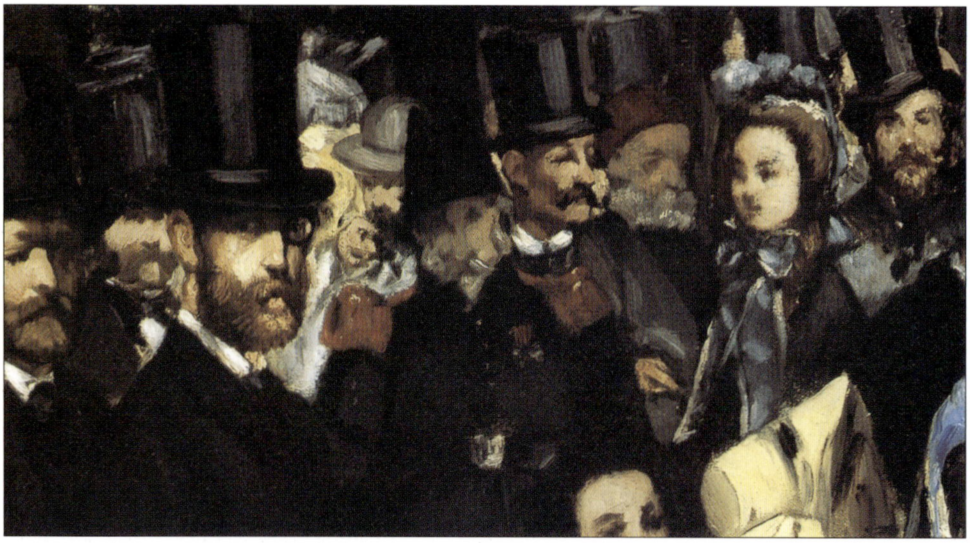

1

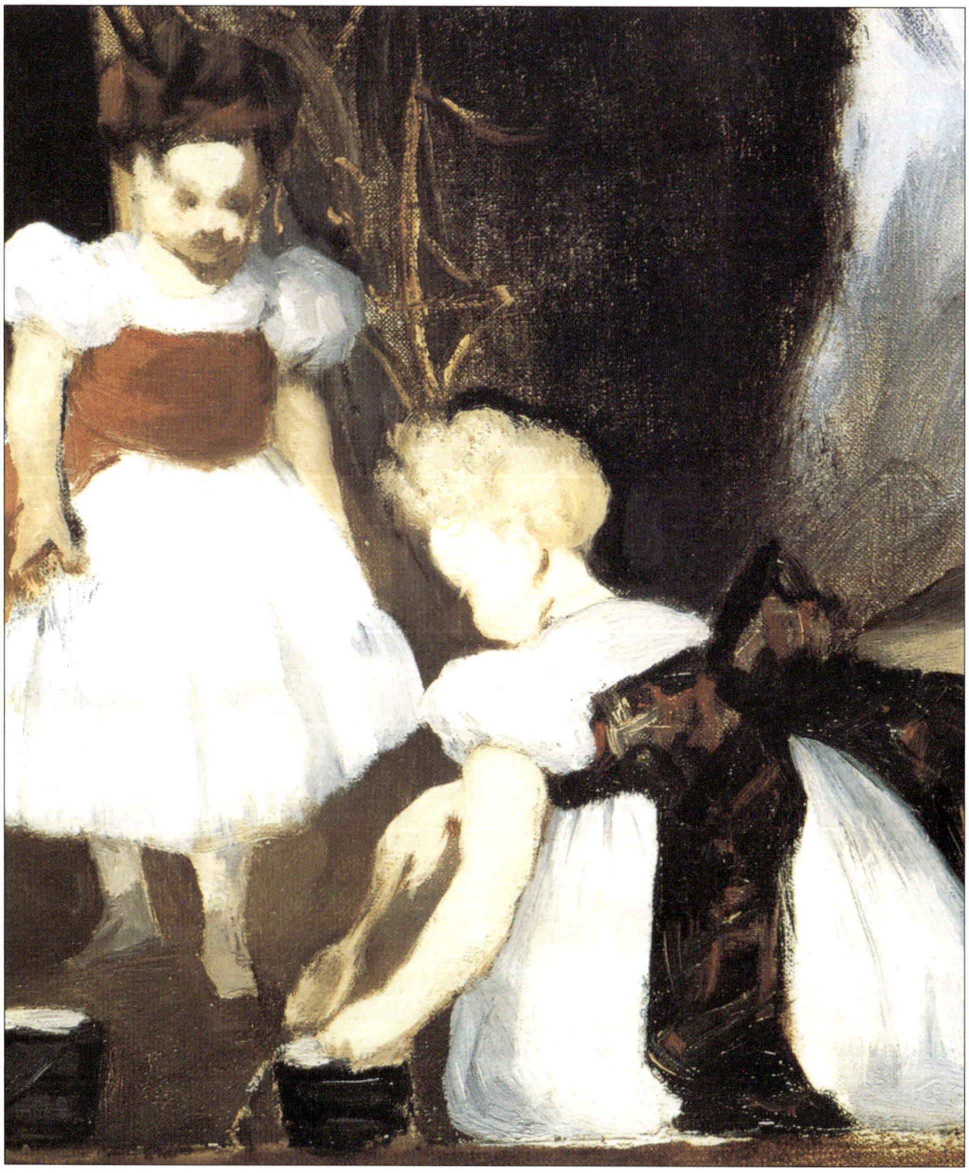

2

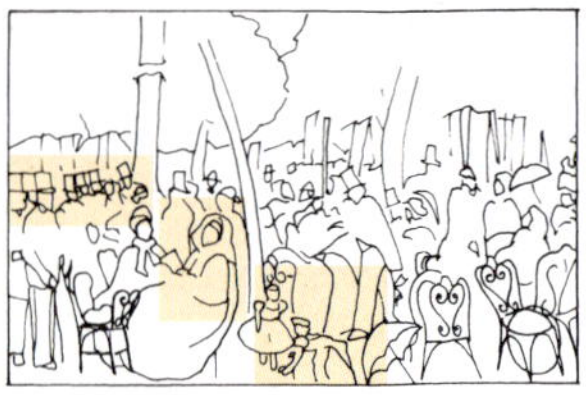

1 The figures in the crowd are all portrait studies of the artist's friends. On the extreme left is Manet himself, standing next to Albert de Balleroy, the animal painter with whom he shared a studio. Seated is Zacharie Astruc, the journalist whose lines were inscribed on the frame of *Olympia* (see page 341). The mustachioed figure immediately behind him may well be that of the journalist Aurélien Scholl, the epitome of the young dandy. Between Manet and de Balleroy can be glimpsed the head of the writer Champfleury, for whose *Cats* Manet produced an illustration and poster.

2 This central foreground detail offers a charming vignette of two very young girls playing on the ground with buckets and spades, and provides a small central focus of activity in a setting of enforced leisure. Their white dresses and huge sashes tied in big bows create the kind of bold dash of detail that Manet was to further develop in his Spanish-style works.

3 *Actual size detail* The veiled seated figure is most probably that of Madame Loubens. The brushwork is loose and free, with the strokes following the direction of the flowing folds of the dress. The artist has worked quickly, with a loaded brush, leaving small areas of bare canvas uncovered in places. The gray-blues of the veil were produced by dabs and streaks of black, painted wet-in-wet.

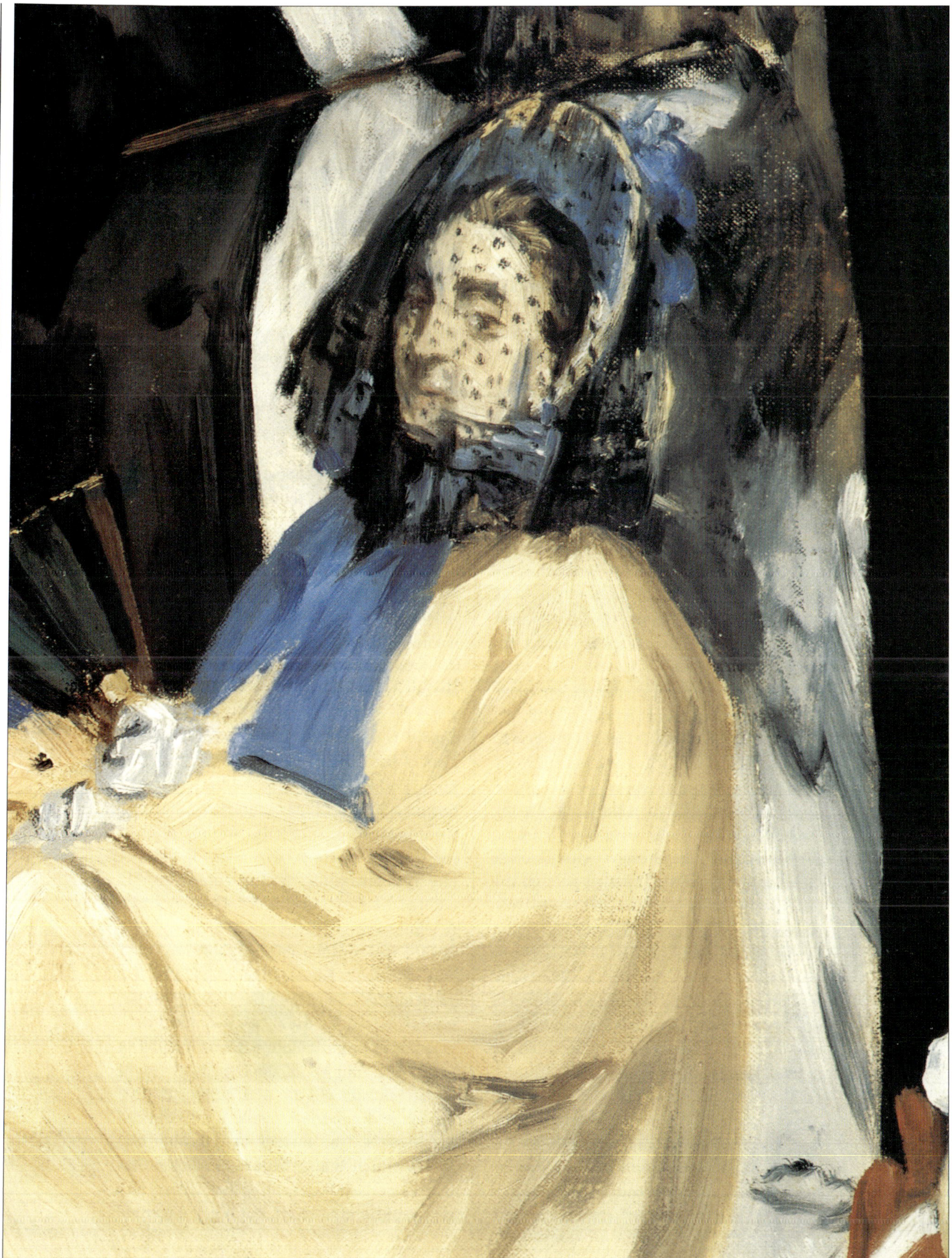

3 *Actual size detail*

Dejeuner sur l'herbe

(The Picnic)

1863

$81\frac{3}{4} \times 104$in/208×264.5cm

Oil on canvas

Musée d'Orsay, Paris

"This nude has shocked the public, which has been unable to see anything but her in the picture. Good Heavens! How indecent! What! A woman without a stitch of clothing seated between two fully clad men! Such a thing has never been seen before! But this belief is gross error; in the Musée du Louvre there are more than fifty pictures in which clothed people mix with the naked. But no one goes to the Louvre to be shocked." These words are taken from Emile Zola's article entitled *A New Way of Painting: Edouard Manet,* in which he championed the painter's work.

"It was considered," Zola continued, "that the artist's choice of subject was obscene and showy, whereas all the artist had sought to do was to obtain an effect of strong contrasts and bold masses." But Manet, while grateful for the praise from an influential young writer, would not have been happy with the assessment of his work as an arrangement of colored shapes. He refused Zola's offer to write the catalog to his private exhibition, giving the polite excuse that such fulsome praise would seem immodest. But what Manet actually felt was that he had been misunderstood. "Already many people speak well of me," he said, "but I feel they don't understand me. They don't grasp what there is in me or at least what I try to show."

Zola described this painting solely in formal terms. "What you have to look for in the painting is not just a picnic on the grass, but the whole landscape, with its bold and subtle passages, its broadly painted, solid foreground, its light and delicate background and that firm flesh modeled in broad areas of light, those supple and strong materials, and, particularly that splash of white among the green leaves in the background . . ." Zola makes no reference to traditional sources of inspiration for the painting, but Antonin Proust maintained in his memoirs that Manet's initial source was Giorgione's *Concert Champêtre* in the Louvre (possibly completed by Titian). He recorded how he and Manet were strolling along the banks of the Seine at Argenteuil discussing their work. "It seems that I've got to paint a nude," declared Manet. "Very well! I'll do 'em one . . . I copied a picture of some women by Giorgione – the women with the musicians – but it's too black . . . I would like to redo it and make it translucent, using models like those people we see over there."

Feeling that a nude was expected of him, Manet chose to reinterpret a classical theme in a modern idiom. Giorgione's depiction of an Arcadian idyll, which is further developed in Titian's *Sacred and Profane Love,* may have provided Manet's original theme and the oblique allegory, but the iconography derives directly from an engraving by Marcantonio Raimondi of Raphael's *Judgement of Paris* (opposite below).

In spite of its outdoor setting, the picture is very obviously a studio work, and shows a self-conscious anti-naturalism both in the lack of modeling, especially evident in the girl's flesh, and the strange rendition of space. There is little traditional perspective: the figure of the bather, behind the main group, is out of scale, and the background is reminiscent of a stage backdrop, which implies recession while simultaneously showing an obvious lack of it. The flash-lit effect, flattering the forms and eliminating half-tones, suggests that photography may have been influential in its conception, as was probably Manet's familiarity with Japanese prints, which emphasize contour and pattern and use no tonal modeling. Both these art forms sustained Manet's assertion that "light appeared to the human eye with a unity such that a single tone was sufficient to render it, moreover it was preferable, crude though it might seem, to pass suddenly from light to darkness rather than accumulate features the eye does not see."

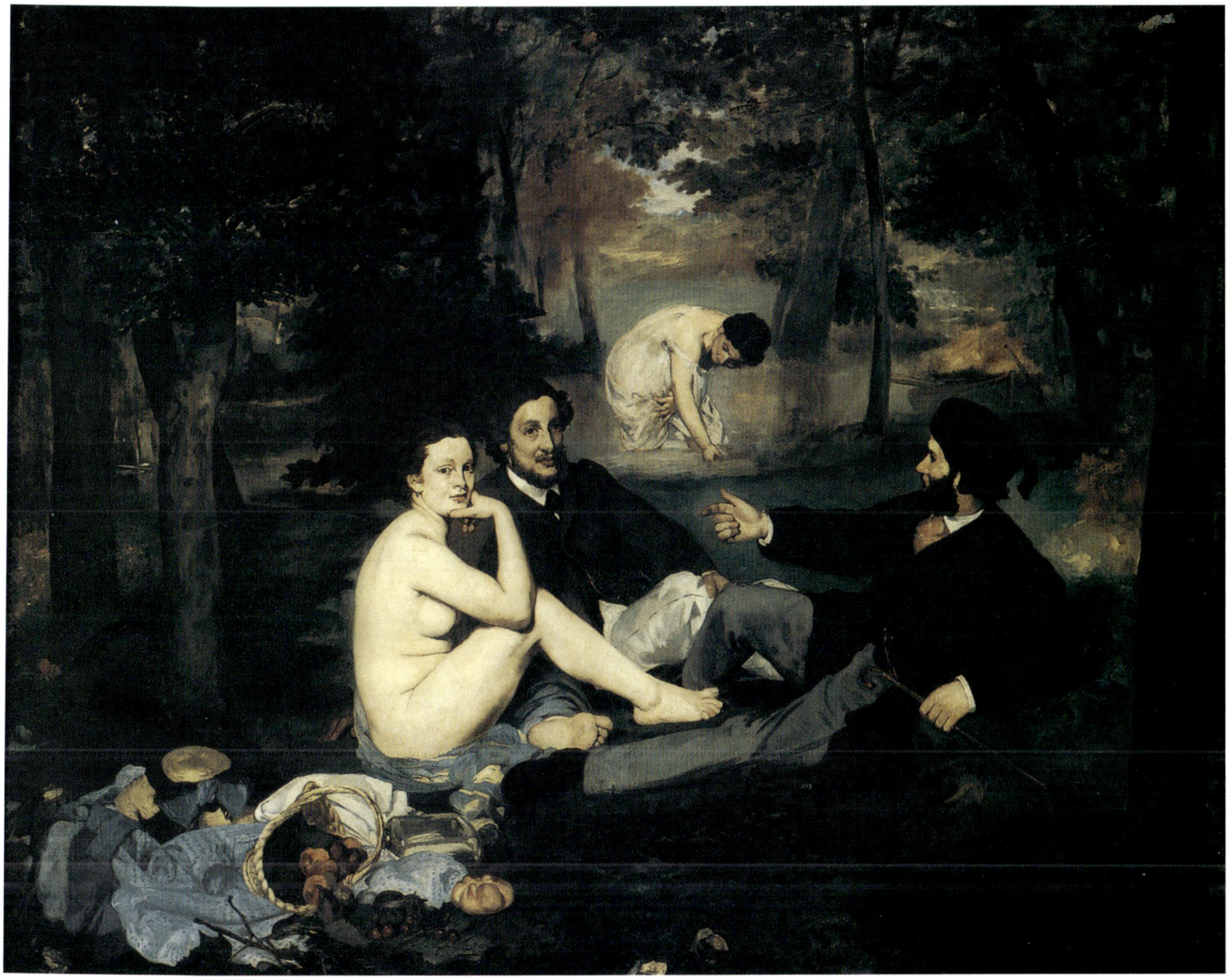

The subject matter, while no longer arousing the hostility it did in Manet's lifetime, is still enigmatic. It is seen by some as a symbolic landscape in which dualities of town and country, male and female, past and present, purity and sensuality are alluded to. Manet's close friend Antonin Proust suggested that the original inspiration came when Manet saw some bathers in the Seine, and said he would like to paint them, but this claim may have been the result of Proust's desire to assert his friend's status as one of the forerunners of outdoor painting. Manet revealed almost nothing of his reasons for experimenting with new ways of depicting form and space, claiming that "I only paint what I see in front of me, with sincerity."

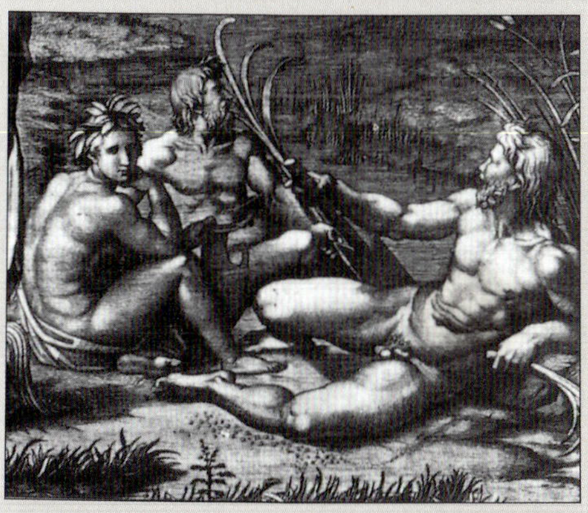

MARCANTONIO RAIMONDI
The Judgement of Paris
(detail) after Raphael
British Museum, London

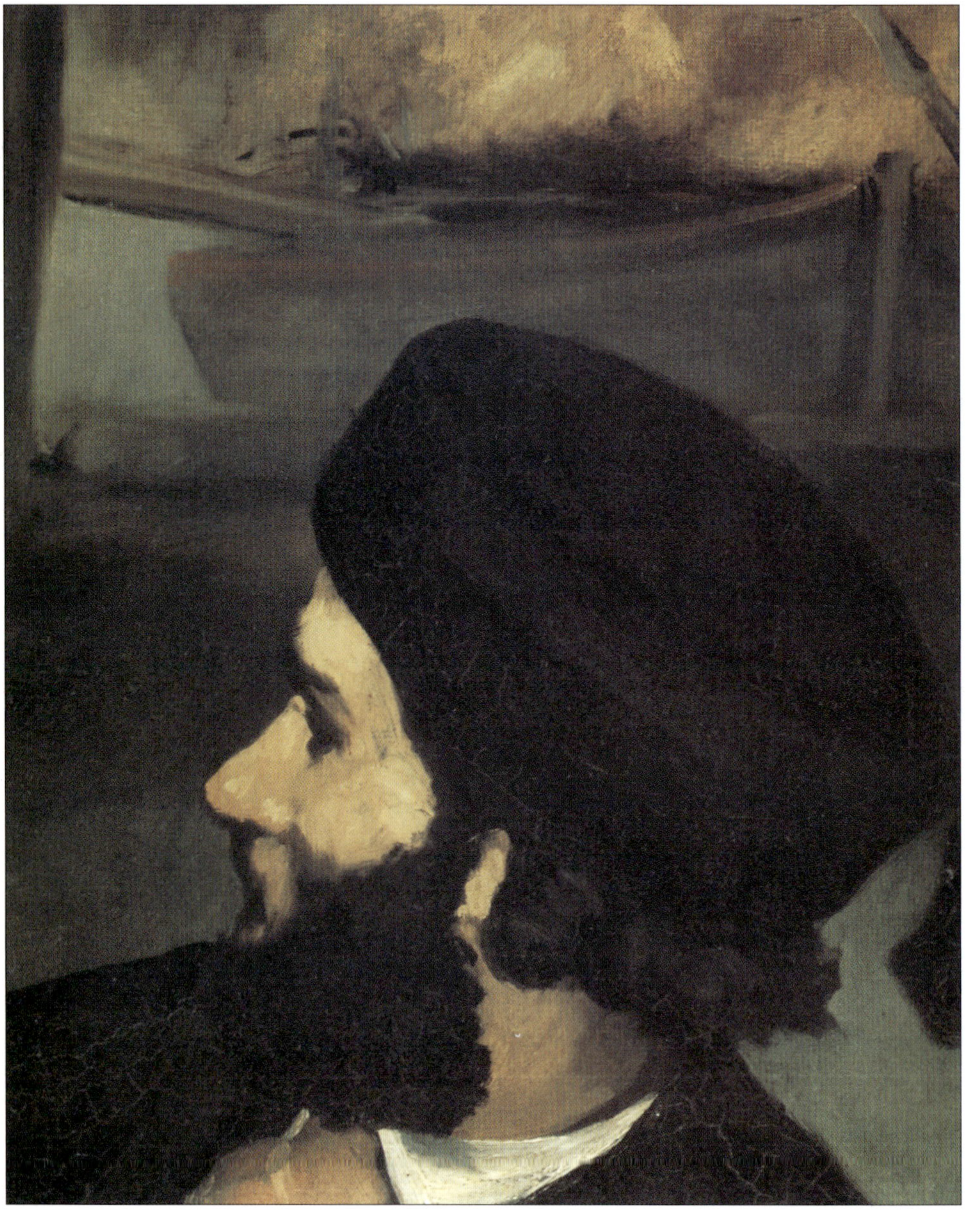

1

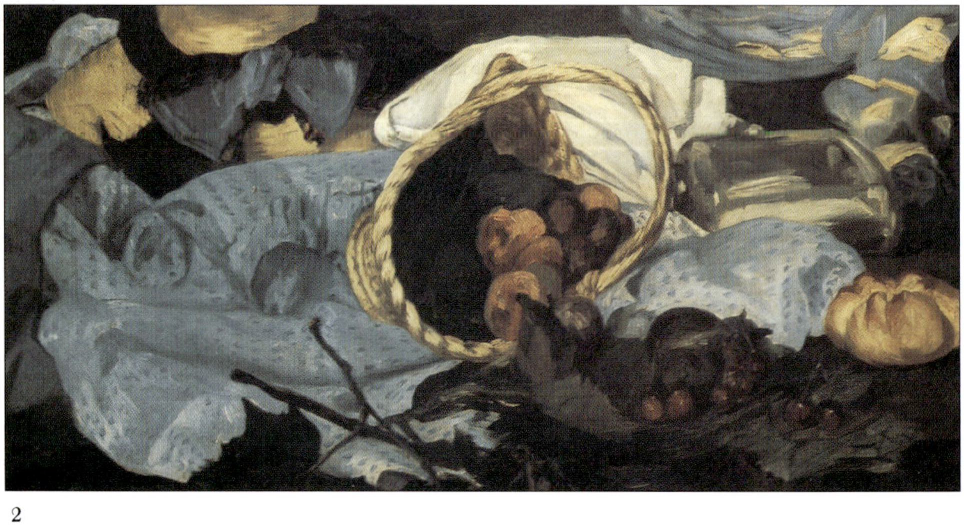

2

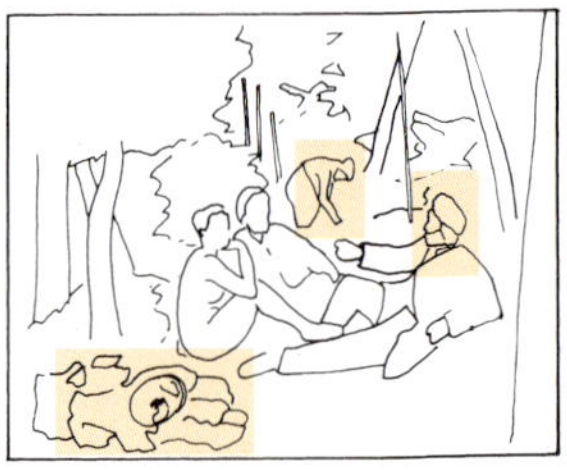

1 According to Antonin Proust, both Manet's brothers – Eugène and Gustave – posed in turn for this figure. The tasseled cap worn by students at the time contributes to the flavor of a bohemian picnic, a modern equivalent of a *fête champêtre,* which offended contemporary critics. The heavy use of black in the cap, hair, beard and coat, striking against the light, even color of the face, contrasts strongly with the paler tones of the boat behind.

2 The selection of foodstuffs essential to a picnic lunch provided Manet with the opportunity of composing a luscious still life at the lower left of the canvas. The fact that the assemblage of ripe fruit is unrealistic – June cherries with September figs – suggests that there may be a symbolic element, possibly relating to the naked woman on whose discarded dress the picnic lies. The silver flask at the right enhances the sense of luxury and liberality, another cause for complaint among the critics.

3 *Actual size detail* The pose of this semi-clad wading figure may derive from that of St John in Raphael's tapestry cartoon of *The Miraculous Draught of Fishes.* Out of proportion in spatial terms, she occupies a space which was traditionally placed in the middle distance. Here she looks as though she inhabits the lower half of a backdrop to a stage set.

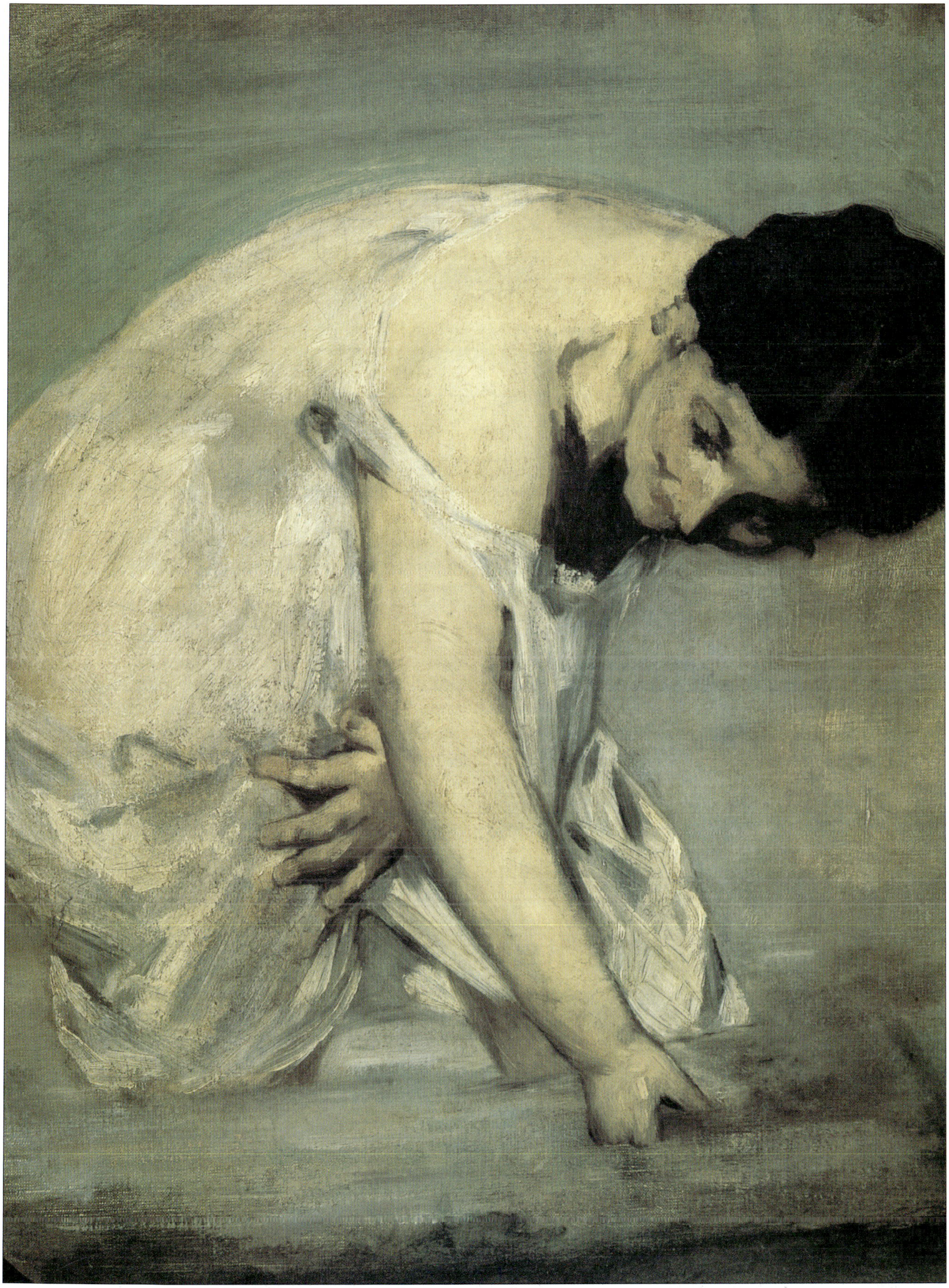

3 *Actual size detail*

Olympia

1863

$51^3/_8 \times 74^3/_4$in/130.5×190cm

Oil on canvas

Musée d'Orsay, Paris

The year of 1863 was an important one for Manet. He married his mistress of eleven years, Suzanne Leenhoff, and painted what are probably his two most famous works, *Déjeuner sur l'herbe* (see page 337) and this painting. *Olympia*, however, was not exhibited until two years later, in spite of the encouragement provided by Manet's close friends, as he was reluctant to invite a repeat of the scandal that had followed the showing of the *Déjeuner*. But Baudelaire continued to press him to exhibit the nude, and it was duly submitted to the Salon of 1865.

Its critical reception confirmed Manet's misgivings. It was condemned as an outrage to public morality. "Nothing so cynical has ever been seen as this *Olympia*," wrote the critic of *Le Grand Journal*. "... A sort of female gorilla, an india-rubber deformity, surrounded by black, lying on a bed, completely nude ... Her hand is clenched in a sort of indecent contraction. Truly women about to become mothers, and young maidens, would do well, if they were prudent, to run away from this spectacle." It was Manet's detachment, reflected in the cool gaze of his model, that shocked people. This nude is very different from the titillating variety, such as Cabanel's *Birth of Venus* (see page 322), which received high acclaim. It is an unsentimental and not particularly graceful portrayal of a young prostitute, looking out at us as though summing up the next client. The hissing cat, its back arched, indicates the arrival of a third party – the spectator – unseen beyond the confines of the frame. The black maidservant, a character who traditionally appears as companion-procuress of such women, emphasizes the nature of the subject's profession, as does the bouquet of wrapped flowers she is offering, presumably just received from a gentleman who has enjoyed her favors.

Zola expressed to Manet the main objection to the painting. "She has the serious fault of resembling young ladies of your acquaintance. Isn't that so?" This nude, while deriving in pose from classical Venuses, is not looking wistfully away or feigning sleep. No modest blush rises to her cheek, and the gesture of the hand, unlike that in Titian's *Venus of Urbino* (opposite below), was seen as a means of drawing attention to her sex rather than concealing it. Manet was disappointed that none of the critics mentioned his use of traditional references, although the painting clearly derives from Titian's masterpiece, with an amusing inversion in the exchange of the lapdog, a symbol of fidelity, for the cat, associated with lasciviousness.

The model was Victorine Meurent, who also posed for *Déjeuner*. Slight and elegant, Manet had picked her out in a crowd, and she became his favorite model for some ten years. In the 1860s, slenderness was the vogue for female beauty, and Baudelaire explained the attraction of the currently typical *femme fatale* by saying that "there is in thinness an indecency which makes it charming ... Thinness is more bare, more indecent than fatness." Mallarmé saw *Olympia* as a "wan and wasted courtesan, showing to the public for the first time the non-traditional, unconventional nude ... captivating and repulsive at the same time, eccentric and new." She is posed awkwardly on her silken cushions, and the stiffness of her upper torso has nothing of the voluptuous relaxation of Goya's *Naked Maja*. This may have been a further inspiration for the work, while the oriental shawl associates it with the Odalisques of Ingres. Ironically, although at the time the public would have disclaimed any connection with the revered master, when *Olympia* became a modern icon and was placed in the Louvre, she was hung next to an Ingres nude. An observer remarked how strange it was that after all that fuss the difference between the two was barely discernible.

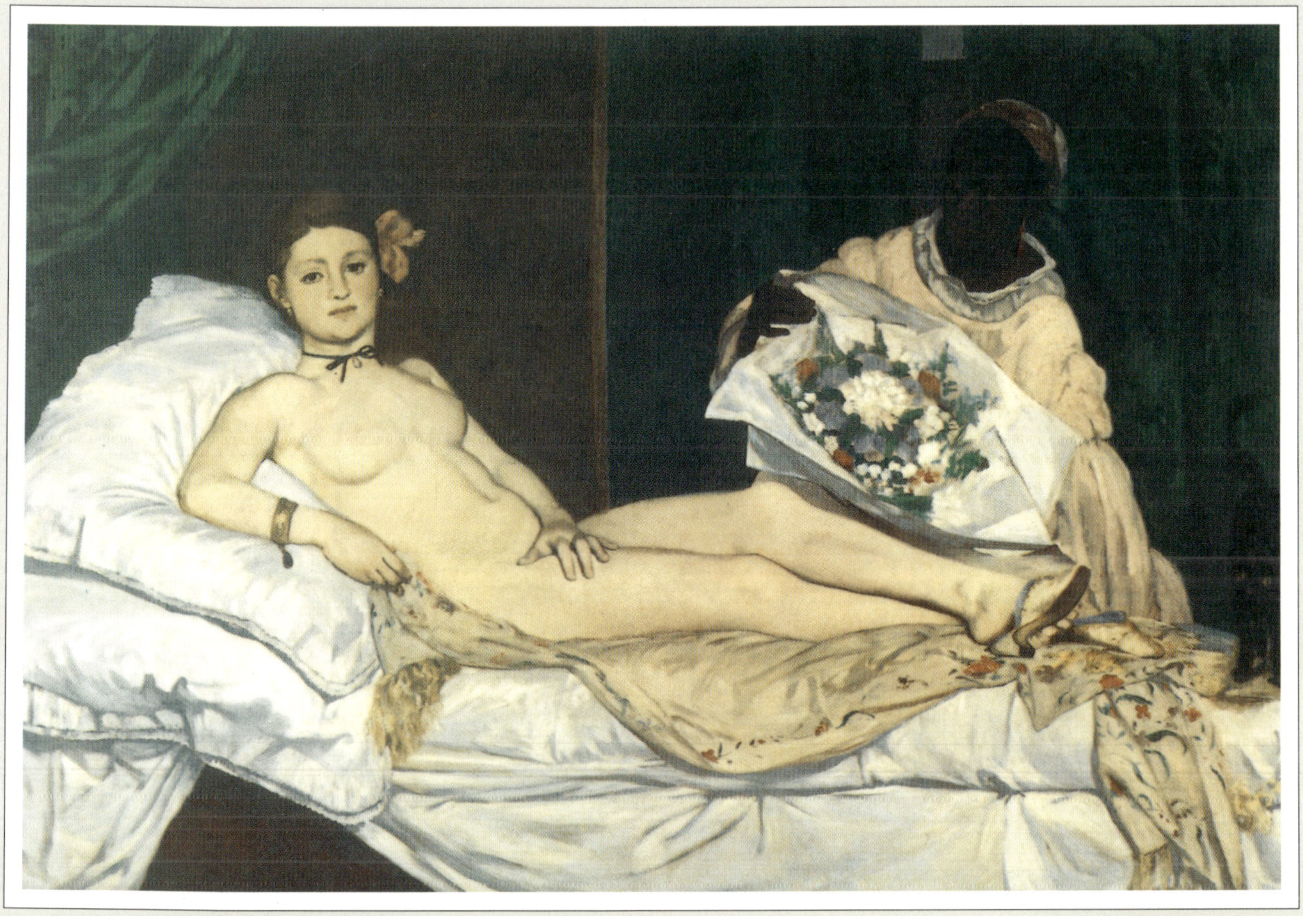

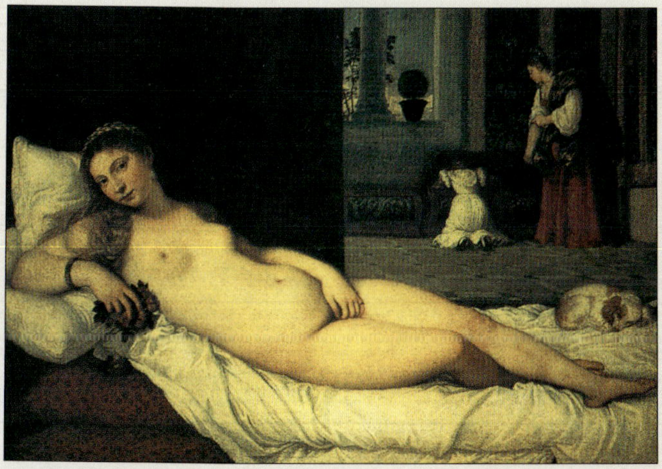

Painted largely in monochrome planes of even color, light in the foreground and dark in the background, the picture is enlivened by touches of polychrome detail. The contrast between foreground and background is accentuated by the silhouette of the figure, which divides the painting into two halves, the lower one stressing the horizontal and the upper one the vertical. Just as Titian's *Venus of Urbino* (left) was the model for Manet's painting, *Olympia* itself became an icon for subsequent painters. Faithfully copied by Gauguin and interpreted more freely by Cézanne, it has also been affectionately parodied by artists as diverse as Picasso, Dubuffet and Larry Rivers. Strangely, although the painting is imbued with the spirit of Baudelaire's poetry, the words inscribed on the frame are those of an inferior poet, Zacharie Astruc. Perhaps Manet felt he owed a debt of gratitude to Astruc, who had defended his work in 1863.

TITIAN
Venus of Urbino
1538, Uffizi Gallery, Florence

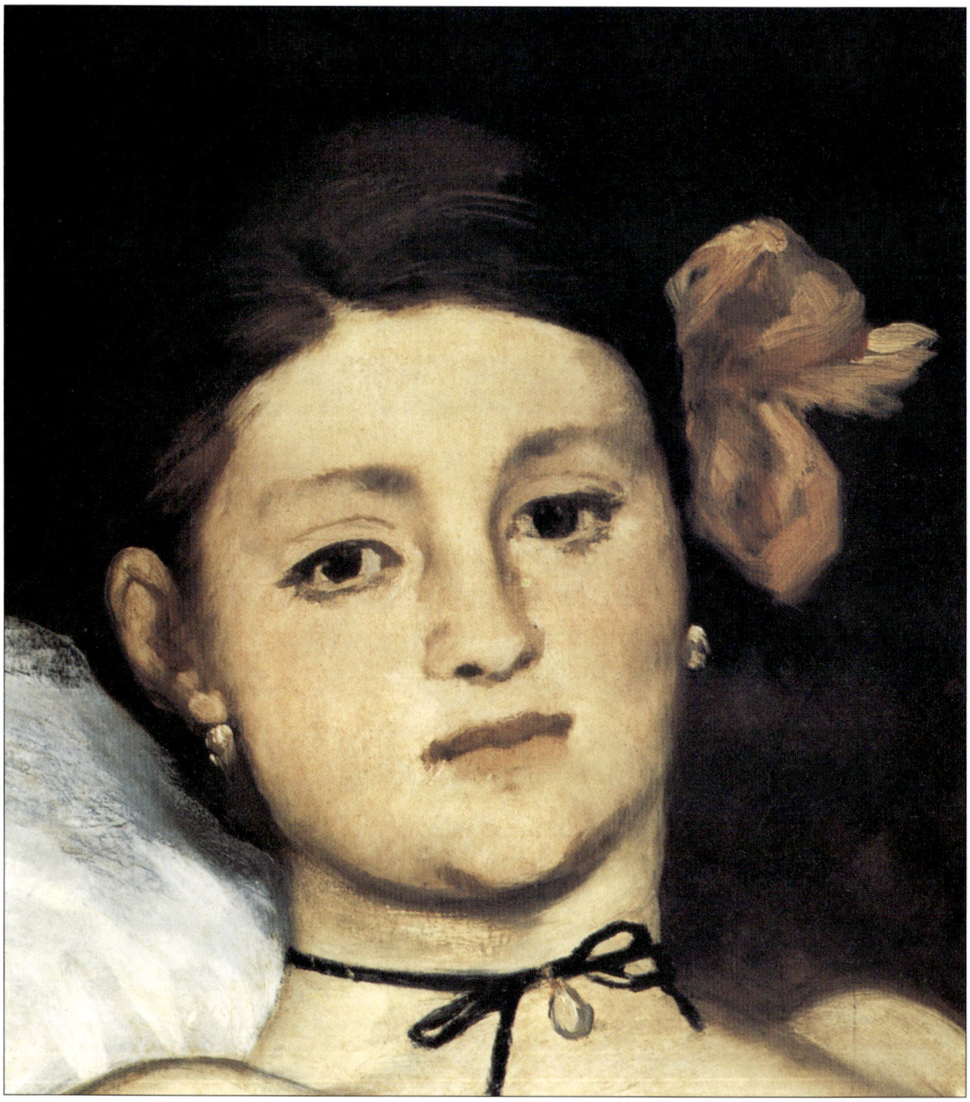

1

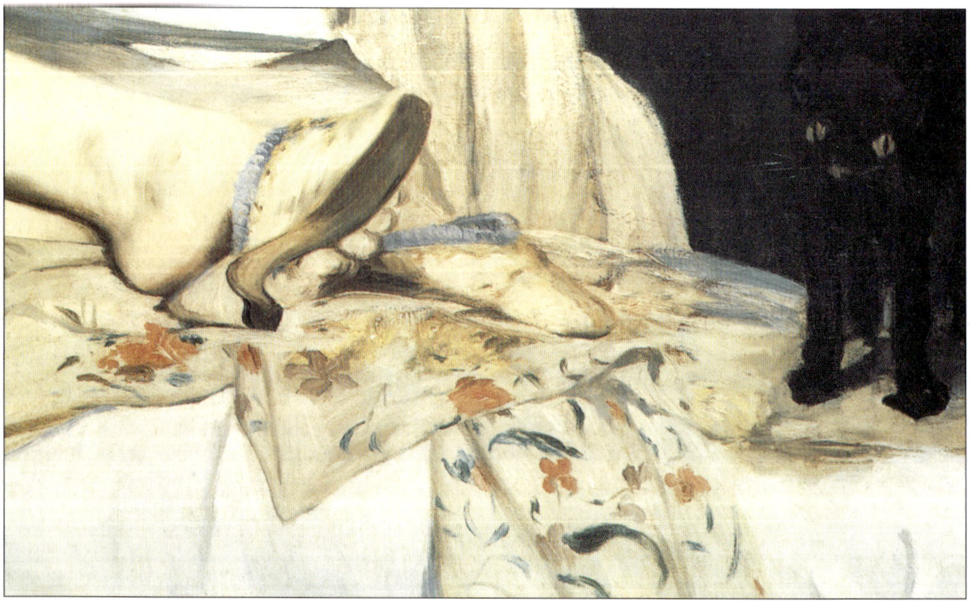

2

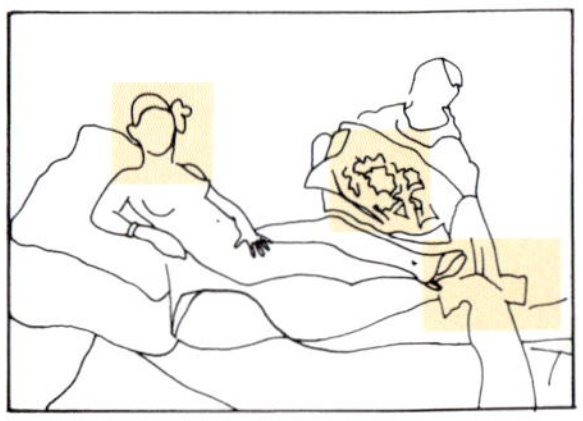

1 Like the bloom in her hair, the pearl earrings and black velvet choker emphasize Olympia's nakedness. The head, with its cool gaze trained on the spectator, is scarcely modeled, although a light, semi-transparent brown has been used to trace the model's pointed chin. Contemporary critics regretted the way the artist had upset traditional values, "esteeming a head no more highly than a shoe, and assigning more importance to a bunch of flowers than to the face of a woman."

2 Like the oriental shawl, which discloses rather than conceals, the slippers accentuate the artificiality of the figure. The colors in the floral bouquet are echoed in the blue trim on the slippers and the red and green of the embroidered flowers.

3 *Actual size detail* The bouquet, which provides a counterbalance to Olympia's head, is composed of a central large white flower immediately surrounded by alternating dashes of light blue and dark green. These are encircled by touches of white, offset by four evenly spaced red accents. Sprays of fern, painted wet-in-wet, encompass the bouquet. By way of contrast to the thin application of colored pigment on some of the flowers, the wrapping paper has been created with a bold sweep of thick white paint, which in places overlaps the foliage.

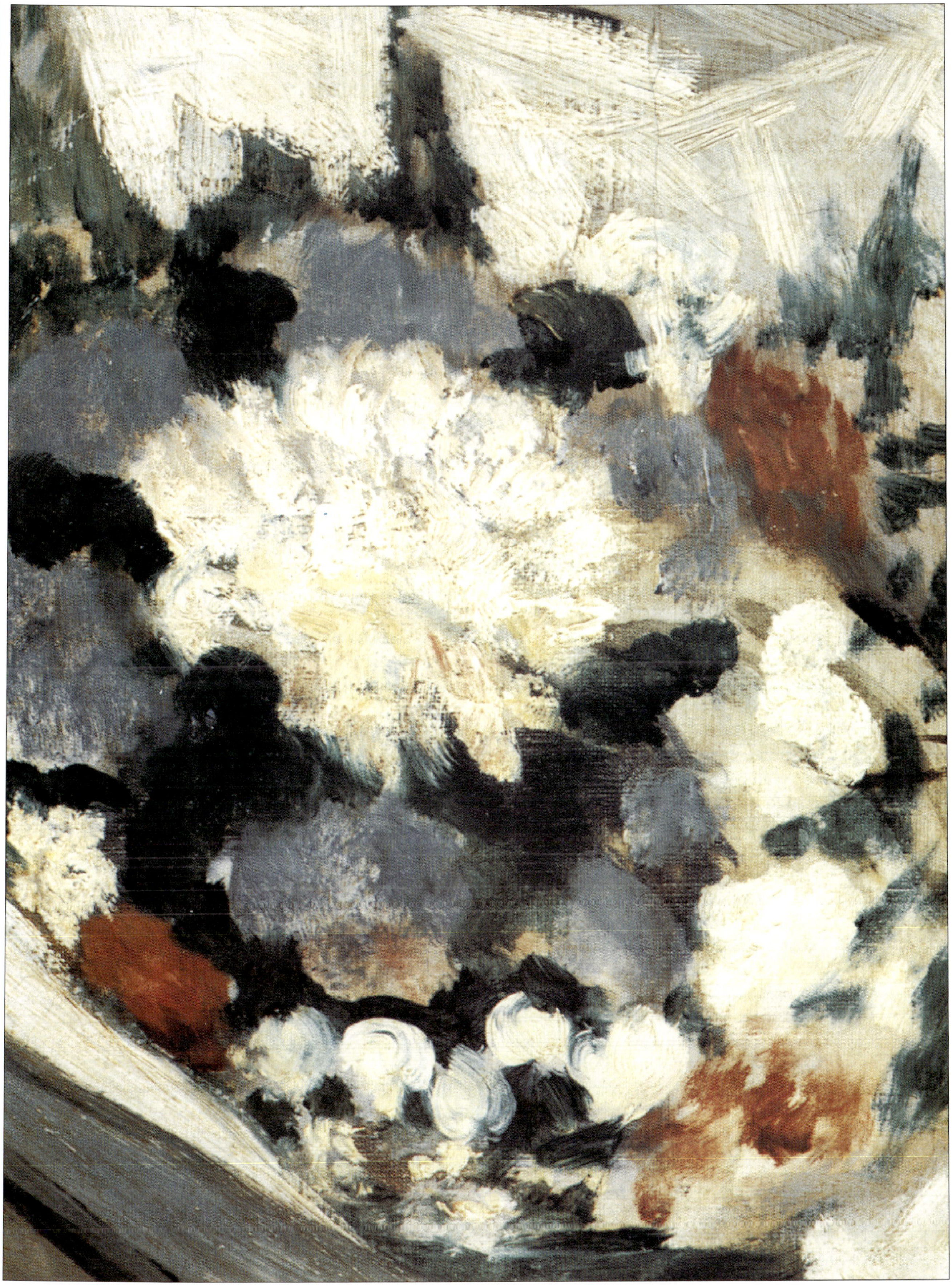

3 *Actual size detail*

Portrait of Emile Zola

1867-68

$57^1/_2 \times 44^3/_4$in/146×114cm

Oil on canvas

Musée d'Orsay, Paris

Grateful for the support of the young Zola, who had defended the *Déjeuner sur l'herbe*, (see page 337). Manet contacted him and offered to paint his portrait. Zola discussed sitting for this portrait in an article published on May 10, in *L'Evénement Illustré.* "The public is becoming used to Manet's work; the critics are calming down and have agreed to open their eyes; success is on its way . . . Manet's originality, which had once seemed prodigiously comic, now occasions them no more astonishment than that experienced by a child confronted by an unknown spectacle . . . When they see the name Manet they try to force a laugh . . . They go away, ill at ease, not knowing any more what to think; moved, in spite of themselves by the sincerity of his talent, prepared to admire it *next* year.

"From my point of view the success of Manet is assured. I never dared dream that it would be so rapid and deserving. It is singularly difficult to make the shrewdest people in the world admit a mistake. In France, a man whom ignorance has made a figure of fun is often condemned to live and die a figure of fun . . . there will still be jokes at the expense of the painter of *Olympia.* But from now on intelligent people have been won over, and as a result the mob will follow.

"From time to time, as I posed, half-asleep, I looked at the artist standing at his easel, with features drawn, clear-eyed, engrossed in his work. He had forgotten me, he no longer knew I was there, he simply copied me, as if I were some human beast, with a concentration and artistic integrity that I have seen nowhere else. And then I thought of the slovenly dauber of legend, of this Manet who was a figment of the imagination of caricaturists, who painted cats as a leg-pull.

"What, personally, astonished me, was the extreme conscientiousness of the artist. Often, when he was coping with a detail of secondary importance, I wanted to stop posing and give him the bad advice that he should 'make it up.' 'No,' he answered me, 'I can do nothing without nature. I do not know how to invent . . . If I am worth something today, it is due to exact interpretation and faithful analysis.'

"There lies all his talent. Before anything else, he is a naturalist. His eye sees and renders objects with elegant simplicity. I know I won't be able to make the blind like his pictures; but real artists will understand me when I speak of the slightly bitter charm of his works. The color of it is intense and extremely harmonious. And this, mark you, is the picture by a man who is accused of being able neither to paint nor draw."

This portrait broke new ground. It is an informal portrayal of the writer viewed from the side, in a study which contains references to both sitter and artist. On the wall a frame displays three pictures which hold special significance for Manet himself. Most prominent is a monochrome version of *Olympia* (see page 341), the most notorious work in the painter's *oeuvre*. In this version, a lock of hair falls over the nude's brow, and her head is turned to the writer as though in recognition of his praise for her and her creator. Above this can be seen the upper half of Velasquez's *Drinkers,* to which Manet had first been introduced by means of the copy shown here, and then seen in the original at the Prado when he visited Spain in 1865. To the left is a print of a wrestler by the Japanese artist Kuniaki II, an eastern contemporary of Manet. Manet was one of the earliest collectors of Japanese art in Paris. Directly below the framed display, amid the pamphlets on the desk, is Zola's article on Manet, and it is possible that the open book — which the sitter is holding but not reading — is Charles Blanc's *History of the Painters,* a work frequently consulted by the artist.

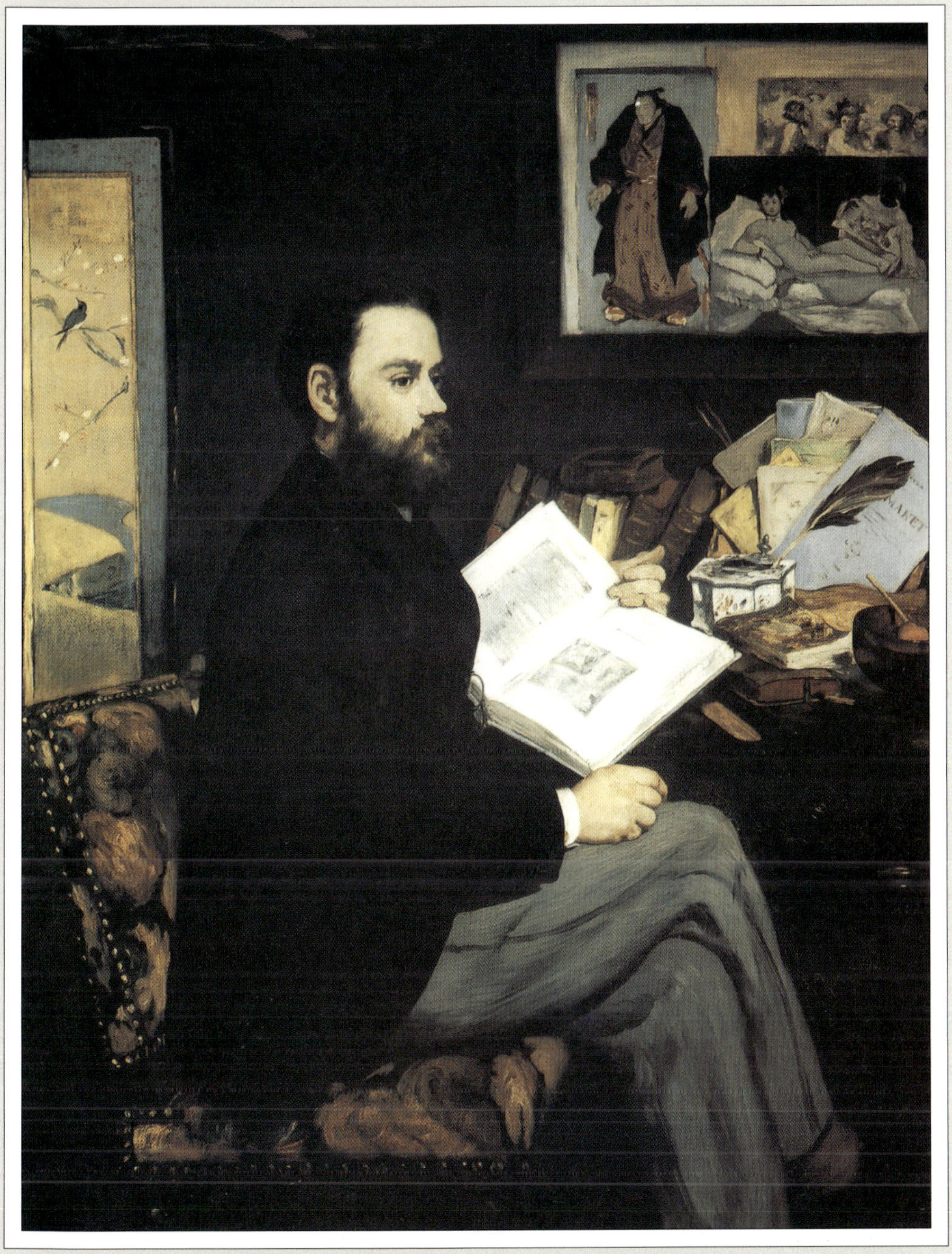

Manet's portrait of the young Zola corresponds closely to the novelist's own description of himself in his novel *L'Oeuvre,* in which he appears under the name of Sandoz. "Dark complexion, heavy set but not fat — at first. Head round and obstinate. chin square, nose square. Eyes soft in mask of energy. Neckpiece of black beard." The erect L-shape of the pose, and the distant, unengaged look of the sitter were remarked upon by contemporary viewers. The critic Jules-Antoine Castagnary praised the portrait as one of the best at the Salon of that year but regretted that "the face lacks modeling, and looks like a profile pasted onto a background," adding that Manet "sees black and white, and only with difficulty gets objects in the round." In fact, X-rays reveal initial modeling of the face which was subsequently deliberately overlaid, so clearly the flattening effect was intentional.

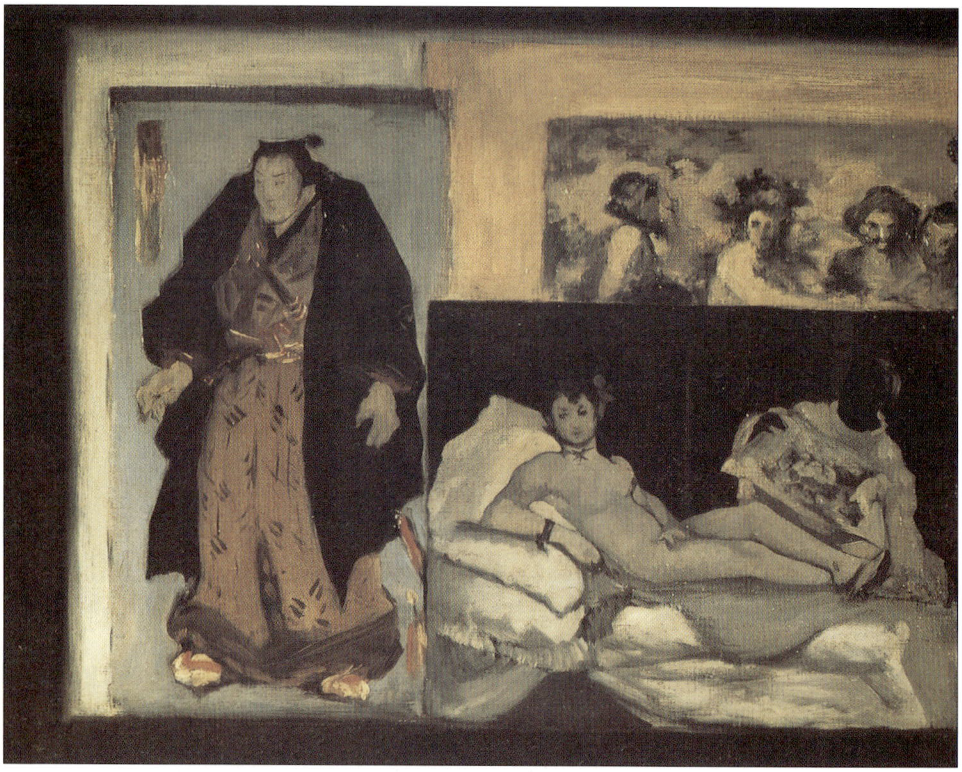

1

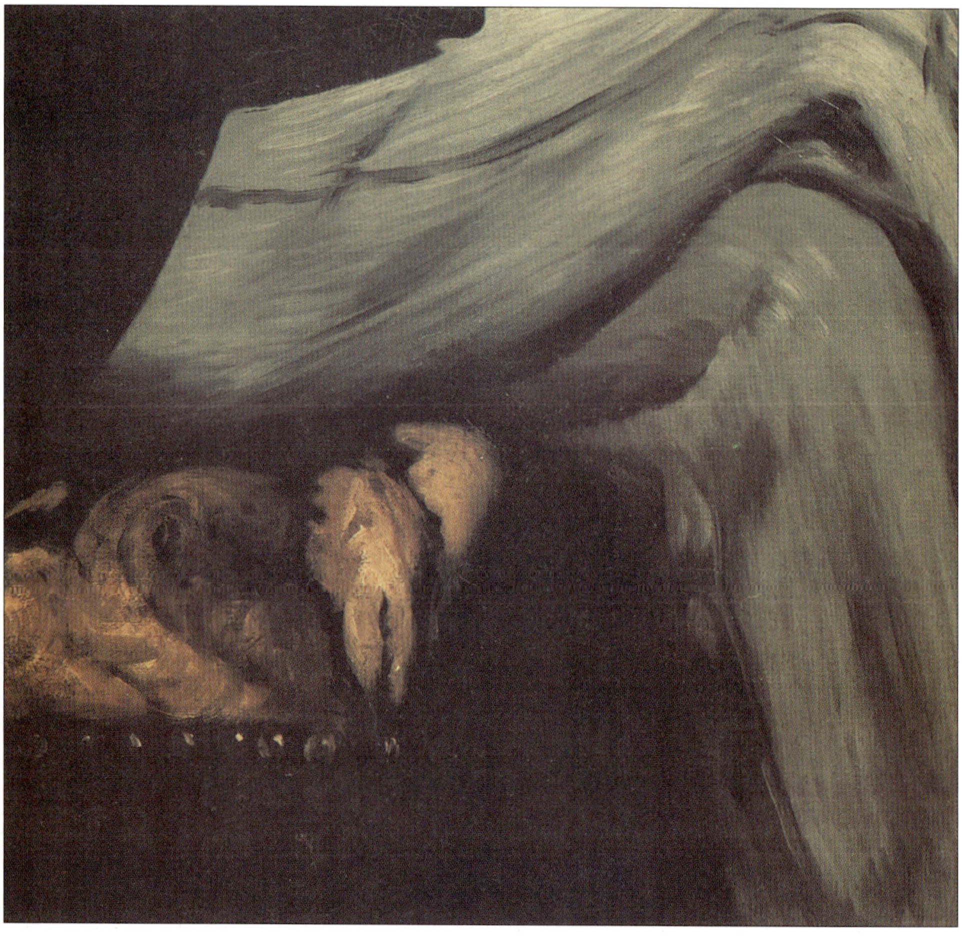

2

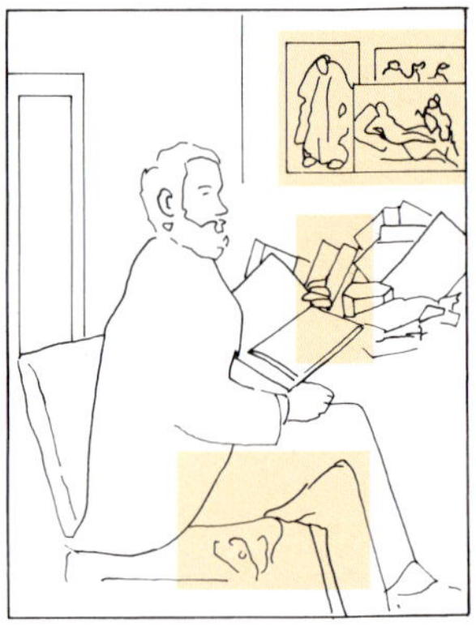

1 Degas had included a framed collection of prints in his picture *The Collector of Prints* painted the previous year. Here the three identifiable works, including Manet's own *Olympia*, are included for their importance for the artist rather than the sitter, although the position of Olympia's head, turned towards Zola, may suggest a mute gratitude for his defence of the painting. The juxtaposition of the Japanese print with the painting reveals the influence of Eastern art: in both works there is a dominant, flattened image whose silhouette is darkly outlined against paler tones. In the original print the robe was blue, but Manet altered the color to brown to harmonize with his gold and black color scheme.

2 The lower section of the canvas is much the most freely painted. While this treatment is admirably suited for suggesting the pattern and texture of the chair, certain contemporary reviewers criticized the artist for his neglect in not faithfully recreating the texture of the trousers.

3 *Actual size detail* Zola himself drew particular attention to the depiction of the hands in this work, remarking, "In short, here is skin, but real skin, without ridiculous *trompe l'oeil . . .*" When the painting was shown at the Salon, it met with a mixed reception, but the collection of books and objects cluttering the wall and table were admired as "astonishingly real."

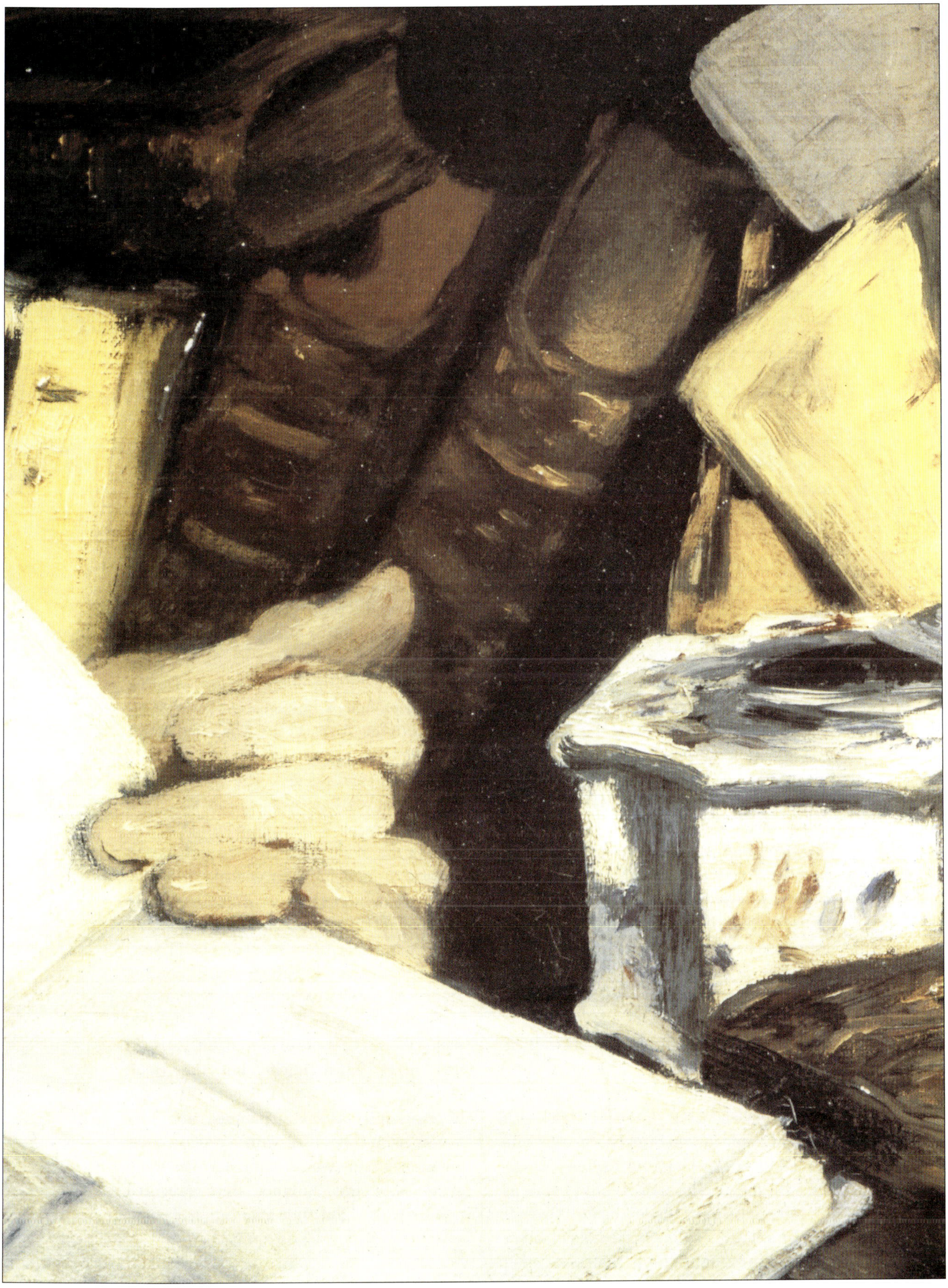

3 *Actual size detail*

The Seine Banks at Argenteuil

1874
24×39¾in/61×101cm
Oil on canvas
National Gallery, London

During the summer of 1874, Manet worked closely with Monet and Renoir, the two arch-exponents of Impressionism, painting on the banks of the Seine. His family had a house at Gennevilliers, on the south bank, while Monet then lived at Argenteuil on the opposite side. The area is now an industrial suburb, but in Manet's day Argenteuil was a riverside retreat of country resorts and cottage gardens. Monet had settled there in 1871, and the place became popular with the Impressionist painters throughout the decade. It was close enough to Paris to allow visits to exhibitions, social gatherings and artist's suppliers, while simultaneously offering a range of landscape subjects, particularly the river. Although principally attracted to the pleasures of the city, Manet also delighted in working outdoors directly from nature. He had spent holidays at Argenteuil from childhood, and it is much in the holiday spirit that he approached the outdoor scenes painted at this time.

Manet's association with Monet led to a change in his work, but it was very much a cross-fertilization, with each artist learning from the other at different times. Some years earlier, when Monet had shown his *Camille,* a portrait of his wife-to-be, at the Salon of 1867, critics had noted the influence of Manet. This gave rise to André Gill's jest: "Monet or Manet? Monet. But we owe this Monet to Manet. Well done Monet. Thank you Manet." Seven years later the names could easily be inverted.

Manet's palette now lightened considerably; he had spent the summer of 1869 with Degas at Boulogne, and the beach scenes he painted there show a strong feeling for light and atmosphere. This new *peinture claire,* as it is called, also owed something to his friendship with Berthe Morisot, a talented member of the Impressionist group. His paintings of this period show none of the contrived quality of the previous studio works, and he largely abandoned the stark contrasts of light and dark and the perplexing compositions in favor of a more spontaneous approach — an attempt to catch the fleeting effects of light and water that so entranced Monet. Manet described his friend as the "very Raphael of water," adding that he had "an understanding of its mystery and of all its moods." Here he has attempted to catch something of the same effect, and he was to further his study of water on a brief trip to Venice in the following year, when he painted two highly Impressionist waterscapes.

Monet later recalled a summer afternoon in his garden, where Manet, "beguiled by the color and light, had begun a painting *en plein air* with the figures under the trees. During the session Renoir arrived. Captivated in his turn by the charm of the hour, he asked me for my palette, brushes, a canvas, and began to paint at Manet's side." The subject was Camille, now Monet's wife, and their son Jean. The couple in Manet's painting, standing on the river bank looking out at the moored boats, is probably one and the same. The subject matter is pure Impressionist. In Manet's work, figures usually form the main subject, but here the woman and child, seen from the back, are almost incidental, serving mainly to point up the real subject of the painting — the river. The broken brushwork, which conveys a sense of movement, is also in the Impressionist idiom, but the color, although light and bright, is not used in the Impressionist prismatic manner, nor does Manet seem concerned with a precise color notation. All the works painted by the three artists over this summer were executed rapidly, with a light, fluid application of paint, and this picture is no exception.

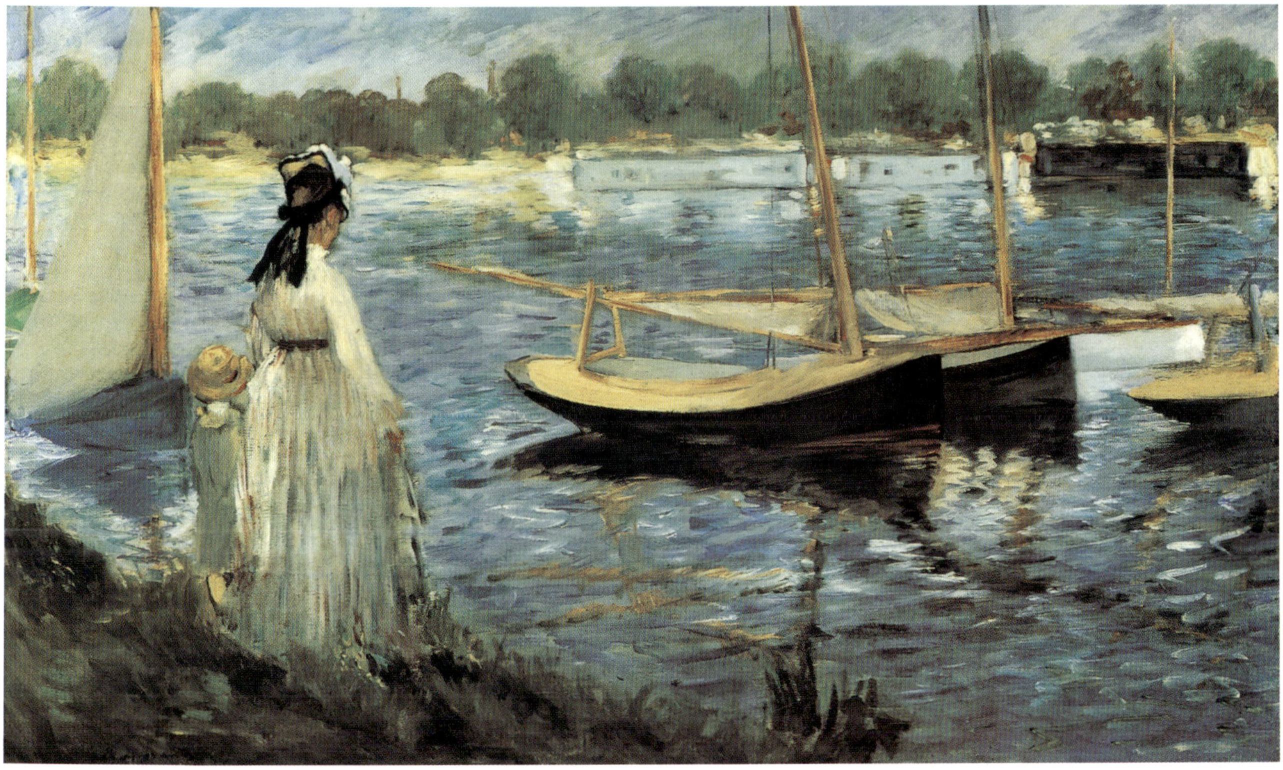

During the summer of 1874 Manet worked out of doors with Monet and Renoir, painting in Monet's garden and on the banks of the Seine. The influence of the Impressionists is evident in his treatment and choice of subject. The figures, usually of paramount importance in Manet's paintings, are here merely an incidental part of the landscape. But although he lightened and brightened his palette in response to his friends' theories, he did not restrict himself to primary colors, continuing to use black and some earth colors. Impressionism was largely concerned with rendering the fleeting effects of nature by means of touches of pure color that approximated to the way light broke up the shapes and planes. Manet found this approach interesting up to a point – and was to use **Impressionist technique to spectacular effect in the *rue Mosnier* series — but light and atmosphere were not his main concern. Nor was the countryside his natural** habitat. Unlike Monet, he was not a committed landscape painter, preferring to draw his inspiration from the drama of city life.

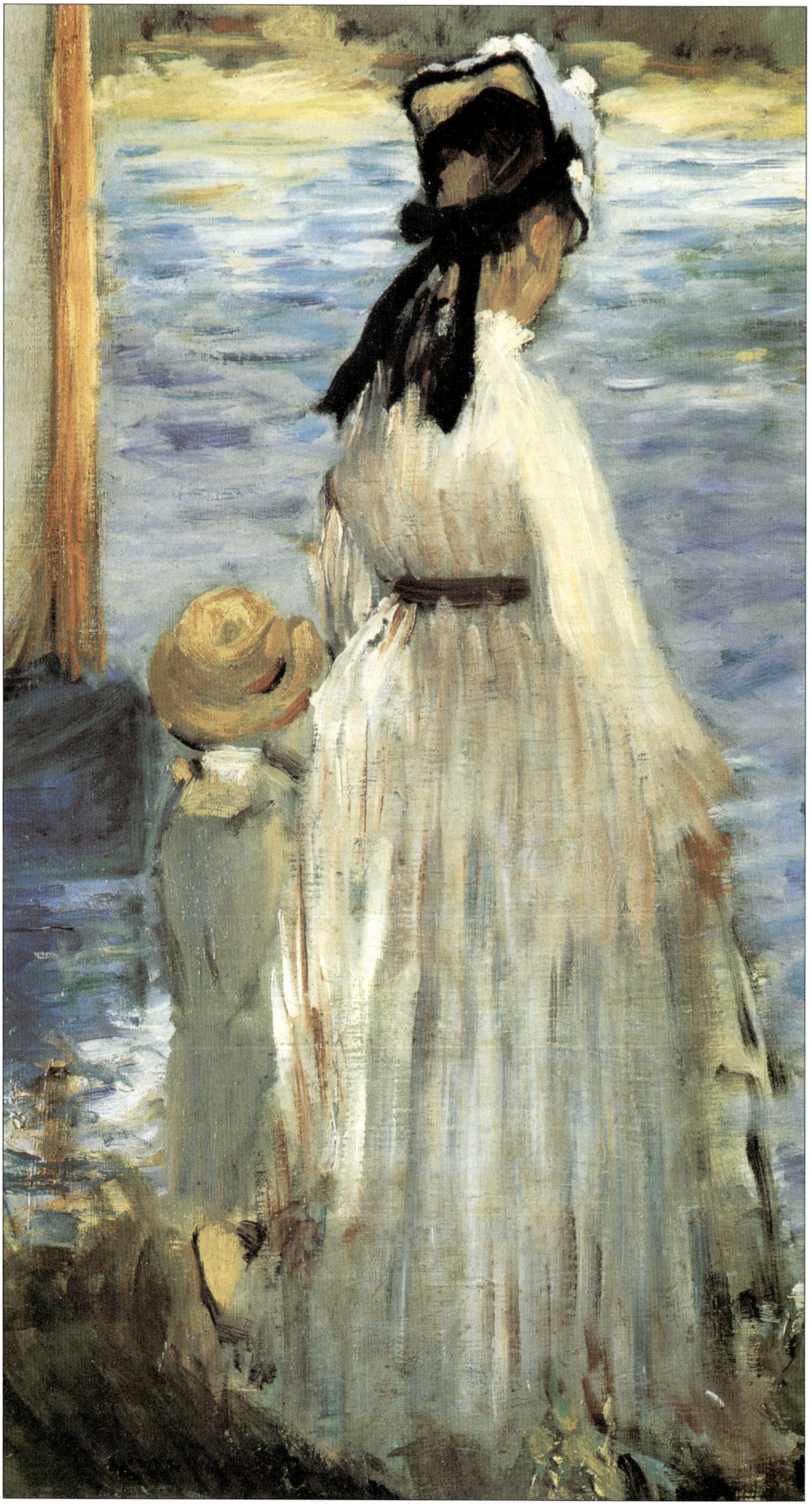

1

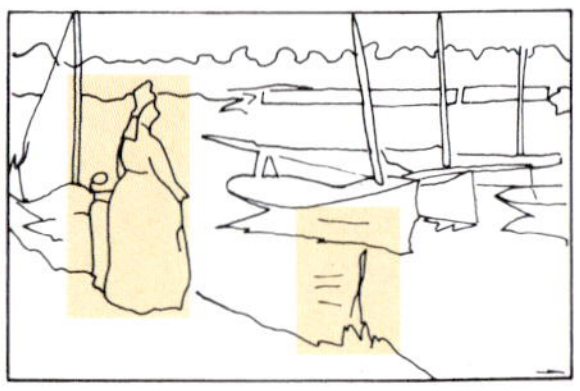

1 The models for the two figures were probably Camille and Jean, Monet's wife and child. Although painted largely in an Impressionistic style, the treatment of the hat is different, and stands in bold defiance of the Impressionist use of broken brushwork and prismatic color. Manet was master of the use of luminous black, and unlike the Impressionists, he never banished the color from his palette. Here he has used it to delineate the trim and ribbons of the woman's tilted hat. By contrast, the texture of her white dress is created by means of light touches of color laid on in vertical sweeps, suggesting both reflections of local color and the folds of the skirt's fabric.

2 *Actual size detail* Manet has used bold dashes of pure color to suggest the movement of water. Horizontal and diagonal strokes of unmixed cobalt and ultramarine create the overall local color, the glancing light is described by strokes of white, painted wet-in-wet, and yellow ocher, applied in diagonal brushstrokes, becomes the broken reflection of the boat's mast and rigging. The green clump of weed closest to the water shows the white canvas beneath and we can see both the fluid use of lighter color and a stiffer, drier use of darker pigment.

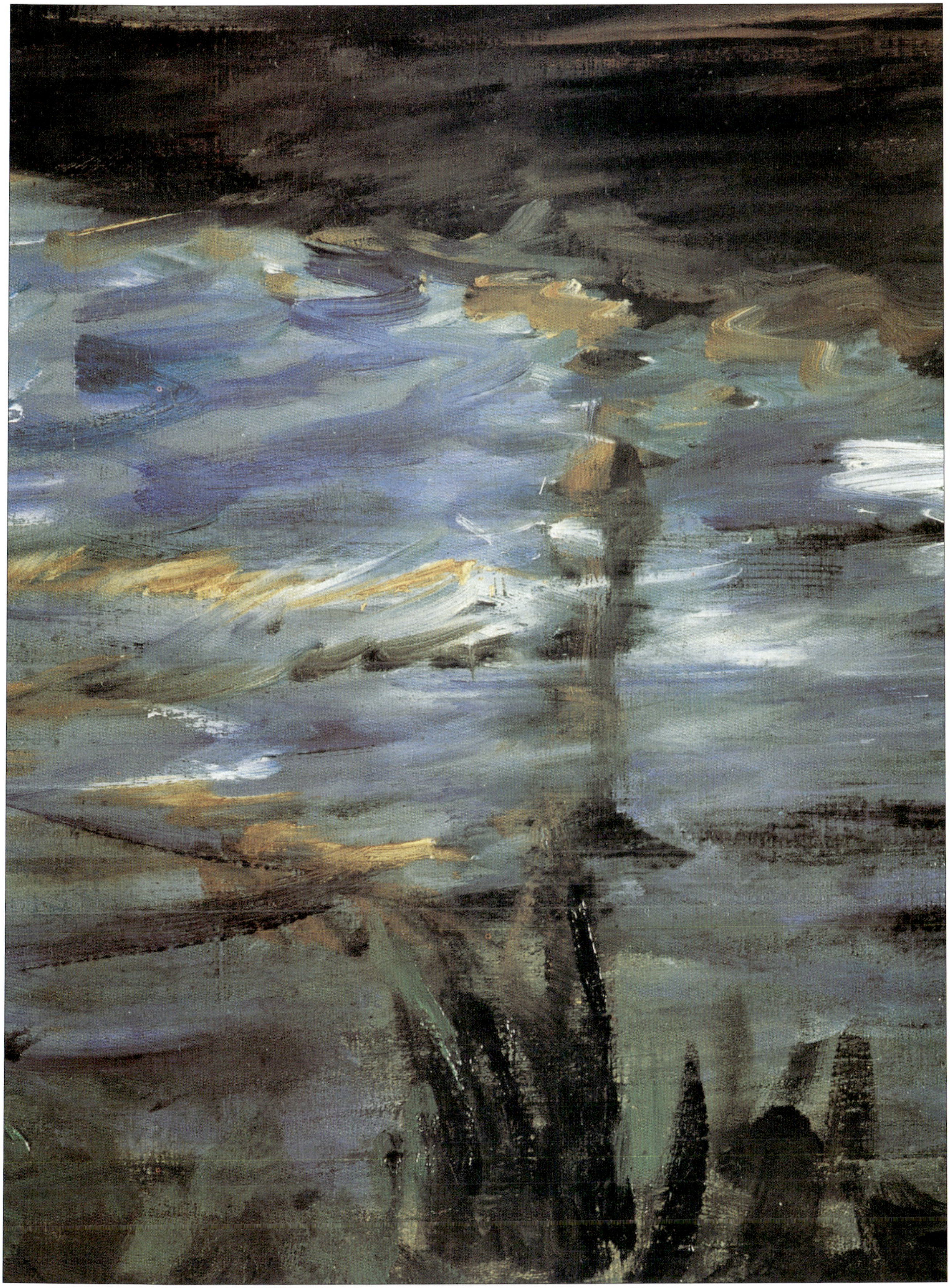

2 *Actual size detail*

Girl Serving Beer

1878-79
$30\frac{1}{2} \times 25\frac{5}{8}$in/77.5×65cm
Oil on canvas
Musée d'Orsay, Paris

The café lay at the heart of French social life, particularly towards the end of the last century, increasing in importance as a response to a rapidly growing urban population, often living in overcrowded, cramped conditions. The café provided more than simply relaxing and congenial surroundings in which to take a drink. It was the very center of metropolitan popular culture: a place where newspapers were read, letters written – and often received – old friendships kept up and new ones formed. Class differences were temporarily suspended, allowing the poorest laborer to rub shoulders with affluent men-about-town, and prostitutes to seek temporary refuge as well as clients. Most important for the artists and writers of the period was that cafés gave them somewhere to meet and discuss their work. Manet was closely associated with a number of Parisian cafés: in his twenties and early thirties he frequented the fashionable Café Tortoni and the literary Café de Bade; from 1866 he favored the Café Guerbois, where the proprietors reserved two tables every Thursday evening for "Manet's band"; and ten years later, the Café de la Nouvelle-Athènes became his preferred venue. The 1870s saw a new development, with the introduction of the café-concert, a light musical entertainment aimed at a working-class audience. Manet and Degas both based paintings on the theme of these popular concerts, and the café was also treated in literature, notably by Zola, whose *L'Assommoir* (1876-77) was widely circulated among Manet's circle.

This painting relates directly to the *Waitress Serving Beer* (opposite below), and the two are often confused. Both works show the same two principal figures, but in the London version they are placed inside a larger space, which includes a glimpse of the double-bass player, the dancer on stage, the marble counter cluttered with glasses, and a section of the clientele. The lower half of both figures is also visible. It is not known definitely which painting is the earlier, although it seems more likely that this is a later revision of the London work. X-ray photographs and traces of earlier painting *(pentimenti)* reveal that the London painting underwent many revisions in the course of its production. It is itself the right side of a larger picture which Manet cut in two (the left side is now in the Oscar Reinhart Collection, Winterthur, Switzerland.) A comparison between the two works suggests that Manet has, to use a photographic term, "zoomed in on the original shot," stripping extraneous detail for a more revealing close-up. The London version shows a busy barmaid deftly depositing glasses of beer with her right hand while looking across to her left, presumably toward the table where she is to take the remaining glasses. *Girl Serving Beer* focuses on the face of the woman herself, who engages us in the same way as did Victorine Meurent in *Déjeuner* (see page 337) and *Olympia* (see page 341), and prefigures the frontal gaze of the waitress in the *Bar at the Folies-Bergère* (see page 357).

The paint is handled with relish. Manet was a master of the seemingly effortless still life, giving flowers, fish and vegetables a freshness that makes them seem almost alive, and here the impression of two mugs of beer is created with consummate skill – no more than a few vivid strokes of freely handled paint. The waitress herself has a voluptuousness absent in the earlier work, a sensuality brought out by the delicious blue of her scarf and the charm of the flowered background which frames her. However many times Manet scraped down and repainted areas of a picture, he seldom failed to achieve the freshness and immediacy that was his ideal, and this painting, with its expressive brushstrokes and fluid lines, glows with life and animation.

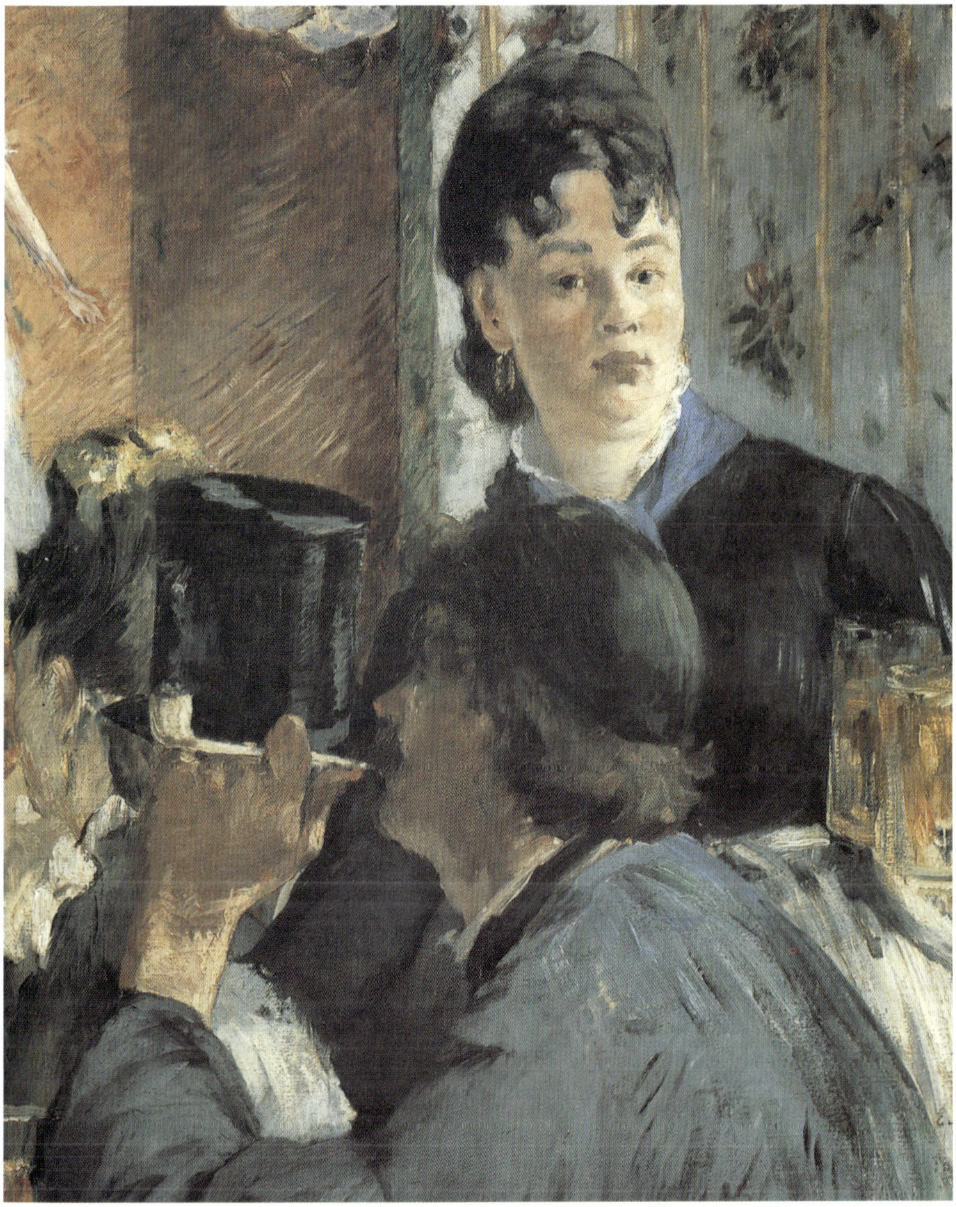

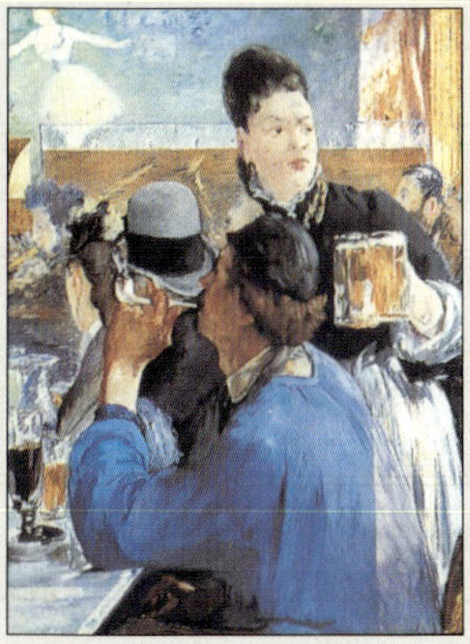

EDOUARD MANET
Waitress Serving Beer
1878-79, National Gallery, London

Other related works show this establishment to be the Café Reichshoffen, and the model for the waitress, in both versions, was the actual serving girl at the café. The writer Théodore Duret recorded that "Manet had noticed the position of the waitress, who, while with one hand placing a beer on the table in front of a customer, knew how to hold several others in the other hand without spilling any . . . Manet approached the one at the café whom he believed the most skillful." The girl evidently agreed to go to Manet's studio in the rue d'Amsterdam on condition that her young man went with her, and it is he whom Manet has placed in the foreground, elbow on bar and smoking a pipe. It seems likely, although it is not known for certain, that the London version (left) was the earlier of the two.

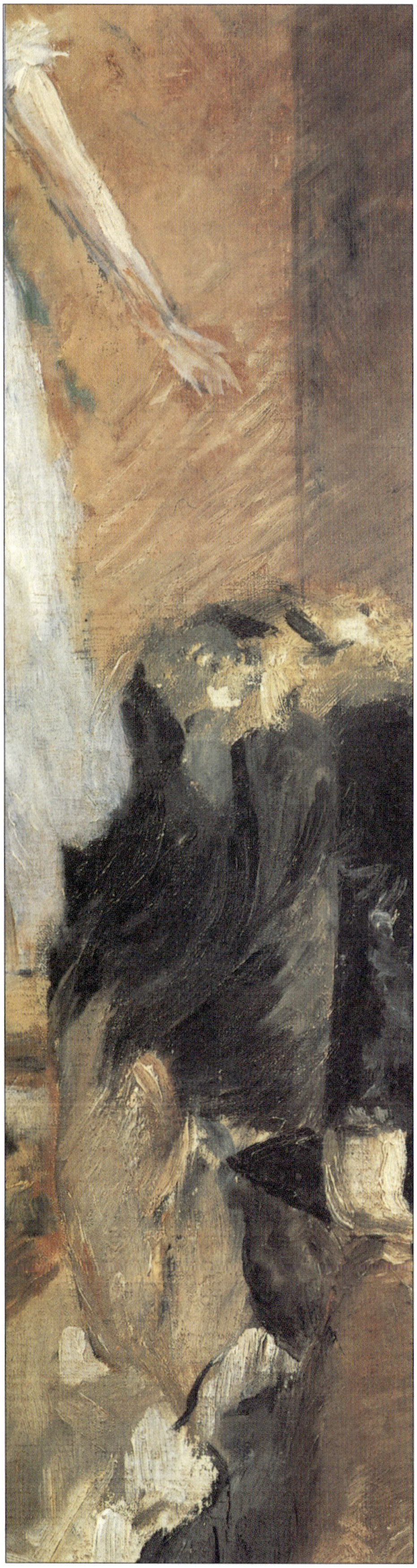

1

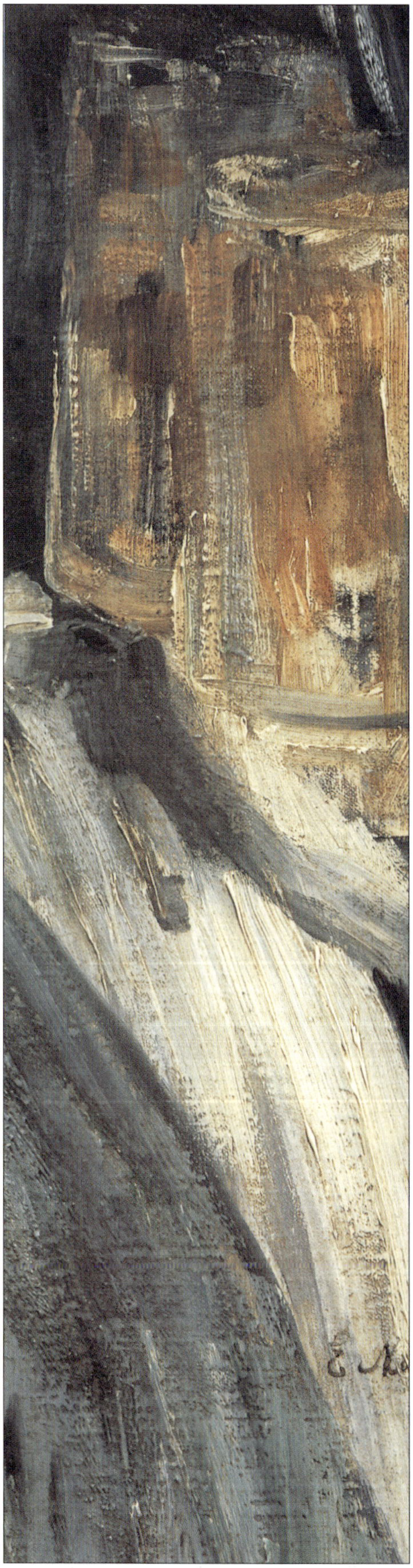

2

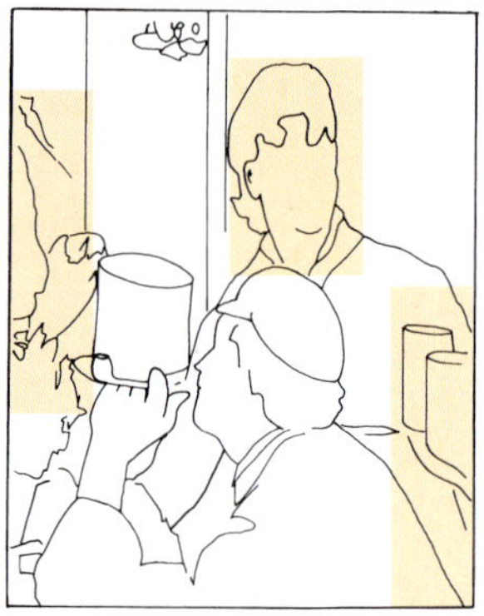

1 The dramatic cropping of the stage performer was a device frequently used by Degas. Warm touches have been achieved by the use of a red halo effect which can be seen around the performer's left hand and on the left of the cool, bluish contour formed by the profile of the woman.

2 This detail shows the most freely worked area of the canvas. The overall blue effect of the man's smock has been created with bold sweeps of stiff Prussian blue overlaid with a lighter blue into which white and green have been worked more wetly. Long strokes of thickly applied white pigment have left a thin impasto line on either side of the brushstroke, suggesting the highlighted folds of the apron. The working-in of yellow ocher over the underpainting gives the impression of the semi-translucency of the glasses and of reflected local color.

3 *Actual size detail* The execution of the face is much tighter than that of other areas of the canvas. Like the waitress in *Bar at the Folies Bergère* (see page 357), the model here also has a high coloring. The deep pink tones of her mouth and the left side of her face are repeated in areas on either side of her. The tonal contrasts are relatively small, but white highlights have been used on the right side to indicate the source of light and also to give a luminosity to her complexion.

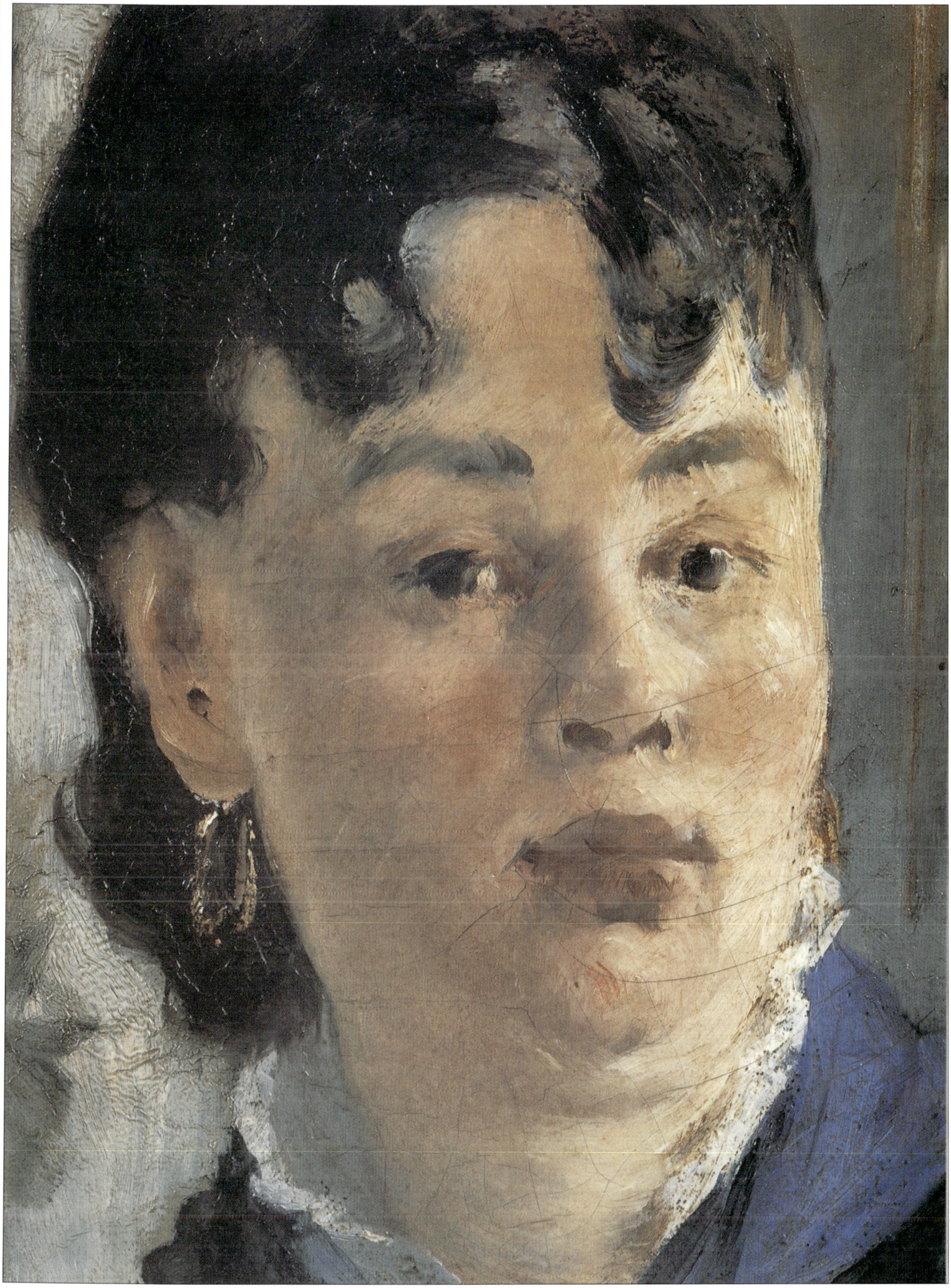

3 *Actual size detail*

Bar at the Folies Bergere

1881

$37^3/_4 \times 51^1/_4$in/96×130cm

Oil on canvas

Courtauld Institute Galleries, London

This was Manet's last great work, painted a year before his death. Seriously ill with locomotor ataxia, a degenerative disease of the nervous system which prevented him from moving with ease, his cast of mind was tending increasingly towards the melancholic. "Sorrow," he remarked, "is at the root of all humanity and all poetry." The painting is suffused with sadness as, isolated amid the splendor of the café, the young woman looks out with an unfocused and reflective gaze. The work draws together all the elements of Manet's work from the previous two decades: the contemporary subject matter, the single isolated figure, the idiosyncratic depiction of space, and the reference to a spectator beyond the picture plane. We are given, not only a demonstration of his virtuosity as a painter of still lifes, but also an invitation to probe beneath the surface at what remains always oblique and poetic.

Manet, who loved Parisian café life and the entertainments of the city, was drawn to fashionable haunts such as the now legendary Folies-Bergère, which opened in 1869. The novelist Huysmans described it as "stinking sweetly of corruption," seeing in such places a symbol of the times, and Guy de Maupassant was to describe the waitresses as heavily made-up women who "sold refreshments and love." But Manet's central figure has a freshness and innocence which recalls another literary source. She resembles Lisa, the *charcuterie* girl in Zola's novel *Le Ventre de Paris*, of which Manet owned an autographed copy. As Zola describes her standing behind her counter in the market of Les Halles, "she had a superb freshness, the white of her apron and sleeves continuing the white of the platters up to her rounded neck, to her rosy cheeks, where the tints of tender hams and pale translucent fats lived again . . . the mirrors . . . reflected her from the back, the front, the side . . . There a host of Lisas showed the breadth of shoulder, the full bosom, so still and soft that she aroused no carnal thought, and might almost have been a side of bacon." The high coloring and roundness of face certainly reflect Zola's description, and Manet's painting also emphasizes the same quality of being removed from her environment.

Isolated from the glitter of her surroundings, the expression of the waitress invites a multiplicity of interpretations, and is made still more ambiguous by the duality implied in the reflected image. Although the painting was received with acclaim at the 1882 Salon, its bizarre optical effects were commented on. The entire background presents a mirrored reflection of a gallery of seated figures, the counter of the bar at the front of the painting, and the waitress herself. Yet the reflection is deliberately inaccurate, not only in the positioning of the reflected figure but also in the pose, which shows her smaller and leaning slightly forward. Manet's denial of naturalism is provocative: he seems to have deliberately used the distorted reflection as a means of presenting another aspect of the subject

Like *Olympia* (see page 341), this work involves the viewer directly. In the earlier painting, the hissing cat alluded to the arrival of an unseen visitor, and here the spectator is presented directly with himself in the form of the reflected male figure at the top right. In a contemporary caricature of the picture, the image was "corrected" by the inclusion of the back of this figure, deliberately excluded from the painting. The modernity of the setting and the simple grandeur and detachment of of the woman herself evokes one of Baudelaire's strictures on art. He held that the artist should interpret his own time while also recreating the magnificence of earlier art. "He must sift from fashion what is poetic in the historical, and extract the eternal from the transitory."

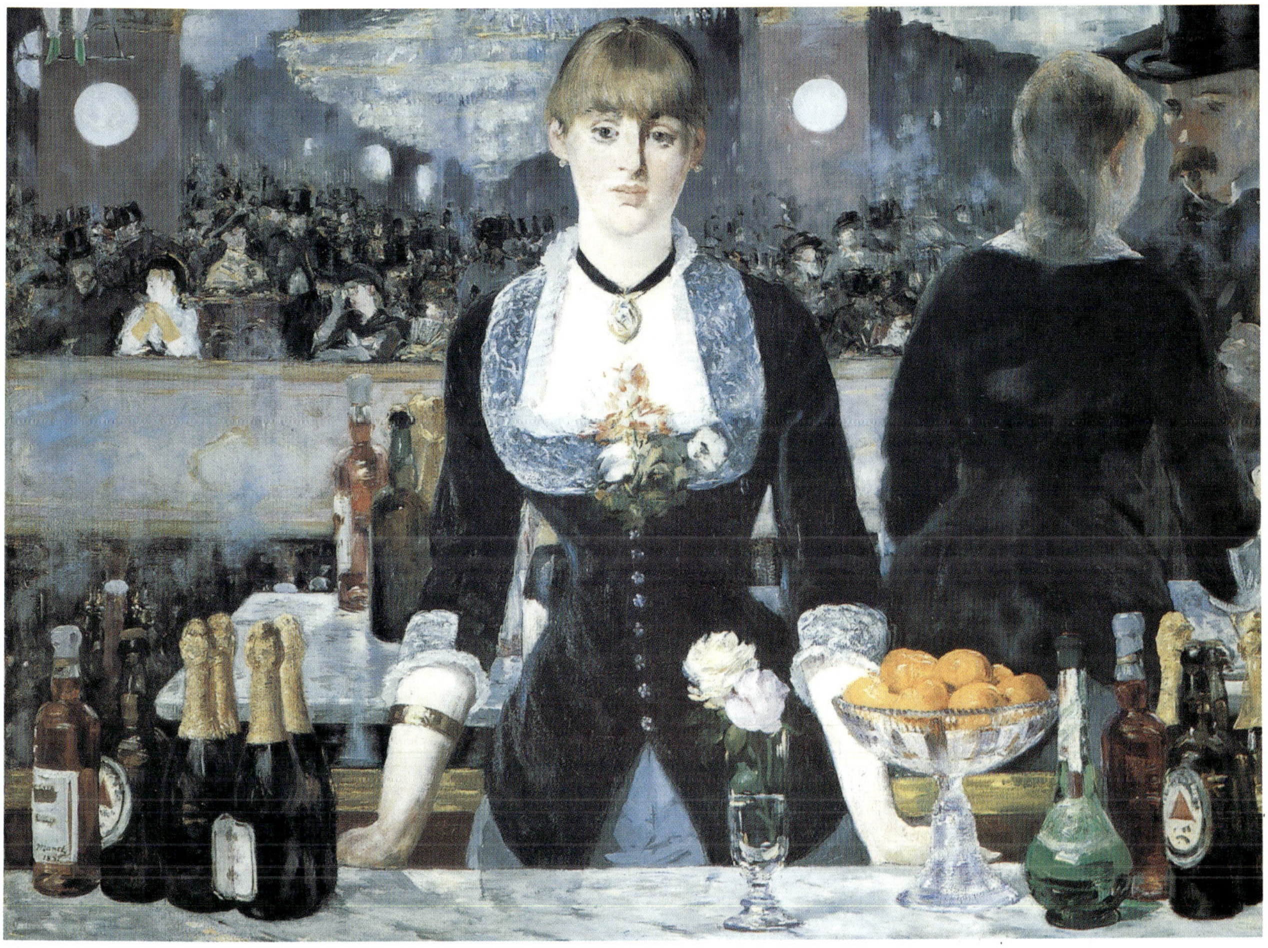

The Folies-Bergère was the embodiment of the type of establishment a contemporary Anglo-Saxon tourist guide warned against. "You cannot go into any public place in Paris without meeting one or more women that you will recognize at a glance as belonging to the class known in French society and fiction as the *Demi Monde.*" The model for the painting, whose freshness and innocence belies de Maupassant's description of the waitresses as heavily made-up women who sold "refreshments and love," was an actual barmaid at the establishment. Her name was Suzon, and she was doubtless picked for her prettiness. Manet posed her in his studio, where he had built a reconstruction of the marble bar, while the background, which includes a number of Manet's friends, was painted from studies made at the Folies-Bergère. The painter Gaston Latouche admitted to having posed for the gentleman on the right, while the woman in yellow gloves, recognizable from a pastel portrait, is the dazzling Méry Laurent, an intimate of the artist. Jeanne Demarsy, behind, in brown, has also appeared in portraits.

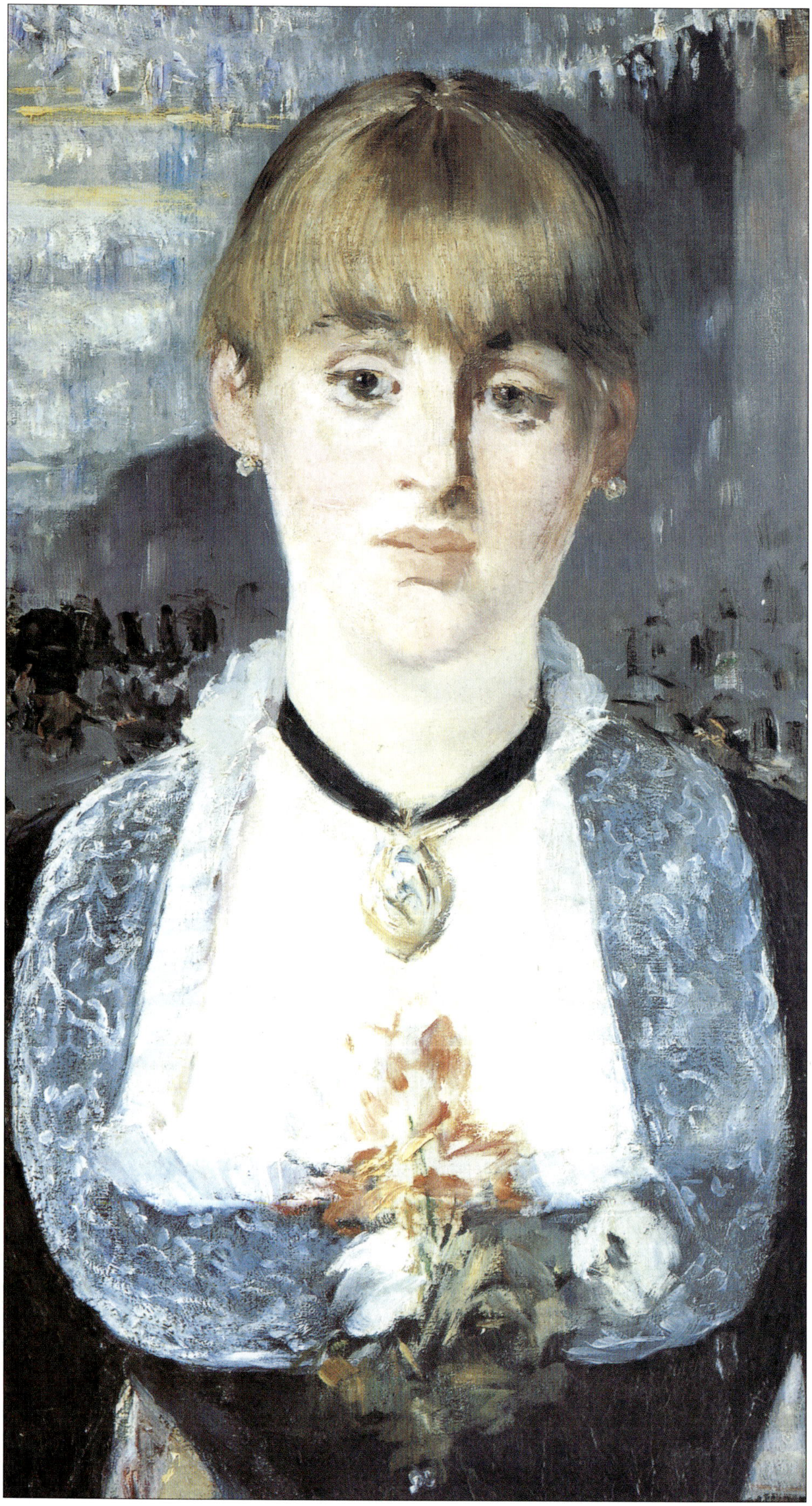

1

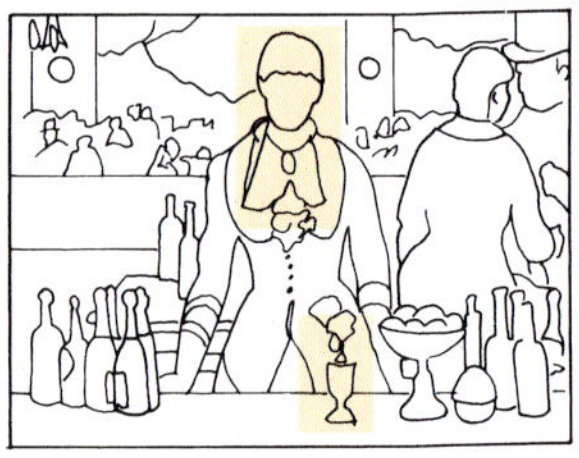

1 Manet has used painterly effects to create the texture of the model's hair, skin and clothing. The richness of the velvet costume has been achieved with a deep Prussian blue into which a lighter blue, or possibly white, has been worked in wetly to produce the effect of light on the folds of the fabric. For the lace trim of the dress, a transparent, thinned white has been laid lightly over the dark blue and then overlaid with denser swirls of pigment to suggest the patterns. The corsage of flowers picks up the girl's skin tones and echoes the still life motif in the foreground of the painting.

2 *Actual size detail* Manet painted a large number of fine still lifes, sometimes of nothing more than a loaf of bread, a few sticks of asparagus or a ham, and sometimes more elaborate flower pieces, which are among the loveliest of his paintings. This arrangement of two full blooms in a slender glass provides a delightful arrangement at the forefront of the picture as well as linking the immediate foreground to the figure of the girl in the center. The bottom of the glass above the stem is indicated by a bold sweep of stiff white pigment, while impasted white paint is used for the light-struck edges and top rim.

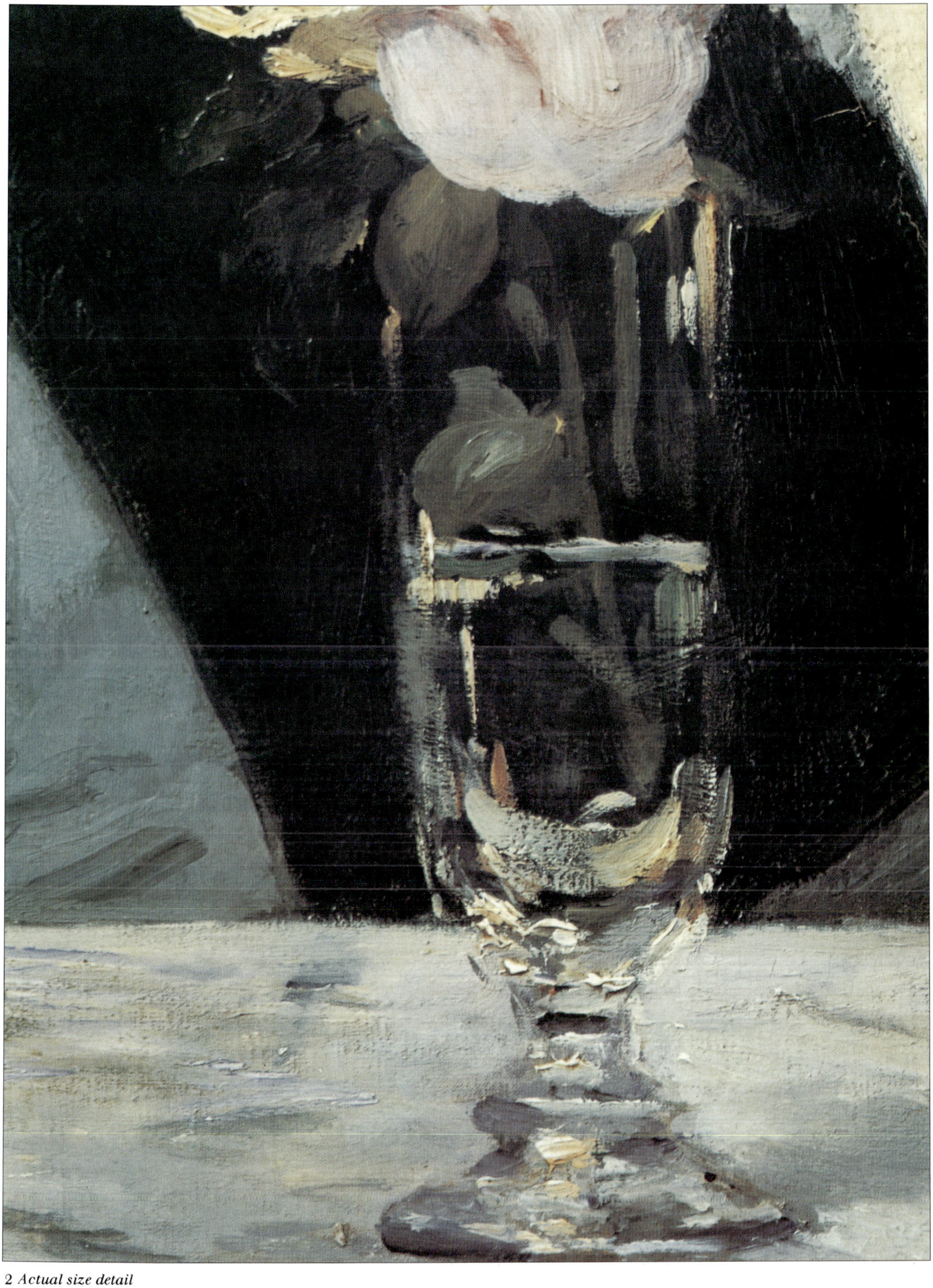

2 *Actual size detail*

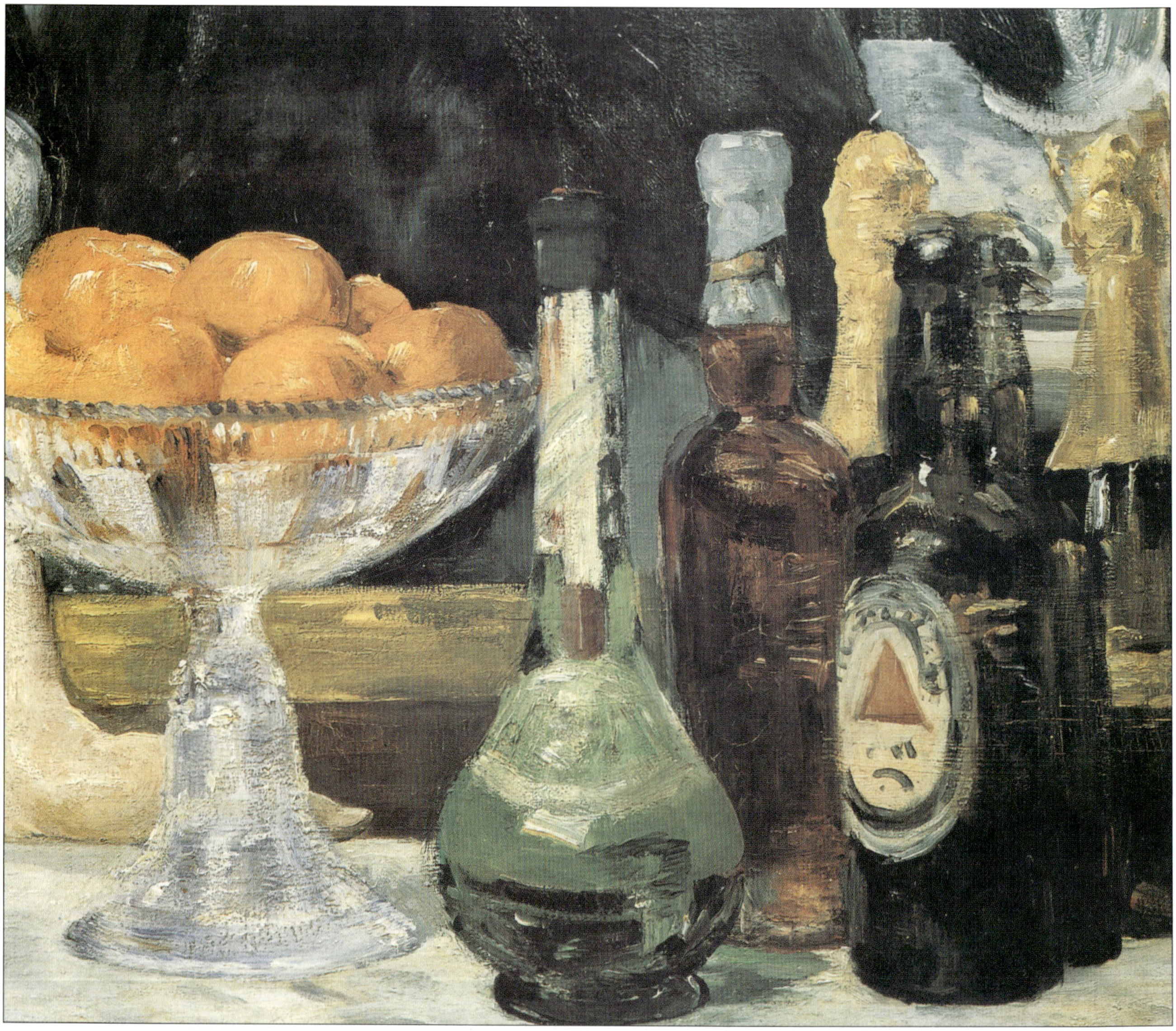

3

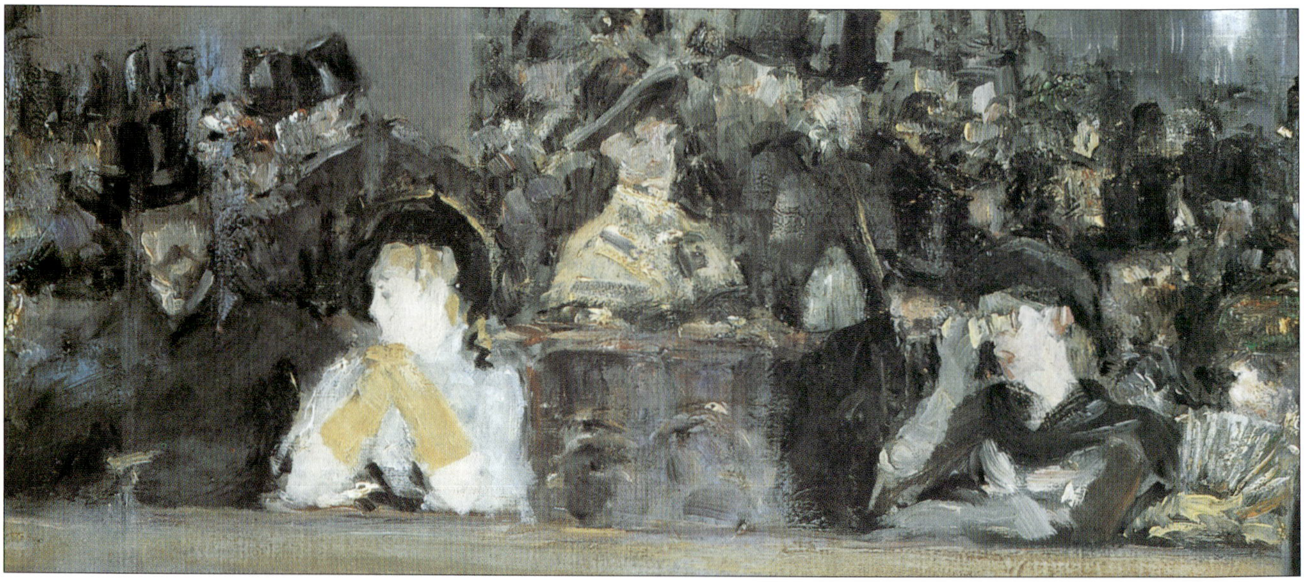

4

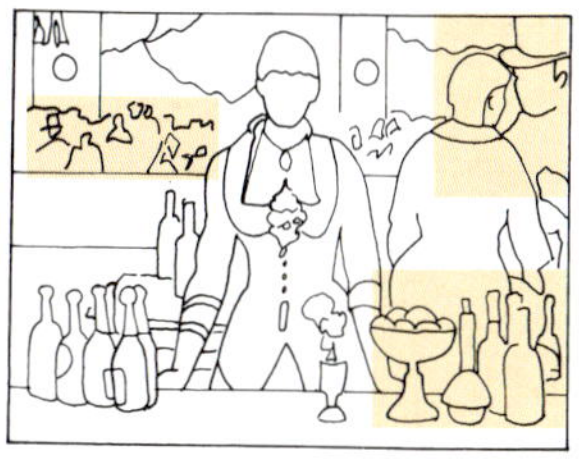

3 Manet arranged the bottles and dish of oranges on the replica of the bar that he set up in his studio. Clearly identifiable are the bottles of champagne, crème de menthe and Bass Pale Ale, recognizable through its distinctive red triangle. The bottles are painted freely, wet-in-wet, while for the less reflective surface of the multi-faceted glass dish on the left, Manet has dragged white paint over a dry surface, highlighting the shiny skins of the mandarin oranges with small touches of thick white paint.

4 Clearly recognizable from other portraits is the celebrated beauty Méry Laurent, depicted here in yellow gloves. Kept by a series of wealthy men, she enjoyed the company of artists and musicians, and remained one of Manet's closest friends. Behind her, in beige, rapidly and sketchily painted, is Jeanne Demarsay, a young beauty whom Manet painted a number of times. The haze of smoke which de Maupassant described as hanging over the hall is suggested by the thin transparent overlay of blue paint. The fluid, free brushwork and lack of fine detailing of the seated figures, each realized with a few staccato strokes, evokes the bustle and animated chatter of the crowd in the gallery.

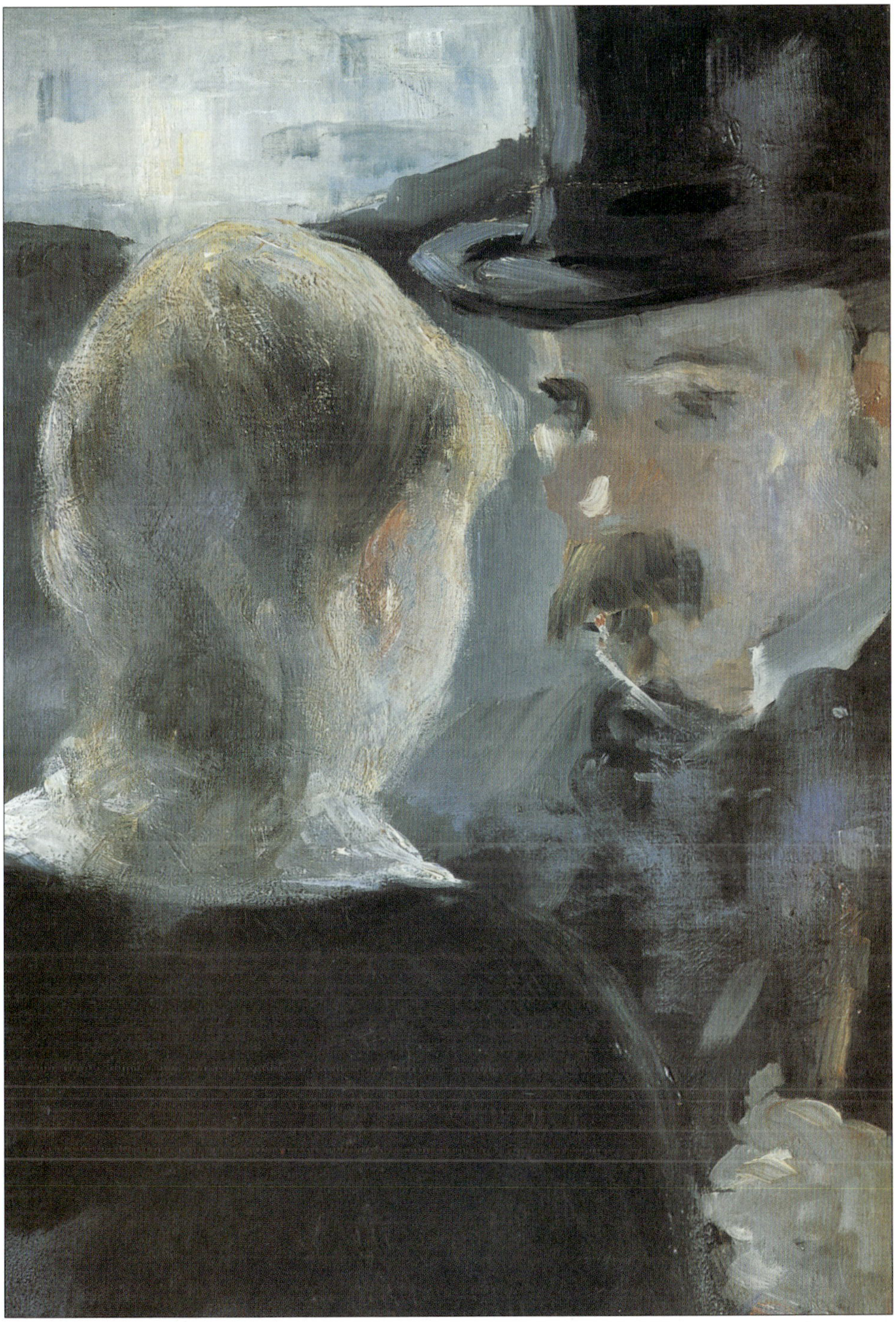

5

5 The smoke-dimmed mirrored reflection of the barmaid's back and the face of the man talking to her (who can only be seen in this reflection) have been laid in with thin paint and then overlaid with broad dashes of blue-gray paint, also thin. The barmaid is positioned immediately beneath a bright chandelier, and the sides of her head in the reflection are highlighted in pink, as are the cheekbones and nose of the man's face.

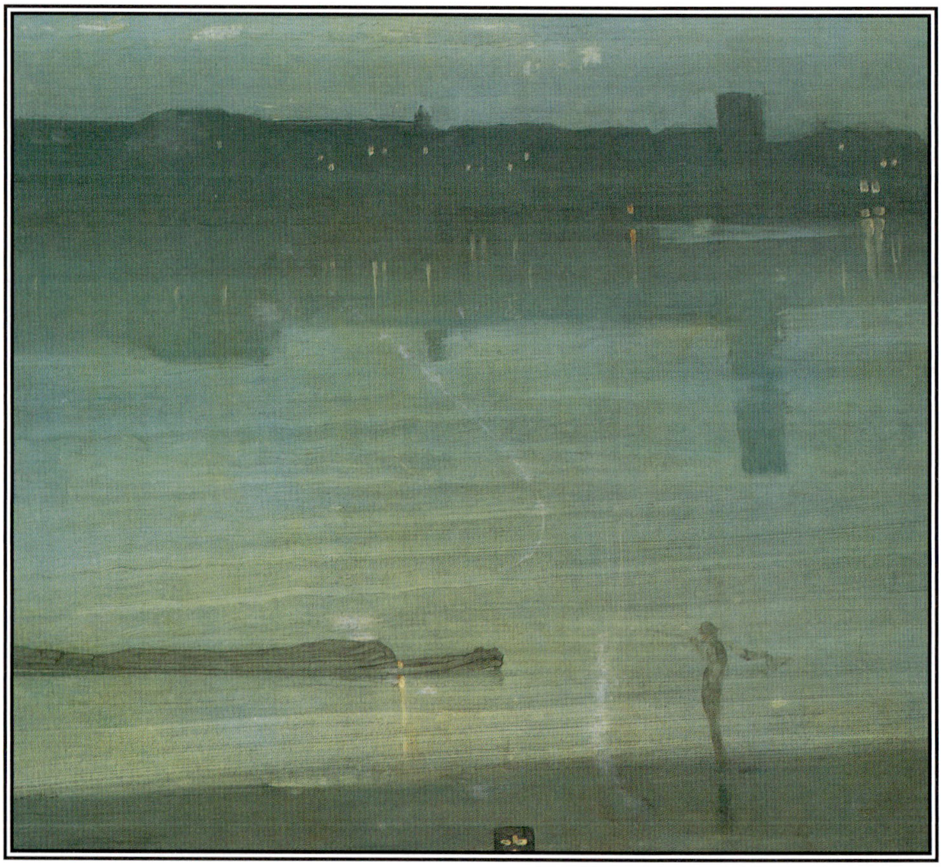

WHISTLER

Introduction

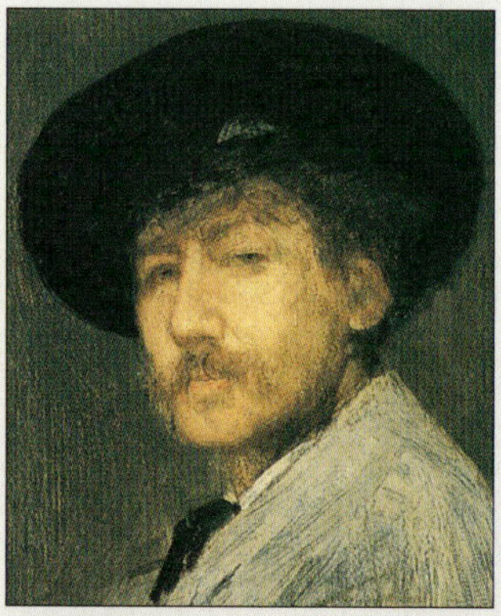

James McNeill Whistler
Arrangement in Gray: Portrait of the Painter (detail)
1872-73, Detroit Institute of Art

The words of a contemporary neatly encapsulate the self-projected image of James Abbott McNeill Whistler as one of the major eccentrics of his time. "A prince among men . . . he wore a short black coat, white vest, white ducks and pumps; a low collar and a slim black tie, carefully arranged with one long end crossing his vest." Whistler's brilliant wit, exquisite taste and tetchy rivalry with Oscar Wilde are part of folklore, but his place in the history of art is less easy to assess. Writers, critics and even fellow artists have regarded him as an outsider, a fugitive from tradition, never quite able to find a home among the many avant-garde factions of his day. His life and art present us with a tangle of paradoxes, and the very flamboyance of his personality has always tended to overshadow a real appreciation of his very remarkable work.

Possibly the only great artist to attend West Point Military Academy, Whistler was born in 1834 in Lowell, Massachusetts. He spent a substantial part of his childhood, however, in St Petersburg, Russia, where his father, a civil engineer, was employed by Czar Nicholas I to supervise the development of the St Petersburg-Moscow railway. In 1849 Whistler's father died unexpectedly, bringing to an end the family's affluent ex-patriate lifestyle, and they returned to America. The young Whistler bowed to his mother's wishes and enrolled at West Point in 1851, but his commitment to a military career was less than total; he later remarked of his (probably deliberate) failure to complete his studies, "If silicon had been a gas, I'd have been a Major-General."

Student years in Paris

He then spent a year as a cartographer in the US Coastal Survey Office in Washington, where he gained a sound introduction to the techniques of etching. But he was drawn to the Bohemian life, particularly after reading Henri Mürger's colorful novel, *La Vie de Bohème* (1848), and in 1855 he left for Paris, never to return to the land of his birth. There he became friendly with other artists, notably Gustave Courbet and later Edgar Degas and Henri Fantin-Latour, and after six months he enrolled at the Académie Gleyre, where several of the painters later to become the Impressionists also studied. Charles Gleyre specialized in the popular Neo-Grecian style which drew on antique subject matter, both as a pretext for displaying the skill of the artist and as an acceptable means of introducing an erotic element into paintings. Gleyre's studio maxims, such as "Black is the basis of all" and "Style is everything," were famous, and his influence on Whistler's subsequent painting was stronger than is often acknowledged.

Although the young Whistler did not neglect his studies, he was satirized as the "idle apprentice" in the novel *Trilby* by George du Maurier, who was in Paris at the same time. In the book, Whistler featured as one Jos. Sibley, whose lazy southern ways, outlandish dress and self-consciously idiosyncratic behavior set him apart from the rest of the "Paris Gang," which included the subsequent President of the Royal Academy, Edward Poynter. (Whistler quite rightly objected to his portrayal in the serialization that ran in *Harper's Monthly Magazine,* and after the inevitable lawsuit, references to him in future editions of the book were excised.)

Formative years: the 1860s

Whistler's first major canvas, *At the Piano,* was rejected by the Paris Salon of 1859 and, following its acceptance and success at the Royal Academy the following year, he decided to move to London, where he felt he had a better chance of artistic and financial success. This was a period of transition and experimentation in the arts, and Whistler's work of the 1860s reflects elements of the new concerns shared by the avant-garde at the time, as well as revealing the twin influences of Courbet and the pre-Raphaelites. Gustave Courbet, the leading painter in the Realist movement, which took everyday life as its subject

JAMES MCNEILL WHISTLER
Symphony in White No. 1: The White Girl
1862, National Gallery of Art, Washington

Whistler has left us his own description of this painting. His mistress and model Jo is seen "standing against a window which filters the light through a transparent white muslin curtain, but the figure receives a strong light from the right, and therefore the picture, barring the red hair, is one gorgeous mass of brilliant white." Despite the artist's subsequent reworking of the canvas, notably the face, hands, wolfskin and carpet, his description still holds true.

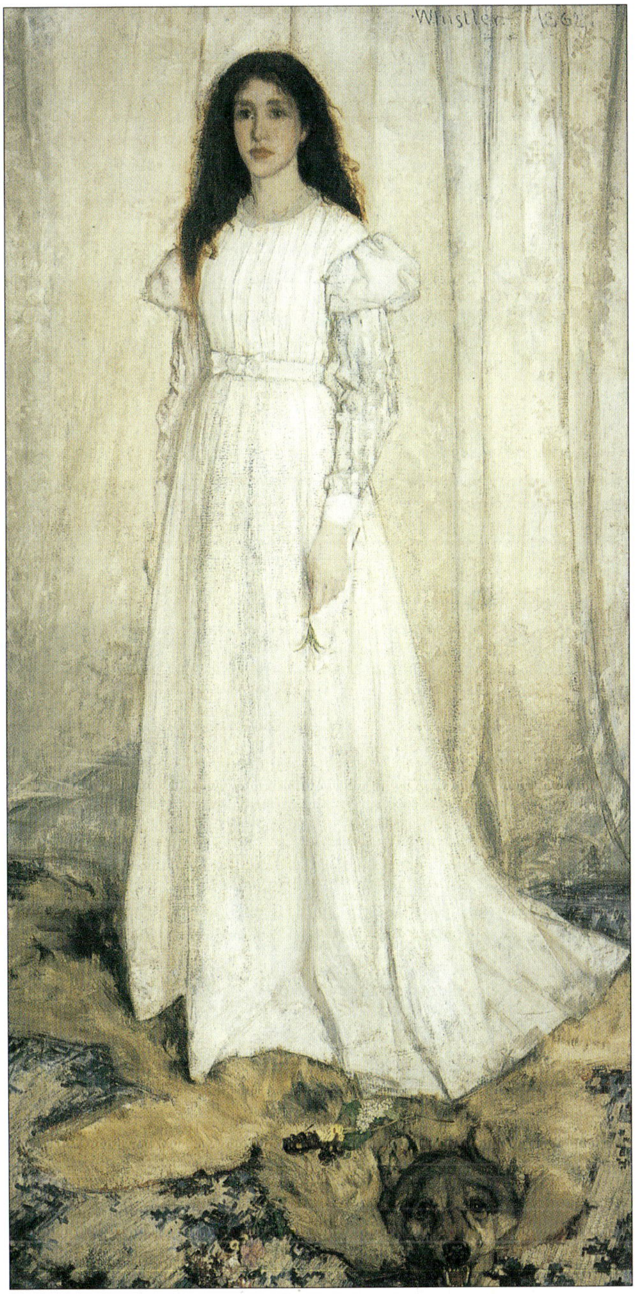

matter, was admired by all the young painters who were seeking a new direction for art. Whistler's contact with the pre-Raphaelite painters, especially Millais and Rossetti, encouraged him in his belief that the fundamental purpose of art was the creation of beauty. Velasquez, whose work he had seen at the Manchester Art Treasures Exhibition in 1857, was to provide a lasting influence, and his presence can be felt in all Whistler's work throughout his career.

In 1862 he painted the *White Girl* which, like his earlier work, *Wapping*, featured Jo, his Irish model. The painting was rejected by the Academy, and Whistler, enraged, sent it to the Paris Salon of 1863. The French jury that year refused over 4000 works, and such was the outcry from the rejected artists that the Emperor Napoleon III instituted a Salon des Refusés, where Whistler's picture shared a *succès de scandale* with Edouard Manet's innovatory canvas, *Déjeuner sur l'herbe.*

Whistler's painting, like the *Little White Girl* of the following year (see page 380), illustrates his concern to minimize the narrative implications of his subject matter, his unusual use — or non-use — of color and his penchant for pre-Raphaelite images of dreaming women. As the decade progressed the solid Realist characteristics of Courbet's art became increasingly modified by the influence of Rossetti and Millais.

After a number of years of crossing and re-crossing the Channel, Whistler eventually settled down in London — although the word "settled" is not entirely appropriate to one for whom permanence could never be more than a relative state — and in so doing he decided his fate. Had he remained in France with friends and colleagues such as Degas (to whom he later gave a copy of his collected writings, *The Gentle Art of Making Enemies*) his art and his place in the art history books would have been very different. Not only had he rejected the heritage of Courbet's Realism, he had also cut himself off from immediate contact with progressive Parisian art. It is possible that he might have found the competition from the French capital too daunting; he was always very uncertain of his own technical prowess.

In 1865 Whistler came into contact with the work of the English painter Albert Moore, whose languid and harmonious paintings of women in Greek dress exerted a profound effect upon him. Japanese prints had already begun to make a strong impact on painting, and now Whistler saw the arts of Greece and Japan as the cornerstones of his theory of a new art based on the twin qualities of harmony and beauty. "It seems to me," he wrote to Fantin-Latour in 1868, "that color ought to be, as it were, embroidered on the canvas, that is to say, the same color ought to appear continually here and there, in the same way that a thread appears in an embroidery . . . In this way, the whole will form a harmony. Look how well the Japanese understood this. They never look for contrast, on the contrary they're after repetition." Whistler was one of the first collectors of Oriental artefacts, but his attempt to assimilate Japanese prints into his work led to a series of uneasy paintings in which the various elements vied with each other in canvases that sought a modernity very different from that of Courbet's earthy Realism.

Toward the middle of the decade Whistler adopted Albert Moore's practice of signing his paintings with a symbol instead of his name, and the one he chose was a butterfly, developed from his own initials and drawn in the Japanese manner. Millais also used a distinctive monogram, and Moore himself signed his work with a scallop shell motif. Aubrey Beardsley was later to use a three-stemmed candlestick as his signifier, by way of homage to Whistler.

Painting and music

In 1867 Whistler painted a picture of two girls dressed in white, placed in an all-white setting, and entitled it *Symphony in White No. 3*. This was his first use of a

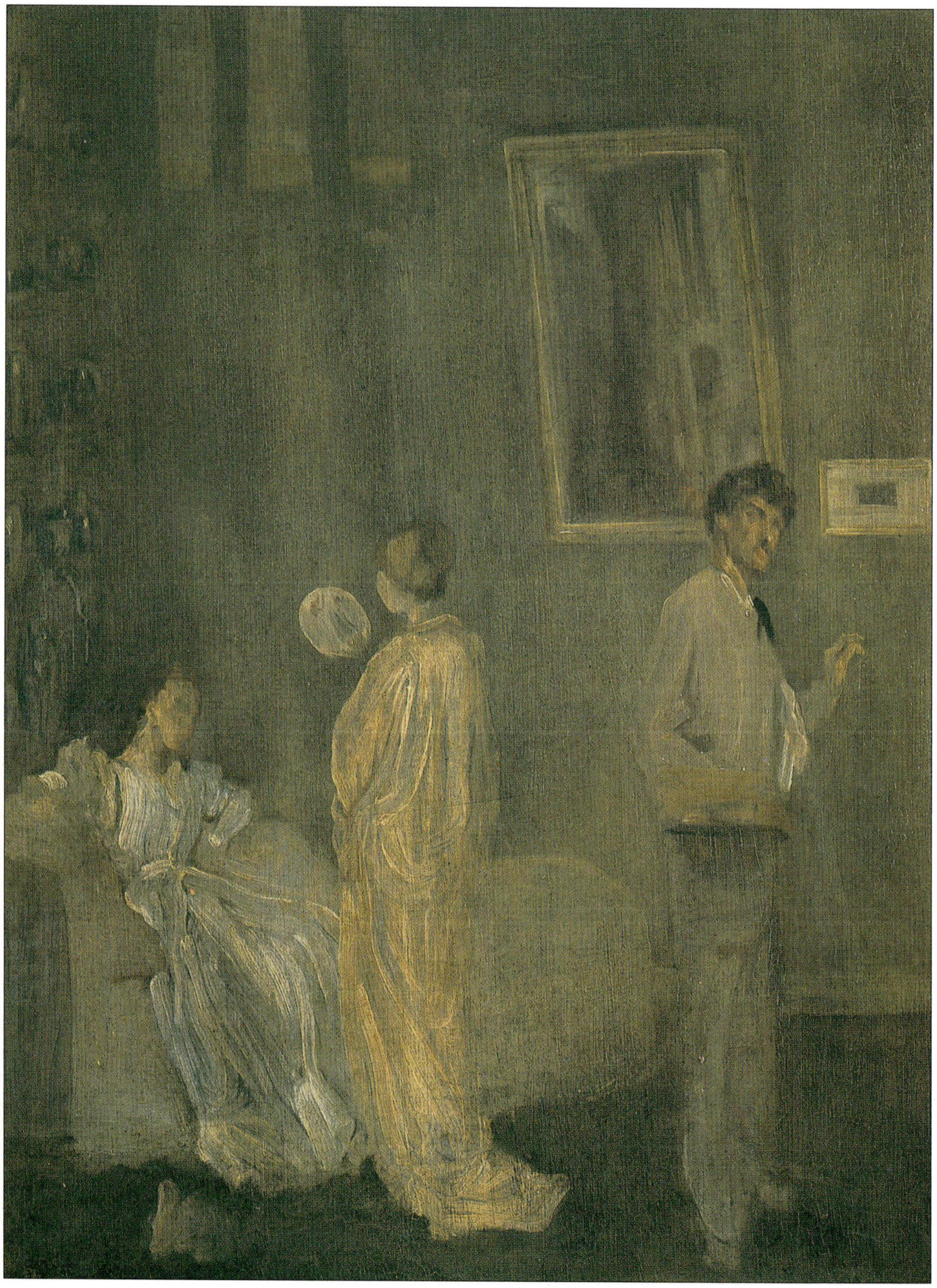

JAMES MCNEILL WHISTLER
The Artist's Studio
c1865, Municipal Gallery of Modern Art, Dublin

Whistler intended to paint a monumental canvas for the Paris Salon of 1866 featuring his friends Albert Moore and Henri Fantin-Latour in his own studio. His ambition was to produce a work equal to Courbet's *The Artist's Studio* and Fantin's two group portraits (one of which features Whistler). But this was never realized, and all that remains of his idea are two modest-sized sketches, of which this painting is one.

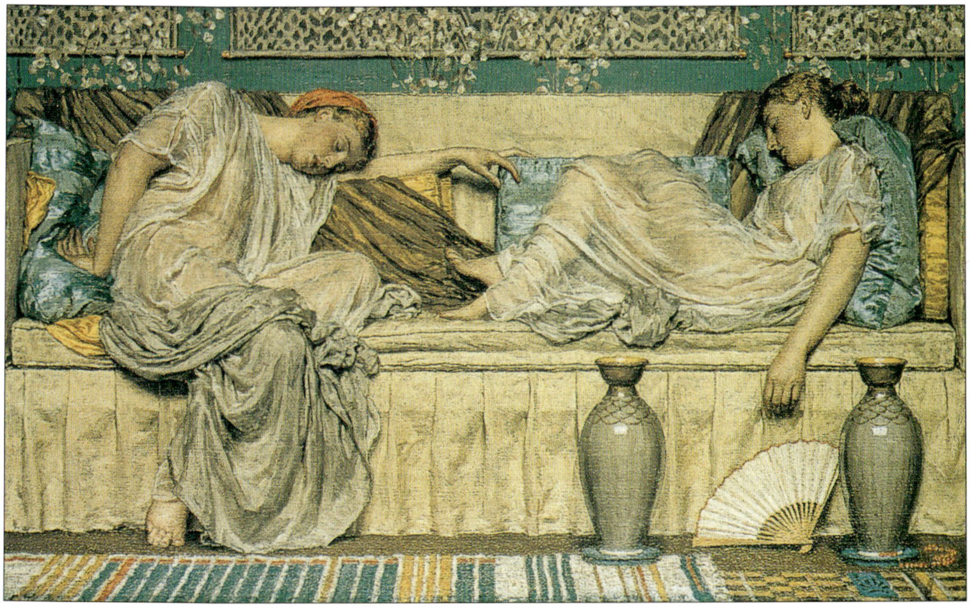

ALBERT MOORE
Beads
c 1875, National Gallery of Scotland, Edinburgh

Albert Moore's work, stressing the formal arrangement of pictorial elements, had a great influence upon Whistler, and foreshadows the well-known dictum of the French symbolist painter Maurice Denis. Denis wrote in 1890 that "a picture, before being a battle horse, a nude woman, or some anecdote, is essentially a flat surface covered with colors assembled in a certain order."

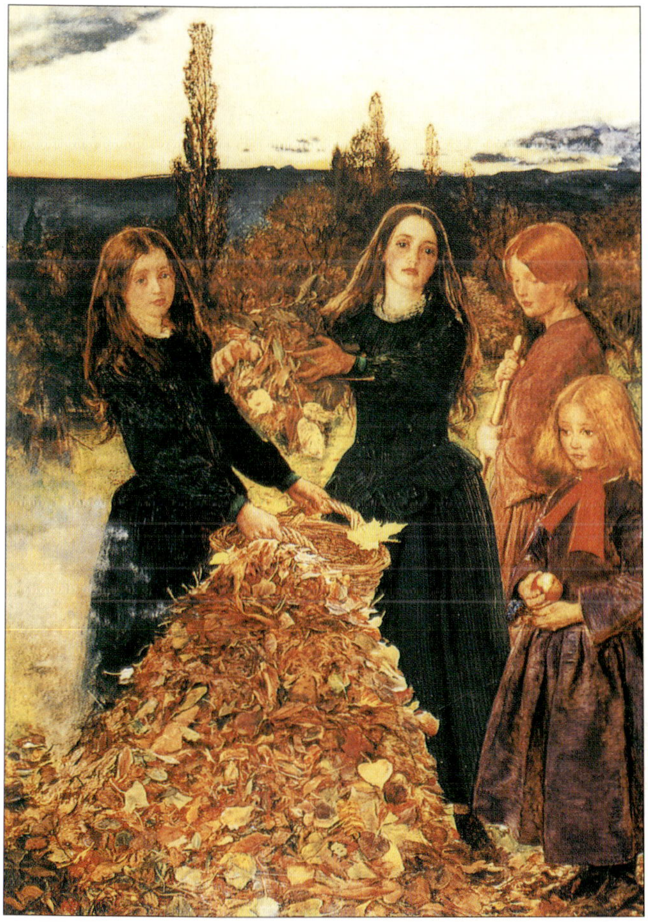

JOHN EVERETT MILLAIS
Autumn Leaves
1856, Manchester City Art Gallery

Whistler was very impressed with Millais' early work, drawn to its powerful symbolic content and evocative use of color to convey a sense of moody melancholy. A subtle erotic element which underpins much of the pre-Raphaelites' work also appears in Whistler's paintings.

musical term to highlight a picture's abstract qualities, a practice that would last until the end of his life (the earlier paintings were re-titled accordingly). Many of his paintings were called "arrangements" or "harmonies," and his views of the Thames were "nocturnes," a term borrowed from Chopin and suggested by one of Whistler's patrons, Sir Francis Leyland. The parallel between painting and music was one of the major debates among members of the avant-garde at the time, and Whistler's titles stress the musical analogies he tried to evoke in the mind of the viewer.

In the 1870s Whistler "came of age" as a painter; he finally threw off the influence of Courbet, abandoned the depictions of antique luxury suggested by Moore's classicism, and returned to the themes of the city and the river, producing many of the works for which he is best known today. The opaque paint surface, rich detail and human interest of his earlier paintings, such as *Wapping*, were replaced by a number of relatively small works in which a thin translucent wash of paint was used to evoke the atmosphere of London, and particularly the river, seen by night and transposed into a series of harmonious relationships of line, color and form. There is no moral or social element in Whistler's work – he did not consider comment or criticism to be the goal of art. Mundane reality, in his view, should be studied only in order to be transformed by the artist's vision into something possessing both flawless beauty and universal significance.

The society portrait painter

By this time Whistler was beginning to make his mark as a portrait painter, although his extreme perfectionism in every project he undertook resulted in a relatively small

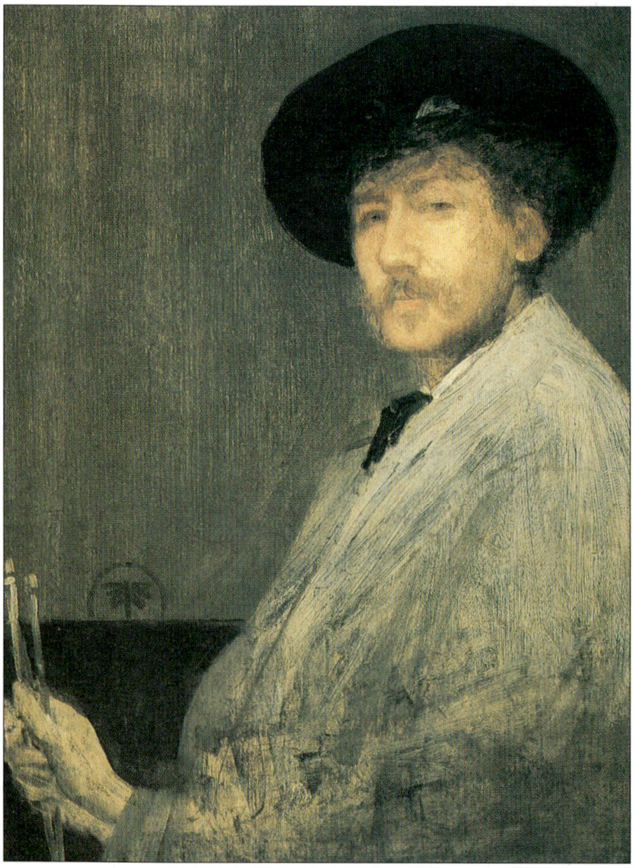

James McNeill Whistler
Arrangement in Gray: Portrait of the Painter
1872-73, Detroit Institute of Art

Titian and Rembrandt were very important to Whistler, and this self-portrait contains elements from the work of both masters. It is the first portrait to feature his famous single lock of white hair. Whistler has scraped down the jacket area, which has led to an odd visual ambiguity: is it the artist's left or right hand that grasps the paintbrush?

number of surviving paintings. He made intolerable demands on his sitters; poor Miss Cicely Alexander (see page 396) had to endure over seventy sessions before Whistler pronounced himself happy with the result. Every element associated with his creations had to be exquisite in conception and appearance, and Whistler planned each painting to have only a single skin, or surface, of paint, which meant that every one must, in effect, be completed in a single session. In practice, this involved a continued series of separate attempts to produce the ideal work, since each time a painting fell short of the artist's own high standards it would be scraped down and begun afresh at another sitting, instead of being corrected and reworked in the conventional way. When successful, as in the portrait of Miss Cicely Alexander, this approach has a freshness and a unity of surface that is comparable to Velasquez, whose paintings Whistler always hoped to equal.

The artist as interior designer

Following pre-Raphaelite practice, Whistler designed his own frames, which were invariably simple, often arrangements of fine reeds, painted with a variety of Japanese-inspired motifs in various shades of gold. As a picture should be a perfect piece of decoration on a wall, it was inevitable that he should treat the frame as a means of continuing and refining the decorative aspects of the painting, and the logical extension to this was to take his principles of design into the environment itself. Most of his ventures into the area of interior design have sadly long since vanished, although Claude Monet's house at Giverny may well have been inspired by Whistler's ideas. His reputation as an interior designer of genius must rest on the reconstruction by Washington's Freer Gallery of his Peacock Room.

In 1876 Sir Francis Leyland commissioned the artist to make some minor alterations to his dining room, which housed a collection of porcelain and Whistler's portrait of Christine Spartali of 1864. The result was one of the most famous interiors of the 19th century. Essentially, Whistler got carried away. Instead of merely repainting the small red flowers on the priceless 16th-century hand-tooled leather that covered the walls of Leyland's room, he obliterated it with blue paint on which he introduced swaggering blue peacocks, which strut about their blue-green and gold enclosures quivering with pride. A priceless Persian carpet with a red border which he saw as clashing with the new color scheme was trimmed to remove the offending red, and poor Leyland returned home to find that not only had his walls been completely overpainted without his permission, but that his private residence had been the stamping ground of Whistler's entourage throughout that winter. He never forgave Whistler this infringement of his privacy – nor did he appreciate the artist's close relationship with his wife – and accordingly withdrew his hitherto generous support of the artist and paid only half of his bill for 2000 guineas.

The artist versus the establishment

Whistler's relationship with the British art establishment had never been a happy one, and it reached breaking point in 1877 when John Ruskin made a disparaging reference to Whistler's painting of *The Falling Rocket* (see page 400), exhibited at the opening exhibition of the Grosvenor Gallery. Ruskin wrote that he had "seen, and heard, much of Cockney impudence before now; but never expected to hear a coxcomb ask 200 guineas for flinging a pot of paint in the public's face." Although Ruskin was by now an old man, he was still the most respected and feared of all Victorian critics, and Whistler was forced into an attempt to protect his reputation, and hence his portrait practice. He sued Ruskin for libel. The case was a farce and the result of the court action was public humiliation – technically, Whistler won but was awarded a derisory farthing, the smallest coin in British currency at the time – for damages.

The artist, already impoverished by Leyland's withdrawal of support, was declared bankrupt, and he still had to pay his legal costs. With characteristic aplomb, he hung the farthing from his watch fob and set out to recoup his losses, turning again to etching in which he had always enjoyed both popular and critical acclaim and which could be considered as a sound commercial enterprise. He left England for Venice, where he stayed from 1879 to 1880, and produced a series of etchings and pastels of the city, seeking out moody subjects and unfamiliar corners. He had earlier used his skill in etching to capture the bustle of London's dockside in sharp-focused detail in his justly famous *Thames Set* of 1859, but now he exploited the medium in a different way, producing evocations rather than literal descriptions.

James McNeill Whistler
Harmony in Blue and Gold: the Peacock Room
1876-7, Freer Gallery of Art, Washington

Hanging on the far wall and acting as a key to the decorative ensemble, Whistler's painting *La Princesse du Pays de Porcelaine* (1863-64) reigns over the sole surviving example of the artist's genius as an interior designer. During the creation of this interior he was described as "spending his days on ladders and scaffolding, lying on a hammock, painting with a brush fastened to a fishing-rod."

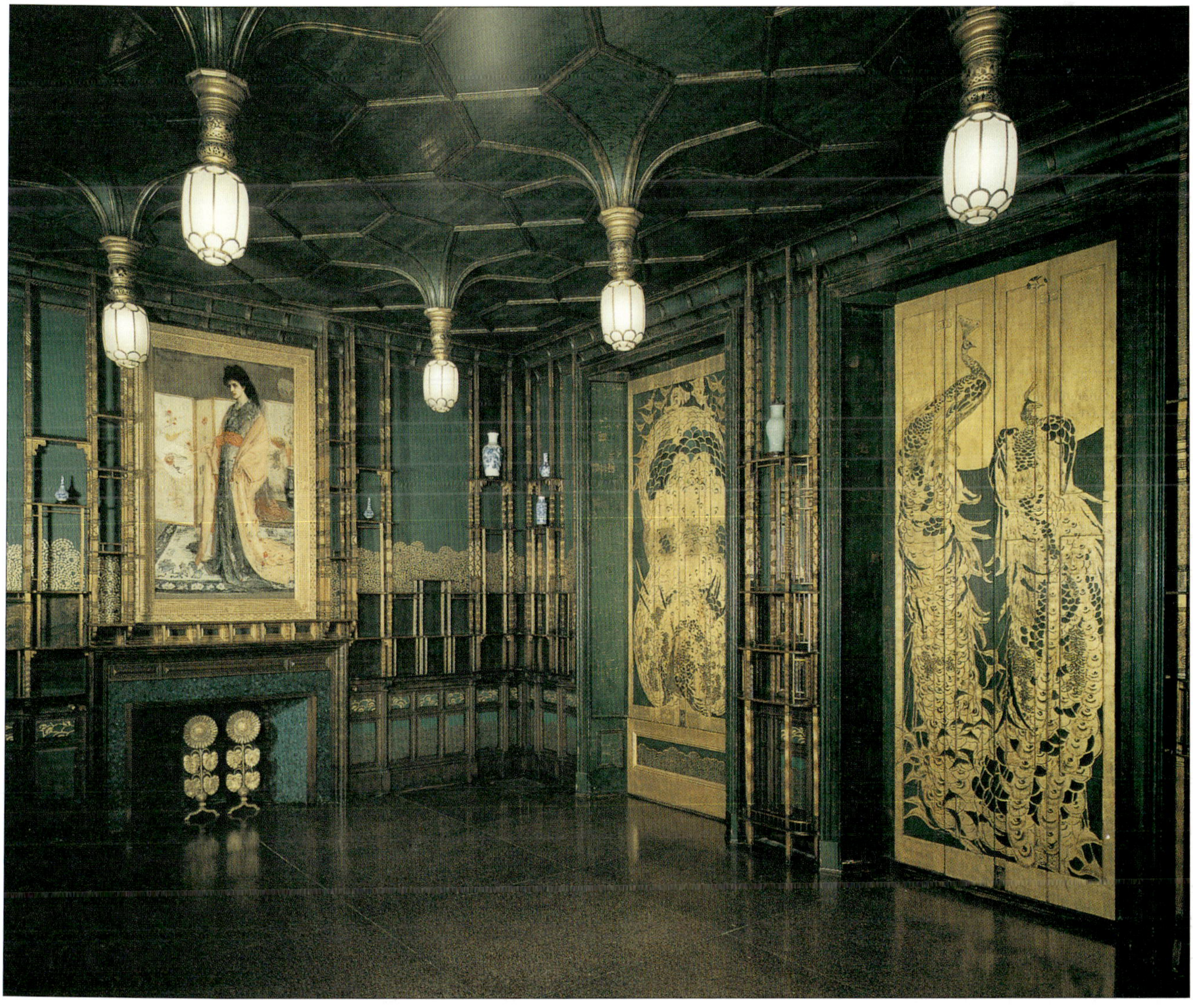

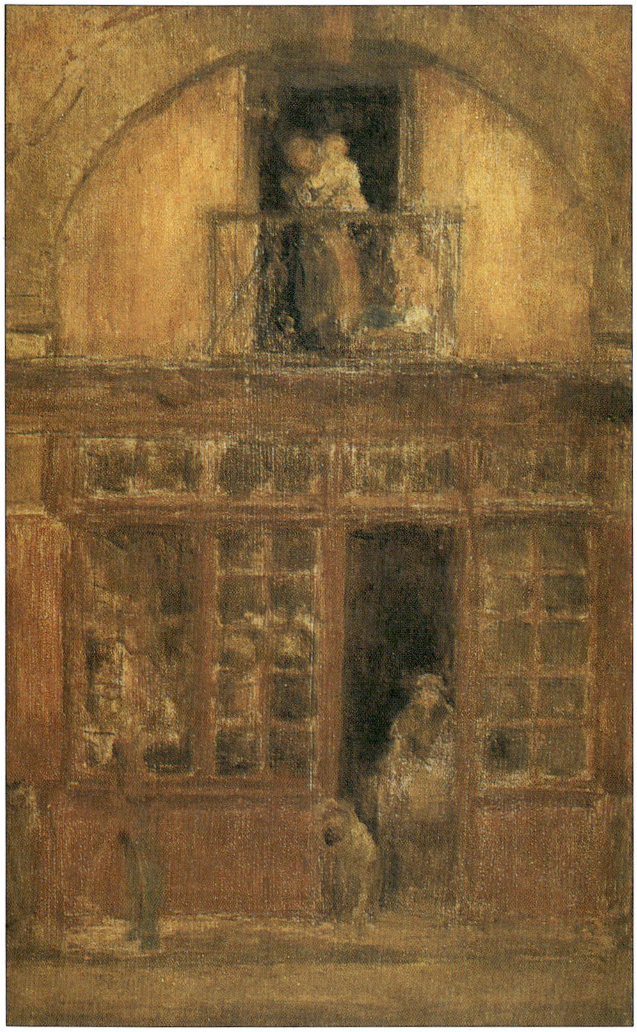

JAMES MCNEILL WHISTLER
A Shop with a Balcony
c1897-79, Hunterian Museum and Art Gallery, University of Glasgow

This delicate sketch, painted in Dieppe, was executed on a gray-primed panel the size of a cigar box. It could almost be a watercolor. Its mood of quiet intimacy, its color and geometry suggest the paintings of the younger generation of French avant-garde artists of the period, Bonnard and Vuillard, who also found poetry in unpretentious street scenes such as this.

The aesthetic position

A year later he returned to England to pick up the pieces of his shattered career. The process was a slow one, but Victorian values were waning, the intellectual climate was more favorably disposed to his ideas, and his Venetian etchings were popular. In 1885 he publicized his theories of aestheticism in the famous *10 o'clock Lecture,* which he delivered to select audiences in London, Oxford and Cambridge. This was a clear, witty and occasionally poetic exposition of his creed. He protested vehemently against the accepted belief that "Nature is always right" by putting forward the contrary view that Nature is usually wrong, "that is to say, the condition of things that shall bring about the perfection of harmony worthy of a picture is rare, and not common at all ... Nature contains all the elements, in color and form, of all pictures, as the keyboard contains the notes of all music. But the artist is born to pick, and choose, and group with science, these elements, that the result may be beautiful – as the musician gathers his notes, and forms his chords, until he brings forth from chaos beautiful harmony."

It is not surprising that an artist who took such care with his paintings, frames and settings should take equal care with the arrangement of his exhibitions. The rooms in which his works were hung were invariably designed with great simplicity and elegance. In 1881 the gallery in which his Venetian pastels were shown was decorated with a high-placed dark green dado which was separated from a narrow frieze of pink by a gilt moulding, the gold being repeated in a deeper tone across the skirting board. He designed a different decorative scheme for each of his subsequent exhibitions and his concern for achieving the best possible lighting of his works led to his invention of a muslin hanging which filtered the direct sunlight throughout the interior to create an acceptable level of dispersed light.

By the 1890s Whistler's position as a master of the evocative and the beautiful was established. In 1885 Stéphane Mallarmé translated his *10 o'clock Lecture* into French, and appreciative pieces by other leading writers began to appear in the French press. By the 1890s he had become a cult figure for the young artists and writers of the day; Oscar Wilde modeled his cult of the self on Whistler and attempted – not always successfully – to outwit and outdress the American dandy.

In 1892 a retrospective exhibition featuring forty-three of his works was held at Goupil's London Gallery. It was a public and critical success. Shortly after the exhibition, which had given him the satisfaction of reversing the tables on the English art establishment, Whistler left the country to settle once again in Paris, and in the same year his *Portrait of the Artist's Mother* was bought by the French state and entered the Luxembourg Museum.

In the summer of 1888 he married Beatrix (Trixie), the widow of the architect, E. W. Godwin, ungallantly abandoning Maud Franklin, his mistress of fifteen years standing, and he and his new wife resumed the pattern of restless traveling. In 1898 he was elected first President of the International Society of Sculptors,

WHISTLER'S PAINTING METHODS

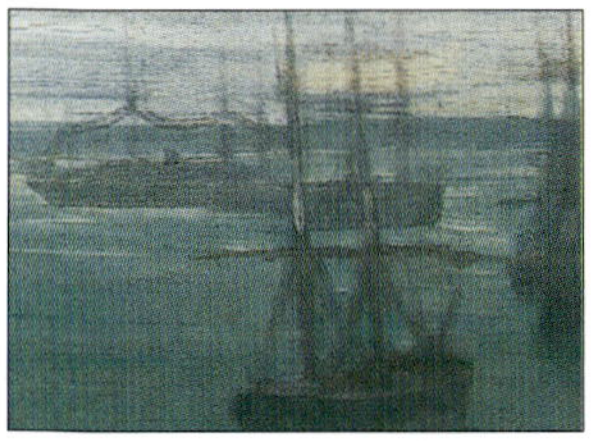

In *Valparaiso,* Whistler used very dilute pigment, thinned with a mixture of gasoline or turpentine.

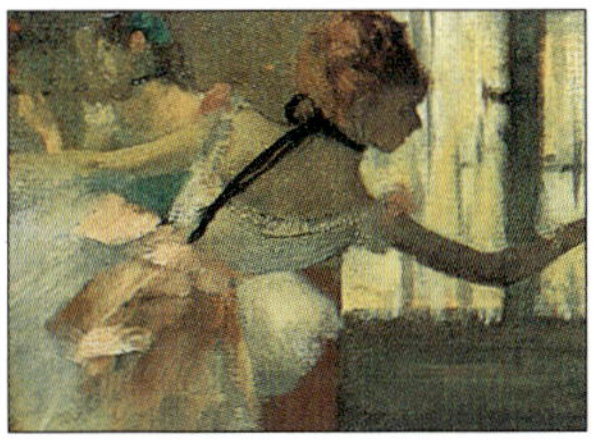

The transparent dress in the portrait of Miss Cicely Alexander was finalized only after continual rubbing down of previous attempts.

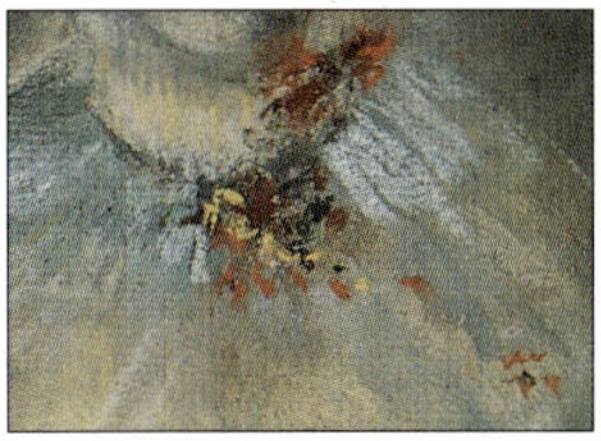

The head of Thomas Carlyle reveals nothing of the anguished hours of scraping down and reworking.

Whistler's technique was a quirky mixture of methods of painting learned at Gleyre's academy in the 1850s together with a series of improvisations directly onto the canvas. When working on large paintings, he used a three-foot long mahogany table as his "palette," arranging an array of mixed colors and tones on it with meticulous care, saying on one occasion, "If you cannot manage your palette how are you going to manage your canvas?" He worked with a fully loaded brush, holding it firmly and applying paint to canvas in a single confident sweep, standing at a distance from the canvas in order to balance the emerging forms with his subject. His long-handled brushes were specially made for him, and he also had a particular liking for large house-painter's brushes, his favorite being one to which he gave the name of Matthew. In place of the traditional mahlstick he preferred to use a walking cane.

Whistler always strove for a restrained and harmonious effect, avoiding excessive color and strong tonal contrasts, and unlike the Impressionists he never worked on a white canvas, always pre-tinting his ground a mid-gray, warm brown, red or sometimes even black. He would not begin a painting until he had prepared it, tone for tone, on his table-top "palette." In his portraits, the accents of tone would become sharper and sharper as the session progressed, and at the end of it the painting was either declared finished, or it was washed down with spirits in preparation for a fresh start the following session. His perfectionism was such that his unfortunate subjects often had to endure endless sittings.

For his *Portrait of Miss Cicely Alexander* (detail below), Whistler organized his table-top palette in the following way. In the center he placed a large mass of flake white. To the left of this were ranged light yellow to browns, and to the right were the reds, gradating to blues at the cool end of the color-temperature scale. Below the central white was a band of black, the extremities of which were used for mixing flesh and background hues.

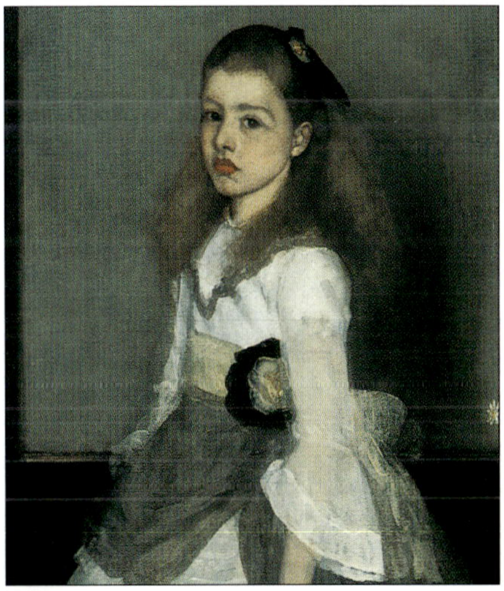

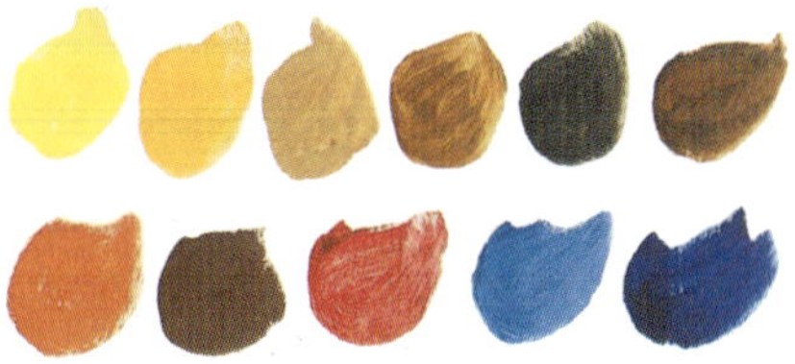

1 lemon yellow; 2 cadmium yellow; 3 yellow ocher; 4 raw sienna; 5 raw umber; 6 burnt sienna; 7 vermilion; 8 Venetian (or Indian) red; 9 rose madder; 10 cobalt blue; 11 Antwerp (mineral) blue

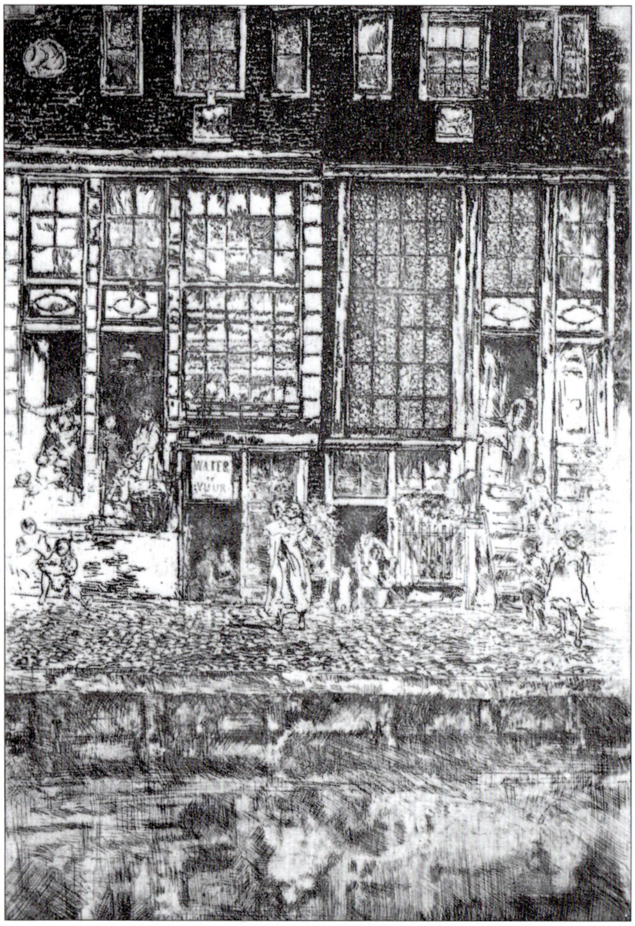

JAMES MCNEILL WHISTLER
The Embroidered Curtain
1889, Freer Gallery of Art, Washington

Whistler is generally acknowledged to have been one of the finest printmakers of the modern period. His graphic work reveals a control over the technical aspects of the medium that is sometimes lacking in his oils. This etching not only shows his debt to Vermeer and 17th-century Dutch art, but also provides evidence of his love of children.

Painters and Gravers, a position which he held until his death.

Whistler's last years were weighed down with official honors from the continent, but it is sad to record that his paintings received no serious recognition from the official art institutions of the United Kingdom – with the notable exception of the Glasgow City Art Gallery.

Since the 1860s Whistler had always found it difficult to sustain a cordial relationship with anyone for long, and his friendships often resulted in quarrels and litigation. But before his wife died in 1896 after a prolonged illness, he made a number of touching drawings, lithographs and paintings of her that suggest a more sensitive side to his personality than that recorded in anecdote and print, and a sense of loneliness pervades most of his late works. The final decades of his life, during which he continued to travel, were dogged by ill health and a growing sense of isolation, despite the adulation accorded him by his acolytes to whom he was simply "the Master." He died on July 17, 1903 and was buried beside his wife in Chiswick cemetery not far from the tomb of Hogarth, whose works were the first that he is known to have admired.

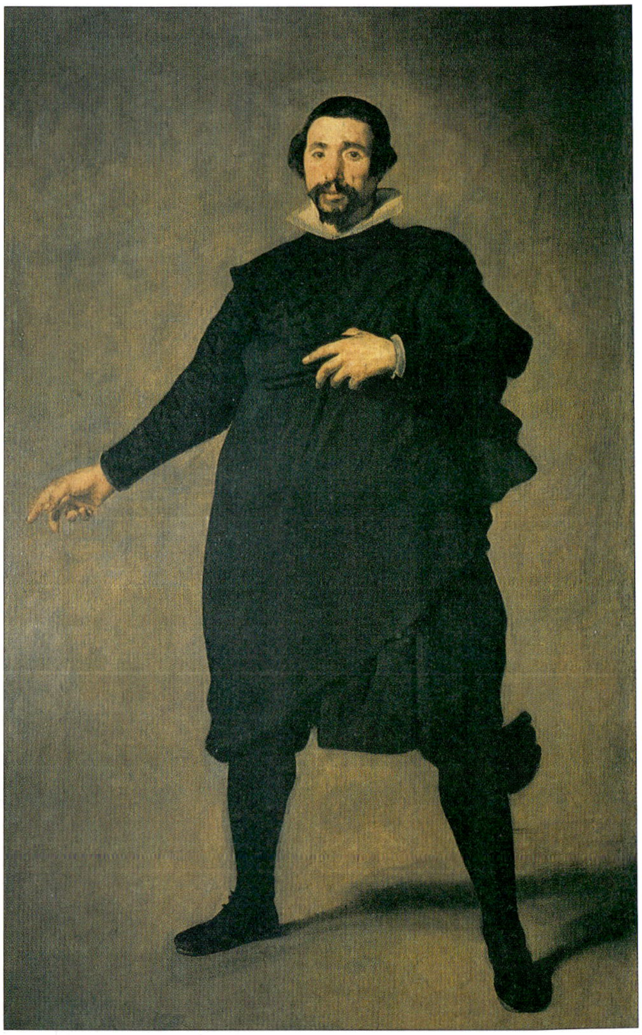

DIEGO VELASQUEZ
Portrait of Pablo de Valladolid
c1632-33, Prado, Madrid

The unity of characterization and formal harmony made Velasquez' full-length portraits a model for generations of portraitists. A photograph of this painting was found in Whistler's studio at his death, and his own late self-portrait (right) was obviously based on it.

JAMES MCNEILL WHISTLER
Brown and Gold: a Self-portrait
c1896, Hunterian Museum and Art Gallery, University of Glasgow

This poignant self-portrait, barely visible, is all that remains of a more finished work that Whistler rubbed down in 1900. It is a powerful image of the effect of time upon an individual, and has all the melancholy dignity of the Velasquez portrait it is based upon (left). It gives the modern viewer a very different picture of the artist than the one handed down by anecdote and contemporary description.

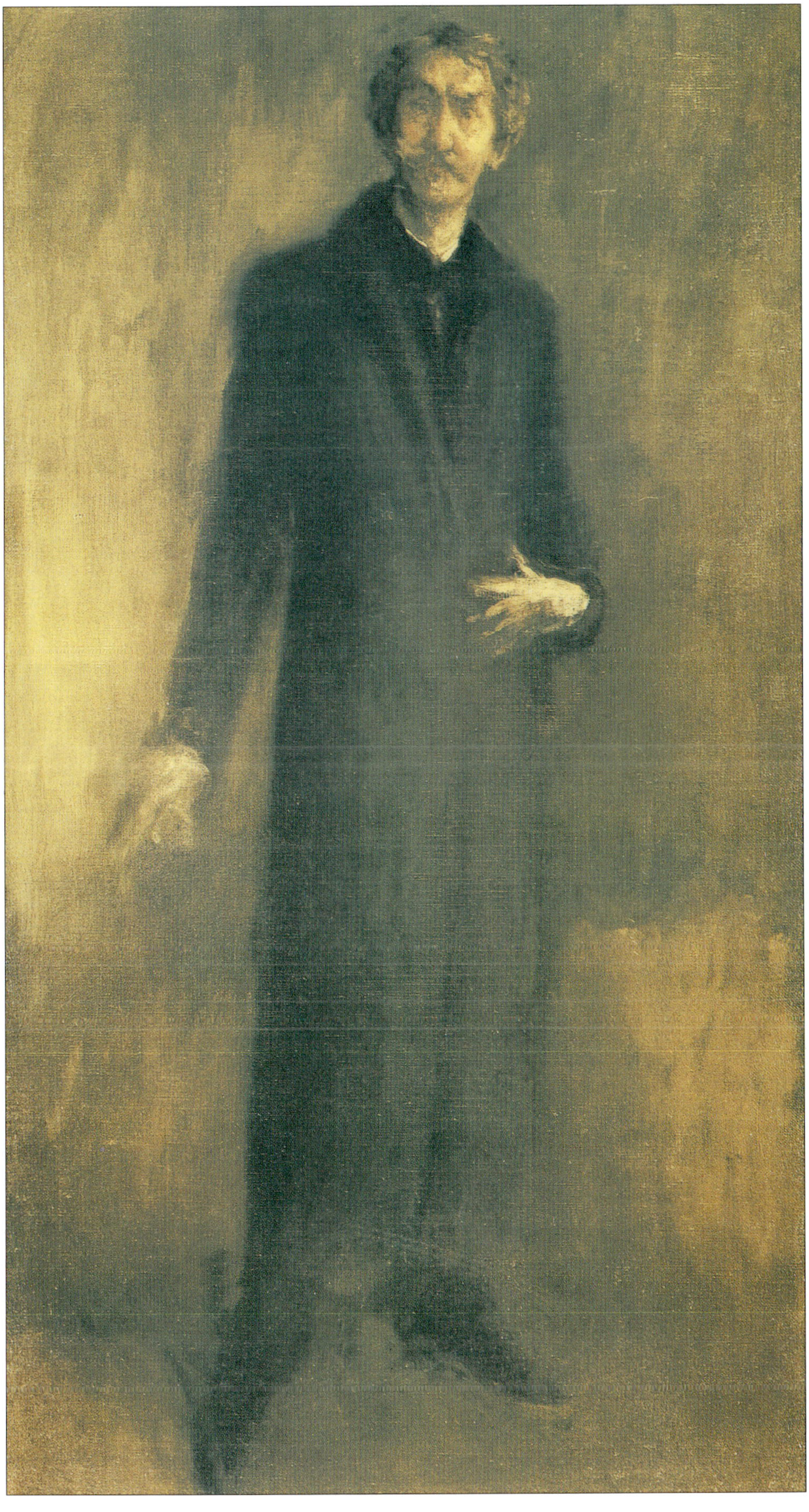

CHRONOLOGY OF WHISTLER'S LIFE

1834 July 11: James Abbott Whistler born in Lowell, Massachusetts.

1842 Major George Washington Whistler employed as engineer on Moscow-St Petersburg Railway; takes his family to Russia.

1851 Whistler enters West Point Academy, adds mother's maiden name, McNeill, to his own.

1854 Discharged from West Point for failing chemistry examination.

1855 November 2: Whistler arrives in Paris.

1856 Enters Charles Gleyre's studio, meets George du Maurier, Edward Poynter. Becomes close friend of Degas and Courbet.

1857 Visits Manchester Art Treasures Exhibition at Manchester, where he sees the work of Velasquez, the pre-Raphaelites and a selection of Japanese prints.

1858 *Twelve Etchings from Nature,* first major set of graphic work.

1860 *At the Piano* shown at Royal Academy.

1862 Settles in London.

1863 *The White Girl* shown at Salon des Refusés together with Edouard Manet's *Déjeuner sur l'herbe.*

1866 Travels to Valparaiso, Chile; paints first nocturnal scenes.

1871 Begins work on *Arrangement in Gray and Black: Portrait of the Artist's Mother* (bought by Musée du Luxembourg in 1891).

1876 Works on decorations for Francis Leyland's house at Prince's Gate, London, completed February, 1877; Leyland is displeased, only pays him half the '2000 guineas the artist claimed as his fee.

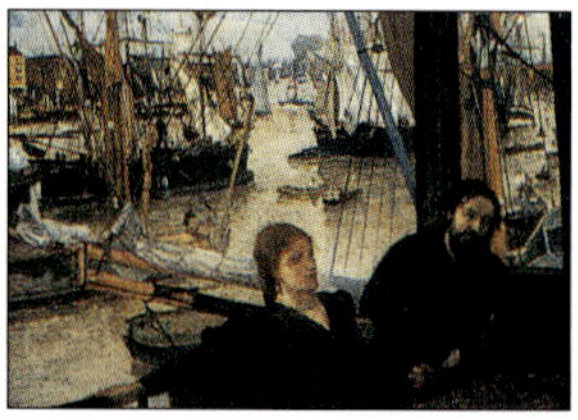

Wapping

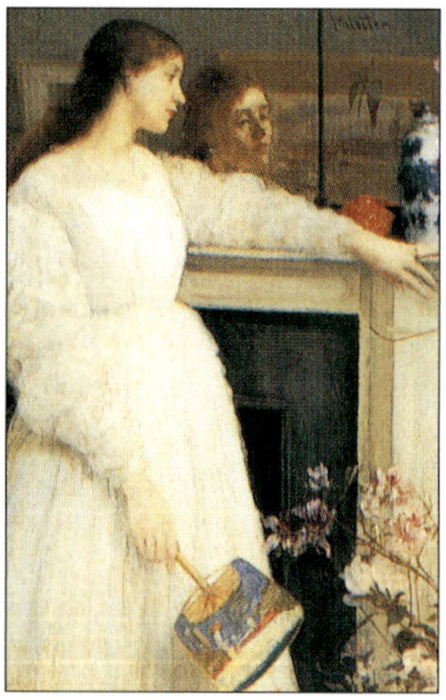

Symphony in White No.2: the Little White Girl

Nocturne in Black and Gold: the Falling Rocket

1877 Exhibits eight paintings at newly opened Grosvenor Gallery, including *Nocturne in Black and Gold: The Falling Rocket,* which is criticized by Ruskin. Whistler sues the critic for libel.

1878 November: Whistler awarded a farthing's damages without costs in his libel action against Ruskin; in severe financial difficulties.

1879 Leaves for Venice, stays for a year working on etchings and pastels of the city.

1881 Beginning of friendship with Oscar Wilde.

1885 February 20: First delivery of the *10 o'clock Lecture* at Prince's Hall, London.

1888 Through Claude Monet, meets Stéphane Mallarmé, the French Symbolist poet, who translates the *10 o'clock Lecture* into French. Marries Beatrice Godwin, widow of architect E. W. Godwin, designer of Whistler's former Chelsea home, the White House (1878-79).

1889 Major exhibition in New York; awarded first-class medal at Munich and Cross of St Michael of Bavaria.

1890 Publishes *The Gentle Art of Making Enemies.*

1892 Made Officer of Légion d'Honneur; major retrospective at Goupil Gallery in London.

1896 Wife dies, after long and painful illness.

1898 Teaching at Académie Carmen in Paris.

1903 July 17: Whistler dies in London.

1904 Memorial exhibition in Boston.

1905 Large memorial exhibition in London and Paris.

THE PAINTINGS

Harmony in Green and Rose: the Music Room

1860

Oil on canvas

$37^5/_8 \times 27^7/_8$in/95.5×70.8cm

Freer Gallery of Art, Washington

The setting for this picture was the music room in the London home of Whistler's brother-in-law Seymour Haden. Haden was an influential printmaker of the period, specializing in drypoint and *plein-air* techniques (working outdoors, directly from the subject), and his influence on Whistler's work was considerable.

While it was being produced, the painting was referred to as *The Morning Call*, a title which links it to the work of some of the more conventional painters of the period, such as Alfred Stevens, who depicted the social round of the elegant upper middle-classes. The standing figure, Isabella Boott, a friend of the family, is dressed *"à l'Amazone"* as the fashionable ladies who rode their horses in the parks of London and Paris were called. Having fulfilled her social obligations, she is now making her farewells to her hostess, whose reflected image can be seen in the mirror. The young girl dressed in white, sitting absorbed in her book and taking little notice of the proceedings, is Annie Haden, Seymour's daughter.

The painting owes much to the Dutch art of the 17th century, and its interest in spatial depth suggests a close study of the work of Ingres. But like so much of Whistler's work, it has the quality of evoking a mood rather than presenting the viewer with an easily readable narrative, despite the number of figures and the rich detail. When the artist saw the painting again at his retrospective in 1892 he wrote to his wife that it looked, "quite primitive – but such *sunshine*! None of the Dutchmen to *compare* with it – and such color!" Whistler painted this with the work of Parisian avant-garde artists very much in mind, and his innovatory treatment of space parallels the work of artists such as Degas and Manet. Degas noted the similarity of their artistic ambitions at this time. "In our beginnings," he said, "Fantin [Fantin-Latour], Whistler and I were on the same road, the road from Holland." Dutch landscapes and *genre* scenes offered a serious alternative to the vast historical or mythological canvases, known as *machines*, that were favored by the artistic establishment of the day. They were an inspiration to the new wave of artists who were beginning to reject academic subject matter in favor of depicting scenes of everyday life. This ambitious painting was clearly conceived in these terms, and represents a major achievement for an artist who was then only twenty-six years old.

Whistler repainted the head of Annie, and it seems that the mirror-reflection of the hostess, Deborah Haden, Whistler's sister and Seymour's wife, was a later addition. Certainly her presence makes the painting easier to interpret. The work is painted on a very coarse canvas, although its texture is only apparent in the thinly painted area of the skirt. Nearly a third of the canvas surface is taken up by the cream, green and deep pink of the chintz drapery, and this emphasizes the flat decorative quality of the work and contrasts with the powerfully realized deep space of the picture. The daring divisions of space and the continuance of the picture's action beyond the confines of the canvas anticipate Whistler's later use of Japanese compositional motifs and Degas' later and possibly more familiar works.

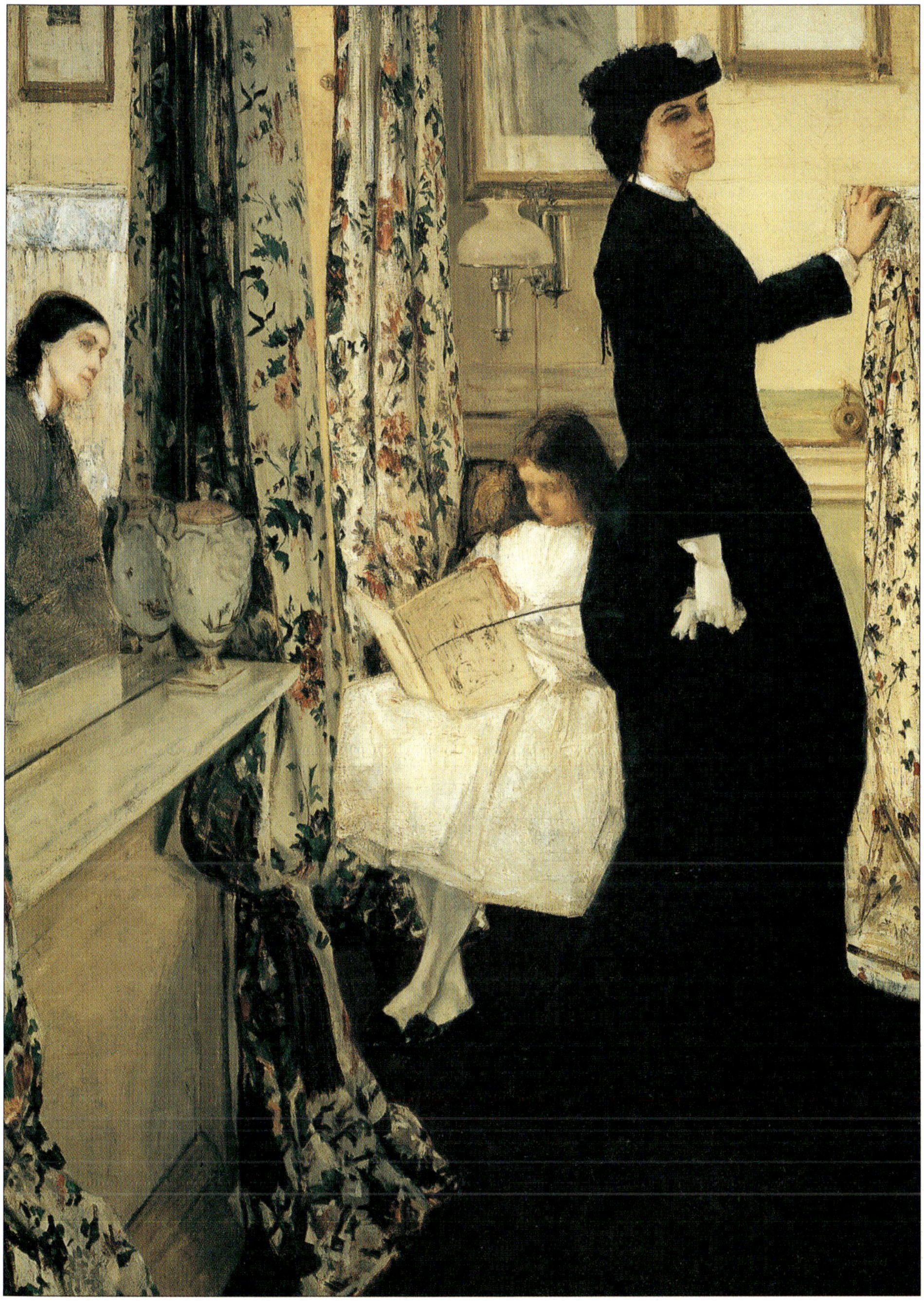

The painting is characterized by a Vermeer-like organization of pictorial space. The clearly defined silhouettes and strong light source are stylistic features typical of the work of the Dutch master. A sharp diagonal leads the eye to the hidden window through which the clear morning light streams, casting white highlights upon the brilliantly patterned chintz which animates what would otherwise be a rather monochromatic picture.

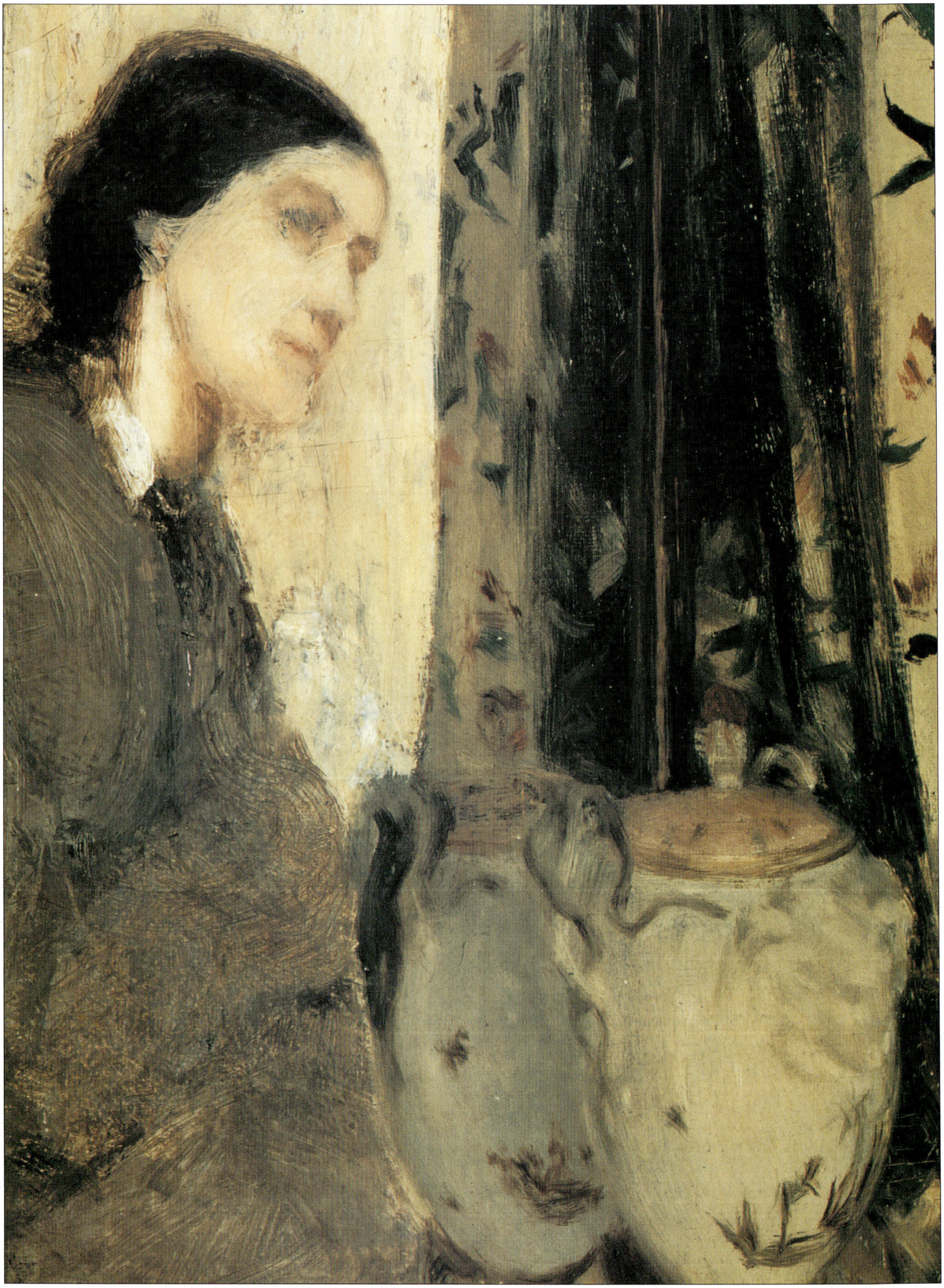

1 *Actual size detail*

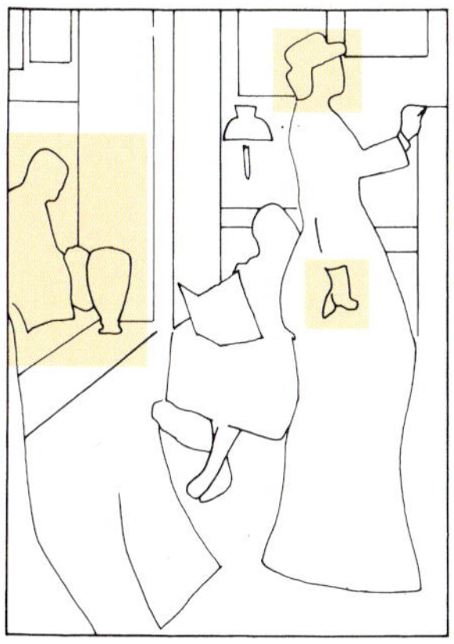

1 *Actual size detail* The head of Deborah, Whistler's sister, is seen reflected in the mirror, a motif that fascinated the artist. The figure, worked in thin glazes of loosely brushed paint, is seen against an area of light and opaque paint which highlights the reflective nature of the mirror surface and gives a tonal balance to the painting. By reversing the color balance of the chintz, Whistler has used greens to suggest shade. The fluency with which the snake-handled pot is drawn is unusual in his work, and suggests the suave handling of his American admirer William Sargent, whose portraits owe much to Whistler's example.

2 The figure of Isabella Boott, a friend of Whistler's brother-in-law, has a sharpness of focus that contrasts with the soft modelling of her features and the scumbled paint that describes the edge of her hat. Her body is crisply delineated and reduced to the simplest of tonal contrasts. In comparison with the work of the Impressionists, working a decade later, the form is relatively unaffected by the fall of light.

3 The starkness of the contrast between the gloved hand and the black dress acts as a perfect foil to the subtle modulations of tone and spatial ambiguities of the rest of the painting.

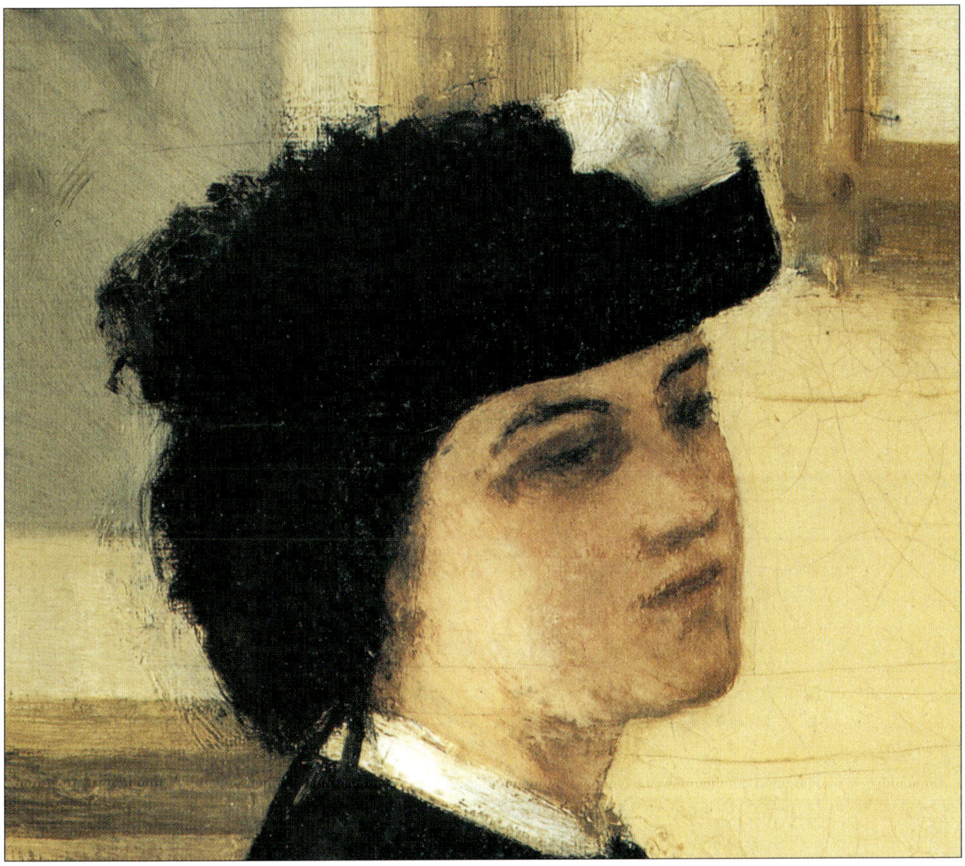

2

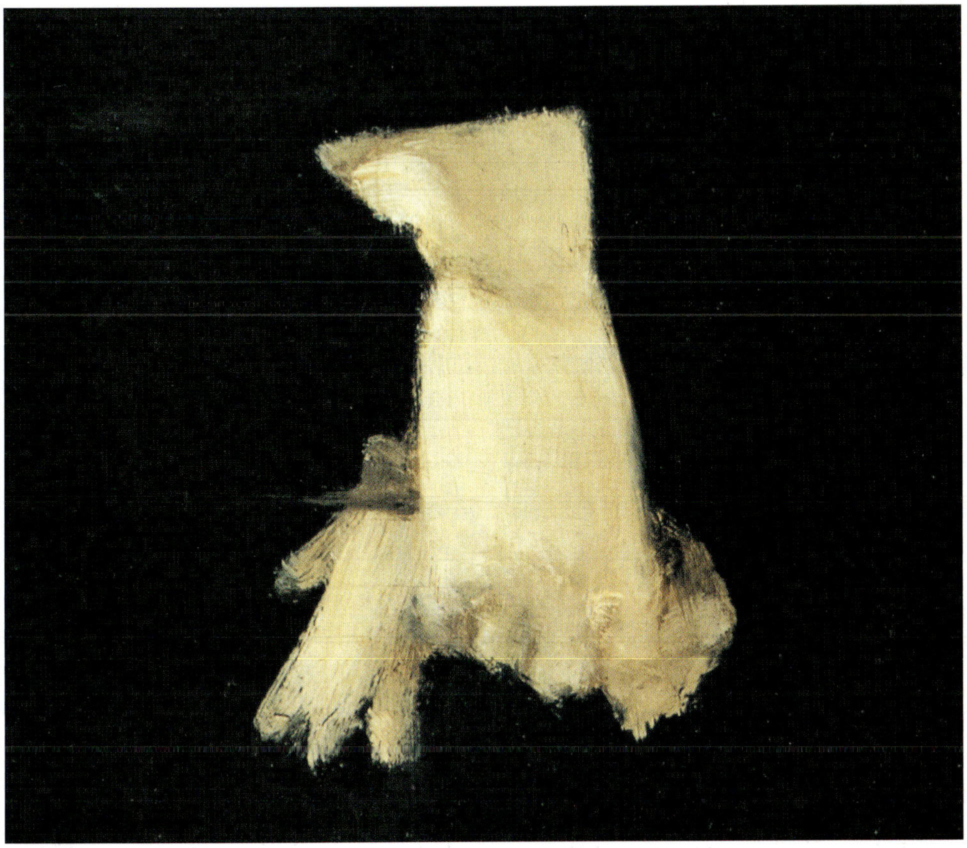

3

Symphony in White No. 2: the Little White Girl

1864
Oil on canvas
30×20in/76×51cm
Tate Gallery, London

This is one of the most exquisite of all Whistler's paintings. His mistress Jo Hiffernan is seen in a mood of wistful reverie, gazing into a mirror which reflects in subdued tones the gentle melancholy of her face. This quiet interpretation is very much Whistler's own creation, and suggests little of the fiery nature of the Irish girl who was his constant companion, favored model and occasional business manager. In 1863 Whistler's mother came to London from America to live with her son, and Jo had to move out of the household, but when, a little later, his mother made a trip to Torquay to recover her health, Jo moved back to her former position. When Whistler went to Valparaiso in 1866 (see page 30) he made a will in which he ignored the rights of his mother, leaving all his possessions to Jo. Soon after his return to London the lovers parted on amicable terms, and Whistler's mother returned to her former place in her son's affections.

The Little White Girl marks a very definite move away from the art of Courbet who, in a letter of 1865 described Whistler as an "Englishman who is my pupil." Two years later the so-called "Englishman" wrote to Fantin-Latour revealing a somewhat different view of their relationship. "Courbet and his influence was disgusting... I am not complaining of the influence his painting had on my own. He did not have any, and it can't be found in my canvases. It is because that damned Realism made an immense appeal to my painter's vanity, and, disregarding all traditions, cried aloud to me the assurance of ignorance: 'Long live Nature! Nature, my dear fellow, that cry was a great misfortune to me."

The formal qualities of the picture are masterly, the simplicity of the girl's white dress is the dominant feature of the canvas, while the Japanese fan and the chrysanthemums counterpoint the weight of the picture's interest, which is placed in the upper portion of the composition. Jo's head, her reflection and the oriental pots fill this upper register in a fascinating amalgam of differing textures, colors and forms. The model's neck and arm sweep down to the lower area of the painting, taking the viewer's eye back to the sketched-in details of the fan loosely held in the girl's right hand. Both this painting and the *White Girl* of 1862, which had been rejected by the French Salon, could be grouped, in pose and mood, with the work of such artists as Millais and Rossetti, who also had a fondness for images of women lost in tranquil reverie. Both artists had become good friends of Whistler, and encouraged him in his belief that the fundamental purpose of art was the creation of beauty.

The picture was exhibited at the Royal Academy show of that year. Attached to the frame was a poem by Algernon Swinburne entitled *Before a Mirror,* a shortened version of which appeared in his *Poems and Ballads* of 1866. In 1902 Whistler remarked that it was "a rare and graceful tribute from the poet to the painter — a noble recognition of a work by the production of a nobler one."

It was retouched at least once in 1900, when the artist removed the date which followed his signature, and either at this time or earlier he reduced the number of chrysanthemums and made other alterations, which can be seen on the canvas. The fireplace — which although it serves the composition well enough, is imperfectly drawn — was thought by Whistler's biographers, the Pennells, to have been the one in his own house in Lindsey Row. The mirror reflection may owe something to Ingres' use of similar motifs, but in handling suggests more the influence of Velasquez' famous *Rokeby Venus.*

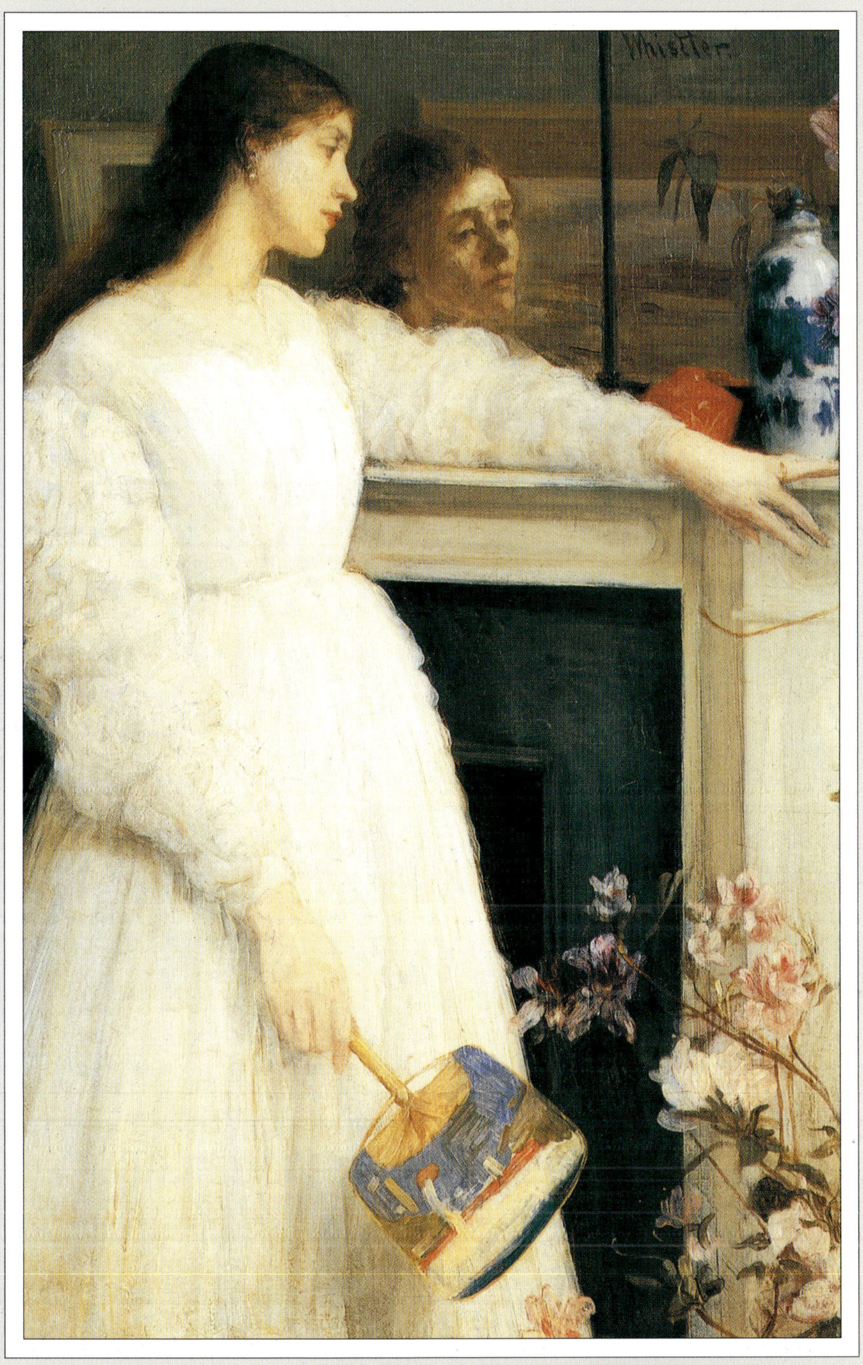

The painting's musical title suggests that this image of a pretty young girl should be regarded as a piece of "visual music" to delight the eyes. The picture's structure is founded on the simple T-shape formed by the model's dress. The whole picture is essentially an arrangement of cool grays, soft ochers and subtly modulated passages of white set off by sharp accents of red and blue.

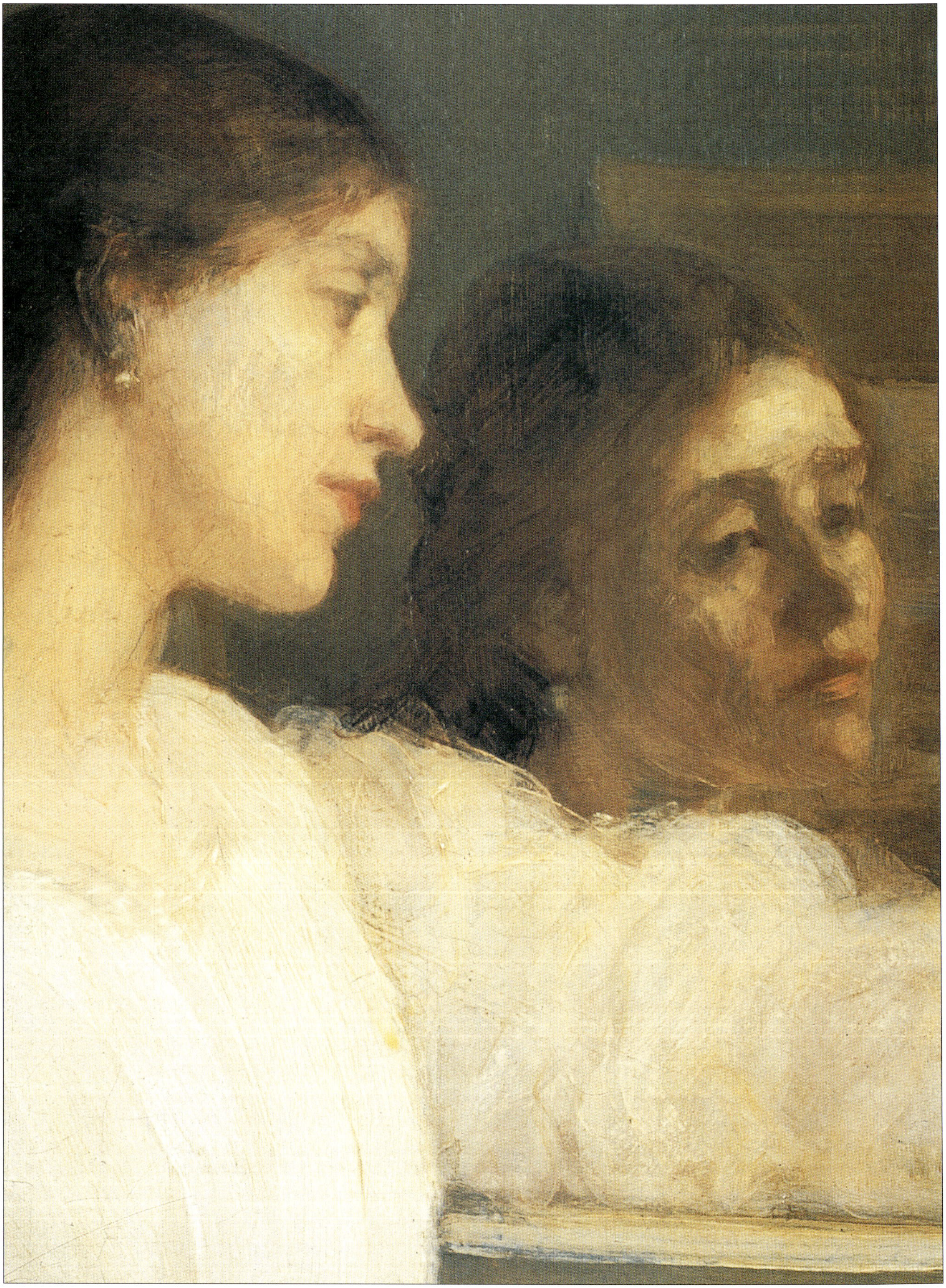

1 *Actual size detail*

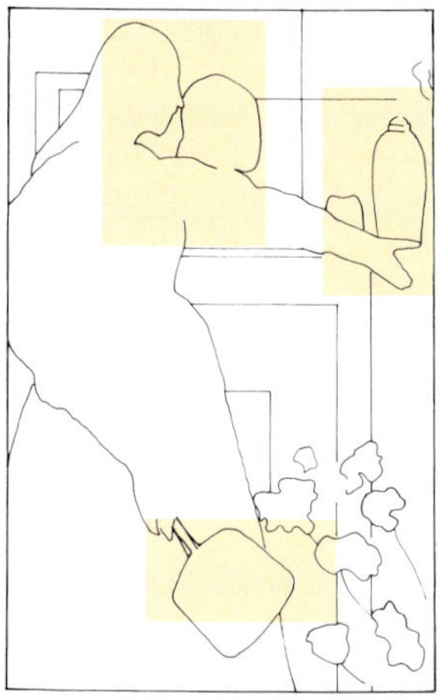

1 *Actual size detail* Like a piece of music, a work of art is as significant for what it suggests as for what it describes. Whistler's model Jo looks not at her own reflection but into the depths of the mirror itself, oblivious of the gaze of the viewer. In this detail the role of the mirror can be clearly appreciated: it provides a device which has allowed the artist to unite several disparate painting methods in the same image. The smooth handling of the girl's face contrasts with the bolder, more direct treatment of the reflection. As in Velasquez' famous *Rokeby Venus*, the reflected face is relatively crudely modeled, with directional brushwork and a few simple tones.

2,3 Contrasting with the smooth ochers and greys of the mirror area, the brilliant color of the small red pot and its reflection, together with the blue and white of the porcelain jar, echo the colours of the Japanese fan (3). The pot is painted wet-in-wet, the colors dragging into each other so that the brushwork suggests the smooth rounded form. A single vertical stroke of pure white made with a square brush describes the highlight and sets off the blue-white modulations of the pot, its design a forerunner of the butterfly that Whistler later adopted as his personal cypher. Against the pot, and picking up some of its color, is a delicate chrysanthemum bloom.

2

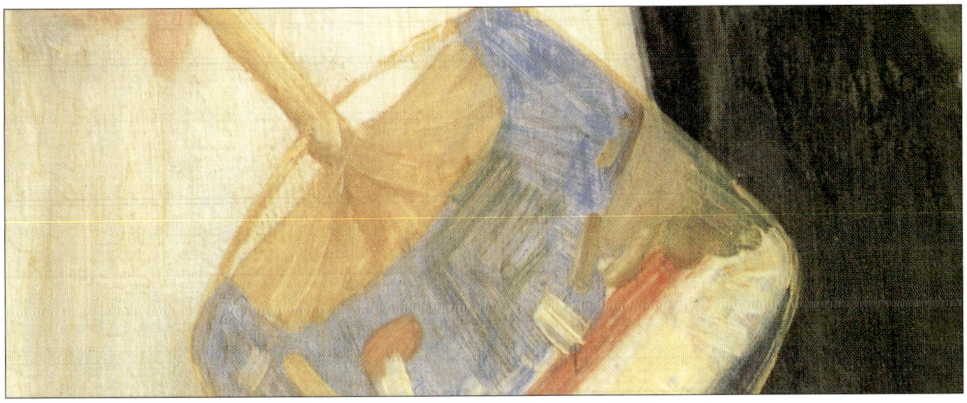

3

Variations in Flesh Color and Green: the Balcony

1864-7

$24\frac{1}{4} \times 19\frac{3}{8}$in/61.6×49cm

Oil on wood

Freer Gallery of Art, Washington

This painting is an example of one of Whistler's many attempts to paint his way out of the difficulties he found himself in during the 1860s. Its intention is clear enough: he hoped to produce an art of timeless beauty, motivated by his response to reality, but carefully ordering that reality by means of Japanese costumes and the conventions of Greek art. The results were not always successful, and by the end of the decade, he had abandoned this rather contrived approach and returned to the more natural theme of the river and its environs.

In this painting, the inclusion of a woman playing the Japanese three-stringed instrument called the *samisen* is a clear visual reference to music, as is the piano in his first major canvas, *At the Piano,* of 1859. Whistler wanted his paintings to be appreciated in an abstract way as pieces of visual music rather than for any narrative or descriptive qualities, and in 1867 he began to give them musical or abstract titles such as "nocturne" or "arrangement" (later retitling the early works). The relationship between music and art was the subject of great debate among avant-garde writers and painters throughout the 19th century. In 1834 the poet and novelist Théophile Gautier had published a short novel, *Mademoiselle du Maupin,* and in the preface of this influential and deliberately paradoxical book occur the following lines. "Things are beautiful in inverse proportion to their utility. The only thing that is truly beautiful is a thing that serves no purpose at all." Beauty, it was believed, should stand proud and aloof from the world, its deadliest enemies being the twin evils of utility and progress. Whistler himself reacted strongly against the Victorian idea that the artist's purpose was to provide a blueprint for public morality, believing that a work of art should exist in its own right, independent of prosaic reality.

By utilizing aspects of Oriental art in his work, he was able to create images that contained attractively mysterious and exotic qualities corresponding to his Western audiences' preconceptions of the East. The Japanese borrowings are obvious, and have been identified by a number of authorities. Four women, dressed in Oriental robes, are shown in a setting that relates directly to the work of the printmaker Harunobu, who like other artists of the Ukiyo-e school, depicted life in the brothels of Edo. The European features of Whistler's women and the view over the Thames to Battersea, however, situates the painting firmly in the West.

Like many 19th-century artists, Whistler has here presented the women as no more than passive decorative objects. In this respect the painting's true antecedents are Ingres' odalisques and Delacroix's *Women of Algiers.* The quirky mixture of stylistic elements is only just held in check. The railings are shown parallel to the picture surface, balanced by the two half-furled blinds. The expanse of the balcony floor suggests the artist's high viewpoint, recalling the directness of his *Wapping* painting and also vividly suggesting the presence of the artist – and hence the viewer. The standing figure looking out over the river links the foreground with the tonally correct backdrop of the far side of the river, complete with its warehouses and chimneys. The tension contained between these two very different worlds is complemented both by Whistler's realistic treatment of the wharfside architecture on the far bank of the river and the strong surface pattern of the foreground. This tension is further amplified by the "realistic" butterflies crossing the rectangular enclosure that contains Whistler's distinctive mark, which appears in this painting for the first time. Whistler signed his work with a butterfly motif developed from his own monogram, and the same visual pun appears in *Miss Cicely Alexander* (see page 397).

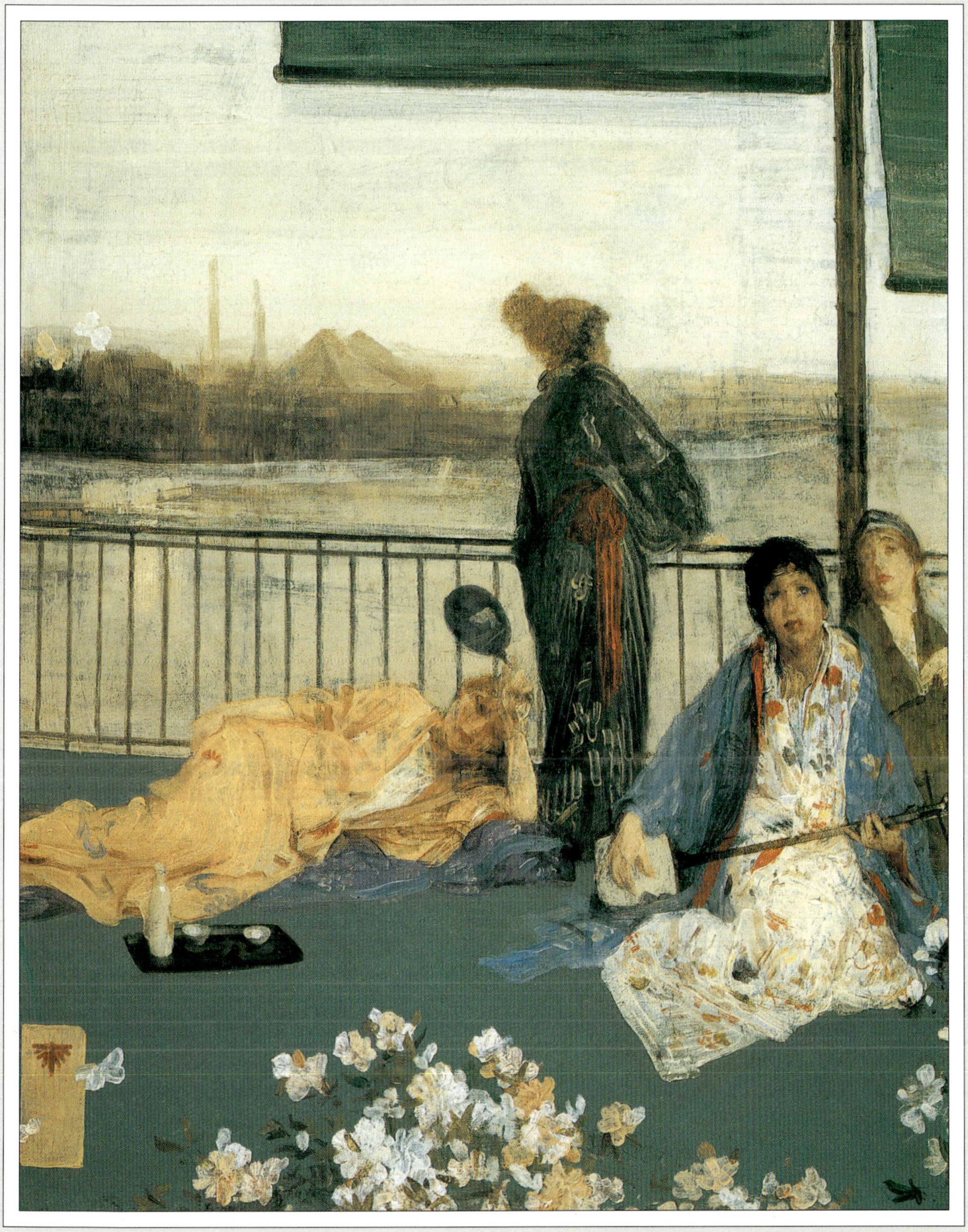

This is one of Whistler's Japanese "fancy dress" pictures, an intriguing medley of semi-erotic fantasy with the everyday setting of the bank of the Thames at Battersea. The contrived nature of the subject matter is matched by a wide range of stylistic mannerisms and visual puns, but these painterly devices do not destroy the melancholy and evocative mood of the painting, somewhat reminiscent of Degas' history and theater paintings of the early 1860s.

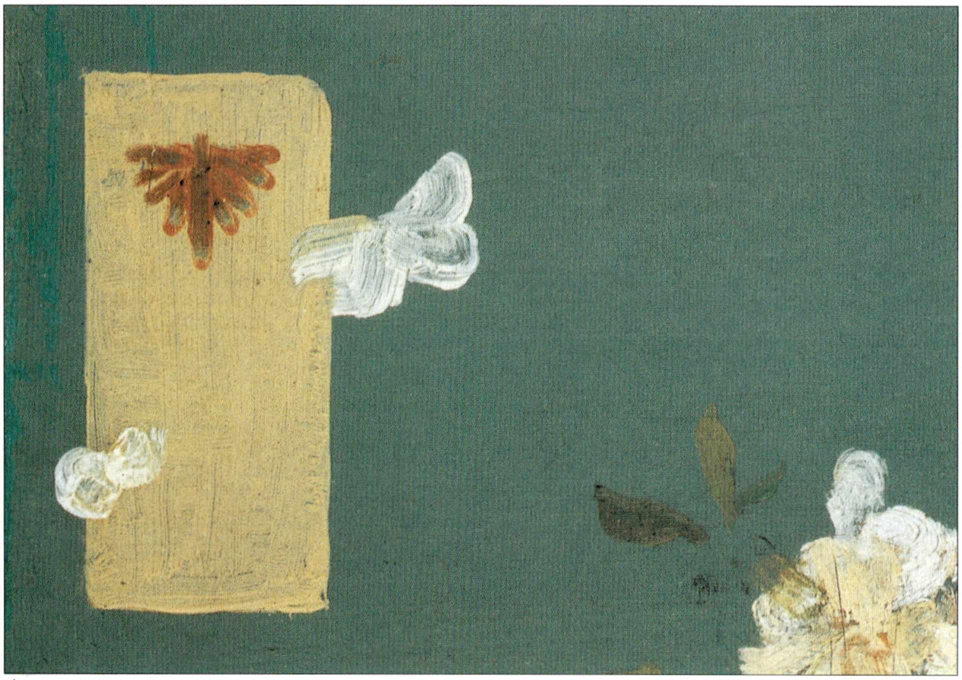

1

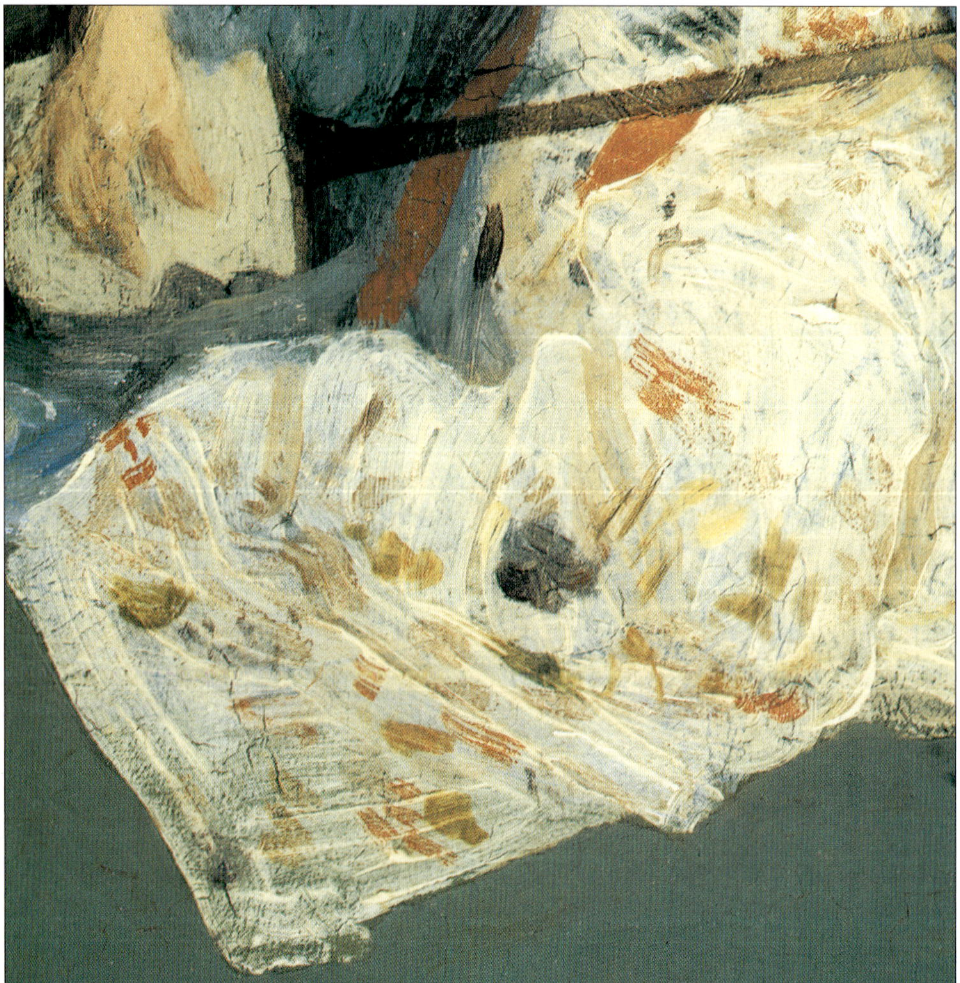

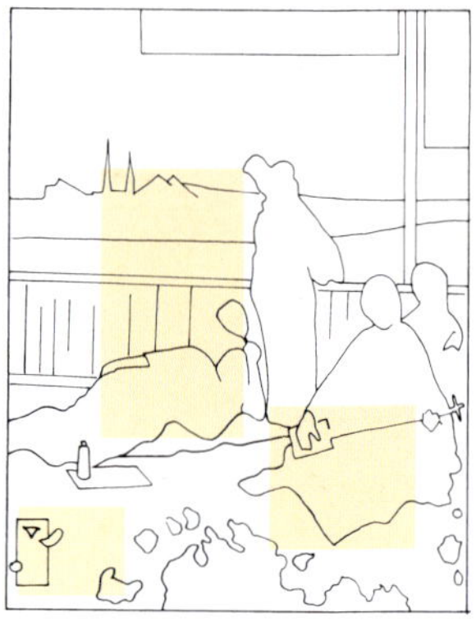

1 Whistler has here repeated the colors of the reclining figure of the cartouche which contains his butterfly insignia. Against this are seen two of a group of butterflies which, in their turn, are made up of the same brushmarks seen in the blossom which fills the lower area of the composition.

2 Whistler has again used the lilac blue and warm, deep red of his *Wapping* painting. His lack of concern for anatomical exactitude relates to the stylizations seen in Japanese prints, and the same influence is discernible in the crisply drawn folds and edges of the kimono. The lightly painted garment reveals the gray of the floor beneath, and the delicately rendered pattern picks up color found elsewhere in the picture.

3 *Actual size detail* The surface of the panel shows the effect of the artist's habitual practice of scraping down previously worked areas before repainting. The grain of the panel can be clearly seen in places, and part of the river area has been painted on top of the uniform mid-gray of the floor. The reclining figure has been loosely brushed on top of the railings painted earlier, and traces of them are still visible beneath the kimono.

2

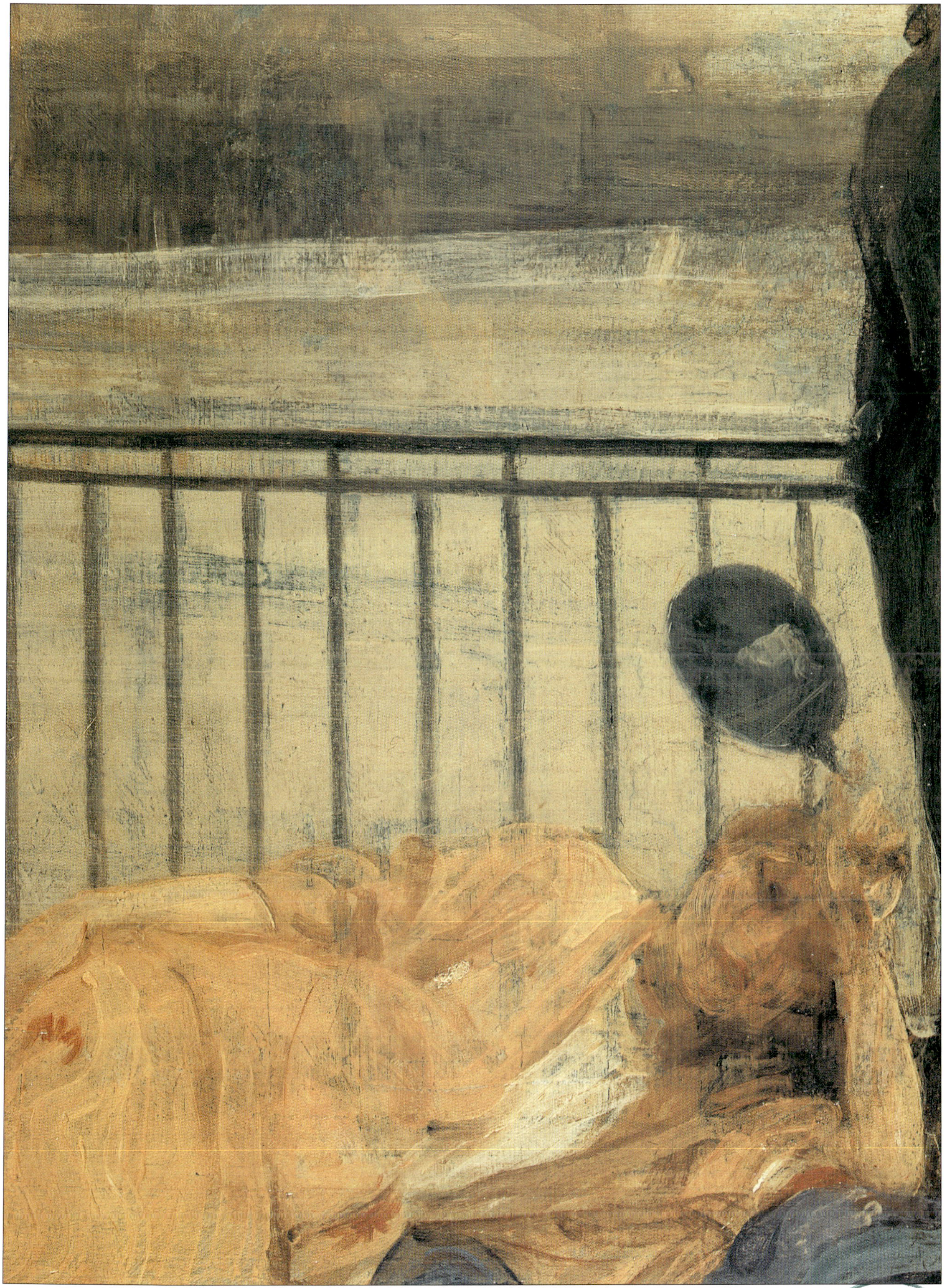

3 *Actual size detail*

Harmony in Flesh Color and Red

(formerly *Symphony in Red*)
c 1869
$15^{1}/_{4} \times 14$in/38.7×35.6cm
Oil on canvas
Museum of Fine Arts, Boston

During the mid-1860s Whistler became obsessed with the idea of producing a series of paintings that would combine the grace and simplicity of the Greek terracotta statuettes known as Tanagra figures with the stylish exoticism of Japanese design as he knew it from Oriental prints and artefacts. The woodcuts of the Japanese artist Kiyonaga seemed to have served as the fundamental model for his designs; but as his entire collection of prints was sold after his bankruptcy in 1879, it is impossible to say what his collection consisted of at this time.

Whistler's work of this period contains strong elements of the French Neo-Grecian school of painting, of which his first master, Charles Gleyre, was one of the best-known practitioners, but it was seeing the work of Albert Moore in 1865 that spurred him on to attempt an art of a similar abstract power. Moore's paintings invariably depicted groups of young "flower-like women," as Swinburne referred to them. They were placed either in an enclosed setting or on a seashore, engaged in doing nothing in particular, their dress and manner deliberately non-specific, but suggesting at once an Oriental, Classical and modern character. The fashions of the women in *Harmony in Flesh Color and Red,* despite their generalized nature, are actually those current in the late 1860s. The painting was produced about 1869 and relates to the series of decorative paintings that he called the *Six Projects,* which are now in the Freer Gallery of Art, Washington, but were originally intended for Sir Francis Leyland. Unfortunately Whistler was unable to bring his designs to completion. The one that was finished he felt unhappy about, and he tried repeatedly but unsuccessfully to buy it back from its owner.

The title of this painting is not Whistler's own, but no doubt he would have approved of its musical associations. It shows three women dressed in a vivid red conversing in an interior or on a terrace; their manner is relaxed and casual, they could almost be models in the studio of a Royal Academy member, waiting to pose for one of those sentimental canvases so popular with the 19th-century public, and which Whistler professed to despise so much. In fact the painting could relate to his own unsuccessful attempts to produce a large version of Courbet's *The Painter in his Studio.* Certainly the figures have the air of quiet expectancy that we find in Degas' images of ballet dancers waiting to go on stage or the models of Seurat's painting of his studio, known as the *Poseuses.* The figure reaching down with an extraordinarily long arm to fit her shoe is an especially happy invention.

The lightness and delicacy of the technique could not be more distant from the earthy Realism of Courbet, an influence that had colored the artist's earlier paintings. It was at this time that Whistler was writing to his friend Fantin-Latour deploring the influence of Courbet and expressing his wish to overcome some of his shortcomings in the technical aspects of his art. He had expressed the regret that he had not trained with the artist Ingres, a consummate draughtsman, whom Degas admired above all others. But although some of Whistler's work does suffer from a lack of incisiveness in the drawing, in this example the fluidity of the brushwork used to block in the elegant forms of the women is perfectly matched to its role as a conveyor of the work's formal delights.

The butterfly monogram was a later addition to the painting, and it has been suggested that it was painted on by another hand, as the form it takes here relates to the work of the mid-1880s.

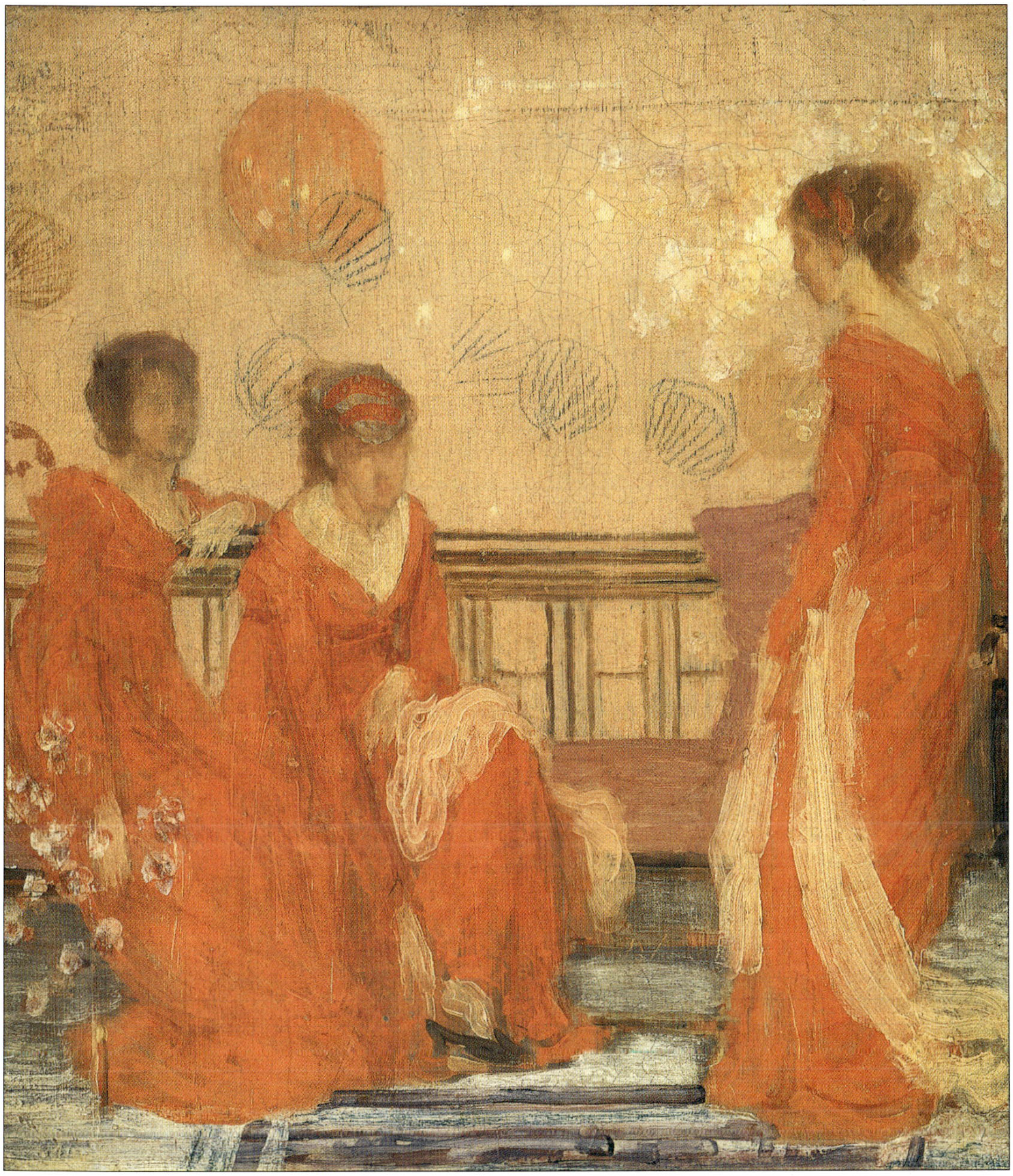

Like musical notations, rhythms of color, line and form move across this small canvas in harmonious counterpoint. No dominating central motif or detailed characterization disturb the picture's visual flow, and the viewer's eye moves across and around it. Regular intervals are provided by the uprights of the bench, balanced by the rise and fall of the models' heads and the scallop-like decorations on the wall that move in melodic progression across the picture surface.

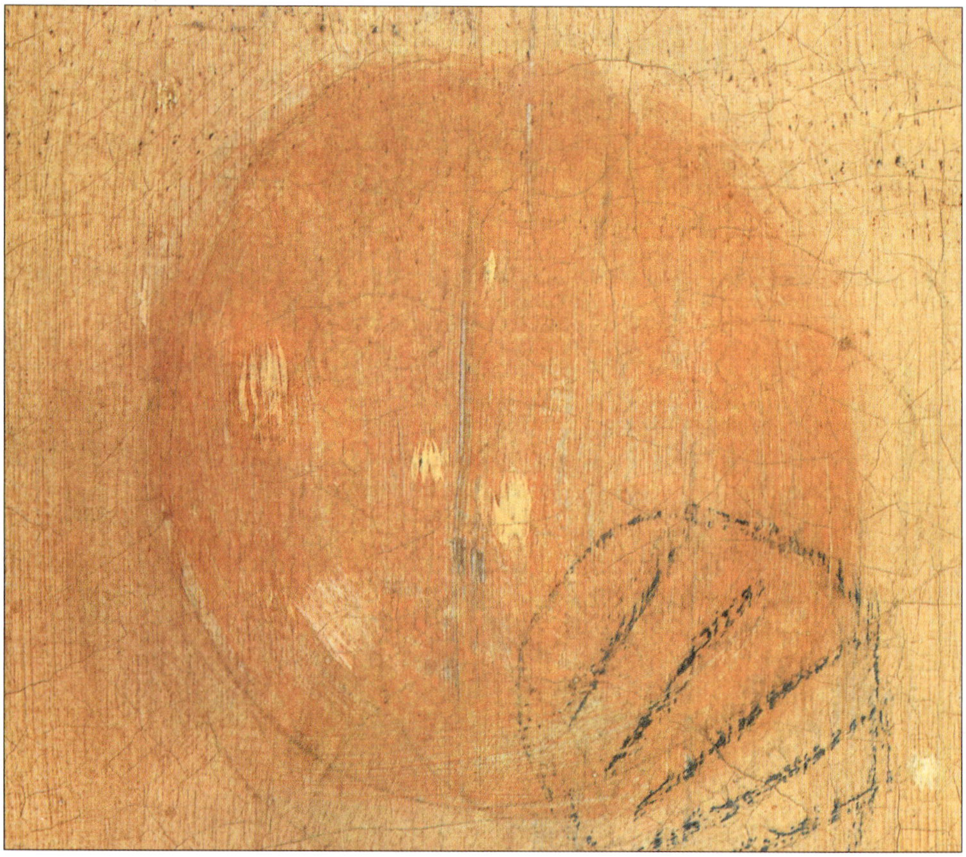

1

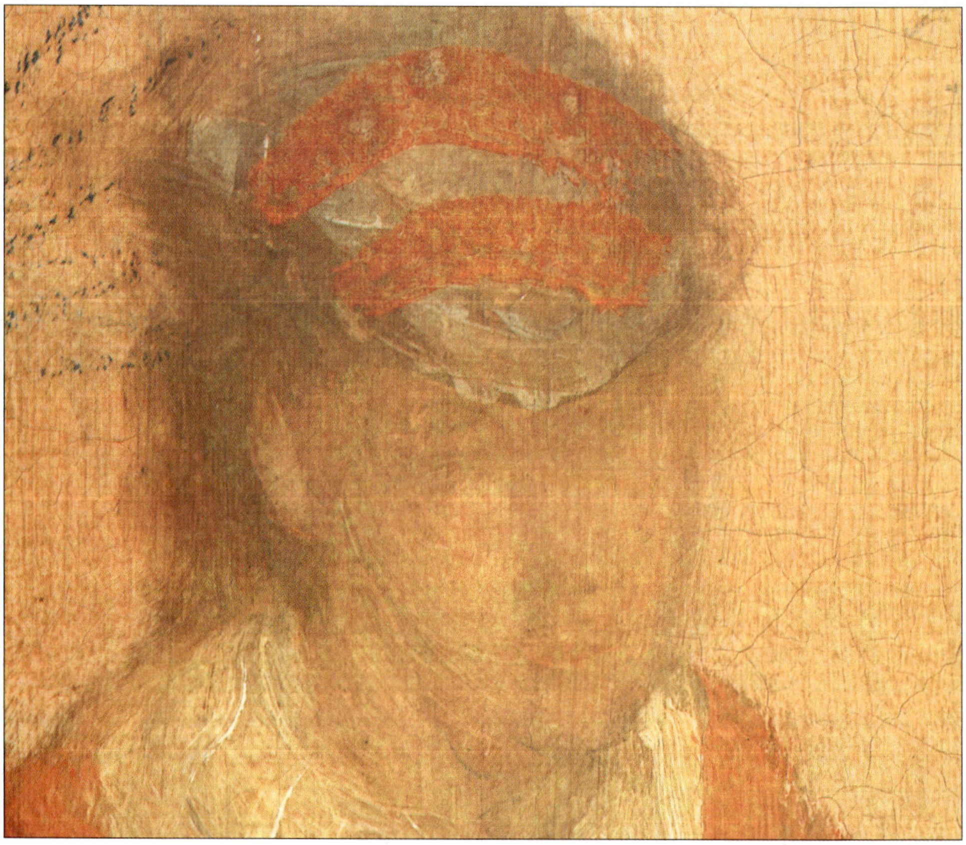

2

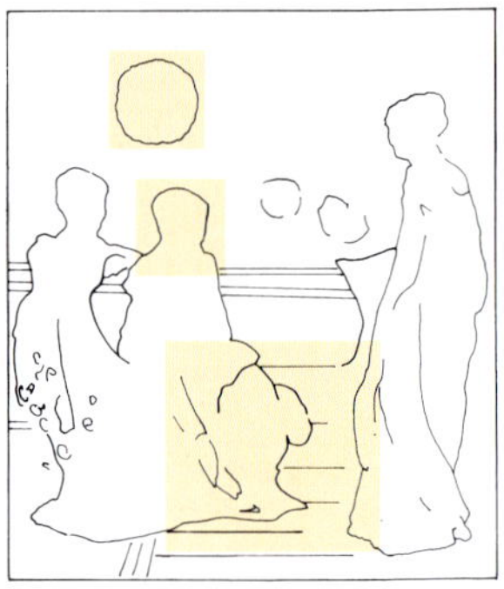

1 The circular orange design on the wall is only one of the several ambiguous elements in this composition. Its color is brushed on in thin vertical strokes, allowing the peach of the wall to show through in places. Touches of yellow and pink enrich the coloration and refer to the color harmonies in the picture as a whole. The pencil-drawn fan or scallop shapes that flit like butterfly wings across the wall create further textural interest.

2 The painting has a richness of color and texture that we associate with late Degas, while the musicality of design is comparable to Matisse's decorative works such as *La Danse* of 1909. The facial characteristics of the models are left undefined, in order not to disturb the aesthetic balance of the composition. Two simple areas of red pick up the barely discernible red of the lips and act as a visual link across the empty central portion of the composition.

3 A square brush leaves an easily recognizable trace in a series of staccato movements which complement the much more fluid painting of the drapery resting on the central figure's lap. Peaches, oranges, reds and browns are made to harmonize with a shrill mauve color that is softened with white on the bench.

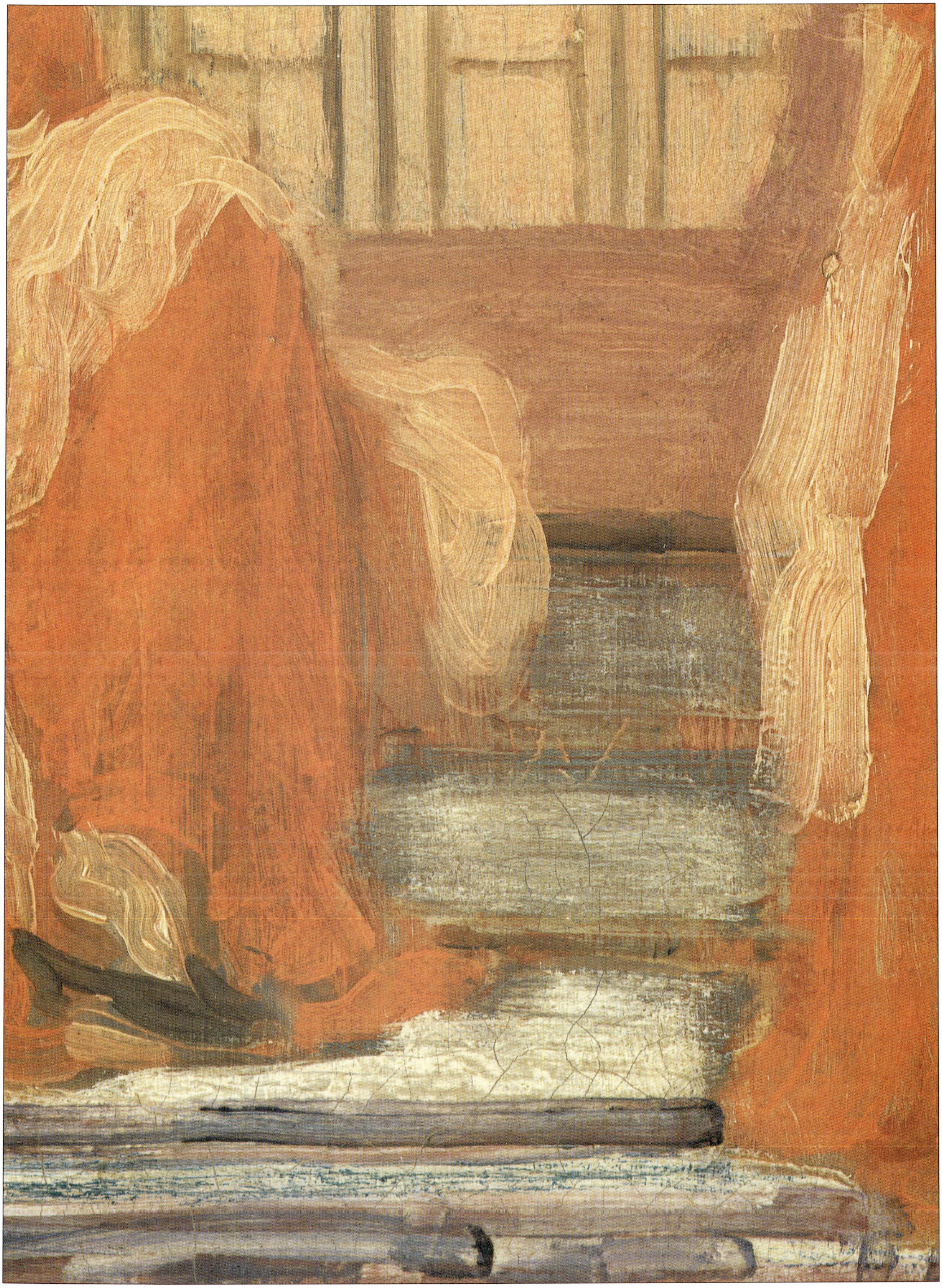

3

NOCTURNE IN BLUE AND GREEN: CHELSEA

1871
Oil on canvas
$19^3/_4 \times 23^1/_2$in/50×59.5cm
Tate Gallery, London

One of the earliest of Whistler's Nocturnes, this is a view across the Thames in London, seen from Battersea, with the tower of Old Chelsea Church in the distance. The exclusion of all inessential details, together with the almost monochromatic coloration, make it a typical example of the genre for which Whistler is today best remembered. The base colors were swept in over a dark ground and, as usual in Whistler's work, the details of the Japanese-inspired boatman, barge and butterfly signature were added later with sinuous ribbons of paint. Every element of the picture's composition is balanced against one against the other to create an exquisite and harmonious design that, like a piece of music, appeals directly to our senses.

Whistler had a special love of the twilight, which he saw as perhaps the only time when nature approached his own high standards of aesthetic perfection. He described his feelings in his famous *10 o'clock Lecture* of 1888. "And when the evening mist clothes the riverside with poetry, as with a veil, and the poor buildings lose themselves in the sky, and the tall chimneys become *campanili*, and the warehouses are palaces in the night, and the whole city hangs in the heavens, and fairyland is before us . . . Nature, who, for once has sung in tune, sings her exquisite song to the artist alone . . ."

"I can't thank you too much," he wrote to his friend and patron, the shipping magnate, Sir Francis Leyland, "for the name Nocturne as the title for my Moonlights. You, have no idea what an irritation it proves to my critics, and consequent pleasure to me, besides it is really so charming, and does so poetically say all I want to say and no more than I wish."

Despite the originality of his own art, Whistler made it clear in the closing remarks of his lecture that he saw the artist's task as one of continuing what had gone before, not searching for some unique style for the mere sake of novelty. "We have then but to wait — until, with the mark of the Gods upon him — there come among us again the chosen — who shall continue what has gone on before. Satisfied that, even were he never to appear, the story of the beautiful is already complete — hewn in the marbles of the Parthenon — and broidered, with the birds, upon the fan of Hokusai — at the foot of Fujiyama."

The lithographer T. R. Way has described Whistler's idiosyncratic manner of producing his wonderfully evocative works. ". . . Pointing to a group of buildings in the distance, an old public house at the corner of the road, with windows and shops showing golden lights through the gathering mist of the twilight, he said, 'Look!' As he did not seem to have anything to sketch or make notes on, I offered him my note-book, 'No, no, be quiet,' was the answer; and after a long pause he turned and walked back a few yards; then with his back turned to the scene at which I was looking, he said, 'Now see if I have learned it,' and repeated a full description of the scene, even as one might repeat a poem one had learned by heart."

Thus the elaborate paraphernalia of actuality would be reduced to its essential characteristics, those that had initially caught the artist's imagination. This distillation would then be used as the model for the subsequent painting, which was produced, not before the subject itself, vainly attempting to capture a fugitive effect, but in the confines of the studio, working from memory and the imagination. As Whistler saw it, mundane reality was to be studied only in order to be transformed by the temperament or vision of the artist into a thing of flawless beauty and universal significance.

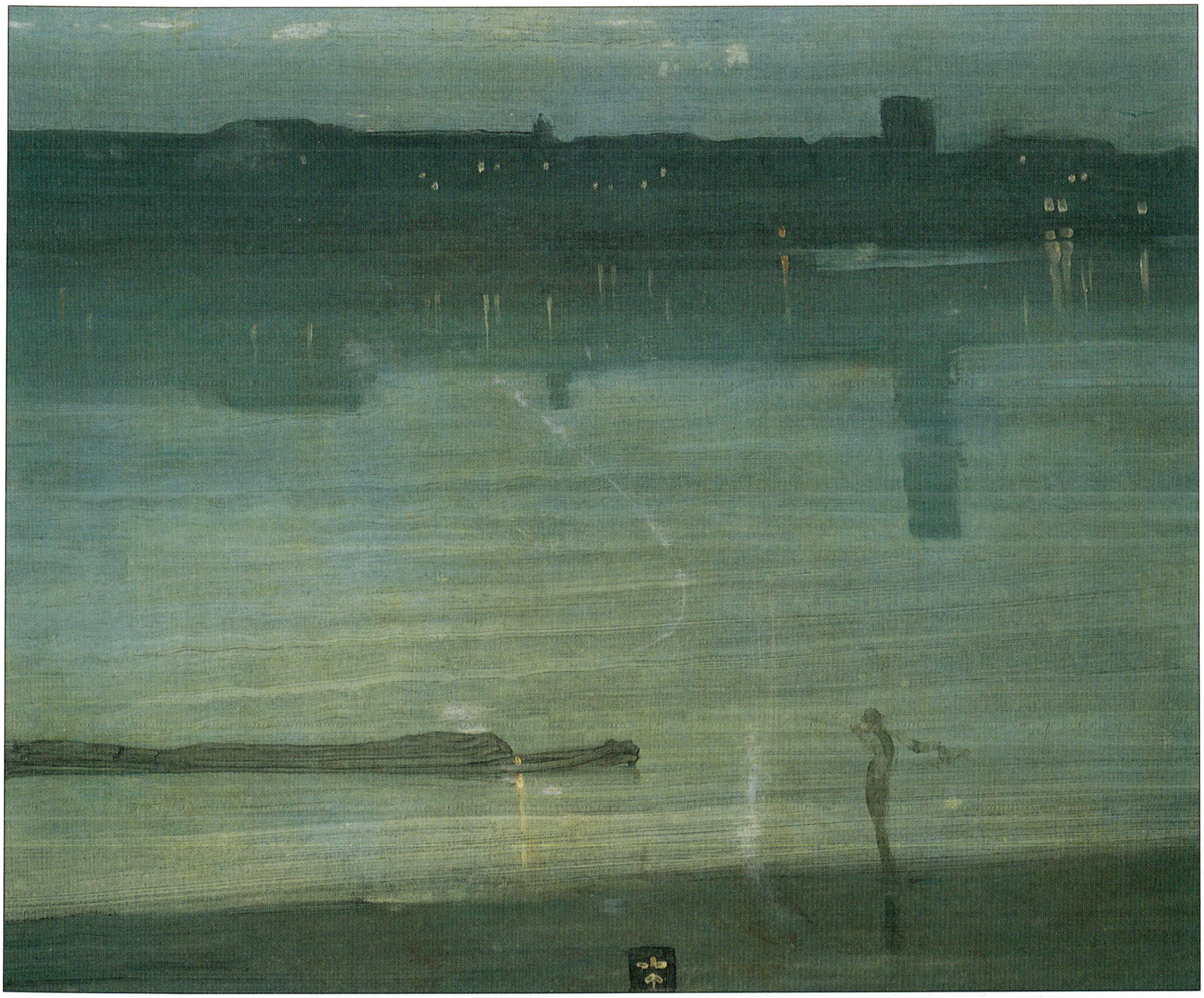

Few other of Whistler's paintings so perfectly illustrate the belief he expressed in his *10 o'clock Lecture.* "Nature contains the elements, in color and form, of all pictures ... But the artist is born to pick and choose, and group with science, these elements, that the result may be beautiful — as the musician gathers his notes ... To say to the painter, that Nature is to be taken as she is, is to say to the player, that he may sit at the piano."

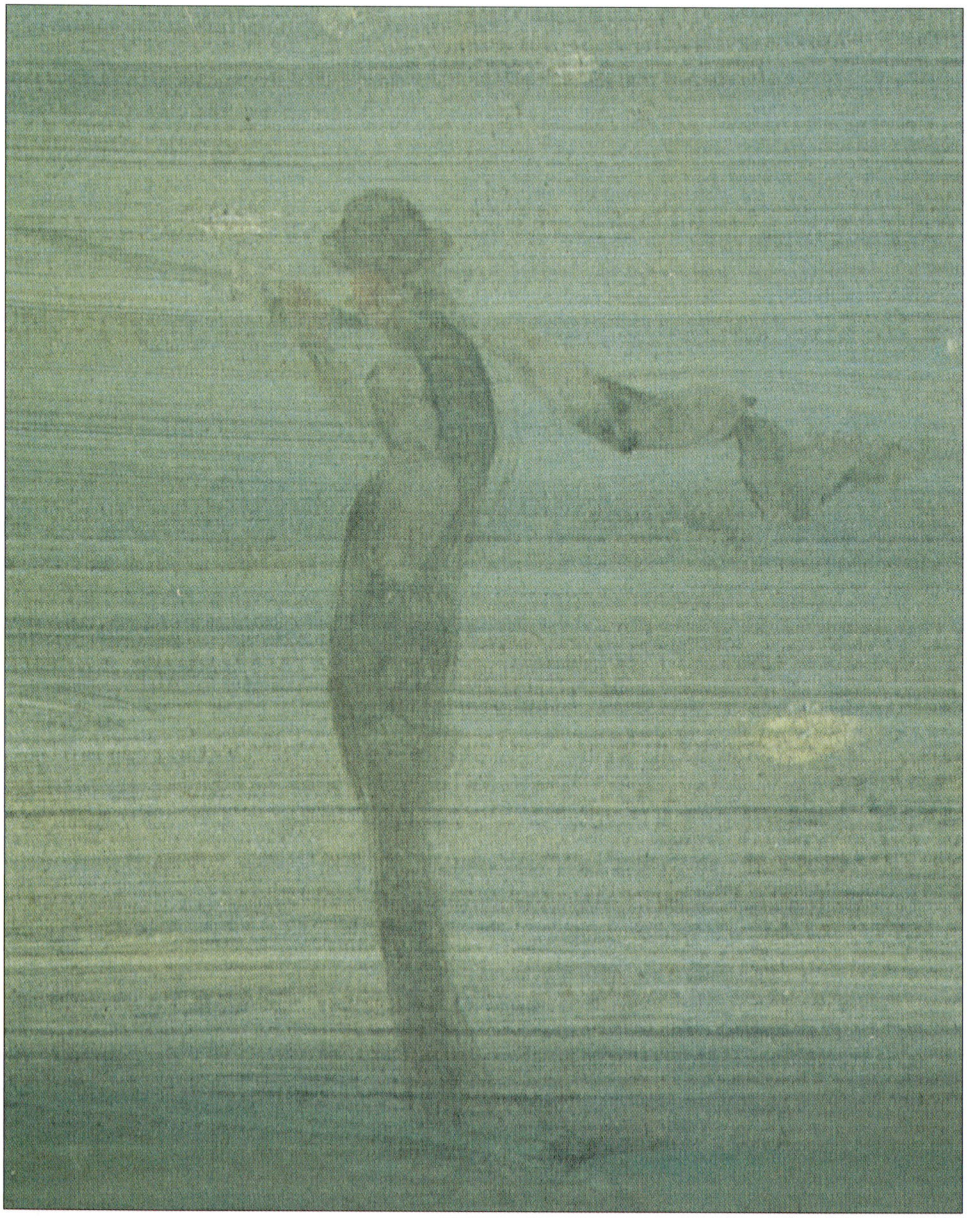

1

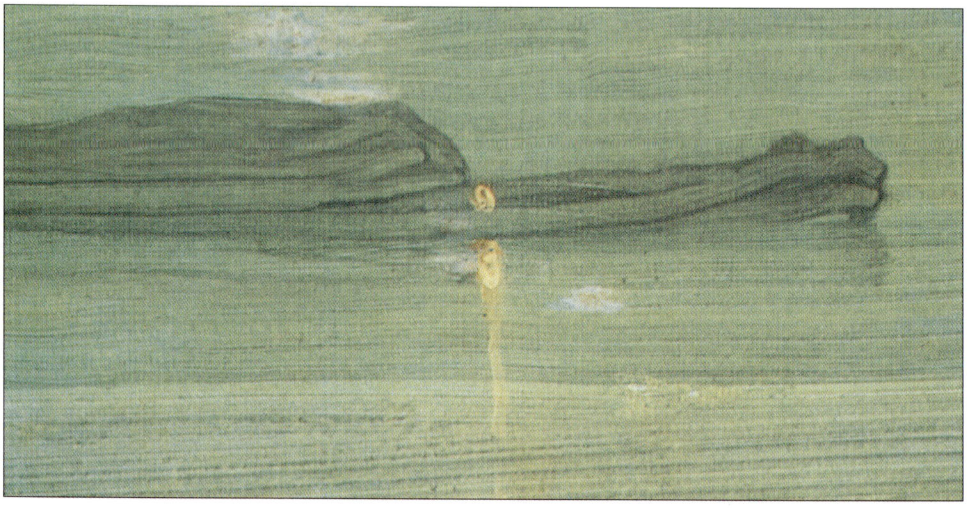

2

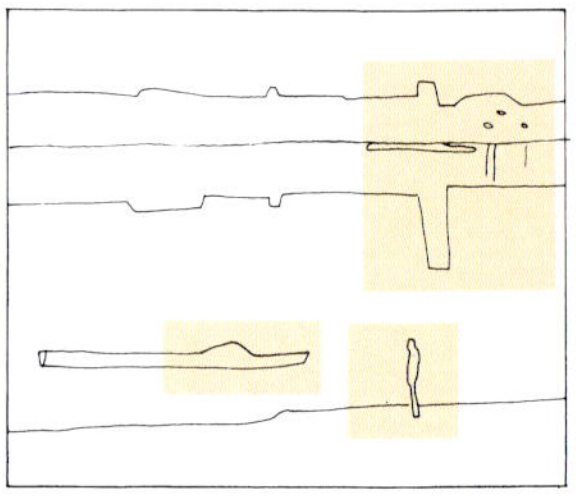

1 A single figure as delicate and decoratively imagined as one on a piece of Chinese porcelain stands on the shore, marking the asymmetry of the major compositional elements. The figure, like the cartouche, reiterates the decorative nature of the painting and shows the influence of the Japanese habit of making signatures part of the overall design of a picture.

2 The composition is founded on bands of subtly modulated color, shifting from blue-grey to blue-green. Simple block-like shapes are played off against dots and dashes of gradated yellow tones.

3 *Actual size details* The paint is swept on in broad swathes, with the brush taken from one edge of the canvas to the other. Nothing is centrally placed; the pictorial elements weave around the central spread of water. The thin paint leaves the trace of brushmarks in places, contrasting with more broadly handled areas from which the forms appear to emerge. Like Monet's paintings, this work hovers between the figurative and the abstract and, also like Monet, it captures perfectly the subdued luminosity and all-enveloping atmosphere characteristic of twilight.

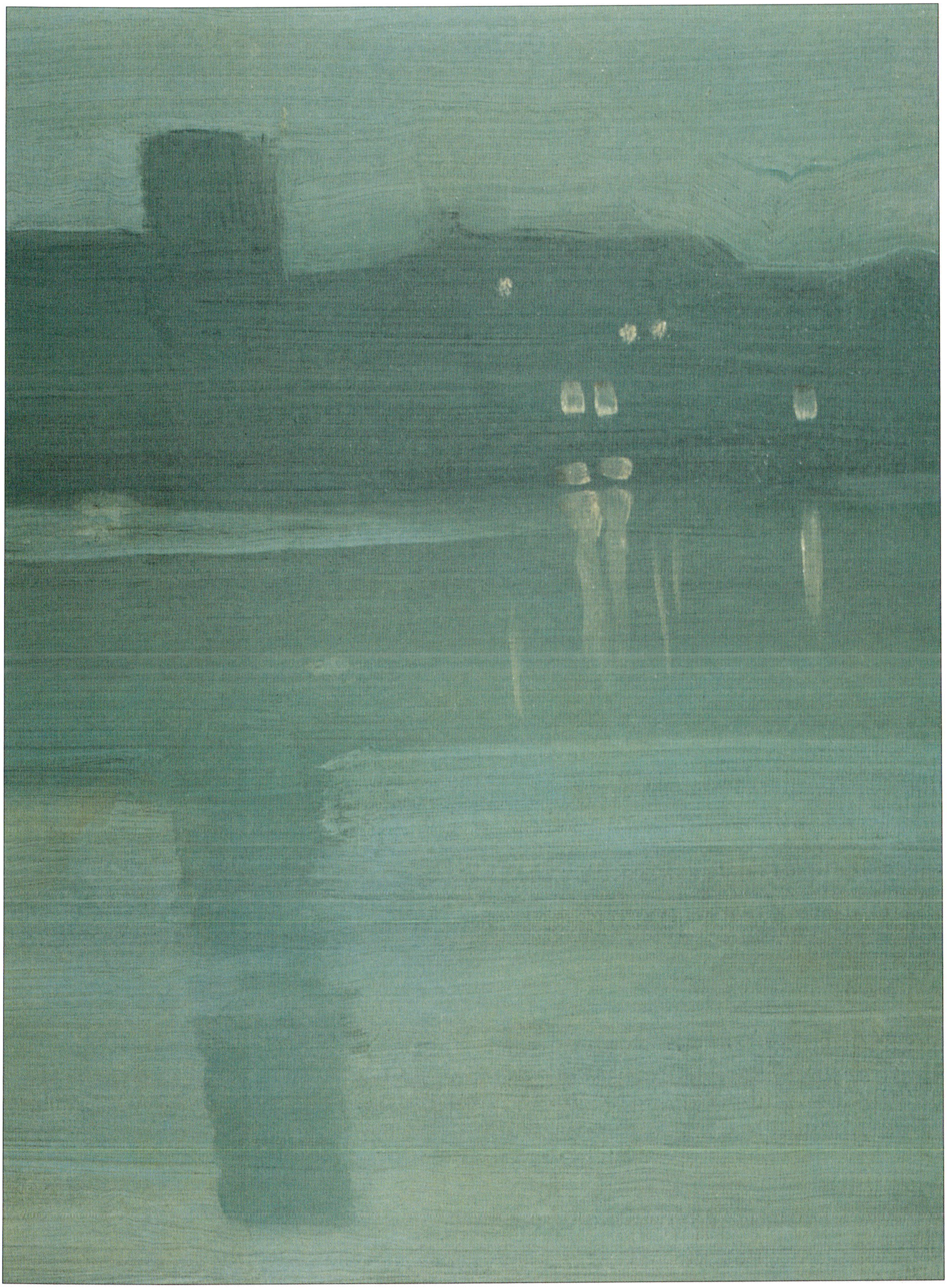

3 *Actual size detail*

Harmony in Gray and Green: Miss Cicely Alexander

1872-3
Oil on canvas
$74^{3}/_{4} \times 38^{1}/_{2}$in/ 189.9×97.8cm
Tate Gallery, London

This painting could easily be retitled "Homage to Velasquez." This banker's daughter, like one of the Spanish painter's young *infantas,* looks out of the canvas with an air of haughty disdain. Or could it be merely the discomfort and boredom she felt after having endured a reputed seventy or so sittings? Her pose, too, is reminiscent of Velasquez, although it was actually taken from the little boy holding the censer in Courbet's *Burial at Ornans* of 1850. The whiteness of the boy's robe is here exchanged for a white dress of Whistler's own design, which was specially starched by his mother to make the frills and skirt stand out.

The sitter later described the sessions to Whistler's biographers Joseph and Elizabeth Pennell (*The Life of James McNeill Whistler,* 1908). "I'm afraid I rather considered that I was a victim all through the sittings, or rather standings, for he never let me change my position, and I believe I used to get very tired and cross and often ended the day in tears . . . [he] never noticed the tears; he used to stand a good way from his canvas, and then dart at it, and then dart back, and he often turned around to look in a looking-glass that hung over the mantelpiece at his back – I suppose to see the reflection of his painting . . ."

While Whistler was painting this portrait he was also working on one of Carlyle, and the story is told of a meeting between "the old man coming out and the little girl going in, 'Who is that?' he asked the maid. 'Miss Alexander, who was sitting to Mr Whistler,' he was told. Carlyle shook his head, 'Puir lassie! Puir lassie!' and, without another word, he went out."

The ground of the painting is dark brown, and the transparency of the dress was formed by the continual rubbing down of previous attempts to paint the skirt until several carefully judged touches of the brush delivered the desired effect. Writing of another portrait of the same period, the Pennells give us an interesting insight into the artist's working methods. "Whistler carried out his method of putting in the whole picture at once. The background was as much part of the design as the face. If anything went wrong anywhere the whole picture had to come out and be started again . . . the system taught by Gleyre, and developed in the Nocturnes was perfected in the portraits . . . The tones, made from a very few colors of infinite gradations, were mixed on the great palette, with black as the basis." The "great palette" is a reference to the three-foot-long polished mahogany table Whistler used instead of a palette when working on large oils. He prepared the painting on this, tone for tone, the final painting being an exact counterpart to his unorthodox palette, and he would spend as much time on this stage as on the canvas itself. At the end of a portrait sitting the painting was either declared finished or it was washed down with spirits in preparation for a fresh start the following session – usually the latter. Gradually over the twenty or so sittings that were the norm for a full-length portrait, a ghostly image of the sitter would appear, its presence enriching the final touches of paint. When successful, as in this work, the result has a marvelous freshness and unity of surface.

When the art critic of *The Times* saw this portrait he remarked that the upright line in the paneling of the wall was wrong, and the picture would be better without it, adding, "Of course it's only a matter of taste." To which Whistler replied, "I thought that perhaps for once, you were going to get away without having said something foolish; but remember, so that you may not make the same mistake again, it's not a matter of taste at all, it is a matter of knowledge. Goodbye."

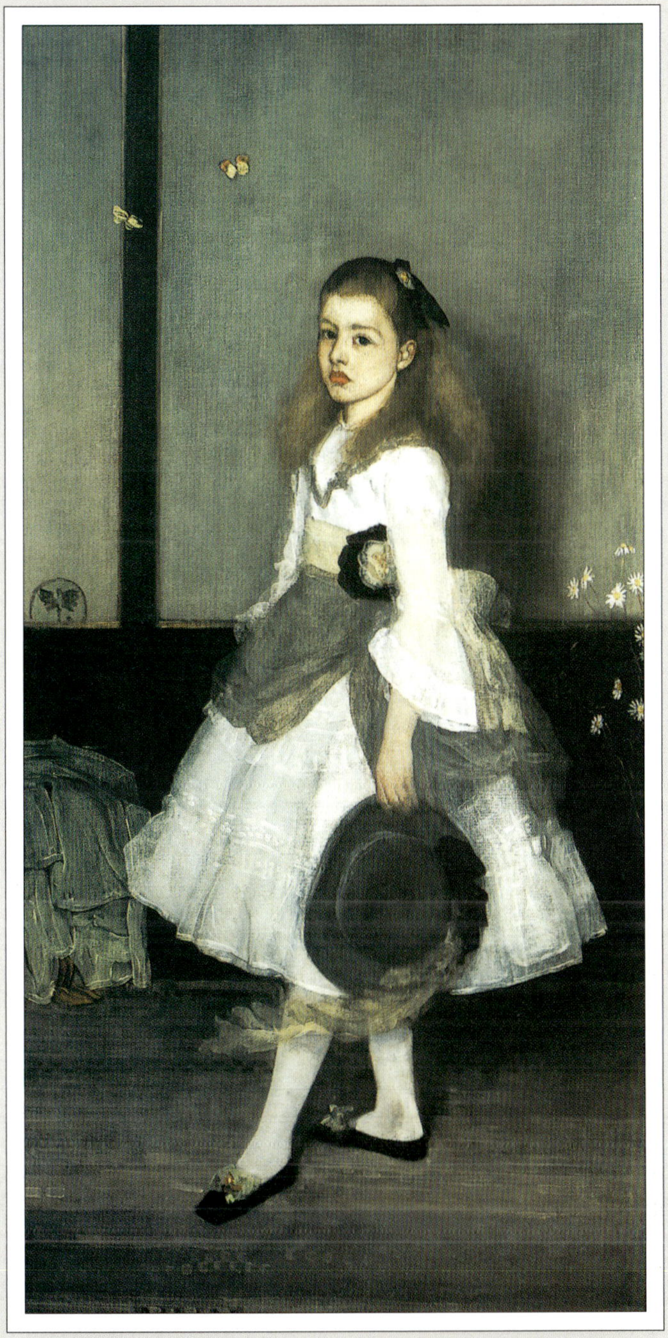

Despite Whistler's often-repeated assertions to the contrary, his successful portraits are often visual documents of great psychological insight. It is hard to see this painting as nothing more than an arrangement of tones and colors, although it certainly displays the artist's powers as a creator of exquisitely balanced formal inventions. Many of the most solid-looking areas of his mature works reveal the texture and color of the canvas ground beneath, which has the effect of subtly modifying the tonal values of the painting and thereby adding a further unifying effect to the composition. Whistler always strove to create above all an aura of harmony and restraint.

1

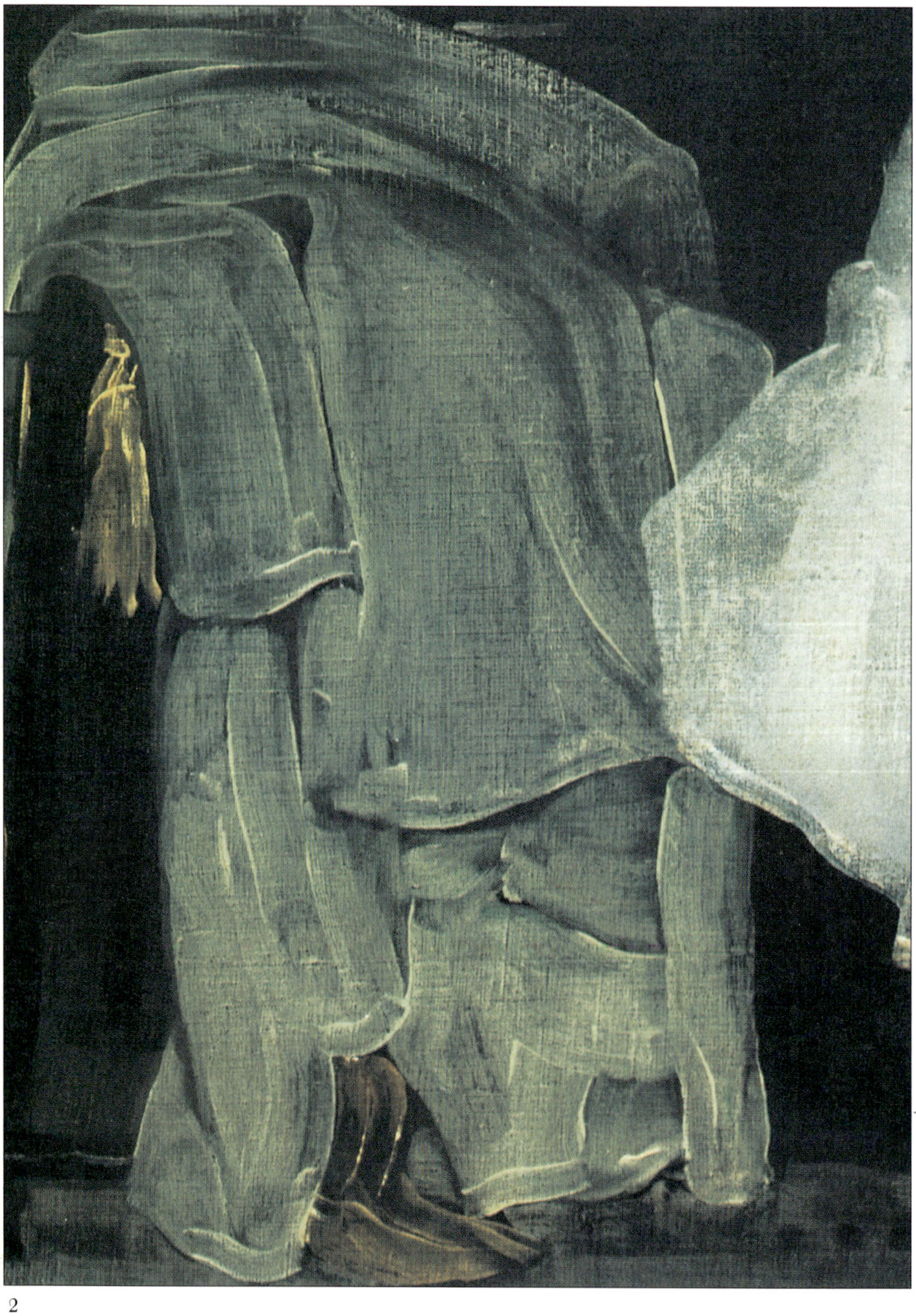

2

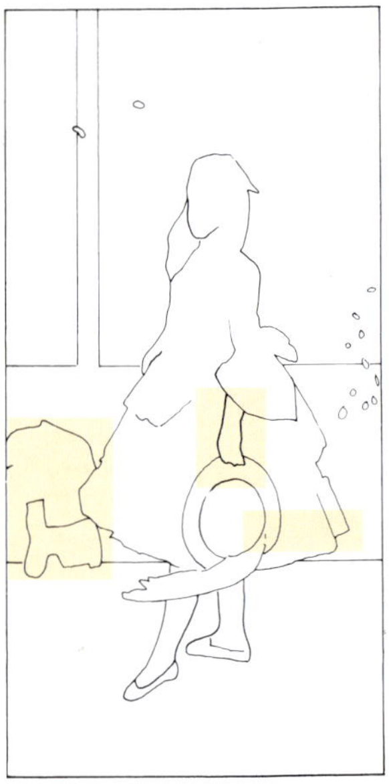

1 The painting is the result of a series of superimposed layers of excessively thin paint washed over a dark ground. This technique was particularly effective for rendering the semi-transparent white muslin, which only partially obscures the sitter's form. The black of the dado area can be clearly seen, modified by the various layers of paint which describe the dress and petticoat. If Whistler was dissatisfied with the painting at the end of a sitting, the day's work would be scraped down or mopped in order to allow him to begin afresh the next day. In this way he could impart to the final image a sense of freshness and immediacy which belied the labor that went into its creation.

2 This detail is a testimony to Whistler's ability to use paint descriptively in rapid gestural movements. Here he uses the minimum of brushstrokes to convey the weight of the sitter's coat as it hangs over a stool. The structure of the fabric is suggested by the thinness and transparency of the applied color modified by the presence of the dark underpainting.

3 *Actual size detail* Traces of the previous positioning of the sitter's arm can be clearly seen in this detail.

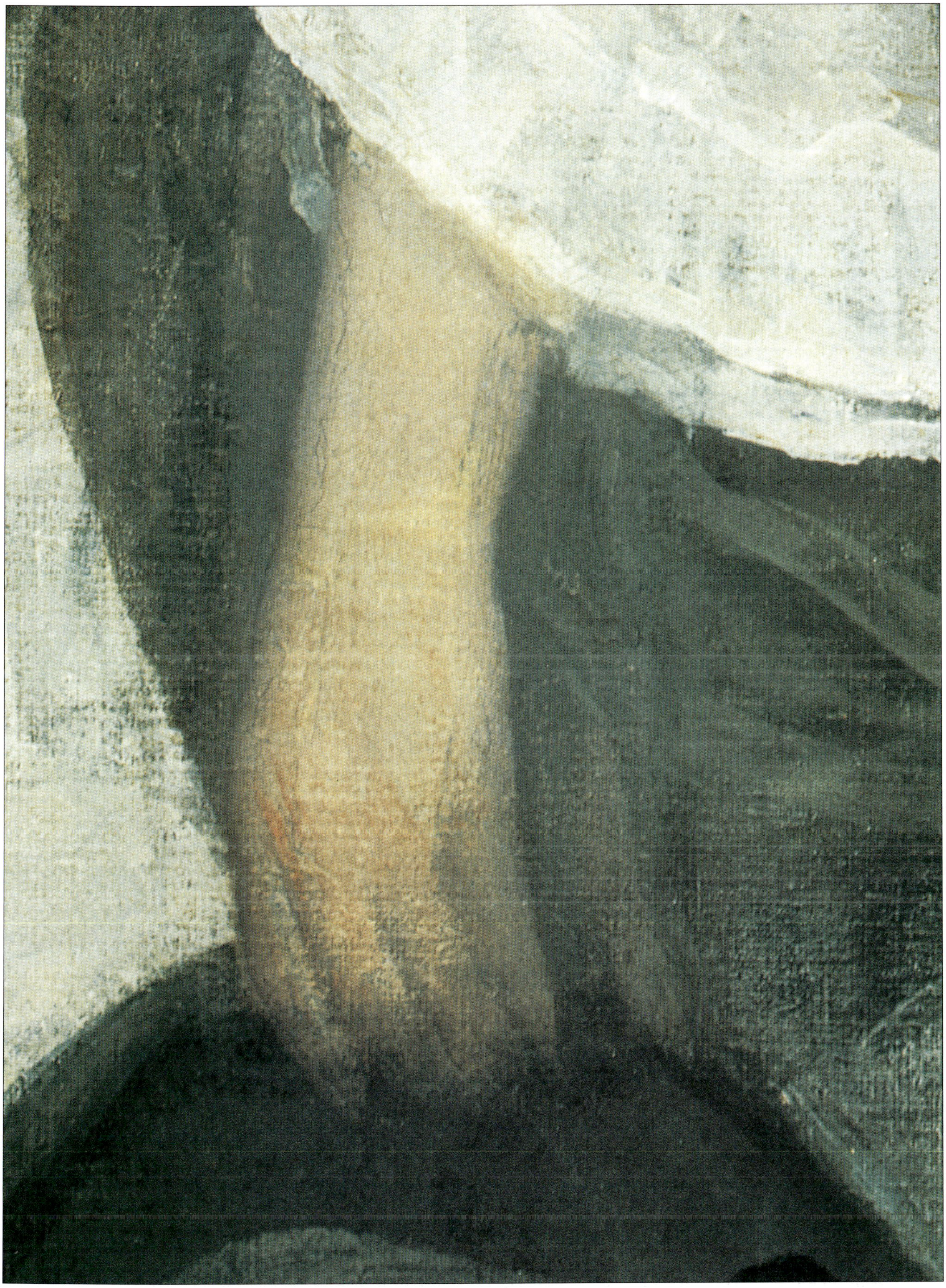

3 *Actual size detail*

Nocturne in Black and Gold: the Falling Rocket

c1875

Oil on wood

$23^3/_4 \times 18^1/_8$in/60.3×46.6cm

Detroit Institute of Arts

This is one of Whistler's most dramatic and effective canvases, painted with a freedom and verve unusual in both his art and that of his contemporaries. When it was exhibited at the Grosvenor Gallery in 1877 it attracted the attention – and wrath – of the elderly art critic John Ruskin. He considered the price of 200 guineas for "flinging a pot of paint in the face of the public" a gross impertinence, and said so in his review. The point in question was whether the time that the artist had spent on a painting was reflected in its monetary value. Ruskin felt that the public was not being given value for money, and was duty bound to say so. Whistler, not only quarrelsome by nature, but also worried at the potential damage to his status as a portrait painter, sued the critic, and although the technical winner of the case, was made to pay costs, which is the legal way of saying that the case should not have been brought. The trial was a farce. Ruskin was too ill to attend, and Whistler's friend Burne-Jones, who appeared against his will to help Whistler, at one point made an unintentional indictment of the artist's work by saying that he "... evaded the difficulties of painting by not carrying his work far enough." "This," said *The Times* in its leader of November 27, "would probably be accepted as a fair representation of the truth by everybody." The trial bankrupted Whistler but ensured the painting's place in history.

The Grosvenor Gallery, which was made gentle fun of in Gilbert and Sullivan's operetta *Patience,* was opened as an alternative to the over-commercialized Royal Academy. Whistler exhibited eight works there in the company of Burne-Jones, Rossetti and others associated with the Aesthetic movement. In court Whistler was asked to describe the painting which had caused such offense. "The picture represents a distant view of Cremorne, with a falling rocket and other fireworks. It occupied two days and is a finished picture. The frame is traced with black, and the black mark on the right is my monogram. What is the particular beauty of the picture? I dare say I could make it clear to any sympathetic painter, but I do not think that I could to you [i.e. the Attorney-General], any more than a musician could explain the beauty of a harmony to a person who had no ear."

William Rossetti, the critic and brother of Dante Gabriel Rossetti, wrote of the picture, "The scene is probably Cremorne Gardens; the heavy rich darkness of the clump of the trees to the left, contrasted with the opaque obscurity of the sky, itself enhanced by the falling shower of fire-flakes, is felt and realized with great truth. Straight across the trees, not high above the ground, shoots and fizzles the last and fiercest light of the expiring rocket." Whistler may well have been helped in visualizing this scene by the print of a similar subject by the Japanese artist Hiroshige, but the major means which enabled him to translate the scene so directly was his technique of memorizing experience so thoroughly that he could recall its essentials later in the quiet of his studio.

The ground is reddish brown, which gives a warm glow to the blue-black of the night sky. The particular milky quality of the sky is the result of Whistler's method of introducing transparent blue-gray washes into the painting. The general thinness of the paint enhances the thickly impasted horizontal strokes of yellow-red that establish the setting of the display and help to define the architectural details half hinted at in the middle distance. The fireworks are brilliantly described by firmly placed dabs of orange and green, which stand out in dramatic contrast with the rest of the painting. The figures are established by the color of the background rather than by any direct application of paint, their flat, modish silhouettes once again bringing Japan to mind, quite appropriately, given the subject of the painting.

Because this painting initially achieved fame through the infamous court case between Whistler and Ruskin, its artistic qualities are sometimes under-appreciated. As with so many of Whistler's paintings, its beauty lies not only in the formal inventions and the painterly innovations, but also in the courage of the artist in breaking new ground. Whistler and other avant-garde artists of the late 19th rcentury were engaged in a similar struggle to develop new and more truthful ways of recording their sensations before an ever-changing nature.

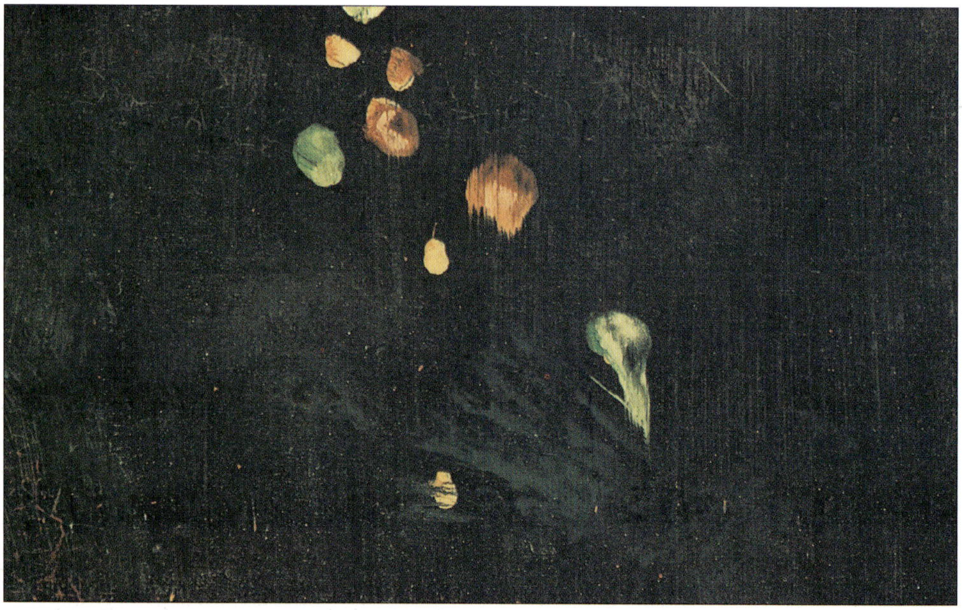

1

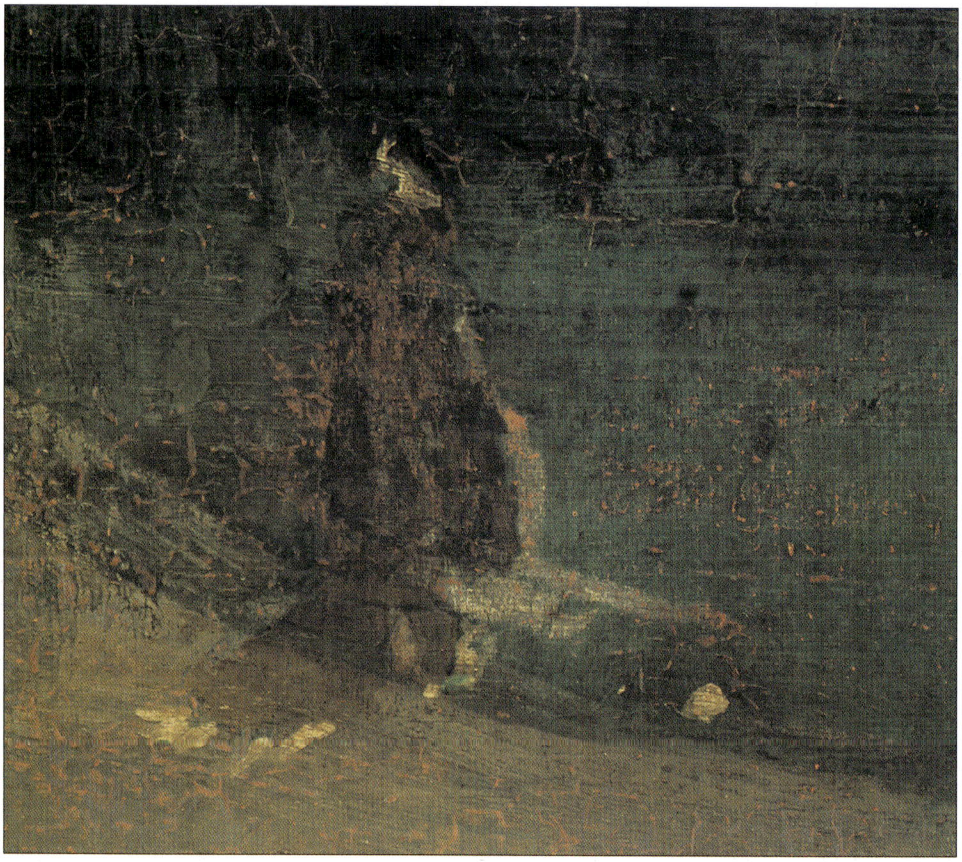

2

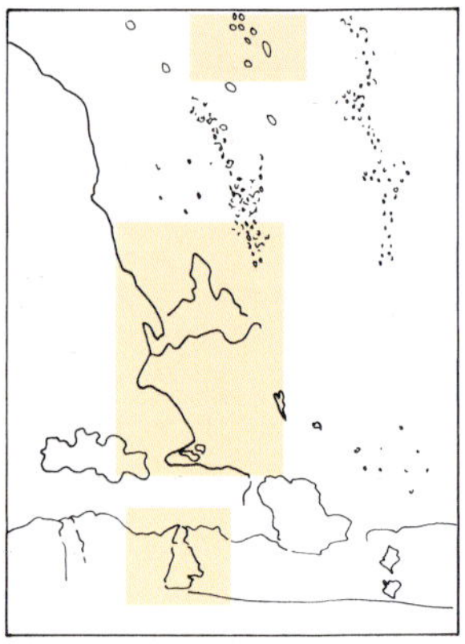

1 Details of this painting reveal the extent to which Whistler abstracted from nature. Here one can almost feel the twists and turns of his wrist as he placed the varied dots and dashes that describe the sparks thrown off by the exploding fireworks, blazing with light as they tumble down to earth.

2 The painting was done on a red-brown ground, and the only color of the foreground figure is that of this underpainting. When the Attorney General was told at the trial that the picture had probably taken "one day to do the work and another to finish," he asked whether "that is the labor for which you asked 200 guineas?" The artist replied, "No, it was for the knowledge of a lifetime."

3 *Actual size detail* A vivid horizontal flash of impasted yellow paint moves across the picture, losing itself in the darkness only to reappear as a parti-colored blob of red-yellow. This is repeated in the bands of yellow lights that mark the verticals of the fantastical buildings of the Pleasure Gardens, which, by their very regularity, contrast with the flecks of paint that describe the falling sparks. Paint has been washed on and dabbed out to create the impression of mystery inherent in such a scene, brilliantly but sporadically lit by short-lived flashes of color.

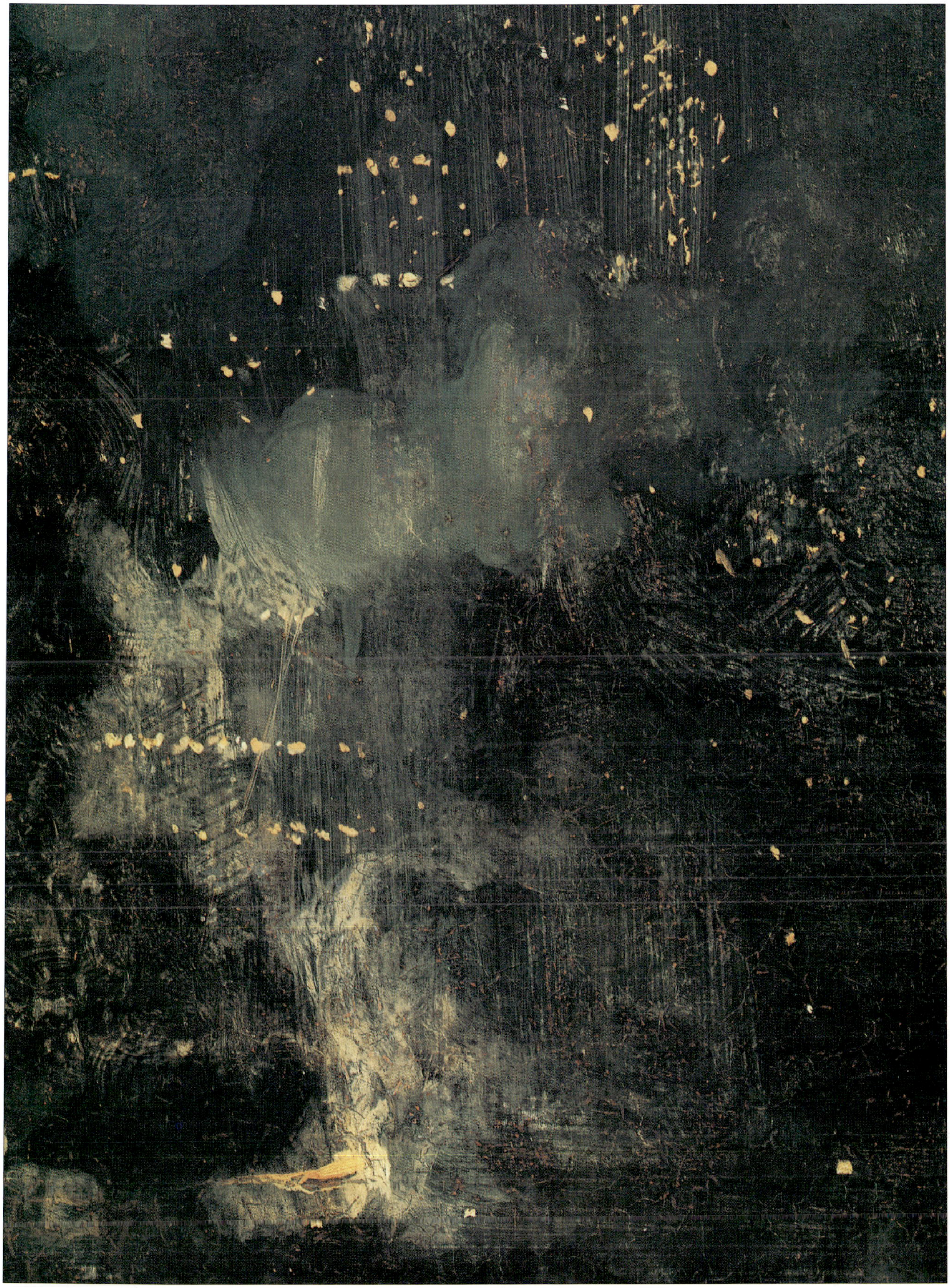

3 *Actual size detail*

Bathing Posts, Brittany

1893

Oil on wood

$6\frac{1}{2} \times 9\frac{1}{2}$in/16.6×24.5cm

Hunterian Museum and Art Gallery, University of Glasgow

Water had always fascinated Whistler, and in the 1880s he began to produce a series of paintings *en plein air* — directly studied from nature — which are very different from either his earlier Courbet-inspired canvases or his near-monochromatic Nocturnes. These tiny panels were produced with the aid of a small box of oils, which contained panels of wood cut just large enough to fit inside the box itself.

For an artist who is most often remembered for his skill in balancing nuances of grays and blues, silvers and opals, these small panels are surprising in the exactitude with which they capture the kind of light and color revealed by full daylight. From his earliest paintings Whistler had preferred to situate himself so that the subject of his composition was fixed in terms of a series of horizontal and/or vertical accents that echoed the sides of his support, in this case, the rectangular shape of his panel. This served both to reduce the problems of perspective and to allow his flat areas of subtly modulated color to give maximum assistance to his intention, namely to create a formal balance made up of a few simple geometrically based forms.

Here he has produced such a formal arrangement, and in some of his late paintings he was to push this trend even further, paring away all detail until all that remained was a series of horizontal bands. These, by their tone and color, are made to suggest with the utmost economy of means the vastness of the sea and sky.

Here the long, delicately drawn lines of thin paint cover the panel from side to side, the broad description of the scene being created by no more than the pressure of the artist's hand and the gradual emptying of his brush, while a few flicks of muted color and carefully placed triangles of white serve as the small details that complete the illusion of actuality. In their somewhat over-fulsome biography of the artist, the Pennells described his procedure. "When the wave broke and the surf made a beautiful line of white, he painted this at once, then all that completed the beauty of the breaking wave, then the boat passing, and then, having got the movement and the beauty that goes almost as soon as it comes, he put in the shore or the horizon."

Paintings like this one reveal a carefree desire to paint with freedom and lack of inhibition that could only with great difficulty have been achieved in the larger and more carefully planned pictures of the artist's earlier career. Working on a small scale directly from his unpretentious subject matter imposed technical limitations that gave him new scope for improvisation, and the enjoyment he clearly felt in producing these works has an impact that belies their physical size. Whistler called these tiny miracles of painting his "little games," and their rigorous, if unassuming geometry and controlled application of color and tone make them some of the most delightful of all his productions. Sickert observed that "Whistler expressed the essence of his talent in his little panels — *pochades,* it is true, in measurement, but masterpieces of classic painting in importance." The modest size of these *pochades* (sketches or studies), whether they depict a row of shops, a seascape or group of humble farm buildings, allowed the artist to sidestep many of the problems he confronted in larger projects and to express some of the concerns that he found so difficult to give voice to in other, perhaps more taxing, undertakings. In a letter to the Pennells towards the end of his life he said, "I could almost laugh at the extraordinary progress I am making and the lovely things I am inventing — work beyond anything I have ever done before."

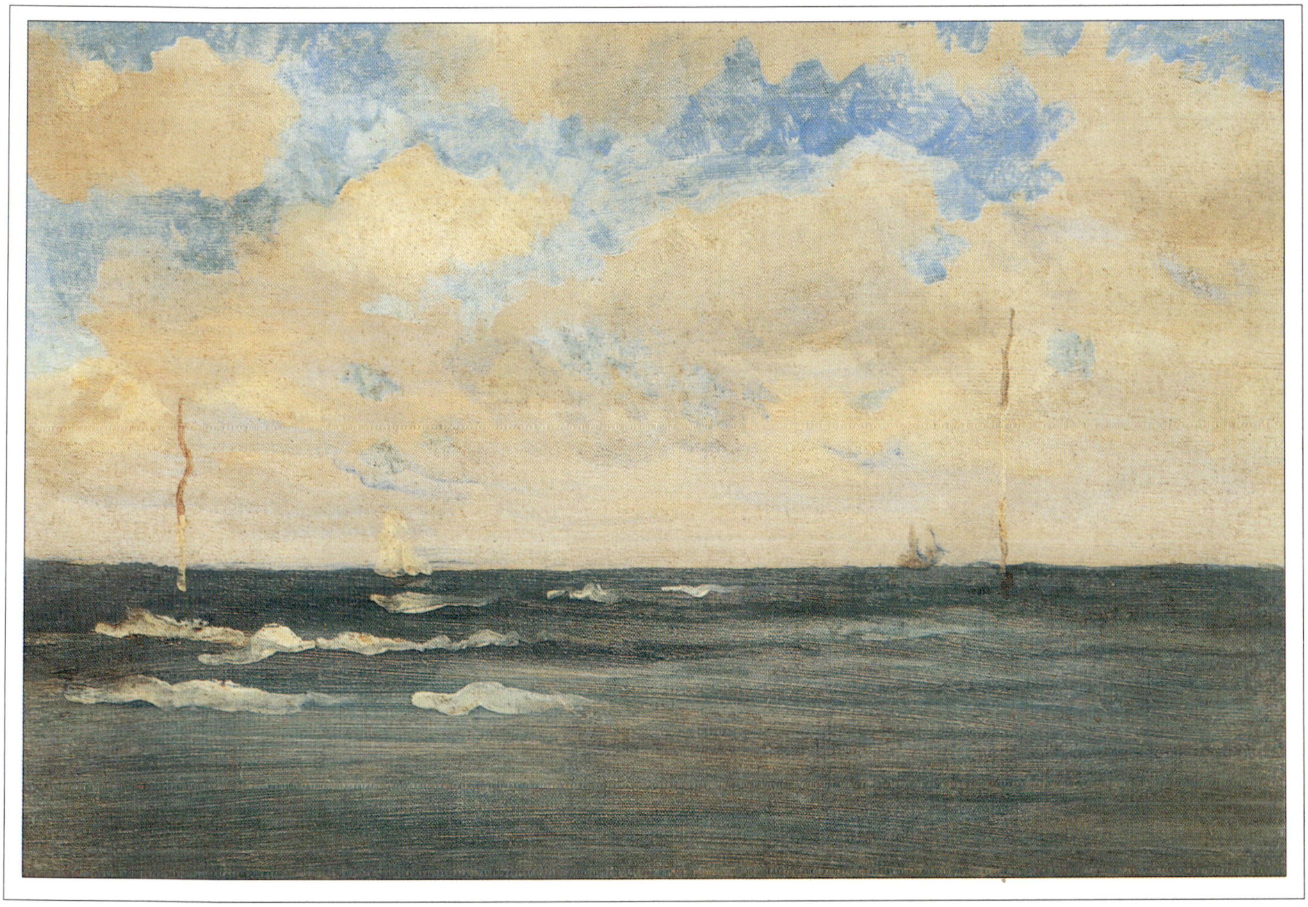

The panel is divided horizontally into almost equal portions, each of which has been painted quite differently. This tiny seascape could easily be mistaken for a detail from a larger work by one of the Impressionists, although the techniques employed are very different. However, the thinness of the medium and fluidity of handling in the picture recalls the seascape in the background of Degas' painting, *On the Beach* (National Gallery, London), which may well have owed something to Whistler's paintings of the 1860s.

1

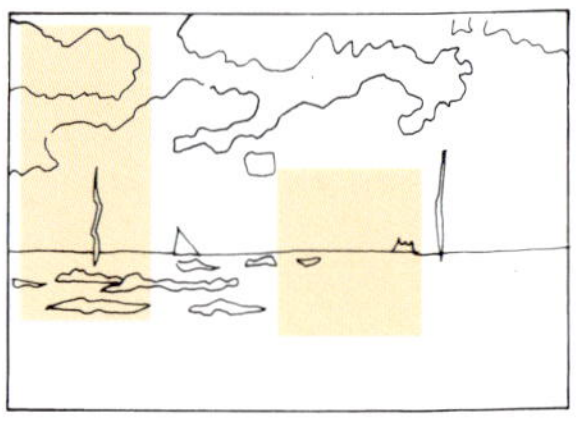

1 Ultramarine mixed with white is dabbed in single brushmarks on a gray ground in a manner traditionally associated with watercolor, leaving the ground to show through to suggest the color and form of the clouds. The structure of the clouds is tightened by the addition of a richer mixture of the ground color. The far distance is suggested by a thin wash of pinkish lilac which brings out the delicate colors of the bathing posts.

2 The sea is described with a translucent wash of paint that appears to have been wiped to suggest the gentle movement of waves. Where it recedes into the distance the paint has been left undisturbed, its stronger color indicating the broader, flatter expanse. The series of waves have been brushed on and then taken off with the brush, allowing the grain of the wood to show through to suggest the darker undersides, while single perfectly controlled dabs of paint describe the white tops of the breakers.

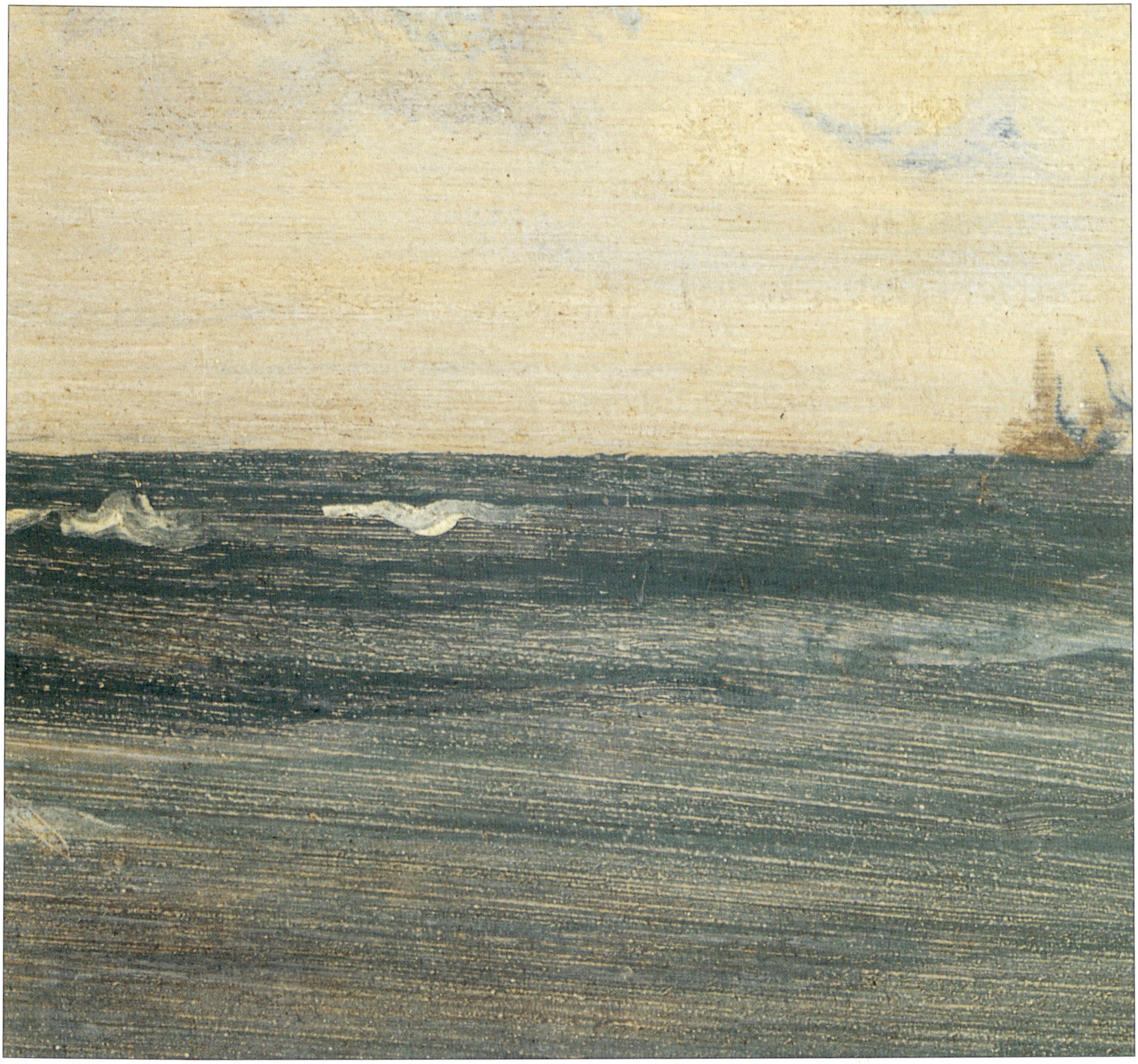

2

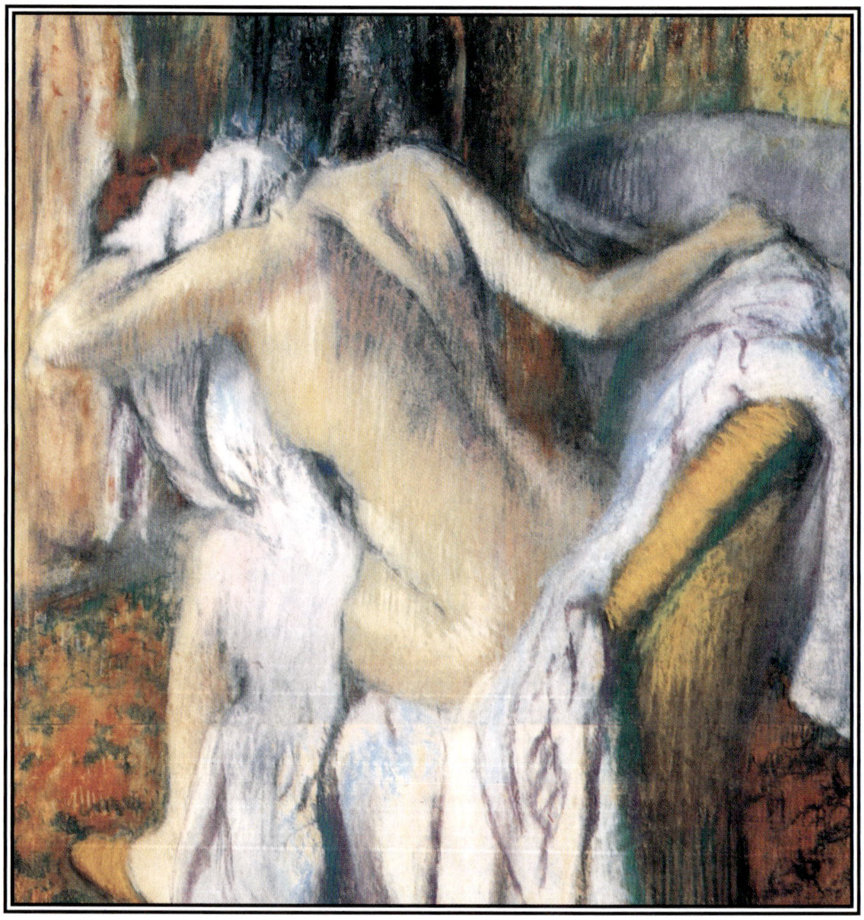

DEGAS

Introduction

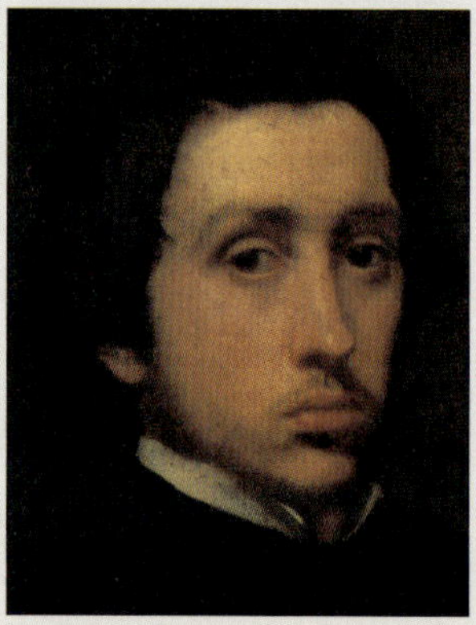

Edgar Degas
Self-portrait
1885
Louvre, Paris

"Art is vice," wrote Degas, "one doesn't take it in lawful wedlock, one rapes it." This passionate statement from a man whose art and character are customarily described as detached exposes the paradox of Edgar Degas. It also describes the artist's radical and dramatic approach to picture making, which made him one of the greatest artists of the nineteenth century.

Degas the man

"An original fellow, this Degas, sickly, neurotic, and so myopic that he is afraid of losing his sight; but for this very reason an eminently receptive creature and sensitive to the character of things." Edmond de Goncourt's journal entry expresses something of Degas' contradictory nature: a reactionary with radical ideas, an anti-Semite whose closest friends were Jewish, and a misogynist whose life was spent observing and painting women. He was a man who wished to be simultaneously famous and unknown.

Demanding, difficult and exacting, Degas commanded reverential respect among a small group of close family friends, who put up with his authoritarian stipulations, such as this one, for dinner: "There will be a dish cooked without butter for me. No flowers on the table, very little light...You'll shut up the cat, I know, and no one will bring a dog. And if there are women there, ask them not to put smells on themselves...Scent, when there are things that smell so good! such as toast, for example. And we shall sit down to table at exactly half-past seven."

Degas himself was well aware of the problems of his difficult nature. He remarked to Renoir that he had "one terrible, irreconcilable enemy." "And who," asked Renoir, "is that?" "Why, don't you know? Myself, of course." To another friend he apologized for his harshness while attempting to explain it: "I was, or appeared to be, hard with everyone, owing to a sort of tendency towards roughness that originated in my doubts and my bad temper. I felt I was so inept, so badly equipped, so flabby, while it seemed to me that my calculations regarding art were so accurate, I was sulky with the whole world and with myself."

Degas shielded himself from certain emotional responses. He felt a lack of passion for what is generally held to be the proper sphere for emotion, such as romantic love, baldly stating, "I have no passion." This was, of course, untrue: his emotion was roused by what might be termed the negative passions; he possessed, in inversion, an overendowment of spleen. Should he disagree with a point made in argument his sarcasm was lacerating, and eventually he had to keep silent for fear of exploding.

Those who knew him well saw Degas' brusque exterior as a form of protection. "He carefully hid his sensibility under a mask of iron. He did not easily give his friendship, but when given, his affection was deep, certain, devoted," wrote Pierre Lafond.

"What a creature he was, that Degas!" remarked the picture dealer Paul Gimpel to Renoir, who replied, "All his friends had to leave him; I was one of the last to go, but even I couldn't stay till the end. The incomprehensible thing is that Monet, so gentle and affectionate, was always attacked, whereas Degas, so vitriolic, violent and uncompromising, was accepted from the very first by the Academy, the public and the revolutionaries." "People were afraid of him," was Gimpel's succinct explanation.

Famous for his intellectual rigor, his quick wit and acerbic quips, Degas was a formidable figure respected throughout the artistic world; an artist's artist who was also popular with the picture-buying public. His artistic integrity also made him a frequently emulated artist. "Everyone copies Degas," remarked Gauguin.

In many ways Degas' character and his art are comparable to that of Michelangelo. Both were widely held to be the greatest artists of their day. Both seemed to have suppressed the channels receptive to romantic love ("I

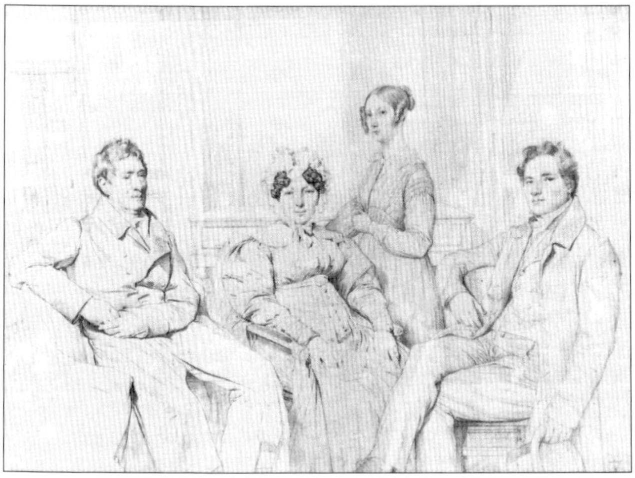

AUGUSTE-DOMINIQUE INGRES
The Gatteaux Family
1850
Louvre, Paris

Degas had a lifelong admiration for Ingres. First introduced to his work through pictures owned by family friends, his respect for the master was fostered at the Atelier Lamothe. By the end of his life he owned some twenty paintings and ninety drawings by Ingres, and he often recounted the story of their one meeting, when Ingres had advised him to "draw lines, young man, a great many lines."

am blocked, impotent," Degas stated). Both appear to have possessed melancholy, prickly characters, prone to spasms of irritation, and both suffered the loss of a mother at an impressionable age, giving rise in this century to posthumous Freudian analysis of the damaging consequences on the psyche occasioned by such dramatic maternal deprivation. Both assumed protective masks, and put all their energy into their art. Furthermore, both men reveal, in their art and in their poetry, a positive leaning toward distress, tension and countertension.

The artist's early life

The events of Degas' life, unlike those of Delacroix or Gauguin, are not of dramatic or romantic interest. He abhorred bohemianism, retaining, to the end of his life, the reserve of his *haute-bourgeoise* upbringing. Born Hilaire Germain Edgar de Gas in Paris on July 19, 1834, Degas, as he later chose to modify his aristocratic surname, was the eldest of five surviving children. His earliest years seem tinged with the melancholy which was to color his life, and which seemed to overshadow the whole Degas household. He appears to have passed a privileged but joyless childhood. His mother, a Creole of French descent, born in New Orleans, educated in France and married at the age of sixteen, also reflects this melancholy as she felt her youth passing "without a single ball." Her married life, given over to childbearing and domestic duties, ended when Degas was thirteen; she died after the birth of her seventh child.

From the age of eleven Degas boarded at the Lycée Louis-le-Grand, one of only three schools which prepared its pupils for France's élite educational establishment, the Ecole Normale Supérieure. It was here that Degas met other pupils from the same social background, the Halévys, the Rouarts and Paul Valpinçon, with whom he remained lifelong friends.

Education at the lycée was entirely in the classics, with a conspicuous absence of science or math. The poet Paul Valéry described its atmosphere as follows. "Neither cleanliness, nor the smallest notion of hygiene, nor deportment, nor even the pronunciation of our language, had any place in the program of that incredible system, conceived as it was to exclude carefully every-

EDGAR DEGAS
Marguerite Degas in Confirmation Dress
1854
Louvre, Paris

Degas was one of five surviving children, and made many drawings and sketches of his siblings. This early portrait of his sister demonstrates why Degas' father believed that portraiture would become the finest jewel in his son's crown. Like Ingres, Degas used a hard pencil to create light, clear line drawings with little shading.

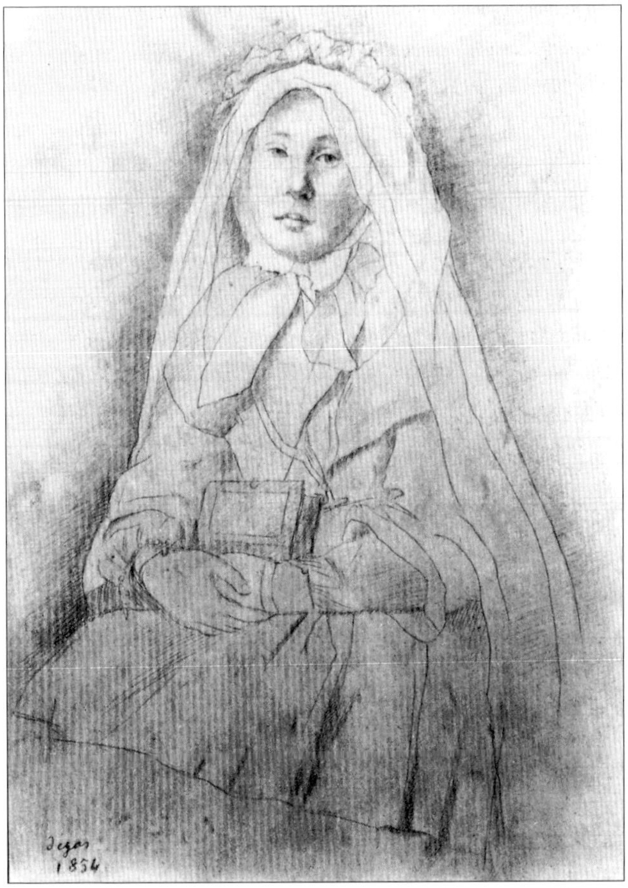

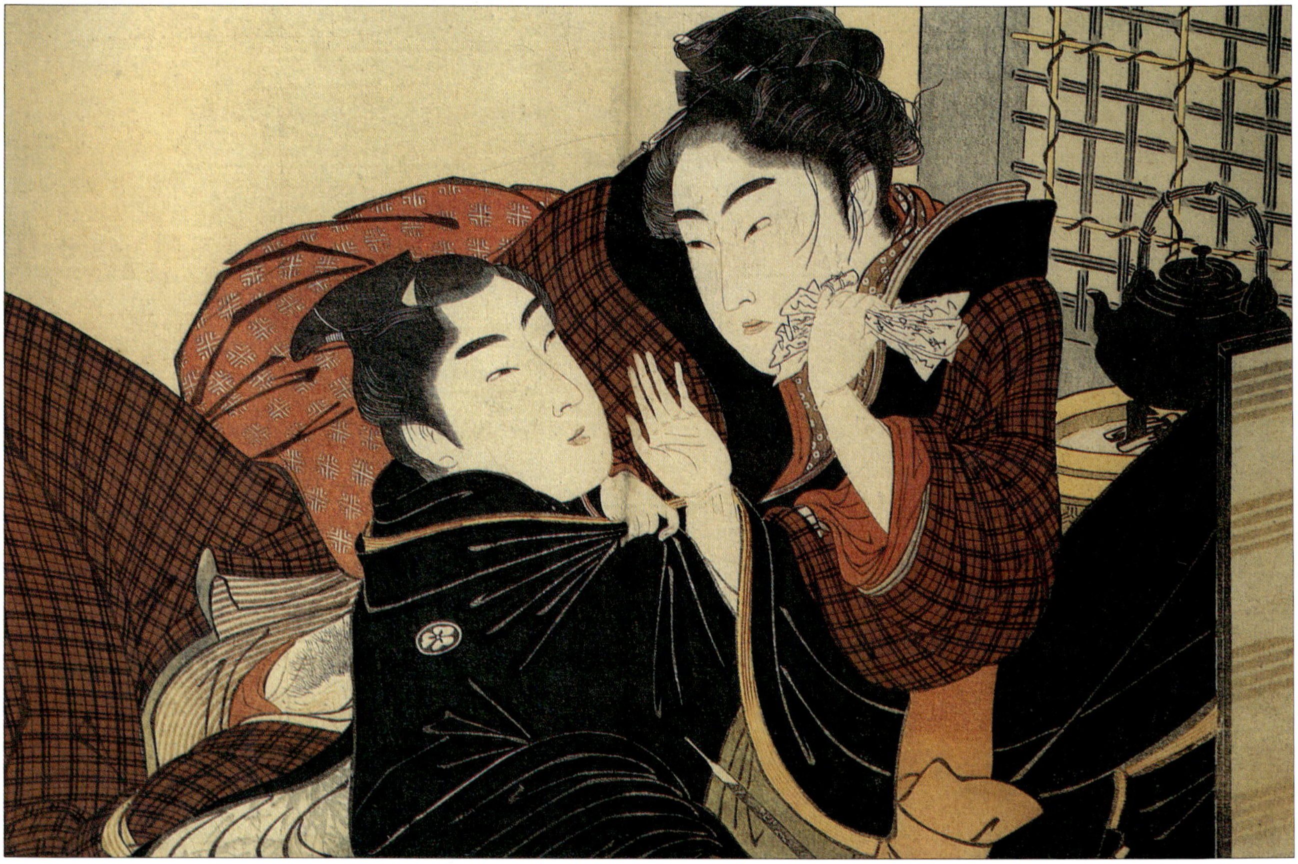

UTAMARO
The Poem of the Pillow
1788
Victoria and Albert Museum, London

Degas, like many avant-garde artists, found a source of inspiration in the Japanese prints which were beginning to come into the country in large numbers in the mid-nineteenth century. The dramatic cropping of figures, the use of color and pattern and the rejection of tonal modeling and shadow can all be seen in Degas' work.

thing to do with the body, the senses, the sky, the arts, or social life." It did, however, engender a profound respect for the intellect.

On leaving the lycée, Degas complied with his father's instructions to study law, but after only a year he discontinued his studies, determined to become an artist. Such was his devotion to his calling that, following a family row, he is reputed to have abandoned home for a draughty garret. His father was sufficiently impressed with his single-mindedness to agree to him following an artistic training, and seems henceforth to have taken his son's endeavors seriously, as his letters to Degas in Italy testify. In 1855, at the suggestion of Henri Valpinçon, father of his schoolfriend Paul, Degas entered the studio of Louis Lamothe, an obscure artist who had in his youth been a pupil of Ingres.

Artistic training

The year spent in the Atelier Lamothe evidently inculcated in the young Degas a profound respect for Ingres, whom he met through M. Valpincon. This never diminished, and was fostered in the following months by a stint at the principal academic art institution in Paris, the Ecole des Beaux Arts. Although he did not enjoy the Ecole, he was happy with the instruction, which placed great weight on drawing and the copying of engravings and plaster casts of antique works. In the Louvre Degas studied not only the works of the Old Masters, but also those of the more modern painters, absorbing the lessons of Ingres and, to a lesser extent, Delacroix's use of color and Courbet's realism. In 1856, abandoning the Ecole, Degas set off for Italy to complete his artistic tuition independently.

The three years spent in Italy were, wrote Degas "the most extraordinary period of my life." It was the birthplace of his father and home of many Italian relatives. Degas spent his time principally in Naples and Florence, where he had relatives, and Rome, where the French artistic colony grouped around the French Academy in the Villa Medici. Italy was the artistic goal for all aspiring artists, and Degas, of independent means and now free from the pressures of the art institutions, studied the paintings in the galleries, drew his relatives and discussed art and life with fellow countrymen. By his return to France in 1859 he had passed a self-regulated period of observation and study, and had seen at firsthand the European masterpieces in the principal Italian collections.

Degas' earliest finished paintings are highly accomplished family portraits showing considerable psychological insights. Established in Paris, he now dutifully embarked on the large-scale history paintings which were considered, in the mid-nineteenth century, to be the most elevated art form — until the challenge of the avant-garde brought about a reconsideration of the role of this kind of painting. His early works in the genre, *The Misfortunes of the City of Orléans*, *Jephthah's Daughter*, *Spartan Boys and Girls Exercising* and *Semiramis Constructing a City*, all painted between 1860 and 1864, can be loosely termed academic, in the established tradition of nineteenth-century French Salon painting, though *Spartan Boys and Girls*, painted in 1860, shows something of the Degas to come. In this work he has attempted to reinterpret a classical subject in a more modern way, displaying a deliberate ungainliness, a lighter palette and visible brushwork.

The realist painter

By about the mid-1860s Degas had rejected history painting, and had become what he was to remain — a painter of contemporary life. Inspired by the new currents in French painting and by his friendship with Manet — whom he met in the Louvre in 1862 — and the circle of artists at the Café Guerbois, later to become known as the Impressionists, Degas completely changed his subject-matter. He executed fewer portraits, and began to frequent the popular haunts of the man-about-town, making the racecourse and the ballet very much his own.

Although Degas is seldom regarded as an Impressionist painter, he did exhibit with the group, and was

EDGAR DEGAS
Vicomte Lepic and his Daughters, Place de la Concorde
c 1876

This painting, which was lost — presumably destroyed in World War Two — reflects the influence of Japanese prints in the way the figures are cropped at the edge of the canvas. It is both a picture of contemporary life and a lively portrait of a friend, out walking with his daughters and his dog, and captured with the artificially contrived naturalism that became the hallmark of Degas' work.

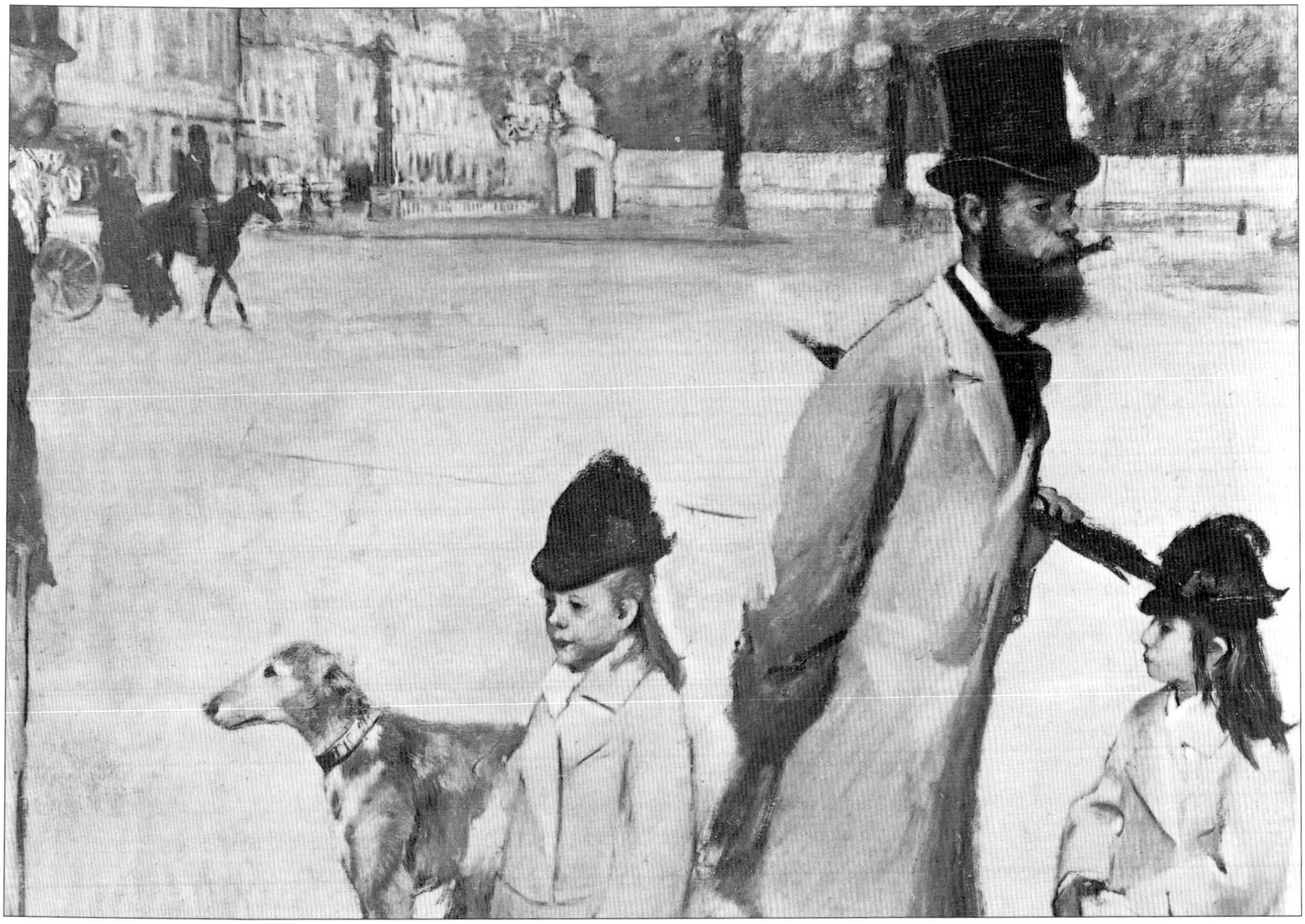

instrumental in organizing the Impressionist Exhibitions in the 1870s and '80s, which posed a challenge to the accepted artistic standards of the Salon. He shared with the Impressionists an interest in depicting contemporary subject matter, in painting techniques, in Japanese prints, and in light. Where he differed from them was in his preference for artificial lighting and his active dislike of outdoor *(plein-air)* painting, which caused him to remark "The gendarmes should shoot down all those easels cluttering up the countryside."

As an intellectual painter and an artist preoccupied with formal qualities of abstraction, he was not interested in the Impressionists' attempts to record the immediate and transient effects of light, and he had a strong preference for painting people. A classically educated, native Parisian, he had no interest in landscape painting; the calm of the countryside bored him profoundly. Apart from two series of landscapes, the first made around 1869 in Boulogne and a second late in his life, in his studio, his racing scenes are the only works which include a rural background. He also found the painting of still lifes incomprehensible. It is part of the Degas paradox that, while he needed to work alone, it was people and movement only which interested him. To a greater extent than the Impressionists he strove to reinvent the Old Masters. "Oh Giotto," he implored, "show me how to see Paris, and Paris show me how to see Giotto."

Always dissatisfied with his pictures, he would frequently borrow back sold canvases and rework them — owners of Degas' paintings were rumored to chain them to the wall. Within his chosen range of subjects he repeatedly painted the same thing, making pairs or threes on a single theme, and drawing the subject countless times. One entire notebook was used for a study of the hands for a portrait. He often repeated the remark Ingres had made to him: "Draw lines, young man, a great many lines." Degas himself voiced similar sentiments: "One must treat the same subject ten times, a hundred times." It was part of his working method. He had not time, he maintained, for inspiration. "What I do is the result of reflection and study of the great masters; of inspiration, spontaneity, temperament I know nothing."

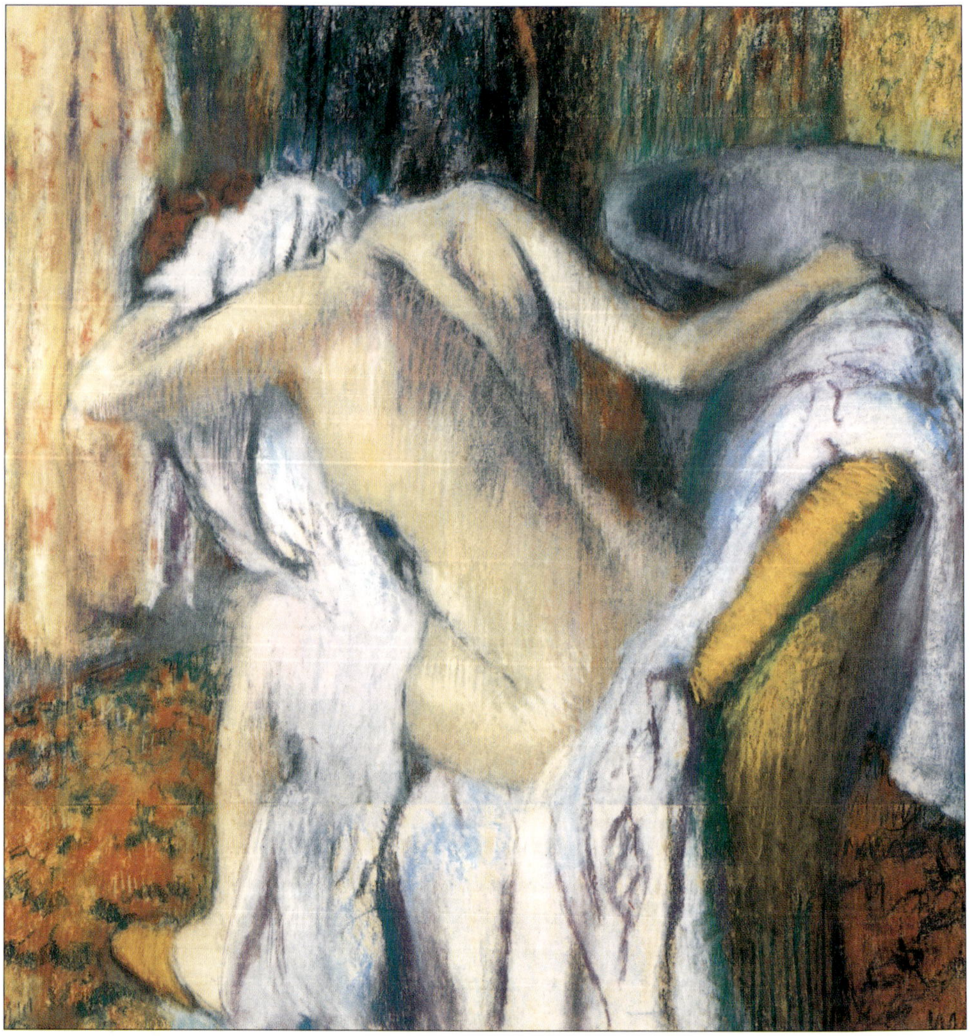

EDGAR DEGAS
After the Bath
1880
National Gallery, London

Women washing or bathing was one of Degas' favorite themes, and he painted every aspect of their most intimate ablutions. This is a late work, done in pastel, a medium Degas favored more and more as his eyesight deteriorated. The use of cream-colored paper has given a pervading sense of warmth and unified the colors, while the varied marks of the pastels evoke the different textures.

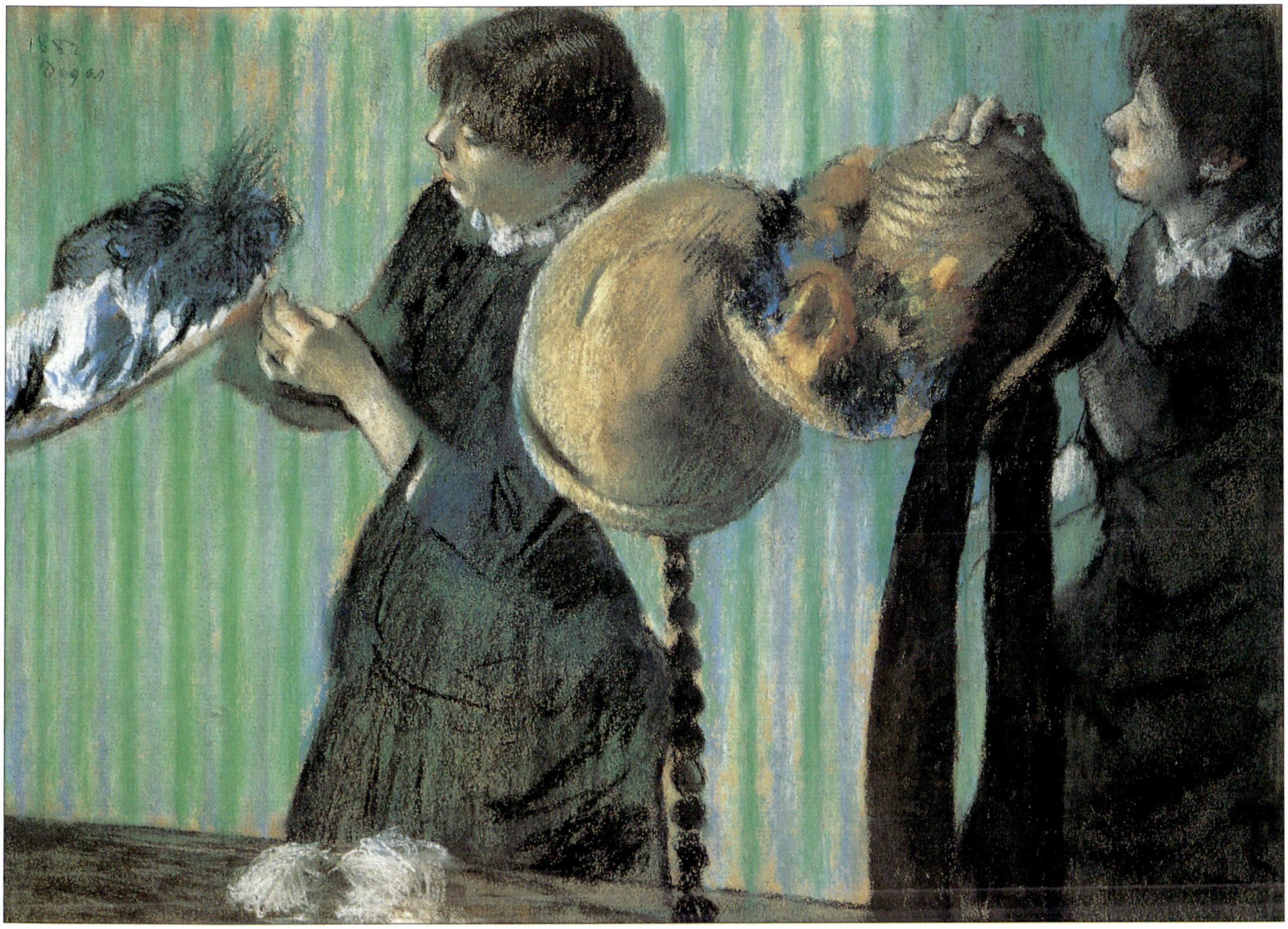

EDGAR DEGAS
At the Milliners
c 1882
Nelson-Atkins Museum of Art, Kansas City

Degas was fascinated both by the young milliners themselves and by the customers trying on hats in front of the mirror. When asked by a woman who had accompanied him to the hat-shop what he found so interesting he replied, "the little milliners' red hands." As in many of Degas' paintings, we feel that we are spying on an intimate scene, with the subjects quite unaware that they are being watched.

Drawing was the prime concern. It was drawing which led to an understanding of the subject so that the artist could synthesize and stylize. The model should be scrutinized and then painted from memory. "Place the model on the ground floor and paint her from the first floor," he once advised an aspiring artist. He regarded as regrettable that too many artists followed color instead of line, and told the English artist Walter Sickert, "I always tried to urge my colleagues along the path of draftsmanship, which I consider a more fruitful field than that of color." It was through line only, Degas felt, that an understanding of underlying forces could be achieved. Yet toward the end of his life the great draftsman had liberated himself from "the tyranny of line" to become a truly great colorist.

Experiments with media

In the 1870s Degas began to experiment with pastel, a medium which had at the time fallen into disfavor. It offered him the possibility of simultaneous line and color: "I am a colorist with line," he maintained. This aphorism also played upon the apparent contradiction of uniting the two, highlighting the battle between divergent artistic camps — the classical Ingrists and their stress on line, and the Delacroix school of Romantics, who upheld the expressive, emotional effect of color. Degas' liberation derived, in part, from his relentless experimentation, during his forties, with the picture-making process, and with the media of painting and printing techniques.

Degas disliked the shine and consistency of thick oil pigment. He applied his paint thinly, often removing the oil from it, and applying it with turpentine in thin washes of color. He softened his pastels over steam, often making them into paste, and used them in novel combinations over gouache and monotype. He frequently painted with oils on paper, rather than canvas, which not only gave his preferred matte surface as the paper

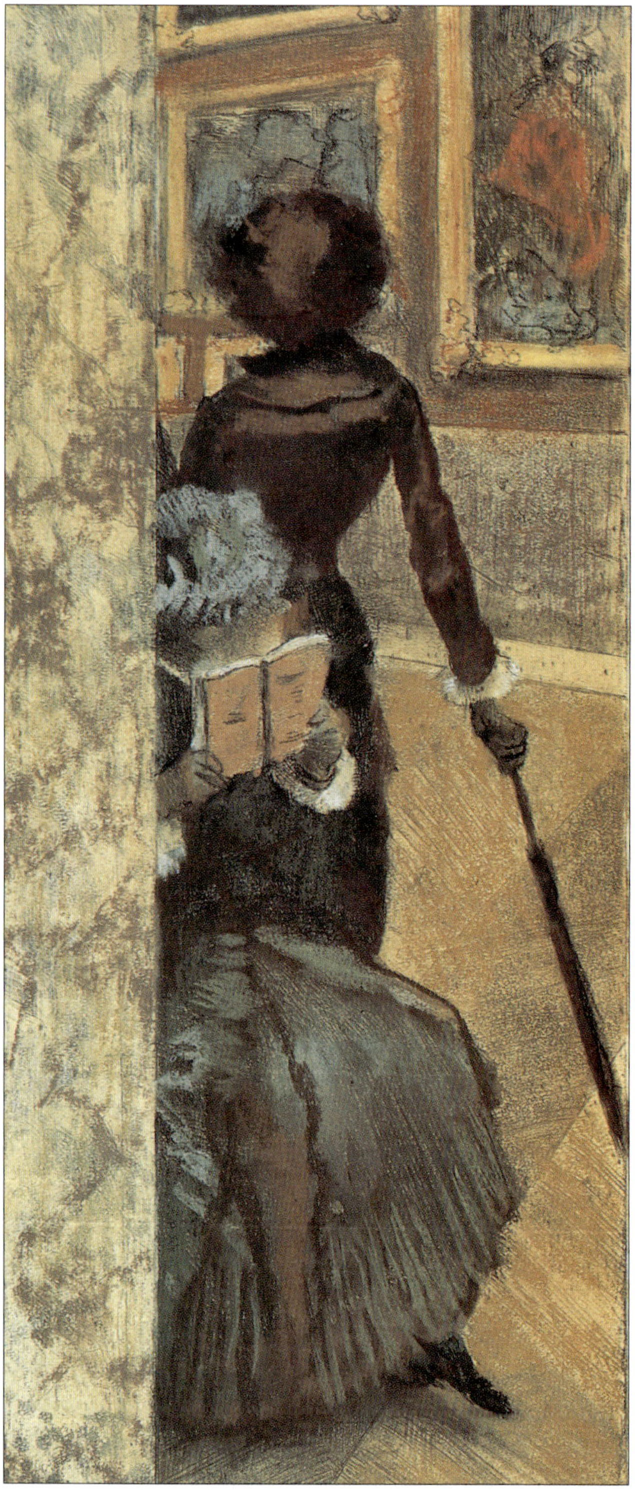

EDGAR DEGAS
Mary Cassatt at the Louvre
1879-80
Chicago Art Institute

This print shows Degas' radical approach to picture making – both in its dramatic composition and in the range of printing techniques used. From the mid-1870s Degas experimented with every known printing technique, continually exploring their possibilities, and here he has combined etching, aquatint, drypoint and "electric crayon" on a single plate.

absorbed the oil, but also offered the possibility of easily cut or added to, a feature which develope approach to the effects of design and perspective c composition.

He was also interested in printing techniques and experimented with every known one, from etching, drypoint, aquatint, lithography and monotype to "electric crayon." The latter was the carbon filament from an electric light bulb, used first at a friend's house when bad weather prevented him from leaving. He applied color washes or pastel on top of a print reworked his frequently excellent first impres Henri Rivière maintained that, "If Degas has just satisfied to draw on his plates quite simply, he w have left behind him the finest engravings of the teenth century."

Degas' eyesight had always been poor, and this have prompted the use of pastel, as well as the cho begin modeling in clay. From 1870 Degas had sculptures in wax or clay, having begun by moc horses to help him with his racecourse pictures figures of ballerinas evolved in a similar way, as m to aid his paintings, but later they became as impc as the paintings themselves. Modeling was an inval tactile discipline to an artist like Degas, whose cor repetition of the same theme gave him such famil with his model at every angle that he was able to r duce the subject from memory. Using clay allowec to feel his way around the forms which his eye scrutinized so thoroughly. In sculpture, too, he ex mented with mixed media: for instance, his wax s ette of a fourteen-year old ballerina has a blue ribbon and muslin tutu – he had searched also for hair and satin ballet shoes. Mixed-media sculptur commonplace today, but this "clothed" bronze sh the public in a way that his paintings had not.

Last years

Much of Degas' late work with its bold, sweeping and overlay of rich color springs from his failin sight. No longer able to create fine line drawing later work is a vehement slashing of color ont roughly executed forms which years of exper examination and sketching had etched on his Blind in one eye, with the sight in the other dim, was quite unmoved by the pre-war sharp rise in th price of his pictures, saying he felt "like a horse w has won the Grand Prix and been given another b oats."

DEGAS' PAINTING METHODS

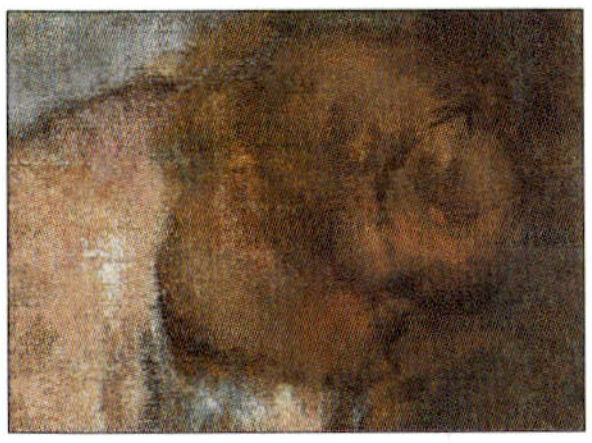

This detail from Two Laundresses *shows Degas' use of loosely handled, thinned oil paint.*

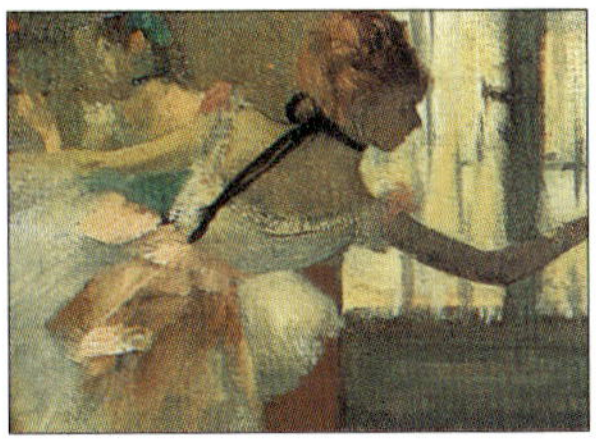

In general, Degas disliked thick paint, but he used areas of impasto to good effect, as can be seen in this detail from The Ballet Rehearsal.

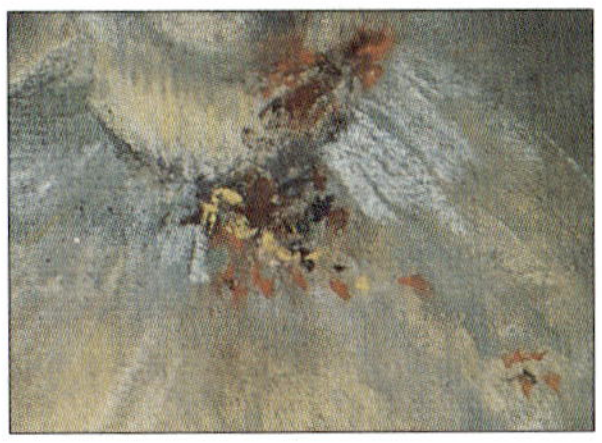

The medium of pastel over monotype, seen in this detail from Dancer Curtseying, *allowed Degas to create stunning effects of color.*

Degas, unlike the Impressionists, did not favor working directly from life or painting out of doors. His concerns were with drawing, form and composition, not with the rapid recording of transient effects of light, and his chosen subject was people, not landscape. He made endless studies for his paintings, filling whole notebooks with drawings of hands, or a particular architectural feature for a background, and for his racecourse scenes he studied horses in close quarters at the Haras-du-Pin stud as well as making small clay or wax models to help him understand the animals' anatomy and the effects of motion. He believed in committing a subject to memory through repeated drawing, and when he felt he had arrived at a full understanding of it he would synthesize his many studies into a thought-out composition.

He experimented endlessly with media, often using oil paints in an unconventional way, much thinned with turpentine and applied to paper or cardboard rather than canvas. He was also greatly interested in all the printing methods – etching, lithography, drypoint and aquatint – and he virtually invented the technique of monotype, which has been popular with artists ever since. He was at his most innovative with pastels, which he frequently used in combination with monotype, softening them over steam or mixing them with fixative to form a paint-like paste which he could then work into with a stiff brush or his fingers.

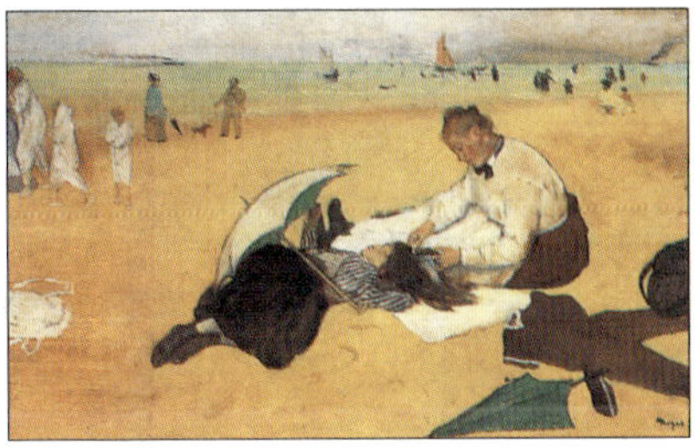

On the Beach, *1876. This work, an outdoor subject but done in the studio, was painted on paper in a medium called* peinture à l'essence. *This is oil paint drained of oil by drying and then mixed with refined turpentine, giving a matte, gouache-like consistency. It was especially suitable for preparatory studies, because it dried more quickly than ordinary oil paint, but here Degas has used it for a finished picture, with the paper mounted on canvas. He was always concerned with finding the best medium for a particular painting, and the matte paint is particularly well-suited to the flat, print-like effect, with no shadows and the minimum of modeling.*

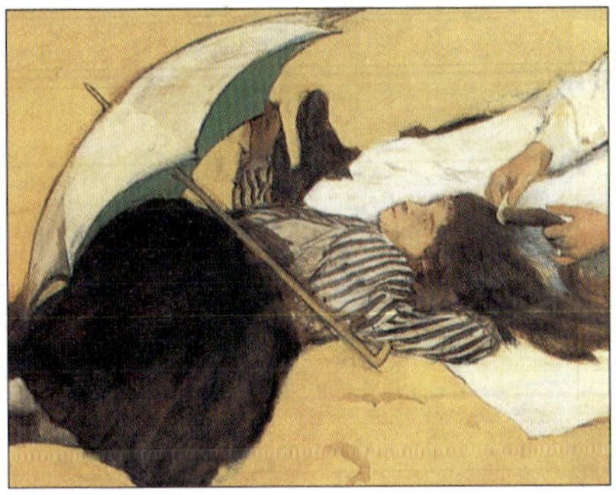

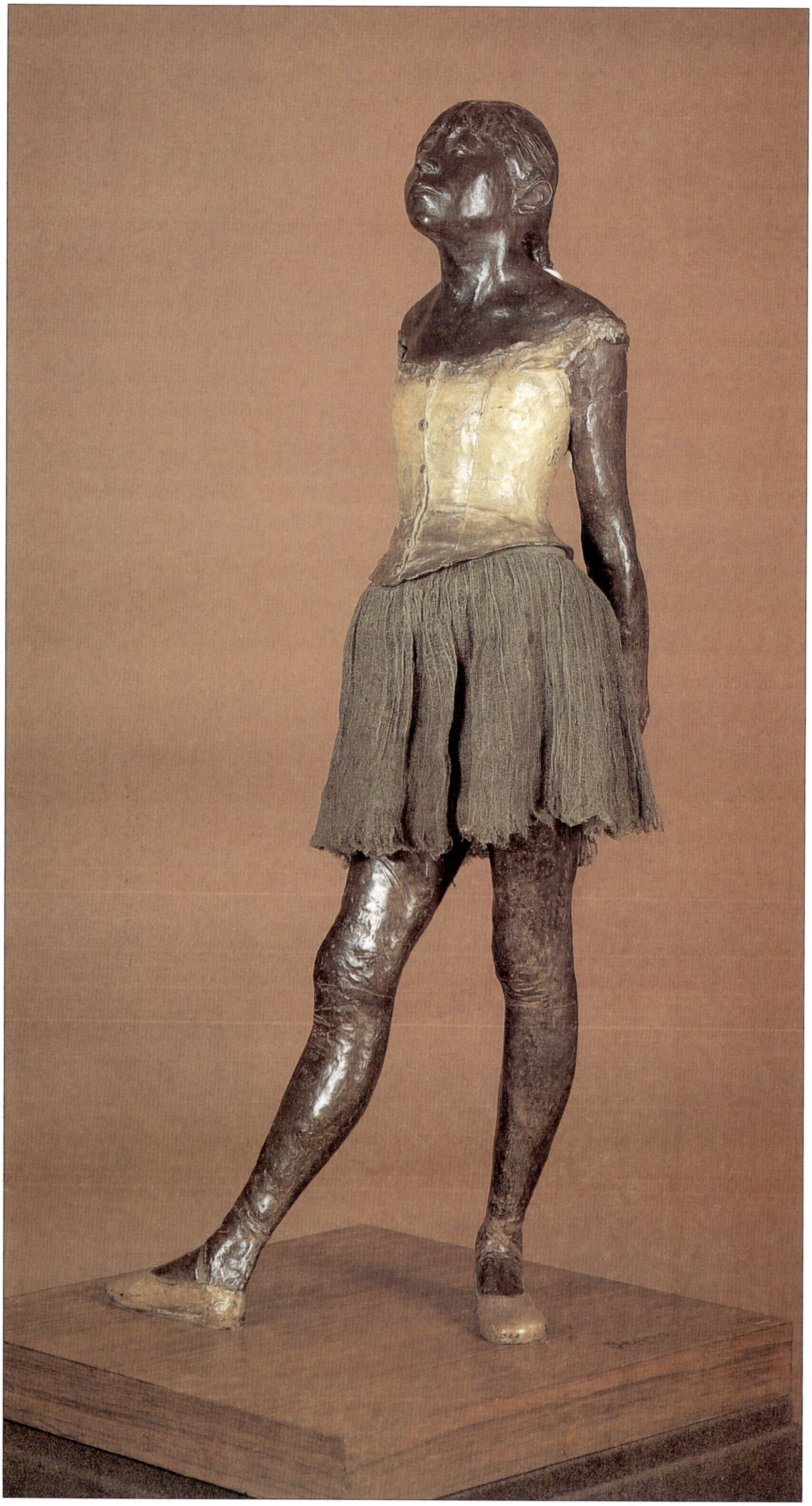

EDGAR DEGAS
Little Dancer
c 1878-80
Tate Gallery, London

Degas began to make wax or clay sculptures in the mid-1870s. Their initial purpose was to help him to understand and paint the figure in motion, but by the 1880s modeling had begun to interest him as an art form in itself. This figure of a fourteen-year-old dancer, first exhibited in lifelike wax and clothed in a real muslin tutu, shocked a public accustomed to sculptures in stone or bronze.

Opposite page
EDGAR DEGAS
Autumn Landscape
1890-3
Museum of Fine Arts, Boston

Landscape did not often form part of Degas' subject matter, but he did execute two series, one in the middle of his life and another toward the end. This almost abstract work, showing the Burgundy countryside, is one of the later series, which he observed from a moving train and then worked up in the studio, using one of his favorite techniques of pastel over monotype.

In 1912 his house was demolished as part of a redevelopment project, and he was obliged to move. "But since I move I no longer work,' he told Daniel Halévy. "It's odd, I haven't put anything in order. Everything is there, leaning against the walls. I don't care." As his sight faded his isolation increased. "I think only of death," he confessed. A familiar, now white-bearded figure, Degas was often seen, always alone, feeling his way through the streets of Paris. Blind, solitary, but always dignified, his old age has been compared to that of the poet Homer. He died at the age of eighty-three on September 27, 1917, and his funeral, which took place toward the end of the war, was attended by those family friends who had pierced through his mask of brusqueness to the deep tenderness beneath.

Artistic aims

Degas' artistic aims were complex; he wished, he said, to produce beauty and mystery. It is not the sort of description immediately associated with the racecourse and the rehearsal room, exhausted washerwomen, deferential milliners, café-concerts, and women at their ablutions. Furthermore, this reinvention of beauty in a modern idiom is an idea that seems to fit a radical artist, not one who, born into the *haute bourgeoisie*, remained always a conservative. Degas was, in fact, a man who viewed with regret the changing society, and mourned the old values which were becoming outmoded in the new "embourgeoisement" of the capitalist class. With his intellectual astuteness, he fully realized the futility of slavishly copying the Old Masters, and he saw Symbolist art as a form of escapism, commenting derisorily that the Symbolist painter Gustave Moreau "showed us that the gods wore watch chains." It is part of the Degas paradox that the artist reared by the staunchest conservative class, from which he showed no wish to escape, should be the modern artist *par excellence*. Edmond de Goncourt observed that, "among all the artists I have met so far, he is the one who has best been able to catch the spirit of modern life."

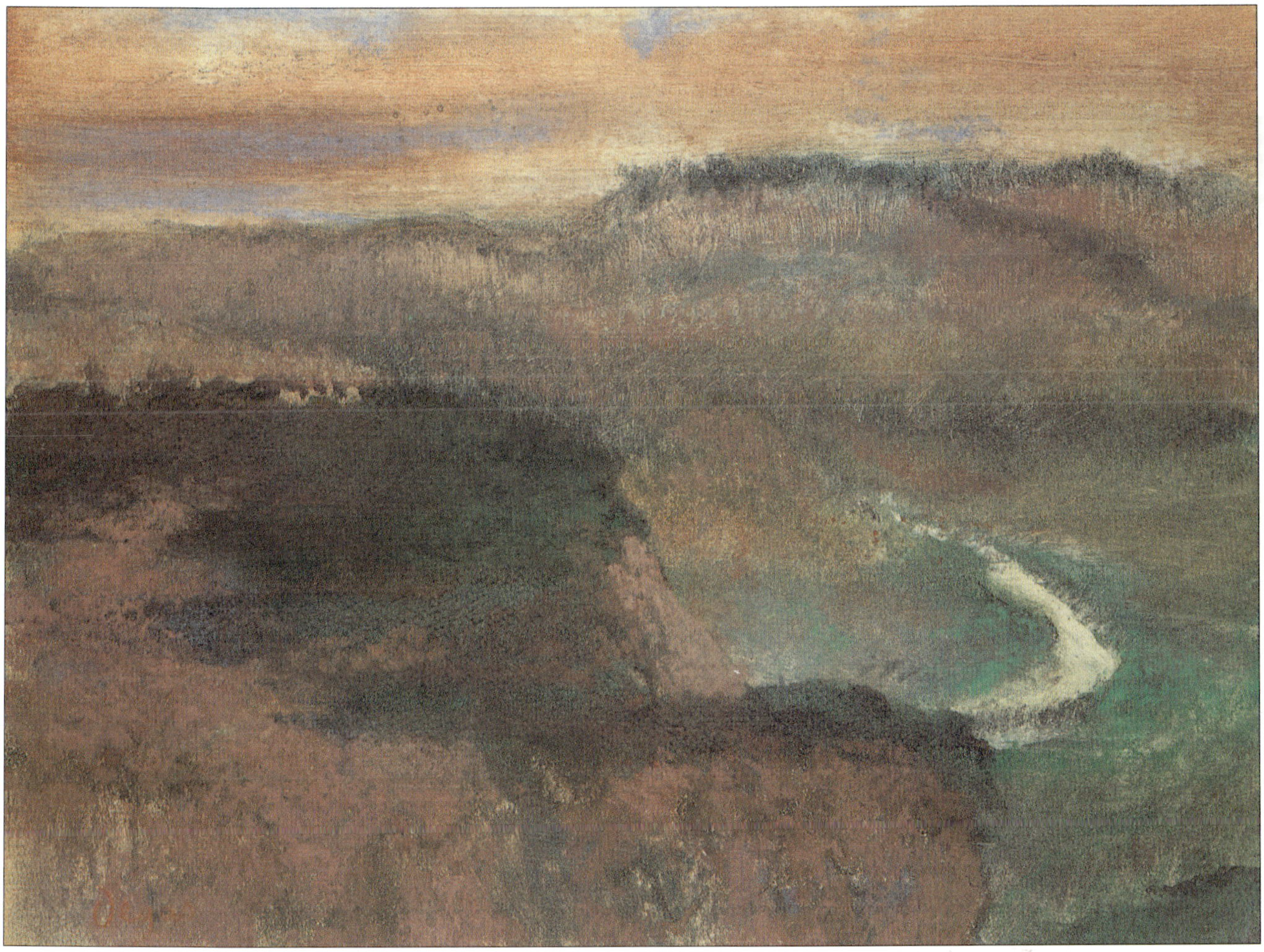

CHRONOLOGY OF DEGAS' LIFE

1834 July 19: born in Paris, son of Auguste de Gas, a banker.

1845 Attends Lycée Louis-le-Grand.

1847 Mother dies. Father takes him to museums and fosters his gift for drawing.

1853 Studies law for a short time, then enrolls in studio of Louis Lamothe, an ex-pupil of Ingres.

1855-6 Enrolls at Ecole des Beaux Arts, Paris. Meets Fantin-Latour.

1856 Travels to Italy, staying at Rome, Naples and Florence.

1858 Visits Italy again and stays with his uncle in Florence, where he makes first studies for portrait group, *The Bellelli Family.*

1860-5 Produces several history paintings, including *Spartan Boys and Girls Exercising.*

1868 Paints *In the Orchestra Pit.*

1870 Franco-Prussian War. Called up and serves in an artillery unit in a fortress near Paris.

1872 Begins to paint the ballet, visiting rehearsal rooms of dancers.

1874 Takes part in organizing the first Impressionist Exhibition, and shows ten paintings.

1875-7 Paints *Dancer Curtseying* and *Café-concert at the Ambassadeurs.*

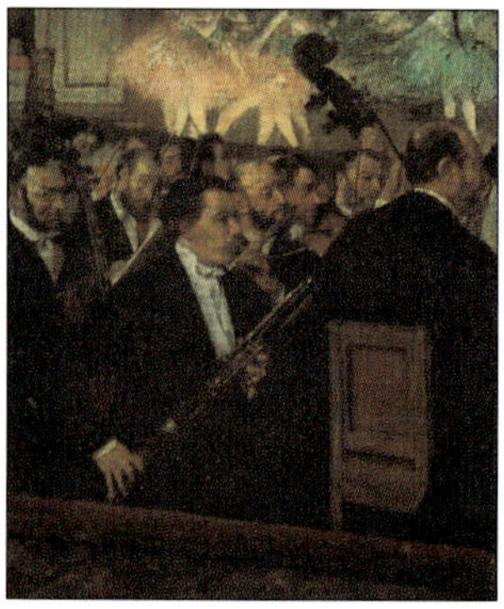

In the Orchestra Pit

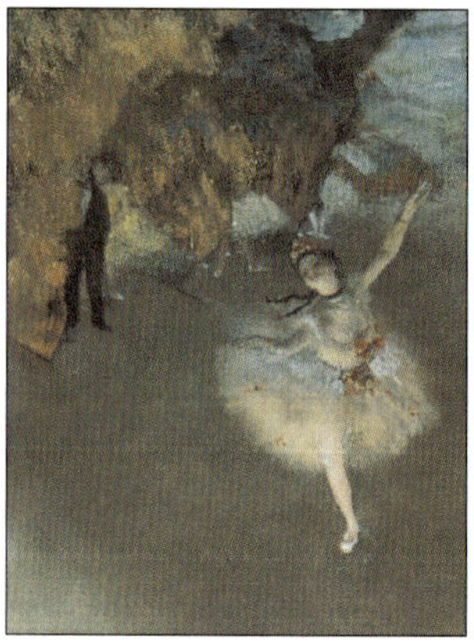

Dancer Curtseying

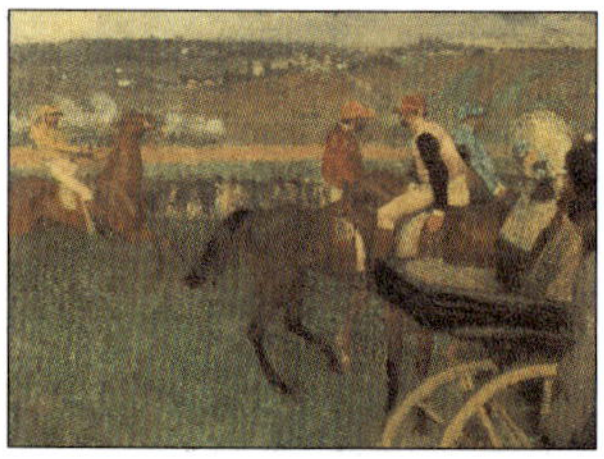

The Tub

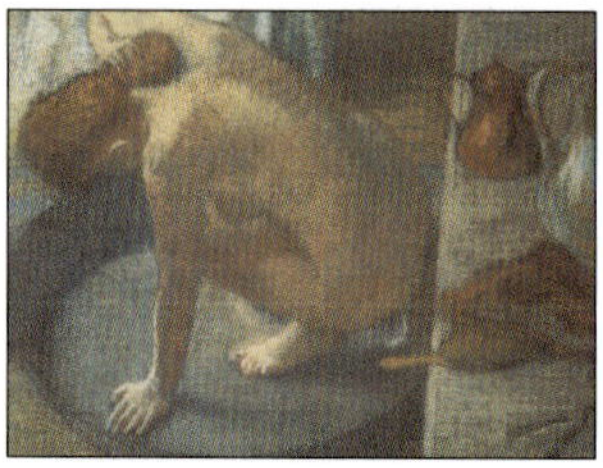

Carriage at the Races

1876 Paints *Absinthe.*

1877-90 Visits Spain. Works on etchings with Mary Cassatt and Pissarro. Paints racecourse scenes and *Miss Lala at the Circus* (1879).

1881 Shows wax statuette of dancer at sixth Impressionist Exhibition. Produces sculptures, lithographs, monotypes and pastels.

1882 Produces paintings and pastels of milliners and laundresses.

1885 Visits Le Havre and Dieppe and meets Gauguin. Eyesight worsens. Experiments with different media and concentrates on painting dancers and women at their toilet.

1886 Eighth and last Impressionist Exhibition. Shows pictures of women washing.

1893 Shows series of pastel landscapes. Eyesight continues to deteriorate, and works only with great difficulty.

1898-1912 Lives in seclusion, almost blind. House in the rue Victor Massé is demolished in 1912 and he is forced to move. His paintings are now fetching very high prices.

1917 September 27: dies at the age of eighty-three.

THE PAINTINGS

In the Orchestra Pit

1868-9

21×17¾in/53×45cm

Oil on canvas

Musée d'Orsay, Paris

This painting reflects Degas' attraction both to Japanese art and to photography. As a draftsman and admirer of Ingres he responded to the way in which the Japanese print made use of contour line, and was struck by the way in which the eastern system of perspective often silhouetted foreground objects which obscured those behind them, as happens in reality. He made the foreground obstruction something of a hallmark of his art: his café or racing scenes are often sliced by intrusive vertical devices, and in many of his pictures of the theater and ballet, columns, heads, fans or the tops of the instruments in the orchestra pit partially obscure the middle ground.

He was also attracted by the way figures in Japanese prints were often cropped, rather than being neatly contained within the picture space, and he admired the same effect in the snapshot photographs of city views which were being produced from the 1860s, which caught figures in motion moving in or out of the photo. This painting, which includes the visually blank area of the side of the orchestra box at the bottom of the painting while excluding the heads of the ballet dancers on stage, anticipates the random snapshot which has not managed to get everything in, and gives an approximation of the "frozen" view from a pair of opera glasses.

It is an artificial device used to create a reality of experience; involving the viewer by giving the sensation that we ourselves are scanning the theater, and our opera glasses have alighted on the orchestra pit. Degas maintained that, "A picture is an artificial work, something apart from nature, that demands as much cunning, astuteness and vice as the perpetration of a crime, do something artificial and add a touch of nature." The seemingly natural setting of the Paris Opera House orchestra pit has been used as a stage for a group portrait of some of the musical friends of the Degas family, not all of whom were actually in this orchestra.

The full title of the work, *Portrait of Desiré Dihau in the Orchestra Pit of the Paris Opéra*, indicates more clearly that the focus of attention is the bassoonist, a close friend of Degas' father and the main subject of the group portrait, who occupies the space usually reserved for the leader of the orchestra.

Unlike the Impressionists, with whom he dissociated himself, although exhibiting with them on numerous occasions, Degas was not interested in the effect of natural light on objects. It was artificial illumination, from gas lamps or footlights, which caught his imagination, as can be seen here, with the lower parts of the ballerinas' bodies lit to ghost-like effect by the illumination from the footlights, providing a dramatic contrast to the darkness of the orchestra pit below.

The painting, a portrait genre picture, reveals much about Degas' complex picture-making process, one which began with observation and repeated sketching until the subject was committed to memory, and was followed by the organization into a composition of his own invention. The ballerinas show the setting to be the Paris Opéra, which also housed the ballet. This is the first appearance of the dancers who were to become Degas' best-known subject.

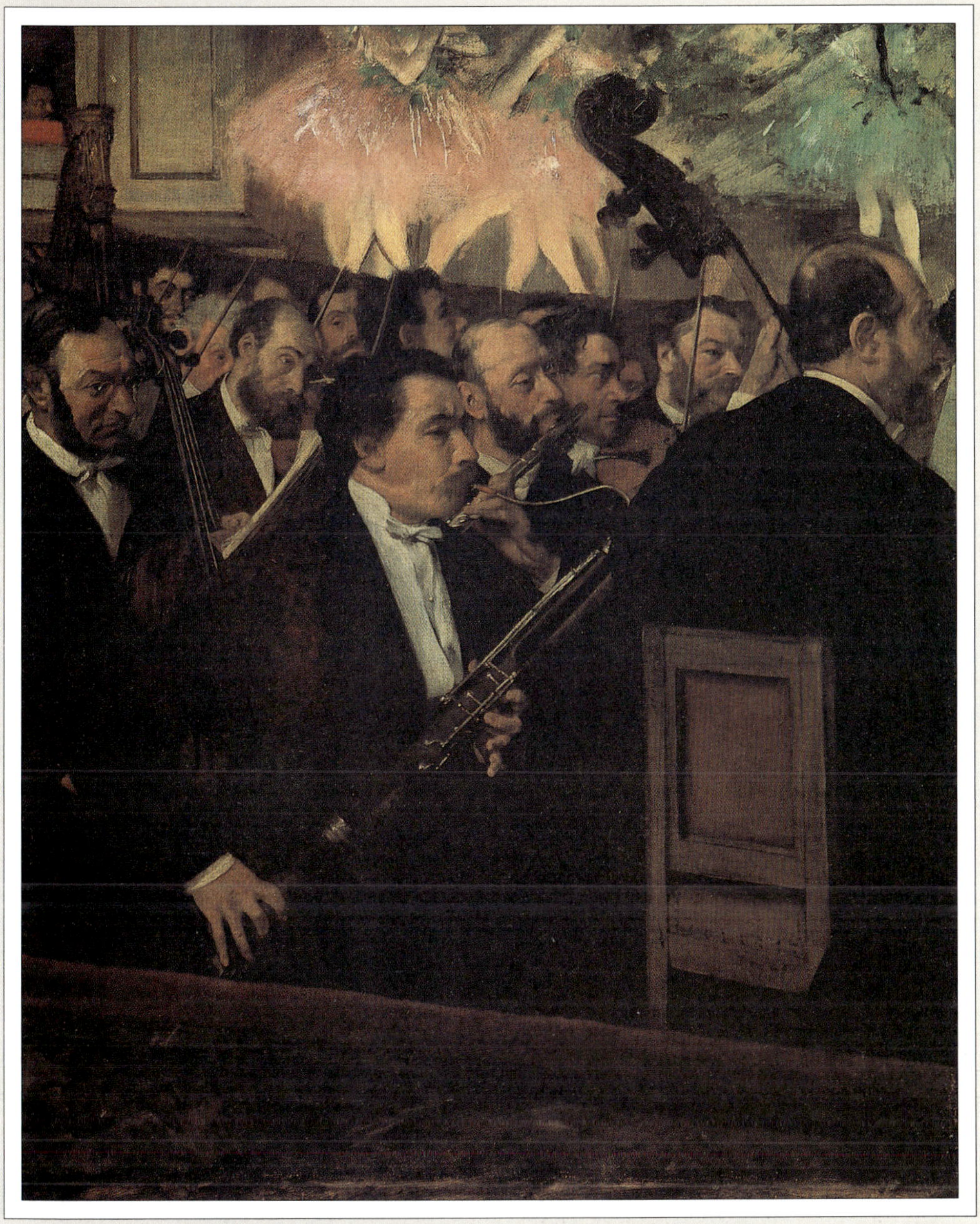

The orchestra pit of the Paris Opéra is the setting for this portrait of Degas' friend, the bassoonist Desiré Dihau, who features prominently in an orchestra of the artist's own invention. This highly experimental composition, which dramatically decapitates the dancers and slices both sides of the orchestra, approximates to the random view from a pair of opera glasses, and suggests that this is an image the artist has actually seen rather than invented. Degas' compositions, however, were never random or unconsidered, and he was contemptuous of the notion of "instantaneous art," remarking that "what I do is the result of reflection and study of the great masters; of inspiration, spontaneity, temperament I know nothing."

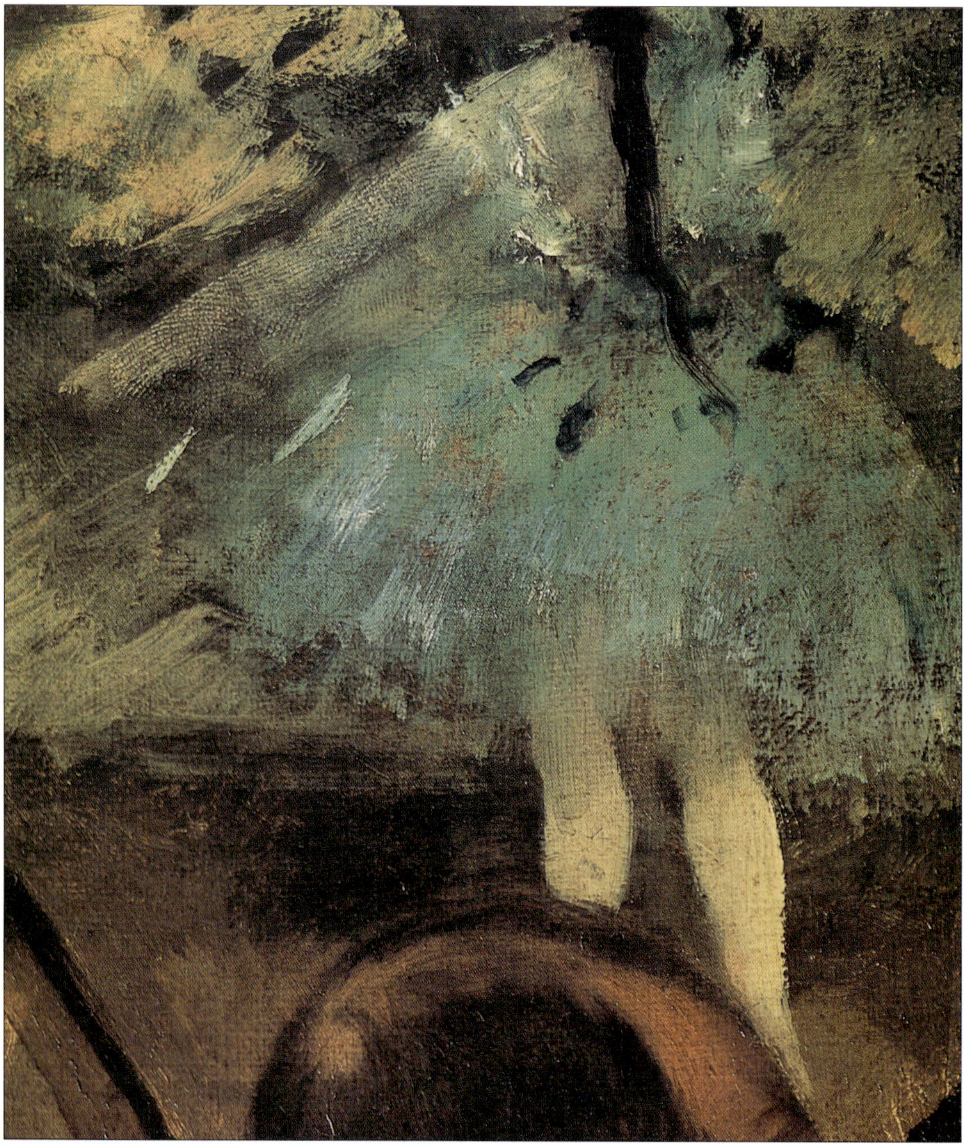

1

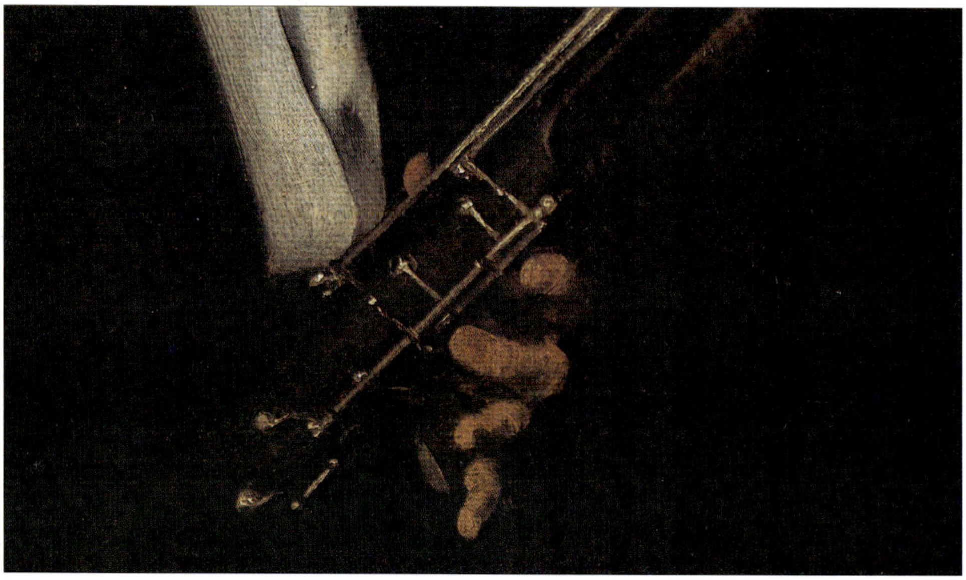

2

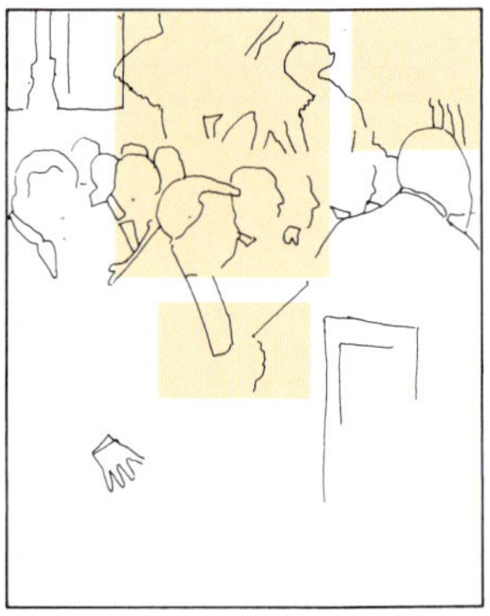

1 This top corner presents an impressionist cameo, intruded upon only by the bald pate of the musician. The texture of the canvas is visible beneath the dabs of thinned blue paint overlaid with touches of thicker white. Degas has evidently manipulated paint with his hands, as he did later with pastels; thumbprints are visible on the dancer's left arm.

2 This detail demonstrates Degas' fine draftsmanship as well as his virtuosity in handling paint. Dots and lines of thick white pigment have been applied over a dark area to create the effect of the instrument's metal keys and pipes. The contrast of gleaming metal on dark fabric and the contrast of white against black were effects Degas admired in the Old Masters.

3 *Actual size detail* Degas' notebooks record his interest in the effects of stage lighting. In the study of this painting he observed that near the footlight only the skirt of the dancer is lit, creating a "piquant effect." Here the ballerinas, lit to luminous intensity, provide a dramatic contrast to the prosaic figures below. In technical terms too, the divide is stressed, by the looser and more impressionistic treatment of the dancers, where shades of premixed, thinned pink pigment have been overlaid with thicker touches of white and green. The faces of the musicians are more lightly painted and fully modeled.

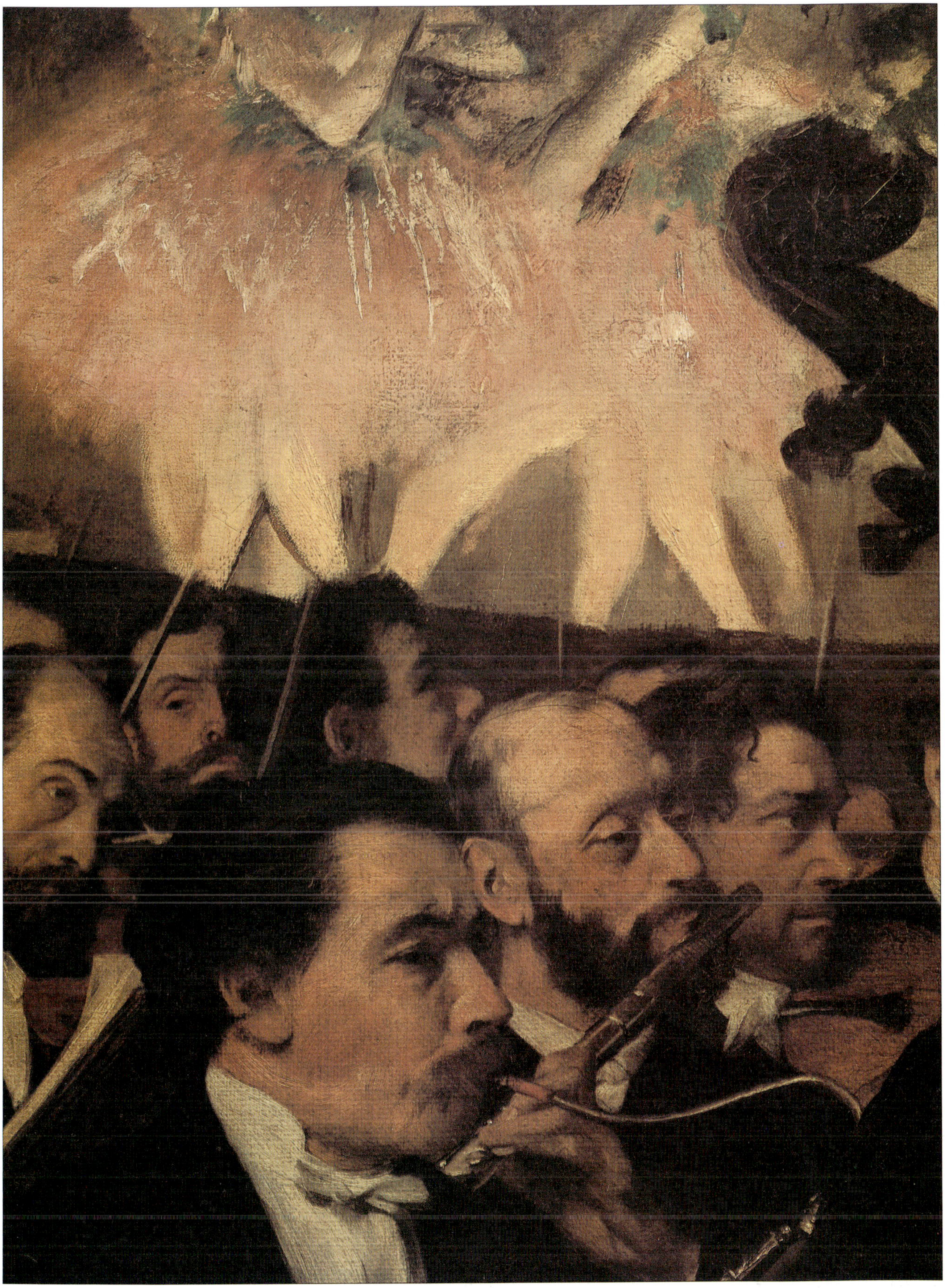

3 *Actual size detail*

Dancer Curtseying

c1875
$22\frac{3}{4} \times 16\frac{1}{2}$in/$58 \times 42$cm
Pastel on monotype on paper
Musée d'Orsay, Paris

When asked by Mrs Havemeyer, the American collector, who bought this work in 1875, why he had concentrated on the ballet to such an extent, Degas replied, "Because I find there, Madame, the combined movement of the Greeks."

As well as full-length performances, short ballets were put on between the acts of operas. It was the moment when the talking stopped. Degas, like every Parisian gentleman of a certain rank, was a thrice-weekly visitor to the Paris Opéra. Like the majority of the audience, it was the dancers in particular he had come to see, not only on stage but behind the scenes: "From green room to wings, from the footlights to the practice-room, runs this seer, pencil in hand, hiding under his evening cloak the sketchbook where he hurriedly records some movement he has glimpsed. Then, when the lamps have been put out, he returns to his studio and there, in the sternest withdrawal, transcribes on canvas or paper the spoils gathered by his ardent eyes."

The subtle effects of tone, the contrast between the lambent delicacy of the young ballerina and the indistinct background, make this one of the artist's best-loved works. Technically it is reliant for its effect on the same technique used in the *Café Concert at the Ambassadeurs* and *At the Terrace of a Café* (see page 435), namely pastel over monotype. Monotype was a process which Degas had developed from standard printing techniques. The print was used rather like an underdrawing, with the pastel color applied on top, a technique which he found ideal for reproducing effects such as the ballerina's gauzy tutu, lit from the footlights and semi-transparent to reveal the lower thigh of the dancer; the sheen on her stockinged leg and the satin of her ballet slipper. The paper onto which the print has been laid is itself highly successful in approximating the patina of the stage floor.

Degas' technical achievements did not go unnoticed by the British audience when his ballet scenes were exhibited in England. The *Manchester Guardian*, in May 1876, singled out Degas' merits as a technician. "M. Degas possesses an almost perfect mastery over the secrets of tone, and he delights to exhibit the subtle changes which colour undergoes as it passes under varying conditions of light and shade. He can measure with almost absolute precision and delicacy of touch the strength of a bright sash or ribbon on the costume of the dancers as the colour flashes in the foreground or recedes into the furthest recesses of the long interior."

The composition of this work is a daring one. Now freed from the landscape format of his early history paintings, in which the action was placed squarely in the middle foreground, Degas experimented with composition, from the late 1860s preferring to use the close-up form to create a startling and immediate effect. Here we are struck by the angle from which this work is taken. If one looks at the lower triangle of the painting which contains the ballerina, she appears to be curtseying to the audience to the left of the auditorium. However, the audience seated on the left would be unlikely to see the stage wings, which would only be visible from a high point in the wings opposite or possibly from a box to the right. Clearly Degas was manipulating naturalistic detail in the interests of picture making, as he frequently did. "All art is artifice," he said, "and needs to be perpetrated with the cunning of a crime."

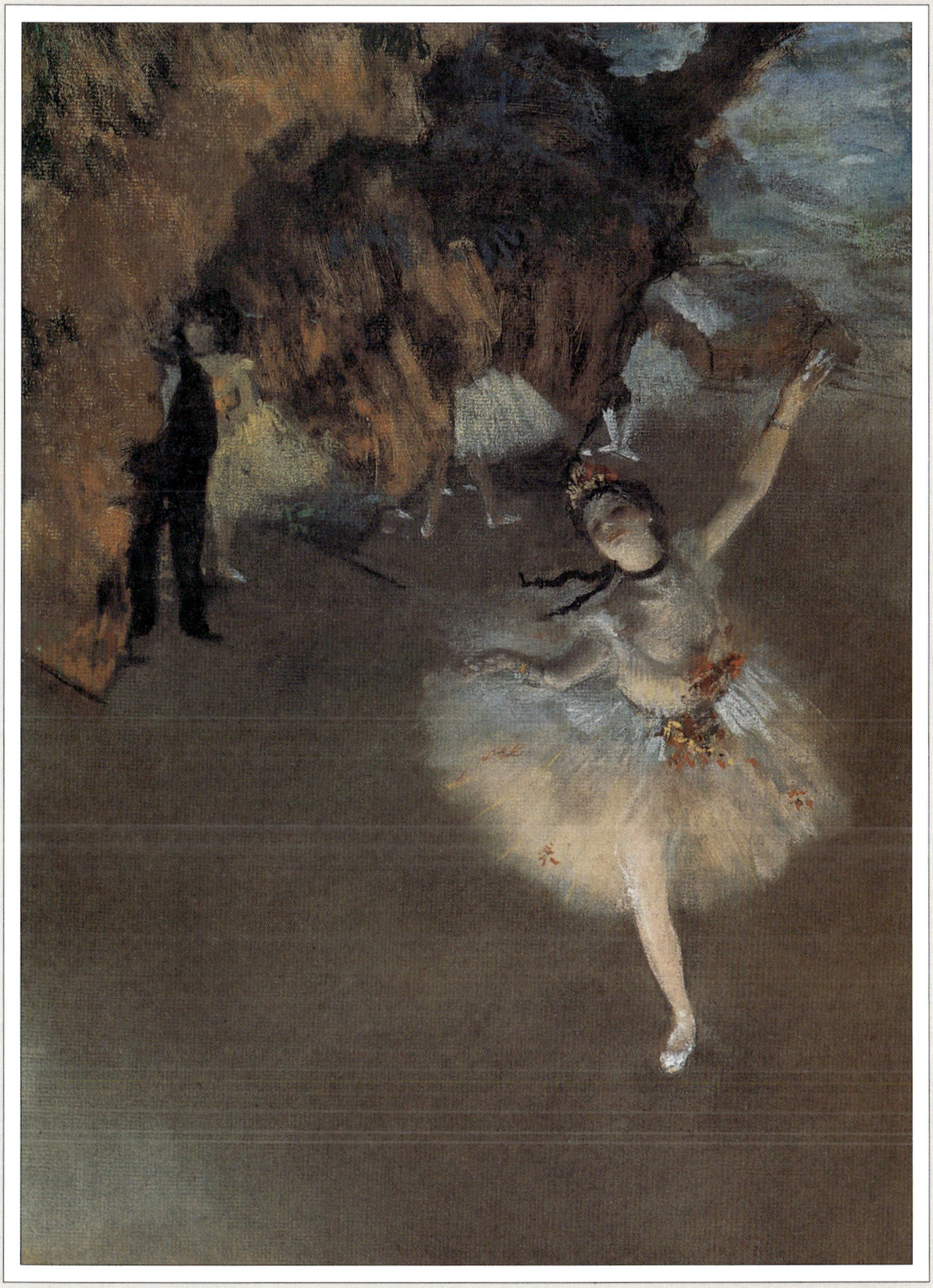

Degas invented what came to be called the monotype (a name he disliked) around 1874. It originated from experiments with moving printer's ink around an etching plate, either removing ink to create an image out of the blackness or drawing an image directly onto the plate and then printing. Etching itself was enjoying a revival in the 1860s, as artists were becoming dissatisfied with the dry, mechanical results of the professional printer. The works which were the result of Degas' experiments are truly innovatory, giving the lie to Renoir's remark that if Degas had been content to leave his plates alone he would have left some of the best prints of the nineteenth century. Although the name monotype suggests that only one p int was taken, Degas often took two. This second impression, the one used in this work, was paler, and provided almost a "tonal map" onto which color was added. Nearly a third of Degas' pastels show a plate mark signifying a monotype beneath.

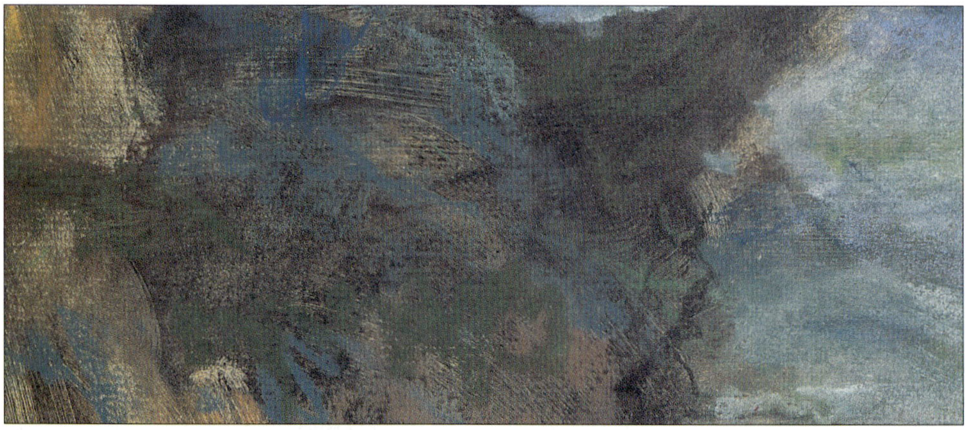

1

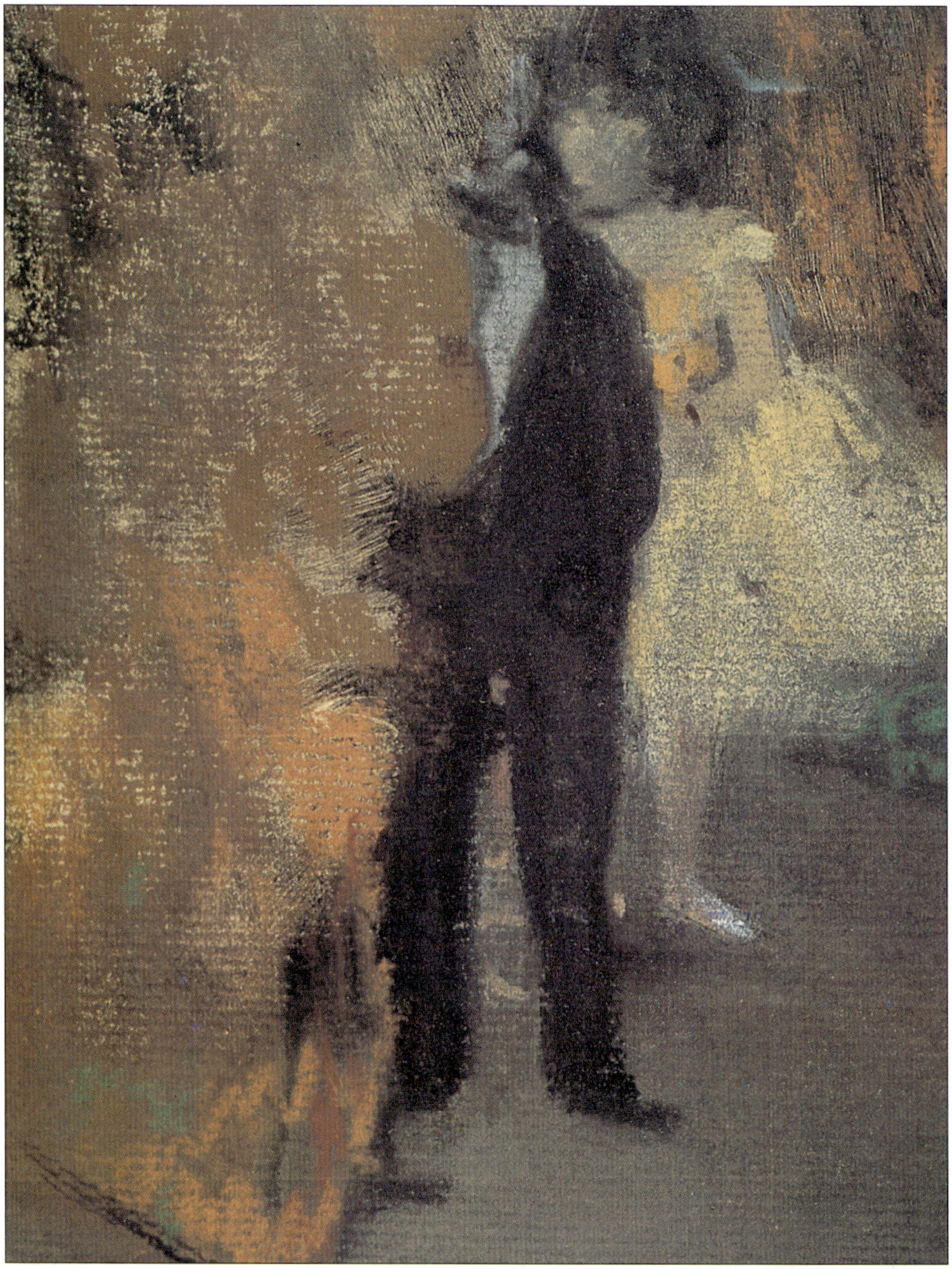

2

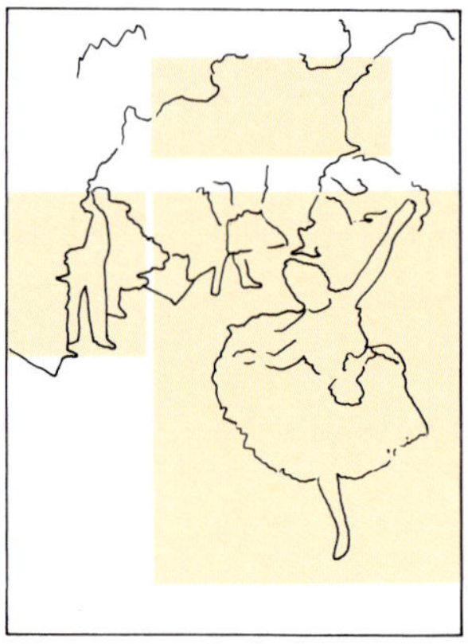

1 The marks of either a thumb or a stiff brush used to wipe away the printer's ink on the printing plate can be seen clearly here, overlaid with bold pastel scribbles of greens and blues. The contrast of technique seen between the loose handling of the background and the exquisite finish of the dancer prefigures the artist's later experimentation with the medium.

2 The brush or finger marks on the monotype and the ridged texture of the paper can both be seen here. The pastel application has been applied in different ways, quite lightly and patchily in the area on the left, and much more densely on the dark figure of the man. He half conceals the dancer, whose shape materializes from a few light and delicate pastel touches.

3 *Actual size detail* Degas has used brilliant white pastel on the ballet slipper, the contour of the thigh, the top of the tutu, and the throat, shoulder and hand to capture the brilliance of the footlights which highlight the dancer from below. Flowers at the waist have been realized with light touches of a pastel stick. The slightly ridged texture of the paper is clearly visible beneath a wash of background color.

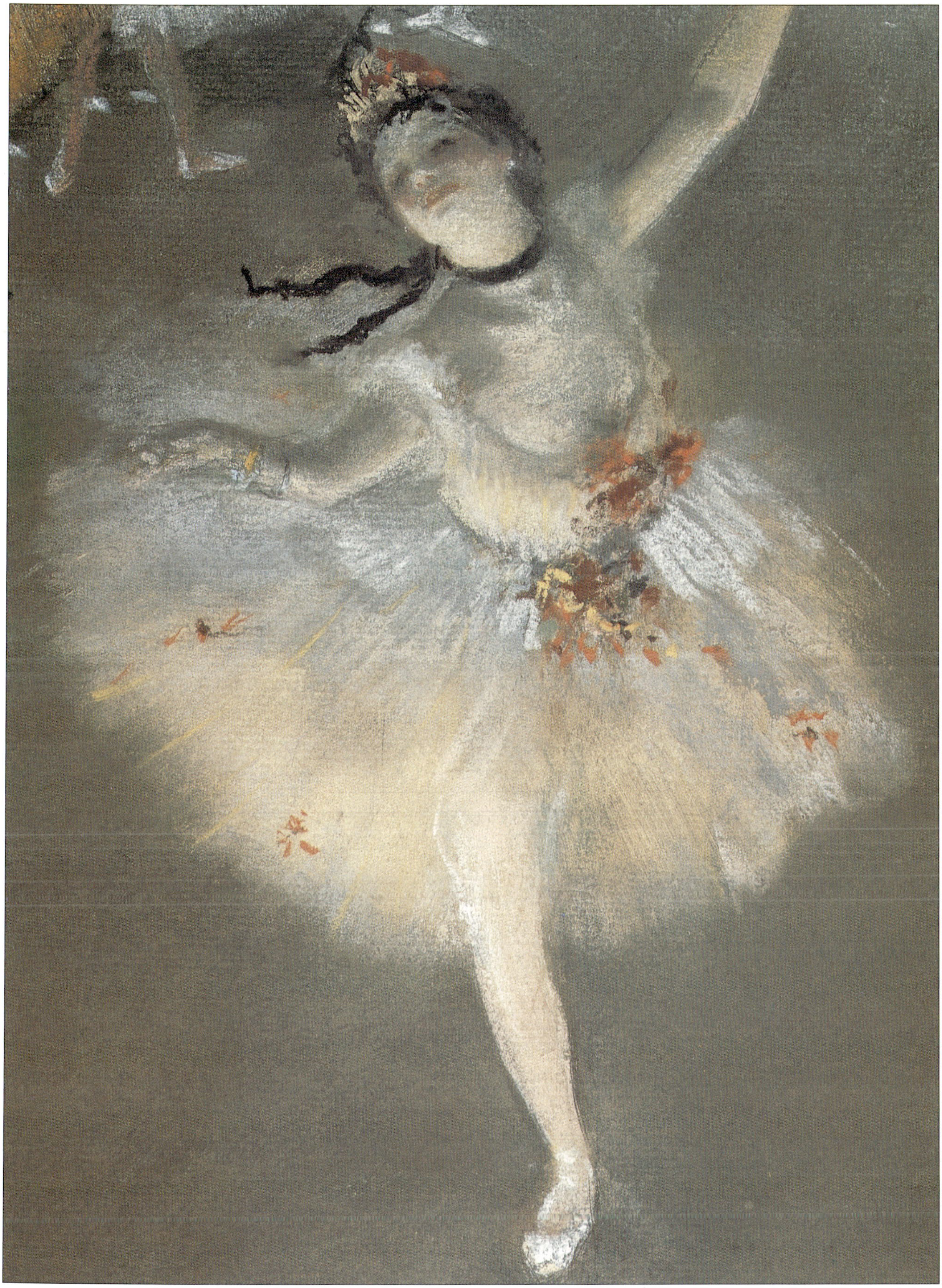

3 *Actual size detail*

Absinthe

c1876
$36\frac{1}{4} \times 26\frac{3}{4}$/92×68cm
Oil on canvas
Musee d'Orsay, Paris

Like *In the Orchestra Pit* (see page 423) this painting, ostensibly a genre work, is in fact a portrait. The subject is Degas' friend Marcellin Desboutin at the Café de la Nouvelle-Athènes, one of his favorite spots, to which he is supposed to have introduced Degas, Manet and their circle. The focal point, however, is the seated woman at his side, the actress Ellen Andrée, who posed often for Degas and Renoir, portrayed here as a *demi-mondaine* seated before a glass of absinthe.

The sadness of this woman's situation, typical of many in both Paris and London who came into cafés either to pick up a customer or to while away the hours of loneliness with a drink, made some impact on the British public when the painting was exhibited in London in 1893. "It is not a painting at all," remarked W.B. Richmond. "It is a novelette – a treatise against drink." Clearly it is not intentionally the latter – Degas was a detached observer, not a propagandist, but the work does have literary qualities, and the woman constitutes a character study of considerable psychological depth. The downward tilt of her hat, eyes, shoulders and arms tells a story of hopelessness, and the ambiguity of her social status is reflected in her very positioning – pushed off one table and half-way between that and the next. Her isolation is intensified by the way the man at her side is turned away from her, with his forearm, a palpable barrier toward communication, occupying much of the shared table and leaving no room for her carafe of water, which is placed on the adjacent table. The tawdry gaiety of her hat and shoes adds a further note of pathos.

In terms of composition, Degas has attempted an extremely daring experiment, one that was noted and appreciated by the French critic Edmond Duranty when this work was exhibited at the second Impressionist Exhibition. "If one now considers the person, whether in a room or in the street, he is not always to be found situated on a straight line at an equal distance from two parallel objects; he is more confined on one side than on the other by space. In short, he is never in the center of the canvas, in the center of the setting. He is not always seen as a whole: sometimes he appears cut off at mid-leg, half-length, or longitudinally. At other times, the eye takes him in from close-up, at full height, and throws all the rest of a crowd in the street or groups gathered in a public place back into the small scale of the distance."

Degas has again drawn our attention to reality, to the way in which people do not sit conveniently between objects. The lower left quarter of the painting is occupied by the barren expanse of table, which not only provides an area of visual bleakness in keeping with the forlorn expression and pose of the woman, but also reflects real life and the effect of the random snapshot. Yet the composition works perfectly; the eye is led in to the figure of the woman, and the newspaper bridging the two tables not only pulls the composition together but also strengthens the naturalistic effect. Degas has placed his signature beneath the ashtray and the newspaper, almost as though claiming ownership of a patent to such a daring device. In fact it has its origins in the Japanese system of perspective, which did not rely on the Western system of distancing space into a vanishing point, but made use of foreground objects, treating the picture surface to an upward zigzag movement to suggest recession.

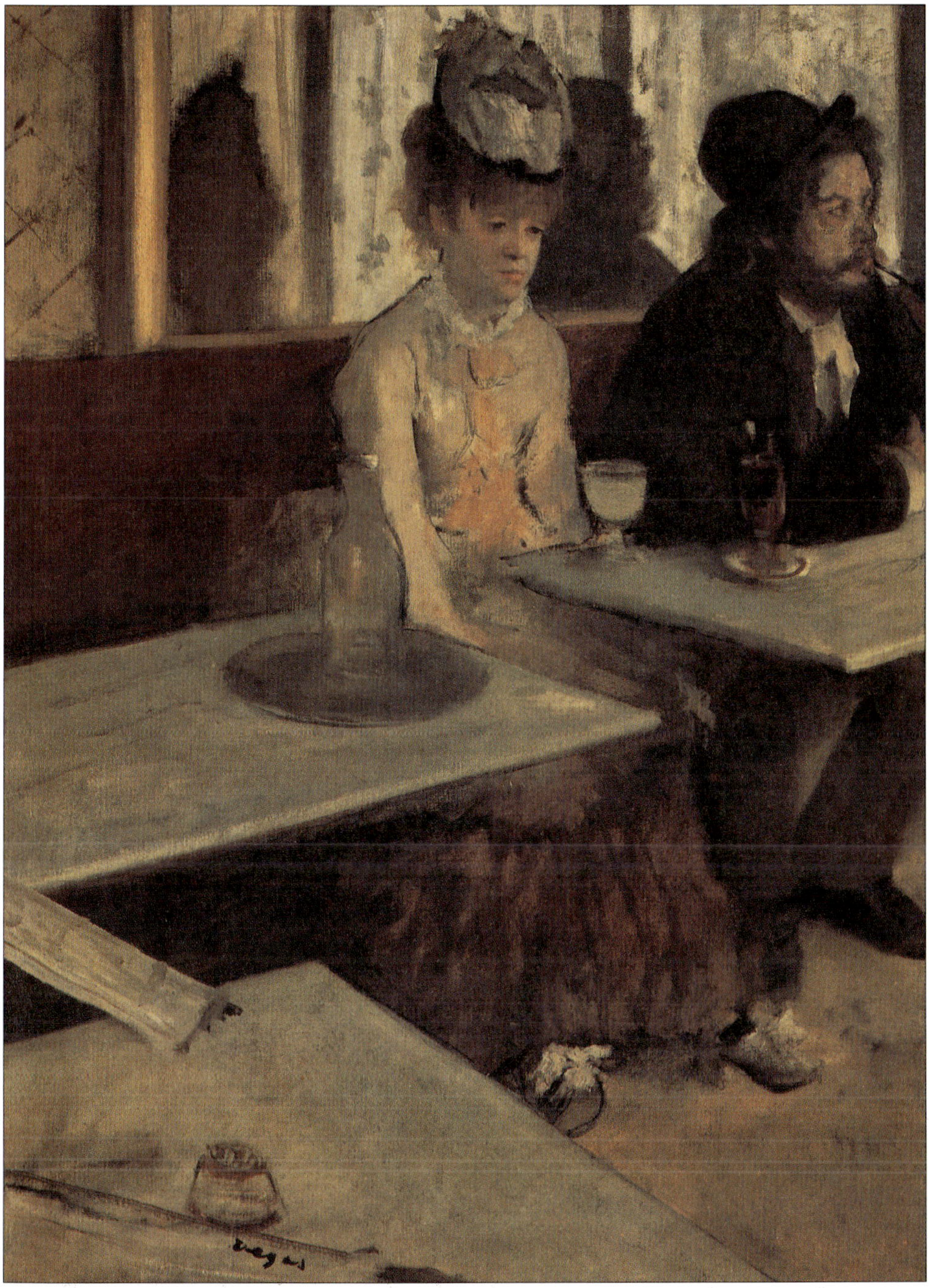

Probably Degas's single best-known work, this aroused strong feelings when it was shown in London. The composition is one of the artist's most daring experiments, in part derived from his observations of the Eastern system of perspective seen in Japanese prints. Degas' often-used motif of a pair of contrasting figures appears again here, but asymmetrically arranged and dramatically sliced at the right. The stasis of the two figures is emphasized by the zigzag movement of the diagonal lines formed by the outer edges of tables and newspaper, an almost abstract arrangement. The scene itself, redolent of despair and hopelessness, provides a negative counterpoint to the gaiety of café life depicted in *Café-concert at the Ambassadeurs.*

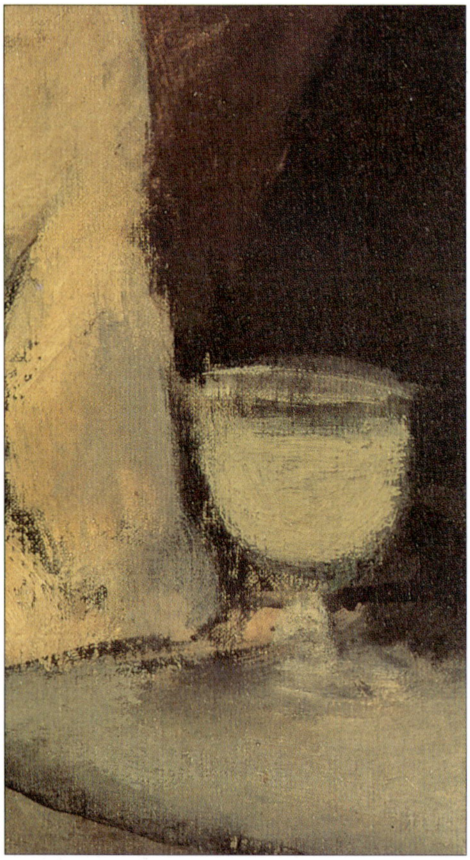

1

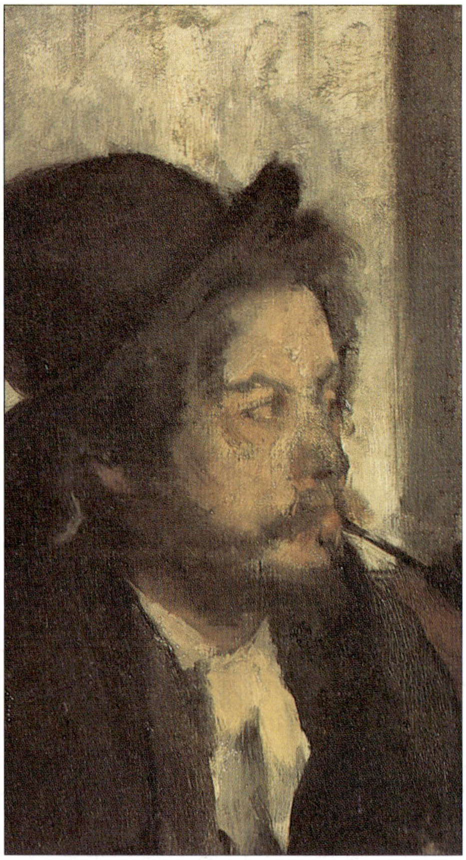

2

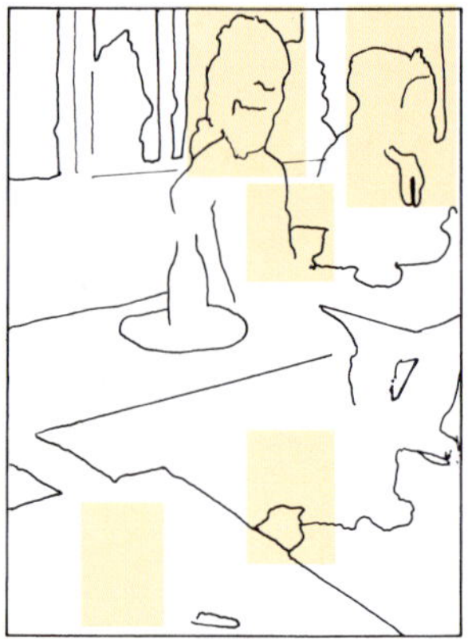

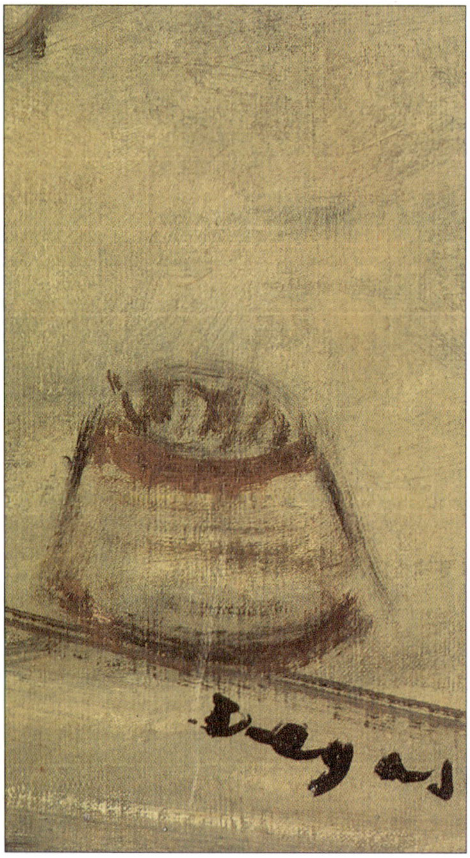

3

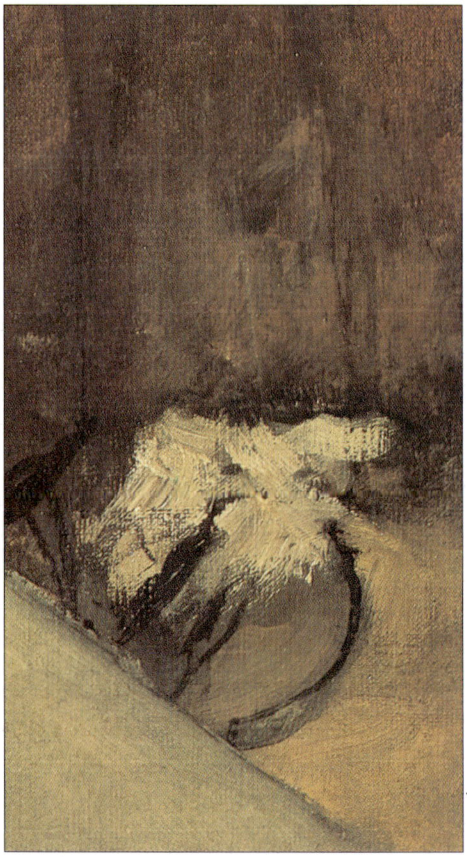

4

1 To create the effect of the absinthe (a cheap but highly potent aniseed drink),light cadmium yellow has been used without modeling over dark contour lines. The stem and base of the glass are no more than a few touches of white pigment applied wet into wet over gray.

2 In this largely monochromatic portrait of Degas's friend Marcel Desboutin the face stares out, away from both his neighbor and the viewer, to a space beyond the confines of the painting. Cast in slight shadow, and more crudely modeled than that of the woman, the expression is also less psychologically probing.

3 Flush to the picture plane, the form of the ashtray is sketched out with a few bold strokes of brown and black. The newspaper bears Degas' signature almost as though it were a printed heading, a device which paradoxically draws attention by its very naturalism to the careful planning of the composition.

4 In contrast to the delicate treatment of the ballerinas' slippered feet in his paintings of dancers, this shoe is heavy and clumsy, offset by the large white bows. It is a study in monochrome, with black used for the contour lines, and touches of white applied wet into wet over gray.

5 *Actual size detail* The model for the woman was the actress Ellen André, who also posed for Renoir's more carefree and lighthearted depictions.

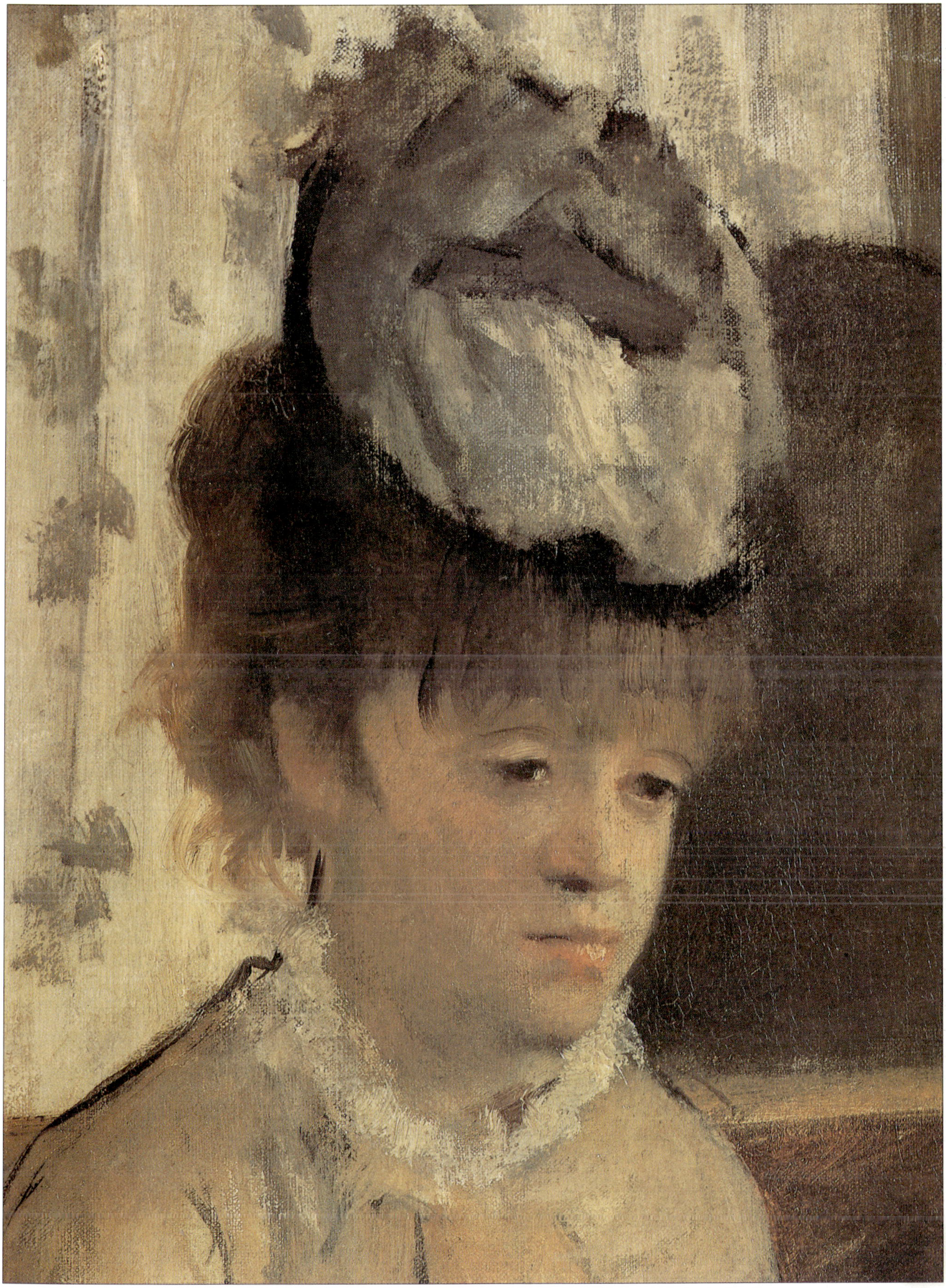

5 *Actual size detail*

At the Terrace of the Cafe

c1877
16×23¼in/41×59cm
Pastel over monotype
Louvre, Paris

Degas encapsulated the gaiety and pathos of lower-class café life; a contemporary recorder observed that "M. Degas is observant, he never seeks to exaggerate, his effects are always obtained by nature itself, with no element of caricature. It is this that makes him the most graceful historian of the scenes he shows us. Here we have some women outside the door of a café, at night: one of them is tapping her teeth with her fingernail and saying 'pas seulement ça,' a poem in itself. Another is spreading out her large gloved hand on the table. In the background is the boulevard, its bustle slowly dying away. This is a very striking historical record."

Degas himself said, "In a single brushstroke we can say more than a writer in a whole volume." His ability to distil the essence of life around him impressed contemporary authors, particularly Emile Zola, who much admired this work of the demimonde, and in 1879 put out in serial form his novel *Nana*, a story about a former laundress turned musical performer-cum-actress and prostitute. However, although Degas' paintings have been described in literary terms, he was far from a literary painter, and was irritated by dinner-party conversations on art. "Let us hope that we shall soon have finished with art, with aesthetics. They make me sick...what interests me is work..." "Degas liked talking about painting," said Paul Valéry, "but could hardly bear anyone else doing so." He derided critics, "thinkers" and the "literary gentry" who wrote about art, maintaining that form and color, not words, were the medium best suited to conveying the artist's intentions.

In this work, as in several others, he has used pastel over monotype, a technique well suited to creating night-time effects, particularly artificially lit ones. "Daylight is too easy," he remarked, "What I want is difficult – the atmosphere of lamps or moonlight." He began here by painting a general outline of the main forms onto a flat surface which he then printed onto paper, adding color and detail with the pastels. The subdued color suggests not only the dimness of evening lighting, but also the somber world of his subject. Painted in the studio from memory, the work is a keenly observed social portrait as well as an attempt at finding fresh ways of looking at contemporary life. Like the female figure in *Absinthe* (see page 431), the expression of the central blue-clad figure speaks volumes.

The vertical slicing of the picture by the pillars of the café provides a dramatic fragmentation of the picture surface, an appropriately startling compositional device for the "shocking" subject-matter of casually observed street-walkers conversing together, and the way figures and chairs at the edges of the picture have been cropped effectively places the viewer in the picture with the women. The severity of the pillars has been offset by the undulating rhythm formed by the tops of the women's hats, their shoulders and chair backs, as well as by the muted but glowing color and texture of the clothing.

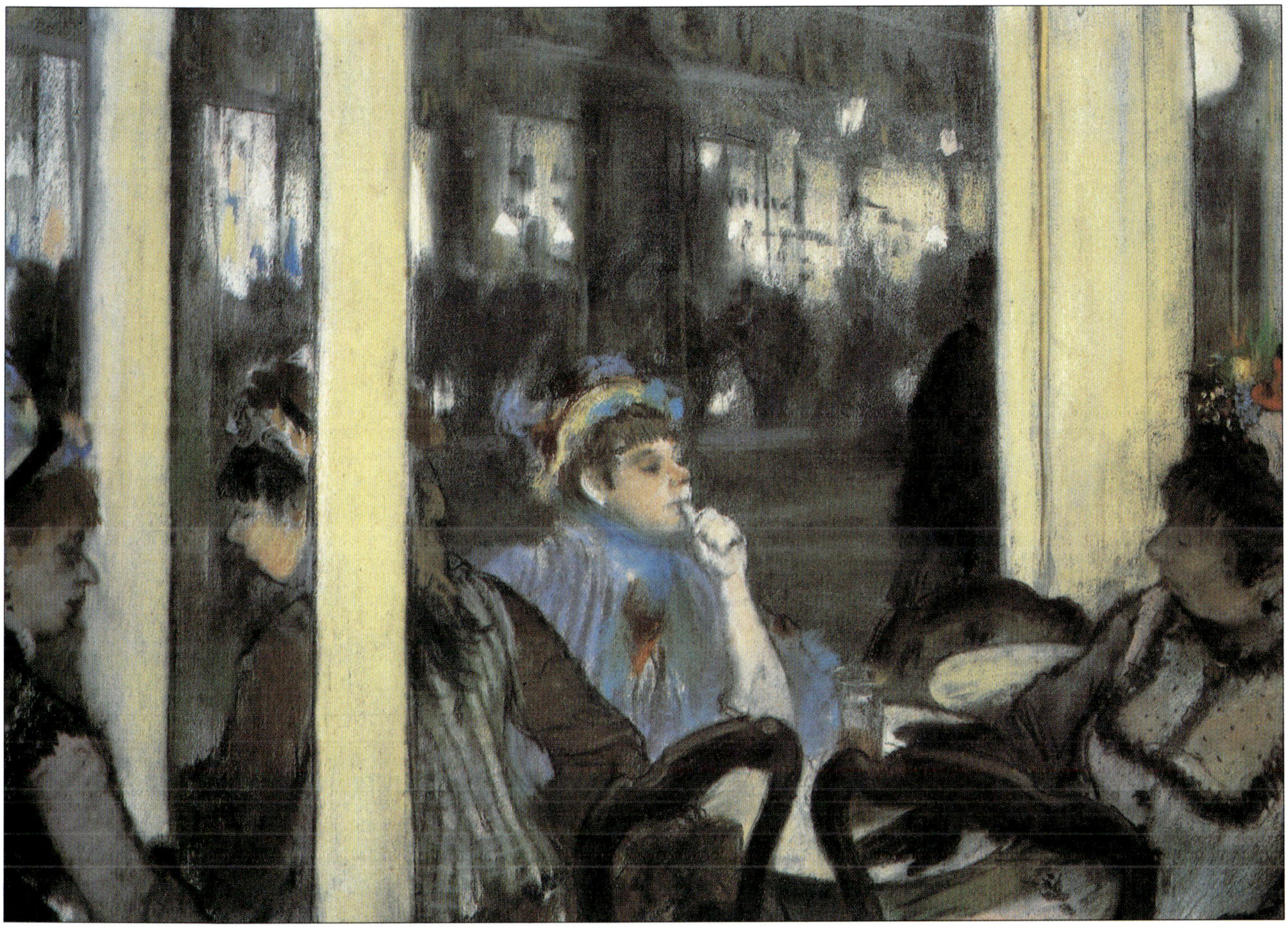

The monotype print beneath the pastel is more in evidence here than in *Café Concert at the Ambassadeurs*, indeed, apart from white highlights and a touch of blue and light brown, the upper half at least is almost monochromatic — essentially a print that has not been transformed by color. Similarly, the lower half of the painting, containing the women, registers as a low-key study in blue and brown with cream lights in the hats and flesh tones of the faces, pure color being reserved for the flowers on the hat to the far right. In collecting material for this work Degas was apparently even more meticulous than in the case of *Absinthe* (see page 431), recording in his notebooks the exact shapes of chairs, hats and figures, and making careful notes of the subtle variations of lighting effects he had observed on the terrace. The narrative quality of the work has evoked a number of literary parallels, among them a suggestion that the work is an illustration from Ludovic Halévy's novel *La Famille Cardinal*, although no passage corresponds very closely.

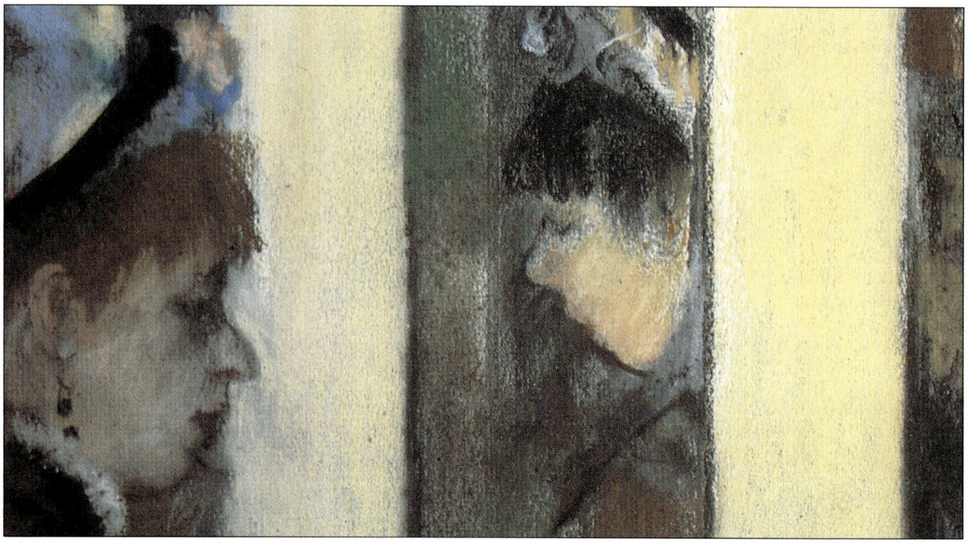

1

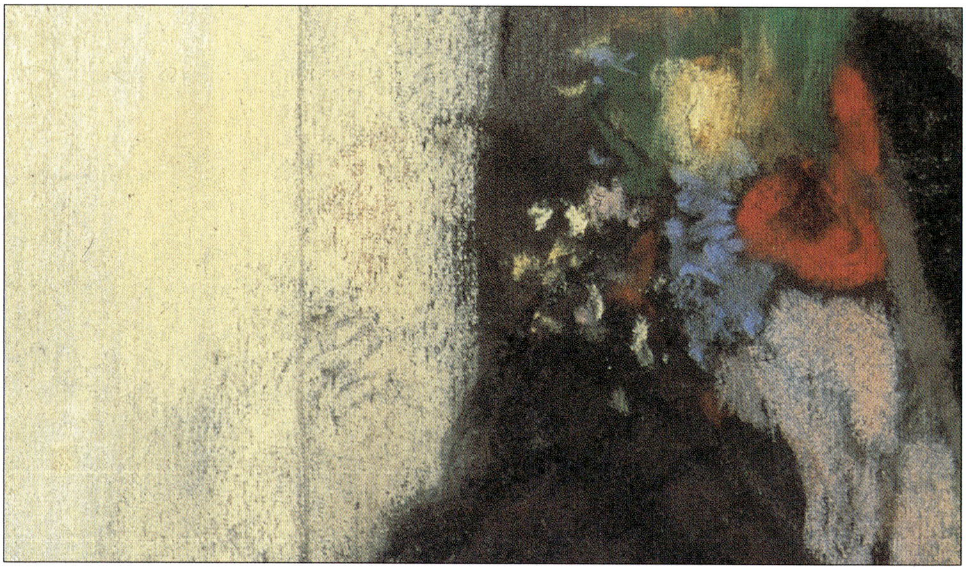

2

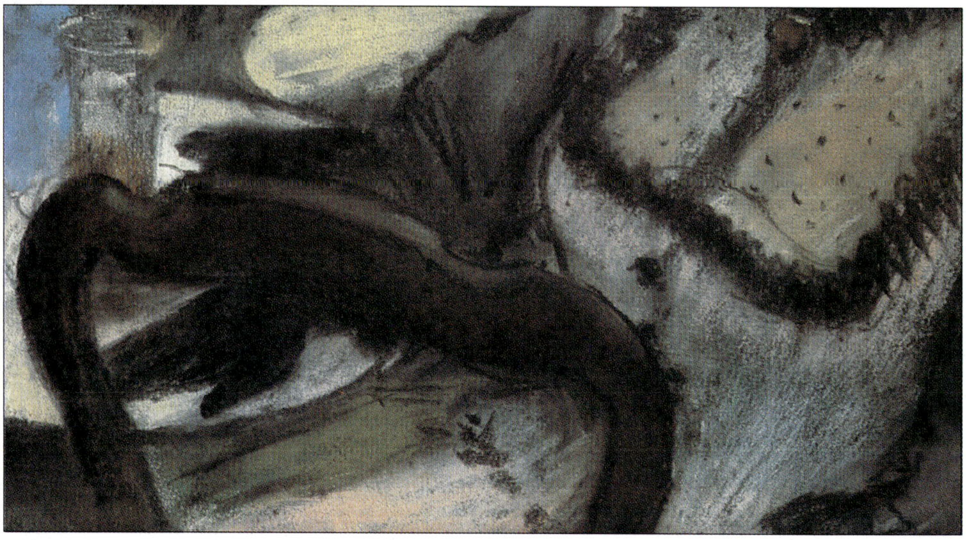

3

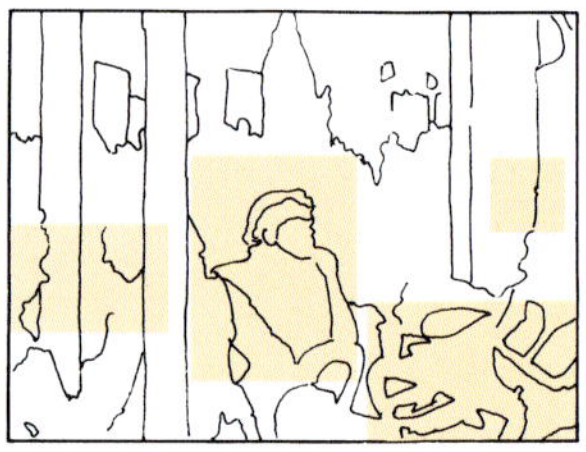

1 The two faces on the left are barely modeled, but that on the extreme left is a good portrait achieved with just a few sure strokes.

2 In contrast to the subdued tone of the picture the artificial flowers on the hat are made up from three primary colors, plus green and lilac, applied with a degree of detail largely absent in the rest of the work. It is the only area of pure color, almost a polychromatic "joke" slapped onto the end of the painting like a punchline.

3 Degas made a great many studies for this work, both of the café furniture and of figures. In one notebook he drew the exact shapes of the café chairs seen from behind and the silhouetted hats and figures of the women, and in another he recorded, above a sketch of the café terrace, the subtle variations in light and dark he had observed there at night.

4 *Actual size detail* This figure is thrown into a pool of light by the darkness of the street behind and the figures in shadow on either side of her. Consequently the treatment of color here is lighter and brighter than in the rest of the painting. A variety of pastel strokes has been used: the lilac of the striped dress is achieved with a simple surface brushing with a pastel stick, the feathers in the hat created with a few sure strokes, and the hat ribbon is a mixture of two shades of blue blurred together by hand.

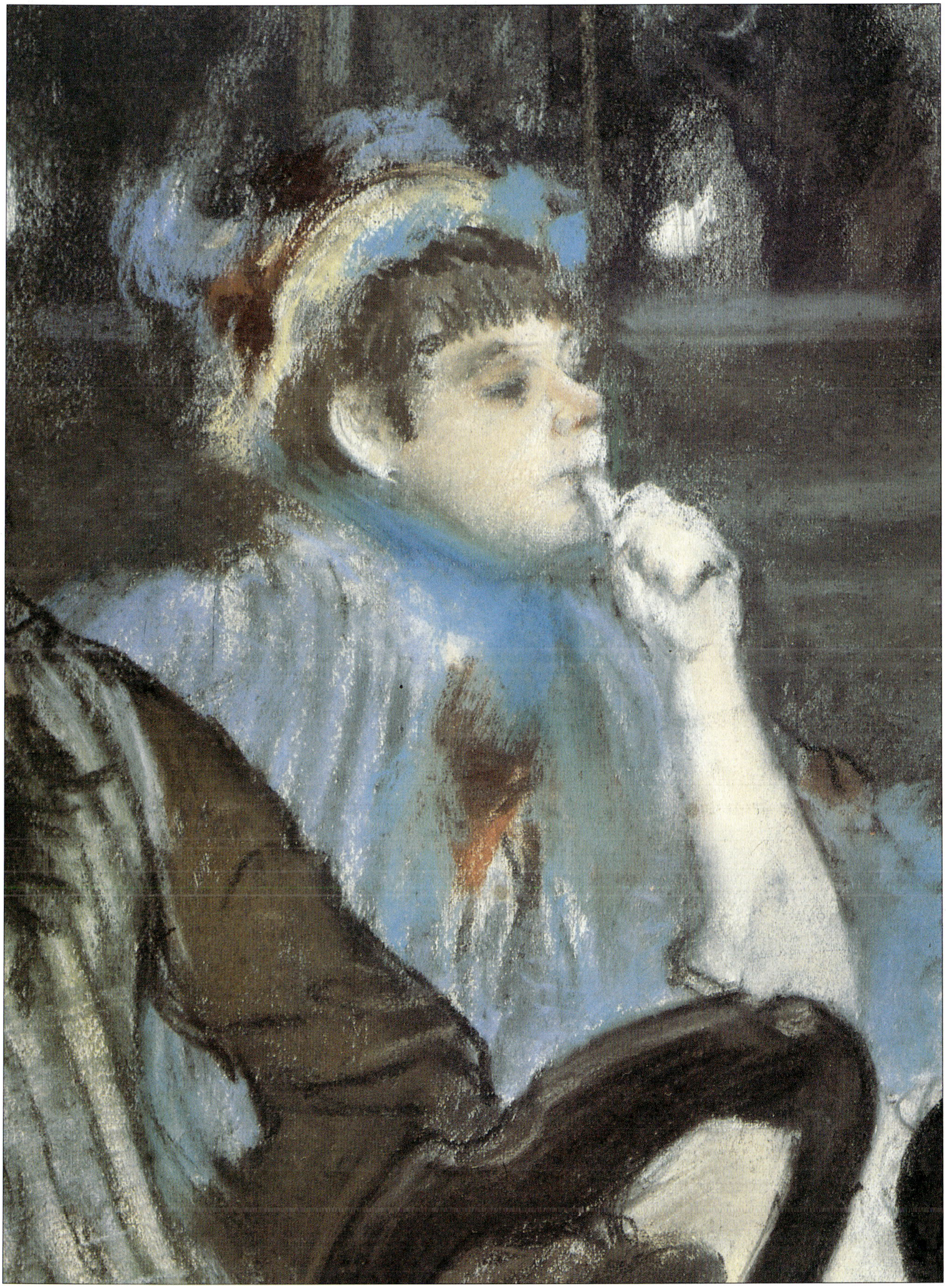

4 *Actual size detail*

Carriage at the Races

1877-80
26×32¼in/66×82cm
Oil on canvas
Musée d'Orsay, Paris

Around 1860-63 Degas had begun to develop new interests and friendships such as those with Duranty and Manet, and the circle of artists at the Café Guerbois. Themes of realism were much discussed in literary and artistic circles, and this climate had an important effect on Degas, leading him toward the kind of contemporary subject-matter advocated by the writer and poet Charles Baudelaire.

Degas was not especially interested in racing as such — he accompanied Manet to the races as another well-to-do young man amusing himself — but he found the horse a wonderful mechanism of moving muscle. He had included horses in his earliest history paintings such as *The Misfortunes of the City of Orléans*, and had studied them in works of the Old Masters. A stay at Menil-Hubert, the chateau of his schoolfriend Paul Valpinçon, where the surrounding countryside resembled that in English sporting prints, and a visit to the nearby stud of Haras-du-Pin, the most celebrated breeding establishment of the day, brought him into close quarters with the animal, which he began to study in detail, making little models in wax and clay to help him understand the effects of motion.

The poet Paul Valéry noted that Degas was "one of the first to study the true forms of noble animal in movement by means of the instantaneous photographs of Major Muybridge." The publication in *The Globe* of Eadweard Muybridge's photographs of horses in motion (see opposite) in 1881 confirmed Degas' own photographic observations that horses did not fly through the air when galloping as English sporting prints had shown them to do. Degas was one of the first artists to show an interest in photography.

Soon after Degas' death in 1917, Jacques-Emile Blanche commented on his innovative system of composition based on the snapshot. "The instantaneous photograph with its unexpected cutting-off, its shocking differences in scale, has become so familiar to us that the easel paintings of that period no longer astonish us...no one before Degas ever thought of doing them, no one since has put such 'gravity'...into the kind of composition which utilizes to advantage the accidents of the camera."

Degas copied his horses from a variety of sources: not only from the stud and racecourse themselves, but from the Parthenon frieze, the paintings of Uccello and Gozzoli, the great Dutch masters, the French Romantic artists, English sporting prints, his own sculptures and, after 1881, from Muybridge's photos published in *Animal Locomotion*. The seemingly arbitrary agreement of mounted horses milling around before or after the race is in fact a "stealthy act of premeditated instantaneity." As Degas said, "Nothing should seem like an accident."

Jean Cocteau expanded on Degas' debt to the photograh in *Le Secret Professionnel* (1922). "Among our painters Degas was the victim of photography as the Futurists were victims of cinematography. I know photographs by Degas which he enlarged himself and on which he worked directly in pastel, marveling at the composition, the foreshortening, the distortion of the foreground forms."

There is no cutting-off in Degas' earlier pictures of racecourse scenes. The device was probably first used in his *Jockeys at Epsom* of 1862, after which it became frequent, especially in the depiction of movement, as in pictures of horses or dancers, where the cropping of figures suggests continuous movement outside and beyond the picture plane. His full mastery of the racecourse as a subject is evident between 1878-91. These scenes of the race are the nearest Degas comes to outdoor painting, until the series of pastels toward the end of his life (see page 419).

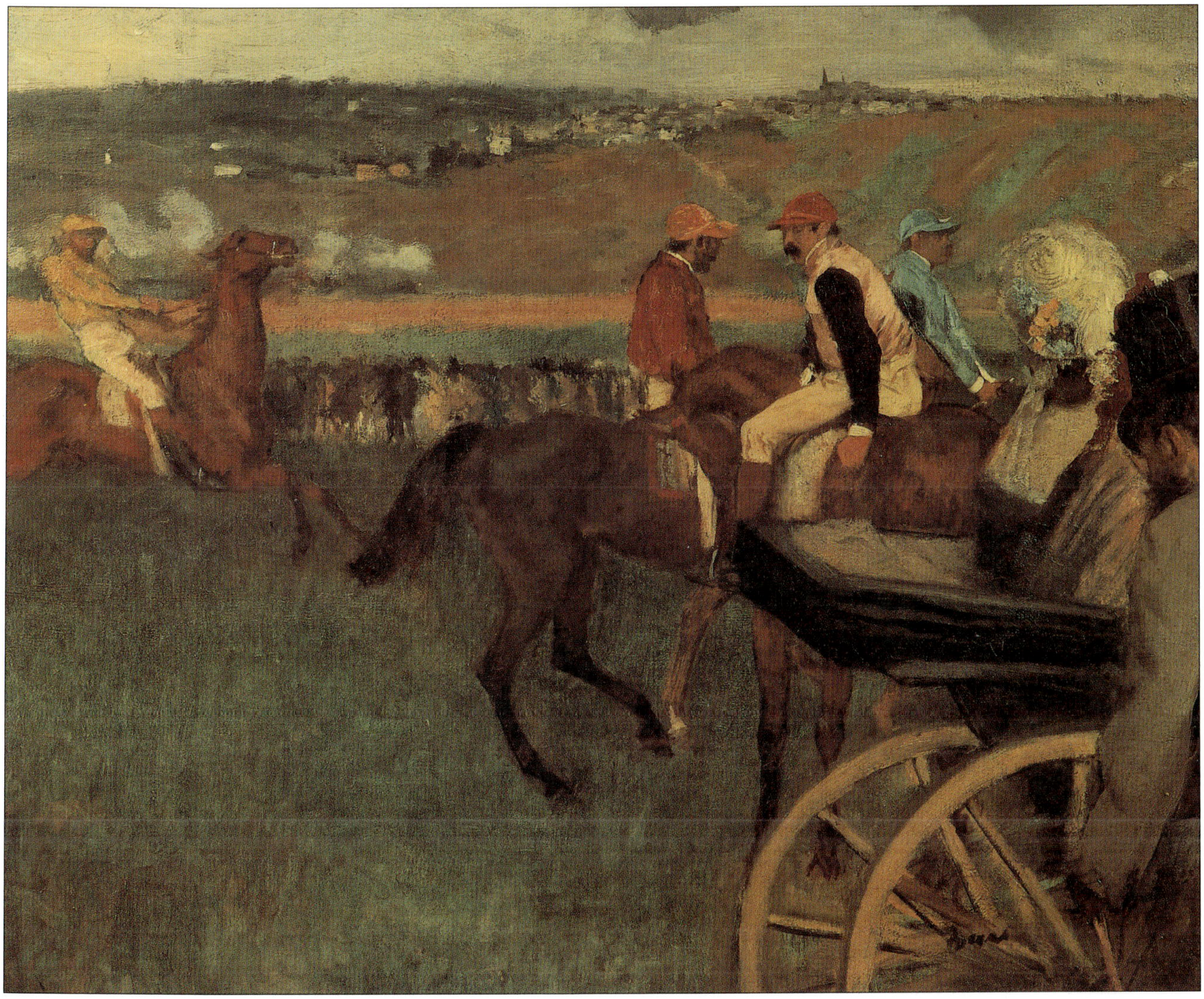

Degas' earliest works on the theme of racing show a broader perspective than this painting, and include not only the jockeys on their horses but also the spectators and racecourse. Here he has included a carriage and just a glimpse of the racegoers, and the composition is not unlike that of *The Ballet Rehearsal* in that the left foreground is totally devoid of figures at precisely the spot where a traditional painter would have placed them.

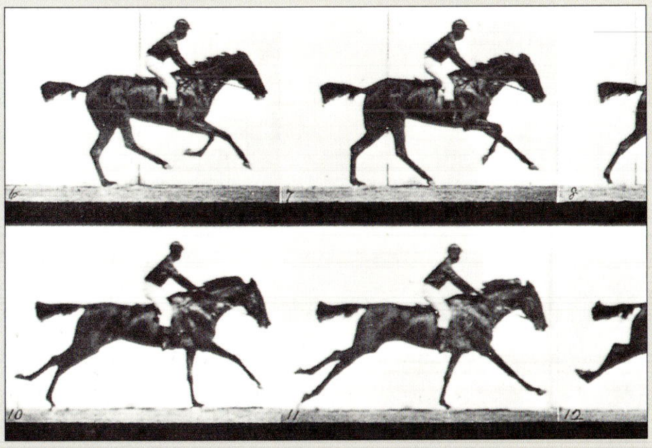

Eadweard Muybridge
Horse in Motion

Muybridge's photographs, published in*Animal Locomotion* in 1881, showed that horses did not gallop with all four legs outstretched as they had appeared in English sporting prints and in Degas' own earlier work. Degas, who was interested in photography and owned his own camera, was quick to adjust to Muybridge's observations and incorporate them into his later depictions of horses.

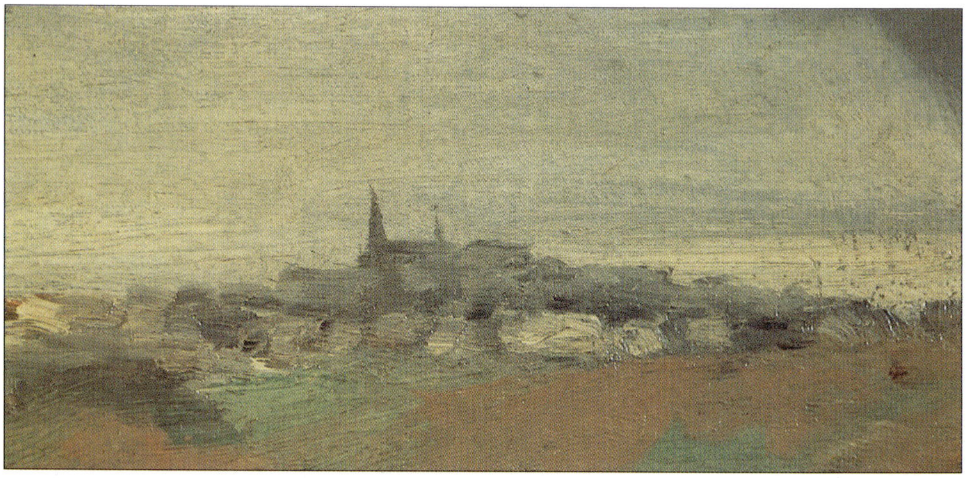

1

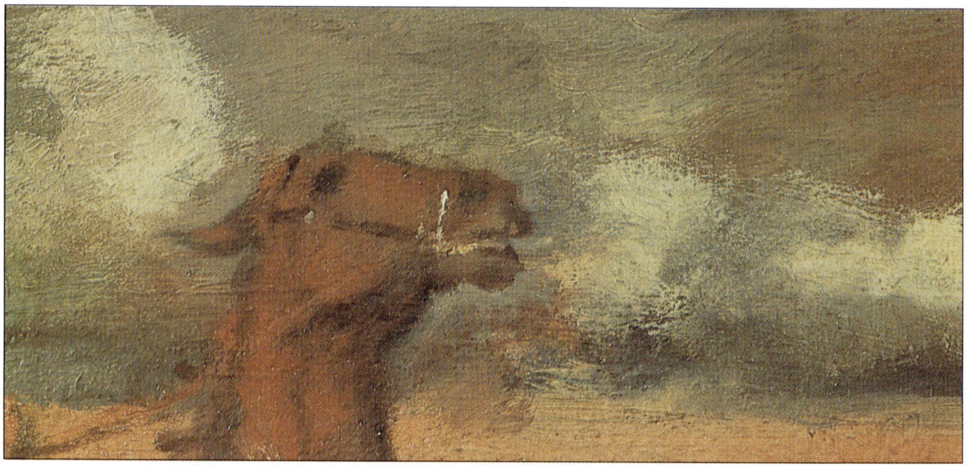

2

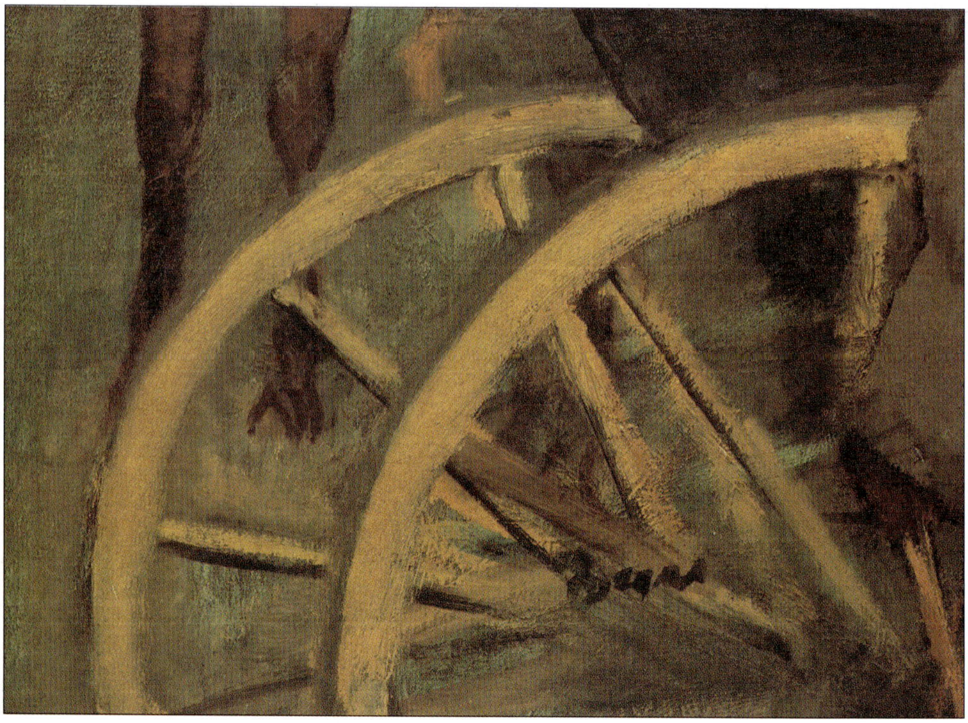

3

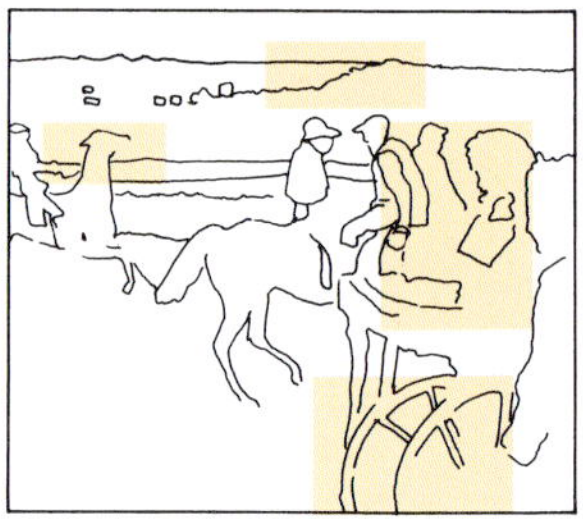

1 Degas' generalized landscape is probably of his own invention rather than a true representation. It is basically a monochrome tonal study, in gray with touches of black and white, but the slope of the hillside is suggested by broad planes of green overlaid with a thin terracotta glaze.

2 During 1859-69 Degas made copies from a wide variety of sources representing the horse, and from the stock of poses he amassed he was able to make a selection for his oils and pastels on this theme. The head of the galloping horse is not unlike one of Delacroix' wild, flared-nostrilled chargers. The billowing steam from a passing train, paralleling the course of the animal, is unique in Degas' work, and provides a neat juxtaposition of modernity and classicism.

3 The lower left corner of the painting is occupied by a cropped close-up of the carriage wheels. The monochromatic use of grays, used in a lighter shade for the man's jacket, is reminiscent of Manet, who was an important influence on Degas in the 1860s.

4 *Actual size detail* Degas was interested in the counterbalance of pairs of figures, and here the two overlapping jockeys create a rhythmic directional thrust which tightens the composition at the right of the picture. The cracks on the man's hat are the result of overpainting before the underlayer was fully dry.

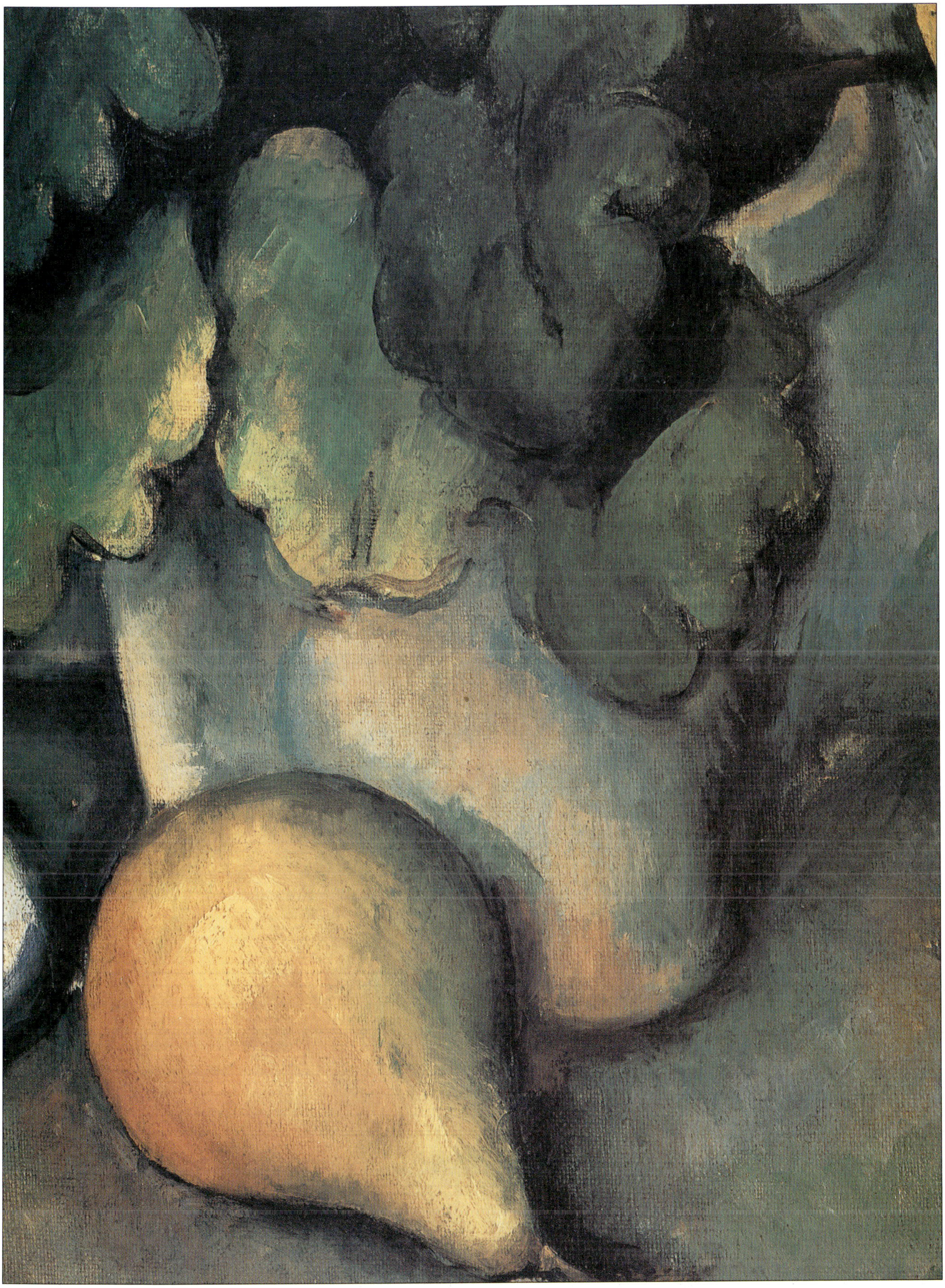

4 *Actual size detail*

Miss Lala at the Circus

1879

46×30½in/117×77.5cm

Oil on canvas

National Gallery, London

Degas made numerous studies of Miss Lala, a mulatto circus artiste whose sensational feats were enthusiastically received when she and her troupe performed in Paris at the Cirque Fernando in January 1879. Known as "La Femme Canon," she held a cannon on a chain between her teeth while hanging by her legs from a trapeze. The cannon was subsequently fired. This and other staggering displays depended principally upon her extraordinary teeth and jaw muscles. Here Degas has chosen to depict her being hoisted to the rafters of the circus pavilion by means of a rope in her mouth. The *Westminster Review* gave a colorful description of Miss Lala's London Performance. "During the past week an additional attraction has been added in the person of a dusky lady know as La La, whose feats of strength fairly eclipse anything and everything of the kind that has gone before. She does all that her muscular rivals have done and a great deal more. She has we believe already astonished Paris, and we have little doubt that her fame in London will rapidly spread."

The choice of the circus as a subject, like that of the café concert, reflects the shift of artistic subject matter from the "elevated" — history or myth — to modern life. Degas was particularly attracted to the artificial in contemporary subject-matter, a preference he acknowledged to an Impressionist landscape painter he met at the circus. "For you, natural life is necessary; for me, artificial life."

His enthusiasm for *The Zemganno Brothers*, Edmond de Goncourt's novel which describes the skilled performance of circus acrobats, demonstrates the inter-dependence of art and literature and the way in which both frequently made use of the same subject matter. Degas, however, was less interested in recreating the atmosphere of places of popular entertainment than in using the settings as a basis for the arrangement of abstract shapes. The exclusion of the audience in favor of a close-up of the performer diminishes the frisson of danger and sense of vertigo which another artist might have stressed.

Like Manet, Degas was basically an abstract artist using the human figure onto which to project form and color. Interested more in the arrangement of shapes than in the exact reproduction of what was before his eyes, he sought to invest his painting with a "magic ingredient." This was the result, not of catching an immediate and passing effect, but of recreating, by a process of observation, sketching and synthesis, something of his own reaction to his subject. Huysmans was impressed by the way Degas had altered the inclination of the circus walls to enhance an effect, and Degas' notebooks show him to have been fascinated by the rafters of the ceiling, its architectural members and surface decoration, for which he made many sketches annotated with details of structure and color. "La Femme Canon" herself appears to have been a useful model for depicting from below, another effect that his notebooks show he was aiming at. "After painting portraits seen from above, I am now going to paint some seen from below."

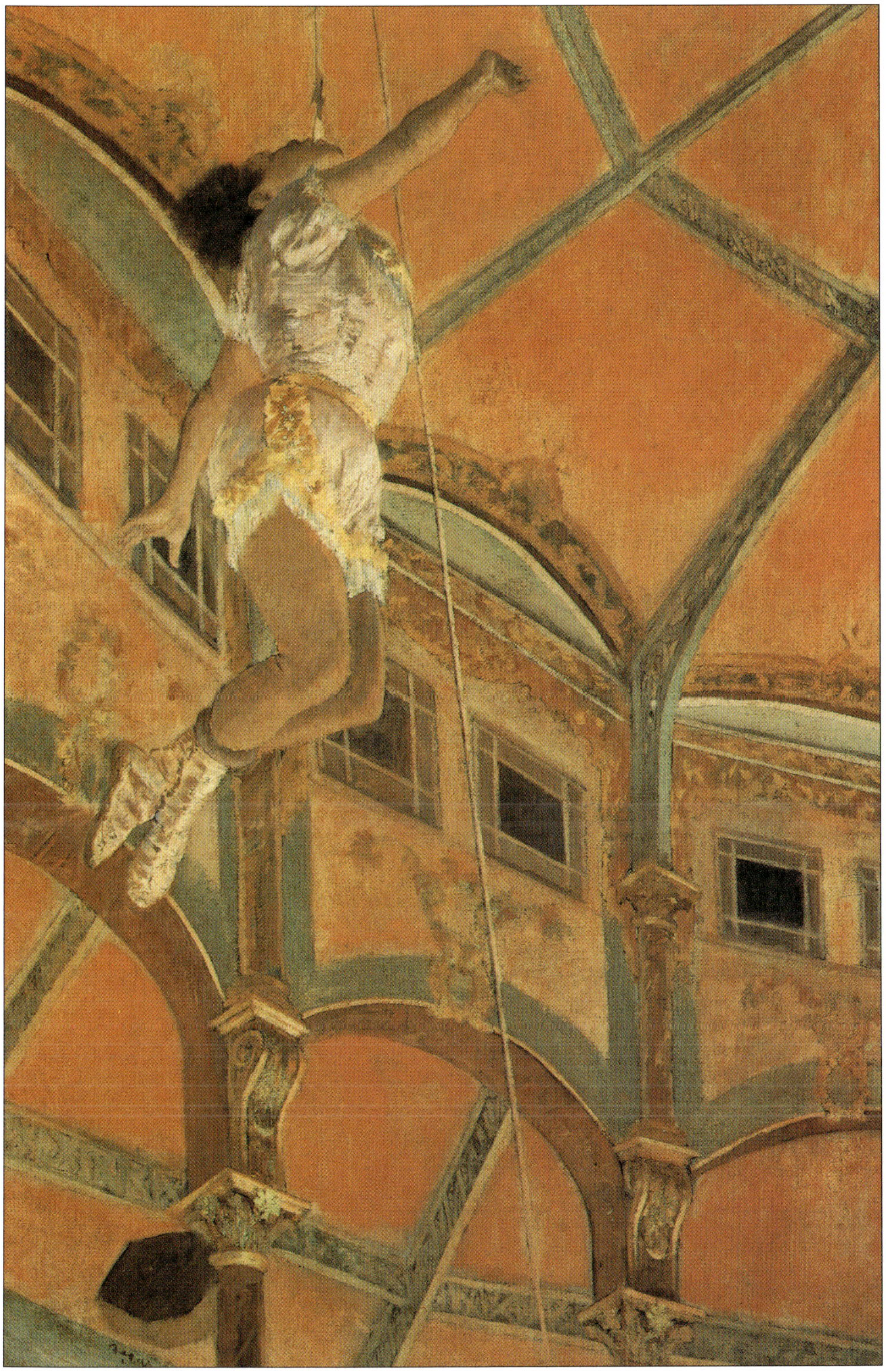

More than any other artist of the last century, Degas was an artist who sought to master his craft by means of experimentation with media. This investigative approach was one that extended to his subject matter, usually the human form, which he sought to understand by means of intense observation and drawings, made from as many different viewpoints as possible. The circus, where the sphere of action is often above the spectator, offered him the perfect opportunity for depicting the model from below as well as providing a contemporary yet exotic note.

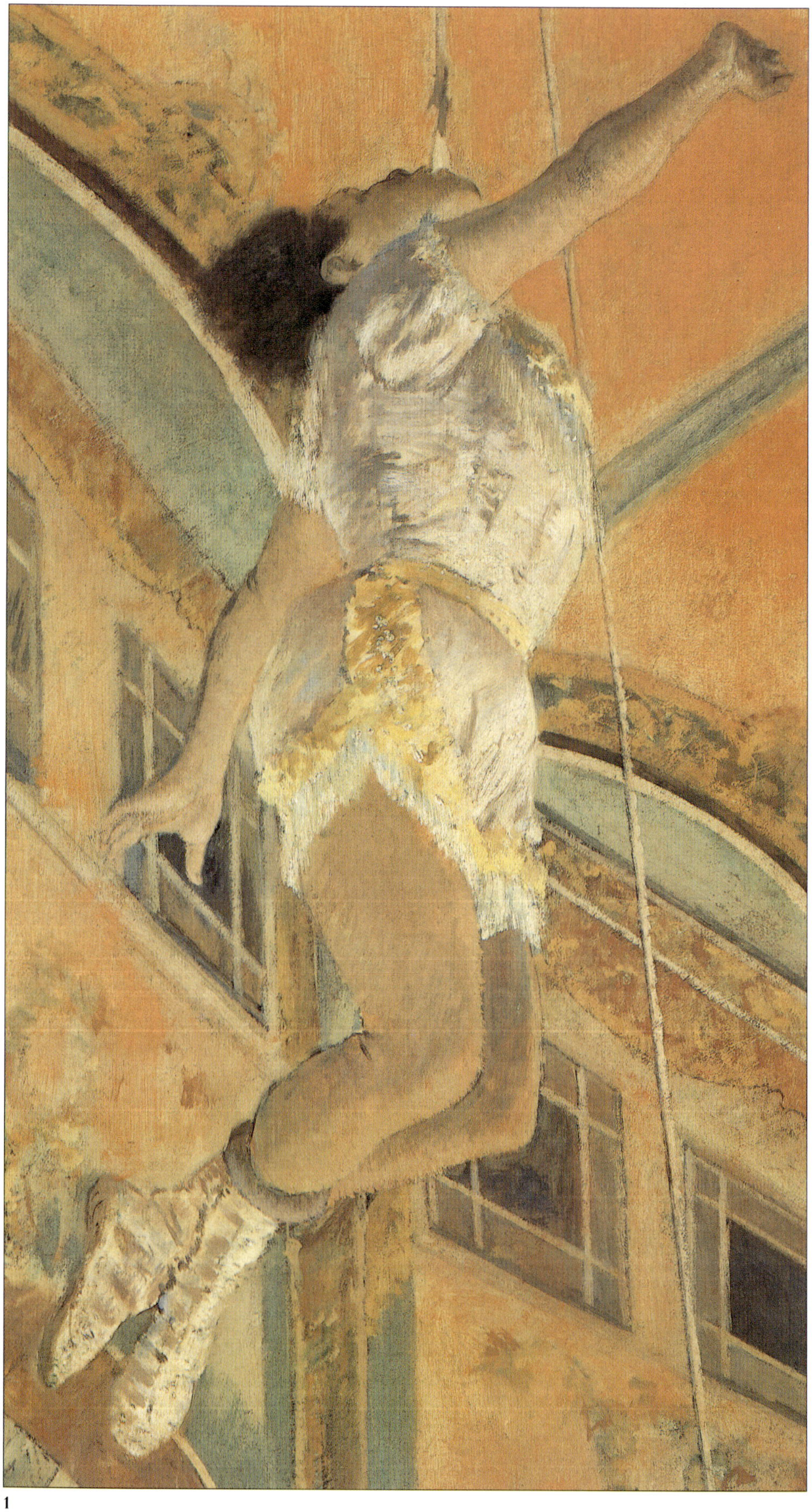

1

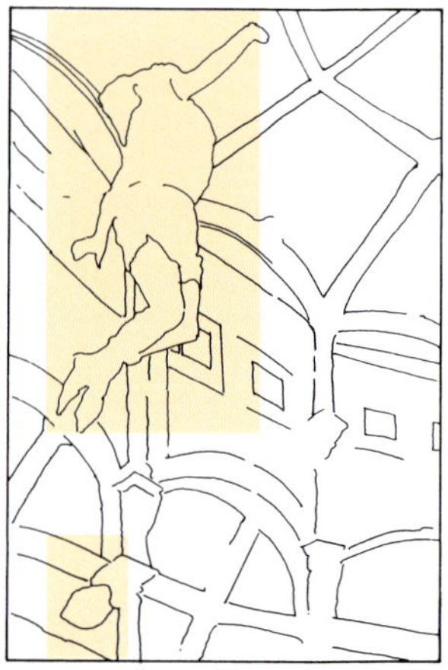

1 Degas was interested in the effect of superimposing the human form over the architectural features, providing an interesting contrast between the rounded forms of the performer herself and the linear, almost gridlike pattern made by the rafters, beams, windows and windowsills. Huysmans, writing in *L'Art Moderne* in 1880 of this work, which was exhibited at the fourth Impressionist Exhibition in 1879, was impressed by the artist's ingenuity. "In order to give the exact sensation of the eye following Miss Lola [sic], climbing to the very top of the Cirque Fernando, Degas dared to make the circus roof lean wholly to one side."

2 *Actual size detail* The artist's notebooks not only reveal his interest in the structure of the pavilion and its gilded stucco decoration but contain detailed annotations of the color harmonies of the interior. Degas made three attempts at the roof, each in a different medium, before bringing together his observations of the artiste in her lofty setting. With a few light, sure touches he has achieved the effect of green-painted acanthus leaf on the slender column.

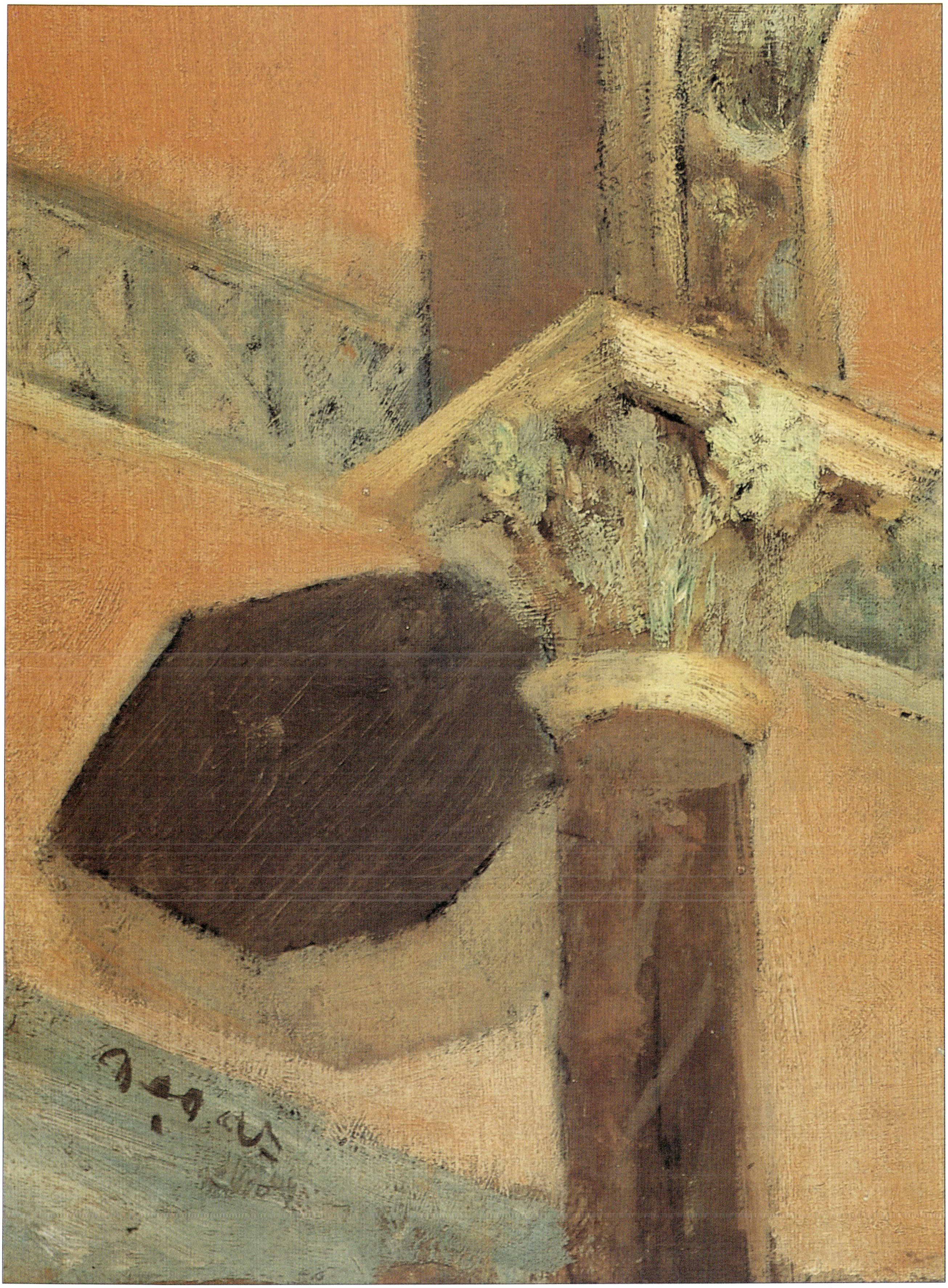

2 *Actual size detail*

The Tub

1886
$23\frac{5}{8} \times 32\frac{5}{8}$in/$61 \times 82.5$cm
Musée d'Orsay, Paris

"The nude has always been represented in poses which presupposed an audience, but these women of mine are honest, simple folk, unconcerned by any other interests than those involved in their physical condition. Here is another, she is washing her feet. It is as though you looked through a keyhole." Degas' remark to George Moore, a rare studio visitor, testifies to his proclivity for depicting scenes as though through an invisible spy-hole. It is an extension of the artist's protective mask to view unseen, as well as a revelation of his often rather harsh voyeuristic characteristics.

The observation of his studies of the female nude was prefaced by the remark, "She is the human animal attending to itself, a cat licking herself." Toward the end of his life Degas confessed that he had perhaps treated the study of women too dispassionately. The novelist and critic Huysmans wrote that Degas had "with his studies of nudes, contributed a lingering cruelty, a patient hatred."

"It seems as though, exasperated by the baseness of his surroundings, he has resolved to proceed to reprisals and fling in the face of his own century the grossest insult, by overthrowing woman, the idol which has always been so gently treated and whom he degrades by showing her naked in the bathtub, in the humiliating positions of her private toilet...Here we have a red-head, dumpy and stuffed, back bent, so that the sacrum bone sticks out from the stretched bulging buttocks; she is straining to curl her arm over her shoulder so as to squeeze a sponge, the water from which is trickling down her spine and splashing off the small of her back.

"Such, in brief, are the merciless positions assigned by this iconoclast to the being usually showered with fulsome gallantries.

"But in addition to this special accent of contempt and hatred, what one should note in these works is the unforgettable truthfulness of the types caught with a simple, basic style of drawing, with lucid, controlled passion, coldly but feverishly; what one notes is the warm, veiled color of these scenes, their rich, mysterious tone, the supreme beauty of flesh turning to blue or pink under the water, lit by closed muslin-draped windows in dark rooms where the dim light from a courtyard reveals washbasins and bathtubs, bottles and combs, the glazed boxwood backs of brushes, pink copper hot-water jugs."

Huysmans has expanded on the way Degas' drawing and subtle color transformed the ugly and everyday, an effect much helped by pastel. Although Degas had used the medium in the 1860s, it was from the '70s onward that he began to take full stock of its possibilities, experimenting with methods of fixing what is essentially colored chalk onto the picture surface. The richness of much of his pastel work was greatly admired by Renoir, who personally found the medium uncongenial, but noted that in Degas' hands it possessed "the freshness of fresco." For a draftsman it was the most successful medium for transforming line into color. The two happened simultaneously: in this work contours are clearly visible, showing that Degas was still working principally with line, but the overlay of white highlight and darker shadow tones mitigate the outline effect.

This nude is a modern-day Susannah at her bath. Degas made this connection himself while at the same time denying it. "See what differences time has brought. Two centuries ago I would have painted Susannah at her bath. Today, I paint only women at their tubs." The work is a successful reinterpretation of the Old Masters in the modern idiom. In a way Degas was a painter of modern life in spite of himself, taking to heart Baudelaire's dictum that "the man who does not accept the conditions of ordinary life sells his soul," while at the same time lamenting an age gone by. "They were dirty perhaps, but distinguished; we are clean but we are common."

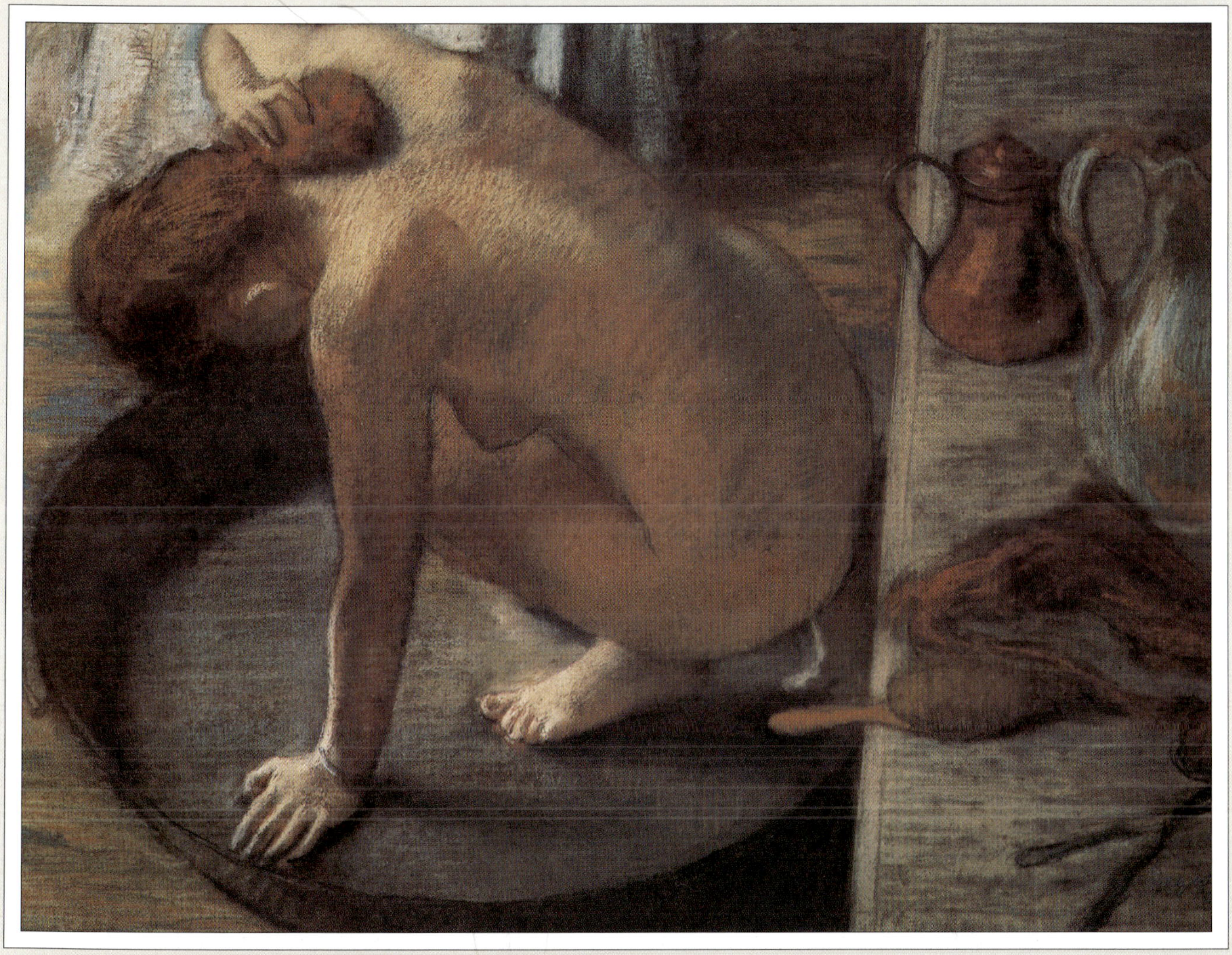

Women at their toilette was one of Degas' most favored subjects at this stage of his life, and he sketched them from many viewpoints and in every aspect – getting in and out of the bath, washing and drying themselves, and having their hair brushed. In this work the angle of the close-up viewpoint is unusual: seen from above, the table and shelf has become an abstract slice of the picture, its strong, almost vertical line which traverses the height of the canvas broken by the handle of the brush and copper jug. This daring compositional device, which is found in a number of Degas' works, is a deliberate break with a classically inspired arrangement. The radical treatment of the nude, not as an idealized thing of beauty but as a working woman washing herself, presented a shock to visitors at the eighth Impressionist Exhibition. In Huysmans' eyes it was a deliberate attempt to shock the *bourgeoisie,* who, he commented, "cried out, indignant at this frankness, struck all the same by the life flowing from these pastels. In the end they exchanged some doubtful or disgusted comments and upon leaving, their parting shot was: 'It's obscene'."

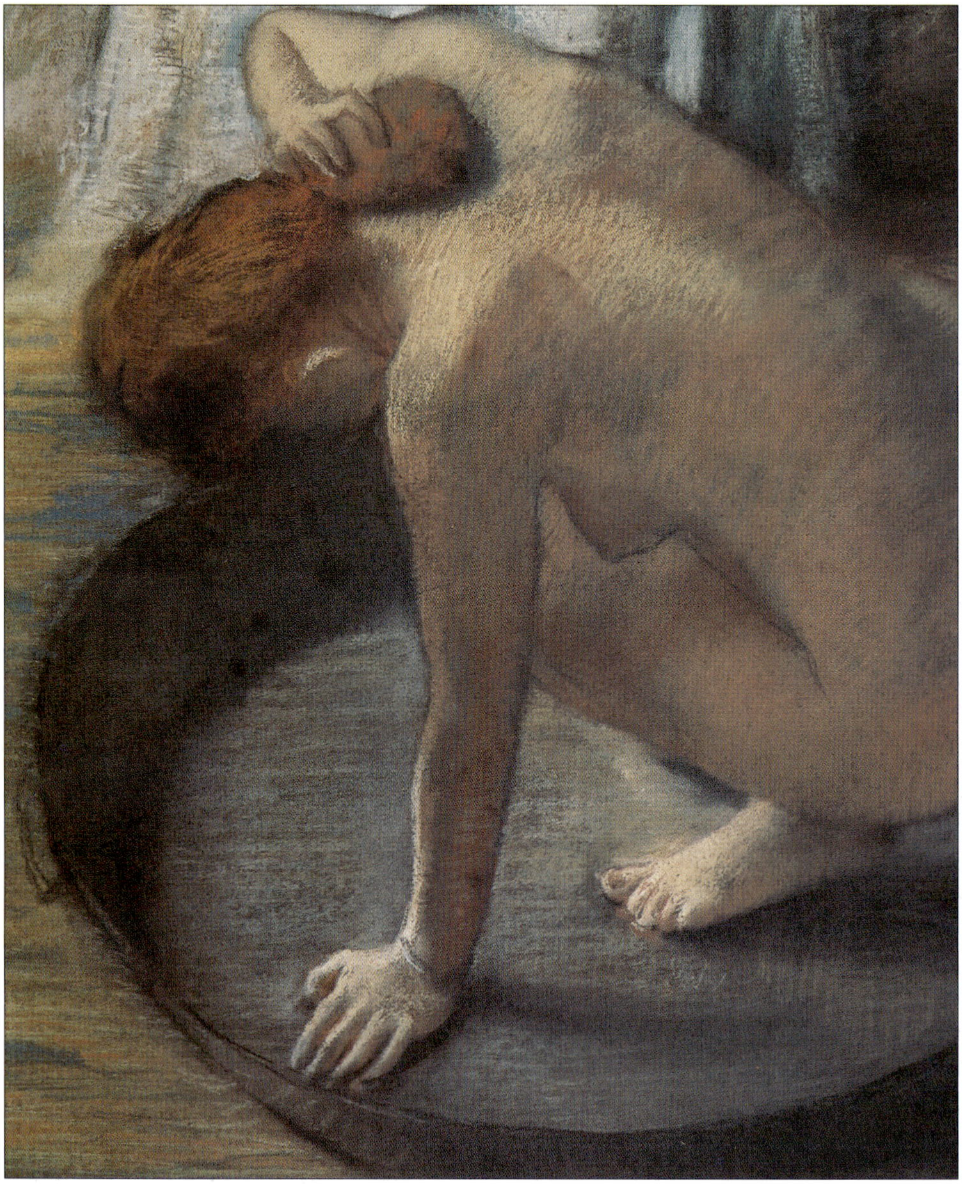

1

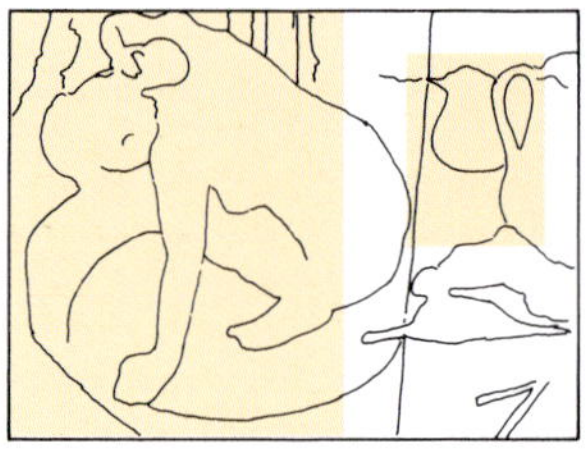

1 Denis Rouart noted that Degas adapted to pastel "the technique of making colors play against each other by superimposition and transparency rather than merely by the opposition of areas of color. Transparency could not, of course, be obtained in pastel as it could be with glazes in oil paint; so he arrived at an analogous effect by working in successive layers, not covering the lower layer entirely but letting it show through." Rouart also described the way in which Degas would lay in his subject in pastel, spray boiling water over it to make the dry pastel into a paste, and then work into it with brushes to varying stiffness. "He took care not to spray the water vapor all over the picture, so as to keep the original surface of the pastel where he wanted to give it variety."

2 *Actual size detail* Gone are the alluring feminine accoutrements of an Old Master "Susannah Bathing," with her ivory-handled scissors, silver-framed hand-mirror and string of pearls. Instead we have the real articles of the female toilette, not intended for public display – the false hairpiece, curling tongs, cheap wooden-handled brush, copper hot-water jug and serviceable cold water pitcher.

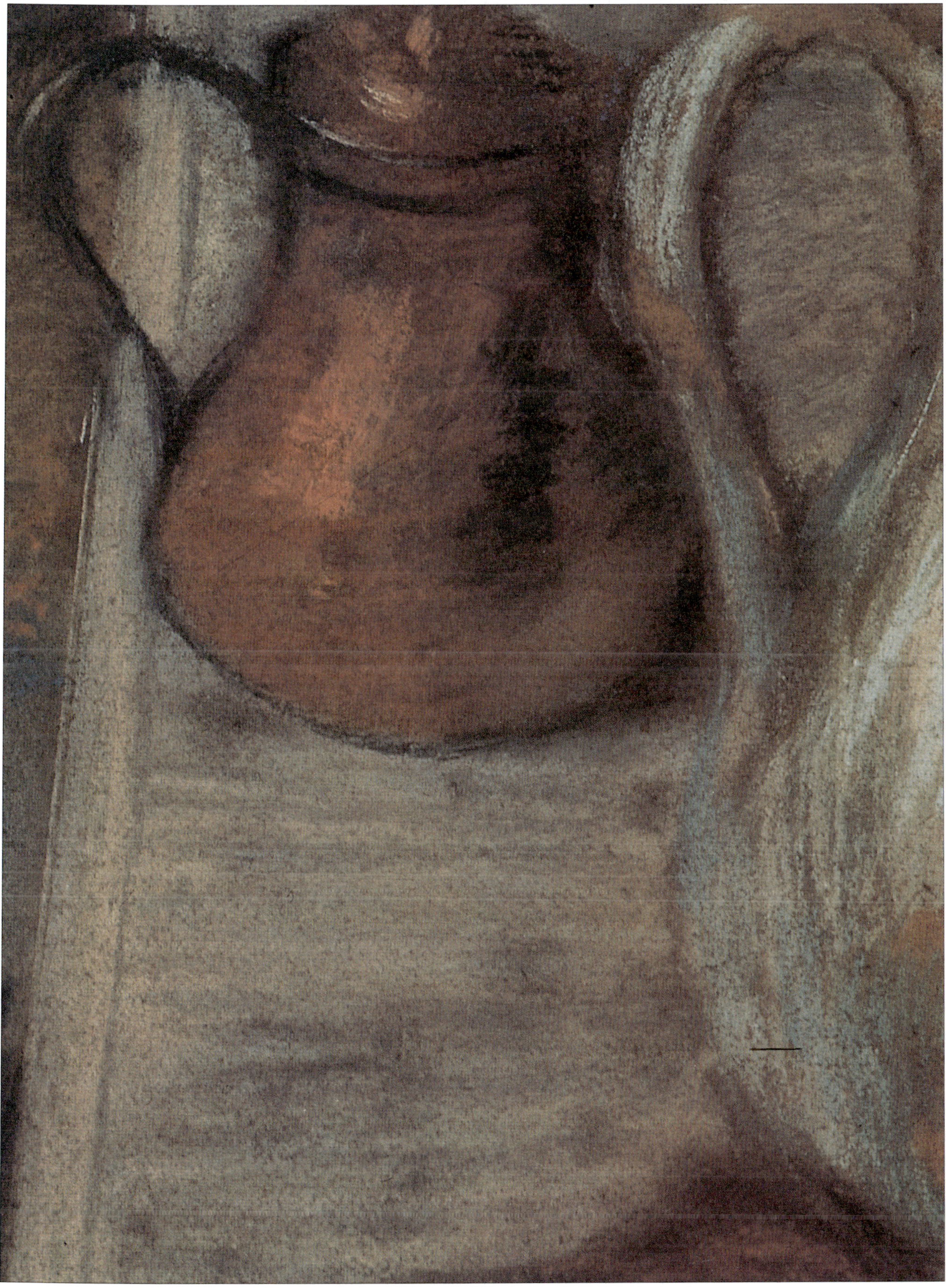

2 *Actual size detail*

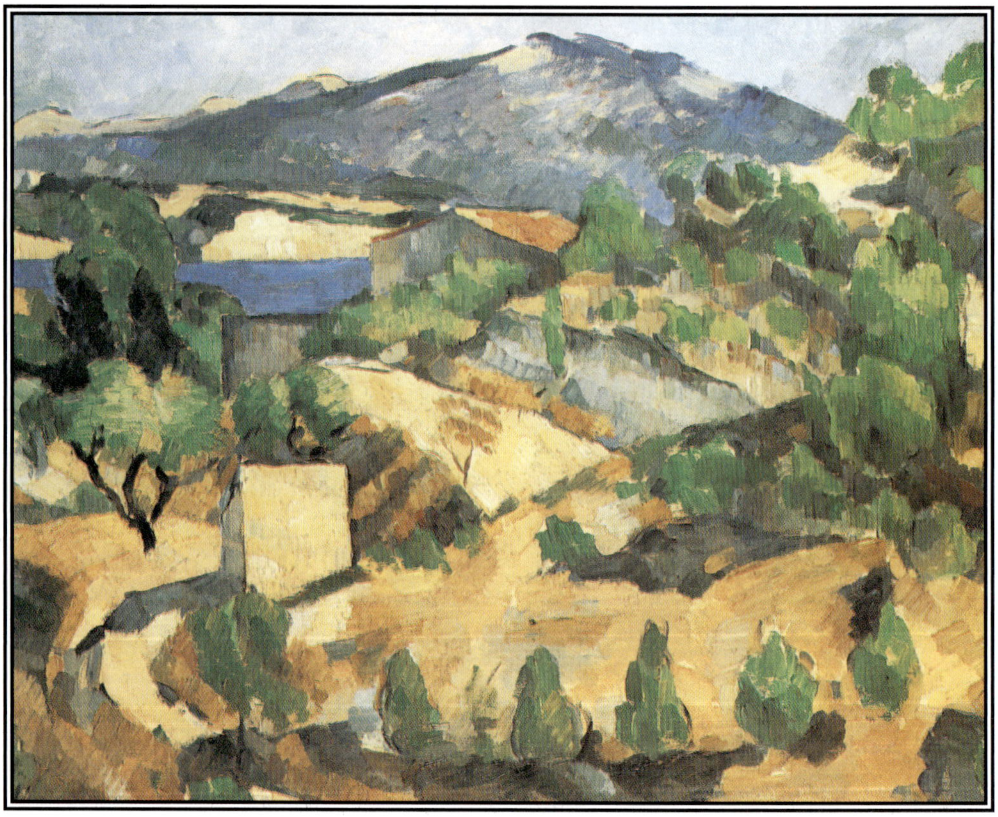

CÉZANNE

Introduction

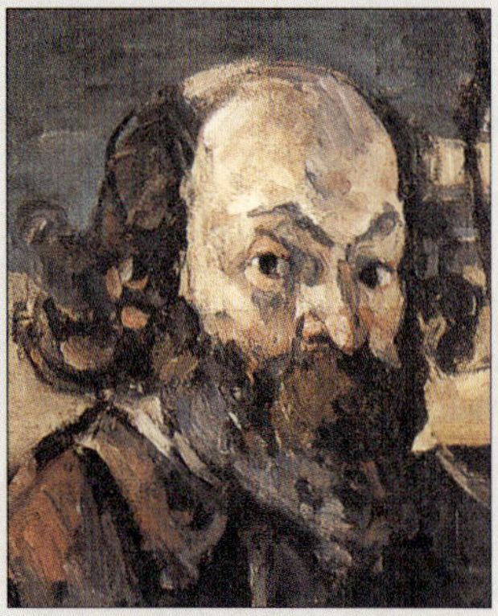

Paul Cezanne
Self-portrait (detail)
c 1872, Musée d'Orsay,Paris

Paul Cézanne's early years appear at first sight to conform almost too easily to the popular mythology of the struggling and misunderstood painter. He fought against the conventional aspirations of his family, escaped to join the bohemian artistic circles of Paris, suffered the indignity of rejection from public exhibitions, and worked doggedly at his painting for many years before tasting any kind of success. There is, however, evidence that Cézanne cultivated this view of himself, flaunting his long hair and abrasive manners in polite society and deliberately submitting violent or erotic pictures to exhibition juries. He could be abrupt and temperamental even with close friends, was savage in his denunciation of critics and cultural bureaucrats, and his commitment to his own art was never less than fierce. There have been few artists as dedicated as Cézanne, but also few whose formative years were so problematic and unexpected.

Early years

Paul Cézanne was born in 1839, and his adolescence and early manhood appear to have been dominated by his father, Louis-Auguste Cézanne, a self-made businessman and banker from Aix-en-Provence in southern France. Paul showed considerable aptitude at school, and was destined to follow in his father's footsteps. As a schoolboy, however, he preferred to roam the countryside with his small band of close friends (one of whom was Emile Zola, the future novelist) talking of art and reading aloud their own and others' poetry. At the age of nineteen, Cézanne started to study at the local drawing academy, where he learned to produce highly disciplined, if rather conventional, studies from the nude male model. Braving his father's wrath, he announced that he wanted to leave Aix for Paris and embark on a career as an artist.

Cézanne senior was accustomed to getting his own way, but on this occasion he met his match. In 1861, after bitter arguments, Paul was provided with a meager allowance and allowed to travel to the capital. Despite the pleasure of meeting up again with his friend Zola, who had preceded him to Paris, the young man experienced a number of setbacks, and more than once had to return to his family home. But the decisive break had been made, and throughout the 1860s, Cézanne worked at his vocation, drawing from models, studying the masters of the past in the Louvre and gradually making the acquaintance of other unknown young artists, such as Camille Pissarro and Armand Guillaumin. His growing self-confidence is reflected in his few surviving letters from this period and in the record of his several submissions to the official Salon.

The character of the pictures he sent in, several of which survive, helps both to explain their rejection by the Salon juries and to summarize something of the young artist's ambitions. The large portrait of 1870 *Achille Emperaire* (see page 465), was not only rejected by the jury of that year, but also lampooned in a contemporary illustration. Emperaire was a lifelong friend of Cézanne's, a fellow painter from Aix, who suffered from a serious condition that left his legs under-developed and feeble. As in his portrait of his father shown opposite, Cézanne has presented Emperaire with extraordinary boldness, almost defying the spectator to turn away from the unlovely creature who completely dominates the large canvas. Another picture from the same period, *The Murder,* shows Cézanne at his most defiant, wilfully distorting the limbs of his figures, and bending the contours of the landscape to accommodate the ferocity of the scene. The paint is thickly applied, the implicit emotion raw and impulsive, as if the artist were giving direct expression to his own passionate temperament.

The idea that an artist's principal function is to express his temperament through his chosen medium seems to have been an article of faith for both Cézanne and Zola. Zola's definition of art as "nature seen through

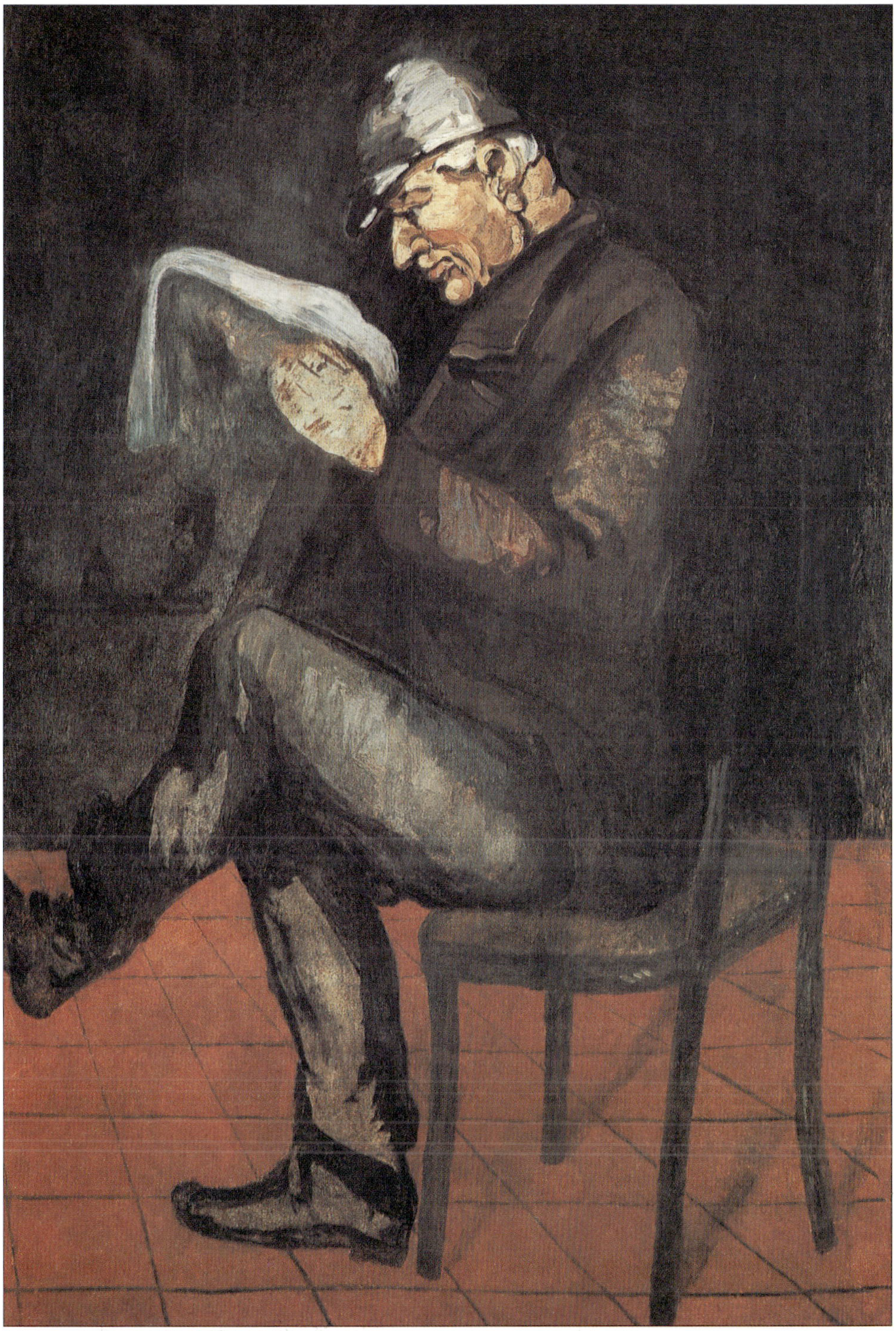

PAUL CEZANNE
Portrait of Louis-Auguste Cézanne, Father of the Artist
c 1862, National Gallery, London

Originally painted directly onto the wall of the family home by the twenty-three-year-old artist, this large picture was later transferred to canvas. The rough handling of the paint and the awkward positioning of the figure say a lot about the young Cézanne's fierce independence and probably as much about his uneasy relationship with his father.

a temperament" emphasizes the uniqueness of the individual's own sensibility and, by implication, the possibility that the most extreme traits of personality can find expression in a novel or a painting. His own books had begun to explore the psychological basis of sexual passion and human violence, often in ways that seem to parallel Cézanne's tormented early pictures. At the same time, both artists knew that such unconventional subject matter could not be expressed within the polite conventions of the day, and each sought for a more authentic, pared-down language for their art.

New directions

Another decisive influence on Cézanne's early career was his contact with the group of artists who were later to exhibit under the name of the Impressionists. A letter of 1865 shows that he had already made the acquaintance of Pissarro, and subsequent letters and paintings

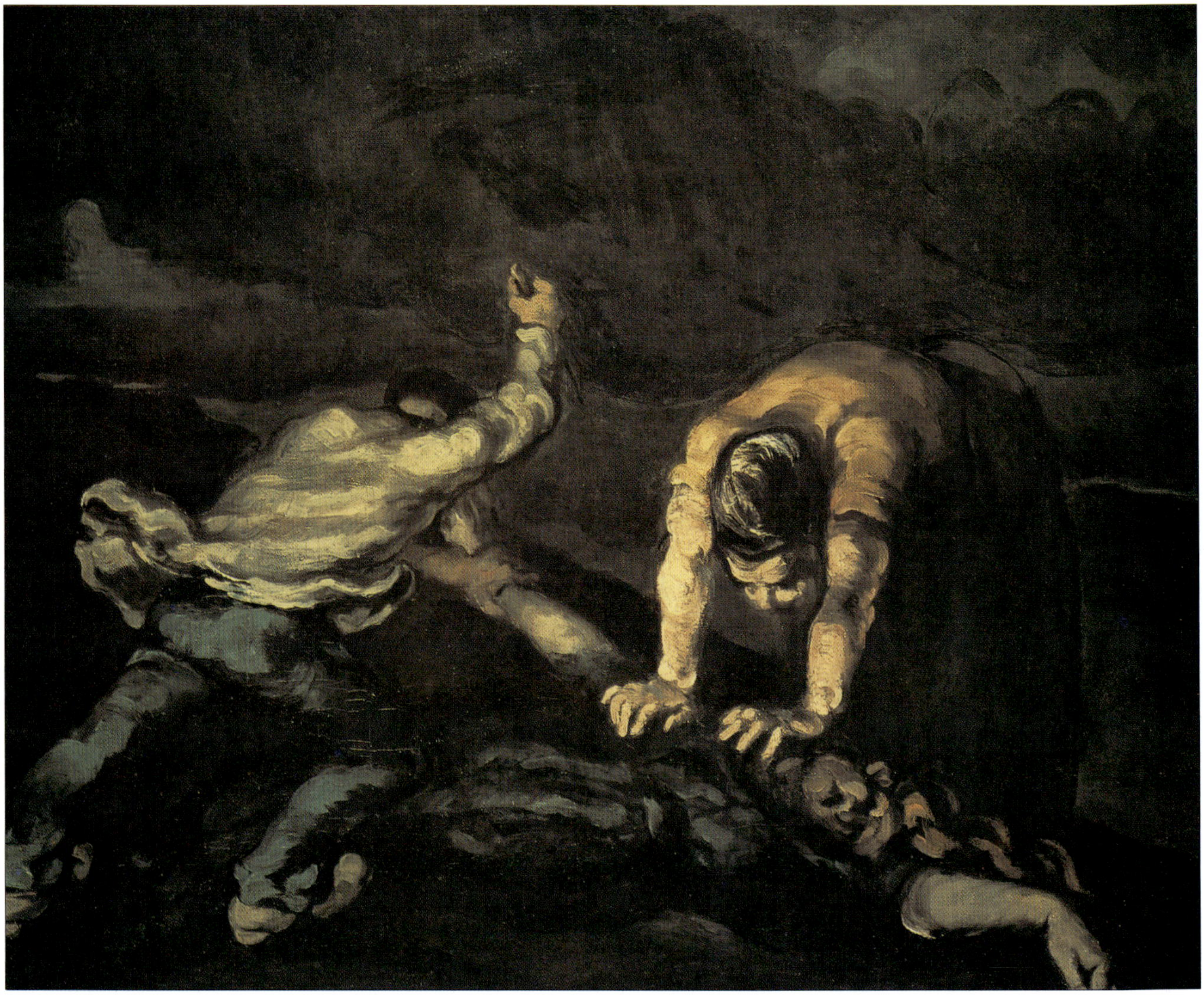

PAUL CEZANNE
The Murder
1867-68, Walker Art Gallery, Liverpool

Scenes of lust, violence and fantasy are common in the first decade of Cézanne's. career, and offer a complete contrast to the apparently serene subject matter of his later years. *The Murder* has parallels in the popular imagery and literature of the day, and appears to be part of an attempt by the artist to express extremes of emotion as directly as possible.

show that the two artists worked together in the country-side, often in front of the same subject. Pissarro was a man of almost saintly character — Cézanne described him as "that humble, colossal Pissarro" — and his patient example and knowledgeable advice affected his younger colleague deeply. For some time Pissarro had devoted himself to outdoor subjects, to the hillsides and farms of his home-town of Pontoise, near Paris. In his company, Cézanne learned to direct his own deeply felt sensations of nature into rich paint textures and strongly conceived compositions, lightening his palette and intensifying his colors in response to his open-air subjects. As if in tribute to Pissarro, two of Cézanne's three submissions to the first Impressionist exhibition of 1874 were landscapes, both influenced by his friend in subject matter and handling, but both recognizably the work of a changed and confident young painter.

Other events had also helped to propel Cézanne's career in new directions. In about 1870 he had begun living with his former model, the twenty-year-old Hortense Fiquet. Two years later she gave birth to a son, also christened Paul, though great care was taken to conceal both the child and the relationship with Hortense from Cézanne's family in Aix. Cézanne appears to have found some fulfilment and stability in his new way of life, but it is a mark of the continuing influence of his father, and perhaps Cézanne's fears for his allowance, that it took more than ten years for him to admit to the existence of his mistress and son.

As a personality, Cézanne continued to shock his con-

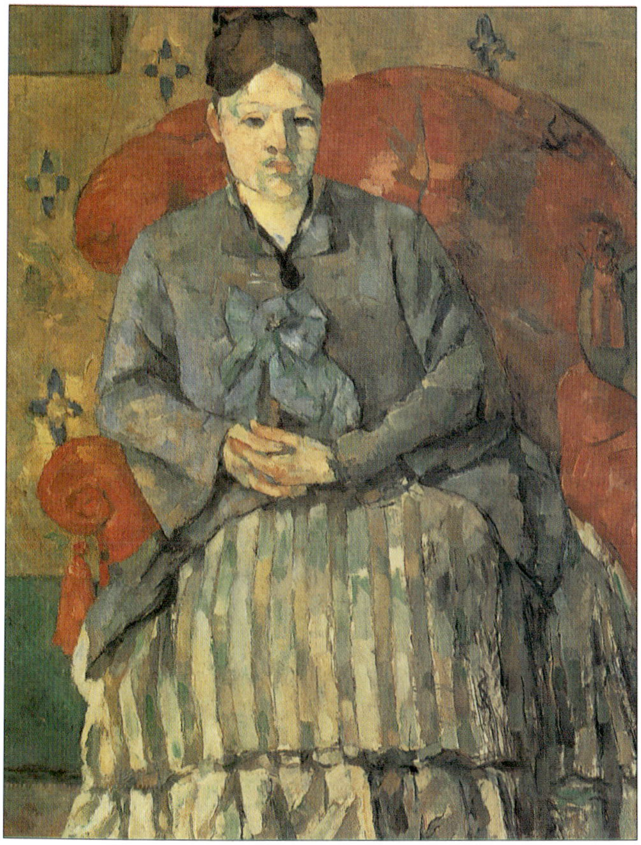

PAUL CEZANNE
Madame Cézanne in a Red Armchair
c 1877, Museum of Fine Arts, Boston

Hortense Fiquet had not yet married Cézanne at the time of this painting, though she had borne their son, Paul, about five years earlier. She had worked as an artist's model in her teens and sat patiently for Cézanne on many occasions. Her dour expression may reflect her boredom at the subsequent hours of immobility.

temporaries by his displays of rough, provincial manners and sudden outbursts of temper, both growing from a fierce determination to remain independent and stay true to what he saw as his "temperament." Cézanne's view of himself, as shown in his many self-portraits, is of an intense, rather swarthy individual whose prematurely balding head enhances the severity of an already stern countenance. His relationship with Hortense was never an easy one and they were to live apart for much of the time, but she seems to have been a compliant model, and is the subject of some of Cézanne's grandest and most subtle portraits. In spite of his attempts to conceal his son's existence, Cézanne was inordinately fond of the

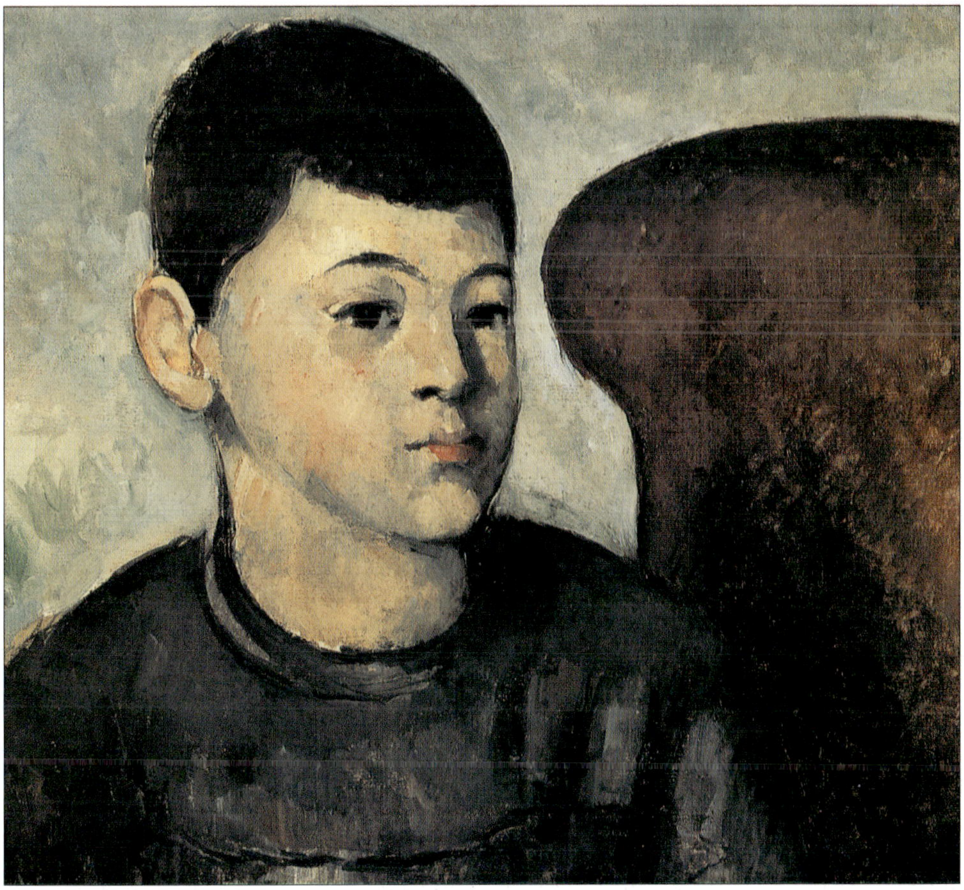

PAUL CEZANNE
Portrait of the Artist's Son
c 1884, Musée de l'Orangerie, Paris

Paul was twelve or thirteen years old when he posed for this portrait, one of more than a dozen painted by his father. Cézanne was always indulgent towards his son, overlooking his youthful misbehavior and allowing him to drift into manhood without training or employment.

young Paul, and there are numerous tender drawings and painted studies of the boy, recording his transition from childhood to adolescence.

The landscape painter

Important though portraiture was to Cézanne, both as an expression of his private world and as a link with a past tradition, the subject that increasingly commanded his attention was landscape. In his mature years, landscapes dominated his output, and it is above all the mountainsides and woodland of his native Provence that reappear in his work. Cézanne was always conscious of his Provencal origins, and his choice of local subject matter was as much a matter of pride as one of convenience. Certain features of the locality, such as the pine trees and reddish-ocher rocks, had a special significance for him, while the towering mountain to the east of Aix, Mont Sainte-Victoire (see page 485), seemed to embody the mysterious, pagan essence of the region. Although he continued to spend time in Paris and elsewhere, and despite financial worries and family disputes, Cézanne returned more and more frequently to Provence to paint the landscapes he had loved since childhood.

As his commitment to the landscape grew, the distinctiveness of his technique became more apparent. During the 1870s, his struggle with the sense of exhilaration he felt in the presence of nature combined with the

CAMILLE PISSARRO
The Edge of the Village
1872, Musée d'Orsay, Paris

Painted at a time when Cézanne was working closely with Pissarro, this canvas summarizes many of the characteristics that he admired in the older man's work. A simple country scene, frontally encountered and lit by clear sunlight, is constructed from bold brushstrokes and a dramatic interplay of horizontal and vertical compositional elements.

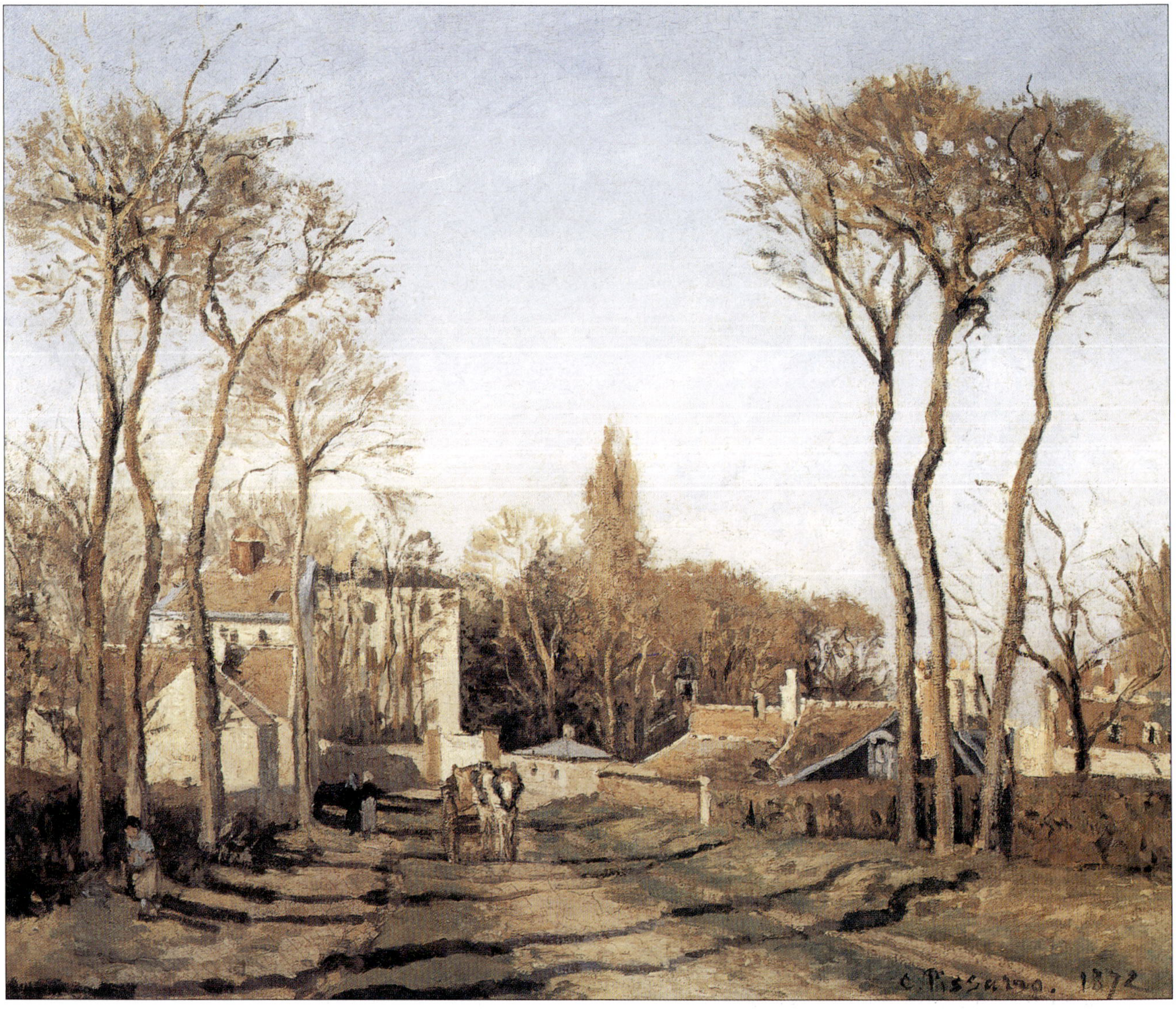

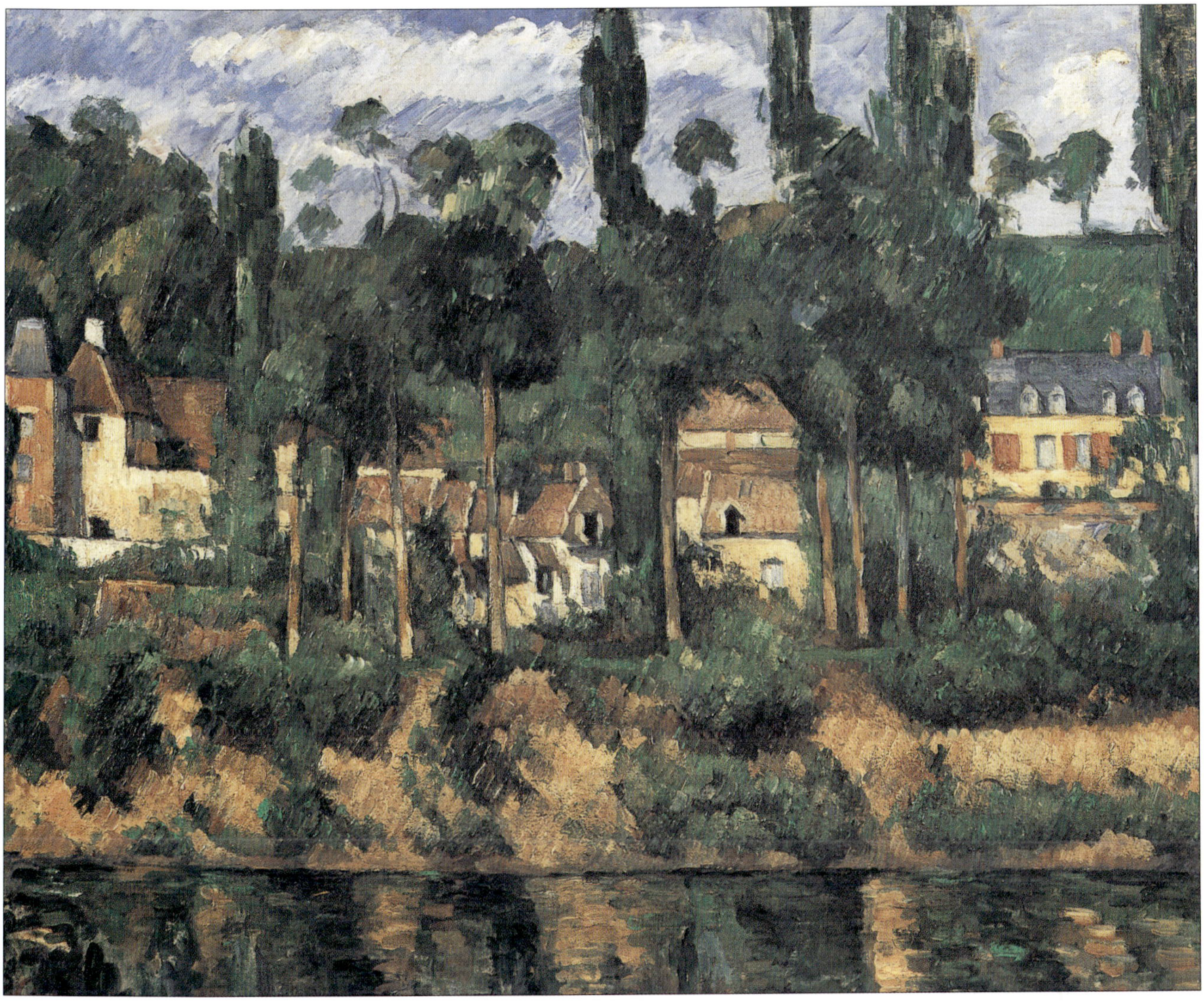

PAUL CEZANNE
Château de Medan
c 1880, Burrell Collection, Glasgow

Cézanne made a number of visits to stay with his friend Emile Zola in his grand house at Medan, before Zola's ostentatious prosperity and declining sympathy for the painter's achievement eventually led to a complete breakdown in their friendship.

demands of painting directly from the chosen "motif," or subject, resulted in some densely worked but increasingly distinctive canvases. Thick flourishes of pigment gave way to organized, regimented sequences of brushstrokes, creating subtle rhythms across the picture surface, echoing the principal elements of the composition. In these works, the dominating principle is a deep sense of deliberation, against which each tree, each rock and each individual leaf is judged. Color, shape, spatial intervals and surface texture all breathe life into the chosen subject, and everything extraneous to the composition is boldly eliminated. This procedural rigor has sometimes been seen as coldness, but nothing could be further from the truth: it is rather that the intensity of Cézanne's delight in "the manifold spectacle of nature," as he once described it, could only be contained within the most resilient of structures.

The landscape and the climate of Provence were ideally suited to an artist who worked out of doors. Cézanne insisted on the need for direct and continuous contact with his subject, and would stride out into the countryside, easel and canvases on his back, and walk for several miles to one or other of his favorite sites, such as the railway viaduct near Aix, the quarry at nearby Bibémus (see page 488) or one of the views of Sainte-Victoire (see page 485). It is noticeable that most of his canvases depict bright or lightly overcast weather. Because he needed time to build up his carefully structured compositions, the steady light of the Mediterranean appealed to him more than the transient effects of light and the seasonal extremes of snow and rain that so attracted his contemporaries, such as Claude Monet. Contemporary accounts describe how Cézanne would gaze intently at his chosen scene, weighing up the evidence of his eyes for several minutes before darting at his canvas with a rapid movement of the brush. At times his patience and his sense of his own achievement deserted him and he would slash the canvas with a knife or hurl it into the bushes.

Cézanne's painstaking approach to his art was rarely compromised by the demands of the market-place, since he was supported by the allowance from his father and by sporadic contributions from the increasingly successful Zola. One or two brave collectors and fellow artists bought his canvases – though at very modest prices – but his decision to stop exhibiting with the Impressionists after the third Impressionist Exhibition of 1877 ensured that his work was entirely unknown to the general public. His life revolved around his painting, and both his journeys to and from Paris and his periods of residence in towns near Aix, such as L'Estaque and Gardanne, were part of a restless relationship with his "motifs."

As Cézanne approached the age of fifty, the modest pattern of his life and his erratic cohabitations with Hortense and young Paul seemed as settled as at any point in his early life. But in 1886, three events occurred that were to affect him profoundly and completely alter his circumstances. Early in the year, Zola published his novel *l'Oeuvre* ("The Masterpiece"), the story of a failed painter who was clearly based on Cézanne. The two men's friendship had already cooled considerably, but Cézanne was deeply hurt, and resolved to sever all connections with his childhood friend. Shortly afterwards,

GUSTAVE COURBET
Still life with Apples and Pomegranate
1871, National Gallery, London

As a young man, Cézanne had been inspired by the vigorous independence of Courbet's personality and also by the flourishing application of paint in some of his pictures. Though he was later to belittle this influence, Courbet's ability to capture the drama of everyday objects unpretentiously arranged must have contributed something to Cézanne's own development of the still life.

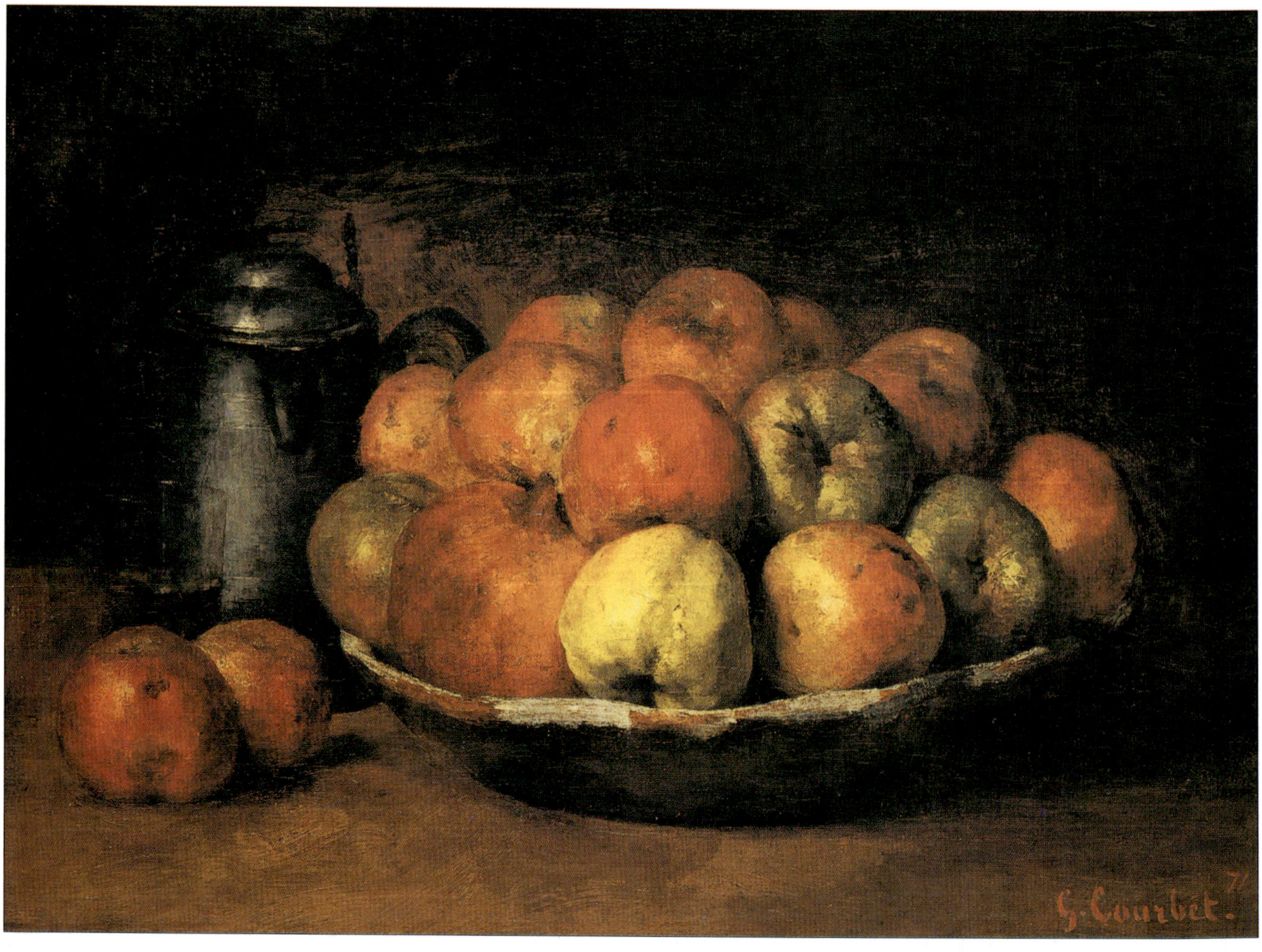

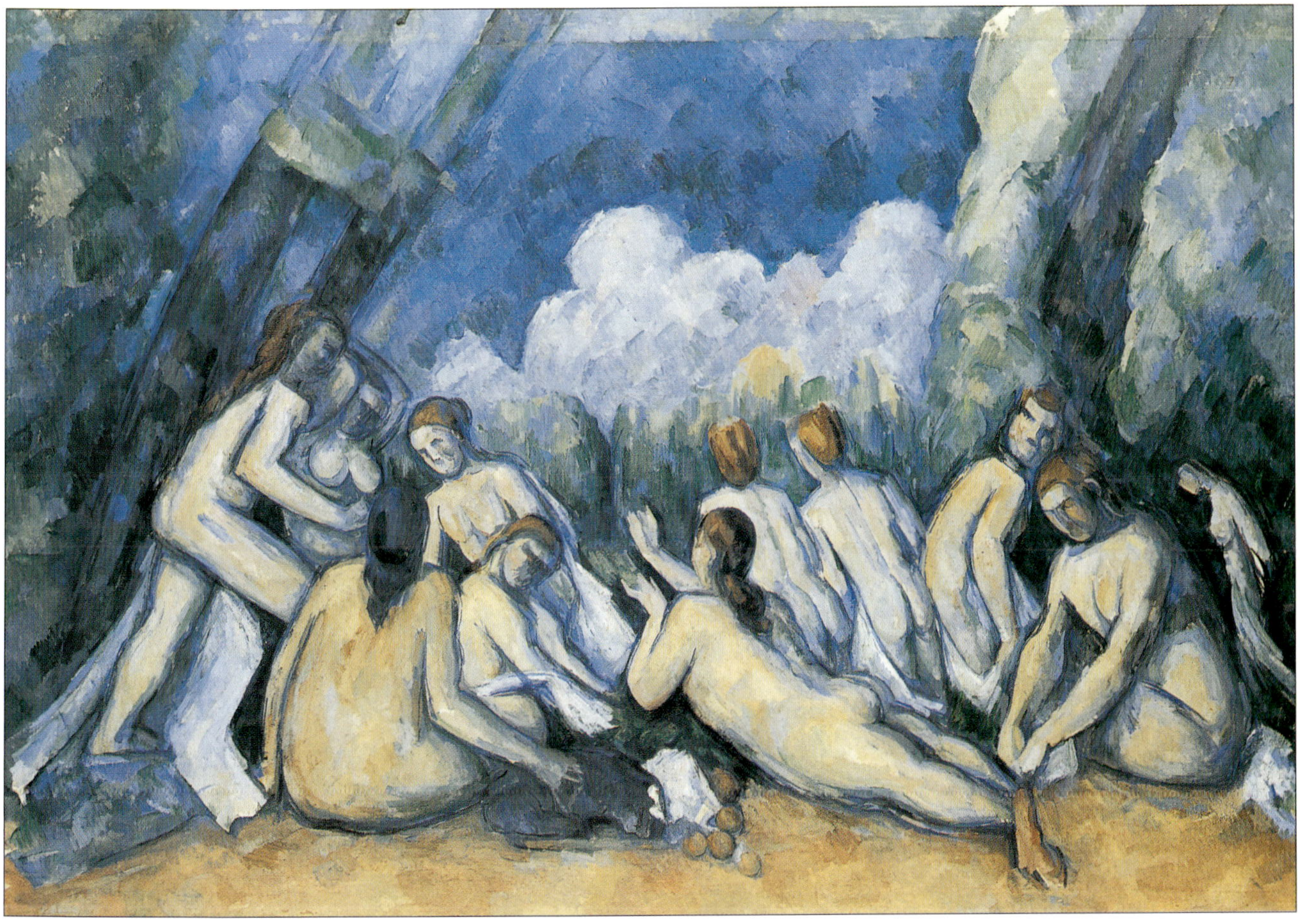

Cézanne publicly married Hortense in a church at Aix, thus legitimizing his son Paul and bringing to an end the years of deceit and procrastination. Within months of the ceremony, Cézanne's eighty-eight-year-old father died, leaving his substantial estate to his son, and so ensuring him a steady income for the remaining thirty years of his life. Released from the dominance of his parents, reconciled with his family and with the demands of conventional propriety, Cézanne was now free to follow his vocation and to live the life he chose.

PAUL CEZANNE
Bathers
c 1905, National Gallery, London

Still in his studio at the time of his death, and probably unfinished, this large canvas is one of a monumental group of three that Cézanne worked on in the early 20th century. The subject is improbable, the figures vacant and anatomically brutalized, but the composition achieves an extraordinary frieze-like gravity that reminds us of Cézanne's admiration for classical art.

Still life and the nude

In spite of his dedication to landscape and portraiture, two other subjects continued to preoccupy Cézanne throughout his mature years. The best known is still life, a *genre* with which his name will always be associated. Gathering together a few simple household objects, such as wine bottles, plates and water jugs, and interspersing them with the common fruit, vegetables and flowers of Provence, he constructed magical worlds of sensation that are amongst his most admired achievements. He would spend hours arranging these little groups, and days or even weeks painting them, rendering each of the subtle relationships of form and color that revealed themselves to his analytical eye. Conscious, as always, of tradition, Cézanne saw himself as a descendant of both the 18th-century still life painter Jean-Baptiste Chardin and of Gustave Courbet, one of the heroes of his youth. But in his hands still-life painting was transformed, the previously humble *genre* becoming one of the great modern vehicles of artistic innovation.

The idea Cézanne had of himself as part of a continuing tradition in Western art is particularly evident in the other recurring subject of his career, the nude. From his earliest years he had drawn the human figure, from models, from paintings and sculptures, and from his imagination. He returned time after time to certain

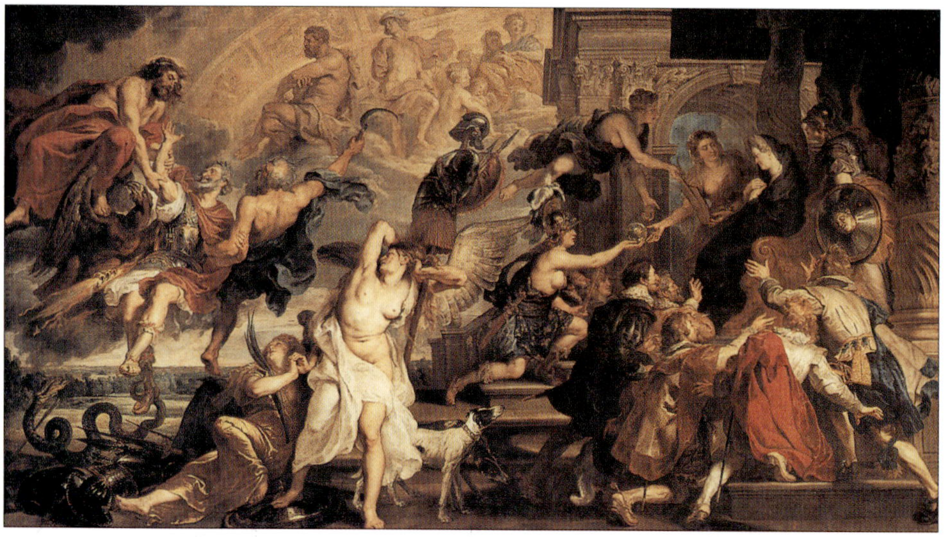

PETER PAUL RUBENS
The Apotheosis of Henri IV
c 1621, Louvre, Paris

When asked to nominate his favorite painter, Cézanne chose the Flemish Baroque master, Rubens. On a number of occasions he studied and copied Rubens's pictures in the Louvre, and the central figure with the raised elbow in this *Apotheosis* occurs in a number of guises in his own compositions.

poses based on the works of Rubens, Michelangelo and Poussin, and even claimed a lifelong ambition to create a large composition of nudes, such as those of Poussin, but to paint it in the open air, an ambition he was never able to fulfil. For a number of reasons he appears to have had trouble hiring models, and in his mature years he worked almost exclusively from earlier drawings or from memory. The subject, however, lost none of its significance, and in the early years of the 20th century he embarked upon a group of huge, spirited, almost visionary compositions of female nudes, their bodies subordinated to the demands of pictorial orchestration.

The "grand old man" of painting

Cézanne's reputation among a small group of artists, critics and collectors had been quietly growing for some time, and in 1895, when he was fifty-six, the insularity of his existence was effectively ended by the first retrospective exhibition of his work, held at the Paris gallery of the dealer Ambroise Vollard. He was now able to enjoy an unexpected, belated celebrity, and a steady stream of writers and fellow painters began to make the pilgrimage to Aix. Although still defensive of his working routine, he could be surprisingly warm towards younger artists, and explained to them, sometimes in letters which survive today, a number of his views on art. He insisted on nature as his primary inspiration and on the need to recognize the intensity of visual experience. Art was not a copy of nature, but a "parallel" to it, and even in his last years he recorded his continuing frustration as he tried to "realize" his motif.

In spite of deteriorating health, Cézanne persisted in his habitual and obsessive routines until his death in 1906. Hardly leaving the Aix area, he still preferred to work in the open air from his favorite vantage points, often returning to subjects he had painted dozens of times before. His sense of the complexity of art, of its intimate but paradoxical relationship to the perceived world, had deepened, and he continued to experiment with new techniques and ideas until his last months. At times he would strip down the shapes of his chosen subject to a few spare lines and forms, like the ellipses of a bowl of fruit or the parallels of branches and tree trunks, while at others he would build up dense and subtle reverberations of color, texture and surface incident. In his late paintings, the language of his art announces itself with increasing clarity, insisting on its separateness from observed nature while moving closer to the "vibrating sensations" of the scene that he himself described.

Among the young artists who discovered Cézanne's painting in the years before his death were some of the major figures of the Parisian avant-garde, notably Matisse, Braque and Picasso. A series of exhibitions of the elderly master's work was held in Paris at the turn of the century, and his influence can be felt in the younger artists' choice of subjects, color harmonies and stylistic devices. Georges Braque went as far as to travel to Provence to paint in front of some of Cézanne's subjects, while Picasso was principally attracted to the great bather pictures. His admiration for Cézanne is openly acknowledged in his *Demoiselles d'Avignon* of 1907, one of the cornerstones of Cubism and of early 20th-century art. Although Cézanne did not live to see these developments – and might not have approved of them if he had – he was clearly gratified by the attentions of the younger generation. Sensing the significance of his work for the future of painting, he declared at the end of his life that, "I am the primitive of a new art."

CEZANNE'S PAINTING METHODS

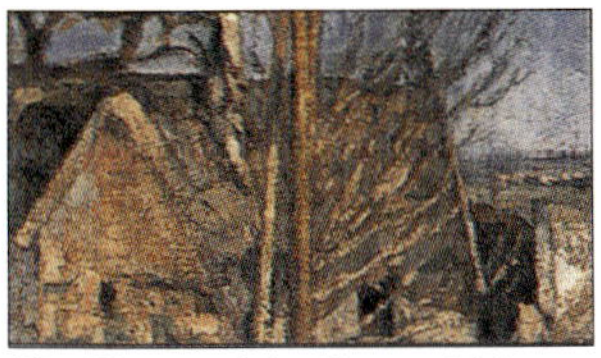

The House of the Hanged Man is one of Cézanne's most densely worked canvases. The encrusted paint seen in this detail is suggestive of the building's weathered texture.

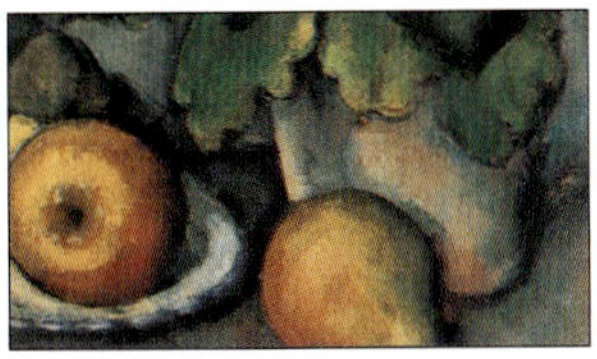

This detail from *Still Life with Apples and Pears* shows the marvelous variety of different colors Cézanne used for each area of a painting.

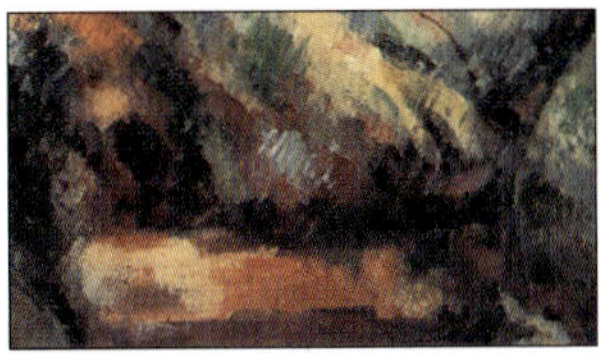

In Cézanne's mature works, such as *The Red Rock*, each brushstroke is carefully planned. One incorrectly judged color or tone would destroy the harmony.

Although Cézanne's name is often linked with the Impressionists, and he exhibited with the group in the first three Impressionist Exhibitions, his preoccupations and technique were very different. After painting side by side with Pissarro in the 1870s, he became deeply committed to working outdoors, directly from his "motif," or subject, but unlike the Impressionists, who were concerned with immediate and transient effects, and painted rapidly, Cézanne was a slow and laborious worker, and his studies from nature were sustained over a period of time. Because he often returned to the same canvas months or even years later, the relatively stable light of the south of France suited him, as did still life painting, which gave him total control over the lighting and arrangement of his subject matter. All the compositions of his mature years, whether landscapes, still lifes or portraits, are carefully thought out. His fastidious concern for finding the exact tone or color for each brushstroke reflects his desire to construct an overall harmony of color, tone and surface pattern in which no note was out of tune — a painterly equivalent to the harmony seen in nature. For his oil paintings, he used a relatively limited palette, usually working on a pale cream ground which he left uncovered or lightly covered in places to read as a color in its own right. His characteristic broad brushstrokes are used not only to express volume and solidity but also to shape the composition, his most quoted advice, to "see nature in terms of the cone, the cylinder and the sphere" being matched by an equally strong sense of the structure of the painting.

Mountains in Provence was painted on primed paper, the equivalent to today's oil-sketching paper. It was later mounted on canvas. The choice of support was unusual, as Cézanne normally worked on canvas; he may have chosen it for reasons of portability, as the painting, one of his sustained studies from nature, was clearly not regarded as a sketch. His palette probably consisted of the colors shown below.

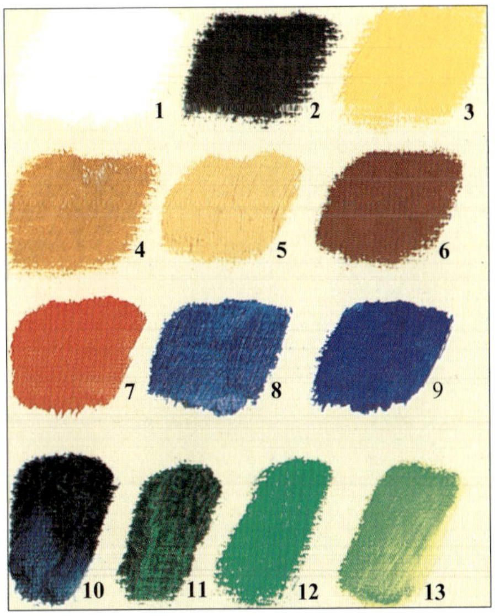

1 zinc white; 2 black; 3 chrome yellow; 4 yellow ocher; 5 Naples yellow;
6, 7 red earth or vermilion;
8 cobalt blue; 9 ultramarine; 10 Prussian blue;
11 viridian; 12 emerald green; 13 chrome green

CHRONOLOGY OF CEZANNE'S LIFE

1839 January 19: Paul Cézanne born in Aix-en-Provence.

1849-52 Attends Ecole St Joseph in Aix-en-Provence.

1852-58 Attends Collège Bourbon in Aix. Beginning of friendship with Emile Zola.

1858-59 Works at drawing academy at Aix.

1859 Father acquires house, Jas de Bouffan.

1861 First residence in Paris.

1863 Exhibits at the Salon des Refusés.

1870 Stays at L'Estaque with his mistress Hortense Fiquet. Submits *Portrait of Achille Emperaire* to Salon, but it is rejected.

1872 Birth of Cézanne's son, Paul. Lives near Pissarro at Pontoise. The two artists work together.

1873 Moves to Auvers-sur-Oise, meets Dr Gachet, who later befriended Van Gogh.

1874 Cézanne shows three pictures in the first Impressionist Exhibition.

1875-86 Lives intermittently at Aix, L'Estaque, Gardanne, Pontoise, Paris and elsewhere. Several visits to Zola at Medan.

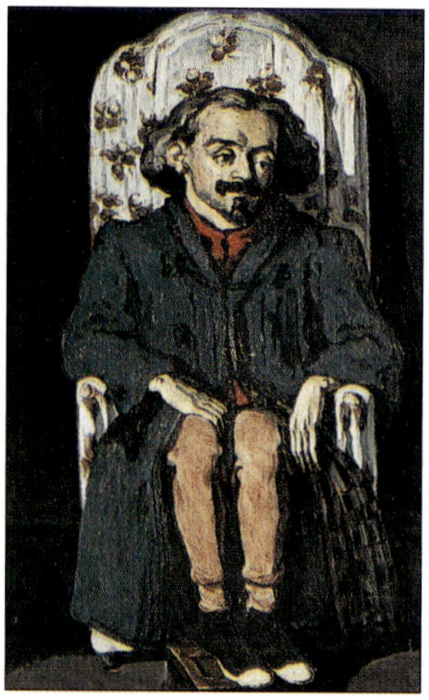

Portrait of Achille Emperaire

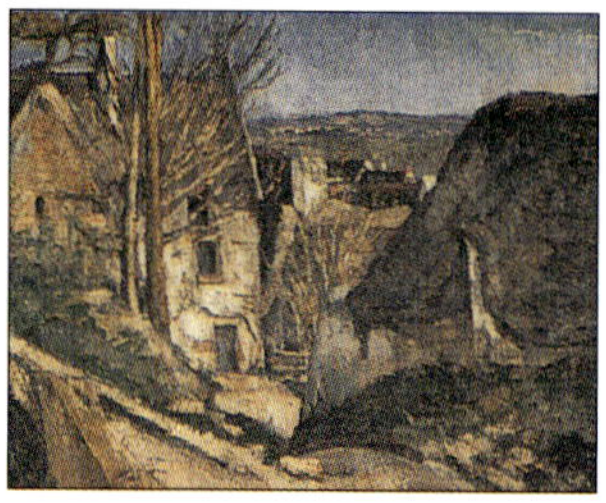

The House of the Hanged Man

1877 Exhibits sixteen pictures at the third Impressionist Exhibition.

1886 Cézanne marries Hortense Fiquet, mother of his son Paul. Louis-Auguste Cézanne, the artist's father, dies, leaving him a substantial legacy.

1889 Renoir visits Cézanne in Provence.

1890 Invited to exhibit in Brussels. Travels with his family for a holiday in Switzerland.

1894 Visits Monet at Giverny.

1895 First one-man show at Vollard's gallery in Paris.

1896-99 Residence in Paris and Aix.

1897 Death of Cézanne's mother.

1899 Sells Jas de Bouffan to settle father's estate. Rents apartment in Aix. Paints portrait of Vollard.

1901 Plans the building of a new studio overlooking Aix.

1904 Exhibitions of Cézanne's work in Brussels and Paris.

1906 Exhibits in Paris at the Salon d'Automne. October 15: collapses while painting outdoors, and has to be carried home. Dies on October 22, aged sixty-seven. Buried in Aix-en-Provence.

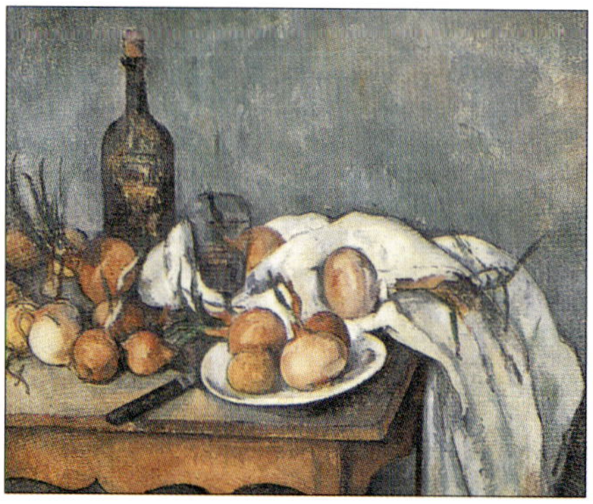

Still Life with Onions

THE PAINTINGS

Portrait of Achille Emperaire

c1868-70
$78\frac{3}{4}\times 48$in/200×122cm
Oil on canvas
Musée d'Orsay, Paris

One of the largest and most haunting of Cézanne's early canvases, this picture was important to him both as a personal document and as a milestone in his artistic development. It is an ambitious, fully resolved and large-scale work, testifying to the emergence of a confident and aspiring young artist.

Achille Emperaire, a painter friend of Cézanne's from his home town of Aix-en-Provence, was about a decade older, but a curious affinity united them from their earliest meetings at the drawing academy in Aix. Little is known about Emperaire, but his few surviving paintings and drawings are small, intense and often erotic studies of human figures which clearly had a considerable influence on Cézanne. On a number of occasions in later life, Cézanne became fiercely defensive about his friend, contrasting his seriousness and integrity with the pretentiousness of contemporary art. He even wrote to Zola in Paris in 1878, pleading with him to find a job for Emperaire, who seems to have been in continual financial difficulties throughout his life.

In contrast to many of Cézanne's large pictures begun in the late 1860s, the portrait of Emperaire is a study of a real subject rather than one drawn from the artist's imagination, and its great strength derives from the abrupt confrontation with an image so familiar and of such personal significance. The figure is centrally placed, the chair parallel to the picture-plane, the body symmetrical except for minor inflections of head, hand and feet. A brilliant source of light illuminates both sitter and chair (the same chair appears in a number of pictures of Cézanne's home), and the primitive lettering added at the top of the canvas suggests a heraldic, almost regal image of authority. Emperaire's hair and beard, more 18th- than 19th-century in style, contribute to this effect, suggesting the enthronement of a neglected genius — or possibly a pun on the sitter's imperial-sounding name.

Several preparatory drawings for the picture survive, notably for the monumental head of the subject. These have something of the elegance and refinement of Rubens, an artist Cézanne admired deeply, and they give an idea of the complex stylistic maneuverings that Cézanne was involved in at this stage in his career. His early life drawings show that he could produce conventional, disciplined studies when required, but much of his art from the 1860s shows a rejection of contemporary style and a search for a more challenging, personal way of working. The thick, textured paint of this portrait and the boldly outlined contours, as well as the aggressive directness of the image, are all part of a public assertion of the artist's uncompromising temperament.

Not surprisingly, when Cézanne submitted the portrait to the Government-sponsored annual Salon of 1870, along with a picture of a reclining nude (subsequently lost), both pictures were rejected. The painting provoked a largely satirical response amongst those present at the judging, and the cartoonist Stock produced a caricature of a monstrous, bearded Cézanne with his grotesque submissions. Stock also claimed to have interviewed Cézanne, and drawn from him such views as "I paint how I see and how I feel" and "I have the courage of my convictions, and he who laughs last, laughs loudest." The portrait of Achille Emperaire was one of the last group of pictures which Cézanne intended as gestures towards an uncomprehending establishment, and it is the majestic and deeply felt realism of this study that points the way to the future.

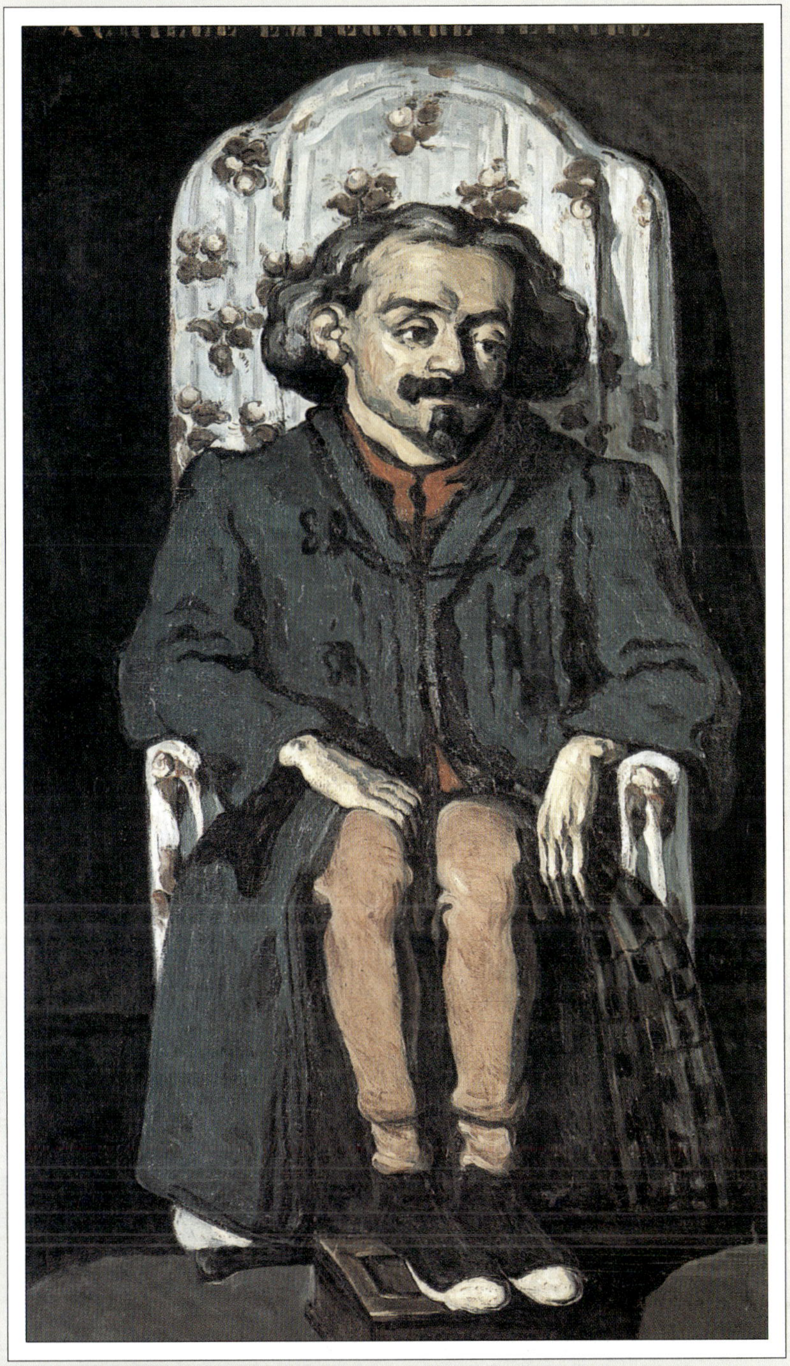

The surface of the canvas is thickly encrusted with paint over much of its surface, and many areas, such as the face and hands, show evidence of considerable over-painting. Some of Cézanne's pictures from this period emerged only after a long struggle, both with the medium and with the demands of the subject, but the artist was always capable of displays of great fluency, such as the painting of the floral chairback.

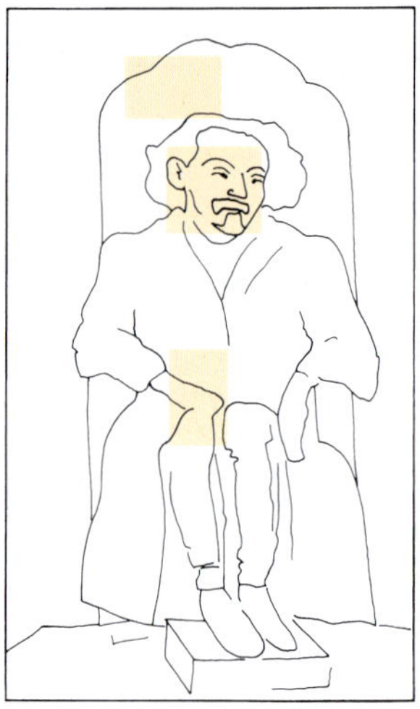

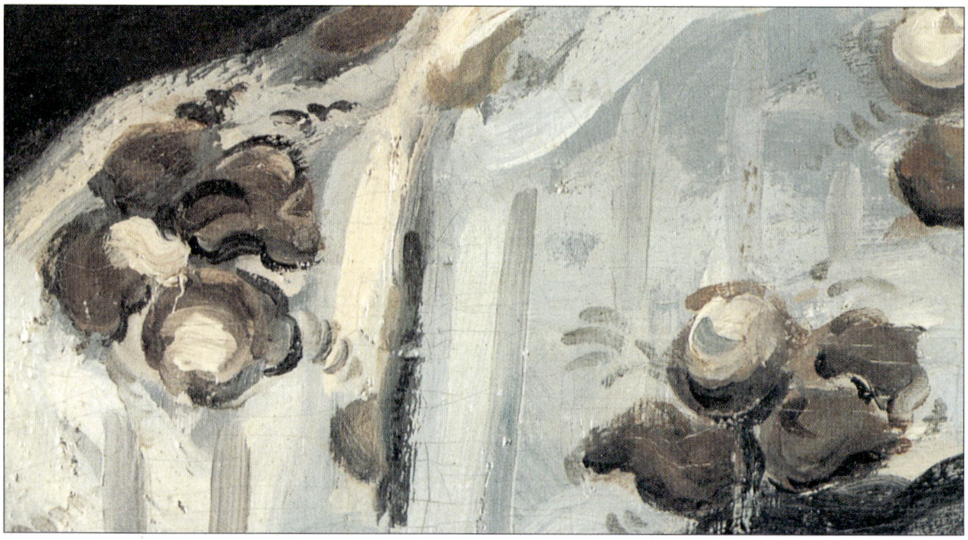

1

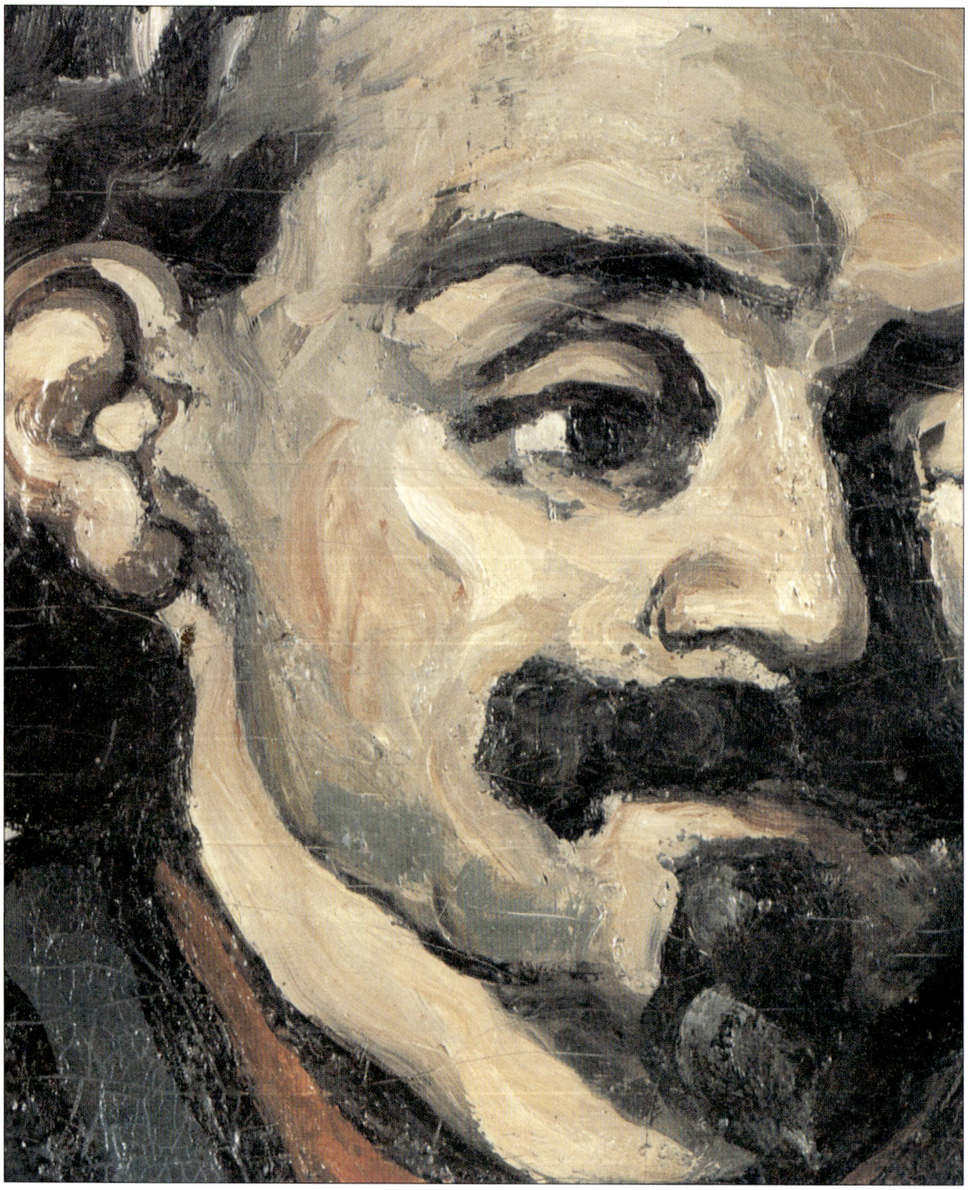

2

1 The patterned fabric of this upright and rather uncomfortable-looking chair appears in several of Cézanne's domestic portraits, most famously in an identically sized study of his own father begun two or three years earlier. In this picture the boldly depicted floral motif and the heavily impasted paint help to draw attention to the flatness and frontality of the painting, as do the stencilled lettering and the symmetrical pose.

2 The thick crust of oil paint almost appears to be out of control in some areas of the picture, but in Emperaire's head the vigorous black outlining and modeling give it strength and purpose. It is noticeable how a rhythmic flow directs the movement of the brushstrokes, following the contours of chin, bone-structure and facial features.

3 *Actual size detail* Emperaire suffered from a debilitating condition that left his legs and body underdeveloped, thus making his head appear abnormally large. Cézanne has chosen to celebrate his friend by drawing particular attention to those parts of him that were most deformed, thrusting the legs forward and emphasizing the pale hands by contrast with the dark background. The slender, limp fingers seem quite pitiful against the rest of this vigorously constructed painting.

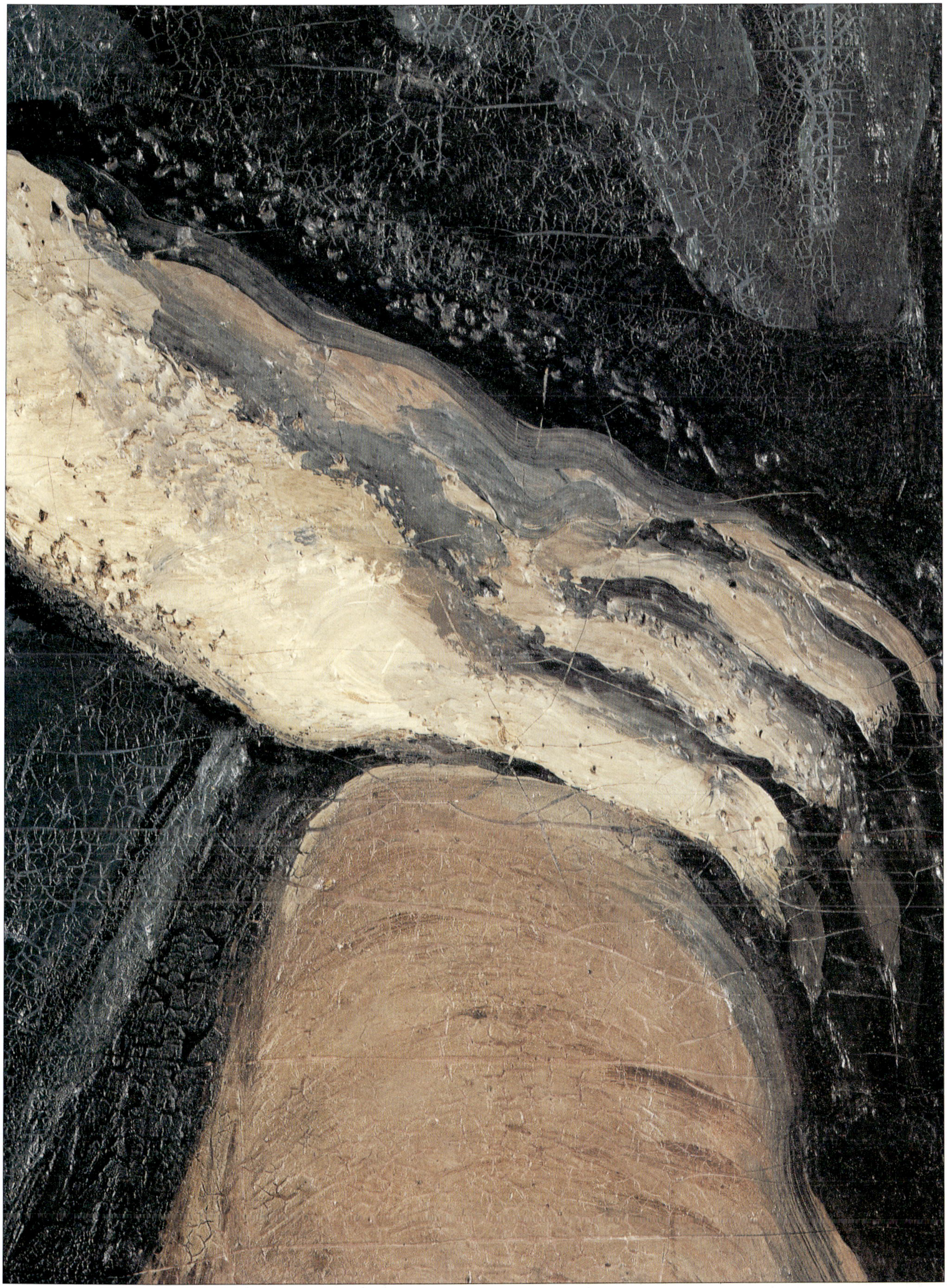

3 *Actual size detail*

Self-portrait

c1872
$25^{1}/_{4} \times 20^{1}/_{2}$in/$64 \times 52$cm
Oil on canvas
Musée d'Orsay, Paris

It is hard to believe that Cézanne was only thirty-three years old when he painted this picture. The description of his stocky torso, dramatically balding cranium and unruly sidelocks all suggest either a ruthless honesty in his presentation of himself or an almost theatrical attempt to shock the viewer. Cézanne was either careless about his appearance or deliberately cultivated a wild bohemian look, and it is said that children threw stones at him in the street.

At the time this portrait was painted, Cézanne was going through one of the most challenging phases of his career. Behind him lay his struggle to find independence from his family and his desperate attempts to assert himself as an artist in a society where, as he saw it, only polished technique and superficial display were admired. His early pictures of gruesome or fantastical encounters between imaginary human beings had inevitably suffered rejection, but slowly he had been turning to other ideas and other possibilities for his future. Under the influence of Pissarro, Guillaumin and other members of the emerging Impressionist group, he was experimenting with a more direct approach to painting, based on firsthand observation and a fresh encounter with the notion of Realism. Painting outdoors, side-by-side with his friends, he re-assessed the rich textures, vivid colors and infinitely varied shapes that he saw in nature, bringing these new discoveries back into the portraits and still lifes developed in his studio.

His personal circumstances had also changed; this self-portrait coincides with the year in which his only son, Paul, was born out of wedlock to his mistress Hortense Fiquet. It is more than likely that the exceptional gravity of the portrait marks a moment of self-assessment, and we see the artist surveying himself in the role of father and breadwinner to his small family. The gaze is implacable, the eyes black and severe, the pose little short of truculent. Little is known of the private relations of Cézanne with his immediate family, but it is worth reflecting that this formidable man had attracted the attentions of the pretty and fashion-conscious Hortense, even though she was more than ten years his junior, and that he was to become an affectionate father.

The technique of the *Self-portrait* vividly illustrates the transitional stage of Cézanne's painting. The heavy nature of the paint-surface and the extensive use of black both belong to the previous decade, and were rarely to be seen again in his mature work. Even the gestural flourishes of the brush, almost scribbled over thickly painted underlayers or smeared across still-wet color, suggest an impatience that was soon to be mastered. But the handling of the face suggests analysis rather than intuition: the subtle shifts of tone and color are carefully scrutinized, and the brushwork organized — albeit in a rudimentary manner — to echo the structure of the face. The fresh touches of color, the greens in the shadow and the pinks in eyelid and nostril, show that Cézanne's discoveries while painting in the open air were now beginning to bear fruit in his studio works. The face is alive with suggestive nuance and tense energy, the fluid paint evoking hazardous decisions and bold improvisation.

As if to summarize his own change of direction, Cézanne has posed himself in front of a canvas by his friend Armand Guillaumin, a picture that was probably included in the first Impressionist Exhibition in 1874. It has a double significance: not only is it a landscape, a subject that Cézanne was increasingly to adopt during this decade, but it was also associated with that radical group of young artists who were soon to present a new kind of art to the Parisian public.

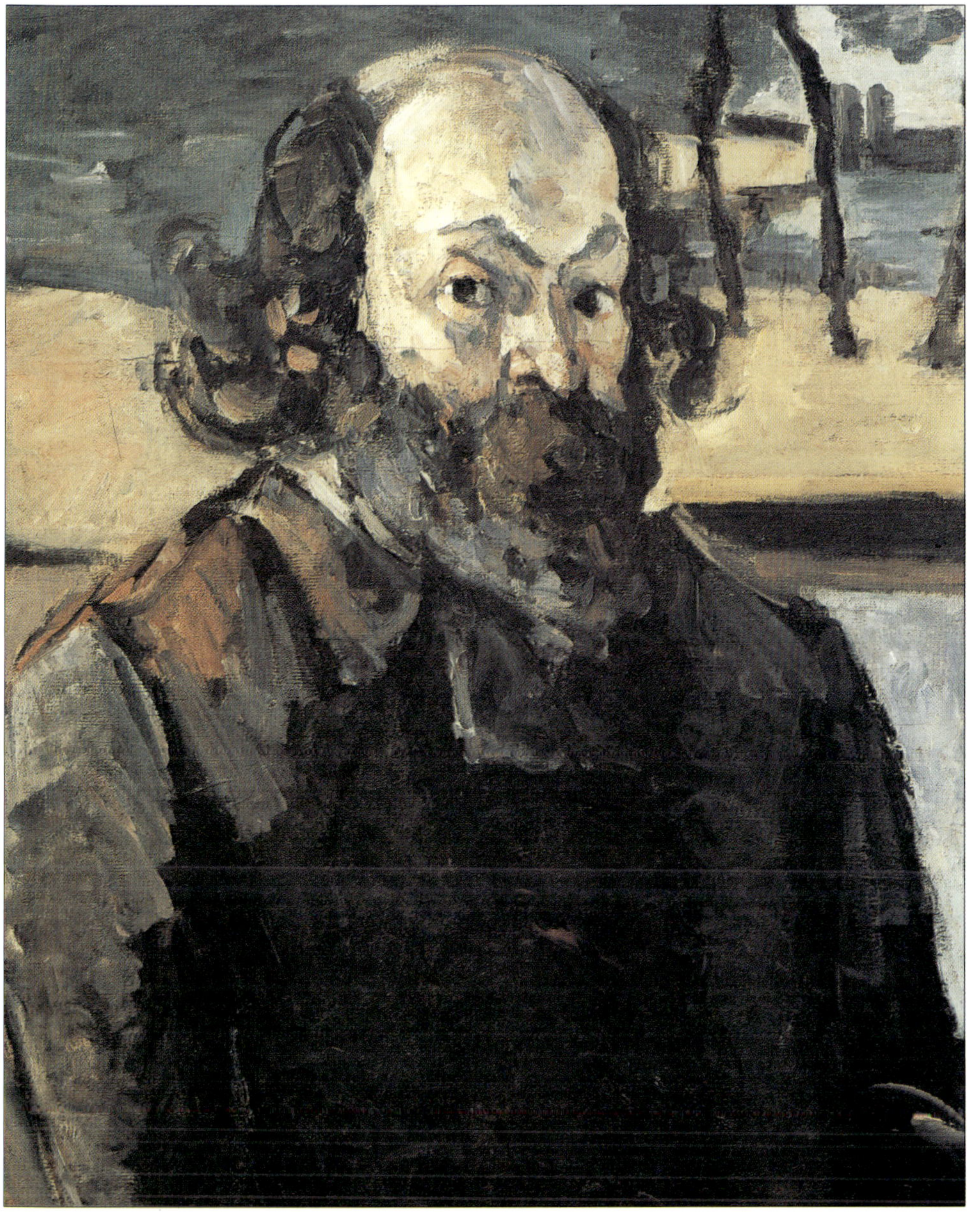

Cézanne painted more than twenty self-portraits in the course of his career, though this is perhaps his most disconcerting. In later examples he adopts a more distant expression, and emphasizes the subtle play of light and color on his own features, but here he is defiant. Inspired perhaps by the dramatic self-scrutiny of Rembrandt or the posturing of Courbet, he has placed his face in a central pool of light and surrounded it with a riot of unkempt hair. The result is authoritative, messianic and entrancing. The penetrating gaze of the eye reminds us of Monet's description of Cézanne as "Only an eye, but my God, what an eye!" The act of looking and analyzing had by this time become increasingly central to his art, and in this portrait he has given vivid form to the center of his own visual world through the rich manipulation of pigment and the sharp juxtaposition of colors and tones.

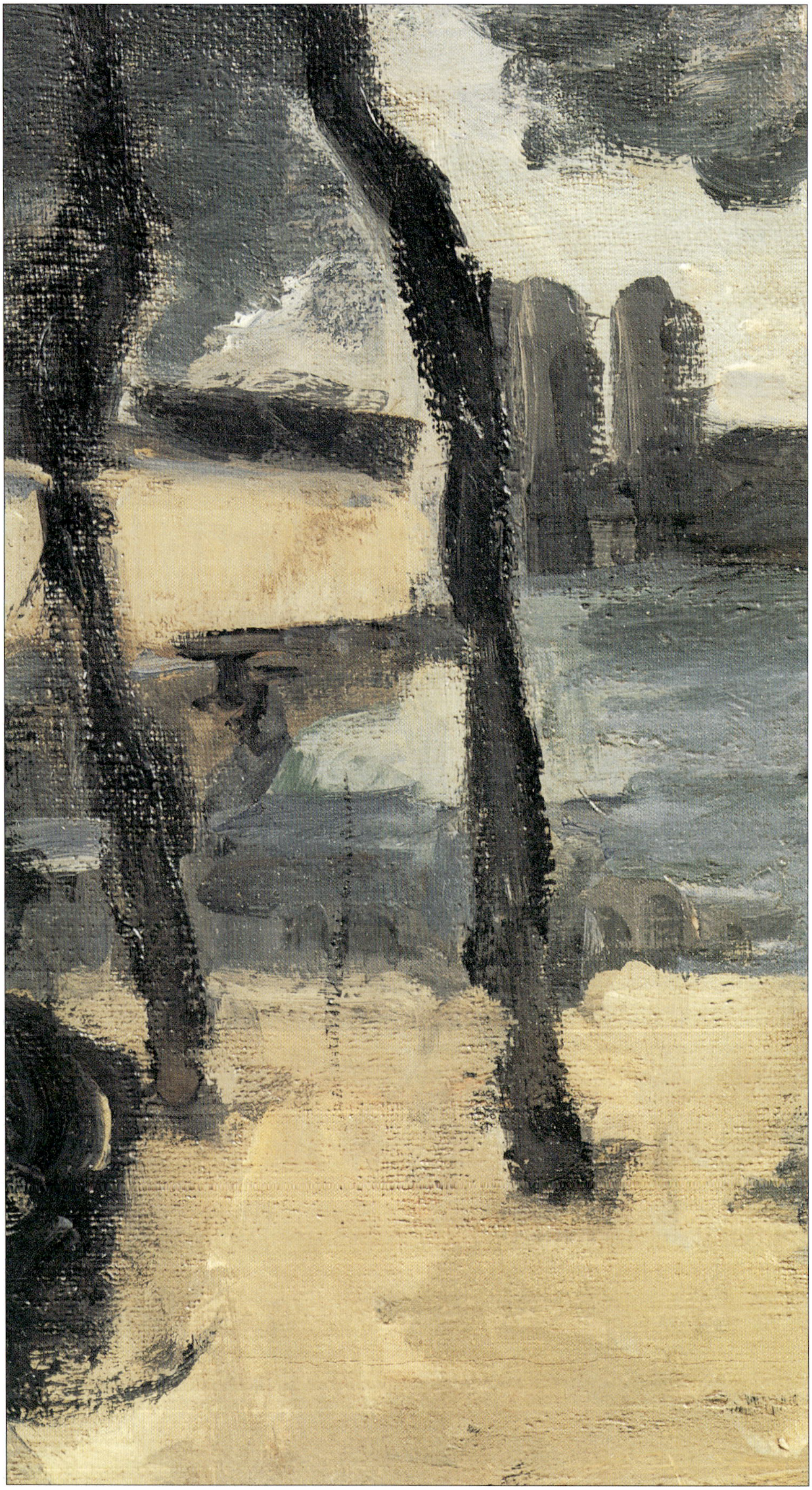

1

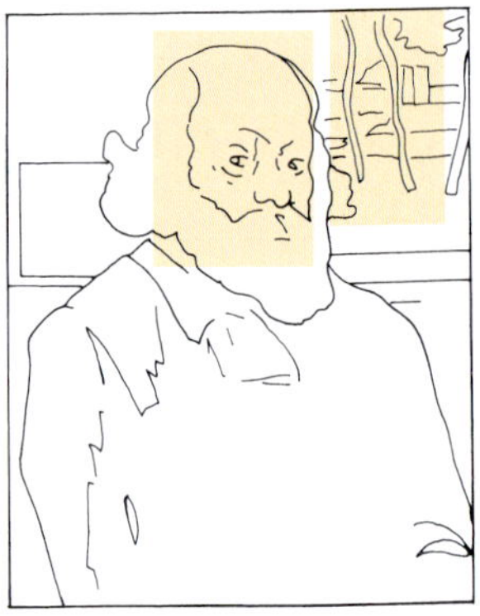

1 The painting by Guillaumin that Cézanne has placed behind his head is in reality a detailed study of the embankment of the Seine, complete with figures, boats and a distant Notre-Dame. In order to concentrate attention on his own features, Cézanne has shown it in simplified form. The painting, which is reversed by the mirror used in the self-portrait, is here reduced to a few blocks of color, with Notre-Dame merely suggested by two vertical brushmarks.

2 *Actual size detail* In places the weave of the canvas can be glimpsed beneath the paint, but most of the face has been built up quite heavily with thick, undiluted paint. Much of it has been applied while earlier brushmarks were still wet, allowing adjacent colors to blend into each other but retaining a few streaks of pure, unmixed hue.

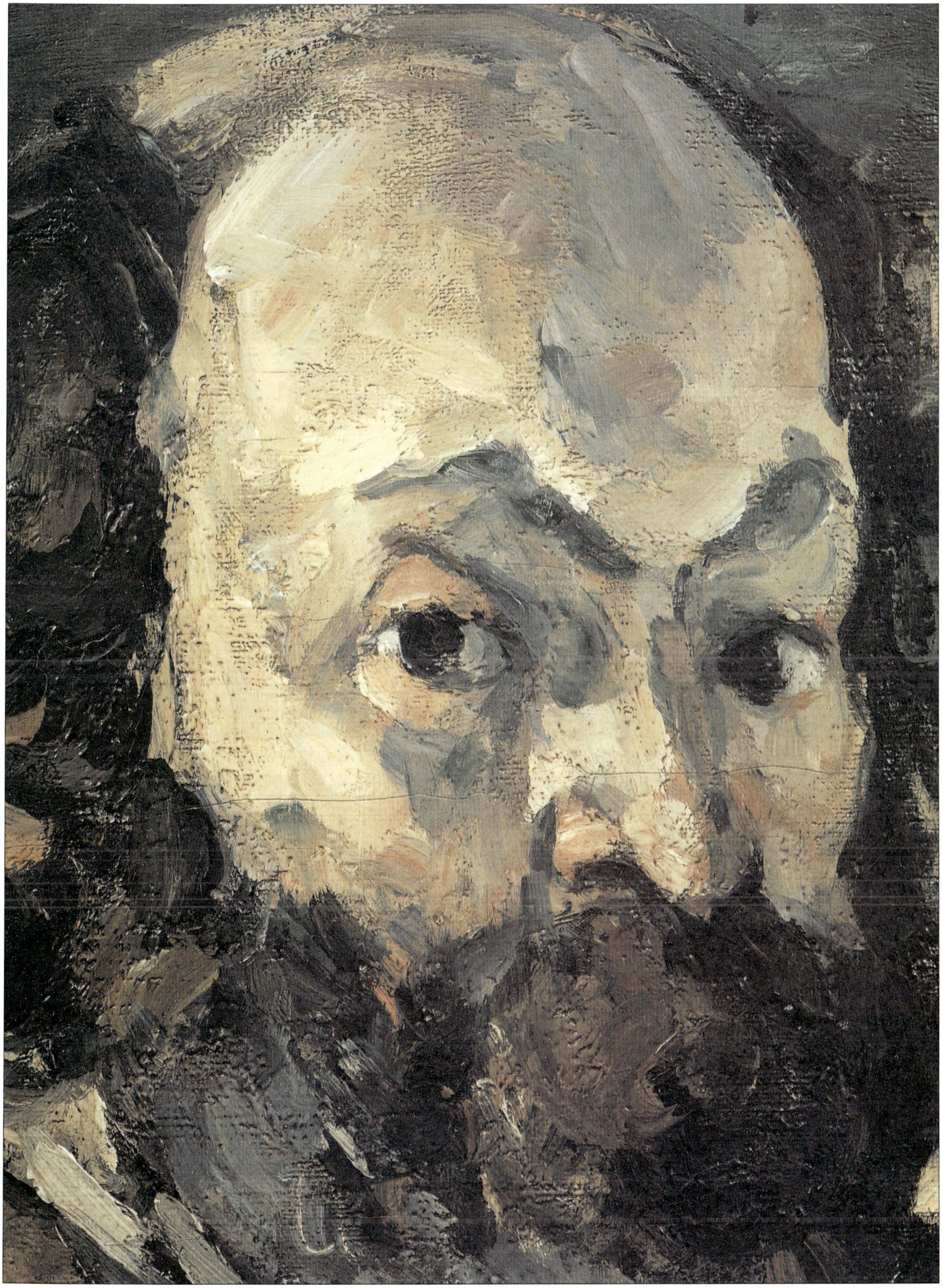

2 *Actual size detail*

Three Bathers

c1877
$7^1/_2 \times 8^5/_8$in/19×22cm
Oil on canvas
Musée d'Orsay, Paris

It was one of the great ambitions of Cézanne's career to create large-scale compositions based on the nude. For centuries the nude had been regarded as the ultimate challenge for the artist, and the masters Cézanne most admired, such as Michelangelo, Veronese, Rubens and Poussin, were all supreme exponents of the European figure-painting tradition. Cézanne saw himself as part of this continuing tradition, and regularly visited the Louvre to study and copy the works of his predecessors.

The nude appears in his art from the beginning to the very end of his career. He put down hundreds of small studies of male and female figures in his sketchbooks, produced oil paintings varying in scale from the minute to the monumental, and devoted a number of watercolors and even lithographs to the subject. Hardly a year seems to have gone by when he did not develop a new variation on the theme and record his admiration for a painting or sculpture by another artist. But despite all these preparations, Cézanne's ambition to paint epic nude subjects was thwarted, and it was not until the end of his career that he embarked on a group of large-scale canvases appropriate to his vision (see page 459). By that time his health was failing, and the great *Bather* canvases were all left in states of partial completion, heroic fragments of a declining tradition.

The *Three Bathers,* an early and almost miniature example of his obsessive theme, forms part of a distinctive group of small-sized canvases devoted to open-air nudes from the decade of the 1870s. A small pencil drawing, lightly colored with watercolor and identical in almost every respect with the painting, was used to work out the composition of the figures, allowing Cézanne to proceed very directly with the oil painting. Virtually the whole picture surface appears to have been painted wet-in-wet, and there is every indication that the painting was executed at a single sitting, perhaps in a matter of hours.

The subject is both simple and highly complex. At an immediate level, we are presented with one of the most innocent and pleasurable of human occupations, bathing or idling beside a stretch of water in a country setting. One woman may be drying her foot, another rising to attend to her hair and a third squatting on the grass and stretching out her arms. The fact that we, as viewers, are implicitly invading the private space of these bathers seems relatively unimportant here, there being no apparent emphasis on the sexual or erotic possibilities of the scene. But as we look further at the picture, this initial, innocent interpretation begins to lose ground. It is noticeable that the two figures to the right appear to be scowling darkly, and the face of the woman on the left is just an intense streak of reddish-brown. The absence of any pictorially plausible stretch of water reopens the question of the "bathers'" activity, and their poses seem urgent, troubled. A sense of unease begins to pervade the picture, heightened by the alarmingly tilted tree on the left-hand side, and finally vindicated by the discovery of a brownish, mask-like male face amongst the foliage.

Reference to the preliminary drawing shows beyond doubt that Cézanne originally intended a fourth figure for this composition, an intrusive male, whose presence explicitly introduces the notion of voyeurism or even aggression into the tranquil scene. In Cézanne's work, sexual subjects are often shown as tense or violent, but here it is probable that a more specific allusion was intended. The archetypal theme of the beautiful woman discovered in her nakedness by a predatory man has surfaced in a number of guises in Western art, from Diana and Acteon to Susannah and the Elders, and here Cézanne appears to be rediscovering it.

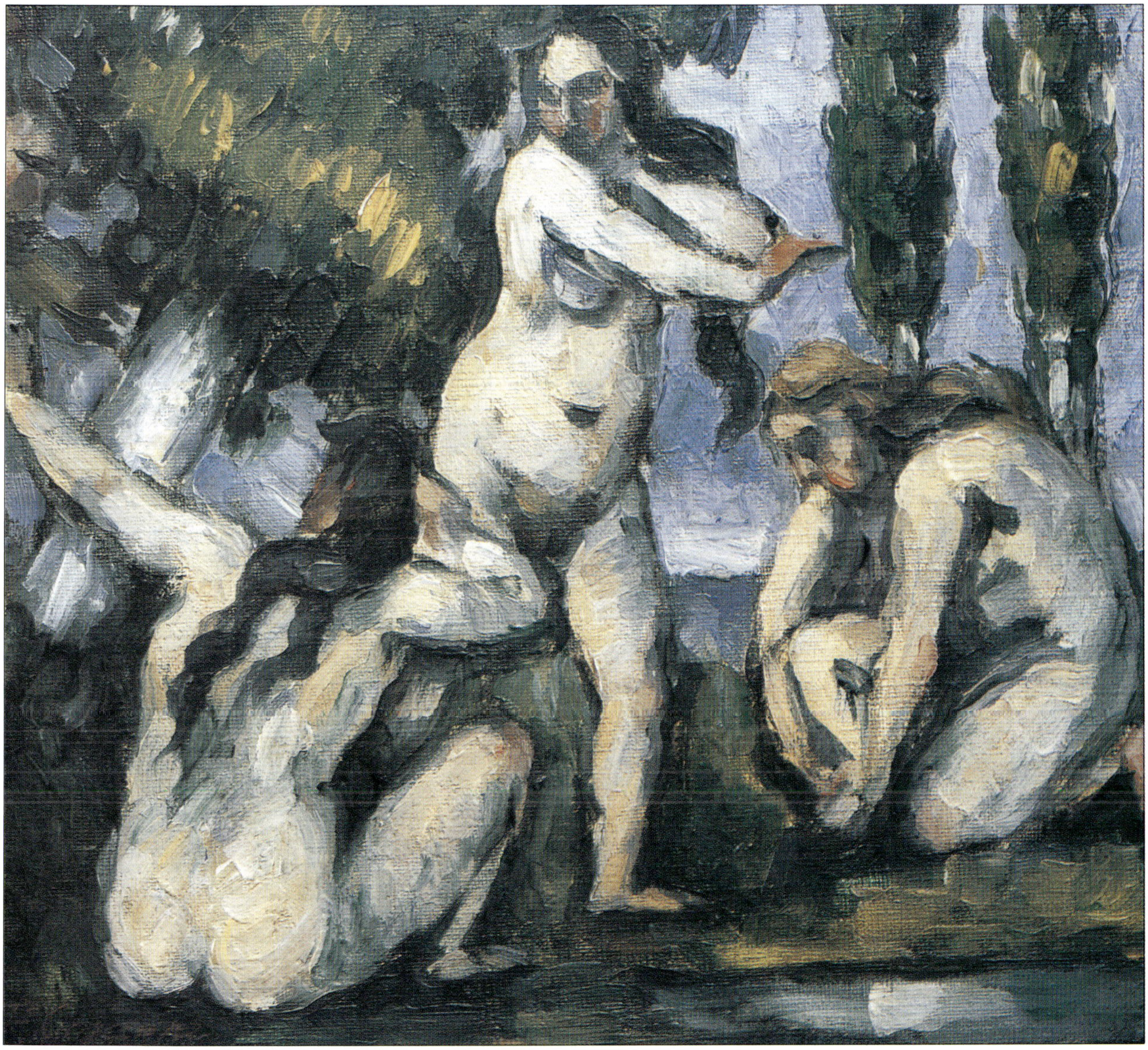

The canvas texture can be seen clearly throughout the picture surface, showing how lightly the paint was applied and how few second thoughts Cézanne had. The main forms of the painting were roughly "drawn" in using dilute dark-green paint and a small brush, after which thicker paint was applied in flickering, nervous touches. An exceptional liveliness and tension animates the picture surface, unprejudiced by a traditional sense of "finish."

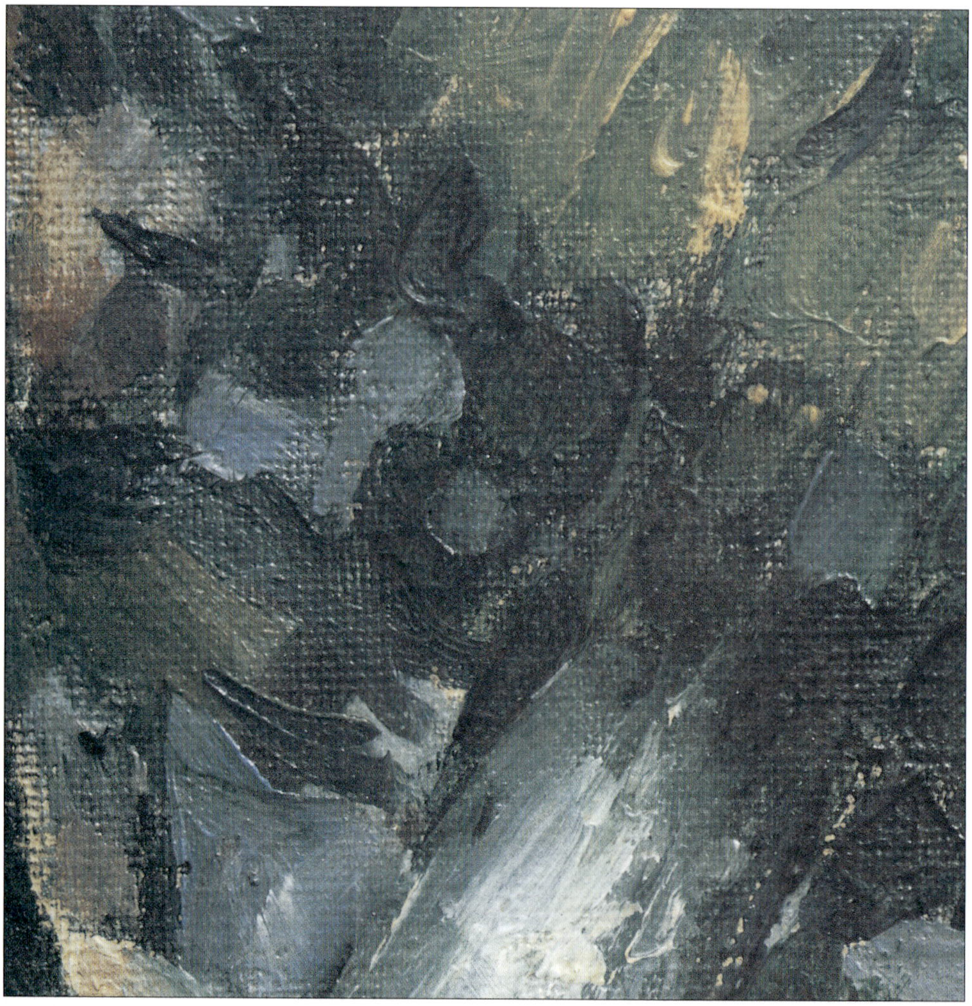

1

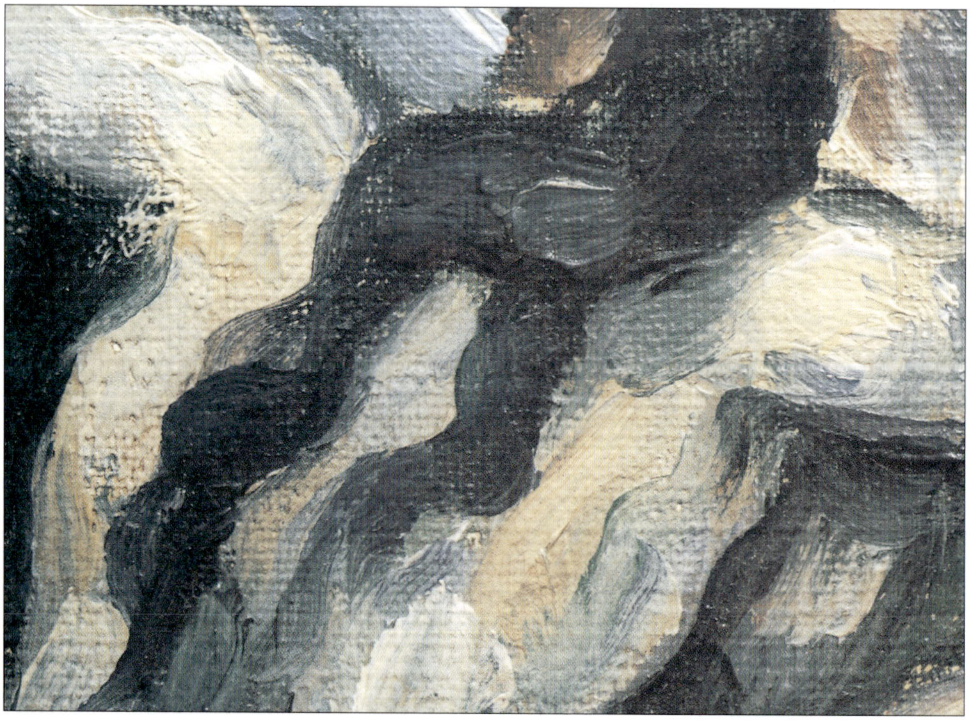

2

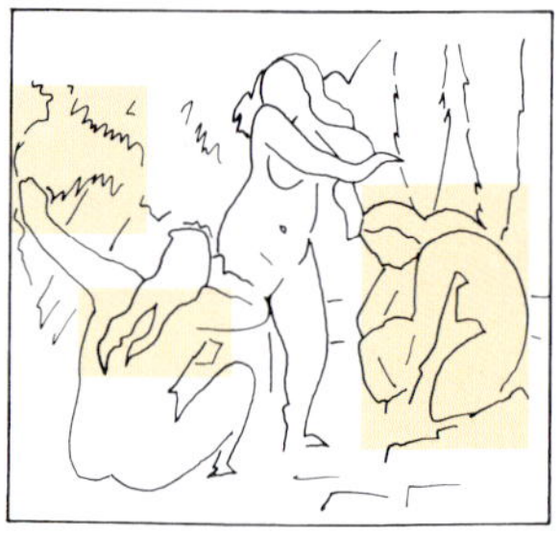

1 Only the coarse flesh-color betrays the male presence amongst the trees. It might have even remained unnoticed had it not been indicated in the working drawing. The drawing shows an adolescent face, while in the painting it seems milder and more bucolic. Such overt references to voyeurism were to disappear in Cézanne's later nude studies.

2 The rhythmic, liquid quality of the brushstrokes is well illustrated in this detail; the woman's back and hair seem to flow or tremble in a single movement. The thin dark green paint of the original underdrawing can be clearly seen, as well as the improvised merging of one wet area of paint with another where later colors were applied.

3 The subject of nude women bathing was taken up by several of Cézanne's Impressionist contemporaries. Renoir, late in his life, was to paint a number of highly popular, idyllic scenes of plump girls on river banks, and Degas had already embarked on his extraordinary paintings and pastels of women washing or bathing. Degas owned one of Cézanne's small nudes, and was perhaps inspired by him to produce a group of outdoor bathing scenes in the 1890s.

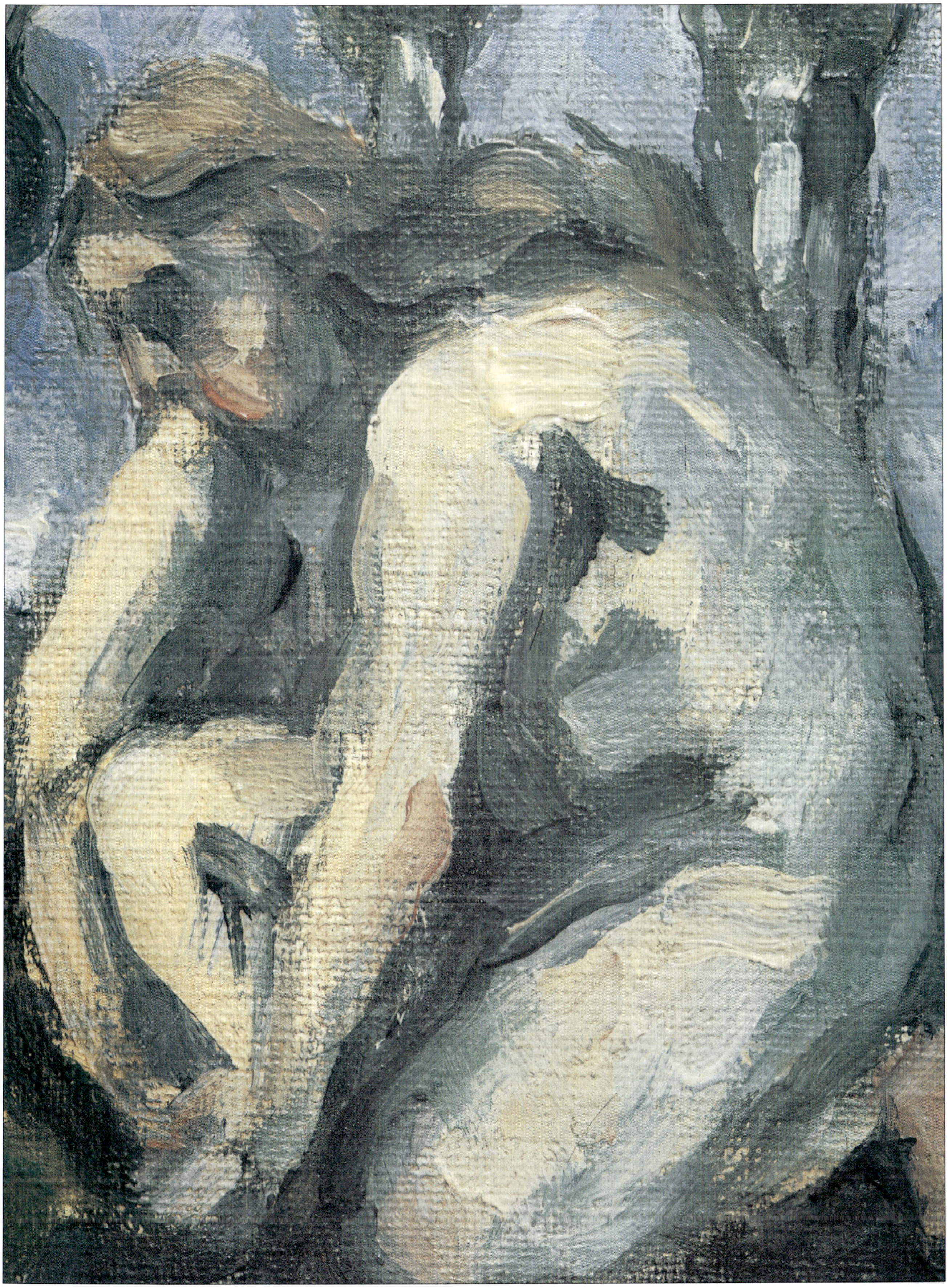

3

Mountains in Provence

c1885

21×28in/53×72cm

Oil on paper, mounted on canvas

National Museum of Wales, Cardiff

The Provençal landscape provided the subject matter for hundreds of Cézanne's paintings. The hot, dry weather of the region suited his way of working, changing little with the advancing seasons, and he noted that even the evergreen shrubs made painting easier by keeping their leaves throughout the year. But his attachment to the landscape was also a historical and emotional one. As a boy he had spent days wandering with his friends in the countryside around Aix, where they would fish, bathe and act out impossibly ambitious plays of their own devising. In later life he wrote nostalgically to his former companions, recalling their days beside the river. As he matured, Cézanne developed a fierce pride in his Provençal origins, stressing the importance of artists from the region, such as Granet and Puget, in his development and encouraging a revival of local literature among his young admirers. Every representation of Provence by Cézanne carries within it some of these associations, and there is always a suggestion of the grown man reliving the memories of a distant youth.

Mountains in Provence is neither large nor ambitious in subject, but it is a perfect summary of the preoccupations and achievements of Cézanne at the beginning of his maturity. The scene encapsulates the Provençal terrain, here looking back from the coastal region of L'Estaque towards the distinctively barren mountainsides of the area. In the middle distance there is a glimpse of water and some modest farm buildings; in the foreground the terraced slopes and stunted shrubs so typical of the Mediterranean landscape. Cézanne has chosen a scene without a central subject, allowing our eyes to wander from area to area within the picture. The line of foreground bushes establishes a sweeping incline that curves back to the block-like cabin, then is picked up again in the diagonals of the hillside. The blue of the water draws the eye back to the left of the painting, and finally the distant mountain swings us back and the circuit begins again. By means of a gentle zigzag from foreground to distance, the artist establishes the necessary space, while a circling movement keeps attention within the picture rectangle.

Cézanne's concern to give expression to the qualities of the landscape was always balanced by an equal concern for the language of the painting. The rhythms and relationships within his pictures came about after long scrutiny and the careful assessment of each tone, contour and color both in his subject and on the surface of his canvas. His aim was to create a unity within the picture in which each element had a clearly defined role and a specific relation to its surrounding elements. He once likened the workings of a picture to the intertwined fingers of two human hands, each locked securely into its neighbour and allowing no gaps or weaknesses to interrupt the pattern. In *Mountains in Provence* all the features of the composition can be seen in this way, every bush and every building taking its place in the overall harmony in such a way that their removal would destroy the equilibrium. While remaining true to his experience of the site, Cézanne has selected, manipulated and directed his observations into a pictorial network of forms that takes on a life of its own.

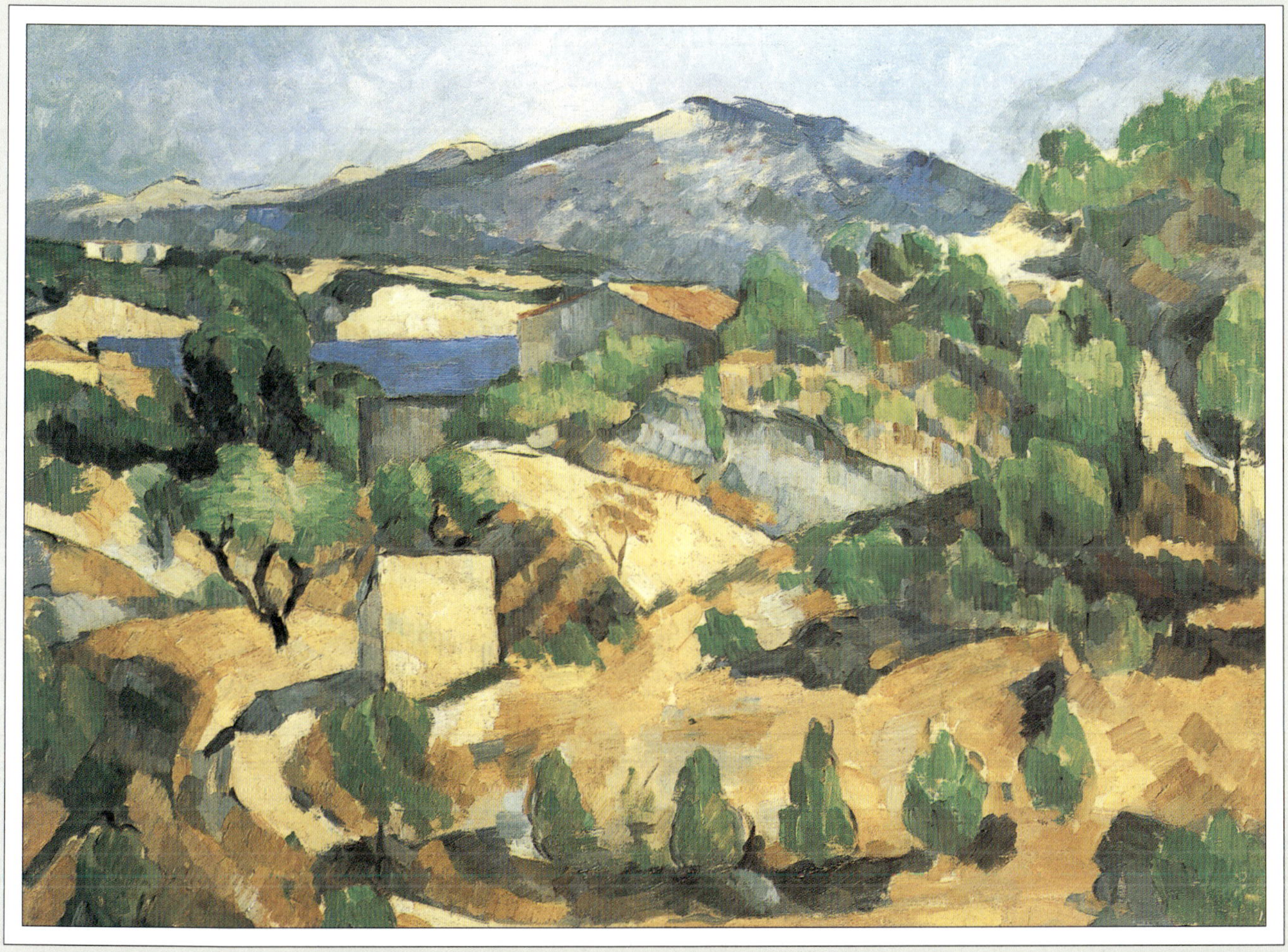

Prominent in this painting is Cézanne's use of the directional brushmark to emphasize the rhythms and structures of his composition. In the foreground, the ochers and whites of the soil follow the sweep of the rudimentary road, curving back as they flow between tree and cabin. In other areas, brushstrokes accentuate the curve of a hillside or the roundness of a bush, or simply assert themselves as flat planes on the surface of the canvas. Unusually for Cézanne, the picture was painted on a commercially prepared paper rather than on canvas. Such papers were available, then as now, from artists' suppliers and were generally associated with rapid outdoor sketching rather than with finished paintings. All the evidence suggests that this scene was executed by Cézanne in the open air in front of the subject, the prepared paper pinned to a board on his easel and the oil-colors applied quite thickly from his palette. The paper was laid down onto canvas at a later date.

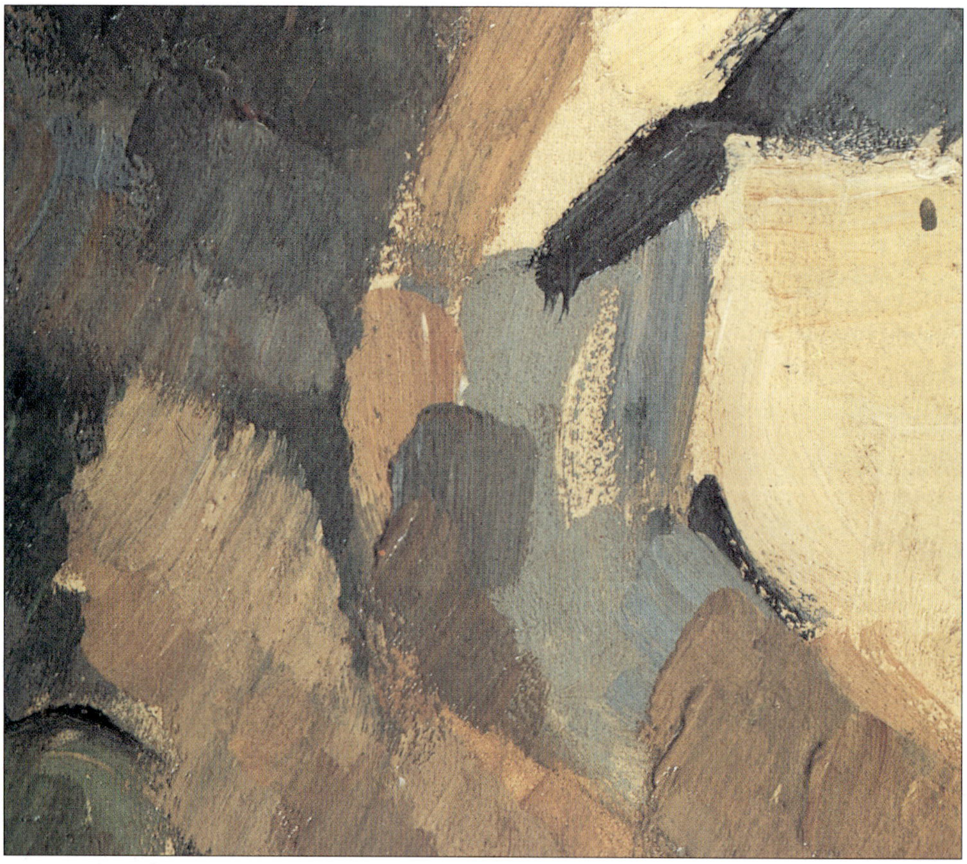

1

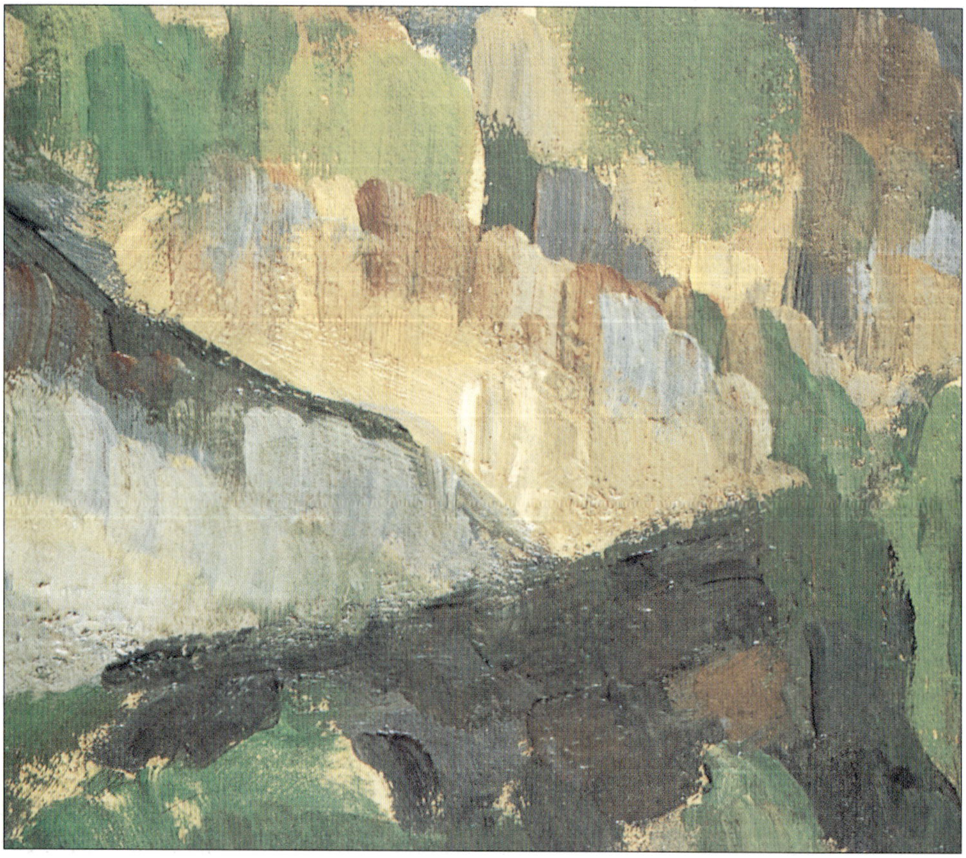

2

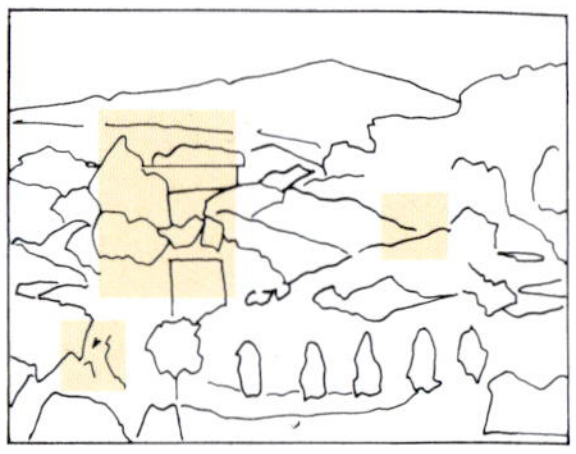

1 The directional, or constructive, brushmarks can here be seen building up the embankment beside the road as well as drawing the viewer's attention away from the corner and back into the picture. The paint is applied quite thickly, and some superimposition over previous colors can be clearly seen, a practice that has led to cracking in some parts of the paint surface.

2 Parallel strokes of several colors, applied while the paint was still wet, are allowed to merge in this central area. Unlike most of the surrounding hillside, this terrace is cooled down with touches of pale blue, perhaps added as an afterthought by the artist to introduce contrast into the hillside.

3 *Actual size detail* The bright sunlight in this scene creates a number of brilliant highlights and saturates the natural colors of earth and foliage. Cézanne is selective in his depiction of shadows, accentuating that of the cabin wall but omitting that of the tree altogether. The intense blue of the distant water animates the middle distance while acting as the perfect foil for the browns and ochers of the foreground.

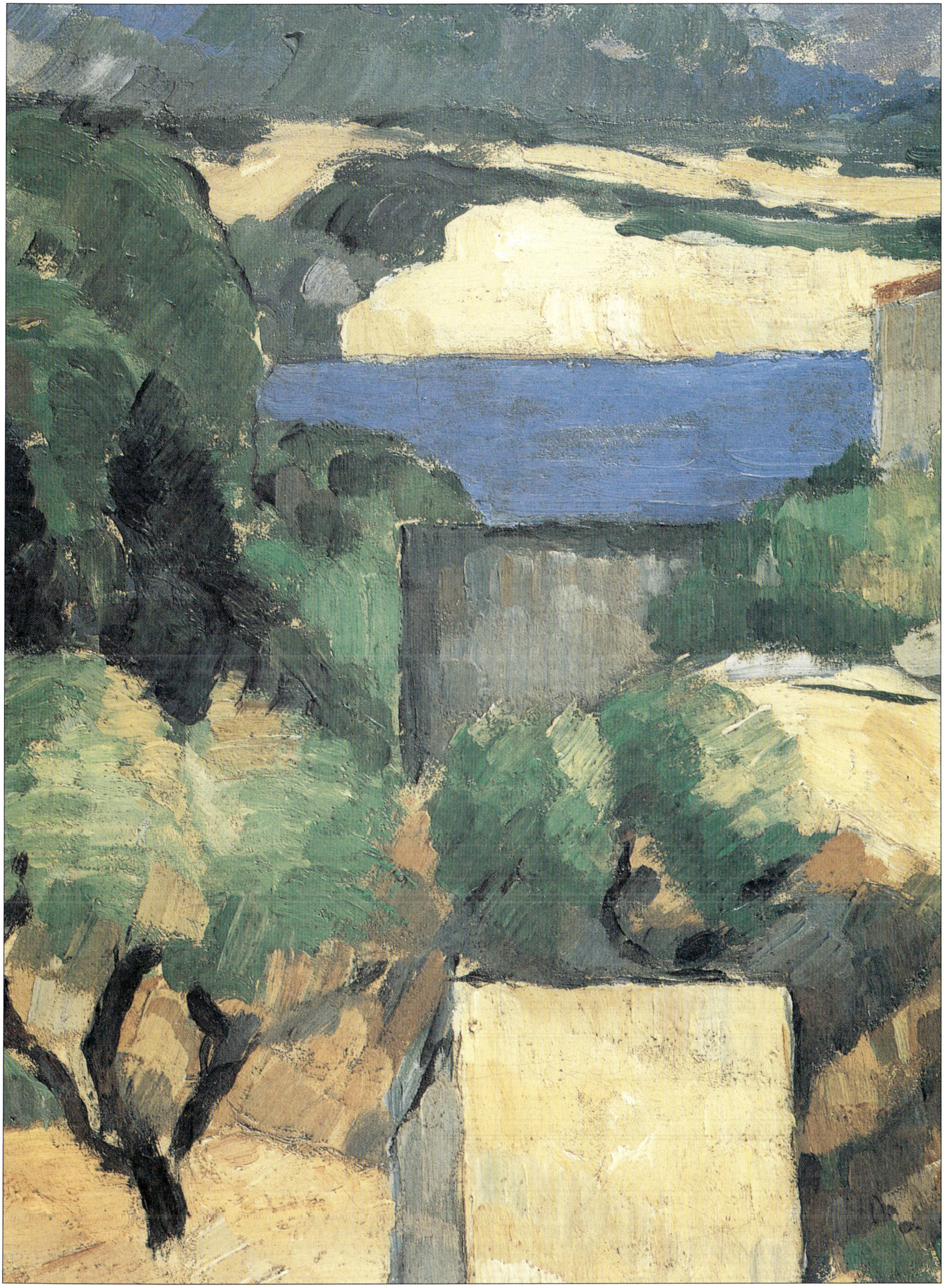

3 *Actual size detail*

Pot of Flowers and Fruit

c1888-90
$18^1/_8$×22in/46×56cm
Oil on canvas
Courtauld Institute Galleries, London

Still life had a special importance for Cézanne, more so than for any of his Impressionist contemporaries. Traditionally, still life had been regarded as an inferior category of painting, unequal to the morally elevating historical scene or the psychologically profound portrait. Some artists, such as the 18th-century French painter Chardin, had become famous principally for their still lifes, but generally the subject was left to obscure specialists or to the occasional demonstration of skill by masters better known for their other work. At least two of the 19th-century artists whom Cézanne admired, Delacroix and Courbet, had produced ambitious and original still lifes, but Cézanne could claim to be the first major artist to have raised the *genre* to the same level as his portraits, nudes and landscapes. In the course of his career he produced several hundred examples, principally in watercolor or oils, and he single-handedly promoted a neglected subject into a major medium of artistic expression.

The reasons for Cézanne's near-reverence for the still life were complex, but principal amongst them was its potential for order. With any other subject, from landscape to the human face, the artist is in the hands of nature and must edit or modify the forms that are presented to his eyes. When arranging a still life, these rules are reversed: shapes can be added, lighting changed at will, even colors altered to suit the demands of the composition. We know from contemporary accounts that Cézanne took full advantage of this God-like power over nature, painstakingly adjusting the positions of the humblest object and propping plates or jugs up to the required angle with piles of coins. It is also known that he amassed a large miscellaneous collection of household utensils, such as coffeepots, sugar bowls and a variety of jugs, to provide him with precisely the right contour or touch of color in a particular configuration. Certain objects, like the famous blue ginger-jar or the plaster cast of Cupid, recur in a number of different pictures, and others, most conspicuously a dark green olive pot, must have been painted scores of times.

Having established the arrangements of objects to his fastidious satisfaction, Cézanne was then able to exploit the other great advantage of the still life, its relative permanence. Unaffected by the vagaries of weather, free from the demands of a human subject, the group of apples or the arrangement of crockery becomes the perfect model. Unchanged from day to day, impassive and self-effacing, it was the ideal subject for an artist who worked slowly and needed to return to precisely the same disposition of forms and tones day after day, even week after week. For Cézanne, with his meticulous, intensely self-critical approach to painting, the dense web of visual relationships to be found in a group of ordinary household objects was equal to the challenge of a landscape or a human figure.

Paintings such as *Pot of Flowers and Fruit* have an extraordinary intensity which only comes from hundreds of hours spent in direct engagement with the subject. Simple though the objects are, every nuance of tone and every inflection of hue has been scrutinized, and every interval and relationship between adjacent objects tested. No leaf is the same color or has quite the same character as another leaf, no square inch of table-surface is unquestioningly tinted with the same tone as its neighbour. Contours and boundaries of objects have been crisply defined and as often redefined, marking the progress of the painting in a sequence of colored halos or reverberations. While the identities of the modest plant and its attendant fruit are vividly characterized, the spectator is everywhere conscious of the functioning of the artist's perception.

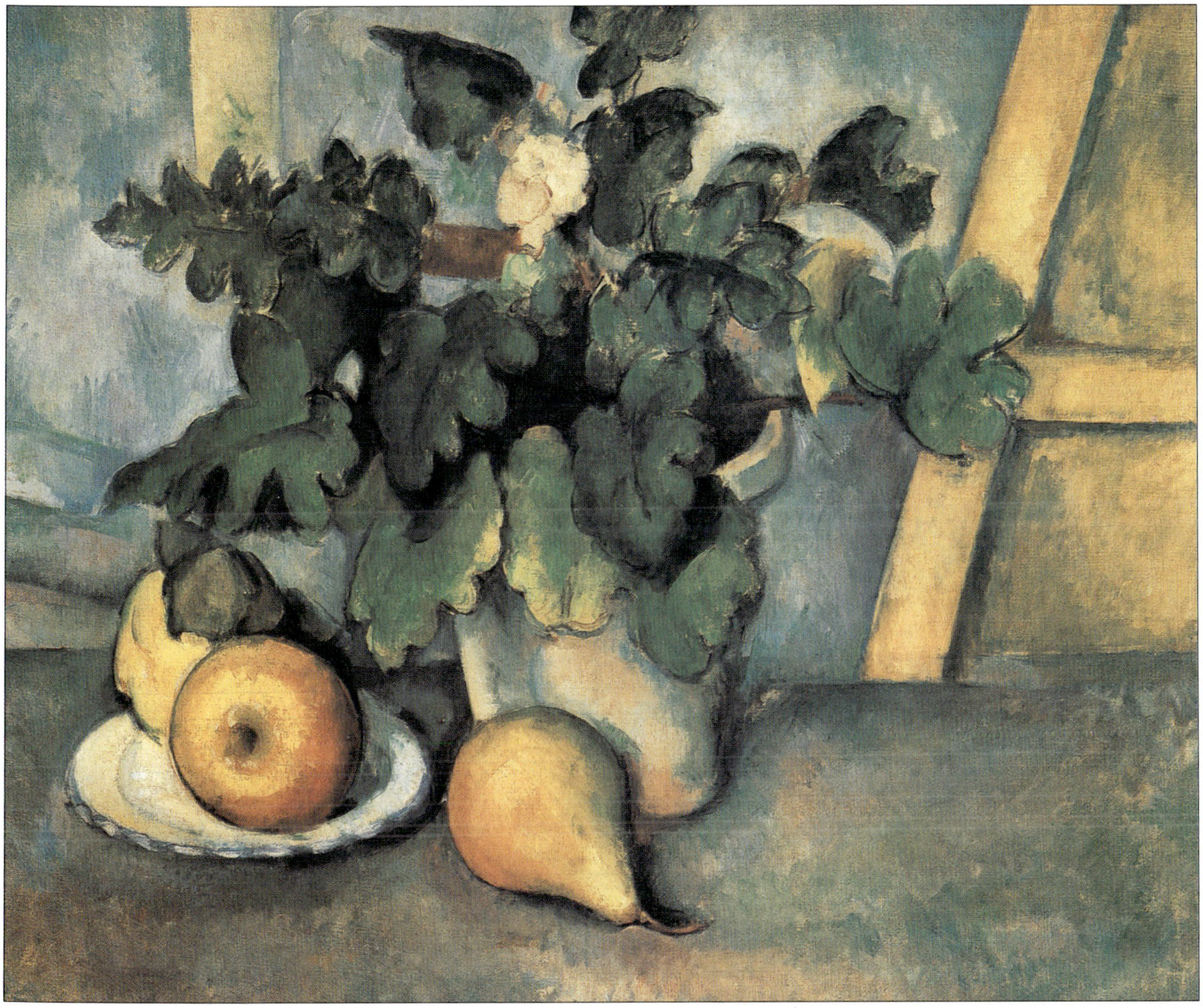

Cézanne's delight in nature extended to the simplest fruit or vegetable, and the forms and colors of this picture bear witness to this delight in the most emphatic way. We are offered both underside and profile view of the almost-too-perfect pear, and the ellipses of plate and plant pot suggest multiple viewpoints within a single object. Even the table top, conventionally expected to run straight across the picture, is broken into a series of steps as if to respond to three varying perceptions. By the middle of his career, Cézanne was using paint with considerable discipline, building the picture from thin washes as he established his initial composition, to more opaque strokes of paint in the last highlights. In this picture, the original "drawing" of the forms with a fine brush can be seen — the artist favored a deep blue for this operation. Some areas of color, such as the grays of the table top, were then brushed in with thinned paint, while the objects themselves were worked more solidly.

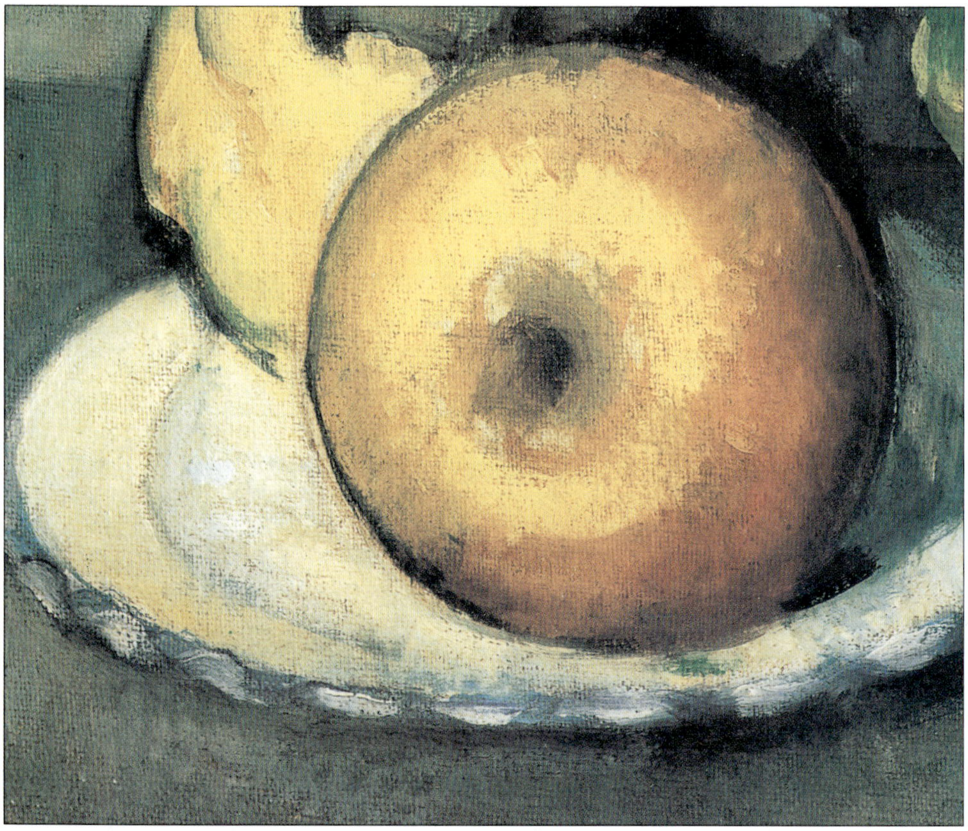

1

2

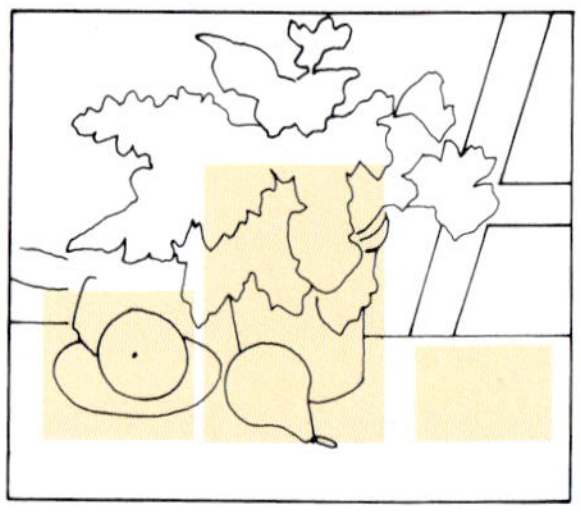

1 Cézanne included pears or apples in hundreds of his still life pictures, perhaps because of their easy availability and rich coloring but also conceivably for their symbolic overtones. Here the fruit is an ideal specimen, unblemished and arranged to conform as nearly as possible to a perfect sphere. Skillfully manipulating the density of his colors, Cézanne fills out the roundness of the form and stresses its autumnal ripeness.

2 In this small area of apparently neutral foreground, it is possible to identify browns, purples, greens and blues. Even though they are tonally very close, their combined effect is to bring an unexpected intensity into what might otherwise have been a lifeless stretch of gray.

3 *Actual size detail* Color is given unparalleled license in some of Cézanne's still lifes, and here touches of virtually every primary and secondary hue are visible within inches of each other. The shadows on the plant pot include blues, greens, red-browns and pinks, while the pear runs through the spectrum from red through yellow to green. Touches of black are still in use to strengthen a curve or subdue a wayward tint, but it is color that effectively describes the forms.

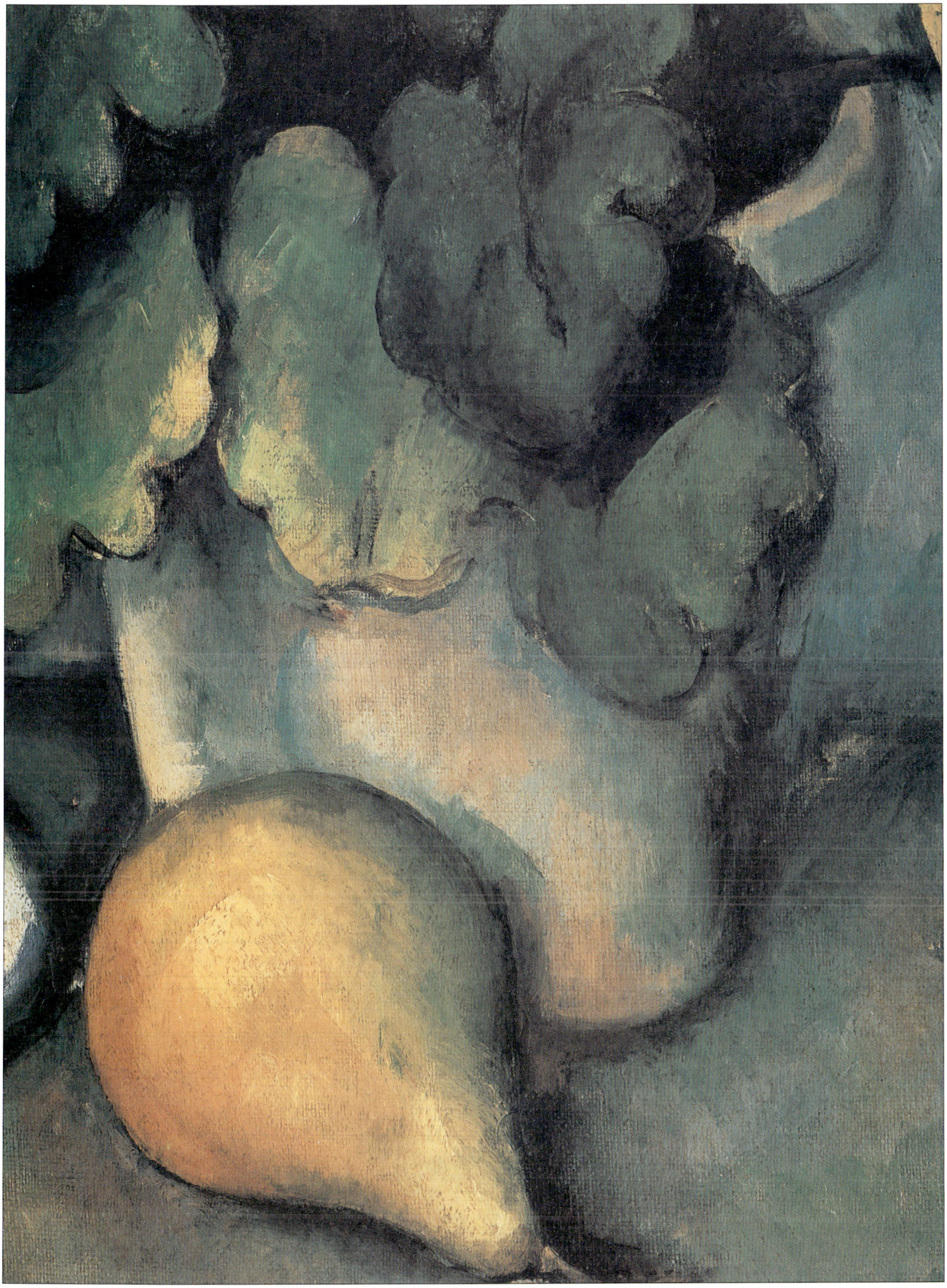

3 *Actual size detail*

Mont Sainte-Victoire

c1902-6
$14^1/_4 \times 21^3/_4$in/36×55cm
Watercolour
Tate Gallery, London

This mountain at the heart of Provence, dominating Cézanne's birth place at Aix, acquired an almost mystical significance for him in his later years. It first appears in the distant background of certain early pictures, and then recurs repeatedly until the final months of his life, developing from a remote landscape feature into a central motif. Just as Monet returned time after time to his water-lilies and the aging Degas to his dancers, Cézanne seems always to have found fresh possibilities and inspiration in this mountain, which was both subject matter and private obsession.

In the later part of his career, Cézanne turned more and more towards watercolor. Although he also did watercolors in his early years, these tended to be small studies related to more ambitious oil paintings; it was not until his maturity that he used watercolor as a medium in its own right. For an artist of Cézanne's habits and temperament, it had a number of advantages. It is easily portable and can be carried on walks into the landscape, often without the need for an easel and other cumbersome equipment. Being water-based, it is extremely quick-drying, especially in the warm air of the Mediterranean where successive strokes of the brush will dry as soon as they are put down. Given Cézanne's insistence on working outdoors and his need to paint and re-paint certain areas of his picture, it is not surprising that many of his most remarkable late landscapes were executed in this medium.

Mont Sainte-Victoire, painted in the last years of his life, is an example of Cézanne's fully developed watercolor technique. The whiteness of the paper was used to establish the tone of the picture, and then systematically inflected and modified by fine touches of dilute color. Initially, a light pencil drawing indicated the broad outlines of the composition, followed by pale washes of paint as areas of tone or color were identified. As soon as the first marks appeared, the painting took on a rudimentary existence, and relationships between one form and another began to grow. Cooler colors, such as blues, tend to recede, suggesting depth, while the warmer reds and ochers advance toward the picture plane. Here the blues of the mountain locate it firmly in the distance, while touches of other colors are introduced to maintain the overall harmony of the picture. Nearer to the viewer, the denser web of yellows, greens, purples and browns gives substance to the foliage, but again touches of blue are used to link this area with the distant mountain.

As the painting progressed, further washes of color were laid over those already dry, suppressing an over-warm hue or giving greater weight to an area of shadow. In places, this superimposition of veils of color has been repeated as many as ten times, and it is possible to glimpse pale reds, greens, blues and yellows within the same block of tone. Every touch of color represented for Cézanne another moment of perception, another observed nuance in the scene which must be translated into the language of his picture. Modifying, adjusting and refining his image, Cézanne advanced in a series of infinitely patient steps towards that unified and harmonious representation of nature that he had pursued for more than thirty years. Looking at his mountain once again, he added another pale thread of blue watercolor to the half-dozen already on its flank, endlessly re-defining the shape he must have known as intimately as anything he painted.

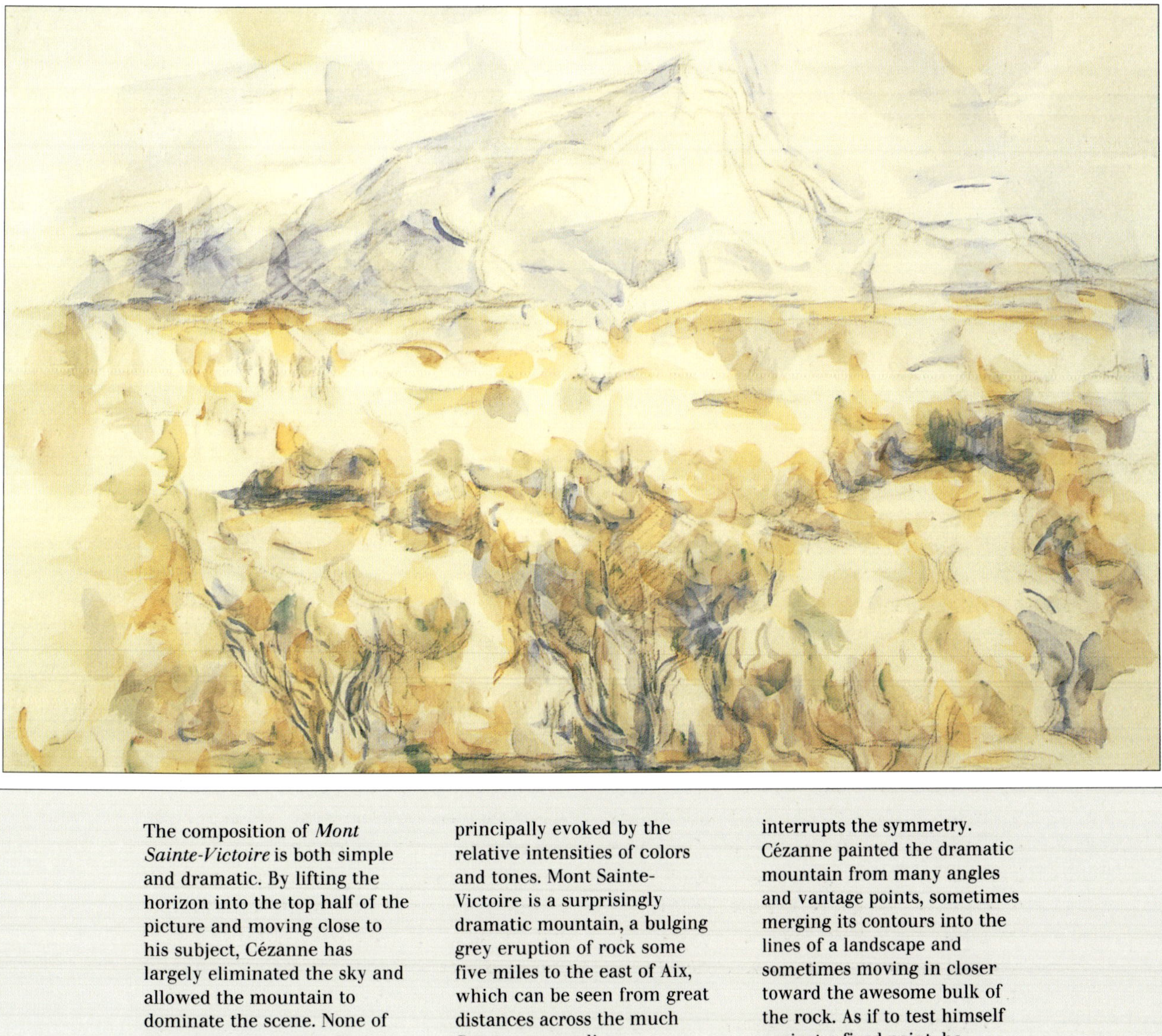

The composition of *Mont Sainte-Victoire* is both simple and dramatic. By lifting the horizon into the top half of the picture and moving close to his subject, Cézanne has largely eliminated the sky and allowed the mountain to dominate the scene. None of the usual perspective devices, such as receding roads or angled buildings, are allowed to clutter up the middle ground, and space is principally evoked by the relative intensities of colors and tones. Mont Sainte-Victoire is a surprisingly dramatic mountain, a bulging grey eruption of rock some five miles to the east of Aix, which can be seen from great distances across the much flatter surrounding countryside. To the north it curves fulsomely down towards its lower slopes, while in the south a cliff-like face interrupts the symmetry. Cézanne painted the dramatic mountain from many angles and vantage points, sometimes merging its contours into the lines of a landscape and sometimes moving in closer toward the awesome bulk of the rock. As if to test himself against a fixed point, he depicted it at every season, on every scale and in all the media he had at his disposal.

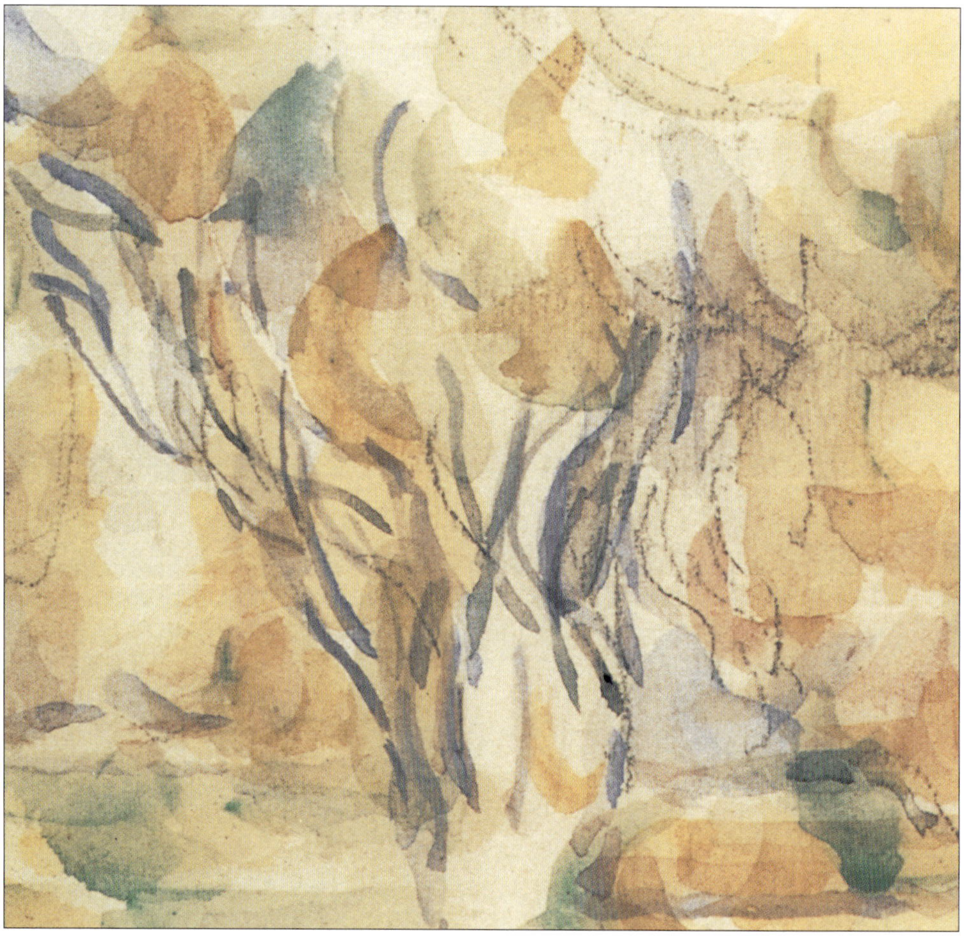

1

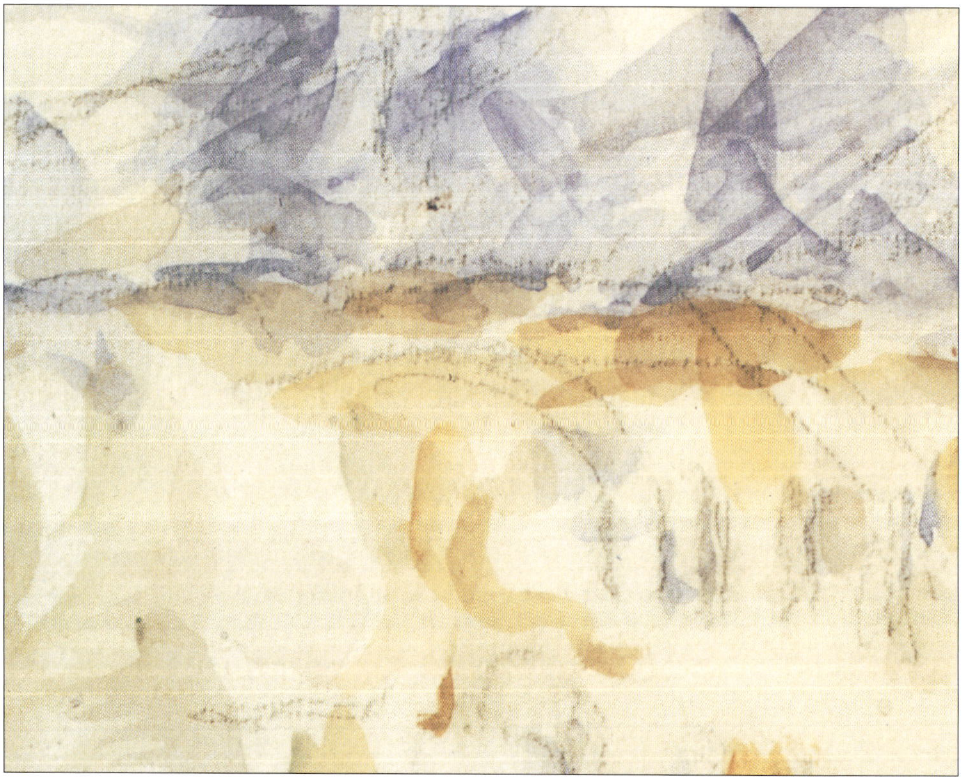

2

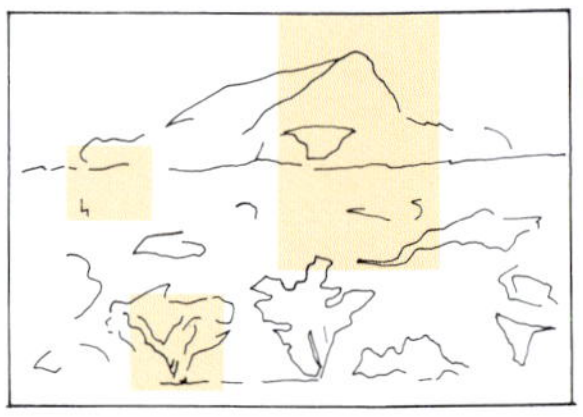

1 Much of the energy in this painting comes from the wide variety of brushmarks that Cézanne employed, from rectangular blocks of pale color in the earlier stages to nervous, flickering strokes of greens and yellows in the foliage. The broader marks would be achieved with the side of the brush, the fine blue lines with the tip, while some of the final touches appear to have been almost jabbed onto the paper.

2 Cézanne's technique of superimposing thin veils of color can clearly be seen in this detail, where a number of brushstrokes have been applied in several different directions on the same area of paper. The delicacy and animation of the successive paint layers prevents the surface of the painting from becoming deadened, while the varied angles of the brushmarks suggest dynamic forces at work in both the landscape and the picture.

3 *Actual size detail* In many of Cézanne's paintings, the shapes of the subject are either chosen or modified in order to "rhyme" with each other. A piece of fruit may echo the shape of a dish or jug, or in this case the mountain is reflected in the forms of the landscape beneath it. Cézanne has artfully emphasized a plunging curve in the foreground foliage, matching the curve of the mountain and giving greater unity and resonance to the picture.

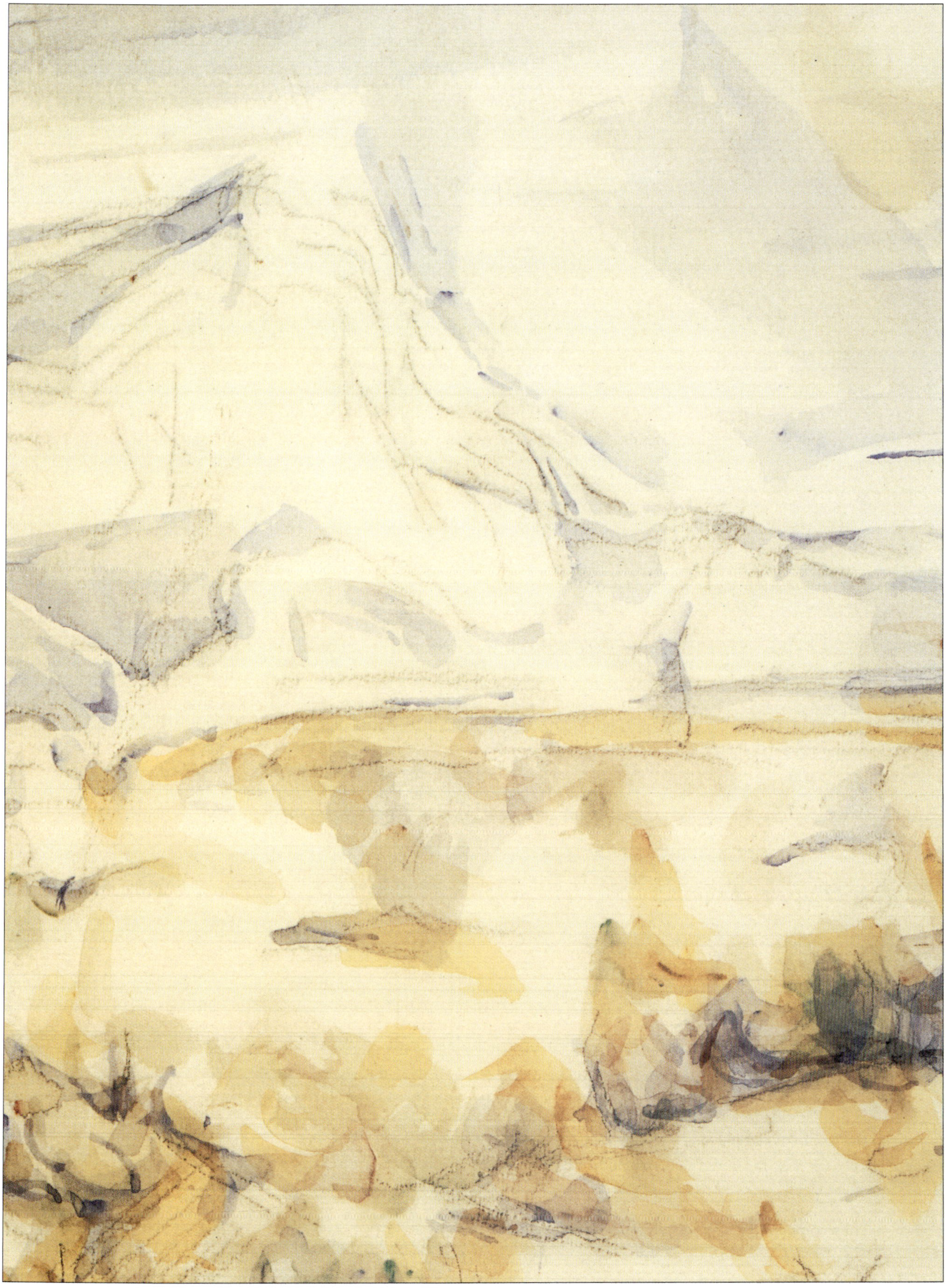

3 *Actual size detail*

The Red Rock

c1897
$25\frac{1}{2} \times 31\frac{1}{2}$in/$65 \times 80$cm
Oil on canvas
Musée de l'Orangerie, Paris

One of the local sites most associated with Cézanne's last years is Bibémus quarry, situated a little way out of the town of Aix-en-Provence in the direction of Mont Sainte-Victoire. The quarry had been dug into a wooded ridge within sight of the mountain and used as a source of stone for the buildings in Aix in earlier times, but was already overgrown by trees and shrubs in Cézanne's day. At Bibémus, Cézanne could work alone and undisturbed within walking distance of his studio, and he was able to produce a large series of drawings, watercolors and oil paintings of its red-brown rocks and wild vegetation.

Cézanne's inclination towards strongly stated forms and grid-like structures in his paintings seems to have found a natural subject at Bibémus, where the sharply cut verticals and diagonals of the rock-faces impose a sense of order on the surrounding vegetation. Many of his Bibémus paintings exploit the opposition between the block-like rocks and the more organic curves of bushes and trees, and in *The Red Rock* we find one of the most startling of these confrontations. In the distance, the quarry workings have become choked with greenery and only glimpses of rock can be seen, but in the foreground a vast ocher-red slab of cut stone looms into the picture. Much of the rock at Bibémus was cut at an angle, so that the abandoned faces appear to lean outward in this way, and a number of similar features still survive in the quarry today.

This brilliant red intrusion into the painting challenges both the symmetry and the integrity of the composition. Much of Cézanne's handling of the rest of the picture, such as the arrangement of the foliage and the balance of colors, can be seen as an attempt to accommodate the red rock within a more general harmony. The strong red-brown of the foreground, for example, as well as the touches of the same color in the trees and even sky, help establish continuity with the rock, while certain lines among the trees echo its triangular shape. Cézanne's delight in the underlying rhythms of nature is clearly demonstrated in the curving, wave-like pattern of the foliage, and again the rounded forms that emerge, such as the spherical bush at lower left, seem designed to complement the angular rock. Such a flat, uncompromising and geometric intervention into a landscape strains the capacities of the medium, but it is difficult to imagine any other artist either taking on the challenge or coming so close to its resolution.

Cézanne's ideas about painting were never systematically written down and have been the cause of much subsequent debate. Many letters to his friends and family survive, though he had a marked aversion to theoretical discussion and tended to refer to the mundane and the domestic. At about the time he was working on *The Red Rock*, however, he had attracted the attention of a group of young artists and writers, and his correspondence with them contains a number of remarks about art that have subsequently become much quoted. Writing to the painter Charles Camoin, Cézanne advised him "You do well above all to study from nature," and admitted that "The understanding of the model and its realization is sometimes very slow in coming for the artist." To another admirer, Emile Bernard, Cézanne insisted that "One must look at the model and feel very exactly, and also express oneself distinctly and with force," and (only a year before his death), "we must render the image of what we see, forgetting everything that existed before us."

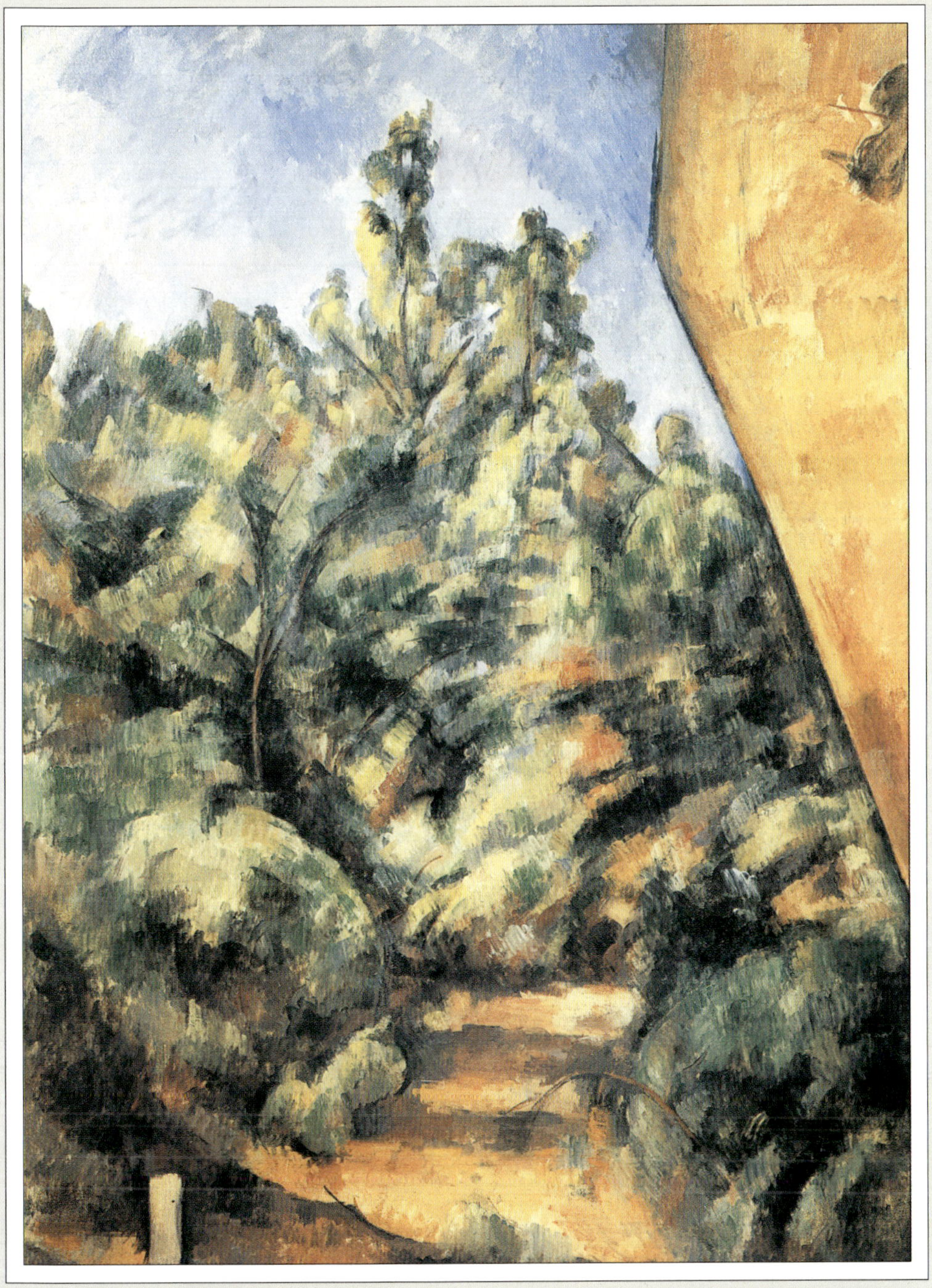

The redness of the rock is as shocking today as when Cézanne conceived the painting. The brightness of the Provencal sunlight conspires with the intense natural pigment of the local stone to produce a rich reddish-ocher hue which can still be seen in some of the stone-built houses of Aix-en-Provence. Such warmth of color also thrusts the rock face to the front of the picture, in contrast to the receding greens and the cool blue of the sky. This interplay between the surface qualities of color and brushwork on the one hand with the naturally recessive tendencies of landscape elements on the other is a constant theme of Cézanne's late painting.

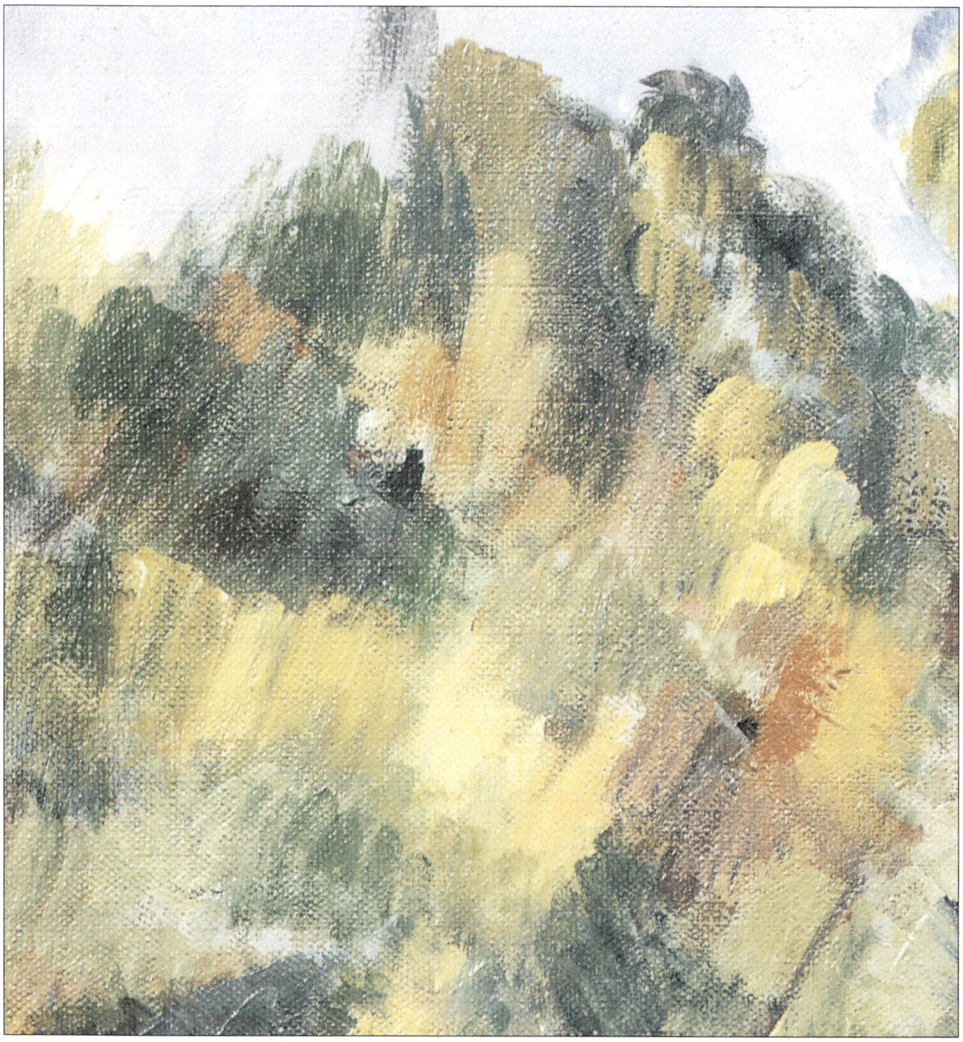

1

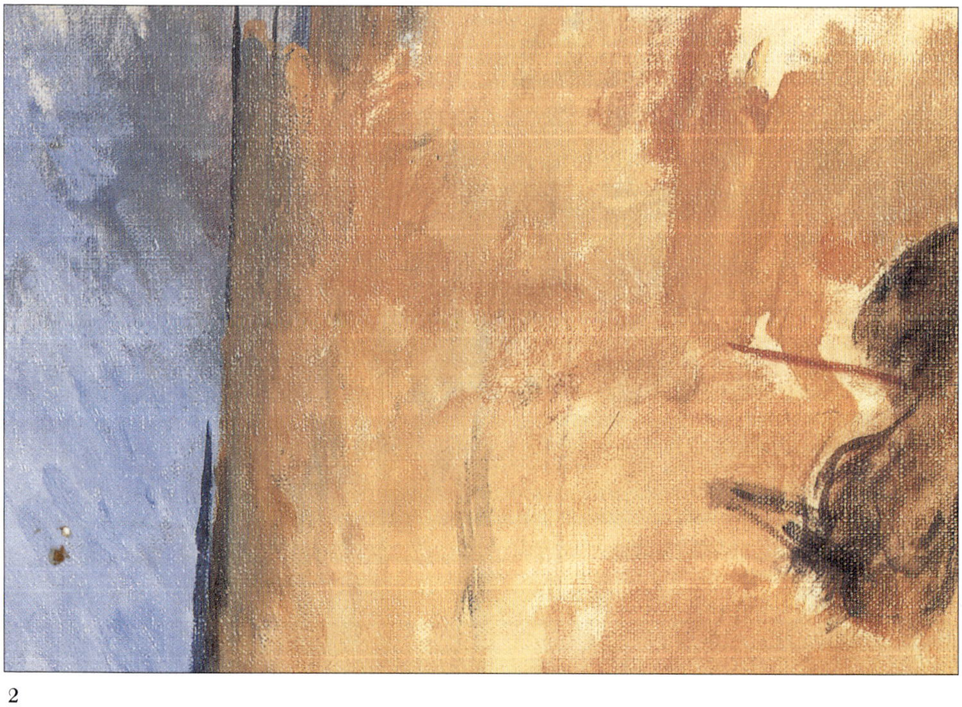

2

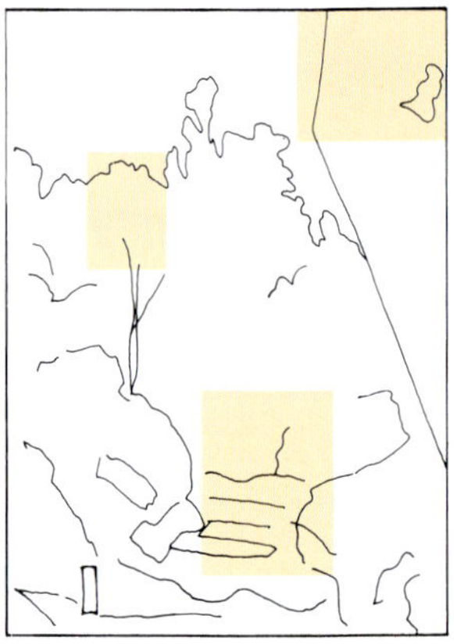

1 Cézanne used greens with great confidence in his pictures, often preferring the sharp acid tints of emerald and chrome green or the heavier hues derived from viridian. Here the mixture of greens with touches of the earth-browns of the Bibémus quarry produces a broad spectrum of contrasting hues, suggesting the lushness of the wild vegetation.

2 Despite the picture's title and the apparent brightness of the rock, the "red" is largely made up of natural earth pigments, such as burnt sienna and yellow ocher. The paint is brushed onto the canvas with an abandon that seems almost careless, though the careful redefinition of the edge of the rock emphasizes its importance in the picture.

3 *Actual size detail* The masterly skill Cézanne had achieved in his old age can be seen in the way he tackles this largely featureless area of foliage and transforms it into a vibrant series of colors and forms, each of which resonates within the general harmony of the picture. The identity of path and bushes is firmly insisted upon, but their integration into a larger whole is equally pronounced.

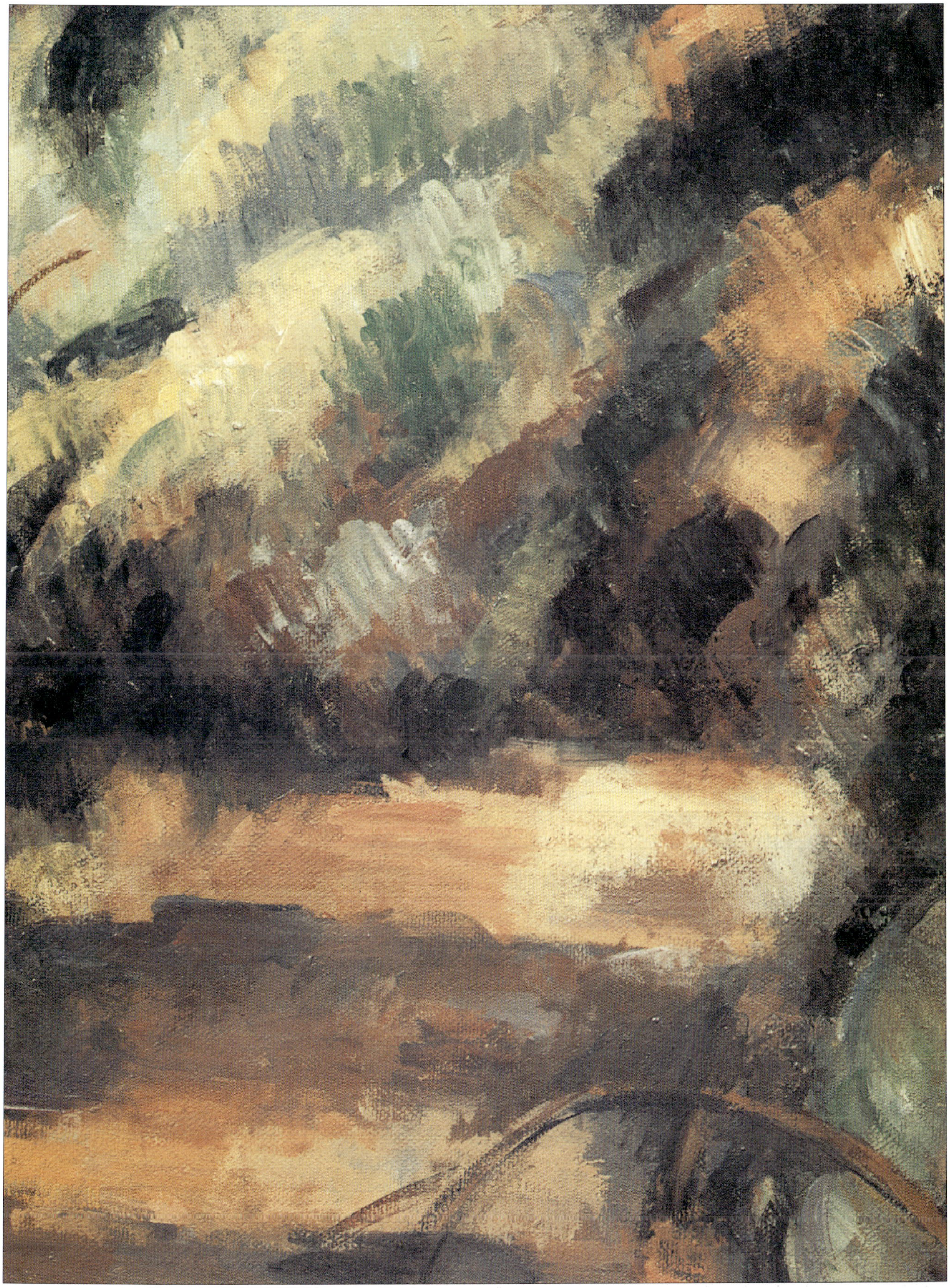

3 *Actual size detail*

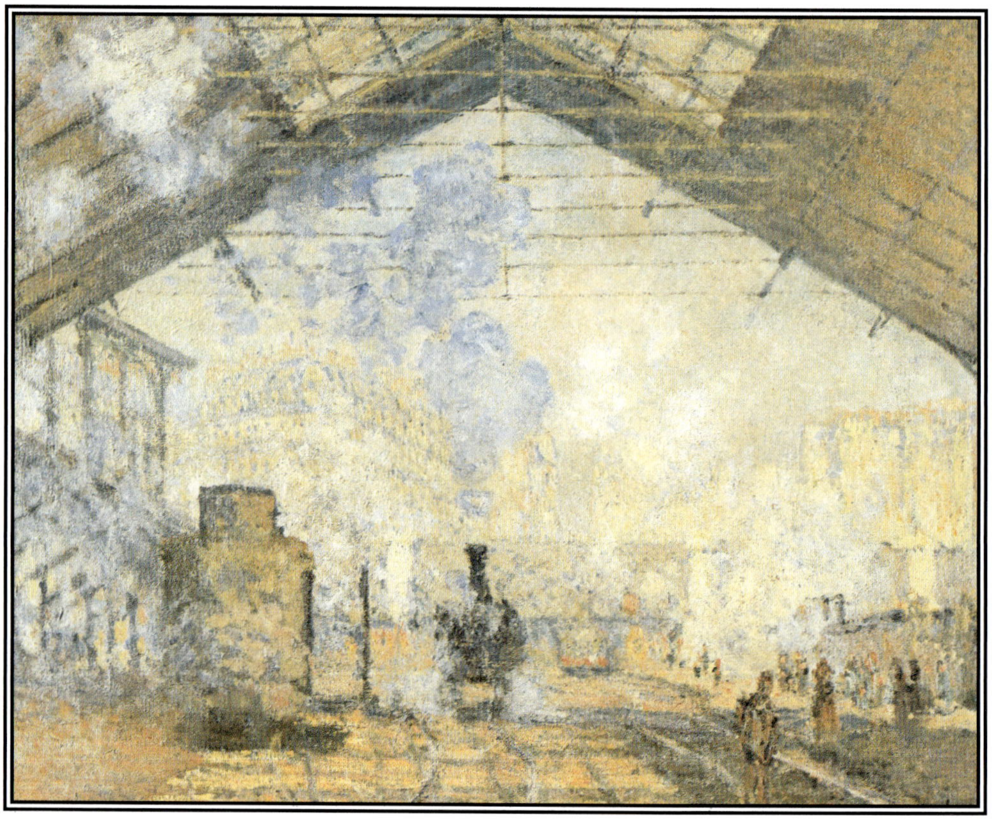

MONET

Introduction

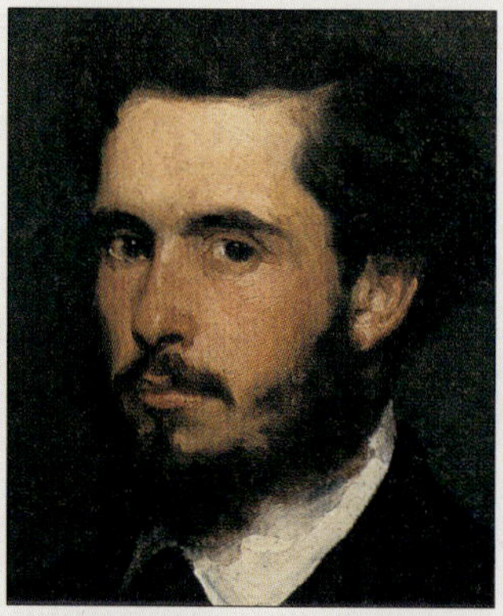

Carolus-Duran
Portrait of Claude Monet
1867
Musée Marmottan, Paris

Monet's paintings carry a peculiar magic. They are ordinary enough in subject matter, consisting almost exclusively of basically direct treatments of landscape — figures rarely appear, and after 1890 not at all. The paintings have little obvious drama or planned appeal to the emotions, and they make no kind of political or social statement. Nevertheless they evoke a constant delight from most viewers, and this very delight in many ways obscures Monet's really extraordinary achievement. It could be claimed that Monet, more than any of the Impressionists, opened the path to a new understanding of the nature of painting.

At first sight Monet appears as an uncomplicated, non-intellectual painter, constantly excited by the world around him, drawing his subjects from nothing more ambitious than his local countryside, and dedicated to exploring the effects of light on the natural landscape. We think of him as a simple, direct person leading a quiet life and blessed with an equable temperament, unbeset by any of the tensions and anxieties that afflicted painters such as Van Gogh and Gauguin. He seems to personify, not just the "happy painter" but also the nature of the Impressionist movement itself, and indeed it was one of his paintings, *Impression, Sunrise* (see page 511), exhibited at the First Impressionist Exhibition in 1874, that gave the movement its name. (The word "impressionist" was in fact intended as a derisory comment, but was taken by most of the group as an acceptable description of its aims.)

In fact Monet's main characteristics were determination and single-mindedness, and his nature was much more complex than his paintings would lead us to believe. His life was a constant struggle with what he saw as insoluble technical problems, and he was frequently so dissatisfied with his work that he would not allow it to be taken from the studio. In his home life he was an autocrat, demanding total punctuality from both his family and his servants. With his friends he was more relaxed, and he enjoyed parties and the café life that was such an important part of the Parisian artistic scene. Although a Parisian from commercial necessity, he always loved the countryside, which he treasured for its infinite variety as well as for the solitude it offered. The landscape, and particularly the sea coast and water, was his passion throughout his life.

But passion is not really the word that provides the key to either the Impressionist movement as a whole or to Monet in particular. Perhaps the most significant thread running through the movement and unifying its varied strands is a concern with vision rather than with emotion or social statement. When Degas painted his laundresses he was not concerned, as Dickens would have been, with the sweatshop conditions in which they worked, but with colors and the effects of light on sharply pressed, clean fabrics. Similarly, it would be unwise to assume that because Monet painted the façade of Rouen Cathedral many times it was because of any strong attachment to the faith it embodied.

Despite the absence of dramatic, emotional and social involvement on the part of its central figures, the Impressionist movement initiated a great artistic revolution, and one that has had a lasting effect, not only on artists, but also on the art-aware public. It changed all the ideas of what constitutes a painting, distinguishing, in effect, between a "picture" and a "painting." Any appreciation of what the movement achieved hinges on an understanding of Monet's own achievement; he was its pivot and its center, and his long life documents its development and evolution well into our own century.

Monet's intention, developed over his entire painting career, was to paint what he saw. This may seem to us a straightforward, even commonplace ambition, but it is important to realize that it was far from being a universal preoccupation of artists of the past, nor is it often a primary concern of artists today. In Monet's own time the well-known academic painters were concerned, not with painting what they saw, but with producing highly finished, often idealized works with a social or religious message, and it was the Impressionists' emphasis on vision that not only distinguished them but gave rise to the hostility and ridicule that greeted their first public appearance.

The simple presentation of landscape or still life was regarded in the nineteenth century as an inferior, if attractive, form of painting, although the beginnings of a change could be discerned with such painters as Constable and Turner in England and the Barbizon school of painters in France. However, even though these painters exerted a considerable influence on the Impressionists they were less concerned with color and light than with tone and form; even Eugène Boudin, Monet's first mentor, built his open-air paintings on a tonal base, seeing his forms in terms of light and dark rather than of color. The Impressionsts, on the other hand, saw the whole of nature in terms of color and light: color was everywhere, even in the deepest shadows, which traditionally had been rendered simply as dark brown or gray. This preoccupation with color made their paintings quite startlingly different from any that had gone before, and no one was more determined in the pursuit of color than Monet himself.

The struggle to record nature

Monet came up against one essential problem presented by the observation of nature: the constant changes caused both by an ever-moving light source and by the movement of the forms themselves — clouds, trees, grasses and water were perpetually in flux. What he saw never stayed the same long enough for the painting of it. For an artist dedicated to painting what he saw the challenge was relentless, and the problem ultimately insoluble.

Thus Monet's apparently commonplace ambition was actually a much greater task than it seems, and it caused him both mental anguish and physical exhaus-

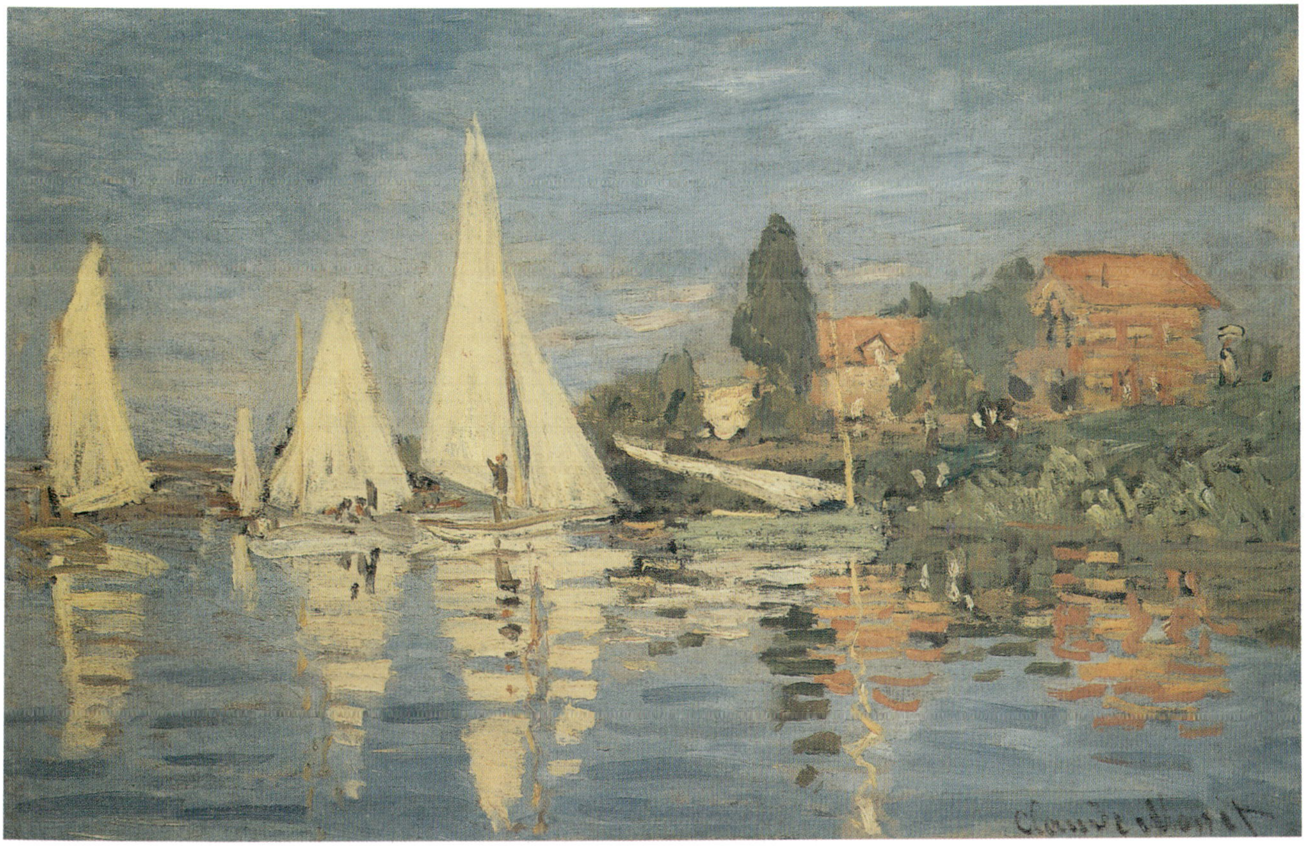

CLAUDE MONET
Regatta at Argenteuil
1872, Musée d'Orsay, Paris

Monet's painting during his settled life at Argenteuil has a particular joy, freshness and visual delight, reflecting his pleasure in the small town and surrounding country, especially the river. This painting, a small *esquisse*, or preliminary sketch, is constructed of broad directional, form-following brushstrokes creating the impression of sunlight with great immediacy. The luminosity of color and the flat patterning both show the influence of Japanese prints, of which Monet owned many at this time. The painting was almost certainly bought by his friend Gustave Caillebotte, a rich collector and painter who exhibited in the Impressionist Group Exhibitions.

tion. Also, however, it transformed his paintings from the hard, Japanese-print-like shapes of his early works such as *Women in a Garden* (see page 19) to the evanescent, ethereal images of the water gardens in the late *Nymphéas* (*Waterlilies*) panels (see page 57).

As his studies and experiments advanced, Monet perceived a further, even more daunting complication. In consciously attempting to paint what he saw, he was actually seeing himself observing the changes of light, and thus was chasing not what he had seen but what he himself had retained of what he had seen. He could never catch up with himself.

CLAUDE MONET
The Bank at Gennevilliers
About 1870, Private collection

Gennevilliers was a small town on the opposite side of the river from Argenteuil, the two being linked by a bridge.

This small sketch, almost certainly done rapidly on the spot, presages the bold brushwork of *Rue Montorgeuil* (opposite), particularly in the treatment of the path, though this was painted at a much earlier date.

But during the process he unconsciously made the most far-reaching discovery of all. His vision, which permitted him only to translate a sensation of color to the canvas, was not spatial but flat, but in spite of this a spatial element did appear on the canvas. By the time he had begun work on the *Waterlilies* paintings the problem had been compounded by the surface of the water he was painting, which was both visually present and transparent. So where was the canvas surface — under the water, on its surface, or in the air space in between?

Monet's painting from 1872, when he settled at Argenteuil (near Paris on the banks of the Seine) onwards, could be seen as the presentation of the direct sketch from nature as the finished work. From this period until his death his basic method was established. Although in his later paintings representationalism and the clear delination of volume became less important, he continued the brush and paint application he had learned when painting with Renoir, Pissarro and other artist friends. Energetic and varied, his technique

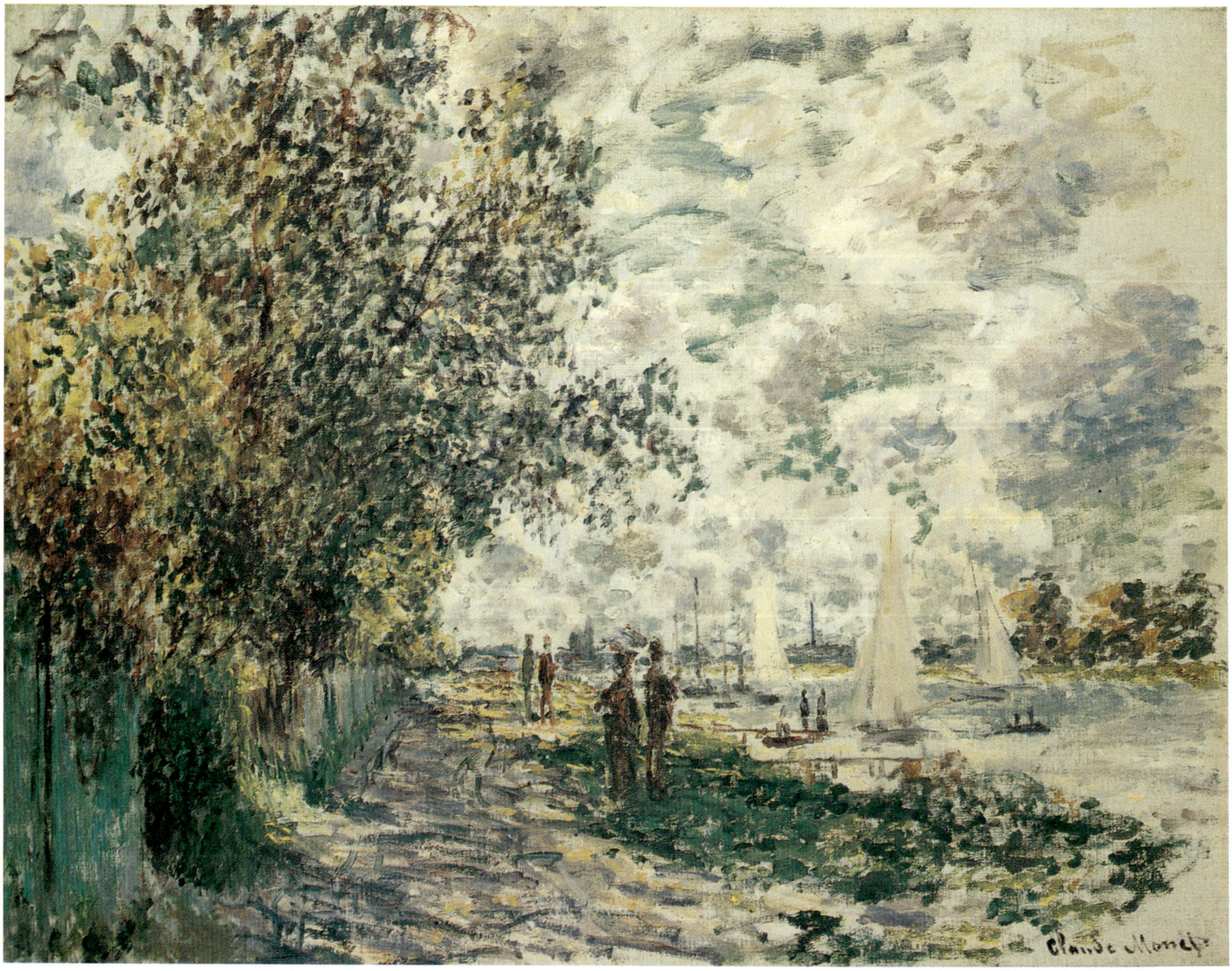

ranged from heavy impastos built up in short, jabbed strokes to long, thick "drawn" brushstrokes. His color was broken into small, fluttering areas where dense foliage was being described, or tense, long, thin or broad strokes where water or sky was treated. He was not a technician by temperament, but his painting methods were marvelously appropriate to his needs.

The artist's early life

Monet's early life was beset by the usual lack of recognition and attendant financial problems, but unlike Van Gogh he did not remain unrecognized, and was relatively affluent when he died in 1926. Although his early life had been disrupted by the great social and political upheavals of late nineteenth-century France, he played little part in them. Throughout the First World War he remained in his house at Giverny, and the great artistic movements of the early twentieth century, Fauvism, Cubism, Futurism and Surrealism, completely passed him by; when Monet died, Picasso was forty-five and already famous.

Claude Monet was born in 1840, the son of a successful wholesale grocer in Paris who moved with his family to Le Havre when Claude was five. He grew up there and was conscripted into the army in 1861, being sent to Algeria but invalided out the following year.

He had already begun to paint before his conscription, and was introduced to open-air painting by the seascape painter Eugène Boudin, whose canvases have a fresh directness, with great luminous sweeps of sky. At the same time he met the Dutch landscape painter J.B. Jongkind, and it was not long before he decided that he wished to become a professional painter. His father somewhat reluctantly agreed to support him provided he studied in the *atelier* of a reputable academic artist in Paris, and accordingly he joined Charles Gleyre's academy in 1862. Some academics gave little or no attention to their students, but Gleyre's reputation was high and he had many students, among whom at the time were Bazille, Sisley and Renoir.

Frédéric Bazille was Monet's first close friend in the art world, and his studio was the focus for a group of young painters from Gleyre's academy who were impatient with the academic processes and teaching methods. They were also dismayed by the commercial ambitions they encountered in the official painting world, where success was more important than achievement, and reputation than quality of work.

Monet and his friends left Gleyre's when it closed in 1864, but Monet, still attracted by the idea of painting in the open air, stayed in Paris and painted in the nearby countryside or on the Normandy coast. At the same time he began living with Camille Doncieux, and in 1867 she bore a son, Jean. This was a lean period for Monet, and when he and Camille finally found themselves penniless he was forced to return home to Le Havre.

In 1870 Monet and Camille were married in Paris, but in autumn of the same year the Franco-Prussian war broke out, and this was to have a dramatic effect on

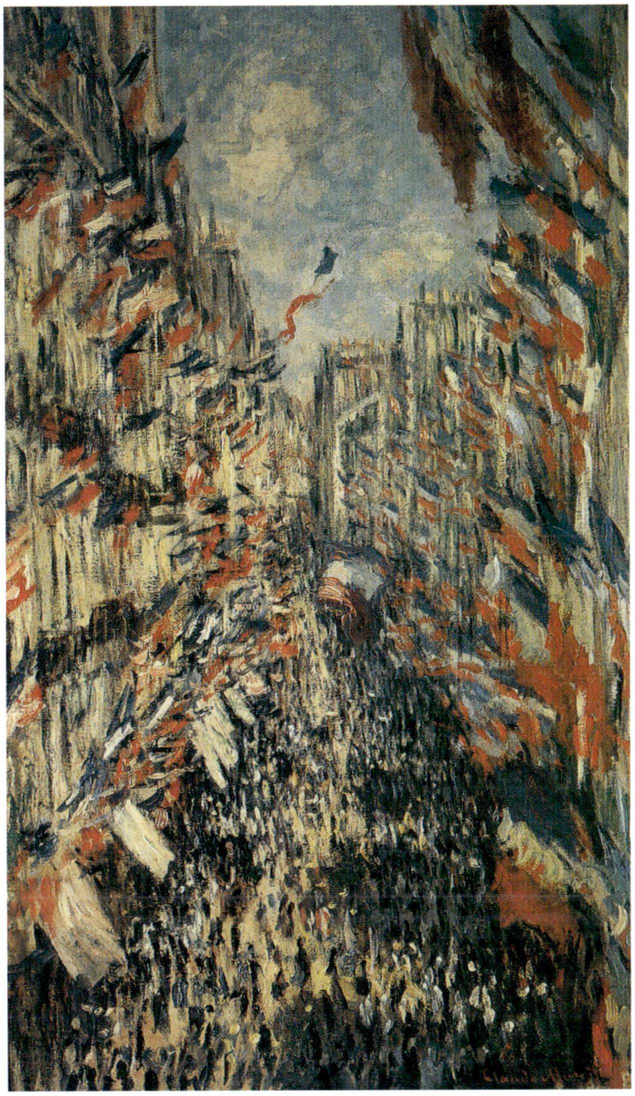

CLAUDE MONET
Rue Montorgeuil: Fête Nationale
1887, Musée d'Orsay, Paris

In his series of paintings of the *Gare St Lazare* (see page 519) Monet had begun to handle paint and color in a way that made the paint surface itself the subject of the painting, with figures and details often described with just a flick of the brush. This is one of a series of paintings of Paris done in 1887 in which this concept was taken even further; here the individual details, such as figures and flags, are seen as a pattern of inter-relating verticals, diagonals and areas of color.

French cultural life, particularly in the aftermath of the siege of Paris. The young painters working in and around Paris were dispersed, and Bazille was killed in a futile engagement early in the war. Degas joined the National Guard and participated in the siege of Paris, but Monet took Camille and Jean on their honeymoon, after which they went to London, avoiding both war and siege. In 1871 they returned to France and settled in Argenteuil.

CLAUDE MONET
The Seine at Porte-Villez; Winter, Snow
1885, Private collection

The river and its different moods was a source of endless fascination for Monet, and here the effects of snow and icy water are captured with singular effectiveness. The earlier form-following brush strokes seen in *Regatta at Argenteuil* (see page 495) have now given way to the *tache* method of building the painting. A darker laying in of thin green-brown underpainting is covered with a thick white, near white or blue dashes of dry paint. The warmest color is in the house behind the trees and the strongest is found in small touches of cobalt blue in the water.

Argenteuil is now a suburb of Paris, but then it was a charming country town sufficiently close to Paris to provide the twin benefits of café life and the delights of the countryside and river banks. It became Monet's home for the next six years as well as a home from home for his artist friends, among whom was Renoir, who often stayed with Monet and frequently painted the same subjects as they sat together on the river bank. These paintings were the real beginnings of Impressionism, and this was one of the most formative periods of Monet's art as well as one of the happiest in his life.

New beginnings

It was also a period of great expansion and prosperity in France, in the aftermath of the Franco-Prussian war. During the 1870s the country, and particularly Paris, established the artistic pre-eminence which it was to hold right up to the Second World War. The feeling of a

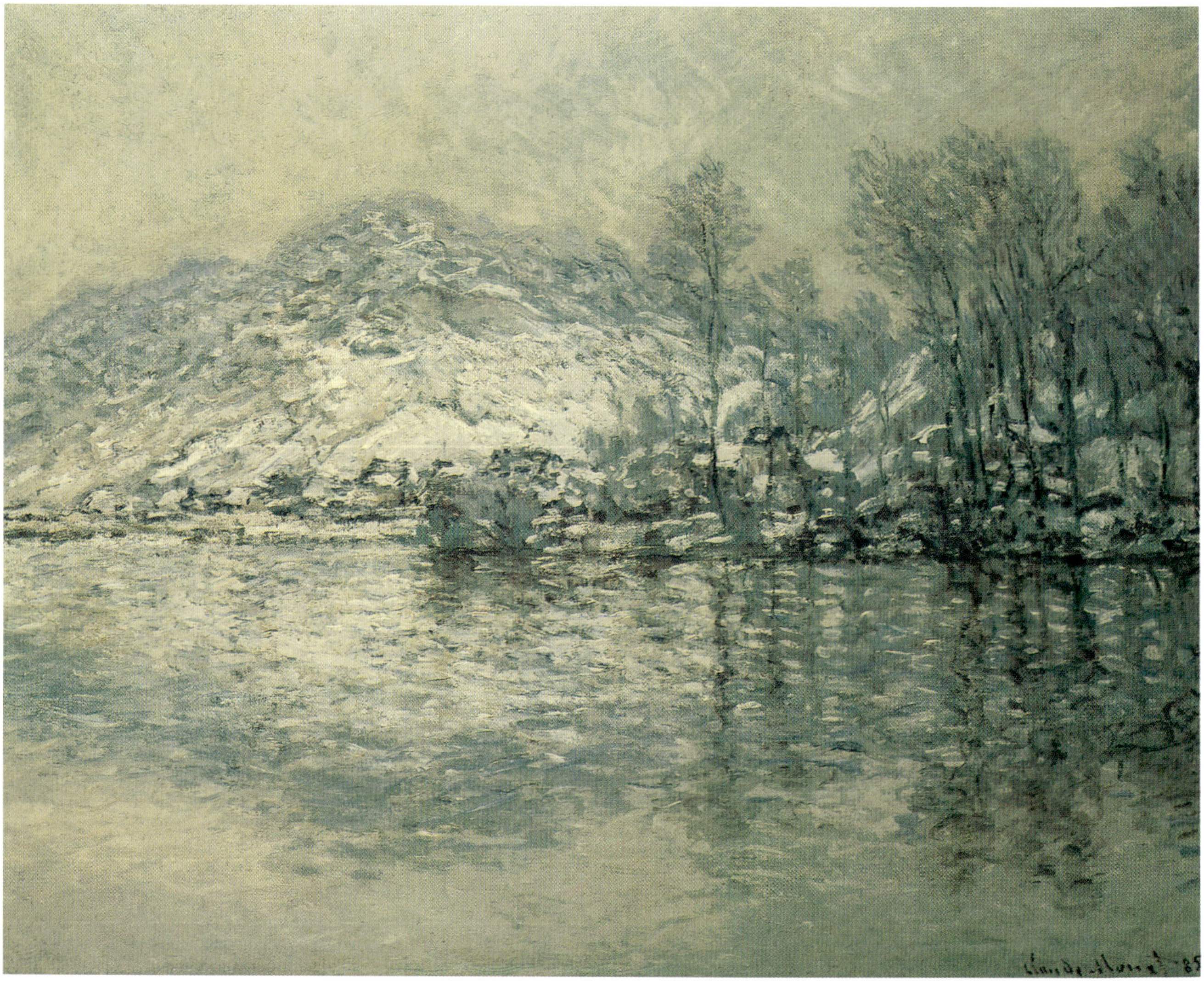

new beginning was heightened by the rebuilding of Paris which had been carried out during the 1860s at considerable expense. All signs of past conflict were obliterated, and a new age had dawned, not only in art but in literature, with such names as Victor Hugo, Flaubert, Balzac, George Sand, Stendhal and de Maupassant leading an impressive rollcall.

When we look at Monet's work during this period it becomes obvious that the old academic tradition represented by such artists as Gleyre and Adolphe Bougereau were no longer relevant to the new creative energy. Undoubtedly society was not conscious of new needs — it seldom is — but the needs were there, and Impressionism, with its directness and immediacy, was able to fill them, at least after the first shock of unfamiliarity had worn off.

At this time the important annual art exhibition in Paris was the Salon, which had opened in the seventeenth century to exhibit the works of the newly formed French Academy. By the nineteenth century the Salon had become so restrictive that even to exhibit was difficult for a non-Academician (so many were rejected that in 1863 a Salon des Refusés was inaugurated as a short-lived alternative). Nevertheless, all young and aspiring painters wished to exhibit, since not only did it bring public recognition, it was also the best marketplace, and Monet was no exception. In 1865 he had been accepted with two seascapes (which he appears to have sold), and a year later a portrait of Camille and a landscape were also hung. But despite this *succès d'estime* he was rarely able to sell his work and often had to rely on funding from his father and his friends.

A change came in 1870 when Monet met Paul Durand-Ruel in London, where both had taken refuge from the war. Durand-Ruel was a picture dealer, one of a newly developing breed of sophisticated and well-educated men who appreciated good paintings, bought them themselves, and were able to persuade potential buyers of their worth. Hitherto, picture dealing had been largely a sideline for shopkeepers selling artists' materials, stationery and so on, and they were little interested in the quality of the works they sold. Durand-Ruel became the most important supporter of the Impressionists during the 1870s and 1880s, and Monet was one of his most successful painters. By the end of the century other dealers had become interested, and Monet and the other Impressionists could afford to ignore the Salon route to success.

Sadly, in 1873, Durand-Ruel found himself in financial straits and was forced to stop buying, causing problems for Monet too. However, at much the same time Monet struck up a friendship with an apparently wealthy businessman, Ernest Hoschedé, and his wife Alice, and the relationship was to have a long-term effect on his life. For the present, it gave him some income from sales to Hoschedé, as well as loans from him.

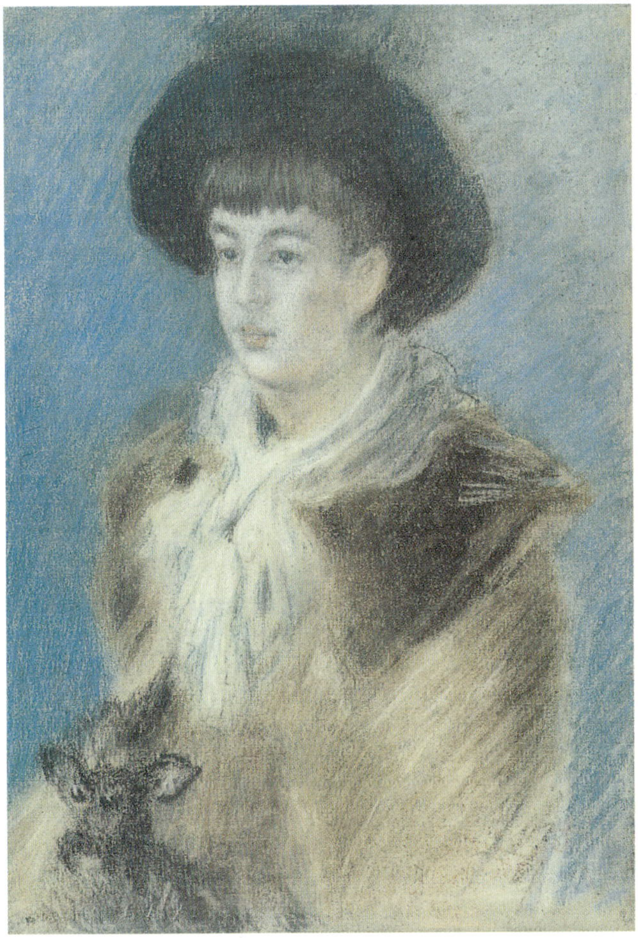

CLAUDE MONET
Suzanne Private collection

Although pastels did not form a large part of Monet's body of work, he produced a number of them, both early and late in his career, finding the medium well suited to his self-imposed task of capturing rapid impressions. This portrait, done in the Giverny period, is of Suzanne Hoschedé, Alice's daughter. In 1892 she married an American painter, Theodore Butler, but became ill after the birth of a child and died in 1899, causing great grief to Monet and his wife.

Monet's life at Argenteuil with Camille and his son provided the stability of a settled household, enabling him to concentrate on the development of his art. In 1874 he became one of the organizers of the First Impressionist Exhibition. Called the "Société Anonyme des Artistes, Peintres, Sculpteurs et Graveurs," the group held its first show in Paris in the studio of the photographer Nadar. The critic Louis Leroy attacked it, suggesting in his article that a "real" (i.e. academic) painter would be driven mad by the works to be seen. Subsequent reviews of other group shows were no more favorable. Another critic, Ballou, reviewing the work of Monet and Cézanne in 1877, wrote: "They provoke laughter and are altogether lamentable. They show the most profound ignorance of design, composition and color. Children amusing themselves with paper and paint could do much better."

But in spite of the poor reception the group shows became an annual event, and Monet exhibited in the first four, the seventh and the last, after which he had "arrived," and was able to sell his work and arrange one-man shows whenever he wished.

His domestic life was again disrupted when in 1877 Ernest Hoschedé became bankrupt. The two families decided to pool their resources, and they moved to Vetheuil, also on the Seine but considerably further — forty miles — from Paris. Monet managed to keep a small *pied à terre* in Paris to show his paintings, since he could not bring his customers so far from the capital.

The Giverny years

Soon after their arrival at Vetheuil Camille, who had recently borne a second son, Michel, died. Monet became distraught and was unable to work. Alice Hoschedé looked after Monet's children as well as her own six, and the families remained linked, moving together first to Poissy and then to Giverny in 1883. While they were still at Poissy, Ernest Hoschedé, disenchanted with poverty

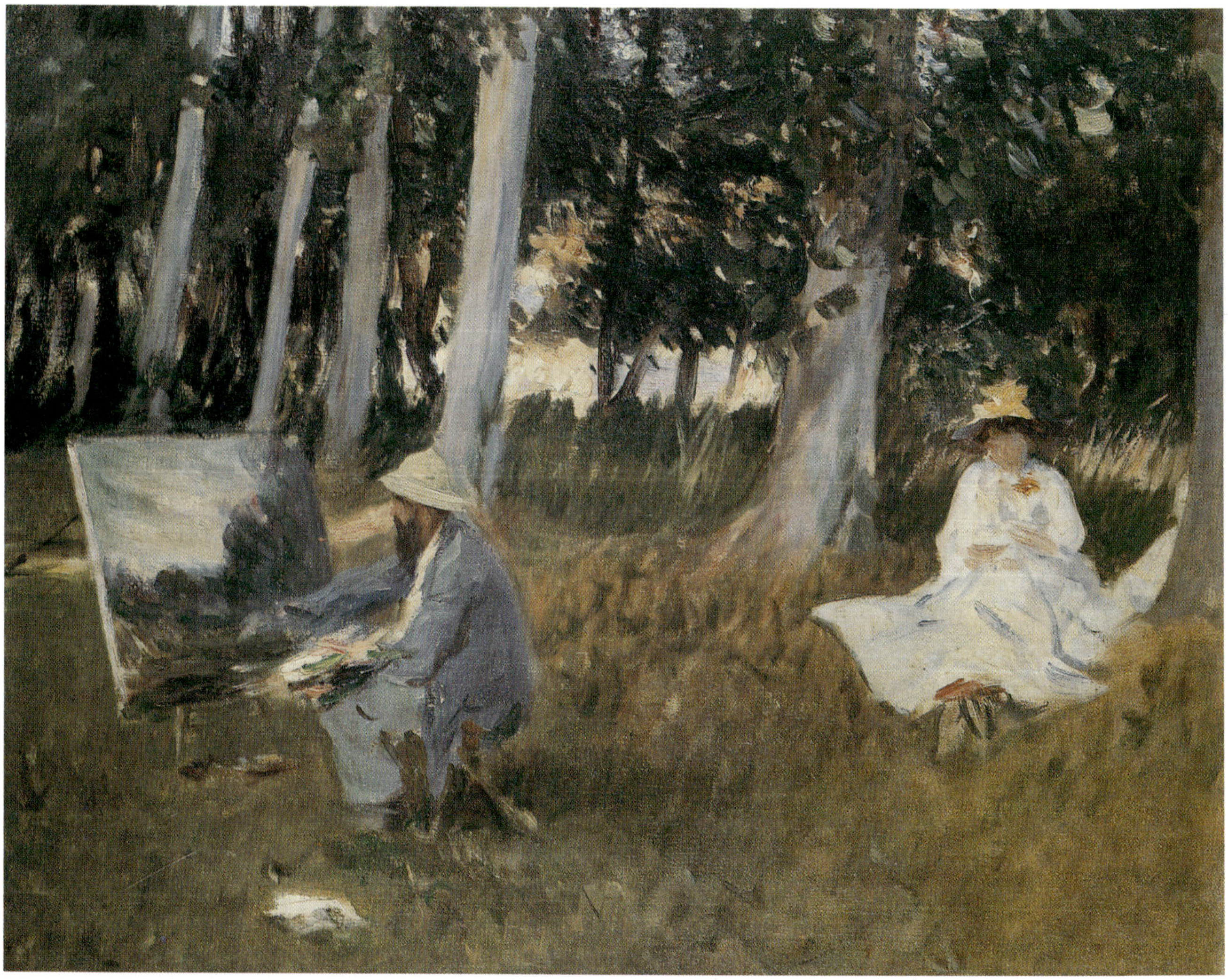

JOHN SINGER SARGENT
Monet Painting on the Edge of a Wood
1885/7, Tate Gallery, London

Monet became friendly with Sargent after they met at Durand-Ruel's gallery around 1884/5, and Sargent became a regular guest at Giverny in the later 1880s. The two artists painted together in the open air during this period, and this direct sketch, showing all Sargent's considerable virtuosity, is a most convincing impression of Monet at work. The other seated figure is probably Blanche, Monet's daughter-in-law, who often carried his equipment and was his most attentive assistant.

MONET'S PAINTING METHODS

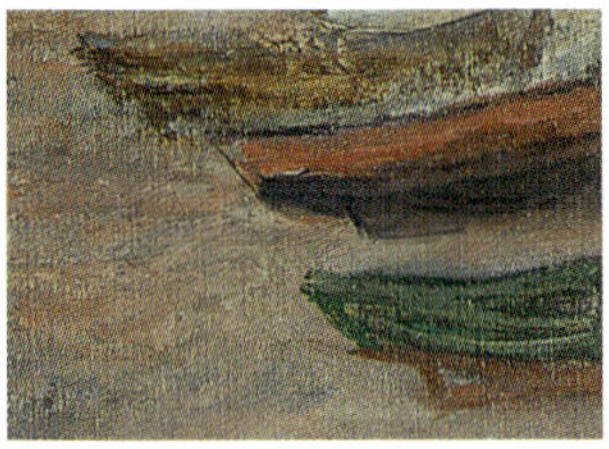

In Morning at Etretat *Monet used a gray-tinted canvas, here visible through the thinly applied paint in the shore area.*

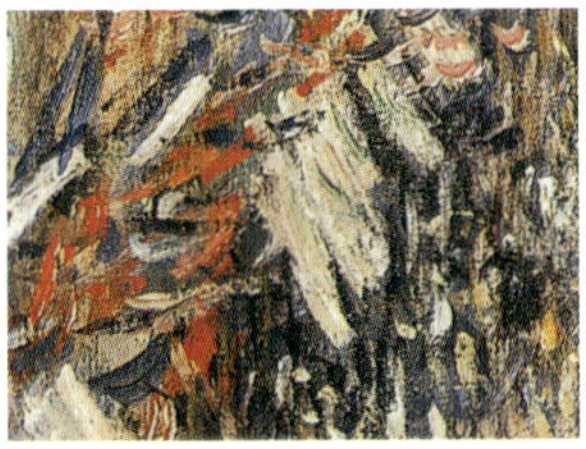

In paintings such as Rue Montorgeuil *Monet has used his brushstrokes to form a vibrating pattern of verticals and diagonals.*

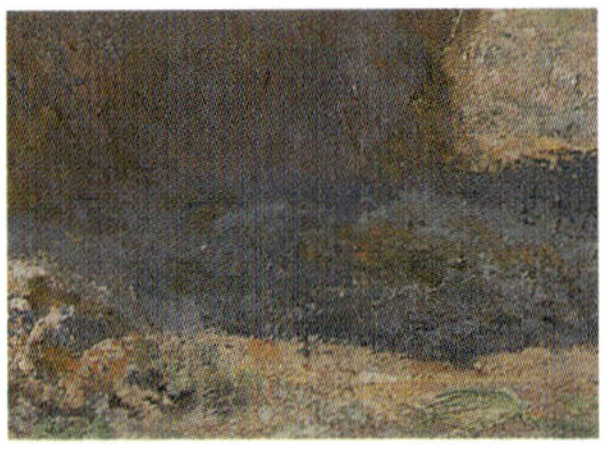

This detail of the foreground of Grain Stacks *shows how Monet saw each area as composed of many different colors of the same tonal value.*

Monet usually painted on standard-sized canvases with a white priming, a break from earlier tradition, in which forms and tones had been built up from dark to light on a dark-toned ground. However, although he said in 1920 that he "always insisted on painting on white canvases, in order to establish on them my scale of values," this statement is not entirely true; in fact he used a wide range of mid-toned primings, often a warm beige or light gray. From about 1860 the color of these primings became an element in the paintings, with small areas either being left unpainted or very lightly covered.

Monet always stood up to work, whether outdoors or in the studio, and he never believed his paintings were finished, frequently reworking them in the studio in spite of his often-stated belief in instantaneity. Except in the earlier works he did little or no underdrawing or tonal underpainting, beginning each painting with colors approximating to the finished ones, and working all over the canvas at the same time with long thin bristle brushes. His brushwork varied from painting to painting as well as through the course of his long career, but one of the main characteristics of his work, and of other members of the group, is the use of what is known as the *tache*, the method of applying paint in small opaque touches, premixed on the palette with the minimum of mixing medium. This provides a patchwork-like fabric of all-over color, described by Zola as "as ensemble of delicate, accurate *taches* which, from a few steps back, give a striking relief to the picture."

The colors shown here, plus lead white, are those used in Bathing at La Grenouillère, *and are typical of Monet's palette at the time. In early paintings he also used black, and it is probable that he sometimes extended his range with yellow ocher, burnt sienna and ultramarine.*

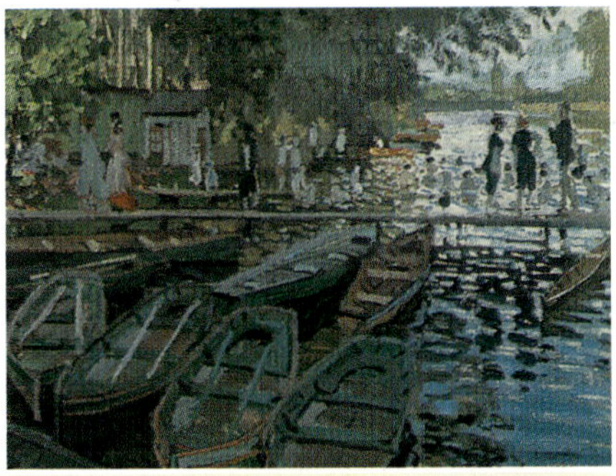

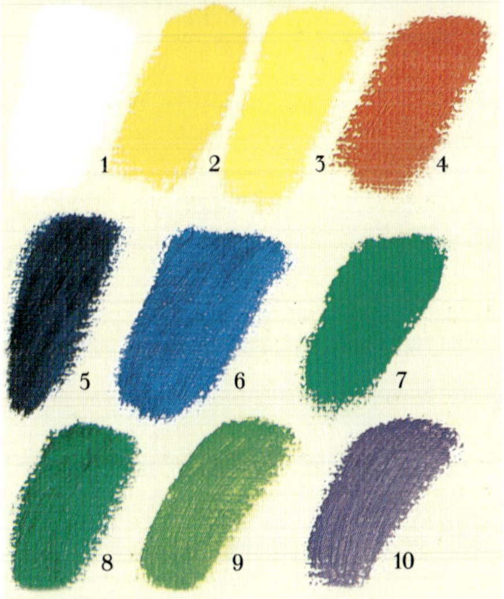

1 White; 2 Chrome yellow; 3 Lemon yellow; 4 Vermilion; 5 Prussian blue; 6 Cobalt blue; 7 Emerald green; 8 Viridian; 9 Chrome green; 10 Cobalt violet

and provincial family life, gradually disengaged himself and took up a bachelor life in Paris, where he built up a new business from the sale of a few paintings he had managed to keep.

The move to Giverny coincided with the death of Manet, and Monet went to Paris to be a pallbearer, but his close association with the city was now over, and Giverny became the focus of his life and the subject-source of most of his later paintings. He had purchased a farmhouse on the outskirts of the village, which is about fifty miles from Paris on the banks of the Seine. The house was close to the river and set in water meadows, and here Monet made the water garden that became the subject of his last great paintings. He gradually became isolated from his friends, a semi-recluse.

Ernest's desertion of the family had created a somewhat unconventional situation in the household, since Alice had remained to look after the children. Neither of them was happy about it: Monet was deeply conventional in such matters and Alice was devoutly religious, so for some time there was an undercurrent of tension in the Giverny establishment. However, in 1892 Ernest died, and a quiet wedding ceremony took place.

All the reports of Monet's life at Giverny — and there were many because by this time he was famous and the subject of considerable public interest — reflect the image of a complex and moody man whose humors affected the whole household. He was irascible and

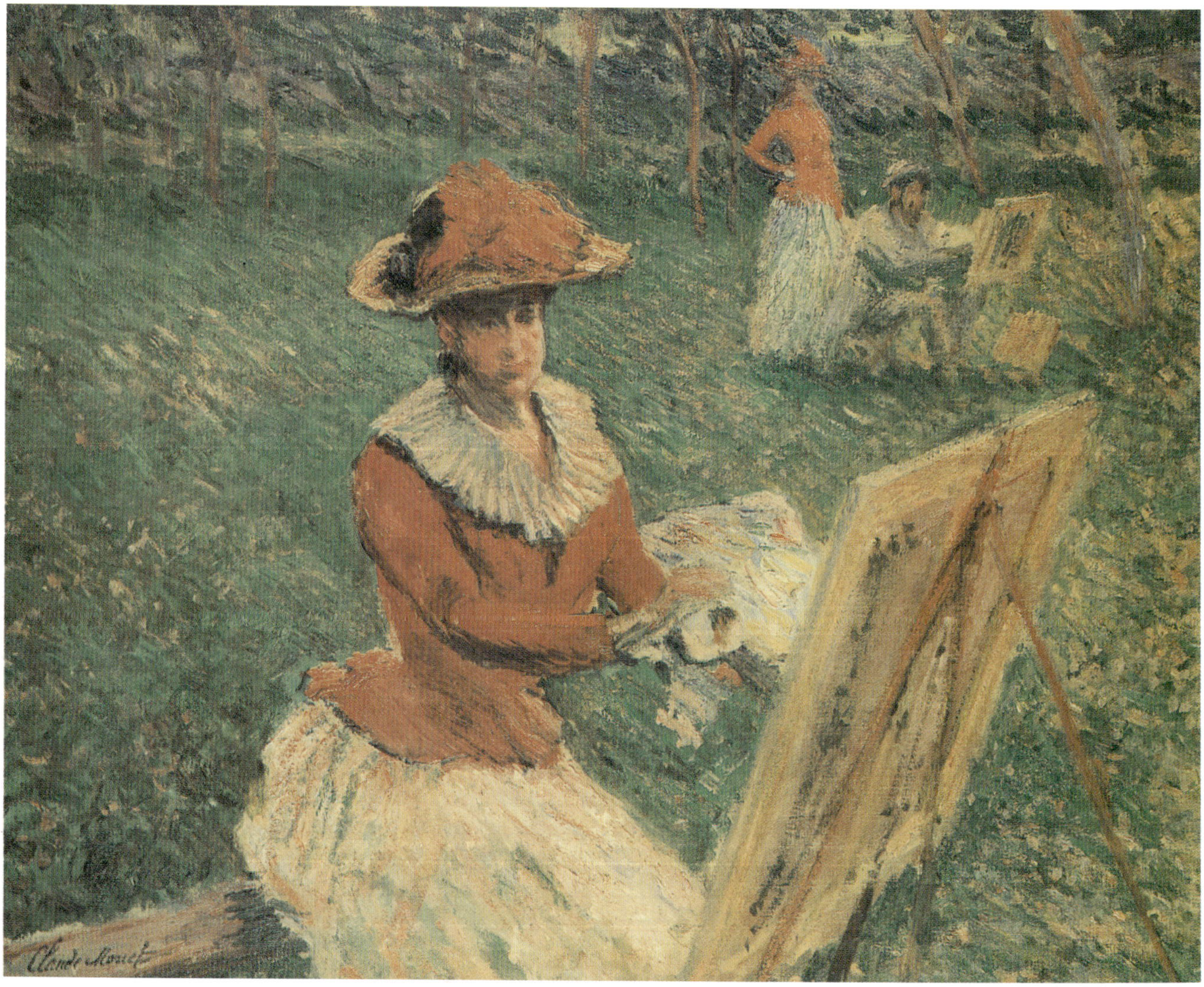

CLAUDE MONET
Blanche painting
1892, Private collection

Blanche Hoschedé, Monet's daughter-in-law, became quite a competent painter under his instruction and often accompanied him on local painting trips. On this one they were joined by another painting friend, probably Caillebotte. The woman in the background is probably Blanche, whose figure was repeated while she took a break from her own painting — a little joke perhaps. This was a private study, and unusual in that Monet rarely painted figures after the 1880s. It shows a good deal of overworking in the head and near arm, and there is less of the fluid assurance which he shows in his landscapes.

unbearable when thwarted, particularly when the weather prevented him from painting – and would sometimes stay in bed all day refusing any attention. He was only forty-three when he bought the house, with exactly half his life still to live, yet he had already become an autocratic patriarch, and clearly fostered the image. Altogether, he lived exactly as he wished, with scant respect for the wishes and needs of others; for instance, he forbade the marriage of Alice's daughter Germaine to Pierre Sisley, the painter's son, on the grounds that Pierre's occupation, as an inventor, was too insecure. Odd behavior from a once-impoverished painter, one might think.

The planning and development of his garden became his major preoccupation and demanded much of the not inconsiderable income he was now making from his painting. Six gardeners were employed, one of whom looked after the water garden exclusively. This, filled with a great variety of waterlilies and surrounded by willows, was developed from the purchase of some nearby land, and across its narrower part Monet constructed a Japanese bridge he had designed himself, based on a Japanese print he had bought in the 1860s.

Monet's house and garden became a place of pilgrimage for friends and admirers. In spite of his reclusive tendencies, friends still played a part in his life and he was deeply distressed as one by one they died, suffering periods of fierce melancholy which prevented him from working. The gravest blow of all was the death of Alice in May 1911, and he did not work until the end of the year.

The most important friend of his late years, and one who survived him, was Georges Clemenceau, the statesman and journalist, whose support during the time after Alice's death was crucial. But Monet's troubles were not over; he had begun to suffer from failing eyesight some years before the loss of Alice, but it was not until 1912 that he was persuaded to see an eye specialist, who diagnosed a double cataract, requiring an operation. Fearing both the operation and its effect on his vision, Monet refused, and even Clemenceau could not persuade him. (He did finally have the operation, in 1923.)

The last great works

Yet another blow for Monet was the death of his older son Jean in 1914 just before the outbreak of war. Jean's widow, Blanche, one of Alice's daughters, came to live with him and cared for him for the rest of his life. She was also a painter, and they often painted together.

Blanche and Clemenceau formed a mutually supportive alliance, and it was through Clemenceau that Monet's last great commission was secured, for the panels known as the *Nymphéas*, or *Waterlilies* (see page 533), destined to decorate a specially constructed room in the Orangerie, Paris. Clemenceau was devoted to Monet and continued to visit him up to his death, though there were, of course, strains in their relationship, mainly caused by Monet's failure to meet his deadlines. His dissatisfaction with his work, partly the result of his failing vision, prompted violent physical attacks on his work, including the *Nymphéas* panels, which he altered constantly. He would not allow them to leave the studio, and there was a real danger that he might even destroy them, since it was his habit to make bonfires in the garden of paintings that he found inadequate. The panels were not, in fact, put in place until the year after Monet's death.

Clemenceau was present at Giverny on December 5th, 1926 when, around noon, Monet died. As he had wished, he was given a quiet funeral, with Clemenceau and the painters Pierre Bonnard, K-X Roussel and Edouard Vuillard as pallbearers.

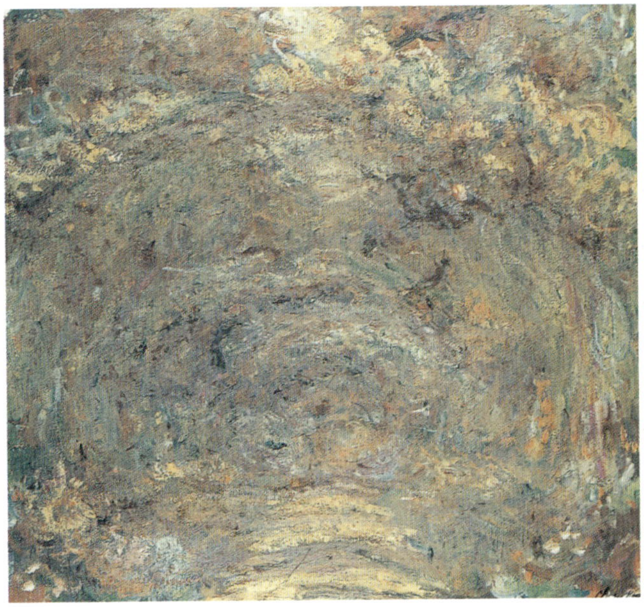

CLAUDE MONET
A Shady Walk
1920, Private collection

Monet created, as part of his garden at Giverny, a walk from the main entrance to the farmhouse itself, which included about six arched pergolas. He liked a controlled wildness, and as time passed this walk became a riot of color, with flowers spreading across the path itself to produce the effect of a shaded, multi-colored grotto. This late painting, done when his eyesight had so deteriorated that he could see the swirling motion of color but few distinct forms, is probably of this walk; he rarely left his garden in his last years. The work is a moving expression of his devotion to his painting, and constitutes a triumph of experience over physical limitation.

CHRONOLOGY OF MONET'S LIFE

1840 November 4th: Claude Oscar Monet born Paris. Auguste Rodin born in same year.

1845 Family moves to Le Havre.

c.1856/7 Meets Eugène Boudin.

1859 First visit to Paris; meets a number of painters including Pissarro.

1861-2 Military service in Algeria. Discharged because of ill health. Meets Dutch painter Jongkind.

1862 Enters Gleyre's studio where he meets Bazille, Renoir and Sisley.

1864 Leaves Gleyre's studio. Paints at Fontainebleau.

1865 Shares studio with Bazille in Paris. First exhibits at Salon.

1866 Portrait of Camille success at Salon.

1867 First son Jean born. Financial problems force him to return to family in Le Havre.

1868 Lives with Camille Doncieux at Etretat during winter.

1870 Marries Camille. Outbreak of Franco-Prussian war causes visit to England where he meets Durand-Ruel.

1871 Returns to France and settles at Argenteuil. Rejected by Royal Academy, London.

1872-4 Durand-Ruel buys paintings.

1874 First Impressionist Exhibition.

1876 Meets Hoschedé family.

1877 Ernest Hoschedé becomes bankrupt. Works in Paris on *Gare Saint-Lazare* paintings.

1878 Moves to Ventheuil and is joined by the Hoschedé family. Second son Michel is born.

1879 Camille dies. Alice Hoschedé takes charge of household.

1880 Exhibits at Salon.

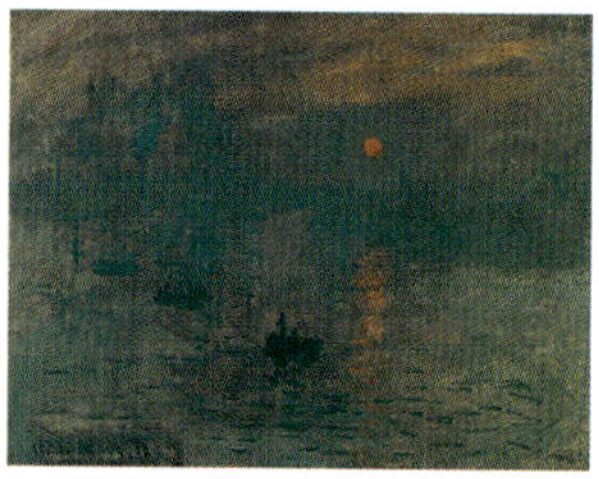

Impression, Sunrise

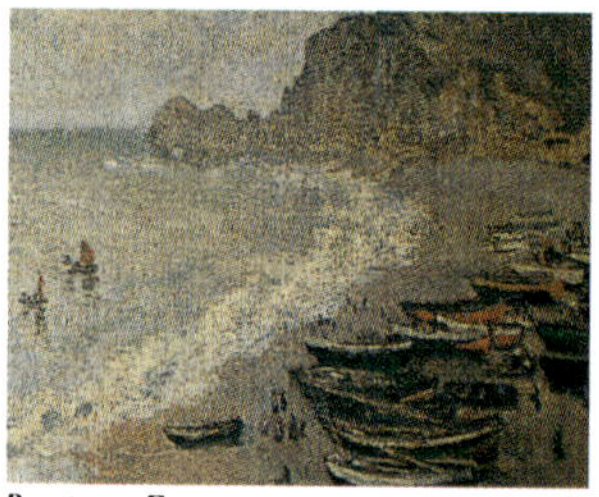

Boats at Etretat

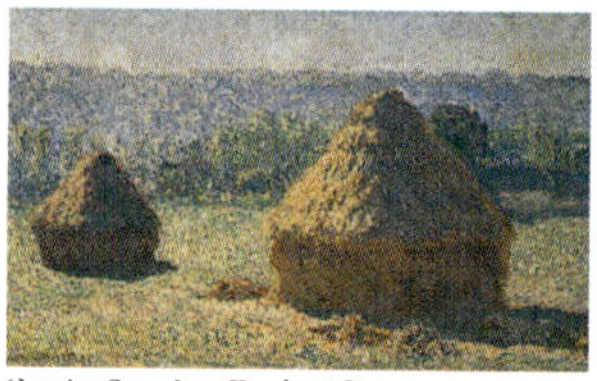

Grain Stacks, End of Summer

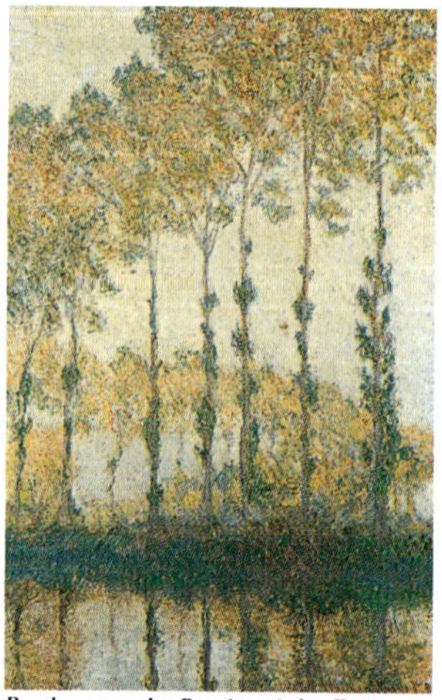

Poplars on the Banks of the Epte

1881 Moves to Poissy. Durand-Ruel resumes purchase of work after earlier financial problems.

1882 Exhibits in seventh group exhibition.

1883 Moves to Giverny. One-man show at Durand-Ruel gallery. Summer: makes first paintings of Giverny region.Trips to the Midi and Italian Riviera with Renoir. Visits Cézanne during trip.

1884-7 Paints at Giverny and northern French coast.

1888 Paints at Antibes. Refuses Legion d'Honneur.

1889 Exhibits with Rodin at Georges Petits gallery. Organizes private subscription list to purchase Manet's *Olympia* for the State.

1890 Begins "series" paintings with *Grain Stacks*. Purchases home at Giverny.

1892 Begins *Rouen* series. Marries Alice Hoschedé.

1893 Begins making water garden.

1895 Painting trip to Norway.

1896 *Early morning on Seine* series.

1899 Begins first paintings of water garden and Japanese bridge. Painting trip to London.

1900-1 Works on *Thames* series in London.

1903 Begins second *Water Garden* series.

1908 Painting journey (last) to Venice. Trouble with eyesight.

1911 Death of Alice.

1914 Builds new studio for *Waterlilies* panels. Death of son Jean.

1921 Deterioration in his sight..

1922 Bequest of *Waterlilies* to state.

1923 Has cataract operation, which is partially successful.

1926 December 5th: death at Giverny.

THE PAINTINGS

Women in the Garden

1866/7

$100\frac{3}{4} \times 81\frac{3}{4}$in/$256 \times 208$cm

Oil on canvas

Musée d'Orsay, Paris

Monet planned this painting as a major exhibition piece for the Salon of 1867. The Salon was still at this time the place where artistic reputations were made, and no young artist could afford to ignore it. Monet had previously shown small works in the manner of Boudin and a full-length portrait of his wife Camille, but this painting, a very large-scale work more than eight feet high, was clearly intended as a publicity work designed to gain commissions, and the size of the signature suggests that Monet wanted to fix his name in the mind of the public.

The work, however, was rejected, which perhaps did not surprise Monet unduly; since his time at Gleyre's studio he had had no very high regard for academic judgement. Although the painting might have appeared to conform to the pattern of figure composition that was acceptable to the Academicians it lacked one important element: the figures in the group have no dramatic relationship with each other, that is, there is no "story line" in the painting. This was then regarded as the *raison d'être* of a painting, whether it be historical, literary, religious or social, but in Monet's work the people simply exist. Also they all look somewhat alike – not surprising, as Camille posed for all of them.

But this was not the only reason for the rejection of the painting. Monet's technique itself left much to be desired in terms of academic practice. As in other early works the paint handling is close to that of Manet, with the shapes of the figures, the shadows and the foliage clearly defined, and little range of tonal modeling. This treatment may well have reminded the judges of the public scandals caused by Manet's work, first by the *Déjeuner sur l'Herbe* displayed in the Salon des Refusés in 1863 and then by the equally offensive nude, *Olympia*, two years later. Monet had intended to submit his own version of a "Déjeuner sur l'Herbe" in 1866, but failed to complete it in time, so *Women in the Garden* was his first major attack on the citadel of the Salon.

The academic method of painting was essentially one of building form by means of tone. The painting was built on a lightly colored neutral ground, beginning with an underpainting of dark tones, usually brownish in hue. Into this dark underpainting the highlights were added in white or near-white, and the local color of the object or figure (its actual color) was introduced into the middle-toned areas. This method produced a strong sense of volume and solidity of form, but color played a secondary role, being diminished or sometimes even lost in highly illuminated or deeply shadowed areas. The method adopted by Manet, sometimes called *peinture claire*, was first to determine color areas through mid-tones and then to add highlights and darks into the wet paint, thus emphasizing shapes at the expense of form. This resulted in a strong color pattern, reminiscent of the then-popular Japanese prints, and also gave more importance to color itself, since the real colors of highlights and shadows could be given more consideration.

Monet went a stage further in this painting, giving a clear color identity to each shadow, such as that falling across the path and onto the dress of the seated figure. The resultant mauve-blue on the dress is one of the dominant colors in the work, and gives "uplift" to the tonal pattern. In the painting of the foliage there is a great variety of greens and yellows but no dark-toned shadows, and very little black is used, a color Monet was soon to abandon altogether.

The whole effect of the painting was thus antipathetic to standard academic practice, and the Salon judges were the reverse of artistically adventurous. The rejection, although undoubtedly disappointing for Monet, in no way deflected him from his chosen course.

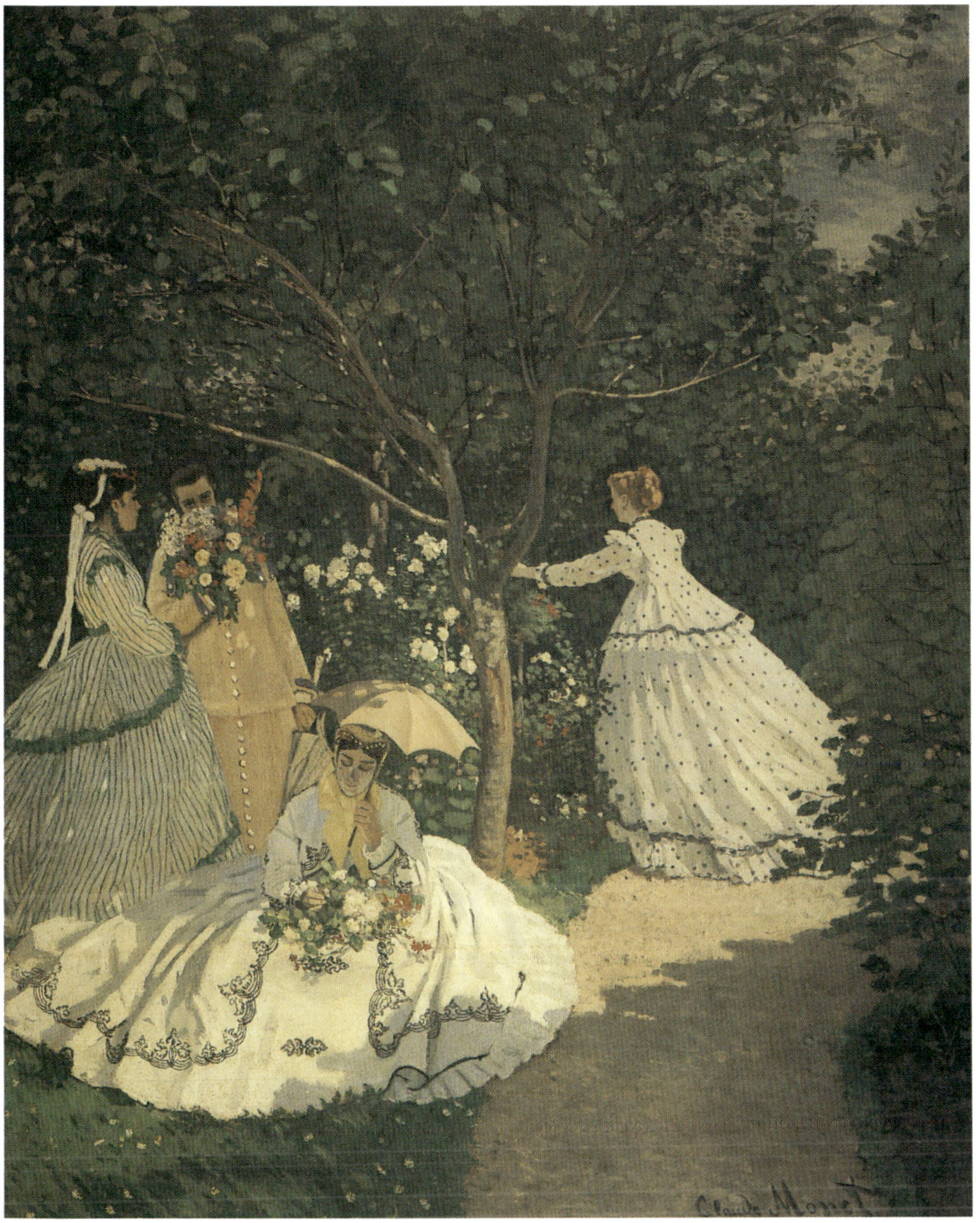

Compositionally the painting is divided into quarters, pivoting on the springing of the branches of the small tree — an almost central spot in the work. The top half of the painting is in deep tone almost entirely occupied by foliage, while three or four figures, static and preoccupied, are concentrated in the left lower quarter. The moving figure is lit from the right and this light, falling across both the path and the dress of the seated figure, also strikes the flowers she is holding. The second bunch of flowers and flowering shrubs provide a moving ellipse through the outstretched arm, the lefthand figure, the skirt of the seated figure and across the path, giving a touch of animation.

The large scale of this work necessitated the digging of a trench into which the canvas was lowered to enable Monet to work on the top of the painting in the open air.

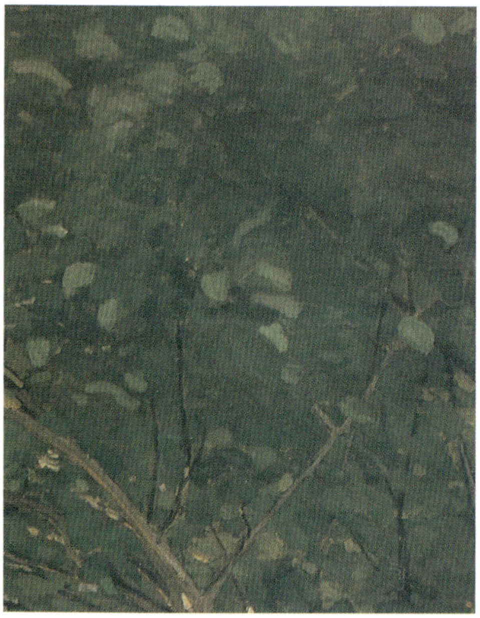

1

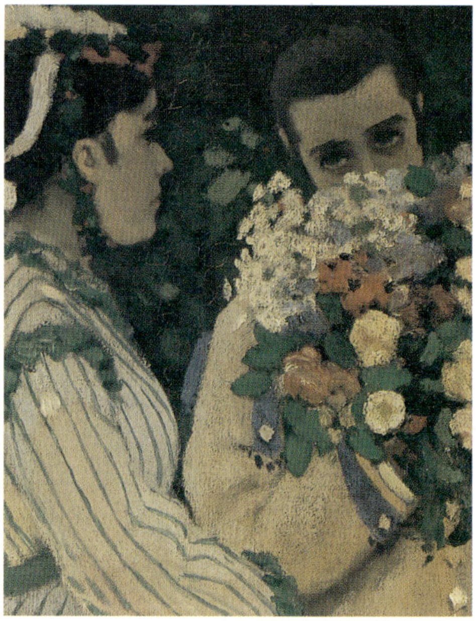

2

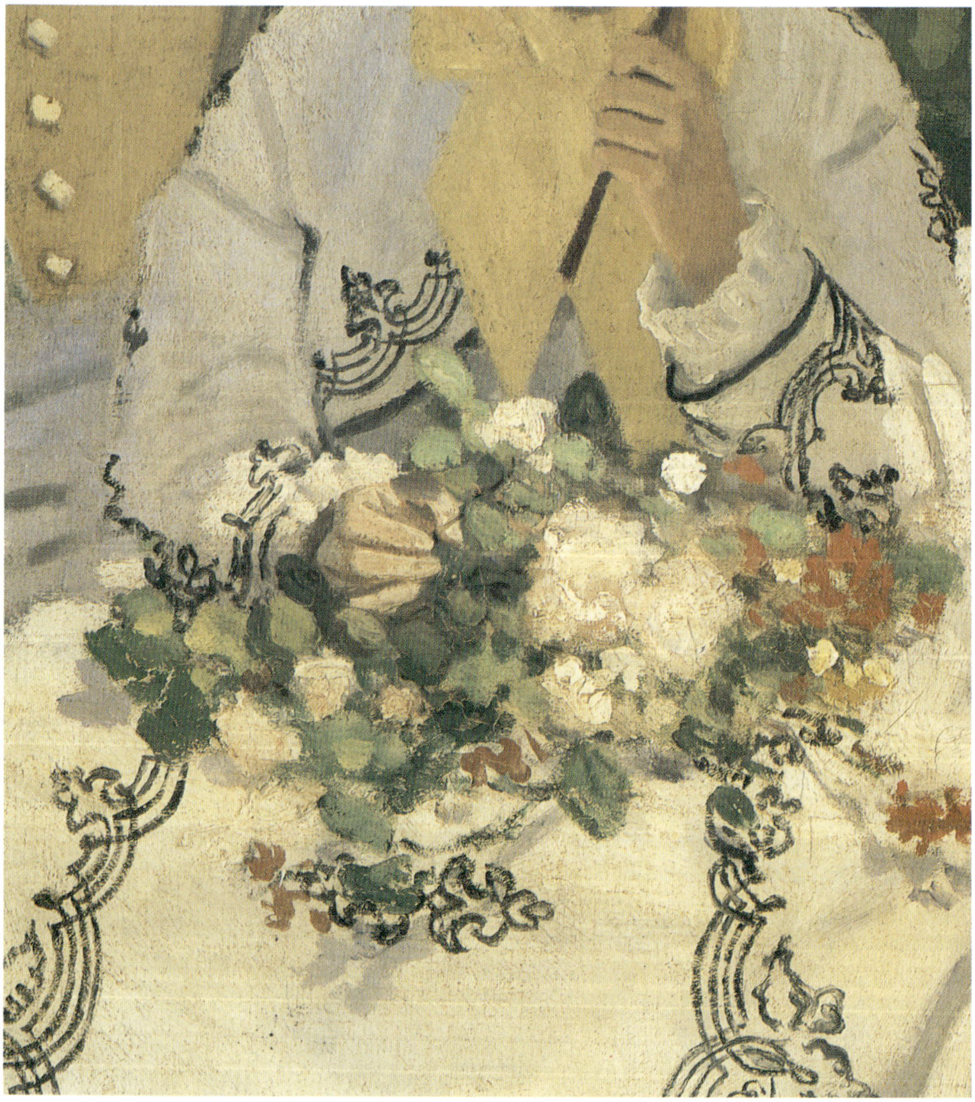

3

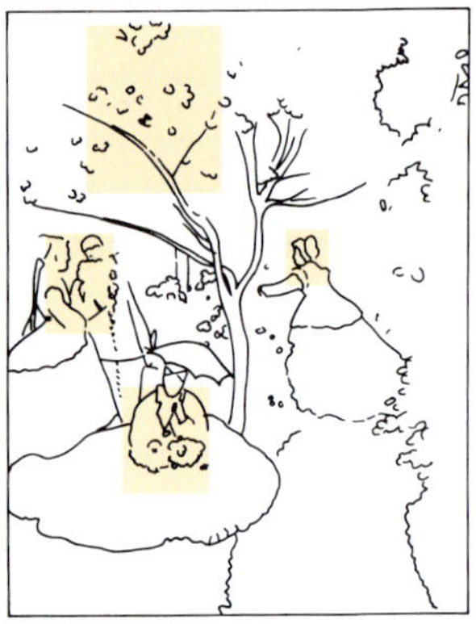

1 The foliage in this part of the painting is done in a variety of greens and brown with touches of black (Monet later abandoned the use of black). Some leaves are given emphasis with emerald green heightened with white and modified with yellow ocher, chrome yellow or cadmium yellow.

2 There is a curious quality about these two heads: the coyness of the eyes seen over the flowers and the pertness of the lefthand figure suggest that some dramatic relationship, or "story line," is intended, but nothing is explicit. The whole group is lower in tone, with these flowers quite muted in comparison with the others.

Painted thickly and freely, the flowers provide an enlivening note of warm color in a part of the painting which is largely cool and shaded.

3 This is the liveliest piece of virtuoso brushwork in the whole painting, and reminds us that this large work was in part an advertisement of the artist's skill, designed to establish his ability at handling large-scale compositions. The cast shadow from the flowers is a delicate mauve-violet, a departure from the usual academic practice and the beginning of Monet's search for true color equivalents, as distinct from tones, in every part of a painting. The blue-mauve tint of the upper part of the dress, sharpened by the warm yellow-brown hat ribbon, a near complementary, provides a lively background.

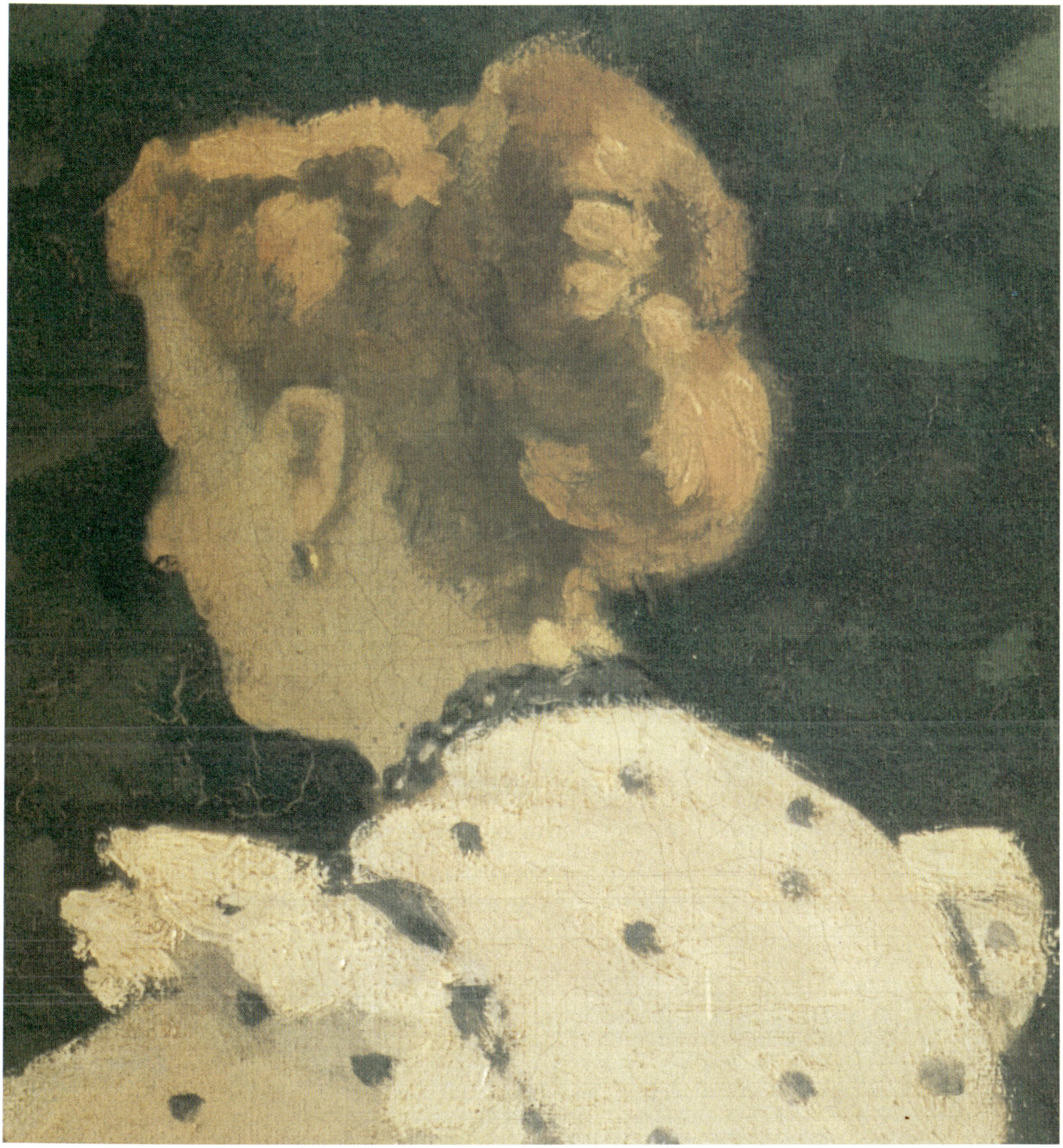

4

4 *Actual size detail* The solid blocked paint can be seen clearly in this detail. The basis for the color is probably burnt sienna with white. The blue-green halo effect heightens the hair color, and the flesh is treated in a grayish tone, as deep as possible to retain the head shape while still laying emphasis on the hair.

Impression, Sunrise

1872

19×25in/48×63.5cm

Oil on possibly reused canvas

Musée Marmottan, Paris

This small painting has become one of Monet's most important works by virtue of the title he chose for it, and to fully understand Monet's work it is necessary to understand the significance the word "impression" had for him. One of the canvases submitted for the First Impressionist Exhibition in 1874, this was singled out by an antagonistic critic as typifying the "half-finished" look of all the works on show, and he dubbed the group "Impressionists."

In the personal terminology Monet used to describe his various types of paintings he would normally have called this work a *pochade* (sketch). However, as he said himself, he called it "impression" because "it really could not pass as a view of Le Havre," and he subsequently used the same word for a number of his paintings, all of them quick atmospheric sketches capturing a particular light effect. An "impression" for Monet was a special and limited form of sketch, and although the other Impressionists accepted the word as a reasonable description of their aims, Monet himself used it only when he felt it appropriate to a particular work.

Thus it appears that he did not really regard himself as an "Impressionist," and as a description of the diversity of aims of the other painters who exhibited in 1874 it hardly seems very revealing. However, it is the term universally adopted of the movement which became one of the most popular in the entire history of art, and is also frequently applied to painters — and even sculptors — only remotely connected with the original group.

Impression, Sunrise is a slight sketch, almost certainly completed on the spot in a single sitting, depicting the harbour at Le Havre as the sun rises over the cranes, derricks and masts of the anchored ships. The only evidence of life is the lazy action of the oarsman in the most sharply defined part of the painting. The painting gives a suggestion of the early morning mist, at that time clogged with the industrial smoke of the city, and has a strong relationship to the earlier views of mist and fog done in London in 1870. Monet had only recent returned from London, and his abiding impression of the city, recalled later, was of its fog. While there, he had seen the work of J.M.W. Turner (1775-1851), who is generally thought to have been an important influence on Monet and the other Impressionists, and he may also have seen some of the early *Nocturnes* by his contemporary Whistler.

At this time Monet was still painting scenes of urban and industrial life, though his vision was entirely that of a landscape painter and his interest mainly in the effects of light rather than in any specific architectural features or the social significance of the manifestations of industry. The most obvious characteristic of *Impression, Sunrise* is its immediacy of execution and the way it captures just one perceived instant. The forceful, clear shape and strong color of the sun provides the keynote for the work, with the dense, muted pale blue surrounding it providing the opposition of complementary colors which enhances the brilliance of both. The dark note of the nearest boat identifies and stabilizes the color key, the darkest element in the whole painting being the single near-black accented horizontal defining the waterline. With the passage of time, underpainting sometimes begins to come through, and here we can see some early drawing in the lower left- and righthand areas, further evidence of the urgency and immediacy of the painting.

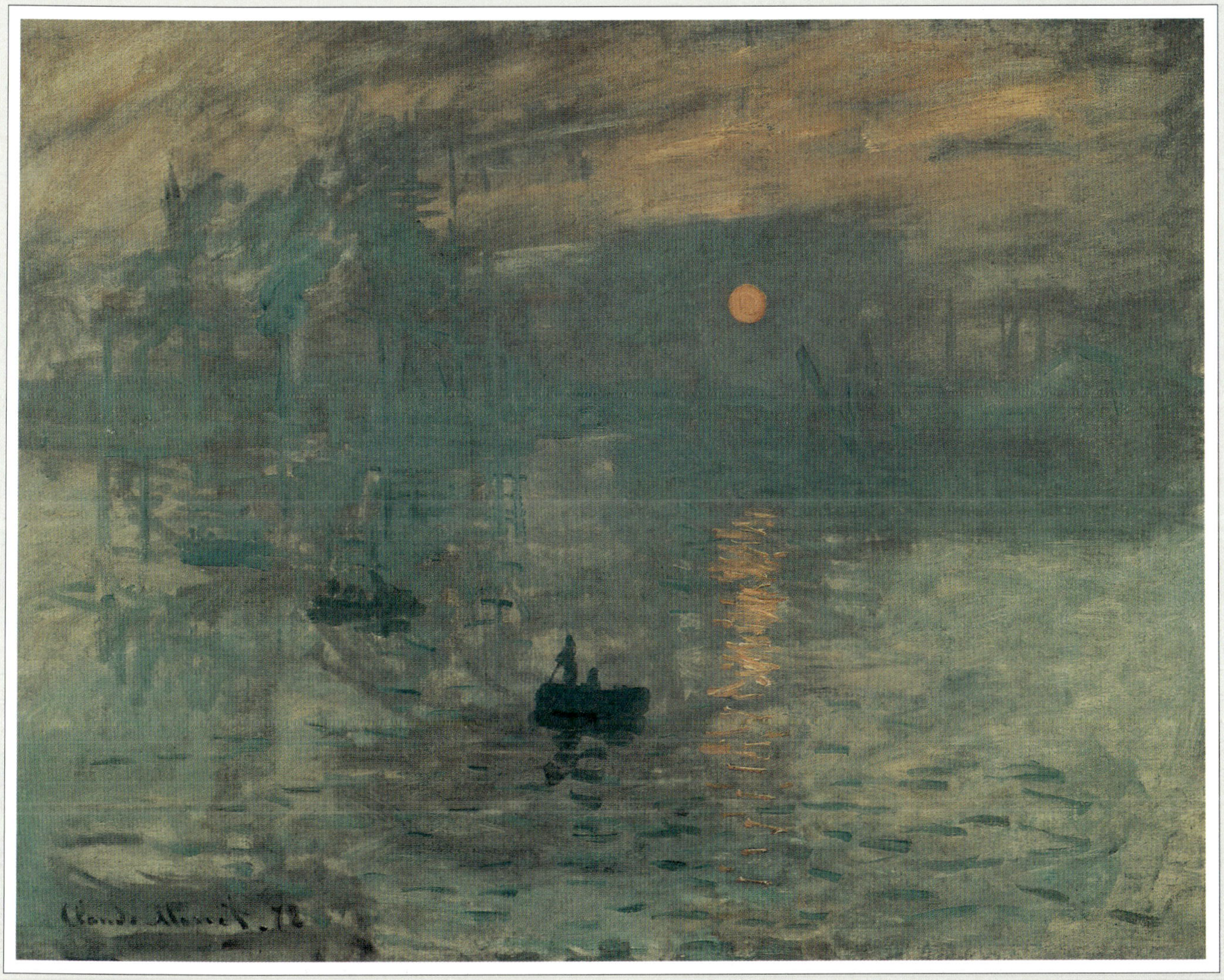

The color character of this painting relies on the opposition of complementaries or near complementaries — orange and blue. In the top left a brown (a mixture of the same orange and blue) gives a linking color note. The composition, though simple, like that of most Impressionist paintings, is nevertheless dramatically effective. The indistinct forms of the port run across the canvas at Golden Section height, and a diagonal from the left edge through the three small boats emphasizes the positioning of the orange sun, while the middle small boat repeats the sun's position in the alternative quarter. The effect is a dynamic balance in which the reflection of the sun in the water contributes the enlivening element.

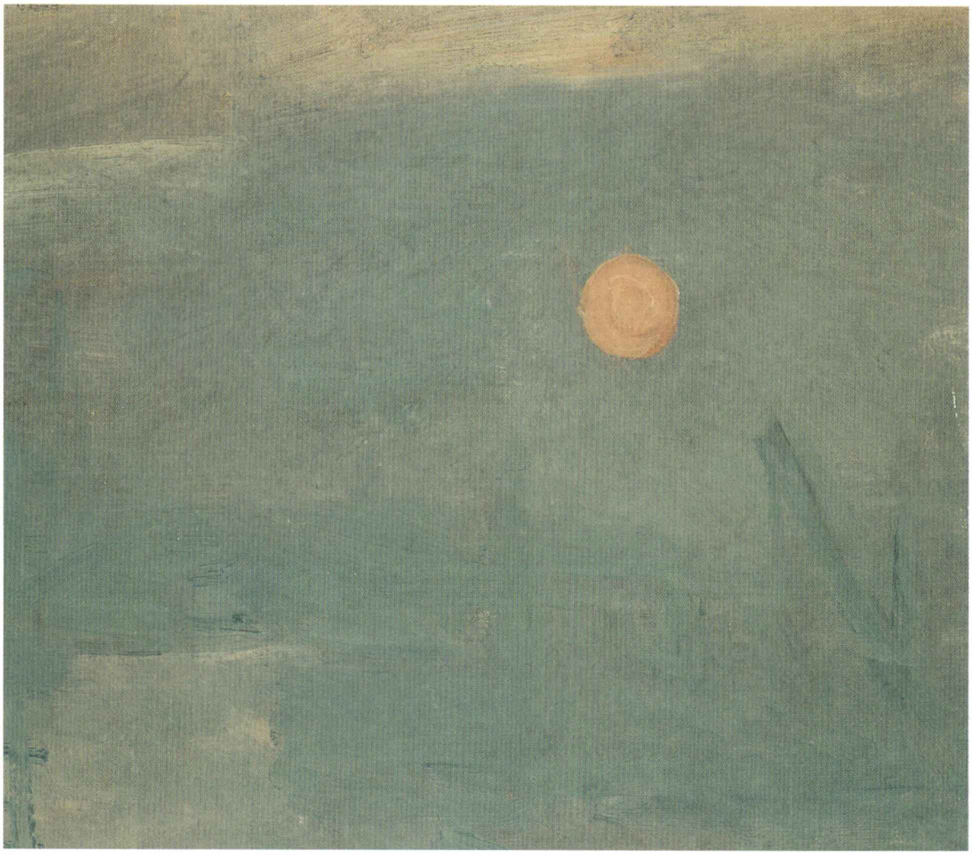

1

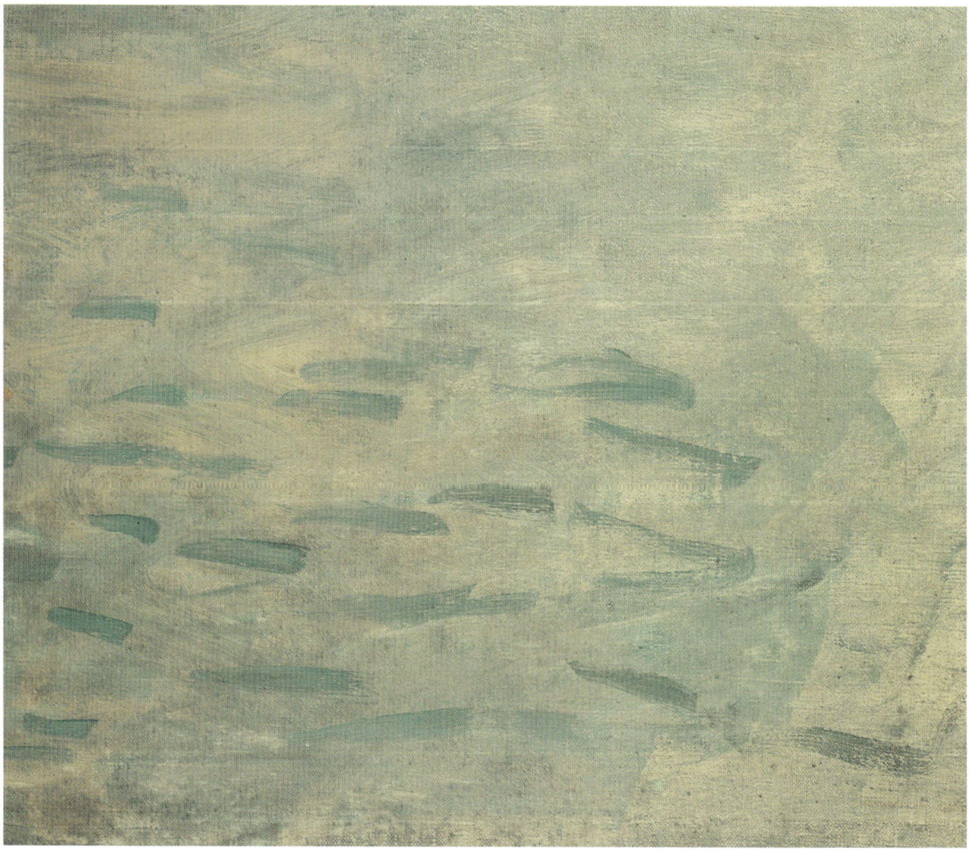

2

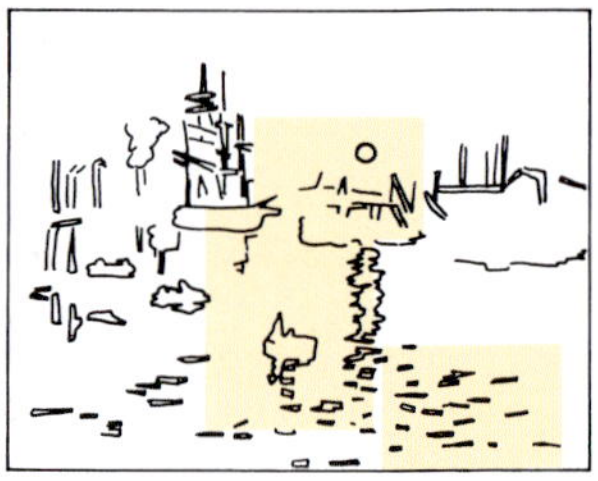

1 Most of the rest of the painting is thin, but the sun is surrounded by an opaque blue – of cobalt and white – which emphasizes the brilliance of the sun in a way that thin, transparent paint would not have done. The sun itself, a strong orange, probably a mixture of cadmium yellow and vermilion, provides the dominant color note, and all the other forms are indistinct.

2 Although it is not easy to see in reproduction, there is some suggestion in this area of overpainting of another subject. With passage of time, underpainting sometimes begins to show through the top layer of paint. The warmth of the underpainting – an orange-pink tint – is overlaid with strong dashes of blue-green, providing a transparent effect presaging Monet's later preoccupations with water surfaces. The paint is thinly applied over a neural ground.

3 *Actual size detail* Although the sun is the dominant note, all the spatial and color patterns are set by this boat, whose waterline is the darkest note in the painting. Viridian is used to strengthen the shapes in the blue surrounding, and this also appears in both the signature and the water area leading from the boat, with white producing the intermediate tone of the middle small boat. Some touches of ultramarine are also evident.

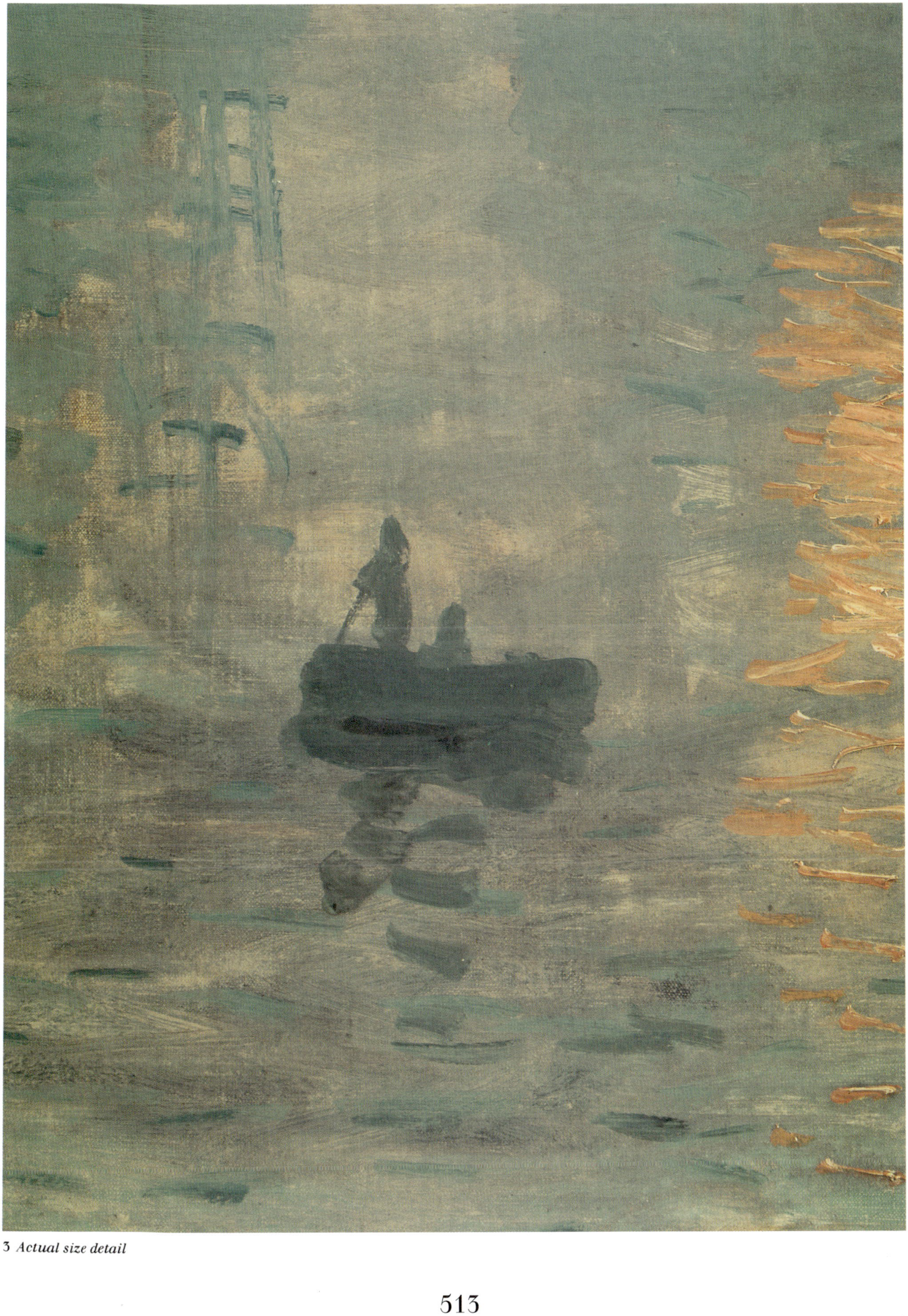

3 *Actual size detail*

Autumn at Argenteuil

1873
Oil on canvas
22×29in/56×75cm
Courtauld Institute Galleries, London

Monet's home at Argenteuil was his first really settled place since leaving the family house at Le Havre. With a new wife and a young son he needed a stable base, and his choice of Argenteuil gave him what proved to be some of his happiest years. Arriving in December 1871, when he had just turned thirty-one, he settled into the rented house near the railway bridge which formed the subject of a number of his paintings. During the next six years the countryside around Argenteuil and the town itself became the center for the development of the Impressionist movement, as his fellow-artists came out from Paris to work with him and to discuss their new ideas.

Monet's life at Argenteuil was more comfortable than is sometimes believed. He was beginning to sell his paintings and made a reasonable income — on a par with an office worker and about five times more than any local laborer. Dealers, too, visited him, particularly Durand-Ruel, and bought his work. Nevertheless, he was always short of money and often borrowed from his friends so that he could entertain them well.

Once settled, he painted with great enthusiasm, in the first year alone (1872) producing forty-six paintings, of which thirty-eight were sold. Most of these were views of the Seine, the town and the surrounding landscape; he had now changed from being a much traveled painter to being one who explored his own locality to the exclusion of all else.

Autumn at Argenteuil is typical of the lyrical painting technique he was developing to explore the light effects which excited him so much. This is a much more worked painting than *Impression, Sunrise*, and shows the new range of his oil-painting method. From the strong directional brushstrokes found in *Bathing at La Grenouillère* or the nervous delicate sketchiness of *Impression, Sunrise* Monet had now moved to a denser, more light-catching paint surface. Here the scene is shown bathed in the consistent and unified light that Monet believed should pervade every part of the painting and enclose it. He used the word *enveloppe* to describe this effect. It is difficult to define, but a comparison between this and *Bathing at La Grenouillère* makes it clearer. In the latter, each part seems to some extent separately painted, whereas in this painting there is total unity — it all seems to have come together under the all-pervading light.

As in many of Monet's paintings of water done at the time, the division between it and the sky is defined only by the strong blue horizontal which holds the delicate balance between the lefthand and righthand foliage forms. The darkest area, in ultramarine, on the righthand edge, is the hinge on which the painting sits — much as the dark line of the boat in *Impression, Sunrise* (see page 511) provides a spatial focus for the painting. There is also something of the same use of complementary colors, orange and blue, with the orange predominating, and there is opposition, or contrast, in the paint surface itself, with the broad areas of sky and water painted fluidly and the foliage done with dense dots of drier paint. It is interesting to see the change in painting technique between the actual foliage and its reflection. The foliage has a quality of solidity which in the slightly deeper color of the reflection is given a vertical floating look. The tall tree on the right reveals a further characteristic of Monet's method. The form is crossed by a number of dragged strokes made with the brush handle which slightly lighten the density of the form, an improvisation which shows a concern with effect rather than with traditional finish.

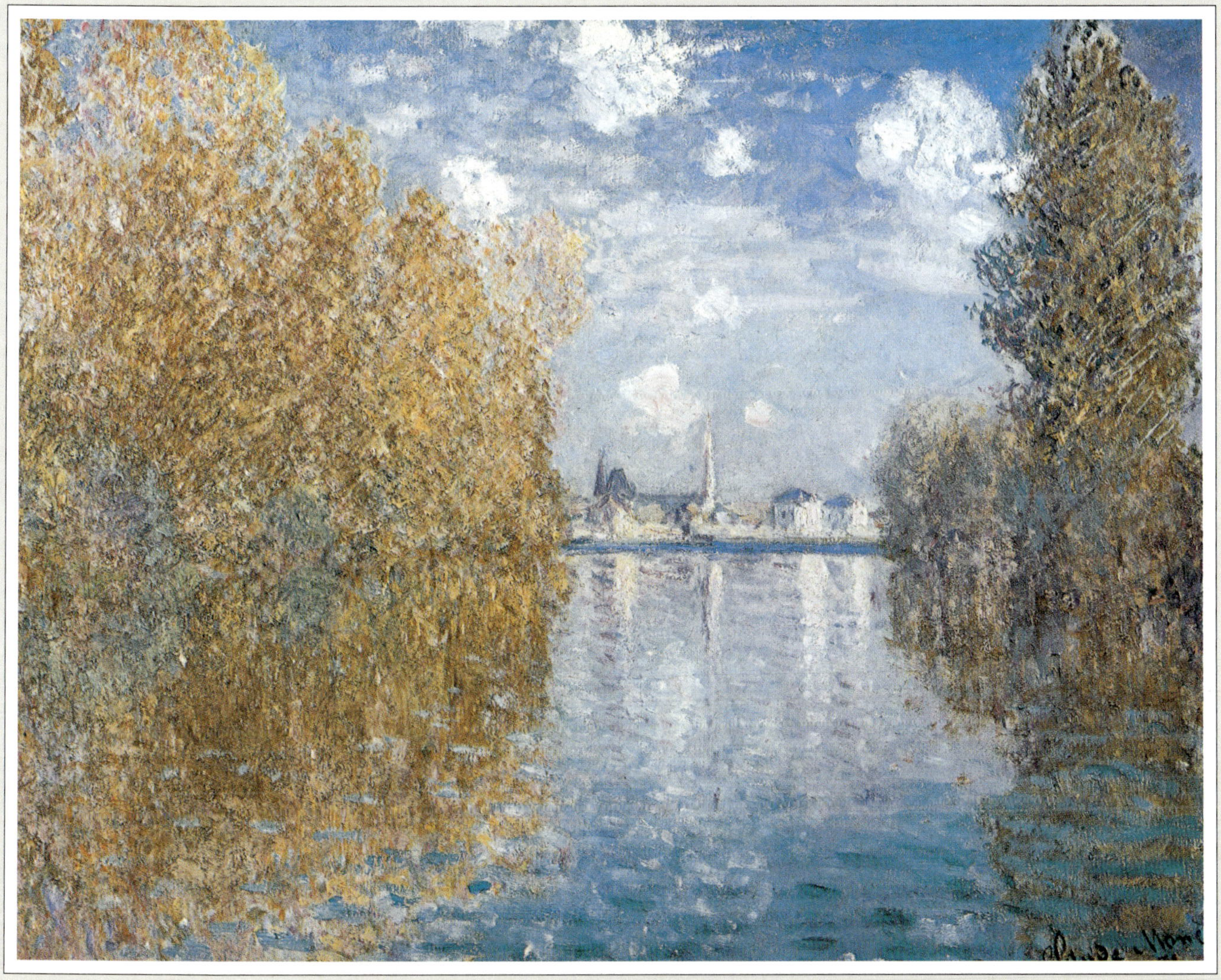

The mass of foliage on the left almost reaches to the center of the painting — the dark spire — and dominates, with its reflection, the left half of the work. A soft, almost amorphous shape, it contrasts with the sharper colors and more definite form of the tree on the right, the lower foliage on the right being indeterminately treated. Apart from the signature, the darkest tone is found, as a note of emphasis, on the middle right edge. The central section showing the town sits on a strong, thick blue line, stabilizing the whole composition. This line, although visually artificial, adds a sharp middle between water and sky, containing something of both.

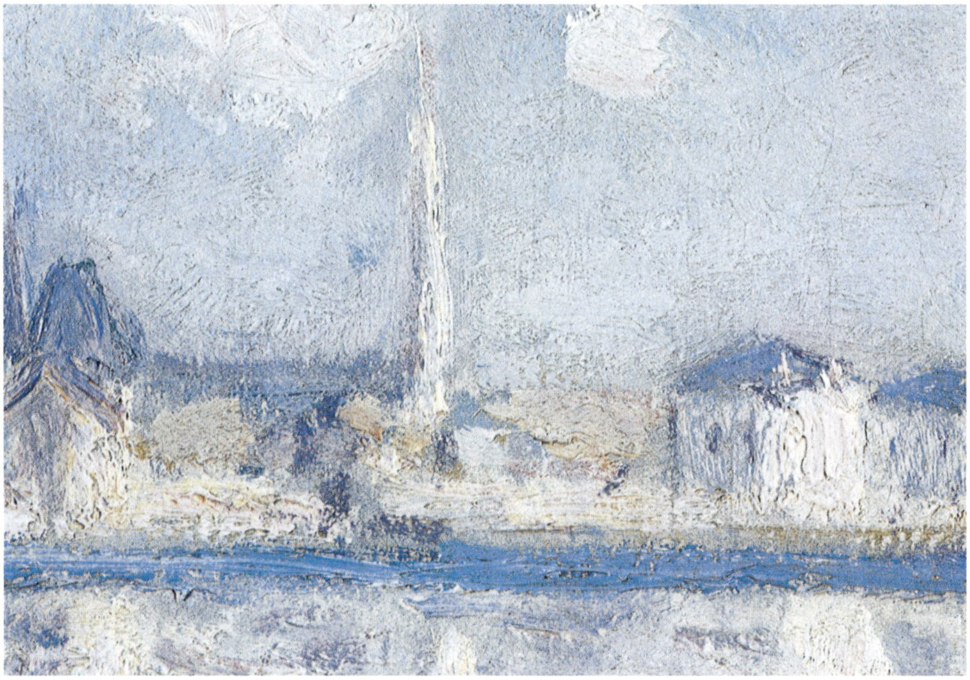

1

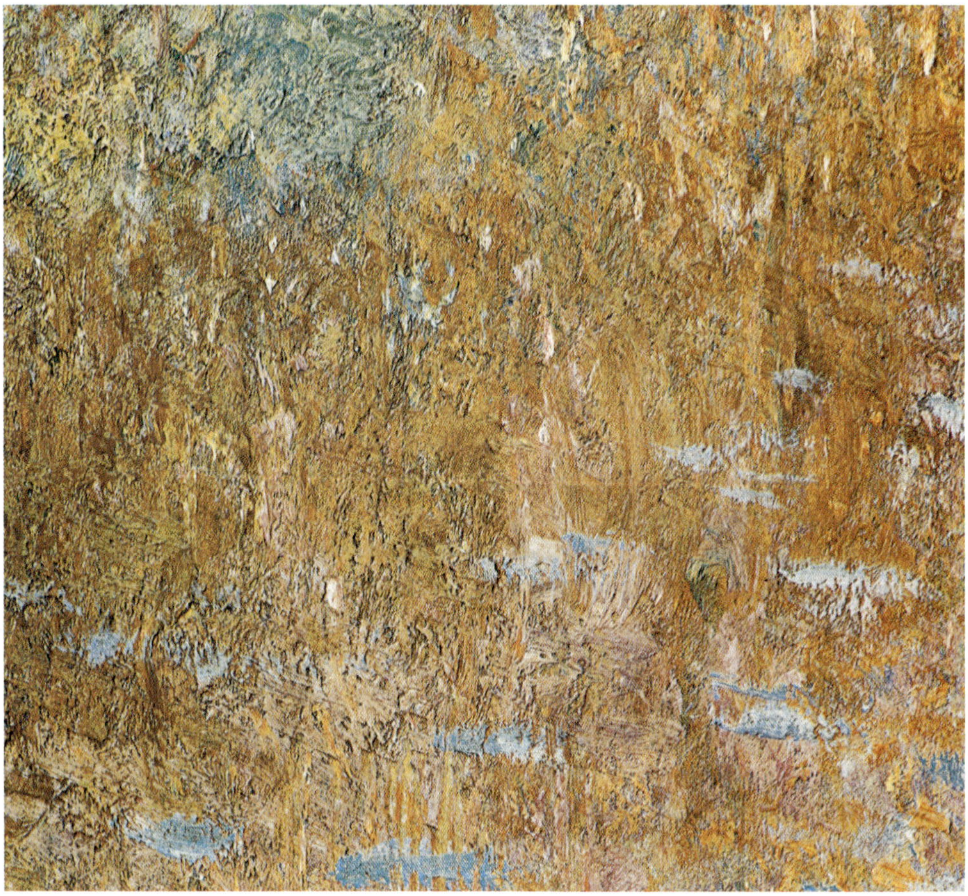

2

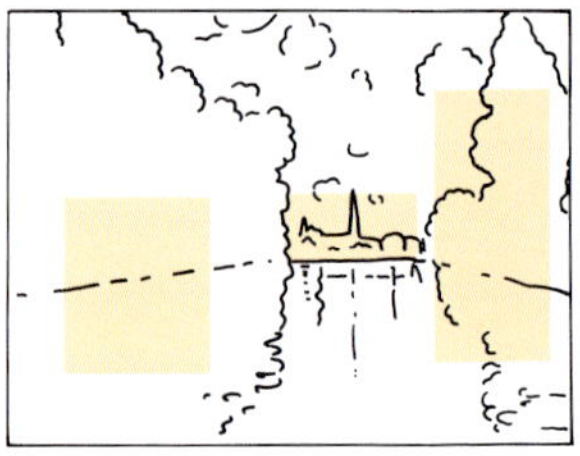

1 The main interest in this detail is perhaps the revealing fact that the density of paint in these distant features is the same as in the foreground, although recessive colors — blues and violets — have been used. This similar treatment of the paint surface over the whole picture has the effect of emphasizing unity, so that it is seen as a coherent painted surface rather than a depiction of space.

2 There is a marked difference in the paint surface of the trees and that of their reflections, although they are both heavily worked, thick paint. There is no precise division between foliage and water, but there is vertical smeared brushwork in the water area which is crossed by horizontal blue dashes which determine the surface, whereas the foliage itself is worked with close, stabbed brushstrokes. Monet's usual palette can be discerned in this detail. It included viridian, cadmium yellow, vermilion and cobalt blue, in mixture and with white. Some delicate vertical strokes of yellow-orange crossed by blue enliven this area — a characteristically Monet touch.

3 *Actual size detail* Monet's impasto technique, with overlay on overlay of dry dragged paint, is clearly revealed in this detail. Flecks of wet blue and cloud white suggest fluttering movement. The thick paint, which could have been too solid, is relieved by scoring into it with the handle of the brush so that the underpainting is revealed in places. The great number of colors used, from Prussian blue to vermilion, produce a characteristic density of effect.

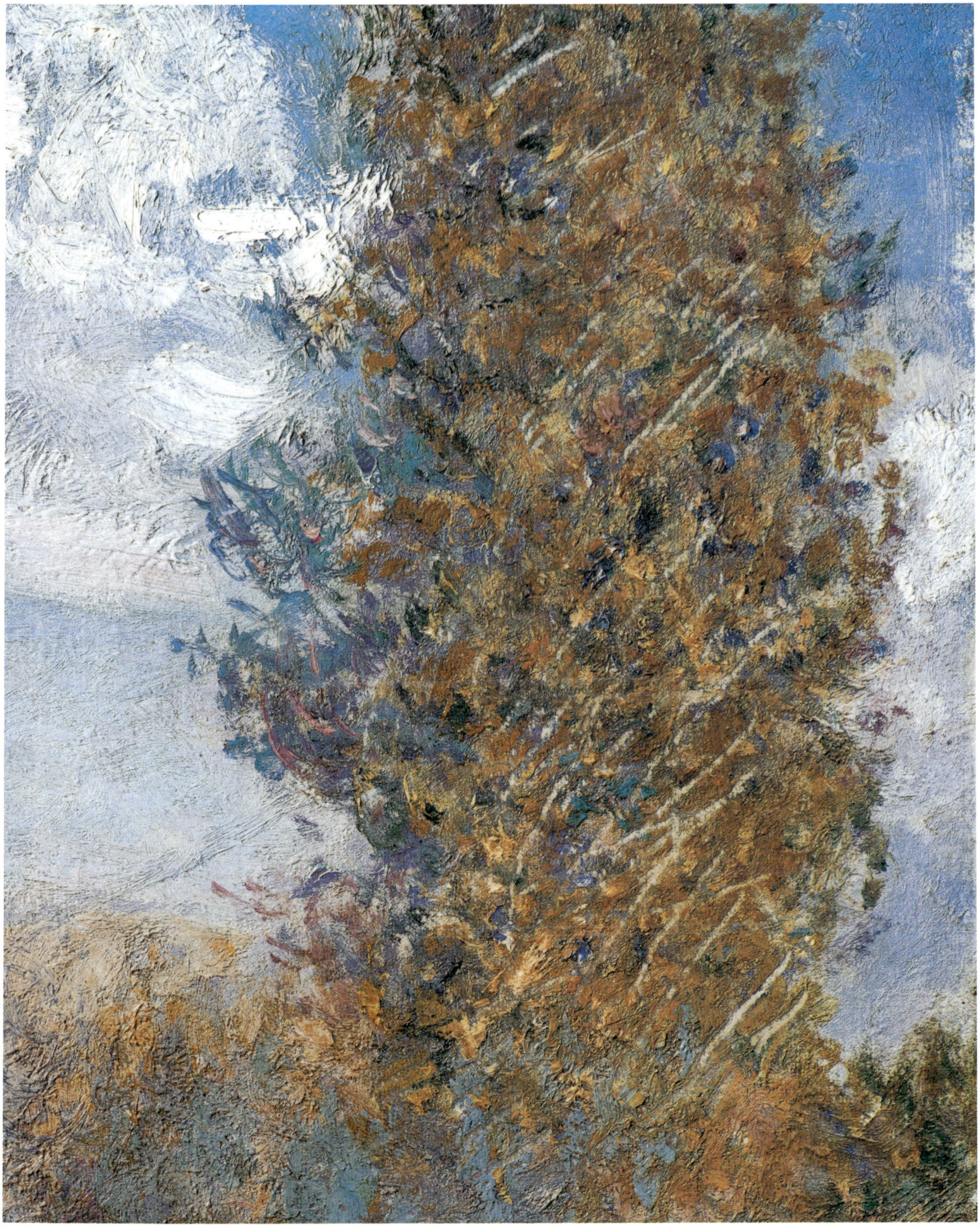

3 *Actual size detail*

THE GARE SAINT-LAZARE

1877

$29\frac{1}{2} \times 41\frac{1}{3}$in/$75 \times 104.7$cm

Oil on pale primed canvas

Musée d'Orsay, Paris

Saint Lazare station was the Paris railway terminus which served what might now be called "Monet country." It was the station not only for Argenteuil but also for most of Monet's favorite locations in northern France, including Le Havre, Chatou, Bougival, Louveciennes, Ville d'Avray, Rouen and Vernon (for the branch line to Giverny).

In 1876 Monet took a studio apartment in Rue Moncey close to the Gare Saint-Lazare, and from there, in 1877, between January and March, completed twelve paintings of the station. At this time he also had an apartment in the Rue d'Edinbourg, even closer to the station, so including his house at Argenteuil he actually had three residences. Evidently he was far from being poor.

As a group, these twelve paintings represent the last of his modern-life subjects, after which he turned completely to the natural landscape. The railway station was at that time the single most powerful reminder of the importance of industrialization to modern man, and a number of painters had treated the subject, the most emotive and romantic version being Turner's *Rain, Steam and Speed* of 1844. Turner had seen the train as a powerful force thrusting itself unfeelingly through a protesting nature, a dark and menacing beast, but Monet's train is very different — a delicate shape contained in an atmospheric web made of the intricate ironwork. His concern is with light and atmosphere, just as it would have been in a landscape of trees and water, but here they have been given a special character by the presence of the smoke and steam filtering the sunlight. The subject had an obvious fascination for a painter with his interests, and the fact that he made twelve paintings in such a short time is a testament to his enthusiasm. Another reason for his haste was that the wanted to include the paintings in the Fourth Impressionist Exhibition and the closing date was in April. In the event he exhibited only eight of the twelve. Once he had completed the group he seems to have been creatively exhausted, and only produced four other paintings that year.

Although they are a sequence of paintings, they are not, in Monet's terms of reference, a series, since they show a number of different views of the station rather than exploring the changing effect of light on the same view. The treatments vary from the oil-sketch to the studio-finished work, this painting having been done on the spot. He set up his painting stand centrally under the canopy, and the symmetricality of the composition is broken by both the large carriage shape on the left and the placing of the engine a little to the right of the center of the canopy of iron girders. The directional movement in the composition is provided by the movement toward the right of the foreground figure. Again, complementary colors have been used to enhance one another, this time the mauvish smoke and the pale yellow glowing sunlight, and the carefully constructed smoke pattern is both the whole color key and the element that gives life and rhythm to the work. The brushwork is no longer directional; it is a dense impasto laid on with such delicacy that even the harsh shape of the engine is softened into a steam-bathed form. The almost ethereal light makes the figures appear more as points of movement than as actual people going about their business.

This is a carefully constructed composition which avoids too much symmetricality by simple devices of balance and placing. Although the canopy is exactly central (reflecting Monet's painting position), the engine is a little to the left, and the bulky shape of the carriage and the direction of the smoke from the engine continue the emphasis on the left side of the painting. The framework of the side of the shed extends this further, while the right side is left open, filled with light sharpened by the small dabs of sharp color suggesting figures and objects. The general warmth of color is emphasized by the floating areas of steam and smoke in white and cobalt violet tints — at once exciting and surprising. As Monet's painting developed it became increasingly high in key until the time of the later water garden series (see pages 532-537), when the deep blues and greens returned, used with an even greater mastery.

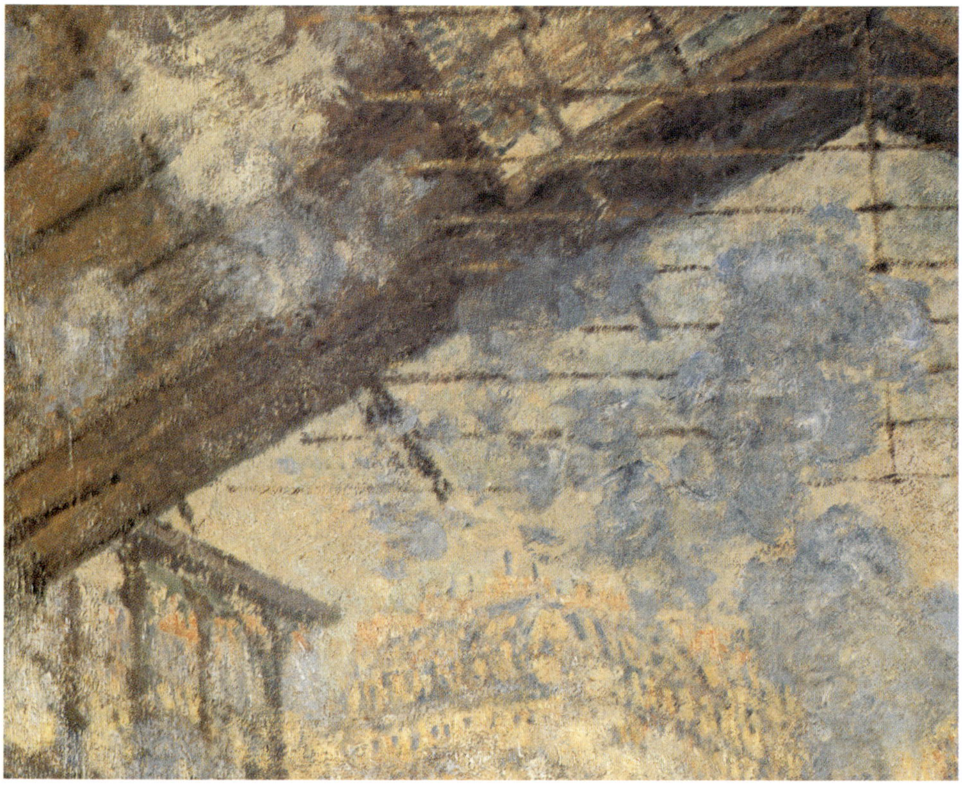

1

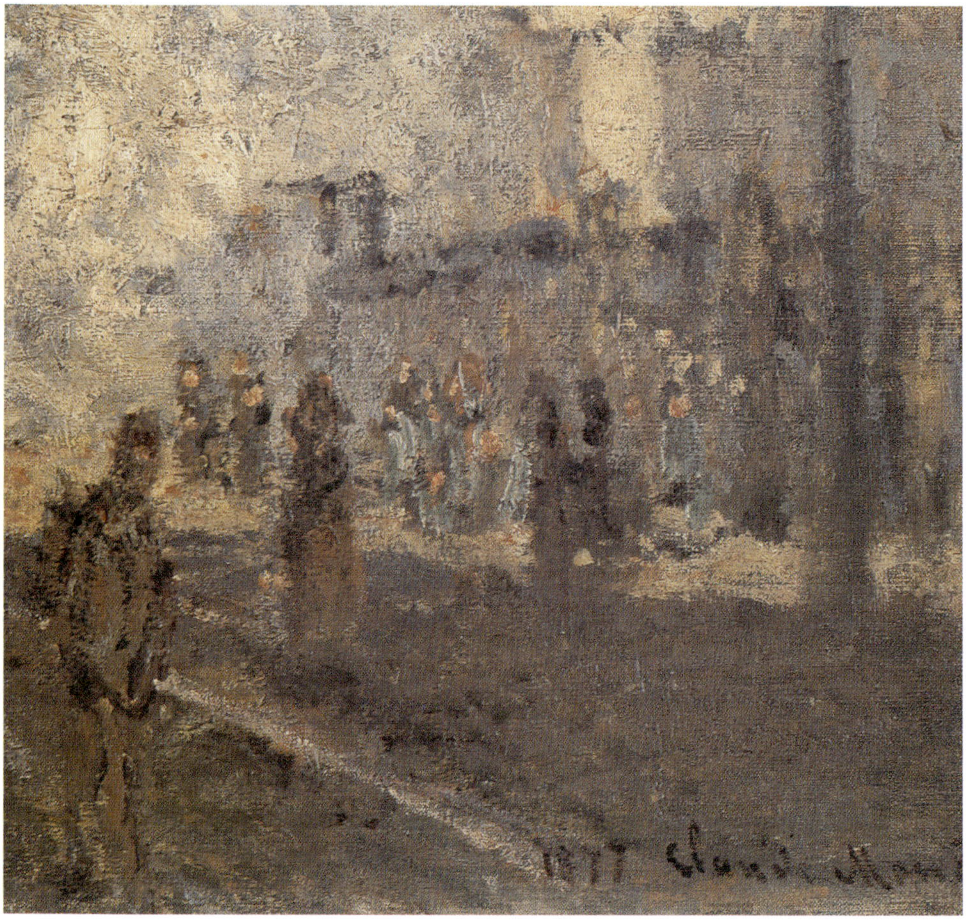

2

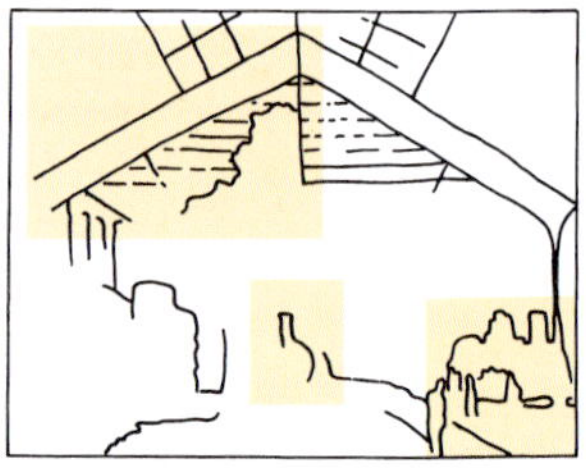

1 In this area Monet is accurate to an unusual degree, and the structure is clearly defined, providing a firm framework for the delicacy of the distant sunlit apartment buildings. The strong forms of the canopy are softened by the wisps of smoke which direct the eye to the dark engine smoke-stack.

2 This detail shows how roughly and sketchily the figures have been treated, with single blobs of flesh tint standing for faces and hands. The carefully placed pattern of dark brown and light red on the lefthand figure of a woman suggests the shape of the dress, but no precise description has been attempted.

3 *Actual size detail* The characteristic density of overpainting and the spatial implications it can acquire are very evident here. No form is precisely delineated but everything is seen, statically and in painterly terms. Although the brushstrokes are no longer form-following, as in *La Grenouillère*, each one nevertheless relates to form, for instance, the engine shape is specifically identified. The apparent use of black dryly overpainted on a dry underpainting is significant in suggesting Monet's desire for a deep, dark luminosity — he had not yet begun to reject the use of black on principle. The surrounding area, with orange and blue in lively conjunction, adds a forceful contrast.

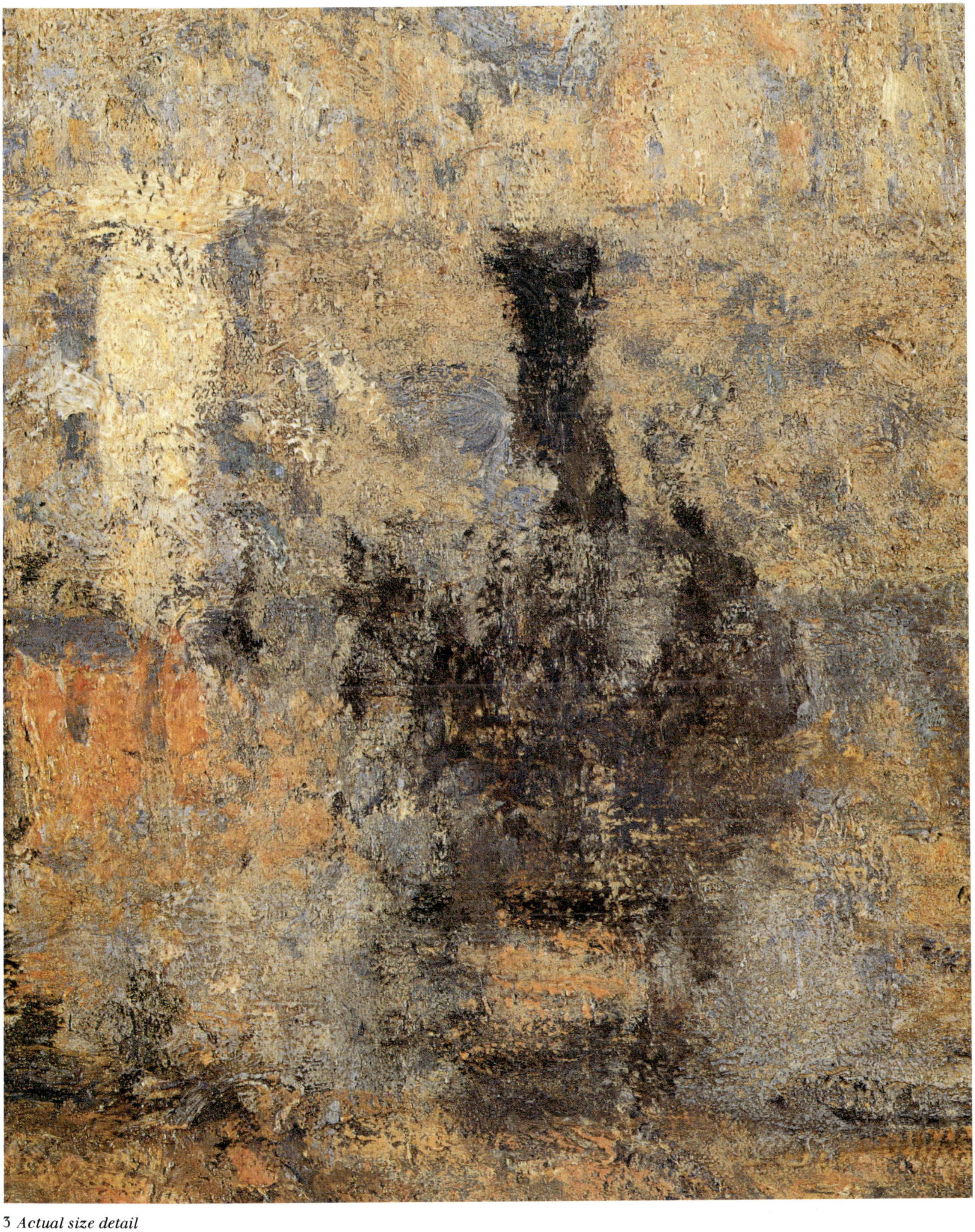

3 *Actual size detail*

Boats at Etretat

1883
26 × 32in/66 × 81cm
Oil on canvas
Musée d'Orsay, Paris

Throughout his painting life Monet was fascinated by the effect of water. From his earliest seascapes at Le Havre and Trouville, inspired by his first mentors Boudin and Jongkind, to the last great *Waterlilies* panels (see page 533) of his water garden at Giverny, he pursued his obsession with the surface of water. Its opaque restlessness in a choppy or rough sea, its reflectivity in strong sunlight, and its paradoxical non-presence in still dark ponds, all fascinated him. This is not surprising since the most constant concern of Monet and the other Impressionists was with the ever-changing surfaces in nature.

This is one of several paintings done between 1883-86 during visits to the cliff coast near Etretat, north of Le Havre. Unlike the later true "series" paintings, such as the *Grain Stacks* or the *Poplars,* where the same view was seen under different lights, Monet chose a variety of viewpoints and locations for the Etretat paintings.

During his first three-week visit in February 1883, he started but did not finish a number of paintings intended for an exhibition at Durand-Ruel's gallery in March. After a period of estrangement Durand-Ruel had again become Monet's dealer, but in the event Monet was unable (and unwilling) to supply any Etretat paintings for this show. This particular view was probably the one that was eventually taken by the dealer in 1886 after it had been further worked on in the painter's studio. There is a degree of finish in the foreground boats that suggests studio work.

The writer Guy de Maupassant, a valued friend of Monet's, stayed with him at Etretat in one of his visits in 1885 and he has left an interesting and revealing account of Monet's working methods at the time. "Off he went, followed by children carrying his canvases, five or six canvases representing the same subject at different times of the day and with different light effects. He picked them up and put them down in turn, according to the changing weather."

Etretat also had many artistic associations. Monet later owned a Delacroix watercolor of it; he knew Courbet's painting of boats on the beach there (one of his paintings used a similar composition) and Boudin had also used it as a subject. By 1883 Etretat had become a popular resort and, although Monet usually stayed later in the year after the Parisian trippers had left, he was nevertheless aware of its popularity with the Parisian public to whom, eventually, his paintings would be exhibited.

Fishing was an important means of livelihood all along the Normandy coast, a constant battle between the uncompromising power of the sea and the courage of the fishing folk with their small but sturdy boats, and this painting gives an impression of impending activity, with bustle on the beach and the sea choppy. The treatment of the hard forms of the boats, painted directionally as in *Bathing at La Grenouillère,* is at variance with the looser, more atmospheric treatment of landscape and sea. It should also be noted that there is a curious inconsistency of scale in the painting: the boats on the right, whose size is established by the standing foreground figures, suggest that the two sailing boats on the left are very small indeed, while the figures in the middle distance seem out of scale with those in the foreground. The overall effect of this is to thrust the cliffs forward in the painting and to make the shore, as it approaches them, rather unconvincing. Altogether, although it may be possible to see what the artist's intentions were, the result is not completely convincing or unified.

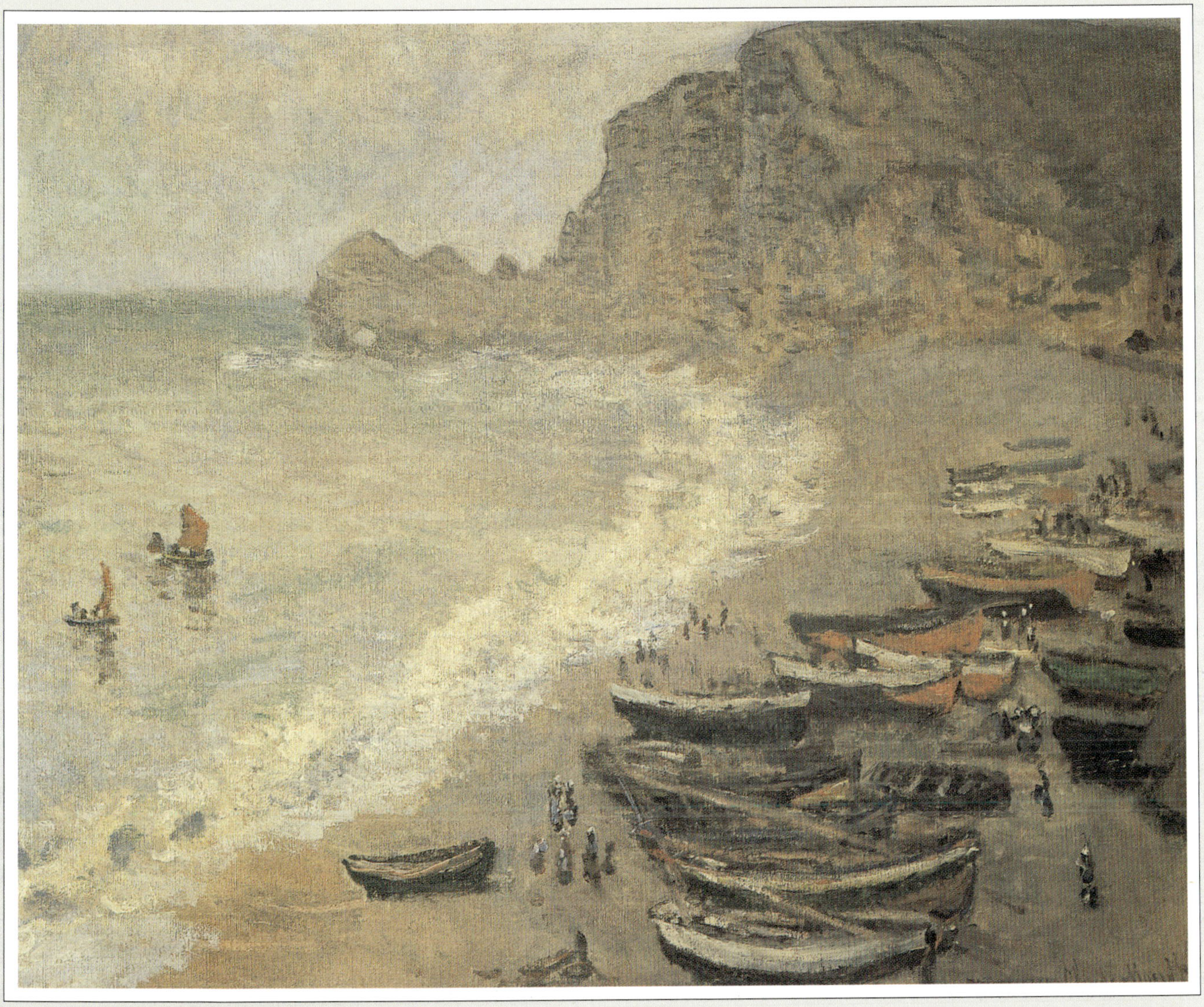

The work is thinly painted on a pale-tinted primed canvas without, for the most part, the thick impasto of the earlier *Gare Saint-Lazare* or the later *Grain Stacks*. It is essentially a small open-air sketch with all the vibrant quality of direct observation. Compositionally it is rather unbalanced, the strength of the boat forms pulling to the right. A diagonal taken from the bottom left to the top right shows two different painting procedures, with that on the left being much looser and more luminous.

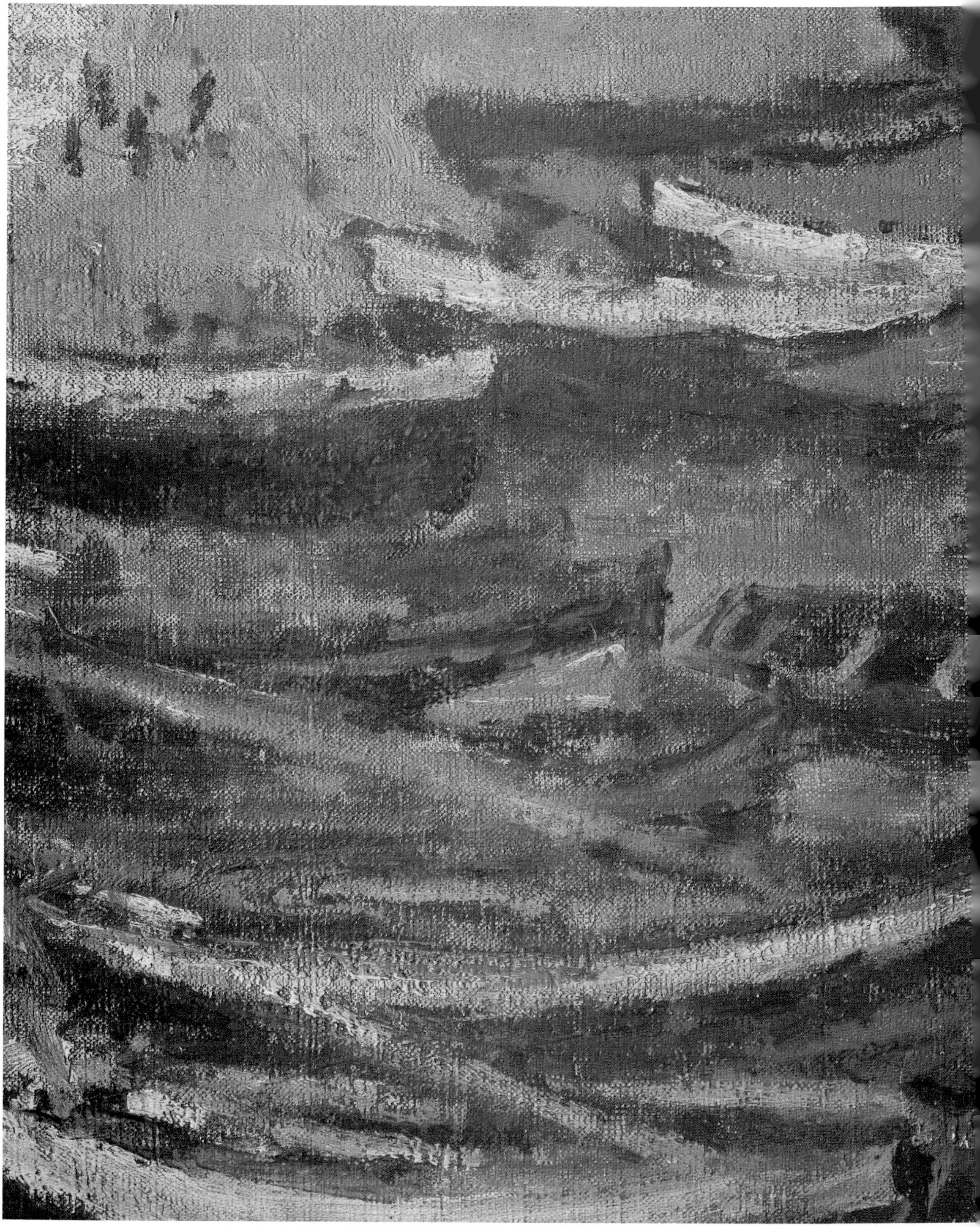

1 *Actual size detail*

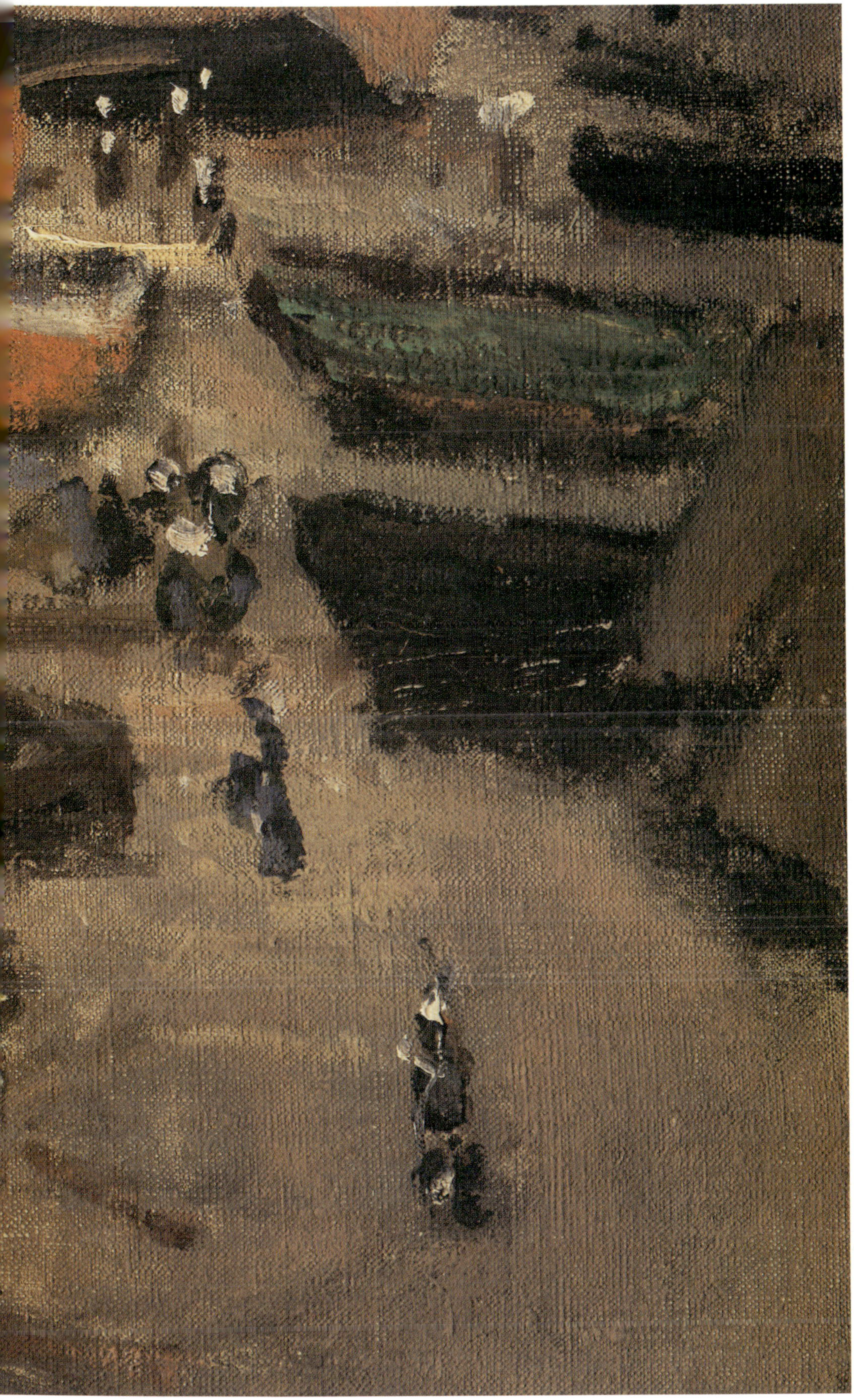

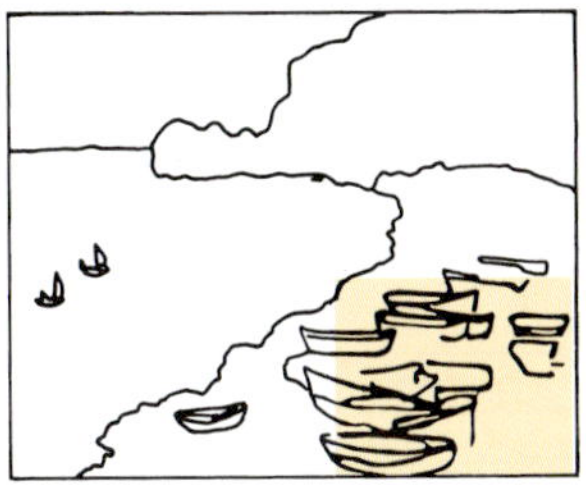

1 *Actual size detail* The strength of this detail lies in the full colors – viridian, cobalt, ultramarine, vermilion and cadmium yellow combined with a dark near-black Prussian blue-vermilion mixture for the shapes and shadows. The strokes are form-shaping and directional, and the figures are indicated simply and with touches of near-white for emphasis. The unity of color is helped by the fact that the tinted ground has been allowed to show through in places.

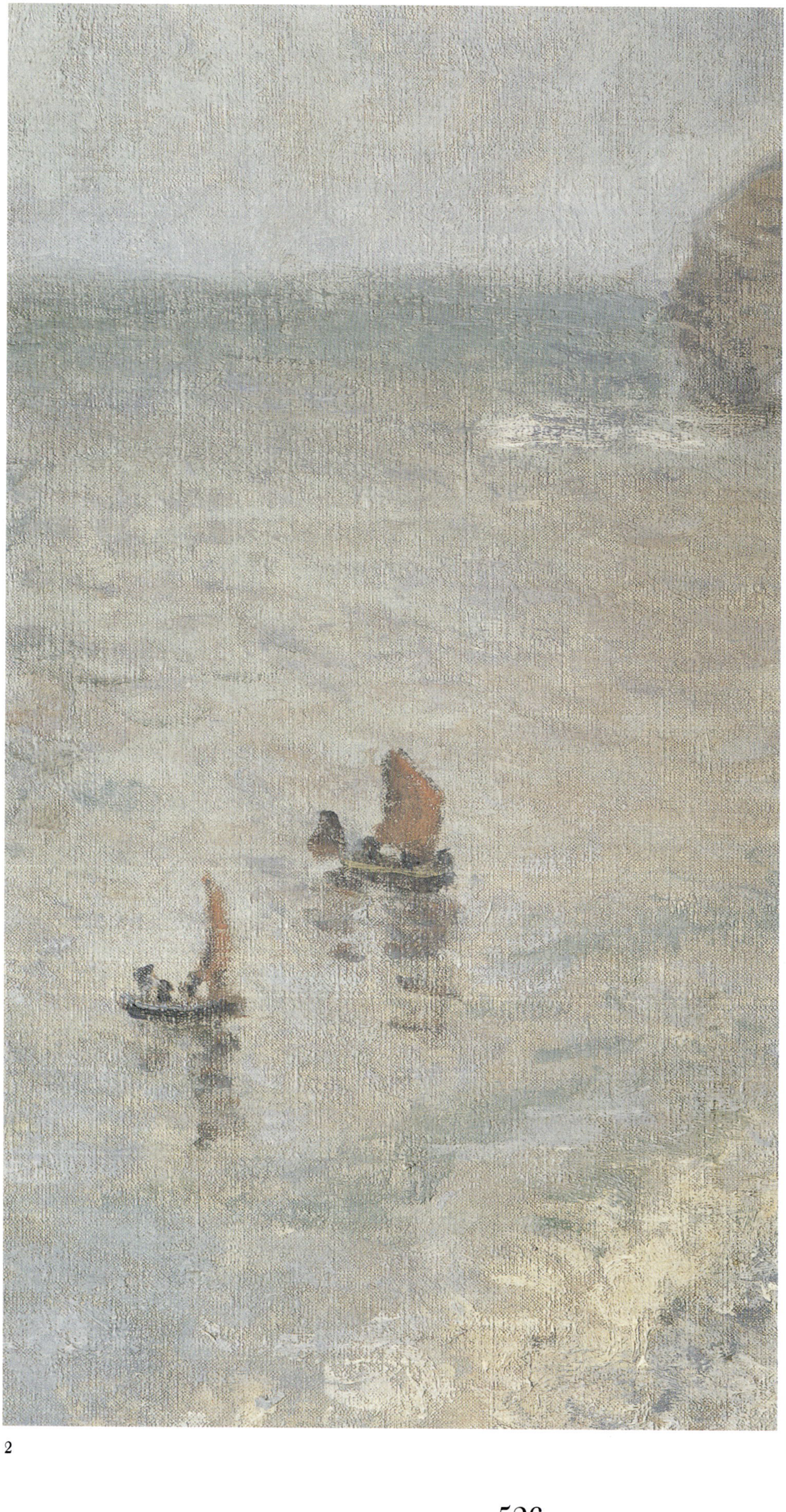

2

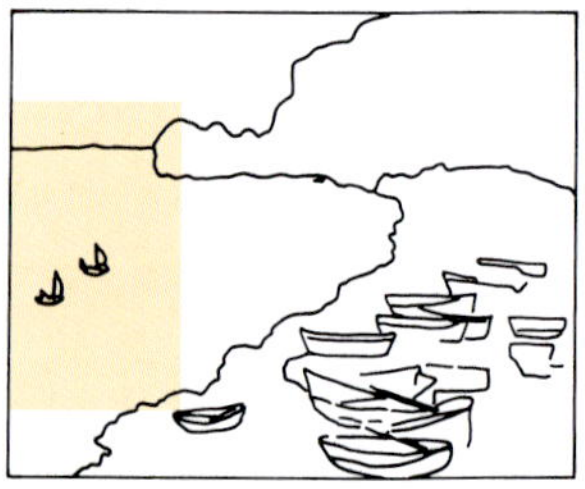

2 The sea is painted quite thinly, with the warm, creamy tint of the canvas ground being allowed to show through. The red sails, their color echoing that of the foreground boats, are composed of just one or two rapid brushstrokes of vermilion, with a little darker red-brown blended in to suggest form.

Opposite page Monet painted a great many studies of Etretat and the coastal villages nearby. *The Sea at Fecamp* is essentially a sea study, the cliffs being sketched in without, it seems, great analytical interest, but the sea evidently carefully studied to create the feeling of the great Atlantic rollers as they follow each other in quick succession to break on the beaches. *Morning at Etretat*, taken from the same position as *Boats at Etretat*, and painted on a pale gray-tinted canvas, shows a different mood and treatment. A rougher, more changeable weather pattern with sunlight on the cliffs and shadows on the sea is treated in nervous, jerky brushstrokes. There is more overpainting on the left and the color contrasts in the water are stronger — viridian, Prussian and cobalt blues with touches of yellows.

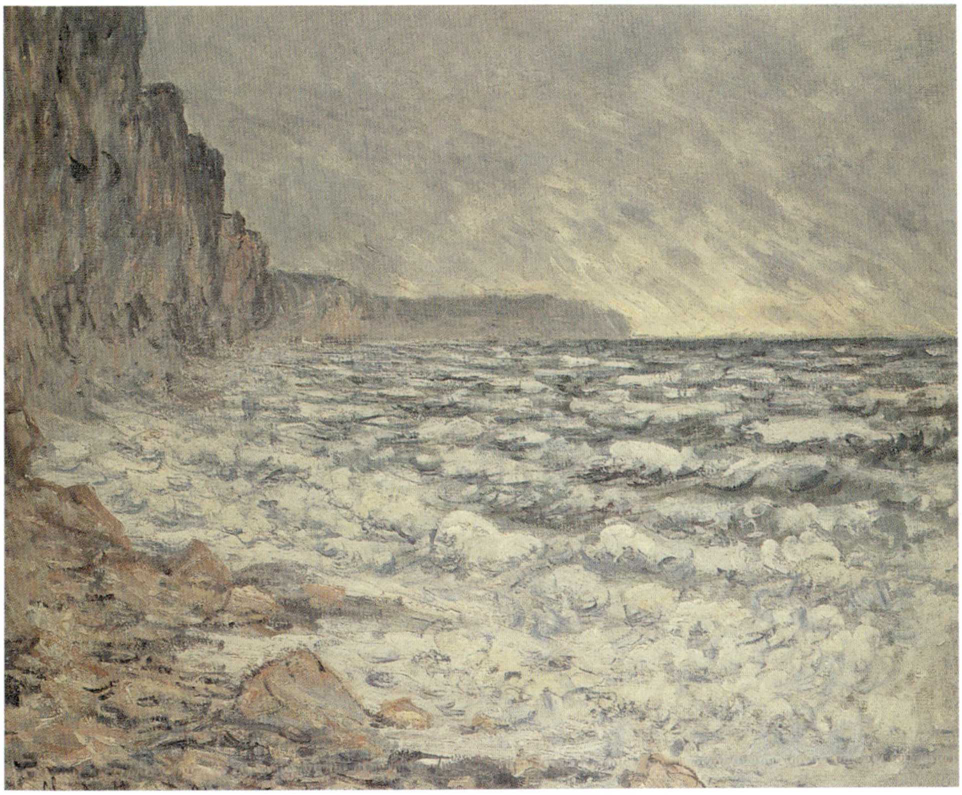

The Sea at Fecamp 1881, Private collection

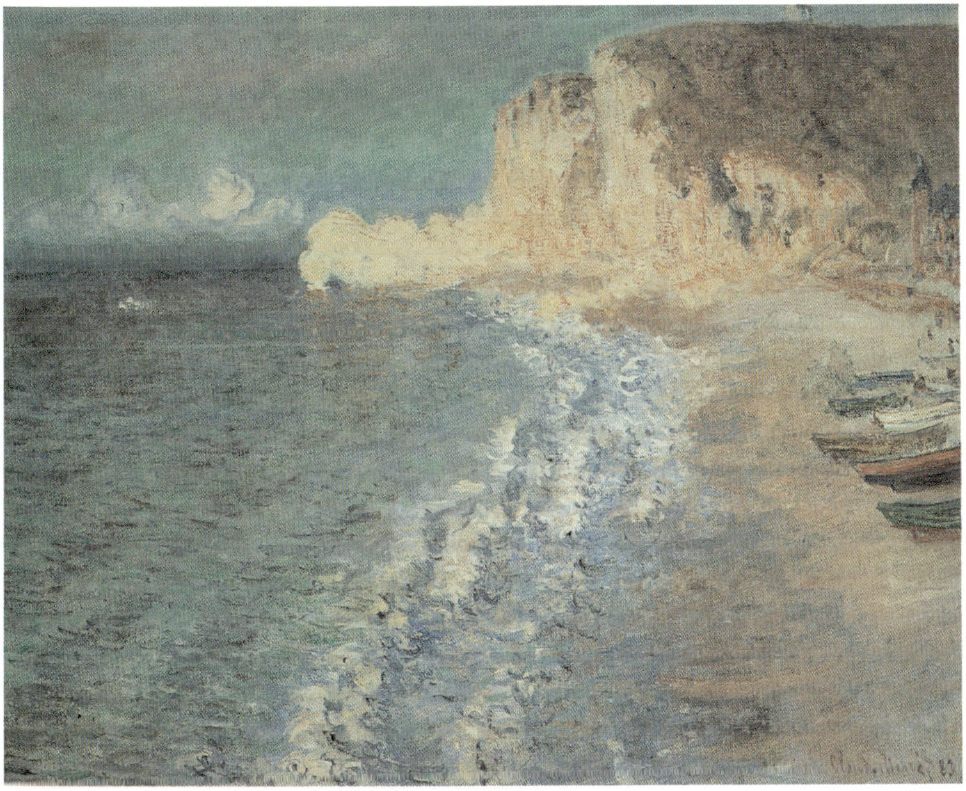

Morning at Etretat 1883, Private collection

Poplars on the Banks of the Epte

1891

39¾×26in/101×66cm

Oil on canvas

Private collection

After his first Giverny series of *Grain Stacks*, with their bulky, solid forms, Monet chose a linear subject – a row of poplar trees by the side of a small river. The delicate tracery of foliage around the sharp vertical lines of the trunks and the strong horizontal emphasis of the river bank gave him the opportunity for new exercises in light. Here his *enveloppe* presented a new and exciting challenge; there was more air and sky than solid form.

Monet found the poplars marked for felling and paid their owner to leave them standing until he had finished painting them. He started in July 1891 and worked on the paintings until October, choosing mainly afternoon and evening effects, with the light falling from the right. The weather was poor at Giverny that year, and Monet, always bad-tempered when prevented from painting, became frustrated and irascible, fearing also that the trees would have to be felled before long. He complained about "this appalling weather which makes me fear for my trees."

As with his other series, he worked on a number of canvases during the same painting session, moving from one to the other as the light changed. His speed of working is astonishing: he allowed himself only seven minutes on one of the poplar paintings – "until the sunlight left a certain leaf," were his own words.

The compositions are generally of two types. The first is a vertical pattern of bars – created by the trunks – opposed to the single horizontal of the river bank, usually placed low on the canvas with the reflections carrying the line of the trunks right down through the horizontal. The second, as in this painting, takes the form of a single sweeping zigzag of foliage set against the sometimes broken verticals of the tree trunks. Here again the river bank provides a firm horizontal, and both foliage and tree-trunks are continued in the reflection.

The pictorial effect, very unusual and often very dramatic, emphasizes a characteristic which was to become a significant element in Monet's influence on later painting. It demands a positive effort of visual interpretation to turn the dramatically effective pattern of a painted surface into acceptable three-dimensional representation of a particular landscape. Because the surface is so insistent, the painting tends to thrust forward instead of receding in space. The consciousness of surface, of the paint texture rather than illusionist space, is so much a part of twentieth-century pictorial consciousness that it is easy to forget the importance of Monet and the Impressionists in the formation of this concept. The poplar series is much concerned with space, and this element is very evident.

Poplars on the Banks of the Epte was probably painted in the flat evening light, the time when the direct sun has left the scene but dusk has not yet begun to remove the color. We cannot be sure of this, as the time of day is not indicated in the title as sometimes it is, but there is a very closely related painting in Philadelphia which is clearly in full sunlight, and it is likely that this version was painted soon afterward.

Monet's signature, which he came to consider a significant part of his paintings, is in red, which echoes the red on the tops of the trees and provides a balancing note at the base. The signature here is used as an element in the composition rather than being an "advertising" feature, as it is in *Women in the Garden* (see page 507).

The whole series of popular paintings was exhibited at Durand-Ruel's gallery in February 1892 – the only one of Monet's exhibitions which was devoted to a single series. This painting was included and was brought to what Monet considered "exhibition standard" by later work in his Giverny studio. Durand-Ruel was quite firm with Monet in insisting on the need for "finish."

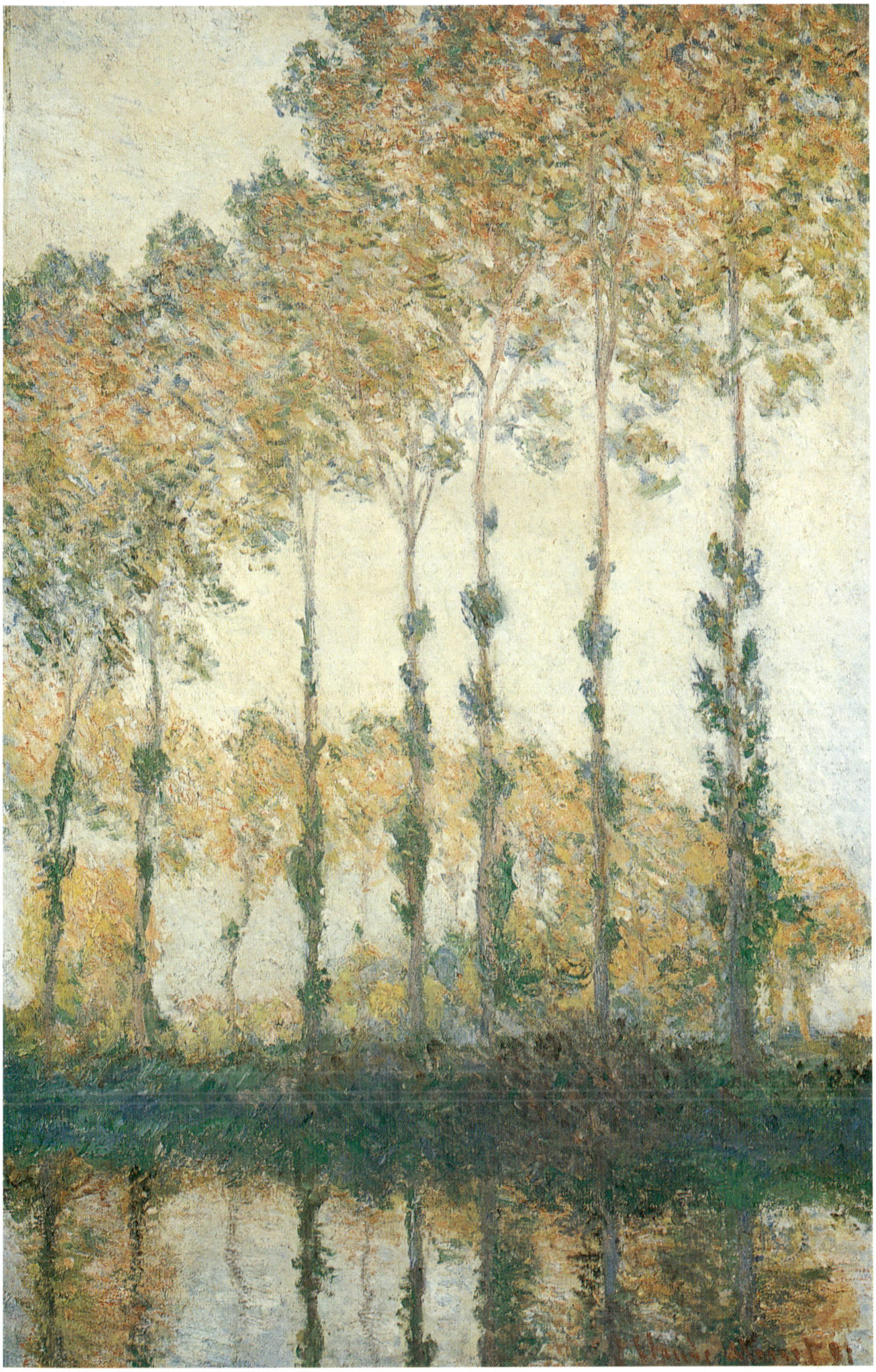

This is one of several treatments of the same view of trees, one of which shows more of the linear direction of the trees as they follow the bends of the river. Monet must have been interested in the criss-crossing of the lines as they receded along the banks to provide a pattern of receding tones and tints with a consequent loss of detail and narrowing range of tone. All these elements are to be discerned in this work, and particularly evident is the change of tone where the near bank meets the distant foliage. On the lower right the deep Prussian blue and viridian in the bank are thrust forward by the warm area, enlivened by touches of vermilion. This is the darkest and most intense area of the painting, and the foliage appears almost to float away from it.

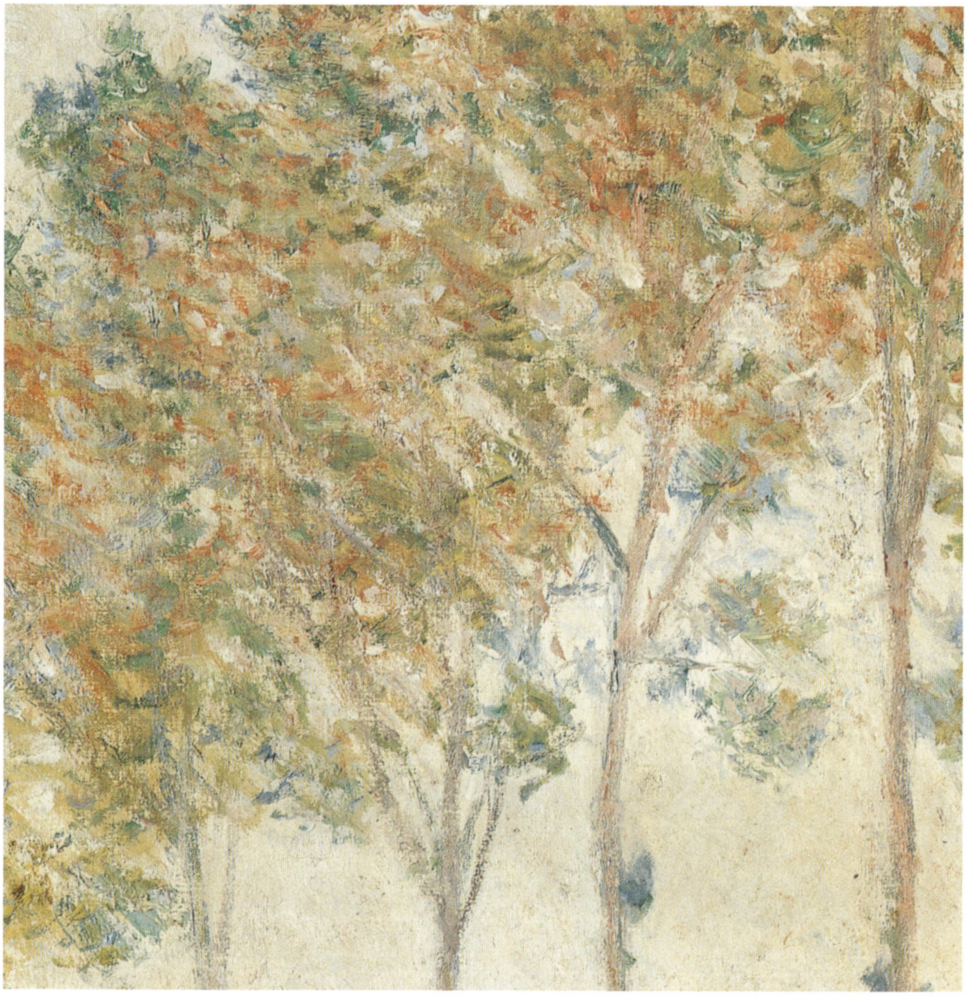

1

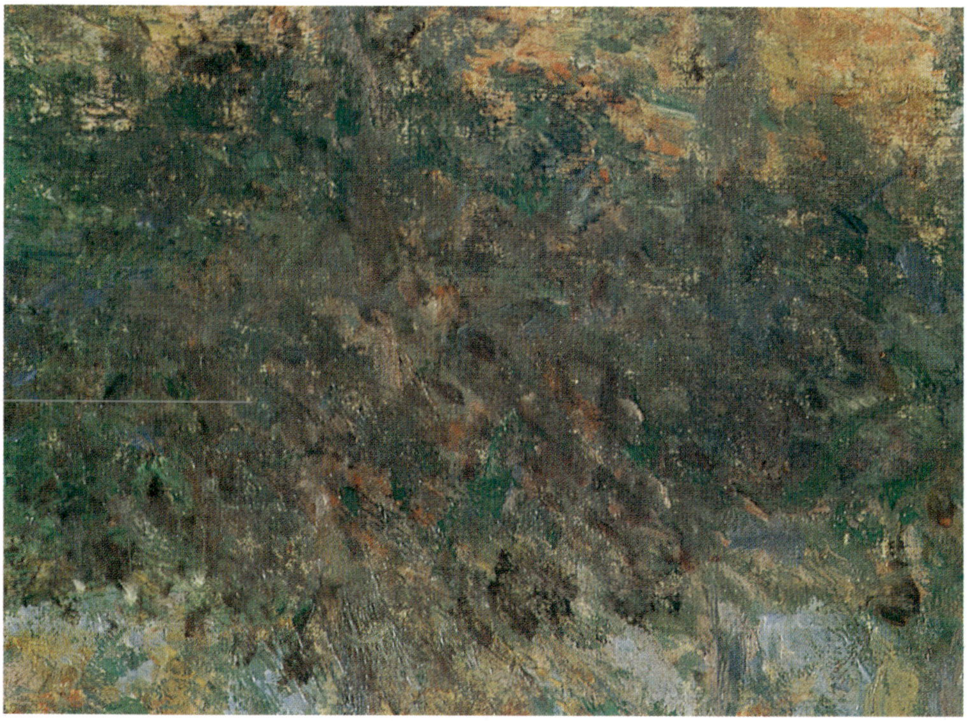

2

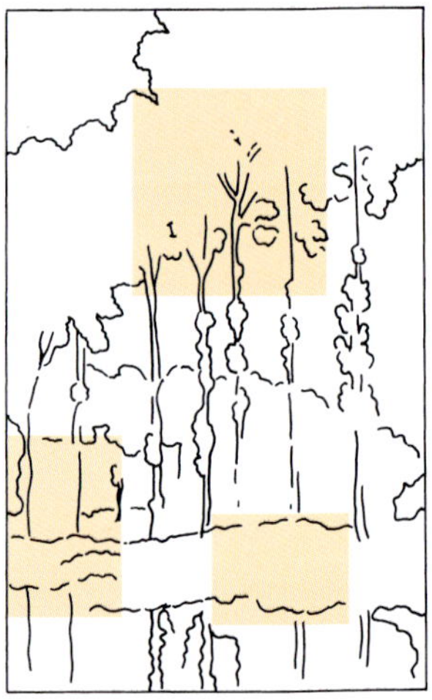

1 There is a delicate energy and visual delight in this area. Monet's experience in painting leaves in fluttering movement at differing times of the day enabled him to tackle this in a way that suggests enthusiasm and pleasure. Though the paint is solidly opaque, it is not heavily worked and contains flecks of many colors, deftly placed. The thin trunks of the poplars, although giving a strong vertical emphasis to the painting, are also delicately painted.

2 The density of overpainting, done in sharp, nervous, directional strokes, suggests that the resolution of this area of the painting presented the greatest difficulty. The waterline is not precise, and the bank must have been in deep shadow. The relationship of the enshrouding *enveloppe* of light with the freely painted upper area must have given problems.

3 *Actual size detail* A surprisingly separate detail — another tree or group of trees, standing apart from the poplar row, casts its reflection in the water. The color range is strongest here: bright blue-green (cobalt and viridian tints) provides a complementary balance for the strong if amorphous yellow-orange shape of the tree form and also for its darker reflection. This is painted with crossing horizontal and vertical brushstrokes expressing the water surface.

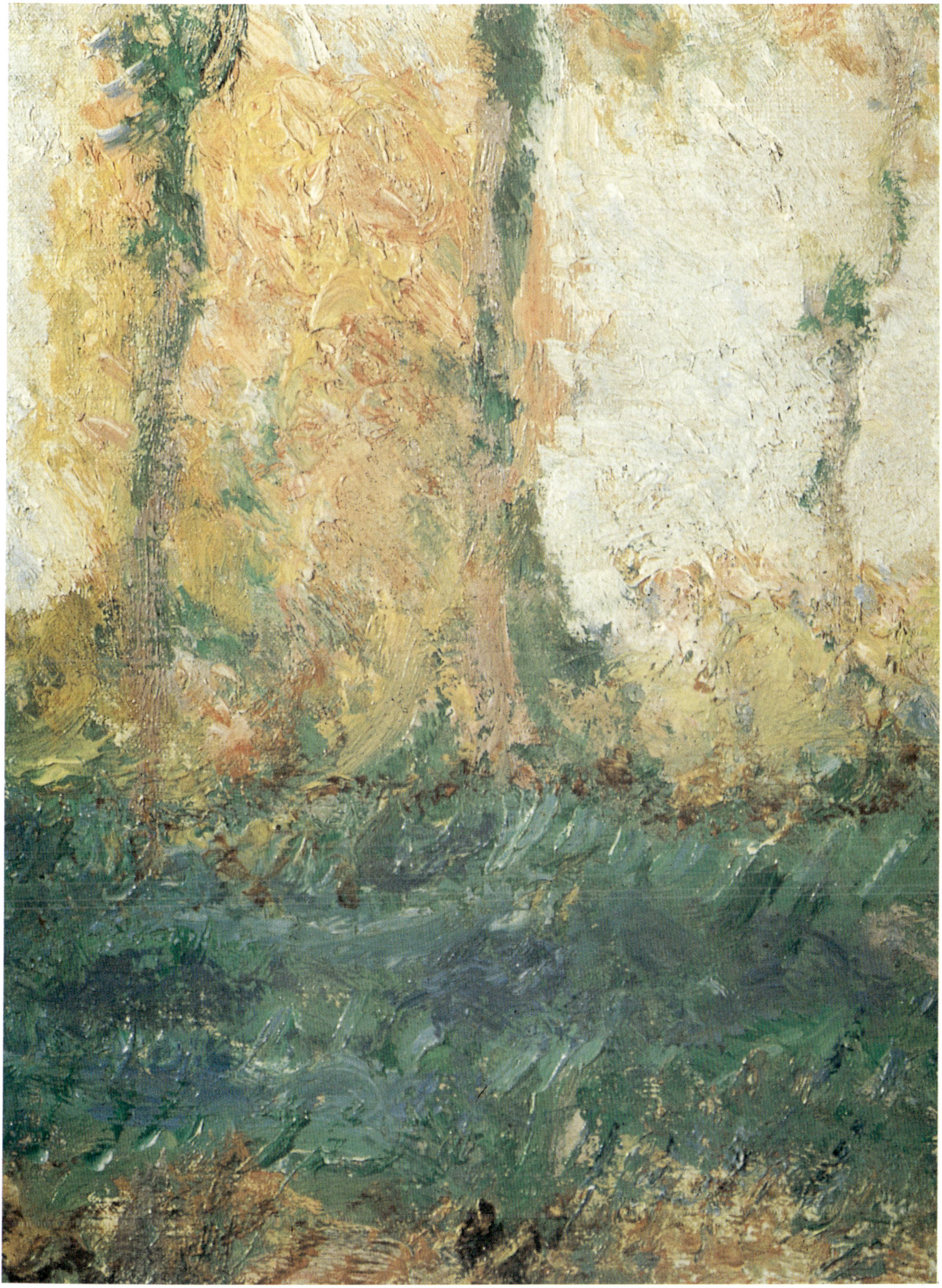

3 *Actual size detail*

Morning with Willows

One panel of the *Décoration des Nymphéas (Waterlily Decorations)*
1916-26
6ft 8in×42ft 6in/2m 3cm×12m 95cm
Musée d l'Orangerie, Paris

After his second wife Alice's death in May 1911, Monet was distraught and unable to work, shunning his friends and even losing interest in his garden. He was close to despair, which was exacerbated by concern for his failing eyesight, shortly to be diagnosed as caused by a double cataract. Although by the end of the year he had begun to paint again, he seemed to feel none of the dedication and purpose that had typified him in the past. When his son Jean died in 1914 at the age of forty-seven Monet became almost a recluse, his only human contact being with his friend Clemenceau and Blanche, Jean's widow, who cared for him until his death.

Clemenceau, at this time Prime Minister and in charge of the French war effort, still managed to find time to support and encourage Monet and to give him a new enthusiasm which carried him through the last decade of his life. Clemenceau persuaded Monet to reconsider an idea that the artist had projected earlier — for a series of large mural-sized water landscapes. Monet financed this project through the sale of old works; he had few newly painted canvases to sell since he had produced very little for the previous three years. He had a large new studio designed and built especially for the project (although with the shortage of labor caused by the war it was not completed until 1916.) Although Monet disliked the look of this huge, factory-like structure in his idyllic garden setting he nevertheless worked in it on the *Waterlilies* panels for the next ten years. The work tormented him; at moments he felt like destroying everything he had done and starting again, while at others he was buoyed up by the success of his efforts. He painted and repainted, employing thick impasto underpainting and thin wet over-painting; he spent hours in contemplation and then worked either furiously or steadily for short periods. He felt he had never completed the paintings and that he never would, but nevertheless they became an ever-deeper expression of his vision.

Although he had concentrated on water-lilies and the water garden since 1905 these panels marked a new departure for Monet. Firstly they extended horizontally to provide a much wider field of vision than he had considered before, and secondly they were on a much larger scale than anything he had previously attempted. These two factors alone might have daunted even an energetic young

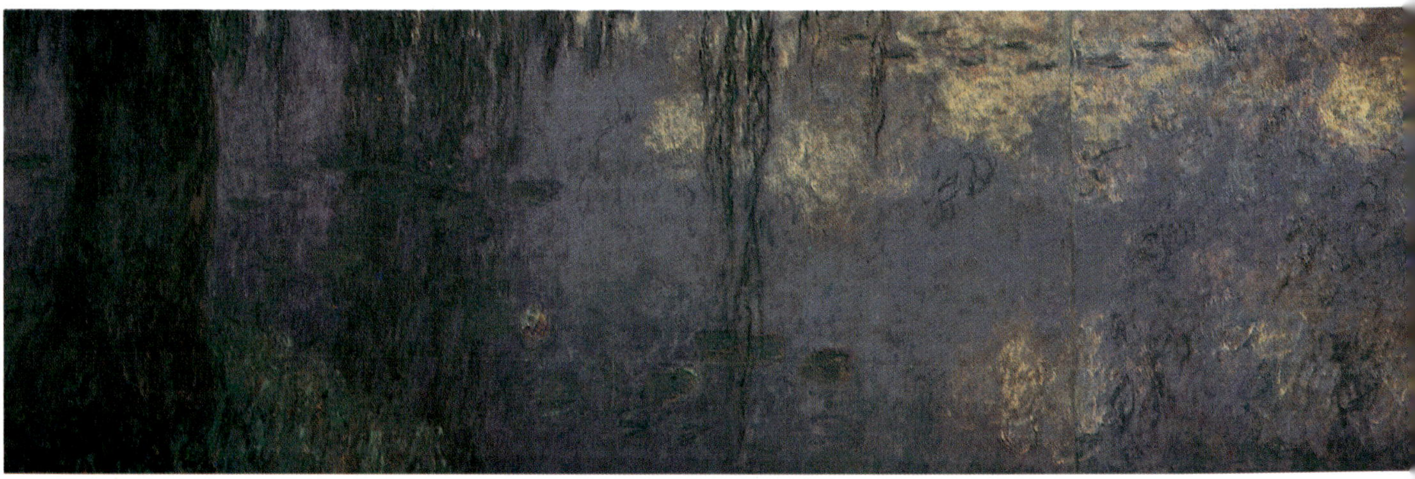

painter, but Monet was old and his eyesight was poor and failing.

But the problems were not only physical and emotional. Much later Walter Sickert (1860-1942) expressed the view that Monet had "yielded to a fatal enlargement of scale that called for the strictest limitations of area." What he meant was that the paintings were on a huge scale while the subject — the surface of the water in his own water garden — was not. There are twelve panels, all exploring the same subject, this one alone being over six feet high and over forty-two feet long. No other large mural project in the history of art has attempted such concentration on one limited subject.

Sickert's comment gives rise to the question of whether the scale is actually too large for the content. Monet's obsession with water surfaces, particularly those he observed in his own water garden, can possibly be seen in the last analysis as a program of decoration, more of a record of obsession than a progressively renewing sense of discovery. Even so, the achievement is immense. No one can be in the presence of these panels without a feeling of spiritual enlargement as well as a pure physical delight in the paint surface and color. The very presence of the works is affecting and their scale is such that no reproduction can really convey their atmosphere.

The paint quality contributes enormously to the feeling of this floating world, as consisting of points of light over a varying blue depth; dense overpainting combines with lightly drawn-on color to pull the eye across the surface with constant pleasure. What is so captivating is the paradox of flat depth; the consciousness of the painting surface, mentioned earlier, here becomes palpable.

Monet donated these panels to the nation by an agreement signed in 1922 and they were placed in the Orangerie in 1927, a few months after his death. He never believed that he had finished them.

The subject matter of these panels is a panorama of the water surface of Monet's water garden, and the color consists for the most part of cool blues, greens and deep mauves, given heightened value by the luminous yellows and pinks and by the flowers picked out in sharp contrast. Monet saw the whole decoration as a continuous horizontal for a circular room.

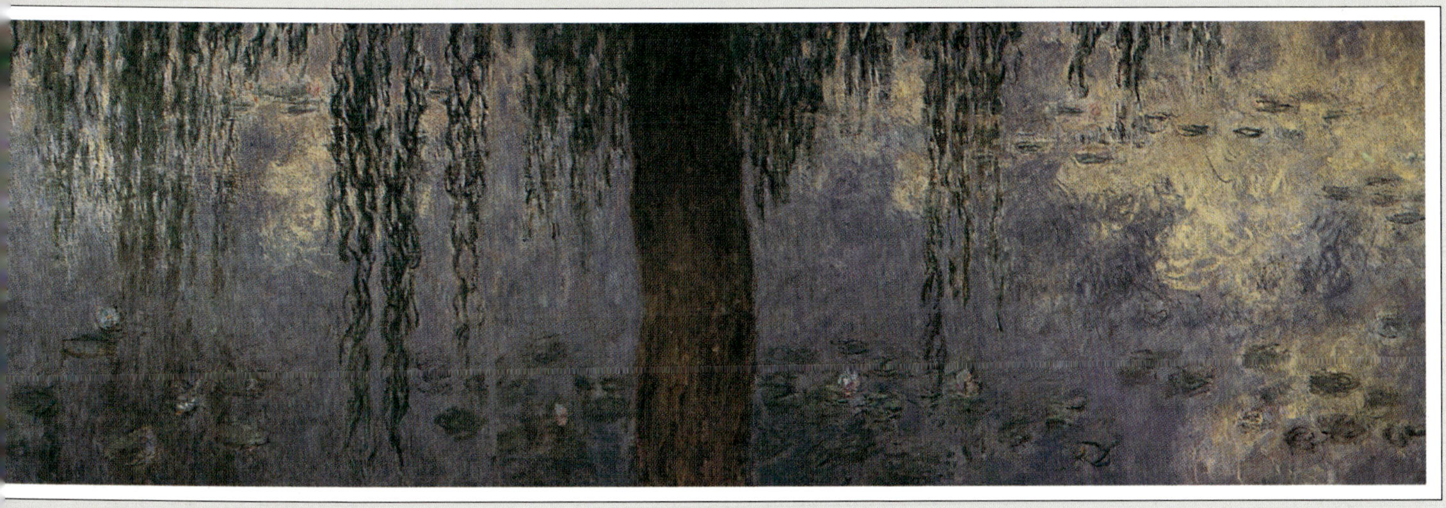

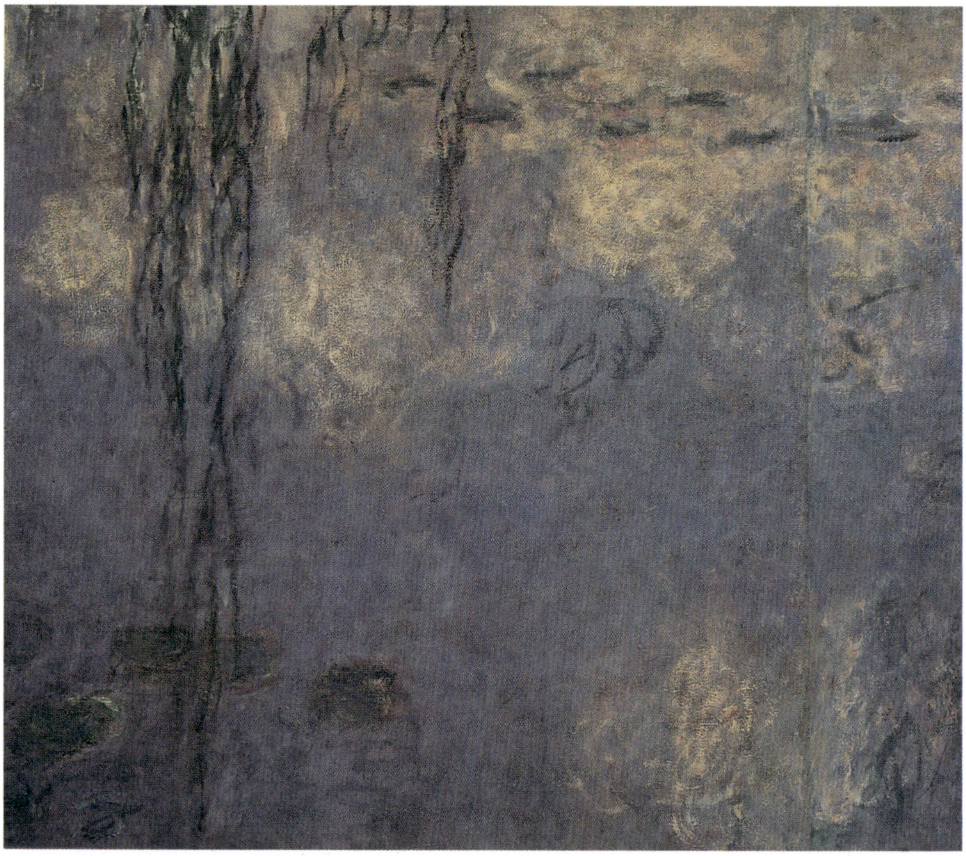

1

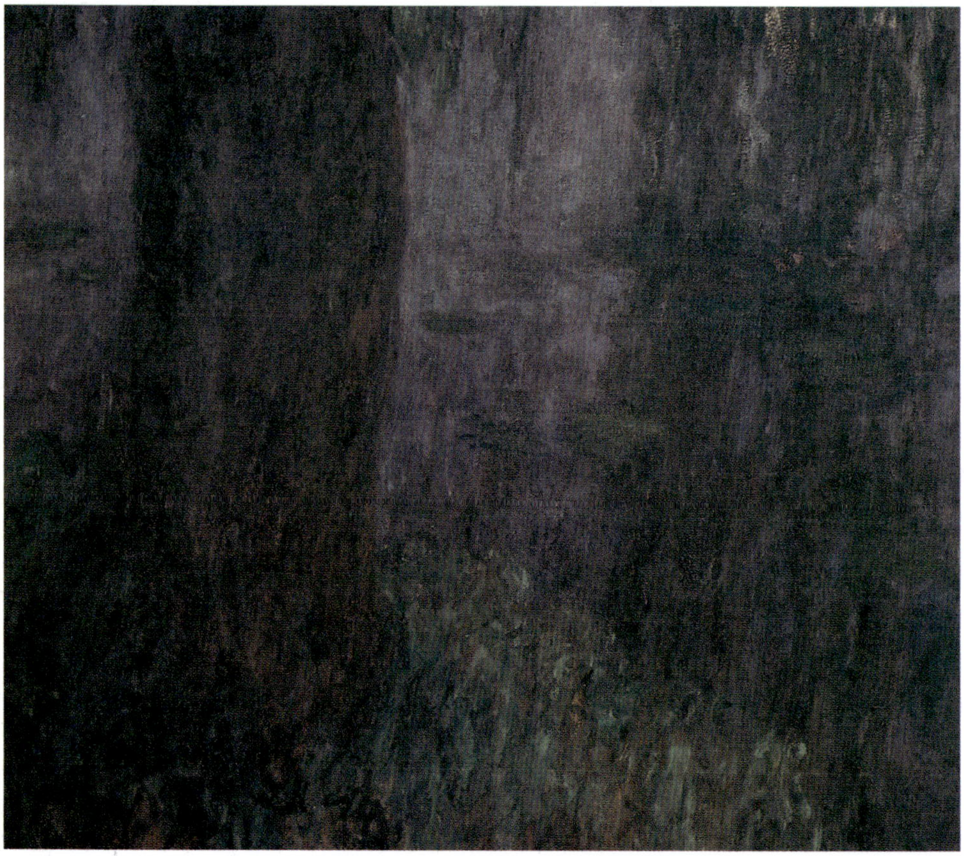

2

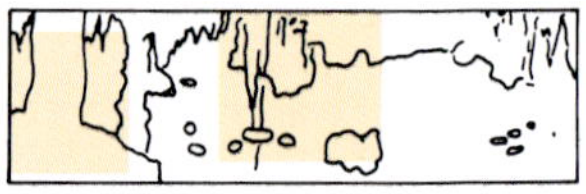

1 "The essence of the motif is the mirror of water whose appearance alters at every moment thanks to the patches of sky that are reflected in it, and which give it light and movement." This detail exemplifies Monet's comment, suggesting the sky within the water, sunlit with roseate clouds. Painted with thick paint in large action strokes and delicate touches, it expresses the controlled mastery achieved after a lifetime of experience.

2 The predominating paint quality of Prussian blues, ultramarine and viridian, mixed in the light areas with white, is balanced by the introduction of warm browns on the trunk of the tree and points of sharp yellow in the grasses. The deep, almost mysterious, shadowed water thrusts the bright green bank into prominence. It is part of the marvelous coherence of these panels that this balance of strong vertical notes and floating and amorphous areas of rich color is maintained in a moving balance throughout the whole project.

3 *Actual size detail* This detail of a single waterlily flower painted in sharp color in a dense impasto pigment gives, by implication, an insight into the great physical tenacity Monet showed in the production of these immense panels. When one reflects that this work was carried over hundreds of square feet of densely painted canvas, with layers of overpainting and repainting one can only be amazed at Monet's physical and mental reserves.

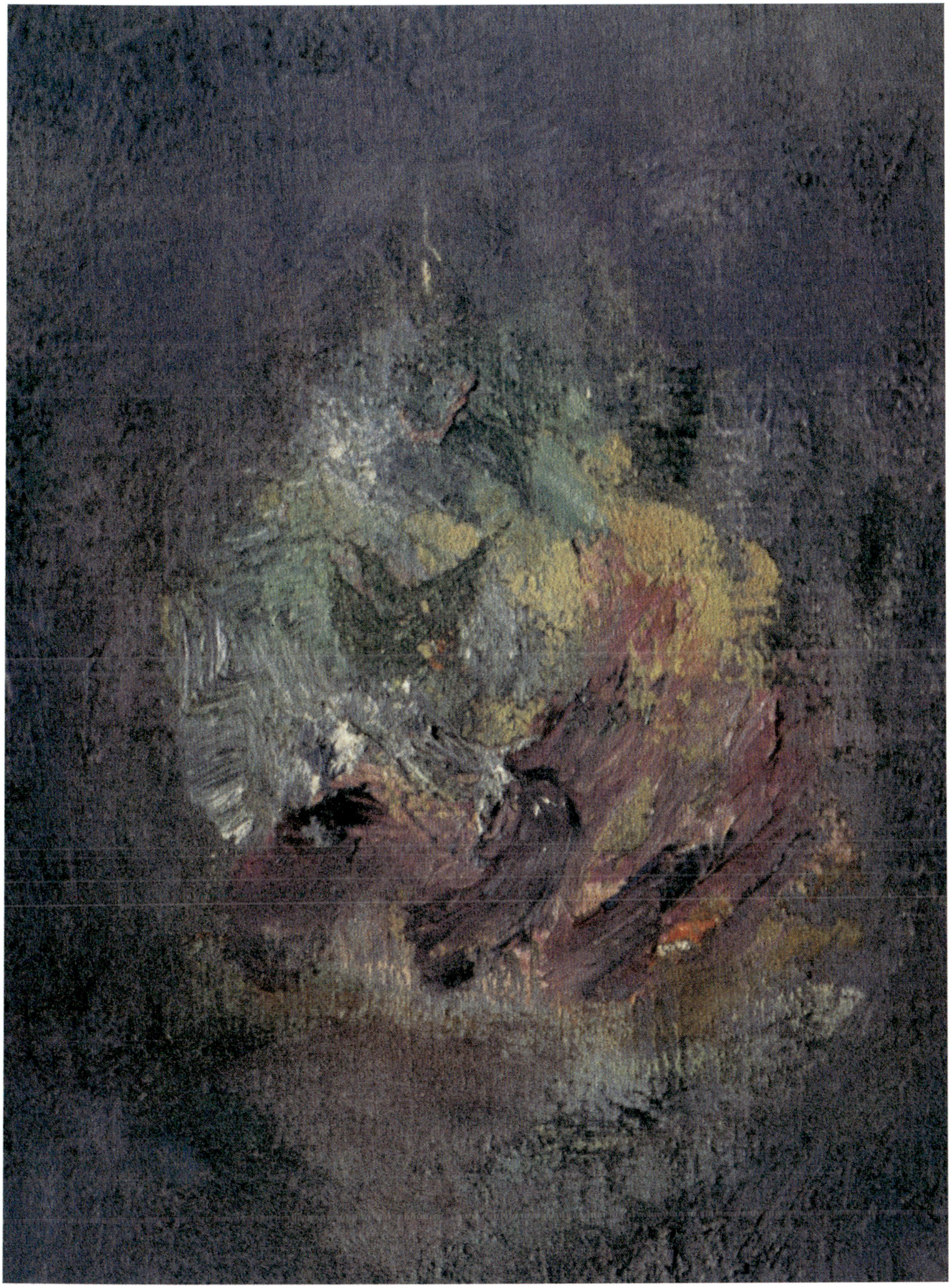

3 *Actual size detail*

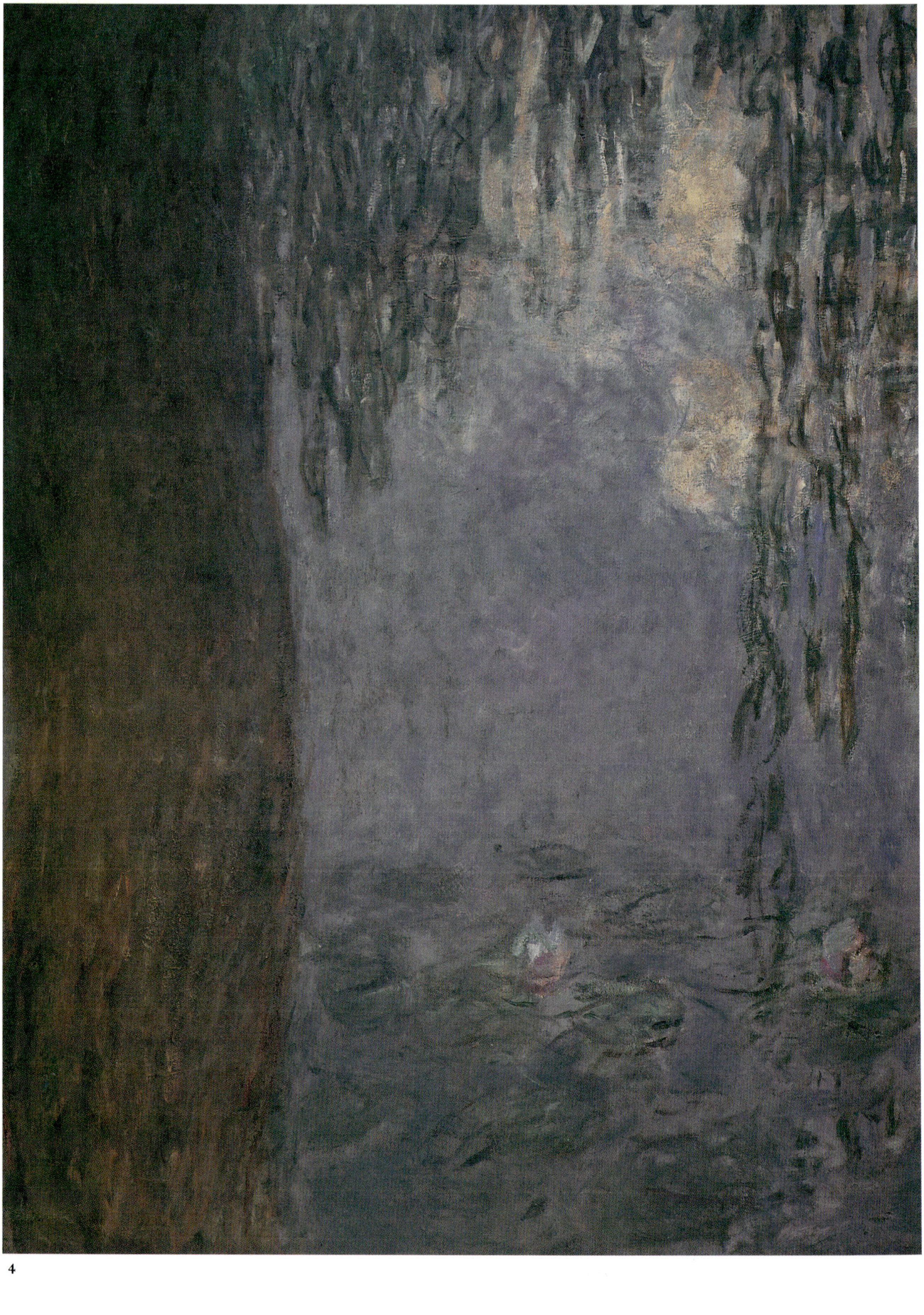

4

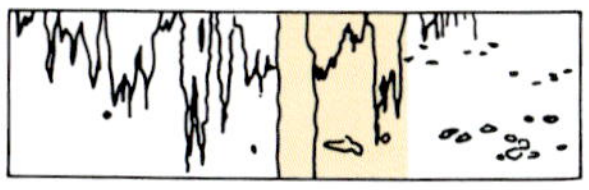

4 The floating indeterminate surface is thrust into its proper relationship with both the edges and the picture plane by the use of solid forms either in the water or on the banks. In this detail the falling fronds of weeping willow send the cloud reflection into a steep perspective recession which is brought back to the water surface through the use of dark and strong color on the lower edge.

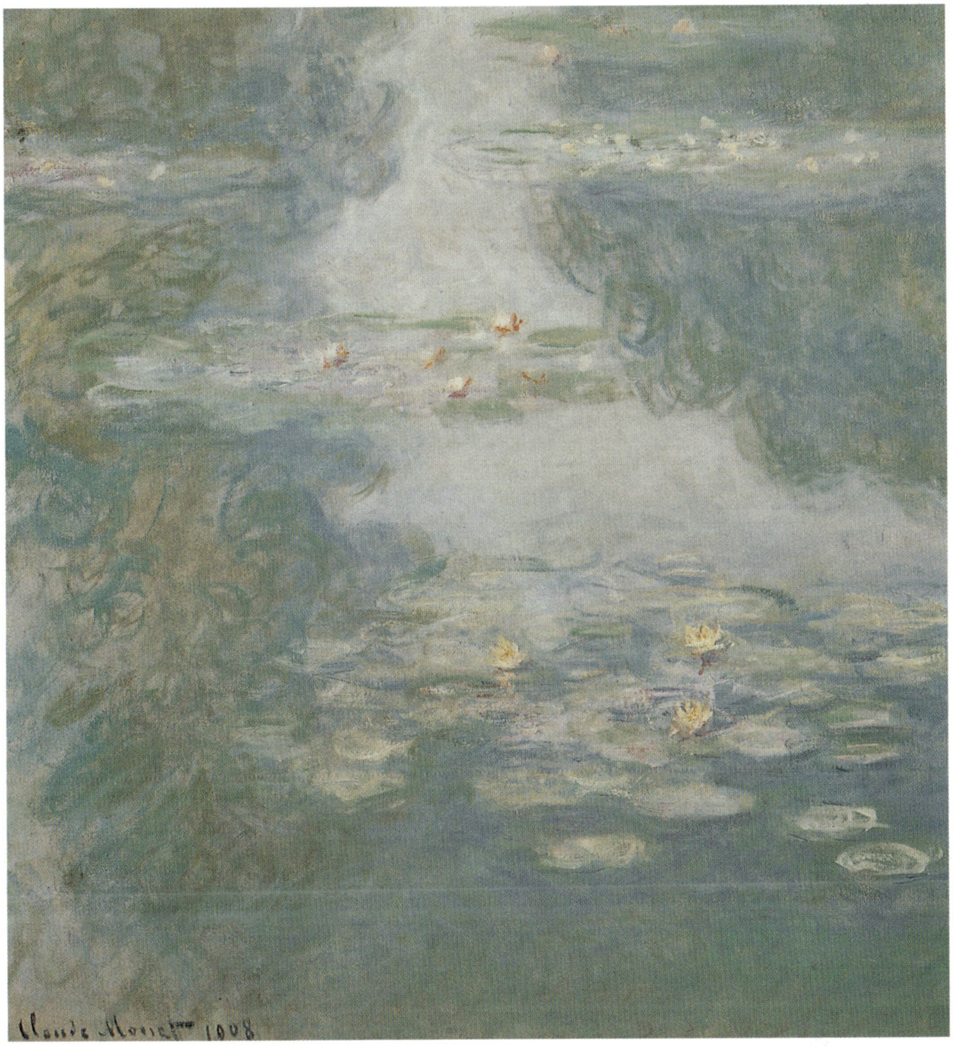

Waterlilies, 1908

Right Monet made his first paintings of the water garden in 1892, and by 1900 it had become his main subject. The earlier paintings, of the Japanese bridge spanning the pond, had taken a standard eye-level perspective, but now he began to concentrate more and more on the water itself, looking down from a high viewpoint, with nothing visible except the water, the floating flowers and water plants and the ever-changing reflections of the sky. In 1909 a group of forty-eight of Monet's waterlily paintings was shown as the Durand-Ruel gallery, and it was at this time that the idea of the great decorative panels began to take shape in his mind.

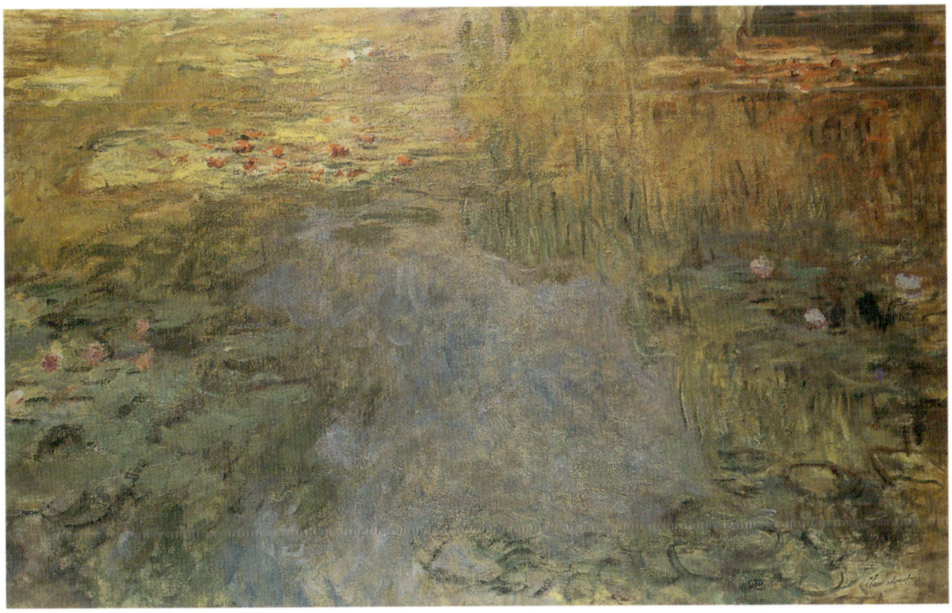

Waterlilies, 1919

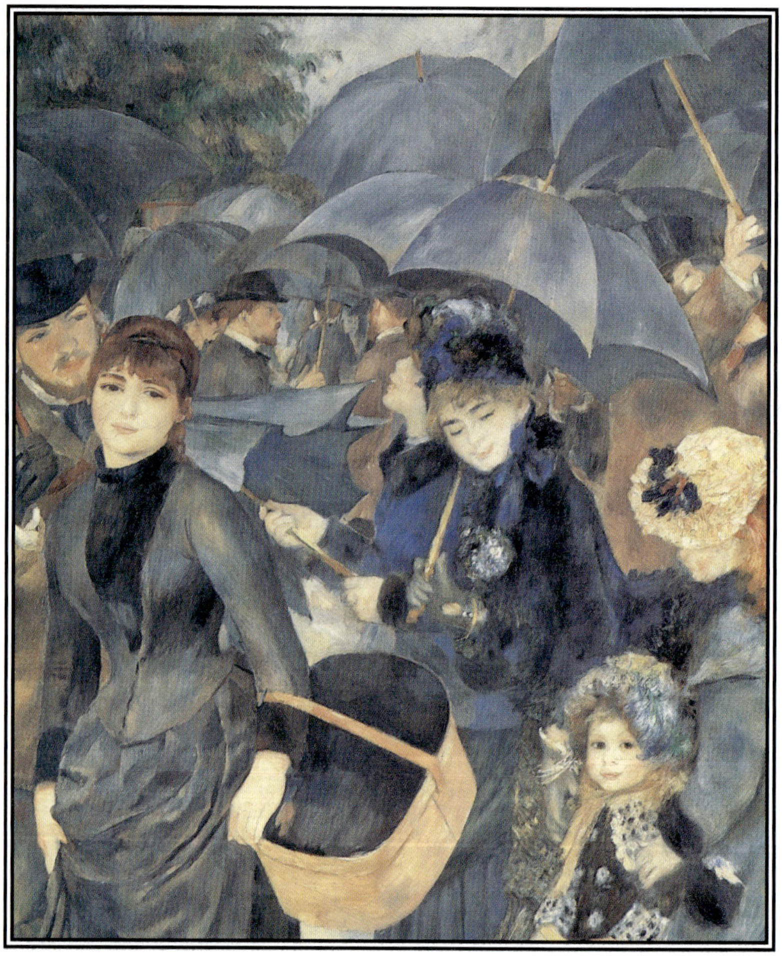

RENOIR

Introduction

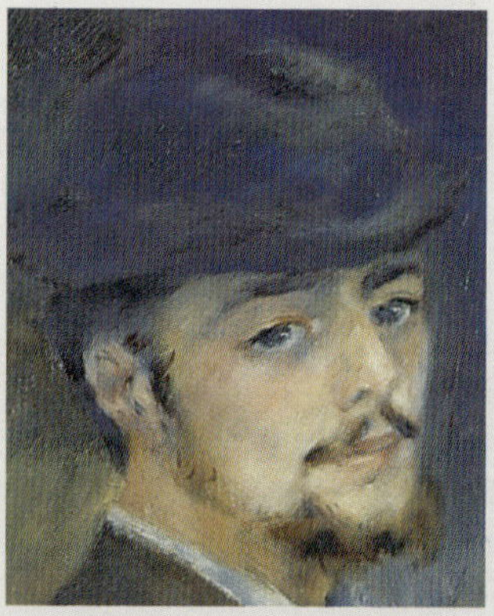

Pierre-Auguste Renoir
Self-portrait
1876
Fogg Art Museum, Cambridge, Mass.

Late nineteenth-century France witnessed the flowering of a school of painting which, although initially derided, is now probably the best known and most loved in the entire history of art. The group of painters who became known as the Impressionists, rejecting the traditional, old-fashioned and established standards set by the Ecole des Beaux Arts, began the process of turning the world of art and aesthetics on its head which continued until the emergence of a school of truly modern painters by the end of the century. Artists such as Edouard Manet, Edgar Degas, Claude Monet, Alfred Sisley, Camille Pissarro and Pierre-Auguste Renoir each in their own way contributed to a change in technique, subject matter and handling that paved the way for a new understanding of art and its aims.

Of all these painters Pierre Auguste Renoir is perhaps the most familiar and in many ways the most readily appreciated, but in other ways he is also less easy to understand than some of his contemporaries, and his pictures less straightforward than they often appear. Renoir, although rightly classified as an Impressionist painter, indeed sometimes seen as one of the driving forces in the development of the movement, does not in truth fit easily into it. Landscape does not dominate his work as it does that of Sisley, nor did he share either Monet's fascination with the ever-changing effects of light and weather or Pissarro's concern for experimentation with form, light and the human figure within the landscape. Renoir, like Degas and Manet, was a painter close to Impressionism but never quite of it. He borrowed many of the techniques of the new younger artists, such as the lighter preparations and the stronger, brighter palette, but for much of his subject matter and inspiration he had more in common with the artists of the eighteenth century than with those of the late nineteenth.

The early years 1841-1868

Pierre-Auguste Renoir was born on February 25, 1841, son of Léonard Renoir, a tailor of modest means in the city of Limoges in the southwest of France. In 1844, the Renoir family moved to Paris in search of a better living and settled in the rue d'Argenteuil in the center of Paris not far from the Louvre, and it was here, in the shadow of the great museum, that the young Renoir grew up. He was a happy child with a sunny disposition; a spontaneous talker, who made friends easily, and his uncomplicated attitude to life was later to be reflected in the warmth and gaiety of his paintings. Although poor for much of his life, he would never accept lack of money as a barrier to success or to a happy life, and one of his favorite maxims in later life, "there are no poor people," seems to express a refusal to acknowledge poverty of means as a justification for poverty of spirit or imagination.

As a child in school Renoir showed a natural inclination toward scribbling and drawing, but in early life his greater talent appeared to be for singing, and he was for a time a pupil of the composer Charles Gounod, then choir-master at the Church of St Roch in Renoir's neighborhood. Gounod tried to encourage Renoir's parents to let him follow a musical career, but owing to their poor background (their circumstances had not been improved by the move to Paris), it was necessary for the boy to leave school at the age of thirteen and discontinue his music lessons. Instead, because of his facility for drawing, he was apprenticed as a porcelain painter with the aim of one day decorating the porcelain at the great Sèvres factory on the outskirts of Paris. He quickly displayed a ready talent for his new occupation, but frequently tired of the monotonous subject matter, and would escape into the galleries of the Louvre. Here he could look at the works of the Old Masters, and more particularly those of the great eighteenth-century French painters Fragonard and Boucher, who delighted in depicting the human figure amidst rich and splendid surroundings.

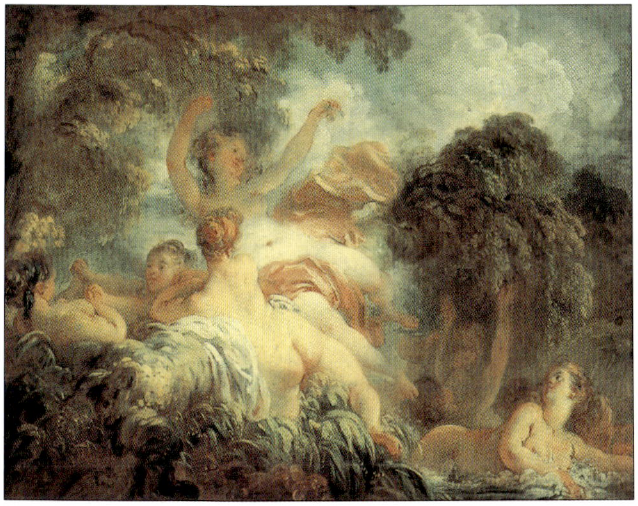

JEAN HONORE FRAGONARD
The Bathers
c.1760
Louvre, Paris

Fragonard's work had been much admired by Renoir ever since his first visit to the Louvre as a young boy. Throughout his life he continued to be inspired by the imagery and subject matter of the eighteenth century, and in particular by the delicacy and opulence of Fragonard's paintings.

The master of the porcelain factory soon recognized his young apprentice's talent, and told his parents that he was too good to be restricted to porcelain painting and should be encouraged to train properly as a painter. In the nineteenth century there were very strict rules regulating art training, and Renoir accordingly began to take lessons to prepare for his entry into the Ecole des Beaux Arts. For a time he continued to maintain himself by porcelain painting, but in 1858 the factory adopted new mechanical reproduction processes, and he was left without employment and had to turn to decorating window shades, fans and various domestic goods in order to continue his studies. His erstwhile employer's encouragement had strengthened his determination to make his career as a painter, and he spent many hours in the Louvre copying the works of the Old Masters, a traditional part of an aspiring artist's training at the time. One of his favorite works was Boucher's *Diana at the Bath*, a subject which was later to reappear frequently in his own paintings.

By 1862 he had saved sufficient money to enable him to study full-time. He enrolled at the Ecole des Beaux Arts and at the same time entered the studio of Charles Gleyre, chosen because Gleyre was more tolerant of modern ideas than some of the more traditional masters and also because he made only a small charge to cover the cost of his pupils' materials. Here Renoir met three painters who were to have an important influence on him — Claude Monet, Frédéric Bazille and Alfred Sisley. Monet had already been introduced to open-air painting by Eugène Boudin and the Dutch painter Jongkind, and in 1864, at Monet's suggestion, the four young artists began to make painting trips to the forest of Fontainebleau, a favorite haunt of the Barbizon school of painters. Renoir, somewhat easily led by his more dynamic friends, was not immediately taken with the idea of painting out of doors, but was carried along by Monet's infectious enthusiasm. Much of his work at this time is somber and dark, with too heavy a reliance on the use of bitumen, but he gradually began to lighten his palette, particularly after meeting the landscape painter Narcisse Virgile Diaz de la Peña, one of the Barbizon group,

PIERRE AUGUSTE RENOIR
Diana
1867
National Gallery of Art, Washington

Like all aspiring artists at the time, Renoir was anxious to gain acceptance at the Salon, and for this work, submitted but rejected, he has chosen a deliberately conservative and classical subject. The handling, however, is more modern, and the influence of Courbet can be seen both in the thick paint, applied with the palette knife, and in the light, airy background landscape.

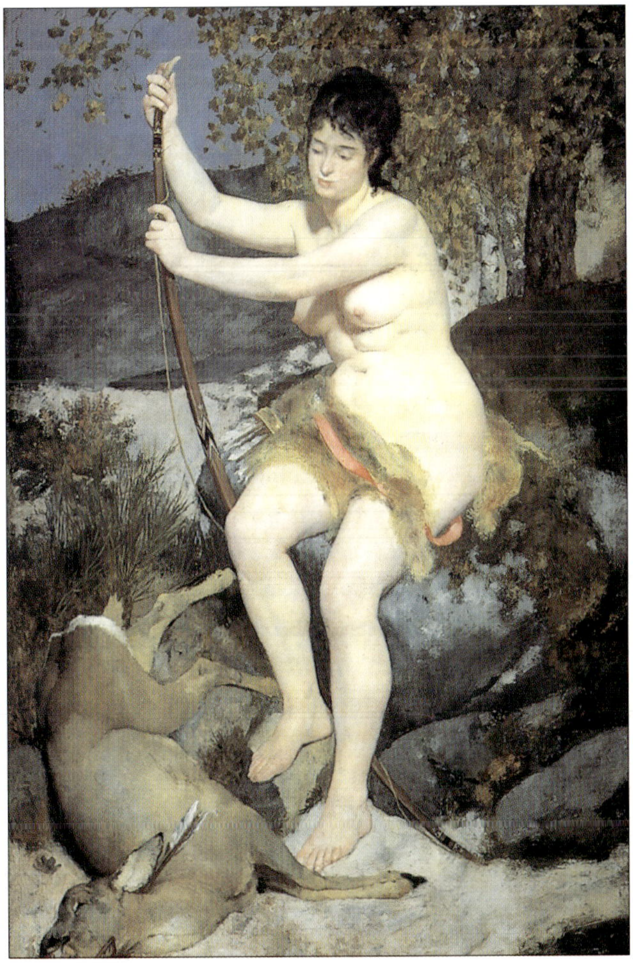

who encouraged Renoir, advised him against the use of black, and was generous enough to let him buy materials on his own account. Renoir was frequently too poor to buy them himself, and throughout the 1860s, in order to make a living, he would take any commissions that came his way, which sometimes meant such humble tasks as decorating a cupboard or doing small caricatures.

In 1865 Renoir returned to Fontainebleau in the company of Sisley, and met Pissarro and Gustave Courbet, who was an influence on his early work. The young painters had by now left Gleyre's studio, which closed shortly afterward, and were attempting to make their own way in the world, and in 1865 Renoir attempted unsuccessfully to win selection for the Salon with a landscape, entering himself as a pupil of Courbet. Later, after seeing Manet's work, he tried to escape from the earlier influence; Courbet's dark colors and heavy use of the palette knife no longer seemed to offer the possibilities of delicacy of touch that was to become such an important feature of Renoir's work.

The summer of 1868 was spent in Paris, with the city providing the subject matter for several important works, one being *The Pont des Arts*, which clearly shows the influence of Monet and the first traces of the style that would come to be known as Impressionism. During this period Renoir was able to live with Bazille and share his studio; Bazille came from a well-to-do bourgeois family in Montpellier in the south of France, and was able to help both Monet and Renoir. He and Renoir became firm friends and painted each other several times. These were difficult times for Renoir: in spite of Bazille's generosity, he could not even afford to stay in Paris, and was forced to go to his parents, who had retired to Ville d'Avray. He said later, "I would several times have given up if Monet had not reassured me with a slap on the back."

But in spite of hardship, whenever they had enough money to buy materials, Renoir and Monet would paint together like men possessed of a great secret, working along the banks of the Seine in the new suburbs growing up on the edge of Paris at Chatou and Argenteuil. They often painted the same subject, for instance both executed versions of *La Grenouillère*, the name of a bathing and boating resort frequented by fashionable Parisians, and it was here that both painted what are now regarded as the first Impressionist pictures (see page 551).

Changing techniques

As the Industrial Revolution gathered pace various technical innovations were made in the nature and preparation of paints and canvas, and these, together with the emergence of photography, were to be important influences on the development of Impressionism. The first crucial technical development was that of ready ground and mixed paints in metal tubes, which meant that the artist no longer had to go through laborious work before he was ready to paint. Previously, painters had had to grind their paints by hand with a pestle and mortar and then prepare them for painting by adding oil, usually linseed oil. This was a long process which could only be carried out in the studio, thus effectively ruling out the use of oil paint out of doors for any but the smallest and thinnest of sketches. The development of ready prepared machine-ground colors in transportable tubes radically altered the position of the landscape painter: artists could now take to the open air fully equipped and ready to paint just as Renoir and his friends did on their first visit to the forest of Fontainebleau.

This was important in itself, but there were also great advances being made in the type of paints and mediums, which affected the way artists used their paints from the 1860s onwards. Because linseed oil tended to yellow the paint as it dried, artists had in the past built up the pictures in very thin layers, waiting for each in turn to dry. This was not only a very slow process, but also one that threatened the long-term stability of the picture. Although the yellowing process could be reduced, the complex chemical reactions of the different layers of paint, some thick and some thinner, some closer and some further from the surface, tended to lead to cracking or shrinking as the picture aged. The spontaneity and immediacy of the Impressionists' work was to some extent stimulated by the ready availability of prepared paint, but was also the result of a desire to avoid painting in many layers, thereby minimizing these chemical reactions.

By the mid-nineteenth century poppy-seed oil was beginning to supersede linseed as the favored binding medium for the machine-ground colors because it tended to yellow less as it dried. A side effect of this was that the paint itself became somewhat stiffer in texture and tended to retain the mark of the brush, something the Impressionists were swift to adopt into their painterly vocabulary. Poppy-seed oil also dried rather more slowly, which allowed the artists to work their colors wet into wet on the surface of the canvas without having to mix them laboriously beforehand. Artists who did not like the buttery texture of the prepared paints would often drain them of oil first by putting them on blotting paper, a method Renoir liked because he found that the

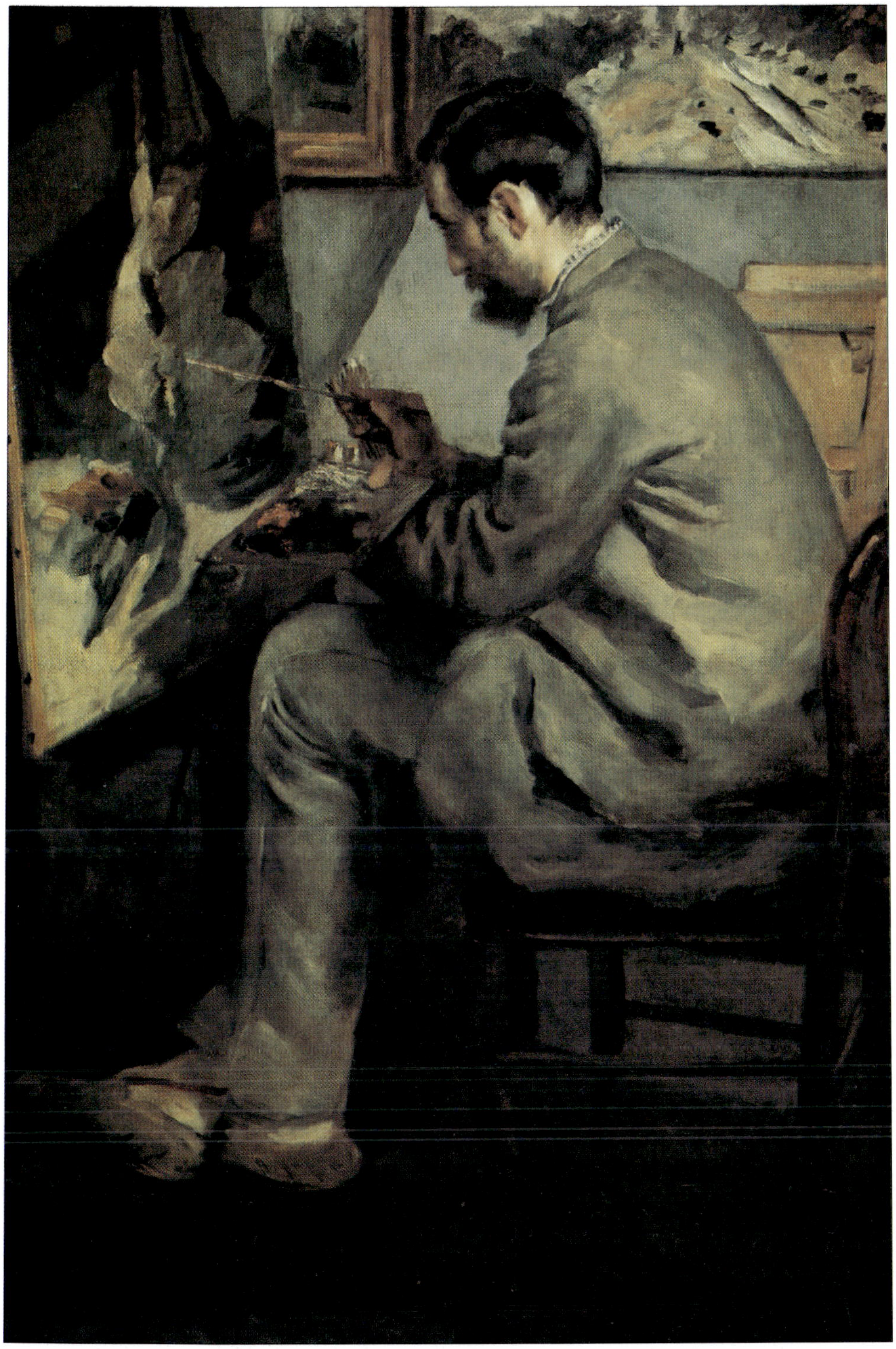

PIERRE-AUGUST RENOIR
Frédéric Bazille at his Easel
1867
Musée d'Orsay, Paris

This portrait of Bazille at work, like his own portrait of Renoir, was probably painted in Bazille's studio, which both Renoir and Monet shared for a time. The sitter is shown at work on a painting which still exists, *Still Life with Heron*. The actual painting is tight and carefully handled, but Renoir's version shows a broad and free treatment that does not match the fine brush he is using.

paint, once dried of its oil, developed a chalky pastel-like quality which could be used to achieve a feathery softness of touch.

Before a painting could begin, the canvas had to be stretched and primed. Until the mid-nineteenth century it had been the tradition to prime the canvas with a somber dark brown, but this slowly began to change, and the Impressionist painters nearly always used canvases primed in white or other pale colors. These light grounds tended to give a painting greater luminosity, and also led to the idea of using the color of the priming as a color or tonal value in its own right. The ground could be left bare in places to show through, or just covered with a thin layer of paint, blending with or contributing to the other colors on the canvas. Moreover, to contribute further to the speed of execution so important to the Impressionists, the priming tint could be chosen in advance to suit a particular effect of light or weather.

The development of photography could not fail to have an important impact on the nature of painting. Despite much atavistic reluctance to accommodate it, photography began to release painters from the demands of painstaking reproduction, freeing them to explore the problems of painting itself. Photographs also changed the way artists viewed composition: the unselective eye of the camera altered the focus of attention, leading to a flatter overall vision which contrasted with the previously more selective painterly vision. The Impressionist painters were quick to become aware of this, and to realize that a painting need not be a concentrated theater of action with a central focal point but, like a photograph, could merely be a "slice of life" hinting at action going on outside the immediate frame. This absorption of the lessons of the photograph led to a new type of painting with a more uniform focus, thicker, more even overall paint surfaces, and flattened pictorial perspectives, confusing the more conservative-minded viewers, who failed to grasp the pictorial intentions of this work which no longer seemed to conform to the traditional Beaux Arts standards.

The search for patrons

The development of Impressionism was temporarily halted by the outbreak of the Franco-Prussian war in 1870. The group became scattered. Bazille was killed fighting at Beaune la Roland; Monet, Pissarro and Sisley sought refuge in England – the latter was of British descent, and his family had become bankrupt as a result of the war – and Renoir himself joined the Cuirassiers. He saw no action, being posted to the remote spot of Pau in the Basses-Pyrénées, but he had little time for painting On being discharged he returned to Paris, and was one of the few painters to remain there during the troubled period of the Commune.

PIERRE-AUGUSTE RENOIR
The Pont des Arts, Paris
1867
Norton Simon Foundation, Los Angeles

As a young man Renoir, like his friend Monet, painted urban landscapes, trying to capture the feel of contemporary Paris with its new bridges and boulevards. This work shows signs of the style that he was later to develop into his own version of Impressionism. The influence of photography can also be seen in the wide angle and the way the action is cropped at the edges of the painting.

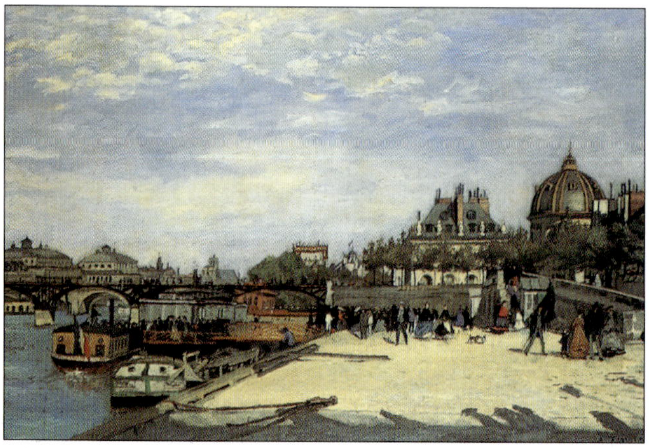

With his friend and benefactor Bazille now gone, Renoir found life far from easy, but in 1873 a turning point came when the dealer Paul Durand-Ruel began to buy his work, enabling him to rent his first studio, at 35 rue St Georges. He continued to send paintings to the Salon, among them his *Diana*, classical in subject matter and concept but rather more modern in handling. This, like most of his entries, was rejected, and his friends Monet and Pissarro were also in general unsuccessful. Both Monet and Renoir did, in fact, have paintings accepted in 1865 and 1866, but simply being hung in the Salon did not necessarily guarantee success – an unknown artist could find his work placed in a dim corner or so high up on a wall as to render it to all intents and purposes invisible.

The difficulty of gaining acceptance at the Salon, then literally the only showplace for an aspiring artist, led to the idea of staging an independent exhibition where the public could see and judge the young artists' work for themselves. Renoir became treasurer of the new-formed group and served on the hanging committee. The first Impressionist Exhibition was held in 1874, with six paintings by Renoir included. Predictably, the show was a financial disaster, and aroused both hostility and derision from the critics, but of the few works that did sell, several were by Renoir.

The dealer Durand-Ruel had been forced to stop buying, being in financial difficulties, and the group of artists had now no source of income or prospects, so the following year Renoir joined with Monet, Sisley and Berthe Morisot and held an auction sale of their work at the Hotel Drouot. This once again was a disaster, although Renoir found a patron in the person of a modestly well-to-do customs official, Victor Chocquet, who had come to the auction quite by chance and was one of the few buyers. Chocquet was to become an important patron, not only of Renoir, but also of other avant-garde painters, notably Paul Cézanne.

Throughout the early 1870s Renoir continued to work with Monet, painting on the banks of the Seine and on

RENOIR'S PAINTING METHODS

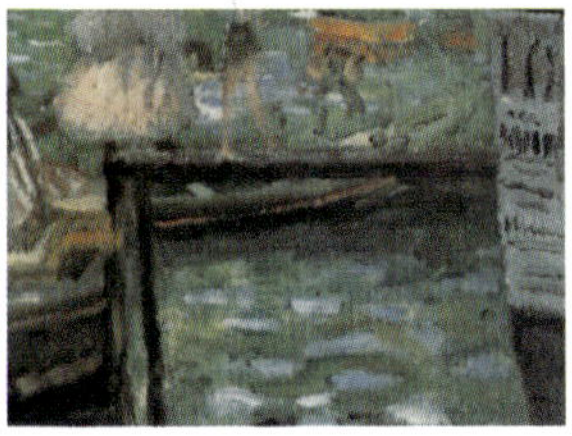

In this detail from La Grenouillère, *we see how Renoir has worked wet into wet to create the effect of the watery reflection.*

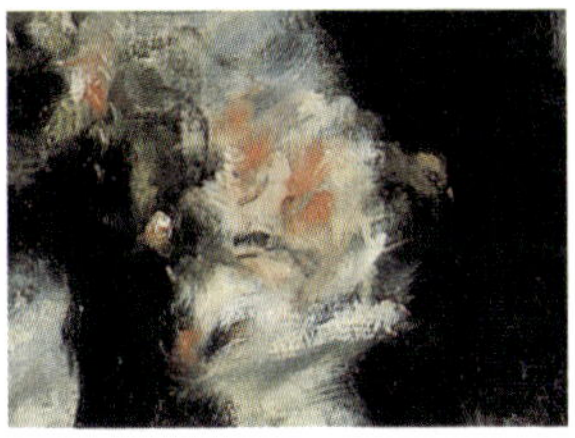

In Box at the Theater *the thickest paint, unusually, is to be found in the dark areas and in the red of the roses.*

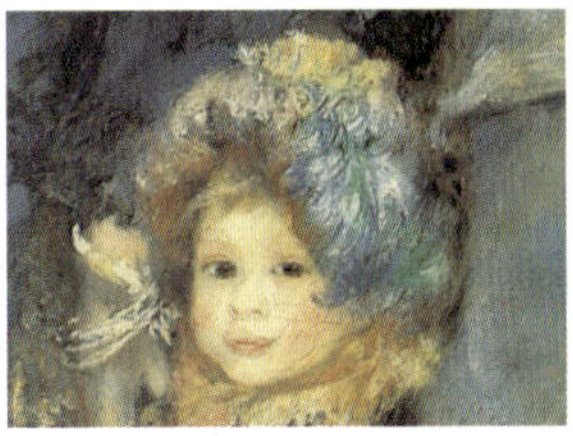

This detail from The Umbrellas *shows Renoir's favorite white ground reflecting back through the thinned paint.*

Renoir's paintings are characterized by a light, feathery and delicate touch (which may owe something to his early training as a porcelain painter) and an obvious delight in the sensual qualities of oil paint. He was always a devoted student of the Old Masters, and his fluid handling of paint owes as much to them as to the Impressionists.

He liked to work on a smooth white or pale-primed canvas, and would often add an extra coating of flake white thinned with oil and turpentine to give extra smoothness. His colors were in general used quite thin, diluted with oil or turpentine, though in places he would build up the paint more thickly, so that each painting shows a considerable variety of paint texture.

He would begin a painting by putting small dabs of thinned color all over the canvas, apparently at random, but actually to give him an idea of the color relationships. After this, he would blend them all together, rubbing all over the canvas so that a soft, shadowy image of the whole painting quickly began to appear. He said himself that he would "arrange my subject as I want it, then I start painting as if I were a child. I want a red to sing out like a bell. If it doesn't, I add reds and other colors until I get there." When the lay-in was complete he would begin to define and build up each area, increasing the proportion of oil to turpentine in accordance with the old maxim, "start lean, finish fat."

The colors shown here, with the addition of flake white, are representative of Renoir's palette at the time of this work, Les Grandes Baigneuses. *He always used black (except for a short time during his outdoor painting phase) but, as he said himself, "in mixtures, as in nature."*

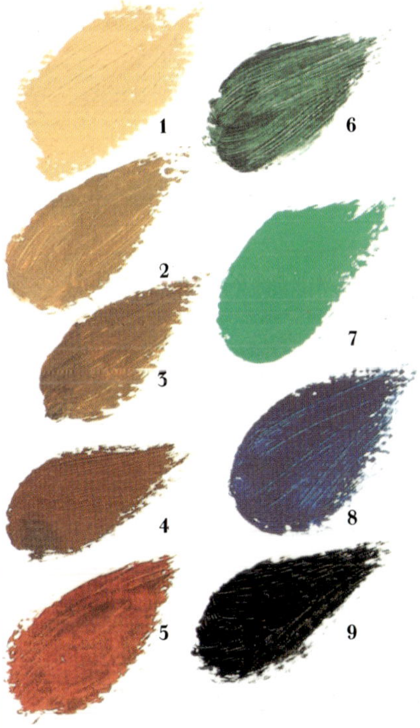

1 Naples yellow; 2 Yellow ocher; 3 Raw sienna; 4 Red ocher; 5 Red madder; 6 Terre verte; 7 Veronese (emerald) green; 8 Cobalt blue; 9 Ivory black

the Normandy coast, but as the need for commissions was ever pressing he began to turn increasingly to portraiture. This found him more favor with the buying public, though it was not until Chocquet introduced him to the publisher Georges Charpentier that he really found success. In 1879 his portrait of *Mme Charpentier and her Children* was not only accepted at the Salon but also enjoyed considerable critical acclaim. Renoir had found that the series of Impressionist Exhibitions, which continued until 1886, did not give him the public platform he needed, and although his return to the official Salon was criticized by some of his fellow artists, he stood firm on his decision. As he said to Durand-Ruel, "I would like to tell these gentlemen that I am not going to give up exhibiting at the Salon. This is not for pleasure, but as I told you, it will dispel the revolutionary taint which frightens me...it is a small weakness for which I hope to be pardoned." In fact Renoir was displaying his inherent conservatism both as an individual and as a painter: now beginning to be accepted as a portrait painter of consequence, he was reluctant to jeopardize his precarious success by too-close association with those the public regarded as revolutionaries. But he had aesthetic reasons too, explaining to his friend Ambroise Vollard that, "I have been to the very end of Impressionism and arrived at the conclusion that I knew not how to paint or draw. In a word I was at a dead end."

A change of direction

Although remaining close friends with the Impressionist group and other associated artists such as Cézanne, Renoir was by the end of the decade developing his own style. In 1881 he traveled through Africa — in the footsteps of Delacroix, as he saw it — and then to Italy. In Rome, Florence and Venice, he studied the Italian Renaissance and post-Renaissance masters, which filled him with doubts about the "mainstream" Impressionism practiced by Monet, Pissarro and Sisley. Although some of his paintings, those owned by Durand-Ruel, were put into the seventh Impressionist Exhibition (1882), he was unhappy about exhibiting with Pissarro and the young Gauguin, feeling that they were becoming too unorthodox in their works. As he later said to his young pupil Albert André, "For my part I always defended myself against the charge of being a revolutionary. I always believed and I still believe that I only continued to do what others had done a great deal better before me."

His style became more refined and traditional, and he began to concentrate on the human form to an even greater degree than he had earlier in works such as the *Moulin de la Galette* of 1876 (see page 559). Landscape became almost totally excluded; in *The Umbrellas* (see page 564), for example, the whole space seems to be defined by bodies and umbrellas. This new trend also helped his reputation with the buying public and with Durand-Ruel who, now back on the scene, was at last beginning to secure him a modest income. He began to concentrate much more on the influence of eighteenth-century painters — his old favorites Fragonard and Boucher — as well as on the Neoclassical nineteenth-century figures, Jean Auguste Dominique Ingres in particular. His great work of the 1880s, and the final statement of how he had moved away from Impressionism, was *The Bathers* of 1887 (see page 581), for which he made many posed and studied preparatory drawings, in keeping with eighteenth-century tradition. He turned his back on the reliance upon nature which had been so characteristic of his earlier work and continued to be of supreme importance to Monet, Sisley and Pissarro. A remark make to Albert André in his old age seems to confirm his essentially conservative approach. "I discovered about 1883 that the only worthwhile thing for a painter is to study in the museums." Renoir took his study of the Old Masters and eighteenth-century painters very seriously, and by the end of his life he possibly felt that he had learned more of value from them than he had from studying nature and working in the open air with his friends.

Material success and declining health

During this period, family life came to be of increasing importance to Renoir, who was by this time well into his forties. Although he did not marry his mistress Aline Charigot until 1890, she had borne him a son, Pierre, in 1885. At the same time he was also becoming more firmly established with the buying public; a new dealer, Georges Petit, was taking an interest in his work, and in 1886 Durand-Ruel exhibited over thirty paintings in New York (although the *New York Sun* did describe his nudes as "lumpy and obnoxious creatures"). Family life provided a new and stimulating range of subject matter which was to remain a popular theme through the birth of two further sons, Jean in 1894 and Claude (or "Coco") in 1901. His wife's cousin Gabrielle came to live with the family in the 1890s, and became one of Renoir's favorite models as well as a studio assistant, carefully preparing his paint and canvases as he became increasingly infirm.

From the mid-1890s Renoir was dogged by constant ill-health. Bronchial trouble and arthritis prompted a move to the south of France at the turn of the century,

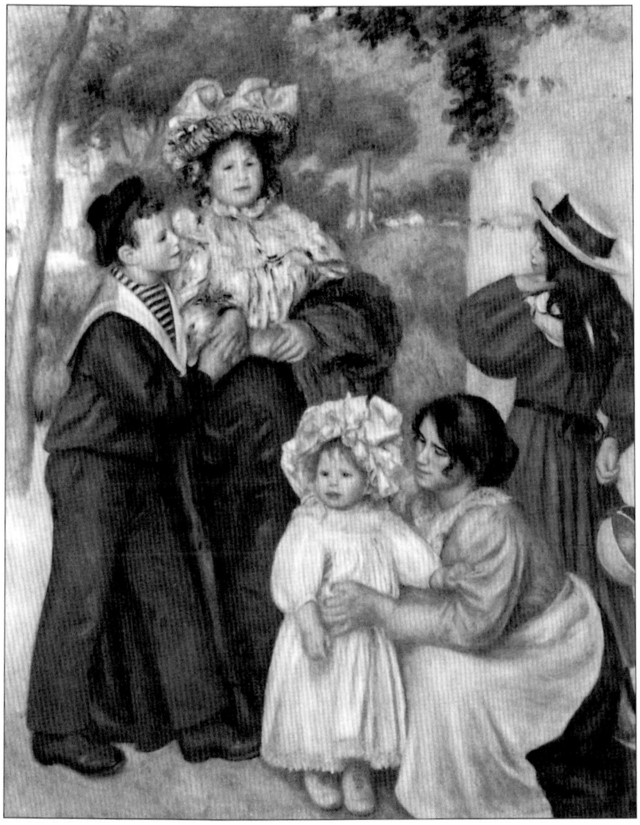

PIERRE-AUGUSTE RENOIR
The Artist's Family
1896
Barnes Foundation, Merion, Pennsylvania

Here Renoir has depicted his wife Aline and her two eldest sons, Pierre and Jean. Claude was not yet born. The kneeling girl is Gabrielle, a cousin of Aline, and a frequent model for Renoir. The other girl is not a member of the family; she is probably a friend or servant.

and the family bought a house at Cagnes. However, at last he had no financial problems; his work was becoming increasingly popular, and he was able to adopt the life-style of the successful professional middle-class. Dealers and private collectors alike competed for his work, and fashionable people sought him out to commission portraits. His enthusiasm for painting never waned, despite a severe hernia in 1908 and a stroke in 1912 which left him temporarily paralyzed. Gabrielle would arrange for him to be carried in a sedan chair to his chosen location in the sunlight or indoors and then prepare the paints on the palette before inserting the brushes between his stiff and arthritic fingers. Despite pain and ill-health Renoir claimed to be very happy in the last years of his life — he now had nothing to do but paint.

Conclusion

Renoir had always had a sanguine appreciation of his own worth as a painter and a great respect for his craft, possibly the result of his working-class background and apprenticeship as a porcelain painter. He saw himself as a workman painter with a job to do rather than as an "artist." Jean Renoir, in his book *Renoir My Father*, lays great emphasis on the particular manner in which his father prepared his paints and his canvases. "Renoir used only eight or ten colors at most. They were ranged in neat little mounds around the edge of the scrupulously clean palette. From this modest assortment would come his shimmering silks and his luminous flesh tones." Renoir never went in for theorizing about painting, leaving this to others around him, and according to Jean, his dislike of such talk once prompted him to complain of critics, "What is to be done about these literary people who will never understand that painting is a craft, and that the material side of it comes first? The ideas come afterwards when the picture is finished." Although he had participated in one of the greatest artistic movements in history, it was his essential modesty and conservatism that came to characterize his work.

In 1919, shortly before his death, Renoir was invited to the Louvre to witness the hanging of his portrait of *Mme Charpentier*. Arriving in his wheelchair, he was treated with the greatest respect. After the ceremony he commented, "If I had been presented at the Louvre thirty years ago in a wheelchair I would have been shown the door. One has to live a long time to witness such changes. I have had that chance." In fact Renoir had become a pillar of respectability, even being made a Chevalier of the Légion d'Honneur in 1900, and had written to Monet asking forgiveness for his willingness to pander to the establishment. It is, however, the key to Renoir's appeal that his ability to make changes led him to combine many of his Impressionist techniques with a more formal sense of pictorial subject matter and style derived from the traditions of the eighteenth-century, producing a style uniquely suited to him and much admired to this day. It is also a tribute to his warm and open personality that, in spite of turning away from Impressionism, he nevertheless retained the affection of his fellow painters, and that he contrived a peaceful, successful and satisfying life in spite of his early tribulations.

CHRONOLOGY OF RENOIR'S LIFE

1841 25 February: born in Limoges, sixth child of Léonard Renoir and Marguerite Merlot.
1844 Family moves to Paris.
1856 Becomes apprentice porcelain painter to Lévy frères.
1862 Enters studio of Charles Gleyre and meets Monet, Sisley and Bazille.
1863 Meets Courbet and Pissarro.
1866 Lise Trehot becomes his model and mistress.
1869 Frequents Café Guerbois and meets Degas, Manet and Zola.
1868 Paints *La Grenouillère.*
1870-71 Franco-Prussian War and Paris Commune.
1872 Introduced by Monet to Paul Durand-Ruel.
1874 First Impressionist Exhibition. Paints *Box at the Theater* and *The Dancer.*
1875 Meets Victor Chocquet and Georges Charpentier.
1876 Second Impressionist Exhibition. Paints *The Ball at the Moulin de la Galette* and *The Swing.*
1878 Paints *Mme Charpentier and her Children.*
1879 Enjoys first critical success at the Salon with *Mme Charpentier.* Meets future wife, Aline Charigot.
1881 Begins *The Umbrellas.*
1881-82 Travels in North Africa and Italy.

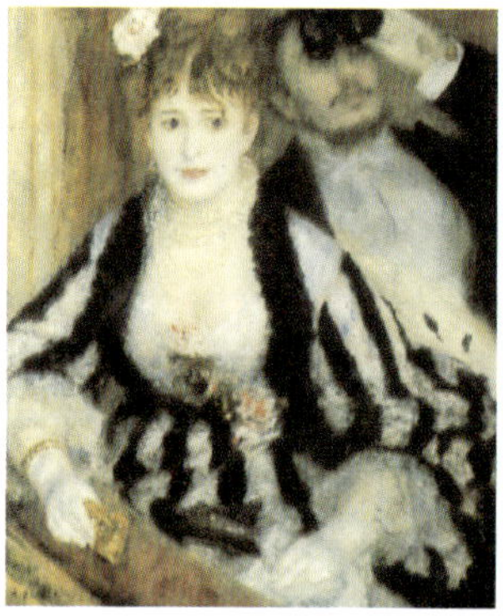

The Box at the Theater

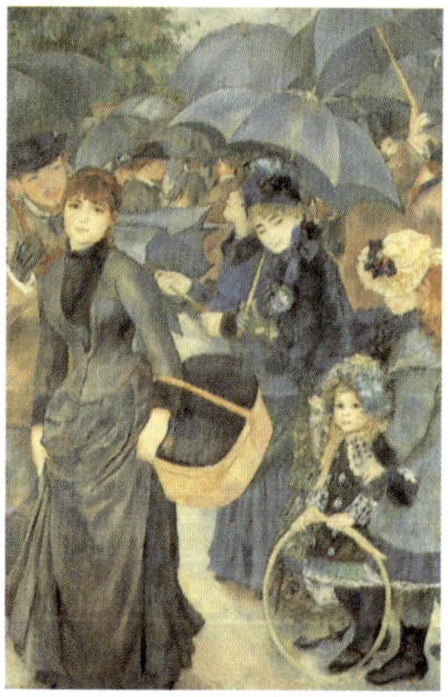

The Umbrellas

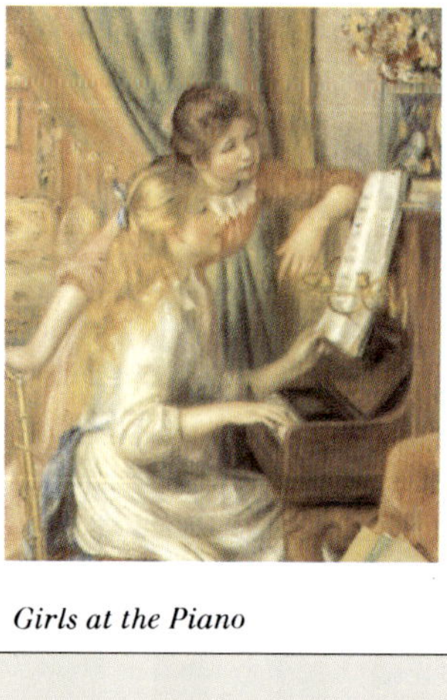

Girls at the Piano

1883 First exhibition of paintings in the US.
1885 Aline gives birth to first son, Pierre.
1887 Paints *The Bathers.*
1888 First attack of rheumatoid arthritis.
1890 Marries Aline.
1892 Paints *Girls at the Piano*, which becomes the first purchase of his work by the French state.
1894 Birth of second son, Jean. Death of Gustave Caillebotte; Renoir appointed executor.
1897 Caillebotte bequests partially accepted by French state.
1898 Buys house in Essoyes in South of France.
1900 Appointed Chevalier of the Légion d'Honneur.
1901 Birth of third son, Claude ("Coco").
1906 Paints portrait of Misia Natanson.
1907 Buys house, "Les Collettes," in Cagnes and has a special studio built.
1912 Suffers a stroke but recovers.
1914-18 First World War. Sons Pierre and Jean wounded. Aline dies (1915).
1918 Begins *Les Grandes Baigneuses.*
1919 Made Commander of the Légion d'Honneur.
1919 December 3: dies and is buried next to Aline in Essoyes.

The Paintings

La Grenouillere

1868

26×37in/66×94cm

Oil on canvas

National Museum, Stockholm

A contemporary description of the riverside resort of La Grenouillère in *L'Evénement l'Illustré*, June, 1868, describes it thus: "Trouville on the banks of the Seine; a meeting place for the noisy well-dressed crowds that emigrate from Paris and set up camp in Croissy, Chatou or Bougival for the summer...on a well-tarred old barge firmly moored to the bank...stands a wooden hut." The pictures that Renoir painted here are perhaps the most Impressionist of his whole *oeuvre*, indeed it was here that he and his friend Monet, painting side by side in the summer of 1868, developed the new ideas about painting that had been growing in them throughout the decade. Monet wrote to Bazille a few weeks before they began work, "I have a dream, a painting, the baths of La Grenouillère for which I have done a few bad sketches, but it is a dream. Renoir, who has just spent two months here, also wants to do this painting." Each executed three different versions of the scene, casual moments in the life of the resort caught with swift and sudden strokes of the brush to give a strong sense of immediacy — a few minutes caught before the light changed or the party broke up.

For such outdoor work Renoir used some special equipment: a folding easel, wooden palette, traveling paintbox and ready prepared canvases on stretchers. These were not primed with the traditional dark brown ground used by his predecessors, but with a white or warm, pale ground which helped to enhance the luminosity of the painting. This work would have been done very swiftly, certainly in a day and possibly even less. The rapid brushstrokes are large in the foreground and smaller in the distance, giving a feeling of depth to the scene. Light grounds make it more difficult to create depth, but it was not long before the Impressionists came to appreciate and cultivate that sense of flatness because they were more interested in the picture surface than in traditional perspective. As can be seen here, Renoir has deliberately blurred detail, dissolved clear lines and avoided giving solidity to his figures, thus encouraging the viewer to participate in the painting and interpret it for himself. He has used variations in the size and intensity of the brushstrokes to express form, so that the figures are not so much drawn as created by the merging of colors and brushstrokes.

The thicker paint resulting from mixing with poppy-seed oil rather than linseed oil stands up on the canvas instead of sinking into it, enabling Renoir to work wet into wet, as in the red boat in the middle distance. Short horizontal strokes have been used to indicate the light shimmering on the water, while wavy vertical strokes describe the reflections of the foreground boats. The brushwork is an important part of the painting, and he has made no attempt to achieve the kind of smooth finish which more academic painters strove for. The palette is fairly muted, with browns, greens and blues set off in places with reds, but more generally just highlighted in white. It is interesting to compare this work with Monet's version (opposite). Renoir has placed greater emphasis on figures, while in Monet's painting they have been allowed to recede into the distance and become absorbed into the landscape. Also, Monet's chief preoccupation has been with the shimmering water, which seems almost to dominate his work. Each artist has expressed his own feelings and rendered his own particular and intimate vision, but neither was attempting objectivity — the uniqueness of approach was of paramount importance.

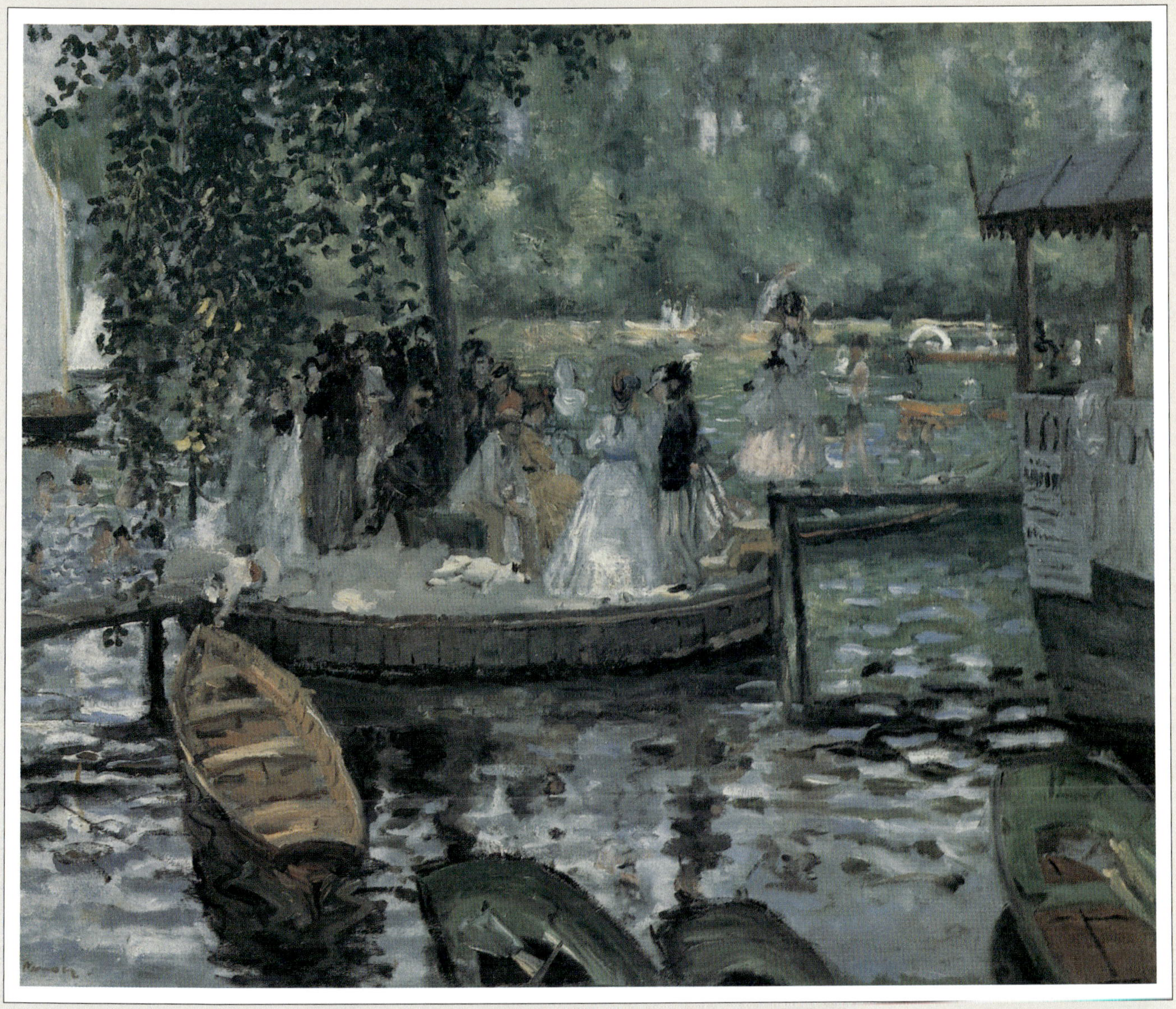

La Grenouillere was a fashionable place for eating, swimming and boating on the outskirts of Paris — now absorbed into the suburbs. In the summer of 1868 Renoir and Monet each painted several versions of the place from different viewpoints. As can be seen from a comparison of the two paintings, each had his own particular vision, but both were concerned with capturing an immediate moment in swift, bold brushstrokes. This picture, painted directly onto the canvas with no preliminary drawing, would have been completed in a matter of hours in order to be finished before the light changed.

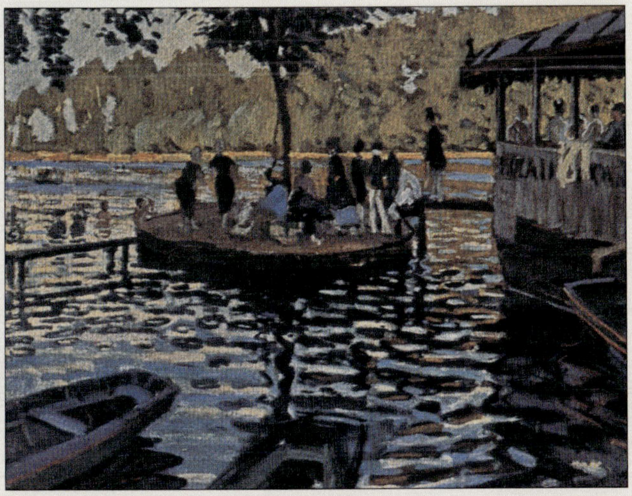

CLAUDE MONET
La Grenouillère
1869
Metropolitan Museum, New York

Monet and Renoir painted together at La Grenouillère (the name of which literally means "the frog-pond"), placing their easels side by side, but comparison of the two paintings clearly shows their different preoccupations. Monet was most interested in the effects of water; the figures have been pushed away from the foreground and play a less prominent role than in Renoir's painting of the same scene.

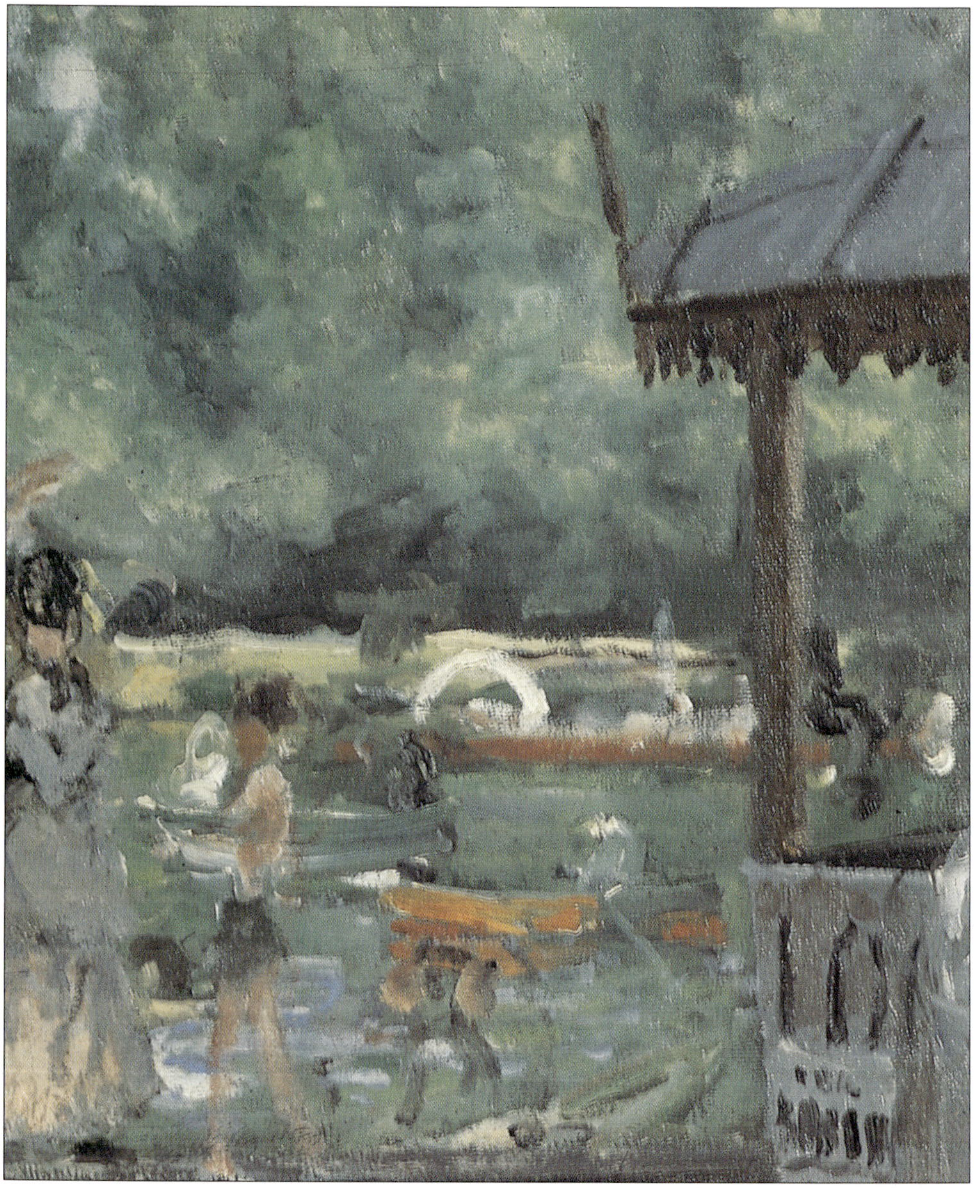

1

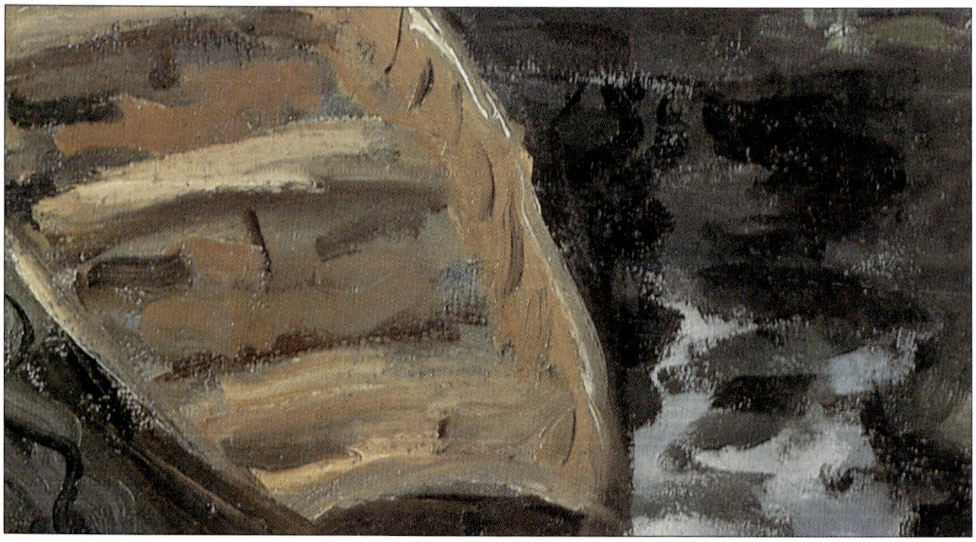

2

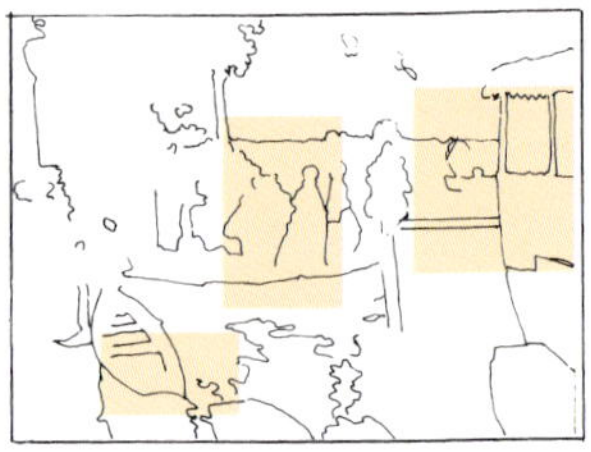

1 Swift, firm brushstrokes have been used to create the figures and the boats, which merge almost indistinguishably into the water, with the reflections and the objects reflected becoming blurred in blobs of vivid color. The poster on the side of the barge and the tablecloth hanging over the edge are painted loosely, hints rather than literal descriptions.

2 Larger strokes of the brush have been used in the foreground, and the water is built up with a series of horizontal strokes which contrast with the vertical of the boat's stern.

3 *Actual size detail* In contrast with Monet's painting (see previous page) the figures play a dominant role, but they are still very loosely painted. In a rapidly executed work such as this, the paints are applied over and beside one another while still wet, so that they blend into and modify each other. This is particularly noticeable in the stripes of the man's trousers.

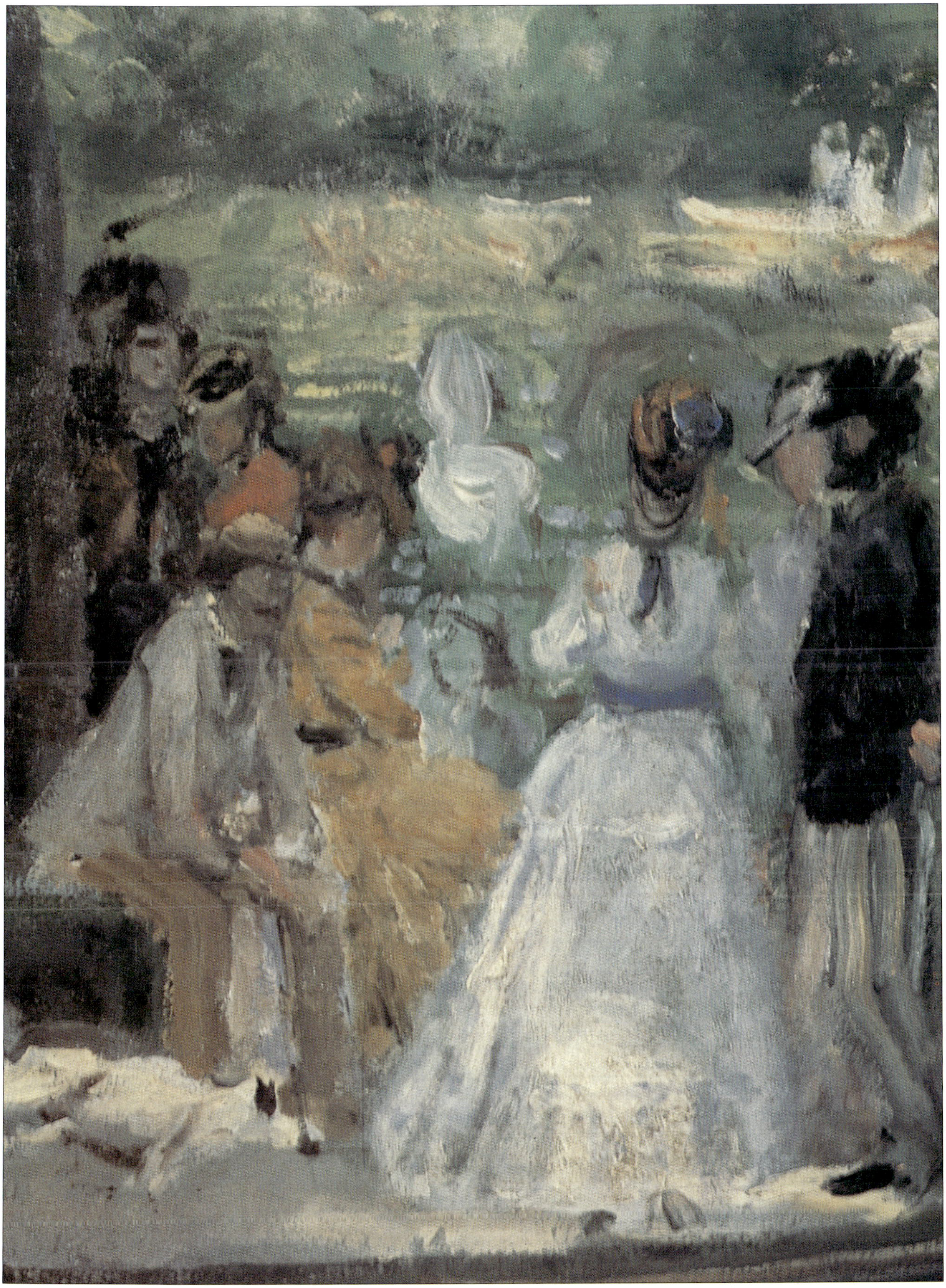

3 *Actual size detail*

The Dancer

(La Danseuse)
1874
$56\frac{1}{8} \times 37\frac{1}{8}$in/$142.5 \times 94$cm
Oil on canvas
National Gallery of Art, Washington

The critic Louis Leroy, whose mockery of Monet's work *Impression, Sunrise* at the first Impressionist Exhibition in 1874 unwittingly coined the word "impressionist," had only one comment to make about this offering of Renoir's in the same exhibition. He singled out *The Dancer* as an example of Renoir's lack of form and depth, complaining that "his dancer's legs are as cottony as the gauze of her skirt." But Leroy's damning opinions did not deter the dealer Durand-Ruel, who bought the painting, sold it two years later for 1000 francs to Charles Deudon, a wealthy clothing manufacturer, and bought it back again in the 1890s.

In fact this lovely painting marvelously exhibits Renoir's talent and the subtlety of his technique. It differs greatly in both method and presentation from *The Box at the Theatre*, painted in the same year. The composition is straightforward and direct, and seems to have been influenced by Manet's work of the 1860s, *The Fife-player.* Like Manet, Renoir has used a full-face light falling evenly and directly on the model, but with less of the harshness and strong tonal contrast of Manet, so that the outlines become softer and more diffused. The figure is indistinctly located, with an absence of floor or wall angles to define the room, and only a minimal shadow cast by the dancer herself. Degas' influence can also be seen in this work, but although using the same subject, Renoir has taken a very different approach. This is not a dancer appearing on stage, nor one practicing exercises or lacing her shoes preparatory to dancing, but one who, having danced and left the stage, is once again ready to resume her character as an ordinary person.

Renoir has used a very restrained palette here; the small touches of pink and blue seem almost to leap out from the subdued tones of the dress, which itself merges gently into the background. Once again a pale ground has been used to give a sense of warmth and lightness, and this can be seen showing through the paint, which has been applied very thinly by mixing with turpentine on the palette. Only the most delicate of highlights have been used on the pink shoes, the ribbons and the handkerchief, which helps to emphasize the lack of recession in the painting and give a feeling of intimacy which a formal staged setting would have lost. The blue of the waistband is echoed in the frilly gauze of the dress. This does indeed have the "cottony" texture remarked on by Leroy, but despite the softness of the work the figure does not lack solidity, which has been achieved by the minimal use of shadows around the feet and legs.

The model for this work was Ninette Legrand, the sister of Alphonse Legrand, who had worked for Durand-Ruel, but in 1874 had established a gallery of his own. Legrand was a close friend of Renoir and tried by auctions and other means to interest the buying public in his work. In 1877 he became the agent for Maclean's, a London-based cement company. Renoir, who had conceived the idea of executing large-scale murals, experimented on Maclean cement, which contained a fine white plaster that gave the works considerably heightened luminosity. This may well have influenced the increasingly smooth white grounds which he began to use as canvas priming in the 1880s.

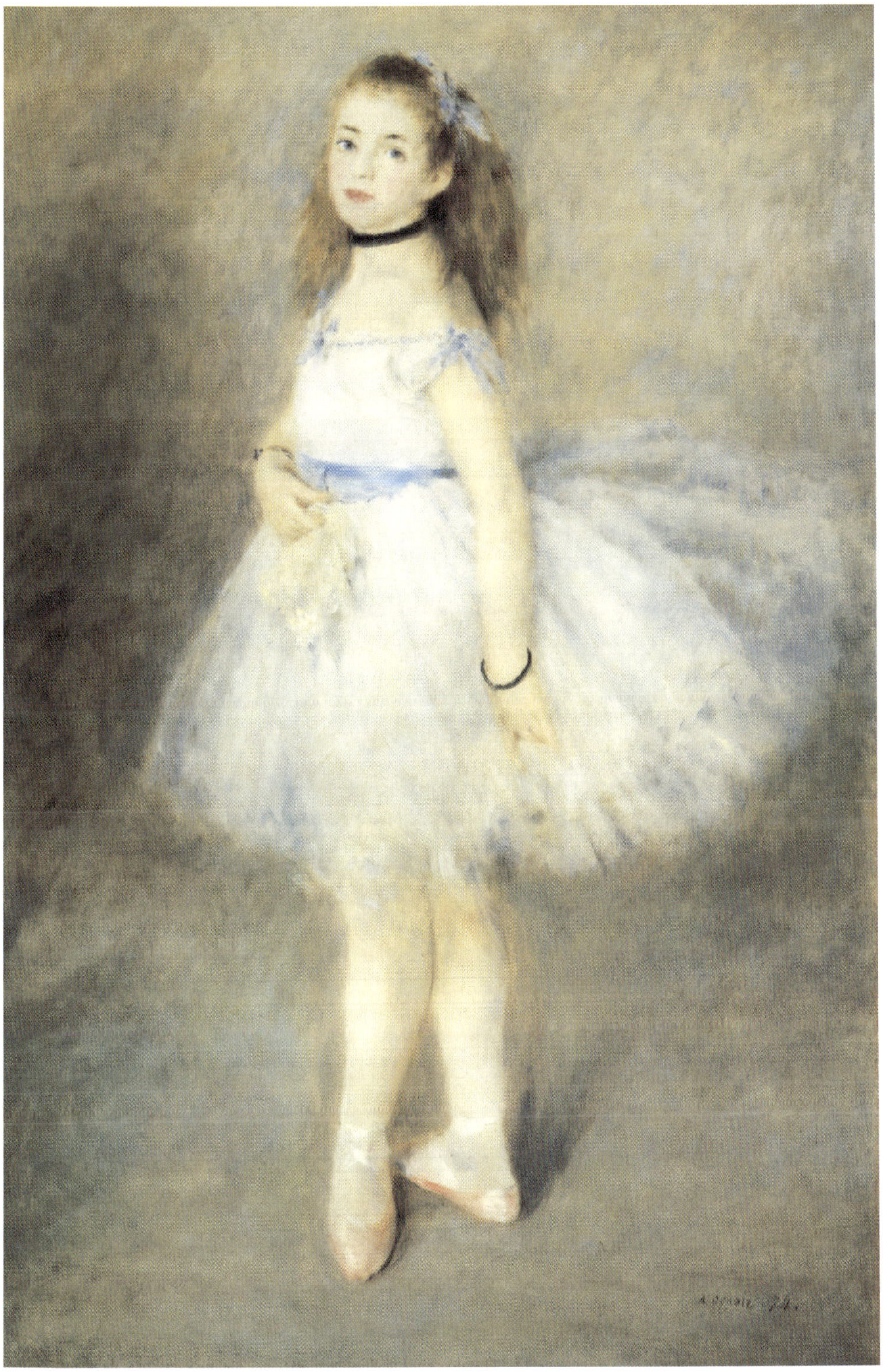

This painting shows the influence of the more figurative side of Impressionism as practiced by Manet and Degas, both of whom were associated with, but not strictly part of, the movement. The composition owes a debt to Manet's painting *The Fife-Player* and the choice of subject matter to Degas, though Renoir's treatment is quite different to Degas', the lines being much softer and the paint handling typically light and feathery. The palette itself is restrained, but the painting is nevertheless full of light and warmth. Like *The Box at the Theater*, this painting was one of those exhibited at the infamous first Impressionist Exhibition held at the studio of the photographer Nadar, and it was bought by the dealer Durand-Ruel.

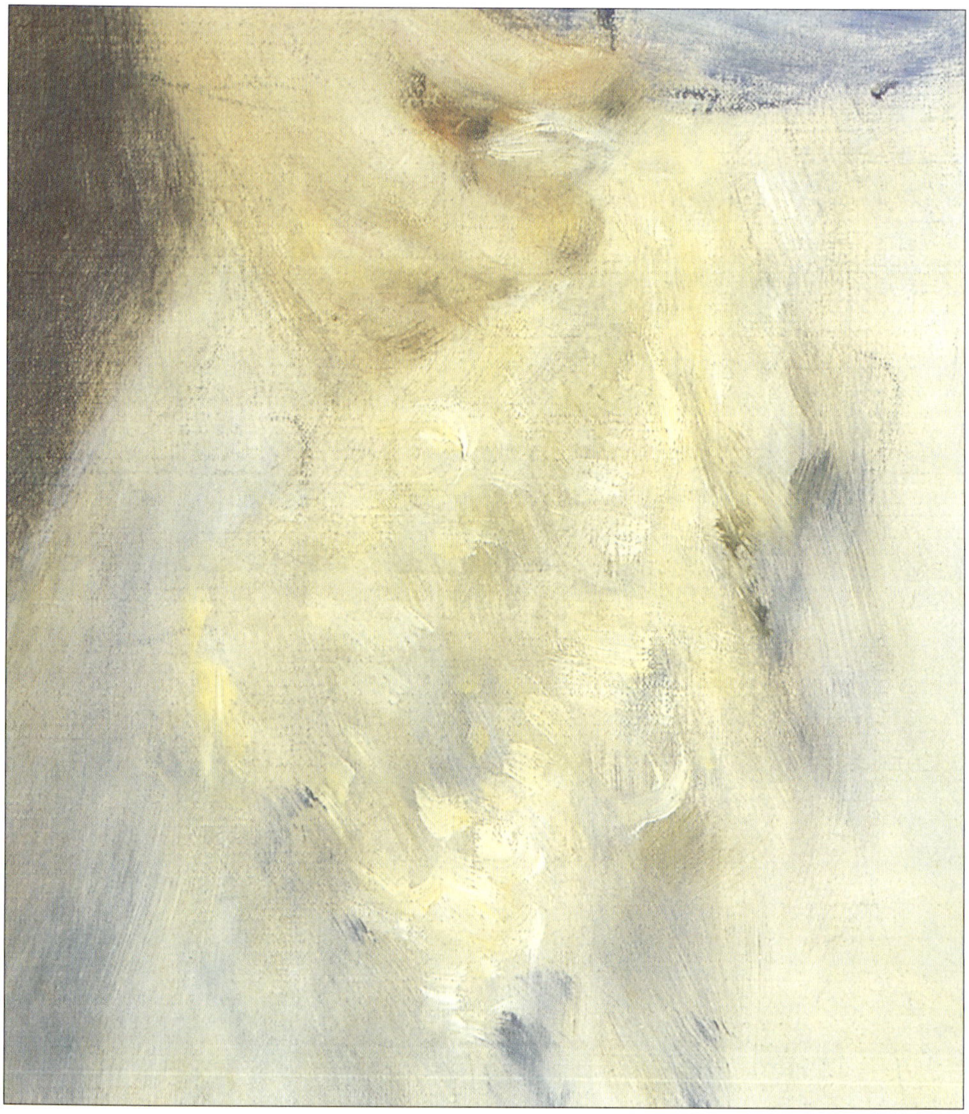

1

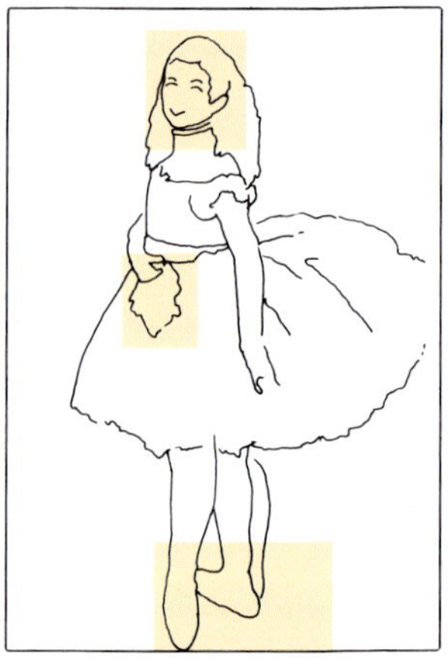

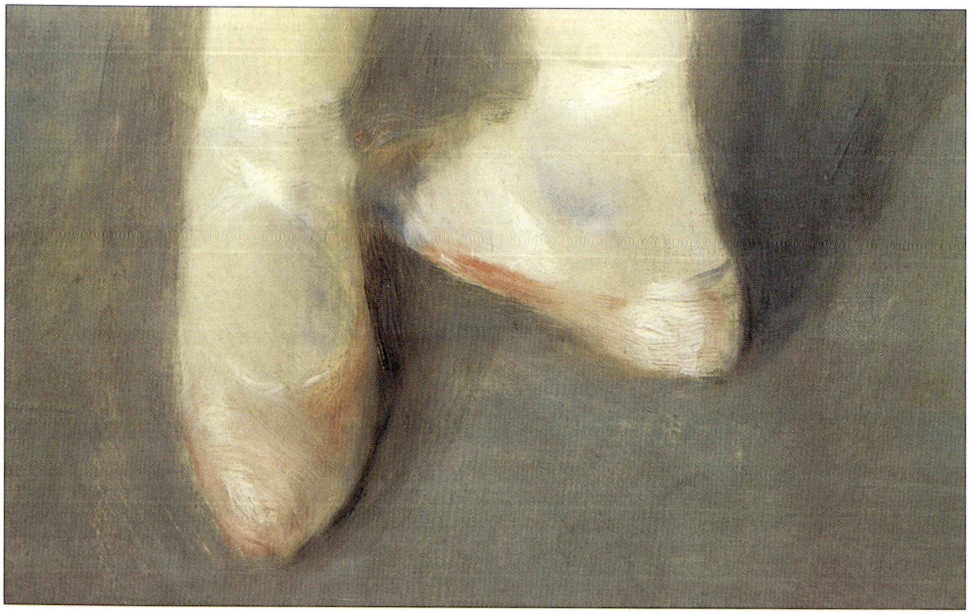

2

1 When looked at from a close viewpoint, as here, the ring of the bouquet shows scarcely any modeling and looks almost insubstantial, but on standing back from the painting one can see the contrast between the short, firm strokes of white and the slightly bluer hues of the skirt. This gives exactly the impression Renoir wanted — one that is destroyed by close examination.

2 The strokes of white have been worked into the pink of the shoes while still wet, enhancing the soft modeling and structure of the slippered feet. The shadow around the feet has been kept to a minimum, but there is just enough to give the figure a sense of solidity against the shadowy, empty background.

3 *Actual size detail* The dancer's head has been more firmly modeled than anything else in the painting other than the shoes. Using soft, feathery strokes of thin paint, Renoir has built up the hair and face so gently that the marks of the brush are almost indiscernible, while in the eyebrows and the ribbon the paint is thicker and the brushwork more noticeable.

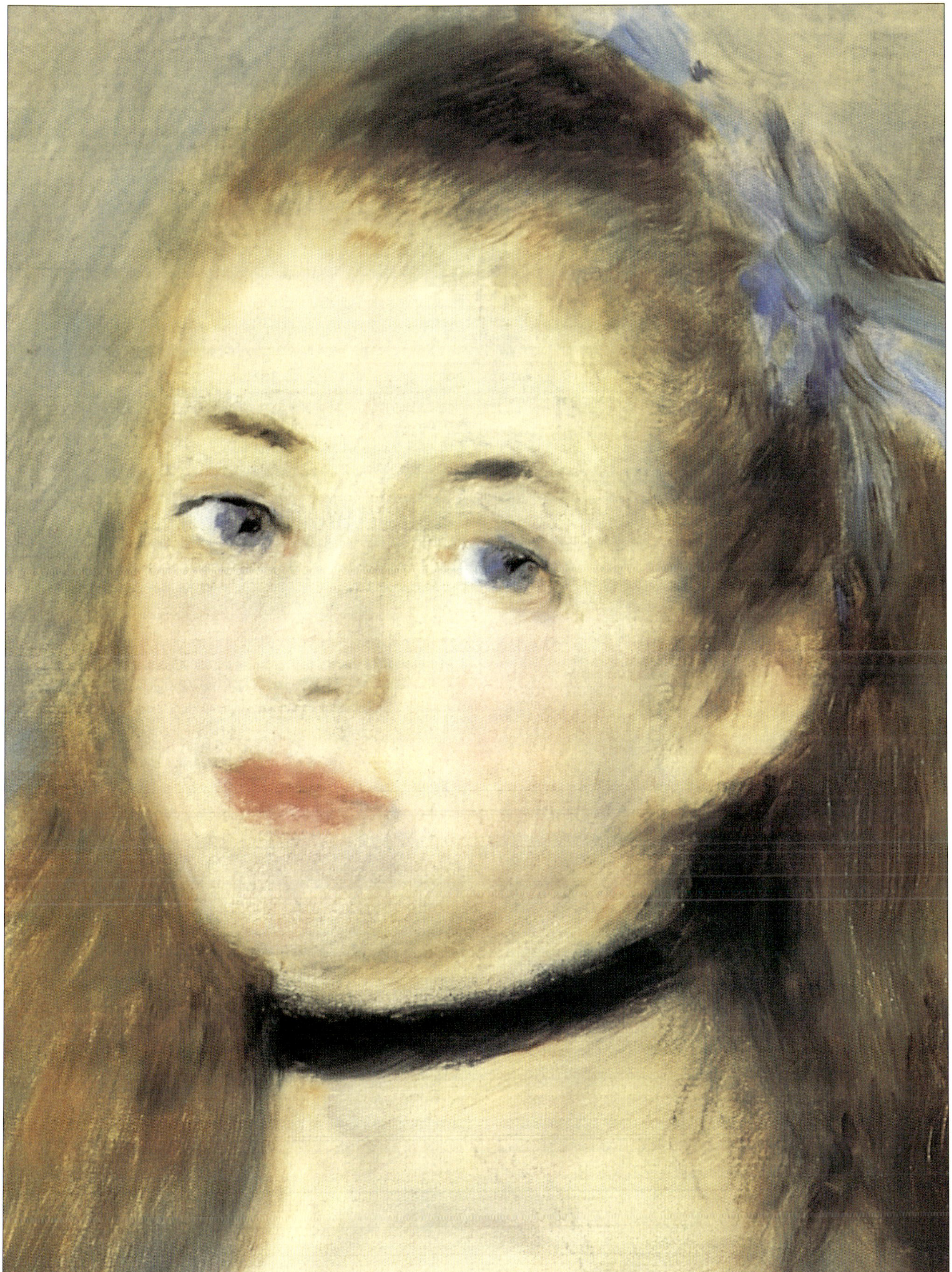

3 *Actual size detail*

Ball at the Moulin de la Galette

1876

$51\frac{1}{2} \times 69$in/130.75×175.25cm

Oil on canvas

Musée d'Orsay, Paris

This painting, Renoir's most ambitious Impressionist genre work, was the fulfilment of an idea that had been maturing for several years. The Moulin de la Galette was a dance hall in a converted mill on the top of Montmartre (then a village on the outskirts of Paris) which specialized in "galettes," sweet thin wafers. It had a large shaded garden, a covered dancing area and a small bandstand. In order to paint the picture Renoir rented a studio in the nearby rue Cortot and went every day to the Moulin to draw and study his subject. His brother Edmond described the process. "How does he go about painting Le Moulin de la Galette? He goes to live there for six months, makes friends with all that little world that has its own style, which models copying their poses would not render, and in the midst of the whim of the popular merry-go-round he expresses wild movements with a dazzling verve." In fact Renoir painted several sketches in oil and one finished smaller-scale version (now in the collection of Mrs John Hay Whitney of New York) which was carried to and from the Moulin every day by Renoir and his friends. Many of these friends are featured in the painting: dancing with the figure in pink, Marguerite Legrand, is the painter Don Pedro Vidal de Solares y Cardeñas, and around the table to the right are seated Franc Lamy, Norbert Goeneutte and Georges Rivière. The final version was painted in the garden of the rue Cortot studio as the canvas was too large to move, and his friends came there to pose for him.

This is a very sophisticated and complex painting showing an impressive grasp of depth and perspective. The preparatory ground is a warm pink, contributing to the overall tone, although here it is not left to show through the paint. Renoir's chief concern, and the one that gives the painting much of its pictorial interest and charm, is the effect of dappled sunlight on the moving figures. This has been achieved by scumbling, mixing colors on the surface of the canvas while still wet, and by introducing occasional white highlights into the wet paint of the clothes and hats. Unlike in some earlier works, for example *The Box at the Theatre*, the highlights and brighter areas of the picture are actually loaded with thicker paint, and the whole texture of the surface is much thicker than in *The Dancer* (see page 555). The vigorous brushstrokes help to convey a sense of movement and excitement in the figures, and the light seems almost to be moving on the surface of the canvas as it flits over the dancers.

The painting was exhibited at the third Impressionist Exhibition in 1877, and was afterwards acquired by Renoir's friend and fellow-painter Gustave Caillebotte who bequeathed it to the French nation on his death in 1894. Georges Rivière, a critic and one of the sitters for the painting, wrote an appreciation of it in his review of the exhibition which probably expressed to some extent Renoir's own feelings about the work. "In a garden inundated with sunlight, barely shaded by some spindly acacia plants whose foliage trembles with the least breeze, there are charming young girls in all the freshness of their fifteen years, proud of their light homemade dresses fashioned of inexpensive material, and young men full of gaiety...noise, laughter, movement, sunshine in an atmosphere of youth. Such is 'Le Bal au Moulin de la Galette' by Renoir."

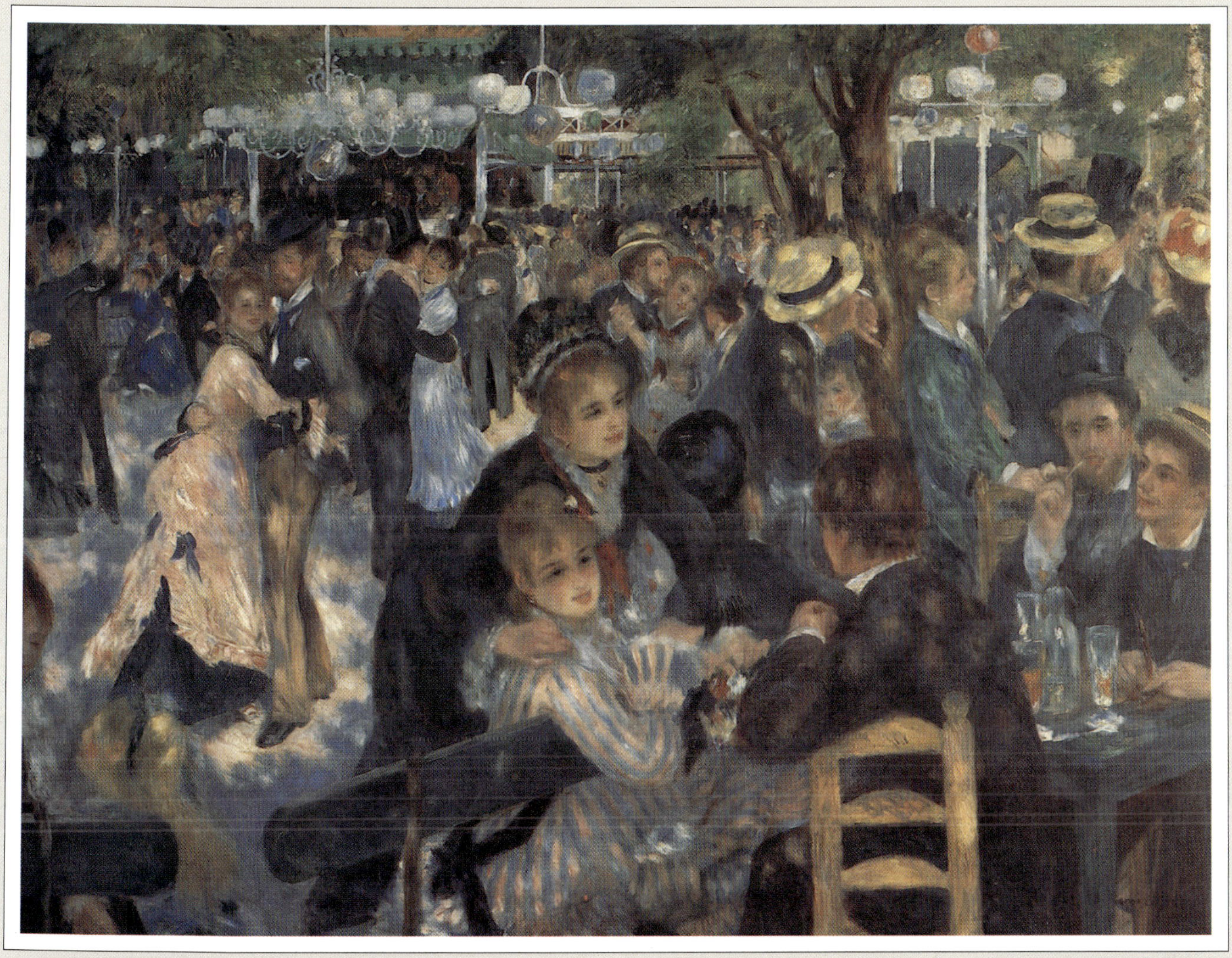

This is Renoir's most ambitious Impressionist genre painting. It is a sophisticated, complex work combining tremendous movement and excitement with the wonderful effect of broken sunlight filtered through the overhanging trees and dappling the figures as they dance or sit talking at the tables. The proceeds of a portrait commission had enabled Renoir to rent a studio in Montmartre, near the dance hall, and he worked on the preliminary oil-sketch for the painting for several months, carrying the canvas from the studio to the Moulin so that he could paint on the spot and lose nothing of the immediacy of the scene. The final,full-scale version was painted in the garden of the studio, where his friends came to pose for him, as the canvas was too large to be moved.

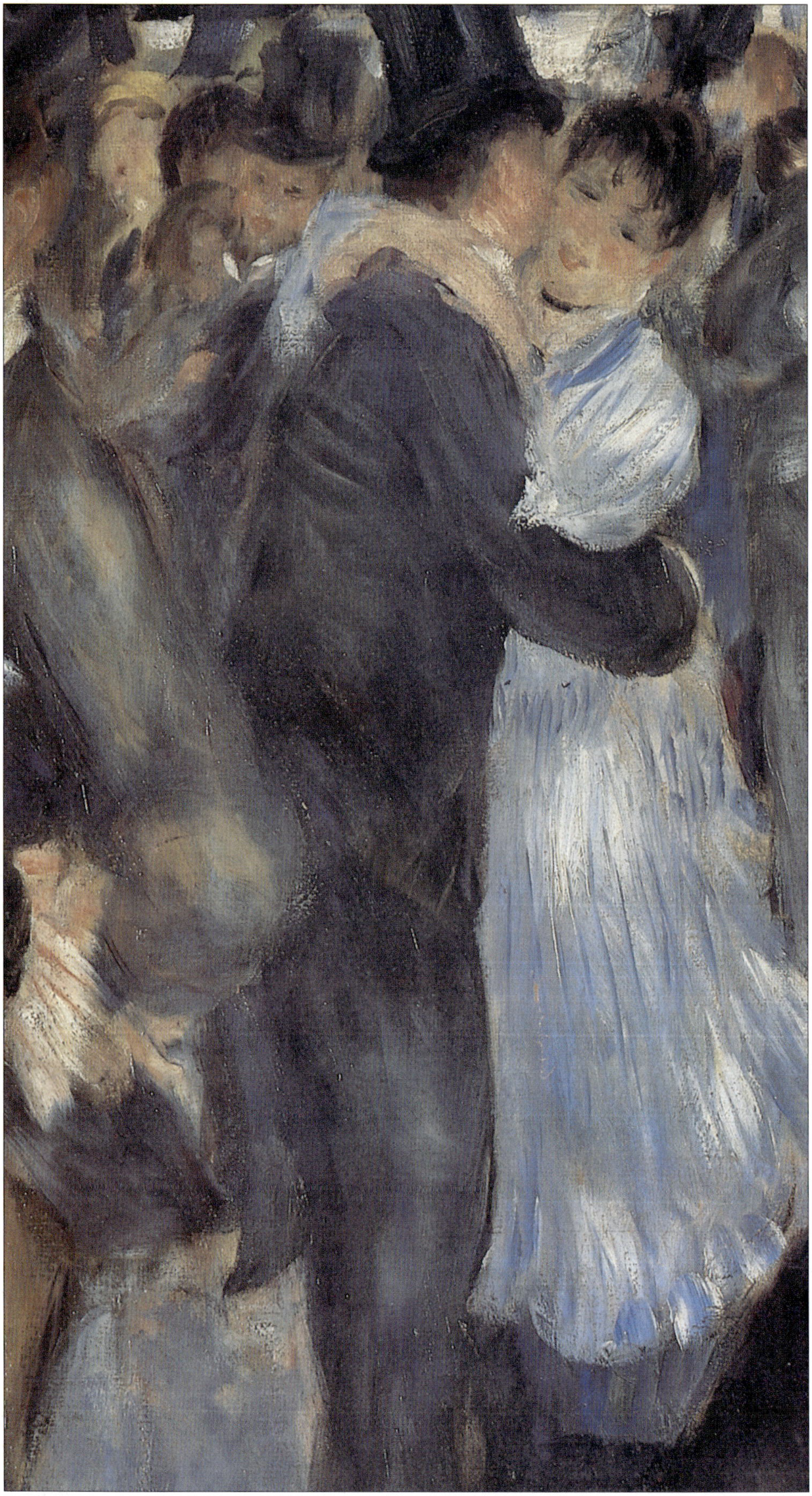

1

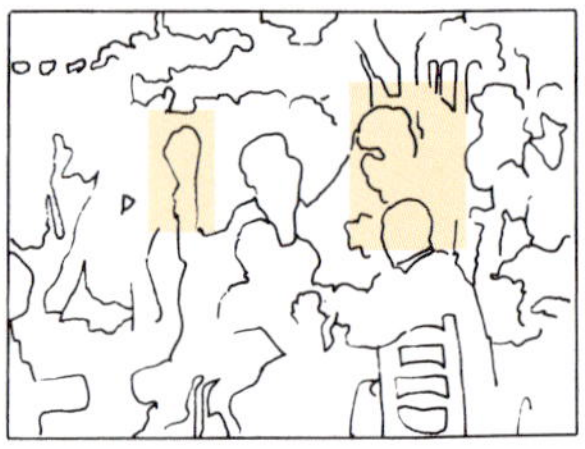

1 The dancing couple in the middle distance have been painted with long, swift strokes that create a strong sense of movement. The woman's arms have been quite loosely executed, and on her dress, the colors have blurred into one another, with blue mixing into the white, evoking the feel of the rapid, whirling dance.

2 This detail is a marvelous study of dappled sunlight, full of color, not only in the man's yellow boater hat with its touches of blue, yellow, red and white, but also in the head of the small boy. This, framed by objects on various different pictorial planes, seems to glow out at us, and even the woman's blue dress in the shade of the trees reflects a spectrum of other colors.

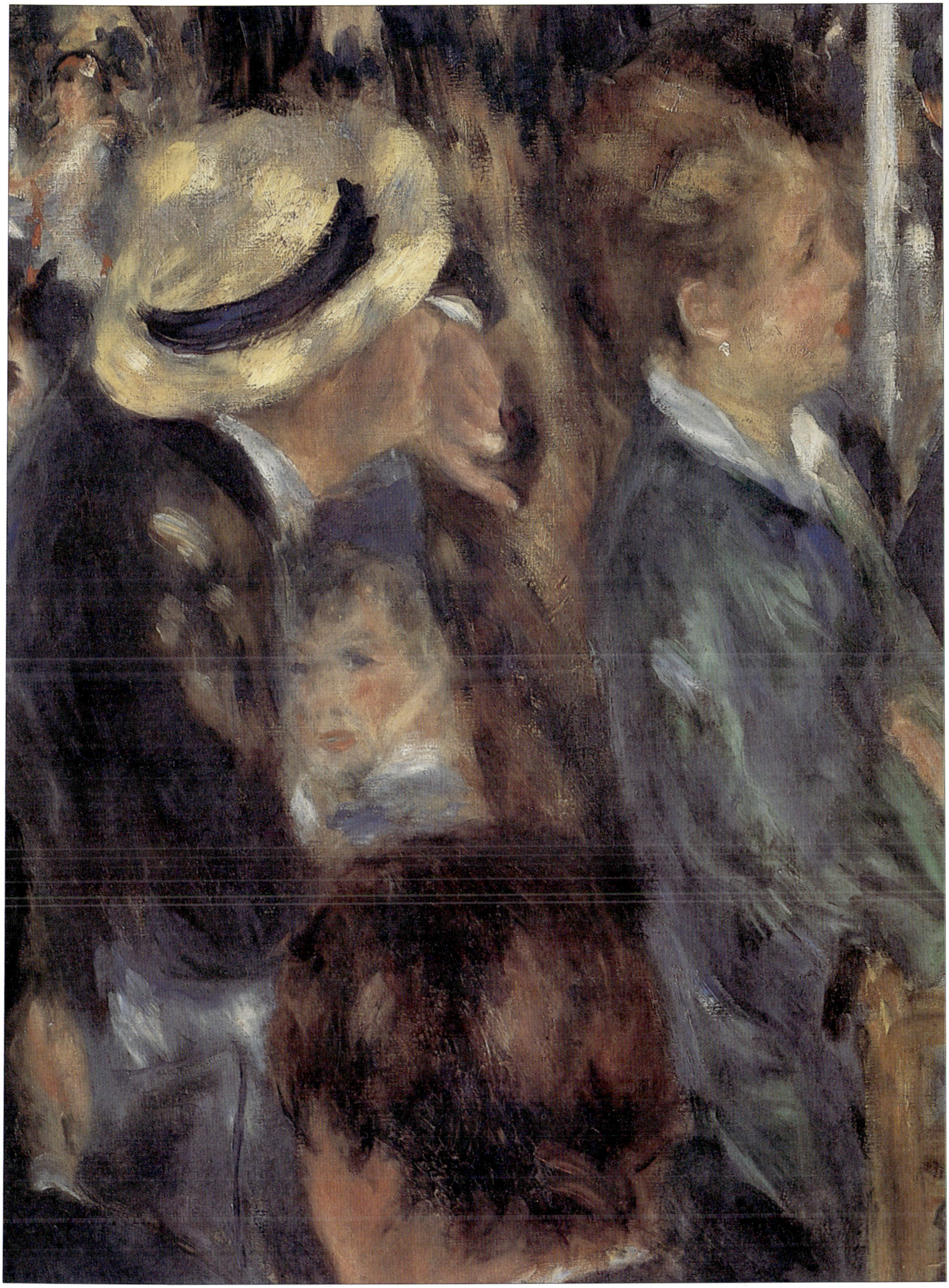

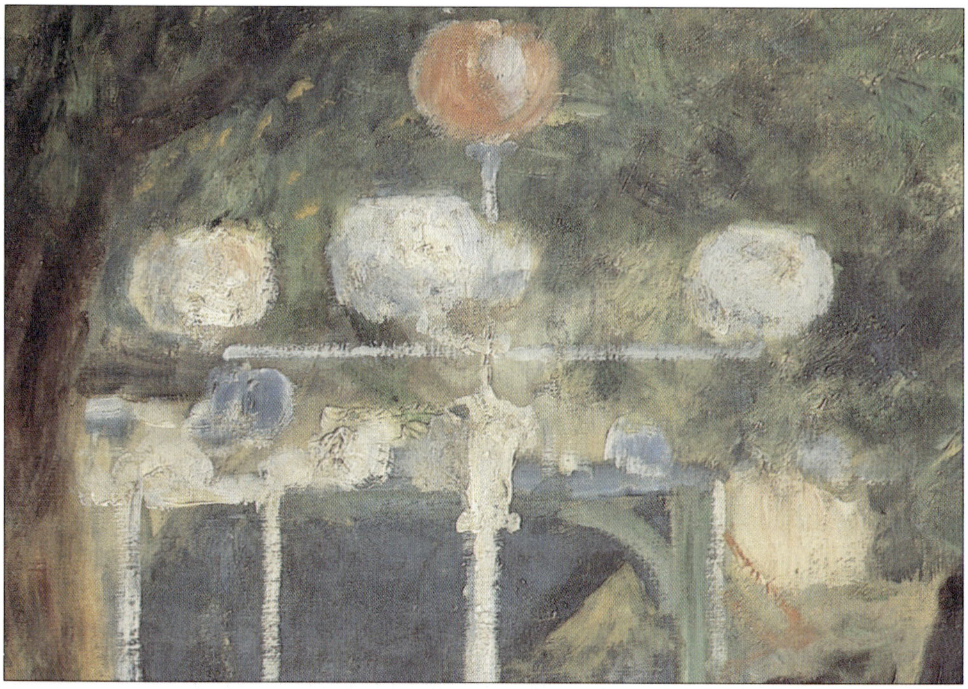

3

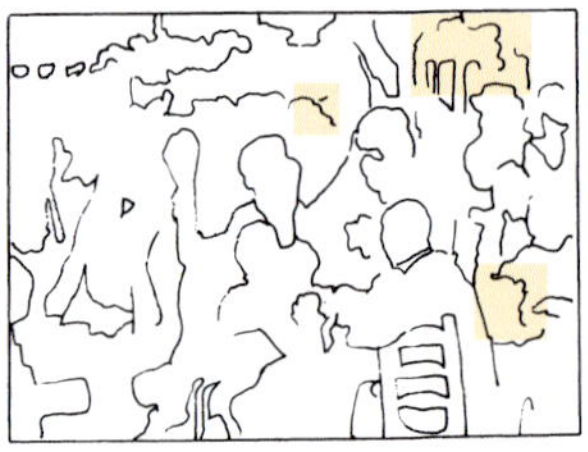

3 The strong pinks and whites of the lamps stand out against the green of the background, contributing to the sense of depth without which the picture would not have worked so successfully.

4 Here, with the two figures turned toward the viewer, Renoir has created a feeling of intimacy as well as conveying the movement of the dance. The hats and ribbons add color to the faces, which are painted more tightly than their surroundings.

5 *Actual size detail* The glasses on the table have absorbed all the color of their surroundings, but Renoir has nevertheless given them definition, achieved by the use of small highlights in white. Because the paint has been applied wet into wet, however, even these highlights have taken on some of the surrounding blue, so that they are subtle and delicate.

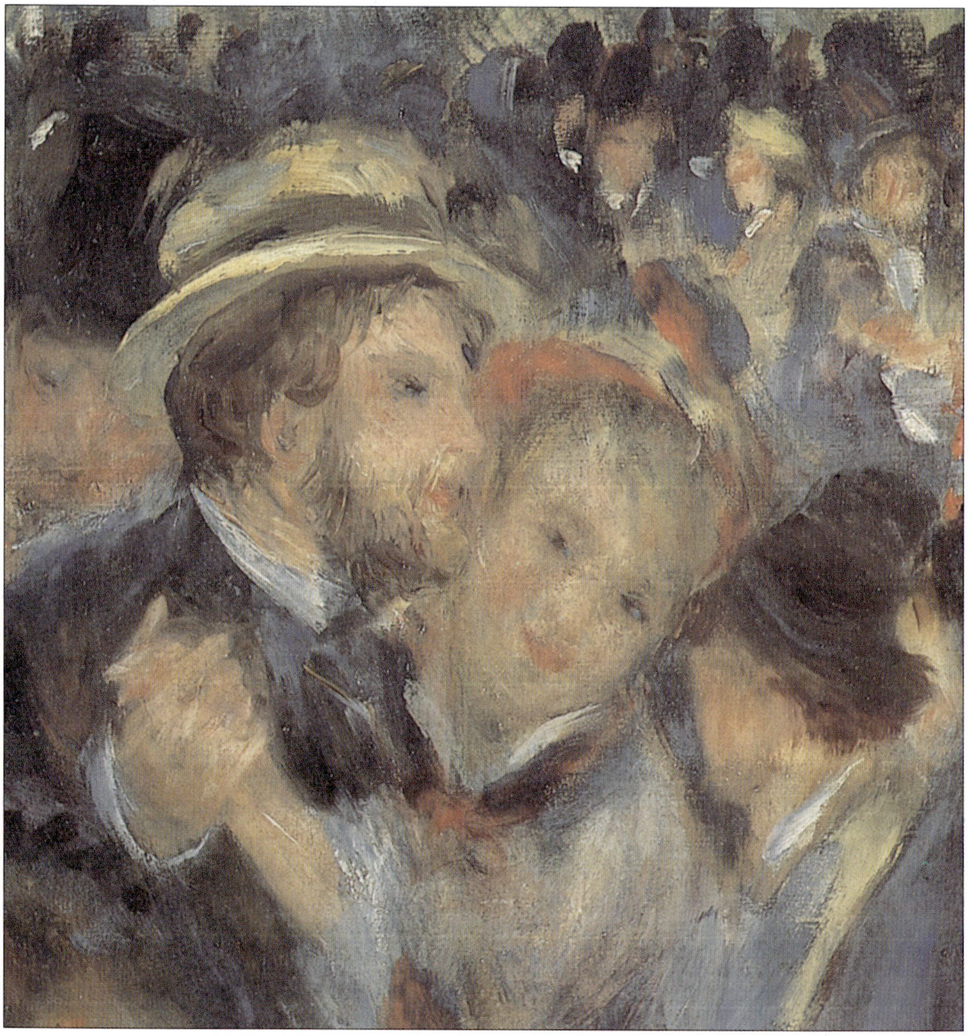

4

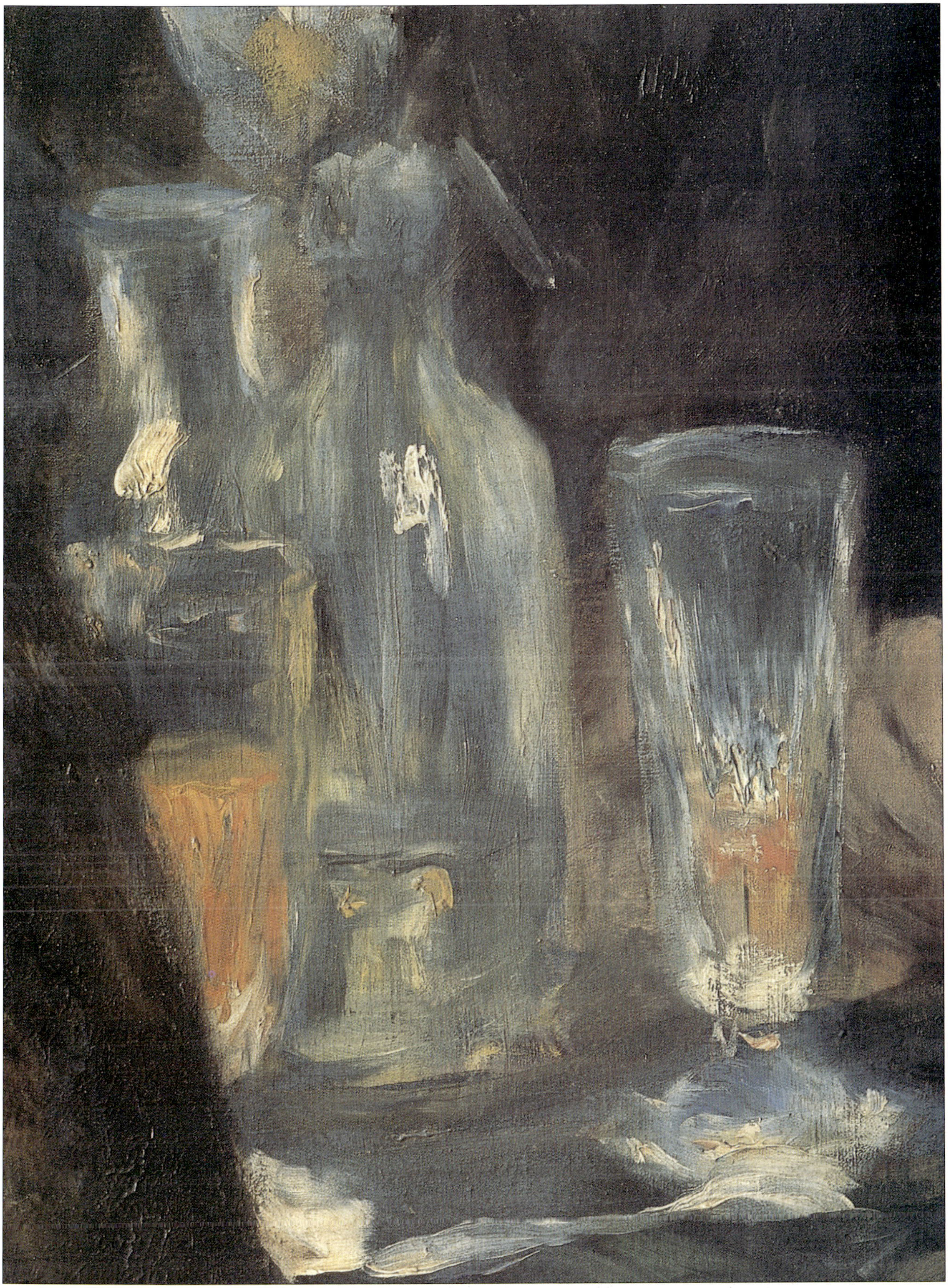

5 *Actual size detail*

The Umbrellas

(Les Parapluies)
1881 and 1885
71×45in/180.25×114.25cm
Oil on canvas
National Gallery, London

The Umbrellas has become for English audiences one of the most familiar and best loved of all Renoir's works, since it entered the National Gallery collection as a result of the Lane Bequest in 1917. It is also one of Renoir's most modern paintings in structural terms, and reveals a great deal about his changing styles between the beginning and middle of the 1880s.

The picture was begun in 1881 but not completed until four years later, and it seems likely that it is the result of two separate periods rather than four years of continuous work. The right-hand foreground side of the painting — which includes the girl with a hoop, the other girl half-turned away to her right and the two women beyond — is the earlier. The later part is the left-hand side and background, including the foreground woman with a basket, the man behind her and all the umbrellas through to the top of the painting. These two separate periods add great interest to a work that is in any case full of pictorial complexity. The bold construction is as modern a one as Renoir ever attempted: there is little sense of the figures actually being set in a landscape, as only the very slightest hint has been given at foreground or background. The subject is viewed from above so that the figures are almost tipped to the front of the painting, and the jostle of umbrellas with the many faces beneath further distorts the traditional perspective.

The date of the first period of painting can be arrived at both by comparison with other works of similar handling of the same date and by looking at the women's dresses. Those on the right display the latest fashions of 1881, and the brushwork has the soft, feathery quality which marks Renoir's work before his trip to Italy in 1882 and which gives a certain insubstantiality to the contours and the modeling. The colors are full, fresh and varied, and have been mixed wet into wet on the surface of the canvas. The left-hand and upper part of the painting could not provide a greater contrast. The dress of the woman with the basket — the model for whom was his future wife Aline — is of quite a different cut and much more severe in its lines, a fashion which only came in in 1885 and would have passed out again by 1887. The handling is also different, with the figures much more precisely drawn and the modeling and colors clearer and firmer. Renoir's usual white-primed canvas has been used, which accounts for the luminosity of the light colors coming out through the blue on the right, but on the left, the paint has been appled drier and with greater solidity, which does not allow for the same luminosity. The umbrellas have also been worked more solidly, giving the group on the right the effect of being surrounded in a small bright corner of their own.

Renoir did not enjoy great success with the painting. Durand-Ruel took it into his gallery in 1890 but did not actually buy it until 1892, and it was only acquired by Sir Hugh Lane in 1907. The cause of dissatisfaction was probably the unhappy marriage of two recent women's fashions which, set against each other in such a tightly constructed composition, must have appeared incongruous to contemporaries familiar with the styles of the day. To us, a hundred years later, this is unimportant, and although we can see the sharp contrasts in painting style that characterize the work, we can also appreciate its complex and stimulating construction.

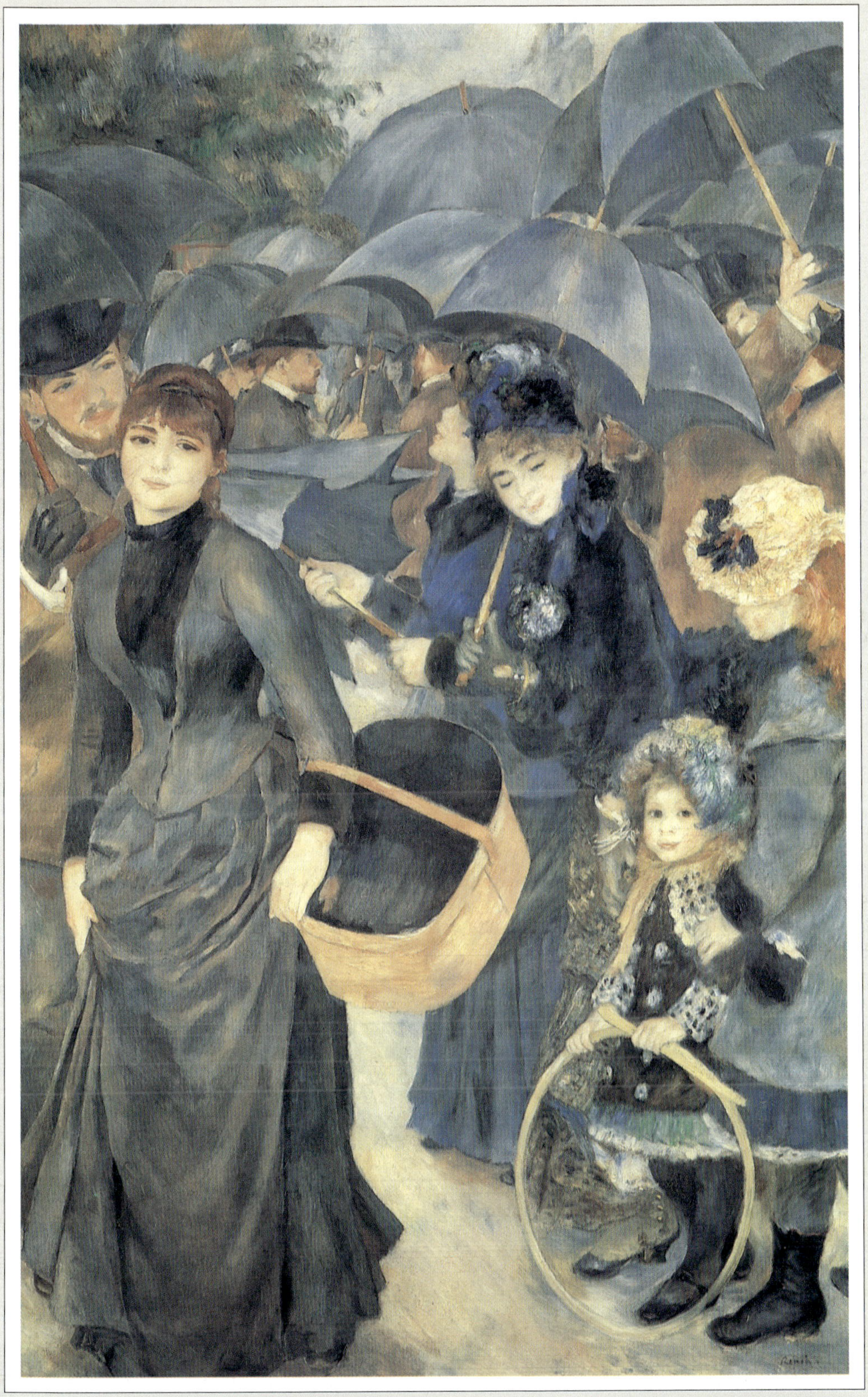

This painting is particularly interesting because Renoir worked on it in two distinct periods, giving us an insight into his changing style at the time. The right-hand side was painted in 1881, and shows the light, feathery brushwork of the previous decade, while the left side was completed four years later. Here the paint has been used much more solidly so that it completely covers the light ground, a technique he began to favor after his long trip to Italy had caused him to doubt the basic tenets of Impressionism.

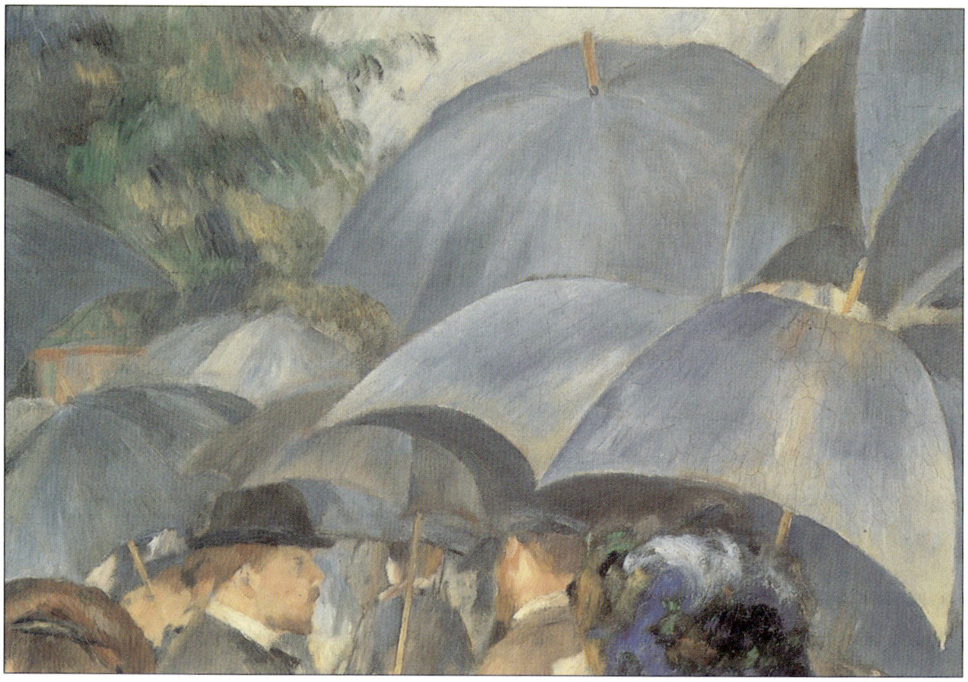

1

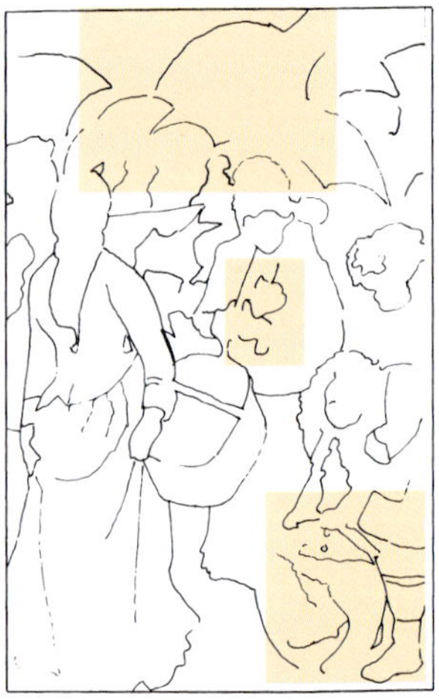

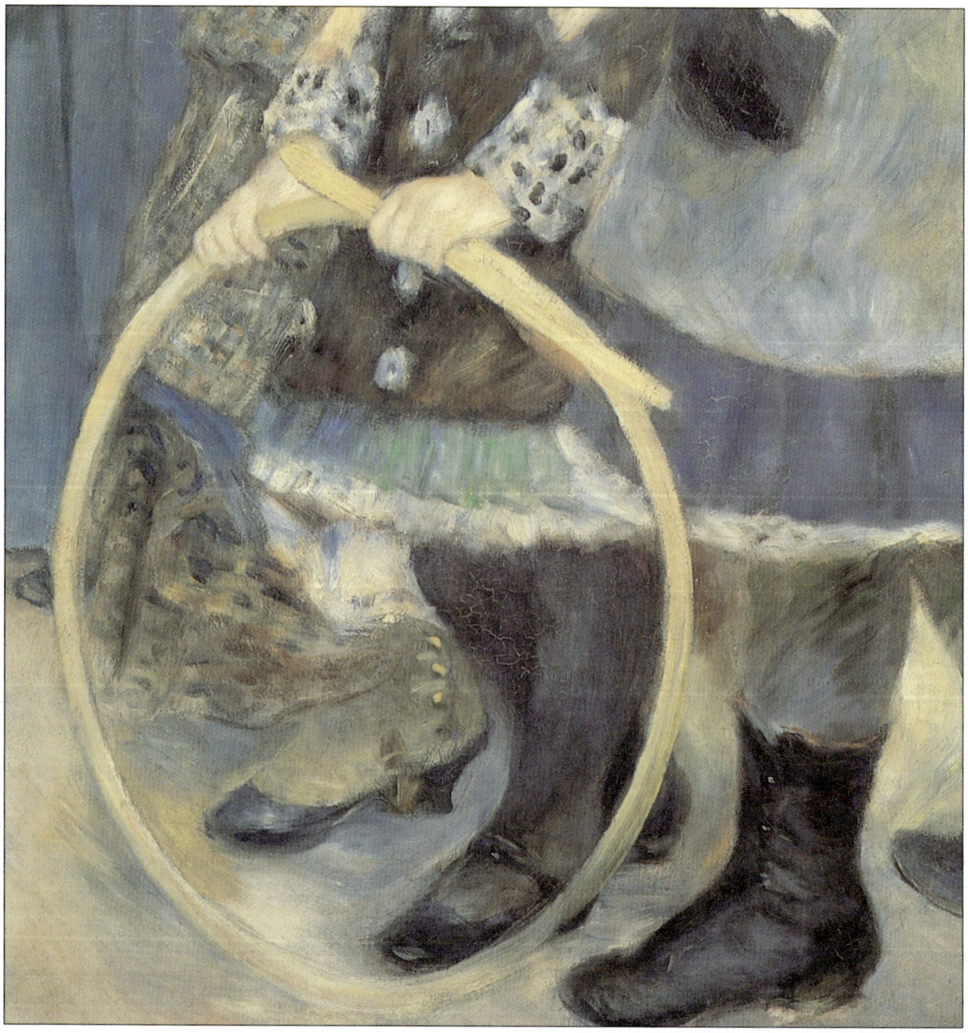

2

1 Renoir's favorite white priming has been allowed to show through the blue in places to describe the surface of the umbrellas. The faces beneath the umbrellas have been painted tightly in contrast to the broad, loose treatment of the sky and trees, whose very sketchiness serve to emphasize the tighter technique of the later parts of the painting — the left and upper sections.

2 In the right-hand part of the painting, done earlier than the left, Renoir is still using the loosely applied, soft, feathery brushstrokes that characterize his work of the 1870s. Blue appears strongly in the shadows, setting off the warm and luxurious colors, another feature of Renoir's earlier work which ceased in his later paintings.

3 *Actual size detail* The bouquet has been created with short, wide brushstrokes that when seen at a distance combine to give the sense of wholeness Renoir sought. By the subtle use of light on the hand and thumb he has given a complete sense of the form and roundness of the flesh beneath the glove.

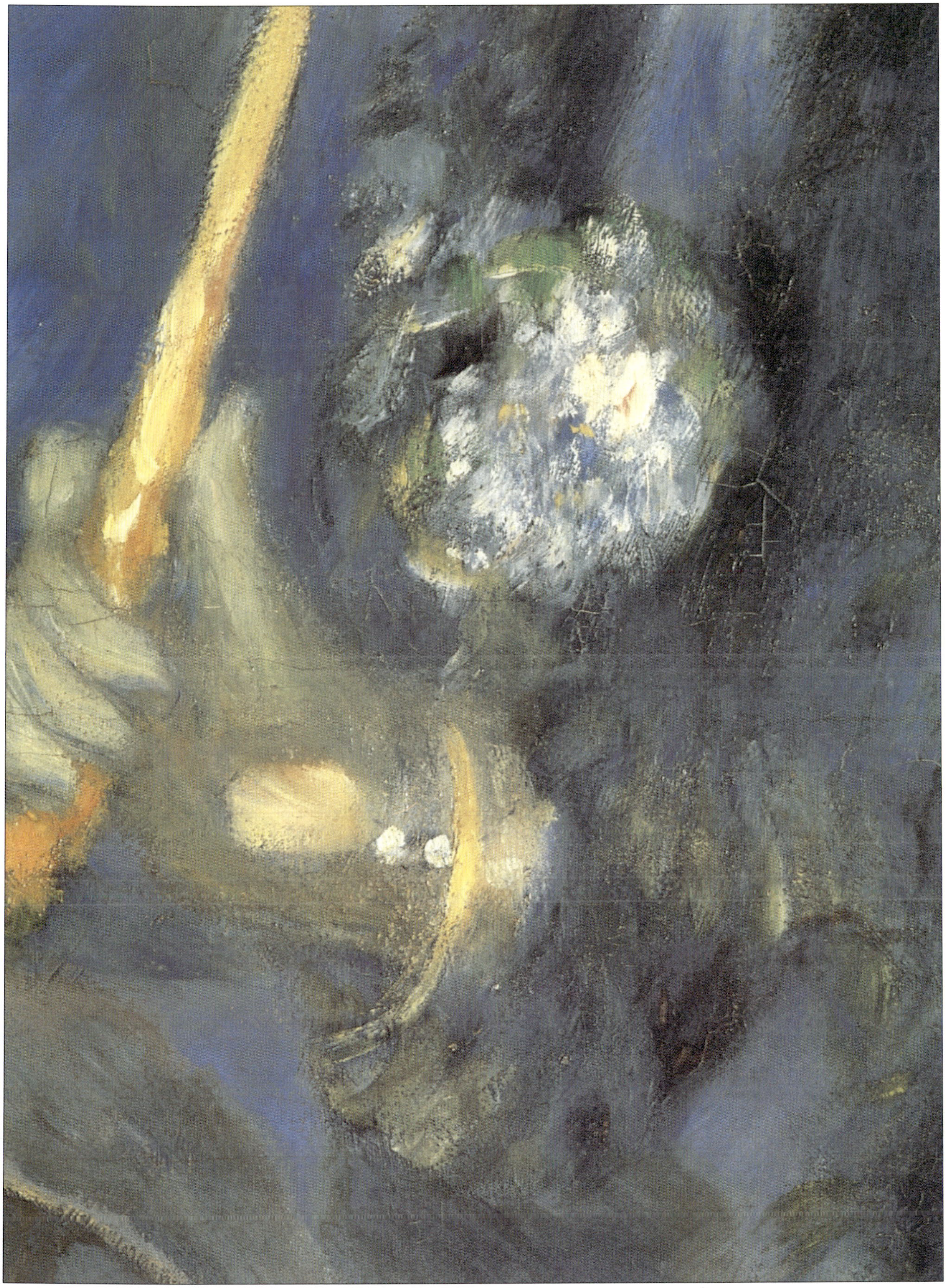

3 *Actual size detail*

THE BATHERS

(Les Baigneuses)
1887
46½×67¼in/118.25×170.75cm
Oil on canvas
Philadelphia Museum of Art

The painting, Renoir's most ambitious work of the 1880s and the one by which he set greatest store, was executed for an exhibition of his works being prepared by the dealer Georges Petit. Petit had a reputation for providing for the somewhat limited and traditional tastes of the bourgeoisie, and Renoir was conscious of the concessions he might have to make.

The Bathers was meticulously worked on and prepared. There are still over twenty preparatory drawings which show the long struggle that Renoir had with the form and posture of his nudes. Even the foreground, the trees and the drapery were worked on in advance, for Renoir was determined not only to make his name with the public but also to show that his new creed of "irregularity" was appropriate to the execution of a great painting. He had tried to explain this creed to Durand-Ruel in a letter of 1884: the idea was an attempt at escape from symmetry and unity in both architecture and painting, although he was in favor of clear lines, a structured composition and realistic details derived from nature. The adoption of these standards did not preclude the use of loose brushwork or the bright colors and light of Impressionism.

Another important influence on *The Bathers* was the classical treatment of the nude. Since his travels in Italy, where he had seen the monumental frescoes of Michelangelo and Raphael, Renoir had been determined to produce a major work glorifying the female nude in a manner that could rank with the Old Masters. The work of Ingres, too, has a bearing on this painting, for he had contorted the bodies of his nudes in an attempt to emphasize decorative qualities over representational accuracy (though he himself denied that he did anything other than copy nature). Renoir was similarly ambivalent on this subject. "How hard it is to find exactly the point at which imitation of nature must cease in a picture. The painting must not be too close to the model and yet we must be conscious of nature."

In order to achieve some of the effects of fresco Renoir painted *The Bathers* on a specially prepared white-lead oil ground, which gave a very smooth surface. Onto this he first painted the figures with their silky-soft, almost porcelain-smooth skin, followed by the surrounding landscape and the two smaller figures, for which he used much more vigorous brushstrokes reminiscent of Impressionism. Because the landscape is entirely artificial, having been painted around the figures in the studio rather than out of doors, there is a certain lack of vitality, especially in the ripples on the water, which gives the painting a rather leaden, stiff appearance. The linear, classical emphasis of the nudes contrasts with the looser handling of the rest of the painting, but this may be an example of the sort of "irregularity" that Renoir was trying to achieve. The bright colors on the smooth white ground have also combined to give the painting an orange sheen, which may explain why this is sometimes known as Renoir's "sour" period. In many ways he was attempting too much in this work, and apart from Monet and one or two others who spoke favorably of it the picture was not well received when it was exhibited at the Georges Petit gallery. It was eventually sold for 1000 francs to Jacques Emile Blanche, a friend and fellow painter. The combination of his attempt to accommodate bourgeois taste and to emulate the example of the Old Masters had caused Renoir to paint an unhappy, unbalanced picture in which he was able neither to abandon the influence of Impressionism nor to submit fully to the discipline of traditional painting.

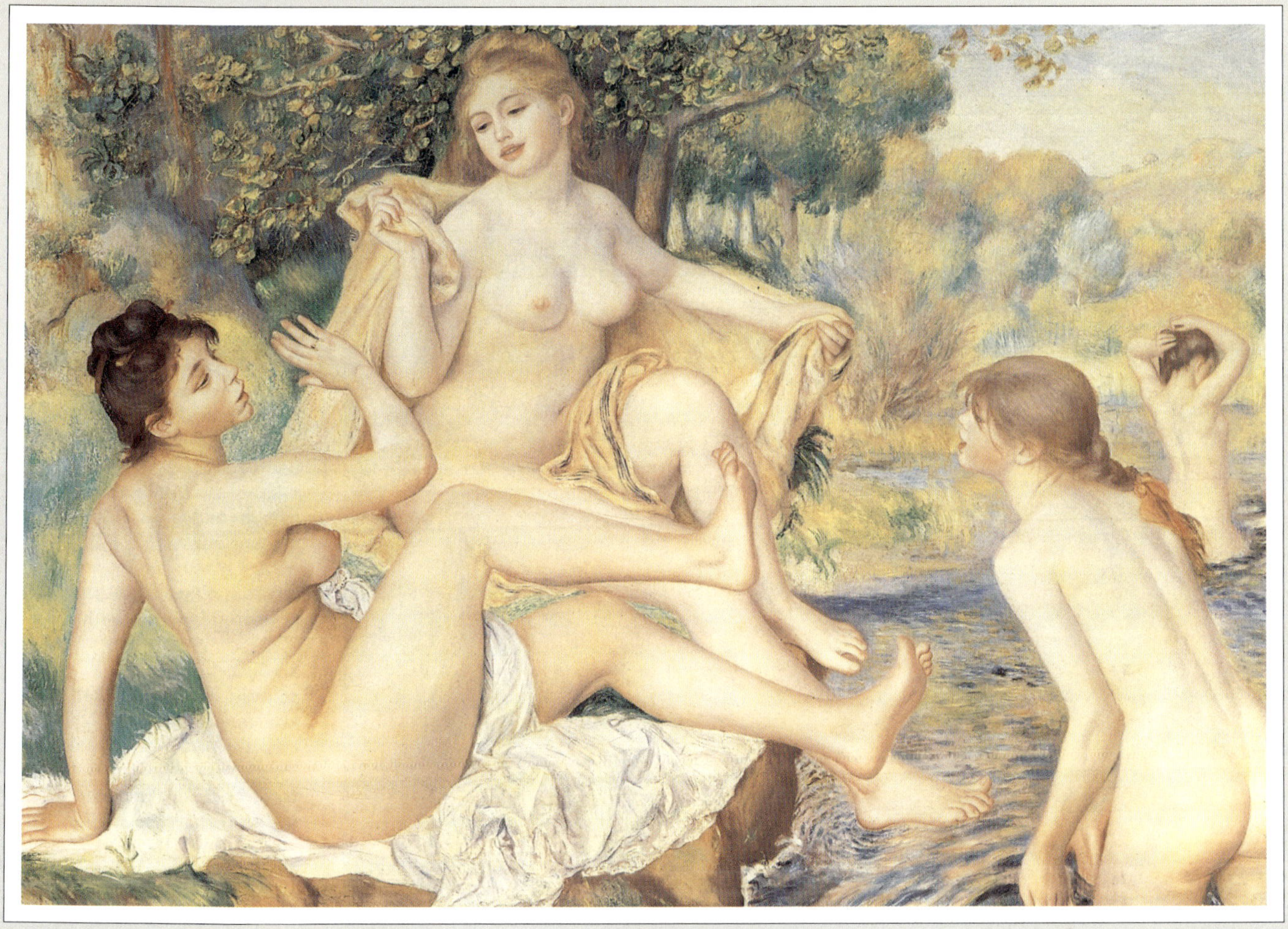

In this ambitious composition derived from the classical subjects of the Old Masters, Renoir was attempting to put on canvas some of the theories that had occupied him for the last five years. He had developed a theory of "irregularism," which favored a clear and structured composition but one that was not necessarily bound by rules of symmetry. At the same time he had absorbed the ideas of Impressionism, such as the light grounds and palette, and was unable to abandon them.

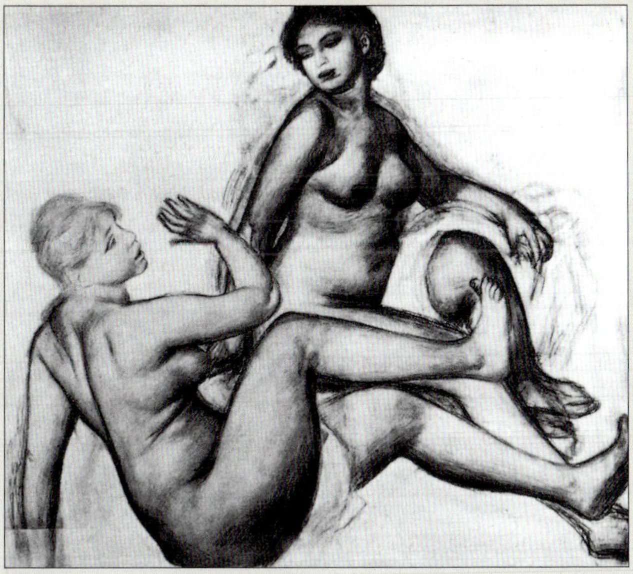

Nude Study
c 1886-7
Art Institute of Chicago

This chalk drawing is one of Renoir's many studies for *The Bathers.* In his earlier works of the 1860s and '70s he had painted his compositions straight onto the canvas, but in the 1880s he was concerned with capturing something of the monumental and classical feeling of Renaissance paintings. He was less than successful, as *The Bathers* neither lives up to the rigorous standards of traditional painting nor has the immediacy and freshness of Impressionism.

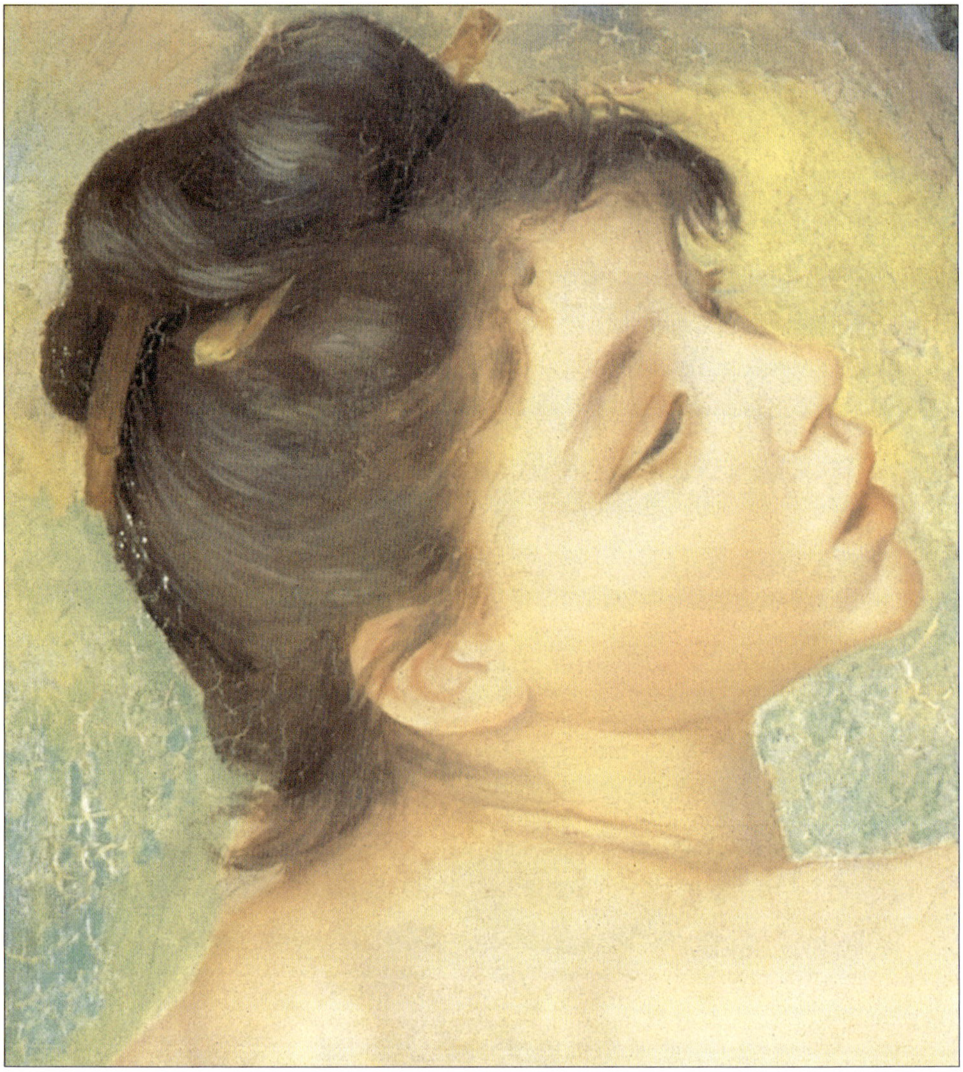

1

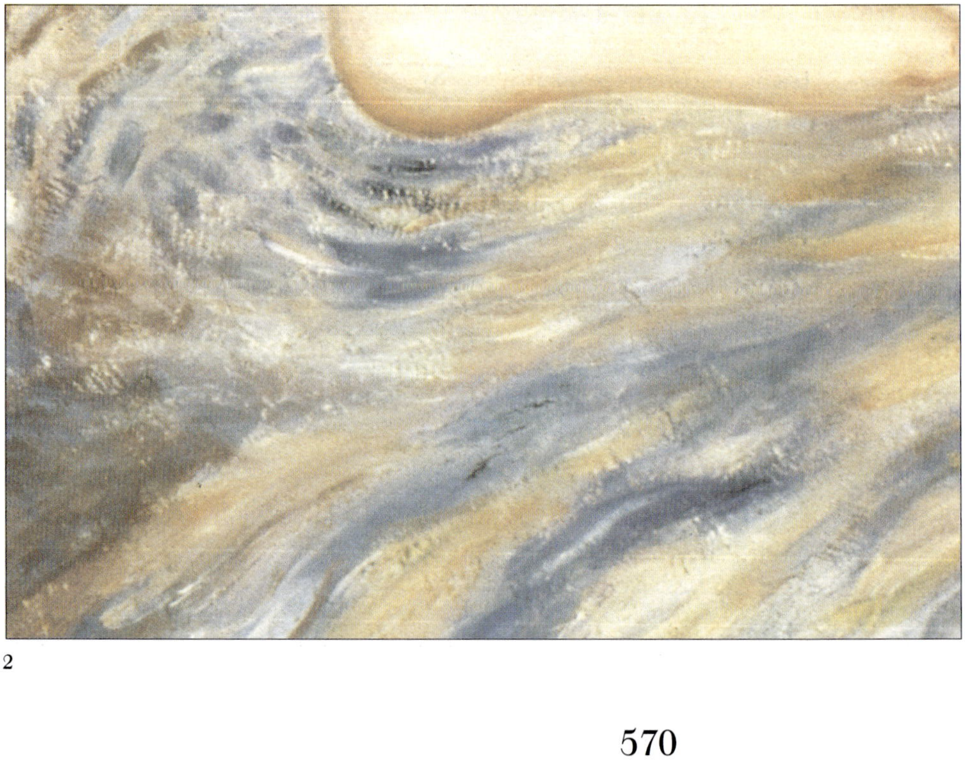

2

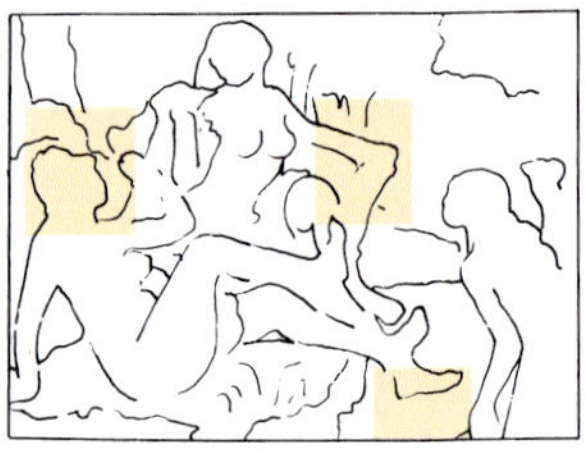

1 The head is the ultimate expression of Renoir's mannered, tight paintwork at this time. The brushmarks are barely visible, and the paint has been worked into an almost porcelain-like finish. The delicate lighting of the hair has been achieved from underneath by allowing the pale ground to limit the contour and shape, with orange worked on top in an attempt to give an impression of warmth and sunlight.

2 This detail shows the contrast between the harsh, academic style Renoir has used for the bodies and the freer use of paint and brushwork for the water. It also illustrates the studied artificiality of the work. Judging from the ripples of the water, the foot should be in contact with it, but in fact it appears to be floating free without any relationship with the water.

3 *Actual size detail* This detail also provides a contrast between the body of the nude, the towel and the background, each being painted in a different way. The skin of the arm is smoothly painted, with an orange glow that is presumably derived from the color of the towel, but the towel itself seems solid and lifeless, with the folds rendered rather clumsily. The background is treated much more loosely and freely, its liveliness emphasizing the dullness of the towel.

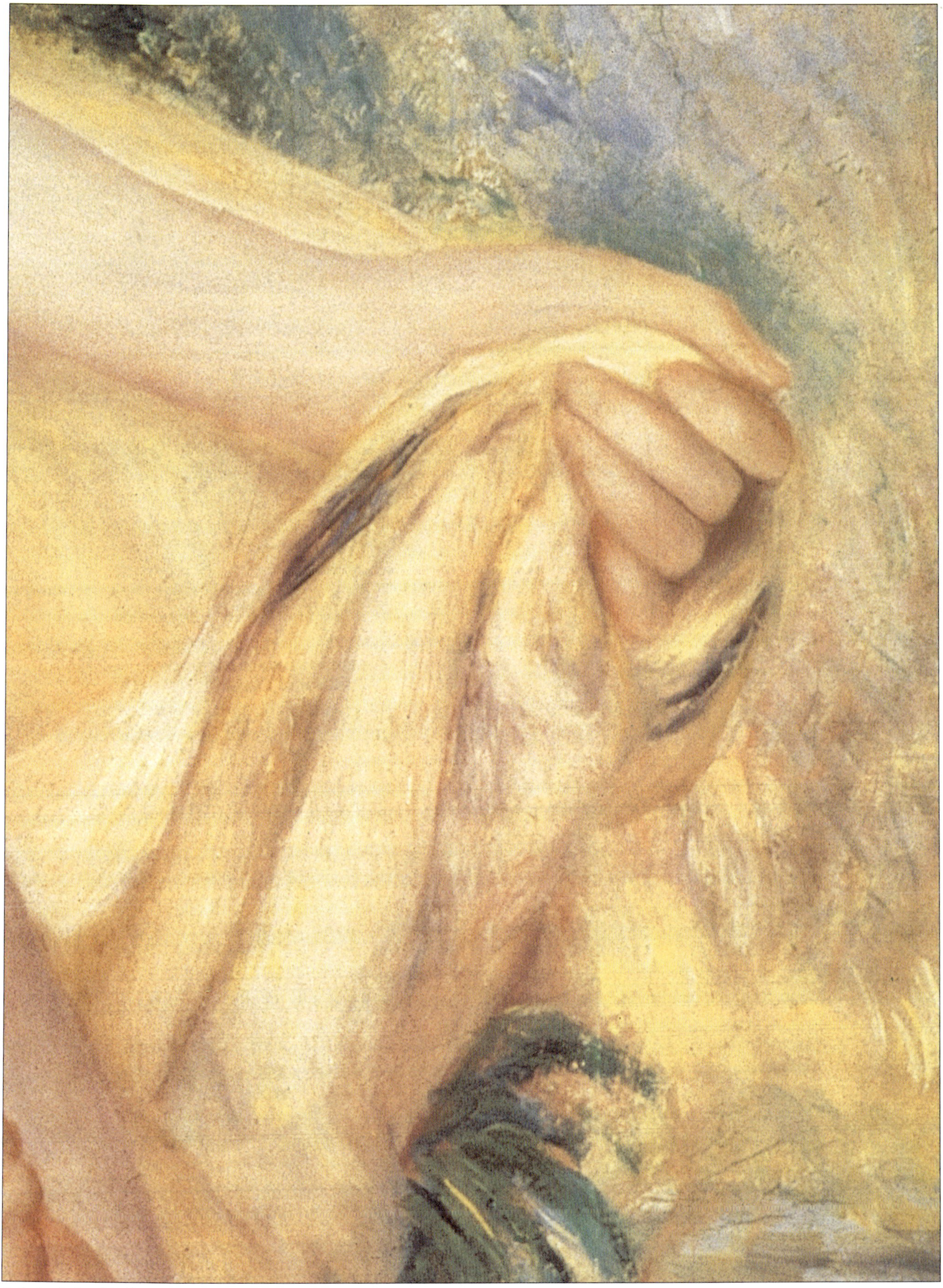

3 *Actual size detail*

Girls at the Piano

(Jeunes Filles au Piano)
1892
$45\frac{5}{8} \times 35\frac{1}{2}$in/115.75×90.25cm
Oil on canvas
Musée d'Orsay, Paris

In 1892, through the influence of his friend, the poet Stéphane Mallarmé, Renoir received an official commission from the government. Mallarmé had been trying to persuade Henry Roujon, the new Director of Fine Arts, who wanted to buy a Renoir of the 1870s, that it would be better to commission a new work. Roujon finally agreed, and the picture, destined to enter the collection of the Luxembourg Palace specially devoted to the work of living artists, was *Girls at the Piano.*

Renoir was very excited by the commission and began work in great earnestness, determined to produce the best he was capable of. The critic Arsène Alexandre, writing in the 1920s, recalled the circumstances of the commission and execution of the painting. "I remember the infinite pains he took in executing the official commission which a well-meaning friend had taken the trouble to gain for him. This was the young girls at the piano, a painting delicate and subtle in its execution, though its color has yellowed somewhat. Renoir began this painting five or six times, each time almost identically; the idea of a commission was enough to paralyze him and to undermine his self-confidence. Tired of the struggle, he finally delivered to the Beaux Arts the picture which is today at the Museum, which immediately afterwards he adjudged the least good of the five or six." Renoir was paid 4,000 francs for the painting, with which he was well pleased, although controversy over which was the best of the several versions continued for some time.

All the works are very similar, with only minor compositional differences, and it is really only a matter of taste as to which is the best. The painting illustrated has a finesse and delicacy which hark back to the 1870s and show that Renoir had emerged from the stylistic and compositional traumas of the 1880s with his style and handling sure and confident. He was to stay with this new, tempered Impressionism until nearly the end of his life, when the restrictions caused by his arthritis forced a change in style.

In order to make the composition consistent from one version to the next, Renoir used tracing paper to transfer the figures rather than re-drawing the same figures freehand each time. Since the 1870s blue had no longer appeared in his shadows — very much a technique of Impressionism — and the shadows here are much warmer, using instead oranges and yellows. The paint is thinner than in the 1870s but not so dry or smooth as in *The Bathers* (see page 569), although the highlights on the clothes and the brackets on the piano have been painted quite thickly. A longer, more curvaceous brushstroke has been used in the hair and clothes to create a more intimate rounded impression.

Before going on view at the Luxembourg, which was currently being restored, *Girls at the Piano* was loaned to Durand-Ruel for a one-man exhibition of Renoir's work. Mallarmé wrote to Roujon while it was on view there, "As for myself, and according to the unanimous impression gathered from all sides, I could not congratulate you enough for having chosen for a museum this definitive canvas, so calm and so free, a work of maturity. I see it once the dampness is gone and the painting is done, after a few months, like a feast in the Luxembourg, and completely accessible to visitors." In November the painting was formally admitted to the museum, marking Renoir's final arrival as an established modern painter. The stamp of official patronage ensured him from now on a steady flow of buyers and commissions.

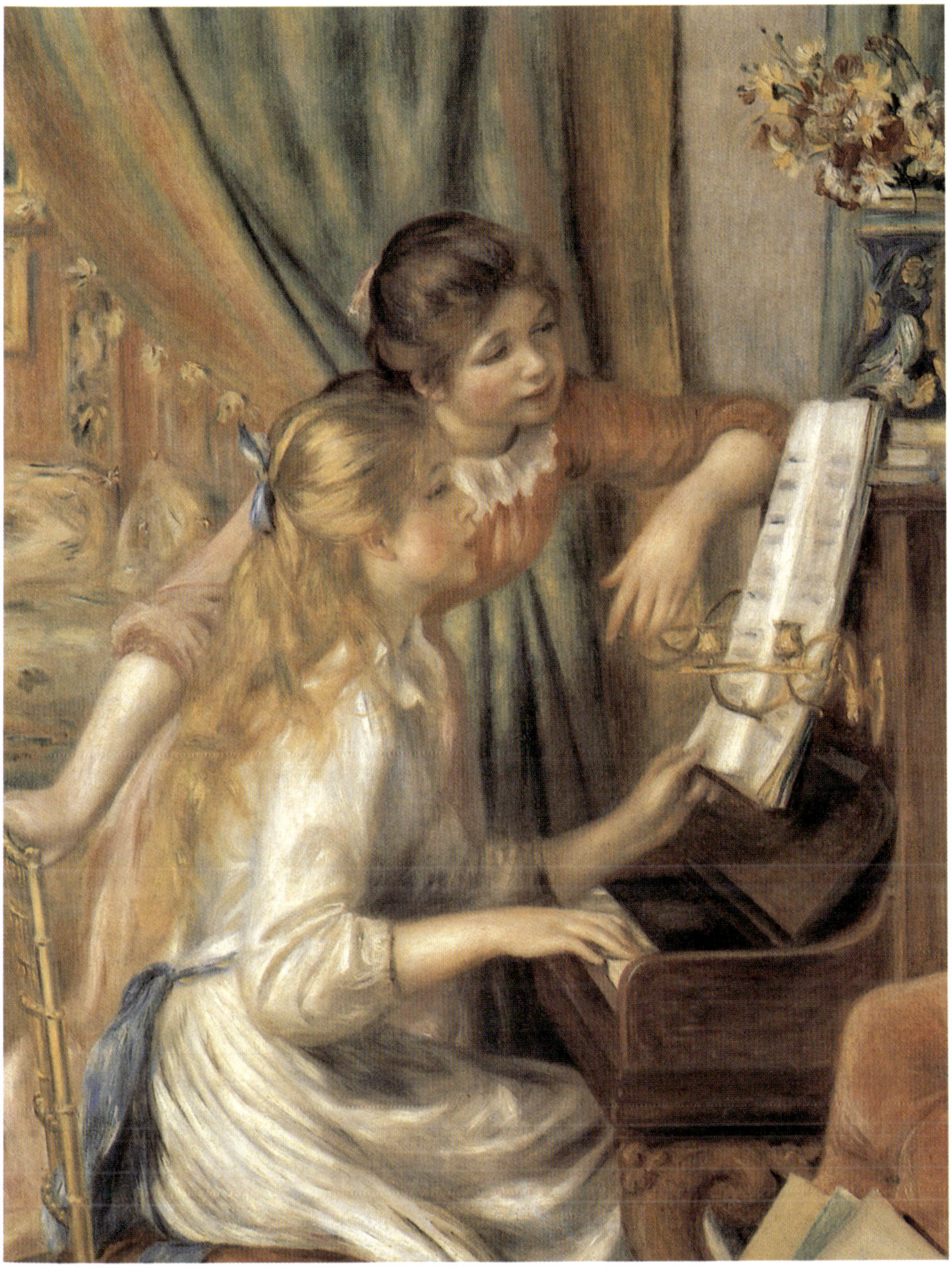

Through his friend Stéphane Mallarmé, Renoir was commissioned by the director of fine arts to produce a painting for the French state, to be hung in the Luxembourg Palace, demonstrating that he had at last gained official recognition for his work. He chose a subject that would not be controversial and would appeal to the tastes of the affluent bourgeoisie, and he worked hard at the commission, painting several versions of *Girls at the Piano*, each almost identical to its predecessor. This is the version that was finally delivered to the museum, and Renoir is reputed to have immediately judged it the least good.

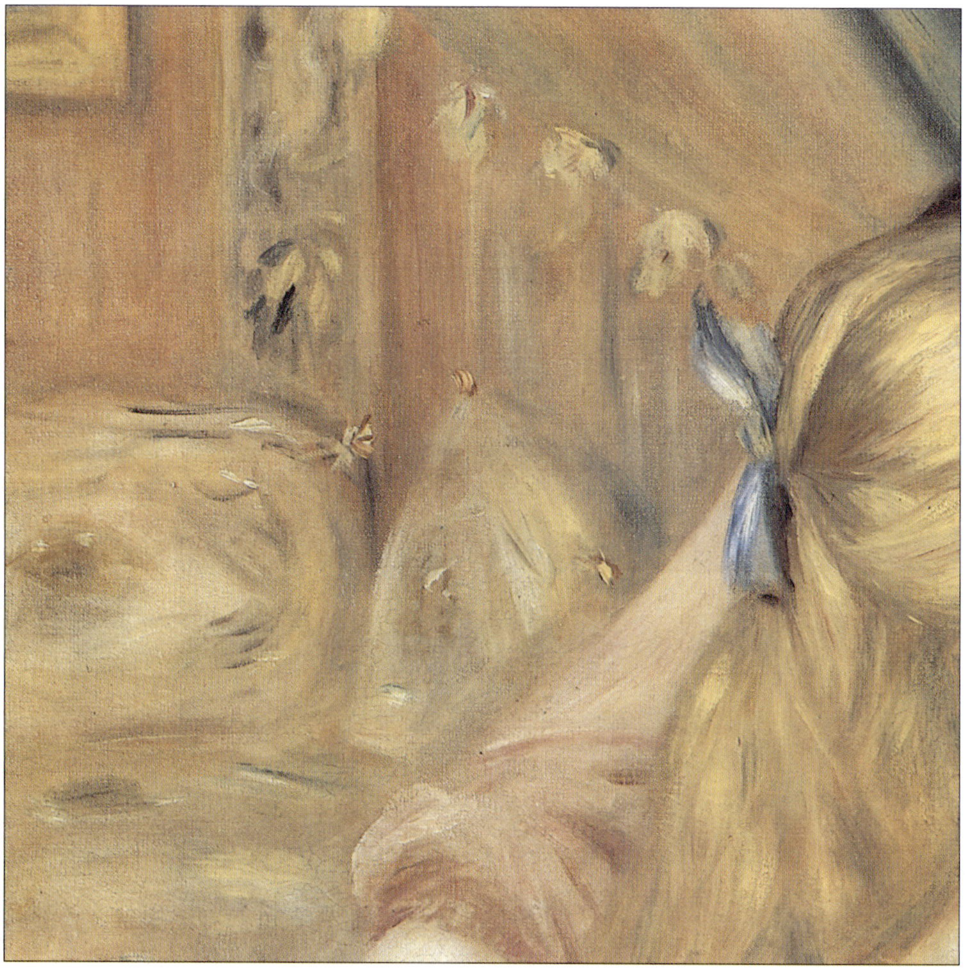

1

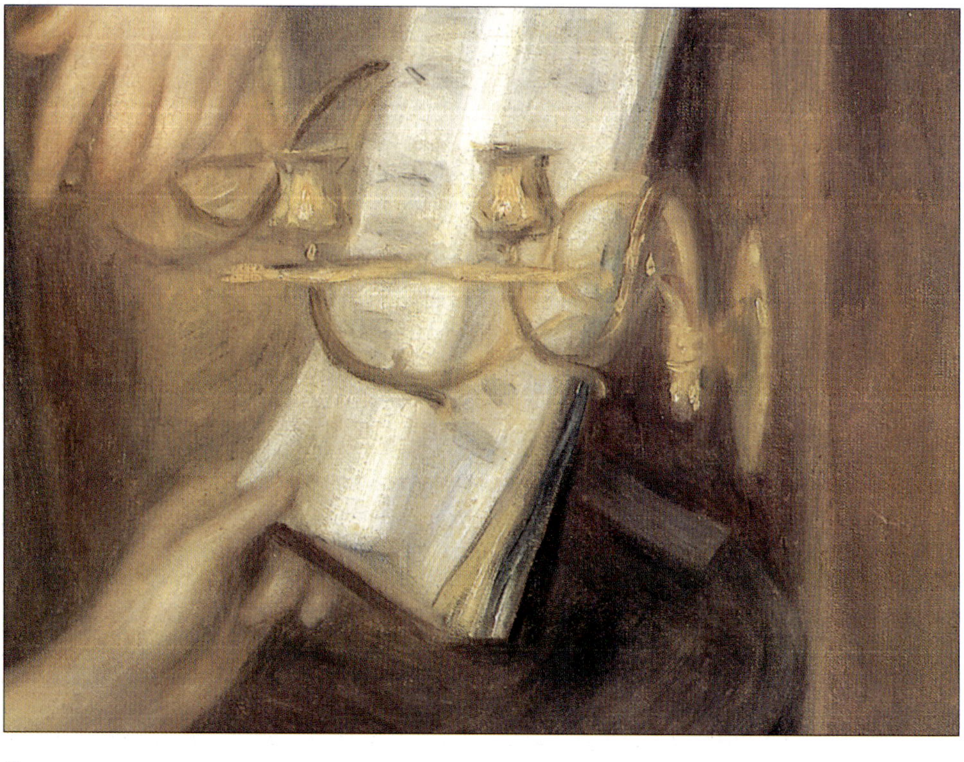

2

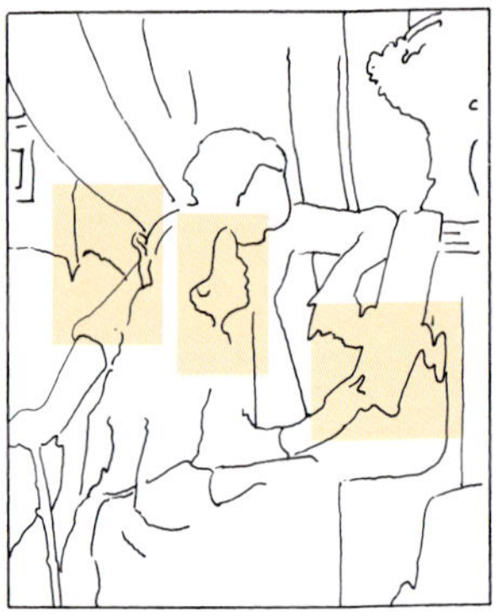

1 Renoir has used a rich array of colors for this work depicting a scene from comfortable bourgeois life. Gone are his earlier blues; these colors are warm and glowing, with the gold of the cushions and the girl's hair split by a wonderful pink on the sleeve of the other girl. The brushstrokes are long and worked to a smooth finish, probably in part due to his desire to please his "establishment" patrons.

2 The brass candle bracket has been swiftly highlighted in yellow, the paint applied on top of a duller yellow outlining. This gives the object a feeling of form and solidity as well as suggesting the hard, shiny qualities of the material itself.

3 *Actual size detail* The features of the young girl's face have been drawn very finely, with soft, smooth brushwork, while the golden hair and white collar show slightly broader strokes. This contrast of brushwork brings out the delicacy of the skin, with the gentle shadows under the chin and the fine pink bloom of the cheek.

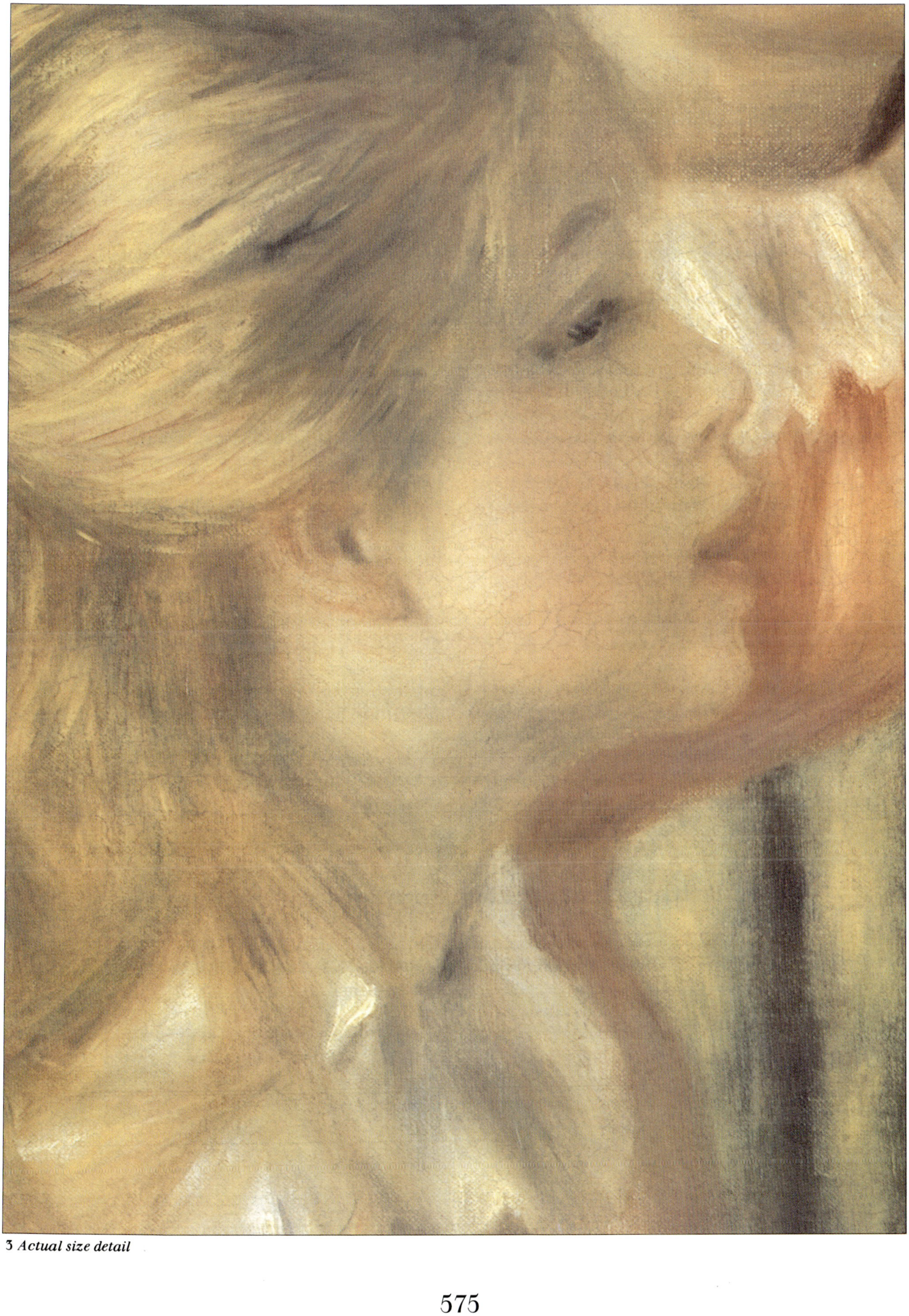

3 *Actual size detail*

Portrait of Misia

1904

$36\frac{1}{4} \times 28\frac{3}{4}$in/$92 \times 73$cm

Oil on canvas

National Gallery, London

Misia Godebska was one of the great society beauties of turn-of-the-century Paris. She was much sought after as a model by painters such as Pierre Bonnard, Edouard Vuillard, Toulouse-Lautrec and Félix Vallotton as well as by Renoir, who painted her at least four times. She was married three times, firstly to Thadée Natanson, then to Albert Edwards and finally to José Maria Sert. At the time of this portrait she was still married to her first husband, who with his two brothers had founded the journal *La Revue Blanche*. Misia's salon was much frequented by many of the young painters and writers, especially the painters of the Nabis school.

By 1904, when this portrait was painted, Jean Renoir, the artist's son, was beginning to watch his father at work, and he has left an interesting account in his book *Renoir, My Father*. "I also mention the coat of silver white which he applied to the canvas before starting to add color. He would ask the model posing for him, or whichever of his sons had been given the task, to increase the proportion of linseed oil. As a result the white took several days to dry; but it gave Renoir a smoother surface to work on. He did not like fine-grained canvases which were softer to paint on, for he thought them less resistant. In addition to this practical reason there was perhaps another one which was unconscious: his admiration for Veronese, Titian and Velazquez, who, it appears, painted on rather coarse-grained canvas. These reasons were complementary for my father was sure that the great masters wanted to produce work that would be lasting...I often prepared my father's canvases with flake white mixed with one third linseed oil and two thirds turpentine.It was then left to dry for several days." This portrait of Misia shows clearly the white ground showing through, which gives the work its fine luminous appearance.

Jean goes on to describe the actual application of the paint. "Renoir began by putting incomprehensible little touches on the white background, without even a suggestion of form. At times the paint, diluted with linseed oil and turpentine, was so liquid that it ran down the canvas. Renoir called it 'juice.' Thanks to the juice, he could, with several brushstrokes, establish the general tonality he was trying for. It covered almost the whole surface of the canvas...The background had to be very clear and smooth...He would begin with little pink or blue strokes, which would then be intermingled with burnt sienna, all perfectly balanced. As a rule Naples yellow and madder red were applied in the later stages. Ivory black came last of all. He next proceeded by direct or angular strokes. His method was round, so to speak, and in curves, as if he were following the contours of a young breast."

It is very interesting to read this firsthand account of Renoir at work in the context of the finished portrait, where one can see the curvaceous quality of the brushwork and the gradual building up of the painting to finish with the yellows, reds and black that give it so much of its vibrancy. But the care with which Renoir prepared his canvases was not simply a matter of pictorial effect; he also had a deep concern for preserving the quality of the paint, regarding himself as a craftsman above all else. As Jean writes, "His concern for durability had nothing to do with the pride of believing his work worthy of eternity."

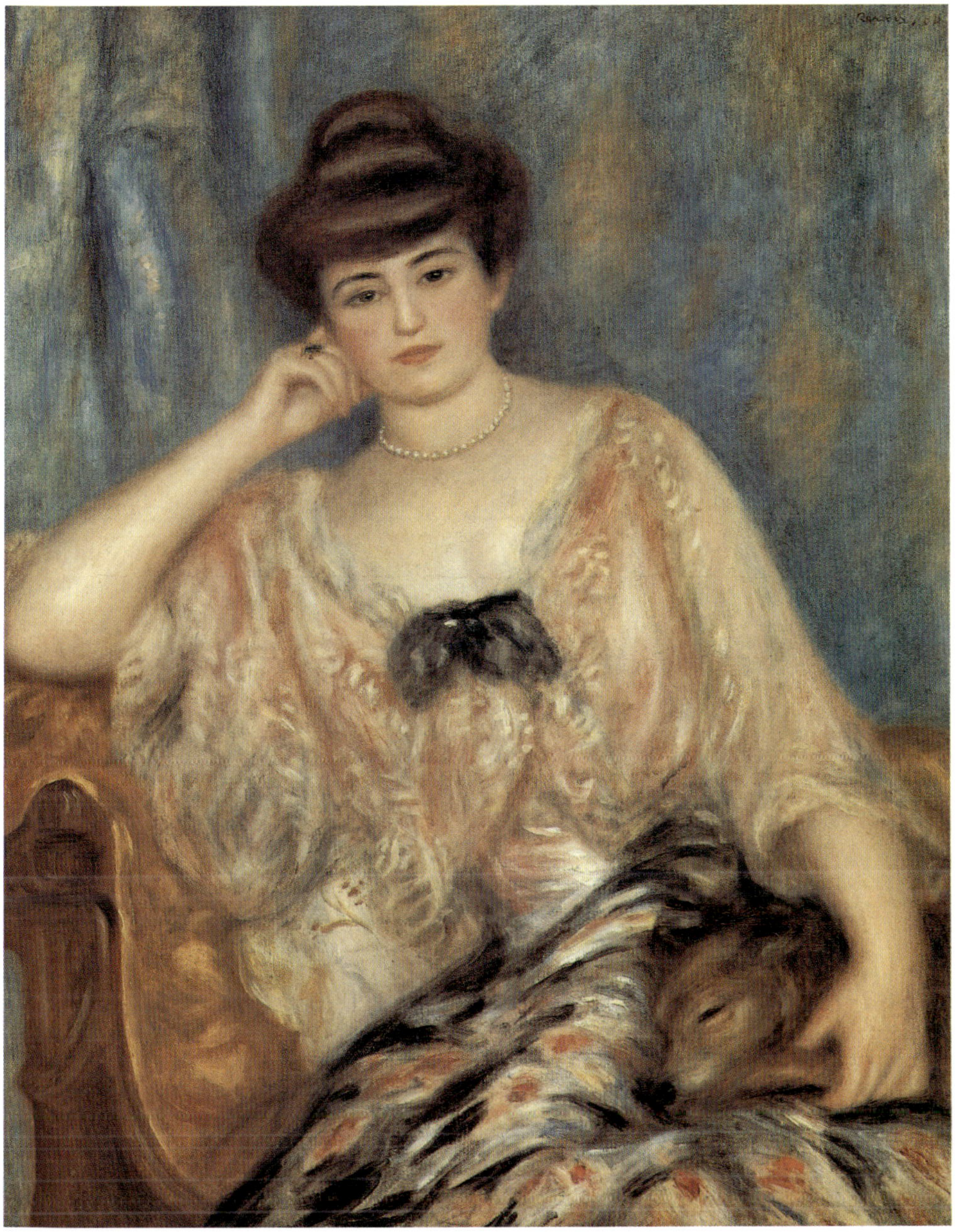

The sitter for this portrait, born Misia Godebska, was of Russo-Polish extraction. At the time of this portrait she was the wife of the journalist Thadée Natanson; later she married an Englishman, Albert Edwards, and finally the Surrealist and Dada poet and painter José Maria Sert. As a society beauty and the toast of intellectual and artistic Paris, she was much painted. Renoir himself did several portraits of her, as did other young artists whose work was championed by Natanson through his literary and artistic journal *La Revue Blanche*.

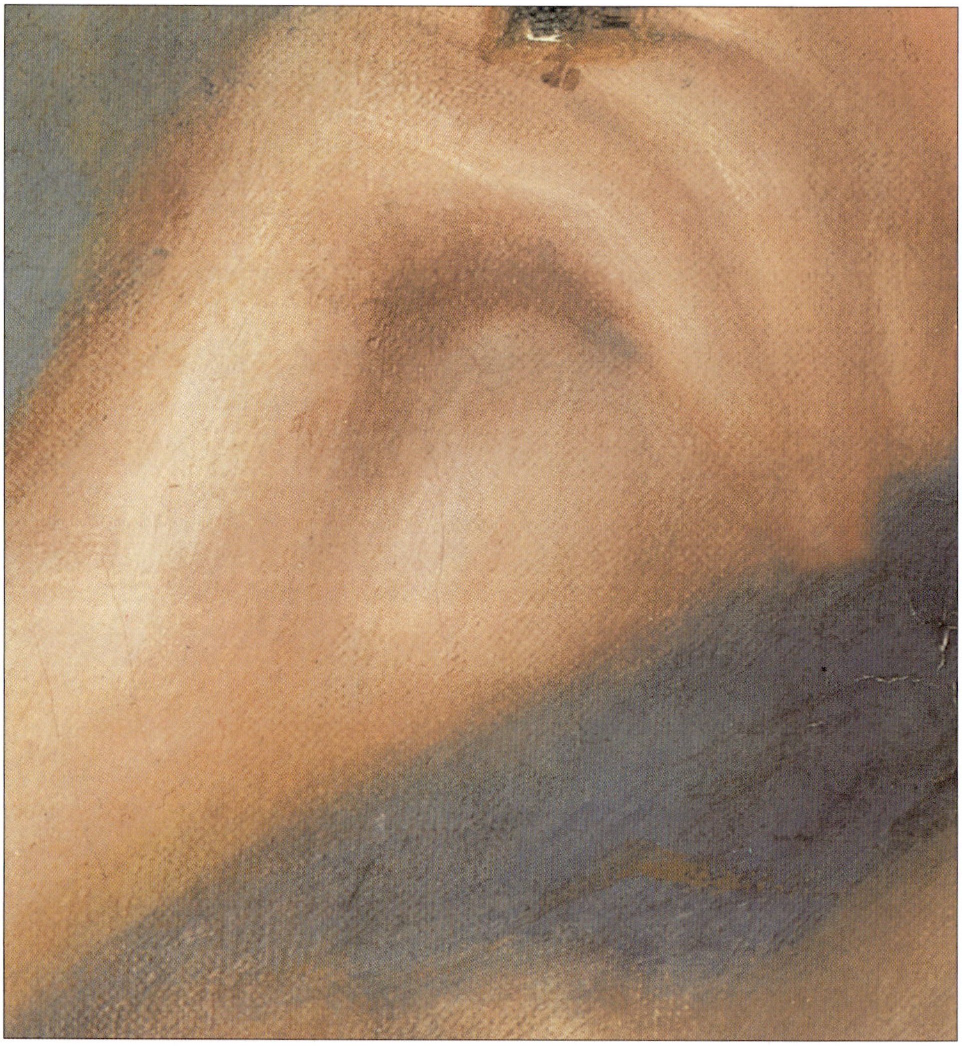

1

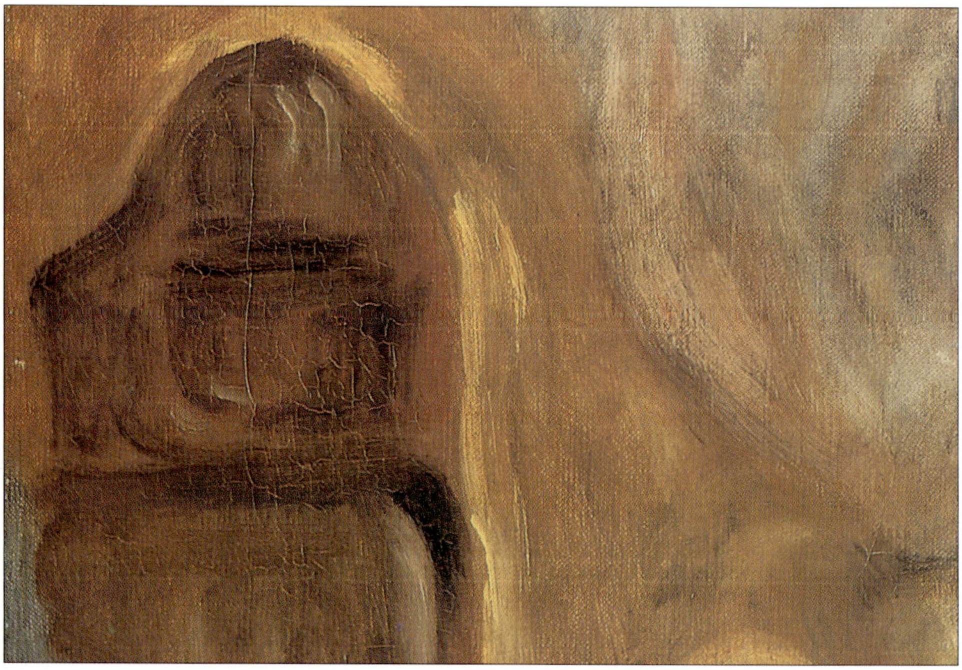

2

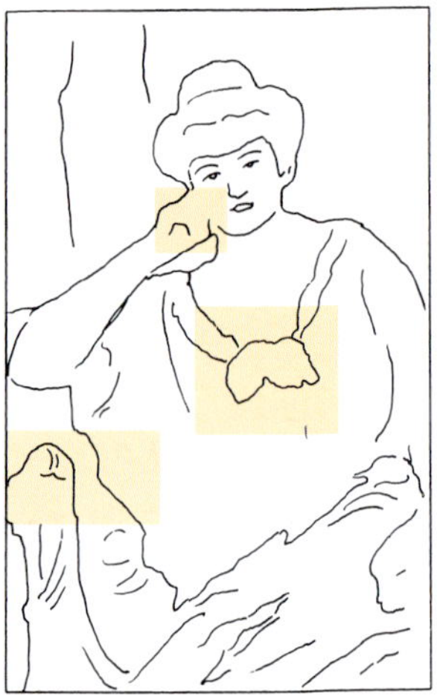

1 A deliberate lack of close-up definition has been created by the warm shadows that rebound from one to the other between the face and fingers of the sitter. The ring has been painted very swiftly with several short, sharp strokes of black, and then given solidity by the simple device of one small stroke of white highlight.

2 The side of the sofa blends its warm colors into the shadows on the folds of the sitter's dress, which in turn throws some of its own color back onto the sofa.

3 *Actual size detail* This detail shows the thinness of the paint, which has been mixed with turpentine to give greater fluidity. The pale ground has been allowed to show through, giving extra light and warmth to the painting, even where the colors are somber.This can be seen most clearly in the bow, where the underpaint has given a warm luminosity even to black, the coldest of all colors.

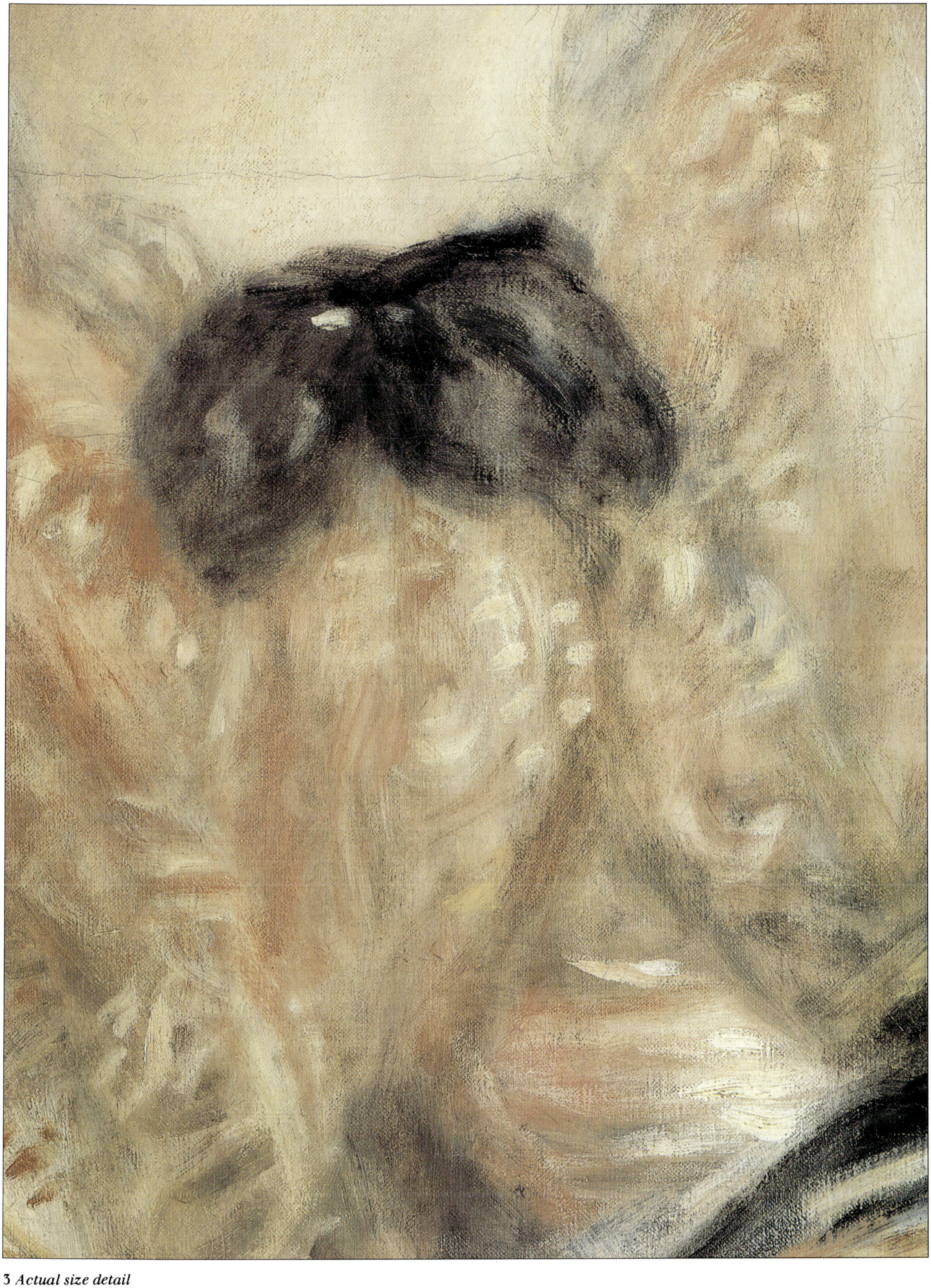

3 *Actual size detail*

Les Grandes Baigneuses

1918-19

43¼×63in/109.75×160cm

Oil on canvas

Musée d'Orsay, Paris

This was Renoir's last large-scale masterpiece, and one which recapitulated and summed up the ideas of the preceding few years. It borrows some of the compositional structure of the earlier work, *The Bathers* (see page 569), but is less awkward in appearence, and the classical motif has been treated with a much looser and more impressionistic brushstroke reminiscent of the works of the early 1870s. Jean Renoir writes of this work that, "He felt that in this picture he had summed up all his researches and prepared a springboard from which he could plunge into further researches." Sadly, Renoir died before he was able to use his self-made springboard.

The immediate inspiration for the painting was reputedly the signing of the armistice on November 11, 1918, and it was painted through the winter of 1918-19. Jean Renoir has once again given some detailed descriptions which give an interesting insight into Renoir's palette. "Towards the end of his life he simplified his palette still further. Here, as nearly as I can remember, is the way he arranged his paints on his palette when he painted *Les Grandes Baigneuses*, now in the Louvre, in his studio at les Collettes in Cagnes. Starting on the lower side, next to the hole for his thumb: silver-white in a thick sausage-roll; Naples yellow in a small dot; and the same for the following colors: yellow ocher, sienna earth, red ocher; madder red, green earth, Veronese green, cobalt blue, ivory black. His choice of colors was not inflexible. On rare occasions I saw Renoir use Chinese vermilion, which he placed between the madder red and the green earth. In his final years he simplified his color range still more and for certain pictures omitted either red ocher or green earth. Neither Gabrielle nor I ever saw him use chrome yellow. His economy of means was very impressive."

It must be remembered that when Renoir painted this work he was a very sick man. His hands were entirely crippled by arthritis and he was suffering with severe bronchial problems as well as being almost paralyzed in his legs. In order for him to paint, Gabrielle or one of his sons had to prepare the palette and then force the brush between his fingers. This accounts for the much wider brushstrokes which delineate the forms and allow the warm priming and coarse canvas to show through. His paint was much thinned with turpentine, which greatly facilitated application but also caused the paints to run on the canvas; this can be seen particularly in the lower corners of the painting. The fiery colors and brightness of the paint make up for some of the unsurprising defects in technique, for the nudes have a lumpy, unnatural appearance and their bodies are rather unresolved. The landscape, like that in *The Bathers* of 1887, was painted indoors, which contributes to the air of artificiality in the work. But despite all the many handicaps, Renoir still loved the work he was doing, and his dedication has contrived to produce a painting of enormous strength, one which captivates the viewer with a sense almost of bewilderment at the beauty and fruitfulness of nature. It is a great irony that as Renoir the man was slowly but surely crumbling into death, Renoir the painter was leaping forward to new heights.

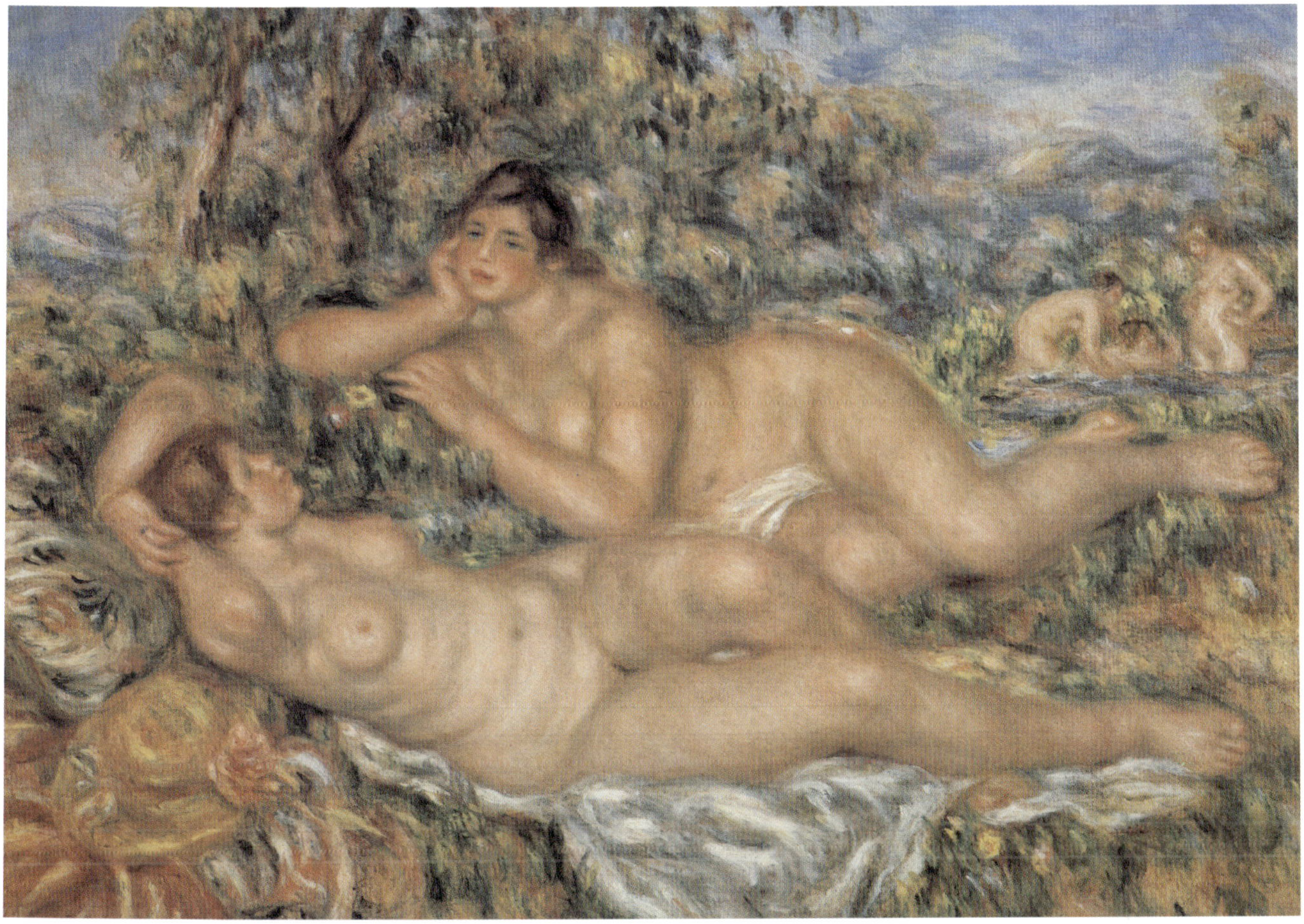

Renoir was inspired to paint this, his last major work, by the signing of the Armistice which brought World War One to a close on November 11, 1918. He was now over seventy-five and severely crippled with arthritis, but in spite of his suffering he has managed to create a work of enormous power. The composition is based on classical subject matter, but the flattened perspective and expressive brushwork both demonstrate Renoir's unabating search for new pictorial possibilities.

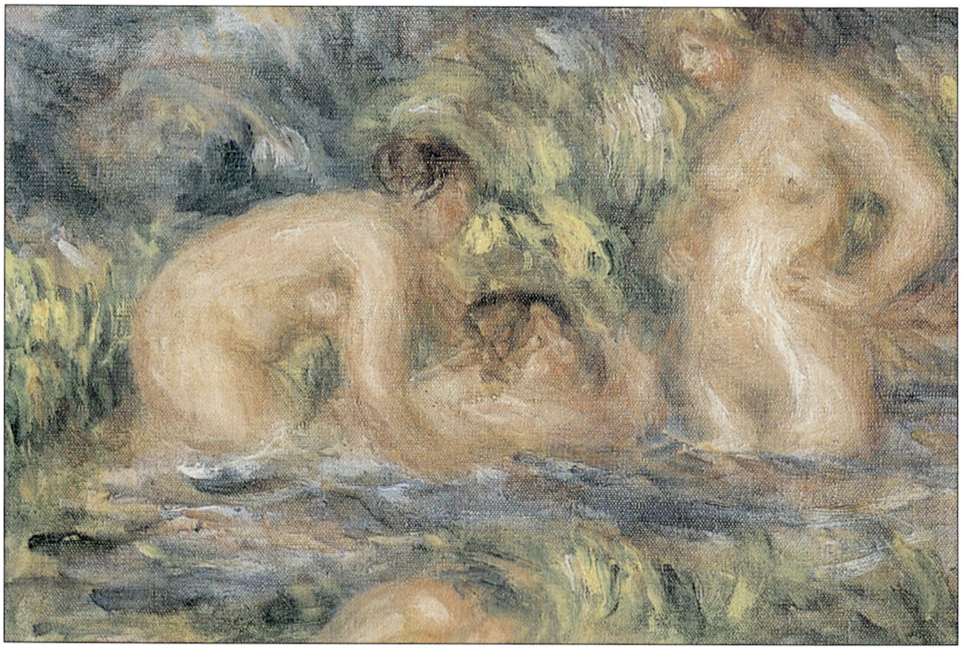

1

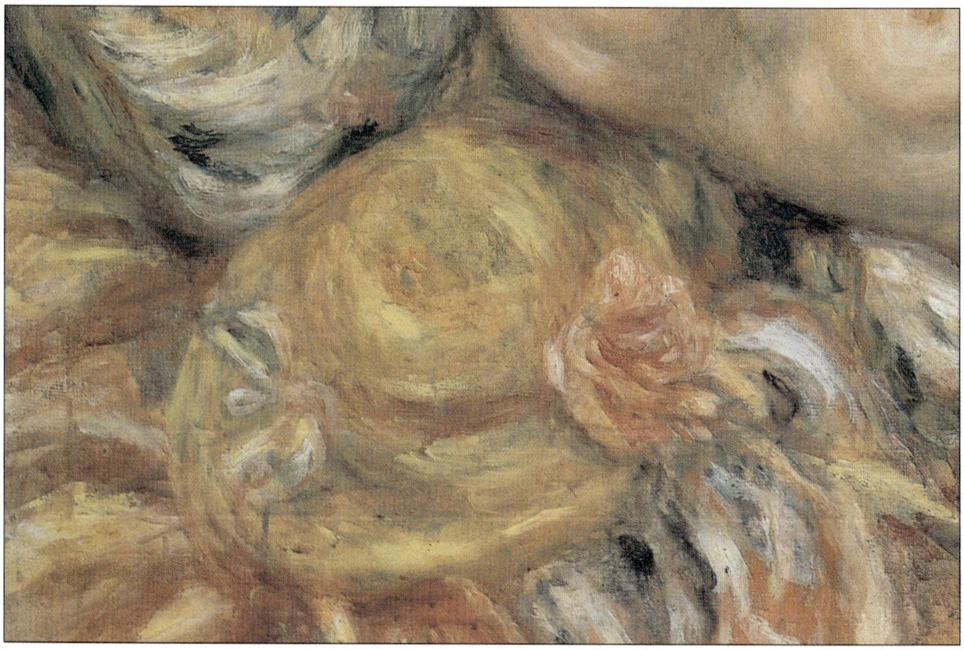

2

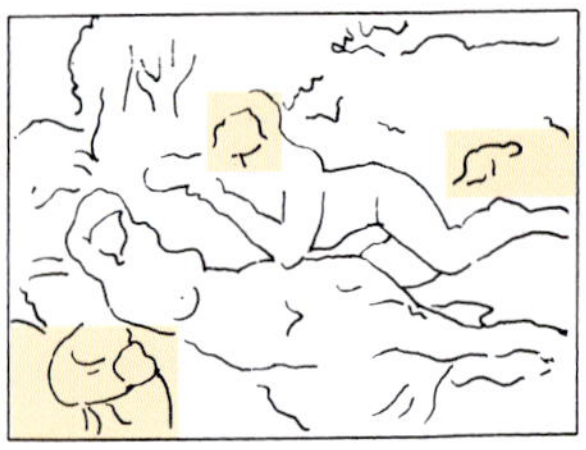

1 By this time Renoir's arthritis made it difficult for him to manipulate his brushes, and the paint has been much thinned with turpentine; the coarse texture of the canvas can be seen clearly beneath it. Small touches of slightly thicker paint have been used for the highlights on the bodies and the light froth of water, while the area of foliage between the figures shows touches of near-impasto in subtly glowing pinks and yellow-greens.

2 The thinning of the paint with turpentine has caused it to run in places, particularly in the reds of the blanket. Despite the increasing stiffness of his brushstrokes, Renoir has lost none of his brilliance of color, which is notable in the golden straw of the hat and the deep pink of the rose.

3 *Actual size detail* The modeling of the face seems to tend toward an exaggerated roundness, giving the cheeks and mouth a rather distorted appearance. Renoir has used a pinkish priming, which strengthens the colors of the face and has given the hair an almost auburn glow in spite of the black paint he has used.

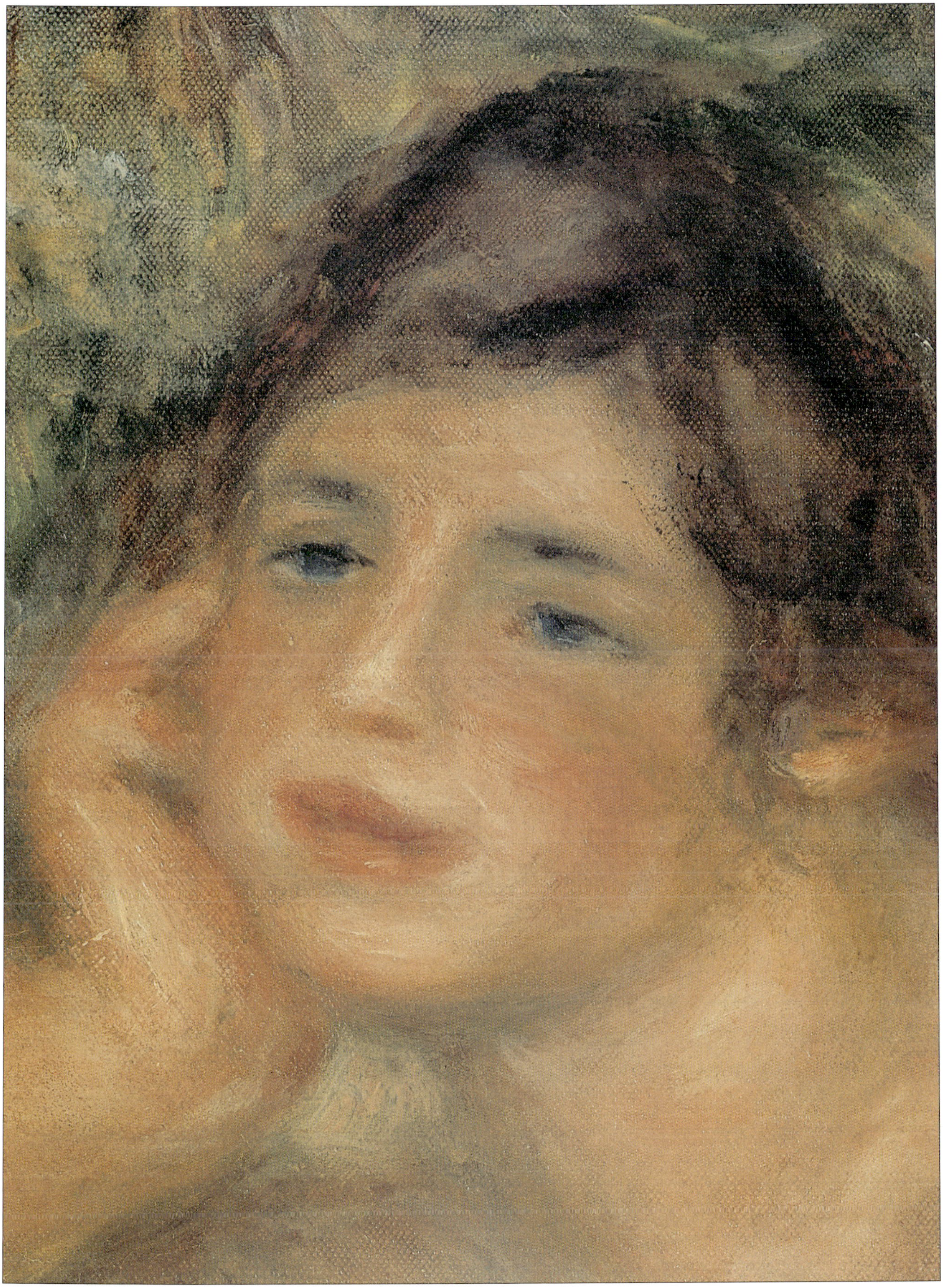

3 *Actual size detail*

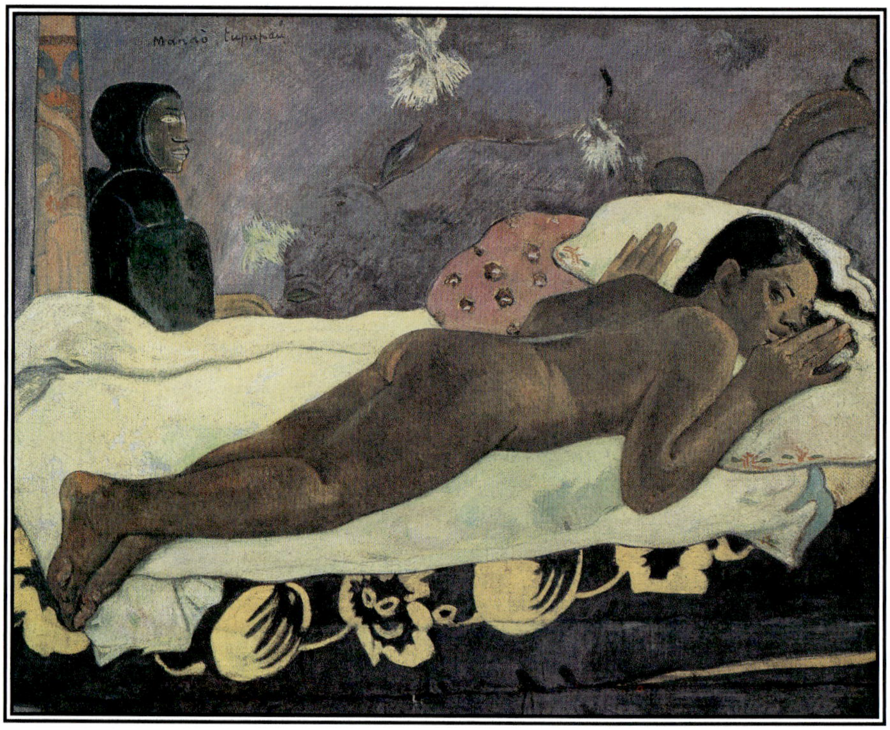
Manaò tupapaù

GAUGUIN

Introduction

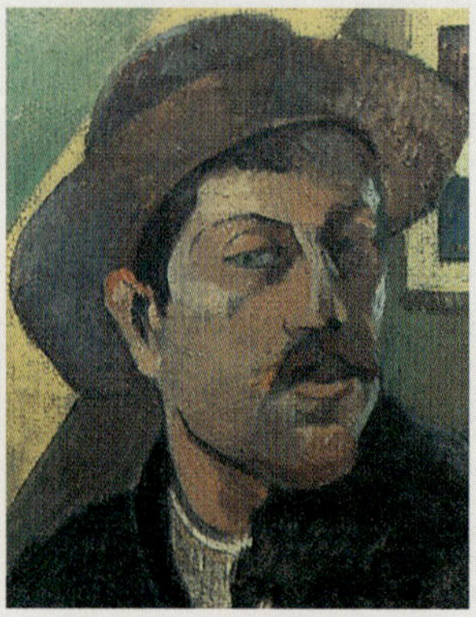

Paul Gauguin
Self-portrait
1893-94
Musée d'Orsay, Paris

"I am a great artist and I know it," wrote Gauguin from Tahiti in 1892. "It is because I am, that I have endured such suffering." The remark is a testament both to the integrity of his artistic vision and to his "monstrous egotism." Gauguin never doubted his talent, attributing lack of financial success to the philistinism of the picture-buying market, or the corruption of dealers living off the backs of artists. "I feel I am right about art," he wrote in the year of his death, "in any case I will have done my duty, and there will always remain the memory of an artist who has set painting free."

Gauguin was always in search of an unspoilt haven where he could paint and live simply and cheaply. It was an elusive quest for a primitive idyll, and drove him ever further from western civilization – from Martinique to Tahiti, from Tahiti to the Marquesas Islands. But he was to find French colonialism had already made inroads into virgin territory like "decrepitude staring at the new flowering, the virtue of the law breathing impurely upon the native but pure unashamedness of trust and faith." Gauguin "saw with grief this cloud of smoke [and] felt ashamed of [his] race."

Illness, lack of funds and bureaucracy made life in Tahiti a nightmare, yet Gauguin was not tempted to abandon South Sea island life for an offer from a Paris dealer to receive a "modest but fixed income" for paintings produced at will. As Degas remarked, "Gauguin is the thin wolf without the collar (that is – he prefers liberty with starvation to servitude with abundance)." Gauguin's "haughty nobility, obviously innate," was, as his friend Charles Morice noted, "a simplicity that bordered on triviality ... aristocracy permeated by the proletariat." It was an image Gauguin approved. He saw his own origins as noble and exotic – "on my mother's side I descended from a Borgia of Aragon, Viceroy of Peru."

Gauguin ascribed immense importance to his Peruvian forebears, even though these connections were tenuous, deriving from a liaison between a young French woman, Thérèse Laisnay, who fled to Spain during the Revolution, and a noble Spanish colonel of Dragoons, Don Mariano de Tristan y Moscoso. This produced Flora Tristan, Gauguin's maternal grandmother. The Tristan Moscoso family had settled early in Peru, and Gauguin fancied that their blood had mingled itself with that of the ancient Incas. In adult life he referred to himself as a "Peruvian savage" and inscribed the frame of one of his works "a gift from Tristan de Moscoso" (see page 602).

Gauguin's Peruvian association encouraged him to consider himself as something of a "noble savage." It also suggested a hereditary urge driving him to follow his destiny in a way his ancestors had, and perhaps mitigated any sense of guilt he may have later felt in rejecting everything for his art. Gauguin revered his maternal grandmother, Flora Tristan, "a socialist-anarchist blue stocking," as he himself styled her, and kept her writings by him until his death. His career parallels that of his mother: having abandoned a spouse to follow her own star, "she spent her whole fortune," Gauguin tells us, "on the workers' cause, traveling ceaselessly." Although her pursuit, unlike Gauguin's own, was philanthropic, he had before him the example of one who had abandoned all material wealth for a cause, which was the way he chose to see his art.

Gauguin was born in Paris in 1848, a year which saw revolutionary activity throughout Europe. Disillusioned with the Second Empire of Louis Napoleon, Gauguin's republican father, Clovis, a political journalist, decided to set out for Lima in Peru, where his wife's great uncle and family lived, intending to start a newspaper. On the journey he collapsed and died of a ruptured blood vessel. His widow Aline traveled on to Lima with her two young children Marie and Paul, and on arrival good fortune attended her, for not only was her great uncle Don Pio a member of the Lima aristocracy (his son was President for some years) but the family was large and welcoming.

The four years Gauguin spent in Lima were never forgotten: "I still see our street with the chickens pecking in the refuse," he wrote in the last years of his life. It was a world of splendor and terror — of shock awakenings by madmen or earthquakes, remembered clearly by Gauguin half a century later. The Lima period ended abruptly with a return to France to settle an inheritance from his paternal grandfather. Life in Orléans after the colorful city of Lima "where it never rained" was gray and unwelcoming. Gauguin saw it as the end of a golden age — "although never in actual poverty, from this time on, our life was extremely simple." It is part of the Gauguin fable that his early memories of his Peruvian days bred a nostalgia for exotic lands and a yearning to seek out undiscovered countries where he could live the life of a "primitive savage." His wanderlust found an outlet in 1865 when at the age of seventeen he joined the merchant navy, sailing to the distant shores of the Atlantic and Pacific oceans. Doubtless it stirred memories of his childhood. Although he did not begin to paint until his mid-twenties, Gauguin evidently responded to pictures from an early age. Sometime around his tenth year, "beguiled" by a picture, he took it into his head to run away to the forest of Bondy with a handkerchief full of sand at the end of a stick which he carried over his shoulder." His introduction to the world of art came from a family friend, Gustave Arosa, who became his guardian on the death of Gauguin's mother in 1867. An important art patron and collector of avant-garde works, Arosa was also responsible for getting Gauguin his position with the banking firm of Bertin in Paris. Here he met Emil Schuffenecker,

PAUL GAUGUIN
Les Lavandières
1886, Musée d'Orsay, Paris

This work shows the Impressionist style Gauguin inherited from Pissarro. It is an example of an intermediate technique characterized by the use of long, thin, curved strokes of prismatic color. This technique is different both from his earlier use of short, wide dabs of pigment in the same tonal range, and from his later use of flat areas of unbroken color and dark outline.

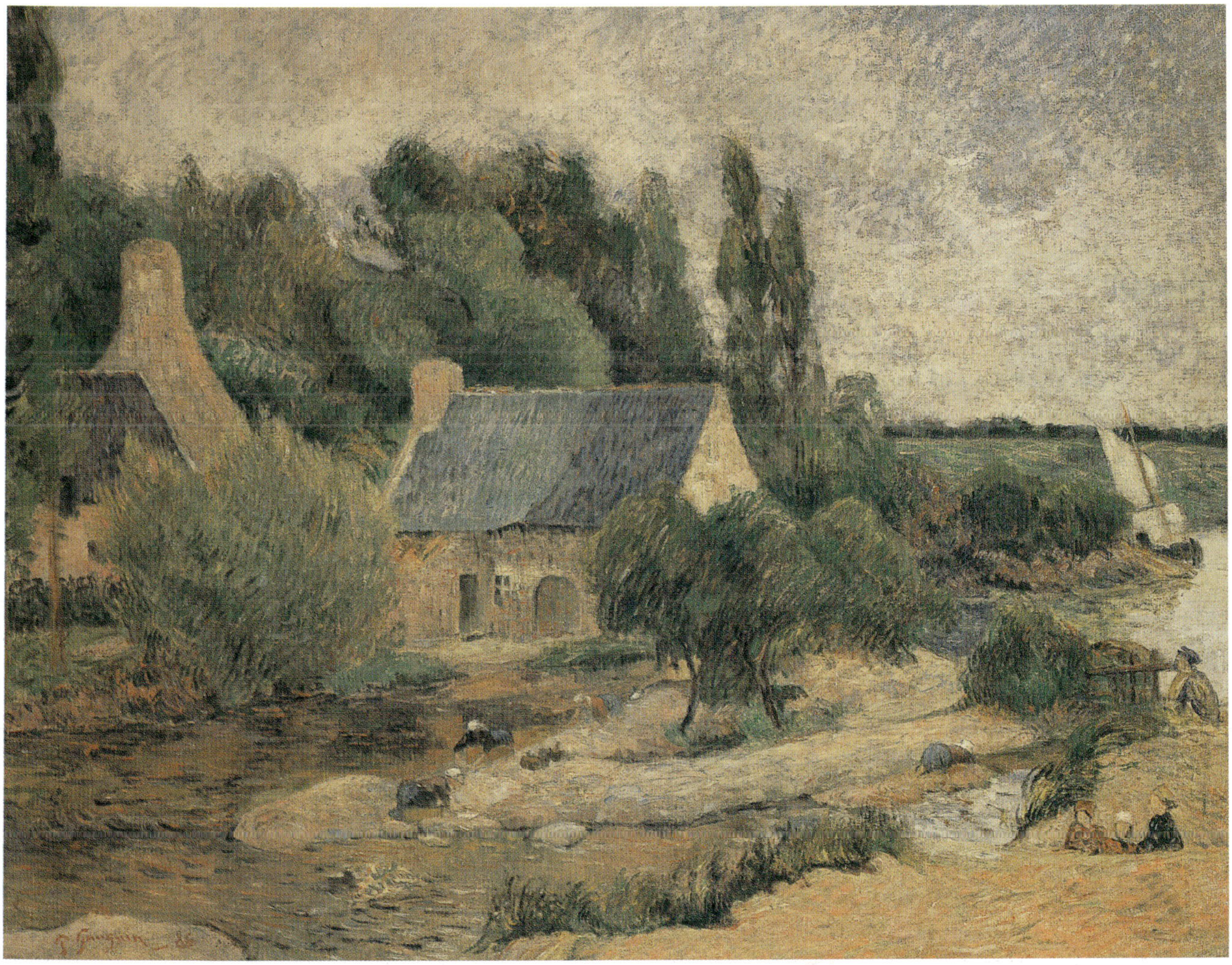

who was to become a loyal and lifelong friend, and who persuaded Gauguin to paint with him on Sundays.

Although he received no formal training, Gauguin's earliest works are remarkably accomplished (a term he would later consider pejorative). He had an eye for the masterpieces of the new Impressionist style; for the yet-to-be fashionable pictures in the collections of "Père" Tanguy and the dealer Durand-Ruel. By 1880 he owned works by Daumier, Manet, Renoir, Monet, Cézanne, Pissarro, Sisley, Guillamin and Jongkind, so that "if his brush hadn't led him, his fame would have rested on his collection."

Through Arosa Gauguin met Camille Pissarro, whose impact on him at the beginning of his career was great, and led to an increasing absorption in painting and involvement with other members of the Impressionist circle. He exhibited with them in 1879, 1880, 1881, and 1882 — against the wishes of Monet and Renoir. Gauguin's landscapes, whose style had previously been conditioned by those of Corot, which he had seen in Arosa's collection, took on an Impressionist flavour under the influence of Pissarro. His immersion in the works of the avant-garde painters of the day provided him with the means of "discovering" the "secret" of expressing nature adopted by those progressive artists. This, combined with occasional visits to the less formally rigid *ateliers* in order to improve his life drawing, formed the basis of Gauguin's art training. His ideas on painting were developing faster than his means of conveying them.

CAMILLE PISSARRO
Diligence at Louveciennes
1870, Musée d'Orsay, Paris

Pissarro was the greatest single influence on the work of Gauguin, and his revolutionary technique earned him Gauguin's respect in the first years of their acquaintance. Later, however, Gauguin scorned him. "You see what has happened to Pissarro... always wanting to be in the vanguard...he has lost every atom of personality."

The pursuit of art

In 1873 he met and married a young Danish girl, Mette Sophie Gad. By 1883 they had had five children, and were living comfortably on Gauguin's salary as a banker. However, there was a serious financial slump that year, and Gauguin abandoned his position at the banking firm with the intention of providing for his family by the sale of his paintings. Unable to make a living in Paris, he

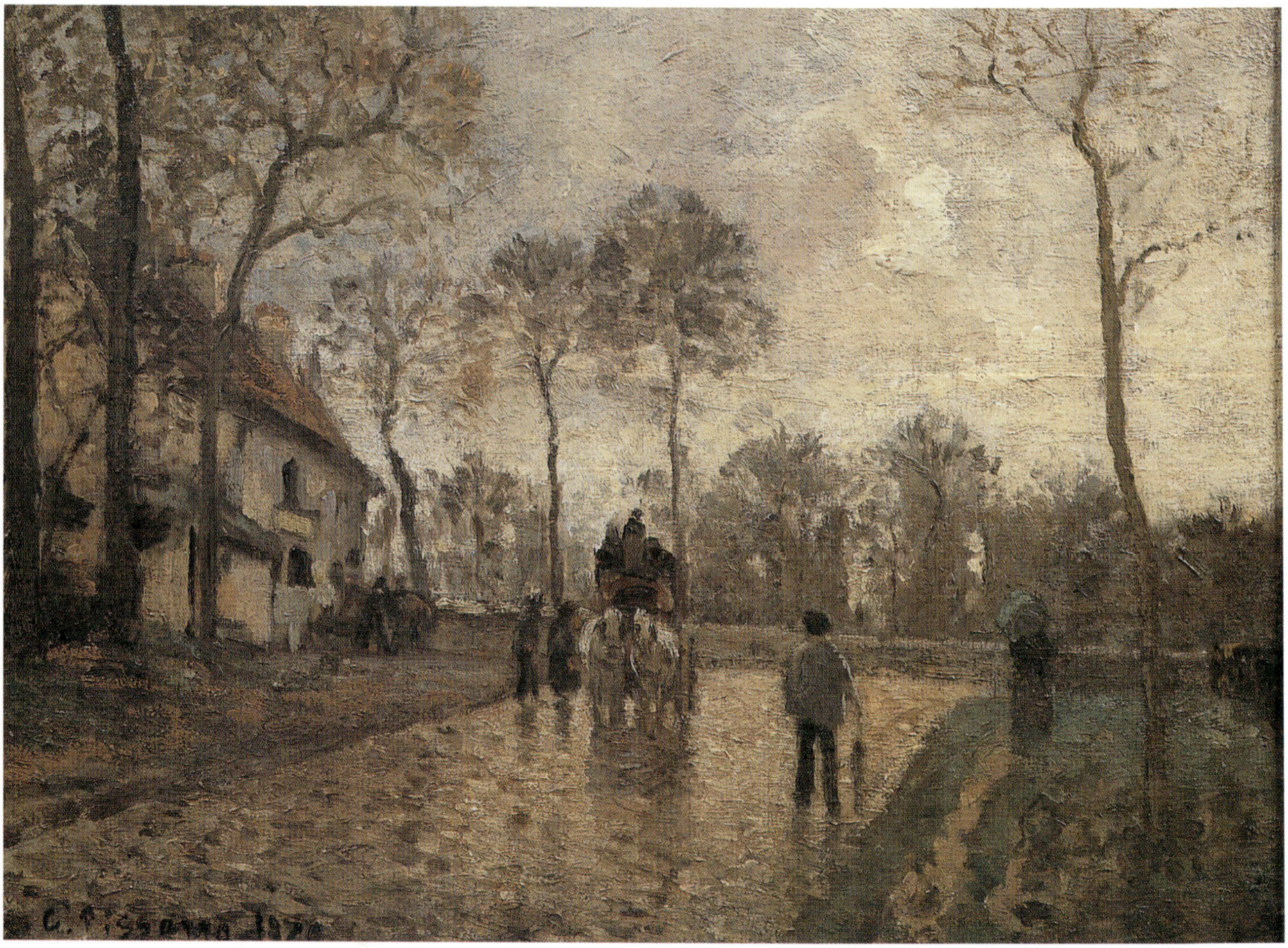

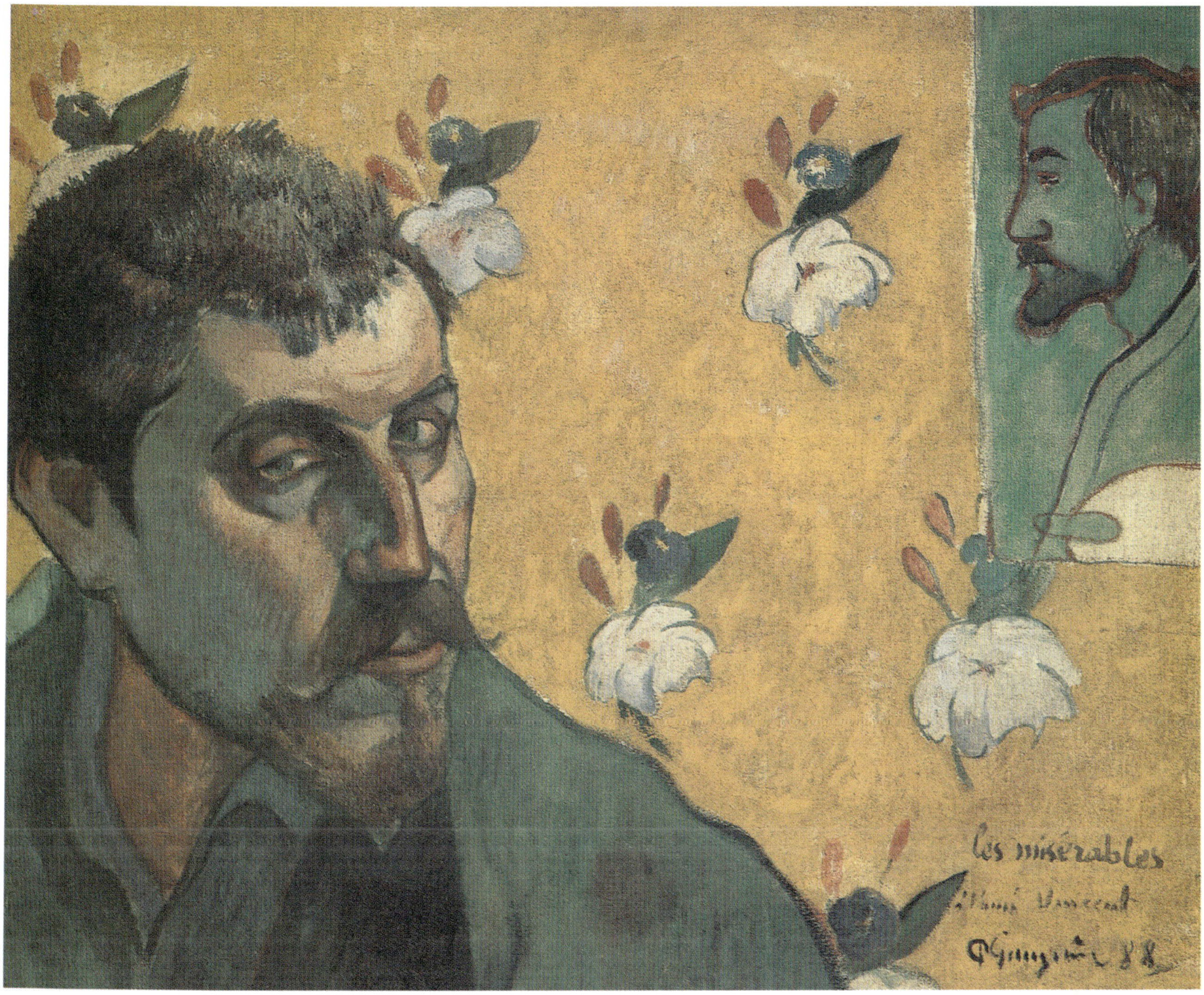

PAUL GAUGIUN
Les Misérables
1888, Van Gogh Museum, Amsterdam

As Gauguin explained to Van Gogh, the title of this self-portrait, was a reference to the "tormented hero" of Victor Hugo's novel. Gauguin saw in his own head "the mask of a... powerful ruffian... who has a certain nobility and inner kindness."

removed his family to Rouen, where Pissarro was working, and the cost of living cheap, and then to Copenhagen, where he tried unsuccessfully to make ends meet by selling waterproof canvas. Humiliations for Gauguin and his wife led to misunderstandings which were never resolved, and bred in Gauguin a hatred of the Danes, and in his wife an equal hatred for painting, as she discovered her best table linen used for canvas and her finest petticoat torn up for paint rags. Their lengthy correspondence of mutual reproach chronicles a constant demand for cash on her part and a statement of direst poverty on his, peppered with remarks from him on the relative ease and comfort of her life among her family and friends in comparison with his. However, although they were never to live together after 1885, Gauguin considered himself bound to her and their children, even occasionally thinking wistfully of their reunion as a family, and he also wrote to her about his painting.

Gauguin returned to Paris with his favorite son Clovis, and for a time lived in extreme poverty, eventually being reduced to bill-sticking to provide enough funds to nurse the boy through smallpox. His pursuit of art to the exclusion of almost every physical comfort; his rejection of family, career and physical well-being for a life of hardship which resulted in an early death from malnutrition exacerbated by syphilis, has become legendary, with Gauguin the exemplar of the heroic artists struggling against all odds in order to communicate his personal vision. As he shook off his domestic commitments Gauguin felt the heroic anima of the "Peruvian savage" assert itself.

The Brittany period

In 1886, having exhibited nineteen paintings in the

eighth and last Impressionist Exhibition, and having placed Clovis in a boarding school, Gauguin moved to Pont-Aven in Brittany. Free from the burden of fatherhood he could at last develop his art in the hard, primeval land to which the "barbarian" in him responded. "I love Brittany," he wrote to Schuffenecker in March 1888, during his second stay there, "I find there the savage, the primitive. When my clogs ring out on the granite soil I hear the dull, muted, powerful tone which I seek in my painting."

Brittany was the turning point in Gauguin's artistic development. Here, away from the influence of Paris and the Impressionists, he found the technical means to express the vision he had long held, intensified by a spell in Martinique in 1887, where he went in search of a tropical haven. He began to move away from naturalism toward suggestion, achieved by symbolic use of line, color and allusion to convey the expressive mood of his response to the subject. He was concerned now with the artist's interpretation of nature rather than with any virtuosity of technique in rendering external appearances.

Gauguin's realization of his personal means of expression reflects the desire of several artists to find new ways of interpreting nature. The avant-garde of the 1880s did not represent a cohesive art movement. The full flower of Impressionism had blossomed. Seurat and Signac, whom Gauguin described as "those petty chemical persons who pile up little dots" were extending an Impressionist concern with light into a more scientific formula. In French literary circles positivism and belief in the supremacy of the science-ideal engendered a reaction against naturalism, and the creation of a new literature based on imagination and feeling was beginning to

PAUL CÉZANNE
Still Life with Open Drawer
Private collection

Gauguin was given a still life by Cézanne and refused to part with it through the years of poverty, describing it as "a pearl...the apple of my eye." He jokingly urged Pissarro to drug Cézanne and make him talk in his sleep in order to discover his "secret," a joke which earned him Cézanne's dislike.

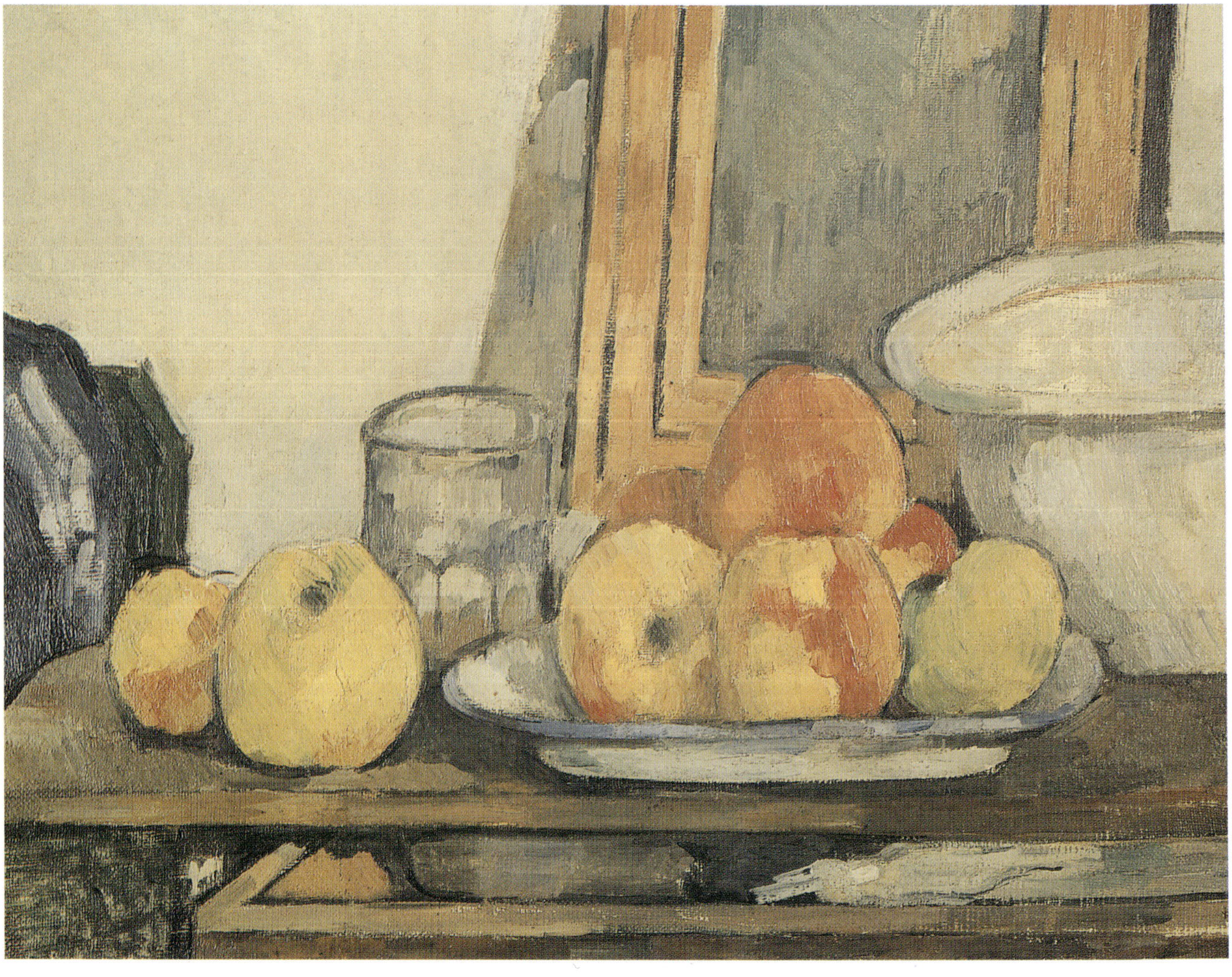

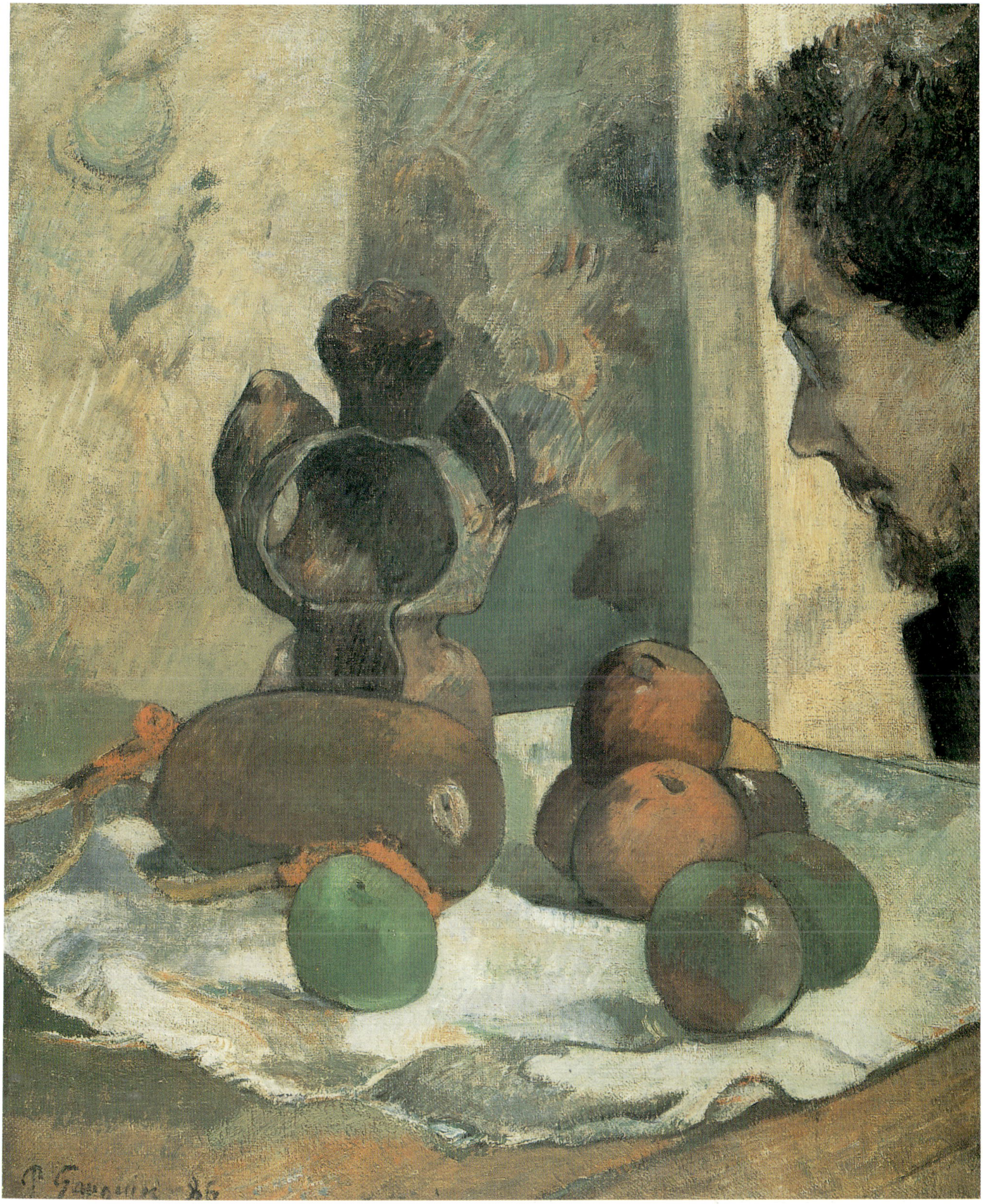

PAUL GAUGUIN
Still Life with Portrait of Charles Laval
1886, Private collection

On starting a new canvas Gauguin would say "Let's make a Cezanne!" The debt to Cézanne is evident here in the brushwork and the modeling of the fruit, but the cropping of Laval's head is a motif directly borrowed from Degas. The remarkable piece of sculpture is one of a number Gauguin made with Chapelet during 1886.

prevail against the dominance of the "sordid realism" of Emile Zola and the de Goncourt brothers. This anti-naturalism had earlier been espoused by the painter Eugène Delacroix and the poet and critic Charles Baudelaire, and now, informed by the literary debates of the 1880s, Gauguin found himself endorsing this position and cursing western society which "has fallen into the abominable error of naturalism."

The dominance of literary symbolism found a responsive chord in both Gauguin and Emile Bernard, a young artist he got to know during 1888 in Pont Aven. Both were moving toward the same resolution — the evolution of a style of painting where "Ideas dominate technique," and the attempt to create a visual poem through the symbolic use of line and color became Gauguin's principal aim. The strength of his taciturn but dominant personality attracted a number of the artists in the Pont-Aven circle, where he assumed the leading role. It was a source of mental anguish to Bernard that the creation of *synthétisme* was attributed to Gauguin just because of this dominance, when Bernard had "proof" of having painted works in the style before Gauguin's. However, Gauguin's remarkably inventive ceramics executed in 1887 — the year before his association with Bernard — show that he was already moving in a similar direction to that of the younger man.

PIERRE PUVIS DE CHAVANNES
The Poor Fisherman
1884, Musée d'Orsay, Paris

Puvis' primitivism and depiction of a simple lifestyle inevitably led to comparisons between his work and Gauguin's. Irritated by the suggestion that he should make his symbolism as clear as Puvis', Gauguin responded, "Puvis explains his ideas but does not paint them," adding, "he is the Greek while I am the savage."

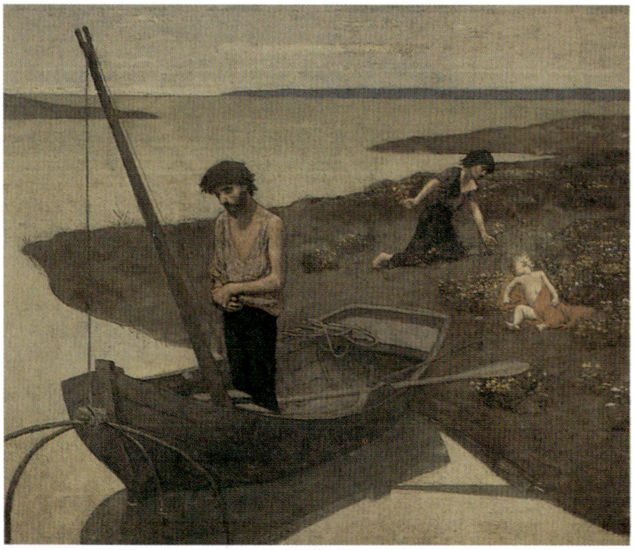

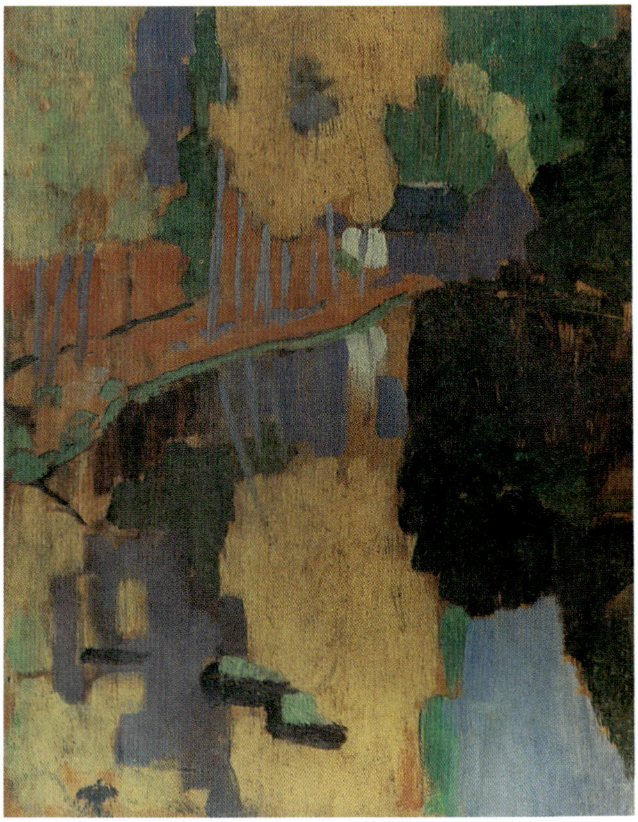

PAUL SERUSIER
The Talisman
1888, Musée d'Orsay, Paris

Serusier painted this tiny panel in the Bois d'Amour outside Pont-Aven under the direction of Gauguin, whom he greatly admired. In Paris it became, as the Symbolist painter Maurice Denis claimed, the key image for the evolution of the second generation of Symbolist artists.

The word synthetism was a catchword of the age, used to convey a sense of "artistic unity, harmonious composition, internal unity of conception, the understanding and the coherence of forms and colors." Bernard's search for a pictorial expression of literary symbolism resulted in the reduction of subject matter to its essentials; forms were simply expressed by means of a few lines; color was applied evenly and flatly, intensified by a dark outline which separated one color from another like a piece of stained glass or cloisonné enamel. Bernard's work was the final trigger in Gauguin's process of working out his artistic credo. "Art is an abstraction," he wrote to Schuffenecker in 1888. "Extract from nature by dreaming in front of it, and think more of the creation which will result ." His *Vision after the Sermon* (see page 603), the first product of the ideas which had crystallized over that summer, shows his individual response to the piety of the Bretons, and presents a personal, imaginary, non-naturalist image of a mental state.

GAUGUIN'S PAINTING METHODS

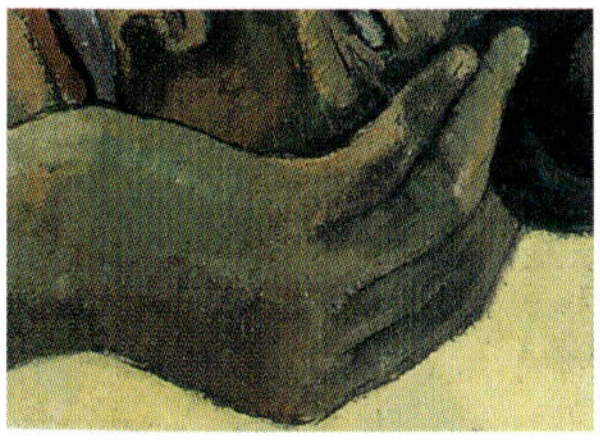

In this detail of Nevermore *we see the deep blue outline Gauguin frequently used to strengthen and define his forms.*

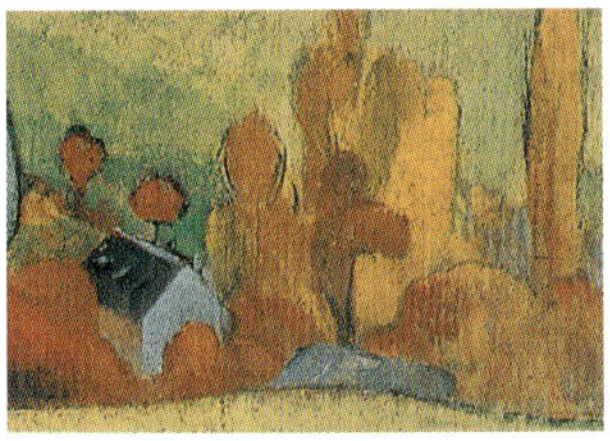

Although Gauguin's paintings give the impression of flat color, there are actually considerable variations in each individual area.

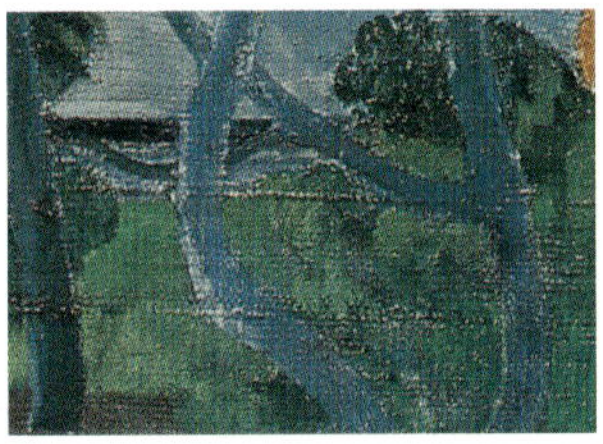

In this detail from Where Do We Come From? *the texture of the rough hessian canvas can be seen clearly. Often the canvas was left unprimed.*

Gauguin's painting technique was quite different from both that of the Impressionists, who applied their colors in small, opaque dabs, and that of Van Gogh, who used thick impastos and bold, expressionistic brushstrokes. Gauguin's paintings in the main are characterized by broad areas of color, relatively flat but nevertheless containing subtle variations of hue that give them a rich glow. He often added wax to his paints to give them extra smoothness and flow, and the paint is seldom thick, being thinnest at the edges of forms, where Prussian blue or earth red is often used to outline and strengthen the shapes. Sometimes parts of backgrounds were applied with a palette knife and then overlaid with thin, translucent paint put on with a brush.

In his Tahiti period he often painted on unprimed hessian, or sackcloth, and in many of the paintings done at the time the weave of the rough fabric is clearly visible through the paint. This was partly a consequence of his poverty, as was the thinness of the paint in some of his works, but he had begun to experiment with coarse canvas with Van Gogh in 1888, and found that the hairy surface of sackcloth enhanced the "barbaric" qualities he so much admired.

We know a good deal about his methods and the colors he used from his own copious writings and the following letter to the picture dealer Ambrose Vollard, written from La Dominique in March 1902, gives us an idea of the palette he favored at the time as well as of his financial problems.

Gauguin's palette in his Tahiti period probably consisted of the colors shown here plus lead white.

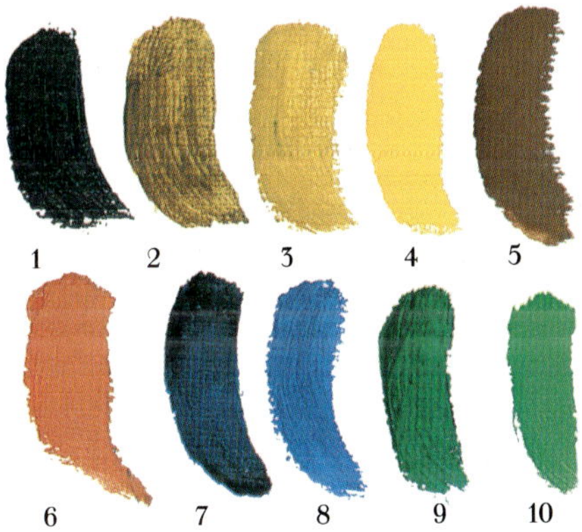

1 Black; 2 Raw sienna; 3 Yellow ocher; 4 Cadmium yellow; 5 Red earth (red ocher); 6 Vermilion; 7 Prussian blue; 8 Cobalt blue or ultramarine; 9 Viridian; 10 Emerald green.

Dear M. Vollard,
I have opened your box.
Canvas and glue — perfect
Japanese paper — perfect
But the colours!!!...What do you expect me to do with 6 tubes of white and terre verte, which I seldom use? I have only one small tube of carmine lake left. So you must send me immediately:
20 tubes of white
4 large tubes carmine lake
2 large tubes light vermilion
10 large tubes emerald green (Veronese)
5 large tubes yellow ochre
2 large tubes Ochre de Ru
2 large tubes red ochre
Powdered colour — Charron blue, ½ litre, large tube
... Now that I am in the mood for work I shall simply devour paints. So buy Lefranc's decorators' colours, they cost a third as much, especially as you get a dealer's discount, and they are much better.

Paul Gauguin

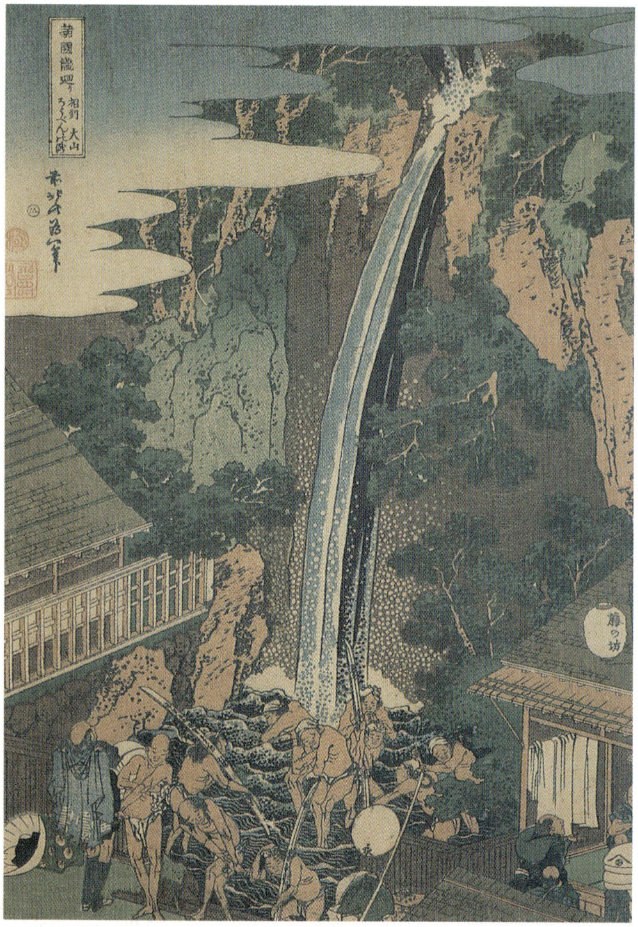

HOKUSAI
Waterfall of Roben
1827, Victoria and Albert Museum, London

Gauguin collected Japanese sketches and Hokusai prints. Like the Impressionists, all of whom were influenced by Japanese prints, he admired the features of this art form which cropped figures, flattened perspectives, used flat areas of unbroken color and dark outline, omitted shadow and simplified form.

The Tahiti period

But although Brittany was certainly the focus for the fermentation of Gauguin's art theory, Tahiti is the place most readily associated with his work. In Tahiti he continued to pursue his aim: "There are transformations every year, it is true" he wrote to his wife in 1892, "but they follow each other in the same direction." His iconography of the Tahiti period incorporates the solid, golden-skinned natives of the islands, with poses borrowed from both traditional western and eastern sources. He borrowed from the Parthenon frieze and pediment; from Javanese and Egyptian temple friezes; from Puvis de Chavannes and Manet; and from the Indian Buddha in his attempt to consolidate and reinterpret his personal symbolism. The harshness of the Brittany works, characterized by dark outlines and sharply angled perspectives, was now replaced by a gentler, more flattened, frieze-like, rhythmic arrangement, as seen in paintings like *The Market* and, *Where do we come from?* (see page 621). Symbolism has become more personal, the works more mysterious. His color range too, is more rich and varied, the jarring rust and yellow contrasts of *The Yellow Christ* being replaced by a light, bright palette, as in *The Market*, or by a rich sonorousness as in *Nevermore* (see page 617).

Gauguin had arrived a century too late to find in Tahiti an undiscovered country. Horrified at the inroads made by missionaries, who had inculcated ideas of sin in the islanders, and by French government officials, who had imposed bureaucracy on their simple way of life, Gauguin was active in urging the natives to resist both. In 1899 he even ceased painting to write about the injustices and corruption he had witnessed on the island. He viewed with horror the French women "dowdy from head to foot, with their superannuated finery, vulgar hips, tumble-down corsets, imitation jewelry, elbows that threaten you or look like sausages," regarding them as "enough to spoil any holiday in this country. But they are white – and their stomachs stick out!" He kept completely away from colonial life, preferring to dress and live "native," and to take as mistresses young Tahitian girls. The young native woman, he said, "even if she wanted to, could not be dowdy or ridiculous, for she has within her that sense of decorative beauty." This was something he had come to admire in the Tahitian's art.

The inner vision

For Gauguin, the artist was a heroic figure, possessed by a desire to reject all that was not connected with his calling. The idea of the artist as a man of inner vision is an important element in any subsequent evaluation of an artist for whom technique was to become subordinate to message. Gauguin saw the sublimity of a work of art as quite unconnected with the kind of manual dexterity admired by the Academicians. He scorned Academy-trained painters, like Bouguereau, who did no more than render the exterior of an object naturalistically, and stressed the artist's sacramental role in giving outward form to the Idea. The discrepancy between the length of time needed for the execution of a work and the inevitable fluctuation in intensity of feeling troubled him: "Where does the execution of a painting come from and where does it end?" The two, he felt, ought to be simultaneous; the result of "that moment, when the most intense emotions are fused in the depths of one's being, when they burst forth and when thought comes up like lava from a volcano ... like an explosion." He believed almost in the pre-existence of a work of art:

"The work is created suddenly, brutally if you like, and is not its appearance great, almost super-human?"

Gauguin realized the quality of his legacy to later painters, remarking, "The public owes me nothing since my pictorial oeuvre is only relatively good, but the painters of today who are benefiting from this newborn freedom do owe me something." By his own admission his technique was only relatively good, but his "inventive originality" was important for the subsequent development of twentieth-century art. He was in the vanguard of those who rejected the naturalist tradition of treating only the exterior world, and regarded the "mysterious center of thought," man's inner response to nature, of paramount importance. His championing of the so-called primitive forms of art, especially that of the South Seas, influenced the vogue for Primitivism in the first two decades of the twentieth century, and his rejection of western materialism in favor of a primitive idyll made a great impact on subsequent generations of artists.

PAUL GAUGUIN
La Plage du Pouldu
1889, Private collection

Gauguin saw in Japanese art the reflection of a simple and composed lifestyle. "The great error is in the Greek," he wrote, "we need to seek the clearest form." He preferred the flatness of Egyptian decorative art or the Japanese woodcut to the classical western tradition, and in this painting the Japanese influence is very evident.

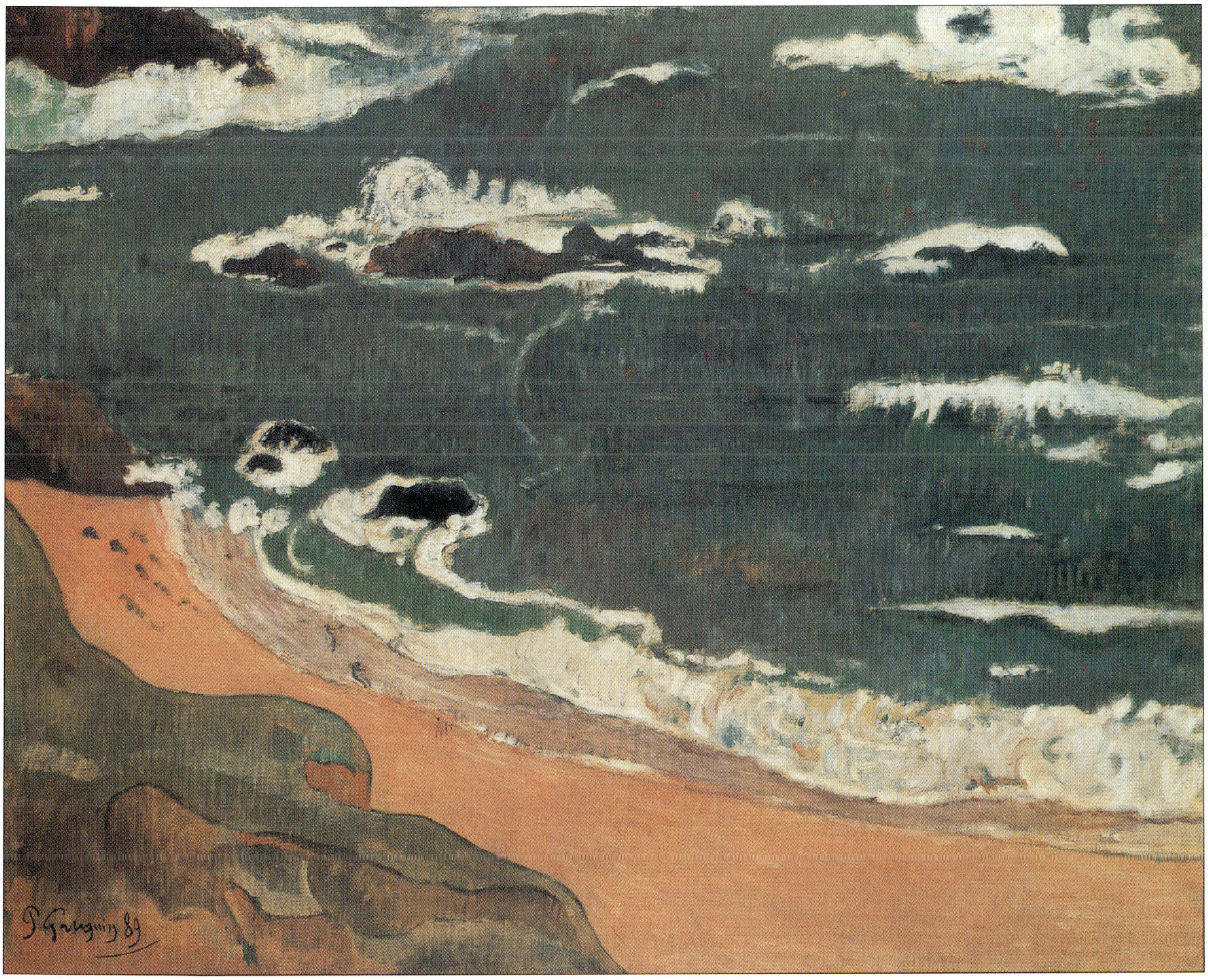

CHRONOLOGY OF GAUGUIN'S LIFE

1848 June: Paul Gauguin born.

1849 Family sets sail for Lima, Peru.

1855-65 Family returns to France. Gauguin joins merchant navy in 1865.

1868-71 Military service in the French navy. Leaves navy in 1871. Gustave Arosa finds him work with the Parisian banker Bertin. Meets Emile Schuffenecker.

1873 Summer: Begins to paint under the tutelage of Arosa's painter daughter Marguerite. November: marries Mette Sophie Gad.

1874 First son Emile is born in August.

1876 *Landscape at Viroflay* accepted by the Salon. Begins to buy paintings.

1877 Meets Pissarro. Starts to collect Impressionist paintings. December: daughter Aline is born.

1879-82 Exhibits with the Impressionists. Two further sons born.

1883 Gives up job to devote himself to painting. December: Fourth son born.

1884 Moves with his family to Rouen..

1885 Joins his wife and family in Copenhagen. June: Returns to Paris with son Clovis.

1886 In desperate poverty. Puts Clovis in boarding school. Shows paintings in 8th and last Impressionist Exhibition. Spends June-November in Pont Aven, Brittany. Breaks with Pissarro. Sees much of Degas. Meets Van Gogh.

1887 April: Sets off for Panama "to live like a savage." June: In Martinique. Becomes ill, works his passage back to Marseilles.

1888 February: Returns to Pont-Aven. October: Joins Van Gogh in Arles, returning to Paris in December.

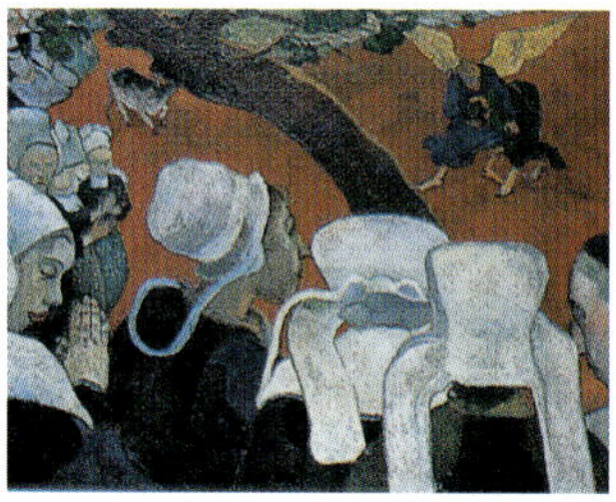

Vision after the Sermon: Jacob Wrestling with the Angel

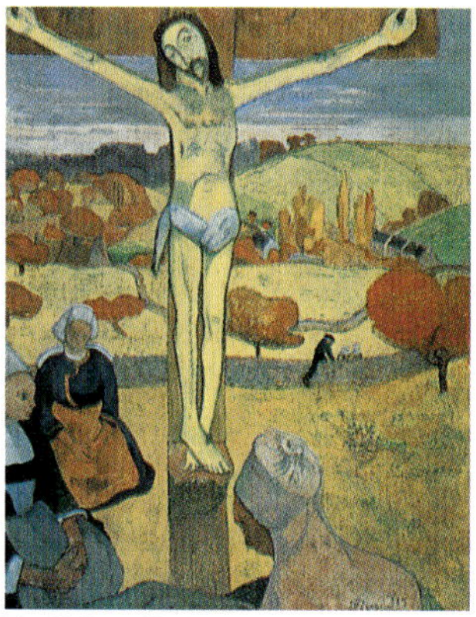

The Yellow Christ

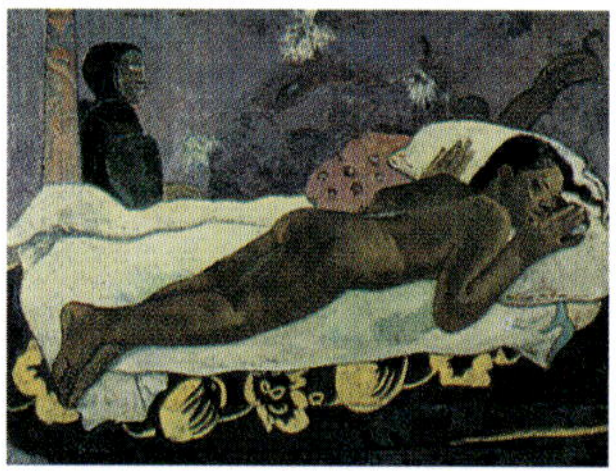

Manao Tupapau: The Spirit of the Dead Keeps Watch

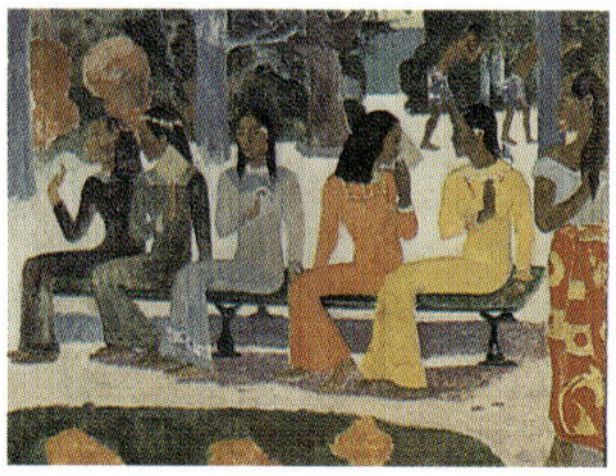

Ta Matete: The Market

1889 June: Exhibits with friends at the Café Volpini. Returns to Brittany.

1890 Working in Paris and Brittany. Close contact with Symbolists.

1891 Decides to leave for Tahiti. Has relationship with Juliette Huet, who later bears him a daughter. March: Goes to Copenhagen to bid his family farewell. Banquet held in his honour at the Café Voltaire, presided over by Mallarmé. April: Departs for Tahiti, arriving in May. August: In hospital, coughing blood.

1892 Begins to compile book about Tahitian folklore. Lives with thirteen-year-old Tehamana.

1893 August: Returns to France. Inherits a small legacy. Lives with Anna "the Javanese." Starts to write *Noa Noa*, an idealized account of primitive life in Tahiti.

1895 Suffering from syphilis, sells up and returns to Tahiti. Settles with fourteen-year-old Pahura.

1897 Ill and depressed, decides to commit suicide after painting his largest picture *Where Do We Come From?*

1898 January: Takes arsenic but fails to kill himself.

1901 Moves to the Marquesas. Settles with fourteen-year-old Vaeoho.

1902 Incites natives against colonial government. Vaeoho bears him a daughter. Starts writing his *Intimate Journals.*

1903 Accused by authorities of libel and stirring up anarchy. Sentenced to three months imprisonment. Appeals but dies on 8 May, aged fifty-five.

THE PAINTINGS

Pont d'Iena

1875

$25\frac{1}{2} \times 36\frac{3}{4}$in/$64.7 \times 92$cm

Oil on canvas

Louvre, Paris

Gauguin did not start to paint until he was twenty-five, when Marguerite, the painter daughter of his guardian Gustave Arosa, taught him the technique of oils in the summer of 1873. Inspired by Arosa's collection of contemporary work, and encouraged by Marguerite, Gauguin's interest in art received a further stimulus from his association with Emile Schuffenecker, who was also an employee of the banking firm of Bertin where Gauguin had worked since 1871. Schuffenecker urged Gauguin to join him on Sunday excursions to the outskirts of Paris to draw and paint, and also to accompany him on occasional evening visits to the Atelier Colarossi to draw from the life model.

Gauguin soon followed Arosa's example and began to amass his own collection of avant-garde paintings, initially the naturalistic but freely handled landscapes by artists such as Corot, Jongkind and Pissarro but later the more revolutionary work by the group of painters who came to be called the Impressionists. The basis of Gauguin's art training was thus the close study of actual works of art rather than a formal studio training, and so he did not feel the same need as other artists to rebel against academic teaching practices or the dominant artistic conventions of the day.

The Impressionists themselves rejected the traditional academic art theories insisted upon by the Salon, preferring to develop the freer painting technique of Delacroix, who had in turn been influenced by the color and freshness of the English landscape painters. Courbet, with his non-academic subject matter, and the outdoor (*plein air*) painters of the Barbizon school were also important influences in the new movement which sought to cut across fossilized tradition. Historical and religious themes, regarded by the Salon as the only proper ones for a serious artist, were now rejected in favor of landscapes or city scenes depicting modern life, and the traditional painting methods, of drawing from a model in the studio, preparing sketches, and then producing contour outlines to be "painted in" were replaced by a much more direct approach. The Impressionists preferred to work out of doors, attempting to catch the impression of a fleeting moment by means of bold dashes of prismatic color.

This painting, done after two years of self-tuition, resembles a Monet of the same date, both in the choice of subject matter and in the handling, particularly of the sky, which is similar to that in Monet's *Westminster Bridge* of 1871. The treatment of the water does not, however, reflect Monet's bold technique of applying dashes of unmixed color; the effect produced here is therefore calmer and more reminiscent of Pissarro's finely handled snow-scenes. The influence of Pissarro was remarked on by the novelist Huysmans, who described Gauguin's paintings exhibited at the Impressionist show as "dilutions of the still-hesitant works of Pissarro." Pissarro was to remain a major influence for over six years, and this work demonstrates how competently Gauguin had absorbed the ideas and techniques he had studied. Small dabs of the gray-violet range laid next to each other give a snow-laden feel to the sky, and snow-capped trees are realized with a few touches of the brush. Although Gauguin was never to acknowledge Pissarro as his master in the way Cézanne had, he learned much from this artist whom he was later to despise for always following artistic fashions to the detriment of his own personal vision.

It was also through Pissarro's influence that Gauguin was able to exhibit at the Impressionist Exhibitions, against the wishes of certain other members, and he became allied with the group until the development of his own artistic credo in the 1880s led him to reject the Impressionists' technique, which he came to disapprove of because it "dwelt too much on the outward form and not on the mysterious center of things."

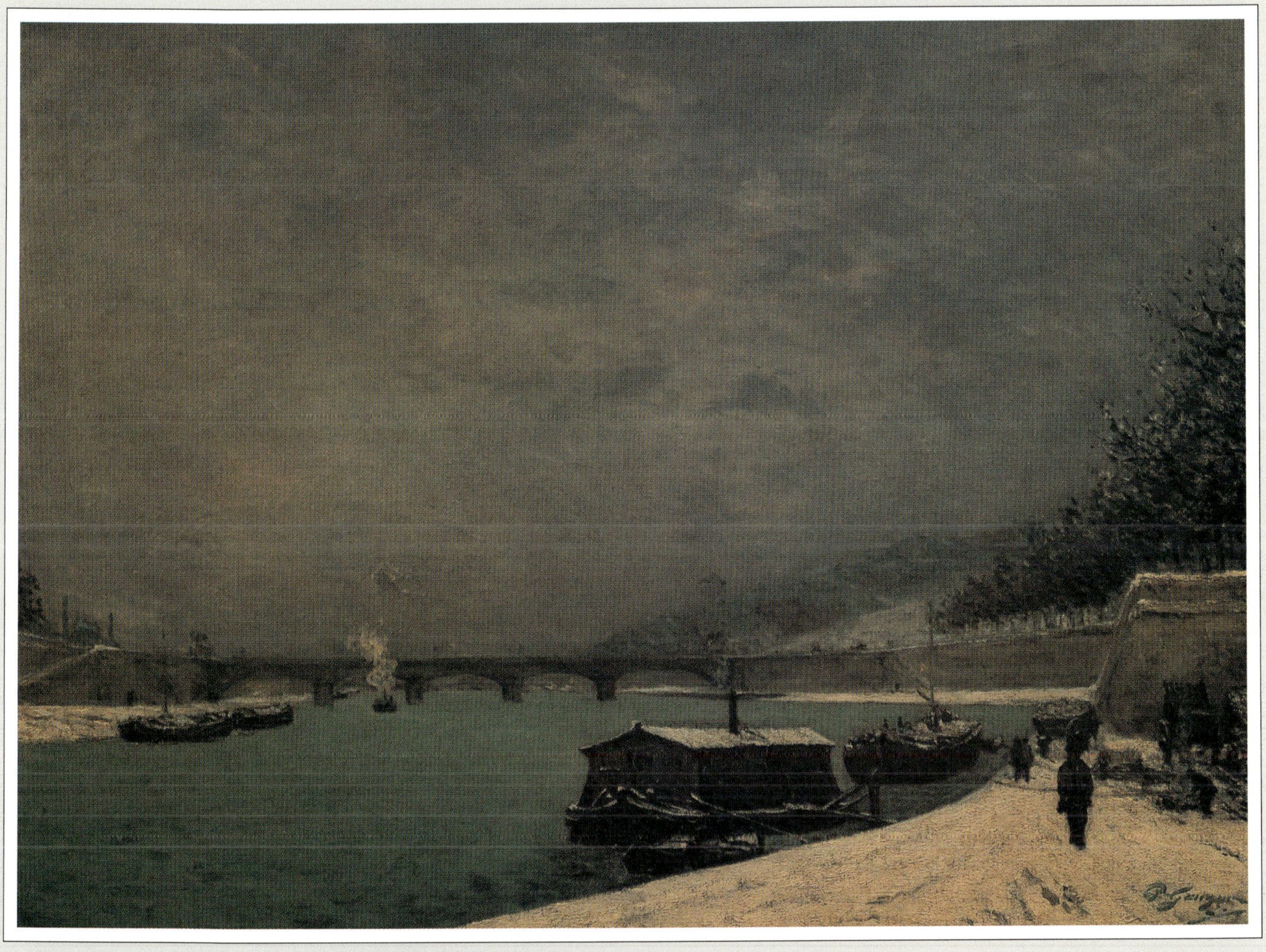

This early work is painted in the idiom of the Impressionists, whose first exhibition Gauguin had seen in 1874. The subject matter is an everday scene: a winter riverscape. Following established tradition, the horizon cuts across the lower third of the canvas, above which the remaining two-thirds of the painting is occupied by sky. The influence of Japanese prints was the principle source of Gauguin's later rejection of this technique; open sky is rarely apparent in his mature work, where perspective is to a large degree flattened. This painting shows how ably he had absorbed the technique and style of Pissarro and the Impressionists.

1

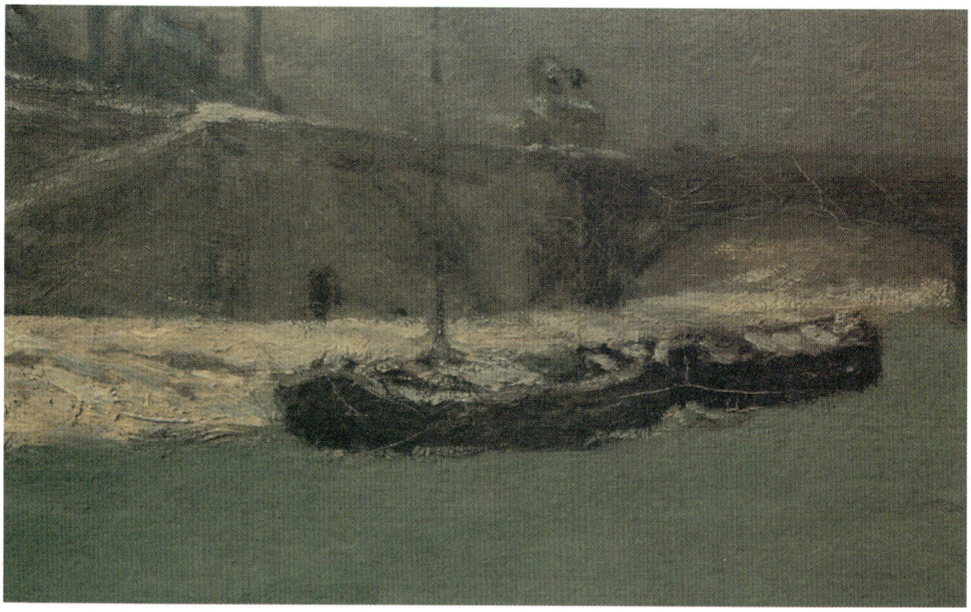

2

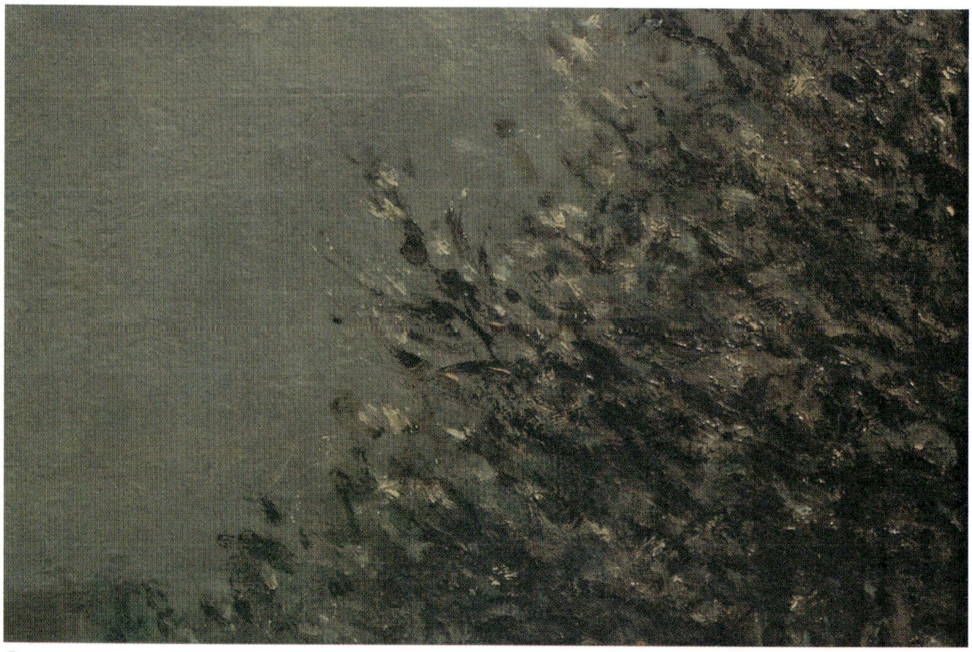

3

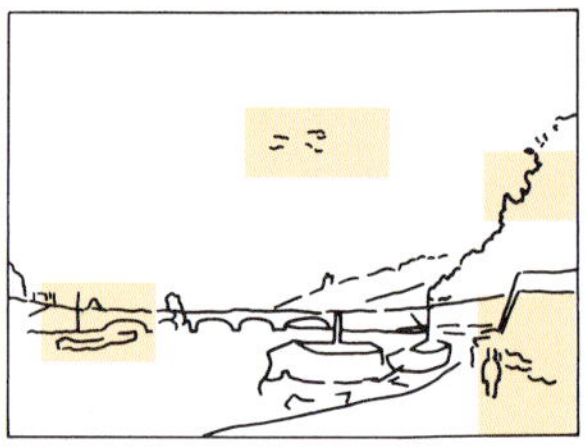

1 The sky is treated with dabs of green-blue, white, cream and pink. Color is less important than tone in this early work. It is reminiscent of Monet's treatment of the sky in his *Westminster Bridge*, although here the paint is not laid down in short brushstrokes of pure color but in dashes of pre-mixed pigment.

2 Unlike the treatment of the sky the river shows a much denser application of thick paint unbroken by brushwork or color harmonies. The effect of snow on the bank is created by dabs of color in the same tonal range, and the wall surface with a thinner application of monochromatic color.

3 The trees are realized with light, impressionistic touches of the brush, but color harmonies are not derived from the Impressionist selection of primaries but taken from a more naturalistic, less experimental tradition which uses the brown-green range, tipped with dashes of Naples yellow and white.

4 *Actual size detail* Highly reminiscent of Pissarro's snow-scenes, these figures are monochromatic and solid, not impressionistic either in color or technique. The effect of ridged snow is created by a thick application of mixed color in the cream, gray and pink tonal range.

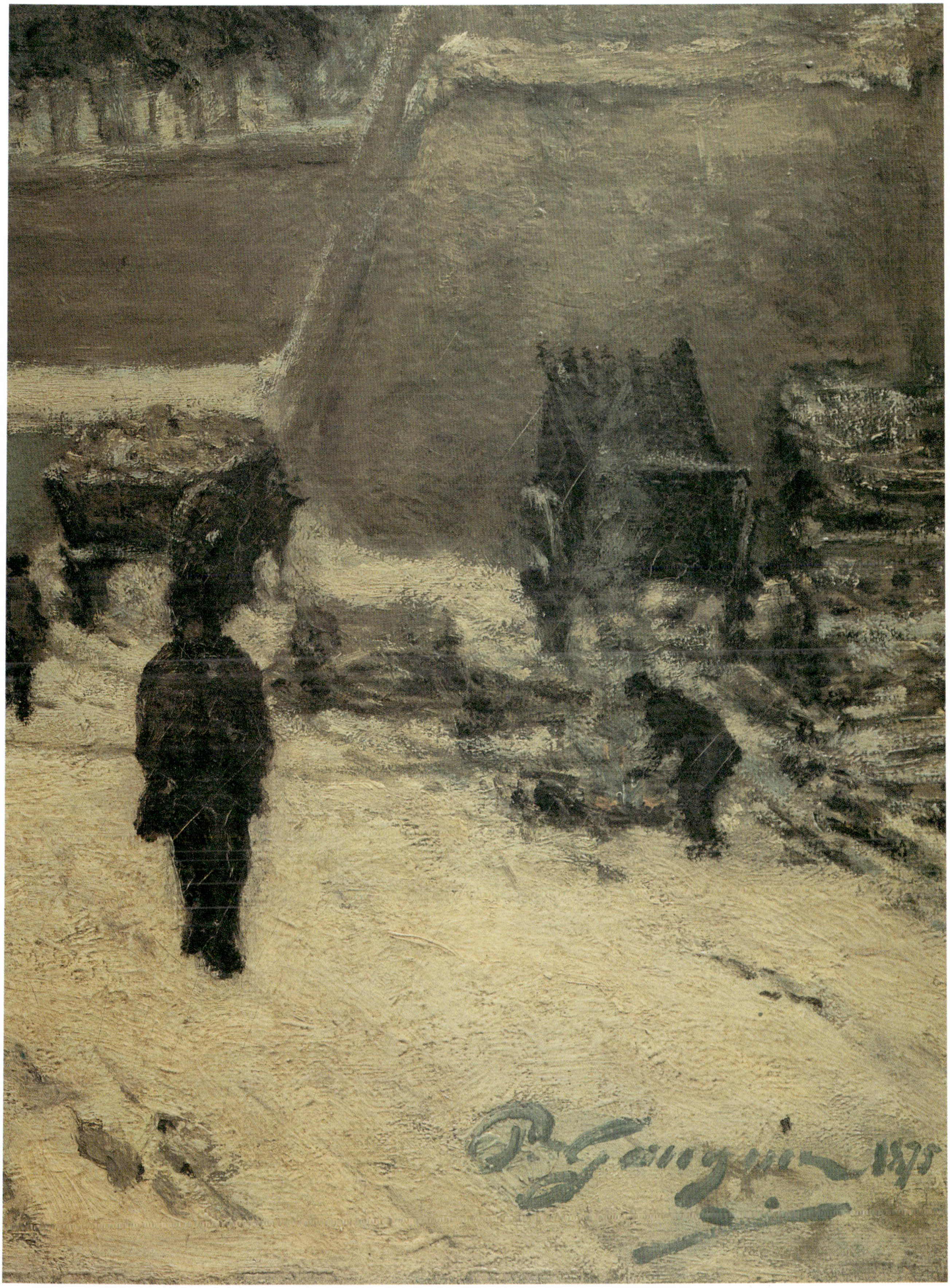

4 *Actual size detail*

Vision After the Sermon: Jacob Wrestling with the Angel

1888

$25\frac{1}{2} \times 36\frac{3}{4}$in/64.7×92cm

Oil on canvas

Jeu de Paume, Louvre, Paris

This work, Gauguin's first masterpiece, is a clear expression of his aims in painting, a crystallization of the ideas on art which he had developed in Pont-Aven that year. It represents not only Jacob's struggles, as seen in the minds of the pious Bretons, but also Gauguin's own struggle, his grappling with technique to convey his newly realized ideas.

Writing to Van Gogh in the same year, Gauguin said "I believe I have attained in these figures a great rustic and superstitious simplicity. It is all very severe ... To me in this painting the landscape and the struggle exist only in the imagination of these real people and the struggle in this landscape which is not real and which is out of proportion."

Although disdainful of the Catholic teaching he had received at school, Gauguin was impressed by the simple faith of the Breton women, whose traditional headdress and bearing reminded him of a religious order. It is not a religious picture so much as a painting of religious people, and more ambitiously, it attempts to show the strength of their faith. The scene was inspired by the piety of the peasant women, whose response to the sermon they have just heard evokes a vision of the struggle with evil.

The biblical scene is sited at the upper right of the canvas, separated from the praying group of women and priest in the foreground and righthand edge of the picture. The diagonal sweep of the apple tree, a pictorial device borrowed from Japanese art, divides the real from the visionary in both a literal and a symbolic way. The cropping of the foreground figures, the rejection of traditional perspective, the flattening of form, and the rejection of shadows also show the influence of Japanese prints, an influence which was felt by all those associated with Impressionism. Simplification of figures and flat unmodeled areas of bright color had already been practiced by Emile Bernard, twenty years Gauguin's junior, and had profoundly influenced Gauguin; both artists had been impressed by folk woodcuts and medieval stained-glass windows. A return to a simpler, cruder, more archaic style, both of life and of art, was what Gauguin now sought.

Stress on composition and form are not accidental in this painting, which was intended as a kind of demonstration of the essentials of a "synthetic" work of art, in which the effect was achieved by the internal unity of color, line, form and composition. The influence of Bernard is apparent in the use of unmixed colors applied in large areas and bounded by a blue-black line to increase their intensity. Bernard had been producing pictures of this sort before Gauguin's masterpiece, but Gauguin's own ceramics of the previous year show that both artists were moving in the same direction, needing to free themselves from the traditional western practice of naturalism in favor of a spiritual quest to discover the inner nature of the subject.

On the frame of his painting Gauguin wrote in blue letters, "a gift of Tristan de Moscoso," and offered it to the local church at Nizon, interested to learn the effect his Vision would produce on the congregation. However, having satisfied himself that the picture was not a hoax, the curé rejected it on the grounds that the parishioners would not understand it.

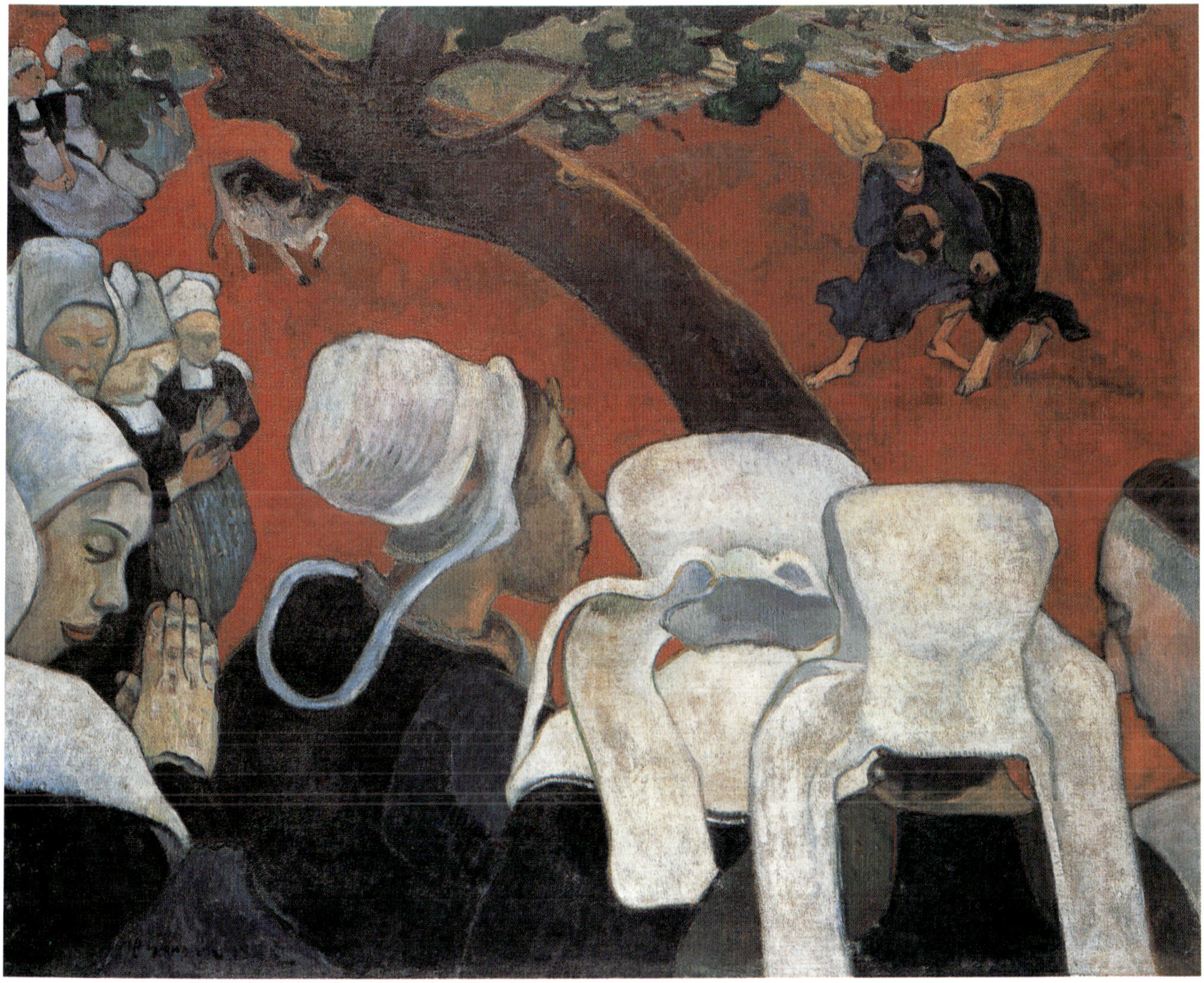

Unlike Gauguin's earlier work this painting depicts an imaginary setting. It represents a definite break from the Impressionists, with whom Gauguin had become increasingly dissatisfied because of their concern with the outward appearance of things. He was seeking a means of expressing abstract emotional qualities in his paintings, and here he is conveying his personal reaction to Breton piety. The assertiveness with which he seems to have embraced this newly found technique is reflected in the work. The composition is dramatically bisected by a strong diagonal, either side of which the imaginary and the actual are boldly realized.

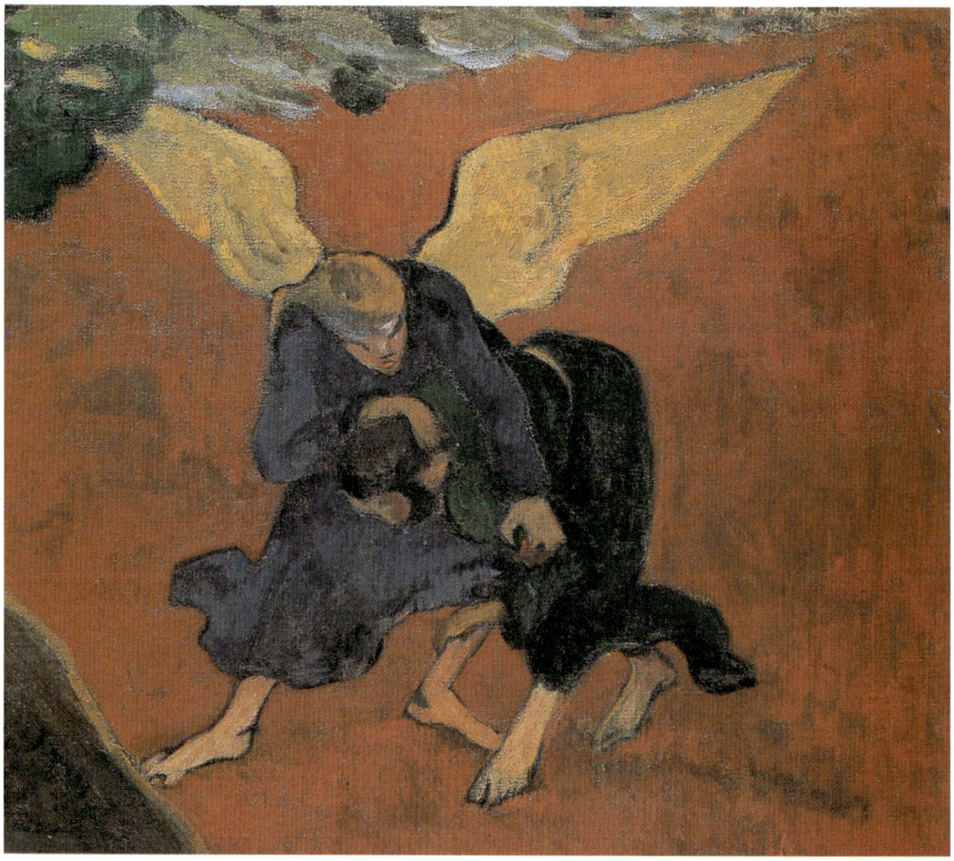

1

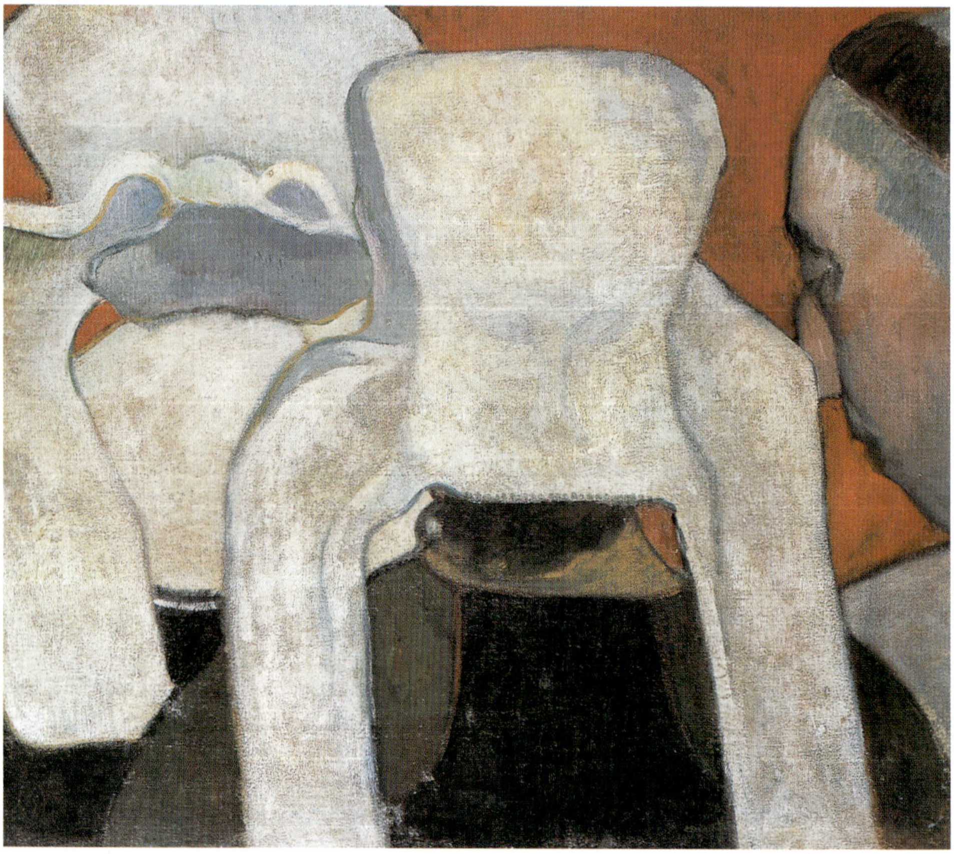

2

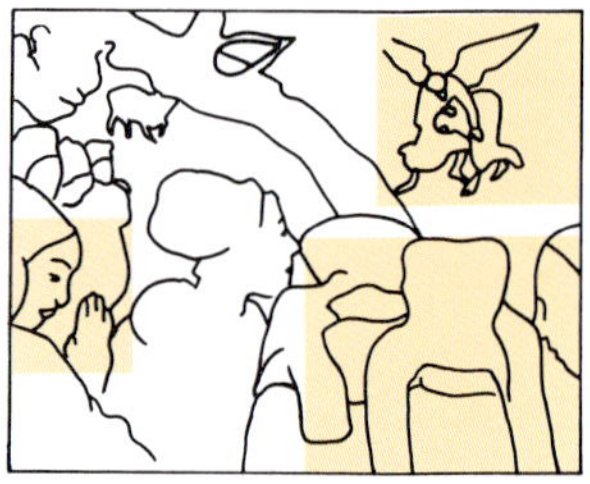

1 The figures of Jacob and the Angel are based on those of the Japanese artist Hokusai, whose art Gauguin greatly admired. Modeling has been replaced by the use of flat areas of color intensified by a dark outline.

2 The cropped profile of the priest is a feature borrowed from both Japanese art and Degas. The headdress and collars are treated as flat white areas, shadowed with pale blue, brushed on in vertical strokes. They are seen almost as abstract forms rather than representations of people.

3 *Actual size detail* This profile of the praying woman shows features borrowed from Japanese prints, folk art, and medieval stained-glass windows. The face is barely modeled, and is boldly highlighted in white. The lower lip, formed with a crimson stroke, takes up the background color. Features, headdress, and hands are outlined in Prussian blue.

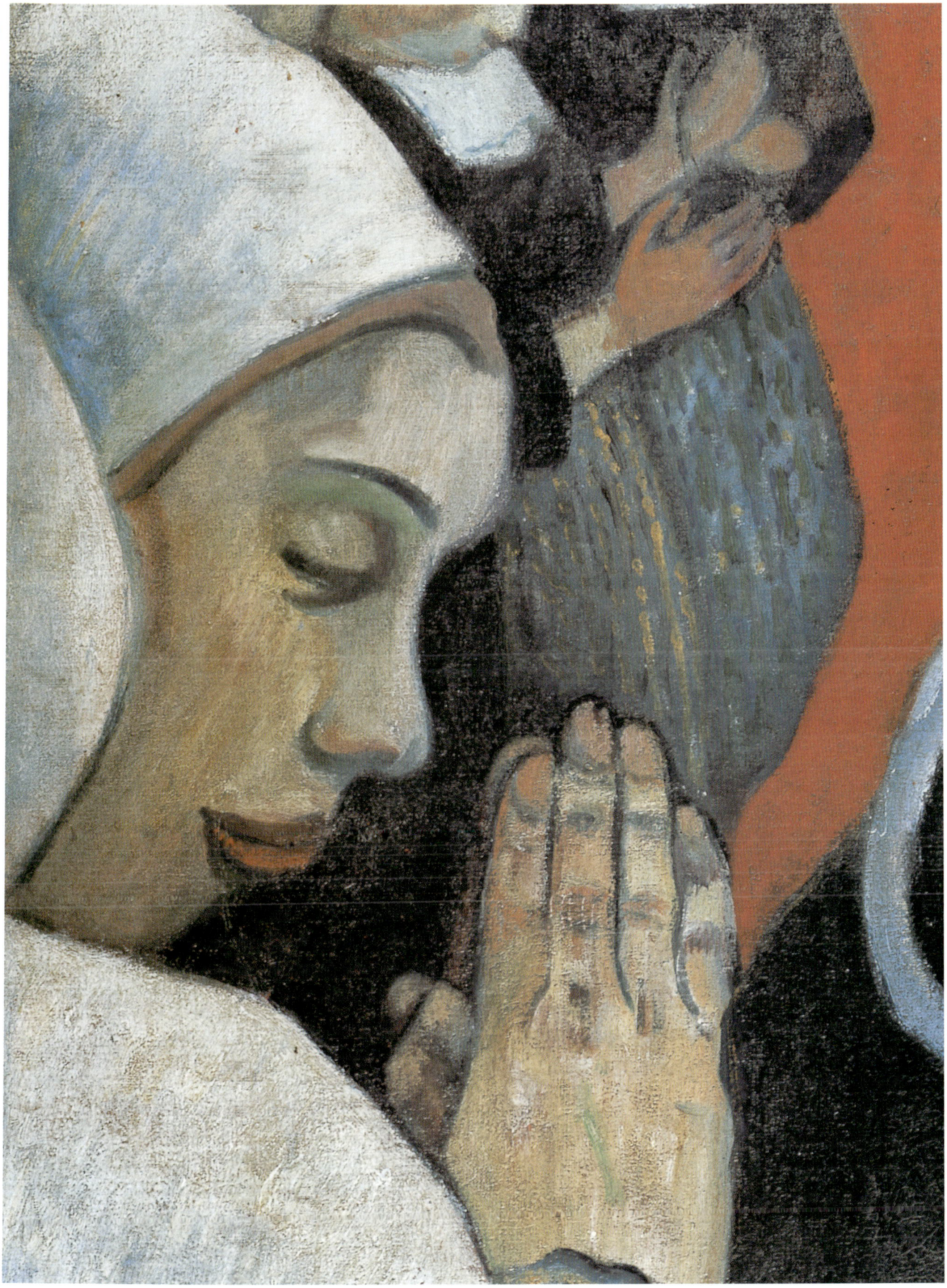

3 *Actual size detail*

Van Gogh Painting Sunflowers

1888

$29\frac{1}{4} \times 36\frac{3}{4}$in/$73 \times 92$cm

Oil on canvas

Van Gogh Museum, Amsterdam

Following Van Gogh's invitation to join him at his studio in Arles, Gauguin arrived from Brittany in October 1888. The "primitive" Gauguin found Vincent's beloved town in the south too "pretty and paltry," and made no attempt to conceal his feelings. Fifteen years later Gauguin wrote of the period the two spent together:

"For a long time I have wanted to write about Van Gogh ... in order to correct an error which has been going around in certain circles." The error referred to was, of course, Gauguin's contributory role in the madness and eventual death of Van Gogh himself and then of his brother Theo. "It so happens," acknowledged Gauguin, "that several men who have been a good deal in my company and in the habit of discussing things with me have gone mad. This was true of the Van Gogh brothers, and certain malicious persons have childishly attributed their madness to me." While Gauguin cannot be blamed for the instability of the Van Goghs — a sister who never met Gauguin also went mad — his visit certainly caused a great strain.

Having formed his own ideas on painting, and assumed the role of "Master" at Pont-Aven, Gauguin "undertook the task of enlightening" Vincent. The relationship was seen by both as that of master and pupil. "Van Gogh, without losing an ounce of his originality, learned a fruitful lesson from me. And every day he thanked me for it."

The lesson lay in instructing Van Gogh not to paint too much after nature but from the imagination. Gauguin also discouraged "all this work in complementary colors [which] accomplished nothing but the mildest of incomplete and monotonous harmonies. The sound of the trumpet was missing in them." He was also critical of Vincent's untidiness: "I found a disorder that shocked me. His colorbox could hardly contain all those tubes, crowded together and never closed."

Gauguin wrote of his painting, "The idea occurred to me to do his portrait while he was painting the still-life he loved so much ... when the portrait was finished he said to me 'It is I, but I gone mad'." The remark was a prelude to the recurring bouts of madness Vincent experienced. "That very evening" wrote Gauguin, "we went to the café. Suddenly he flung the glass and its contents at my head. I avoided the blow and, taking him bodily in my arms left the café." The following evening while taking a walk Gauguin related the events which indicate the intensity of Van Gogh's unbalanced state of mind: "I ... turned as Vincent rushed toward me, an open razor in his hand. My look at that moment must have had great power in it, for he stopped." Vincent's subsequent action with the razor, the incident of the severed ear, washed and consigned to a prostitute to give to Gauguin as a souvenir, is well known. It ended the relationship as far as Gauguin was concerned, although he depended on the efforts of Theo, Vincent's younger brother the picture dealer, for the sale of his paintings. Vincent's suicide in 1892 brought on Theo's despair and death the following year, which dashed Gauguin's immediate financial hopes.

The portrait shows a deliberate flattening of form — Gauguin found modeling a "moral deceit" — the right hand is barely modeled, and the texture of the canvas clearly visible beneath the paint emphasizes this two-dimensional quality. The cropping of the left shoulder, lower arm and chair shows the influence of Japanese prints. Gauguin wrote that he found in Arles "a combination of a colorful Puvis and Japanese art. The women here have elegant headdresses and a Greek beauty." Although Theo was perplexed as to why Japanese and Greek ideals of beauty were continually aimed at in Gauguin's aesthetic, the artist himself saw the art of the Japanese as "simple and composed."

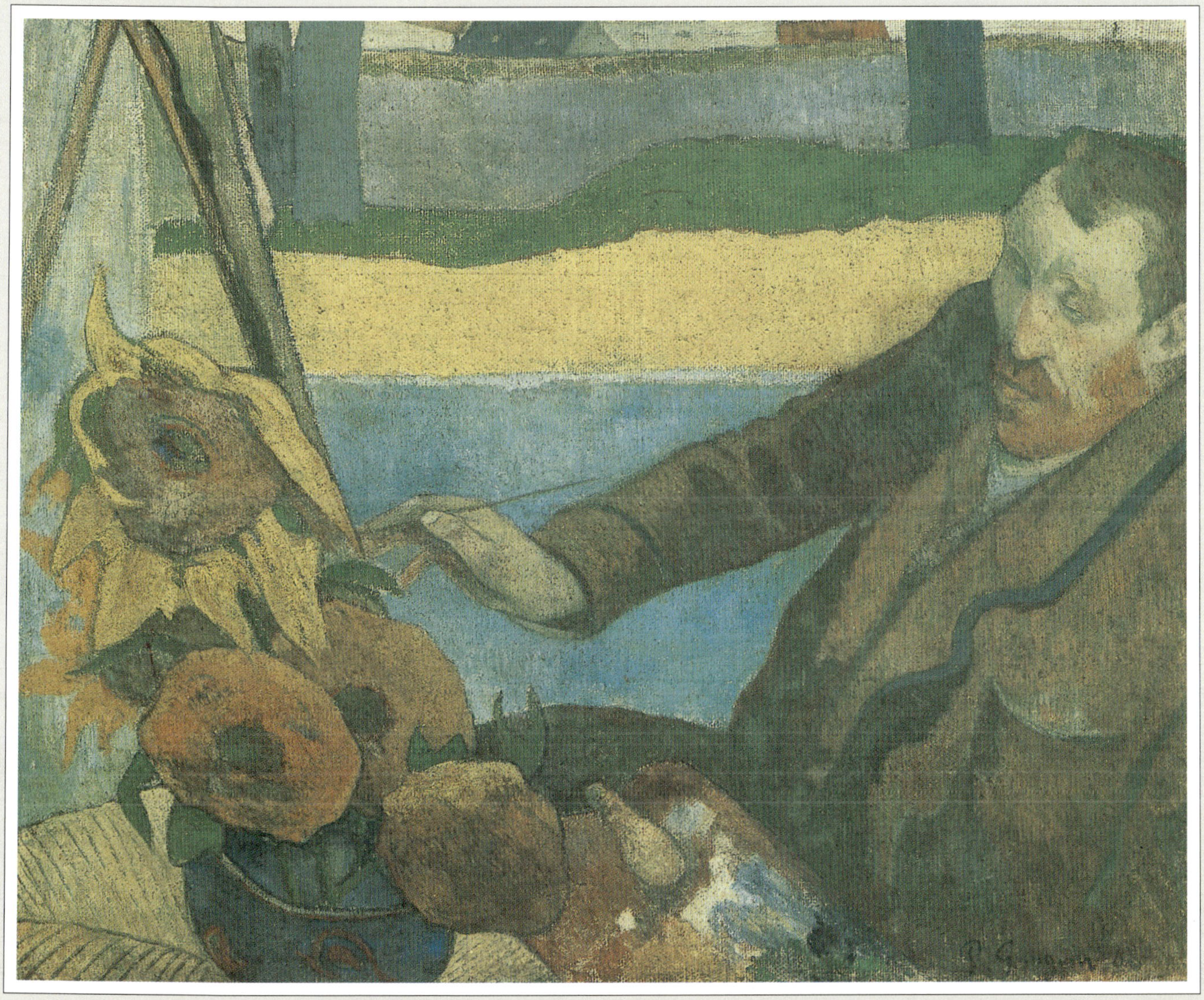

This portrait of Van Gogh at work on his favorite subject was painted during the couple of months the two artists worked together in the south of France. Originally they were both to have painted each other's portraits, but Van Gogh found Gauguin too intimidating a subject to work on. The composition balances two strong diagonals formed, on the right side, by the artist's arm, and on the left by the easel, sunflower petal and palette. The resulting void presents a curious, empty, abstract landscape of layered color, topped by a series of roofs between the blue-gray verticals of the flanking tree trunks. Naturalistic setting has been rejected for a decorative, abstracted background.

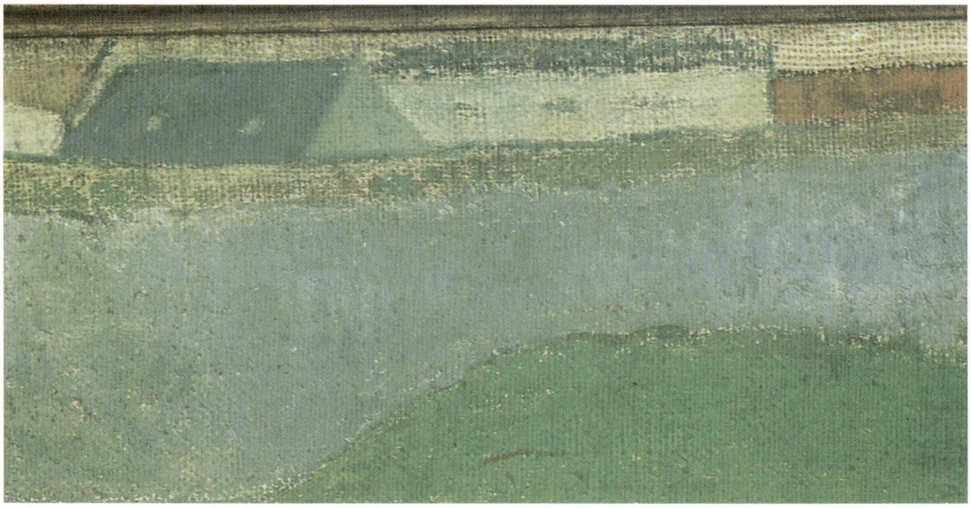

1

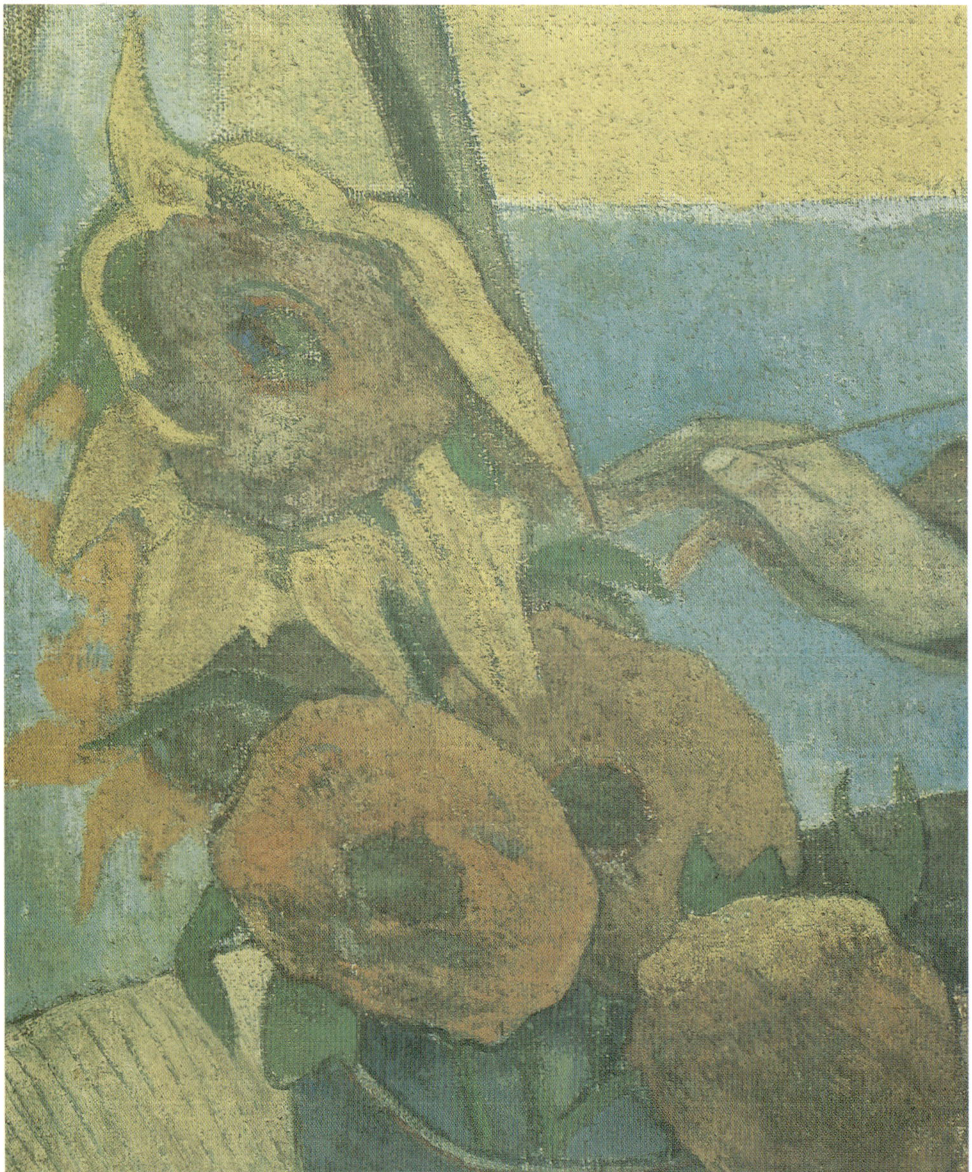

2

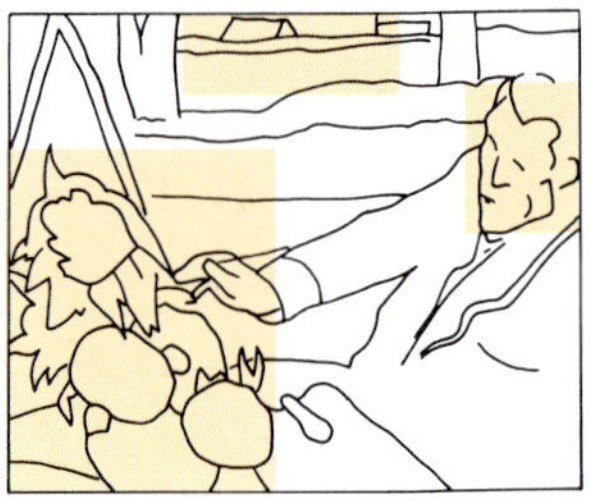

1 The treatment of the background shows how Gauguin rejected modeling in favor of an approach which flattens and does not "deceive" the viewer; he regarded modeling as dishonest. Shapes are outlined, as are the forms in Japanese prints, and the two-dimensional quality is further exaggerated by the way the paint does not conceal the texture of the canvas.

2 Van Gogh's beloved sunflowers give the color key to the painting, which everywhere echoes the yellows, rusts, browns, greens and blues of the flowers and vase. Van Gogh's blue-trimmed brown suit follows through the color harmonies, which are also reflected in the central abstracted landscape.

3 *Actual size detail* It is interesting to note the physical likeness to Gauguin himself in this portrait of Van Gogh. It was possibly not conscious, but Gauguin was evidently identifying himself with another painter, and an earlier letter to Van Gogh reveals that he saw artists as a separate group, oppressed by society.

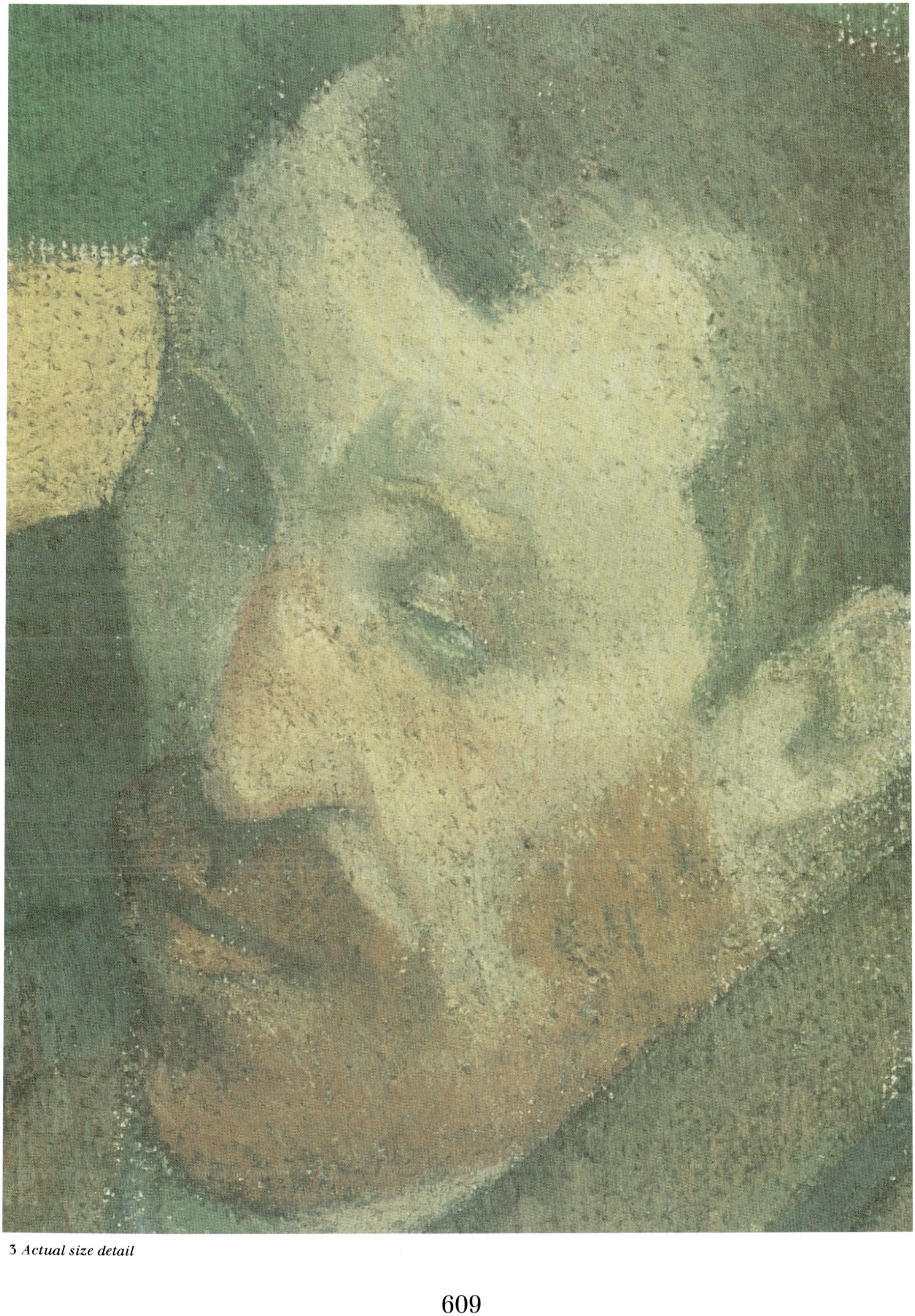

3 *Actual size detail*

Manao Tupapau: The Spirit of the Dead Keeps Watch

1892

$28^{3}/_{4} \times 36^{1}/_{4}$in/$73 \times 92$cm

Oil on canvas

Albright Knox Gallery, Buffalo

The strong religious faith of the Breton peasantry had made a strong impact on Gauguin, and in Tahiti he was similarly impressed by the beliefs and religious secrets of the islanders, which he became familiar with through a book called *Voyage to the Isles of the Great Ocean*, published in 1837 and written by a French consul to the South Sea Islands named Moerenhut. Passages of this book were later used by Gauguin in his own manuscript on the "Ancient Maori Cult," which itself was then incorporated in his work *Noa Noa*.

In this book, the title of which means "very fragrant," he states that his knowledge was received from his wife – meaning his thirteen-year old Tahitian companion Tehamana. This in fact seems unlikely, since women were excluded from knowledge of religious secrets, and these had, moreover, become more or less extinct by the time Gauguin arrived in Tahiti. On one occasion, however, he was struck by an incident which he believed demonstrated the "religious" fear still felt by the Tahitians. Returning home later than expected, he entered his hut to find Tehamana alone in the darkness (the light having gone out), lying face down on her bed, eyes open in terror and dread of the dark. The scene gave rise to this painting, one of his most important Tahitian works, which he frequently described at length. Writing to his wife Mette he said:

"I painted a nude of a young girl. In that position, a trifle can make it indecent. And yet I wanted her that way, the lines and the action interested me. A European girl would be embarrassed to be found in that position; the women here are not at all. I gave her face a somewhat frightened expression. This fright must be pretended, if not explained, and this is the character of the person – a Tahitian. These people by tradition are very much afraid of spirits of the dead. I had to explain her fears with a minimum of literary means, unlike the way it was done in the past. To achieve this, the general harmony is somber, sad, frighteneing, sounding to the eye like a death knell: violet, dark blue, and orange yellow. I made the linen greenish yellow, first because the linen of these savages is different from ours (it is made of beaten bark), secondly because it produces and suggests artificial light (the Tahitian women never go to bed in the dark), and yet I did not want the effect of lamplight (it's common), third because the yellow which connects the orange-yellow and the blue completes the musical harmony. There are flowers in the background but, being imagined they must not be real: I made them resemble sparks. The Polynesians believe that the phosphorescences of the night are the spirits of the dead. They believe in them and dread them. Finally I made the ghost very simply like a small, harmless woman, because the girl can only see the spirit of the dead linked with the dead person, that is, a human being like herself."

As Gauguin explained in his *Intimate Journals*, the Tahitian language has few words but each one possesses many implications and he explained the two meanings of the painting's title, which means either "She thinks of the spirit of the dead" or "The spirit of the dead remembers her."

In Tahiti Gauguin's symbolism developed into a personal vocabulary of line, color, allusion, dream and memory in which he attempted to create an intensity of feeling which in the words of the German philosopher Schopenhauer, "aspired to the condition of music," but which also contained literary resonances. He concluded with a description of the painting's abstract qualities: "The musical part: undulating horizontal lines, harmonies of orange and blue brought together by yellows and purples...which are lighted by greenish sparks. The literary part: the spirit of a living soul united with the spirit of the dead. Day and Night."

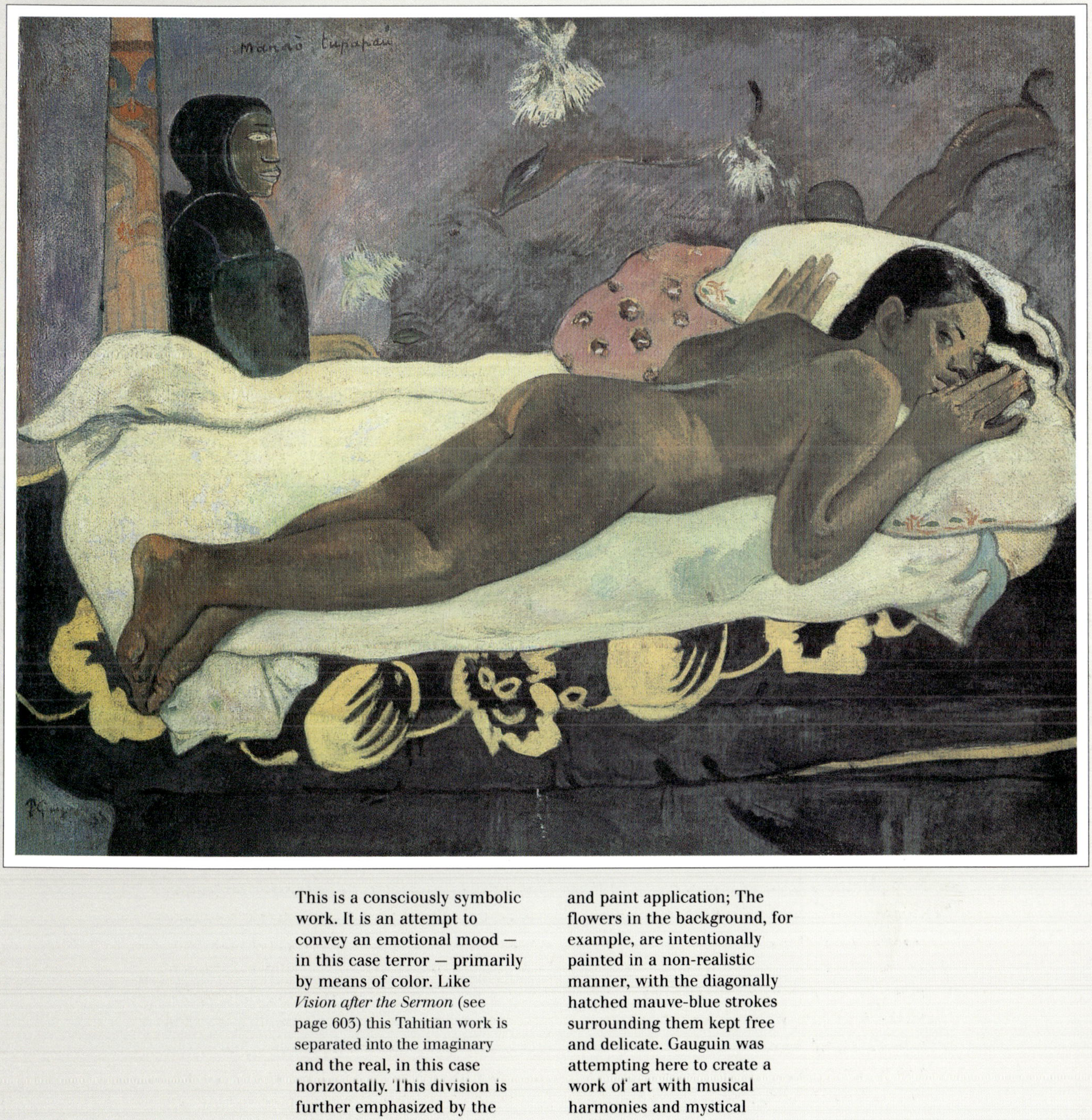

This is a consciously symbolic work. It is an attempt to convey an emotional mood – in this case terror – primarily by means of color. Like *Vision after the Sermon* (see page 603) this Tahitian work is separated into the imaginary and the real, in this case horizontally. This division is further emphasized by the different kinds of brushstroke and paint application; The flowers in the background, for example, are intentionally painted in a non-realistic manner, with the diagonally hatched mauve-blue strokes surrounding them kept free and delicate. Gauguin was attempting here to create a work of art with musical harmonies and mystical associations.

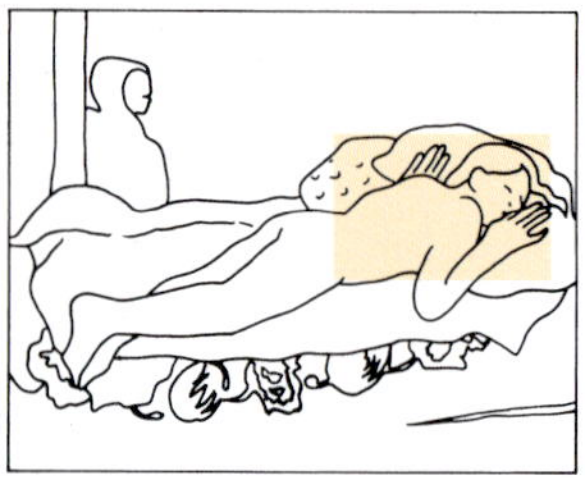

1 *Actual size detail* The face of Tehamana is modeled in green-brown, and the lips take up the pink of the cushion above her arm, while the whites of her eyes echo the greenish tinge of the bedding. Gauguin has used brushwork primarily to model the figure, which is highlighted in yellow ocher.

1 *Actual size detail*

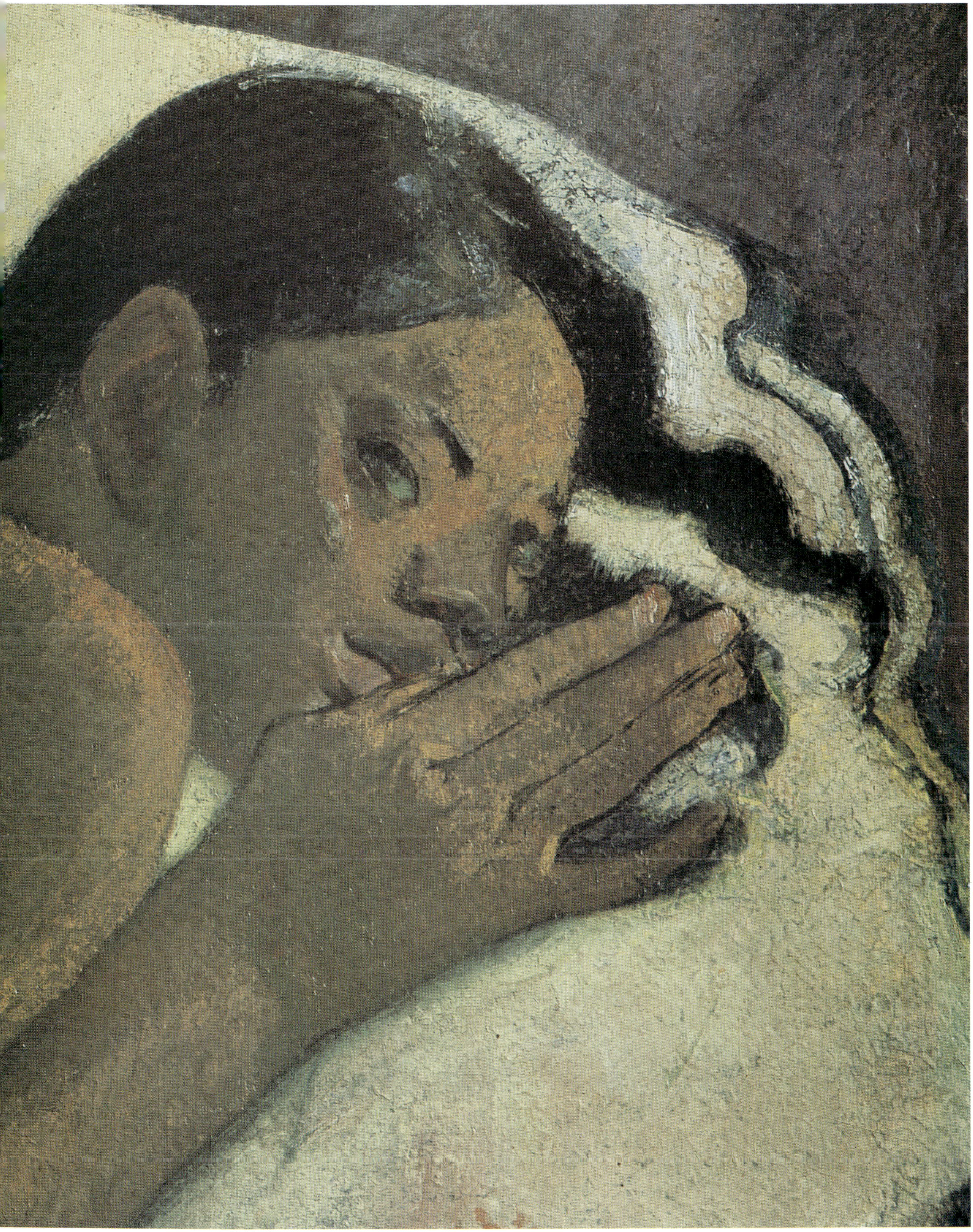

2

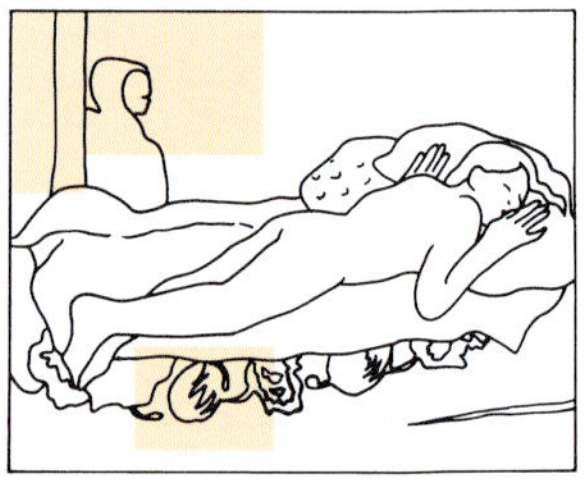

2 The totem pole has given Gauguin an opportunity to depict an abstract pattern. Color is thinly applied to the shapes of the pole and outlined in a thin blue glaze. Brushwork is not visible in this flattened pattern, which seems to incorporate the abstracted face of an idol and the back view of a man. This technique is reminiscent of his **treatment of the headdress in *Vision after the Sermon* (see page 603).**

3 The crude treatment of the ghost contrasts strongly with that of the recumbent living figure, and shows the influence of both Egyptian and native Tahitian art. The background is painted in diagonal strokes of color in the purple-blue range applied wet-in-wet, and creates a less easily apprehended setting, appropriate for the spiritual domain.

4 The flat print-like effect of the yellow flower on a dark blue background which represents the mattress intensifies the foreground area, which is actual, as opposed to the scene behind the bed, which is imaginary. It also forcefully creates a color scheme which Gauguin intended to be somber and frightening.

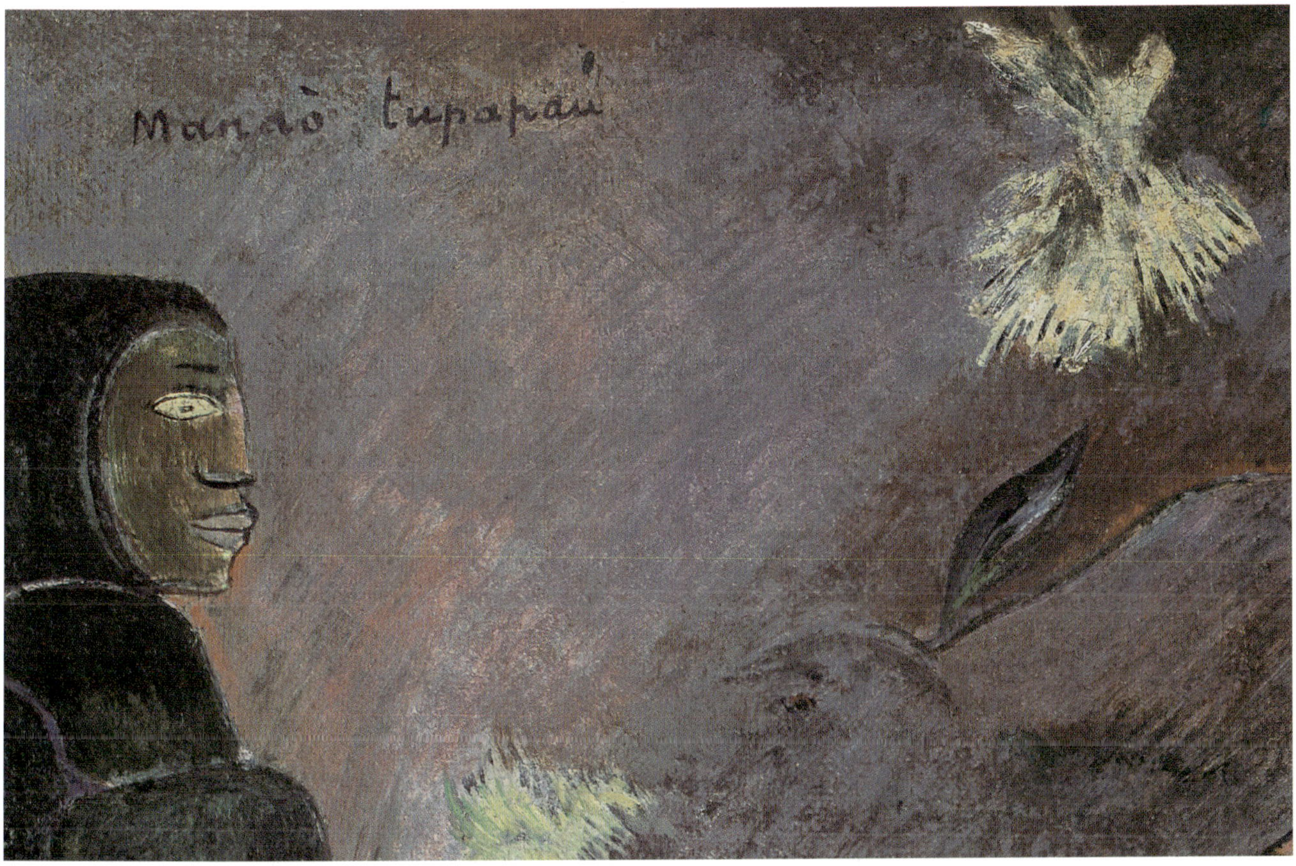

3

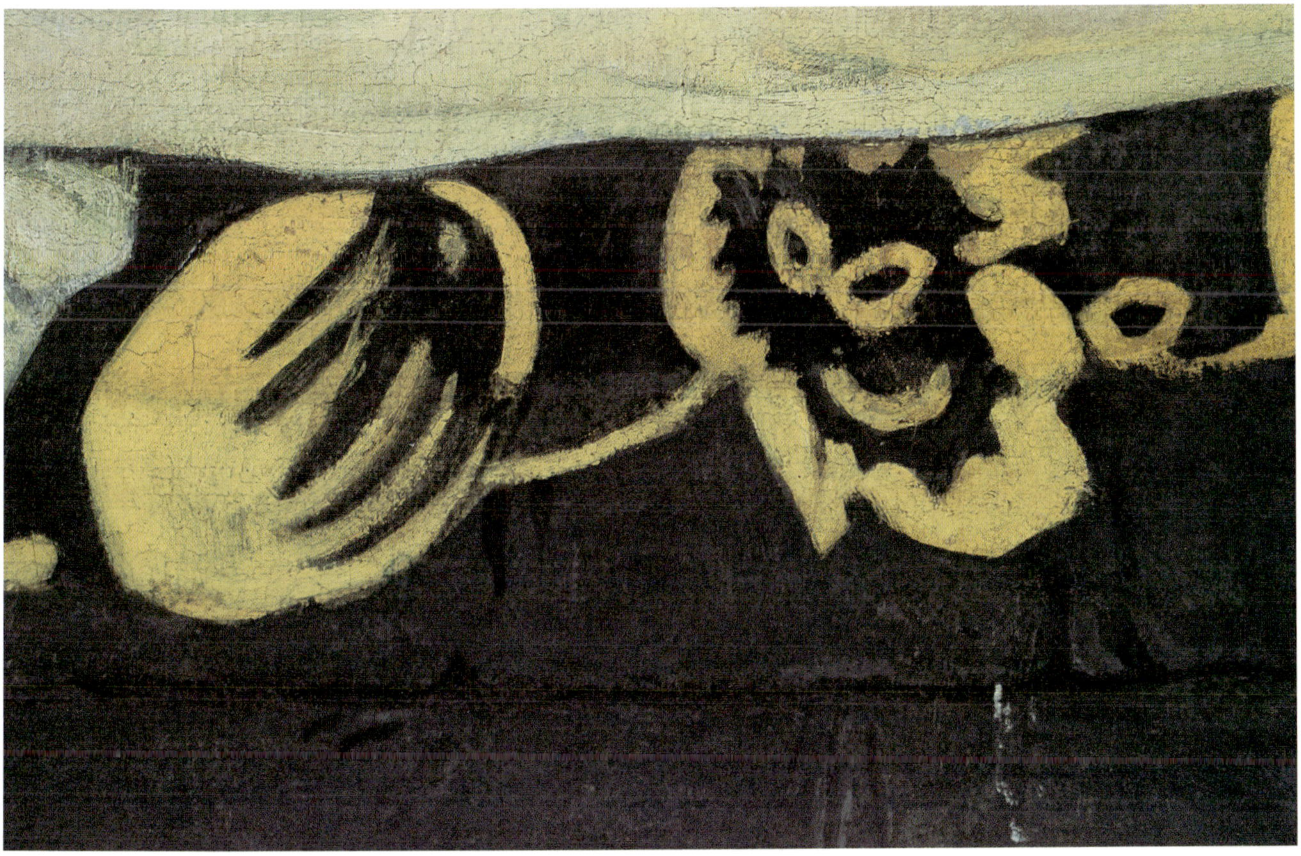

4

Nevermore

1897

$23^3/_4 \times 46^3/_4$in/59.5×117cm

Oil on canvas

Courtauld Institute Galleries, London

In a letter to Daniel de Montfried Gauguin wrote of his work: "I am trying to finish a canvas to send with the others ... I don't know if I am mistaken, but I believe that it's a good thing. I wanted, with a simple nude, to suggest a certain barbaric luxury of former times. The whole thing is suffused with color which is deliberately dark and sad; it's not silk or velvet, or fine lawn or gold which makes the richness of this painting, it is the hand of the artist ... It is man's imagination alone that has enriched this dwelling with his own fantasy."

The title, *Nevermore*, written in English at the top left of the painting is not, Gauguin explained "the raven of Edgar Poe, but the bird of the devil which is keeping watch. It is painted badly (I'm very nervous and work jerkily), it doesn't matter, I think it's a good canvas." Again we see Gauguin's stress on the importance of the "Idea" over all other considerations.

Nevermore is a consciously symbolic work in which the artist has attempted to create a poetic, literary and musical echo. The last word of Edgar Allen Poe's haunting refrain "Quoth the raven 'Nevermore,' brings to mind the words of the Symbolist poet Stephane Mallarmé, who maintained that the essence of a work of art lay in what was left out. Although Gauguin denied direct reference to Poe's poem, the work clearly carries overtones of Poe's lament for a loss, not easily put into words. Poe's poem was one of those read aloud at Gauguin's farewell banquet at the Café Voltaire preceding his first trip to Tahiti.

Translated both by Baudelaire and Mallarmé, Poe's work was of enormous influence on the French Symbolists in the last two decades of the century. Gauguin admired the work of all three men, being particularly attracted to the importance placed on the imagination and instinct over realism. "As in 'The Purloined Letter' [a short story] of Edgar Poe," Gauguin wrote in his *Intimate Journals*, "our modern intelligence, lost as it is in the details of analysis, cannot perceive what is too simple and too visible." The words apply directly to the major part of Gauguin's work.

The direct inspiration for the earlier painting, *The Spirit of the Dead*, done on his first trip to Tahiti, had come from Tahitian legend, which is also a theme in *Nevermore*. Fascinated by island lore, he recorded in his manuscript *Noa Noa* something of a legend told to him by his young companion Tehamana (who he called Tehura in his literary work). There he tells of finding Tehura rigid with fear as she imagined the "tupapas", the spirits of the dead, walking in the darkness, crying out between her sobs, "Never, never leave me alone like this without a light."

Gauguin's own description of *The Spirit of the Dead* reveals that he also considered the role of music important in his painting. It was part of the "synthetist" experience to blend together all art forms to produce a sensation which approximated to the way in which music conveys a mood. It was the aim of all Symbolist art to "aspire to the condition of music." Interestingly, the painting was bought by a musician – the composer Delius purchased it for 500 francs the year after it was painted.

Gauguin's leadership of the Symbolist art movement resulted largely from an article by the influential art critic Albert Aurier, in which he said: "Paul Gauguin seems to me to be the initiator of a new art, not in the course of history, but at least in our time ... The normal and final goal of painting, as of all arts, cannot be the direct presentation of objects. Its ultimate goal is to express Ideas by translating them into a special language. To the eyes of the artist ... objects are valueless merely as objects. They can only appear to him as signs. They are the letters of an immense alphabet which only the man of genius can combine into words."

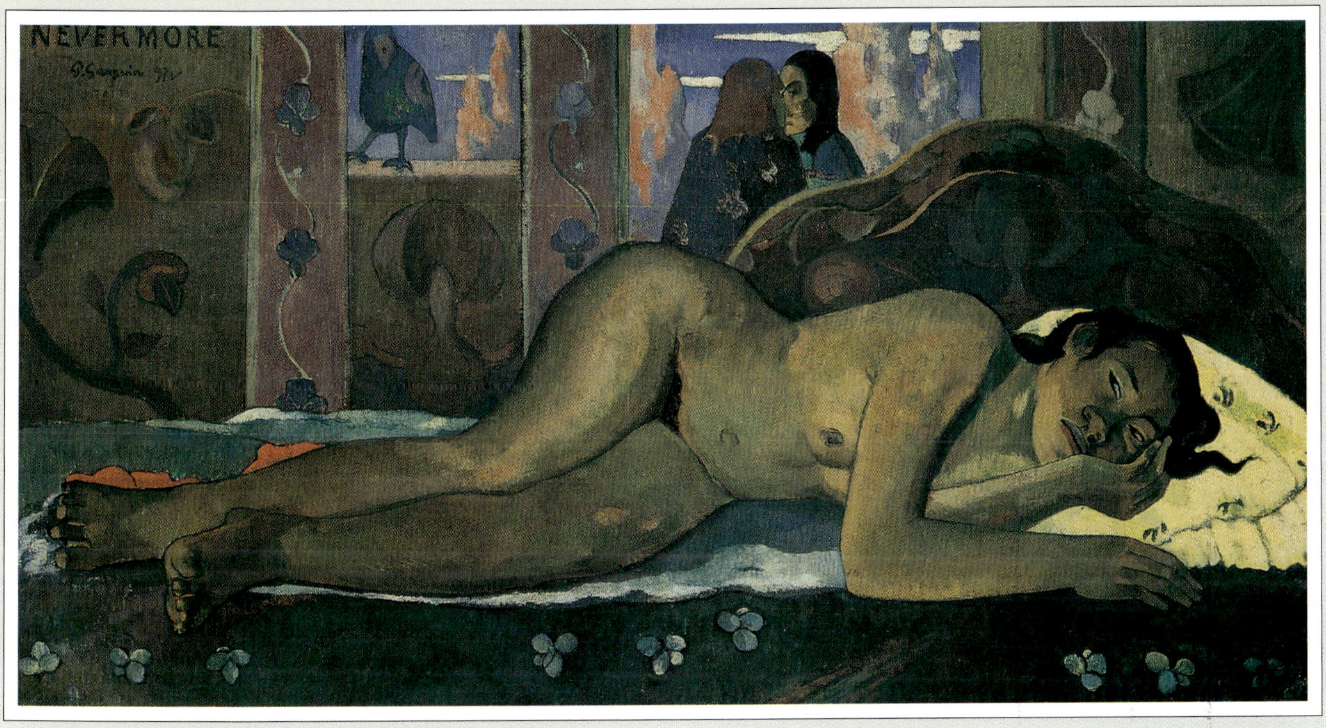

Like *The Spirit of the Dead* (see page 611) this work depicts a naked recumbent female in a setting which combines the real and the imagined. Gauguin found the physique of "Maori" women more aesthetically pleasing than that of the European female, whose "enormous thighs" and turned-in knees he scorned.

"In the Oriental and especially the Maori women," he remarked, "the leg from hip to foot offers a pretty, straight line. The thigh is heavy but not wide, which makes it round and avoids that spreading which gives to so many women of our country the appearance of a pair of tongs."

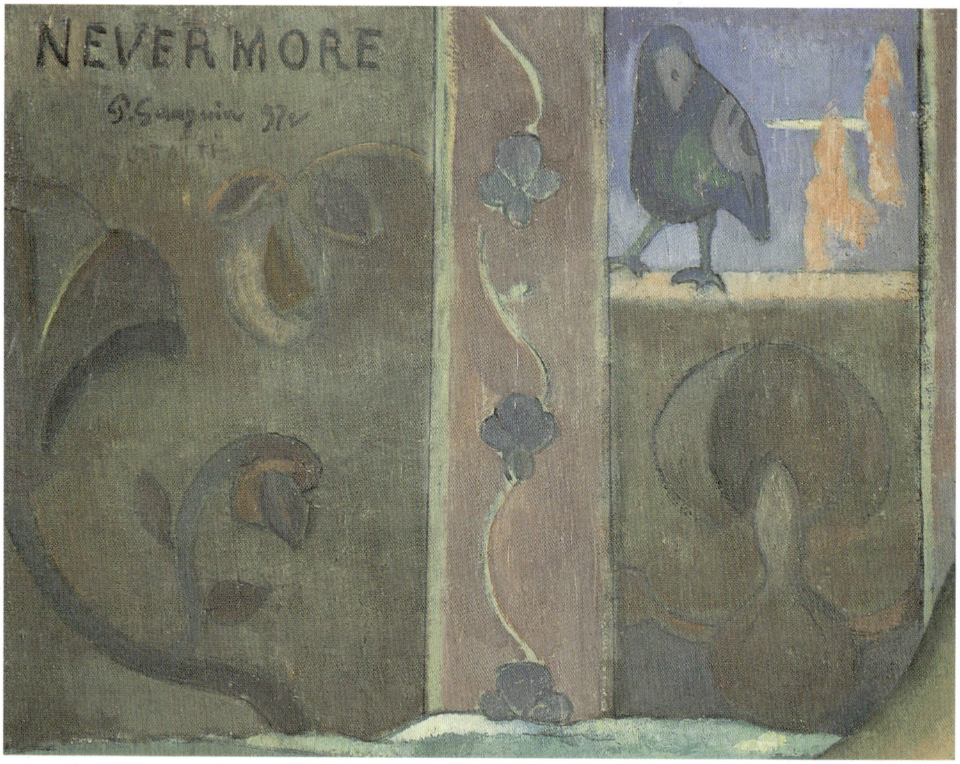

1

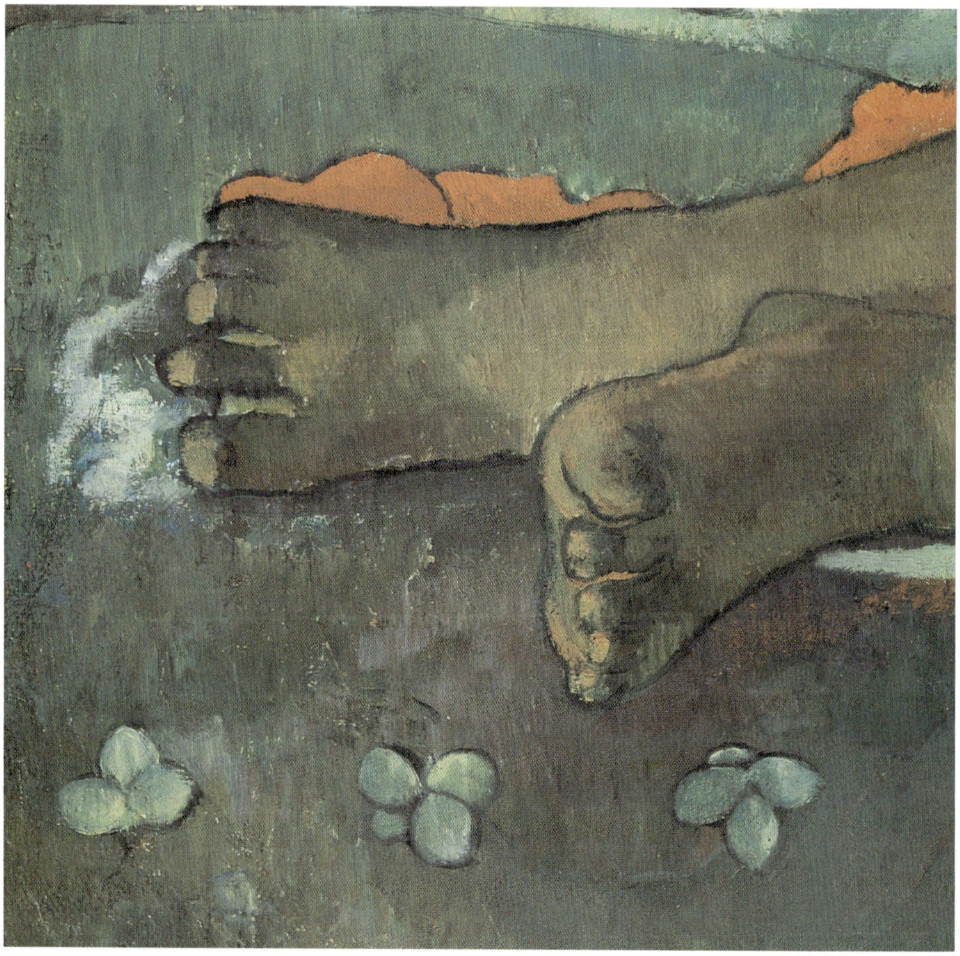

2

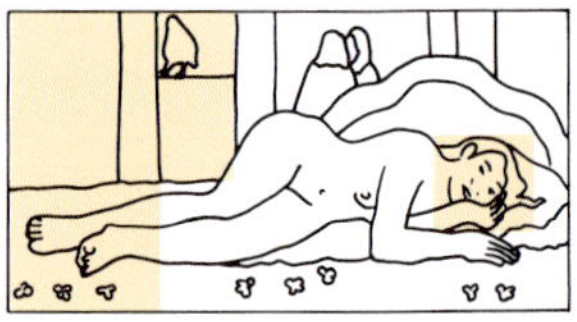

1 As in many of Gauguin's works the title is painted onto the canvas as an integral part of the painting, contributing a "literary" association to the painted poem. Beneath the signature flow the curves of two imaginary exotic flowers, painted wet-in-wet, and outlined delicately in a thin blue glaze. The exotic bird, painted in blue, green and lilac next to an abstracted landscape of muted red, lilac and cream, forms a decorative detail in a highly decorative work. Panels of blue flowers on a lilac background flank the bird and the curious vessel beneath, which is reminiscent of Gauguin's own sculpture.

2 The bedding around the feet shows the patterning effect of vertical brushwork, scumbling and muted color, which contrasts strongly with the flat evenly-painted area of bright red above the right foot. Shadow is almost entirely rejected, and by extending the white of the sheet beyond the right toes the artist has formed a highlight; an ironic inversion of what the western eye is trained to expect.

3 *Actual size detail* The face is modeled in broad sweeps of dark flesh tones, shadowed in green. Features are darkly outlined in a non-naturalistic manner. The contours of the naked from are also drawn in Prussian blue, which flattens the form and produces a less naturalistic and more decorative approach.

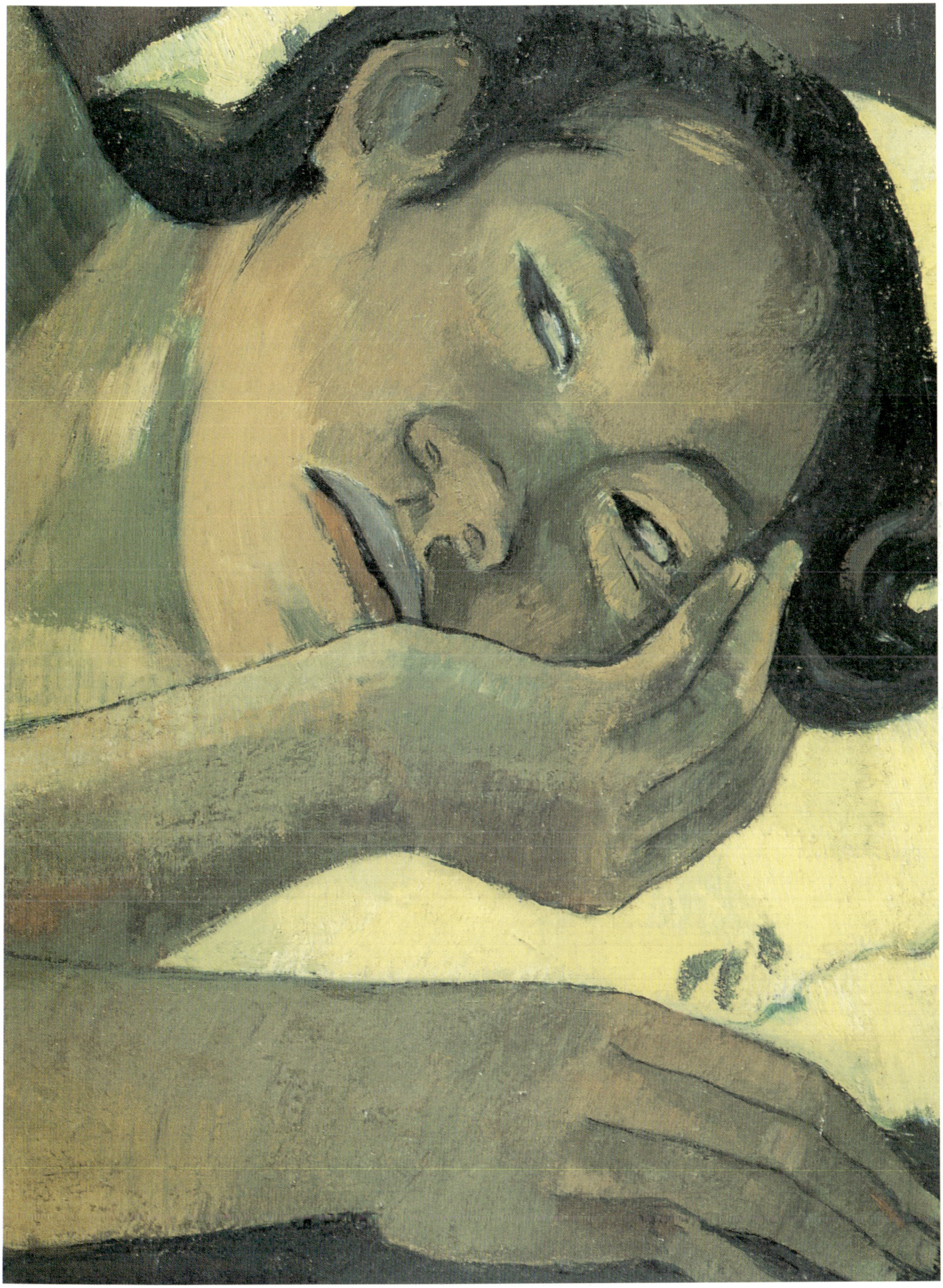

3 *Actual size detail*

Where Do We Come From? What Are We? Where Are We Going To?

1897
$55\frac{1}{2} \times 149\frac{3}{4}$in/139×374.5cm
Oil on rough canvas
Boston Museum of Fine Arts

After years of hardship in Tahiti, suffering dreadfully from eczema, Gauguin prepared to commit suicide after painting his most important work. "Before I died," he wrote, "I wished to paint a large canvas that I had in mind, and I worked day and night that whole month in an incredible fever."

After the painting was finished Gauguin took a huge dose of the arsenic he had hoarded to treat his eczema, but instead of killing him it caused a night of severe and painful vomiting. He survived to leave detailed accounts of this painting, and in February 1898 he wrote to Daniel de Montfried: "To be sure it is not done like a Puvis de Chavannes, sketch after nature, preparing cartoon etc. It's all done straight from the brush on sackcloth full of knots and wrinkles, so the appearance is terribly rough."

"It is a canvas 4 meters 50 in width, by one meter 70 in height. The two upper corners are chrome yellow, with an inscription on the left and my name on the right, like a fresco whose corners are spoiled with age, and which is appliquéd upon a golden wall. To the right at the lower end, a sleeping child and three crouching women. Two figures dressed in purple confide their thoughts to one another. An enormous crouching figure, out of all proportion, and intentionally so, raises its arms and stares in astonishment upon these two, who dare to think of their destiny. A figure in the center is picking fruit. Two cats near a child. A white goat. An idol, its arms mysteriously raised in a sort of rhythm, seems to indicate the Beyond. Then lastly an old woman nearing death appears to accept everything, to resign herself to her thoughts. She completes the story! At her feet a strange white bird, holding a lizard in its claws, represents the futility of words. It is all on the bank of a river in the woods. In the background the ocean, then the coloring of the landscape is constant, either blue or Veronese green. The naked figures stand out in bold orange ... So I have finished a philosophical work on a theme comparable to that of the Gospel. I think it is good."

Gauguin has tried in this word picture to convey, but not interpret, the symbolism of this painting, which had been met with incomprehension. André Fontainas, the critic of *Mercure* (which Gauguin read in Tahiti) had compared Gauguin unfavorably with Puvis de Chavannes, which caused Gauguin to write to his friend Charles Morice in 1901: "Why, before a painting, does a critic find it necessary to make a comparison with the too often expressed ideas of other artists? Not finding that which he believes ought to be there, he fails to understand and is not moved. Emotion first. Understanding follows.

"Puvis ... knew well how to express his ideas ... Puvis explains his idea, but does not paint it. He is a Greek, while I am a savage. Puvis calls a painting 'Purity' ... he paints a young virgin with a lily in her hand — an obvious symbol — and is understood. Gauguin, with the title 'Purity' paints a landscape with limpid waters, unsoiled by the hand of man ... there is a world of difference between Puvis and me."

Gauguin felt impelled to spell out the painting's symbolism as follows:

In the large painting:-
Where are we going?
An old woman nearing death
An exotic stupid bird
What are we?
Daily existence
The man of instinct wonders what all this means
Where do we come from?
The brook
A child
Communal life

The strange bird concludes the poem — an inferior being contrasted with an intelligent one, which is the answer sought in the title.

"Behind a tree, two sinister figures,

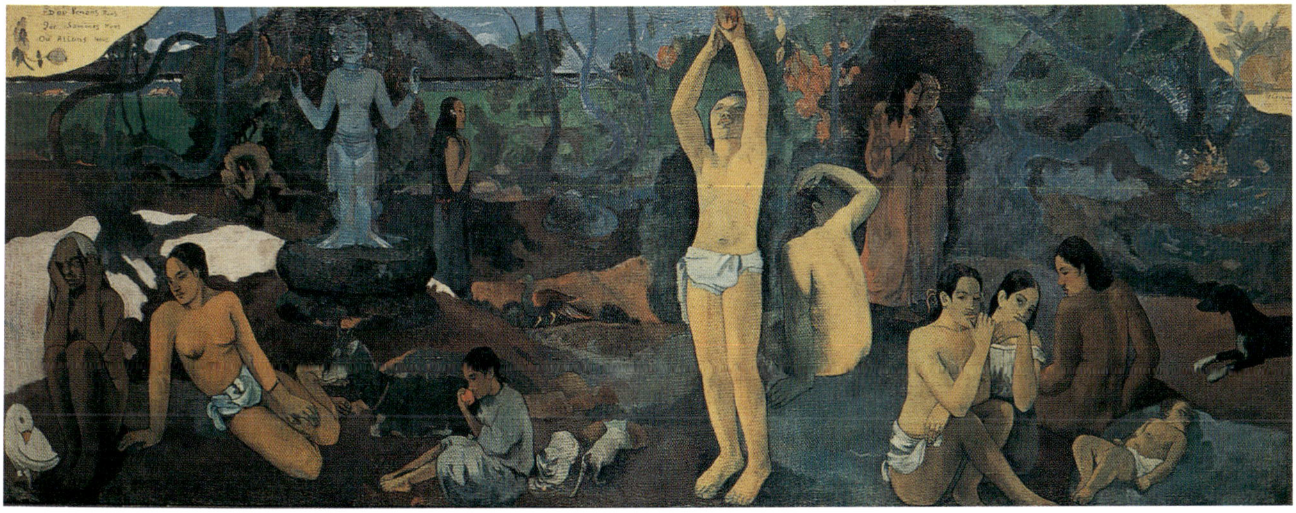

wrapped in gloomy clothing, inject their note of sorrow, near the tree of science, caused by this name science, as compared with the simple beings in a virgin nature, a paradise of human conception, giving themselves up to the joys of living."

Although this seems to proffer an explanation it does not explain the derivation of Gauguin's symbolism.

To Fontainas himself Gauguin wrote in 1899: "If my dream is not communicated it contains no allegory. It is a musical poem; it does not require a libretto. 'The essential work of art,' said Mallarmé, 'consists precisely of that which is not expressed: there result lines, without color or words, which are not materially expressed.' Mallarmé understands my Tahitian paintings [remarking]: 'It is extraordinary that one can put so much mystery into so much splendor.'

"... Coming back to the panel: The idol is not a literary explanation, but a statue ... It all took form in my dream in front of my hut. There all nature dominates the primitive soul; it is the consolation of our suffering, full of the vague and the incomprehensible in the presence of our origin and our future."

Intended as his last, most important work before ending his life, this painting is one of Gauguin's most significant. He has chosen a frieze-like construction which contains no single focus but depicts separate references to the journey of human life. The continuity of action offered by the frieze form is well suited to this concept, and also suggests both an origin and an end which continues beyond the painting itself. It is a translation of a dream on the nature of existence into a "musical poem" without explanatory symbols whose literalism would destroy the essential form. It is painted directly onto a rough sackcloth without preparatory sketches, which Gauguin felt to be the best means of truthfully conveying his idea.

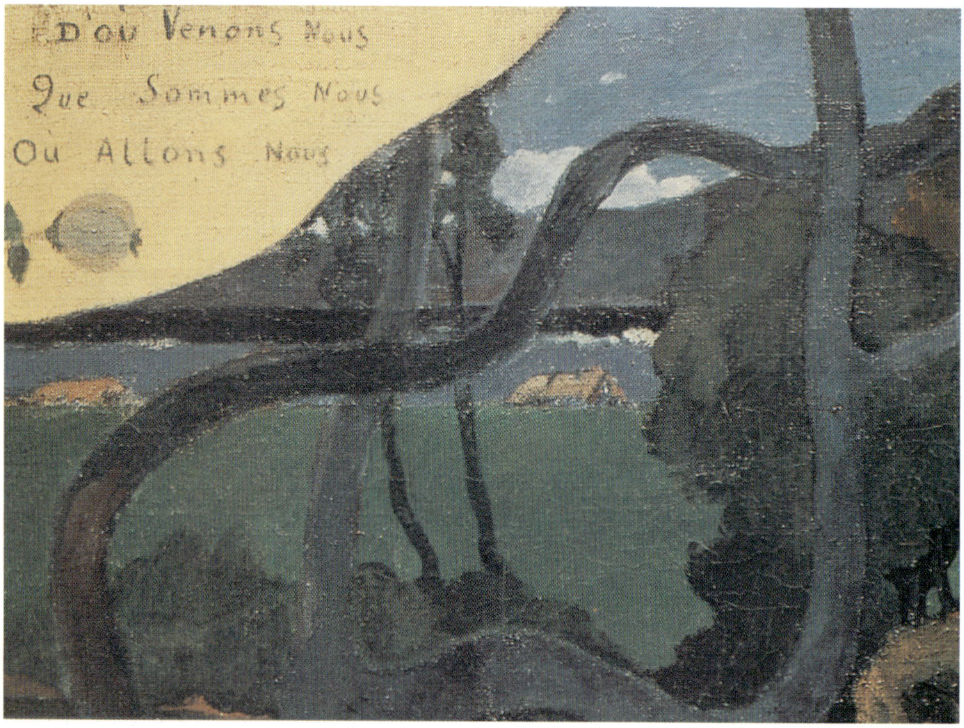

1

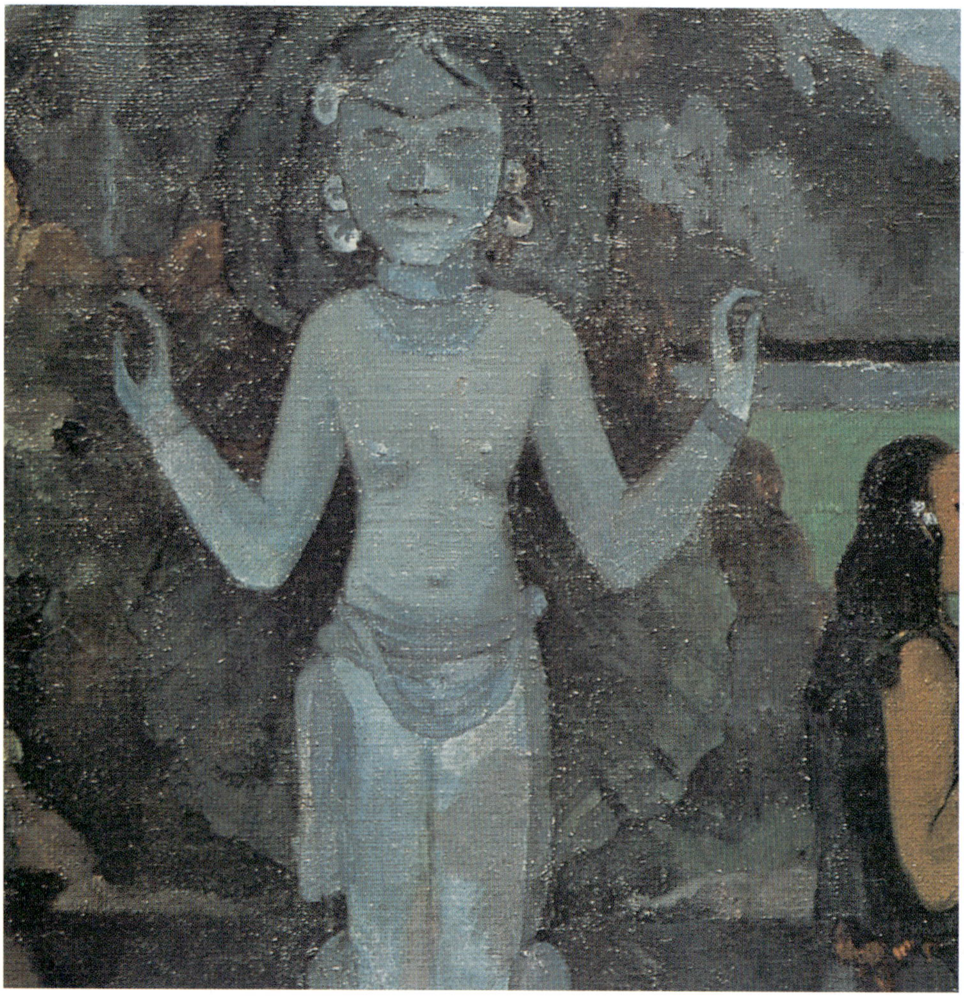

2

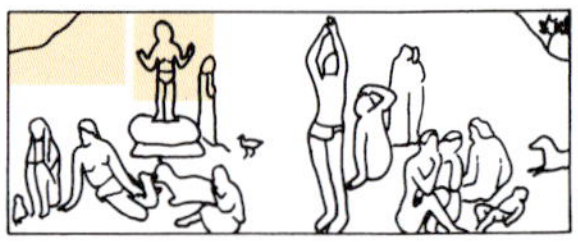

1 The title of the work appears in French on a chrome yellow background, and was intended to resemble the corners of an ancient fresco. To the left of the title an open flower and one in bud provide a decorative curve on the otherwise flat area of color.

2 Painted entirely in monochromatic blues, the figure of the idol shows Gauguin's debt to Eastern art. Fascinated by the cult of the ancient Tahitian gods, he has reworked an emblem of an extinct culture into a work whose theme he saw as comparable to that of the Gospel. The strong vertical of the figure in profile on the right is set against a landscape which comprises the curving trees of a woodland riverbank, beyond which lies the ocean below a strong horizontal of dark blue.

3 *Actual size detail* The old woman on the extreme left of the canvas completes the story of human life begun with the baby on the right. She sits in quiet resignation, accepting the inevitable approach of death.

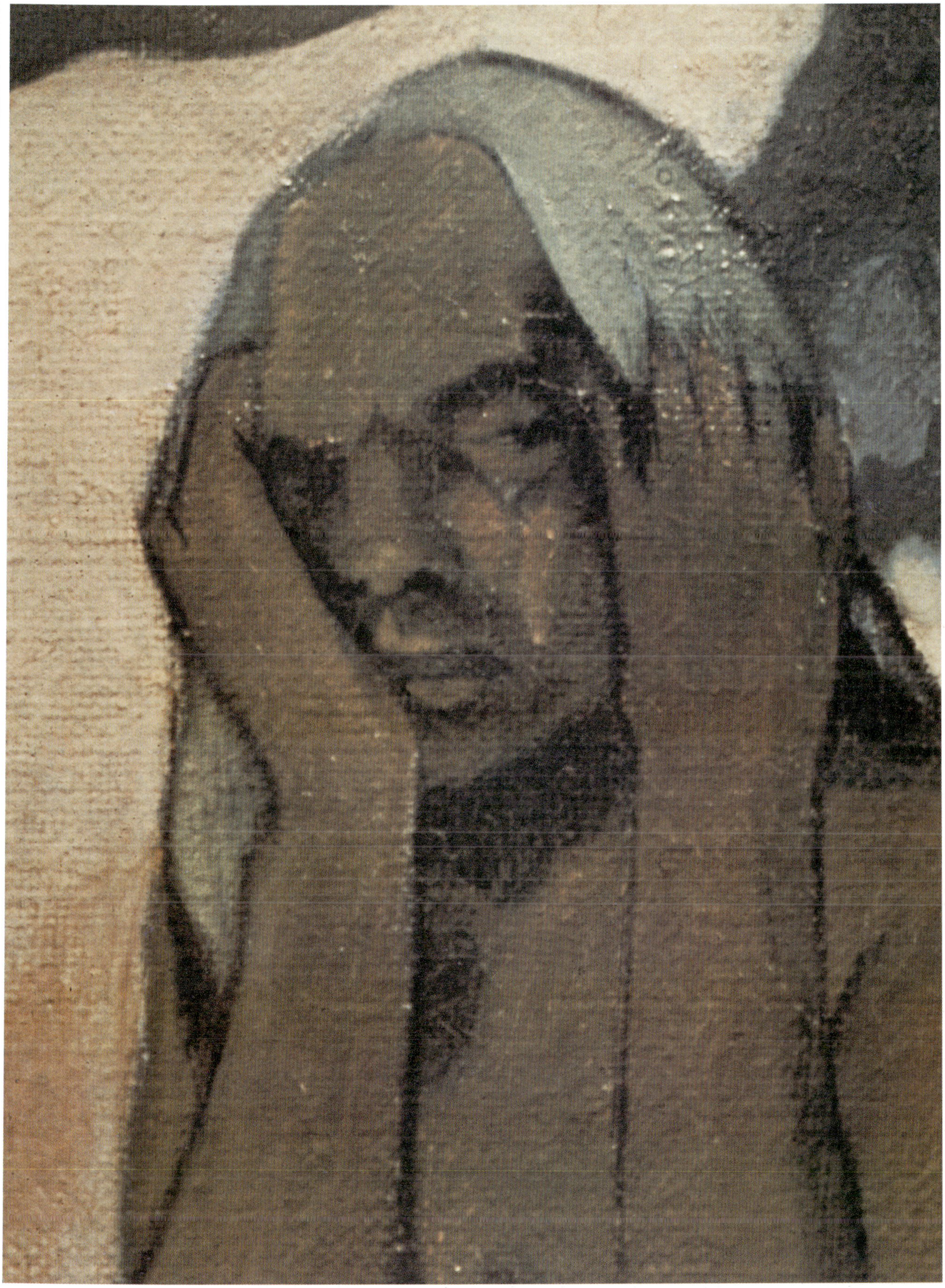

3 *Actual size detail*

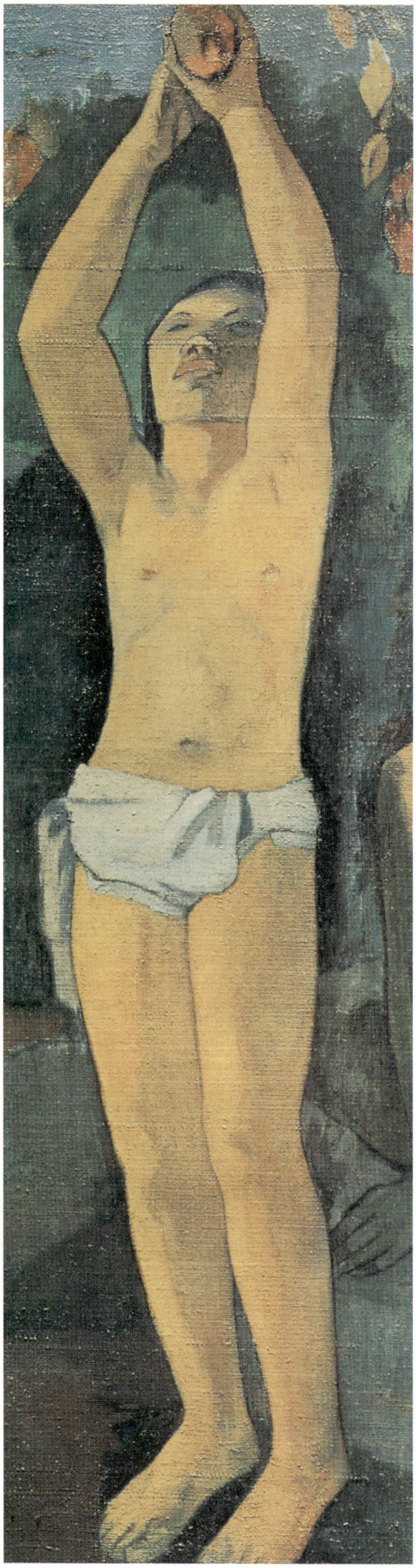

4

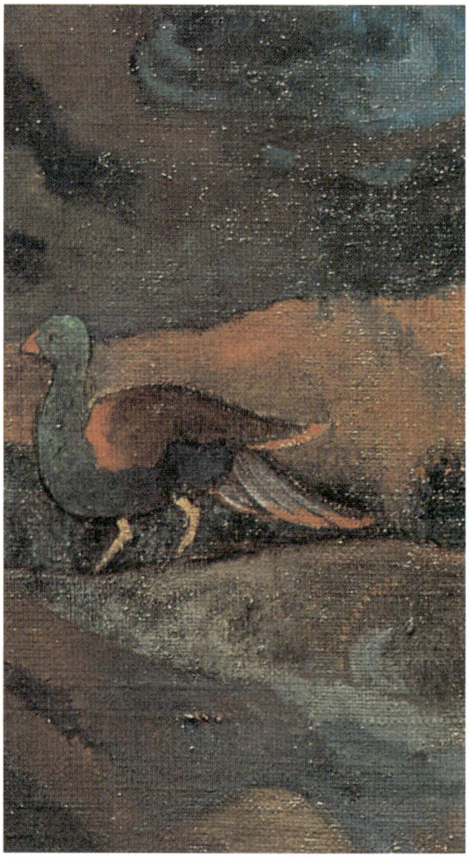

5

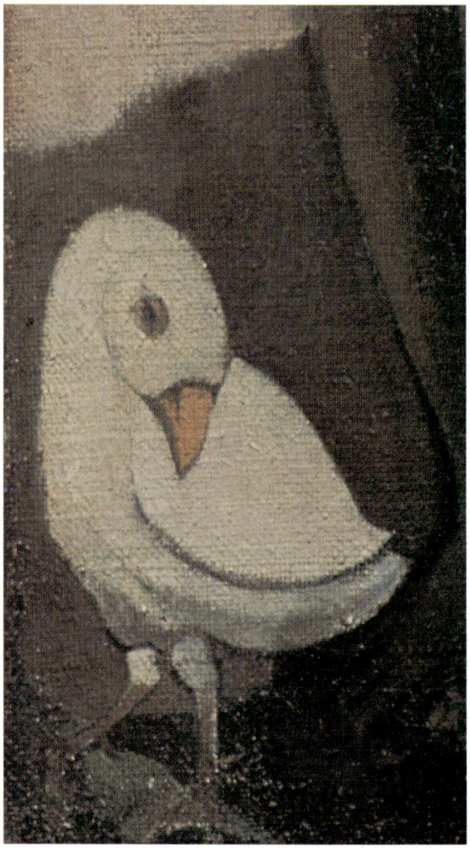

6

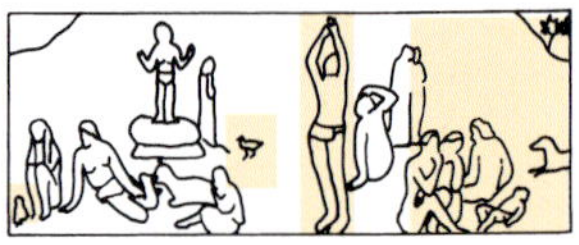

4 More than any other element in the painting this semi-clothed man is the focal point of the work. Not only does he span the whole height of the painting, breaking it into two sections, he also indicates, in reaching for fruit from a tree out of our vision, an extension of space above the boundaries of the picture, which has psychological relevance to a work with the theme of the nature of existence. The weave of the sackcloth support is clear in three separate horizontal lines which run across much of the picture surface but which are most clearly visible over the face of this standing figure.

5 The brilliance of this small, brightly colored exotic bird stands out against a background of red and green, in contrast to the monochrome treatment of the nearby idol and pedestal.

6 The white bird holding a lizard sits at the feet of the old woman at the extreme left of the painting, and both were seen by Gauguin as representing the futility of words and the acceptance of death. In a letter of 1899 he said "Do you see how useless it is for me to understand the value of words...With all the sincerity possible, I have tried...to translate my dream without the aid of literary devices."

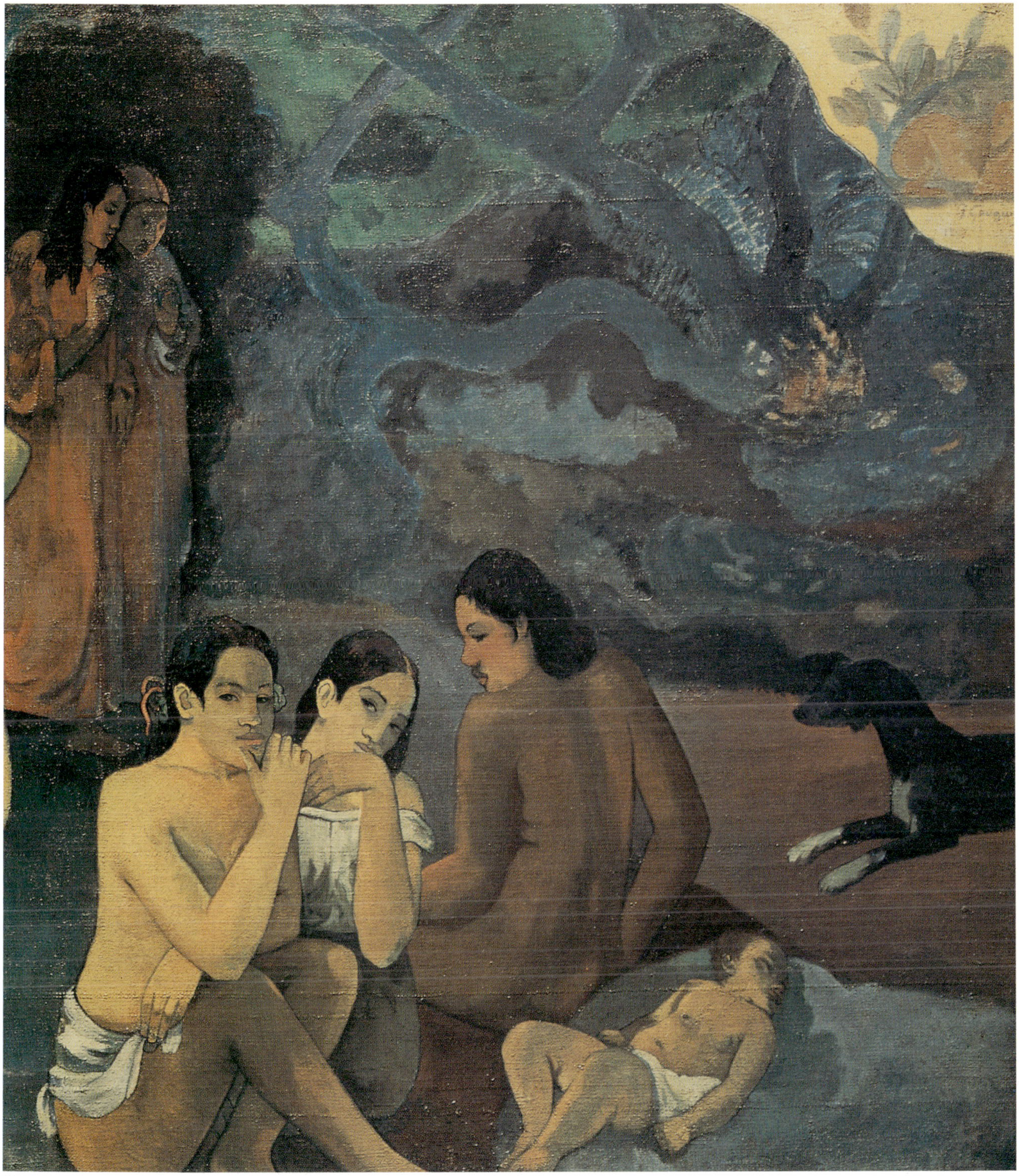

7

7 Although Gauguin painted this quickly and "jerkily" due to pains and illness, the two foreground figures are remarkably clearly executed in flat areas of yellow ocher, shadowed in green. The flat treatment of the muted red background on which the dog sits contrasts with the broken brushwork and dabs of varicolored paint above.

THE WHITE HORSE

1898

56×36½in/140×91cm

Oil on rough canvas

Musée d'Orsay, Paris

This picture shows a return from the horizontal frieze-like arrangement Gauguin had been using to a vertical form, with spatial recession suggested by the way figures are placed one above the other. It unites features of the art of the east, especially that of Japan, with that of the west, fusing together Japan and Greece in a blend Gauguin had often sought. His earlier Impressionist treatment of a similar theme, the *Still life with Horse's Head* of 1885, combines decorative Japanese fans and a puppet with a Classical Greek marble horse's head, derived from one of those on the Parthenon pediment. Gauguin possessed several photographs of Greek subjects, including those of the Parthenon frieze and pediment in the British Museum, which served as models in his paintings.

The White Horse shows a more subtle blending of the two traditions, the influence of Japanese prints being evident in the vertical, asymmetrical arrangement of the canvas, the flat areas of unbroken color and the decorative overlay effect produced by the curvilinear patterning of the branches. The spirit of traditional western classicism is embodied in the emblematic use of the white horse itself; it is still basically the Parthenon horse, but here Gauguin has inverted the head to create an image of a young animal drinking from a brook.

Traditional western techniques are also much more evident in this work than in those done in the preceding dozen years, and we see a return to naturalism in the depiction of the horse itself. This is modeled in tones, unlike the earlier flat-pattern paintings, with the tones taking up the reflections of water and foliage. The image of the horse, whose physical beauty and strength embodies the classical ethos, was frequently employed by Degas, whom Gauguin greatly admired for having "a contempt for art theories," and "no interest in technique." Acknowleding his own debt to the master he asserted that, "people are always borrowing from Degas."

The powerful image presented in this work had an influence on a subsequent generation of artists, particularly the German Expressionists. Although Gauguin himself left no record of this particular work, his personal symbolism, recorded in letters to Charles Morice, Daniel de Montfried, André Fontainas, and his wife, suggest that the image was intended as one of purity, solitude, nobility and power. The white horse stands alone, refreshing itself in the shallow water – an elemental source of life and sustenance often symbolizing purity. It is tempting to interpret the image in terms of the artist himself – the solitary, wild but pure beast over whom no one has control, a feature emphasized by the presence of the two other horses with their naked riders. Such an interpretation is given validity by Gauguin's quotation in his *Intimate Journals* of Degas' remark about him being like the lone wolf – hungry but free.

The painting also presents an idyll, a pastorale where man and beast co-exist in harmony with nature. The harmony is stressed by the stream and waterfall running through the center of the painting and the trees, with their branches encircling the free and naked riders and their mounts. A white lily in the foreground, leading the eye into the body of the canvas, typifies, with its traditional assocation of purity, the symbolism of the work, which Gauguin's personal vocabulary enlarges on.

Painted at speed with decisive brushstrokes and the occasional use of a palette knife, *The White Horse* is one of Gauguin's most harmonious works, communicating, by symbolism and allusion, color and line, the poetry he sought to convey.

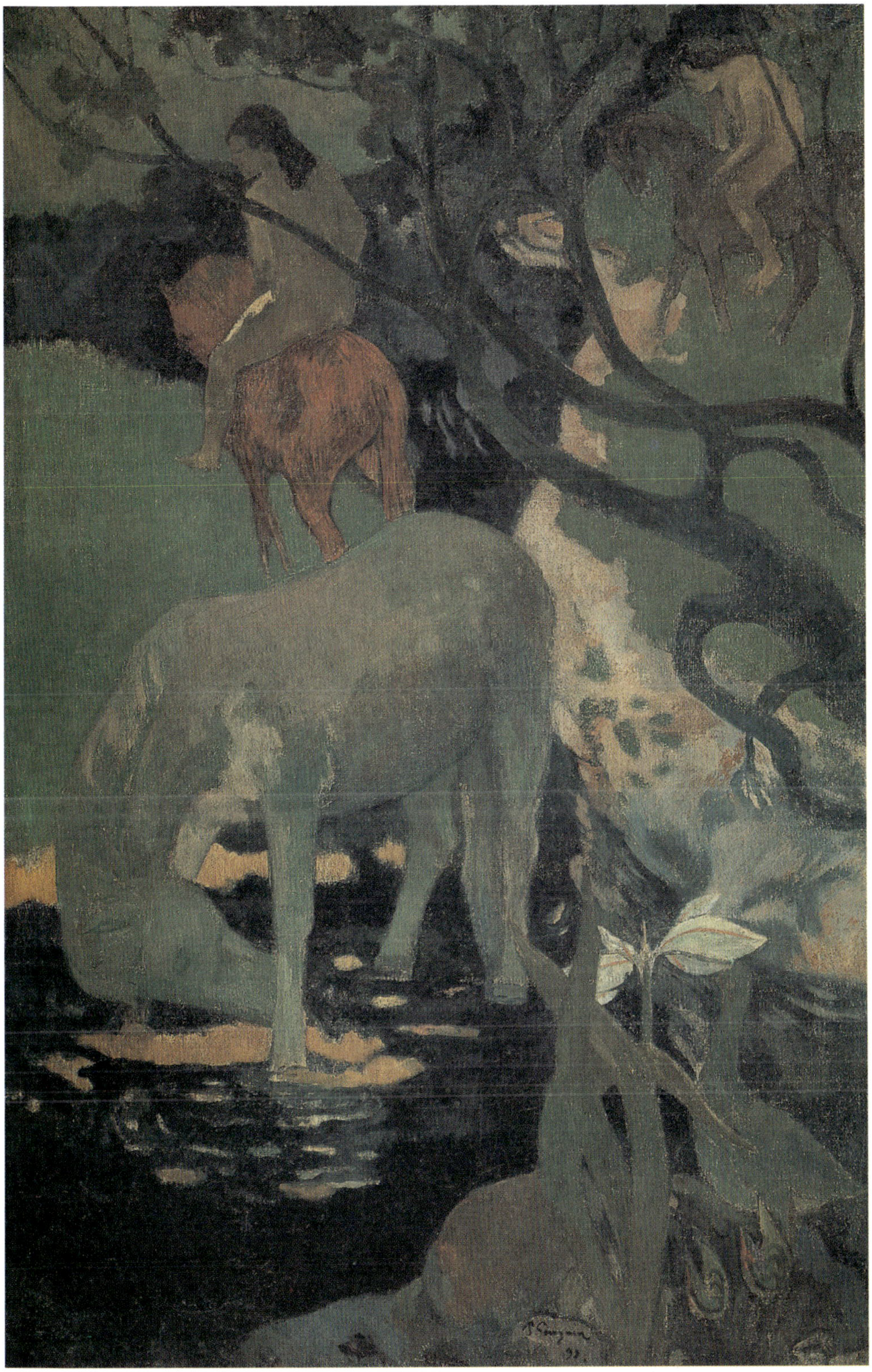

As in *Vision after the Sermon* (see page 603) the picture plane of *The White Horse* is diagonally bisected. Here it is not a single bough which cuts across the surface of the canvas but a series of curvilinear branches overlaying a pattern. This picture shows the diversity of Gauguin's approach to brushwork and modeling, which ranges from the flat, print-like effect on the upper right to the crude hatching of the red horse, the vertical brushwork of its surrounding, and the relatively high degree of color modeling of the white horse itself.

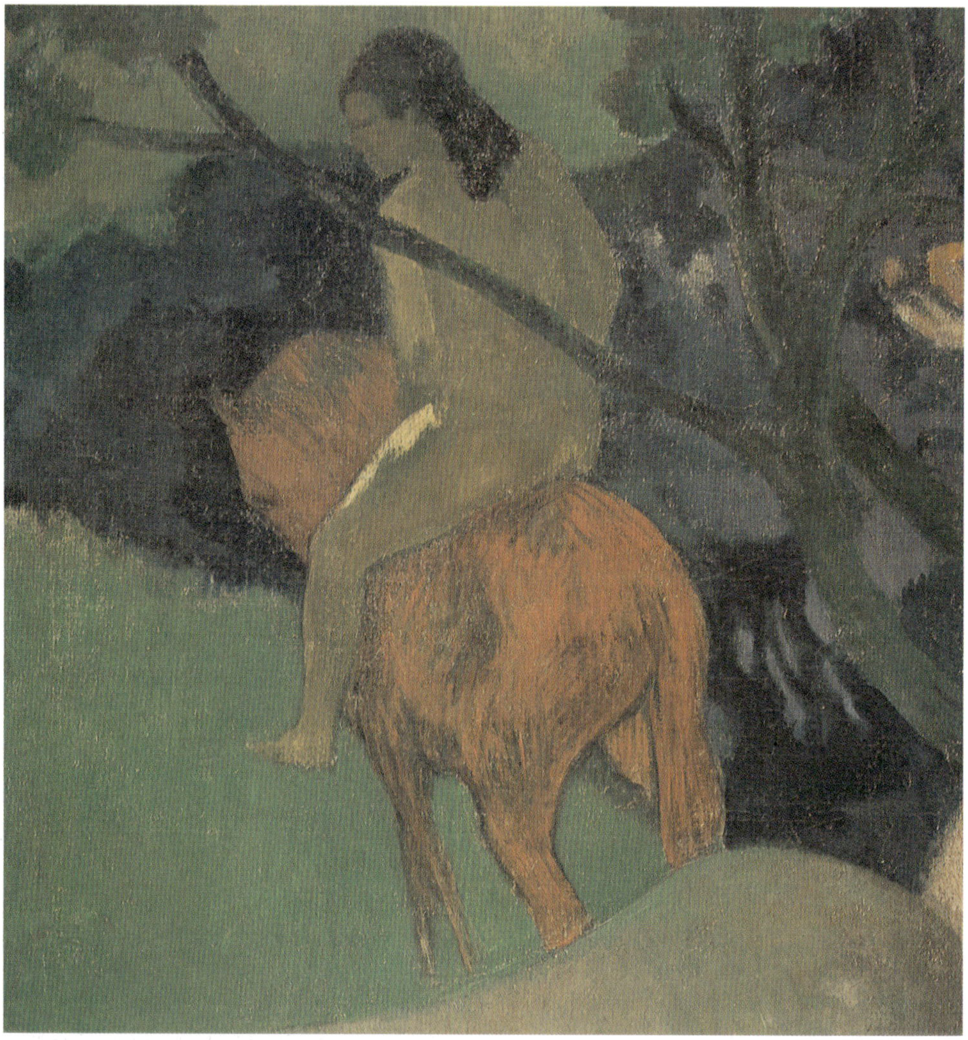

1

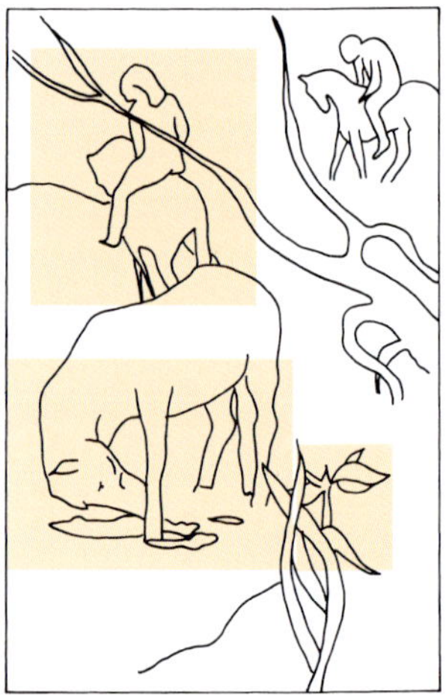

1 Here, in direct contrast to the white horse, Gauguin has hatched green-brown pigment over red. Foreshortening and anatomical precision have been subordinated to decorative effect. The roughness of the canvas he used to paint on is evident in the slightly raised horizontal texturing which runs through the lower back of the rider and is most clearly seen in the blue area to the right.

2 The horse's head, derived from photographs of the Elgin marbles, is crudely modeled in green, its features outlined in dark green instead of the dark blue which is used to silhouette the two other horses. The reflections are painted both as contained areas of pure color and — below the horse's foot — wet-in-wet. The underbelly of the horse shows a greater degree of modeling than Gauguin normally used, though the essential crudeness has been retained in the dark green contour of the belly.

3 *Actual size detail* The green-white tones of the lily reflect those of the white horse. Paint is applied fairly stiffly in contrast to the freer wet-in-wet and wet-in-dry treatment of the area immediately above.

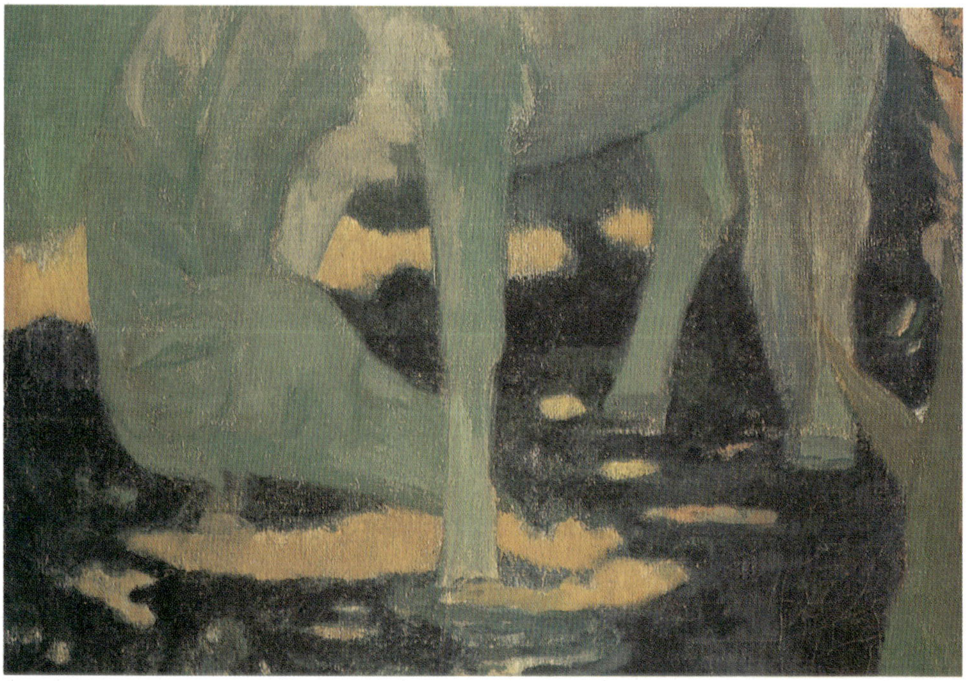

2

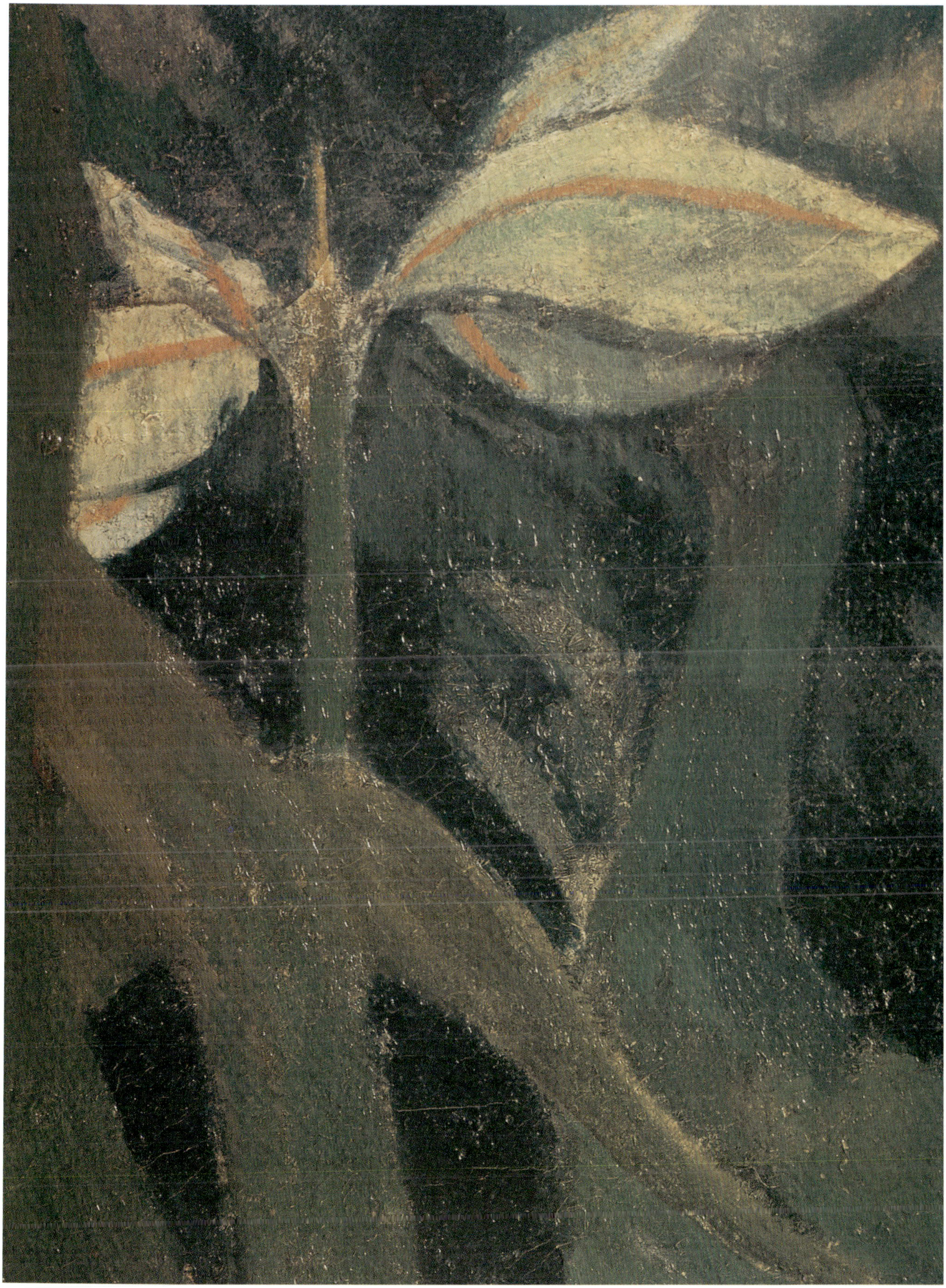

3 *Actual size detail*

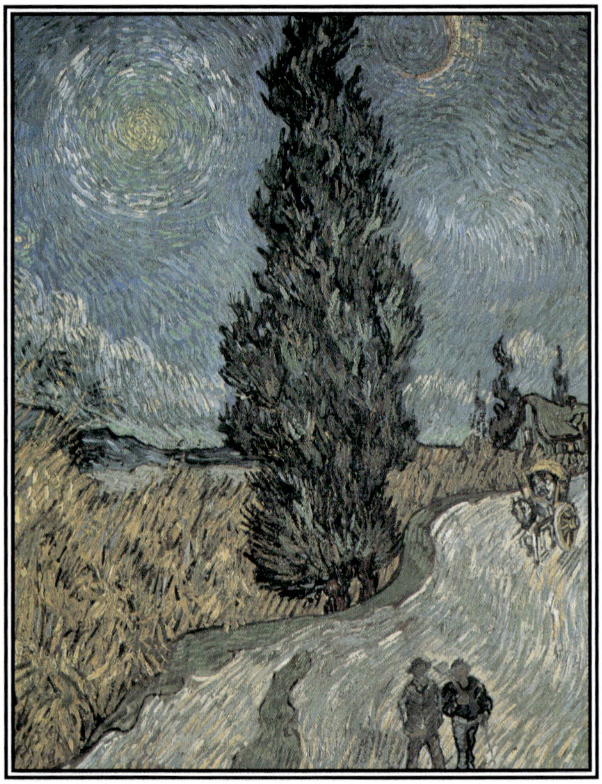

VAN GOGH

Introduction

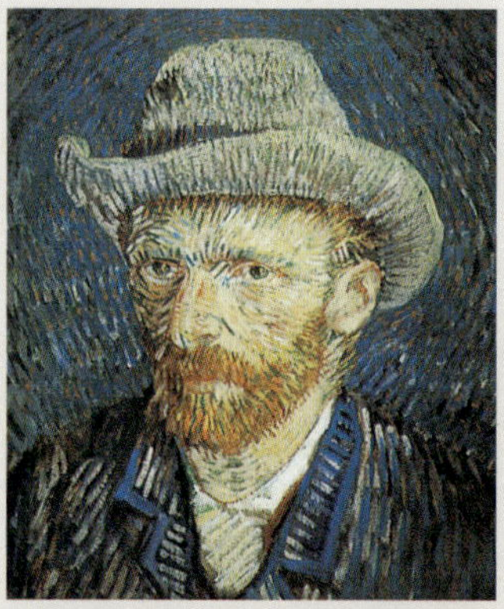

Vincent Van Gogh
Self-Portrait
1888
Van Gogh Museum, Otterlo

Vincent Van Gogh died by his own hand, an impoverished failure in the eyes of the world. He had struggled to succeed in a number of fields: as an art dealer, teacher, missionary and only finally as a painter. He committed suicide at the very time his work was beginning to attract both critical approval and the enthusiasm of his fellow artists, yet today he is probably the most popular and widely known painter in the entire history of art, known to millions through reproductions of his works. The contrast between the obscurity of his life and his universal posthumous acclaim has become in the popular imagination the prototype story of the modern artist: a poor and dejected outcast, descending into madness, but whose genius, inevitably only recognized after his early death, brings him immortality.

Van Gogh would not have despised this popularity, for above all else he wanted his painting to reach ordinary people and be a part of their lives. His great compassion for the suffering of others, together with the pain and loneliness he suffered himself, gave to his art a universality beyond dry intellectual or historical themes, and his life itself seemed to dramatize the very essence of the emotions that we all encounter, albeit less intensely. In this respect his paintings deal with things that are simple to recognize and easy to sympathize with, whatever our own particular experiences have been.

Not only do Van Gogh's paintings address fundamental human emotions very directly, they also depict the real world square on. His subject matter was nearly always what was before his easel — concrete, familiar, everyday reality. Although he was highly literate, deeply absorbed in spiritual issues and had a thorough knowledge of artistic tradition, his work is never complicated by obscure allusions or layers of meaning intelligible only to the few. Although his paintings have great depth, this is never at the expense of direct impact. The obvious sincerity of his work is one of its chief attractions, and its emotional force is very directly conveyed through his painting technique. His brushwork is almost a form of speech, and a highly articulate one.

As well as expressing his own emotional state, Van Gogh's art also tells us a great deal about the events of his life, since everything that happened to him was directly reflected in his subjects and how he painted them. This again makes him very approachable, an artist who keeps nothing hidden from his audience. However, the expression of his thoughts and feelings, and the description of events in his life were not confined to his paintings. Throughout his life he recorded his intimate thoughts in a remarkable series of letters to his brother Theo, who worked as an art dealer in Paris. The two brothers were extremely close, sharing similar temperaments and concerns. Published after Theo's death, this correspondence tells the same story as the paintings, of the many false starts in life, of his struggle for survival as a painter and of his mental collapse and periodic internments in a lunatic asylym. Through these intimate and moving letters it is possible to know Van Gogh as closely as his own brother did, and to follow the struggle of his life and the development of his art.

Background and early life

Van Gogh's life reflected many of the central issues of his time, in particular religion and socialism, the two great formative influences on his life, which were also of crucial importance in the history of the nineteenth century itself. He was the son of a Dutch Protestant minister, and throughout his early life he idolized his father and was himself deeply devout. He began his career, however, following in the footsteps of his uncle Vincent, who had been an important figure in the firm of Goupil & Co., picture dealers with branches in Paris, London and The Hague. Van Gogh worked for short periods at all three of these branches, but after seven years of increasing disillusionment both with his employers and with the business itself, he left, at the age of twenty-three.

He then traveled to England and taught for a while, first at a boy's school on the south coast and then on the outskirts of west London. During this time he became more and more absorbed in the idea of an ascetic way of life and in mystical, evangelical Protestantism. He decided to return to Holland to train for the ministry at a college in Amsterdam, but left after barely a year, disheartened by the need to study for what he saw as irrelevant academic exams. He decided to move to Brussels, where he enrolled in an evangelical missionary college, but managed to alarm the authorities with the extreme fervor of his convictions. After three months he was sent to preach amongst the miners of the Borinage region, but was dismissed for the excessive zeal with which he embraced and emulated the poverty of his surroundings. The intensity with which he approached life drove him to take his religious beliefs to what seemed their logical conclusion, and his desire to lead a life of poverty based on Christ's own at the expense of the usual social or religious conventions led to a parting of the ways with his superiors. By the time when, as a struggling painter in The Hague, he had set up house with a prostitute whom he hoped to save from her former ways, he had quite broken away from the conventional morality of the established Protestant church, and later, when he left Holland for Paris, he even abandoned his belief in God. His early years as a devout Christian, however, were to remain with him in his painting, as was the deeply moral standpoint from which he viewed the world, evidenced by his choice of the poorest of society as his subjects. The

JEAN FRANÇOIS MILLET
The Angelus
1857-9, Musée d'Orsay, Paris

This is typical of Millet's simple and dramatic compositions, many of which feature poorly clad figures set against a stark landscape. The religious element of the picture, however, produces a note of sentimentality lacking from many of his more defiant depictions of peasant hardship, which had a profound influence of Van Gogh.

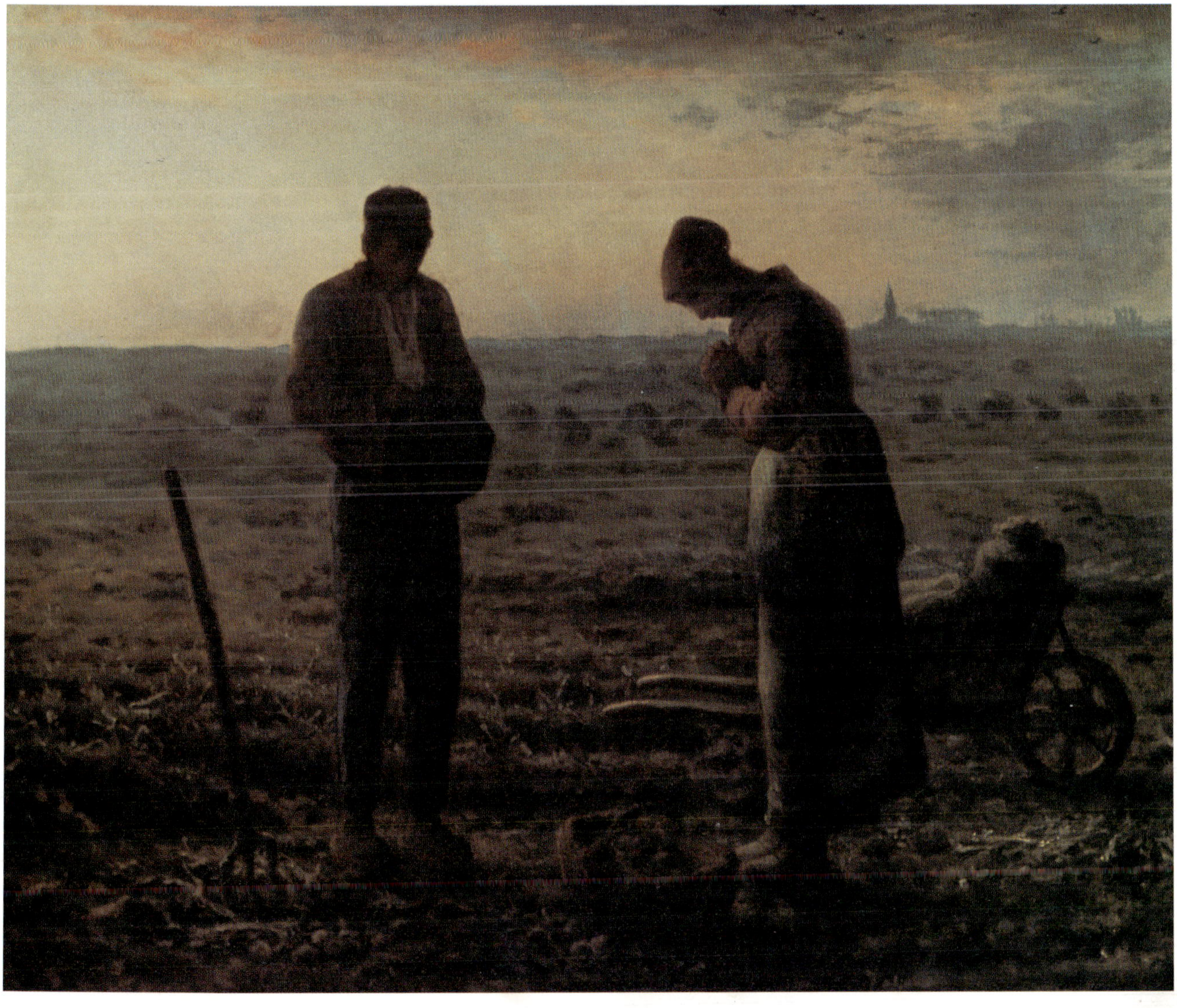

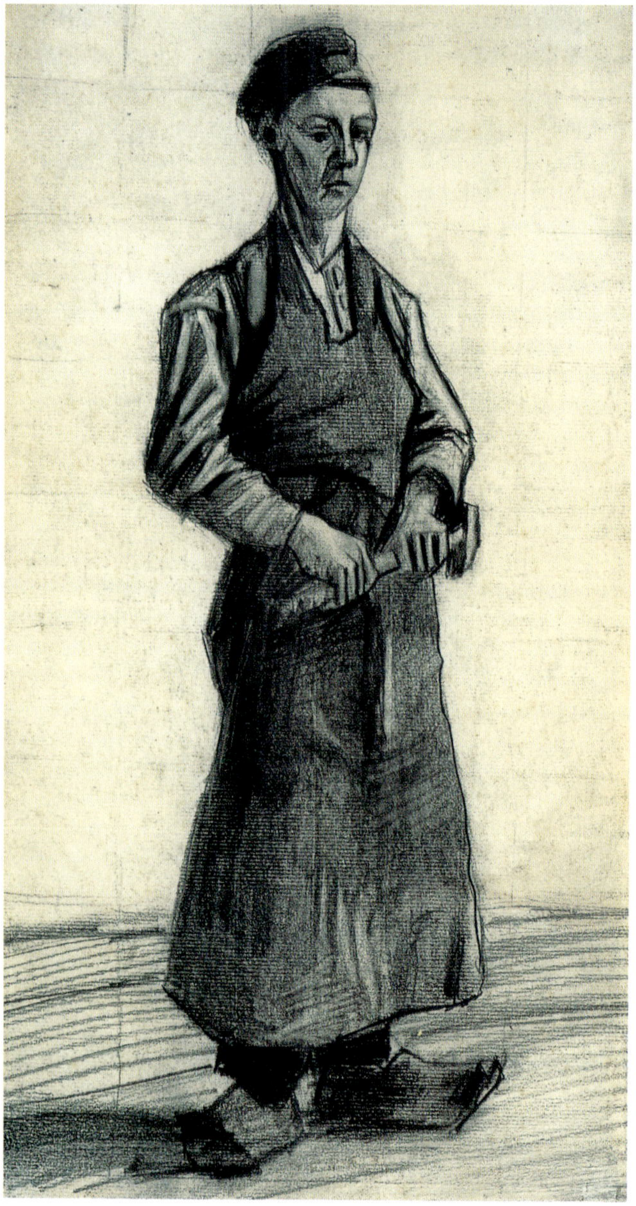

VINCENT VAN GOGH
The Blacksmith
1882, Private collection

This charcoal drawing dates from the period Van Gogh spent in The Hague, when he was influenced by the realistic style and subject matter of the Hague School of painters. He produced many drawings and lithographs at this time, before his love of color was awakened.

manner in which he sacrificed all else to work as a painter also recalled his early life, and he himself compared his life to that of a monk, who lives only for his vocation.

In abandoning a Christian answer to the injustice and suffering of his times, Van Gogh drew closer to a more political stance. Although he was at no time directly involved in the political turmoil of the age, in which socialism was fast developing as a major force, he made it plain, both in his letters to Theo and in his paintings, where his sympathies lay. Even when staying in the relative comfort of his father's parsonage at Neunen after the failure of his attempt to make a career as an artist in The Hague, it was the poor weavers and the farm laborers that he drew. His plans for producing art together with his fellow artists mirrored the socialist ideal for society as a whole. While in The Hague he had developed a scheme whereby he and like-minded fellows would work as a co-operative, mass-producing cheap lithographic prints for the working class. The idea was that all the artists would work with no thought for personal gain, and if the business dissolved the remaining prints would be distributed free. In Paris, where socialist and anarchist views were common among his painter friends, he continued to dream of communities of painters working together.

VINCENT VAN GOGH
Peasant Head
1884, Private Collection

Van Gogh's intense sympathy for the poor is.clearly shown in this portrait. The dark tones and muddy color are typical of his Dutch work, the most famous example of which is *The Potato Eaters* (see page 649). Studies such as this were among the preperations for the painting.

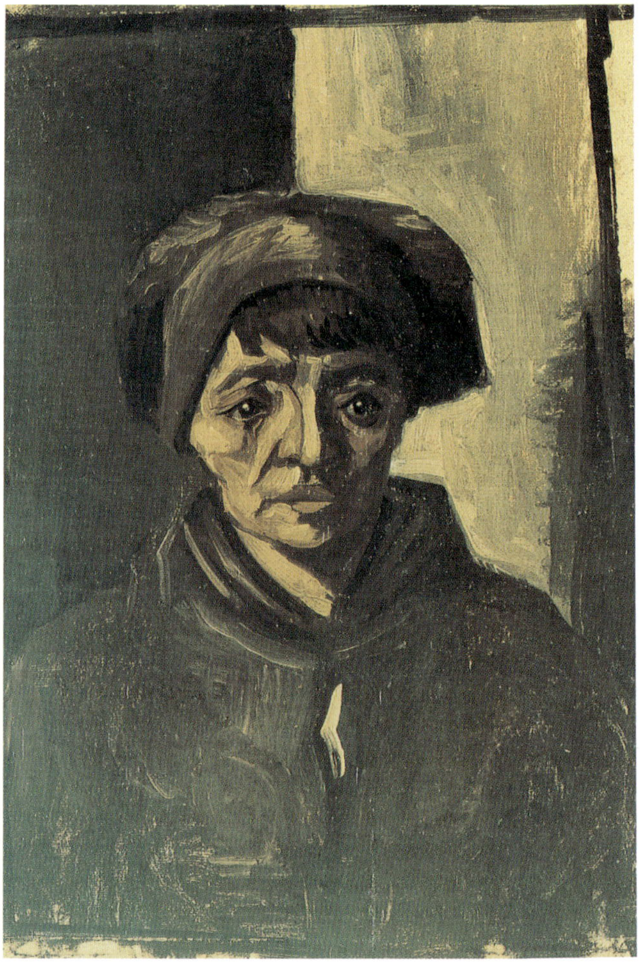

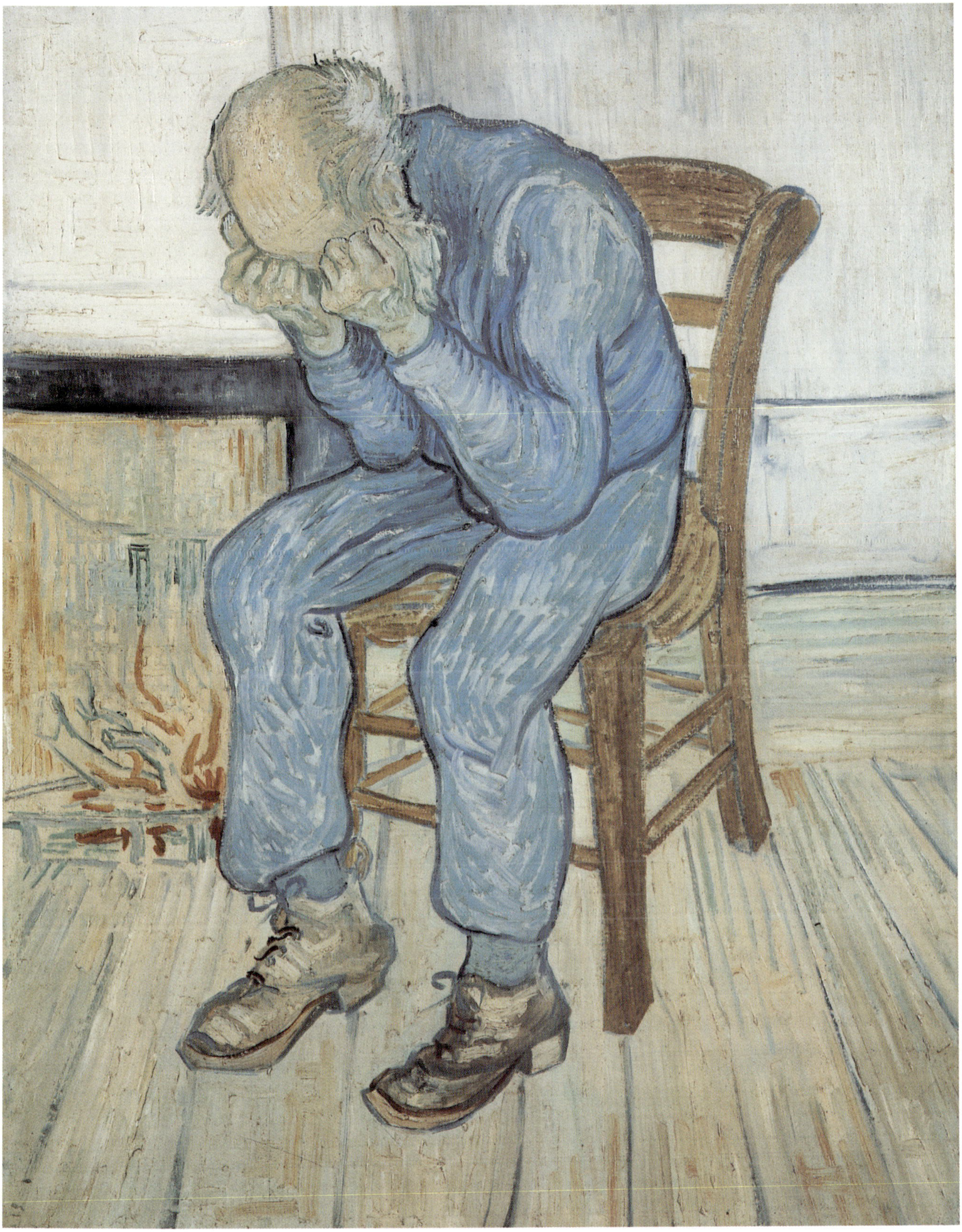

VINCENT VAN GOGH
Sorrowing Old Man
1890, Kröller-Müller Museum, Otterlo

Van Gogh first drew this subject in Holland, but he produced this version in the last year of his life. By this time it had become for him an image of both universal human suffering and the pain of his own life.

The new realism

Van Gogh's drift from radical evangelicism to a secular concern for social issues mirrored the broader issues of the times, notably the shift from the great religious revival of the nineteenth century to the social turmoil of the twentieth. Other artists and writers as sensitive as Van Gogh were moving in the same direction as the nineteenth century drew to a close, Leo Tolstoy's development in terms of social conscience being much of a parallel to Van Gogh's own, although the two never met. The literature of the time sheds valuable light on the influences that helped to form Van Gogh's painting, and the artist was himself extremely well read. A simple, eloquent statement of the role of religion and contemporary literature in his life is given in a painting he produced after his father's death, depicting the large family bible placed next to an extinguished candle. In the foreground is a novel by the French realist writer Emile Zola, a symbol of the future course of Van Gogh's life.

In his correspondence he continually refers to novels by such writers as Jean Michelet, the Goncourt brothers, Zola, Charles Dickens and Victor Hugo, and he saw the common thread between these writers as being the determined, often aggressive, realism with which they depicted contemporary life, particularly the sufferings of the poorer classes. Many of Van Gogh's favorite painters were those who shared his close relationship with literature, who actually worked as illustrators, or who shared the same devotion to realism that he saw in his

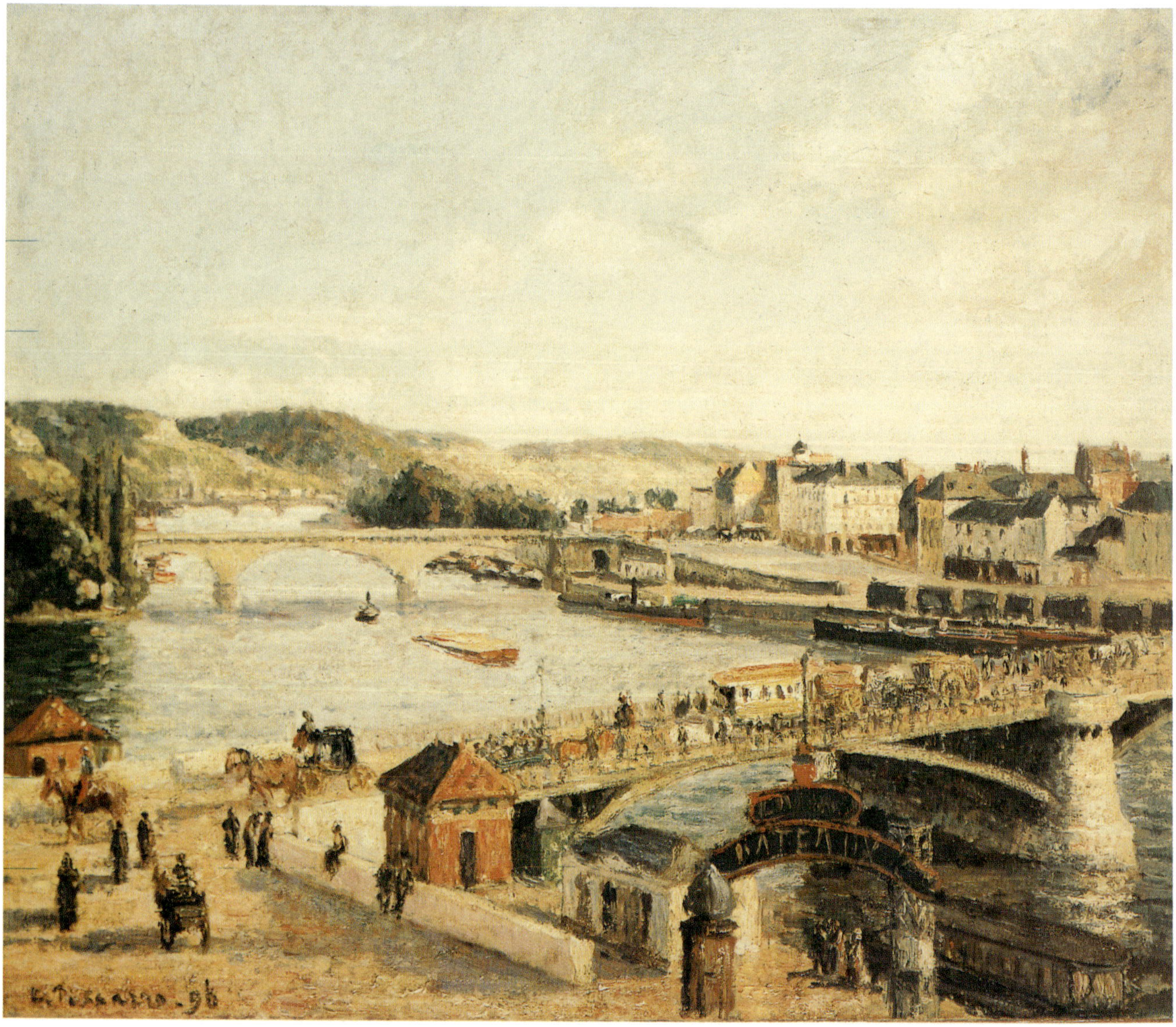

CAMILLE PISSARRO
Sunshine at Rouen
1896, Private collection

Pissarro's kindly nature made him the most approachable of the original members of the Impressionist group. Van Gogh was not the only artist to owe him a debt; he also taught Gauguin and Cézanne how to capture the colors of outdoor light using small dabs of paint, as in this typical painting.

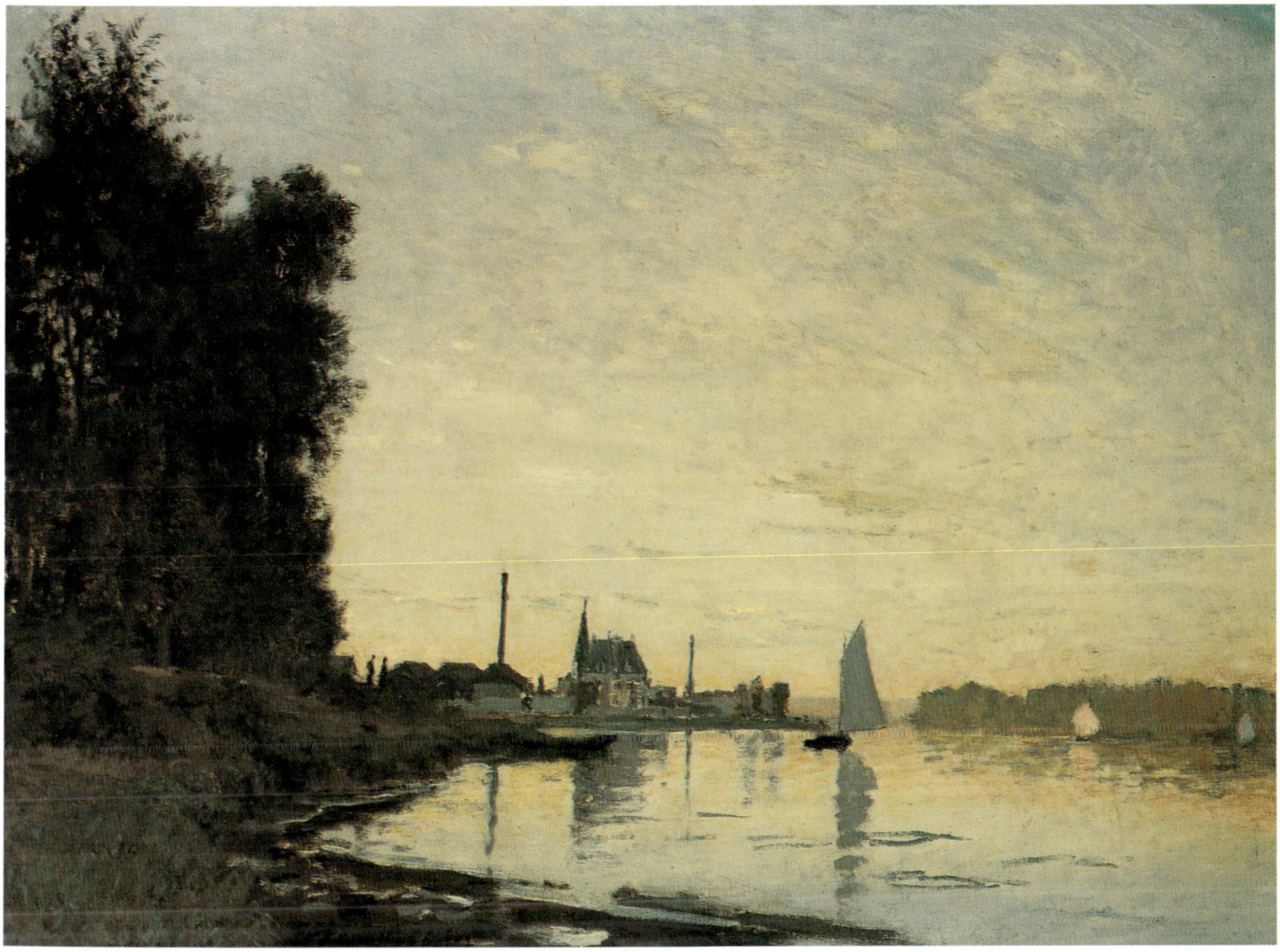

CLAUDE MONET
Evening at Argenteuil
1872, Private Collection

A typical river scene by the master of the Impressionist landscape. Monet painted on the spot to capture the exact colors that made up shadows in particular light conditions. He was particularly drawn to the surface of water as a subject that encouraged him to break up distracting details.

favorite writers. From his own Dutch heritage he admired Rembrandt in particular for the humanity and sensitivity he brought to his Biblical scenes, and the French artist Honoré Daumier (1808-79) struck a chord in Van Gogh for the way he had ridiculed the establishment in his popular engravings. Toward the end of his life, when he had committed himself to the asylum at St Rémy and his choice of subject matter was necessarily limited, Van Gogh produced his own versions of the work of both these artists.

In his emphasis on visual, as well as social, realism, Van Gogh can be seen as belonging to the central tradition of Dutch painting. Since the seventeenth century Dutch painters had chosen their subjects from everyday life, and in the mid-nineteenth century these themes had been given a further significance by The Hague School of painters, led by Josef Israels. Although deeply rooted in the traditions of their own country, these painters were also part of the Realist movement in painting that was current throughout mid nineteenth century Europe. This had started in France where it became the focus of opposition to the Academy, which exerted almost complete control over the style and content of French painting through the monopoly held by its own exhibitions. The Realists, by creating small, pioneering, alternative exhibitions, were able to challenge the conservative Academy and its promotion of historical, mythological and religious subject matter as the only concerns of the serious painter. The Realist painters depicted ordinary working people, often in the fields, and painted the French landscape as they saw it, often working directly from life in the open air, rather than constructing highly embellished studio pieces from sketches as the Academicians did. There were precedents for such innovations in Dutch and English painting, but in France the Realists saw themselves as revolutionaries, and they established the notion of an artistic avant-garde – young painters suffering poverty rather than compromising their style.

The Realists not only rejected the outmoded, idealized and escapist subjects of the Academicians but also the genteel polish they gave to their paintings. One of the leading Realist artists, Gustave Courbet (1819-77), delighted in exploiting the range of textures available with oil paints, and refused to disguise the vigorous brushwork he used to achieve his effects. The vitality and freedom of this sort of painting was to influence many later artists, Van Gogh among them.

But the Realist painter Van Gogh admired above all others was François Millet (1814-75). The hardship of Millet's life was similar to Van Gogh's own; from peasant stock himself, Millet had rejected a career in Paris to live among the peasants, and his pictures were deliberately stark, somber and crude. He gave his peasant subjects, often only a single figure set against a bare, uninviting landscape, a grandeur and dignity quite unprecedented in art history, so that they frequently appeared as heroic, grandiose figures, seemingly far removed from the physical hardship of their lives. Van Gogh loved the simplicity and power of these pictures, and he also found the religious overtones of many of them sympathetic. He was later to comment that although Millet, like himself, was steeped in the Bible, he never chose to paint directly religious subjects, but instead expressed his natural piety through the real world around him and the way he painted it. An aim which was precisely Van Gogh's own.

VINCENT VAN GOGH
A Corner of a Park
1888, Pen and ink drawing
Private collection

During his early months in Arles, Van Gogh used a reed pen in imitation of the Japanese masters. This drawing shows the large vocabulary of different strokes he had at his command, derived from the new knowledge he had acquired in Paris, and it demonstrates the same interest in varied textures and surfaces as his later paintings.

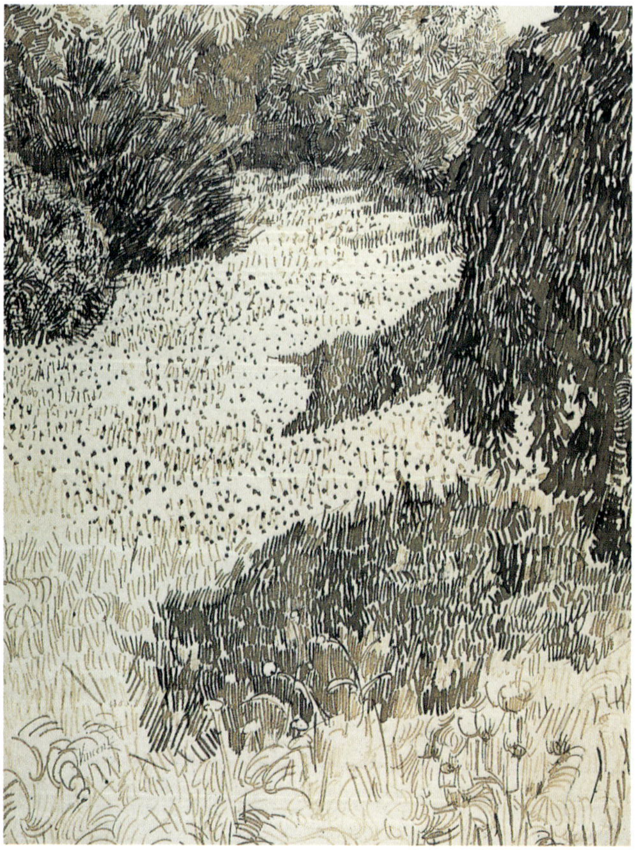

By the 1800s, when Van Gogh began to paint seriously, Millet was dead, but his reputation was established and his works had become popular and widely known through the circulation of engravings. Paris was now the center of avant-garde painting in Europe, and the modern movement set in motion by the Realists had moved far beyond the work of Millet. Van Gogh's brother Theo, who was now working in Paris for Goupil, wrote to tell his brother of the new generation of Realist painters, the Impressionists, and to describe their views of the city and countryside. Without having seen their work, however, Van Gogh was unable to comprehend their significance, and remained absorbed by Millet.

The Impressionists and after

It was not until he joined Theo in Paris in 1886 that he actually saw the work of Monet, Renoir, Degas and Pissarro and realized what the Impressionists had achieved. Building on the same foundations as the Realists, and painting much the same subjects, they had begun to concentrate much more on color and the effects of natural light than on the precise details of the scenes before them. Their palettes became ever lighter and of ever purer colors as they systematically banished the black pigment that had traditionally controlled the tonality of a picture, and began reproducing the hues they saw in nature. Under the influence of the Impressionists, Van Gogh's painting underwent a dramatic change, from the dark and somber colors of his Dutch work to the new vividness of the French landscape style. For a while he

Opposite page
GEORGES SEURAT
Bathing, Asnières
1884, National Gallery, London

The surface of this work is made up of countless tiny brushstrokes of differing colors that merge, when seen at the usual distance, into the subtle hues of a sunlit outdoor scene. Van Gogh was influenced by Seurat and his followers.

Opposite page
HOKUSAI
Temma Bridge at Osaka
c 1830, Victoria and Albert Museum, London

Van Gogh loved the brilliant, pure colors he saw in the work of Japanese printmakers such as Hokusai. Japanese art had been a major influence on the Impressionists for the same reason, and had a large following among Paris artists.

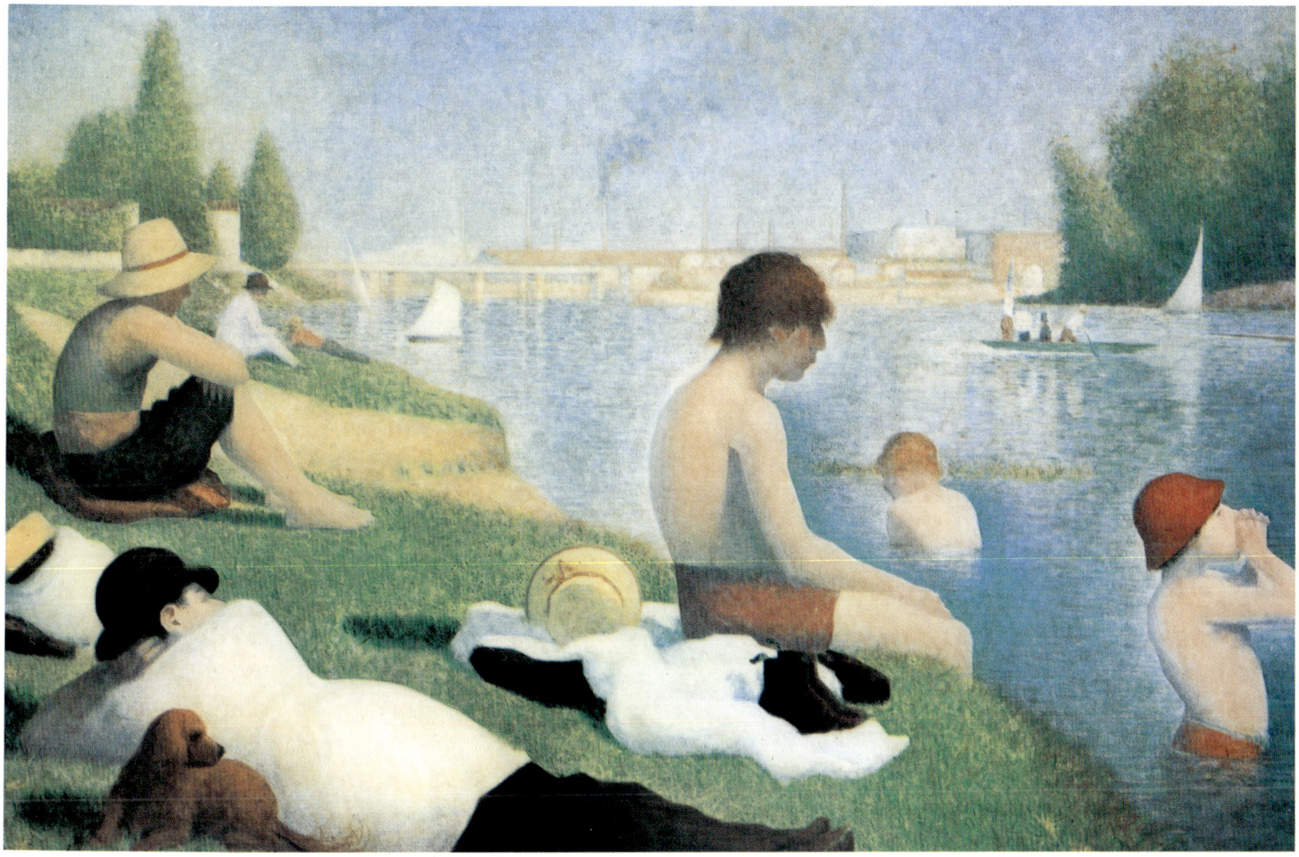

GEORGE SEURAT *Bathing, Asnières*

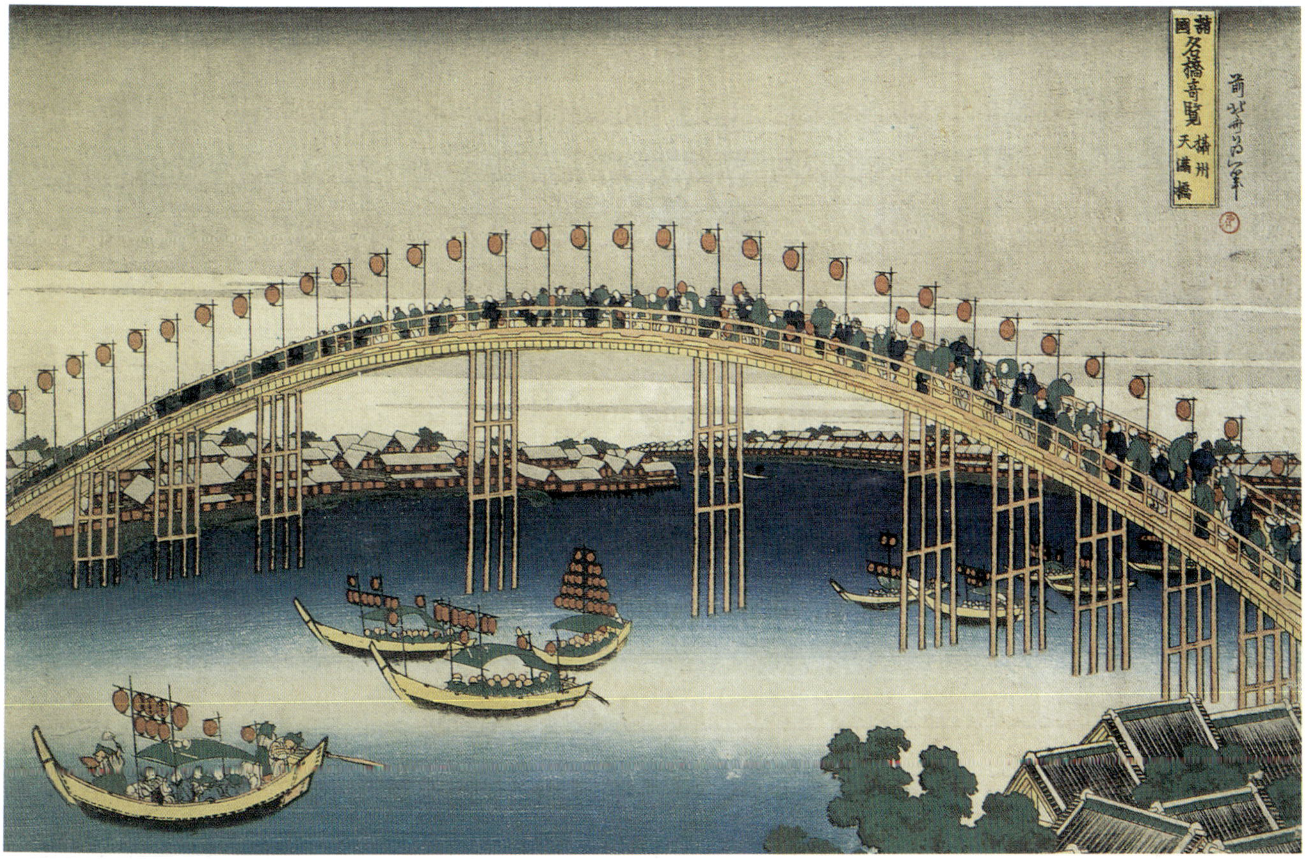

HOKUSAI *Temma Bridge at Osaka*

painted the Impressionist subject matter of parks and riverside scenes, with the same broken brushwork and pure colors, indeed the discovery of bright, sunny colors was a revelation to him and he continued to use them almost until his death. However, he had soon absorbed all that the Impressionists could teach him – they were now becoming rather remote and successful figures – and found himself facing new challenges.

PAUL GAUGUIN
Van Gogh Painting Sunflowers
1888

Gauguin has depicted Van Gogh painting one of his favorite subjects. While Van Gogh used Impressionist brushwork as a starting point to develop his own more expressive form, Gauguin soon rejected it altogether to concentrate on expressing his poetic and visionary ideas through flatly painted areas of color.

As Impressionism became an established style taught by its creators, particularly Camille Pissarro, to younger artists such as Van Gogh, its limitations became clearer. To record contemporary life in its true sunlit colors no longer seemed a compelling task for the avant-garde, but for this new generation, later to be known as the Post-Impressionists, the way forward was not immediately clear. Some became followers of Georges Seurat, who was attempting to create a new form of Impressionism, Pointillism, based on the scientific observation of light and tiny, uniform brushstrokes of pure color. For a while Van Gogh painted with Paul Signac, an ardent convert to Seurat's style, but others, like Paul Gauguin and Emile Bernard, began to turn away from the depiction of mundane reality altogether and to seek objects in religion, mythology or far-away, exotic places.

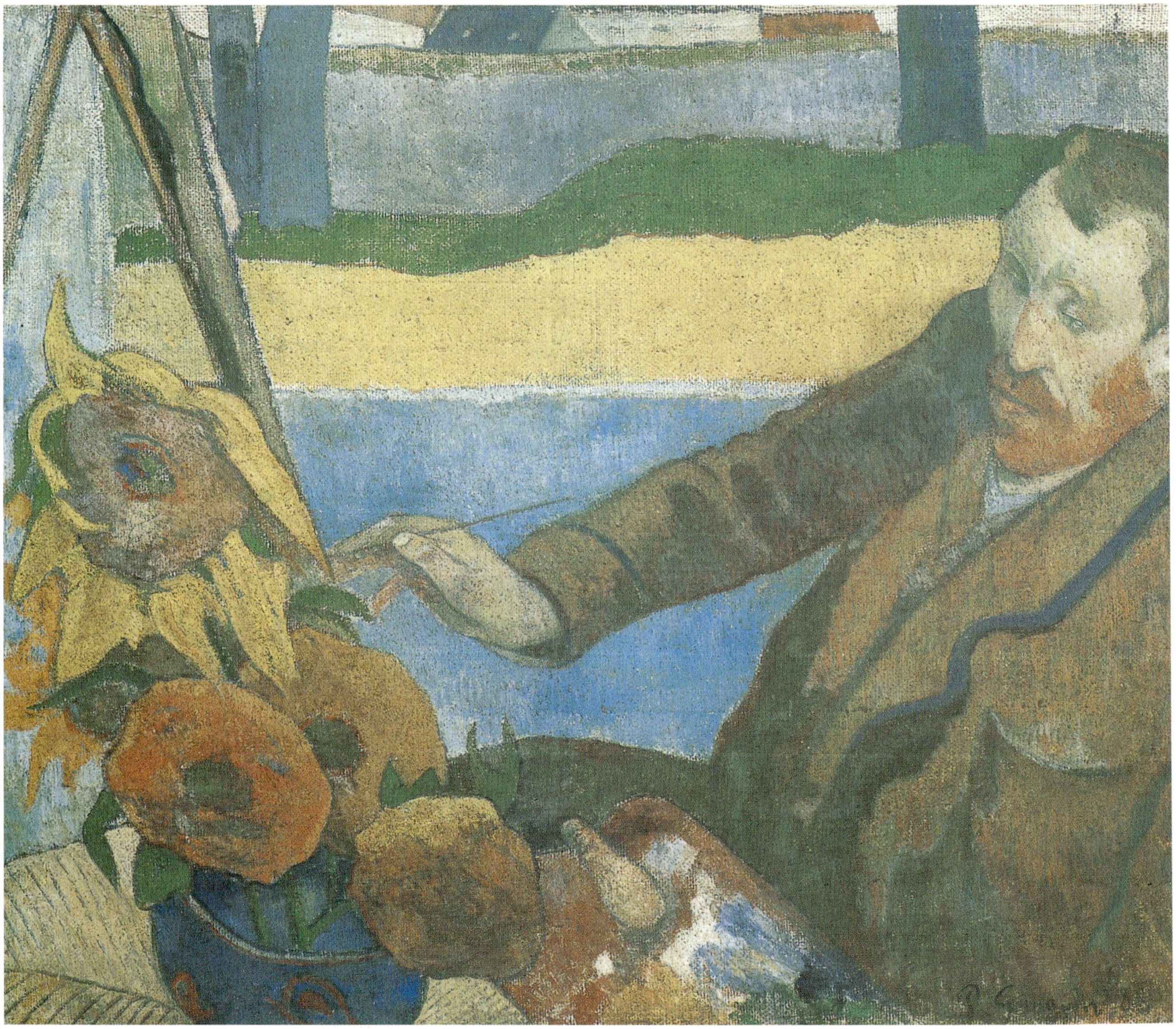

VAN GOGH'S PAINTING METHODS

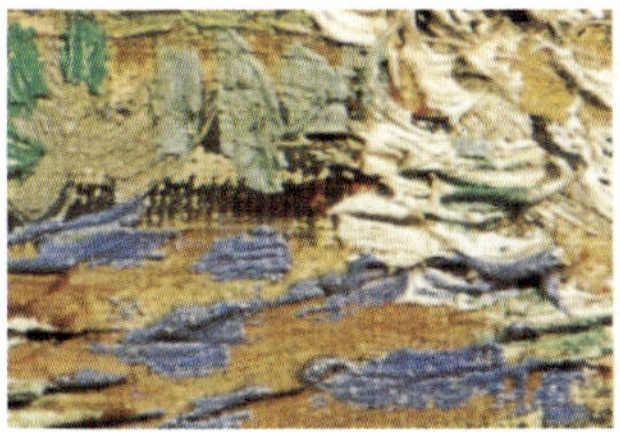

In this detail from Peach Trees in Blossom *the cream-beige of the canvas priming is just visible between the thickly impasted brushstrokes.*

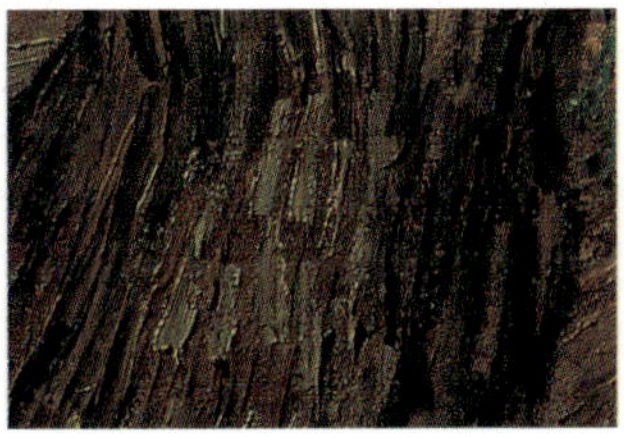

Here, in the painting Hospital Garden at St Rémy, *the brushstrokes describe the form of the tree and suggest the rough texture of the bark.*

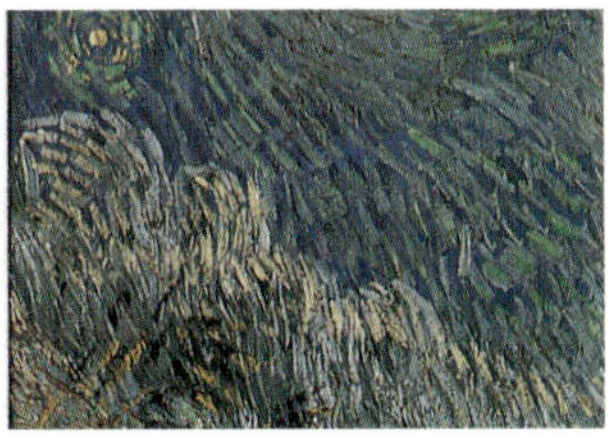

In the sky area of Road with Cypress and Star *the brushstrokes are expressionistic, giving a feeling of restlessness and turbulence.*

For the Impressionists, color was a vital means of conveying optical effects, but for Van Gogh and his successors, the Expressionists, it was much more than that. For these artists, painting was a whole language, in which line and color were called upon to interpret feelings and a personal vision. Van Gogh claimed to be able to express "those terrible things, men's passions" by red and green, and he saw certain colors, juxtapositions and contrasts as having their own symbolic significance. In a letter of 1888 he described an intention "to express the love of two lovers by a marriage of two complementary colors, their mingling and their opposition, the mysterious vibration of kindred tones."

The way he used paint was very personal and equally expressive, the result of much conscious experimentation as well as an instinctive feeling for the creation of a varied paint surface. In his later works he used his bright, vibrant colors in thick, rich impastos, with brushstrokes that echoed the forms of the subject, often working wet-into-wet so that the colors were slurred together, but sometimes dragging dry, thick paint over an already dry underlayer or working in a criss-cross pattern of strokes. He liked a matt surface, and both he and Gauguin experimented with coarse, unprimed canvas such as hessian, which absorbs the oil binding from the paint. The majority of his paintings, however, are on ready-primed canvas which he bought in rolls and stretched himself. The grounds he preferred were off-white, gray, white or warm pink, and in some paintings the ground colors are allowed to show through.

In his mature works of the Arles period, such as Chair with Pipe, *Van Gogh used the small but vivid palette shown here, with lead white and some earth colors.*

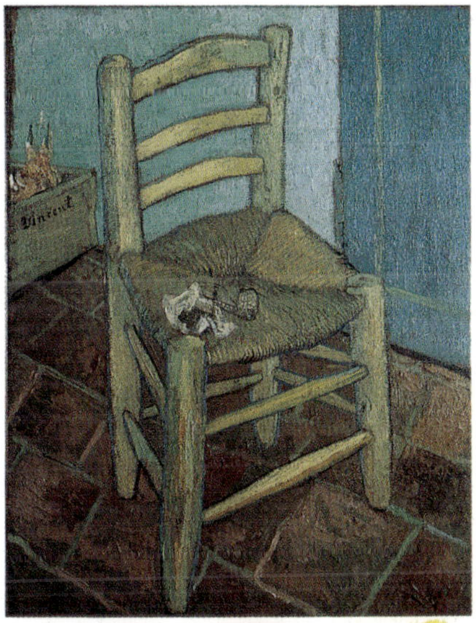

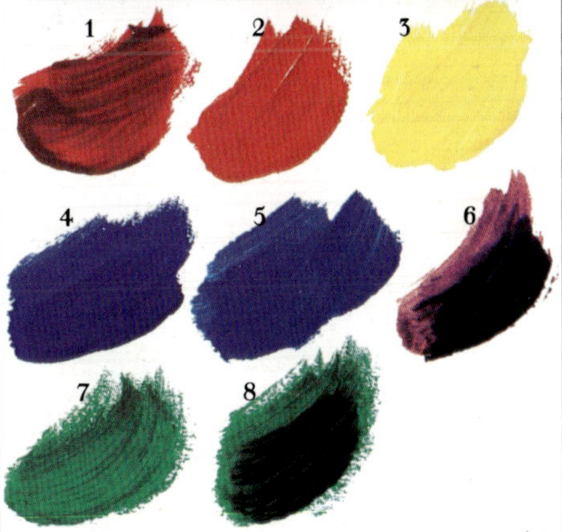

1 Red lake; 2 Vermilion; 3 Cadmium yellow; 4 Ultramarine; 5 Cobalt blue, 6 Cobalt violet; 7 Emerald green; 8 Viridian

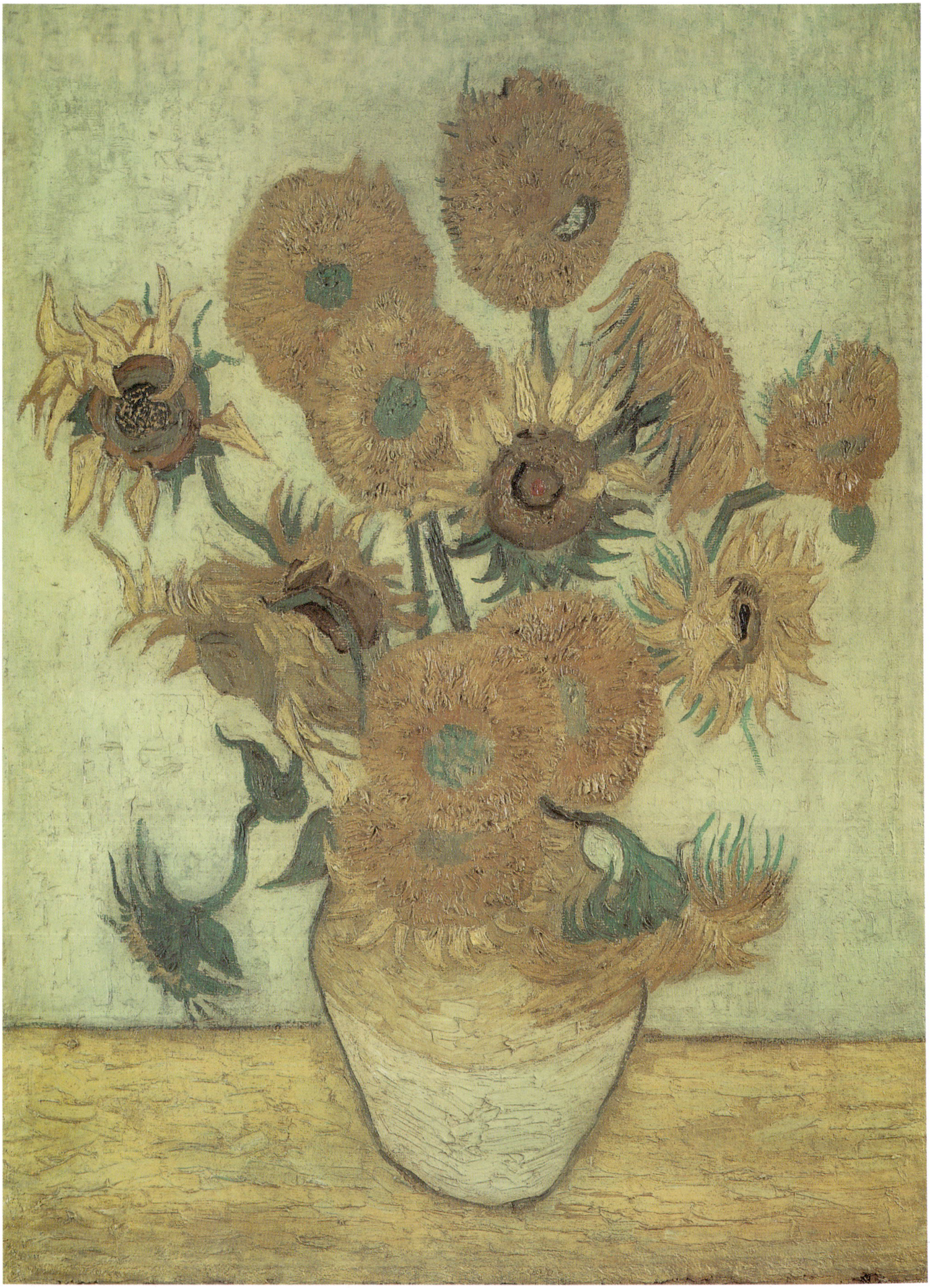

The path to self-expression

Although Van Gogh adopted the color and brushwork of the Impressionists his whole background and character distanced him from their approach. Working with Pissarro or Signac had been essentially part of his artistic education – catching up with the developments in Paris – but he was temperamentally unsuited to making pictures that were dispassionate visual records, and having extended his own technical range he was once again ready to make his own personal statements. He always looked for subjects that had a special significance to him, often a deeper one than their mere appearance, and after he had left Paris in 1888 to paint in the south of France his work became more and more personal, echoing the increasingly turbulent events of his life.

Van Gogh thus became one of the leading figures of Post-Impressionism, building on the work of the Impressionists but moving forward in a totally new direction, and the Post-Impressionist "alternative" that he developed in the last two years of his life was to become one of the most important paths to be followed by painters of the twentieth century. Although still taking his inspiration from the scene before him, his interpretation of it became far freer. The relationship between artist and subject assumed an equality, the artist imposing his own feelings on his subject in a way that had not been done before, by simplifying forms, distorting perspective and altering colors. All this was carried out with brushwork of such vigor and paint of such thickness that the viewer is constantly reminded of the painting's nature as an object with its own flat surface, rather than seeing it as a window through which a "real" scene is perceived. As his mental state became more precarious – from December 1888 onwards he suffered periodic attacks of insanity and had to spend time in the hospital at Arles and the asylum of St Rémy – his technique became increasingly concerned with self-expression rather than the strict recording of visual impressions.

Opposite page
VINCENT VAN GOGH
Sunflowers
1889, Private Collection

Van Gogh painted several versions of this favorite subject, which seemed to him the very essence of the bright sun of the south of France.

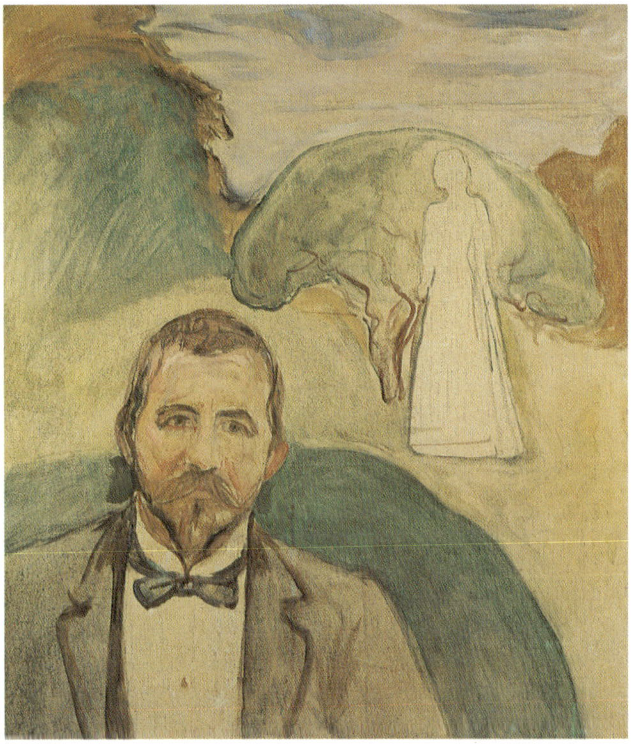

EDVARD MUNCH
Dream Self-Portrait
c 1926, Private collection

Like Van Gogh, Munch explored his inner anguish through a long series of self-portraits. He developed the expressionist elements of Van Gogh's later work to produce pictures that were characterized by a highly subjective use of color and distortion of space.

Van Gogh's heritage

Van Gogh sold only one painting in his lifetime, but his suicide at Auvers, near Paris, in July 1890, coincided with a time when his work was becoming better known and appreciated, at least by his fellow artists. As his fame grew his work appeared in exhibitions throughout Europe, and his influence became discernible in the work of others. It was in northern Europe that his paintings were perhaps best understood. The Norwegian Edvard Munch (1863-1944) shared something of Van Gogh's emotional make-up, for he himself suffered from deep depressions and led a life scarred by trauma. Munch began to employ similar distortions of space and color with expressive brushwork to communicate emotional states. The two artists' backgrounds and concerns were similar enough to suggest that in some respects Munch, who became an important influence on German twentieth-century art, continued Van Gogh's work, thus establishing a thread running right through to the present century. This thread brought a need to describe the new kind of painting, and the term which came to be used, Expressionism, was particularly attached to two groups of German painters working before the First

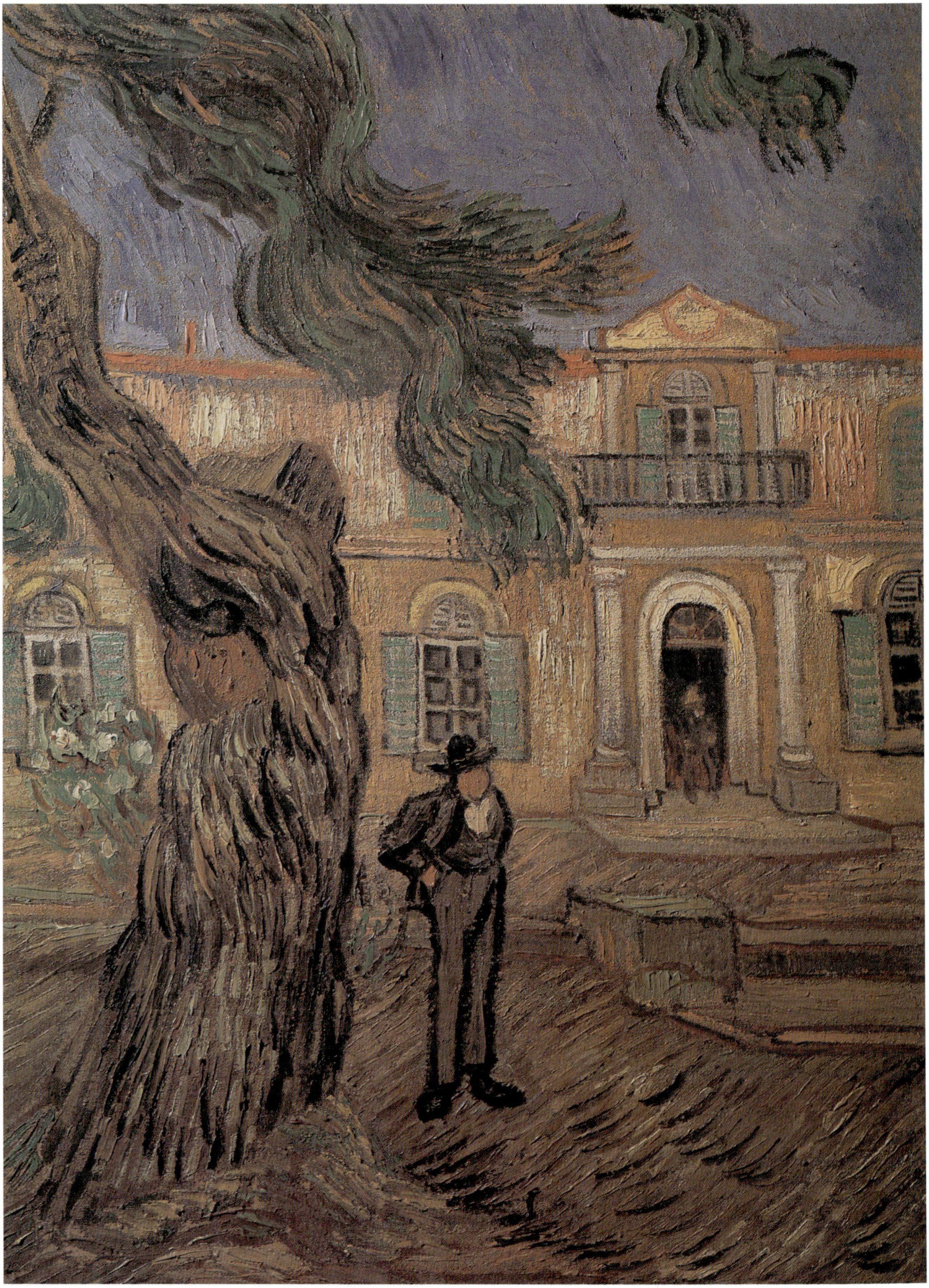

World War, *Die Brücke* ("The Bridge") of Dresden and *Der Blaue Reiter* ("The Blue Rider") of Munich. Although different in style both from each other and from their forebears, these two groups of artists owed their freedom to express themselves directly and non-descriptively to Van Gogh, who came to be viewed with hindsight as the father of modern Expressionism. This has been a recurring theme in modern painting: it emerged, revitalized, in American painting of the 1940s and '50s as Abstract Expressionism, with Van Gogh again acknowledged as the original inspiration. A sequence of books and exhibitions from this time confirmed his status, and the English master Francis Bacon (b.1909) produced a series of paintings derived from Van Gogh's own self-portrait of *The Artist Going to Work* as a direct homage.

Today, a hundred years after Van Gogh's revolutionary paintings in the south of France, modern painting in Europe and America has returned to a form of Expressionism, vigorously and often violently produced but nevertheless recognizable as descending from the same source. Van Gogh himself has become a symbol to the world of the artist struggling to make sense of the pain and hardship that he saw as the human condition. Through his life and work he brought the painter's role to its moral peak as one who works for his fellow man as interpreter of his hopes and as comforter for his suffering. His struggle to express himself through his painting has come to represent modern man's struggle to make sense of a hostile and confusing world.

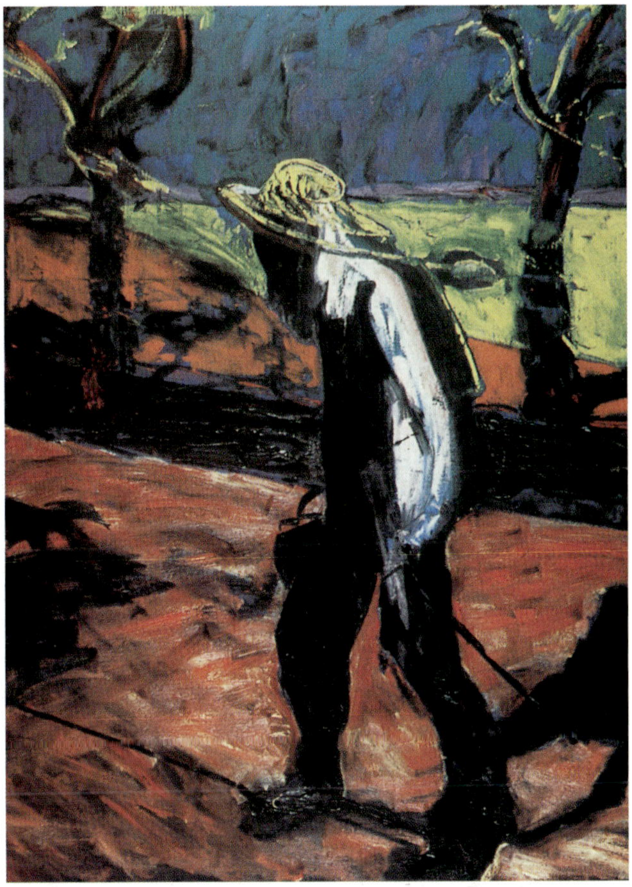

FRANCIS BACON
Study for Portrait of Van Gogh VI
1957, Arts Council of Great Britain

This work is a tribute to Van Gogh by the contemporary English artist Francis Bacon, based on a Van Gogh painting of himself walking to work.

Opposite page
VINCENT VAN GOGH
The Garden of the Asylum at St Rémy
1889, Musée d'Orsay, Paris

In his later works the turmoil of Van Gogh's mind becomes the principal subject of his paintings. Here it is clearly seen in the charged brushwork with which the tree is painted. A disturbing note is added by the faceless figure standing in the foreground, thought to be the director of the asylum.

CHRONOLOGY OF VAN GOGH'S LIFE

1853 March 30th: Vincent Van Gogh born in the parsonage of Groot Zundert, Holland.

1869 Joins Goupil & Co., art dealers, in The Hague.

1873-5 Works for Goupil in London and Paris.

1876 Schoolmaster in England.

1877 Studies in Amsterdam for the entrance exam to the Theological Seminary.

1878 July: gives up his studies in Amsterdam and enters evangelical school in Brussels. December: sent to preach in the mining district of the Borinage, Belgium.

1879 Dismissed from his post but continues to work nearby.

1880 Starts drawing and attends art classes in Brussels.

1881 Working at The Hague, taught by the painter Anton Mauve.

1882 Living in The Hague with a prostitute and her child.

1883 September: moves to Drenthe in east Holland to paint the peasants.

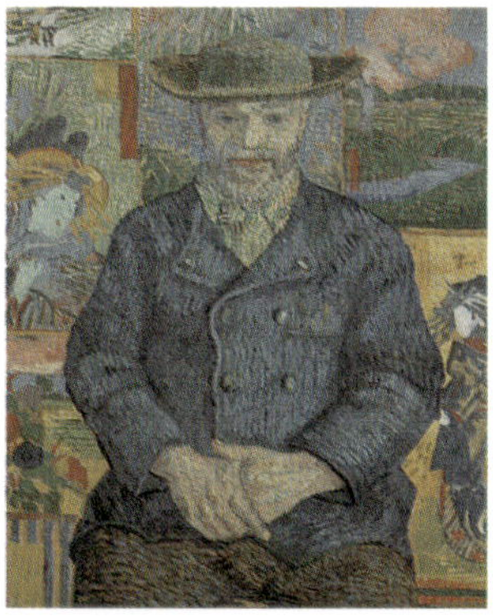

Portrait of Père Tanguy

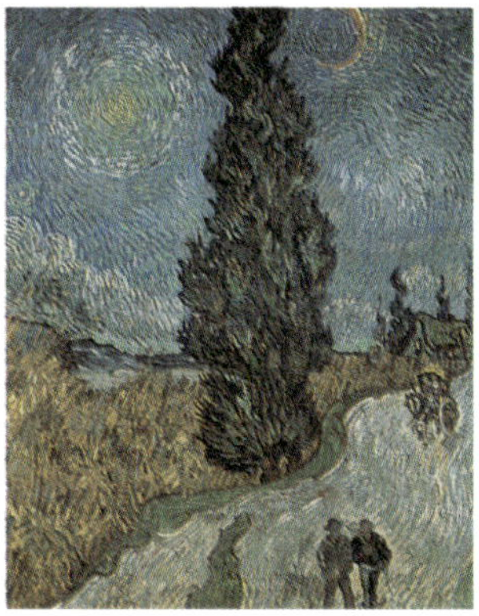

Road with Cypress and Star

1885 September-October: paints *The Potato Eaters.* November: moves to Antwerp.

1886 January: attends the Academy of Art in Antwerp. February: moves to Paris.

1887 *Kitchen Gardens in Montmartre. Portrait of Père Tanguy.*

1888 February: leaves Paris for Arles. October: arrival of Gauguin at Arles. November: *Vincent's Chair with his Pipe. L'Arlesienne.* December: first mental collapse.

1889 January: *Self-portrait with Bandaged Ear.* Further breakdowns — enters hospital at Arles. May: Moves to the mental asylum at St Rémy. *Road with Cypress and Star.*

1890 May: briefly visits Paris and moves to Auvers-sur-Oise.
June: *Portrait of Dr Gachet.*
July: *Crows in the Wheatfield.*
July 27th: shoots himself, but misses his heart.
July 29th: dies at Auvers.

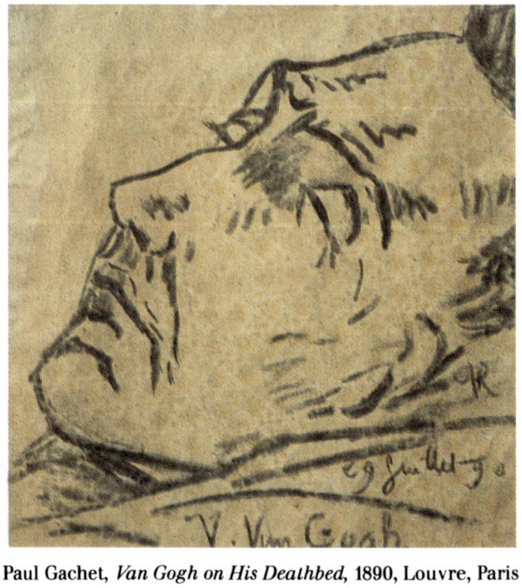

Paul Gachet, *Van Gogh on His Deathbed,* 1890, Louvre, Paris

THE PAINTINGS

The Potato Eaters

1885

$32\frac{1}{4} \times 45$in/82×114cm

Oil on canvas

Van Gogh Museum, Amsterdam

The Potato Eaters was painted toward the end of a period of relative stability in Van Gogh's life. After the difficult time at The Hague, when his first efforts at working as an independent artist with his own studio had been undermined by the stress of setting up a household with his ex-prostitute lover and her child, he made a brief stay in the bare, rainswept heathland around Drenthe in eastern Holland and then, in 1883, returned to live with his parents at Neunen in Brabant. The last time Van Gogh had lived with his parents he had stormed out to move to The Hague, but now, although he acknowledged to Theo that there were still tensions between them, both sides endeavored to avoid actual conflict. Tending an illness of his mother with the same care that he had given to influenza-stricken miners in the Borinage showed his father a different side of his character and helped to draw them together.

He worked hard at his painting while at Neunen and progressed rapidly. *The Potato Eaters* draws together all that he had observed about peasant life in his early years, using the new skills he developed in The Hague. The dark interior recalls the many studies he made of the weavers of Neunen toiling over huge, creaking looms in cramped, poorly lit rooms, and the faces of the family are not direct portraits but a sort of composite, deriving from the many studies of heads he produced at this time. These, like those in *The Potato Eaters*, were painted with deliberately crude strokes, not because Van Gogh was in any way inept in the use of paint, but because he was trying to convey what he saw as the very essence of their way of life. He said himself that he would like to produce paintings of peasant life that looked as if they had been painted with the very soil of the fields.

Although firmly rooted in real social conditions, the painting has a further dimension. The simple dignity of the scene has been likened to a painting of a religious ceremony, even to a Last Supper. Such an impression is given validity by the fact that when asked by a neighbor — an amateur painter — to decorate his dining room with religious scenes Van Gogh preferred to produce scenes from peasant life, including a meal of potatoes.

Throughout this period Van Gogh produced a large number of charcoal drawings, using dark, strong strokes. Although his main interest was still the figure, these drawings also show a strong interest in the effects of chiaroscuro, or light and shade, as does *The Potato Eaters*, which was produced as a lithographic print as well as a painting. Although a dark painting it is not completely reliant on tonality, and even the deepest shadows have color. Van Gogh was able to produce extremely vital "muddy" tones by mixing a number of pigments together to produce variations of dark, neutral colors instead of simply using dark brown or black, which produce a lifeless effect. When blue and shades of brown (in this case raw and roasted sienna) are mixed together they give a luminous and atmospheric near-black, to which blues, yellows and reds can be added to gain the required variations.

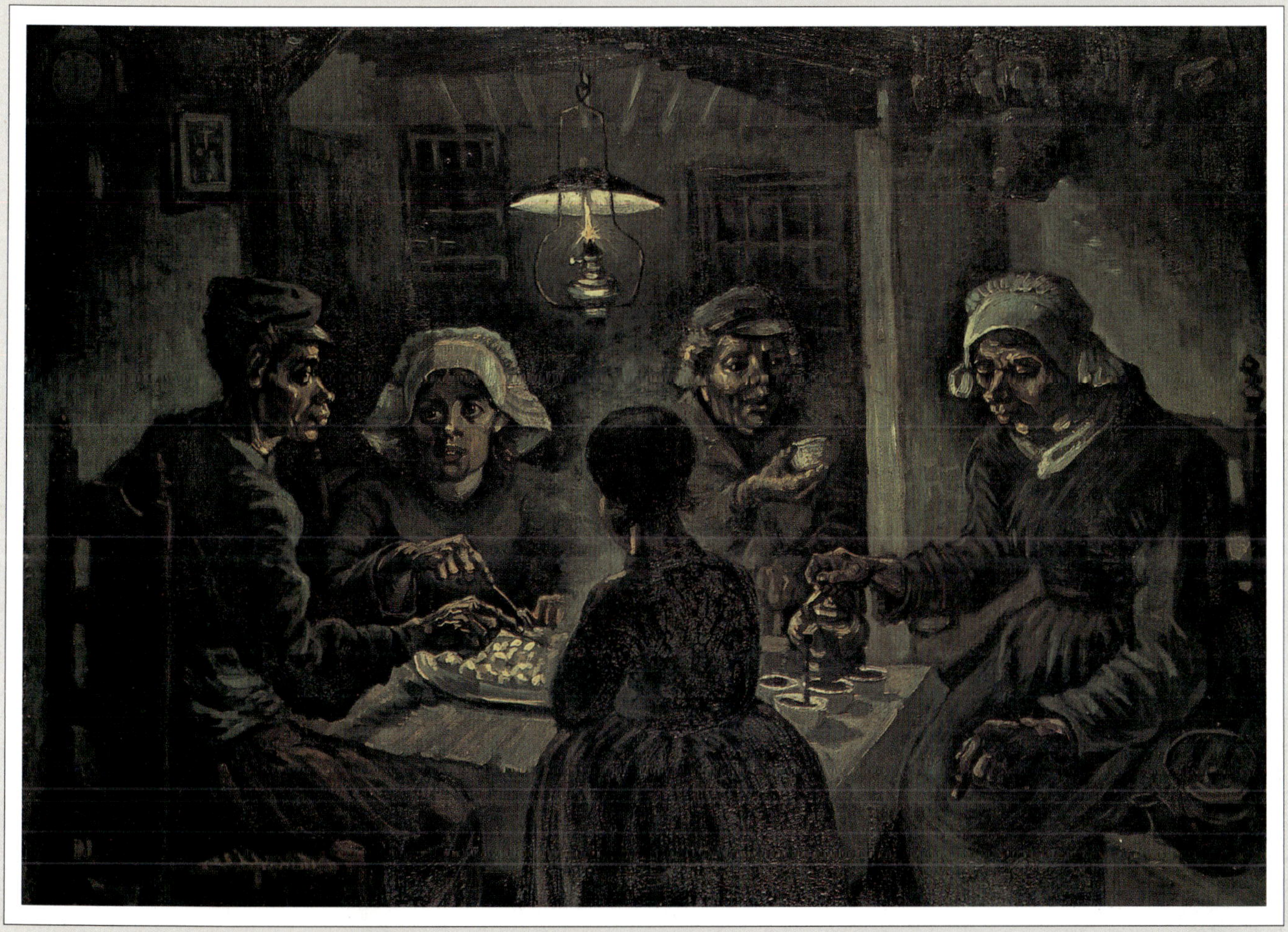

The Potato Eaters is typical of Van Gogh's Dutch interiors in its use of a very few bright highlights against a predominantly dark background. Throughout his career Van Gogh was particularly aware of the dramatic possibility of strong contrasts in his paintings, but as his talent and knowledge of painting developed these contrasts were focused less around light and dark than around cool and warm colors, foreground and background, different textures of paint and so on. It has been suggested that these recurring pictorial tensions and oppositions may help to reveal something about the inner conflicts from which he suffered.

In this case the murky interior is intended to stress the poverty and hardship of the peasants' lives, but the occasional highlights also help to create a feeling of attractive intimacy – the sort of simple fellowship that Van Gogh himself craved.

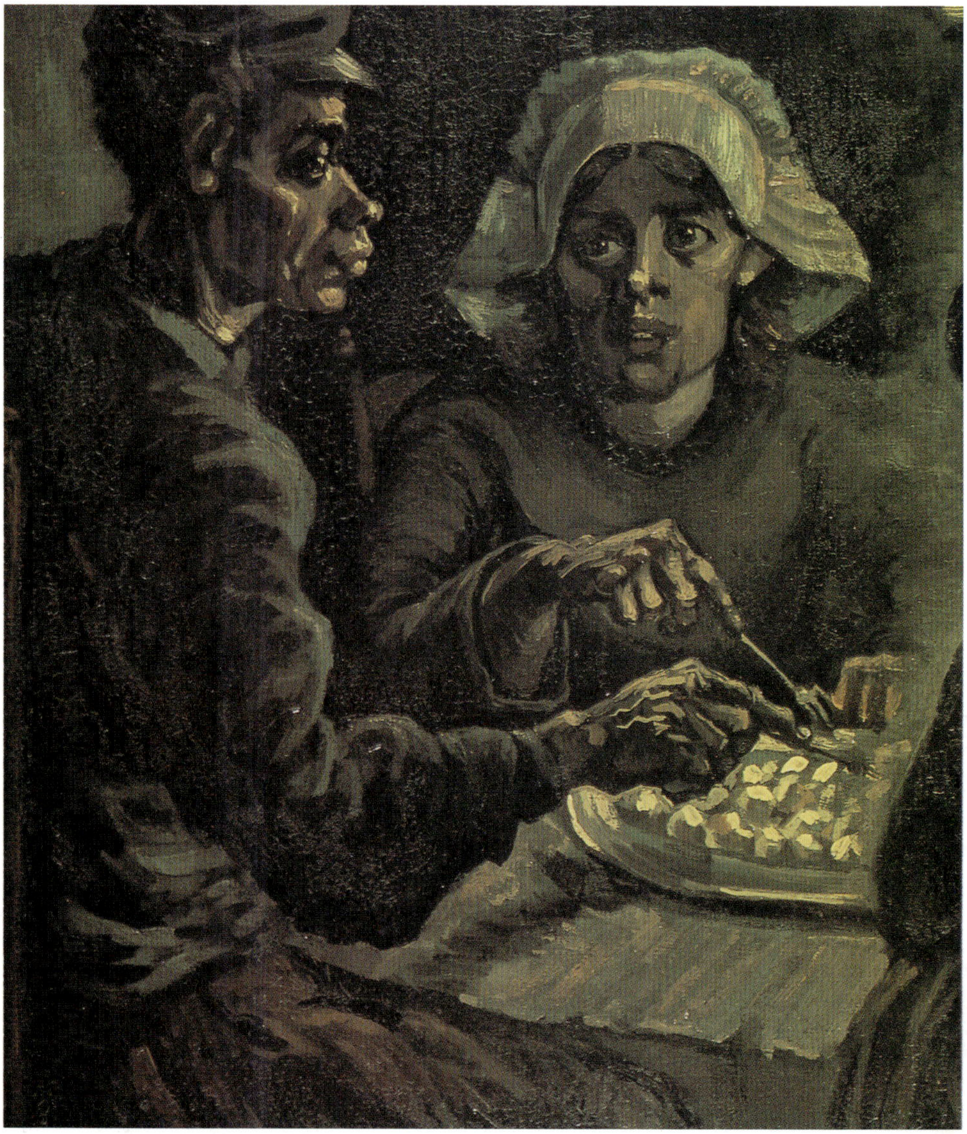

1

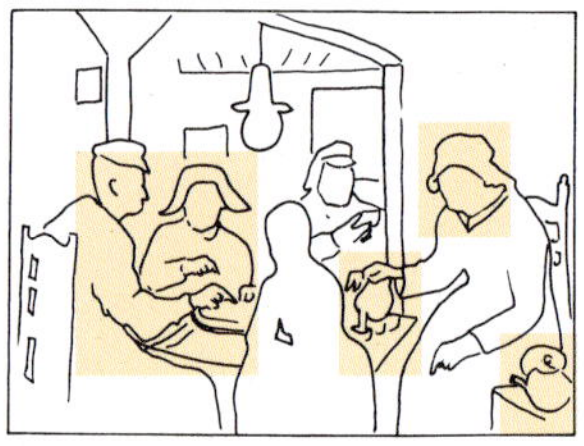

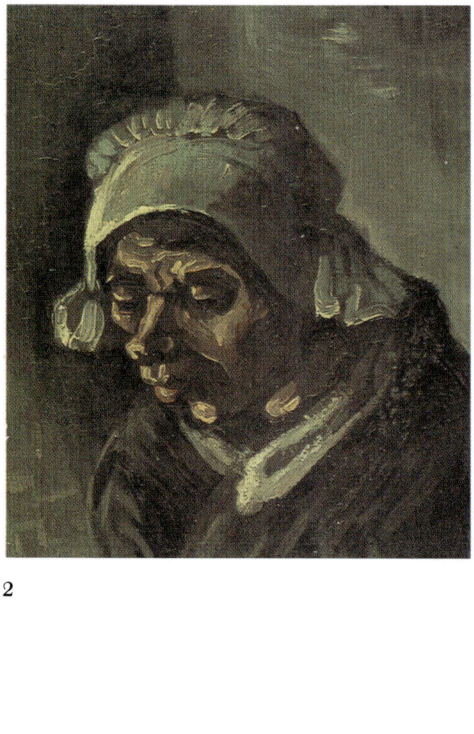

2

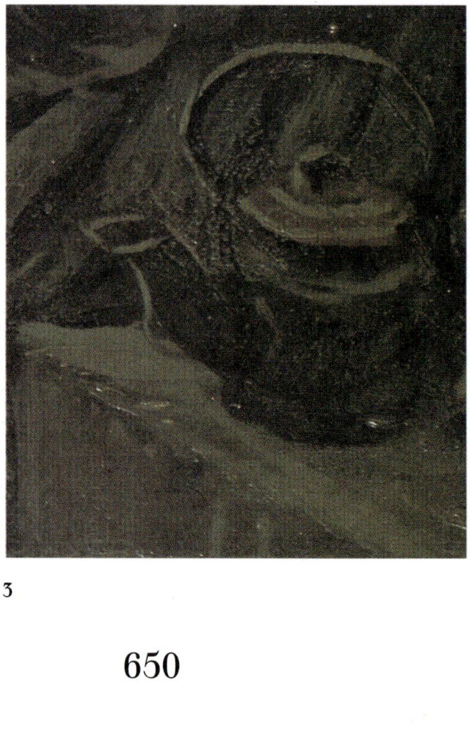

3

1 The apparent crudity of the brushstrokes belies the accuracy and economy of their use. The veins and knuckles of the hands, for instance, are treated with much more care than is seen on the sketches which led up to this work, such as the *Peasant Head* (see page 634). Van Gogh viewed this painting as a major work and devoted his most concentrated skill to it.

2 A sparing use of half-tones creates the very strongly molded face of the peasant woman. The darkest area of her cap demands a correspondingly lighter "halo" of wall behind to create the silhouette. Looser, thinner paint is used for the background to help push the figure forward — again reminding us of Rembrandt's work, where the thinnest paint is in the background.

3 The subtlety of Van Gogh's handling of tone is shown in the form of the pot, lightly painted in an area of what appears to be deep shadow, almost lost against the highlights of the central area. It is also possible to see how the shading is created by a mix of different colors, not a pure black or dark brown.

4 *Actual size detail* Here Van Gogh "draws" with the brush to create the form of the coffeepot with a few directional strokes. The same technique is used on the hands, the painter's concern being more with the texture of his own paint than with those of the surfaces he is depicting.

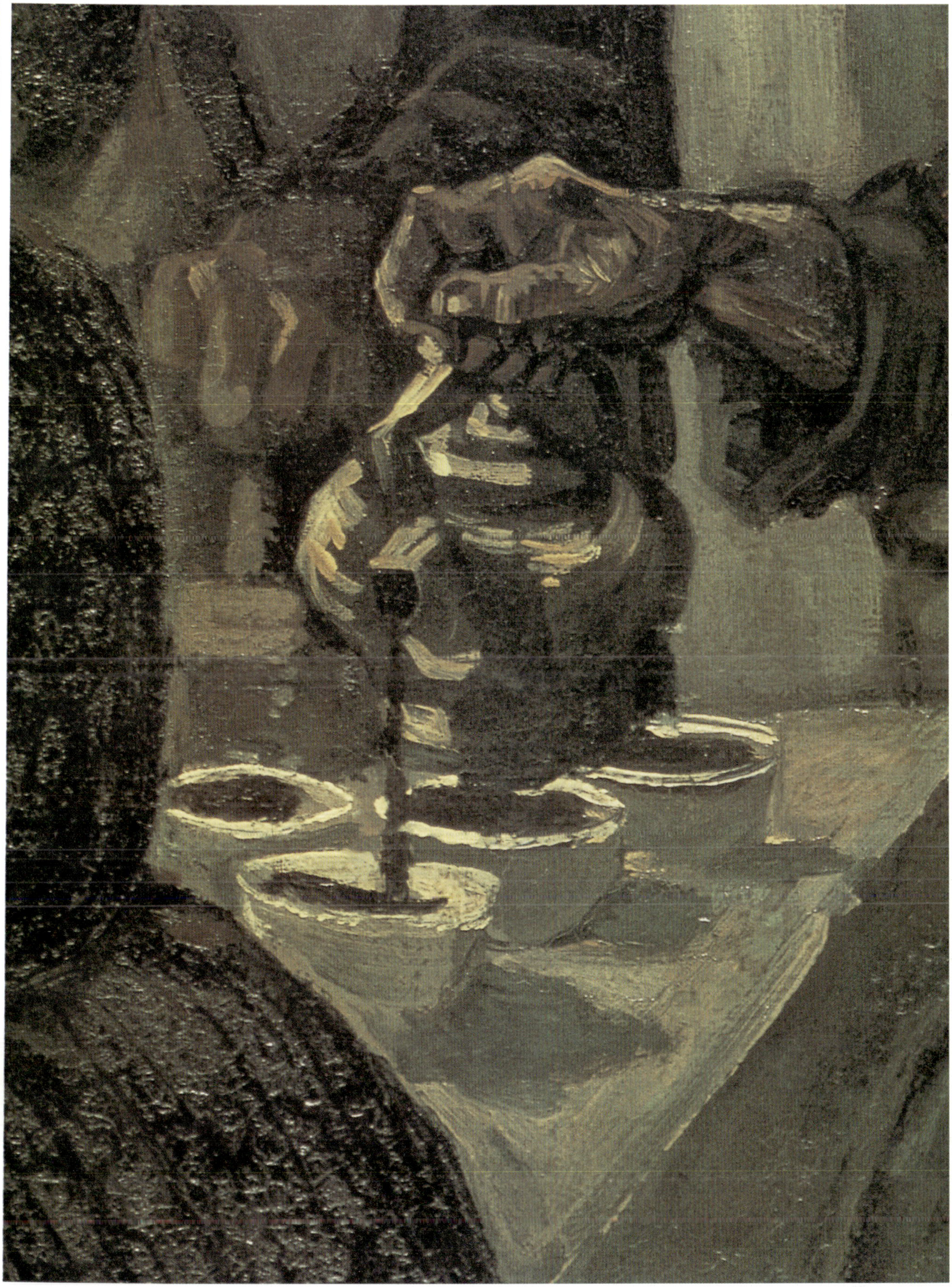

4 *Actual size detail*

Kitchen Gardens in Montmartre

Summer 1897
37¾×47¼in/96×120cm
Oil on canvas
Van Gogh Museum, Amsterdam

Van Gogh arrived in Paris to stay with his brother in February 1886, and at last he was able to see at first hand the work of the artists whom Theo had praised so highly in his letters. Seeing his first Impressionist paintings was the greatest revelation to him, for no amount of written description could have prepared him for the surprise and delight of discovering the purity of their colors. The heavy, expressive shading that he had used so effectively to evoke the poverty and drudgery of Dutch peasant life began to vanish, and like the Impressionists he began to use far less black in his palette, and to concentrate more on landscape painting than on figures.

The apartment he shared with Theo was on the slopes of Montmartre, on the very edge of the city and dominated by the Moulin de la Galette, the original windmill, standing above the more recent dance hall. Beyond were the sheds and smallholdings that blurred the boundary between city and open countryside. Typically Van Gogh chose this area as the subject for several landscapes, just as earlier he had shunned the picturesqueness of The Hague's old buildings to paint the outlying more modern ones. Although his paintings were now more attractively colored he still resisted the lure of the conventionally pretty or the familiar for his subject matter.

The founding fathers of Impressionism, whom Van Gogh admired so greatly, were remote figures to him in personal terms, the painters he met and worked with being the less well established, younger ones. Among these was Paul Signac, the enthusiastic disciple of Georges Seurat and follower of Seurat's Pointillist style – so called because it attempted to regulate Impressionism by the use of tiny point-sized brushstrokes to control precisely the accurate depiction of color. Here Van Gogh's debt to the technique can be seen clearly, yet the effect he creates is one of movement rather than a calm uniformity of brushstroke. He has ignored Seurat's scientific theories, and used his own version of Pointillism to create an exciting surface pattern.

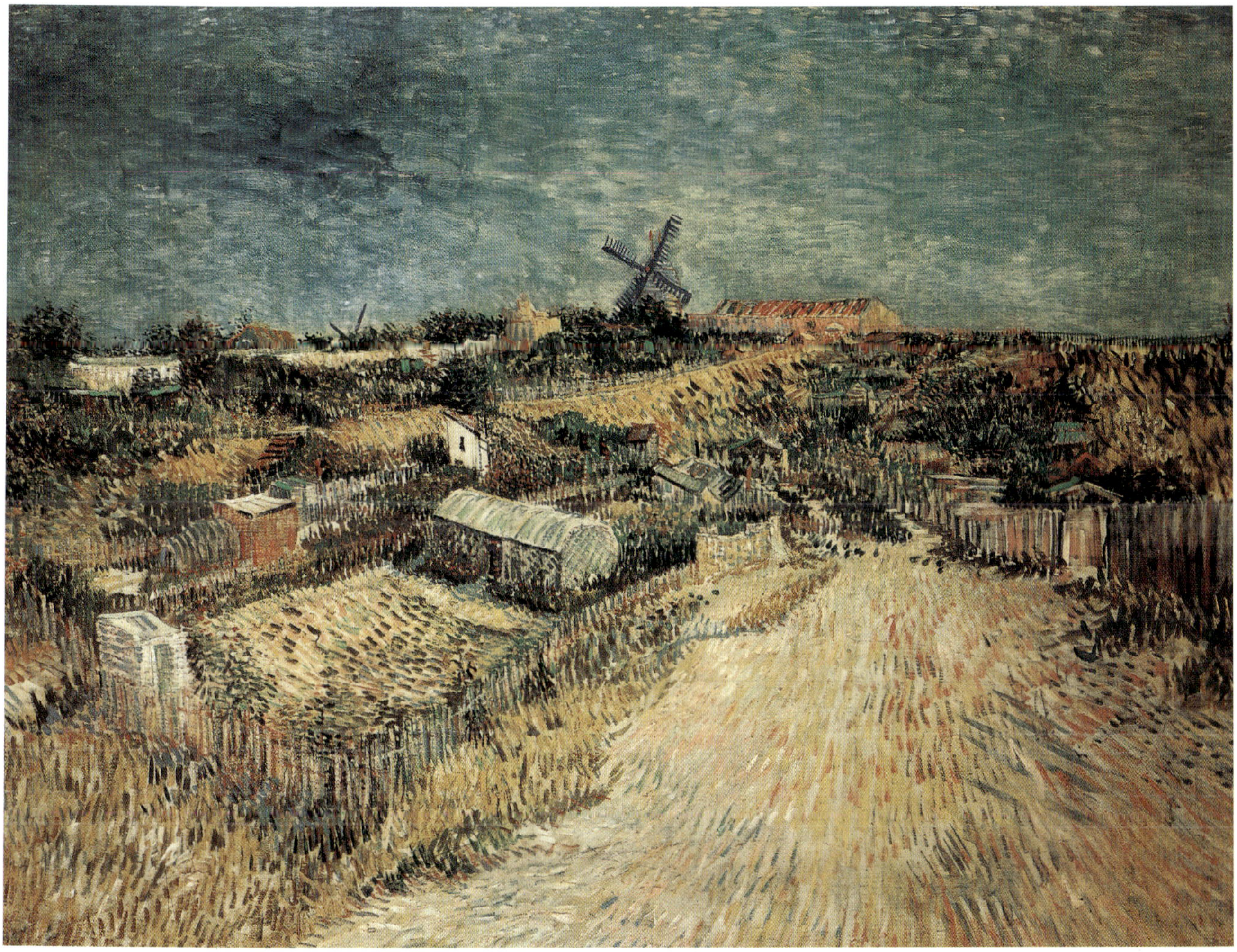

Here Van Gogh conveys an impression of the exhilaration of open space so near the crowded city by the dramatic movement of his foreground path which pushes forcefully into the middle ground. A series of parallel diagonals of paths and fences echo this movement, pointing both toward the distance and toward a remarkably freely rendered area of color in the righthand corner of the landscape. This constitutes a near-abstract celebration of the pure color he had discovered in Paris. From the freshness of these colors it is easy to sense that the work was painted in the open air, in the Impressionist manner, and the openness of the brushwork, through which bare canvas is often visible, creates the illusion of space and light entering the painting.

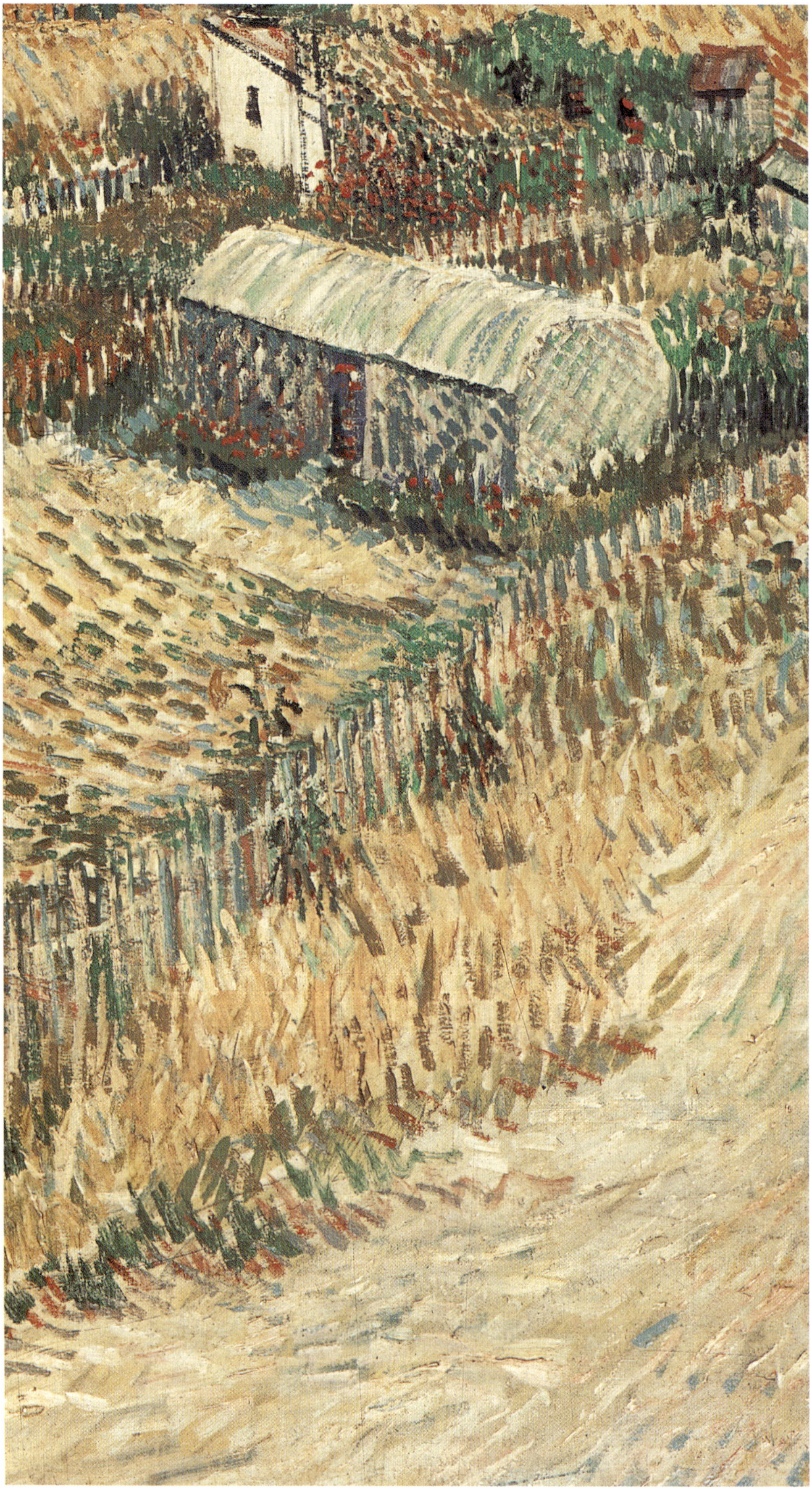

1

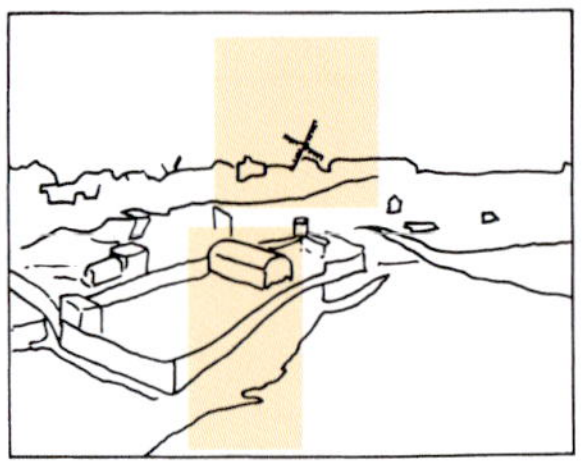

1 The dense dots of the Pointillist style that Van Gogh had seen in the work of Seurat and the younger artist Signac are used only sparingly, as in the wall of the background shed. They are only a part of a pattern of various different strokes used here with a freedom and a lightness of touch new in Van Gogh's work.

2 The thinner and paler paint of the sky toward the horizon suggest recession into space (atmospheric perspective), but are confidently offset by the pure color of the windmill's sails and the roof of the distant shed.

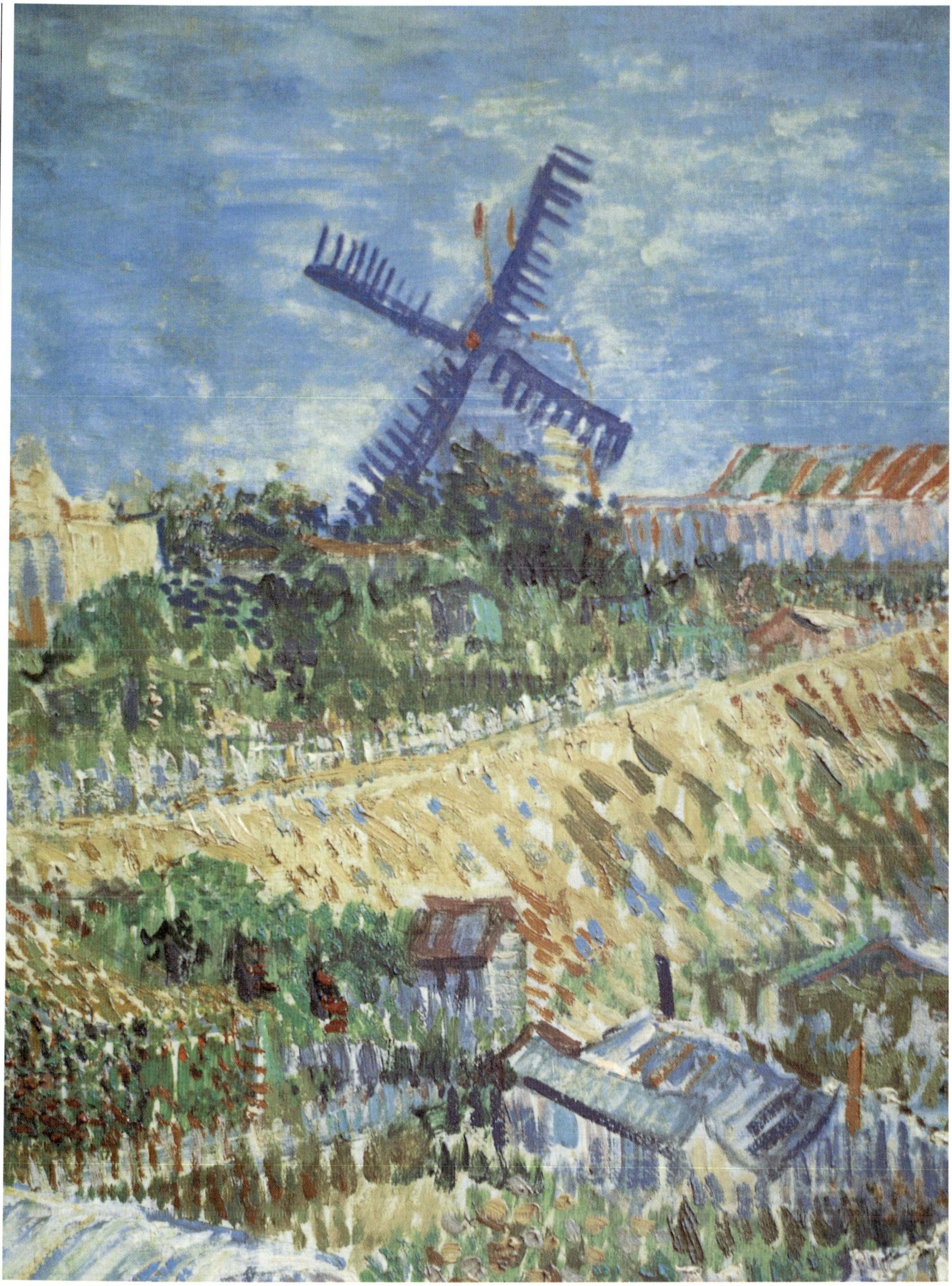

2

Night Cafe

September 1888
27½×35in/69.8×88.9cm
Oil on canvas
Yale University of Art

Sleeping by day, Van Gogh produced this picture after three night's work. He described it as "one of the ugliest I have done," explaining that he had "tried to describe the terrible passions of humanity by means of green and red. Everywhere there is a clash and contrast of the most alien reds and greens." The landscapes that Van Gogh painted in Arles had something of the sunny innocence of the Impressionists, but this work is quite different, and in it he was returning to deeper concerns and conveying much more than superficial appearances. The infernal colors set in painful contrast to each other do indeed create an ugly picture, but they also transform the scene of a dingy café in the small hours of the night into a place of dread, fear and unhappiness. Unlike the Impressionists, Van Gogh wanted his pure colors to stir up a strong emotional reaction in the viewer.

It is not only the violent colors and crude brushstrokes that create the disturbing mood of the painting; the perspective is also dramatically exaggerated. The dimensions of the room are unsettling, with the floor seeming to rush away at our feet, and the possibility of escape through the curtained door seems distressingly distant. The size and position of objects and people are unsure, and familiar things seem distorted and threatening. In a dramatic contrast to the deep space Van Gogh has placed motifs that have an unnatural flatness, like cut-outs. The figure of the landlord, one of Van Gogh's creditors, stands in his white suit like an apparition, hovering behind his billiard table and fixing the painter with an unsettling gaze. The uniform thickness of the paint adds to the picture's atmosphere of heavy foreboding. Van Gogh himself said of the painting "I have attempted to show that the café is a place where a man can ruin himself, become mad, commit a crime . . ."

Van Gogh is most often remembered as a great colorist, but his use of a strong perspective is frequently an equally important element in his compositions. It was often exaggerated for expressive purposes, as in this and in many other of his later works, and the features of this painting, discussed above are in fact a register of the pictorial devices used by the Expressionist painter Munch and his successors.

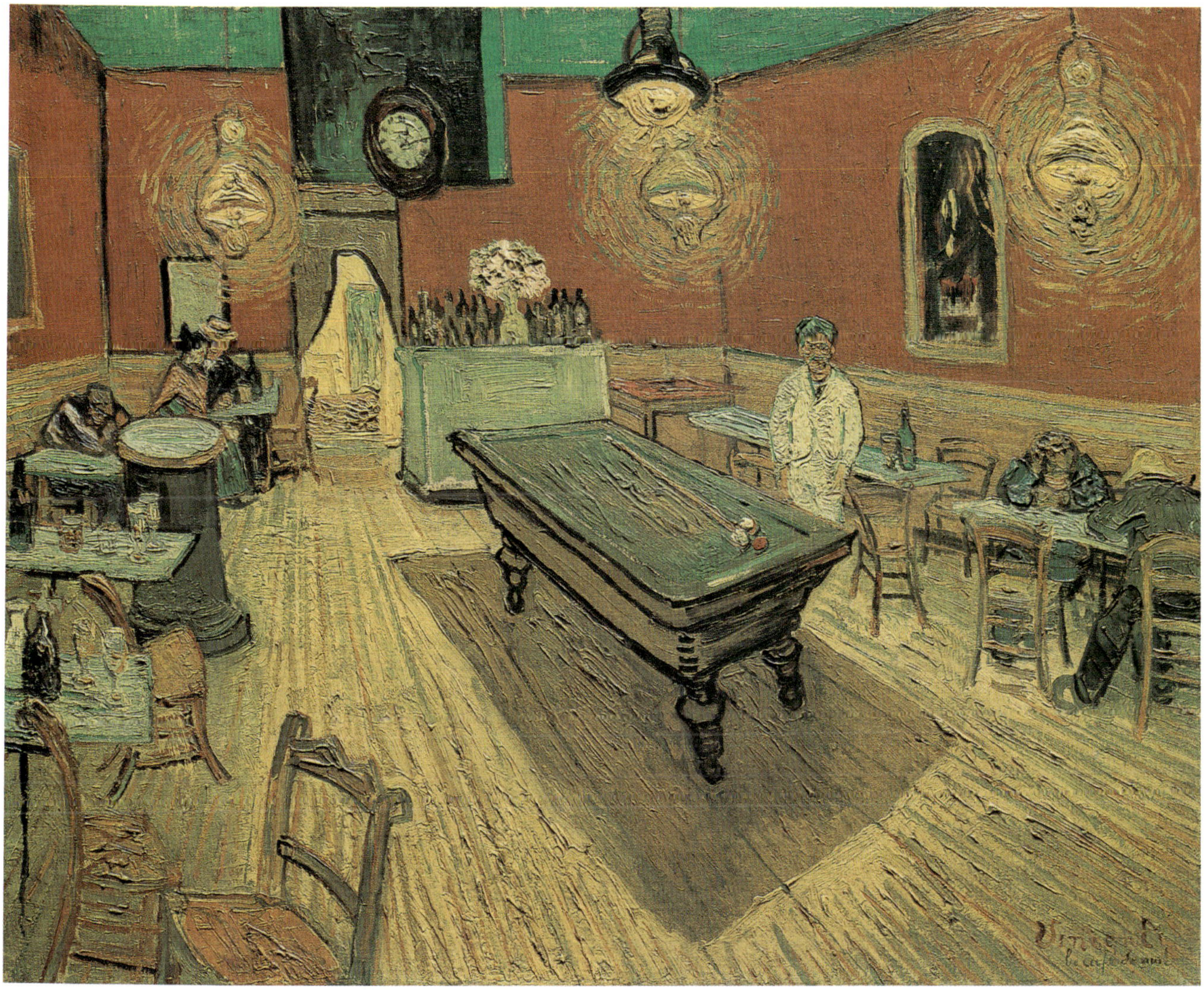

A social scene such as this is rare in Van Gogh's work; more typically, such a comparatively large cast of figures is pushed to the back and sides of the picture and painted in a few summary strokes. Here the characters and appearance of the figures are less important to the painter than the distance which separates him from them. The casually placed chairs in the foreground recall a favorite device of the Impressionist painter Degas, but the bleakness of this gathering could not be further from the lively interest in personality apparent in Degas' work.

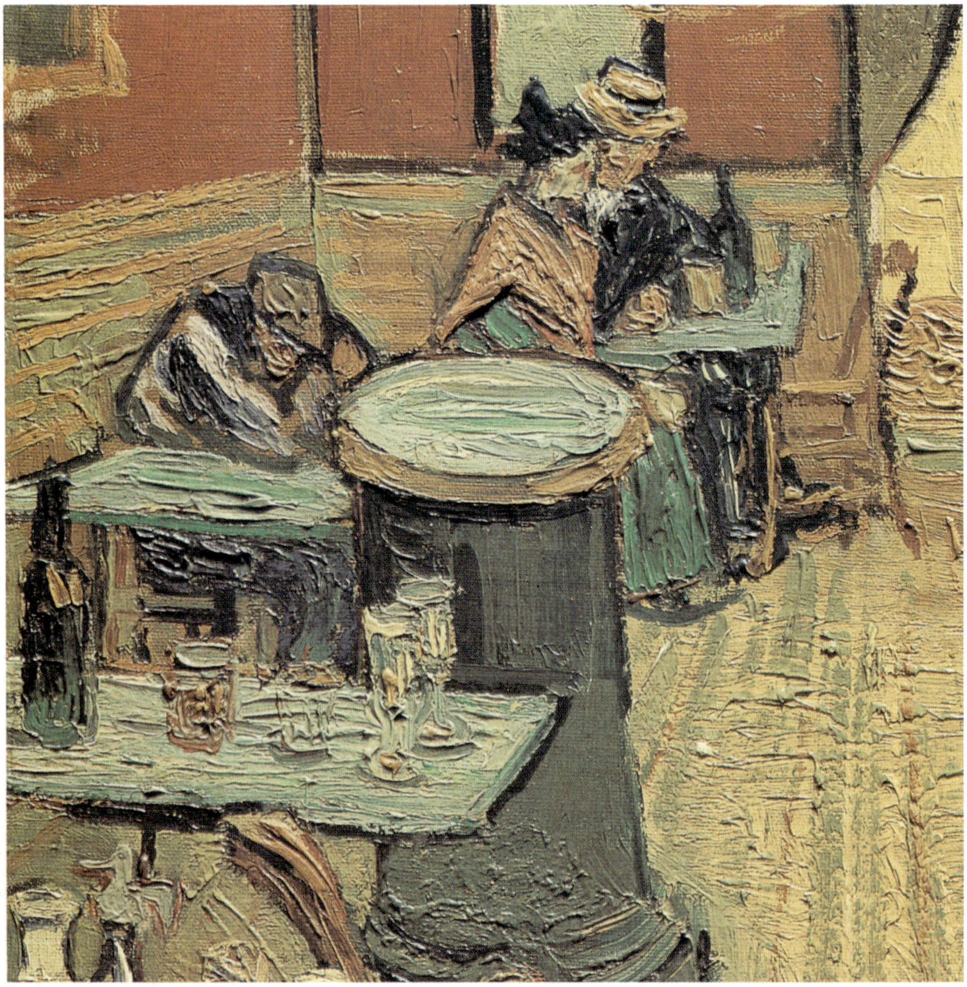

1

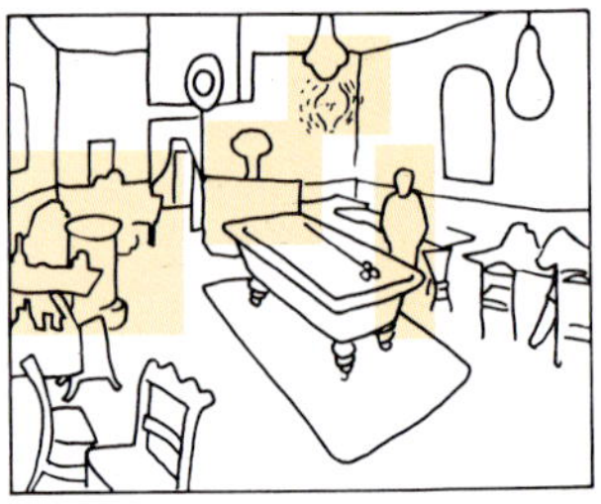

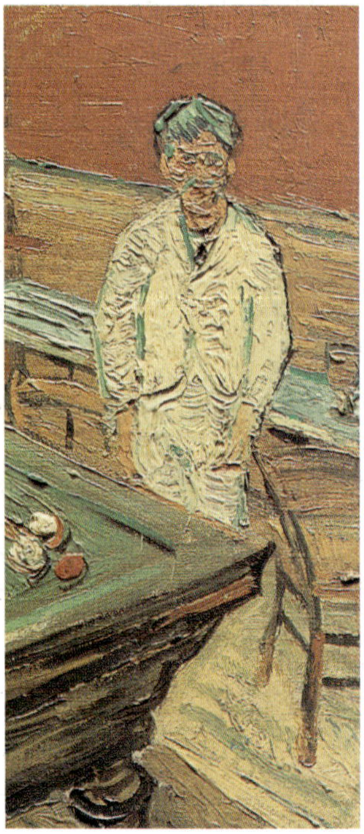

2

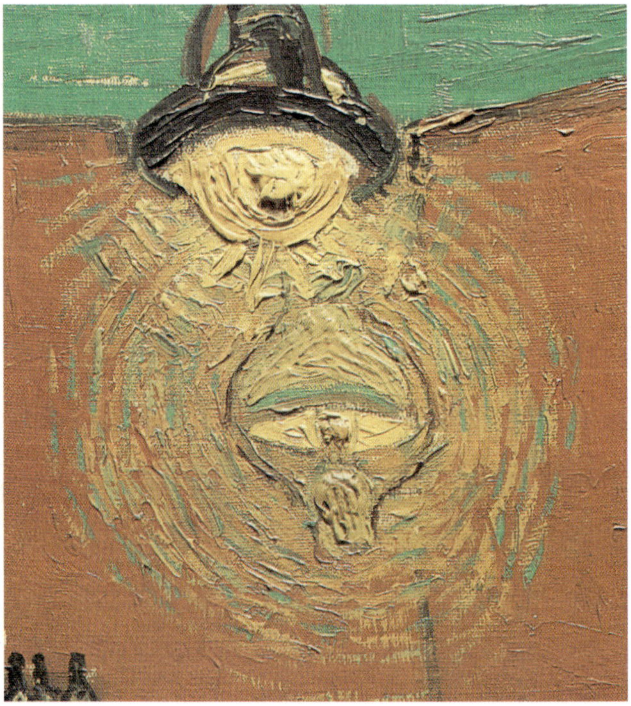

3

1 The uniform thickness of paint adds to the heavy atmosphere of the work. The body of paint left at the side and end of each stroke is best seen on the center table and the top of the neighboring stove, the latter being tilted up in accordance with the distorted perspective of the room.

2 The owner seems squeezed between the two tables, the unrelieved white of his suit helping to flatten him still further.

3 Increasingly separate strokes convey the incandescence of the lamp. Its center is green to bring it out from the surrounding red, another use of the opposition of complementaries seen in much of Van Gogh's work.

4 *Actual size detail* Rejecting distracting detail, Van Gogh has used the simplest movements of his brush to convey the fullness of the blooms and the somber congregation of bottles.

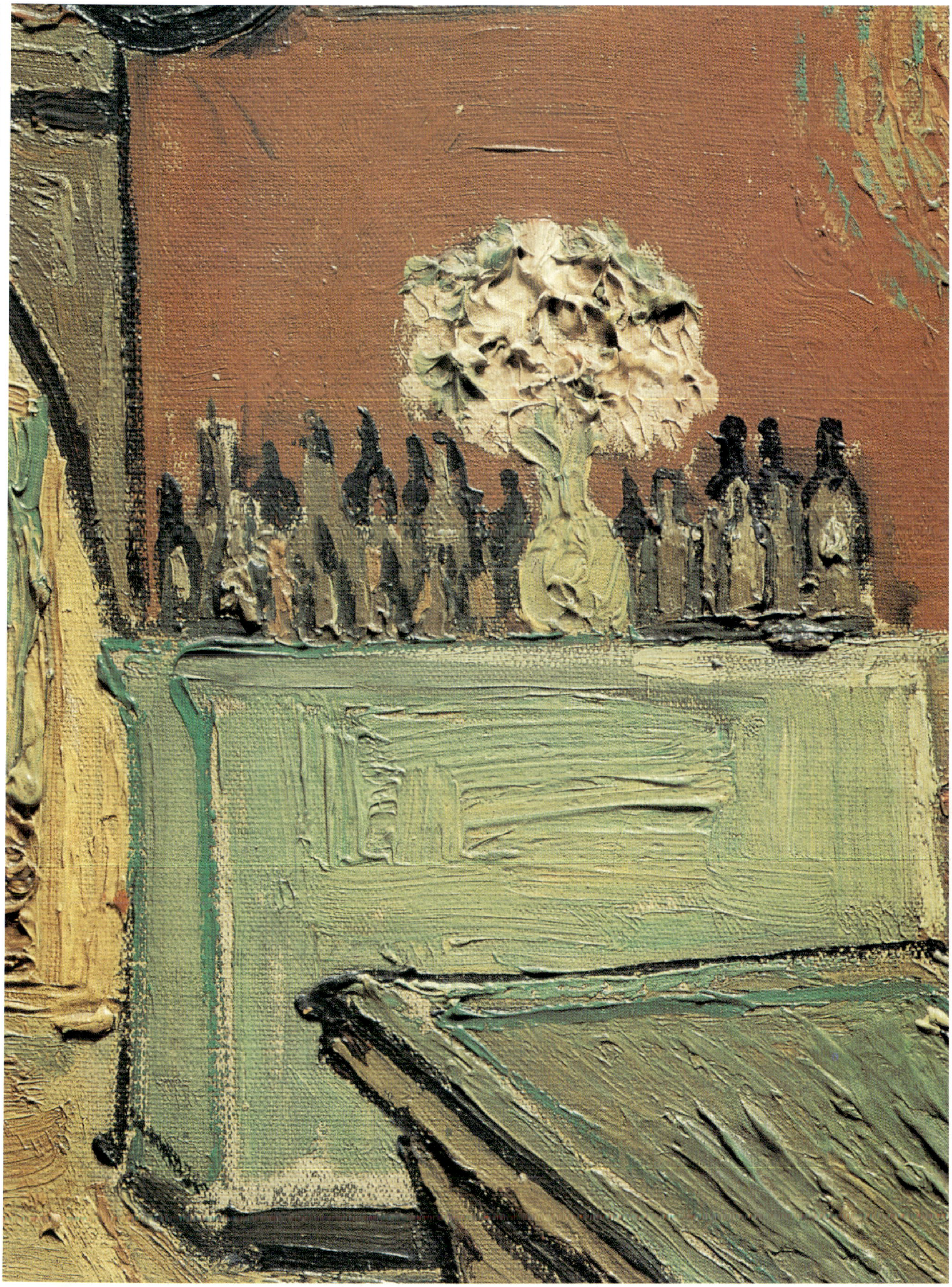

4 *Actual size detail*

Vincent's Chair with his Pipe

November 1888
$28^3/_4 \times 36^1/_4$in/73×92 cm
Oil on canvas
Tate Gallery, London

Van Gogh rented a small house in Arles, buying a respectable bed for the guest bedroom but furnishing his own room with the utmost simplicity. He painted a wide range of subjects during this time, including the room itself, and he described his plans for this picture to his brother. "This time it's just simply my bedroom, only here color is to do everything, and giving by its simplification a grander style to things, is to be suggestive here of rest or of sleep in general. In a word, to look at the picture ought to rest the brain or rather the imagination." A very succinct definition of the aim of his painting – the distillation of a spiritual quality from the most mundane reality.

The chair in this painting is identical to those from his bedroom that had appeared in the earlier work. As a subject it appears at first to be uncompromisingly ordinary, but in fact it is an eloquent parallel to the work and thoughts of a Japanese artist admired by Van Gogh, who devoted himself to the study of a single blade of grass, only to find that this seemingly simple task led him, step by step, to the contemplation of all that is in nature. By including his own pipe and tobacco on the seat Van Gogh connects the chair to its owner, and it thus begins to appear more as a kind of veiled self-portrait. He frequently painted the personal belongings that were particularly close to him – in Paris his battered boots, and in Arles his worn clogs – and these pictures tell us as much about the owner as they do about the objects themselves.

With this knowledge in mind it becomes obvious that the crudity of the drawing is deliberate, expressive rather than arbitrary, conveying the rough "earthenware" nature of both the south and of Van Gogh himself. He referred to this when he expressed the hope that one of his peasant portraits would be hung next to the glamorous, powdered Parisian artifice of a Toulouse-Lautrec work, so that both would be set off to their mutual advantage.

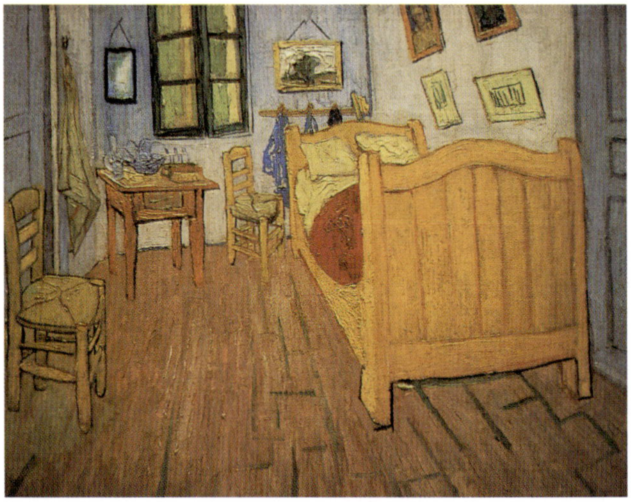

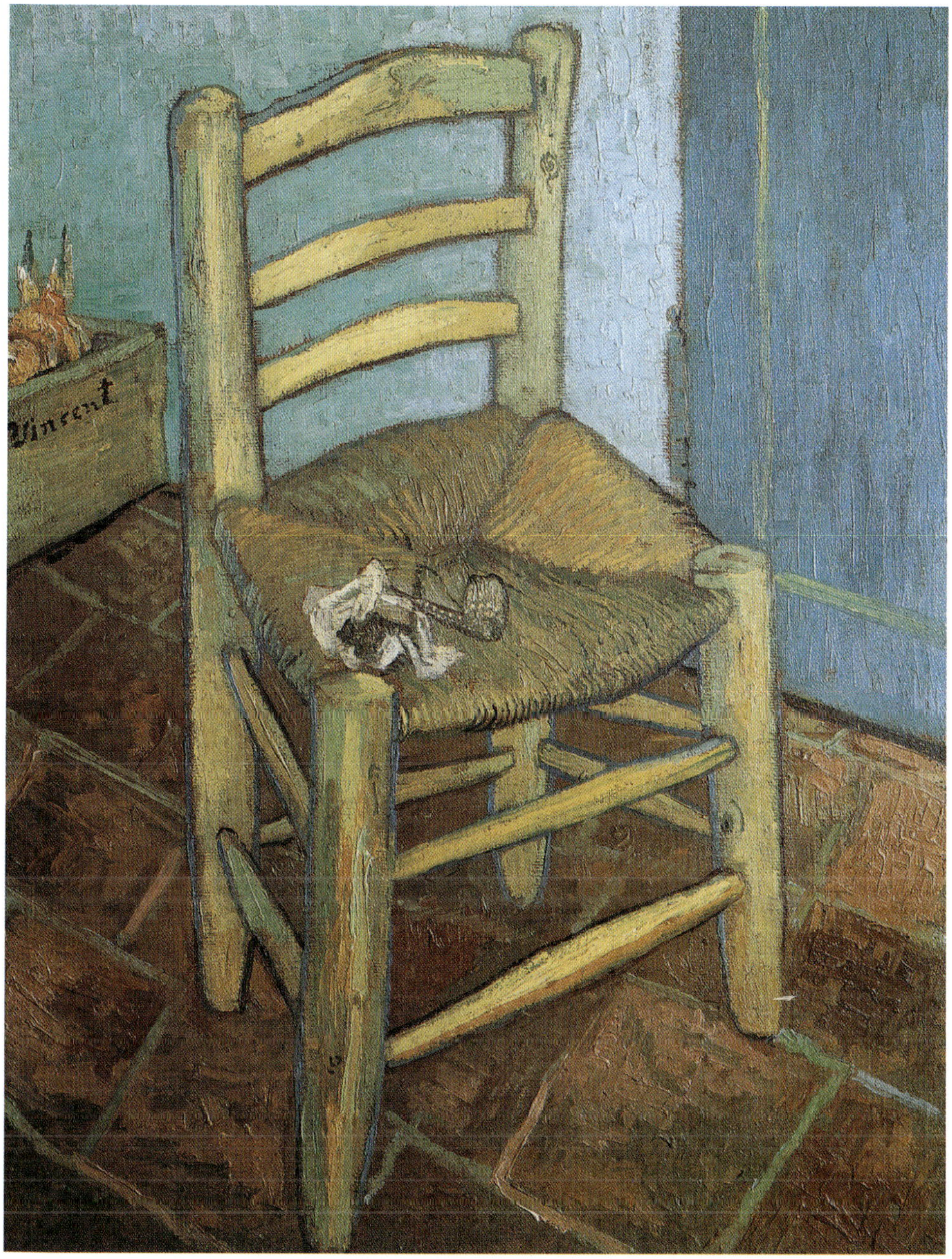

Opposite page
VINCENT VAN GOGH
Van Gogh's Bedroom at Arles
Van Gogh Museum, Amsterdam

The use of color and space in this view of Van Gogh's bedroom is extremely close to that seen in the painting of his own chair. Both paintings are reflections of his personality and way of life, almost forms of "self-portrait."

The color composition of this work is based on variations around the pairs of primary complementaries – blue and orange, and red and green. These appear in their purest form only in occasional passages, to set the keynotes for the composition. Thus the area of purest red on the paving beneath the chair is balanced by touches of green above it and by a further stroke of green on the nearest chair leg. Van Gogh stresses structure through emphatic outlines, added later, that serve to contain areas of pure painting. The strength of these increases the impact of the image but also creates a certain tension between line and color. In distorting the perspective of the floor and the chair leg, Van Gogh imposed his own personality upon the work, stressing the subjectivity of his view.

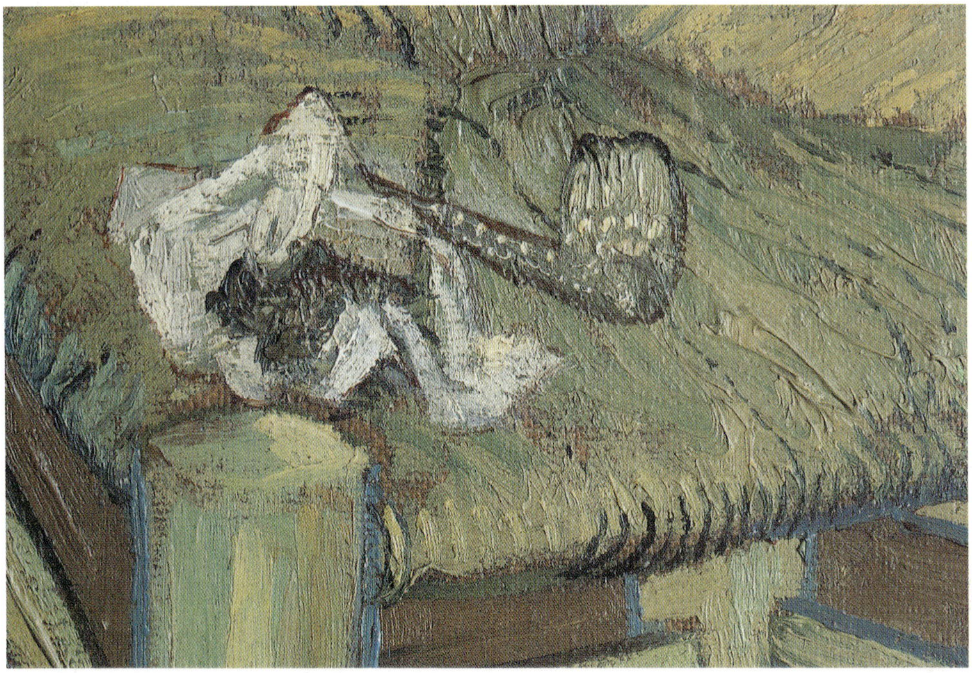

1

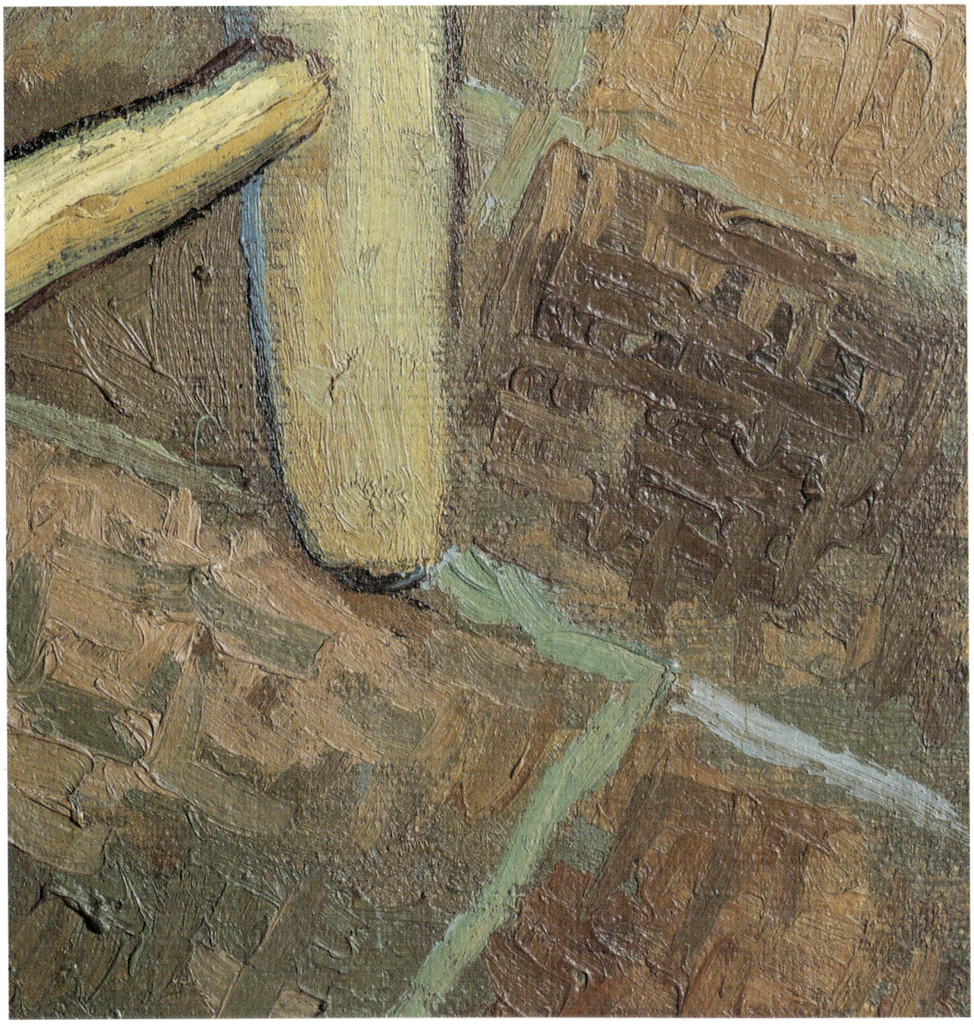

2

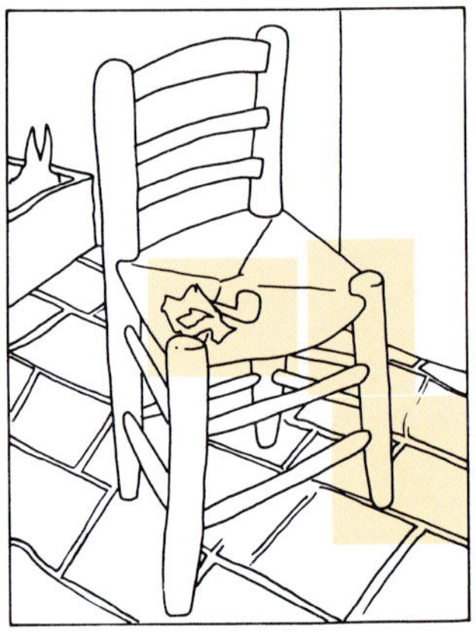

1 The pipe, handkerchief and tobacco give a focus to the picture in both narrative and pictorial terms, providing a note of neutral white at the center of the interplay of cool and warm hues. The use of blue to outline the parts of the chair increases the sense of cool draftsmanship restraining the sensuous handling of paint.

2 The floor tiles are painted with the weaving brushstrokes that Van Gogh often used in the backgrounds of his work at this time. Short horizontal and vertical strokes alternate in a loose mesh of reds, browns and greens. The thickness of the paint used is revealed by the heavy smear from the side of the brush that is left alongside each stroke.

3 *Actual size detail* The inconsistency of Van Gogh's finish can be seen here in the disparity between the caned seat of the chair, given considerable attention and depth of paint, and the sparsely painted top and edges of the chair leg. This adds to the variety and vivacity of the overall paint surface as well as telling us much about the speed with which he worked.

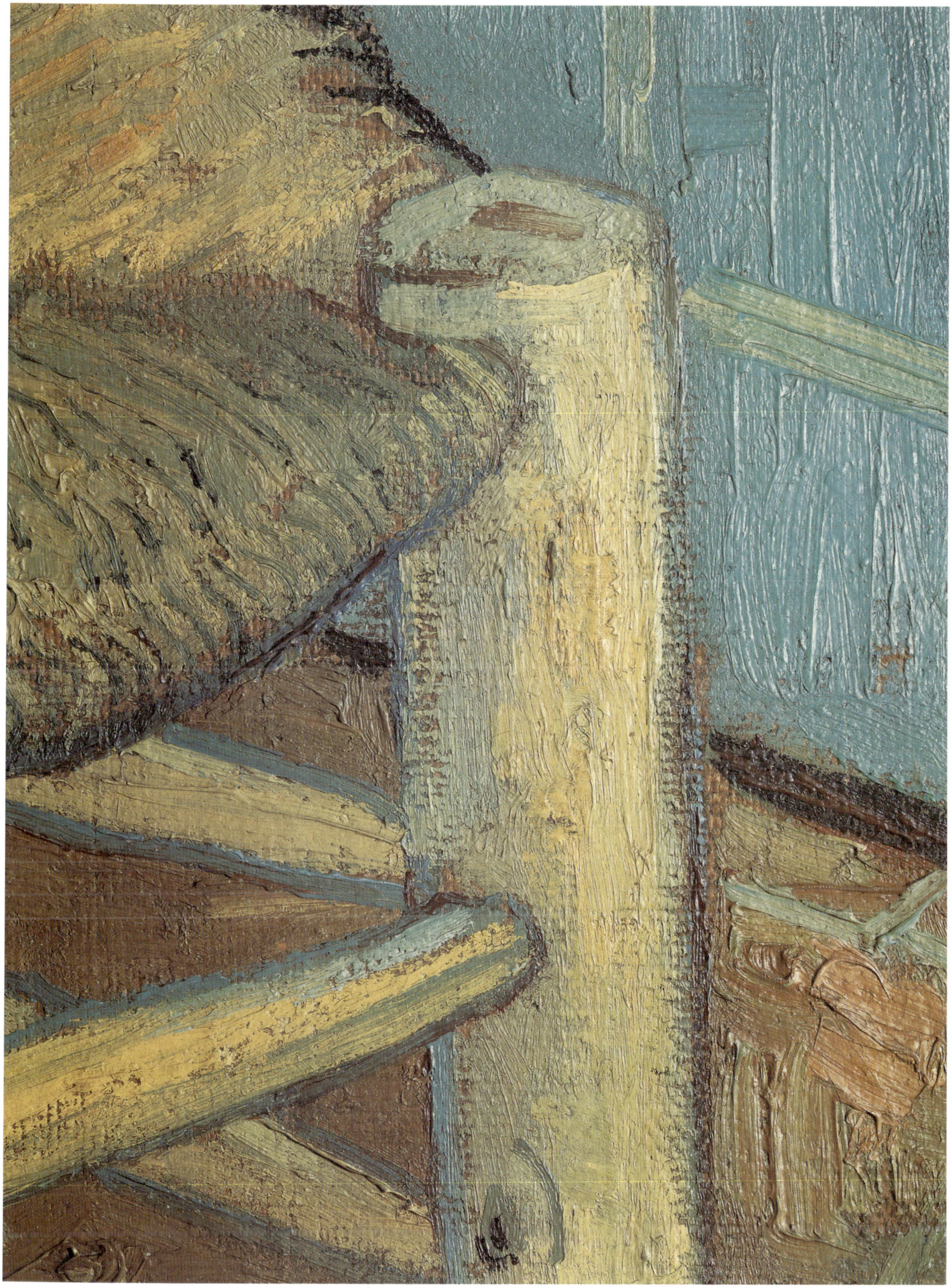

3 *Actual size detail*

Self-portrait with Bandaged Ear

January 1889
$23\frac{1}{2} \times 19\frac{1}{4}$in/$60 \times 49$cm
Oil on canvas
Courtauld Institute Galleries, London

Over and over again Van Gogh returned to his own features as a subject, the number and variety of these self-portraits recalling those of his fellow-countryman Rembrandt. These works reflect both the loneliness of his life and his attitude toward himself and his circumstances; in them he was exploring what it was about himself that formed his unique view of the world and separated him from his fellows.

This is particularly true of this work, in which he presents his now famous bandaged ear to the viewer – himself – to draw attention to the self-mutilation rather than to hide it. There is thus an element of confession in the painting, as well as an urge to come to terms with a very damaging episode.

The severed ear was the climax to the eagerly anticipated visit to Arles of Paul Gauguin. Van Gogh had always hoped to found a community of painters working together and supporting each other artistically and emotionally, a microcosm of his dream of society. As a first step toward this ideal, he exchanged works with many of his colleagues – in imitation of the practice among the much-admired Japanese masters – and he had exchanged self-portraits with Gauguin through Theo in Paris. Now Gauguin had agreed to share Van Gogh's small house, motivated at least partly by the very poor state of his own finances and the knowledge that Van Gogh was being sent money by Theo.

The arrangement worked very well at first. Gauguin was stimulating, and knowledgeable, as well as being a very good cook, but it was not long before important artistic and personal differences began to surface. Both painters had just reached full artistic maturity, emerging from the shade of the Impressionists, but they had grown in different directions. Whereas Van Gogh had developed an extremely direct, emotional and expressive form of landscape painting, Gauguin's view of nature was much more artificial and his paintings incorporated imaginary elements, taken from religion, literature and his own memories. As the more confident and worldly of the two he was able to impose his views on Van Gogh, creating a distressing tension in the latter's work, which had previously been assured and tranquil.

Furthermore, Gauguin lacked Van Gogh's emotional delicacy in personal relations, and was soon encouraging the latter to join him in his frequent expeditions to the local brothels. The tension grew between the two, confined together in the small house, until finally it erupted and Van Gogh broke down, cutting off his ear and presenting it to a prostitute in the brothel. The furore this incident caused brought in the police, who removed Van Gogh to the local hospital, where he was to spend the majority of his time before transferring to the St Rémy asylum. Gauguin left for Paris, having prepared a mendacious version of the events to excuse his own involvement.

This portrait recalls the extreme isolation and depression that followed this affair. Van Gogh was left to absorb the terrible truth of his mental instability, and to confront the lowest ebb of his fortunes at a time when all appeared to have been going well. Thus we are presented with a haggard, shell-shocked figure, shabbily dressed and set against a background bare but for a Japanese print, an ironic reminder of the expectation of Japanese sunshine that had brought him to Arles.

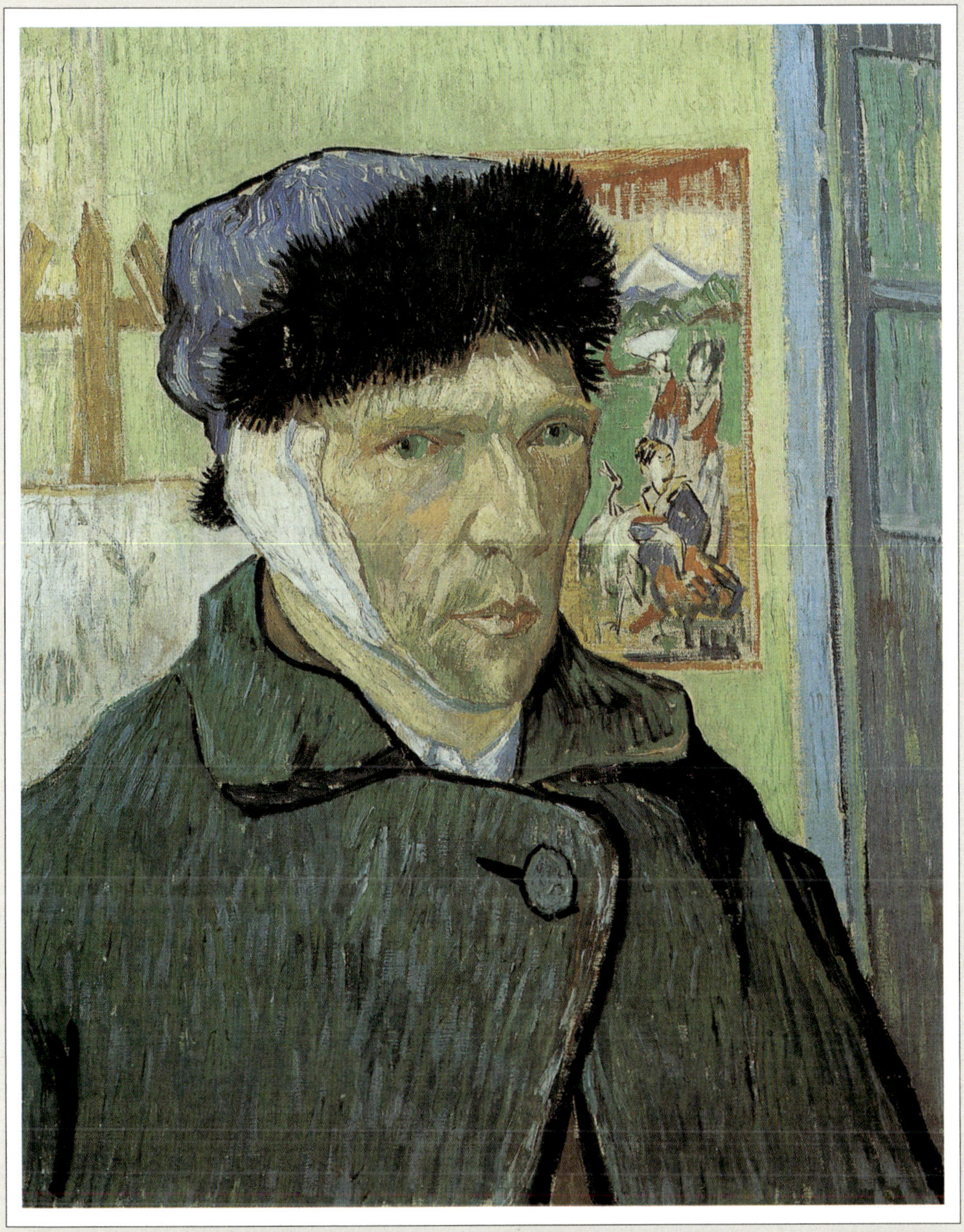

The composition and execution of this self-portrait create the mood as strongly as does the artist's empty gaze. Behind him the easel, print and window appear disjointed, unrelated to each other. The space they occupy seems unclear: it is crowded and rather claustrophobic. On the coat, paint is applied in long, quick strokes pointing toward the face where the brushstrokes are laid in several conflicting directions. The heavily marked outlines no longer contain and counteract the overall restlessness of the surfaces, and although the pose is one of conventional stability — a triangle anchored on the two bottom corners of the picture — it seems to be in danger of imminent collapse from the agitated movement within it.

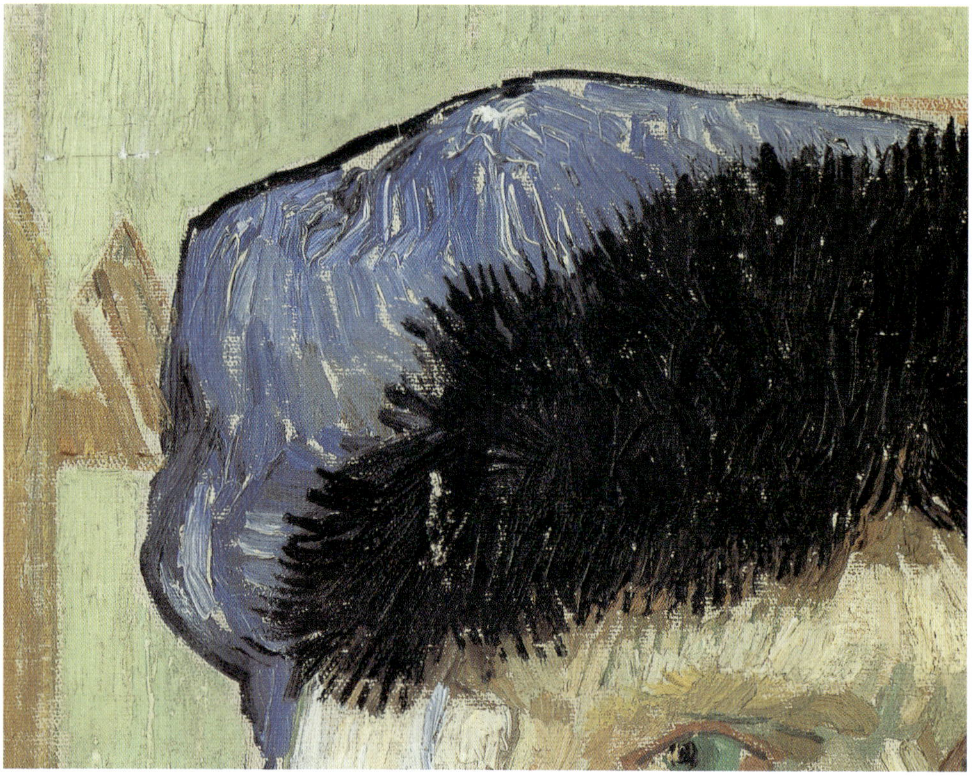

1

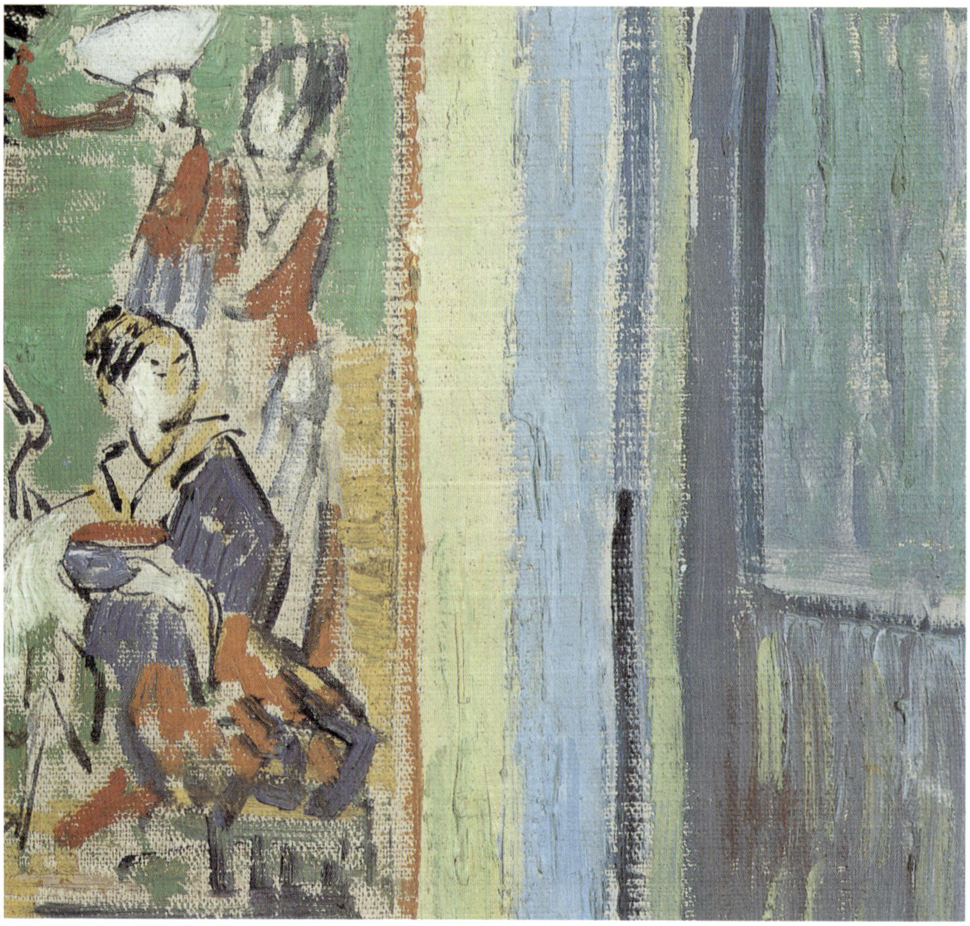

2

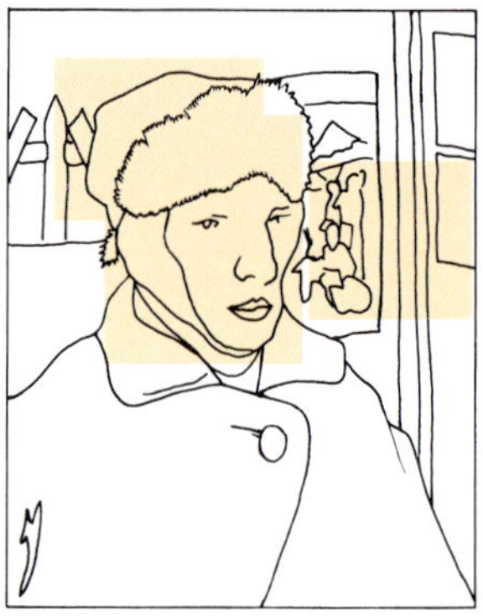

1 Toward the crown of the hat Van Gogh has used the conflicting zig-zag strokes that were to become more frequent in his later work. The outline fails to draw this movement together, nor has the painter tried to disguise the space left beneath it.

2 Few brushstrokes are alike in this area of the painting. Some are completed with the quick flick away at right-angles to the canvas that Van Gogh frequently used, which often resulted in small pinnacles of paint being left at the end of each rapid stroke.

3 *Actual size detail* The face is actually made up of a range of different colors — red eye-sockets, white lips and green chin — but the tonality is controlled with such assurance that it appears pale and drained when set against the rest of the picture. Bare canvas shows on the chin, but elsewhere the paint is thickly applied.

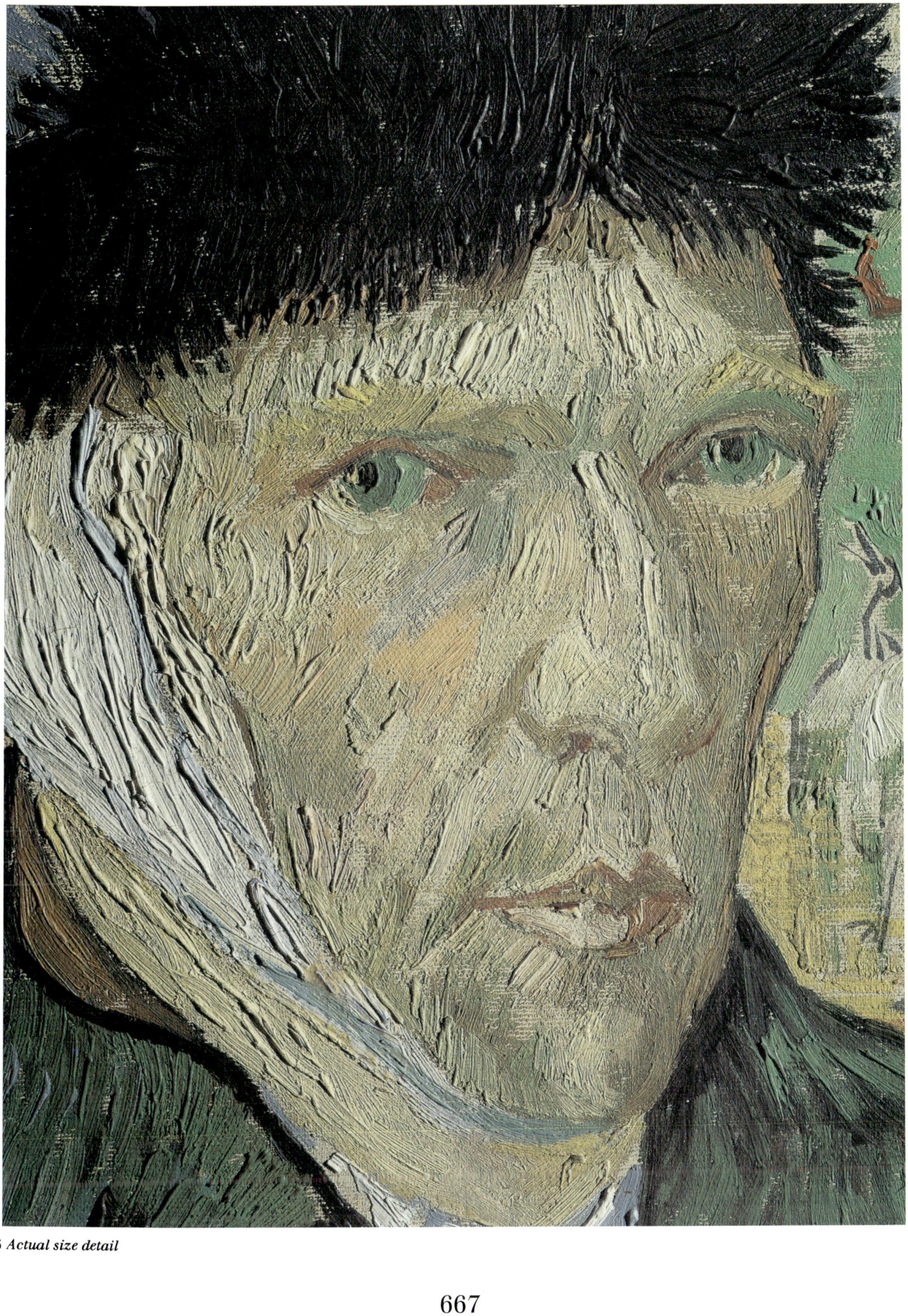

5 *Actual size detail*

Road with Cypress and Star

May 1890
$36\frac{1}{4} \times 28\frac{3}{4}$in/$92 \times 73$cm
Oil on canvas
Rijksmuseum Kröller-Müller, Otterlo

At first Van Gogh had viewed his mental breakdown as the result of external circumstances: the emotional upheaval of Gauguin's visit, overwork and the effect of a poor diet with too much coffee, alcohol and tobacco. However, when he had a further attack, believing himself to be the victim of a poisoner, he was forced to acknowledge that the deeper cause lay within himself, and agreed to move to the asylum at St Rémy.

Here he quickly found that the asylum offered only simple internment rather than any active cure, but he accepted the conditions – the unpalatable food and demoralizing lack of activity – partly because his fits, sometimes violent, left him exhausted and listless for weeks afterward, and partly because he saw his stay in the asylum as a form of ascetic retreat, an austere foundation on which he hoped to reconstruct his life. He also admired the way the patients looked after one another, which echoed his own ideals of fellowship and community.

The exact nature of his illness has never been clear, though the two most plausible diagnoses are schizophrenia or a rare form of epilepsy accompanied by hallucinations. Between attacks he was still able to paint, and was even allowed to make short trips out to do so in the company of a warder. This painting, typical of his developing style, is quite different from his early work in Arles. Vigorous, troubled brushwork has returned, its movement creating restless and conflicting activity, and an expressionistic licence has appeared too, evident in the disturbing angle of the road and the travelers on it. The appearance of sun, moon and stars in his work at this time clearly shows how his search for the truth of what he saw was paradoxically leading him further away from realism toward a mystical vision reminiscent of the medieval world-view. His feeling for the south, associated with an Impressionist preoccupation with light, was changing too. He began to consider returning to northern Europe and, as his passion for the brilliant landscape waned his colors followed suit, becoming less bright and more diluted with half-tones. The image of the cypress tree, a mysterious evergreen link between heaven and earth, provided him with an opportunity to re-introduce into his work the deep, dark hues that had been absent since Holland.

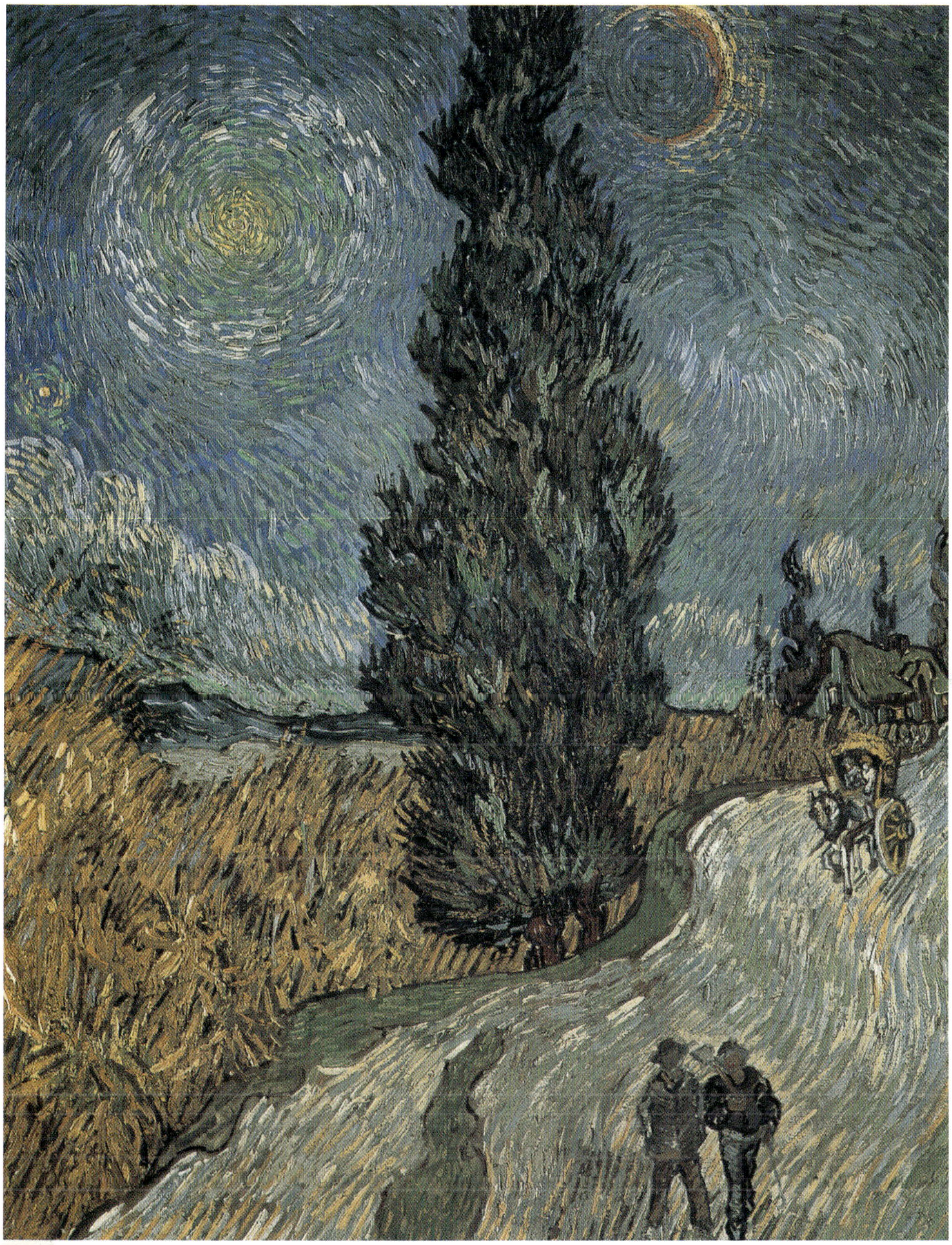

It is the sense of urgency and agitation, not the subjects themselves, that makes Van Gogh's St Rémy landscapes so very remarkable. Here the composition seems to rush off in every direction from the pole of the cypress – to the left through the road, to the right with the rising clouds, and also upward, as the tree has been allowed to "bust" the frame at the top of the picture, which forces the viewer's eye to follow it. Every line of this composition is restless and undulating: each element buffets its neighbor, as the tide of the road rises to swamp the root of the cypress, or the breaking wave of the cornfield threatens to submerge it. The distant sky offers a little relief from these oppressive forces, but is itself turbulent with flowing, spiralling currents.

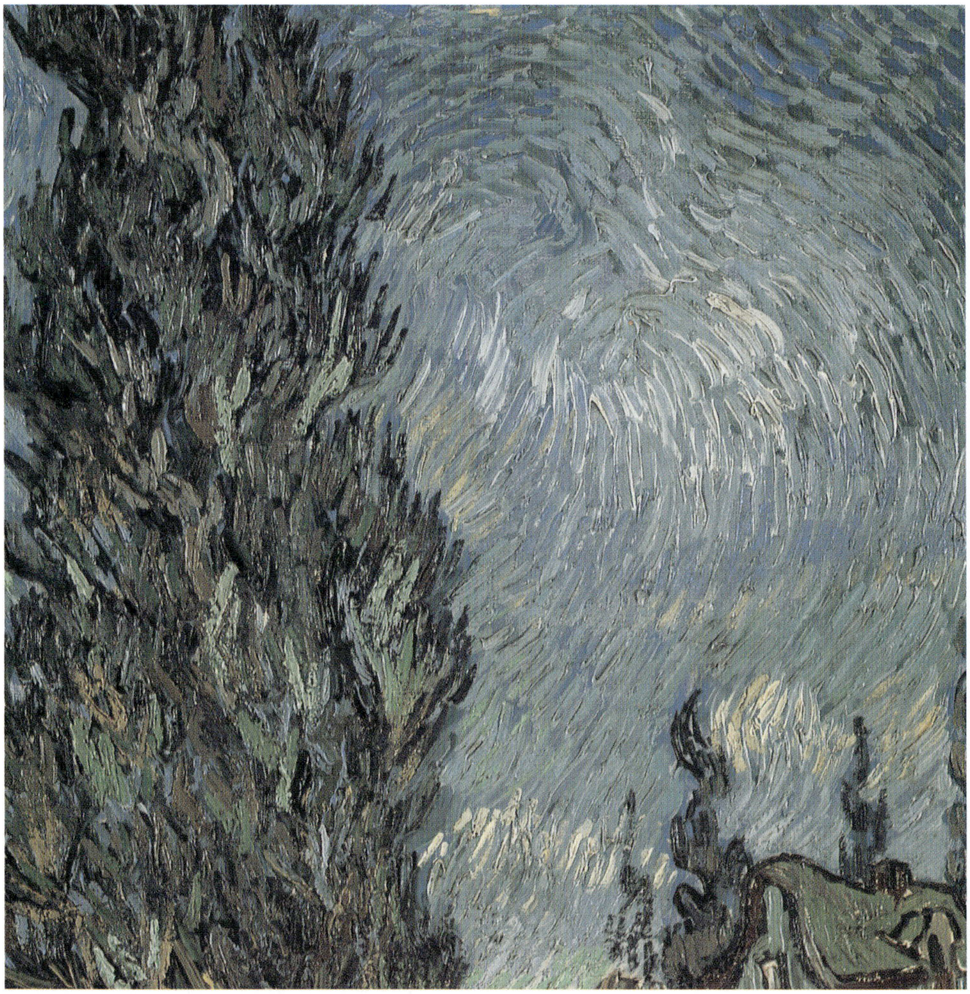

1

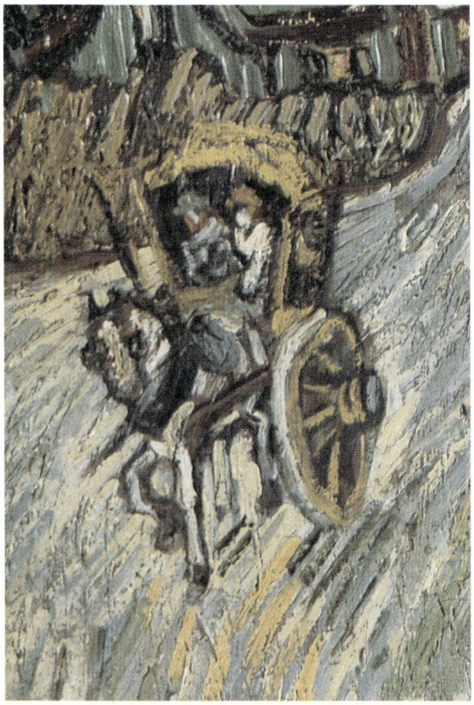

2

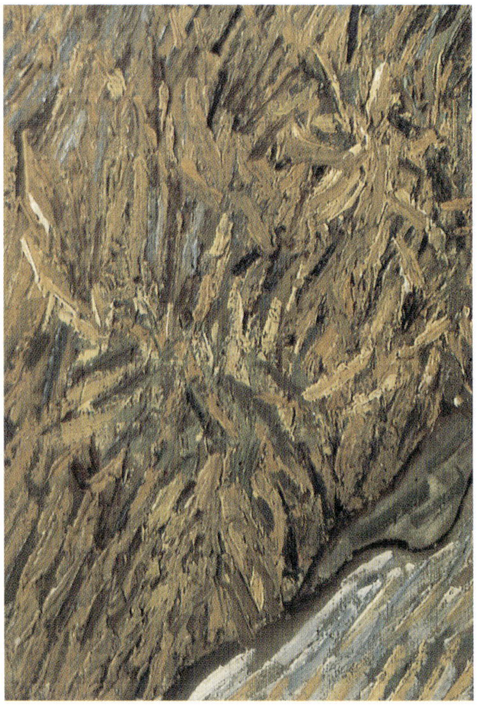

3

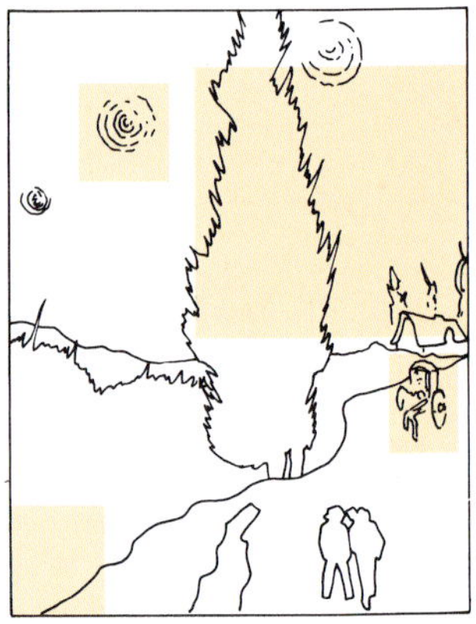

1 The ragged silhouette of the cypress contains a mass of short, angular, vigorous strokes made with a loaded brush. Deep blue helps to cool the dark greens even further, and is echoed in the distant trees, the only element that gives a sense of recession to the landscape.

2 Incongruous in scale, the cart is painted with untypical attention to detail, highlighting the freedom of the rest of the painting. The almost vertical strokes of the road seem to provide an unsure footing for the cart's journey.

3 Here Van Gogh has used less pure color, and in his haste, has allowed paint to mix before drying, as in the corn, thus losing some of the luminosity of his early work at Arles.

4 *Actual size detail* Van Gogh depicts the star as radiating yellow, green and white against the darkening sky. Below, short strokes collide and coalesce into awkward twisting movements.

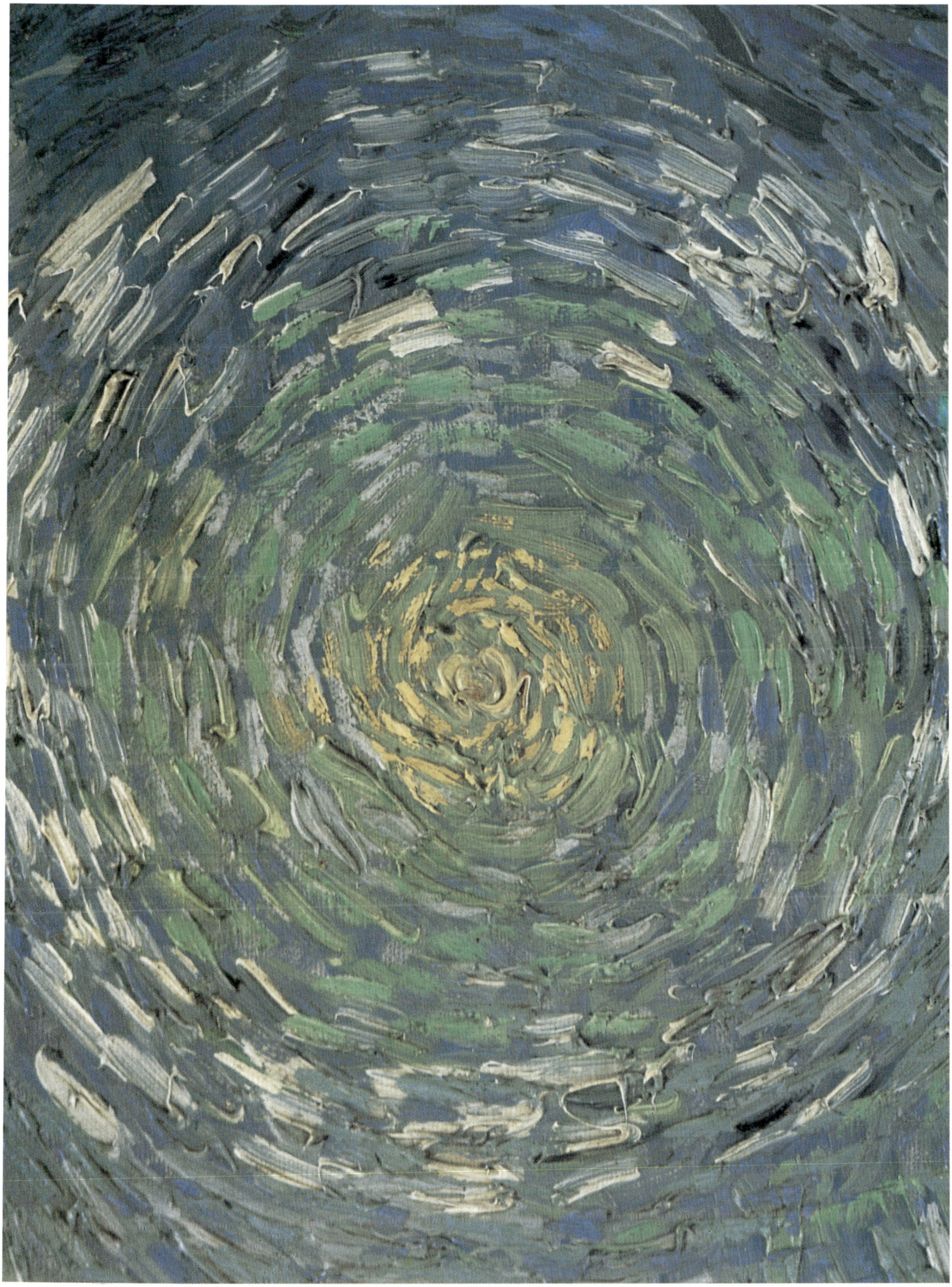

4 *Actual size detail*

Crows in the Wheatfield

Early June 1890
20×39½in/50.5×100.5cm
Oil on canvas
Van Gogh Museum, Amsterdam

Van Gogh was in good spirits when he arrived at Auvers, partly as a result of observing his brother's newfound domestic happiness, but when news reached him of financial troubles threatening Theo and his family he was thrown into dejection. Apart from the threat to his beloved brother, his own future was in question since he was on an allowance from Theo and his unhappiness was increased by a growing sense of guilt about his dependence on his brother and hence his role in Theo's misfortune. (There is evidence that this situation may have contributed to his first breakdown at Arles.) Now fear and guilt began to turn into depression, sometimes even violent rages, and he quarreled with Dr Gachet and was once again reduced to solitude. Although still lucid, he could sense the imminence of despair and madness, and he no longer felt able to fight against them.

He began to paint the great plain of wheatfields surrounding Auvers. When he had approached a similar subject from his window at St Rémy he had included the figure of the reaper, seen as a symbol of death advancing with his scythe, and now similar thoughts returned to him. He wrote of those wheatfield paintings that "They are vast stretches of corn under troubled skies, and I did not need to go out of my way to express sadness and the extreme of loneliness." In this version there is indeed a tangible sense of foreboding, as a flock of sinister black crows approaches in the vanguard of heavy, dark stormclouds. The road ahead is tilted up into an impossible incline and seems to peter out, offering no escape, while the brushwork is at its most expressionistic.

It was in these very fields that Van Gogh shot himself in the chest, and although he missed his target, his heart, and managed to drag himself back to the village where he collapsed into bed, he did not survive long. His landlord discovered him and summoned Theo from Paris to his brother's deathbed. "The sadness will last forever" were among the last words Theo heard him speak, and Theo himself, overcome with grief, died six months later.

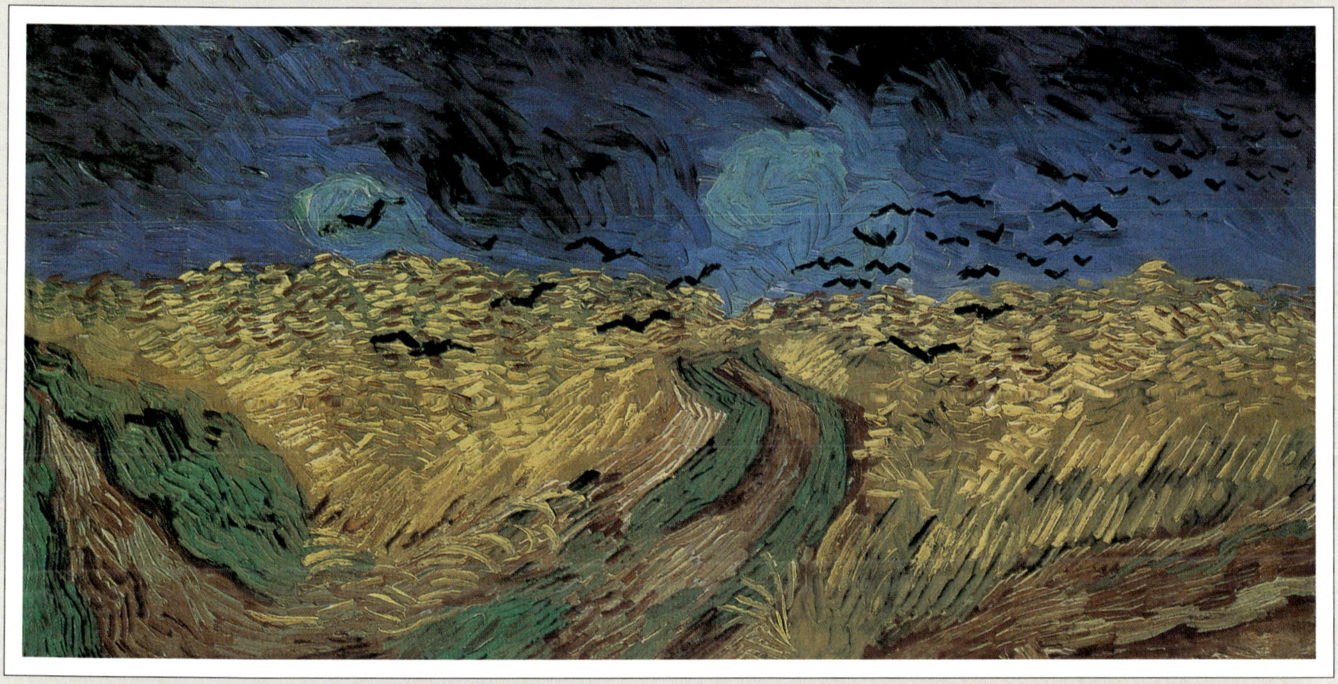

Perhaps the most violently painted of Van Gogh's works, this is the epitome of a subjective, expressionist landscape. Every element of composition, color and brushwork is used in an attempt to arouse in the viewer the same emotions that possessed the artist as he worked. The landscape itself is devoid of any distracting incidents, completely lacking any human presence and with a bare, unrelieved horizon. Distance is extremely difficult to determine as the three tracks seem to be attempting unsuccessfully to scale an almost vertical slope. Nor is there any concern with conveying distance through atmospheric perspective — the color is uniformly intense, and the painting of the sky as thick as that of the foreground.

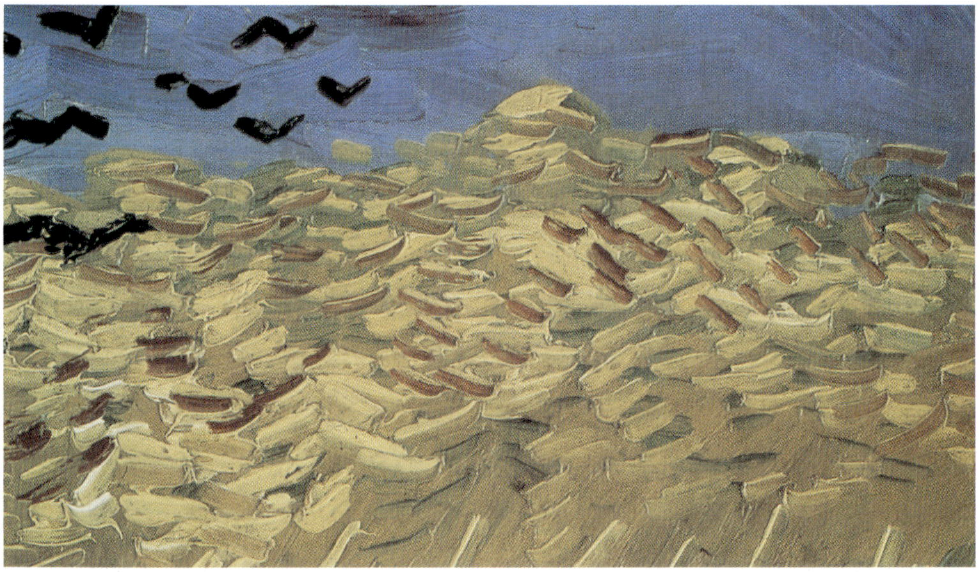

1

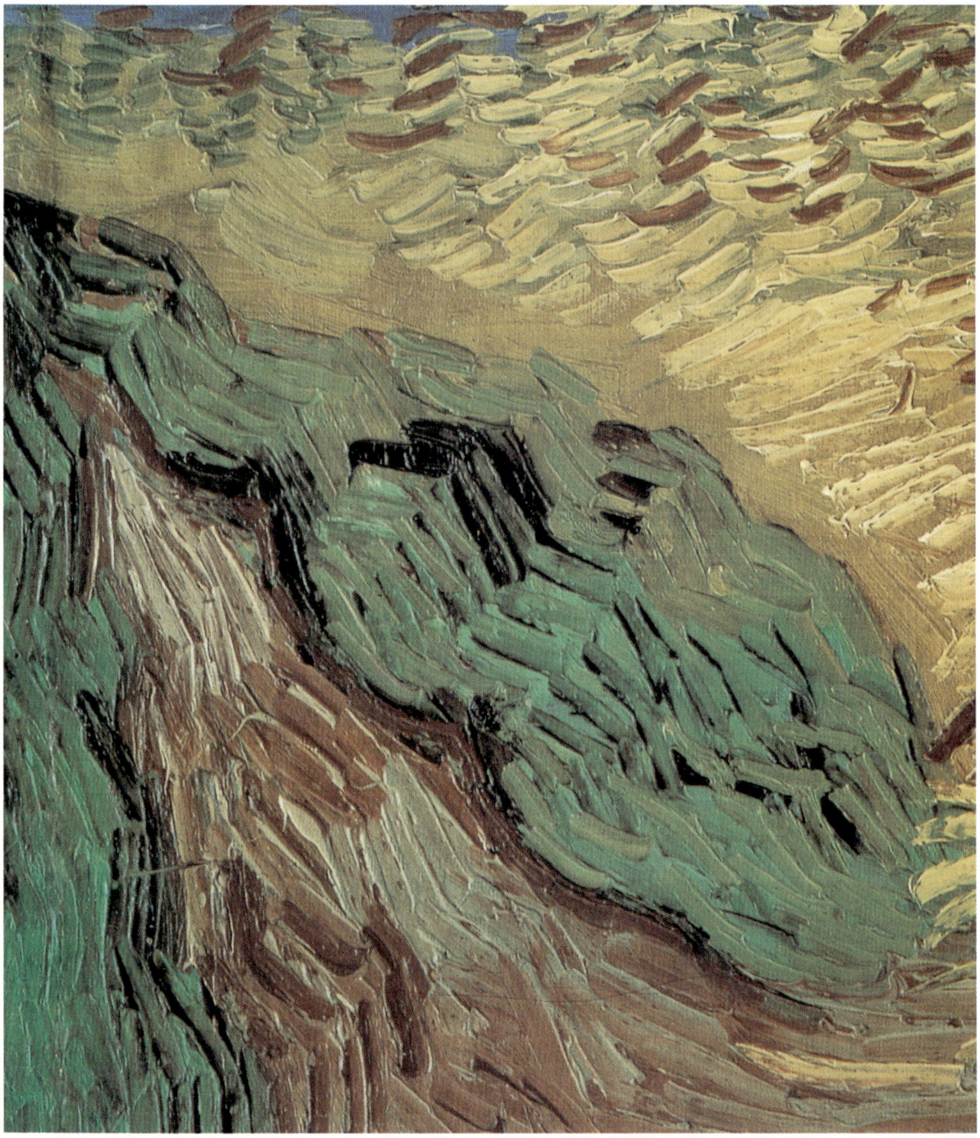

2

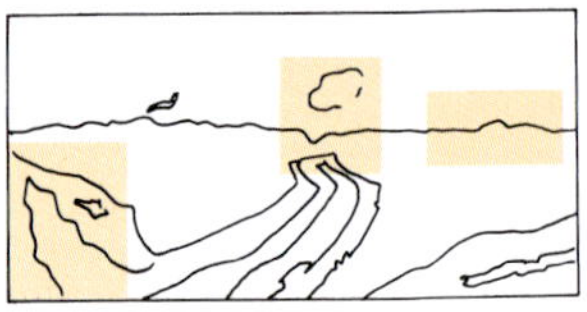

1 The dense mesh of short, rapid strokes that suggest the ears of corn blowing in the wind of the approaching storm are painted rapidly, wet-in-wet.

2 The livid colors used here reflect what Van Gogh felt, rather than what he saw. Darker tones are applied first, building up to lighter and brighter ones in a confused mass of shapeless movement.

3 *Actual size detail* There is no harmony in this painting, either in color or in brushwork; each stroke of the brush clashes with another so that the curves of the road consist of a series of tiny jagged angles. The same zig-zags represent the crows, reduced to the barest elements of the painter's "handwriting." Hues resembling blood and flesh are disturbingly present on the road beneath them.

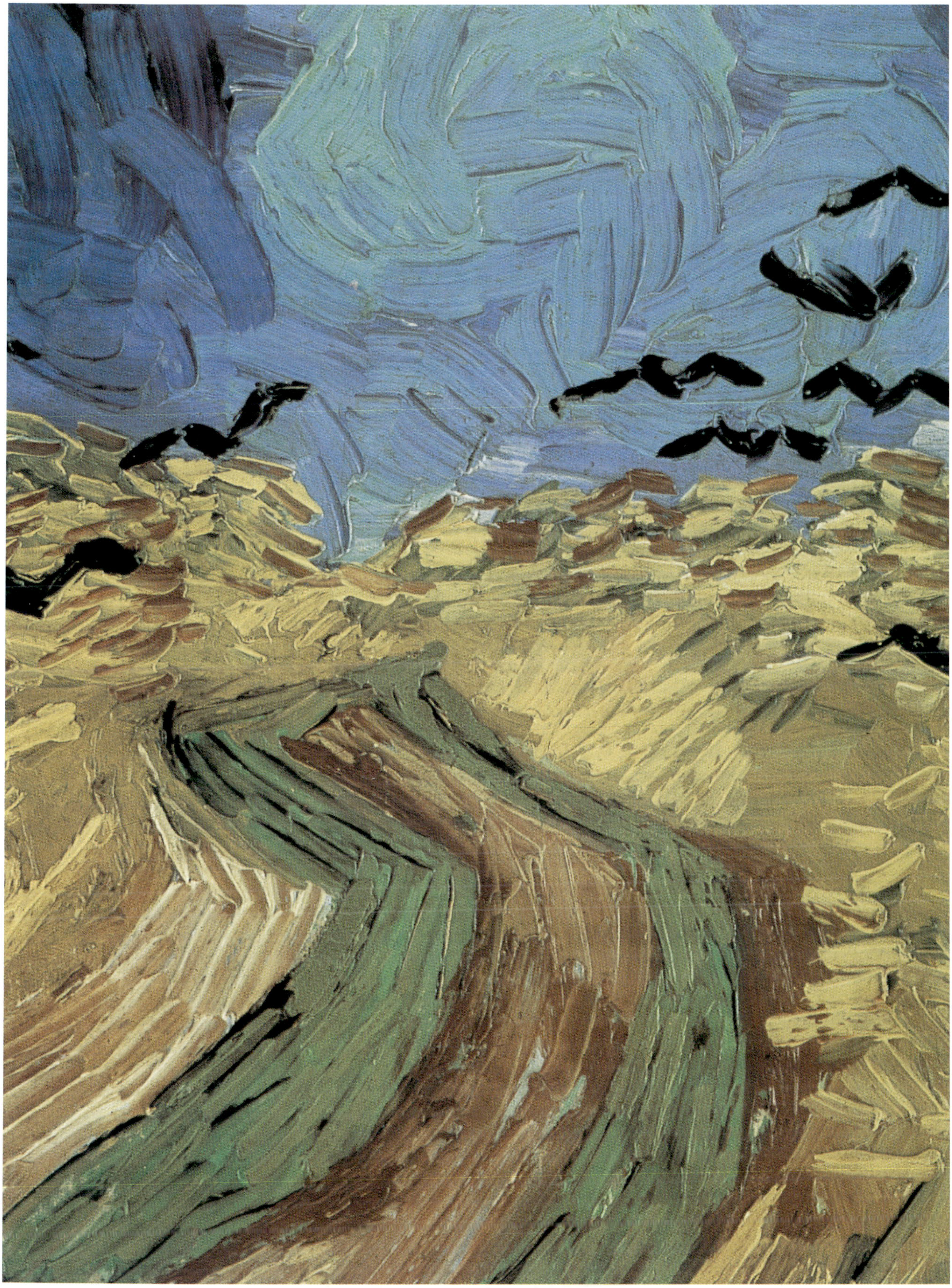

3 ***Actual size detail***

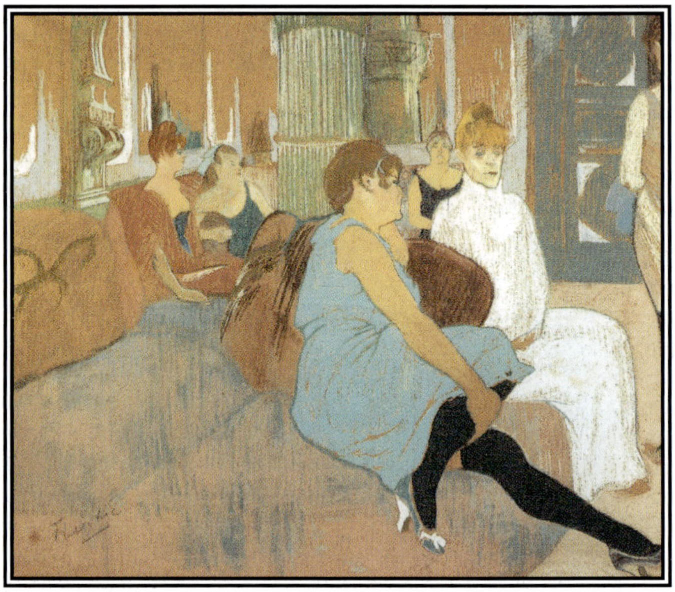

TOULOUSE-LAUTREC

Introduction

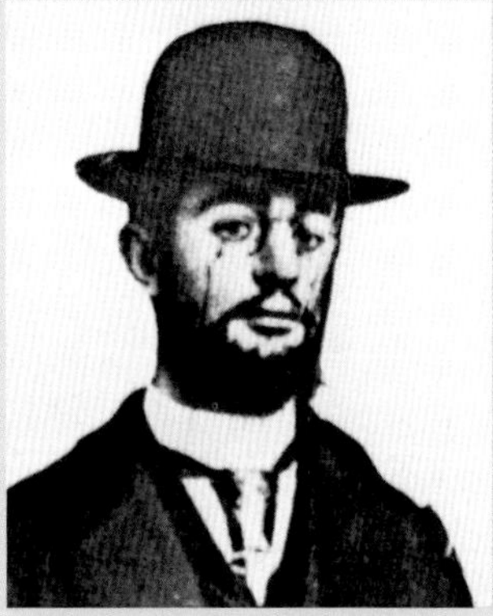

Photograph of Henri de Toulouse-Lautrec (detail)
Date unknown

"At last, I looked Lautrec straight in the eyes. Oh, how fine, large, richly warm and astonishingly, luminously bright they were! I kept on gazing into them and suddenly Lautrec became aware of it and took his spectacles off. He knew his one magnificent feature and he offered it to me with all his generosity. And his gesture showed me his ludicrous, dwarfish little hand, which was so square and attached to extraordinarily short marionettish arms."

This was how the cabaret singer Yvette Guilbert remembered the first of many meetings with Henri de Toulouse-Lautrec. She was not the only one to be won over by the performance of vivacity and wit that deflected attention from his deformity. However, she was more perceptive than some in recognizing so quickly the tragedy behind the eyes. And she was to show a creditable lack of vanity in her realization that the drawings he did of her were not mere representations.

Both were famous by the time he began to work from her, and she ignored the opposition of her various friends and advisers, only mildly reproving him for his most outrageous distortions. Her stage persona was itself a kind of caricature, a medium for satire and innuendo by which she deflated social pretensions and hypocrisy. The aims of artist and performer were thus compatible, Lautrec's primary purpose being an analysis of personality, more particularly of those aspects of human nature revealed when behavioral niceties are discarded. More than any other artist of this period he chose to operate in the seedy areas shared by polite society — the *monde* — and its vulgar counterpart — the *demi-monde,* wilfully specializing in the world of prostitutes, petty crooks, *roués,* and the fashionable men who moved imperturbably among them. To some extent Lautrec shared the latter's air of detached observation, but his involvement was more pronounced — his gleeful bohemianism caused his early death at the age of thirty-six. Ironically, his lifestyle has led him to be identified with the romantic notion of *fin de siècle* gaiety. But although his art does in some ways encapsulate an exuberant period on which Paris still capitalizes, it frequently strikes a note of cautionary melancholy that makes it ultimately impossible to define as either simply characteristic of the milieu or as his own peculiarly private view.

Early life

Lautrec's separateness, the quality that pervades so many of his paintings, was materially affected by the circumstances of his childhood. He was born in 1864 at Albi in southwest France, an aristocrat in a century when the majority of effective power was increasingly controlled by the middle classes. His quixotic father, Count Alphonse-Charles de Toulouse-Lautrec-Monfa, seems to have charged through life from one eccentric gesture to the next, his extravagant adventures outdoing even those of his son in his later, drink-deranged years.

Although neither he nor his parents were aware of it, Henri suffered from a bone deficiency, possibly the result of inbreeding. This was aggravated by the onset of puberty, with its sudden acceleration of growth, and when he broke both thighs in two successive years, each the result of an unspectacular fall, the bones failed to join up properly. The result was that his legs stopped growing, although his torso and head were of normal proportions, and his full adult height was only five feet (152.4cm). When it became clear that the accidents that caused his son's misshapeness would preclude him from a life devoted mainly to horses and hunting, the count ceased to take an active interest in Henri's development. He and his wife were largely estranged, maintaining little more than a marriage of appearances, and so the supervision of the boy's upbringing fell almost entirely to his mother, the Countess Adèle, who withdrew him from school to undergo a variety of cures.

He met his misfortunes with a natural buoyancy of spirit that was to remain as the core of the charm he

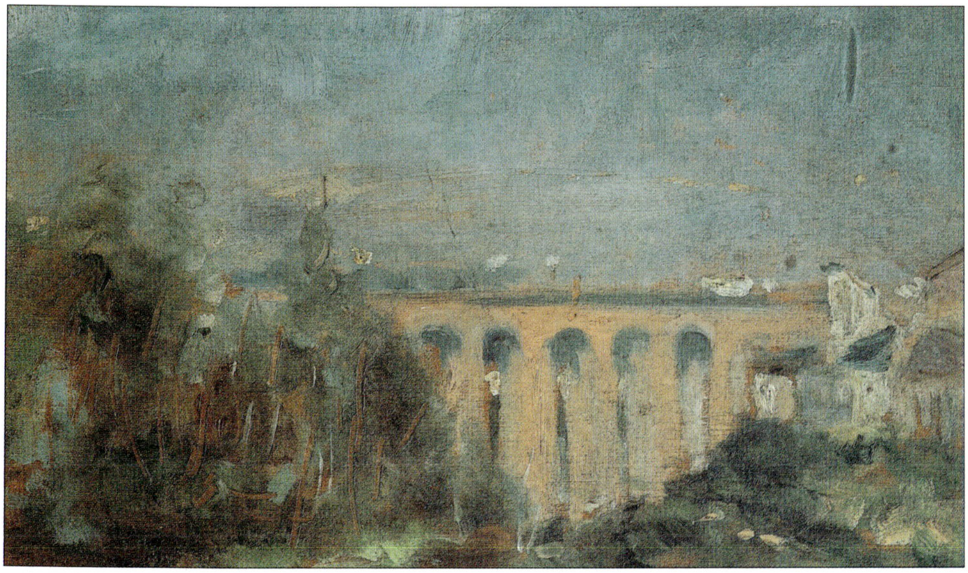

HENRI DE TOULOUSE-LAUTREC
Viaduct of Castel-Vieil at Albi
1880, Musée Toulouse-Lautrec, Albi

Lautrec rarely painted landscapes, declaring once that "only the figure exists," and that nature should be no more than background. This early work was painted from the balcony of the Hôtel du Bôsc, one of several country estates in southwest France owned by Lautrec's family. It is typical of the broadly impressionistic manner he developed before his formal artistic training in Paris.

exerted in later life. Lautrec always disdained self-pity, and even more so the pity of others. One of his most characteristic responses to some setback in adult life was to rasp, "It's of no consequence." Surviving letters to friends and cousins written during the convalescence from his accidents reveal an amazing degree of humor and courage.

Early training

Lautrec had shown a talent for drawing before the accidents. Had they not occurred this would probably have remained at the level of a cultivated hobby, as it was for one of his uncles, Charles. Even Lautrec's father, the count, occasionally attended classes run by a specialist in equestrian subjects, René Princeteau, and visits to this artist's studio in the Rue du Faubourg-St-Honoré constituted Lautrec's first introduction to the professional art world. The enforced sedentary life of the convalescent was made slightly more tolerable by the ability to focus his energy on the skills that remained accessible to him. His earliest efforts reflect his family background and interests: thoroughbred horses, hounds and hawks, fre-

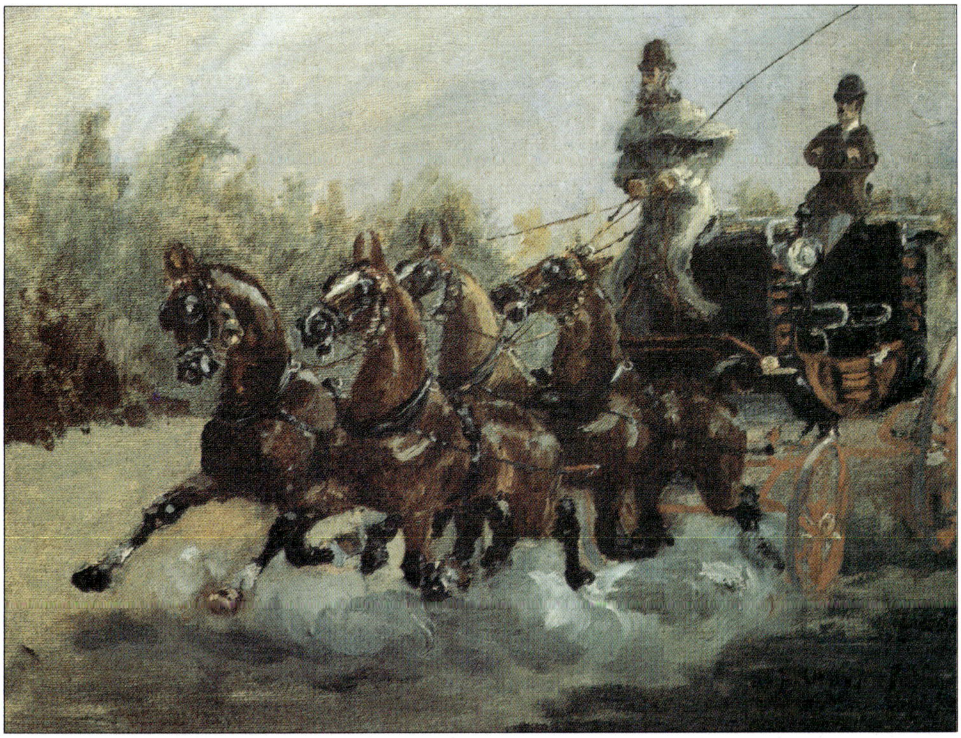

HENRI DE TOULOUSE-LAUTREC
The Four-in-Hand
1881, Musée du Petit Palais, Paris

Spirited horses were one of the main passions of Lautrec's father, here represented driving a coach along the Promenade des Anglais, Nice. Equestrian subjects not unnaturally predominate in Lautrec's early work. In theme and style this example reflects the influence of his earliest teacher, Princeteau, but the vigorous brushwork used to depict movement presages his mature manner.

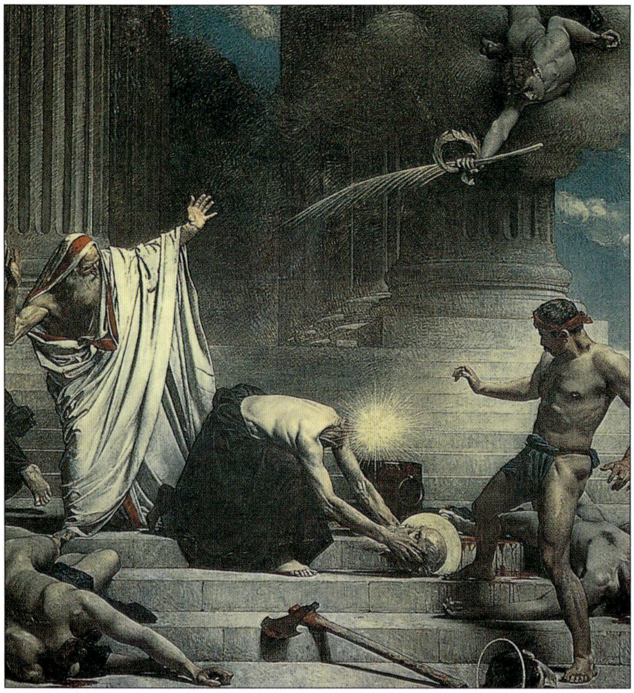

LEON BONNAT
The Decapitation of Saint Denis
1885, Panthéon, Paris

Lautrec studied only briefly under Bonnat, but during the early 1880s he tried hard to discipline his style according to the academic precepts on which a painting of this kind was based. It is an interesting coincidence that Bonnat situated the execution outside the Roman Temple of Mars, on the hill of Montmartre, the very district that was to provide Lautrec with so many subjects of so very different a character.

quently in vigorous motion, and painted in an appropriately boisterous style. By the mid 1880s he had largely abandoned this kind of subject matter, and his tastes were becoming decidedly urban, but he never lost this early ability to capture rapidly the essentials of brisk movement. Strangely, animal themes were to recur in the final years when alcoholic excess had brought him to physical and nervous collapse. These later works are less directly observed and were the products of imagination and memory, as if he were harking back to a period of relatively unsullied optimism.

Princeteau became increasingly impressed by the precocious ease with which his "studio foster child" assimilated his own manner. He was aware too that Lautrec needed and would benefit from more rigorous tuition, and it was arranged that the young man should enter the *atelier* of the academician, Léon Bonnat. In May 1882, a month or so after his commencement, Lautrec reported the comments of his "majestic" new master: "Your painting isn't bad — it's clever, but it still isn't bad — but your drawing is simply atrocious." This opinion is revealing: the essence of Lautrec's painting style is his drawing, but not in the academic sense that Bonnat would have comprehended. The basis of the orthodox system of art training to which Lautrec submitted, first under Bonnat and then, from 1883, with Fernand Cormon, was a respect for classical sculpture and the masters of the High Renaissance. More immediately, it depended on precepts and methods stemming in France from the "School of David" at the beginning of the century. These were perpetuated by the Ecole des Beaux-Arts (where Bonnat became a professor and later director), and the results were annually displayed in their hundreds at the Paris Salon.

Bonnat eventually became a fierce opponent of all modern tendencies in art, and seems to have developed a special dislike of his former pupil. Four years after Lautrec's death he used his considerable influence to get the Commission of National Museums to revoke its decision to accept one of Lautrec's finest portraits, *Monsieur Delaporte at the Jardin de Paris*. Bonnat's style as a painter of grand historical subjects can be gauged from his contribution to the prestigious series of murals for the Panthéon in 1885. But his international reputation was as a painter of portraits, in which powerful realization of character was in part due to a forceful, almost bravura application of paint. Even more relevant to the formation of Lautrec's mature style was Bonnat's recognized brilliance in the rapid execution of oil sketches, both for copies from Old Masters and from the life model, and pupils of the equally conservative Cormon similarly spoke of his encouragement of swift informal copying in the Louvre.

In the second half of the 19th century it was not unusual to find progressive artists incorporating elements of their training into their mature styles. Whistler, for example, made a principle of the importance Charles Gleyre, his teacher, had attached to working from memory, and built a whole aesthetic credo on Gleyre's practice of arranging a picture's color harmonies on the palette before touching the canvas. But the principal purpose of art teaching was to prepare students for entry into the Ecole des Beaux-Arts, and this was probably Lautrec's intention initially; certainly it was the course his family expected him to follow.

But in the early 1880s a number of new ideas were beginning to emerge in the wake of Impressionism, which was itself still controversial. Such developments were keenly discussed in the teaching studios, exacerbating the sense of disenchantment with traditional notions of art practice. In 1886 some of Cormon's students became so openly critical of his methods that he closed the studio, reopening a little later after expelling the worst offenders. (One of these was Emile Bernard, who was introduced to Gauguin at Pont-Aven later in the year.) Lautrec, who three years earlier had found Cormon's teaching insufficiently taxing, was not among the rebels, though he was by now of the same opinion. For two years, since he had taken a studio in Montmartre, he had been attending Cormon's less regularly, and his style had begun to change. He continued for a time to use the somber values and orthodox compositions encouraged by his official teachers, but gradually his naturally vivacious style began to reassert itself in themes redolent of his new surroundings.

Montmartre

In the 18th century, Montmartre, then a village outside Paris, was already known for its cheap taverns, drunkenness and licentiousness. Early in the following century, attracted by low rents and rural picturesqueness, artists began to gather there, along with writers, intellectuals, and political malcontents. Through the century it was gradually transformed from a windmill-dotted, hilltop

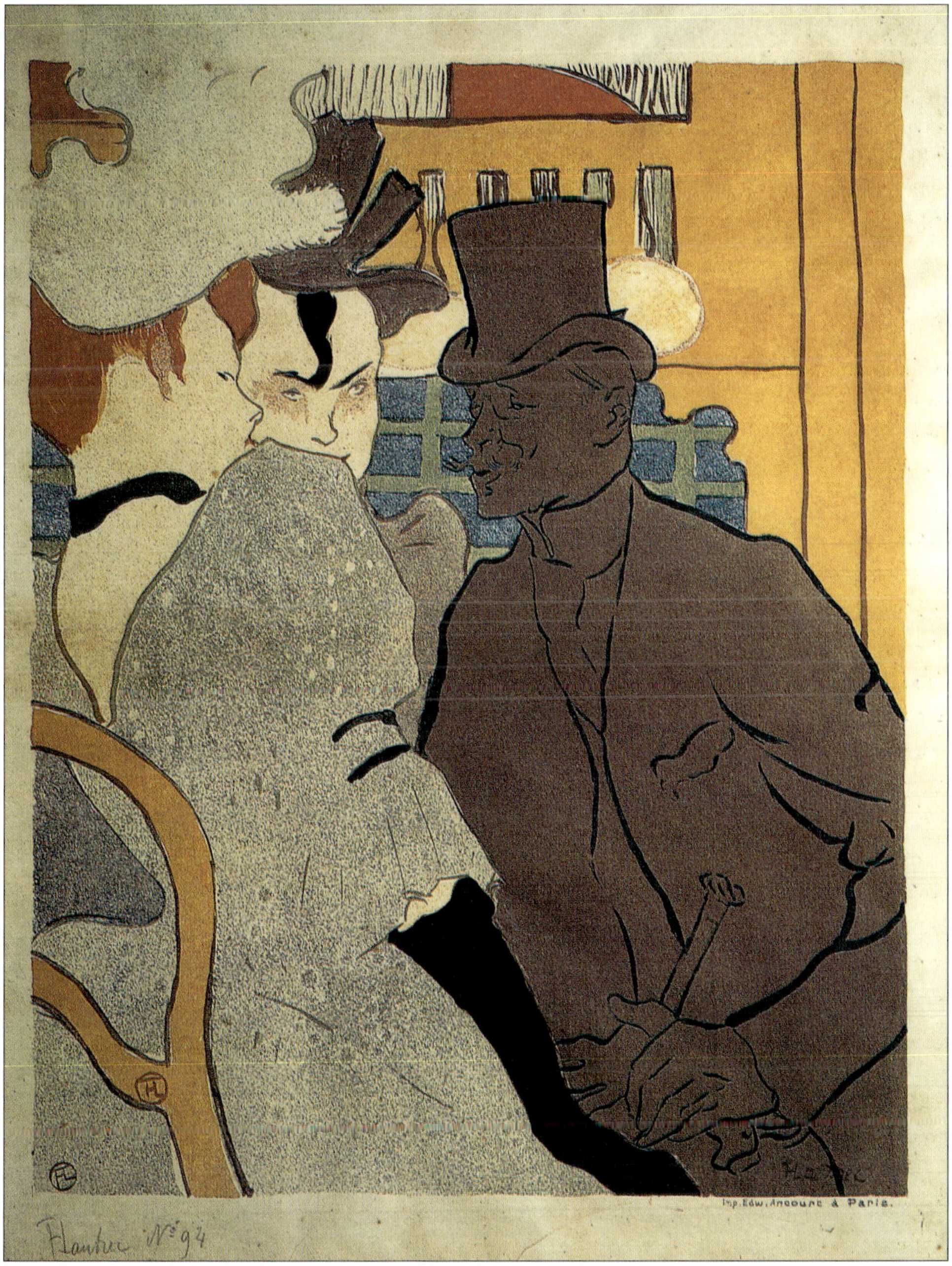

HENRI DE TOULOUSE-LAUTREC
The Flirt — the Englishman Warrener at The Moulin Rouge
1892, Musée Toulouse-Lautrec, Albi

This is one of Lautrec's earliest color lithographs, showing his grasp of the bold pictorial possibilities of Japanese art when combined with his naturally swift draftsmanship. Large, irregular areas of unmodulated color and tone were partly responsible for the success of the poster designs he had begun to produce the year before, and the confidence he gained in this way began to bear fruit in his paintings also.

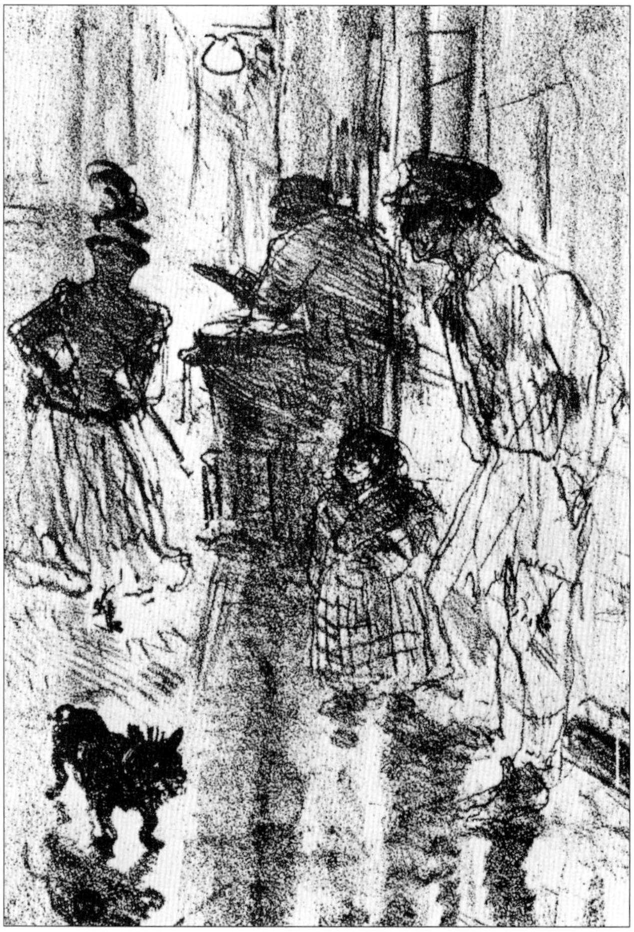

HENRI DE TOULOUSE-LAUTREC
The Chestnut Vendor
1897, Bibliothèque Nationale, Paris

Lautrec was an aristocrat, but paradoxically this, combined with his physical condition, enabled him to identify with the anti-bourgeois sentiments of people such as Aristide Bruant and the graphic artist Steinlen. Overtly proletarian themes, such as this, however, were rare, and his use of the small dog (a frequent metaphor for his own physique) suggests that there may have been a symbolic intent in this unusually atmospheric drawing.

village to a densely populated, lower-class suburb; between 1830 and 1886 the estimated population rose from 6,000 to over 200,000. That it had continued its unsavory character is apparent from a *Baedeker* entry for 1888: "The best cafés [in the center of Paris] may with propriety be visited by ladies, but those on the north side of the Boulevards Montmartre and des Italiens should be avoided, as the society there is far from select."

Lautrec very quickly felt at home in Montmartre, and became identified with some of its notable performers. The first of these relationships was with the satirical singer Aristide Bruant, whose songs expressed his disdain for the fashionable swells out slumming. Lautrec had begun to publish drawings in this vein in 1886, and had accumulated a significant body of illustrations before 1891, when his fame was immediately established through his poster designs, the first commissioned for the newly opened dance hall, the Moulin Rouge. A year later he began to produce fine lithographs, *The Englishman Warrener at the Moulin Rouge* being one of his earliest essays in the medium to which he was to contribute a wealth of innovatory ideas and techniques.

Friendship with Bruant was a crucial phase in

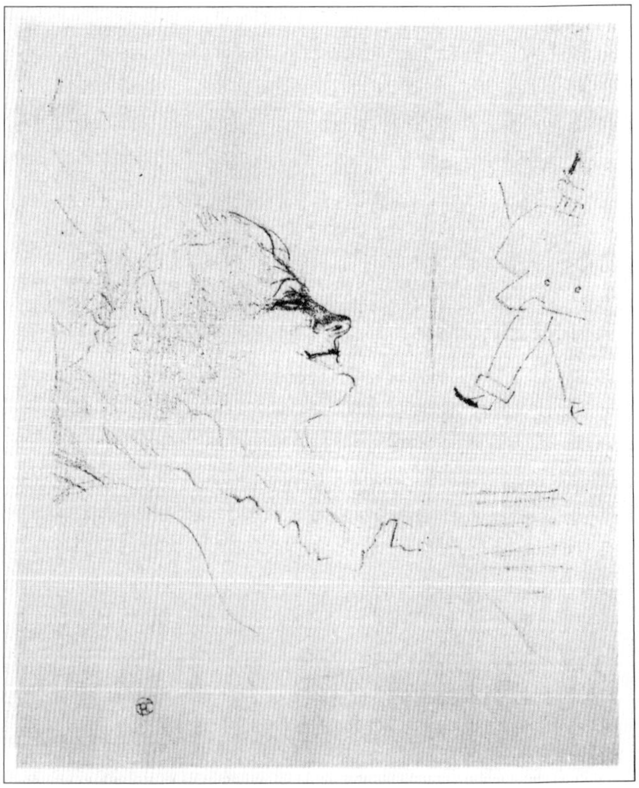

HENRI DE TOULOUSE-LAUTREC
Yvette Guilbert-Pessima
1898, British Museum, London

Lautrec specialized in depictions of popular entertainers. Sometimes (as with May Belfort or Loïe Fuller) his enthusiasm was short-lived, but he worked consistently from both Yvette Guilbert and Jane Avril over a number of years, his depictions reflecting sustained friendships. Here he has caught the jaunty knowingness of the singer's mobile face with a minimum of lines.

Lautrec's education, since much of his subsequent painting and graphic work was dependent on the brilliant realization of the characters of popular entertainers and of the varied types that made up their audiences. His first exhibited works were hung on the walls of Bruant's cabaret Le Mirliton and featured, for example, the singer himself and the riotous dancing of the "naturalistic quadrille" (the predecessor of the can-can) at the Elysée-Montmartre.

Therefore, by the age of twenty-one, Lautrec had already been seduced away from the career in the official art world that his family would have wished for him. His decisive rejection of academicism suggests a degree of certainty about his abilities, but there are indications that throughout his life he was unsure of his artistic stature in relation to the painters he most admired, notably Degas. His family wealth removed the pressure to earn a living from his art that many of his peers felt, and although he clearly had determination, it was not backed by any strong theoretical motivation, as Bernard's was. Nor did he have the sense of great purpose shown by Van Gogh, who had arrived in Paris in 1886 and also studied at Cormon's *atelier.*

Influences

Lautrec avoided attachment to any particular avant-garde group, but he was responsive to some of the leading ideas filtering through his network of acquaintances. Impressionism was clearly an influence on him, lightening and brightening his palette and loosening his brushwork, but his mature works are only minimally analyses of light, which was the main preoccupation of the Impressionists. He also benefited from the notion – not unique to the Impressionists – of sketch-like spontaneity as an equivalent for individuality and self-expression. Several of his friends experimented seriously, if briefly, with variants of Seurat's Pointillism, and some of Lautrec's work of the early 1890s also suggests an interest, though the application of dots of color was much looser and less "scientifically" based than that of the Neo-Impressionists. One of the most obvious stylistic influences is that of Van Gogh, which can be seen in Lautrec's own version of directional brushstrokes, creating a sense of three-dimensional form and space by means of linear striations and cross-hatching. But the painter to whom Lautrec owed most, both in terms of subject matter and technique, was Degas, who was a neighbor between 1887 and 1893. Like Degas, Lautrec experimented with pigment thinned with turpentine, and both artists made use of unconventional supports such as unprimed canvas or brown cardboard, which absorbed the paint and gave a matte quality.

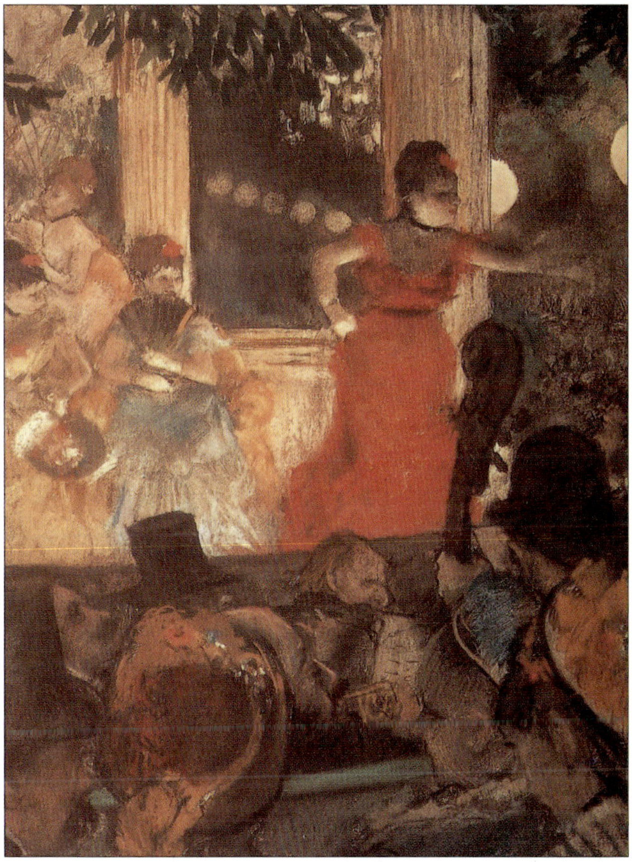

EDGAR DEGAS
Café-concert at The Ambassadeurs
c 1875-7, Musée des Beaux-Arts, Lyon

Lautrec was keenly appreciative of Japanese art, but his adaptation of oriental compositional devices was at least as much due to his admiration for Degas. The critic Gustave Geffroy, writing on Lautrec, coined the term "human landscape." This is equally applicable to Degas who, as here, provided Lautrec with a scheme for combining stage performers and their audience.

As early as 1882 Lautrec had recorded an enthusiasm for Japanese art, a taste shared by many artists of the period, and this led him in time, in paintings such as *Women at her Toilet*, to adopt compositional devices like oblique or elevated viewpoints to give enhanced immediacy to his compositions. This influence is particularly evident in his graphic work; knowledge of Japanese prints, as well as suggesting subjects, encouraged a bold and often asymmetrical disposition of forms, sharp overlapping of figures indicating brief momentary glimpses, and figures and objects cut off dramatically at the picture's edges – devices that Degas also used extensively.

Large, flat areas of color were another feature of Japanese art that painters like Gauguin and Bernard incorporated into their work. Lautrec only rarely used these in his painting – his abstractions were always modified by naturalism – but it was an approach eminently suited to posters and lithographs, in which he was able to exploit simplicity of means even more than in his paintings. This was largely because he accepted the limitations of whatever medium he was working in. For example, he quickly realized the positive nature of blank areas of paper as a foil for the brilliant irregularities of his line, and in such works as *The Englishman Warrener at the Moulin Rouge* he plays off unbroken non-naturalistic areas against atmospheric, textured ones. Although visually this effect is quite different from the styles he was pursuing in his paintings, they too always combine touches of visual realism (usually faces and hands) within a sketchy context whose abstraction is stressed through clearly defined brushstrokes, unpainted ground and unmodulated color.

Lautrec in context

Just as Lautrec had no fixed allegiance to any particular artistic group, his links with the avant-garde critics seem not to have been due to shared aesthetic ideals. For example, two important advocates of Neo-Impressionism and Symbolism, Edouard Dujardin and Félix Fénéon, occur among the *dramatis personae* of Lautrec's paintings, but apart from some youthful allegories, the closest Lautrec came to Symbolism was in the later, sometimes nightmarish, works induced by extreme alcoholism and the effects of withdrawal. Closest to him theoretically were writers like Gustave Geffroy, who promoted the principles of Naturalism, but Lautrec's brand of sometimes bitter realism was less a matter of theory than of instinct and sympathy. When he began to exhibit with the progressive society *Les Vingt* in Brussels in 1888, the often favorable reception he had from such writers was probably partly due to his being recognized as a follower of Degas, and it was the latter's opinion that in many ways mattered to him most.

Lautrec's own politics were vaguely right-wing, and espousal by Anarchist reviewers may have caused him some amusement. However, their interpretation of his work was understandable in view of the evident humanitarian qualities of his depictions of the humbler inhabitants of Montmartre. Above all, it is within the broad context of Naturalism that his art is best understood as a significant contribution beyond purely personal observation. The poet Charles Baudelaire had urged painters to extract the age's "epic quality from the life of today and make us see and understand ... how great and poetic we are in our cravats and our patent leather boots." But he well understood that epic poetry requires a bond between heroism and tragedy. Writers like Flaubert and Zola elaborated on this ambiguity, and it is present too in Lautrec's art. For example, the top-hatted *flâneurs* gratifying their senses among the lower-class women, are sometimes cynical, sometimes impassive, and sometimes lascivious. And yet these men were often modeled on Lautrec's friends, who themselves engaged in such activity with relish, as did Lautrec himself. Images of this kind can be, and were, read as reproaches

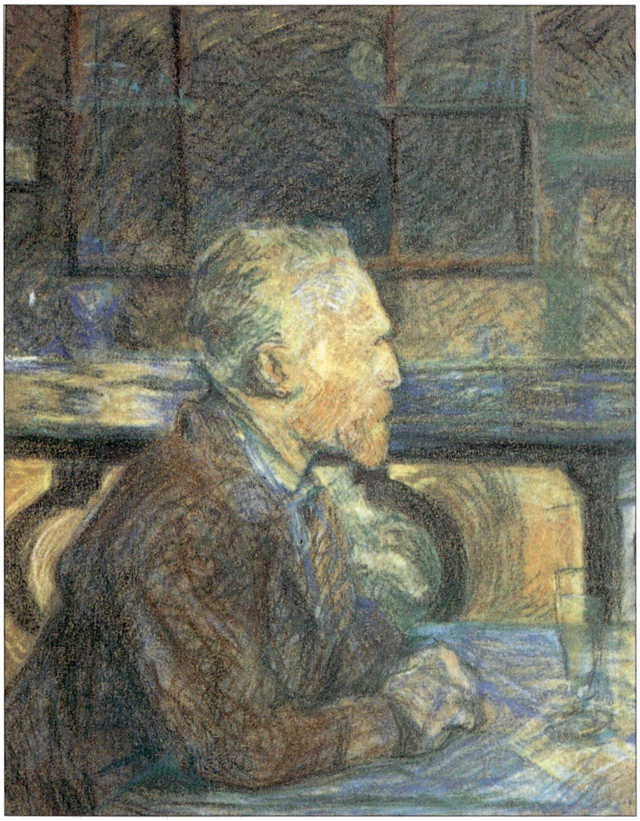

HENRI DE TOULOUSE-LAUTREC
Portrait of Van Gogh
1887, Rijkmuseum Vincent Van Gogh, Amsterdam

Pastel was an unusual medium for Lautrec, but the painting style he developed around this time combined both the linear hatching and the matte coloring apparent in this portrait. Although Van Gogh and Lautrec were dissimilar in temperament, both were outsiders seeking self-fulfillment through art, and they shared both a responsiveness to new ideas and an avoidance of close affiliation with any particular group.

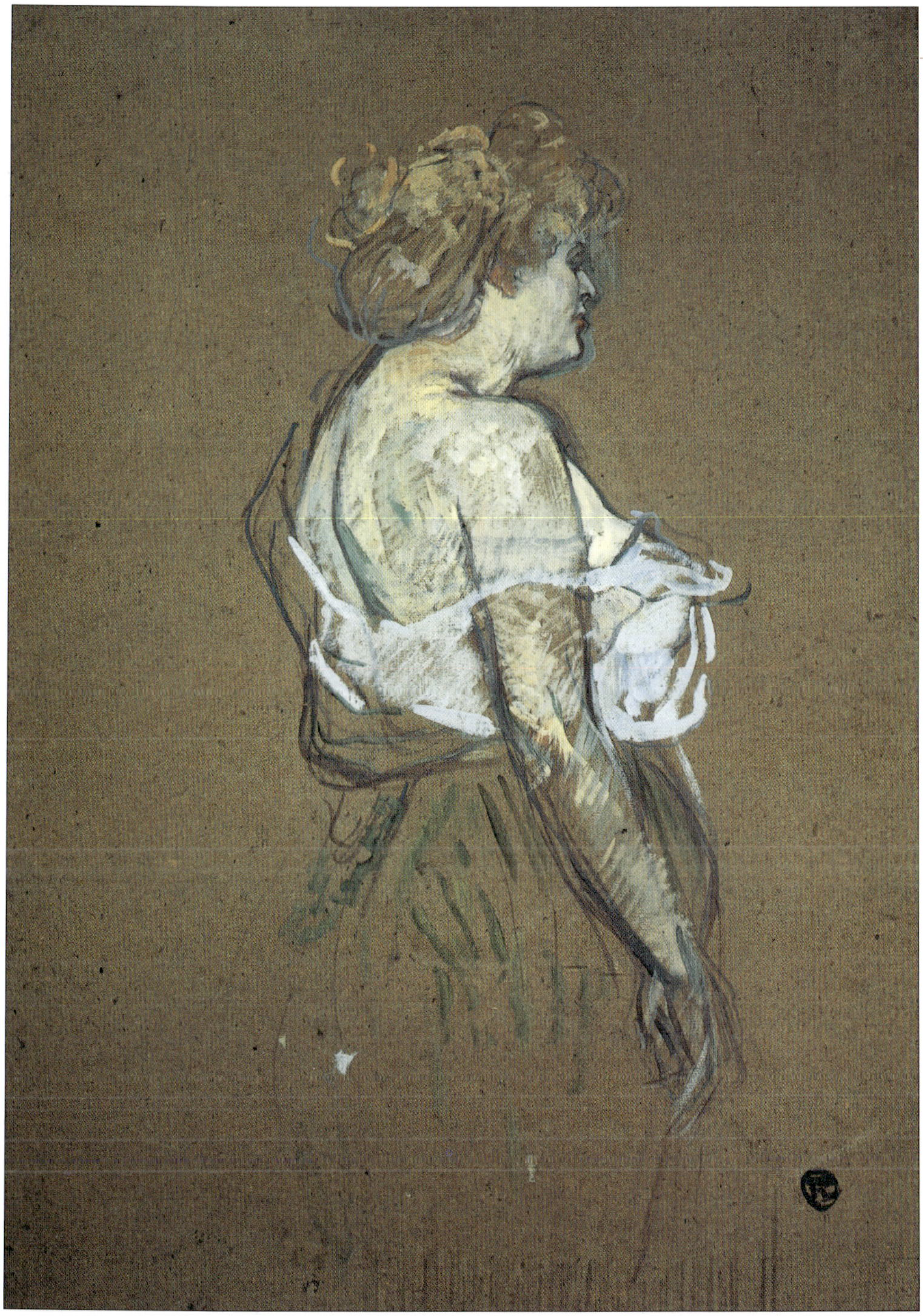

HENRI DE TOULOUSE-LAUTREC
Lucie Bellanger
1896, Musée Toulouse-Lautrec, Albi

This study of one of the prostitutes living in the brothel in the Rue des Moulins is a fine example of Lautrec's exploitation of the qualities of the thinned paint known as *peinture à l'essence.* This allowed him literally to draw in paint, so that despite the sketchy application of line and body color, the result is convincing as a representation of three-dimensional form.

leveled against a social system that produced such inequalities, and Lautrec's sensitive treatment of prostitutes could be seen to support this view. But also his work was and still is characterized as non-judgmental — simply the Naturalist's straight presentation of assiduously collected facts. Neither view is fully adequate. In his paintings and drawings Lautrec presented his own intimate involvement, emotional and physical, in the way of life he depicted, showing us his comprehension of its pleasure and its pain.

New themes and last years

By about 1893 the focus of Lautrec's interests had begun to shift away from Montmartre toward central Paris, and his circle of friends and acquaintances broadened to include the well-known intellectuals and literary and political figures connected with the magazine *La Revue Blanche,* which stood for the most advanced ideas of the day. He began to be increasingly drawn to scenes of the theater and popular operetta, which looked forward to a flurry of paintings based on Isidore de Lara's operetta

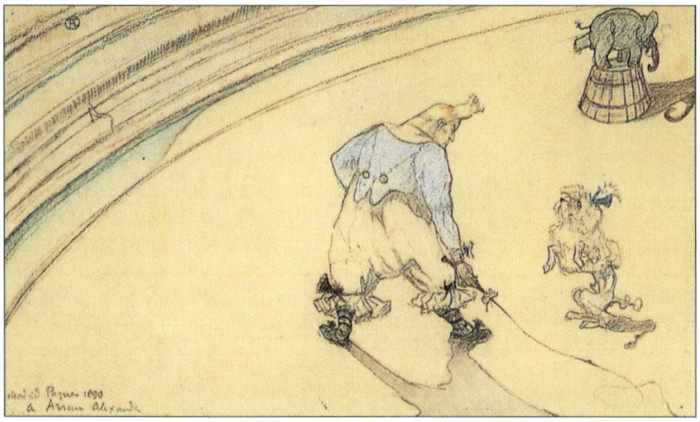

HENRI DE TOULOUSE-LAUTREC
Le Dressage
1899, Statens Museum fur Kunst, Copenhagen

Lautrec's alcoholism led to his confinement in a clinic at Neuilly where, to demonstrate his sanity, he produced from imagination over forty drawings, mainly of circus subjects. This one was dedicated to the critic Arsène Alexandre, who helped secure his release. The series has a dream-like quality and meticulousness of execution unusual for Lautrec, no doubt a measure of his determination to escape.

Messaline, painted in 1900, the year before he died.

By the mid-1890s Lautrec was at the height of his powers, and was now a well-known artist, having held several exhibitions and visited London, where he met Whistler and Oscar Wilde. Even the general public were aware of him through his posters. But his drinking, always excessive, was beginning to take its toll. He had become ill-tempered and was sometimes unintelligible, and by 1899 he was suffering so badly from delerium tremens that he was forced to enter a sanatorium in an effort to cure his drinking problem. While there, determined to prove that he was fit to be released, he made a series of drawings of circus scenes, relying on his impressive visual memory.

The style he adopted in his final years, seen in paintings such as *At the Rat Mort* (see page 715), has perplexed some critics, being painterly and tonal rather than linear, as was his earlier work. The compositions are sometimes more complex (not always successfully) when compared with his earlier manner of focusing around a main — usually female — figure, and the coloring is more exotic and sumptuous. Some have seen this late manner as an attempt to redirect his art, while others have attributed the minimizing of line to his failing powers. Possibly both are correct; he had always been capable of uneven quality, but until the last few months when he could barely put brush to canvas, he could still produce paintings of real merit.

In spite of his stay at the sanatorium, Lautrec's extraordinary capacity for alcohol finally proved too much for a frame enfeebled since birth, and in 1901 his health gave out completely. He asked to be taken to his mother's home, and there he died, on September 9, aged thirty-six. His last recorded words, spoken as he watched his father hovering by his bedside flicking flies from the coverlet with a piece of elastic drawn from his hunting boots, were "the old fool." Jules Renard, one of the writers he had met through *La Revue Blanche,* has left us a moving tribute to his character and his art: "The more one sees of him the taller he grows. In the end he assumes a stature above the average."

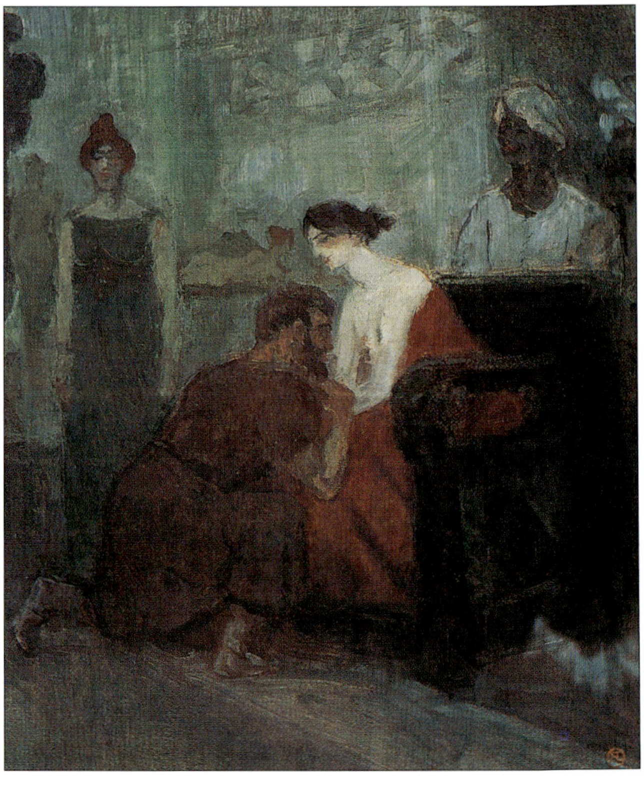

HENRI DE TOULOUSE-LAUTREC
Messalina Seated on her Throne
1900, Musée Toulouse-Lautrec, Albi

The series of paintings based on de Lara's operetta *Messaline,* which Lautrec saw at Bordeaux a few months before his final collapse, was the culmination of an interest in theatrical subjects that had begun earlier in the decade. The uneven quality of his later works reflects both his struggle against failing abilities and a desire, even at that late stage of his life, to develop a more painterly technique.

LAUTREC'S PAINTING METHODS

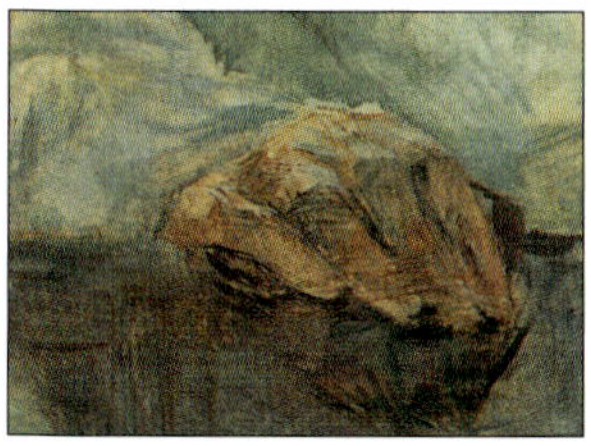

Lautrec's portrait of his mother, *The Comtesse Adèle de Toulouse-Lautrec,* shows an early use of his system of hatched brushstrokes.

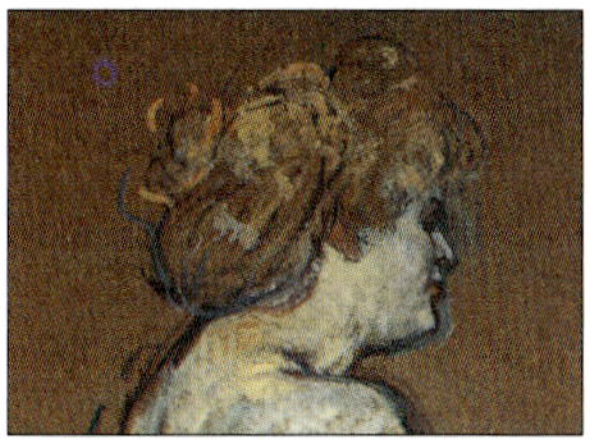

Lucie Bellanger was painted on cardboard in *peinture à l'essence.* The thinned paint dries very fast, allowing the artist to use it almost as a drawing medium.

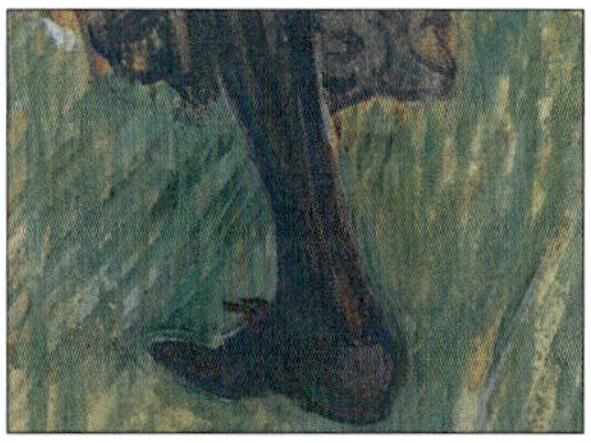

In *Jane Avril Dancing,* also on cardboard, Lautrec achieves an effect of transparency by overlaying layers of different-colored brushstrokes.

Lautrec's early painting style was mainly derived from the Impressionists, but in his later works he developed a freer, more open technique, where fluid, graphic contours outlined blocks of more uniform color, applied with rapid, bold sweeps of the brush. He often varied his brushstrokes, sometimes using dots, lines, hatching, or zigzag marks to create a painterly equivalent for different surface textures.

He was greatly influenced by the subject matter and techniques of Degas, and both artists experimented with pigment heavily diluted with turpentine. This *peinture à l'essence,* as it is called, gives a matte effect that has something of the quality of pastel, quite unlike the buttery consistency and surface sheen of normal oil paint. Lautrec found that this fluid paint enabled him to "draw" with a brush, thus exploiting his genius for linear draftsmanship. Degas used to drain the paints of oil by placing them on blotting paper, and both artists frequently painted on absorbent surfaces, such as brown cardboard or unprimed canvas, instead of the more usual pale- or white-primed support. Lautrec liked this kind of dull, muted ground color, and preferred a palette of broken rather than pure hues, which suited the artificially lit indoor night scenes that he and Degas painted so often.

At the Rat Mort is an excellent example of Lautrec's characteristic thinly worked paint. It is painted on canvas, and shows how skillfully he was able to adapt the technique he had perfected when working on absorbent surfaces to the more conventional support. The canvas is a fine one with a pale commercial priming, and the colors used for the work were probably those shown below.

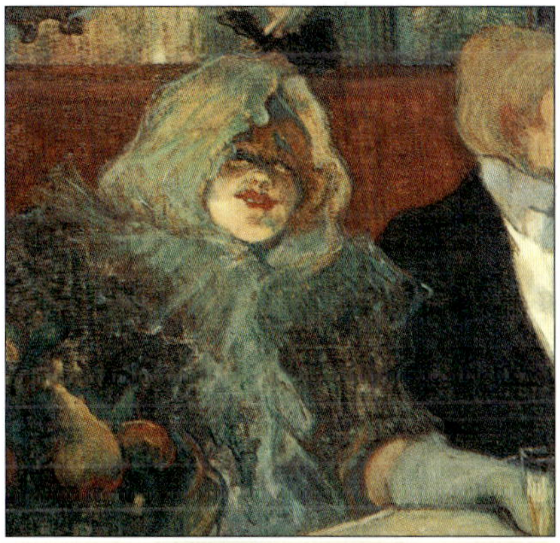

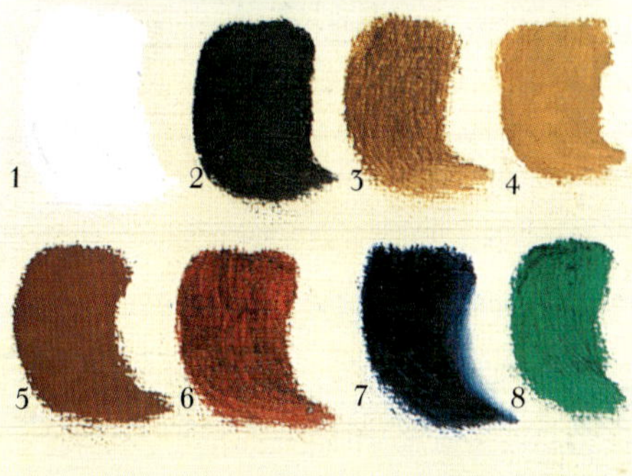

1 lead white; 2 black; 3 raw sienna; 4 yellow ocher; 5 red earth; 6 alizarin lake (possibly); 7 Prussian blue; 8 chrome green or viridian

CHRONOLOGY OF LAUTREC'S LIFE

1864 24 November: Lautrec born in the Hôtel du Bôsc at Albi.

1872 Attends the Lycée Fontanes, Paris.

1875 Poor health causes his mother to withdraw him from school for treatment.

1878-9 Fractures left and then right femur.

1880 Paints *Viaduct of Castel-Vieil at Albi.*

1881 Passes baccalauréat at second attempt. Subsequently concentrates on art, studying initially with René Princeteau. Paints *The Four-in-Hand* and *The Comtesse Adèle de Toulouse-Lautrec.*

1882 Enters the teaching atelier of Léon Bonnat and then that of Fernand Cormon, where he later becomes a friend of Emile Bernard and Van Gogh.

1885 Begins to frequent the dance-halls and bars of Montmartre. Becomes a friend of Aristide Bruant.

1886 Takes his own studio, 7 rue Touraque, which he retains until 1897. First publication of his drawings.

1887 Exhibits in several small exhibitions organized by Theo Van Gogh, the artist's brother. *Portrait of Van Gogh* painted at this time.

1888 Affairs with Suzanne Valadon and "Rosa Le Rouge" — contracts syphilis. February: exhibits with Les Vingt in Brussels.

1889 First exhibits at the Salon des Indépendents *(The Ball at The Moulin de la Galette).* The Moulin Rouge opens; meets Jane Avril.

1891 Lautrec does drawings of the operations of Dr Péan. Becomes member of the hanging committee of the Salon des Indépendents. First poster commissioned by Zidler for The Moulin Rouge. Paints *A la Mie.*

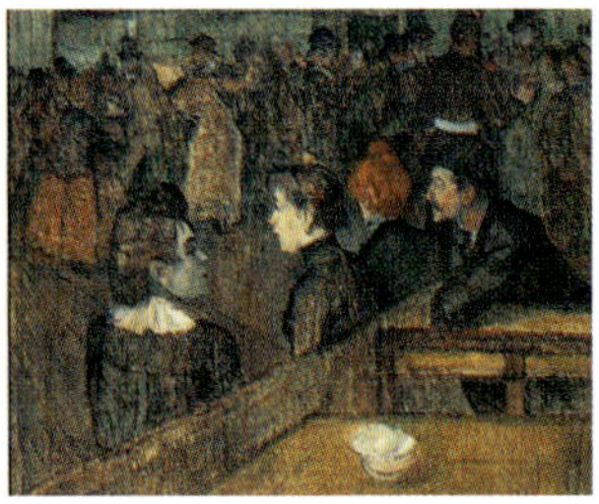

The Ball at the Moulin de la Galette

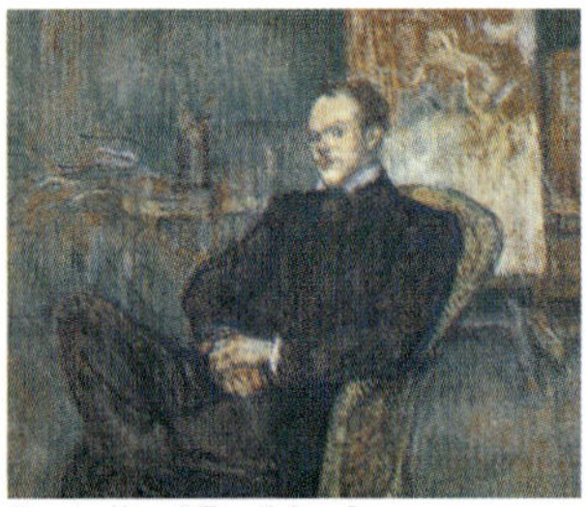

Portrait of Paul Leclercq

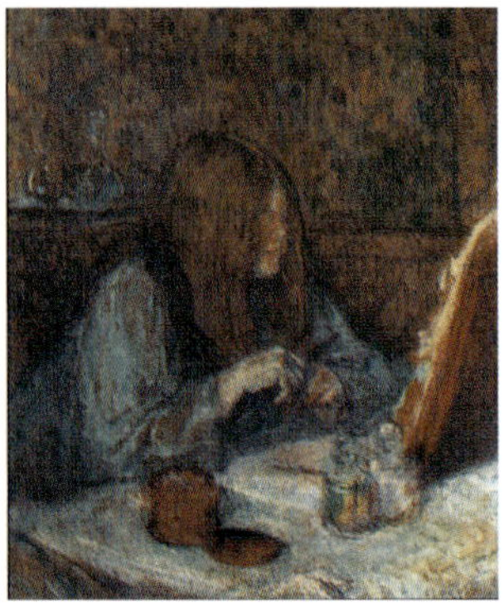

Mme Poupoule at her Toilet

1892 Begins to paint brothel scenes and to publish colour lithographs. Paints *In Bed* and *Jane Avril Dancing.*

1893 Becomes involved with the journal *La Revue Blanche* and begins to use theatrical subjects. His first one-man show is organized by Joyant, but he opts to share it with Charles Maurin.

1894 Begins to stay for periods of time in brothels. Publishes the French series of Yvette Guilbert lithographs with preface by the critic Gustave Geffroy. Paints *Salon at the Rue des Moulins.*

1895 Meets Whistler and Wilde in London. Paints the booth panels for La Goulue. Travels to Lisbon with Maurice Guibert. Begins to frequent lesbian bars and publishes *Elles* series of lithographs.

1896 Alcoholism worsens. Holds one-man exhibition at the Manzi-Joyant gallery. Paints *Lucie Bellanger* and *Woman at her Toilet.*

1897 Moves to Rue Frochot, where he paints *Portrait of Paul Leclercq.*

1898 Exhibition at the London branch of Goupil's. Paints *Mme Poupoule at her Toilet.*

1899 Health deteriorates markedly during the winter. Is confined to a clinic at Neuilly between February and May, but by the year end is drinking again. Paints *At the Rat Mort.*

1900 Makes various trips. At Bordeaux becomes enthusiastic about the operetta *Messaline.*

1901 Returns briefly to Paris to put his studio in order. Has an attack of paralysis while at Taussat in August. Is taken by his mother to the family house at Malromé and dies there on 9 September.

THE PAINTINGS

The Ball at the Moulin de la Galette

1889

$35\frac{1}{2} \times 39\frac{3}{8}$in/$90 \times 100$cm

Oil on canvas

Chicago Art Institute

Lautrec's boisterous personality and style masked a degree of uncertainty about his abilities as an artist. But by 1889 he was more secure in his commitment and consequently more ambitious in his compositions. Previously he had concentrated mainly on scenes involving movement and on portraits of single figures. Here he combines the two interests in a more complex organization which is nevertheless essentially a group of carefully arranged portraits. Subtly dominant is the painting's first owner, the derby-hatted Joseph Albert, presented in surroundings – the dance-halls and café-concerts of Montmartre.

Albert was a friend and fellow painter, and it was he who introduced Lautrec to the organizers of the Salon des Indépendants in the fall of this same year. *The Ball At the Moulin de la Galette* was one of three paintings Lautrec exhibited there. It betrays a hint of the stiltedness of the process of combining separately studied portraits within a relatively complex scheme, but there is a sense of being present; in effect the spectator assumes Lautrec's own seat at the table. "I work in my corner," he once said, meaning that he followed none of the current schools, but the statement applies equally well to his practice of detached observation.

The setting is the Moulin de la Galette, one of the increasing number of dance halls proliferating in Montmartre at the time. It was a less sumptuous venue, with a more down-at-heel clientele, than the Moulin Rouge, which opened for business the day after the exhibition closed, and which soon became Lautrec's favorite haunt. In the 1840s the poet Charles Baudelaire had begun to exhort artists to draw their subjects from modern life, and Manet, Degas, and Renoir, among others, had exploited the potential of this kind of theme – one of Renoir's best-known paintings is of this same dance hall in the 1870s. Over a decade earlier, the Goncourt brothers had written about the novel possibilities of lighting and perspective to be had from theater and ballet themes; the interesting compositional effect of viewing scenes, as it were, over the shoulders of foreground figures; and most important, the way that such devices could be a means of involving the spectator directly in the scene.

Above all, it was Degas whom Lautrec acknowledged in this approach to picture-making, both formally and in terms of subject matter – 1889 was the year the younger artist courted the older man's approval through a family of their mutual acquaintance, the Dihaus. Degas also frequently created a mood of isolated introspection in group portraits. Moreover, in the updating of Japanese spatial conventions in a European context, he provided the example that Lautrec was keenest to follow, so it is not surprising to see his influence in Lautrec's first really successful multiple figure composition.

In several earlier paintings Lautrec had used opposing diagonals as the basis of compositions, but never more daringly than here, where they form the principal structure by which he unites the more or less parallel friezes of foreground heads and background figures. Moreover it is one of these diagonals that draws attention to Albert, who is thrown into further prominence by his proximity to the most brilliant area of color – the red hair of the woman seen from behind – in an otherwise fairly muted harmony of values. One further trick is employed to link the two spatial planes together. The curiously unbalanced pile of saucers on the nearest table (signifying the number of drinks consumed) echoes the motion of the vigorously dancing couple swaying in the distance.

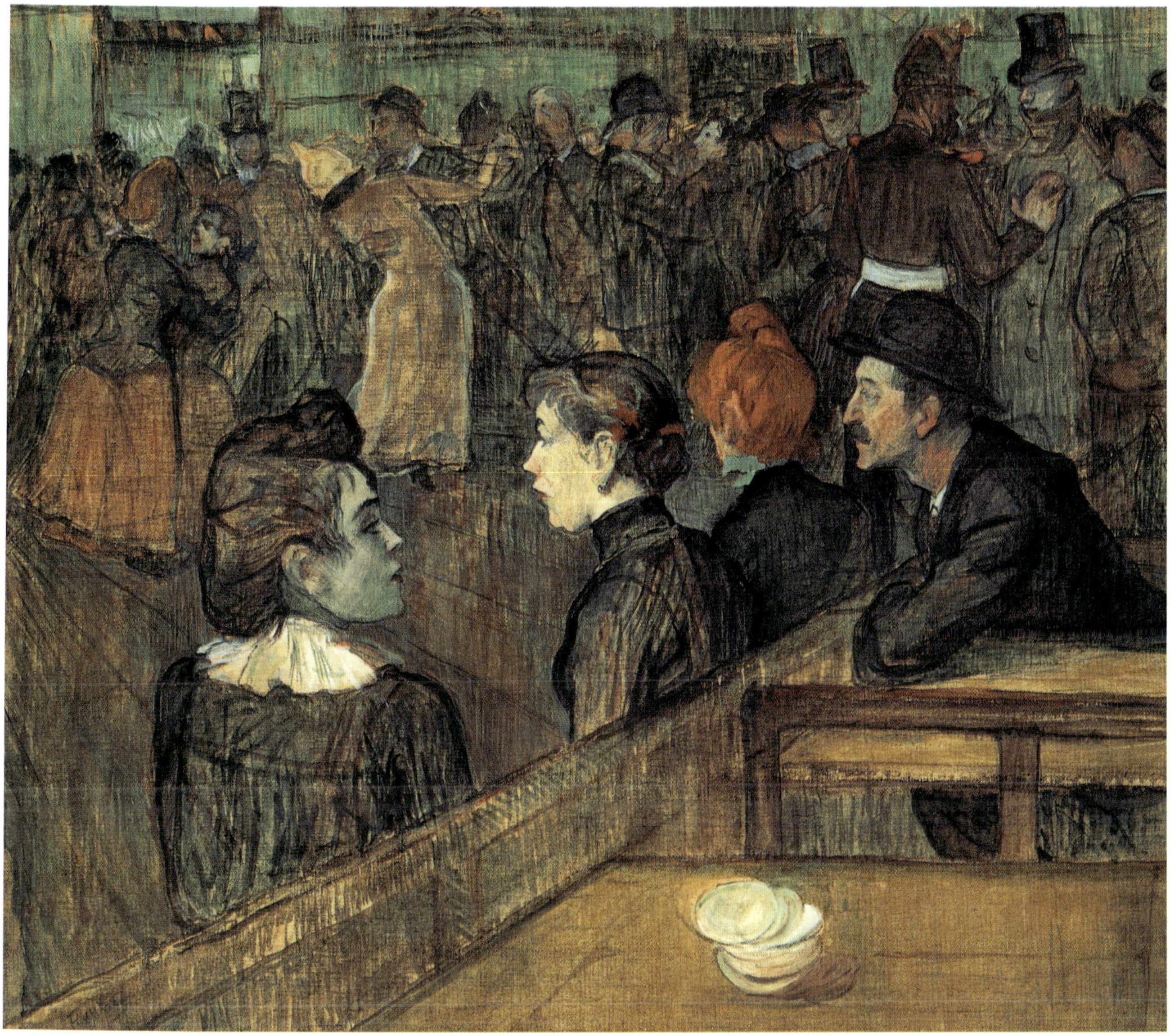

Degas's example was clearly important in this painting, but so too was Van Gogh's. After the brief period of serious tuition in the early 1880s, Lautrec's youthful exuberance of effect began to reassert itself, and Van Gogh, whom he had met at Cormon's *atelier,* evidently encouraged him in his development toward a personal style. In 1887 Lautrec did a pastel portrait of Van Gogh in an apparently characteristic pose (see page 684) and in a manner that suggests the influence of the Dutch painter's strongly directional brushwork and purity of color.

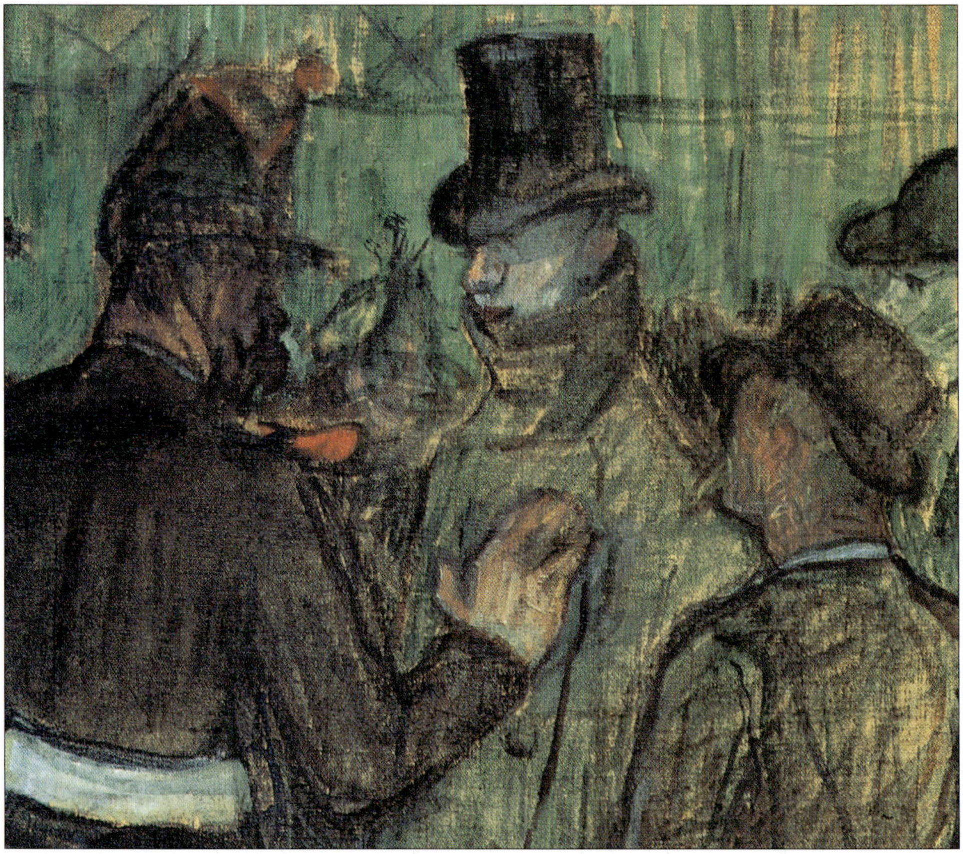

1

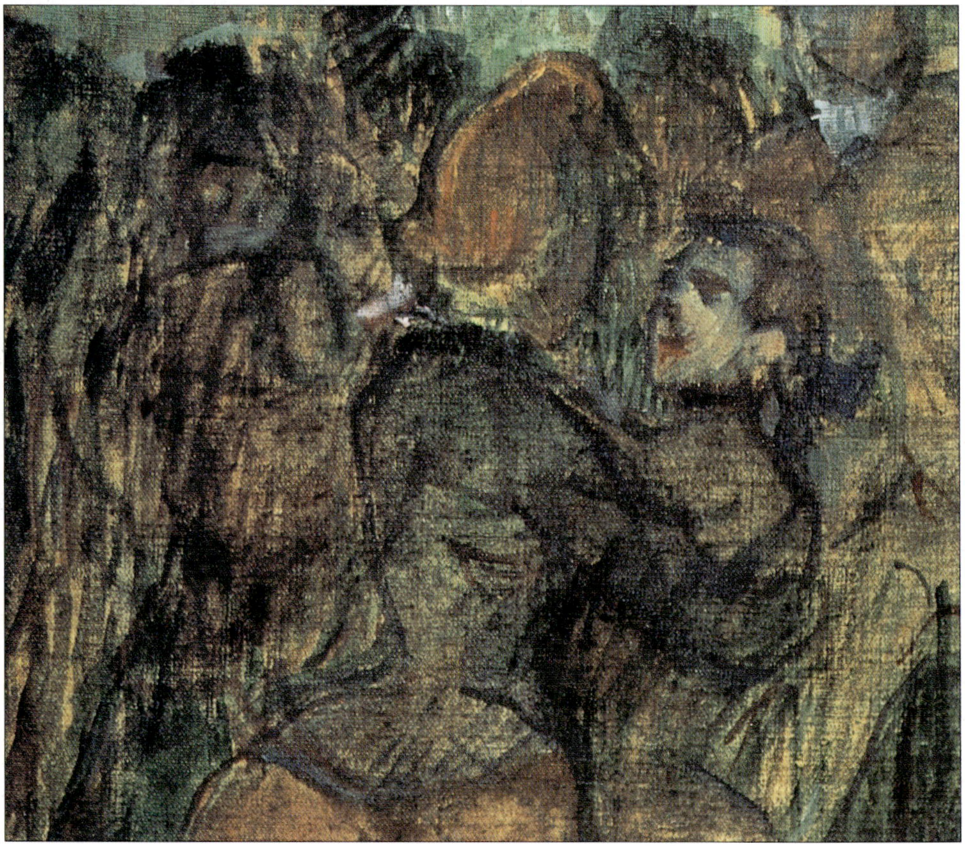

2

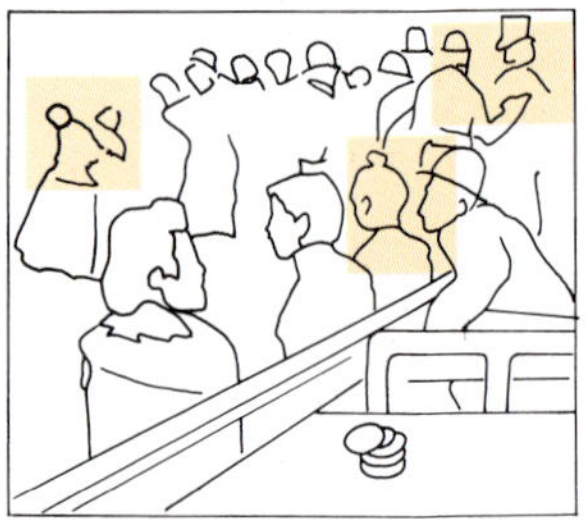

1 The frieze of background figures is made up of individualized types that emerge from the vague suggestion of a crowd beyond. With a few bold outlines their forms are broadly delineated with a brush lightly loaded with thinned paint. Body color has also been applied thinly, and in places the weave of the canvas is scarcely covered, so that it becomes a neutral texture in its own right.

2 Perhaps understandably, Lautrec was keenly aware of physical differences in people, and here he has grouped three contrasting types of manhood. Although the painting bears traces of the somberness of his period of academic training, it is also one of the earliest instances of his mature manner of applying thin paint in vertical overlaid strokes to an absorbent surface. He is reported to have been scathing about the traditional oil-painting method of creating luminosity by means of glazing. In some respects the method he adopted is closer to the transparency of watercolor.

3 This was Lautrec's first serious multiple figure composition, and typically, it combines his two major strengths, portraiture and the rendering of figures in motion. His colouring had become subdued while he was studying under Bonnat and Cormon, and the brilliance of the woman's red hair in an otherwise sombre-toned painting can be seen as a kind of emblem of his rebellion against such conservatism.

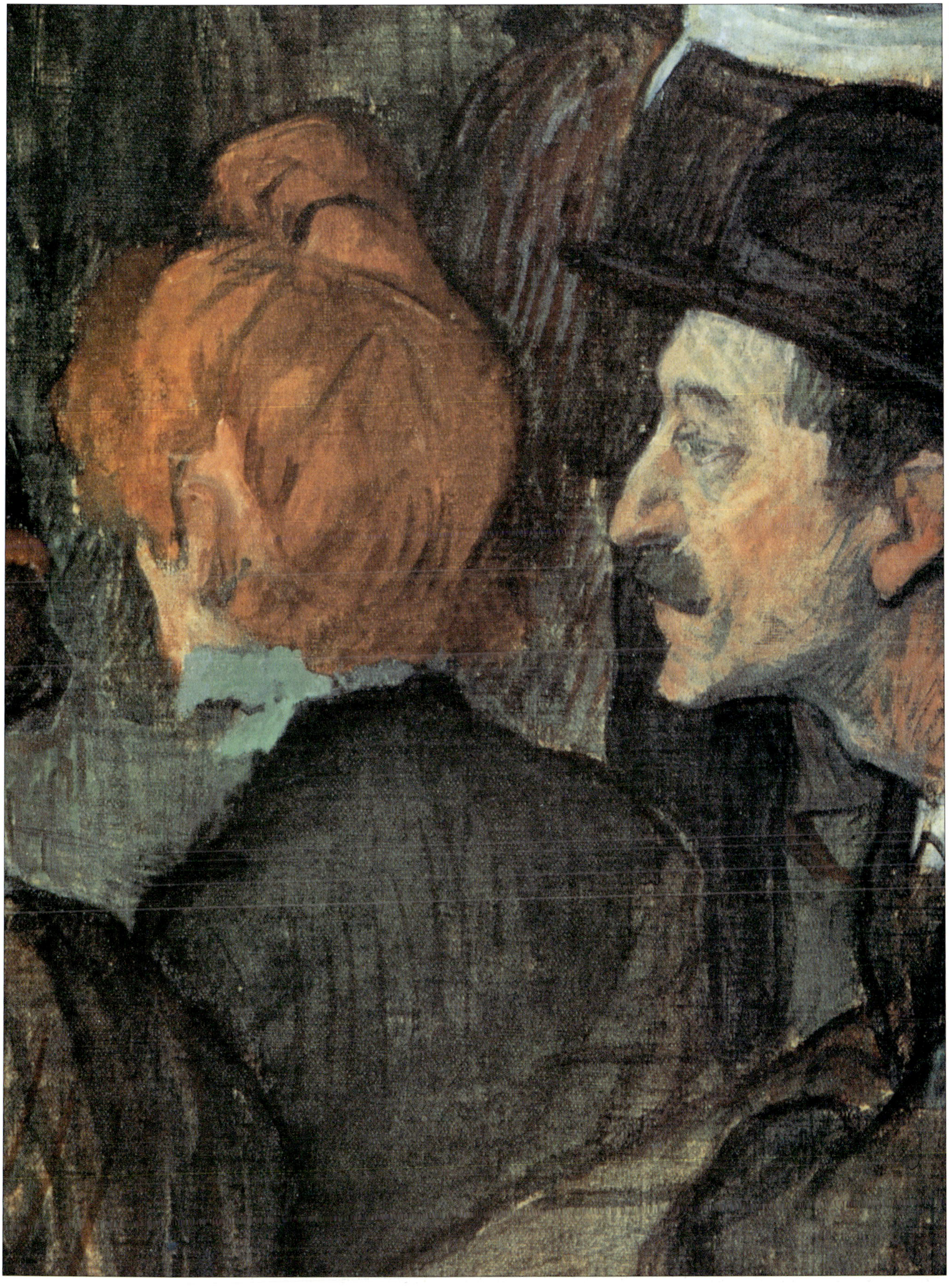

3

A La Mie

1891

$20^{7}/_{8} \times 26^{3}/_{4}$in/53×68cm

Oil on cardboard

Museum of Fine Arts, Boston

As early as 1882 Lautrec had painted an alcoholic slumped in miserable reverie over his glass of wine, and toward the end of the decade he did a series of pictures of single young women similarly preoccupied, morose but attractive. These he gave titles borrowed from the songs of the entertainer Aristide Bruant – *A La Bastille, A Grenelle* – songs that stressed the individuality and humanity of prostitutes and the dehumanizing effect of their trade. In this painting he has placed two figures together, a device that he was to use frequently in subsequent works as it allowed him to exploit contrasting details of character. However, his use of it here is clearly a reference to Degas' *l'Absinthe* of c 1876, and the same mood of dejected *ennui* and isolation pervades both works.

But the circumstances in which the painting was produced raise questions about Lautrec's particular moral and artistic purposes. "This profession of conscientious policemen for the novel is assuredly the most abominable trade that an essentially aristocratic man can pursue." Thus Edmund de Goncourt described the mingled fascination and disgust experienced by the prosperous man-about-town recording the details of low-life – outwardly impassive yet inwardly intoxicated while "spying on the truth." Doubtless Lautrec shared this attitude to some extent, and yet he lacked both the reserve and the distaste implied by de Goncourt. By 1891 he was already known for his hard drinking. Maurice Guibert, who posed for the man, was a close friend of Lautrec's and a familiar *roué* in the bars of Montmartre. In July 1895 the journal *Fin de Siècle* reported that he was "of the whole capital the man who knew the prostitutes best." That same summer the two of them were sampling the brothels of Madrid.

Lautrec was not unusual in making use of photographs as *aides-memoire* to help the process of building a major composition. The photograph he used in this case reveals a number of calculated changes in the painting. Guibert's habitual good humor has been altered to a blend of ruefulness and cynicism. The transformation of the pretty young model is even more startling. Her expression has been coarsened and her physique altered, so that the right arm now hangs in limp resignation. The rendering of hands as an expression of character was especially important to Lautrec; it was one of the criteria he used to judge other artists. Here the mute drama of personalities evident in the faces is played out just as effectively in the contrast between Guibert's bony claw and the girl's bloated, loosened fist.

Victor Fournel had written of his desire "to look into the character indicated by a gait or physiognomy," and to discern "what series of virtues or of crimes have come to engrave an indelible and vivid expression on this or that face one is examining. . ." But like all pictorial artists seeking to convey a multiplicity of visual information in a seemingly momentary observation, Lautrec has had to, as it were, reverse this process, contriving both the psychological point of his scene and the spontaneity of its effect. The latter has been achieved in part by allowing the painting to retain the quality of a rapid sketch, though there is nothing rapid about the technique he used to do this. It is painted with very much thinned oil colors on cardboard, the areas around the figures being built up by a variety of dabs, dashes, and streaks which create a range of textural surfaces that throw the main motif into relief. This method is characteristic of Lautrec's mature manner, and the transparent effect it gives is very different from the loaded impasto used by Van Gogh. Nevertheless, the treatment of the regulated highlights on the woman's skirt is possibly due to the Dutchman's recent influence.

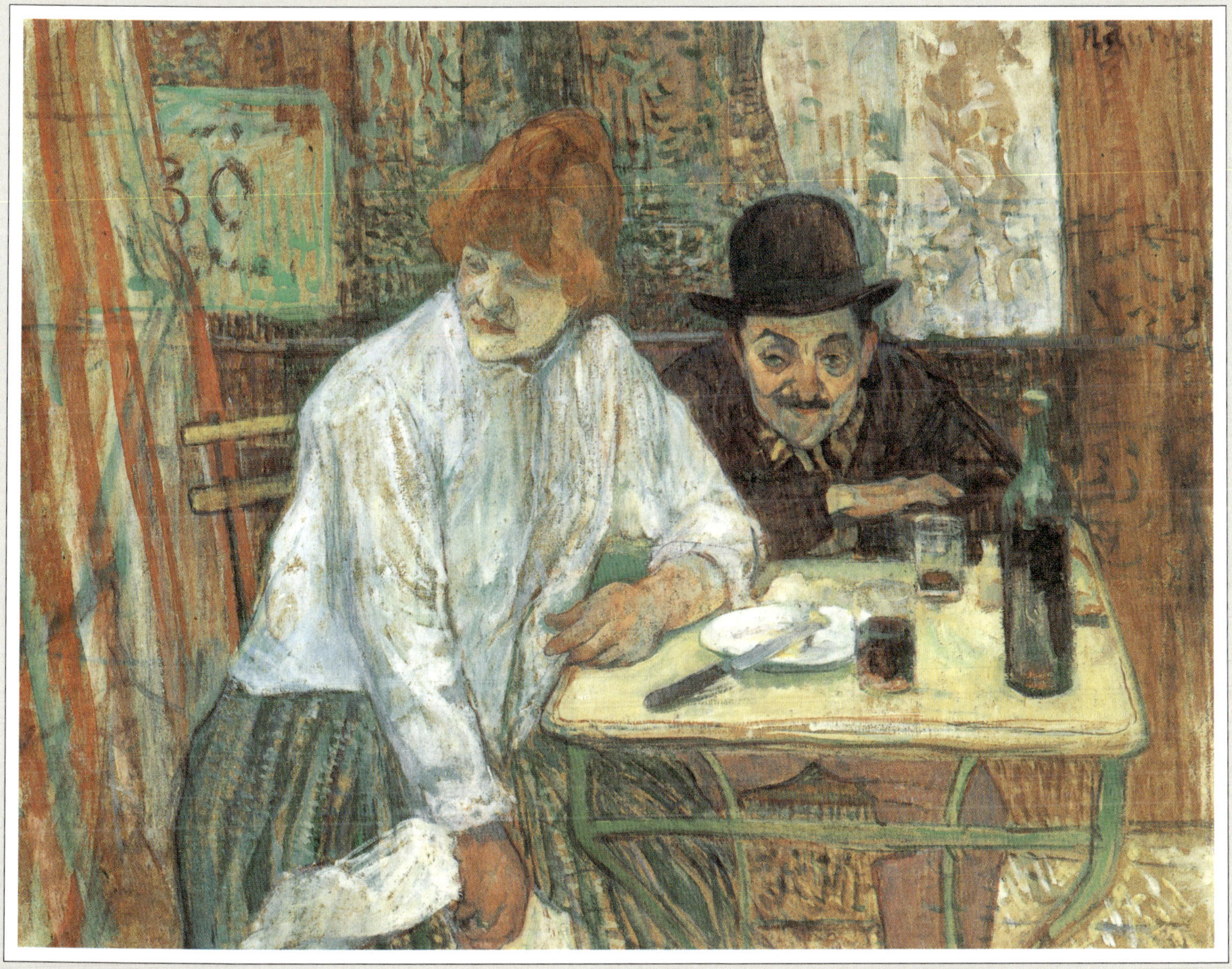

From the 1840s onward, the relation between photography and art had been a matter of controversy. Many artists opposed it as a threat, but others, notably Delacroix and Degas, responded positively and used photographs as an extension of the traditional process of preparatory drawings. Some of Lautrec's friends were photographers, Guibert included, and he occasionally used photographs in this way. The one that relates to this painting, however, is more than a peripheral study since, despite the changes he made in the finished painting, the whole scene has been calculated at the photographic stage. Interesting in this respect is the fact that, rather than exploiting the medium for its capacity to capture transitory effects, Lautrec has contrived a static moment of self-reflection.

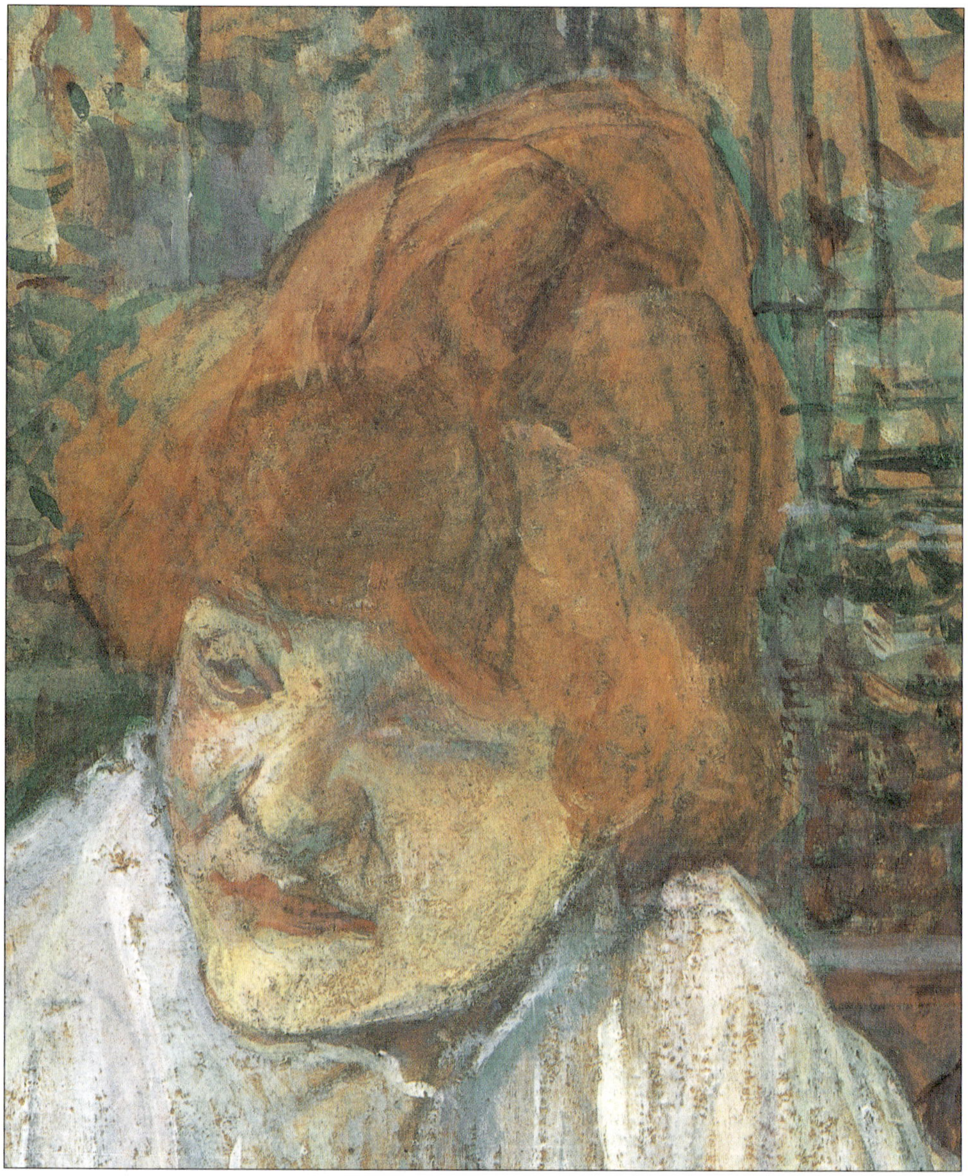

1

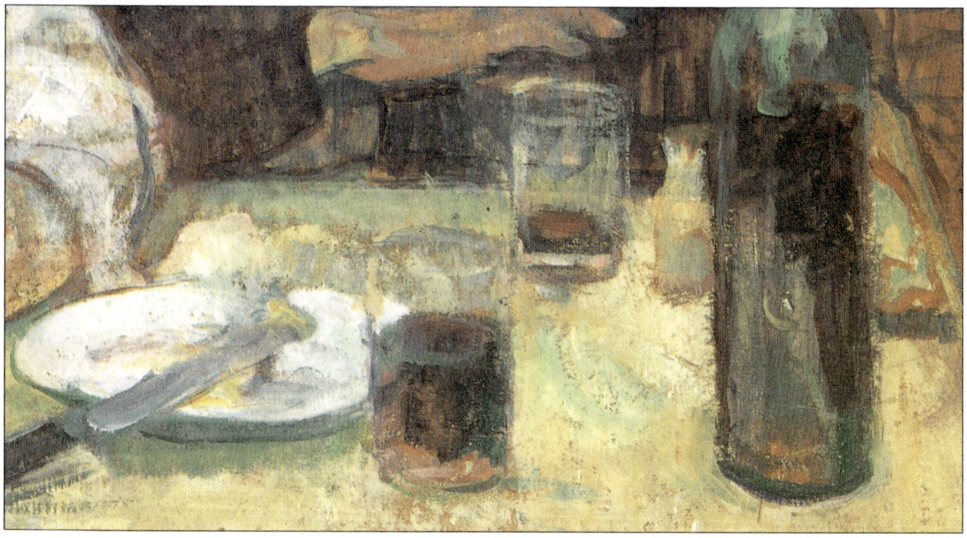

2

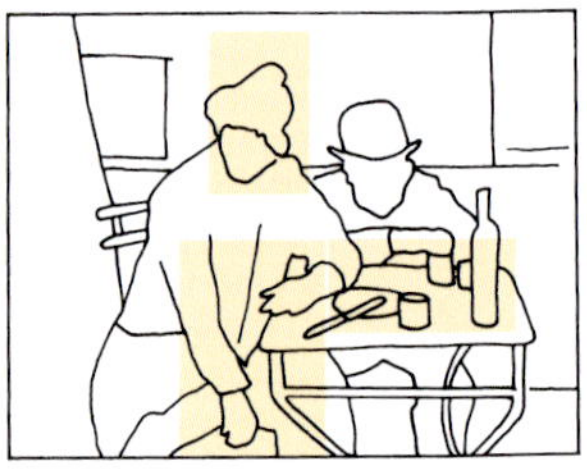

1 A photograph exists of the sitter, taken at much the same time as the painting. This shows how Lautrec deliberately aged the woman by altering and distorting her physique and features.

2 Foreground still lifes in Lautrec's paintings are always significant. They not only form a distinct element in the composition as a whole, but are also used as a device for involving the spectator in the scene. Sometimes, as here, they give a clue to the picture's meaning, which in this case he went to unusual lengths to contrive. Numerous writers have interpreted it as a portrayal of human degradation, but it could be argued that, like Lautrec himself, the pair, being daily confronted by the limitations of their separate fates, find solace only in alcohol and the company of similarly blighted souls.

3 *Actual size detail* The representation of hands was important to Lautrec as a means of conveying character, mood, psychological tension, and so on. In contrast to the sketchiness of the dress and blouse, the coarseness of the pink and swollen fingers has been emphasized by a precisely brushed-in outline. The left hand and right arm add to the woman's general air of dejection, while the right hand quietly suggests regret — both emotions combining in her facial expression. In places the paint has a pitted and chalky quality akin to pastel, a medium favored by Degas, and which, like *peinture à l'essence,* produced matte colors without forfeiting intensity of hue.

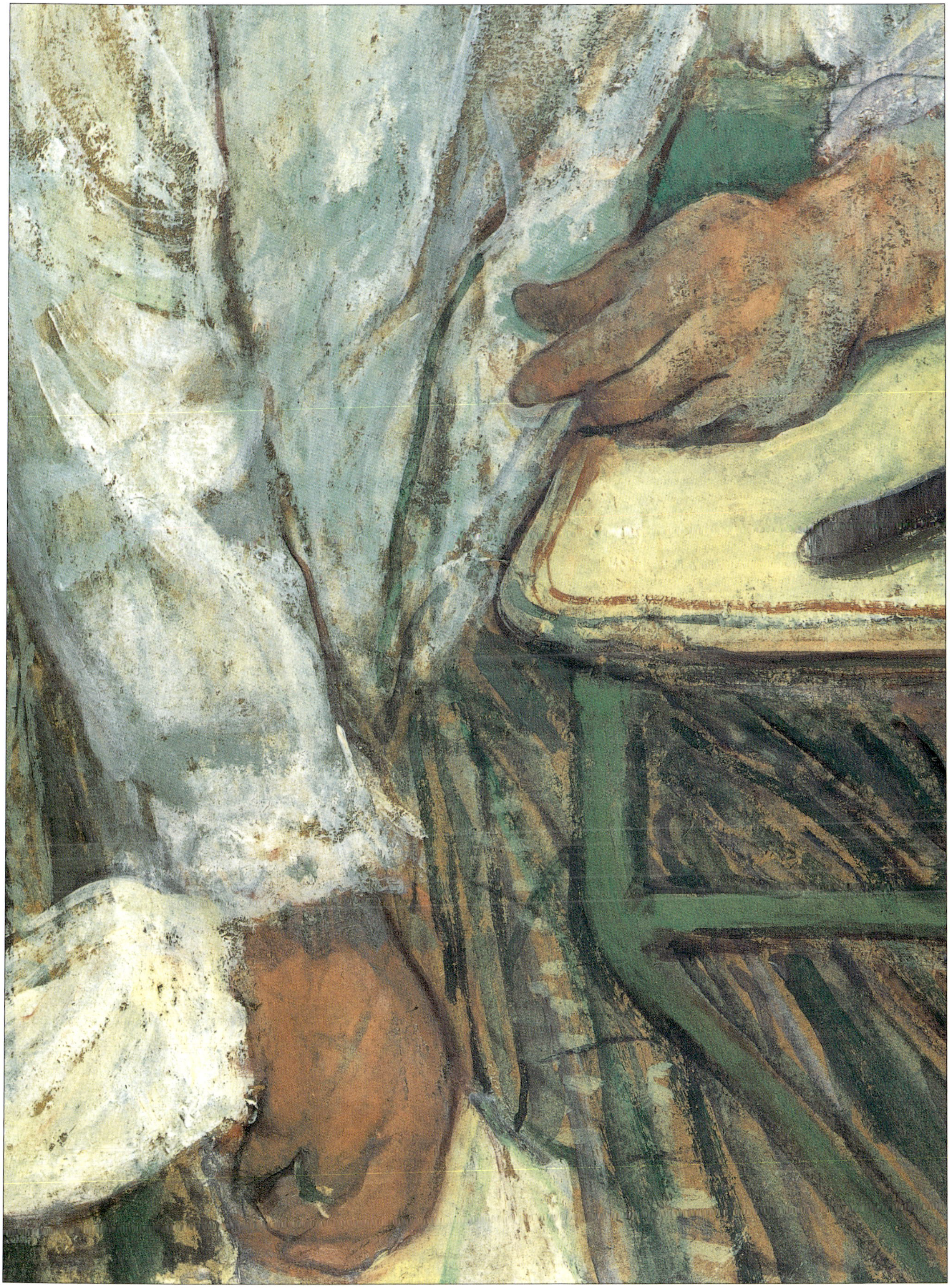

3 *Actual size detail*

Jane Avril Dancing

1892

33×17⅜in/84×44cm

Oil on cardboard

Musée d'Orsay, Paris

Complex figurative compositions like *The Ball at the Moulin de la Galette* (see page 691) occur relatively infrequently in Lautrec's work. More typical is the presentation of a single character in a sketchily defined setting. His quick eye for the revealing outlines of people and animals in vigorous motion found a perfect subject in the wild gyrations of dancers. The popular craze for dancing had begun at least as early as the 1850s, and was an aspect of the official encouragement of organized leisure. Some of the more spectacular dancers achieved considerable popular fame and became the main attractions of dance halls such as Le Bal Mabille (operating in Paris before the full emergence of Montmartre as a center for night-life in the 1880s).

Lautrec's adoption of both the theme and the dance hall itself is evidence of his rejection of the official routes to artistic prestige, and of his increasingly bohemian lifestyle. His involvement with the "minor" art of illustration is significant in this context. The first of the Montmartre cafés and cabarets he became identified with was Aristide Bruant's Le Mirliton, and in the mid-1880s he began to produce cover illustrations for the cabaret's journal of the same name. His subjects, in keeping with the sentiments of Bruant's satirical songs, were similar to the work of the singer's favorite artist, Steinlen, one of whose covers of 1886 featured the high kick of a can-can dancer.

During the 1890s, stimulated in part by the success of his posters, Lautrec began to specialize in similar subjects in his paintings, depicting the dancers and a widening range of café-concert entertainers. Jane Avril's career as a dancer began at the Moulin Rouge in the late 1880s, but like others who made their name in Montmartre – Lautrec included – she was soon taken up by the smarter establishments in central Paris, such as Le Décadents and Le Divan Japonais. The English poet Arthur Symons described her as a "fallen angel" with "an air of depraved virginity." Her refined and often melancholic manner set her apart from the brash vulgarity of the majority of dance-hall stars such as La Goulue. She preferred to dance alone rather than as part of the sexually titillating ritual of the "naturalistic quadrille" or can-can, and her aloofness was resented by the other dancers. Lautrec's delight in individual female entertainers was usually of short duration, but his relationships with both Yvette Guilbert and Jane Avril were more lasting. Their intelligence and sensitive appreciation of his work formed the basis for a sustained friendship, and they occur frequently in his gallery of the personalities of the period. All his depictions of Jane Avril emphasize the withdrawn wistfulness of her features: for example, in the poster he made for her performances at the Jardin de Paris, he transformed the coquettish smile seen in her photograph into a blend of elegant hauteur and strained exertion. Like other artists of the period he often used photographs to supplement his sketches from life.

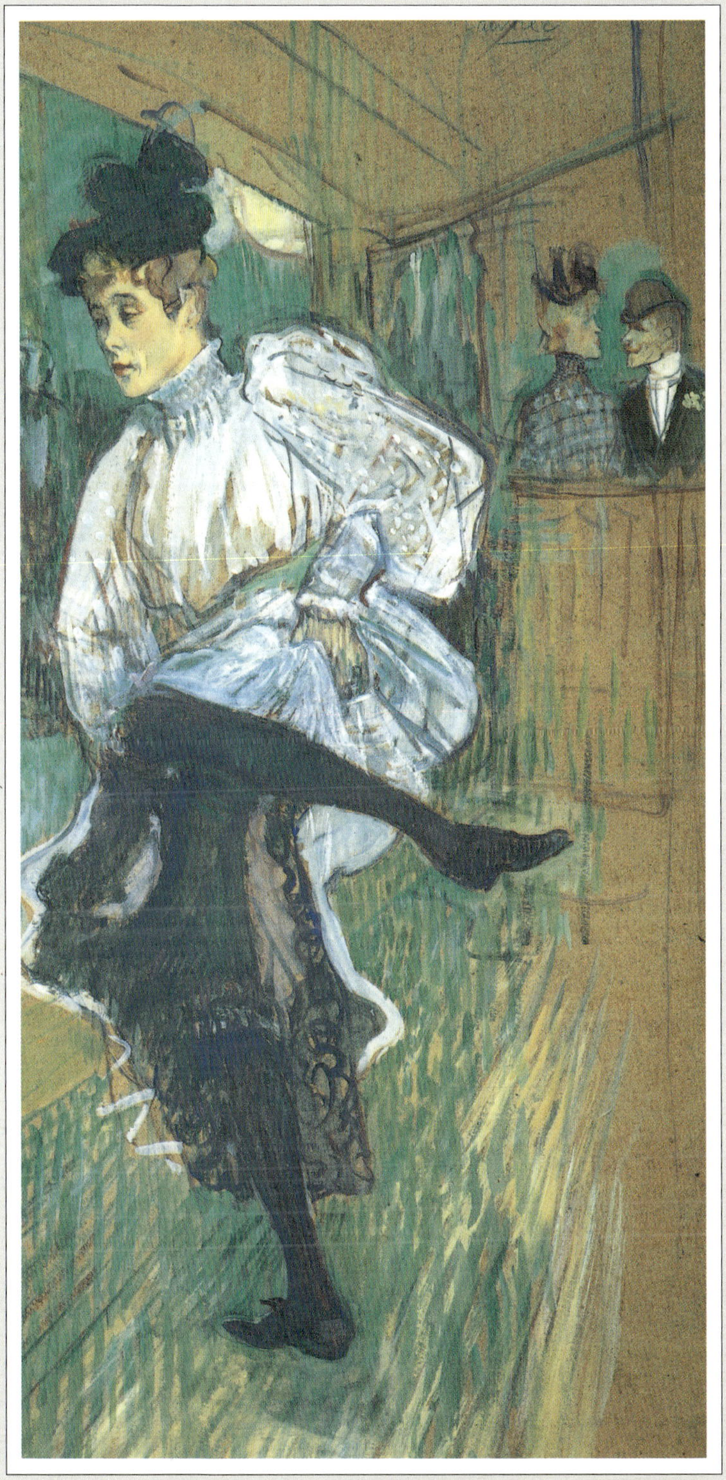

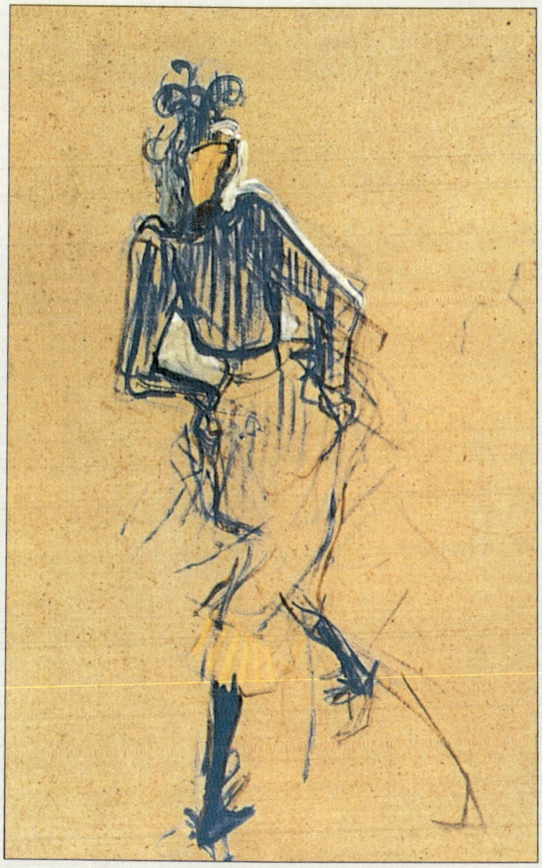

The sketch study for the painting (left) shows Lautrec's amazing ability to catch expressive movements in a few lines, suggesting not only the appearance of a figure in motion but also the personality. This required constant practice, and there are numerous accounts of how he perfected his drawing technique. When he was not satisfied with a sketch he would immediately discard it, repeating it over and over until he had achieved the result he sought. A comparison of the painting with the study indicates his desire to retain the vivacity of the latter and combine it, a little awkwardly perhaps, with a more fully realized portrait.

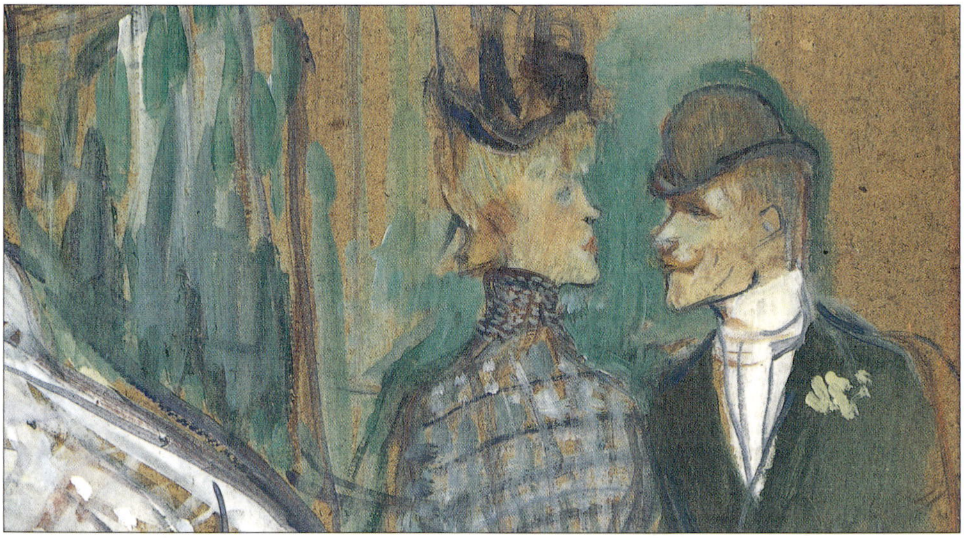

1

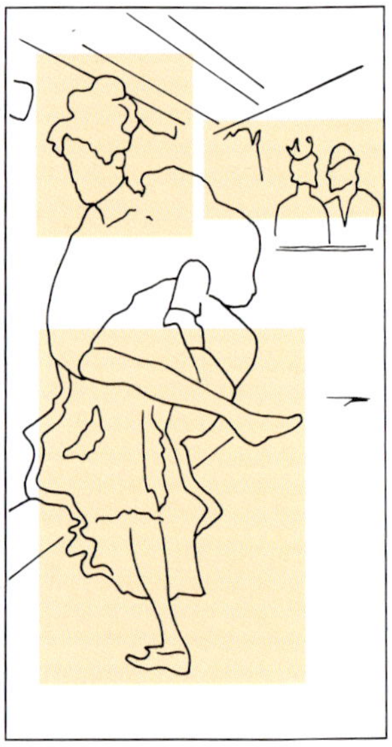

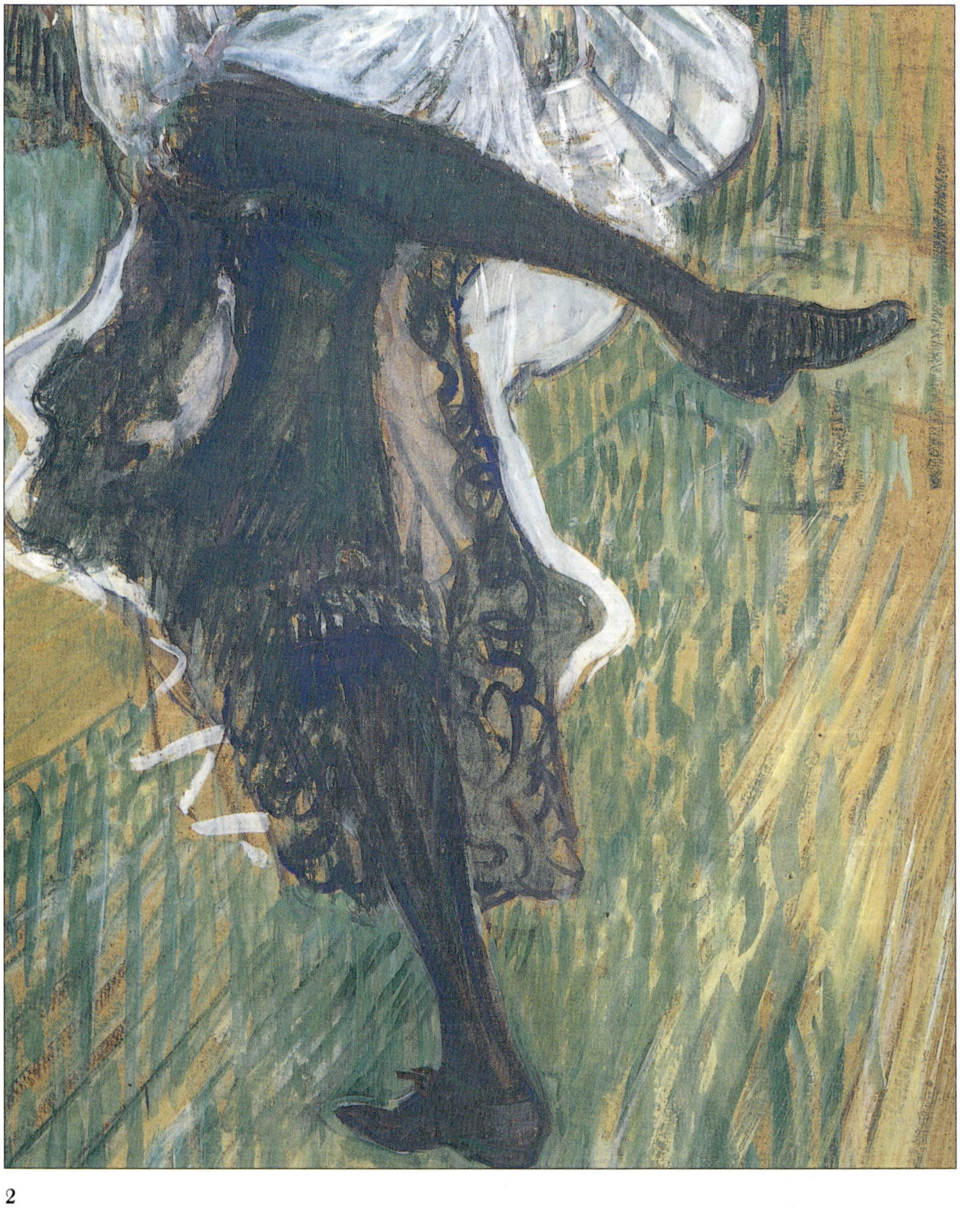

2

1 The man seen here is the same Englishman, Warrener, who featured that year in one of Lautrec's earliest color lithographs (see page 681). He represents the type of man for whom the principal attraction of places like the Moulin Rouge was not so much the dancing as the possibility of picking up a woman.

2 Jane Avril's somewhat superior aloofness extended to her mode of dress: she alone among the dancers at the Moulin Rouge wore colored petticoats and stockings, usually of exotically combined pastel shades — in this case violet and dark purplish blue. Lautrec has built up this color by hatching in some areas with the same aquamarine blue used as a background to the heads. The continuation of the blue in conjunction with greens and yellows shows his method of enlivening surfaces by means of a variety of systematically, if speedily, applied layers of directional strokes in harmonizing colors.

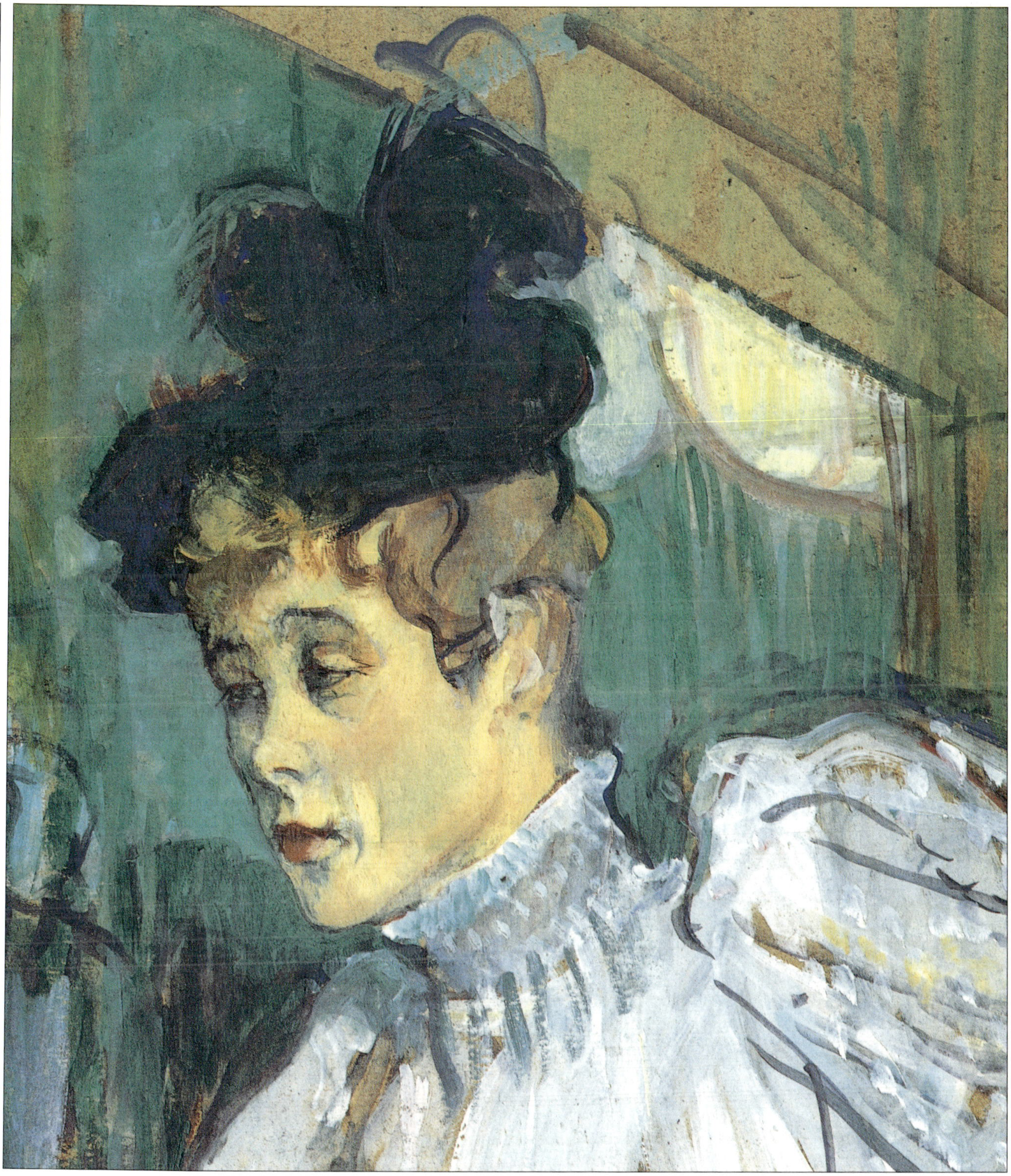

3 *Actual size detail*

3 *Actual size detail* Lautrec once complained of being criticized for not completing his pictures. "All I want to do is paint what I see. Anybody can finish off a painting." In this example, however, some areas suggest he may have left the painting incomplete even by his standards, and it gives a valuable insight into his working methods. The head is the most fully realized part, the features being painted with precision, while the material of bodice and sleeves is sketchy. Lautrec has here exploited the possibilities of *peinture à l'essence*: an initial layer of white has been superimposed with further touches of consequently more substantial white, while elsewhere the cardboard shows through to stand for the color of flesh beneath.

The Salon at the Rue des Moulins

1894

$43^{3}/_{4} \times 52^{1}/_{8}$in/$1.115 \times 1.325$m

Oil on canvas

Musée Toulouse-Lautrec, Albi

In 19th-century France, prostitution was regarded more or less as a social inevitability, and it was accepted as normal for adolescent males to visit brothels. Respectable opinion, however, was offended by public soliciting, so the pragmatic view was taken that it was better to allow prostitutes to practice in the privacy of brothels, known as *maisons de tolérance* or *maisons closes.* The policy never eradicated prostitution from the boulevards, bars and cafés, but in the 1880s and 90s there were renewed attempts at regulation. The question even developed into a point of general political controversy, both right- and left-wing opinion opposing such controls, the latter because the women were virtual prisoners in the brothels.

For the intellectual at the time, the prostitute had become something of a symbol of middle-class exploitation, and Naturalist writers such as Emile Zola frequently dealt with the theme. Lautrec's consistent use of it (often, paradoxically, as a source for subjects that stress the domestic normality of the women's daily lives) is in the same vein, but the regularity with which the theme continued to occur is another instance of his exploration of areas established by Degas. The latter's approach was on the whole more circumspect; his depictions of brothel life emphasized its sexual nature, but were usually on a relatively modest scale and in the more private media of the monotype print and drawings. His paintings of prostitutes are clothed women of the streets, while Lautrec's are more explicit, if curiously asexual.

The Salon at the Rue des Moulins was his largest and most ambitious treatment of the subject, the culmination of numerous related paintings and preparatory studies. This body of work was the result of the artist's habit of taking up residence for several days at a time in one of a succession of brothels – the one we see here was expensively decorated and catered for a variety of sexual tastes. Lautrec adopted this mode of life partly to gratify his own sexual needs and partly because he appreciated the general ambience – he called it, "prostitution palpitating." He complained about the stilted poses of professional models, finding more inspiration in the naturalness of these women who spent most of their time naked or semi-clad.

Lautrec's regular residence in brothels was also another aspect of the thorough and concerted manner in which he conducted his artistic investigations. He was initially secretive about his "lodgings," but in time began to parade the fact, giving 24 Rue des Moulins as his address, and even inviting the prestigious and slightly prudish dealer Paul Durand-Ruel to visit him there. However, when a representative exhibition of his work was held at the Manzi and Joyant gallery in 1896, his more obviously morally dubious paintings were kept in two locked rooms, Lautrec himself selecting those allowed access to them.

Sensitivity in such matters, even when sanctioned by the intellectual climate of Naturalism, is evidenced by the Irish writer George Moore's account of a conversation with Zola. A rivalry had gradually emerged between the relative merits of literature and art in their capacity to portray what Baudelaire called "the drama of modern life" effectively. When Zola asserted that no painters had achieved status comparable to some of the writers of the Naturalist school, Moore suggested the name of Degas. Zola retorted, "I cannot accept a man who shuts himself up all his life to draw a ballet girl as ranking coequal in dignity and power with Flaubert, Daudet and Goncourt." Ballet girls in those days did not have the aura of respectability they have today, and Zola's opinion of someone shutting himself up with whores can readily be imagined.

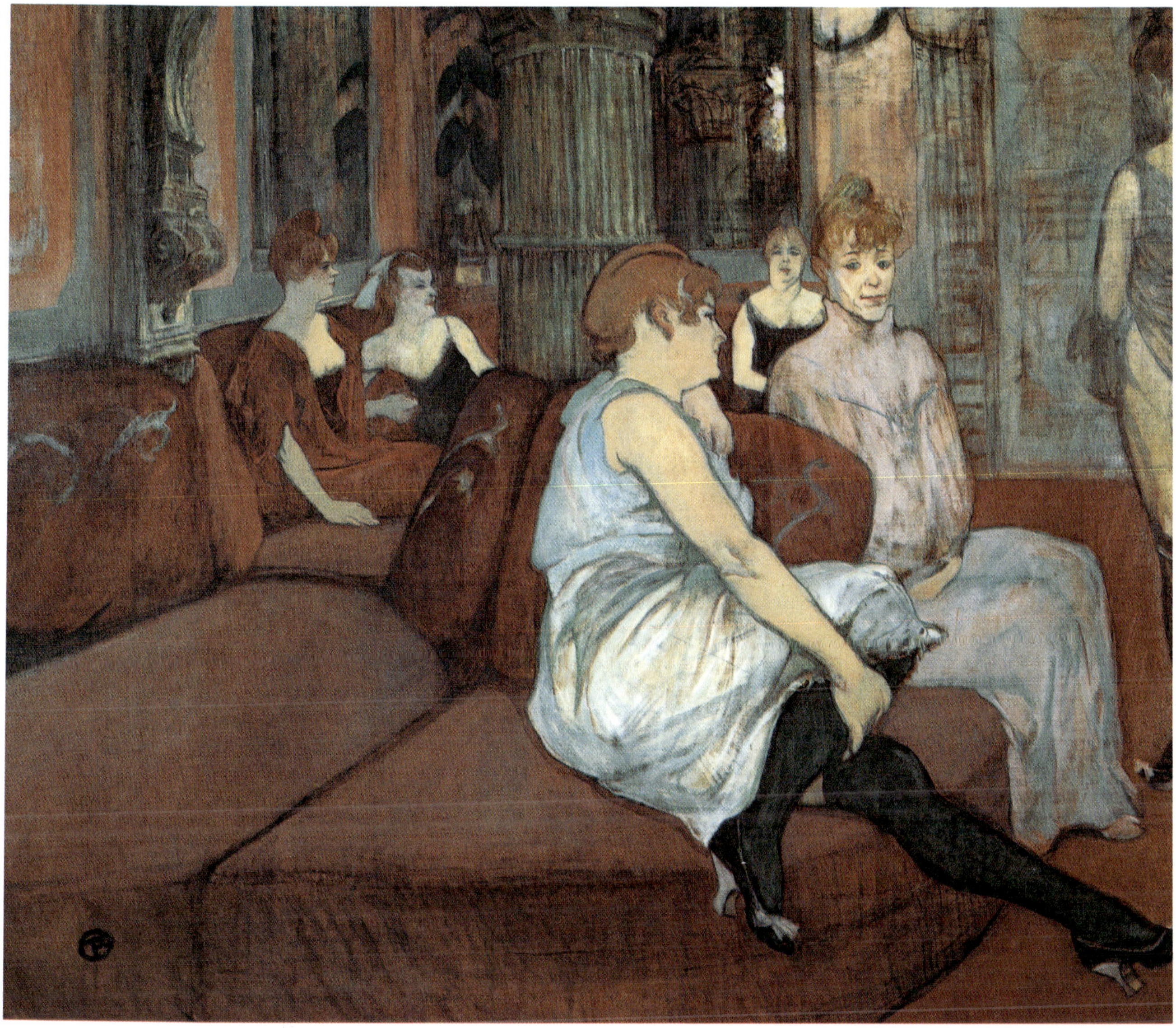

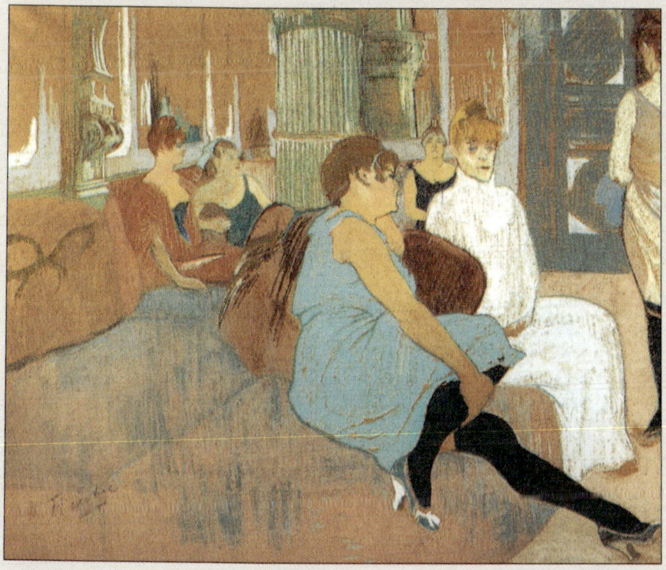

In some ways this is one of Lautrec's most academic compositions. It hinges on the strength of the central column, around which he has asymmetrically arranged the figures of the women. Characteristically, one figure is dominant, and her nearness as well as the pale blue-whiteness of her clothing set against the rich harmonies created by derivatives of red, green, and blue, makes her the focus of interest on which everything else depends. The diagonal emphasis of her striking posture is the major means by which foreground and background are linked. Lautrec's graphic work encouraged in him an appreciation of the positive value of negative spaces, and it is noticeable that the large open areas of the left foreground are treated more flatly than is usual in his work, an effect which adds to the almost tranquil mood of the scene.

One of the preparatory studies for the painting above

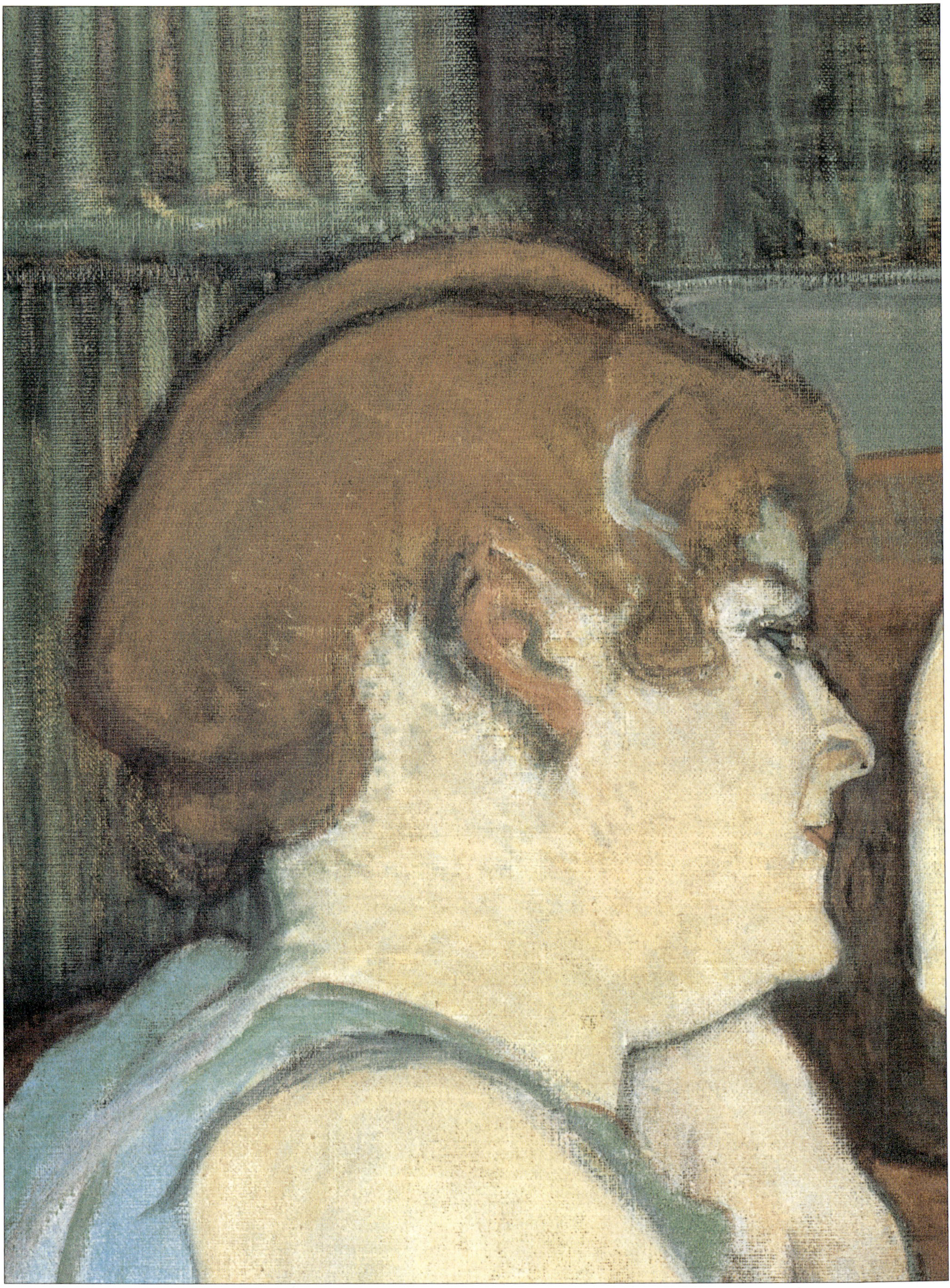

1 *Actual size detail*

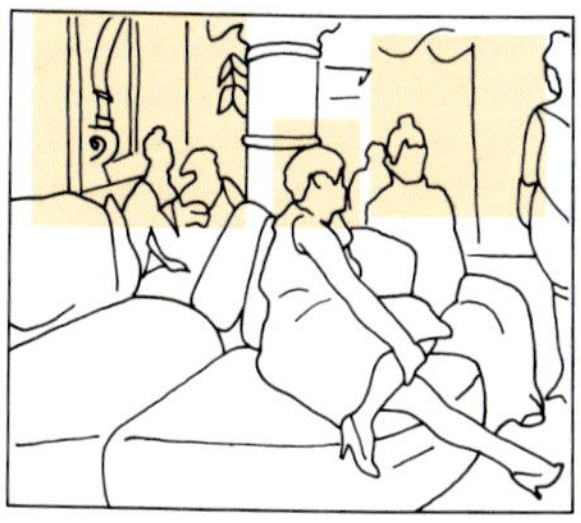

1 *Actual size detail* Perhaps because of the complexity of the design, Lautrec emphasized more than usual the linear structure binding the composition as a whole. This can be seen especially in the woman in the foreground, the prostitute Mireille. Although based on numerous preparatory studies, this head, caught in half profile, retains the quality of a momentary observation. Dark outlines and a relatively even rendering of flesh indicate the tonal flattening of artificial lighting, and a similar approach is used for the areas of seating to her left.

2 The sumptuousness of the interior, with its shot-color effects of plush and gilt, is rendered in part by the opposition of paired hues: reds with softened blues set against gold and greenish yellow (the latter like patina on bronze). Reds are prevalent, varying from touches of flaming intensity through terracotta and dull pinks. The consequent luridness further adds to the air of artificiality by jarring with the dull orange Lautrec uses for all the women's hair.

3 The sketchiness of this area of the painting in one of Lautrec's most considered works indicates how, just as he directs attention to particular details, he can also direct it away from others. Compositionally, the picture is structured around a strong diagonal emphasis from the lower right-hand corner to the upper left, and then, through the direction of gaze of the three women in profile, across to the rearground right, to return, as it were, to the spectator through the expressions of the two women detailed here.

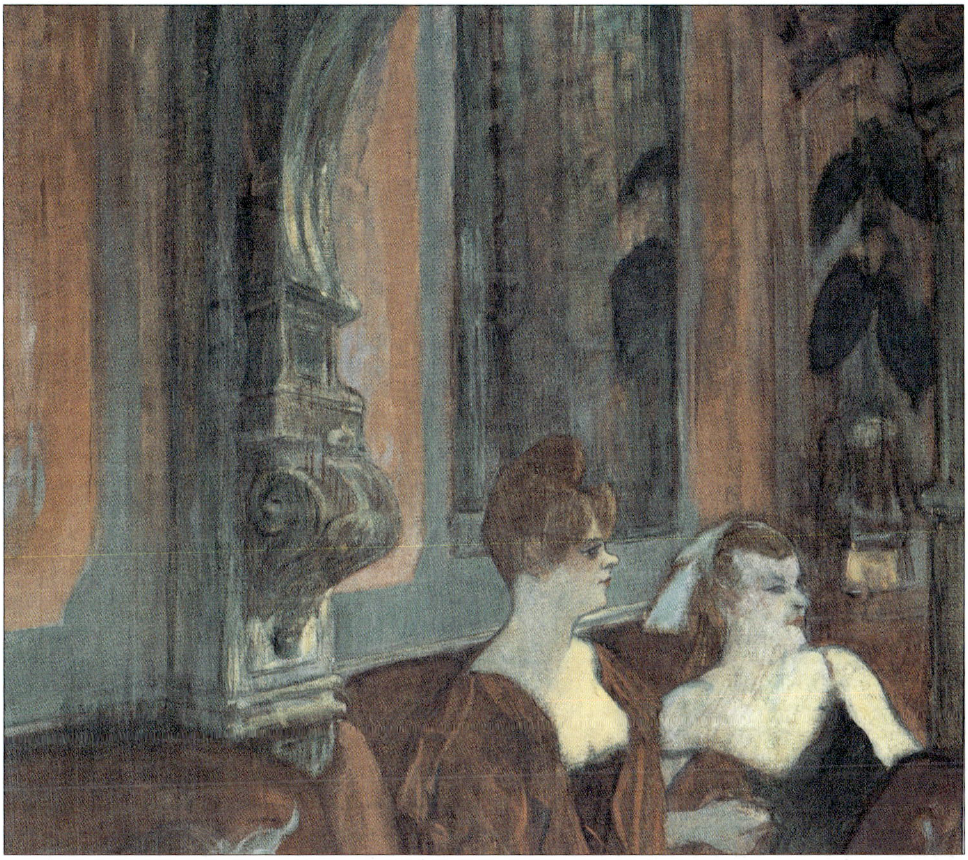

2

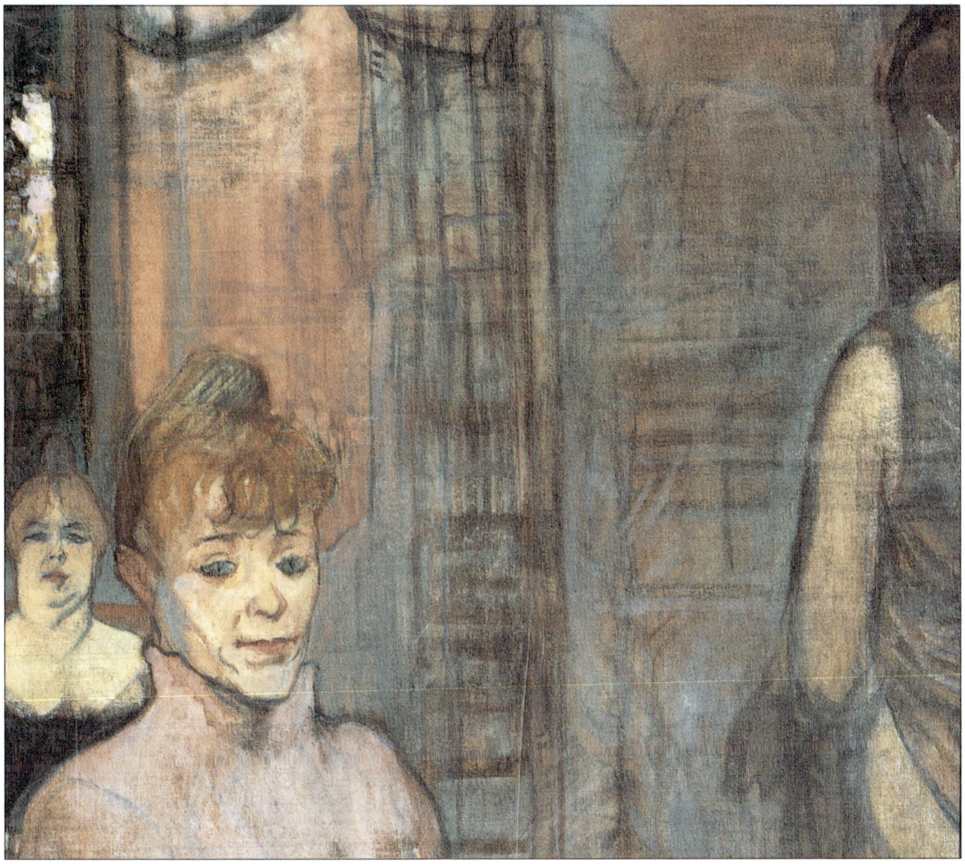

3

Portrait of Paul Leclercq

1897

$21^1/_4 \times 25^1/_8$in/54×64cm

Oil on cardboard

Musée d'Orsay, Paris

The poet André Rivoire, who was painted by Lautrec in 1901, the year of the artist's death, published shortly afterward an account of Lautrec's approach to portraiture. He stressed the importance of getting to know the sitter as part of the sometimes lengthy process of gestation culminating in rapid fruition. "... Two or three sittings, sometimes only one, were enough for him ... To appreciate the extraordinary sureness of touch one must have watched him at work on a canvas or a sheet of cardboard ..." Before commencing the whole painting, Lautrec would sometimes distract himself with some detail in a corner before launching with great speed into the portrait. Rivoire tells us that "... his work was there, all ready in front of him; his eyes could visualize it in its complete form on the canvas as if it existed there beforehand; he seemed to be tracing over invisible lines. He would sing, laugh and chat like a common workman over his task ... Very rarely ... one became aware of a more minute attention."

This account seems to be at variance with what is known of Lautrec's reduced mental and physical condition at this time. Maurice Joyant, who took over the branch of Goupil's gallery from Theo Van Gogh after the latter's premature death in 1891, recorded some seventy-five sittings for his portrait, done a few months earlier than Rivoire's — and Lautrec had been a close friend of his since childhood. However, Rivoire's account, though a little idealized, is probably a reasonable description of Lautrec's methods before the debilitating effects of his alcoholism began seriously to affect his dexterity.

Lautrec himself termed the process, "the technique of leading up," and it tallies with Paul Leclercq's account of the portrait shown here. Leclercq, also a poet, was the founder of the literary and artistic journal *La Revue Blanche* in 1889, and he and Lautrec became friendly in about 1894. According to his account, the portrait of three years later was done over about four to five weeks, though he added that he probably only sat for two or three hours. He noted that Lautrec wore a large floppy hat, in order, as Lautrec put it, "... to concentrate the light and avoid shadows ..." Habitually energetic, Lautrec might daub only a couple of strokes before breaking into some vulgar ballad and then jumping up to lead Leclercq off to a bar.

The painting is an unusual one for Lautrec, who seldom engaged the viewer so directly in his portraits, whether formal or informal. When he did so, as here, the results were often striking psychological penetrations of character. This is one of the finest examples, not least because of the slightly unnerving sensation it gives of being observed by the sitter while at the same time observing him.

Lautrec's connections with *La Revue Blanche* from 1893 onward raised the intellectual level of his immediate social circle. From 1891 Leclercq and the brothers Thadée and Alexandre Natanson shared control of the journal's advanced editorial policy, and through them Lautrec was introduced to a wider range of writers and artists, especially the group known as the Nabis, who followed Gauguin's advice to paint in flat, pure colors. One of the writers was the Anarchist Félix Fénéon who, after his trial, in which he was successfully defended by Thadée Natanson, became an assistant editor of the journal. However, Lautrec did not abandon his former habits. Another writer, Romain Coolus, may have been responsible for his increasing interest in theatrical subjects (see page 686), but Lautrec drew Coolus into his old life by inviting the latter to join him in his extended stays in brothels. Also, as Leclercq noted, Lautrec seemed more interested in the theatrical ambience and the audience than in the plays; his depictions were a continuation of his interest in performers rather than in the interpretation of a text.

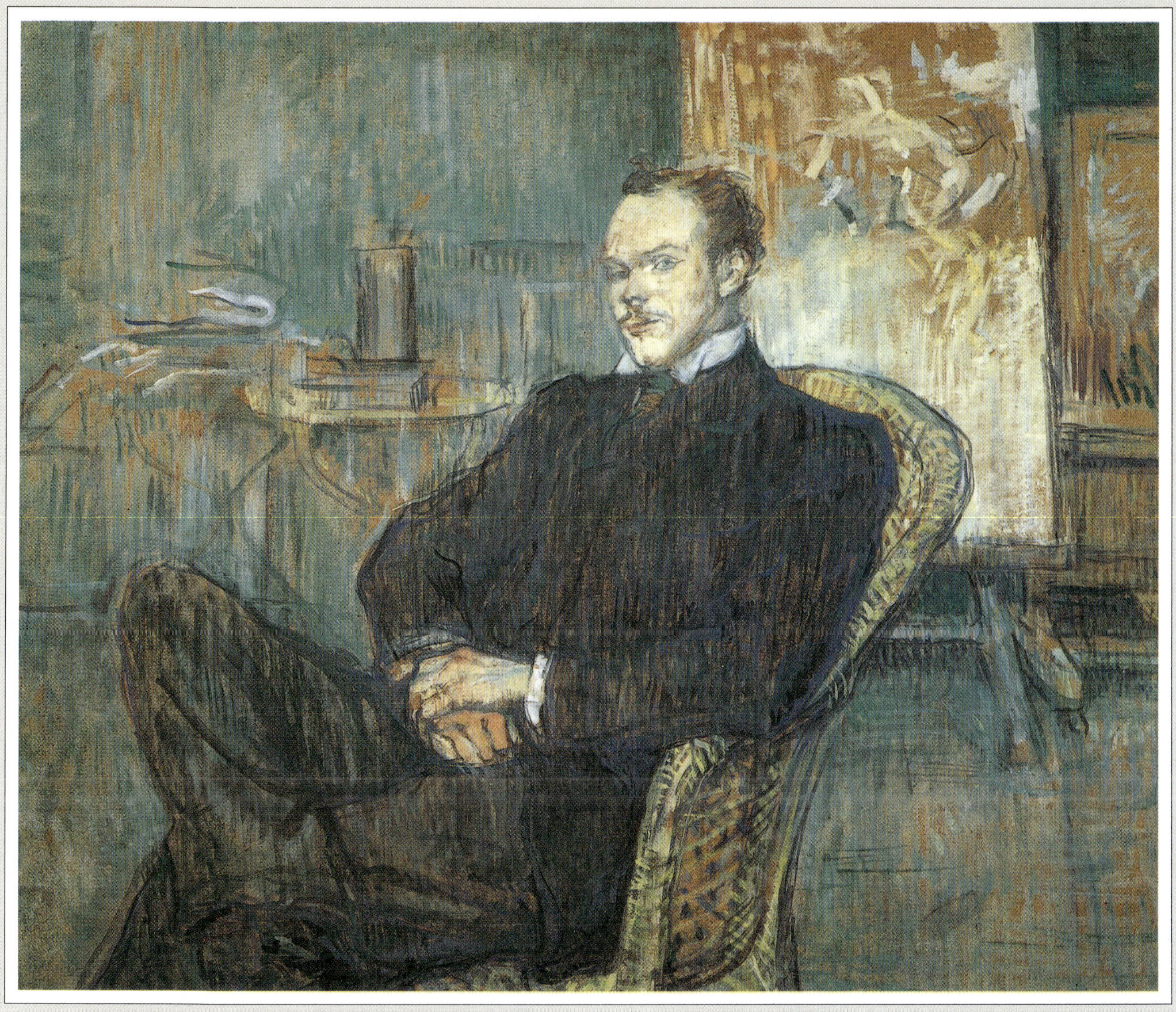

A comparison of the portrait of Leclercq with that of the prostitute in *Mme Poupoule at her Toilet* (see page 711), of about the same time, shows how he could adapt the main features of his style to suit different situations or personalities. The predominance here of soft vertical striations in a harmony of mainly blues and greens creates an air of refined tranquility around the figure. It is a good example of the atmospheric possibilities Lautrec could achieve with thinned oil paint applied to absorbent cardboard. This technique, known as *peinture à l'essence,* which Lautrec adapted from the methods of Degas and Raffaëli, allowed him to overlay lines or webs of different colors to build up a sense of luminosity without resorting to normal *chiaroscuro* methods to depict dark areas and shadows.

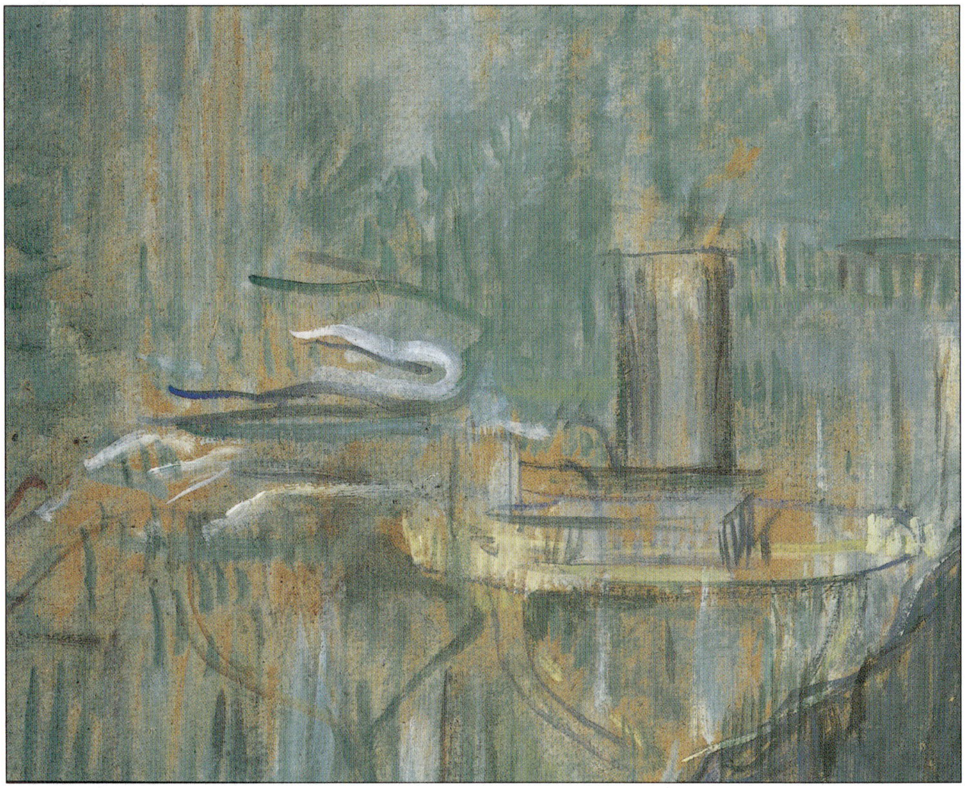

1

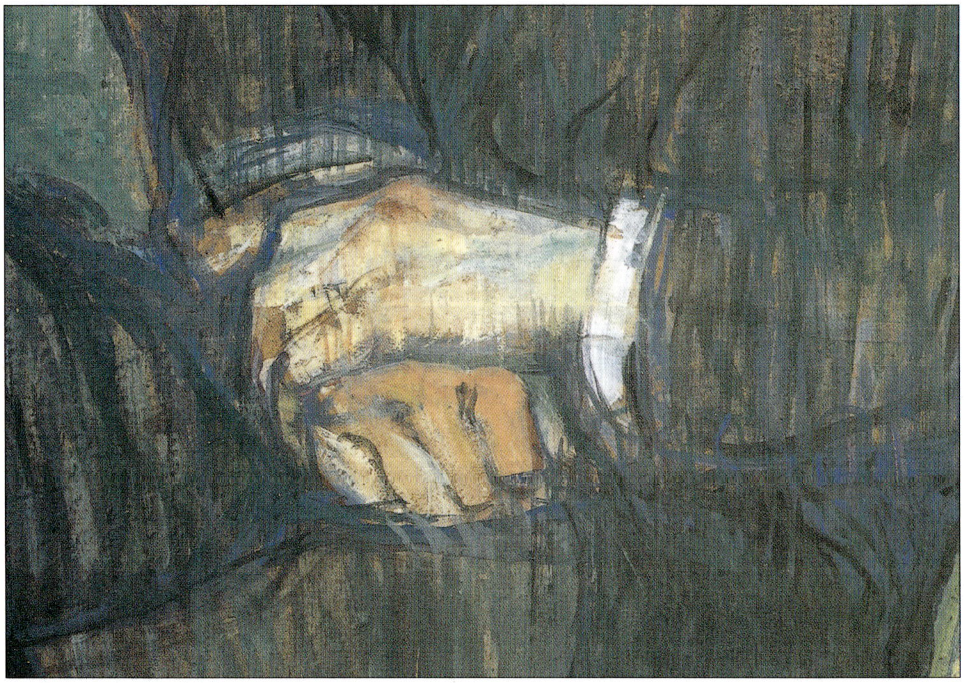

2

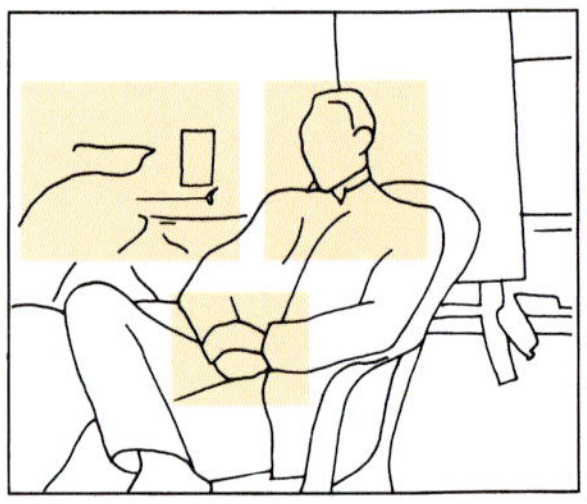

1 Details in the backgrounds of Lautrec's portraits are often most effective when simplest, and therefore less likely to interfere with the main motif. Here an atmosphere of cool luminosity is created by the combination of aqueous blues and greens, within which the tables and their contents shimmer with a translucency that is both fragmented and substantial.

2 A curious aspect of Lautrec's portraiture is that the paintings as a whole can successfully survive occasional weaknesses of one or more of the parts — here Leclercq's right arm and leg. The success of these portraits is partly due to Lautrec's caricaturist's instinct for a convincing overall posture, and partly to the care he took over the dominant elements of head and hands and their placing in relation to the fundamental lines of the composition.

3 *Actual size detail* In his later work Lautrec frequently used a dark blue outline to lay out the basic concept of the figure in its setting. Just how rudimentary this was can be clearly seen here. The detail also reveals the use of the tone of the cardboard support as a lightening element, as well as Lautrec's application of vertical textures. The face is much more thoroughly modeled, and the way the head is tilted to one side adds to the intensity of the gaze.

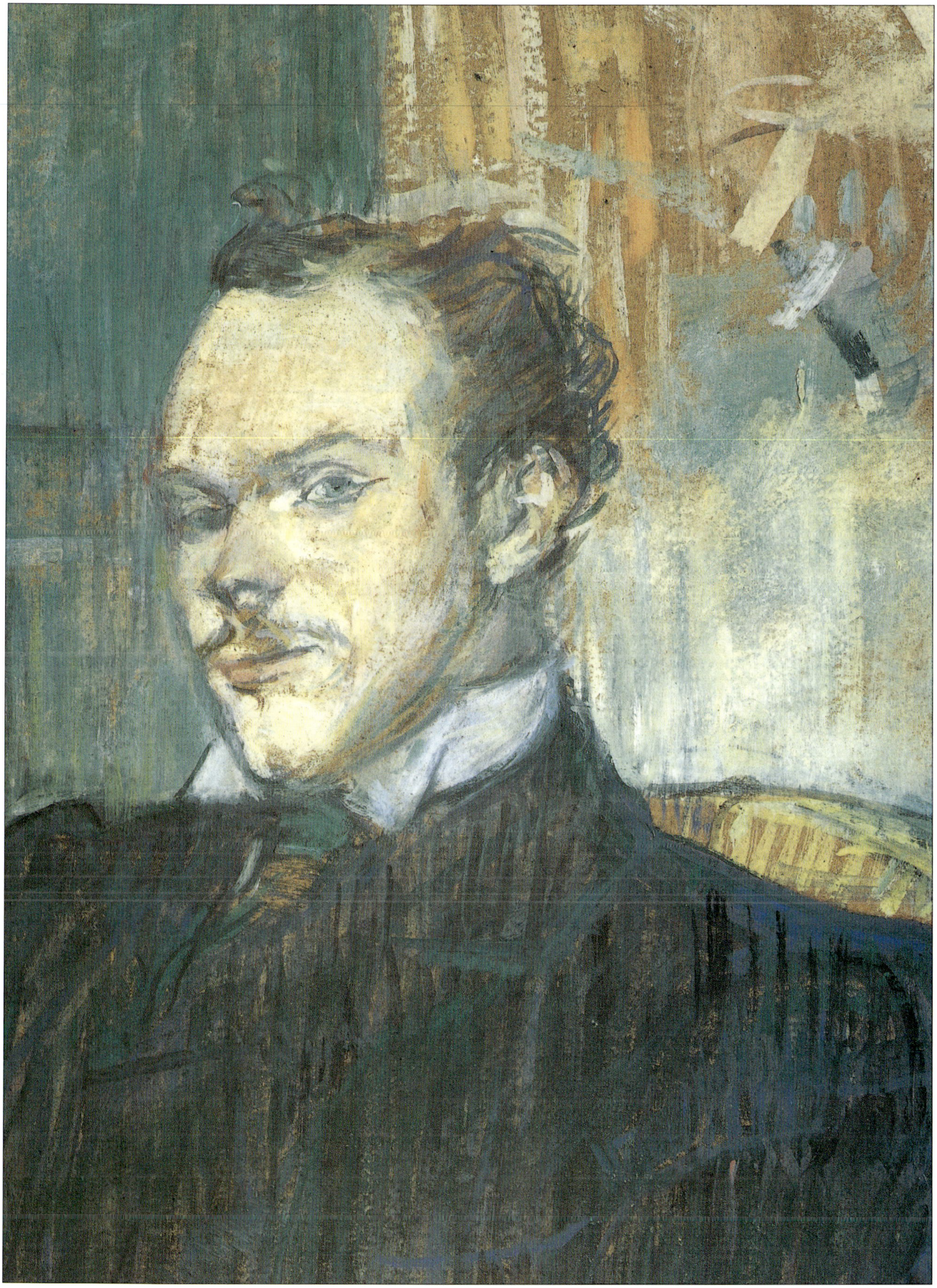

3 *Actual size detail*

MME POUPOULE AT HER TOILET

1898

24×19½in/60.8×49.6cm

Oil on wood

Musée Toulouse-Lautrec, Albi

Lautrec's close contact with *La Revue Blanche* led to friendship with some of the painters of the Nabis group (which included Bonnard and Vuillard), who were helped and promoted by the journal. There are hilarious accounts of a spectacular party held by the Natansons to celebrate the completion of a series of panels by Vuillard at which Lautrec devastated the company by his near-lethal skills as a mixer of cocktails.

The rich coloring and texturing of the background of this painting shows some similarity with Vuillard, who worked up his scenes of domestic interiors with an almost claustrophobic accumulation of decorative surfaces. However, it is clearly a continuation of Lautrec's own thematic interests and stylistic development. As in the early portrait of his mother (see page 19), the observer is placed in close proximity to the self-absorbed sitter via the top of an intervening table on which is a carefully arranged and sensuously painted still life.

Madame Poupoule was a prostitute Lautrec painted a number of times during this period. By the late 1890s, his persistently naturalistic approach was becoming old-fashioned in avant-garde terms, but the theme of prostitutes, which continued to play a crucial role in his art and life, was still popular with writers and the reading public. Two years earlier, for example, he had considered illustrating Edmond de Goncourt's *La Fille Elisa,* published twenty years earlier. Pierre Loüy's *Aphrodite* of 1896 was a paean in praise of prostitution and sold 125,000 copies by 1904. But this is far less obviously a painting of a whore than the earlier brothel paintings, indeed on one level it is simply a private portrait of a woman combing her hair. Lautrec's deformity denied him the kind of conjugal intimacy taken for granted by normal men, but he could enjoy something of the same closeness with women of this kind.

Scenes such as this were common in Degas' work, and it was always to Degas that Lautrec looked for guidance, stylistic, technical, and iconographic. Degas' opinion of his paintings mattered to Lautrec more than anyone else's, and to judge from the older artist's recorded statements, that opinion was somewhat equivocal. After silently perusing the works on show at Lautrec's first major exhibition, at the Boussod and Valadon Gallery in 1893, he is said to have called out on leaving, "One can see, Lautrec, that you know the ropes." Possibly from a lack of confidence, Lautrec had asked to share this exhibition with a now little-known painter, Charles Maurin, and it is ironic that Degas subsequently advised a patron who was considering buying Lautrecs to buy Maurins instead. "Lautrec has a good deal of talent," he said, "but he is merely the painter of a period . . ." Other reported comments indicate irritation at being so closely followed, and in a manner he probably considered too flagrantly immoral. Years after Lautrec's death he said of Lautrec's work as a whole that, "It all stinks of the pox." However, if an incident described by another contemporary is true, he could also be enthusiastically encouraging. The story is that Lautrec and some others encountered Degas in the street on his way back from Durand-Ruel's, where he had been looking at examples of Lautrec's work. Degas praised him at length, concluding, "Work hard! You've got a splendid talent." As he and his friends walked on, Lautrec, visibly shaken, asked whether Degas could possibly have meant it, and one of them crushed him cruelly by asserting that he had been made a fool of. This seems unlikely; although Degas could be unkind and ill-tempered he was known for biting sarcasm rather than for malicious guile. The anecdote is interesting in another way, however, as it provides one of the numerous instances of Lautrec's uncertainty as to the lasting qualities of his art.

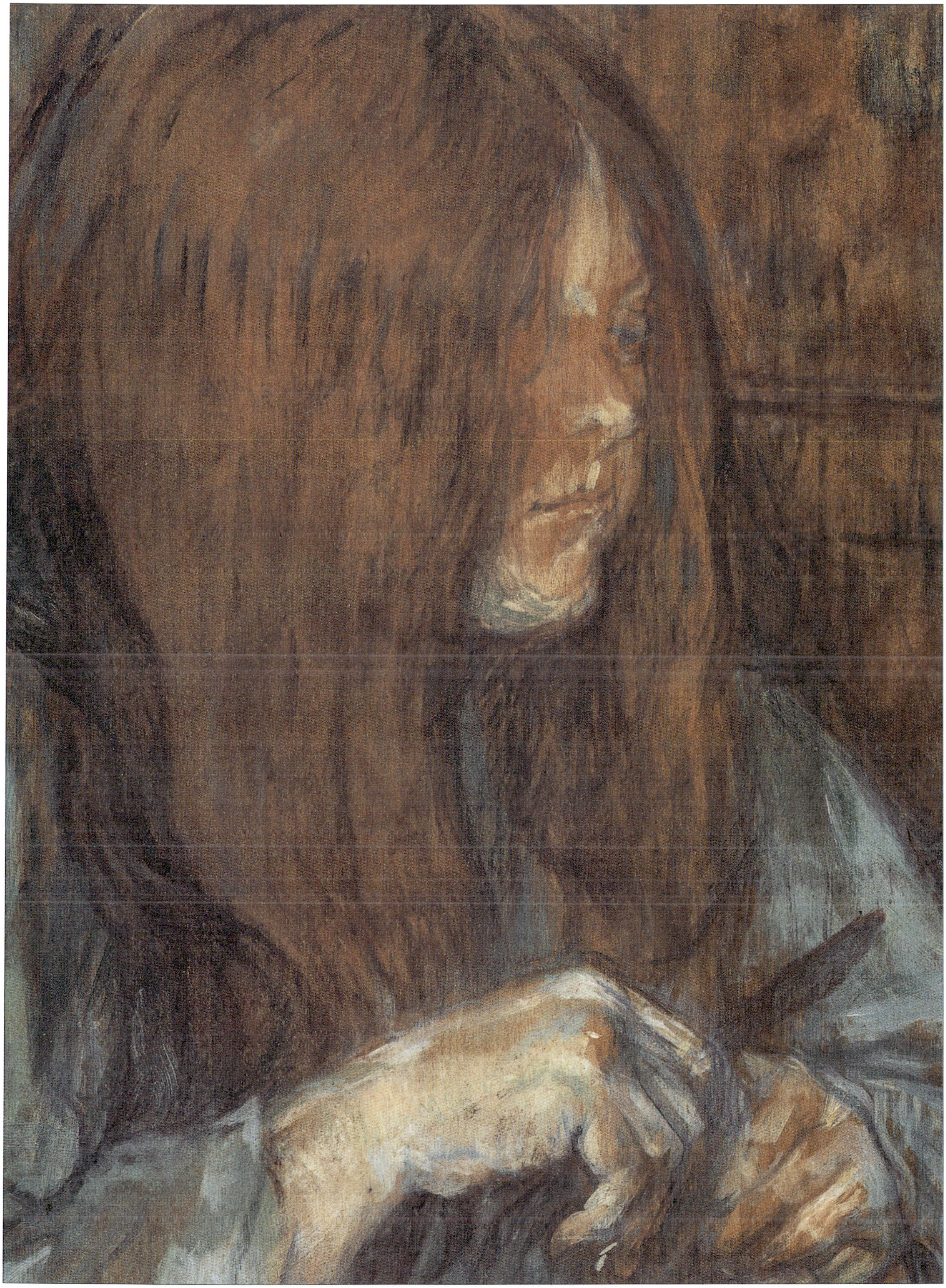

1 *Actual size detail*

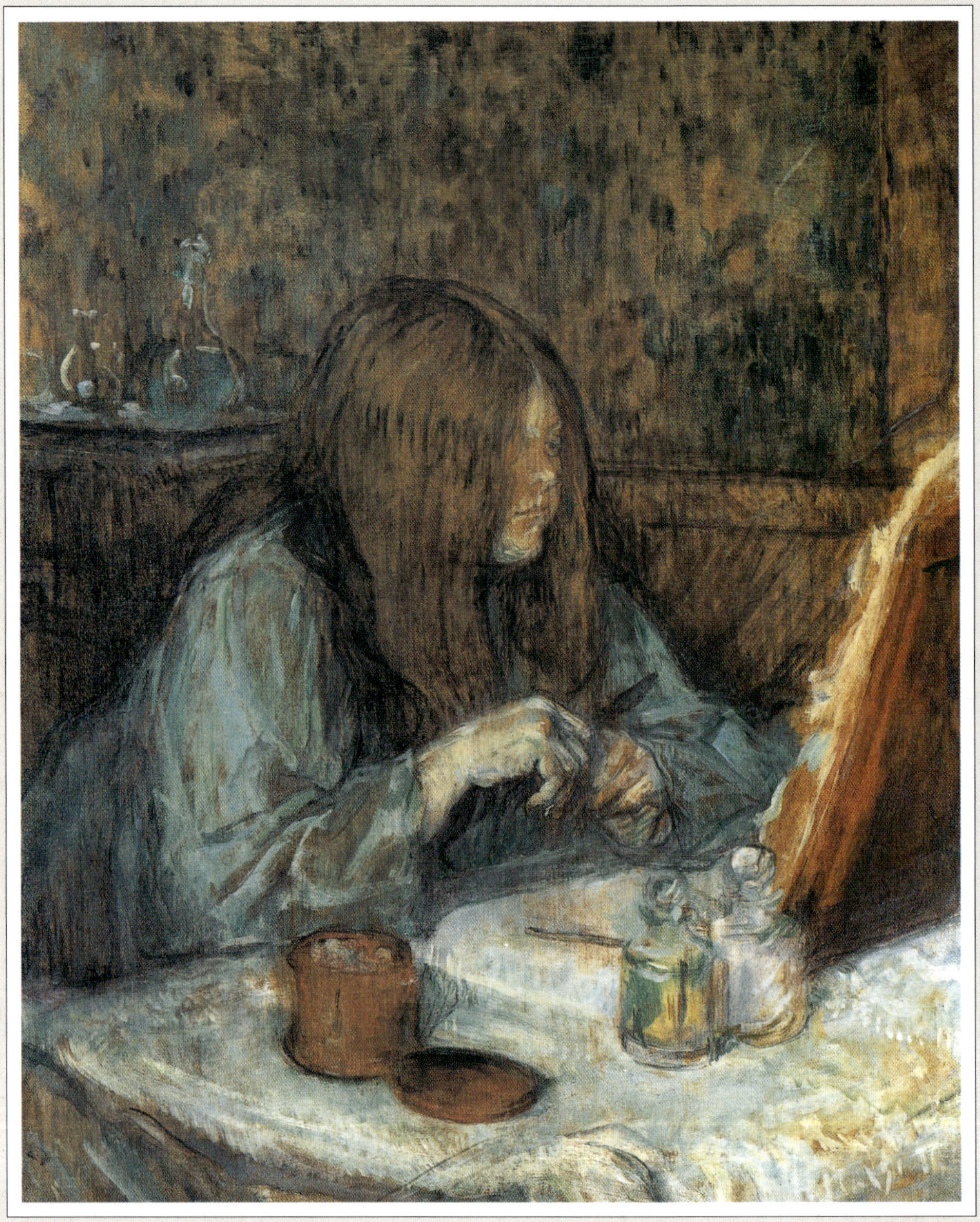

A comparison with Degan's depictions of women combing their hair reveals both the similarities and differences in the two artists' respective approaches.There is the same sense of invaded privacy and of surreptitious access to an exclusively feminine ambience.But Degas was principally concerned with achieving effects of momentary,glimpsed movement,so that the faces, though often clearly visible, indicate little of personality beyond an almost animal lack of self-consciousness. Lautrec, on the other hand, manipulates every facet of the painting to concentrate on the woman's character in a moment of introspection. In this sense he comes closer to the similar representations of the American Impressionist Mary Cassatt.

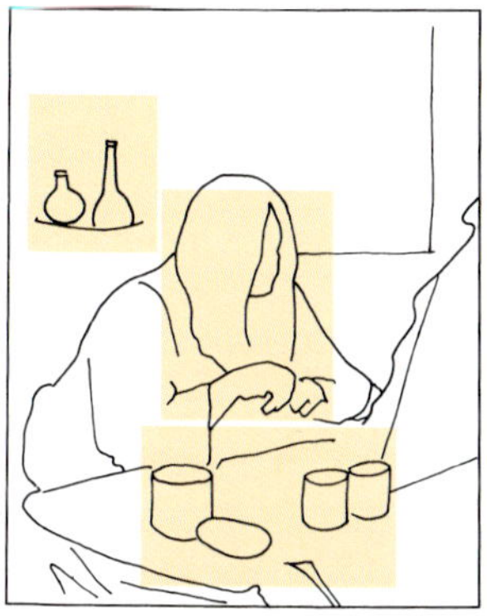

1 *Actual size detail* Mme Poupoule is caught literally in a moment of self-reflection while combing her hair. The positioning of the hands adds to the pervading sense of stillness and the serious thoughtfulness of the expression on her only partially visible face.

2 Lautrec here uses another device learned early in his career, one borrowed from another artist, Jean-Louis Forain, whose specialty was the representation of objects in dimly lit interiors by means of a few deft strokes of highlight. The more than usually claustrophobic feeling of this work also invites comparison with the treatment of similar subjects by Vuillard, but while the latter almost overwhelms his figures by the decorative treatment of wall, floor coverings, and so on, Lautrec's colors seem to create a sense of amorphous depth.

3 Although the head and hands are the main area of psychological interest, Lautrec has here set up a foreground motif which is of almost equal importance. The coloring of the jar and lid is more substantial, because more intense in hue, than any other area of the picture, being a more saturated variant of the color of the girl's hair. Similarly solid in volume, although transparent, are the squat bottles near the mirror, and the physical presence of these objects is enhanced by the echoes of shimmering white highlights on the cloth.

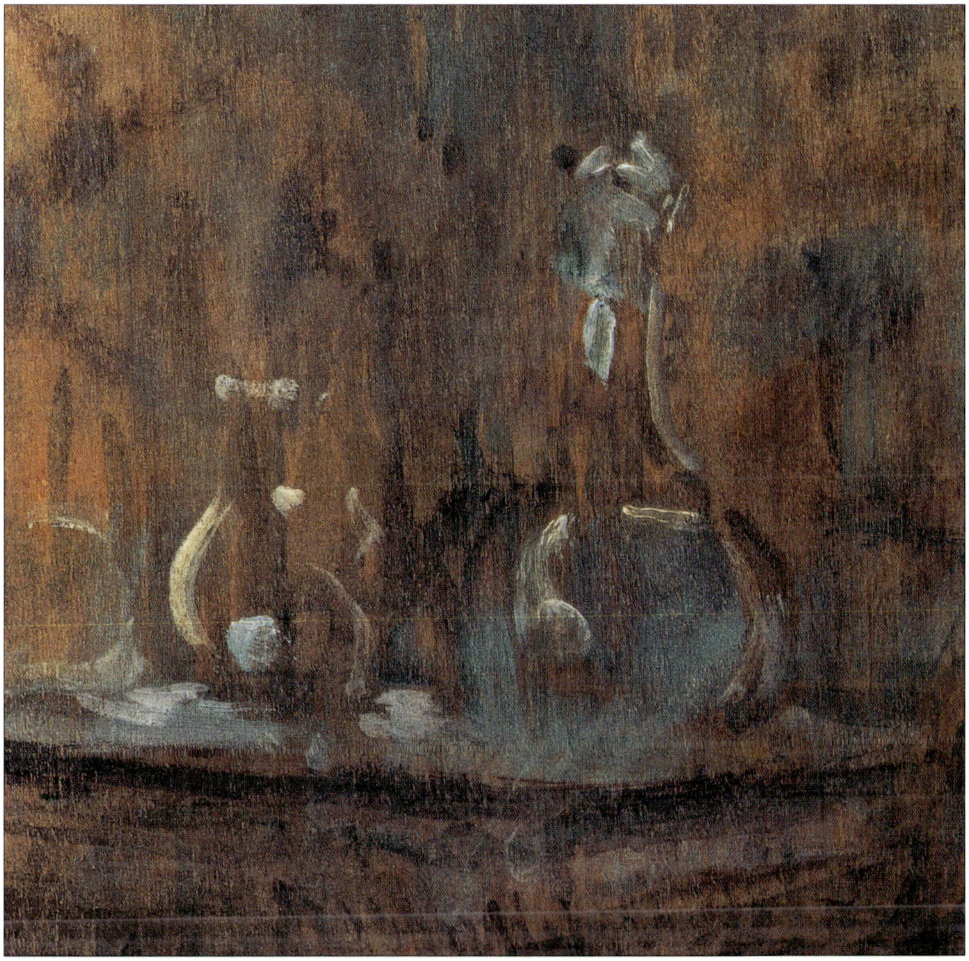

2

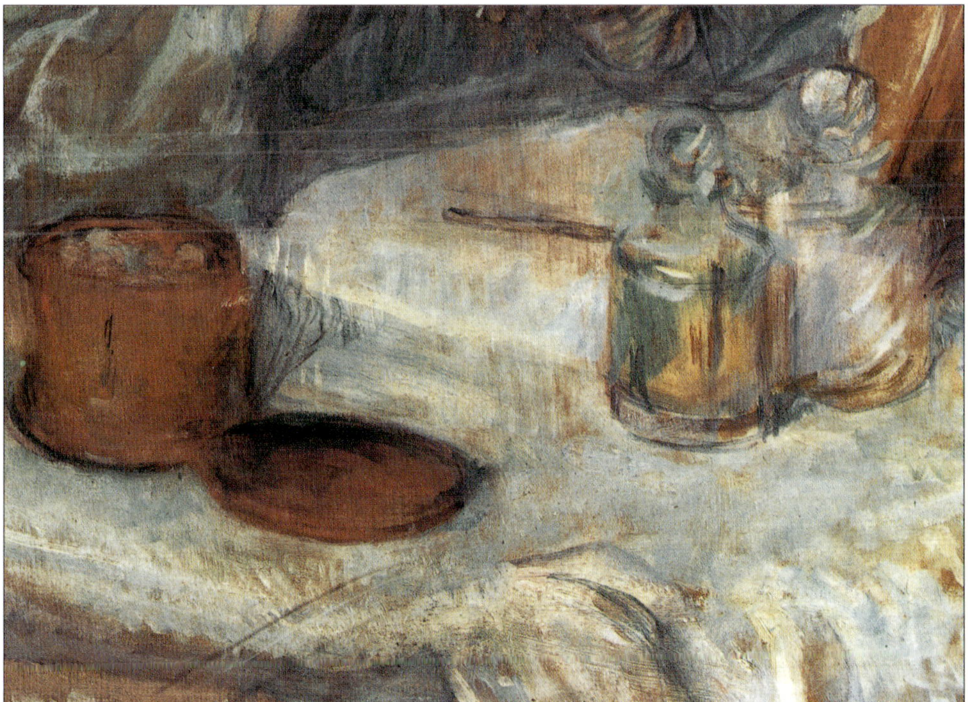

3

At the Rat Mort

(The Tête à Tête Supper)

1899

$21^{5}/_{8} \times 18^{1}/_{8}$in/$55 \times 46$cm

Oil on canvas

Courtauld Institute Galleries, London

The painter William Rothenstein, who documented the artistic life of the period in both England and France, wrote of this restaurant, where he was first introduced to Lautrec, as follows: "The Rat Mort by night had a somewhat doubtful reputation, but during the day was frequented by painters and poets. As a matter of fact it was a notorious center of lesbianism, a matter of which, being very young, and a novice to Paris, I knew nothing. But this gave additional attraction to Conder and Lautrec." He went on to comment on the lesbian and brothel themes Lautrec was already known for (see page 703), adding, "Nor can I imagine anyone else ready to face what Lautrec did in order to get material for his studies."

Earlier in the decade, when staying for periods of time in brothels, Lautrec had been attracted by the affection some of the women could display to one another. The series of lithographs he published as an album in 1896, entitled *Elles,* was for long believed to represent domestic life in the brothels, but it is now thought more likely that the theme is the daily lives of two particular women, only occasionally engaged in prostitution. Montmartre had attracted a number of lesbian bars, and Lautrec began to frequent them in the mid-1890s. Among these were Le Hanneton in the Rue Pigalle and La Souris in the rue Breda, where he began to stay from time to time. Thadée Natanson thought that he was drawn to lesbians because, "they love each other more deeply than men can love them." No doubt a further attraction was that he relished entering places where normal men were shunned but he was welcomed.

Natanson also observed that Lautrec's eyes now shone less brightly, outdone by the glints of his pince-nez. By 1898 his drinking had become even more prodigious, and he no longer seemed to care if it rendered him publicly unconscious. Francis Jourdain was sad to see him at La Souris asleep and dribbling. To others he seemed to be bent on self-destruction; friends noted that his enthusiasm for enticing subjects and even for painting itself was on the wane. Delirium tremens and the breakdown of his health that led to his death was only months away. And yet he was still painting and sometimes producing works that stand comparison with anything he had ever done.

The format of this painting is similar to that of *Mme Poupoule* (see page 711), but the mood could hardly be more different, and the style seems accordingly changed. Moreover, coming so soon after the almost hallucinatory precision of the circus drawings Lautrec had done in the sanatorium at Neuilly, the breadth of handling is remarkable. After about six months abstinence he was drinking again, and some have seen this late manner as the result of a reduced ability to control the line on which his art had always depended. But although it is true that his faculties were greatly impaired, the painting can be seen in a different way. The contrast between the two works suggests that Lautrec might have been consciously taking further a trend that had been evident in his earlier work, and was exploring an idea that had been current for at least a generation, namely that color, value, and even the type of brushstroke used should be in harmony with the psychological content of a picture. Here the tipsy, smiling face of the courtesan Lucy Jourdan is set amid the swaying forms and Baroque rhythms that convey the rolling pleasure of her inebriation.

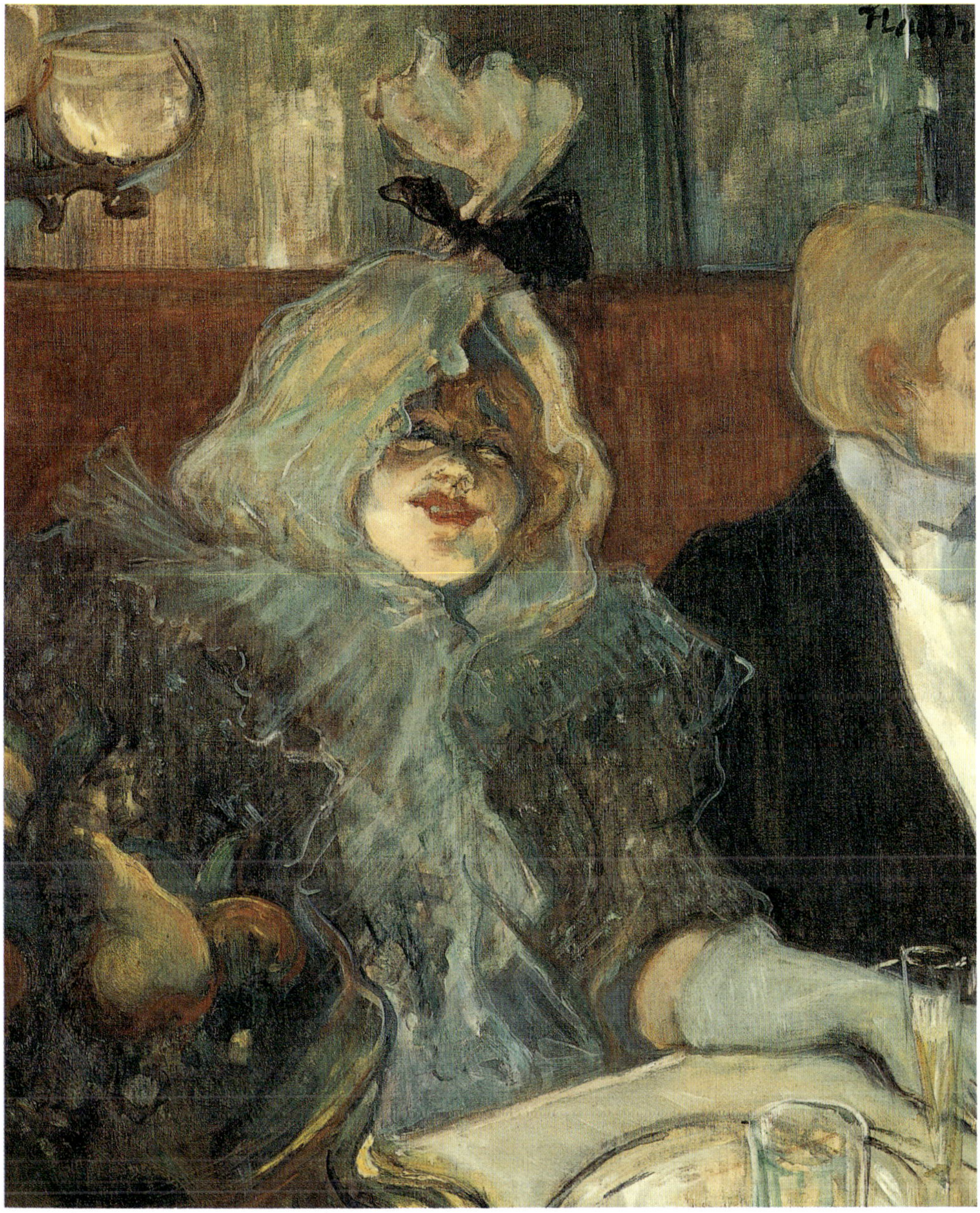

According to contemporaries, Lautrec was only minimally interested in art theory. Technique was a much more engaging preoccupation, whether the term was applied to art or the difficult business of mounting a bar stool. *Technique des Vénitiens* was a frequent expression, and by this he meant a preference for sumptuous color and loose handling as against line, the Florentine and academic preference. Louis Anquetin, a friend who had also trained at Cormon's *atelier,* was also interested in the Baroque tradition and its 19th-century derivatives. *At the Rat Mort* suggests that Lautrec may also have been prepared to take the side of Venetian painting and the freedom of such artists as Rubens and Delacroix against the linear emphasis of Poussin and Ingres.

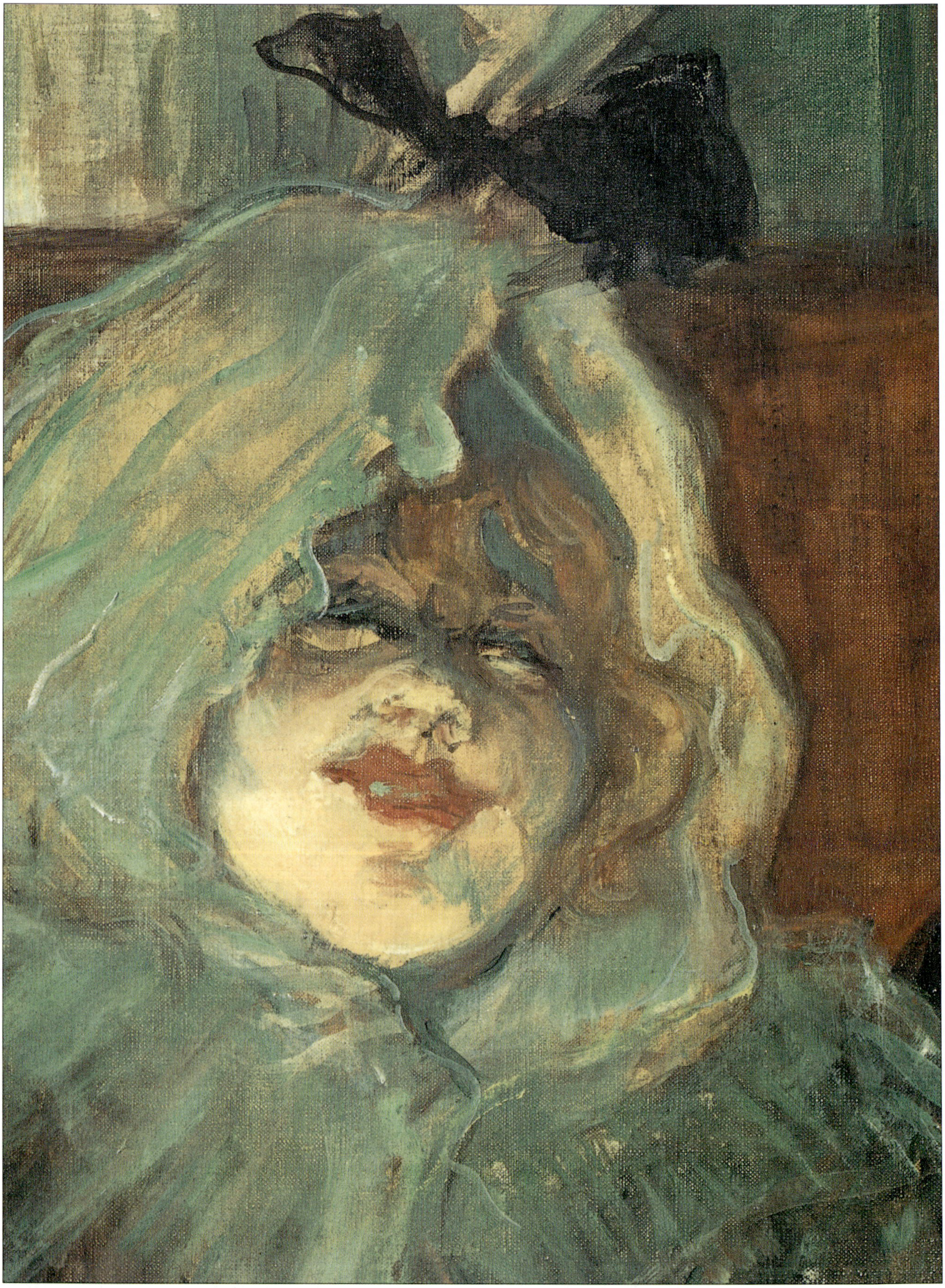

1 *Actual size detail*

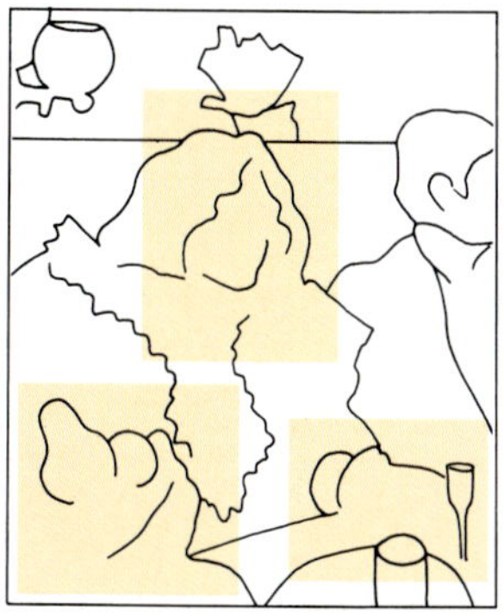

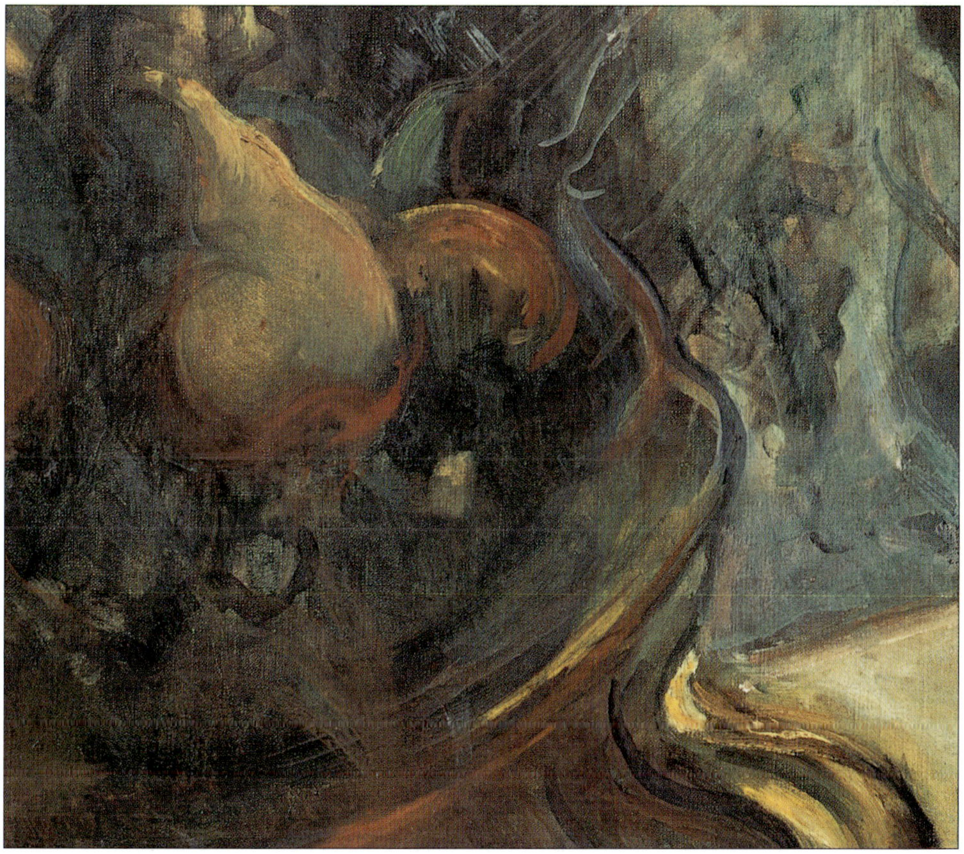

2

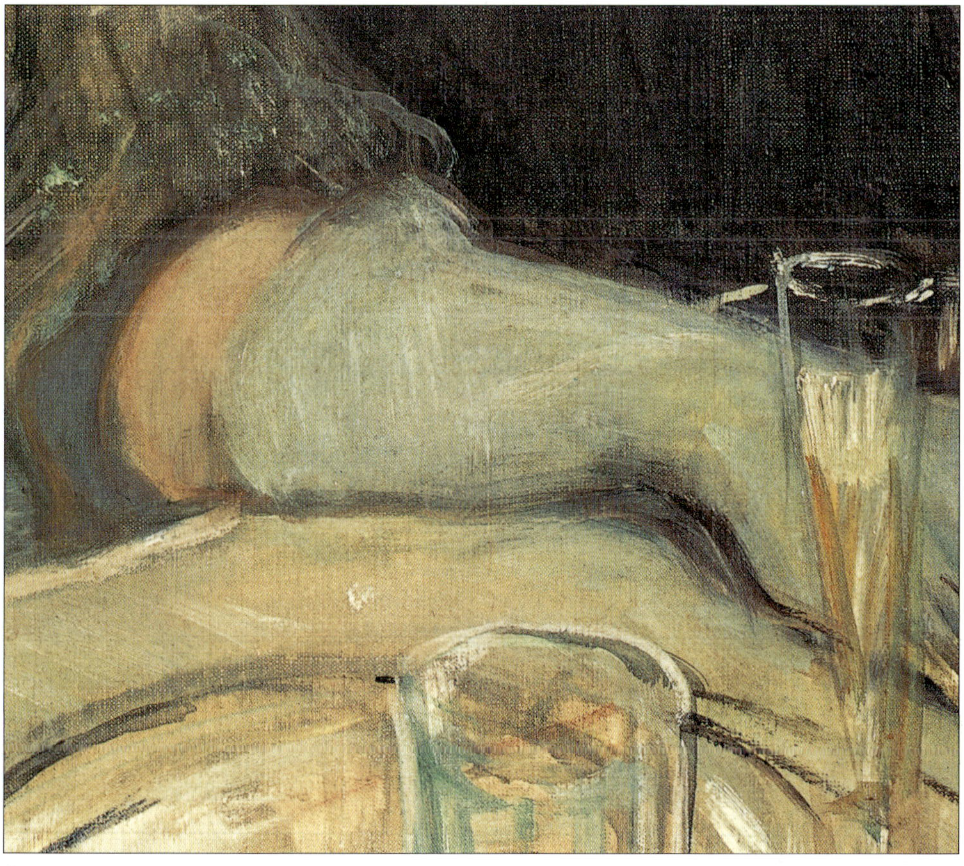

3

1 *Actual size detail* Lautrec excelled in the representation of people in artificial light. His bold technique lent itself well, as here, to the stark demarcation of shaded and illumined areas of the face. With virtually a single stroke of contrasting color he underscores each eye, while the luscious red fullness of the mouth is a concentration of the flourishes and coloring that permeate the whole painting.

2 Always careful in the placing of foreground objects in relation to the figure beyond, Lautrec has here made humorous use of the shape of the pear as a kind of miniature in reverse of the head with its extravagant top-knot of hair. The fruit and bowl have been painted more thickly than the clothing beyond, where the canvas weave is clearly apparent.

3 The cool bluish gray of the woman's gloved hand is echoed throughout the composition. It appears in the glasses and on the wall behind the woman's head, and continues in the exhilarating cascades of her transparent collar and pale blond hair. This relatively neutral tone is combined with touches of equally muted green, and these colors, when set against the areas of deep red, appear stronger in hue, contributing to the air of sensuality.

INDEX

Page numbers in *italic* refer to illustrations and captions

A

A La Mie, 694, *695–7*
Absinthe, 420, 430, *431–3*, 434, 435
Absinthe Drinker, *325*, *326*, 326
Abstract Expressionism, 645
abstract patterns, *614*
abstraction, 414, *419*, *431*, 442, 447
academic painting, 412, 413, 506, 550, *570*
Academicians, 499, 506, 594, 637–8
academicism, rejection of, 322
Académie Gleyre, 364
Académie Suisse, 281–2
Academy of San Fernando (Goya elected to), 194
Adoration of the Kings, The, 67, *71*, 94, 111
Adoration of the Shepherds, The, 154, 178, *179–81*
aerial perspective, *81*, 289
Aertsen, Pieter, 86
Aesthetic movement, 400
aestheticism, 370
After the Bath, *414*
Aix-en-Provence, 456, 457, 460, 488
Alba, Duchess of, 196–7, 197–8
Albert, Archduke of Austria, 111
alcohol, 696
Alexander, Miss Cicely, 368, 396
Alexandre, Arsène, 572, *686*
al fresco painting, 215
Algeria, 497
alla prima (direct) painting, 201
allegory, *66*, 74, *75–7*, 82, 132, *133*, 136
Allegory of Lust, 64, *66*
Allegory of Peace and War, 114, 120, *136-9*
Alpine scenery, *239*, *241*, 254
Alps, 63
altarpiece at Malines, 62
altarpieces, 20, 32
American painting, 645
Amsterdam, 150, 152–3, 164, 633
Anarchism, 288, 304
Anatomy Lesson of Dr Tulp, The, 152, *154*
"Ancient Maori Cult", 610
André, Albert, 546
Andrée, Ellen, 430, *432*
Anna Accused by Tobit of Stealing the Kid, 151, *176*
Anne of Saxony, *105*
Antequin, Louis, *715*
anti-French revolt, 198–9
anti-naturalism, 336
Antwerp, 62, 63, 106, 111
Apple Picking at Eragny-sur-Epte, 287, *289*
aquatint, 416, *416*, 417
architectural detail, 66, *71*, *77*, 82, *83*, *85*, 90
Argenteuil, 348, *349–51*, *495*, 496, 498, 499, 514, 518
Ariosto, Ludovico 28, 168
Arles, 606, 643, 656, 660, 664, 668, 672
Arosa, Gustave, 587, 588, 598
Arosa, Marguerite, 598
Arrangement in Grey and Black No 2: Thomas Carlyle, *371*
Arrangement in Grey: Portrait of the Painter, 368
Arrival of Marie de'Medici at Marseilles, The, *128-31*
art "establishment," 242
Artist Going to Work, The, 645
artist's friends in paintings, *334*
Artist's Studio, The, *366*
assistants, Rubens' use of, 112, 114, 128, *129*, *130*, *131*
Assumption and Coronation of the Virgin, The, 20, 24, 32
Astrue, Zacharie, *334*, *341*
asymmetry, *21*, *32*, *394*, 626, 683, *703*
Atelier Colarossi, 598
At the Milliners, *415*
At the Piano, 364, 384
At the Rat Mort, 686, *687*, 714, *715–7*
At the Terrace of a Café, 426, 434, *435–7*
atmosphere, 90, *283*, 434, 442
atmospheric effects, 239
atmospheric perspective, *298*, 654, 673
atmospheric reality, *194*
Aurier, Albert, 616
Autumn at Argenteuil, 514, *515–7*
Autumn Landscape, *419*
Autumn Landscape with a View of Het Steen, *113*, *118*, *144–7*
Auvers, 643, 672
avante-garde, 637, 638, 640
Avril, Jane, *682*, *687*, 698, *699–701*

B

Bacchus and Ariadne, 22, 24, 36, 37–40, 54
background, 50
landscape, 18
back-lighting, *195*

background(s), 151, *155*, 160, 168, 182, *184*, 222, *306*, 326, 329, 392, 396, *398*, 400, *402*, 426, *428*, 468, *470*, 554, *556*, 564, *570*, 576, 593, *608*, *649*, *650*, *662*, 690, *700*, *708*, 710
background landscape, 66–7, *87*
Bacon, Francis, 645
  Study for Portrait of Van Gogh VI, *645*
Baldinucci, Filippo, 150
Ball at the Moulin de la Galette, The, 546, 548, 558, *559–63*, 701, *691–3*
Balleroy, Albert de, *334*
ballet girls, 702
Ballou, 500
Baltens, Pieter, 62
Balzac, Honoré de, 499
Bank at Gennevilliers, The, *496*
Banning Cocq, Captain Frans, 172
Barbizon School, 281, 495, 541, 598
Bar at the Folies Bergère, 352, 356, *357–61*
Baroque, 132, *133*
Baroque style, 151, 153, 164, 168
Baroque tradition, 193, *201*, 201, 204, 212
Bathers, *459*
Bathers, The, 546, 568, *569–71*, 572, 580
Bathing at La Grenouillère, *501*, 514, *520*, 522
Bathing Posts, Brittany, 404, *405–7*
Battle between Carnival and Lent, The, 65, 74, *75–7*, 78, 86
Baudelaire, Charles, (poet), 322, 324, 340, 356, 438, 446, 592, 616, 684, 690
  Heroism of Modern Life, The, 332
Bayeu, Francesco, 194
Bayeu, Josefa, wife of Goya, 194
Bazille, Frédéric, 282, 497, 498, 541, 542, *543*, 544, 548, 550
  Still Life with Heron, 543
Bazire, Edmond, 325
beach scenes, 348
Beardsley, Aubrey, 366
Bedford Park, The Old Bath Road, *288*
Bellelli Family, The, 420
Bellini, Gentile, 17
Bellini, Giovanni, 17
  Sacred Allegory, *17*, 17
  Young Woman with a Mirror, *18*
Belshazzar's Feast, 153, *155*, 164, *165–7*, 178
"Belvedere torso," 109, 120
Bewitched, The: Priest Pouring Oil on the Devil's Lamp, 208, *209–11*
Bernard, Emile, 488, 592, 602, 640
Bertin, 587, 598
Bibémus quarry, 457, 488, *489–91*
Bible, 150, 160, *179*, 182, 186, 637, 638
black chalk study *285*
Black Paintings," "The, 199, *201*, 226, 232, *233–5*
  originally painted *al secco*, *234*
black, extensive use of, 468
black, use of, 325, *329*, *338*, *350*
black, Monet rejects, 506, *508*, *520*
Blacksmith, The, *634*
Blanche, Jacques-Emile, 438, 568
Blanche painting, *502*
Blaue Reiter, Der, 645
Bles, Herri met de, 63, *64*, 86
Blue Cloak, The, see *The Netherlandish Proverbs*
Boats at Etretat, *504*, 522, 523–6
body colour, 155
Bondy, forest of, 587
bone, deficiency, 678
Bonington, Richard Parkes, 262
Bonnard, Pierre, 503, 576, 710
Bonnat, Léon, 680, *692*
  Decapitation of Saint Denis, The, *680*
Booth, Mrs, 240
Boott, Isabella, 376, *379*
Borgia family 586
Borinage, 633, 648
Bosch, Hieronymus, 150, 226
  The Garden of Earthly Delights, 64, *66*, *67*, *75*
  influence on Bruegel, 62, 65–7
Boucher, François, 540, 546
  Diana at the Bath, *541*
Boudin, Eugène, 495, 497, 506, 522, *541*
Bougival, 518, 550
Bouguereau, Adolphe, 499
Bouguereau, William, 594
Boulevard Montmatre at Night, The, 311, *312–14*
Bouquet of Flowers, 308
Box at the Theatre, The, *545*, 548, 554, *555*
Brabant, 648
Brandt, Sebastian, *Ship of Books*, 64
Brant, Isabella, 111
Braque, Georges, 460
  Demoiselles d'Avignon, 460
British Museum, 626
Brittany, 589–92, 594, 602, 610
Brown and Gold: a Self-portrait, *373*
Bruant, Aristide, *682*, 682–3, 694, 698
Brücke, Die, 645
Bruegel, Jan (son), 69, 70
Bruegel, Jan the Elder, 144
Bruegel, Pieter, 226
  apprenticeship and formative years 62–3
  graphic work, 64
  influences on, *64*, 65–7
  landscape, 62, 63
  the later religious paintings, 67–8
  married Mayken Coecke, 66
  new departures, 68–70
  painting methods 71
  use of earlier style, 86
  visited Italy, 63
Bruegel, Pieter (the Younger), 66
Brunelleschi, 326
brushes, *187*, 371, *390*, 501
  handles, 514, *516*
  hog's hair, 292, *318*
  large, *58*
  soft-haired, *310*
  square-ended, *53*
brushstroke, comma-like, 285
brushstrokes, 113, *113*, 117, 128, *134*, 245, *259*, *264*, *269*, *272*, *273*, 413, *432*, 434, *436*, 501, *501*, *508*, *611*, *612*, *614*, *618*,

625, *627*, 632, 638, *650*, *653*, 656, *665*
backgrounds, *662*
'drawn', 497
drapery 124, *126*
enveloppe, 514
expressionism, *641*, 672
Gauguin's, *640*
impasto, 497, *516*, 518, 532, *534*, 641, *641*
Impressionists, 640
lack of harmony, *674*
landscapes, *256*, *272*, *276*
Pointillism, *639*, 640, 652, *654*
Post-impressionism, 643
and Van Gogh's mental breakdown, 668, *670*
seascapes, 250, *251*, *252*
sketches, 495
tache method, *498*, 501
weather effects, *256*
zig zag, *666*, *674*
brushwork, 16, 19, 23, 24, *30*, *35*, *44*, *48*, 50, *53*, 54, *57*, *58*, *65*, *71*, 71, *77*, *81*, *85*, *89*, *92*, *96*, *101*, 151, 160, *165*, *166*, 172, *174*, 178, *181*, 182, *183*, *201*, 201, 204, *207*, *215*, *217*, *220*, *225*, *226*, 234, *281*, 283, 284, 285, 287, 289, 292, *293*, *299*, 300, *305*, *306*, 308, *309*, *310*, 312, *315*, 316, *317*, *318*, 322, 326, *329*, 329, 332, *334*, 348, *350*, 352, *361*, 371, *379*, 388, *390*, *394*, *398*, *402*, *406*, *461*, *466*, 468, *470*, *474*, *478*, *486*, *489*, *679*, 683, *687*, *691*, *700*, 714
emphasizing structure of composition, 477
Brussels 71, 633
Buckingham, First Duke of, (George Villiers), 132
Buddha, 594
Bulls of Bordeaux, 200
buon fresco technique, 212
Burial of the Sardine, The, 226, *227–31*
Burke, Edmund, 239
Burne-Jones, Sir Edward, 400
Burning of the Houses of Parliament, 238
Butler, Theodore, *499*
butterfly signature, 366, 380, *383*, 384, *386*, 388, 392
Byron, Lord, 242
Byzantine art, influence of, 16

C

Cabanel, Alexandre, *Birth of Venus,* 322, 323, 340
café-concert, 352
Café-concert at the Ambassadeurs, 420, 426, *431*, *435*
Café de la Nouvelle-Athènes, 430
Café Geurbois, 282, 328, 413, 438, 548
Café Voltaire, Paris, 616
Cagnes, 547, 548, 580
Caillebotte, Gustave, *495*, *502*, 548, 558
collection of Impressionists, 316
Calais Pier, 250
Calais Sands, Low Water, Poissards Collecting Bait, 262
Calligraphic black paint, 226, 229
Camille, 348, *349*
Camoin, Charles, 488
can-can, 698
canvas, 136, *137*, 204, *293*, *687*, *717*
diagonal weave, *293*
texture, 593, 606, *608*, *628*
unprimed, 683
canvases, *23*, *30*, 155, *461*, 501, 547, 641
coarse, 376
fine-grained, 576
priming, 543, 545, 550, 554, 564, *566*, 580, *641*
ready-prepared, 542, 550
stretching, 543
texture, *582*
Caravaggio, Michelangelo, 151, 164
Caravaggio, Michelangelo Merisi da, 109, *111*
Death of the Virgin, 109
The Entombment, 109, *111*
"Caravaggisti", 151, 153, *156*
cardboard, 683, *687*, 694, *701*, *708*
Carleton, Sir Dudley, 112
Carolus-Duran, *Portrait of Claude Monet, 494*
Carriage at the Races, 438, *439–41*
Carthage, 241, *244*
cartouche, *394*
Cassatt, Mary, *416*, 420
cassone, 47
Castagnary, A. J. (critic), *284*
Catholic Church, 602
Catholicism, 104, 106
Cecilia (wife of Titian), 20–21
ceiling decorations, 104, 109, *109*, 117, 132, *133*
ceramics, 592, 602
Cézanne, Paul, 24, 280, 281–2, 282, 285, 292, *303*, 500, 544, 546, 588, *591*, 598
approach to painting, 458
ceases exhibiting with Impressionists, 458
early years, 452–3
ended friendship with Zola, 458–9
and his father, 452, *453*
influences on, 452, 453
L'Etang des Soeurs, 300, *301*
marriage to Hortense Fiquet, 459
quoted, 488
Still Life with Open Drawer, 590
temperament, 455
worked with Pissarro, 300
working methods, 461
Cézanne, Paul (son), 454, 458, 468
chalk and glue ground, *77*
Champfleury, *Cats, 334*
Chapelet, *591*
character, psychological penetration of, 706, *711*
characterization, 218, *219*
charcoal drawings, 648
Chardin, Jean-Baptiste, 459, 480
Charigot, Aline, 546, *547*, 548, 564
Charles IV and his Family, 198, 218, *219–21*

Charles V, Holy Roman Emperor, 21
Charpentier, Georges, 546, 548
Charpentier, Mme, 546, 547, 548
Château de Medan, 457
Chatou, 518
Chestnut Vendor, The, 682
chiaroscuro, 42, 151, *151*, *153*, 160, 172, 182, *183*, 648
Children's Games, 65, *75*, 78, *79–81*
Chocquet, Victor, 544, 546, 548
Christ, 154, 178, 633
Christ Appears to the Apostles at the Sea of Tiberias, 63
Christ and the Woman taken in Adultery, 67, 68
chronology, 26, 158, 330, 374, 462, 504, 596
Cirque Fernando, 442, *444*
classical influence, 104, 106, *109*, 112, 120, *125*
classical subjects, 117, 120, 136, 140, 413, 415, *440*, *541*, 544, 568, *569*, 580, *581*
classicism, 626
clay models, 416, 417, *418*, 438
Claude Lorraine, *242*, 243, *259*
Embarkation of the Queen of Sheba, II, The, 243
Liber Veritatis, 270
Clemenceau, Georges, 508, 532
Clothed Majas, The, 196
Clovio, Giulio (miniaturist), 63, 82
Coast Scene near Naples, 247
Cock, Hieronymus (printer and publisher), 62, 63, *66*, 66, 75, 86
Coecke van Aelst, Pieter, 62
The Resurrection of Christ, 63
cohesion of design, 94
Collettes, Les, 548, 580
color, 16, 23, 28, *30*, 32, 36, *38*, *37*, *40*, 42, *44*, *48*, 50, *53*, *55*, *57*, *71*, *77*, *81*, *85*, *92*, *95*, *96*, *98*, *101*, *132*, 140, *141*, *142*, *200*, 201, 204, *207*, *225*, 226, 232, *243*, *264*, 270, *281*, *289*, *295*, 296, 298, *301*, *303*, *306*, 308, *315*, 316, *318*, 326, *342*, 348, *350*, *354*, *361*, 365–6, 376, *381*, *383*, *386*, 392, *394*, 396, 400, *402*, 404, *406*, *424*, 426, *428*, 434, *435*, *436*, *440*, 442, 446, *461*, 468, *478*, 480, *489*, *490*, 547, *562*, *566*, *570*, 572, *574*, 576, *578*, 580, *582*, 593, *593*, 594, 602, *604*, 656, *674*, *681*, 684, *687*, 690, *691*, *692*, *700*, *703*, *705*, *707*, 710, *713*, 714, *715*, *717*
and design, 36
and light, *244–5*, *247*, 258, *267*, *268*
and texture, richness of, *390*
and tonality, 222
and tone(s), 322, *469*
balance, 488
Barbizon school, 541, 542
brilliant, 117
broad washes, *122*
browns, *126*
"color beginnings," *247*
complementary, *658*, *661*
contrasts, *556*, *649*
Courbet, *541*, 542
deceptive, *127*
Delacroix, 412, 415
density of, *482*
depth of, 286
"dead", 155, 164
development of technique, 245, 258, *259*
emotional value, 274
Expressionism, 641
harmonies, 182, *600*, 610
harmony, 444
harsh, *105*, 106, 120, *121*, *122*, *132*, 142
impasto, *417*, 582
Impressionists, 543, 568, *569*, *637*, 638–40, 641, 643, 652, *653*
Italian paintings, 258
Italianate, 120
Japanese prints, *412*
landscape, *255*, *276*
large flat areas of, 684
limited range, *217*
low-toned, 212
machine-ground, 542
matt, *684*, *696*
merging, 550
mixing, 558, *560*, 564
monochrome, 54
muted, *126*, *130*
new theories, 284
oil sketches, 132
overlay, 416
palette(s), 155, *155*, 186, 540, *541*, *545*, 554, *555*, *569*, 580, 641
Pointillism, 652
Post-Impressionism, 643
pure, *260*, *261*, 262, *271*
range, 120, *122*, 124
relationships, 545
rich, 124, 128, 138
seascapes, *253*, *254*
spectrum, *560*
subtle, *89*
subtlety of, 286
superimposition, *448*, 484, *486*
symbolism, *174*
terracotta glaze, *440*
theories, 245, 271, 274
to clarify narrative, *141*
transparent glazes, *448*
unified, *414*
Van Gogh's Dutch paintings, *634*, 638, 648
washes, 415, 416, *428*
color: academic painting, 506
colour range, *530*
complementary, 510, *511*, 514, 518
contrasts, *526*
Impressionists' preoccupation with, *495*
Monet's painting methods, 501
palette, *501*, *516*
recessive, *516*
shadows, 506, *508*
unity of, *525*
color balance, *379*
color harmonies, 18, 32, 46, 390
color harmonies limited, *201*
complementary colors, 510, *511*, 514, 518, *658*, *661*
composition, 32, *113*, 117, *121*, *134*, 140, *141*, 164, 172, 186, *187*, 250, 254, *255*, 275, *276*, *309*, 322, 324, *325*, *341*, *358*, *381*, 404, *405*, 416, *416*, 417, *423*, 426, 430, *432*, 438, *440*, 454, 476, *507*, *511*, 518, *519*, *523*, 528, 554, *555*, 564, 568,

569, 572, *581*, 602, *603*, *653*, *665*, *669*
and technique,Titian as innovator, 23, 24
geometric, 292, *293*, *295*
Comtesse, Adèle de Toulouse-Lautrec, The, *687*, 710
Concert Champêtre, 19
Constable, John, 244, *244*, 283, 296, 495
contemporary life paintings, 332
contemporary settings, 70, 86, 94
contrapposto, 28, 36, *37*, 169
contrast, *29*, *338*, *379*, *649*
dramatic, 326
contre-jour light, 316
Conversion of St Paul, The, 69
Copenhagen, 589
Cormon, Ferdinand, 680, 681, 692
Corner of a Park, A, *638*
Coreggio, Antonio Allegri da, *51*, 193
Corn Harvest, The, 90, *91–3*
Cornelisz van Haarlem, Cornelis, 151
Corot, Camille, 281, 282
Dardagny, Morning, 281, *282*
influence on Pissarro, *282*
Corot, Jean Baptiste Camille, 588, 598
Country Concerns, *65*
country people, life of, 286
Courbet, Gustave, 281, 364–5, *365*, 380, 412, *459*, *480*, 522, *541*, 542, 548, 598, 638
Burial at Ornans, 396
Still Life with Apples and Pomegranate, *458*
The Painter in his Studio, 388
reappraised, 285, 300
courtesans, 340, *341–3*
Couture, Thomas, 323, *326*, *332*
cover illustrations, 698
Cremorne Gardens (London), 400
Crepuscule in Flesh Color and Green: Valparaiso, *371*
cropping, *412*, *413*, 422, 434, 438, *440*
cross-hatching, 285, 683
Crows in the Wheatfield, 672, *673–5*
Crucifixion, *194*
Cruz, Roman de la (dramatist), 204
Cubism, 460, 497

D

Danaë (1545–46), *51*
Danaë (1553–54), *23*, 50, *51–3*
Dance of Death theme, 65–6
Dancer Curtseying, *417*, 420, 426, *427–9*
Dancer, The, 548, 554, *555–7*, 558
Dante, *Divine Comedy*, 82
Daubigny, Charles François, 281, 292
Alders, *281*
Daumier, Honoré, 324, 588, 637
de Granvells, Cardinal (collector and patron of Bruegel), 64, 68, 70
De Loutherbourg, Philip, 254
"dead-color" painting, 155, 164
Dead Toreador, The, *325*
death, 239, 241, 274
Death of Actaeon, The, *23*, 23, 24, 54, 55–9,
Death of St Peter Martyr, 20
Death of the Virgin, The, 67–8, *70*
d' Este, Alfonso, 36
deformity, 678
Degas, Edgar, 283, 286, 304, 322, 324, 328, 348, 352, 364, 365, 376, 388, *390*, *474*, 494, 498, 540, 548, 554, *555*, 586, *591*, *604*, 626, 638, *657*, 687, 690, *691*, *695*, *696*
and prostitution, 702
background and early life, 411, 412
Café Concert at The Ambassadeurs, *683*
experimentation with artistic media, 415, 416, *416*, 417, *418*, 420, *423*, *427*, 430, *431*, *443*, *444*
influences on, 412, *412*, 413, *413*, 414, 422, *423*, *424*, 438, *439*, *440*
L'Absinthe, 694
notebooks, 417, *424*, *435*, *436*, 442, *444*
On the Beach, *405*
painting methods, 414, *414*, 417, *417*
printing methods, 415, 416, *416*, 417, 426, *427*
sketchbooks, 426
study in Italy, 412, 413
Déjeuner sur l'herbe, 322, 323, 326, *329*, 336, *337–9*, 352
Delacroix, Eugène, 128, 411, 412, 415, *440*, 480, 522, 546, 592, 598
Massacre of Chios, 200
Women of Algiers, 384
Delacroix, Ferdinand Victor Eugène, 695
Delius, Frederick, 616
Demarsay, Jeanne, *357*, *361*
Demi Monde, *357*
demi-monde characters, 204, *205–7*
Denis, Maurice, 322, *367*, *592*
Denmark, 589
depth, *267*
Desboutin, Marcellin, 430, *432*
Descent, from the Cross, The, 112, *118*, 124
detail, *106*, 124, 128, *255*, *271*
detail, absence of, 322
Deudon, Charles, 554
diagonals, 78, 86, *89*, 94, 98, 204, *284*, 690, *703*, *705*
Diana, *541*, 544
Diana and Actaeon, 54
Diana and Callisto, 24, *25*, 54
Diaz de la Peña, Narcisse Virgile, 541, 542
Dickens, Charles, 494, 636
Diderot, Denys, on the painting of contemporary dress, 332
Dido Building Carthage, *247*
diffused light, *40*
Dihau, Desiré, 422, *423*
dilute paint, *253*, *256*, *259*
diplomacy, and Rubens, 109, 112–4, 129, 136
Disasters of War, The, 198–9
discipline in use of paint, *481*
disegno, 104
Disparates, Los, 199, 232
distance, *276*
Dix, Geertge, 156

Dogano, The, San Giorgio, 274; (detail), *245*
Doña Isabel Cobos de Porcel, 222, *223–5*
Doncieux, Camille, *see* Monet, Camille
draftsmanship, 280, *285*, 383
dragging, 19, 24, *53, 81, 361*, 383
dramatic narrative, 212, *213–7*
drapery, 124, *126*
drawing technique, *699*
drawings, 107, 154–6, 178, 244, 388, *411*, 412, 414, 415, 416, 417, *443*, 446, 464, 472, 540, 546, 568, *569, 572, 634*, 648
drawings, preparatory, *87*
Drenthe, 648
Dresden, 645
Dressage, Le, 686
dry brush, *53, 57, 299*
drypoint, 376, 416, *416*, 417
du Maurier, George, *Trilby*, 364
Dujardin, Edouard, 684
Duke of Buckingham, The, Conducted to the Temple of Virtus, 118, 132–5
Dulle Griet 65
Durand-Ruel, Paul (art dealer), 282–3, 499, *500*, 514, 522, 528, *537*, 544, 546, 548, 554, *555*, 564, 568, 572, 588
Duranty, Edmond, 430, 438
Dürer, Albrecht, 78, 106
Duret, Théodore, *353*,
  friend and patron, 282
Dutch painting(s), 242–3, 250, *251*, 376, 637

E

early pictures, 452, 453, 468, 474
ébauche, 333
Ecole des Beaux Arts, 323, 680
Edinburgh Earl of, 266
Edinburgh National Gallery, 54
Egremont, Earl of, 266
Egyptian art, 594, *595, 614*
"electric crayon", 416, *416*
Elgin marbles, *628*
Elles, 714
ellipse, 250
Elsheimer, Adam 151
Embroidered Curtain, The, 372
emotionalism, 452, *454*
Emperaire, Achille, 464, *465–7*
engravings, 62, 63, 64, *65*, 67, *70*, 412, 416, 638
England, 495, 633, 637
Englishman, Warrener at the Moulin Rouge, The (lithograph), *681*, 681, 682, 684
Entombment, The, 24, 42, 43–5, *110, 111*
enveloppe, 514, 528, *530*
equestrian subjects, *679*, 679
Erasmus, In Praise of Folly, 64
eroticism, *114, 115*, 117, *125*, 128, *323*
esquisse (preliminary sketch), 495, 496
etchings, 154, 194, *197*, 197–8, 198–9, *199*, 199, 208, 232, 286, 308, 369, 370, *372*, 416, *416*, 417, 427
  techniques, 364
Etretat, 522, *523–7*
European nobility, portraiture of 20
Evening Star, The, 262–5, 274
Execution of Maximilian, The, 327
Exhibitions, 370
Expressionism, 641, *641*, 643–5, 656, 672, *673*
Expressionists, 626

F

faces, *126*
Fall of an Avalanche in the Grisons, The, 254–7
Fall of the Rebel Angels, The, 64, 65, 86
Fallacies of Hope, The (poem), 241–2, 274
Falling Rocket, The, see *Nocturne in Black and Gold: the Falling Rocket*
family portraits, 117
  lost *383*
fans, decorated, 286
fantastic creatures, 64
fantasy, 385
Fantin-Latour, Henri, *366*, 420
Fauvism, 497
female nudes, 446, *447*, 546, 568, *569–71*, 580, *581–3*
Fénéon, Felix, 684, 706
Ferrara, Duke of, 22, 36
Fighting Téméraire, The, 241
figure compositions, 64
figure-painting, 472
figure, 65, 69, 90, *91, 92*, 94, *96, 97*
  foreground, 67, 86, 87
figures, 502, 506, *507*, 518, 520, 656, *657*, 686, 690
fingers, used in painting, 54, *58*
"finish", 250, 258
Fiquet, Hortense, 454, *455*, 458, 468
First World War, 497, 532
Fishermen at Sea off the Needles, 239
Flanders, 164
Flaubert, Gustave, 499
Flemish influence, 120, *122*
  see also Mannerism
Flemish mannerism, 151
Flemish 15th century works, influence of, *66*, 86
flesh-painting technique, 108, 120, *122, 123*, 124, *126*, 132, 139, 140, *142*
Flirt, The – the Englishman Warrener at the Moulin Rouge see *The Englishman Warrener at the Moulin Rouge* (litho graph)
Florence, 16
Floris, Frans, 62
Forain, Jean-Louis, *713*
Forge, The, 197
foliage, *507, 508*, 514, *515, 529*
Folies Bergère, 356, *357–61*
Fontainas, André, 620, 621, 626
Fontainbleau, forest of, 541, 542
forecasting of events, *96*
foreground(s), 296, 426, 430, 438, *439*
foreshortening, *628*
form, academic painting, 506
forms, 416, 417, 434, 442
  animal, 438, *440*
  human, *418, 443, 444*
  and movement, *418, 419*, 422, 426, 430, *431*

Four-in-Hand, The, 679
Fourment, Helena, 114, 117
Fourment, Susanna, *113*
Fournel, Victor, 694
Fragonard, Jean Honoré, 540, 546
Bathers, The, 541
frames, 368
France, 540, 637
Francken, Frans the Younger, 124
Franco-Prussian War, 420, 497–8, 544, 548
Franklin, Maud, 370
Frari chapel, 22
Frari Church, 20, 32
Frédéric Bazille at his Easel, 543
French Academy, 499, 506, 637–8
French painting, 244
French Revolution, 586
French Salon, 380
frescoes 193, 197, 212, *213–17*, 620, *622*
friends, recognized in paintings, *705*
friezes, 594, *621*, 626
fruit and vegetables in still life, 480, *481–3*
Futurism, 497
Futurists, 438

G

Gachet, Dr Theo, 672
Gad, Mette Sophie *see* Gauguin, Mette Sophie
Garden of the Asylum at St Rémy, The, 644
Gare Saint-Lazare, The, 497, 518, *519–21, 523*

Gaugin, Aline (Gaugin's mother), 586, 587
Gaugin, Clovis (Gauguin's father), 586
Gaugin, Clovis (Gauguin's son), 589, 590
Gauguin, Marie, 586
Gauguin, Mette Sophie (Gauguin's wife), 588–9, 610, 626
Gauguin, Paul, 280, 410, 411, 494, 546, 640, 641, 664, 668
as a "noble savage", 586, 589
childhood, 587
early paintings, 588
family background, 586
in Brittany, 589–92
in Peru, 586–7
in Tahiti, 586, 594
influences on, 594, 598, 602
marriage, 588–9
Van Gogh Painting Sunflowers, 640
Gautier, Théophile, 322
Mademoiselle de Maupin, 384
Geffroy, Gustave (critic), *683*, 684
Genouillère, La, 542, *545*, 548, 550, *551–3*
genre painting, *179*
Gentle Art of Making Enemies, The, (writings), 365
German Expressionism, 643–5
German Expressionists, 626
gesso ground, *71*
Gimpel, Paul, 410
Giorgione, 17, 18, 28, 54, 156, 336
Sleeping Venus, 46
The Tempest, 18, *20*
Concert Champêtre, 19
Giotto, 414
Giovane, Palma di, 23
Gipsy Madonna, The, 17, *18*
Girl Serving Beer, 352, *353–5*
Girls at the Piano, 548, 572, *573–5*
Giverny, 497, 500–3, *500, 503*, 518, 522, 528
Glasgow City Art Gallery, 372
glazes, 23, *34, 35, 38, 37, 40, 44*, 54, *57, 71*, 124, *130*, 138, *138, 139, 146, 155*, 160, *162, 165*, 168, *170*, 172, *174*, 182, *183, 184*, 201, 204, 223, 243, 245, 258, *276, 303*, 332, *379*
glazing, *692*
Gleyre, Charles, 364, 388, 396, 497, 499, 506, 541, 542, 548
Godwin, Trixie (became Whistler's wife), 370
Goenuette, Norbert, 558
Goethe, Johann Wolfgang von, 245, 274
Golden Section, *511*
Goncourt brothers, 592, 636
Goncourt, Edmond de, 410, 419, 442, 694
La Fille Elisa, 710
gouache, 286, *286*, 415, *417*
Gounod, Charles, 540
Goupil & Co., 632, 638
Goya, 325
collection of paintings, 199
continued to experiment, 200
deafness, 196
director of the Academy of Fine Arts, 197
early years, 192–3
fame and success, 194–6
as first court painter (*primo pintor de cámara del rey*), 197
graphic works, the, 197–8
illness and introspection, 196–7, 232
influences on *193*, 204
last years, 199–200
left Spain, 200
loyalty to state, 192
mature work, 192
Naked Majas, The, 46, 340
official court painter (*pinto del cámara del rey*), 196
painter to the King (*pintor del rey*), 194–5
painting methods, 201
patronage, 194–5
political conflicts, 198–9
records troubled times, 199
son, Francisco Javier, 198
study of genesis and original state of paintings, *225*
super-natural, and the, 208
tomb, *213*
worked in royal tapestry factory, 194
world of dreams, and, 192
Gozzoli, Benozzo, 438
Grain Stacks, 501, 522, *523*, 528
Grain Stacks, End of Summer, 504
Grandes Baigneuses, Les, 545, 548, 580, *581–3*
Granet, 476
graphic work, *372*
Greek art, 626
grisaille, 67, 68, *70*

ground(s), 113, *113*, 124, 155, *207*, *234*, 245, *251*, *268*, 542, 543, *545*, 550, 554, 558, 568, *569–70*, 576, 578, 641
color of, 204, 226, 229
colour varied, 201
dark, 232
warm, *200*, *201*, *210*, *220*
group portraits, *154*, 172, *173–5*
guerrilleros, 198–9
Guibert, Maurce, 694, *695*
Guibert, Yvette, 678, *682*, 698
Guiccardini, Ludovico, *Description of the Low Countries*, 62
Guild of Arquebusiers, 124
Guillaumin, Armand, 281–2, 452, 468, *470*, 588

H

Haden, Annie, 376
Haden, Deborah (Whistler's sister), 376, *379*
Haden, Seymour, 376
Hague, The, 633, 634, *634*, 648, 652
Hague School, The, *634*, 637
hair, red, 690, *692*
Halévy, Daniel, 411, 419
Halévy, Ludovic, 411, 435
half-tones, *650*, 668
half-tones, not used, 322, *329*
hands, 684, 694, *696*, *713*
Hannibal Crossing the Alps, 254
Hanson, A. C., *Manet and The Modern Tradition*, 332
Haras-du-Pin, 417, 438
Harmony in Blue and Gold: the Peacock Room, *369*
Harmony in Flesh Colour and Red (formerly *Symphony in Red*), 388, *389–91*
Harmony in Green and Rose: the Music Room, 376, *377–9*
Harmony in Grey and Green: Miss Cicely Alexander, 384, 396, *397–9*
Harvesters, The, *285*
hatching, *162*, *183*, 285, 286, *306*, *611*, *627*, *628*, *687*
Havemeyer, Mrs, 426
Hayet, Louis, colour wheel, 287, *289*
Heemskerck, Maerten van 62–3
Helena Fourment and her Children, 116, 117
Helena Fourment as Venus, *114*, *115*, *117*
Henry, Charles, 287
hessian (sackcloth), 593, *621*, *624*, 641
Het Pelsken, *114*, *115*, *117*
Heyden, Pieter van der, *Big Fish Eat Little Fish*, *66*
Hiffernan, Jo, 365, *365*, 380, 381–3
high viewpoint, *309*
High Baroque, 153, 164
highlights, 71, *85*, *101*, 151, 160, *162*, *166*, 178, 217, *234*, 284, 316, *317*, *318*, *428*, *435*, 446, 506, 550, 551, 558, *562*, *578*, *582*, *618*, *649*, *650*
Hiroshige, 400
Hisaka in the Sayo Mountains, *327*
historical paintings, *327*
history paintings, 413, 426, 442
Hoar Frost, the Old Road to Ennery, Pontoise, *284*, *293*
Hogarth, William, *Marriage à la Mode*, 64
Hokusai, 604
Temma Bridge at Osaka, *639*
Waterfall of Roben, *594*
Holbein, Hans, *Dance of Death*, 106
Holland, 150, 172, 186, 633, 637, 648, 668
Honthorst, Gerrit van, *Christ before the High Priest*, 151, *153*
Hoogstraten, Samuel van, 172
horizontals, *293*, *309*
Hoschedé, Alice (Monet's second wife), 499, 500, 502, 503, 532
Hoschedé, Blanche, *500*, *502*, 503, 532
Hoschedé, Ernest, 499, 500–2
Hoschedé, Germaine, 503
Hoschedé, Suzanne, *499*
Hospital Garden at St Rémy, *641*
Houbraken, Arnold, 157
House of the Hanged Man, The, *461*
household utensils in still life, 480
Hugo, Victor, 322, 499, *589*, 636
Humanism, 16
humour, 208, *209*
Hunters in the Snow, The, 90
Huygens, Constantijn, 152
Huys, Pieter, 64
Huysmans, Joris Karl (critic), 304, 356, 442, *444*, 446, *447*, 598

I

Ignudo, *106*
imagery, *199*
imagination, 392
imagination, creations of *197*
impasto, 23, *48*, 54, 124, *130*, 136, *138*, *142*, 144, *146*, 151, *155*, 160, *161*, *162*, 164, *165*, *170*, *174*, *176*, 182, *184*, *201*, *207*, *220*, *222*, *225*, 245, *245*, *260*, *268*, *272*, *273*, *276*, 283, 285, 288, 296, *299*, *306*, *313*, *315*, 316, *318*, *354*, *358*, 400, *402*, *417*, *466*, 497, 516, 518, 532, *534*, *582*, 641, *641*
Impression, Sunrise, 494, *504*, 510, *511–13*, 514
Impressionism, 244, *247*, 683
Impressionist Exhibition (1874), 283–4
Impressionist Exhibition (1882), 304
Impressionist Exhibitions, *461*, 494, 499–500, 510, 518, 590, 598
Impressionists, 155, 322, 328, 348, *349*, 413, 414, 417, 420, 422, 430, *444*, 447, 453–4, 461, 468, 494–5, 498, 499, 510, 514, 540, 542, 543, 544, *544*, 545, 546, 547, 548, 550, 554, *555*, 558, *565*, 568, *569*, 572, 580, 588, 590, 593, 598, *599*, *603*
Impressionists(ism), 282, 283–5, 292, 312, *637*, 638–40

improvisation, 404
In the Orchestra Pit, 420, 422, *423–5*, 430
India, 594
informality, *33*
Ingres, Jean Auguste Dominique, 376, 380, 384, 388, 412, 414, 415, 420, 546, 568
Gatteaux Family, The, 411
Odalisques, 340
innovations, *401*
Inquisition, the, *193*
Inquisition Tribunal, 193
interiors, dim, *713*
Intimate Journals, 610, 616, 626
Interior at Petworth, 266–9
interior design, 368
International Society of Sculptors, Painters and Gravers, 370, 372
insight, in religious works, 24
inventions, formal, *401*
Israels, Josef, 637
Italian influence, 82, 106, 107, 120, *121, 125*, 241, 243, *246*, 258
Italianate composition/style, 62, 63, 68
Italy, 164, 412, 413, 546, 548, 564, *565*, 568
ivory, painting on, 63, 82

J

Jane Avril Dancing, 687, 698, *699–701*
Japan, 400
Japanese art, *594, 595, 599*, 602, *604*, 606, *608*, 626, *638, 639*, 660, 664, *681, 683*, 683
Japanese prints, 327, 336, 365, *412, 413*, 414, 422, *431, 495*, 496, 503, 506
Javanese art, 594
Jepthah's Daughter, 413
Jeremiah Lamenting the Destruction of Jerusalem, 160, *161–3*
Jewish Bride, The, 157
Jockeys at Epsom, 438
Jones, George, Turner
Lying in State in his Gallery, 247
Jonghelinck, Niclaes, 69, 82, 87
Jongkind, Johan Barthold, 497, 522, 541, 588, 598
Jourdain, Francis, 714
Jourdan, Lucy, 714
Joyant, Maurice, 706
Judgement of Paris, The, 106, 107, *120–3*

K

key figures, small, 86
Keyser, Willem de, 152
Kitchen Gardens in Montmartre, 652, *653–5*
Kitchen Garden with Trees in Flower, Pontoise, 285
Kiyonaga, woodcuts, 388
knife painting, 245, *257*, 266

L

labouring class, *197*
La Donna Nuda see The Venus of Urbino
Lafond, Pierre, 410
Laisnay, Thérèse, 586
Lamothe, Louis, *411*, 412, 420
Lampsonius, Domenico, 62, 86, 98
Land of Cockaigne, The, 90
landscape artists, British, 283
Landscape with Trees, 157
Landscape with the Fall of Icarus, 65, 75, 86
Landscape with the Flight into Egypt, 68
landscapes, 17, 54, *65*, 68, 69, 82, *83–5*, 90, 117, *122*, 144, *145*, 154, 238, 239, *242*, 243, 284, *284*, 285, 308, 414, 417, *419*, 420, *440*, 456,–8, 461, 476, *477–9*, 484, *485–7*, 540, *541*, 542, *544*, 546, 550, 564, 568, 580, 637, 652, 656, *669*, 673
and figures combined, 69, *87*
and poetry, 241
composition, 63
imaginary, *282*
innovatory, *21*
Patinir, *64*
Mediterranean, 458, 461
sketches, 63
symbolic, *337*
Lane, Sir Hugh, 564
Language, Tahitian, 610
Laocoön, 21, 24, 37, 109, *109*, 112
Lara, Isadore de, *Messaline*, 685–6, *686*
Large Landscapes, The (engravings), *65*
Lastman, Peter, 150–1
Juno Discovering Jupiter with Io, 152
Latouche, Gaston, *357*
Laurent, Méry, *357, 361*
Lautrec, Henri de Toulouse
alcoholism, 684, 686, *686*, 706, 714
commenting on the social system, *682*, 684–5
death, 678, 686
early life, 678–9
early style, 687
early training, 679–81
education, 678
formation of mature style, 680
influences on, 679–80, 681, *681*, 683–4, 690, *691*, 694, 710
in context, 684–5
new themes and last years, 685–6
painting methods, 687
rebellion against conservatism, *692*
rejected academicism, 683
residence in brothels, 702
Laval, Charles, *591*
Leclerq, Paul (poet), 706, *707–9*
Legrand, Alphonse, 554
Legrand, Marguerite, 558
Legrand, Ninette, 554
Le Havre, 497, 510, 514, 518, 522
Leenhoff, Suzanne, 324, 340
Leroy, Louis, 499–500, 554
les Lavandières, 587
Les Vingts, Brussels, 684
lesbianism, 714
Lévy frères, 548

Leyden, 150
Leyden, University of, 150
Leyland, Sir Francis, 367, 392
Liber Studiorum, 270, 271
Lievens, Jan, 152, 156
light, *16, 28, 83*, 90, *105, 111, 134, 138, 146*, 204, *234*, 245, 270, 283, 292, *295, 306*, 322, 325, *329*, 329, 336, 348, *365, 377*, 414, 417, 426, *435, 436, 566*
  and colour, 244–6, *247*, 258, *267, 268*
  artificial, *195*, 222, 414, 422, 434, *705*
  chiaroscuro, 151, *151*
  footlights, 426, *428*
  Impressionists, 414, 417, 422, 540, 550, 568
  luminosity, 543, 550, 554, 564, 576
  stage lighting, *121*
  symbolism, 178
light effects, *85*
  contrasting, *77*
light sources, 67
Ligne-Arenberg, Margaret de, 106
Limoges, 540, 548
Lima, 586–7
line, *411*, 414, 415, 416, 446
  contour, 422, *432, 438*, 550, *555*, 564, 568
linear hatching, 684
linear structure, *705*
literature, 636, 664
literature, role in paintings, 241–2
lithographs, 199, 200, 472, *681*, 684, *700*, 714
lithography, 416, 417, 420, 634, 648
Little Bridge, The, Pontoise, 285, 300, *301–3*
Little Dancer, 418
Little White Girl see *Symphony in White No 2: The Little White Girl*
London, 282–3, 296, 297–9, 365, 510, 633
Lopez, Alphonso, 168
Lordship Lane Station, Dulwich, 282, 296, *297–9*
Los Caprichos, 197, 197–8, 208
Loubens, Madame, *334*
Louis Napoleon, 586
Louveciennes, 518
Loüy, Pierre, *Aphrodite*, 710
Lucie Bellanger, 685, 687
luminosity *71*, 286, 297–9, *354, 707, 708*
Luzán y Martinez, José, 193

M

machine, 376
Madame Cézanne in a Red Armchair, 455
Madame Poupoule at her Toilet, 707, 710, *711–13*
majaism, 204, 222, *223–5*
Mallarmé, Stéphane, 324, 340, 572, *573*, 616, 621
Man with a Blue Sleeve, 24, 28, *29–31*
Manao Tupapau: The Spirit of the Dead Keeps Watch, 596, 610, *611–15*, 616, *617*
Mandyn, Jan, 64
Manet, Edouard, 226, 283, 284, 292, 376, 413, 430, *438, 440*, 502, 506, 540, 542, *544*, 548, 588, 594
  arranged own showings, 328
  association with Monet, 348
  Chevalier of the Légion d'Honneur, 328
  Déjeuner sur l'Herbe, 282, 292, *365*, 506
  described, 324
  entered studio of Thomas Couture, 323
  Fife-player, The, 554, *555*
  illness and premature death, 328
  influences on *324*, 325–6, 327, 336, *341, 349*
  marriage, 324, 340
  Olympia, 46, 506
  painting methods, 329
  and Parisian café life, 356
  technique, 322
  working outdoors, 348
Manet, Eugène, *338*
Manet, Gustave, *338*
"Manet's Band," 328
mannerism, *55*, 67, 104, *105*, 106, 120, *121*, 151, *385*
Mantua, 107
  Duke of, 42
Maoris, *617*
Marguerite Degas in Confirmation Dress, 411
Market, The, see *Ta Matete: The Market*
Marquesas Islands, 586
Martinique, 586, 590
Mary Cassatt at the Louvre, 416
Massacre of the Innocents, The, 70, 94
mathematical perspective, 326
Matisse, Henri, 285, 460
  La Danse, 390
Maupassant, Guy de 356, 499, 522
Medici, Marie de', 107, 114, 128
Melbye, Anton, 280, 282
Melbye, Fritz, 280
Memling, Hans, *64*
Memorizing of experience, 400
Mengs, Antonio-Raphael, 194
Mennonites, *179*
Mercure, 620
Messalina Seated on Her Throne, 686
Messina, Antonella da, 16
metaphors, use of, *227*
Meurent, Victorine, 340, *341–3*
Michelangelo, 19, *106, 107, 125*, 410, 411, 460, 472, 568
  Ignudo, 107, *107, 108, 109*
  Leda and the Swan, 50, *125*
  The Punishment of Haman, 21
  The Mocking of Christ, 24, 24
Michelet, Jean, 636
Militia Company of Arquebusiers, 172
Milkmaid of Bordeaux, The, 200
Millais, John Everett, 365, 366, 380
  Autumn Leaves, 367
Millet, Jean François, 90, *91*, 281, 286, 304, 638
  The Angelus, 633
miniatures on ivory, 200
Miracle of St Anthony, A, 201, 212, *213–17*

Miserables, Les, 589
Misfortunes of the City of Oreléans, The, 413, 438
Miss Cicely Alexander see *Harmony in Grey and Green: Miss Cicley Alexander*
Miss Lala at the Circus, 420, 442, *443–5*
mixed-media sculpture, 416, *418*
Mme Charpentier and her Children, 546, 547, 548
Mme Pissarro Sewing Near a Window, 283
modelling, *161*, 164, *166*, 172, *176*, 182, *183*, *184*, 506, *556*, 564, 606, *608*, *618*, 626, *627*, *628*
modello, 113, *113*, 124
models, posing of, 323
modern art, 322
modern movement, 638
Moerenhut, *Voyage to the Isles of the Great Ocean,* 610
monde and *demi-monde*, 678
Monet, Camille, (Monet's first wife), 38, 348, 350, 354, 497–9, 499, 500, 506
Monet, Claude, 280, 281–2, 283, 284–5, 292, 308, 312, *313*, 348, *349*, *394*, 410, 458, *469*, 540, 541, 542, *543*, 544, 546, 547, 548, 550, 568, 588, 638
  at Giverny, 500–3, *503*
  character, 494, 502–3
  death, 503
  early life, 497–8
  Evening at Argenteuil, 637
  failing eyesight, 503, 532, 533
  Grenouillère, La, 542, 550, *551*, *552*
  Hyde Park, 297
  Impression, Sunrise, 554
  influences, 510
  painting methods, 496–7, 501, *501*
  struggle to record nature, 495–6
  Westminster Bridge, 598, *600*
Monet, Jean, (Monet's son), 348, *350*, 497, 498, 503, 532
Monet, Michel, 500
monarchy, 104
monochrome, *432*, *435*, *440*, *622*, *624*
monochrome painting, 341
  see also grisaille
monotype, 415, 416, 417, *417*, *419*, 420, 426, *427*, 434, *435*
Monro, Dr, 238
Monsieur Delaporte at the Jardin de Paris, 680
Mont Sainte-Victoire, 456, 457
Mont Sainte-Victoire, 484, 485–7
Montfried, Daniel de, 616, 620, 626
Months, 62, 68–7, 69, *87*, 90, 94, *95*
Montmartre, 558, *559*, 652, *680*, 681–3
Moore, Albert, *365*, *366*, 388
  Beads, 367
Moore, George, 435, 446, 702
Moreau, Gustave, 419
Morice, Charles, 586, 620, 626
Morisot, Berthe, 348, 544
Morning at Etretat, 501, 526
Morning Call, The, see *Harmony in Green and Rose: the Music Room*
Morning with Willows, 532–3, *533–7*
mosaics, 17
"motif," 457, 458, 460, 461, 484
motto (*impressa*), 24
Moulin Rouge, 682, *700*
Mountains in Provence, 461, 476, *477–9*
movement, 36, 68, 69, *87*, *89*, *91*, 117, 226, 295, 680, 690, *699*
Munch, Edvard, 643, 656
  Dream Self-portrait, 642
Munich, 645
Murder, The, 452, 454
Murer, Eugène (patron), 308
Mürger, Henri, *La Vie de Bohème*, 364
musculature, *106*, 109, 120, *125*
music, 616
Music in the Tuileries Gardens, 325, 326, *329*, 332, *333–5*
musical associations, 364, 367, *381*, 384, 388, *389*
Muybridge, Eadweard, 438
  Horse in Motion, 439
mythological paintings, 24, *25*, 36, *37–41*, 50, *51–3*, 54, *55–9*. *See also poesie*

N

Nabis group, 706, 710
Nadar, *555*
Nadar, Felix, 499
Naked Majas, The, 196
Naples, 151
narrative paintings, 164, *173*, *435*
Nativity, 178
Natanson, Alexandre, 706, 710
Natanson, Misia, 548, *576*, *577–9*
Natanson, Thadée, 706, 710, 714
natural disasters, 241, *243*, 250, 254
naturalism, 16, *333*, 356, *413*, 426, *432*, 590–2, 602, 626, 684–5, 702, 710
"naturalistic quadrille", 683, 698
nature, 62, 239, *402*, 454, 461
  as background only, *679*
  painting directly from, 244, 245, *245*
nature, and Rubens, 104
nature, interpretation of, 322
negative space, value of, *703*
Neo-Grecian school, 388
Neo-Impressionism, 684
  limitations of 287
Neo-Impressionists, 280, 286–7, 308
Netherlandish Proverbs, The, 65, *68*, *75*, 78
Netherlands
  hostility towards ideas of Philip II, 69–70
  landscape painting tradition, 63
  troubled state of, 66
Neunen, 634, 648
Nevermore, *583*, 584, 616, *617–9*
Newton, Sir Isaac, 244
Night Café, 656, *657–9*
Night Watch, The, 154, 172, *173–7*, 178
Nizon, 602
Noa Noa, 610, 616
Nocturne in Black and Gold: the Falling Rocket, 400, *401–3*
  court case concerning, 368–9, 400
Nocturne in Blue and Green: Chelsea, 392, *393–5*

Norham Castle, Sunrise, (detail), *270–3*, *245*
Norham Castle, on the Tweed, Summer's Morn, 270, *271*
Normandy, 497, 522
Noort, Adam van, 106
Nude Study, *569*
nudes, 46, *47*, *107*, 128, *323*, 336, *337–9*, *338*, 340, *341–3*, 459, 460, 472, *473–5*
Numbering at Bethlehem, The, 70, 94, *95–7*
Nymphéas (Waterlilies), 496, 503, 522, 532, *537*

O

observation of nature, 244
octagonal composition, *275*
Old Masters, 412, 414, 419, *424*, 438, 446, *448*, 540, 541, 545, 546, 568, *569*
oil on plaster, 232
oil paint, Venetian use of, 16
oil painting,
  unconventional techniques, *245*, *268*, *272*, *276*
  and watercolour, 270
oil paintings, 308
oil sketches, 182
  see also sketches
old age, portrayal of, 160
Old Musician, The, *325*
Old Testament, 182
Olympia, 326, *329*, *334*, 340, *341–3*, 352, 356
On the Beach, *417*
open-air painting, 497, 541, 542, *545*, 546, 550, *653*
open-air subjects, 454, 460
Orange, Prince of, 152
Orangerie, Paris, 503, 533
Oriental art, 384
Orléans, 587
Ortelius, Abraham, 62, 67, *70*
outdoor (*plein-air*) painting, 243, *245*, 414, 417, 438
outlines, 602, *604*, *608*, *665*
outlining, *77*, *101*, *318*
overpainting, *215*, *234*, *512*, *520*, *526*, *530*, 532, 533
  white, *217*

P

paint, dilute, *220*
painting *en plein air*, 348
painting, role of, 322
painting, structure of, 296, 304
painting from nature (*en plein air*), 283, 312
painting technique, change in, 69
paintings
  commemorating the uprising, 198
  disseminating royal authority, 218, *219–21*
  restricted, 234
paints, preparation, *245*
palette, 69, 98, 155, *155*, 186, 195, 289, 296, *303*, *318*, *329*, 348, *349*, *350*, 371, 396, *461*, *501*, *516*, 540, *541*, *545*, 547, 550, 554, *555*, *569*, 580, *593*, *641*, 683, 687
  lightening of, 454
  lighter and clearer, 285
  limited (oils), 54, 461
  Monet, *297*
  restrained, 95
  restricted, 234
  subtlety of 90
palette knives, 182, 285, 286, 292, *295*, *301*, *303*, *541*, 542, 593, 626
Palma Vecchio, 158
Palomino, Treatise on Spanish painting, 212
panel-painting, 124
  see also wooden panels
paper,
  commercially prepared, *477*
  primed, *461*
Parable of the Blind, The, 69
Paris, 370, 430, 497–9, 500, 542, *544*, 548, 550, *551*, 558, 576, *577*, 586, 588, 590, 633, 638, 643, 652, 660
Paris Commune, 544, 548
  overthrow of, 286
Paris Salon, 326, 328, 330, 356, 364
Paris Opéra, 422, *423*, 426
Parisian café life, 352, 356
Parott, S. W., *Turner on Varnishing Day*, *239*
Parthenon frieze, 438, 594, 626
Passage of the St Gotthard, The, *241*
pastel(s), *414*, 415, 416, 417, *417*, *419*, 420, *424*, 426, *427*, *428*, 434, *435*, *436*, 438, *440*, *446*, *447*, *448*, *499*, *684*
patent easel, 288, *289*
Patinir, Joachim, 63, *65*
  The Flight into Egypt, *64*
Paul III, Pope, 22
Pea Pickers, The, *286*
Peace: Burial at Sea, *274–7*; (detail), *245*
Peach Trees in Blossom, *641*
Peacock Room, 368, *369*
Peasant Dance, *99*
Peasant head, *634*, *650*
peasant life themes, 304
peasant subjects, 69, *71*, 90, 98, *99*, *99–101*
peasant types,
  Caravaggio, *111*
Peasant Wedding, A, 69, *71*, 98, *99–101*
peasant-girl studies, 285, 287, 304, 305–7
peasant women, *286*
peasants, 638, 648, *649*, 652, 660
peinture à l'essence, *417*
peinture claire, 348, 506
pen and ink drawing, *65*
Pennell, Joseph and Elizabeth (Whistler's biographers), 396
pentimenti ("ghost" images) 101, 352
people, 192
perceptive observation, 78, *89*, *96*
personality analysis, 678
perspective, 416, *439*, *537*, 544, 550, 558, 564, *581*, *599*, 602, 643, *654*, 656, *658*, 661, *673*
  Japanese prints, 422, *431*
perspective, theory of, rejected by Manet, 326
Peru, 586–7
Pesaro family, 32
Pesaro Altarpiece, The, 20, *23*, 32
Pesaro, Jacopo, Bishop of Paphos, 32, *33*

Petit, Georges, 546, 568
Philip II of Spain, 24, 50, 54
Philip III, King of Spain, 109
photographs, as *aide-memoire*, 694, *695*, *696*
photography, 327, 336, 422, 438, *439*, 542, 544, *544*
Picabia, Francis, 285
Picasso, Pablo, 497, 460
  Duchess of Alba, 195
pientre á l'essence see thinned paint
Pietà, 24
Piette, Ludovic, 296
Pieve de Cadore, 17
pigments, 71
Piles, Roger de, 109, 112
Pink Peonies, 283
Piombo, Sebastiano del, 17
Pissarro, Camille, 420, 452, 454, 468, 496, 540, 542, 544, 546, 548, *587*, 588, *588*, 589, 598, *599*, *600*, 638, 640, 643
  attention to detail, *298*
  death, 288
  Diligence at Louveceinnes, 588
  early life, 280–1
  Edge of the Village, The, 456
  eye infection, 288, 312, *313*
  final years, 288
  fled to Belgium, 288
  friend and teacher, 285–6
  honesty of drawing, 281, 286, *298*
  and the Impressionists 283–5
  influences on, 281, *282*, *283*, 283, *284*, 284–5, 286, 292, 300
  London, 282–3
  new themes and Neo-Impressionism, 286–7
  painting methods, 289
  Paris and new influences, 281–2
  political beliefs, 280, 282, 286, 288
  pupil of Corot, 281
  ruin of many early works, 283
  Sunshine at Rouen, 636
Pissarro, Lucien (son), 280, 282, *288*, 292, 300, 308
Plage du Pouldu, La, 595
plein air (open-air) painting, 497, 598
plein-air technique, 376, 404
Plutarch, 106
pochade(s) (sketch), 404, 510
Poe, Edgar Allen, 616
poesie, 24, 36, 50, 54
poetry, 241–2, 254, 274
Pointillism, 640, 652, *654*, 683,
Poissy, 500
Pont Aven, 590, 592, 602, 606
Pont des Arts, The, 542, *544*
Pont d'lena, 598, *599–601*
Pontoise, 453
Pope Paul III and his Grandsons, 24
Poplars, 522
Poplars on the Banks of the Epte, 504, 528, *529–31*
Porcellis, 158
Portrait of Achille Emperaire, 452, 464, *465–7*
Portrait of the Artist's Son (c 1884), *455*
Portrait of the Artist's Mother, 370
Portrait of Emile Zola, 344, *345–7*
Portrait of Louis-Auguste Cézanne, Father of the Artist, 453
Portrait of Misia, 576, *577–9*
Portrait of Paul Leclerq, 706, *707–9*
Portrait of Van Gogh, 684
portraits, 20, 24, *104*, 117, 150, 152, 157, 194, 196, 198, *200*, 222, *223–5*, 304, *305–7*, 348, 367–8, 368, 370, 371, 372, 396, *397–9*, *411*, 413, *413*, 416, 434, 442, *455*, 461, 464, *465–7*, 468, *469–71*, 546, 547, 680, *687*, 690, 694, *695–7*, 698, *699*, 706, *707–9*, 710, *711–3*, 714, *715–7*
  group portraits, *154*, 172, *173–7*
  portrait genre works, 422, *423*, 430
  royal, 218, *219–21*
  self-portraits, 151–2, 154, 157, 168, *169–71*, *176*, 186, *187–9*, *410*, *540*, 660, *661*, 664, 665–7
portraiture, 28
positivism, 590
Post-Impressionism, 640, 643
Post-Impressionist ideas, 680–1
poster designs, *681*, 682, 684, 686, 698
Pot of Flowers and Fruit, 480, *481–3*
Potato Eaters, The, *634*, 648, *649–51*
Poussin, Nicholas, 460, 472
  The Deluge, 243
pre-Raphaelites, 364
priming, 113, 124, 132, 543, 545, 550, 554, 564, *566*, 580, 641
  canvases, 501
priming, white gesso, *55*
Primitivism, 595
Princesse du Pays de Porcelaine, La, *369*
Princeteau, Rene, *679*, 679, 680
prints, *372*
private patrons, 192
Procession to Calvary, The, 67, *71*, 86, *87–9*, 94
prophets, 150, 160
prostitutes, 687–717, *passim*
prostitution, 19th century attitudes, 702
Protestanstin, 633
Proudhon, P-J, 286
Proust, Antonin, 323, 324, *337*
Provence, 456, 457, 476, *477–9*, 484, *485–7*
proverbs, 64, 68, 69
Puget, 476
Puvis de Chavannes, Pierre, 594, 606, 620, 628
  The Poor Fisherman, 592

Q

Quays at Rouen, The, 288, 308, *309–11*

R

railway stations, 518, *519–21*
railway viadict, Aix, 457
Raimondi, Marcantonio, 106, 120, *121*
  engraving after Raphael, *The Judgement of Paris*, *121*, 336, *337*

The Rape of the Sabine Women, 117, *140–3*; (detail), *113*
Raphael, 36, 106, 109, 111, 156, *246*, *338*, 568
cartoons, 68
The Judgement of Paris, 120, *121*
realism, 28, 42, 250, *251*, 304, 365, 380, 464, 468, 592, 616, 636–7, 668, 684
realism, Caravaggio, *111*
Realist movement, 244, 364–5, 637–8
receding parallels, 296
recession, 298, *301*, 312, *315*
recessive colours, *316*
Red Rock, The, *461*, 488, *489–91*
rederijker kamers, 75
reed pens, *157*, *638*
reflection, use of, *383*
reflections, *303*, 312, *313*, *315*
Regatta at Argenteuil, *495*, *498*
religion, 104, 105, 602, 610, 632, 633–4, *633*, 636, 638, 648, 664
religious paintings/themes, 16, 20, 24, 42, *43–5*, 50, 64, 65, 66–7, 67–8, 69, 70, 82, *83–5*, 86, 94, *95–7*, 194, 195, *201*, 212, *213–17*
religious tolerance, 68
Rembrandt, 24, *51*, 117, 144, *193*, 194, 240, 266, 316, *368*, 637, *650*, 664
chiaroscuro, 151, *151*
early life, 150–2
influences on, 151, *153*, 168, *169*
last years, 156–7
marriage, 153
painting methods, 151, 155
self-portrait, *29*
Rembrandt, Titus (Rembrandt's son), 153, 156, 157
Renaissance, 168, *176*, 546, *569*
Renoir, Claude and Pierre, 546, *547*, 548
Renoir, Edmond, 558
Renoir, Jean, 546, 547, 548, 576, 580
Renoir, Léonard, 540, 548
Renoir, Pierre Auguste, 282, 283, 304, 308, 322, 324, 348, *349*, 410, *427*, 430, *432*, 446, *474*, 496, 497, 498, 588, 638
background and early life, 540
influences on, 540, 541, *541*, 542, 544, *544*, 545, 546, 547
on Pissarro, 287
painting methods, 542, 543, *543*, 545, *545*, 547, 554
patronage, 544
porcelain painter, 540, 541, 545, 547, 548
"sour period," 568
theory of "irregularism," 568, *569*
Repas Champêtre, Le, 286
restoration, *234*
Revue Blance, La, 685, 706
Reynolds, Sir Joshua, 242, 270
Rhine, river, 150
rhythms of nature, 488
Richmond, W. B., 430
Rickox, Nicholas, 124
Rijn, Harman van (Rembrandt's father), 150
River Thames, 262
Rivers of England, 270, 271
Rivière, Henri, 416
Rivoire, André, (poet), 706
Road with Cypress and Star, *641*, 668, *669–71*
Romance of the Rose, The, (allegorical poem) *66*
Romantic artists, 415, 438
Romantic movement, 239
Rome, 16, 21–2, 151
Rome from the Vatican, 246, 258
Rood, Ogden, 287
colour wheel, *289*
Rossetti, Dante Gabriel, 365, 380, 400
Rossetti, William (critic), 400
Rota, Martino, engraving after Titian's *The Death of St Peter Martyr*, *21*
Rothenstein, William, 714
Rouart, Denis, 411, *448*
Rouen, 518, 589
Rouen Cathedral, 494
Roujon, Henri, 572
Roussel, Ker-Xavier, 503
Royal Academy, *239*, 242, 250, 364, 380
Royal Bounty Overcoming Avarice (sketch for), *108*
royal commissions, 194
Rubens, 71
Christ Giving the Keys to St Peter, 70
Rubens, Jan 105–6
Rubens, Sir Peter Paul, 153, 164, 472
Apotheosis of Henri IV, The, *460*
artistic training, 106
as collector, 111–12
as court painter, 107–11
as diplomat, 109, 112–14, 136
early life, 105–6
influences on, 109, 117, 120, 125, 136
marriage, 111
working methods, 112
Rue Montorgeuil: Fête Nationale, *496*, *497*, *501*
rue Mosnier series, *349*
Ruisdael, Jacob van *83*
rural scenes, 292, 308
Ruskin, John, (art critic). 240, 258, 274, 368–9, 400
Ruytenburch, Willem van, 172

S

sackcloth *see* hessian
sacra conversazione, 32
Saint Lazare station, 518, *519–21*
Salon, 413, 414, 499, 506, *541*, 542, 544, 546, 548, 598
alternative to, 283
Salon at the Rue des Moulins, The, 702, *703–5*
Salon des Indépendants, 690
Salon des Refusés, 282, 499, 506
Samson and Delilah, *124–7*; detail, *113*
Sand, George, 499
sarcophagus, 42, *43*
Sargent, John Singer, *Monet Painting on the Ede of a Wood*, 500
Sargent, William, 379
Saskia Lying in Bed, *157*

satire, 198
Saturn Eating his Children, 199
Scale, 522, 533
Scholl, Aurélien, *334*
"School of David", 680
Schopenhauer, Artur, 610
Schuffenecker, Emile, 587–8, 590, 592
science, 244–5
scratching, 160, *162*, 164, *166*, 182, 186
sculpture, *618*
  influence on Rubens, 112, 120
scumble, 315
scumbling, 24, *53*, 113, 144, 168, *217*, 245, 332, *379*
Sea at Fecamp, The, 526
seascapes, 239, 243, 250, *251*
Second of May, The, 198
secular paintings, 16–17, 18
Seghers, Hercules, 156
Seine Banks at Argenteuil, The, 348, 349–51
Seine, river, 496, 500, 502, 514
Seine at Porte-Villez, The: Winter, Snow, 498
Self-portrait, Turner, *238*
Self-portrait (detail), Rubens, *104*
Self-portrait, Titian (c. 1565–70), *16*
Self-portrait, Rembrandt (c. 1629) 151–2, *151*
Self-portrait, Rembrandt, (1640), *150*, 154, 168, *169–71*, 186
Self-portrait, Cézanne (c 1872), 452, 468, *469–71*
Self-portrait, Pissarro, (1873), 280
Self-portrait, Gauguin, (1893–94), *586*
Self-portrait, Pissarro, (1903), 288, 316, *317–19*
Self-portrait after Tintoretto, Manet, 323
Self-portrait with Bandaged Ear, Van Gogh, 664, *665–7*
Self-portrait with Candles, Goya, *195*
Self-portrait with Maulstick, Palette and Brushes, Rembrandt, 186, *187–9*
Self-portrait, Renoir, *540, 632*
Self-portrait, Degas, *410*
Self-portrait with Saskia, Rembrandt, *156*
self-portraits, *104*, 117, 151–2, 154, 157, 168, *176*, 186, *195, 201*, 238, *280,* 283, 288, 316, *317–19*, 364, *368, 373, 410,* 452, 468, *469–71*, 632, 660, *661*, 664, *665–9*
self-scrutiny, 468, *469*
Semiramis constructing a City, 413
Seneca, 106
sensuality, 24, 36, 42, 46, *58*, 352
series paintings, 518, 522, 528, 532–3
  colours, 506, *508*
Sert, José Maria, 576, *577*
Sérusier, Paul, *The Talisman, 592*
Seurat, Georges Pierre, 287, *289*, 590, 640, 652, *654*
  Bathing, Asnières, 639
  Poseuses, 388
Seven Vices, The, 64, *66, 75*
Seven Virtues, The, 64
sfumato, 181
  technique, 18–19
shading, *411*, *650*, 652
shadows, *77, 81*, 90, 182, *234, 284*, 286, 292, *295, 306, 309, 310*, 312, *412, 417, 432, 436, 446, 478, 482*, 484, 545, 554, *556*, *566*, 572, *578*
  chiaroscuro, *151*, 160
  portraits, 186
  rejection of, 602, *618*
Shady Walk, A, 503
Shelley, Percy Bysshe, 242
Shepherdess, The, 287, 304, *305–7*
Shipwreck, The, 250–3
Shop with a Balcony, A, 370
Sickert, Walter Richard, 404, 415, 533
Signac, Paul, 590
signatures, 528
silhouettes, *259, 276*
Sisley, Alfred, 497, 540, 541, 542, 544, 546, 548, 588
Sisley, Pierre, 503
Six Projects, 388
sizing, 71
sketch, *370*
sketches, 107, *108*, 109, *111*, 113, 124, 182, *247, 411*, 416, 422, 426, *432*, 442, *447, 495, 496,* 510, 550, 558, *559, 634*, 650
  oil, 244, *245, 259*, 370
skies, *599, 600*
skin tones, 186
Slavers Throwing Overboard the Dead and Dying, 241
Sleep of Reason Produces Monsters, The, 197
Snow Storm: Hannibal and his Army Crossing the Alps, 244
Société Anonyme des Artistes, Peintres, Sculptures et Graveurs, 283, 499–500
Solimena, Francesco, 193
socialism, 632, 634
Sorrowing Old Man, 635
space, 292, 376, *377*
  illusion of, 315
Spain, 109–111, 150, 172, 586
Spartali, Christine, 368
Spartan Boys and Girls Exercising, 413, 420
spatial depth, *161*, 300
spatial organization, 287
Sperling, Otto, 112
Spirit of the Dead Keeps Watch, The, see *Manao Tupapau*
spiritual comment, 74
Spontaneity, 683, 694
stained glass windows, 602, *604*
Steinlen (graphic artist), *682, 698*
Stevens, Alfred, 376
statuary *see* sculpture
Stendhal, 499
Still Learning, 200
still life, 98, *101*, 328, 338, 352, *358, 361*, 414, 459, 461, 480, *481–3, 696, 717*
Still Life with Apples and Pears, 461
Still Life with Brioche, 328
Still Life with Horse's Head, 626
Still Life with Portrait of Charles Laval, 591
Striations
  linear, 683
  vertical, *707, 708*

Stock (cartoonist), 464
Stoffels, Hendrickje, 156, 157, 182
Stoics, 106
Stradamus, 144
St Rémy, 637, 643, 664, 668, 672
St Thomas, Virgin Islands, 280
studies, *417*, *436*, *634*, *650*
Stylization, *385*, *386*
subject matter, disturbing 196
Sublime, the, 239, 254
Sunflowers, *642*
surface treatment, variety in, 254
Surrealism, 497
Suzanne, *499*
Swanenburgh, Jacob van, 150
Swinburne, Algernon (poet), *Before a Mirror*, 380
Swing, The, 548
symbolism, *20*, 78, 86, 94, 98, 172, 178, *367*, 592, *592*, 610, *611*, 616, 620–1, 626, 641, 684
Symbolists, 616
symmetricality, 518, *519*
Symphony in White No 1: The White Girl, *365*, 366, 380
Symphony in White No 2: The Little White Girl, 365, 380, 381–3, *366–7*
Symphony in White No 3, 366–7
synthetism, 592, 602, 616

T

Ta Matete: The Market, 594, *596*
tache method, *498*, 501
tactile quality, 19, *53*, *55*, *58*
Tahiti, 586, 594, 610, 616. 620, *622*
Tanagra figures, 388
Tanguy, Père, 588
tapestry cartoons, *194*, 194, 195, 204, *205–7*, 232
tapestry designs, 192, 195, 226
technique, 192, *210*, 456–7, 468, 694, 717
Techniques des Vénétiens, *715*
Tehamana, 610, *611–5*, 616
tempera, 16, 164, 204
tempera painting, *285*
tempera painting on linen, 62, 63, *65*
10 o'clock Lecture, 370, 392, *393*
temperament (artist's), expressed through chosen medium, 452–3
terror, atmosphere of, 226, *227–31*
texture *77*, *89*, *126*, *129*, *137*, *138*, 151, 178, 186, 300, *303*, 528, *593*, 606, *608*, *624*, *628*, 638, *638*, 641, *649*, *650*, 684, 687, *692*, 694, *707*, *708*, 710
textured paint, 464
textures, 28, 42, 454
Thames Set, 369
The Times art critic, 396
theatre and operatta themes, 685–6
Theatrum Mundi (Theatre of the World), *75*, *78*
There is no Remedy, *199*
thin paint, 69, 71, *77*, *89*, *92*, 94
thinned paint, 683, *685*, *687*, 687, *692*, 694, *701*, *707*
Third of May 1802, The, *199*
Thomas Carlyle see *Arrangement in Grey and Black No 2: Thomas Carlyle*
Thompson, James, *The Seasons*, 241, 254
Three Bathers, 472, *473–5*
three-dimensionality, 50
Tiepolo, Giambattista, 226
Tintoretto, *51*
Tintoretto, Jacopo, 109
  Minerva and Mars, 136
Titian, 109, 111, *114*, *115*, 117, 136, *138*, 150, 155, *368*, 576
  achievement, 24
  contrast between early and late works, 23
  daughter, Lavinia, 21
  early life, 18
  early religious painting, 17
  Ecco Homo, 136
  Portrait of a Man with Blue Sleeve, 168, *169*
  elected to Florentine Academy, 22
  family, 17
  Girl in a Fur Wrap, *115*, 117
  influences on, 18, *19*, *21*, 28, *55*
  marriage, 20–1
  "painted poetry" (landscapes), 17–18
  painter of kings and princes, 21–2
  painting methods, 23
  Sacred and Profane Love, 336
  Venus of Urbino, 340, *341*
  Worship of Venus, 136
  son, Orazio, 22
  as state painter, 19–21
Tolstoy, Leo, 636
tonal changes, *77*
tonal gradation, *34*
tonal interplay, 36
tonal structure, 18
tone, *681*, 714
  academic painting, 506
  changes in, *529*
  tonal underpainting, 501
tones, 28, *35*, *77*, *101*, 194, *200*, 201, 204, *217*, 232, *234*, 286, 289, *379*, *412*, *426*, *427*, *435*, *436*, *440*, 446, 480, 543, 547, 554, 558, 576
topographical drawing and painting, 238, 242–3
Toulouse-Lautrec, Henri de *see* Lautrec, Henri de Toulouse
Toulouse-Lautrec, Henri de, 576, 660
Toulouse-Lautrec-Monfa, Count Alphonse-Charles de, father, 678
Toulouse-Lautrec-Monfa, Count Henri Marie Raymond *see* Lautrec, Henri de Toulouse
  transparency, 687
Tower of Babel, The, 66–7, *71*, 82, *83–5*
  painted on ivory, 82
Transept of Ewenny Priory, *240*
Trehot, Lise, 548
Tristan, Flora, 586
Tristan y Moscoso, Don Mariano de, 586
Triumph of Death, The, 65–6, *69*
trompe-l'oeil, 168
Trouville, 522, 550
Tub, The, 446, *447–9*

Turner, Joseph Mallord William, 283, 296, 495, 510,
appearance and character, 240
concern for completeness, 246
and criticism, 240–1, 258, *259*, 274
as draftsman, 238
gallery, 246, *247*, 250, 254
influence of, 244, 246
influences on, 242–3
legacy, 246
literary influences, 241–2
poetry, 241–2, 254, 274
as professor of perspective, 242
Rain, Steam and Speed, 297, 518
themes in paintings, 239–41
and tradition, 242, *259*
training in watercolour, 238–9
Two Female Harvesters, 285
working methods, 238, 244, 245
turpentine, to dilute paint, 113
Two Laundresses, 417
Two Old People Eating, 199, 232, *233–5*
Twelve Year Truce, 150
Two Women Teaching a Child to Walk, 154, *156*

U

Uccello, Paolo, 438
Ukiyo-e school, 384
Ulysses Deriding Polyphemus, 258–61, 262; (sketch), 258, *259*
Ulenborch, Saskia van (Rembrandt's wife), 153, 156, *156, 157*
Umbrellas, The, 545, 546, 548, 564, *565–7*
underdrawing, 71, *101, 288,* 426, 501
underpainting, 69, *71,* 77, 92, *113,* 136, 155, *162,* 164, *166,* 168, *174, 188, 207, 210, 215,* 245, 255, *256, 263, 295,* 501, 506, 510, *512, 516, 520,* 532, *578*
monochrome, *333*
unfinished works, *263, 267, 271, 275*
urban/portside themes, 288, 296, 297, 308, *309–11,* 312, *313–15,*
Utamaro
Poem of the Pillow, The, 412
Utrecht school, *151*

V

Valéry, Paul, 411, 412, 434, 438
Vallotton, Félix, 576
Valparaiso see *Crepuscule in Flesh Colour and Green: Valparaiso*
Valpinçon, Henri, 412
Valpinçon, Paul, 411, 412, 438
Van der Velde, Willem, 243, 250
Ship in a Storm, 251
Van Dyck, Sir Anthony 112, 153, 266
Van Eyck, Jan 16
Van Gogh, Vincent, 494, 497, 593, 602, 606, *607–9,* 683, *691,* 694
background and early life, 632–4
influence of, 643–5
influences on, 632, *633,* 636–7, 638, *639*
letters to Theo, 632, 634
mental breakdown, 643, 664, 668, 672
painting methods, 641, *641*
religious beliefs, 633–4
severed ear, 664
social conscience, 634, 636
suicide, 632, 672
Van Gogh, Theo, 606, 632, 634, 638, 652, 664, 672
Van Gogh painting Sunflowers, 612, *607–9*
Van Gogh's Bedroom at Arles, 660
Van Mander, Karel, *63,* 70, 98
on Bruegel, 62, 71, *79, 83, 99*
Het Schilde-Boek (The Painters Book), 62
Variations in Flesh Colour and Green: the Balcony, 384, *385–7*
Vasari, Giorgio, 16, 23
Lives of the Most Excellent Painters, Sculptors and Architects 86
Veccellio, Tiziano *see* Titian
Veen, Otto van (Octavius Vaenius), 106
Velasquez, Diego, 194, 204, 325, 326, 365, 576
Las Meninas, 193, 218, *324*
Little Cavaliers, 325
Portrait of Pablo de Valladolid, *372*
Rokeby Venus, 196, 380
Vellay, Julie, later Pissarro's wife, 282, 292, 316
Venetian painting, 17, 19, 54
a turning point, *33*
Venice, 16
Venus of Urbino, The, 46, *47–9,* 50
Verdonck, Rombout, 106
Verhaecht, Tobias, 106, *145*
Vernon, 518
Vernonese, Paolo, 472
Veronese, 576
Vetheuil, 500
verticals, 204
Viaduct of Castel-Vieil at Albi, 679
Vicomte Lepic and his Daughters, Place de la Concorde, 413
Vidal de Solares y Cardeñas, Don Pedro, 558
View across the Nieuwe Meer near Amsterdam, 157
View from Louveciennes, 281, *283*
View from my Window, Eragny-sur-Epte, 287, *287*
View of l'Hermitage at Pontoise, 292, *293–5,* 300
viewpoint, high 65, 75, 78
Ville d'Avray, 518
Vincent's Chair with his Pipe, 641, 660, *661–3*
Vincenzo I Gonzago, Duke of Mantua, 107, 109
Virgil, *Aeneid,* 242
Vision after the Sermon: Jacob wrestling with the Angel, 592, *596,* 602, *603–5, 611, 614, 627*

visionary compositions, 460
visual music, 384
vitality, *229*
Volckher Ambroise, 546
Volckhertzoon Coornhert, Dierick, 67–68
Vollard, Ambrose, 593, 546
Voragine, Jacobus de, *Golden Legend*, 67
vortex, *253, 275*
voyeurism, 472, *474*
Vuillard, Edouard, 503, 576, 710, *713*

W

Waitress Serving Beer, 352, *353*
Walk in Andalusia, A: Majas and the Muffled Majos, 195, *201*, 204, *205–7*
Wapping, 365, 384, *386*
War, the Exile and the Rock Limpet, 274, 275
Warrener, *700*
wash drawings, 280
water, *130*, 270, 514, 522, 530, 532, 533, *533–7*
watercolour, 238–9, 245, 258, 280, 308, 472
  and oil painting, *245*, 270
  technique, 484
Waterlilies (Nymphéas), 496, 503, 522, 532, 537
Watteau, Antoine, 204
wax, 593
Way, T. R., 392
weather effects, 238, 244, *244*, *251, 256*
wet-in-wet technique, *162*, 178, 182, 186, *188, 201*, 284, *295*, *298, 299, 305, 329*, 329, *354*, *342, 350, 361, 383*, 472
wet-into-wet, *432*, 542, *545*, 550, *552, 556*, 558, *562*, 564, 641, *674*
wet-on-dry, *628*
wet-on-wet, *614, 618, 628*
Weyden, Rogier van der, *Descent from the Cross*, 86
Where Do We Come From? What Are We? Where Are We Going To?, *593*, 594, 620–1, *621–5*
Whistler, James Abbott McNeil, 328, 680, 686
  declared bankrupt, 369, 400
  father's death, 364
  ill health and death, 372
  influences on, 364, 365, 376, 384, 388, 392, *394*, 400
  as interior designer, 368
  marriage, 370
  Nocturnes, 510
  painting and music, 366–7
  painting/working methods, 371, 392, 396, 404
  relations with mother, 380
  society portrait painter, 367–8
  Women in the Garden, 496, 506, *507–9*, 528
White Girl see *Symphony in White No 1: The White Girl*
White Horse, The, 626, *627–9*
Whitehall, Banqueting Hall ceiling 104, 109, *109*, 117
Whitney, Mrs John Hay, 558
Wilde, Oscar, 370, 686
Wilkie, David, 274
William of Orange–Nassau, 105
Wilson, Richard, 243
  The River Dee, 242
Winter, *194*, 195
witchcraft scenes, 208, *209–11*
Wolf, Albert, in *Le Figaro*, 284
Woman at her Toilet, 683
wood panels, preparation for painting, 71
wooden panels, as painting support, 113, *113*, 124, 144
woodcuts, 602

Y

Yellow Christ, The, 594, *596*
Young Woman Bathing, *155*, 182, *183–5*
Yvette Guilbert-Pessima, 682

Z

Zamora, Antonio de, 208
Zapater, Martin, 194
zig zag strokes, *666, 674*
Zola, Emile, 280, 284, 292, 324, 326, 328, 340, 434, 452, 457, 458, 464, 501, 548, 592, 636, 702
  A New Way of Painting, 336
  and the Dreyfus Affair, 288
  definition of art, *453*
  L'Assommoir, 352
  L'Oevre, 458–9
  Le Ventre de Paris, 356
  on Pissarro, 282, *283*
  "Thursdays", 282
Zuccato, mosaicist, 17

PICTURE CREDITS AND ACKNOWLEDGMENTS

The material in this book previously appeared in all titles of:

HISTORY & TECHNIQUES OF THE GREAT MASTERS

TITLES AVAILABLE IN THIS SERIES

BRUEGEL
CÉZANNE
DEGAS
GAUGUIN
GOYA
MANET
MONET
PISSARRO
REMBRANDT
RENOIR
RUBENS
TITIAN
TOULOUSE-LAUTREC
TURNER
VAN GOGH
WHISTLER